HANDBOOK OF ENERGY FINANCE

Theories, Practices and Simulations

HANDBOOK OF ENERGY FINANCE

Theories, Practices and Simulations

Stéphane Goutte

CEMOTEV, UVSQ, Paris-Saclay, France

Duc Khuong Nguyen

IPAG Business School, France & VNU International School, Vietnam

World Scientific

NEW JERSEY • LONDON • SINGAPORE • BEIJING • SHANGHAI • HONG KONG • TAIPEI • CHENNAI • TOKYO

Published by

World Scientific Publishing Co. Pte. Ltd.
5 Toh Tuck Link, Singapore 596224
USA office: 27 Warren Street, Suite 401-402, Hackensack, NJ 07601
UK office: 57 Shelton Street, Covent Garden, London WC2H 9HE

Library of Congress Cataloging-in-Publication Data
Names: Nguyen, Duc Khuong, 1978– editor. | Goutte, Stéphane, editor.
Title: Handbook of energy finance : theories, practices and simulations /
edited by Duc Khuong Nguyen (IPAG Business School, France & Indiana University, USA)
and Stéphane Goutte (University Paris 8, France).
Description: New Jersey : World Scientific, [2019]
Identifiers: LCCN 2019011950 | ISBN 9789813278370 (hc : alk. paper)
Subjects: LCSH: Energy industries--Finance. | Energy policy.
Classification: LCC HD9502.A2 H254 2019 | DDC 333.79--dc23
LC record available at https://lccn.loc.gov/2019011950

British Library Cataloguing-in-Publication Data
A catalogue record for this book is available from the British Library.

For any available supplementary material, please visit
https://www.worldscientific.com/worldscibooks/10.1142/11213#t=suppl

Desk Editors: Aanand Jayaraman/Sandhya Venkatesh

Typeset by Stallion Press
Email: enquiries@stallionpress.com

Printed in Singapore

Preface

Modeling and forecasting the dynamics of energy markets have become a challenging task for energy players, particularly in the oil and gas sectors. The intensification of their financialization since 2004 had made them more complex but also more integrated with other tradable asset classes. More importantly, their large and frequent fluctuations in terms of both prices and volatility, particularly in the aftermath of the global financial crisis 2008–2009, posit difficulties for gauging energy price behavior and are primary sources of concerns for macroeconomic stability and general economic performance. It is worth noting that the high level of energy market volatility is strongly related to the supply uncertainty, storage constraints, short-term inelasticity of demand, and unexpected macroeconomic and geopolitical changes.

The 2019 World Energy Outlook recently published by the International Energy Agency (IEA)[1] has drawn the attention of energy market stakeholders on, at least, three important facts: (i) there are still one billion people worldwide having no access to electricity, which contrasts the willingness of rapid cut in global carbon emissions under the Paris climate agreement to target no more than 2°C increase in global temperature; (ii) under the sustainable development goals, more than half of the growth in energy demand projected by the IEA (1% each year toward 2040), due to global economic expansion and rising world population, would be satisfied by low-carbon sources and another third by natural gas; (iii) despite the increase in US shale output and the rising share of renewables which both reshape the world energy markets, the global economy still relies heavily on oil production and supply from the Middle East with, as usual, a continuing rise on energy security risk and geopolitical complexity.

---

[1] https://webstore.iea.org/world-energy-outlook-2019.

The above-mentioned predictions of changes in global energy market, coupled with the increasing economic uncertainty, the intensity of international trade tension, and climate risk, would lead to significant changes in not only the behavior of market participants but also market designs. Rapid transformations of the energy markets are also expected with a move to more sustainable sources, with however uncertain growth patterns. All these factors affect the price formulation and decision-making processes, which makes the energy price modeling and forecasting extremely difficult.

This handbook thus aims to advance the debate on the theories and practices of quantitative energy finance while shedding light on innovative results and technical methods applied to energy markets, taking into account new challenges and economic circumstances. We organize the 30 high-quality chapters in six different parts to tackle the ongoing issues faced by energy consumers, producers, and regulators: Modeling and Forecasting Approaches; Volatility and Jump Modeling; Regulation, Risk Management, and Network System; Environmental, Green, and Renewable Energy; Pricing and Hedging; and Cross-market Linkages. The readers would also see that the majority of the contributions are dedicated to the recent development and applications of mathematical and quantitative approaches for a better understanding of the stochastic processes that drive energy market movements.

We firmly believe that not only graduate students and researchers but also practitioners and policy makers can greatly benefit from the materials presented in this handbook.

Stéphane Goutte and Duc Khuong Nguyen

About the Editors

Stéphane Goutte has two Ph.Ds., one in Mathematics and one in Economics. He got his Habilitation for Supervising Scientific Research (HDR) in 2017 at Paris Dauphine University. He is Full Professor at CEMOTEV, Université Versailles St Quentin en Yvelines, Paris-Saclay, France. He teaches mathematics and related topics as part of M.Sc. and B.Sc. courses. He is also a Senior Editor of *Finance Research Letters*, an Associate Editor of *International Review of Financial Analysis* (IRFA) and *Research in International Business and Finance*, a Subject Editor of *Journal of International Financial Markets, Institutions and Money* (JIFMIM), and an Editorial member of *European Management Review* (EMR). His interests lie in the areas of mathematical finance and econometrics applied in energy or commodities. He has published more than forty research papers in international reviews. He is a guest editor of special issues of international peer-reviewed journals and the editor of many handbooks.

Duc Khuong Nguyen is Professor of Finance and Deputy Director for Research at IPAG Business School (France). He holds a Ph.D. in Finance from the University of Grenoble Alpes (France) and an HDR (Habilitation for Supervising Scientific Research) degree in Management Science from the University of Cergy-Pontoise (France), and has completed an executive education program in "Leadership in Development" at Harvard Kennedy School (United States). He is also a Non-Resident Research Fellow at the School of Public and Environmental Affairs, Indiana University. His research articles have been published in various refereed journals such as *European Journal*

of Operational Research, *Journal of Banking and Finance*, *Journal of Economic Dynamics and Control*, *Journal of Empirical Finance*, *Journal of International Money and Finance*, *Journal of Macroeconomics*, *Macroeconomic Dynamics* and *Review of International Economics*. Dr. Nguyen has edited many books on corporate finance and financial market issues and serves as subject and associate editor of several finance journals.

About the Contributors

Tiho Ancev is an Associate Professor at the University of Sydney. His main research areas are environmental, natural resource and agricultural economics. He has contributed to *Water Economics and Policy*, and *Economics of Air Pollution and Climate Change Policies*. His wide publications on these topics have led and contributed to several national and international projects in these research areas.

Maria C. A. Balatbat is a Senior Lecturer at the Business School and Joint Director for the Centre for Energy and Environmental Markets at UNSW Sydney. She teaches financial accounting and a course on reporting for climate change and sustainability. Before joining UNSW Australia, Maria was a Teaching Fellow at Nanyang Business School in Singapore, a Lecturer and the RJ Chambers PhD scholar at the University of Sydney. Prior to her academic career, she worked as a consultant and auditor in large accounting firms in the US and Asia. Maria is also a Fellow at CPA Australia.

Christian Bellak is an Associate Professor of Economics at the Department of Economics, WU University of Economics and Business, Vienna (Austria). He has published several book chapters and is the author of articles published in international scientific journals like the *Oxford Bulletin of Economics and Statistics*, *Applied Economics*, *International Journal of the Economics of Business*, *Transnational Corporations*, *Global Economy Journal*, *Economic Dynamics and Structural Change*, *The World Economy*, *Public Finance Analysis*, *Global Economy Journal*, *Transnational Corporations Review*, *Journal of Development Studies* and *Journal of International Economic Law*. His research interests include international factor flows (Foreign Direct Investment (FDI) and Migration) and economic policy.

Marcelo Bianconi, PhD, is a Professor of Economics at Tufts University, in Medford, MA, US. He received his PhD in Economics from the University of Illinois Urbana-Champaign. He has authored academic papers in several professional journals and books including *European Economic Review*, *Journal of Economic*

Dynamics and Control, *Review of International Economics*, *Canadian Journal of Economics*, *International Review of Economics and Finance*, *International Tax and Public Finance*, *Journal of International Money and Finance*, *Macroeconomic Dynamics*, *Emerging Markets Review*, *North American Journal of Economics and Finance* among others. Book entitled *Financial Economics, Risk and Information*, has been published by World Scientific Publishing Co. and is in its current second edition published in 2011. www.tufts.edu/~mbiancon.

Mohammed Bouaddi is an Associate Professor of Economics at the American University in Cairo, Egypt. He holds a PhD in Economics from HEC Business School in Canada. He has published papers in journals such as *Energy Economics*, *The Journal of Dynamics Economics and Control*, *Communications in Statistics-Theory and Methods*, *The International Review of Economics and Finance*, *Studies in Nonlinear Dynamics & Econometrics*, etc.

Kelly Burns is an Early Career Researcher at the Curtin Business School, Curtin University. Kelly's research focuses on the macroeconomic and financial impacts of energy consumption and energy prices, as well as investment in renewable energy. Kelly has multidisciplinary skills in economics, finance and law, with a focus on econometric modeling, forecasting and public policy. She has successfully published over 14 peer-reviewed journal papers and has also coauthored a book and book chapter. In addition, Kelly has been the primary statistical advisor and analyst for several government reports that have informed public policy debates and have been the foundation for evidence-based policy making and law reform.

Julie Carey is an Energy Economist and Director with NERA Economic Consulting. She has substantial experience across the energy sector, power, oil and gas, pipeline, railroad, coal and renewables. Julie frequently provides expert evidence in regulatory proceeding, and in courts and international arbitration about economic analyses of market dynamics (supply, demand and pricing), competition, regulatory economics and economic damages and valuation issues. She frequently studies global energy markets including the US, Asia and beyond. Julie is an Adjunct Professor at Georgetown University where she teaches energy economics.

David G. Carmichael is a Professor of Civil Engineering and former Head of the Department of Engineering Construction and Management at the University of New South Wales, Australia. He is a graduate of the Universities of Sydney and Canterbury; a Fellow of the Institution of Engineers, Australia; a Member of the American Society of Civil Engineers; and a former graded arbitrator and mediator. Professor Carmichael publishes, teaches and consults widely in most aspects of project management, construction management, systems engineering and problem solving. He is known for his leftfield thinking, including that in the monographs *Project Management Framework* (A. A. Balkema, 2004), and with Taylor and Francis, CRC Press: *Project Planning, and Control* (2006); *Problem Solving for Engineers* (2013); and *Infrastructure Investment: An Engineering Perspective* (2014).

Luca Di Persio is an Assistant Professor at the College of Mathematics, Department of Computer Science, University of Verona, where he teaches mathematical finance, stochastic calculus, and SDEs. He has authored dozens of research papers related to stochastic analysis and its applications, spanning from SPDEs theory to energy forecasting and from MFGs to Mathfin, interacting particle systems, stochastic control theory, etc. Luca Di Persio is also the cofounder and Chief of the R&D sector of the University of Verona official spinoff High Performance Analytics (www.hpa8.com).

Rita De Siano is an Associate Professor of Economic Policy at the Parthenope University of Naples. Prof. De Siano holds a bachelor degree in International Trade and Foreign Exchange Markets at Istituto Universitario Navale of Naples, a Master in Economics at the University of Manchester, and a PhD in Economic Sciences at the Istituto Universitario Navale. She has taught political economy, development environment and tourism, international financial markets, territorial and localisation economics, and regional economics. Prof. De Siano's research works have spanned various topics, such as spatial econometrics applications; regional convergence; public expenditure and fiscal decentralisation; human capital migration effects on structural change and Italian dualism; social policy and welfare regimes; migration and pension system; aid, gender, corruption and economic growth; business cycles and financial variables; credit sector efficiency and effects on local growth.

Derya Eryilmaz, PhD is an Economist at NERA Economic Consulting. Dr. Eryilmaz is experienced in applied economic analysis of the power sector including renewables, energy efficiency and demand response. In her work, Dr. Eryilmaz has employed spatial dynamic modeling and various applied econometrics methods (e.g. time series analysis, demand analysis, forecasting, logit regression models) in understanding several energy markets issues. Dr. Eryilmaz received her PhD in Applied Economics from the University of Minnesota.

Mostafa Fallahnejad holds a master's degree in Power Engineering from Technical University of Munich. He is currently a PhD candidate at the Energy Economics Group (EEG) in TU Wien and is involved in the field of energy system modeling as well as heating and cooling planning. His research interest is mathematical modeling within the energy sector.

Zheng Fang is a Lecturer at Singapore University of Social Sciences, Singapore. Prior to the employment, she worked as a Research Fellow at Nanyang Technological University, Singapore; an Associate Professor at Southwestern University of Finance and Economics, China; and an Analyst at Mercer-HRBS, Singapore. She obtained PhD in Economics from Nanyang Technological University in 2012 and has so far published about 25 refereed journal articles including *Energy Economics*, *Energy Policy*, *Economics of Transition*, *Applied Economics*, *Social Indicators Research*, *Journal of Happiness Studies*, *Asian Economic Journal and Singapore Economic Review*.

Roland Füss is a Full Professor of Real Estate Finance at the University of St.Gallen and a Member of the Board of the Swiss Institute for Banking and Finance s/bf-HSG at the School of Finance. In addition, he is a Research Associate at the Centre for European Economic Research (ZEW), Mannheim, Germany. His main research topics are in the field of asset pricing, real estate economics and finance, risk management and applied financial econometrics. Prof. Füss has authored numerous articles in economics, finance and real estate journals such as *Journal of Economic Dynamics and Control*, *Journal of Financial and Quantitative Analysis*, *Journal of Money, Credit and Banking*, *Journal of Banking and Finance*, *Public Choice* and *Review of Finance*.

Vanesa Garcia was born in Cuenca in 1991. She graduated in 2013 in business administration and management, and completed a master's degree in banking and quantitative finance in 2016 — both in the University of Castilla La Mancha. She is currently studying the fourth year of a law course at the National University of Distance Education (UNED) and working at the BBVA bank.

Costantino Grasso is a Lecturer in Business Management and Law at UEL, visiting lecturer at Queen Mary University of London and Global MBA module leader for Corporate Governance and Ethics at the University of London. In 2014, he worked as a corporate governance and compliance specialist for the Serious Fraud Office participating in the first-ever UK Deferred Prosecution Agreement between that prosecuting body and ICBC Standard Bank Plc, which concerned a complex case of transnational bribery. On that occasion, he was awarded as a member of the case team the UK Government Legal Department's Prosecutor of the Year Award. His foremost areas of research are financial crime, corporate governance, corporate social responsibility and business ethics. In particular, in the latest years, he has focused on corporate criminal liability and on the effectiveness of corporate and compliance measures to counter financial crime offences such as bribery and corruption, fraud, tax evasion, money laundering and terrorism financing. He has also conducted comprehensive studies on European criminal law, economic sanctions, transitional justice, as well as energy trade and governance. His research has always been inspired by the necessity of taking into consideration the protection of fundamental rights and, in particular, the right to a fair trial and due process. He is the author of various articles, chapters and volumes both in English and Italian.

C.-Y. Cynthia Lin Lawell is an Associate Professor and the Robert Dyson Sesquicentennial Chair in Environmental, Energy and Resource Economics in the Charles H. Dyson School of Applied Economics and Management at Cornell University. She is the Director of Cornell DEEP-GREEN-RADAR and the Director of the Cornell University TREESPEAR. Professor Lin Lawell has received numerous awards for her research, including the Harvard University Stone Fellow Award. Her research has also been featured in such media outlets as the *New York Times*, the *Washington Post*, the *Guardian*, Platt's blog, and *Bloomberg View*. Professor Lin Lawell received her bachelor's degree, *summa cum laude*, in Environmental Science and Public Policy from Harvard College in 2000 and her PhD in Economics from Harvard University in 2006.

Maik Günther is expert for Energy Economics at Stadtwerke München GmbH and is in charge for long-term analyses of global oil and gas markets. He is also an affiliated researcher at the Center of Energy Markets at the Technical University of Munich and holds lectures at Conenergy Akademie.

Jim Hanly is a Senior Lecturer in the College of Business at Technological University Dublin (Ireland). He also works as a financial trainer and consultant. He holds a PhD and an MSc in Finance from University College Dublin. He has published his work in several journals including the Energy Journal, Energy Economics, Energy policy, the International Journal of Finance and Economics, The Journal of Futures Markets, The Journal of Risk and The European Journal of Finance as well as book chapters and articles in practitioner journals. His research interests focus on risk management and hedging, asset pricing, and volatility modelling in energy, financial and commodity markets.

Wieger Johan Hinderks, MSc has studied mathematics and physics at the University of Amsterdam (the Netherlands) before continuing with a Master's degree in financial mathematics at the University of Kaiserslautern (Germany). Wieger Hinderks' Master thesis focused on the modeling and calibration of factor models for electricity markets. During his studies he was a student assistant at the Department for Financial Mathematics at the Fraunhofer ITWM, where he started working full-time as a research fellow after he graduated. In this position he worked on the implementation of risk-management software for energy utilities and as a consultant for modern Monte-Carlo techniques.

Oleksandr Honchar is a machine learning practitioner and researcher and focuses on the applications in financial technologies. He holds a master's degree in mathematics from the University of Verona. He is the co-founder of the AI boutique Neurons Lab LTD and is currently the CTO. As an independent researcher, he also develops new models for time series analysis and publishes related results.

Tom Houghton is a Adjunct Research Fellow in the Curtin Business School, Curtin University, Perth, Australia where he was previously the Director of the MBA (Oil & Gas). Before joining Curtin, he served as a resident Research Fellow at the University of Strathclyde (UoS) where he straddled the Business and Engineering Faculties. His principal fields of research are sustainable energy economics and financing and, in addition, he has a keen interest in energy for development. He has published widely in energy and economics related journals including *Energy Policy*, *European Journal of Operational Research* and *IEEE Transactions on Power Systems*. He has taken a lead role in a number of significant research projects including the European Union funded TWENTIES and a number of knowledge exchange projects with leading European utilities such as Eon and Scottish and Southern Energy. Tom now works full time for sustainable energy consultancy, E4tech.

Jingze Jiang is an Associate Professor of Economics at Edinboro University. She received her PhD in Economics from Washington State University. Her research has focused on energy economics, risk quantification and management, and environmental economics. Her research has been published in journals such as *Energy Economics and Applied Economics*.

Johnson Kakeu is an Assistant Professor of Economics at the University of Prince Edward Island in Canada. He holds a PhD in Economics from University of Montreal in Canada, a Master's in Statistics and a Master's in Applied Mathematics and Mechanics. He has published papers in journals such as *Energy Economics*, *the B.E. Journal of Macroeconomics*, *the Journal of Sustainable Finance & Investment*, *Environmental and Resource Economics*, *Dynamic Games and Applications*, etc.

Khaled H. Kheiravar is an Economist and Air Pollution Specialist in the Market Monitoring Section at the California Air Resources Board; as well as a Research Associate at Cornell University DEEP-GREEN-RADAR and at Cornell University TREESPEAR. Khaled has won several prestigious awards for his research, including the 2013 ExxonMobil Corporate Affiliate Fellowship, the National Center for Sustainable Transportation 2018-2019 Spring UC-Davis Dissertation Grant, the

2016 ExxonMobil Corporate Affiliate Fellowship, the Henry A. Jastro Graduate Research Award, the USAEE Student Registration Fee Scholarship, the OPEC Fund for International Development IAEE Support Fund Scholarship; the UC-Davis Fellowship for Excellence in Graduate Research, and the UC-Davis Economics Department Job Market Fellowship. Khaled has presented his research at USAEE conferences; at Columbia University; and at AERE @ WEAI. He received his PhD in Economics from the University of California at Davis in 2019.

Trang Kim is a Senior Lecturer of International Finance at Foreign Trade University, Vietnam and she was awarded PhD degree at Middlesex University Business School, the United Kingdom. She won the first prize at "The scientific research contests for students 2004" of Vietnam, and won the first prize of "VIFOTEC prize 2004" of Vietnam. She has published her paper in the top-ranked journal in International Business — *Journal of International Business Studies*. Her research interests include financial performances and financial management of Multinational Corporation (MNCs), risk management, financial derivatives use and institutional theory.

Thai-Ha Le is a Senior Lecturer at RMIT University Vietnam, which is an Australian-based university operating in Vietnam. She obtained PhD in Economics from Nanyang Technological University in 2014. Energy economics is one of Dr. Le's primary research fields. She has published 14 articles in international referred journals, including *Energy Economics*, *Energy Policy*, *Resources Policy*, *Applied Economics*, *Emerging Markets Finance and Trade*, *Research In Economics and International Economics*. Dr. Le has been awarded the Pacific Trade and Development (PAFTAD) Fellowship for Young Scholars and three research grants from RMIT Australia and RMIT Vietnam while working in RMIT Vietnam.

Steffen Mahringer holds a PhD from the University of St.Gallen, Switzerland and an MSc. from the University of Mannheim, Germany. His research interests are commodity markets and derivatives pricing as well as energy market regulation. His work has been published in journals such as *Journal of Economic Dynamics and Control* and *Energy Economics*.

Panagiota Makrychoriti holds a PhD and an MSc in Finance from the Department of Accounting and Finance, Athens University of Economics and Business. She is a Lecturer at the Department of Management, Birkbeck University of London (UK). He did her PhD and her Post-Doc at Athens University of Economics and Business. Her research interests are in the areas of economic 16 sentiment, central bank policies, credit risk and econometrics.

Thomas L. Marsh is the Distinguished Professor of Agricultural and Resource Economics at Washington State University. His research focuses on commodity markets, econometrics and natural resource economics. His research has been published in *Advances in Econometrics*, *Energy Economics* and other journals.

Beatriz Martinez is a Ph.D Assistant Professor at the Department of Business Finance at the University of Valencia (Spain). She obtained her PhD Degree in the Doctoral Programme in Quantitative Finance and Economy from the University of Valencia in 2018. After having received her bachelor's degree in Economics from the University of Valencia, she completed a master's degree course in banking and quantitative finance in a joint programme from the Complutense University of Madrid, University of Castilla-La Mancha, University of the Basque Country and University of Valencia. Her research primarily concerns commodity futures markets and the risk management modeling of energy markets.

Paweł Maryniak is a PhD Student at the Wrocław University of Economics and an Expert at the Ministry of Economic Development, Poland. His research focuses on asset pricing and energy markets. He is the recipient of prestigious scholarships and research grants awarded by the Polish Ministry of Science and Higher Education, including the Diamond Grant.

Charles F. Mason is the H. A. "Dave" True, Jr. Chair in Petroleum and Natural Gas Economics in the Department of Economics and Associate Dean for Research in the College of Business at the University of Wyoming. He is an internationally known scholar who specializes in Environmental and Resource Economics with over 80 publications in peer-reviewed journals and book chapters. He served as the managing editor of the top international journal in the field of Environmental and Resource Economics (the *Journal of Environmental Economics and Management*), from 2006 to 2011. He is currently an Associate Editor of the European Economic Review, Co-editor of Economic Inquiry, and joint Editor-in-Chief of Strategic Behavior in the Environment. He earned a double B.A. in Economics and Mathematics in 1977 and a PhD in Economics in 1983, all at the University of California at Berkeley. He is a non-resident fellow at Resources for the Future, and has been a visiting academic at the University of Cambridge (2003); the London School of Economics (2014, 2015); the University of Oxford (2008, 2009, 2010, 2011, 2012); the Venice International University, Ca' Foscari (2013); and the Toulouse School of Economics (2013). He has been on the faculty at the University of Wyoming since 1982.

Loretta Mastroeni is an Associate Professor of Mathematical Finance at the Department of Economics of Roma Tre University of Rome. Her main research interests focus on pricing of financial derivatives, risk management in energy and commodities markets and risk management in telecommunications. She is the author of many papers published in main peer-reviewed journals (like *Energy Economics*).

She acts as an expert evaluator of European Union projects and as a referee for a number of peer-reviewed journals.

Gérard Mondello is Senior Researcher at the GREDEG, UMR 7321, CNRS at Sophia Antipolis (France). He holds a PhD in economics and a PhD in law. His field of research focuses on the relationship between law and economics in civil liability for industrial, climate change and natural risks. He focuses his main researches focus on the comparison between liability regimes, the liability of lenders in ultra-hazardous activities, the impact of liability on producers' strategic choices and competition.

Georgios Moratis holds a PhD in Finance from the Department of Accounting and Finance, Athens University of Economics and Business and an MSc in Finance and Investments from the Rotterdam School of Management Ranked. He is a Postdoctoral Fellow at Athens University of Economics and Business and has been a Visiting Scholar at the Bank of Greece. His research interests are in the areas of banking, bank-sovereign contagion in the Eurozone and econometrics.

Quang Nguyen joined Business School, Middlesex University in 2013. Prior to that he was a faculty member at the Division of Economics at Nanyang Technological University in Singapore and University of Lyon 2 in France. Incorporating insights from economics and psychology — i.e. behavioral economics — he conducts field experiments to explore behaviors of consumers in the market, as well as employees and managers in the firms. He has published in top academic journals such as the *American Economic Review*.

Prilly Oktoviany, MSc has graduated with a Master's degree in financial mathematics at the University of Kaiserslautern (Germany) and the University Joseph-Fourier in Grenoble (France). During her studies Prilly Oktoviany made her first contact with the energy industry as a member of RWE's scholarship program 'RWE Fellows', followed by her Bachelor thesis which dealt with time series modeling of Germany's reserve market. Recently, as research fellow in the department of Financial Mathematics at the Fraunhofer ITWM, she worked on the implementation of (mainly) analytical risk methods in a risk management software for an energy utility.

Iris Pfarl works as an independent business consultant in the field of corporate finance, specializing in project and export finance. She holds a doctorate degree from WU University of Economics and Business, Vienna (Austria) and has many years of relevant professional experience. She worked for the Austrian Export Credit Agency and headed the department of Structured Finance of the Vienna branch of a global renewable energy company. Besides her work experience in the banking and energy sector she teaches at the University of Applied Sciences BFI Vienna and engages in research projects cooperating with WU Vienna. She has recently published a Case Study book on project financing of renewable energy projects with Gabler Springer.

Marcel Prokopczuk is a Professor of Finance at Leibniz University Hannover, Germany, and Visiting Professor of Finance at the ICMA Centre, Henley Business School, University of Reading, UK. He is an editor of the *Journal of Commodity Markets* and Associate Editor of the *Journal of Banking and Finance*. Prof. Prokopczuk's main research interests are commodity markets, asset pricing, derivatives and risk management. His research has been published in international high-quality journals such as the *Journal of Financial and Quantitative Analysis*, the *Review of Asset Pricing Studies*, the *Journal of Banking and Finance* and the *Journal of Economic Dynamics and Control*.

Lorena Remuzgo is a Postdoctoral Researcher at the Department of Economics of the University of Cantabria (Spain). She obtained her PhD degree in Economics from the University of Cantabria in 2017 for her thesis on the analysis of the inequality in the distribution of atmospheric emissions using the family of generalized entropy measures. Her research interest includes environmental economics, inequality analysis and risk management. She has been a visiting scholar at the Department of Environmental Economics at the IVM Institute for Environmental Studies (VU University Amsterdam) and has participated in various research projects funded by the Spanish Government.

Afees A. Salisu is currently a Senior Research Fellow at the Centre for Econometric and Allied Research (CEAR), University of Ibadan and specializes in macroeconomics and econometrics with special interests in energy and finance and has published same in reputable journals. He teaches applied econometrics courses at both the undergraduate and postgraduate levels and has coauthored books on Introduction to Macroeconomics and Applied Panel Data Analyses with many lecture manuals on applied time series. He has continued to serve as a reviewer to many peer-reviewed journals and a consultant to many organizations on macroeconometric modeling and impact assessments.

Alessandro Sapio is an Full Professor of Economic Policy at the Parthenope University of Naples, and acts as Associate Editor of *Economia Politica — Journal of Analytical and Institutional Economics* (Springer), where he deals with papers on energy economics. He has been awarded a PhD in Economics and Management at Sant'Anna School, Pisa. Sapio's research interests include the econometric analysis of wholesale electricity markets, focusing on the impact of renewables and market integration on prices. On these topics, he has published on the main scholarly journals in the field, such as *Energy Policy* and *Energy Economics*, and guest coedited a special issue of *Energy Policy* on "The regional integration on energy markets" in 2015. He is coediting a *Handbook of Energy Economics and Policy* for Elsevier, to be published in 2019. Prof. Sapio has been a member of FP7 project Impressions — Impacts and risks from high-end scenarios, on climate policy, and a visiting research fellow at the Energy Markets Group, London Business School.

José María Sarabia is a Professor of Quantitative Methods for Economics and Business at the Department of Economics of the University of Cantabria (Spain). He is also a Professor of Statistics and Operational Research at the Complutense University (Madrid, Spain), now on leave. His main fields of interest are: economic inequality, distribution theory and multivariate analysis with applications to risk analysis, finance and informetrics. He has been a visiting professor and a researcher at the London School of Economics, Imperial College London and the International Capital Market Association (ICMA) Centre at the University of Reading (UK). In addition, he is an Associate Editor several journals including *TEST*, *Communications in Statistics* and *Journal of Statistical Distributions and Applications*, among others.

Saleem Shaik is a Professor of Agribusiness and Applied Economics at North Dakota State University and Director of Center for Agricultural Policy and Trade Studies (CAPTS). He teaches Applied Risk Analysis at the undergraduate level and Analytical Methods for Applied Research at the graduate level. His research philosophy is built on answering three questions — (1) what is the issue? (2) why is the issue important and to whom? and (3) how to address the issue? His current research deals with — (1) efficiency, technology and productivity growth analyses, (2) economics of crop yield distributions, (3) US federal farm policy and historical farm bills and (4) trade studies and agreements. Results of his research include the development of several indexes including: (1) an agriculture output, input and productivity index, (2) farm financial ratio indexes, (3) a farm programs, crop insurance, public investments, private patent innovation index for North Dakota and the Northern Great Plains states, and (4) trade export, import and openness index. These outcomes will be available at www.ndsu.edu/faculty/shaik. As the director of CAPTS, in cooperation with US Senators John Hoeven and Heidi Heitkamp and Congressman Kevin Cramer, he organized the 2018 Farm Policy and Bill: Issues and Opportunities Conference.

Takayuki Shiina is a Professor at Department of Industrial and Management Systems Science, School of Creative Science and Engineering, Waseda University,

Japan. He received his B.E., M.E. and Doctor of Engineering from Waseda University. He has been studying in the field of mathematical programming at Central Research Institute of Electric Power Industry (Tokyo, 1991–2008), Northwestern University (Evanston, Illinois, 2000–2001), Chiba Institute of Technology (Narashino, Chiba, Janan, 2008–2016). His main areas of interest are stochastic programming and integer programming. He was awarded the best paper prize with Professor John R. Birge (University of Chicago) from Japan Society of Industrial and Applied Mathematics in 2005.

Spyros Spyrou is a Professor of Finance at the Department of Accounting & Finance, Athens University of Economics & Business. Before that he was at the University of Durham (UK) and Middlesex University Business School (UK). He holds a PhD and an MSc from Brunel University (UK). He is the Director of the Behavioral Finance Lab (BeFin Lab), at Athens University of Economics & Business.

Raymond Swaray is a Senior Lecturer (Associate Professor) in Economics specializing in applied international macroeconomics and finance with particular interest in commodity markets, energy economics, agricultural economics and applied econometrics. He is module leader of the final year econometrics module. Raymond previously served as visiting lecturer of financial economics for the African Economic Research Consortium and as a member of International Panel of Experts for Setting Comprehensive Examinations for the Collaborative PhD Programme in Economics. He has supervised several PhD research and has served as external and internal examination of PhD viva voce examinations in many universities in the UK. He is an Associate Editor of *International Journal of Social Economics* on the editorial board of *Managerial and Decision Economics.*

Anatoliy Swishchuk is a Professor in mathematical finance at the Department of Mathematics and Statistics, University of Calgary, Calgary, Canada. He is a holder of two doctorate degrees in Mathematics and Physics (PhD and DSc) from the prestigious National Academy of Sciences of Ukraine, Kiev, Ukraine. Dr. Swishchuk is the finance and energy finance seminar "Lunch at the Lab" chair at the Department of Mathematics and Statistics. He is a steering committee member of Global Association of Risk Professionals (GARP), Canada (since 2015). He is the author of more than 150 publications, including 13 books and more than 100 articles in peer-reviewed journals.

Hipòlit Torró is currently a Professor of Financial Economics at the Universitat de València, Spain, where he has held an appointment since 1991. He has a BA in business administration from the Universitat de València, an MSc in financial mathematics from the universities of Edinburgh and Heriot-Watt, and a PhD in financial economics from the Universitat de València. He has published a number of referred articles in academic financial journals, and contributed to several books and conference proceedings. He has participated in research projects funded by the Generalitat Valenciana, Fundación Caja de Madrid, Instituto Valenciano de Investigaciones Económicas and the Spanish Ministry of Education and Science.

Carmen Trueba is an Associate Professor of Quantitative Methods for Economics and Business at the Department of Economics of the University of Cantabria (Spain). She is also member of the Spanish Network of Development Studies (REEDES). She obtained her PhD degree in Economics from the University of Cantabria in 2011. Her research interest includes distribution theory, inequality, multivariate analysis, informetrics, risk management and development studies. She has been a visiting researcher in the Department of Economics at the Ibero-American University (Mexico) and the University of Alicante (Spain) and has participated in various research projects funded by the Spanish Government.

Pierluigi Vellucci received an MSc degree in robotic engineering in 2013 and a PhD degree in Mathematical Models for Engineering, Electromagnetics and Nanosciences from Sapienza University of Rome, Italy, in 2017. He is currently a Postdoctoral researcher at the Department of Economics of Roma Tre University of Rome. His main research interests focus on the application of mathematical models in energy and financial markets.

Andreas Wagner is the head of the Department for Financial Mathematics at the Fraunhofer ITWM in Kaiserslautern (Germany). After studying mathematics and business administration at the University of Augsburg (Germany) and the University of Sheffield (UK) he moved to Fraunhofer ITWM, where he initially worked on interest rate models and the valuation of structured products. After a PhD in Energy Finance developing electricity price models with a focus on the integration of renewables he worked as a Senior Analyst at an energy utility in Austria on fundamental price models and their application. Since 2015 he is back at Fraunhofer ITWM and leads several projects on risk management for energy utilities.

W. D. Walls is currently Professor of Economics at the University of Calgary, Canada. After completion of his Doctoral Degree in Economics from the University of California, Dr. Walls was an Assistant and then Associate Professor at the University of Hong Kong. Dr. Walls has published widely in *Energy Economics* and on the implications of extreme uncertainty for the organization of industry. His work is widely cited, with a Wu-index and H-index in the top 5% of economists in the world.

Xue Wang, M.S. received degree from Tufts University, Research Program in economics. At Tufts, has been awarded the Henken Family Endowed Graduate Research scholarship for graduate thesis research and the Varkey Family Endowed Fellowship fund. Bachelor in economics with major in Finance at Renmin University of China; awarded National Scholarship of China and the Chinese Scholarship Council.

Rafał Weron is Professor of Management Science and Head of the Economic Modeling and Forecasting Group at the Wrocław University of Science and Technology, Poland. Over the last 20 years he has built an impressive international reputation in modeling and forecasting power market processes and computational statistics as applied to finance and insurance. Rafał is the author of the widely acclaimed *Modeling and Forecasting Electricity Loads and Prices: A Statistical Approach* (Wiley, 2006), coauthor of four other books and has published over 80 peer-reviewed book chapters and articles in top-tier journals (including *Energy*, *Energy Economics*, *Energy Policy*, *IEEE Transactions on Power Systems*, *International Journal of Forecasting* and *Renewable & Sustainable Energy Reviews*).

Neil A. Wilmot is an Associate Professor in the Department of Economics at the University of Minnesota Duluth, and an Associate of the Institute on the Environment at the University of Minnesota. He received his Ph.D. in Economics from the University of Wyoming, after the completion of a Master's degree from Lakehead University. Dr. Wilmot's research interests include energy economics, stochastic processes and applied econometrics. He has published numerous articles, several of which appear in leading economics journals, including *The Energy Journal, Energy Economics* and *Journal of Economic Behavior & Organization.*

Wei Zhang is currently Senior Corporate Economist at the City of Calgary, Canada. Ms. Zhang holds Advanced Degrees in Economics and in Marketing, and an Undergraduate Degree in Physics. Ms. Zhang has been instrumental in applying the tools of statistics and economics to the management of resources in public enterprises.

Liangxu Zhu is a Financial Economist who holds a PhD degree from the University of Sydney. His main research areas are energy economics, environmental policy and financial market. After completing his Masters degree in Finance, Accounting and Economics at Georg-August University of Göttingen, he worked as an Analyst for Non-Core Exotic Derivatives at the head office of Deutsche Bank in Frankfurt,

Germany from 2009 to 2012. Since 2013, he has been researching about the effect of carbon pricing policy on energy market and commodity market. His research provided insight into policy issues that are highly relevant to researchers and practitioners in the field of financial markets. His work has been presented widely and contributed to diverse projects in these areas.

Contents

PART I

Modeling and Forecasting Approaches

Chapter 1

Evolution of Forecasting Techniques for Dynamic Energy Markets

Julie Carey*,† and Derya Eryilmaz*

NERA Economic Consulting, Washington, DC, USA

†Georgetown University, Washington, DC, USA

We are in a very dynamic period in our domestic and global energy markets. Market forces are at work in both the shale oil and gas revolution and the development of renewable energy, which are dramatically impacting the energy industry. Transformation of global energy markets highlights the importance of understanding various forecasting methods and technical methods to accurately forecast in such a dynamic market structure. This chapter provides a comprehensive review of the forecasting techniques for energy markets and illustrates them through a case study. This chapter can potentially be utilized by academics and industry practitioners for understanding the evolution of the energy market dynamics.

Keywords: Energy forecasting; energy markets; time series analysis; applied econometrics methods.

1. Introduction

Forecasting in the energy sector is similar to other industries that require forward-looking estimates of supply, demand, price in order to plan and operate the businesses. Forecast energy supply, demand and price has long been recognized as an important component of long-range energy planning and investment decision-making by energy companies.

However, the energy industry is more complicated than other industries in many respects, including the highly capital-intensive nature of the industry, the regulatory and policy oversight aspects that exist because of the importance of energy in our daily lives as a basic good and the unique economic attributes inherent in the energy industry. The energy industry includes energy products that are used in daily activities, such as gasoline for transportation (which uses crude oil as a feedstock), natural gas for home heating and as an input fuel to generate electricity in the power sector and electricity for heating, lighting and air conditioning.

In addition, the operation of energy sector is highly technical. The oil and gas business requires sophisticated upstream operations, including development of underground or deep ocean crude oil and natural gas fields, drilling and operating the wells that recover crude oil and natural gas to the surface that then utilizes a sophisticated pipeline network (and other transportation options, such as vessels, barges, rail and trucks for crude oil) to deliver products to downstream refineries, power plants, other industrial, commercial and residential customers utilizing distribution networks to deliver energy products to the end users. Electricity is the most complex energy product due to the non-storable nature and other engineering complications with the transmission of power that relies on instantaneous generation of power that must exactly match the moment-to-moment changes in demand from the changes in our daily activities. Further technical operating complications have grown with the integration of renewable energy resources into the electricity sector, which are non-controllable and generate electricity when the renewable energy is accommodated (i.e. when the sun shines and when the wind blows). Further, distributed energy such as residential solar Photovoltaics (PV) enables consumers to produce some of their own electricity demands and sell excess power back to the electricity market, which shifts power flows from traditional paths [SEIA, 2017].

Due to the importance of the energy industry to the economy as well as the high capital cost and technical nature of the energy industry, historically there has been substantial governmental focus on energy forecasting. Many developed nations have governmental agencies responsible for developing long-range forecasts of energy demand and supply that may aid in the development of government policies to ensure adequate capital investments to provide reliable supply of energy in order to meet the country's needs with the lowest possible cost (i.e. energy security). Governments of industrialized nations typically use these forecasts and other agencies focused on the implementation of regulation of the energy sector (rate, environmental, etc.).

In addition, energy market participants develop their own forecasts which can be shared (e.g. BP and Exxon) or used solely for their own business decision-making. Academics, think tanks, consultants and other independent entities may conduct energy forecasts for industry use and decision-making.

Forecasting has become even more critical for various energy markets in the recent years. The development of competitive wholesale electricity markets, in the

US and elsewhere rely on demand forecasting as a key component for dispatching the available generators at the minimum cost. Furthermore, technological innovations and other developments across the energy sector not only create additional challenges in forecasting energy markets but also increase the importance of forecasting to aid in energy planning and business decision-making [Hong, 2014; Armstrong and Brodie, 1999].

We will highlight the econometric methods used in forecasting energy markets. Econometrics methods are appealing because these methods are built upon the economic theory [Bhattacharyya and Timilsina, 2009]. Econometric methods have been widely used by academic researchers and industry practitioners. This chapter will provide an in-depth review of the challenges of dynamics for various energy markets and econometric models on forecasting market dynamics using a case study.

Majority of the forecasting studies in the literature often focus on the forecasting approaches developed for a single energy source (e.g. natural gas forecast). This chapter differentiates from the existing literature by providing a comprehensive review of the market trends for multiple energy sources and highlights the importance of forecasting methods from different energy market perspectives. We cover the market dynamics of multiple energy sources and address the challenges for forecasting these markets. Further, this chapter contributes to an understanding of the complex nature of the energy markets by presenting an overview of various energy market dynamics and the use of forecasting in these dynamic market environments. We also introduce the fundamentals of the underlying economic theory of general equilibrium in this chapter in addition to a practical industry example.

Finally, we studied a practical industry example of forecasting prices for Renewable Electricity Credits (RECs) using the time series method. This is a widely used forecasting method in both academic and industry studies. This practical example provides a forecast for the movement of the future REC prices along with the changing commodity prices under the changes in federal policies. The approach we employed also considers the causal relationship between the dependent and independent variables. Overall, we found that the regional electricity prices in NEPOOL affect future REC prices but not regional electricity prices in PJM. We also found that there is no significant impact of REC prices on the wholesale electricity prices.

The purpose of this example is to introduce how one can analyze and understand the characteristics of time series data for forecasting as well as to introduce an approach to model construct, model testing and estimation outcomes. Thus, this example should guide the readers on the basic steps for forecasting using a specific time series model. It is important to note that we provided this as an illustrative example for the application of time series models and the analysis could substantially be expanded with additional model specifications and robustness testing.

The remainder of the chapter covers the evolution and challenges in forecasting energy markets in Section 2. Applied Methods for forecasting energy markets are discussed in Section 3. Finally, Section 4 provides a case study from renewable energy markets to illustrate a practical application of the forecasting methods.

2. Evolution and Challenges of Forecasting Energy Markets

Substantial developments in the energy industry have occurred across the energy sector, including technology innovations, policy/regulatory reforms, resource shifts and other market dynamics.

Heightened recent focus on energy market forecasting methods have resulted due to the recent substantial development in the energy industry. These development take the form of both market and non-market changes, which have created tremendous variability in market dynamics across the energy sector. Market dynamics affect supply and demand as well as market prices. More accentuated market dynamics, in terms of the order of magnitude of unpredictability or the increased number of factors affecting supply, demand and prices, create an ever-challenging environment to forecast energy markets. Therefore, forecasting energy markets has become more challenging.

Further, due to the interrelated nature of the energy sector, changes in one energy sector can affect other energy sectors. In another example, since natural gas is an input fuel to generate electricity, any change to the economics of natural gas will impact the economics within the electricity markets. Consequently, these collective substantial changes have and can be expected to lead to changes in energy market dynamics, characterized by significantly greater uncertainty in supply, demand and pricing.

By way of background, energy forecasting has evolved tremendously in the past 40 years since the 1970s oil crisis brought focused attention to the impact of energy on consumers and the economy. [Bhattacharyya and Timilsina, 2009]. In the 1980s, simplified methods of energy demand forecasting had been documented in numerous countries, including reliance on energy intensities or an elasticity of energy demand with respect to national income or GDP [Westoby and Pearce, 1984; Codoni *et al.*, 1985]. For example, simple measures of GDP elasticity and energy intensities have been used to forecast energy demand and develop energy policies in China and India [GOI, 2006; Berrah *et al.*, 2007].

The forecasting techniques developed generally comprise three categories of approaches as follows [Bhattacharyya and Timilsina, 2009]:

- econometric models grounded in the economic theories that seek to validate the economic rules empirically;
- engineering-economy models (or end-use models) that attempt to establish accounting coherence using detailed engineering representation of the energy system;
- combination or hybrid models that combine the features of the two traditions of econometric and engineering models.

As discussed above, the focus of this chapter is on econometric methods used to forecast energy. An econometric model is a quantitative approach to establish a statistical causal relationship between the dependent (i.e. outcome) variable and the selected independent variables by using historical data. The statistical relationship can be used to forecast changes in the independent variables and determine their effects on the dependent variable [Varian, 1992].

Econometric estimations are frequently used to forecast energy demand. Major developments in econometric estimation methods have occurred particularly since 1990. According to Griffin [1993], there are three major developments in energy forecasting, including the trans-log revolution, the panel data methods and the discrete choice method [Wirl and Szirucsek, 1990]. These methods are evolved from the basic ordinary least squares approach and allowed researchers to analyze complex energy data empirically. This allowed investigations into capital energy substitutability and technical change questions. A large number of studies applied the trans-log model at the aggregated and disaggregated levels, including Christopoulos [2000], Dahl and Erdogan [2000] and Buranakunaporn and Oczkowsky [2007]. Even the econometric analysis has been applied to the entire energy system using the energy balance framework (e.g. see [Adams and Shachmurove, 2008]). Below, we provide a short overview of primary energy sources and related challenges for predicting the future for these energy sources.

2.1. *Crude oil*

Crude oil is currently the single most dominant energy product consumed for the entire global energy industry. On a global basis, crude oil has a more than 30% share of the primary energy [BP Energy Outlook, 2016]. Within the US, crude oil products accounted for 36.6% of the primary energy consumption in 2015 [EIA, 2017]. An important economic characteristic of the crude oil industry is that it is a global market with significant trade occurring among countries.

Forecasting global crude oil markets has always been challenging due to the difficulties in understanding the supply and demand outlook for all of the distinct economies across the globe along with the difficulties in forecasting the decision-making of the OPEC cartel in its goals to control prices through production limits.

However, with the game-changing oil production technological developments that occurred over the last decade in the US, forecasting crude oil markets has become much more challenging. The oil and gas industry has enabled cost-effective extraction of oil and gas resources from shale rock using hydraulic fracturing and horizontal drilling which led to substantial production increases in the US. Shale rock holds substantial oil and gas resources but without the technological breakthrough, it could not be economically extracted. This abrupt shift led to the US substantially reducing imports of crude oil to meet US refinery demand and to begin to export crude oil production that extends beyond domestic needs. This technology breakthrough has materially impacted the global crude oil markets in terms of market supply and pricing, therefore, introducing challenges for forecasting global crude oil prices. Figure 1 presents the historical global crude oil prices.

Fig. 1. Historical Brent and West Texas Intermediate ("WTI") spot crude oil prices ($/bbl).

Notes: Global crude oil prices showed a precipitous decline in mid-2014 with prices falling from a peak of $115 per barrel in June 2014 to under $35 per barrel in February 2016. Prices have begun to stabilize in more recent months with the figures largely fluctuating around $50 per barrel since late 2016 [EIA, 2018].

There are numerous economic factors that have contributed to the free fall in crude oil prices. First, on the supply side of the equation, the large increase in production from the US shale producers added substantial quantities of supply to the global crude oil market beyond historical levels. In the US, the primary shale crude oil production basins include the Bakken basin located in North Dakota, numerous basins located in Texas including Eagle Ford and the Permian Basin as well as Niobrara (Colorado and Wyoming). Since 2008, US unconventional shale oil production increased substantially from approximately 0.5 million barrels per day (BPD) in 2008 to over 4.5 million barrels per day in 2014 [EIA, 2017]. All else equal, an increase in supply will reduce the market-clearing price.

Importantly, OPEC decided not to make a cut in production levels as it had historically done which would have caused prices to rise by offsetting the increased US production. OPEC's reversal of its past cartel behavior could have been driven by its desire not to help the US shale producers with higher prices (while it lost sales volumes). In addition, OPEC had an economic incentive to maintain its market share in the growing Asian economies.

On the demand side of the equation, lower-than-expected demand resulting from slowing growth in emerging markets, most importantly in China, caused demand growth to lag behind historical levels. The stunted demand was exasperated by the strong US dollar. Crude oil is traded in US dollars and a strong dollar translates to reduced purchasing power of countries that are consuming crude oil. No major energy forecasting organization that we are aware of predicted the precipitous fall in crude oil prices that occurred in the middle of 2014. Figure 2 shows crude oil spot prices and crude oil forward price curves during the period January 2014 to December 2014.

Within the global crude oil market, the prices of crude oil futures contracts traded on exchanges such as the New York Mercantile Exchange or the Intercontinental Exchange are commonly perceived to reflect the expectations of market participants about the future course of crude oil prices [Alquist and Arbatli, 2010]. The futures market provides an important role in information aggregation and price discovery available. The price discovery process involves the interactions of buyers and sellers in the market prices to determine the market price of an asset. The futures market serves an important function of price discovery as informed individuals with judgement participate in these markets to take advantage of new and emerging industry information, which causes price movements to occur commensurate with timely actions taken by market participants in response to new and relevant information. Future markets react quickly to forward-looking information and the transaction cost is much lower in these markets than in the spot market, which

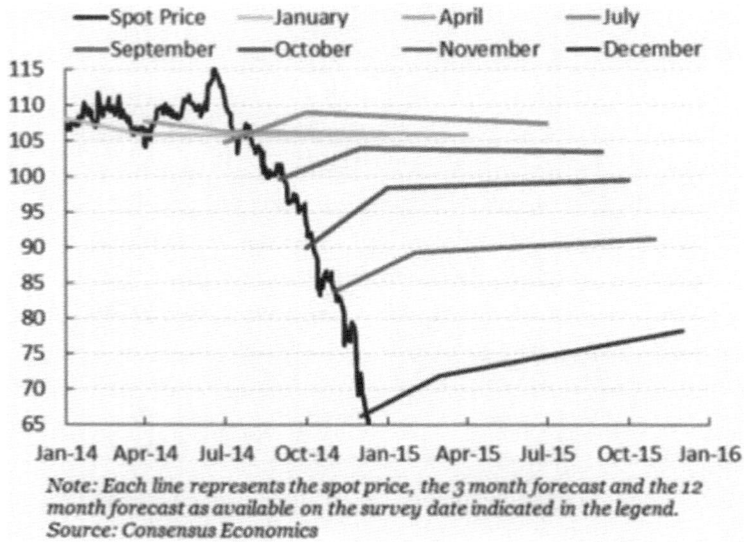

Fig. 2. Evolution of Brent crude oil price forecasts ($US/barrel).

Notes: The forward price curves reflect actual market transactions by market participants that show their then current short-term forecast of crude oil prices. This figure highlights the free fall of crude oil prices, even when market participants continued to believe prices would bottom and rise somewhat and then remain flat [*Financial Times*, 2014].

further facilitates activities in the futures markets, leading to robust evidence of what is likely to happen and therefore relevant information for price discovery. However, as discussed above, market participants did not anticipate the substantial decline in crude oil prices during the precipitous fall in prices that occurred in the middle of 2014.

2.2. *Natural gas*

Natural gas has become an increasingly important fuel source in recent years as a result of technology developments, including the improving economics of shale gas, increasing production of natural gas and liquefied natural gas (LNG) processing, facilitating global trade of natural gas. In addition, the attractiveness of natural gas has increased because it is the lowest carbon-emitting fossil fuel and the US and other countries are becoming increasingly desirous of reducing carbon emissions.

Natural gas markets have historically been regional in nature because of the challenges of transporting natural gas over long distances. There are limited transportation options for natural gas transportation, including pipelines for land-based transportation of natural gas and expensive LNG transportation for waterborne deliveries, which requires liquifying the gaseous product at the origin location and completing a regasification process at the destination location, along with specialized vessels to carry LNG.

Since there is currently no globally integrated market for natural gas, pricing mechanisms vary by regional markets. Understanding the natural gas pricing regimes and trends provides important economic characteristics to inform forecasting of natural gas markets. To put it into more regional context, we provide the analysis of US and Asian natural gas markets.

2.3. *US regional natural gas markets*

Natural gas price formation is driven by the regional natural gas markets, also referred to as pricing hubs in the US. Deregulation of upstream portion of the natural gas industry and the natural gas commodity process facilitated natural gas price formation in the regional markets.

Forecasting US regional natural gas markets has always been challenging due to limited storage capabilities, which exposes supply and demand to equilibrate more contemporaneously in each market. In addition, other factors that affect natural gas markets include weather conditions, proximity to demand, liquidity of supply at that point and current available capacity on pipelines within the system. Another factor that can impact prices is potential fuel competition, specifically with regard to electrical generation that occurs when the price of gas becomes more expensive than the next cost-efficient alternative, i.e. coal or solar power. This fuel competition can occur in the daily energy markets as well as for long-term energy supply/capacity decision.

Similar to crude oil markets, the US Energy Information Administration (EIA) did not forecast the price decline. US regional natural gas price forecasting became more complicated with the development of US shale gas. In early 2008, the potential of US shale gas to become a viable economic resource to be extracted and produced in substantial quantities was simply not on the radar as a feasible solution to the vast majority of energy industry professionals. The development of the US shale gas resources began in earnest around 2008 as a result of numerous factors.[1] The impact

[1]Long-run energy forecasts projected insufficient quantities of natural gas for the US in close proximity and recorded-high natural gas prices during the time period, 2006–2008, creating strong economic incentives to find alternative sources of natural gas. As a result, some industry participants sought to determine if new (i.e. unconventional) methods of extracting natural gas could become economically viable with record-high natural gas prices and depressed outlook for future natural gas supply. With a focused effort, substantial technological innovations were rapidly observed in drilling horizontal wells in conjunction with a vertical well as well as injecting a specialized liquid substance

Fig. 3. Historical Henry Hub natural gas spot price ($/MMBTU).

Notes: Henry Hub is a location in Erath, Louisiana, whose price is synonymously used with the NYMEX price of gas and is generally considered the benchmark price of natural gas in North America. In the US, natural gas spot prices have dropped 79% since 2008 from almost $14 per MMBtu to about $3 per MMBtu currently. The historical prices demonstrate numerous price spikes in the years 2001, 2005/2006 and 2008.

Source: Energy Information Administration (EIA).

of this development was substantial as the US has been able to substantially increase domestic production of natural gas rather than become heavily reliant on imported natural gas via LNG to meet domestic demand. Further, the US has enough natural gas supply to meet domestic needs and export excess to other countries. Since the shale revolution took hold in 2008, overall US natural gas production increased from about 55 Bcfd to 75 Bcfd by 2016, with the production estimated to double from 2015 to 2040.[2] The expanded natural gas supply resulting from the abundance of economically extractable natural gas resources has led to a general trend of reductions in natural gas prices. Figure 3 shows the US Henry Hub location.[3]

into the rock to fracture (or break) the shale sediment into small pieces, and loosen and capture the natural gas in a cost-effective manner. Substantial technological learnings occurred in years preceding 2008, with substantial breakthroughs in 2008 and further improvements since that time.

[2]The proportion of natural gas production made up by shale gas has increased from about 12% in 2008 to 53% by 2016, with a forecast of 65% by 2040. While shale gas plays are geographically distributed throughout much of the country, adding the Northeast, Rocky Mountains, Great Plains, the Southwest and even areas of the South to the traditional Gulf and Midcontinent production areas, the prime region of interest is the Appalachian Basin focused in the US Northeast. The oft-noted Marcellus play centered in Pennsylvania has been the main focus of the shale revolution to date, while the partially coextensive Utica play currently focused in eastern Ohio should comprise the next wave of shale gas growth. It should also be noted that there is much increased conventional natural gas production occurring in the Permian Basin in the Southwest, as evidenced by the strong 11% annual growth over the last 5 years to almost 6 Bcfd currently.

[3]Natural gas cost savings to consumers over this period could be more than $175 billion, while associated electric cost savings could be more than $200 billion. Further, the combination of low natural gas prices and abundant supply has helped foster increases in demand such as for industrial

2.4. *Asian regional natural gas markets*

Natural gas prices in Pacific Basin have historically been tied to crude oil prices. This phenomenon resulted because the historical contracting practices for natural gas products within Asian markets typically included those indexed to crude oil or petroleum product prices [EIA, 2015]. Internationally traded natural gas has been largely indexed to crude oil prices such as North Sea Brent or Japan customs-cleared crude (JCC) because of the liquidity and transparency of crude oil prices and the substitutability of natural gas and petroleum products in certain markets [EIA, 2015].

Numerous locations in Asia, including coastal China, Japan, Taiwan, South Korea, are particularly dependent on more expensive LNG because there are limited regional natural resources of economic natural gas. Further, the interrelated nature of current crude oil and natural gas markets in Asia means that a supply shock affecting crude oil markets also affects the natural gas markets in Asia. Therefore, forecasting methods must address the interrelated nature of different energy products.[4]

As a result of the substantial reductions in crude oil prices beginning in late 2014, LNG prices in Asia also showed reductions. Figure 4 shows the recent historical trends in prices of LNG delivered to Japan. Numerous market-related factors affected supply and demand over this extended period, and there was substantial impact from macro-economic related factors as well.

Major energy forecasts of LNG prices are completed by government agencies and are mostly produced from the large-scale simulation tools they use to replicate the market function under a variety of scenarios to depict the future of the energy sector. For example, the International Energy Agency (IEA) conducts a World Energy Outlook which includes three primary modules to represent the economic characteristics of future energy consumption (by sector for industry, transport, building and agriculture and non-energy use), energy supply (fossil fuel and bioenergy) and energy transformation (power, heat generation, oil refining and others). The primary outputs from the model for each region are energy demand, supply by fuel and investment needs as well as CO_2 [IEA, 2014].

---

uses in feedstock and process applications. A new manufacturing renaissance has already begun, as petrochemical and other projects have been announced to take advantage of these recent natural gas industry benefits.

[4]To the extent that new market approaches are developed for natural gas, these would need to be incorporated into the forecasting methodology. For example, while long-term crude oil-indexed contracts have been Asia's dominant pricing mechanism, to the extent that natural gas trades on the spot market as one-time transactions, or under short-term contracts which more closely reflect international natural gas supply and demand balances becoming more prominent, forecasting methodology will need to reflect the underlying economic conditions.

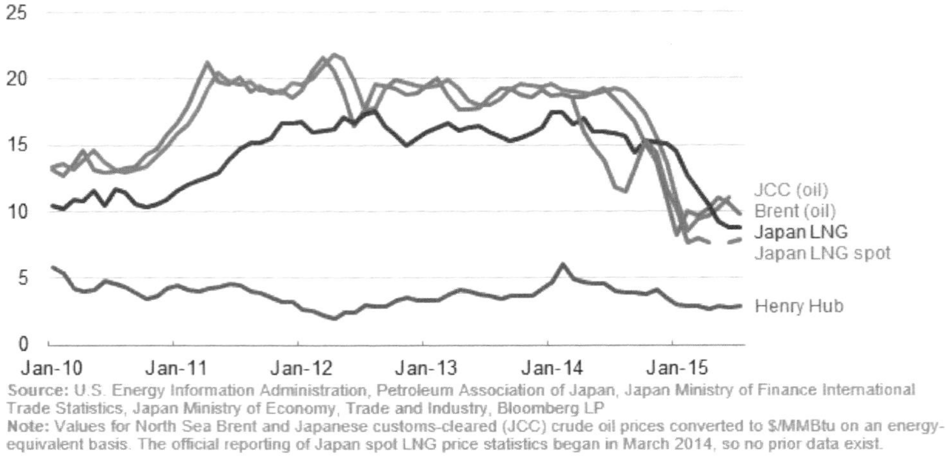

Fig. 4. Historical LNG Japan prices ($/MMBTU).

Notes: The declines in Japan LNG largely track the Brent crude oil prices as well as the observed price declines in Brent crude oil and relatively stable trend of the US regional Henry Hub natural gas price index.
Source: Bloomberg, LNGJLNP Index-Closing Price.

The recent declining trends in LNG prices have impacted the IEA's forecast of LNG prices. In the 2014 forecast, the IEA forecasted an approximately $14/mmbtu price for LNG delivered to Japan in 2020 in its New Policies Scenario [IEA, 2014]. In the 2015 forecast, the IEA reduced its forecast price for LNG delivered to Japan to $12.2/MMBtu price [IEA, 2014]. As discussed above, the interrelated nature of current crude oil and natural gas markets in Asia requires forecasting methods to address the interrelated nature of different energy products.

2.5. *Electricity*

Over the past three decades, electricity markets in the US and many international countries have progressed from a fully rate-regulated regime to wholesale deregulated electricity markets and to some extent deregulated markets. The historical context of deregulation is helpful to put today's challenges into perspective.

In the US, the Energy Policy Act of 1992 [IEA, 2014] was a significant step that allowed for more competition in the electricity industry. Among other changes, this Act allowed electricity to be sold at market prices, as opposed to a heavily regulated rate, and allowed for unregulated firms to independently buy and sell electricity on the open wholesale market. This greatly increased the incentives for trading. It also provided for a new category of market participants, electric power marketers.

Marketers were allowed to buy and sell electricity at whatever price the market would bear, similar to traders of stocks on Wall Street or traders of commodities on the Chicago Board of Trade.

The regulatory responsibility for implementing these changes fell to the Federal Energy Regulatory Commission (FERC). FERC issued orders in 1996 that required utilities to make their transmission systems available to others to move electricity and reach customers, and the detailed rules providing for these changes were adopted in 1998 [FERC, 2010]. Systems with independent system operators, such as PJM, New York and New England, were well positioned to create open markets for electricity. In late 1999, FERC issued an order that provided incentives for the utilities it regulates to join newly-defined Regional Transmission Organizations, or RTOs [FERC, 1999]. The RTOs would support increased trading and could decide to take the further step of becoming independent system operators, but there was no requirement for utilities to join RTOs, nor for RTOs to take on the full responsibility of becoming independent system operators. When not required, many RTOs have been formed and the shift toward increased independent system operators continues to this day. Even without the independent system operator function, RTOs have helped improve the efficiency of the markets by supporting competitive market structure, lowering the cost of moving electricity over longer distances.

Meanwhile, states took action to promote more competitive retail electricity markets, with considerable variation among the actions taken at the state level. State laws called for a fundamental restructuring of the industry in, for example, California [EIA, 1998] and Texas [EIA, 2014]. Provisions allowing for retail competition, where homeowners and other customers could decide which supplier they wanted to provide energy to (which would be transmitted to their homes on their traditional utility's wires), were adopted in many states [DOE, 2007]. At the wholesale level, it became easier for private companies that were not subject to sell-at-cost-based state regulation to build power plants and sell their electricity at market prices. The old system of vertically integrated utilities has been breaking down, particularly with increased competition among electricity generators.

Fast forward to today, the US has continued to develop wholesale power markets but new challenges have emerged. The lower commodity prices of natural gas, resulting from the abundant shale gas resources, has put downward price pressure on natural gas which has led to price reductions of power as well. Lower market-clearing prices for power result because the lower natural gas fuel costs substantially lower the short-run marginal cost (SRMC) of natural gas-fired power plants because fuel costs comprise the majority of the SRMC. Further, natural gas power plants have historically been the marginal power plant that set the overall market-clearing price where total supply equals total demand for power in a geographic market for a specific time period. The lower market-clearing prices for power have raised concerns of financial adequacy of power generation facilities, such as nuclear, coal and natural gas plants. In addition, rapid integration of intermittent renewable resources, particularly wind that is generated at almost zero cost, raised grid reliability issues [Deng *et al.*, 2015; Dillig *et al.*, 2016]. These shifting supply-side market dynamics create uncertainty and additional risks. Further, slower growth in the demand for power than historically observed has further depressed the market-clearing prices for power and created additional demand-side market-based risks [EIA, 2016].

2.6. *Renewable, emerging technologies and energy efficiency and climate policy*

The domestic and global energy industry is inextricably linked to political and regulatory systems that collectively implement government objectives for the energy industry, including economic incentives for investment and regulatory oversight. We will use the US state REC prices to understand the impact of federal policy on the future prices of RECs employing time series forecasting methods in Section 4.1.

In recent years, increased US regulatory intervention and requirements associated with environmental policy goals have created preferences for heavier reliance on cleaner sources of energy. US Regulatory and policy initiatives have increased and are expected to further increase the demand for renewable power and, to some extent, natural gas-fired power plants (which is the lowest CO_2 emission fossil fuel). Specifically, Energy Policy Act of 2005 fostered renewable energy investments, including wind and solar energy, through tax incentives, such as Production Tax Credits (PTC) and Incentive Tax Credits (ITC), which drove the increasing demand and supply of renewable energy investments [Bolinger *et al.*, 2009]. The PTC policy provides financial compensation on a unit of output basis (dollar per kWh) of wind generation produced during the first 10 years of operation. Wind capacity installations have grown substantially across the country with the support of federal incentives [Eryilmaz *et al.*, 2016]. In addition to the federal support, US states have initiated various incentives for renewable energy generation. Renewable Portfolio Standards (RPS) is one of the most well-known energy regulatory mandates specifically designed to increase production of renewable energy generation. This policy requires a certain percentage of electricity generated from renewable resources (e.g. 20% of electricity generated from renewable resources by 2020). The application and achievement goals of RPS policies are distinct for every state.

Although the implementation and the required goals vary in each state, the common goal of these standards is to develop a REC market. RECs are tradable commodities that reflect the environmental attributes of electricity being produced and credits are earned with the production of renewable electricity that are also used to comply with the RPS mandates. RECs that are administered in the compliance market receive a unique tracking number from the state agency (e.g. MRETS in Minnesota) and they can be traded in the RECs market among the generators and utilities [Heeter *et al.*, 2011]. In other words, a qualified generator can produce and sell RECs to retailers or retailers can buy RECs from a utility that has excess amount of RECs due to overproduction. Although RECs provide incentives for the renewable energy generators, price uncertainties in the RECs market affect the renewable electricity sector [Fell *et al.*, 2012].

An additional and recent policy is the state-level policy surrounding Net Energy Metering (NEM). NEM is the state-level incentive specifically for distributed generation, referred to as behind-the-meter because it resides at customer locations. The NEM policy enables residential solar consumers to generate solar electricity for their own consumption and to be able to sell excess amount of electricity generated back to the wholesale power grid and to be compensated for the sale of the excess power generation [EEI, 2016].

These policies have promoted the integration of renewable resources, particularly in power generation. The intermittent nature of renewable power (i.e. only when the sun shines or the wind blows) and limited energy storage capabilities make forecasting renewable energy more challenging [Hong, 2014]. The difficulties in accurately predicting wind and solar generation is one of the biggest challenges in renewable energy forecasting. It becomes particularly more challenging because of the wide geographical distribution of these resources and unpredictable nature of their share in the electricity generation mix. To give an example, wind generation during times when the grid is congested (i.e. when energy generation is more expensive) is a more cost-effective resource for the generators. However, wind is intermittent and it is highly uncertain to predict the cost of generation from this resource during grid congestion. On the other hand, large amount of electricity generated from distributed solar energy during times when the electricity demand is low may result in extremely low voltage, which could create reliability issues at the feeder level of the transmission network [Palmintier *et al.*, 2016].

Tremendous research and development has occurred and continues, and the predictability of the changes and the order of magnitude on impact and timing are not easy to anticipate. All of these technological developments have created discussions about the appropriate utility regulation and business model going forward to meet the future energy needs under policy and market uncertainty.

3. Applied Methods for Forecasting Energy Markets

3.1. *Energy demand*

Changing policy and regulations in energy has been one of the important drivers of the changing trends in energy demand. In fact, policy is not the only factor that influences energy demand. Choice theory in traditional economics is the foundation of demand for economic matters, such as consumption, investment and savings. In energy economics literature, energy demand is also based on traditional economic utility theory. Traditional economic theory suggests that price of a good is the main driver of its demand. Therefore, economists have conducted extensive research to understand the relationship between energy demand and energy prices.

Demand for energy resources has been widely studied in applied research. Early research by Deaton [1974], Houthakker [1970, 1974] and Bohi and Zimmerman [1984] have demonstrated the dynamic nature of energy demand. Further, predicting future demand is critical for planning the allocation of resources and meeting energy needs of future generations.

Demand for energy is mostly derived from the demand for energy services, such as oil for transportation, natural gas and electricity for lighting, heating and cooling [Platchkov and Pollitt, 2011]. The utility function of an economic agent (i.e. household and businesses) includes the energy services and the economic agent maximizes its utility subject to its budget constraints. Equation (1) illustrates the utility maximization problem of the economic agent i.

$$\max_{\{e_i\}} \mathrm{u}_i(e_i) = \max \prod_{i=1}^{N} e_i^{(\alpha_i)} \text{ subject to } y_i = \sum_{i=1}^{N} p_i e_i \tag{1}$$

The solution of the utility maximization problem yields a demand function that is a function of income (y) and energy prices (p_1, p_2), as shown in Eq. (2) [Mas-Collel *et al.*, 1995; Levin and Milgrom, 2004; Alberini and Flippini, 2011],

$$e_i^* = f(y_i, p_i) \tag{2}$$

For the sake of simplicity, we assume Cobb–Douglas functional form (i.e. linear) throughout this chapter. We define demand model in Eq. (3), where e_i represents the energy demand for economic agent i, P_i represents energy prices, Y_i represents income, X_i represents other factors affecting energy demand such as Gross Domestic

Product (GDP) or home size of an household and finally, ε_i is the identically and independently distributed error term. In this econometric regression equation, a_0, b_1, b_2 and b_3 are the estimated coefficients to predict energy demand.

$$e_i = a_0 + b_1 \cdot P_i + b_2 \cdot Y_i + b_3 \cdot X_i + \varepsilon_i \tag{3}$$

Considering the dynamic nature of the energy demand, the model specification adjusts for the short-term and long-term response to income and price changes. In the case of energy users who are unable to adjust instantly for the optimal amount of energy consumed due to production or technological constraints, Eq. (4) accounts for this adjustment with $e_{t-1,i}$ and the estimated coefficient b_4 is the adjustment factor to the optimal energy demand based on the actual demand.

$$e_{t,i} = a_0 + b_1 \cdot P_{t,i} + b_2 \cdot Y_{t,i} + b_3 \cdot X_{t,i} + b_4 \cdot e_{t-1,i} + \varepsilon_{t,i} \tag{4}$$

Depending on the research focus and study objectives, model specification can be modified [Bhattacharyya and Timilsina, 2009]. For example, this modeling framework can also account for regional variation, home size or seasonality. In Section 3, we provide concrete application of this modeling framework with the examples from the energy industry.

3.2. *Energy supply*

Energy supply is also primarily driven by the energy prices [Fezzi, 2007]. The law of supply suggests that an increase in price of a good leads to an increase in the quantity offered (or supplied) of that good. The energy supplier solves the profit maximization problem that is shown in Eq. (5) to produce a given amount of energy [Varian, 1992; Jebaraj and Iniyan, 2006],

$$\max_{\{e_j\}} \Omega_j(e_j) = \max \sum_{j}^{N} p_j e_j \text{ subject to } m_j = f(e_j). \tag{5}$$

The solution of the profit maximization problem yields a supply function that is the function of units of output (m_j) and energy prices (p_j), as shown in Eq. (6),

$$e_j^* = f(e_j, w_j). \tag{6}$$

Another way of expressing the energy supplier's problem is the cost minimization such that the supplier produces a certain amount of energy with the least cost. Equation (7) shows the minimization problem, where e_j is the amount of inputs needed to produce m_j quantity of energy, q_j is the input prices for energy production (e.g. technology, labor, water) that is subject to the quantity of energy to be produced m_j.

$$\min_{\{x_j\}} C_j(x_j) = \min \sum_j^N q_j x_j \text{ subject to } m_j = f(x_j). \tag{7}$$

In this case, the solution of the minimization problem yields the conditional demand equations where e_j becomes a function of input prices to produce energy and the total output of energy as shown in Eq. (8):

$$e_j^* = f(x_j, m_j). \tag{8}$$

3.3. *Overview of general equilibrium*

After deriving energy demand and energy supply, market equilibrium can be defined as the point where the amount of energy demanded is equal to the amount of energy supplied in a competitive energy market. A competitive energy market can be defined as the economic agents are price-taking, meaning that individual economic agents cannot directly influence the market price, as shown in Eq. (9).

$$\sum_i^N e_i^*(p) = \sum_j^M e_j^*(p) \tag{9}$$

There is a significant amount of research on general equilibrium modeling using numerical methods. In this chapter, we focus on partial equilibrium analysis using empirical methods while encouraging readers to explore structural models and applications in computational general equilibrium models (CGE) from General Trade Analysis Project (GTAP) by Purdue University and the relevant resources.

4. Case Study

4.1. *An example from renewable energy market: Forecasting REC prices*

The relationship between renewable energy policies has received little attention of researchers. In this example, we evaluate the interaction between these two renewable energy policies in the US: federal PTC and the market for RECs from state RPS policy. This example provides a forecast for the movement of the future RECs prices along with the changing commodity prices under the changes in federal policies. It is important to understand the impact of the federal PTC policy on state policy is because the PTC policy was set to be retired by the federal government several times in the past. The decision by the federal government had implications on renewable energy every time it announced to retire and enact the policy. Table 1

Table 1. Legislative history of PTC policy.

Date announced	Duration	Effective duration
08/08/2005	24 months	01/01/06–12/31/07
12/20/2006	12 months	01/01/08–12/31/08
10/03/2008	12 months	01/01/09–12/31/09
02/17/2009	24 months	01/01/10–12/31/12
01/02/2013	12 months	01/02/2013–12/31/2013

Note: Most recently, the PTC pays for the renewable energy investors 2.2¢/kWh for wind and geothermal resources and 1.1¢/kWh for other renewable resources (PTC is adjusted to the inflation over time).
Source: Lou (2011) and Wiser *et al.* (2007).

provides the legislative history for the PTC policy. As shown in the table, this policy was announced at a certain date and had an effective time period. After the time period ended, the government had an option to enact the policy again or retire it completely. This created uncertainty in the renewable energy markets because the investors who rely on the federal incentive were unsure whether their investment was going to be subsidized due to the uncertainty in the policy.

RECs are market-based and PTC policy is a price-based policy (i.e. subsidy paid per MWh generation in the next 10 years of investment) for increasing the supply of the renewable energy. However, there is uncertainty about the future renewable energy policies (i.e. REC market and PTC) after mandatory requirements are met. Understanding the impact of this federal policy as well as the relationship between state and federal policies is important for forecasting and future decision-making. Moreover, PTC is a federal tax program, whereas the RPS which generates the market for RECs are at the state level. Therefore, identifying the interaction between the state-level and the federal-level policies are important since the design of these policies is different in terms of cost paid by the government. This example evaluates the policy and the impact of the federal policy on future REC prices. We also test the causal short-term impact of electricity prices on the RECs prices based on historical time series data.

Data are obtained from the EIA and the MarexSpectron Company. Our data include the daily spot prices for the national REC market and the spot prices for the electricity prices. The REC market data include daily historical data on both the compliance and the voluntary[5] market bid and offer prices. We only used the compliance market data for this analysis. We also contracted a policy variable based

[5]Compliance Markets for RECs: RPS goals drive the RECs trading, utilities and the power-generating companies to buy and sell RECs to meet their state-level requirements. Voluntary Markets for RECs: Consumers and institutions purchase renewable energy on a voluntary basis [Heeter and Bird, 2011].

on our knowledge on when the government announced the PTC and when the PTC is set to expire. Therefore, a dummy variable (i.e. a 0/1 variable) will be generated based on this historical information. Table 1 summarizes the legislative history of the PTC policy.

Table 2 provides the descriptive statistics of our data and Fig. 5 includes the historical daily prices for the REC compliance and voluntary markets.

We used time series data for two regions that have a market for RECs, PJM and NEPOOL, where the average daily prices differ across the regions. Regional REC markets cover multiple states. The PJM region includes the trading states: Delaware,

Table 2. Descriptive statistics for the market price data May 2006–November 2012.

Region	Wholesale electricity prices ($/MWh)	REC prices ($/MWh)
NEPOOL	62	32
PJM	58	86

Note: All variables are in daily format.

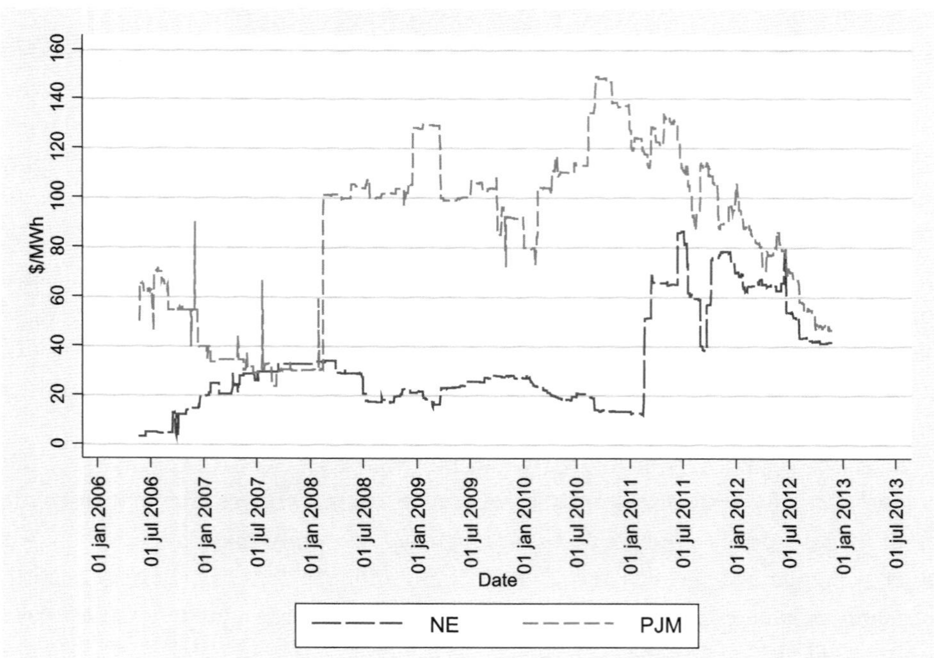

Fig. 5. Daily REC prices.

Ohio, Maryland, New Jersey, Pennsylvania, Texas and Washington D.C. NEPOOL region includes the trading states: Massachusetts, Maine, New Hampshire, Rhode Island and Connecticut. PJM region had the highest average REC prices ($86/MWh) and NEPOOL average prices were ($32 MWh).

Prior to developing a forecasting model with any time series data, we need to determine whether it is suitable for forecasting. More specifically, in order to proceed with the analysis, we need to determine whether price series are "stationary". By definition, stationary time series is defined as the series with constant mean, variance and autocorrelations can be well approximated by sufficiently long time averages [Enders, 2010].

As a first step, we plotted the actual spot prices and the lagged REC prices as in Fig. 5. After visually inspecting the data series, we see that daily REC prices are fluctuating between 2006 and 2012; however, there is a downward trend in the last couple of years. Visual assessment of the price series is useful but not sufficient to determine stationarity. Therefore, we need to employ formal statistical tests. Dickey–Fuller and KPSS tests are the most commonly used statistical tests for stationarity. The null hypothesis for Dickey–Fuller test statistic is that "the time series is non-stationary". It essentially tests whether the relationship between the time series and its lags are statistically significant (i.e. tests whether the coefficient δ is statistically different from zero in equation

$$y_t = a_o + \delta y_{t-1} + \varepsilon_t. \tag{10}$$

We present the results for Dickey–Fuller test, as shown in Table 3. We found that REC prices are non-stationary because the Dickey–Fuller test statistic is not sufficiently greater than the p-value [Wooldridge, 2009; Brockwell and Davis, 1986]. In addition, the test statistic was not sufficiently greater than the 1%, 5% or 10% critical value, suggesting that the series is non-stationary. We also tested whether the REC prices are trend stationary, have a drift (i.e. constant term) and whether there is a significant dependency on the lagged values. We found that the estimated coefficients on trend, constant and lagged REC prices are statistically different from zero, except for the second lag of REC prices in PJM. The estimated coefficients are also presented in Table 3.

The most common method to convert non-stationary data into stationary data is differencing (i.e. $\Delta y_t = y_t - y_{t-1}$). Although differencing converts the data into stationary, stationary data from the first differencing also eliminates the information about the causal effects of the federal policy in such frequent time series data. The differenced data are stationary, but we cannot estimate the change in the slope or the intercept of the time series based on policy intervention. Therefore, we have used

Table 3. Dickey–Fuller Test Statistic for REC prices.

Region	**Dickey–Fuller test statistic**	**1% critical value**	**5% critical value**	**10% critical value**	***p*-value**
NEPOOL	−1.183	−3.960	−3.410	−3.120	0.9139
PJM	−1.243	−3.960	−3.410	−3.120	0.9013

	NEPOOL	PJM
REC [t–1]	−0.006 (−1.18)	−0.0072 (−1.24)
REC [t–2]	−0.027 (0.037)	−0.123** (−2.73)
Trend	0.00003 (0.0001)	−0.00004 (0.0002)
Constant	0.212 (0.162)	0.906 (0.504)

Notes: *t*-statistics in parenthesis. $^{*}p < 0.05$, $^{**}p < 0.01$, $^{***}p < 0.001$.

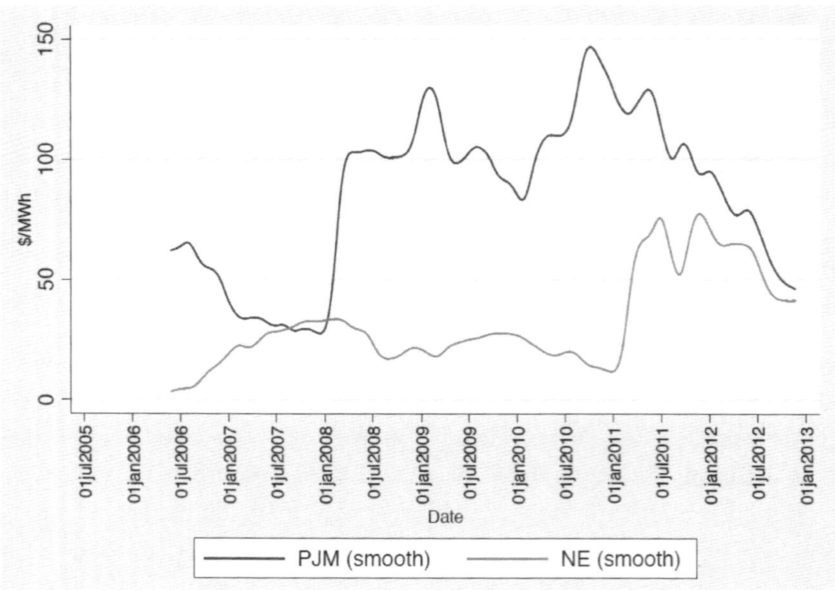

Fig. 6. Daily detrended REC prices.

Hodrick–Prescott smoothing method, which is a common method to remove trend movements in non-stationary time series data in business cycle literature [Baum, 2006]. The detrended series and the historical prices are shown in Fig. 6.

Using the detrended data, we now introduce the policy intervention, the federal PTC policy and see whether there is an effect of the policy on the REC market. These policy decisions are often perceived as shocks to the market and we test whether the changes in policy intervention have an impact on REC market prices.[6] The most recent PTC expiration was set for December 2012 and in early January 2013, the policy was reactivated until January 2014. We define "intervention" as the time when the federal policy is announced to be effective (i.e. no time lapse in the PTC policy and investors are certain they will receive the tax credits), which makes it a dummy variable that takes the values of "1" for the associated month and takes the value of "0" in the remaining days. We are interested in the effect of the PTC policy on the REC market prices.

Federal government announces the day that the PTC will be effective and the day it will expire. PTC was announced and expired many times in the past, therefore we divided the historical price data into two different time segments and included the continuous "time" variables, into the regression: t is a continuous time variable, which takes the time values where the PTC is not announced. When $PTC_t = 1$, we estimate $\hat{\alpha}_2$ which denotes the time that the PTC is effective. We estimate the following linear equation with Ordinary Least Squares (OLS) approach, which is a method to predict an outcome variable by minimizing the sum of squared errors.[7] We also included the time trend and an indicatory variable taking value 1 for the associated month of a year and otherwise 0. The monthly dummy (i.e. indicator) variables control for the seasonality and the unobserved time effects associated to each month on REC prices.

$$\log(REC_t) = \alpha_o + \alpha_1 PTC_t + \alpha_2 t + \sum_{i}^{12} \alpha_{3,i}\,\text{Month}_t + \varepsilon_t \tag{11}$$

Our results are shown in Table 4. The estimated coefficients on the policy variable (PTC_t) are positive and highly significant for each region, indicating that after the announcement of the continuation of the policy intervention, REC prices are higher. More specifically, compared to the REC prices in NE, it is approximately 0.02% higher and PJM is approximately 0.017% higher after the federal government announced that the PTC policy will be continued. This could be explained by the increase in the supply of renewable electricity with the incentives offered to the investors. We have tested the change in slope as well as the change in the intercept using standard t-tests. Based on the regression results, we can conclude that the estimated coefficients are significantly different from zero, which suggests that there are differences in the REC price market before and after the "event". Moreover,

[6]This method is also known as Interruptible Time Series, which predicts the impact of a policy intervention in high-frequency time series data.

[7]For more detailed information about this modelling approach, see Wooldridge [2009].

Table 4. Estimations results.

Variable	NEPOOL	PJM
PTC_t	0.0208***	0.0169***
	(0.00124)	(0.000831)
t(trend)	0.00000568	0.00000287*
	(0.00000348)	(0.00000126)
2 month	0.0975*	0.0427
	(0.0414)	(0.0453)
3 month	0.114**	0.0503
	(0.0420)	(0.0453)
4 month	0.163***	0.0797
	(0.0443)	(0.0447)
5 month	0.0961	0.061
	(0.0536)	(0.0440)
6 month	−0.125	0.0466
	(0.0657)	(0.0425)
7 month	−0.123*	0.0239
	(0.0585)	(0.0429)
8 month	−0.121*	0.00319
	(0.0550)	(0.0442)
9 month	−0.0902	−0.0332
	(0.0524)	(0.0460)
10 month	−0.0365	−0.0265
	(0.0494)	(0.0481)
11 month	0.00333	−0.0105
	(0.0510)	(0.0489)
12 month	0.0254	0.0523
	(0.0503)	(0.0475)
Constant	10.03***	11.10***
	(0.0324)	(0.0352)
N	2374	2374

Note: REC prices are in natural logarithm form and the values presented in the brackets are standard errors.

these results suggest that the detrended series are stationary and still include the information of interest.

Note that the intervention (i.e. PTC_t in this example) could have been defined differently based on the researcher's interest such as taking the value 1 during the lapse period. Additionally, effects of different interventions (i.e. effect of government announcing period, lapse period and effective period) could have been tested in the same model specification as well. We presented the simplest model as a reference. An important assessment, which we did not discuss in this chapter, is the assessment of the autocorrelation, which is the delayed correlation of a

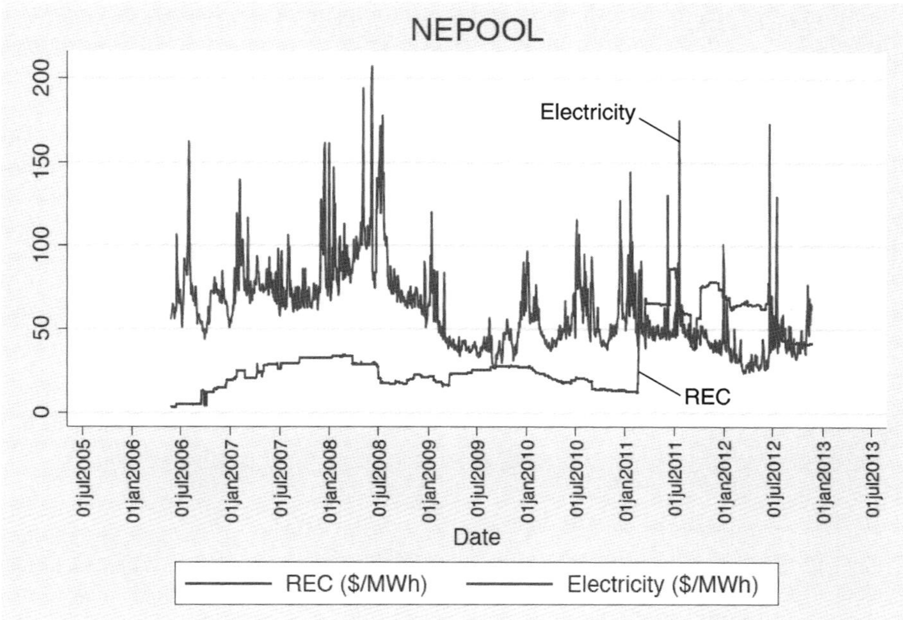

Fig. 7. REC prices and electricity prices in NEPOOL and PJM regions.

given series. We recommend Enders [1995] as an invaluable resource for further information.[8]

4.2. *Vector Autoregression model*

The second empirical method that will be employed in this study is the Vector Autoregression (VAR) model. VAR models are mostly used with the time series data that are stationary to understand the dynamic relationship between the two series [Enders, 1995]. In this example, we examine the future relationship between REC prices and electricity prices in NEPOOL and PJM as well as the causal impact of PTC policy on the REC prices.

The VAR method allows us to answer the question: Does existence of PTC cause decrease/increase on the prices of the market for RECs in the future given there are other markets affecting the RECs prices? Granger causality test will be applied to test for the future causal relationship between the policy of PTC and the RECs [Enders, 1995]. A potential limitation of this approach could be the identification

[8] An example alternative specification could be
$\log(REC_t) = \alpha_0 + \alpha_1 \log(REC_{t-1}) + \alpha_2 PTC_t + \alpha_3 t + \sum_i^{12} \alpha_{4,i}\,\text{Month}_t + \varepsilon_t$.

problem and the strong assumption that announcing PTC is the primary shock for the REC market, whereas there can be other potential shocks that are omitted from the analysis — that could be tested in future research (e.g. economic recession and level of renewable energy investments decrease significantly or there is a sudden high amount of purchase/sell in the REC market). We define a system for both REC and electricity prices, where REC price series can be affected by the current or lagged values of the electricity prices, or vice versa. Equation (11) presents the estimated VAR model. As shown in the equation, we specify REC prices as a function of its lags and the electricity prices while the electricity prices are specified as a function of REC prices, lagged electricity prices. To ensure stationarity, we take the first difference of the REC and the electricity prices for VAR analysis. We tested the differenced series with Dickey–Fuller test and confirmed that both the first difference of electricity and REC price series result in stationary series.

$$\Delta REC_t = \alpha_{10} + \alpha_{12}\Delta REC_{t-1} + \alpha_{13}\Delta Elect_{t-1}$$
$$\Delta Elec_t = \alpha_{20} + \alpha_{21}\Delta Elec_{t-1} + \alpha_{22}\Delta REC_{t-1} \tag{12}$$

The results from VAR analysis include estimated coefficients for the variables specified in Eq. (11) and presented in Table 5.

We found that the regional electricity prices in NEPOOL influence future REC prices and the estimated coefficient is statistically significant at 95% significance level. More specifically, a dollar increase in wholesale electricity prices in NEPOOL

Table 5. Estimations results.

	NEPOOL	PJM
Equation 1: REC		
ΔREC [t–1]	−0.03	−0.174***
	(−0.02)	(−5.10)
ΔElec [t–1]	−0.0133*	−0.0107
	(−2.43)	(−1.15)
Constant	0.035	0.10
	(0.59)	(0.84)
Equation 2: Electricity		
ΔElec [t–1]	0.0268	0.0304
	(0.76)	(0.06)
ΔREC [t–1]	0.188	0.131
	(0.81)	(1.01)
Constant	0.177	0.43
	(0.65)	(0.96)
Number of Observations	908	934

Notes: t-statistics in parenthesis. $^{*}p < 0.05$, $^{**}p < 0.01$, $^{***}p < 0.001$.

is associated with a cent decrease in future REC prices. Similarly, a dollar increase in PJM wholesale electricity prices is associated with about one cent decrease in REC prices in PJM. We found that there is no significant impact of REC prices on the wholesale electricity prices. This could be explained by the fact that REC market is not large enough to influence the prices in the wholesale electricity market.

We assumed that the first lag of prices is appropriate for this VAR model, however, in order to compare the model goodness-of-fit, we recommend using Akeike Information Criterion (AIC) and/or Bayesian Information Criterion (BIC) [Gujarati and Porter, 2009] to select between competing models.

One of the primary outcomes of the VAR model is impulse-response function, which illustrates the direction and significance of the future relationship between the REC and electricity prices using the estimated coefficient from Eq. (11). The confidence intervals in the impulse-response function are created using the standard errors of the estimated coefficients. These impulse-response functions show that the impact of electricity prices on REC prices is short term, i.e. the next 1–5 days depending on the region. Figure 8 presents the impulse response function between REC and electricity markets in both NE and PJM regions. This figure illustrates the short-term future relationship between REC prices and electricity prices. In this specific example, we considered the 10-day forecast and we see that the increase in REC prices is associated with an increase in the electricity prices. Remember that we used the first difference of the REC and electricity price series that are stationary, and the observed shock prices will not be persistent. When the impulse is the regional REC prices, the response of the electricity prices is positive the next day for PJM, but then the response goes down to zero indicating there is no impact after a day. For NEPOOL, the response of the electricity prices is fluctuating for the following 5 days, where we see a positive response on the second and fourth days, while response is negative on the next and third days. These impulse-response functions show the short-term impact of electricity prices on REC prices, i.e. for the next 1–5 days, depending on the region. These graphs are produced using Stata software, and they include the 95% confidence intervals, as shown in the figures.

This practical exercise helps us understand the statistical relationship between the REC prices and electricity prices in the near future. Findings suggest that the policy interventions have an impact on the REC market prices. Changes in policy decisions and government actions on policy announcements influence the markets. Further, renewable market is highly affected by the wholesale electricity prices in the short term. This short-term relationship is important to understand as more renewables are being integrated in the system and the causal relationship between the electricity prices. However, long-term relationship between the REC prices and

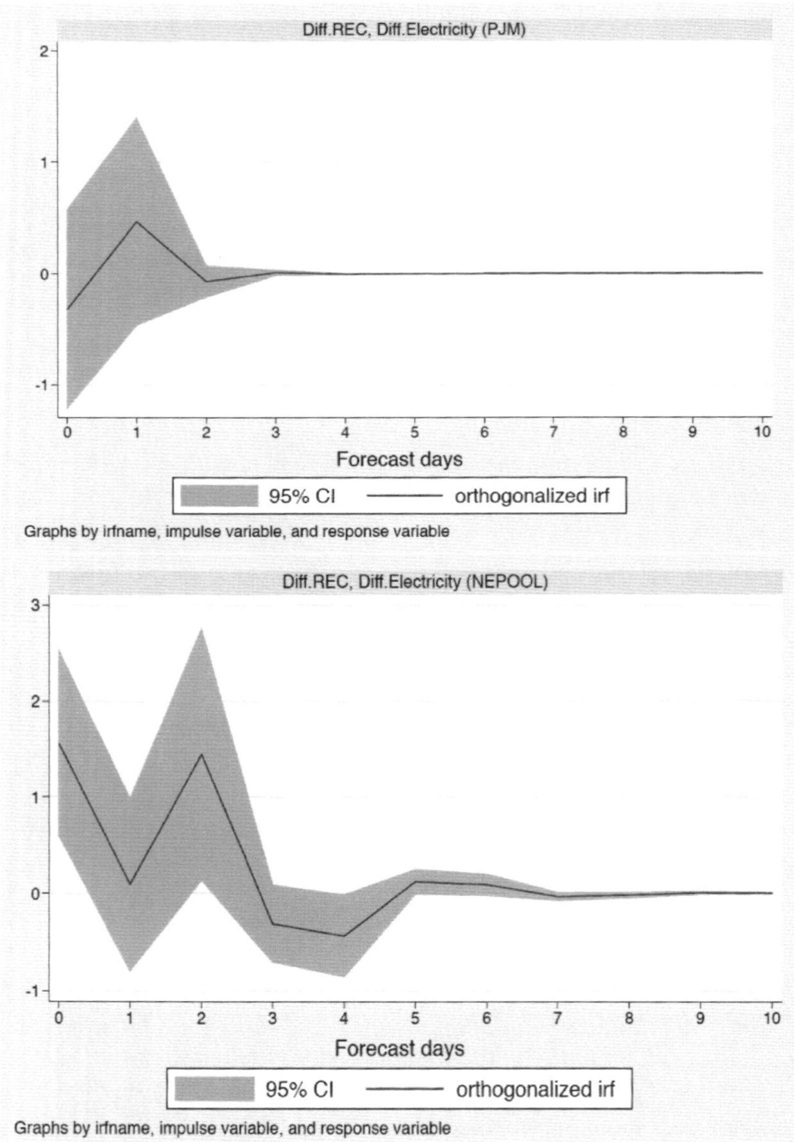

Fig. 8. Impulse response functions.

electricity prices are kept outside the scope of this analysis and deserves attention in future research. Consequently, this study should be expanded with additional model specification testing in order to derive specific policy recommendations. As our purpose is to illustrate the basic steps to analyze time series data for short-term forecasting with this exercise, we do not draw any policy conclusions from this analysis.

5. Concluding Remarks

This chapter covers the evolution of market dynamics for multiple energy markets, including crude oil, natural gas, electricity and renewables. We provide an overview of markets for these energy sources and challenges for forecasting prices or quantities with changing market dynamics. Understanding these markets is the key for employing the appropriate forecasting methods that can provide the most accurate and reasonable results for decision- and policy-making efforts and we aim to provide this knowledge to the readers in this chapter.

We would like to conclude by highlighting that the objective of the practical example is mostly illustrative. Note that there are many alternative specifications available and also options for the number of lags that can be utilized. Statistical fit should provide guidance and appropriate statistical tests should be completed to ensure a robust and reliable model. Therefore, our examples in this chapter serve as an illustration of fundamentals of these discussed methods and similar research questions should not limit their analyses to the approaches and statistical tests presented in this chapter.

References

Adams, F. G. and Shachmurove, Y. (2008). Modeling and forecasting energy consumption in China: Implications for Chinese energy demand and imports in 2020. *Energy Economics* **30**, 1263–1278.

Alberini, A. and Flippini, M. (2011). Response of residential electricity demand to price: The effect of measurement error. *Energy Economics* **33**, 889–895. Available at: http://faculty.smu.edu/millimet/classes/eco6375/papers/alberini%20filippini%202011.pdf.

Alquist, R. and Arbatli, E. (2010). Crude oil futures: A crystal ball? *Bank of Canada Review* **2010** (Spring): 3–11.

Alquist, R., Kilian, L. and Vigfusson, R. J. (2013). Forecasting the price of oil. In G. Elliott and A. Timmermann (eds.) *Handbook of Economic Forecasting*, 2A, North-Holland, Amsterdam, pp. 427–507.

Armstrong, S. J. and Brodie, R. J. (1999). Forecasting for marketing. In Graham J. Hooley and Michael K. Hussey (eds.), *Quantitative Methods in Marketing, 2nd edn.* International Thompson Business Press, London, pp. 92–119. Available at: http://forecastingprinciples.com/files/pdf/Forecasting%20for%20Marketing.pdf.

Armstrong, S. J. (2001). Selecting Forecasting Methods. Available at: http://repository.upenn.edu/marketing_papers/147.

Baum, C. F. (2006). Time-series filtering techniques in Stata. Presentation. Department of Economics, Boston College. Available at: https://www.stata.com/meeting/13uk/baumUKSUG2007.pdf.

Baum, C. F. (2007). Instrumental Variables: Overview and advances. Presented in Boston College and DIW Berlin.

Berrah, N., Feng, F., Priddle, R. and Wan, L. (2007). Sustainable energy in China: The closing window of opportunity, The World Bank, Washington, D.C.

Bhattacharyya, S. C. and Timilsina, G. R. (2009). Energy demand models for policy formulation. *A Comparative Study of Energy Demand Models*. The World Bank Development Research Group, Environment and Energy Team. Policy Research Working Paper. Available at: https://openknowledge.worldbank.org/bitstream/handle/10986/4061/WPS4866.pdf.

Bloomberg, https://emp.lbl.gov/projects/renewables-portfolio.

Bloomberg, LNGJLNP Index-Closing Price.

Bohi, D. R. and Zimmerman, M. B. (1984). An update on econometric studies of energy demand behavior. *Annual Review of Energy* **9**, 105–154.

Bolinger, M., Wiser, R., Cory, K. and James, T. (2009). PTC, ITC, or Cash Grant? An Analysis of the Choice Facing Renewable Power Projects in the United States. Lawrence Berkeley National Laboratory. Available at: https://www.nrel.gov/docs/fy09osti/45359.pdf.

BP Energy Outlook: Outlook to 2035. (2016). Available at: https://www.bp.com/content/dam/bp/pdf/energy-economics/energy-outlook-2016/bp-energy-outlook-2016.pdf.

Brockwell, P. J. and Davis, R. A. (1986). *Time Series: Theory and Methods*. (Springer-Verlag New York, Inc., New York).

Buranakunaporn, S. and Oczkowsky, E. (2007). A dynamic econometric model of Thailand manufacturing energy demand. *Applied Economics* **39** (17), 2261–2267.

Codoni, R., Park, H. C. and Ramani, K. V. (1985). Integrated Energy Planning — A Manual, Asia Pacific Development Centre, Kuala Lumpur.

Dahl, C. and Erdogan, M. (2000). Energy and interfactor substitution in Turkey. *OPEC Review* **24** (1), 1–22.

Deaton, A. (1974). A Reconsideration of the Empirical Implications of additive Preferences. Empirical Implications of Additive Preferences. Economic Journal — The Quarterly Journal of the Royal Economic Society, London: MacMillan. This paper is a complete revision of "Additive Preferences and Pigou's Law," which was read at the European Meeting of the Econometric Society in Oslo, August 1973. Available at: https://www.princeton.edu/_deaton/downloads/A_Reconsideration_of_the_Empirical_Implications_of_Additive_Preferences.pdf.

Deng, L., Benjamin F. H. and Piet Renson. (2015). What is the cost of negative bidding by wind? A unit commitment analysis of cost and emissions. *IEEE Transactions on Power Systems* **30** (4), 1805–1814.

Dillig, M., Jung, M. and Karl, J. (2016). The impact of renewables on electricity prices in Germany — An estimation based on historic spot prices in the years 2011–2013. *Renewable and Sustainable Energy Reviews* **57**, 7–15.

Enders, W. (1995). *Applied Econometric Time Series*. Wiley, New York.

Eryilmaz, D. and Homans, F. R. (2016). How does uncertainty in renewable energy policy affect decisions to invest in wind energy? *The Electricity Journal* **29** (3), 64–71.

Eryilmaz, D., Smith, T. M. and Homans, F. R. (2017). Price responsiveness in electricity markets: Implications for demand response in the Midwest. *The Energy Journal* **38** (1), 1–46.

Federal Energy Regulatory Commission (FERC) 1999. Docket No. RM99-2-000 - Order No. 2000. http://www.ferc.gov/legal/maj-ord-reg/land-docs/RM99-2A.pdf.

Federal Energy Regulatory Commission (FERC) (2010). History of OATT Reform. http://www.ferc.gov/industries/electric/indus-act/oatt-reform/history.asp.

Fell., H., Linn, J. and Munnings, C. (2012). Designing Renewable Electricity Policies to Reduce Emissions. Resources for the Future DP 12-54. Available at: http://www.rff.org/files/sharepoint/WorkImages/Download/RFF-DP-12-54.pdf.

Fezzi, C. (2007). Econometric Models for the Analysis of Electricity Markets. Doctor of Philosophy Thesis in Statistical Methods for Scientific Research, XIX Cycle. Available at: http://amsdottorato.unibo.it/433/1/tesi_dottorato_carlofezzi.pdf.

Financial Times (2014). The dark side of the oil shock. http://blogs.ft.com/gavyndavies/2014/12/14/the-dark-side-of-the-oil-shock/ GOI, 2006, Integrated Energy Policy – Report of the Expert Committee, Planning Commission, Government of India, New Delhi, 2006 (see http://planningcommission.nic.in/reports/genrep/rep_intengy.pdf, last visited on 28 March 2008).

Gujarati, D. N. and Porter, D. C. (2009). *Basic Econometrics*. (McGraw-Hill, Boston, Mass).

Heeter, J., Armstrong, P. and Bird, L. (2011). Market Brief: Status of the Voluntary Renewable Energy Certificate Market (2011 Data). National Renewable Energy Laboratory. Technical Report. Available at: https://www.nrel.gov/docs/fy12osti/56128.pdf.

Hong, T. (2014). Energy Forecasting: Past, Present and Future. *Foresight*. https://forecasters.org/pdfs/foresight/ForesightWinter2014_Hong_Energy_Forecasting.pdf.

Houthakker, H. S. (1974). Dynamic demand analyses for gasoline and residential electricity. *American Journal of Agricultural Economics* **56**, 412–418.

International Energy Agency (IEA) (2014). Word Energy Outlook 2014. https://www.iea.org/publications/freepublications/publication/WEO2014.pdf.

Jebaraj, S. and Iniyan, S. (2006). A review of energy models. *Journal of Renewable and Sustainable Energy Reviews*, **10** (2006), 281–311. Available at: http://aoatools.aua.gr/pilotec/files/bibliography/renew_models-1547752705/renew_models.pdf.

Levin, J. and Milgrom, P. (2004). Introduction to Choice Theory. Lecture Notes. Available at: http://web.stanford.edu/~jdlevin/Econ%20202/Choice%20Theory.pdf.

Mas-Colell, A., Whinston, M. D. and Green, J. R. (2006). *Microeconomic Theory* (Indian edn). (Oxford University Press, New Delhi; New York).

"Order No. 2000," *FERC*, accessed February 26, 2014, http://www.ferc.gov/legal/maj-ord-reg/land-docs/RM99-2A.pdf.

Palmintier, B., Robert, B., Barry, M., Michael, C., Kyri, B., Fei, D., Matthew, R., Matthew, L. and Ashwini, B. (2016). *On the Path to SunShot: Emerging Issues and Challenges in Integrating Solar with the Distribution System*. Golden, CO: National Renewable Energy Laboratory. NREL/TP-5D00-65331. http://www.nrel.gov/docs/fy16osti/65331.pdf.

Platchkov, L. M. and Pollitt, M. G. (2011). The Economic of Energy (and Electricity) Demand. University of Cambridge, Electricity Policy Research Group. Cambridge Working Paper in Economics No. 1137. Available at: http://www.econ.cam.ac.uk/research-files/repec/cam/pdf/cwpe1137.pdf.

Solar Energy Industry Association (SEIA) (2017). Net Energy Metering. Available at: https://www.seia.org/sites/default/files/resources/Net%20Metering%20Facts_Feb17.pdf.

Uri, N. D. (1982). The demand for energy in the transport sector in the United States. *Journal of Transport Economics and Policy* **16** (1), 65–84.

U.S. Energy Information Administration. (2014). Texas Restructuring Active. http://www.eia.gov/electricity/policies/restructuring/texas.html.

U.S. Department of Energy. (2014). So you have questions about_Renewable Portfolio Standards. Resources and Technical Assistance. Second in a series of Policy Basics. Available at: https://www.nrel.gov/docs/gen/fy14/62350.pdf.

U.S. Energy Information Administration, based on information in Advanced Energy Economy PowerSuite and Database of State Incentives for Renewables & Efficiency (DSIRE) https://www.eia.gov/todayinenergy/detail.php?id=32332.

U.S. Energy Information Administration. (2017). What is Energy? Explained. http://www.eia.gov/energyexplained/index.cfm?page=about_home.

U.S. Energy Information Administration. (2017). Natural Gas Explained. Where Our Natural Gas From. https://www.eia.gov/energy_in_brief/article/shale_in_the_united_states.cfm.

U.S. Energy Information Administration. (2015). Natural Gas Prices in Asia Mainly Linked to Crude Oil, but Use of Spot Indexes Increases. https://www.eia.gov/todayinenergy/detail.php?id=23132.

U.S. Energy Information Administration (EIA) (2017). The United States now produces nearly all of the natural gas that it uses. Available at: https://www.eia.gov/energy_in_brief/article/shale_in_the_united_states.cfm.

U.S. Energy Information Administration (EIA) (1998). Provisions of AB 1890. Adopted from: California Energy Commission, *"New Options For Agricultural Customers: California's Electric Industry Restructuring"* (Sacramento, June 1998), pp. 10–13. http://www.eia.gov/electricity/policies/legislation/california/assemblybill.html.

U.S. Department of Energy (2007). Report to Congress on Competition in Wholesale and Retail Markets for Electric Energy. http://energy.gov/oe/downloads/report-congress-competition-wholesale-and-retail-markets-electric-energy.

Varian, H. (1992). *Microeconomic Analysis*. 3rd edn. (W.W. Norton & Company Inc, New York).

Westoby, R. and Pearce, D. (1984). Single equation models for the projection of energy demand in the United Kingdom 1954–80. *Scottish Journal of Political Economy* **31** (3), 229–254.

Wirl, F. and Szirucsek, E. (1990). Energy modelling — A survey of related topics. *OPEC Review*, Autumn, 361–378.

Wooldridge, J. M. (2009). *Introductory Econometrics: A Modern Approach*, 4th edn. (South-Western CENGAGE Learning, Mason, OH).

Zivot, E. and Wang, J. (2006). Vector Autoregressive Models for Multivariate Time Series. In: Modeling Financial Time Series with S-PLUS®. (Springer, New York, NY).

Chapter 2

Econometric Modeling of the World Oil Market as a Dynamic Game

Khaled H. Kheiravar* and C.-Y. Cynthia Lin Lawell†

**Market Monitoring Section, California Air Resources Board, Sacramento, CA, USA*
†Charles H. Dyson School of Applied Economics and Management, Cornell University, Ithaca, NY, USA

The decisions made by petroleum producers in the world oil market are both dynamic and strategic, and are thus best modeled as a dynamic game. In this chapter, we review the literature on the world oil market and discuss our research on econometric modeling of the world oil market as a dynamic game. Our research builds on the previous literature by combining three erstwhile separate dimensions of modeling the world oil market: dynamic optimization, game theory, and econometrics. Our results show that dynamic behavior and strategic interactions are important aspects of the world oil market that must be accounted for in empirical analyses of the world oil market.

Keywords: Structural econometric model; dynamic game; world oil market; petroleum production; dynamic; strategic; dynamic optimization; game theory; OPEC; econometrics.

1. Introduction

The decisions made by petroleum producers in the world oil market are both dynamic and strategic, and are thus best modeled as a dynamic game. In this chapter, we review the literature on the world oil market and discuss our research on econometric modeling of the world oil market as a dynamic game. Our research builds on the previous literature by combining three erstwhile separate dimensions of modeling the world oil market: dynamic optimization, game theory, and econometrics.

In Lin Lawell [2019], we develop and estimate an empirical dynamic model of the world oil market based on optimal control theory, and use this model to test market power.

In Kheiravar *et al.* [2019], we develop and estimate a structural econometric model of the dynamic game among petroleum-producing firms based on dynamic programming and game theory, and we apply this model to firm-level panel data on oil and gas exploration, development, production, mergers, acquisitions, and reserves. We then use the structural econometric model to analyze the effects of government policies, changing geopolitical landscapes, and new technologies on the petroleum industry.

Our results show that dynamic behavior and strategic interactions are important aspects of the world oil market that must be accounted for in empirical analyses of the world oil market.

The balance of this chapter proceeds as follows. In Section 2, we explain why the world oil market should be modeled as a dynamic game. We review the related literature in Section 3. In Section 4, we discuss our research in Lin Lawell [2019], in which we develop an empirical dynamic model of the world oil market based on optimal control theory. In Section 5, we discuss our research in Kheiravar *et al.* [2019], in which we develop and estimate a structural econometric model of the dynamic game among petroleum-producing firms based on dynamic programming and game theory. Section 6 concludes.

2. The World Oil Market as a Dynamic Game

The decisions made by petroleum producers in the world oil market are both dynamic and strategic. The production decisions of oil and gas producers are dynamic because petroleum is a nonrenewable resource; as a consequence, current extraction and production affect the availability of reserves for future extraction and production. The exploration, development, merger, and acquisition decisions of petroleum producers are dynamic because they are irreversible investments, because their payoffs are uncertain, and because petroleum producers have leeway over the timing of these investment decisions. Since the profits from investment and production decisions depend on market conditions such as the oil price that varies stochastically over time, an individual firm operating in isolation that hopes to make dynamically optimal decisions would need to account for the option value to waiting before making these irreversible investments [Dixit and Pindyck, 1994].

The decisions of petroleum-producing firms are not only dynamic but strategic as well. Petroleum producers consider not only future market conditions but also their competitors' investment and production activities when making their current decisions. Since the production decisions of other firms affect the prices of oil and natural gas, and therefore affect a firm's current payoff from production, and since the investment and production decisions of other firms affect future values of state variables which affect a firm's future payoff from producing and investing, petroleum-producing firms must anticipate the production and investment strategies of other firms in order to make dynamically optimal decision. As a consequence, there are strategic interactions between petroleum-producing firms.

Because the decisions made by petroleum producers in the world oil market are both dynamic and strategic, they are best modeled as a dynamic game. In our previous work in Lin [2011], we show that assuming the world oil market is static and perfectly competitive yields unrealistic empirical results, and therefore that econometric models of the world oil market should incorporate the dynamic and strategic dimensions of the world oil market.

3. Related Literature

Economists have long been interested in the world oil market. The theoretical model of optimal nonrenewable resource extraction was first examined by Hotelling [1931], who developed the insight that dynamic optimization and dynamic behavior are critical for analyzing the world oil market.

The dynamic optimization model and framework for the world oil market developed by Hotelling [1931] has since been expanded upon by many others to allow for such features as stock effects in extraction costs [Solow and Wan, 1976; Hanson, 1980; Farzin, 1992]; exploration [Pindyck, 1978; Pesaran, 1990]; market imperfections [Stiglitz, 1976; Khalatbari, 1977; Sweeney, 1977; Crémer and Salehi-Isfahani, 1991]; technological progress [Farzin, 1992, 1995; Lin *et al.*, 2009; Lin and Wagner, 2007]; outward-shifting demand [Chapman, 1993; Chapman and Khanna, 2000]; uncertainty [Hoel, 1978; Pindyck, 1980]; risk [Young and Ryan, 1996]; drilling activity [Anderson, Kellogg and Salant, forthcoming]; stochastic and volatile output price and production cost [Almansour and Insley, 2016]; tax policy [Leighty and Lin, 2012]; and oil contracts [Ghandi and Lin, 2012; Ghandi and Lin Lawell, 2019].

Gaudet [2007] provides a recent review of factors that can potentially help bridge the gap between the basic Hotelling rule of natural resource exploitation and the historical behavior of resource prices. Lin [2009] shows that even the most basic Hotelling model yields insights.

Recognizing the importance of strategic interactions in addition to dynamic behavior in the world oil market, the dynamic optimization model and framework for the world oil market developed by Hotelling [1931] has also been expanded upon to allow for such features as Nash-Cournot behavior [Salant, 1976; Ulph and Folie, 1980] and OPEC behavior [Hnyilicza and Pindyck, 1976; Pindyck, 1976; Crémer and Weitzman, 1976].

Until recently, much of the empirical literature on the world petroleum market was from over three decades ago [Adelman, 1962; Kennedy, 1974; Nordhaus, 1980; Gately, 1984; Griffin, 1985; Lin, 2011; Espinasa *et al.*, 2017]. Crémer and Salehi-Isfahani [1991] provide a survey of models of the oil market. Many previous empirical studies of world petroleum market use a static model. Lin [2011] shows that assuming the world oil market is static and perfectly competitive yields unrealistic empirical results, and therefore that econometric models of the world oil market should incorporate the dynamic and strategic dimensions of the world oil market.

There is also a literature analyzing strategic behavior in the world petroleum market, and particularly the behavior of OPEC [Griffin, 1985; Matutes, 1988; Golombek *et al.*, 2014; Gulen, 1996; Farzin, 1995; Alhajji and Huettner, 2000a, 2000b; Kaufmann *et al.*, 2004; Almoguera *et al.*, 2011; Hochman and Zilberman, 2015; Okullo and Reynès, 2016; Baumeister and Kilian, 2017; Genc, 2017; Asker *et al.*, 2017; Ghoddusi *et al.*, 2017]. For detailed background information on the world energy industry, see the classic text by Dahl [2015]. For a detailed review of the literature on oil market modeling and OPEC's behavior, see Al-Qahtani *et al.* [2008].

4. An Empirical Dynamic Model of the World Oil Market

The mission of OPEC is to "coordinate and unify the petroleum policies of its Member Countries" [OPEC, 2017]; however, it is unclear whether OPEC behaves as a cartel. As a step towards better understanding and modeling the world oil market and OPEC in particular, our work in Lin Lawell [2019] estimates a Hotelling model of the world oil market and tests whether OPEC countries colluded and whether non-OPEC countries behaved as price takers or oligopolists over the period 1970–2004.

Our research in Lin Lawell [2019] makes several important contributions to the existing literature. First, it takes to data the theoretical model of optimal nonrenewable resource extraction that was first examined by Hotelling [1931], and later expanded upon by many others (see e.g. [Pindyck, 1976; Cremer and Weitzman, 1976; Solow and Wan, 1976; Pindyck, 1978; Hanson, 1980; Pindyck, 1980; Pesaran, 1990; Farzin, 1992; Farzin, 1995; Lin, 2009; Lin *et al.*, 2009; Lin and

Wagner, 2007; Leighty and Lin, 2012; Ghandi and Lin, 2012; Anderson, Kellogg and Salant, forthcoming; Ghandi and Lin Lawell, 2019]).

Unlike many previous empirical studies of the petroleum market, which use a static model, in Lin Lawell [2019] we estimate a Hotelling model of the world petroleum market, which is a dynamic model. The dynamics in Lin Lawell [2019] arise from the nonrenewable nature of the resource.

A second contribution is that our work in Lin Lawell [2019] builds upon existing empirical studies of nonrenewable resource markets by addressing the identification problem that arises in empirical analyses of supply and demand. Because the observed equilibrium prices and quantities are simultaneously determined in the supply-and-demand system, instrumental variables are needed to address the endogeneity problem [Lin, 2011].

The third contribution is that our work in Lin Lawell [2019] develops a Hotelling model that enables one to test for the market conduct of OPEC and non-OPEC producers.

Our empirical dynamic model in Lin Lawell [2019] is based on taking an optimal control theory-based Hotelling model to data. In particular, we use the first-order conditions from an optimal control theory model of optimal nonrenewable resource extraction under different market conditions to formulate a general supply-side first-order condition that we then estimate with data.

According to our results in Lin Lawell [2019], results of the analysis by decade support OPEC countries colluding as the dominant cartel producer and non-OPEC countries behaving as an oligopolistic fringe. Market demand has become more inelastic over time over the period of study. The estimated shadow prices are jointly significant, which is consistent with the hypothesis that a Hotelling model, which accounts for the nonrenewable nature of the resource, is a more appropriate model for the world oil market than a static model.

Our results in Lin Lawell [2019] therefore show that dynamic behavior and strategic interactions are important aspects of the world oil market that must be accounted for in empirical analyses of the world oil market.

5. A Structural Econometric Model of the Dynamic Game Among Petroleum-Producing Firms

In Kheiravar *et al.* [2019], we develop and estimate a structural econometric model of the dynamic game among petroleum-producing firms in the world petroleum market. Our model allows firms that are at least partially state-owned to have objectives other than profit maximization alone. We apply this model to panel data on firm-level oil and gas exploration, development, production, mergers, acquisitions, and reserves along with data on oil and gas prices to study the behavior of the top 50 oil and natural gas producing companies in the world.

We then use the parameters estimated from our structural econometric model to simulate counterfactual scenarios to analyze the effects of changes in OPEC membership, the privatization of state-owned oil companies, a ban on mergers, and demand shocks on the petroleum industry.

There are several advantages to using a dynamic structural model to analyze the investment, production, merger, and acquisition decisions of petroleum-producing firms. First, unlike reduced-form models, a structural approach explicitly models the dynamics of these decisions. The production decisions of oil and gas producers are dynamic because petroleum is a nonrenewable resource; as a consequence, current extraction and production affect the availability of reserves for future extraction and production. The exploration, development, merger, and acquisition decisions of petroleum producers are dynamic because they are irreversible investments, because their payoffs are uncertain, and because petroleum producers have leeway over the timing of these investment decisions. Since the profits from investment and production decisions depend on market conditions such as the oil price that varies stochastically over time, an individual firm operating in isolation that hopes to make dynamically optimal decisions would need to account for the option value to waiting before making these irreversible investments [Dixit and Pindyck, 1994].

A second advantage of our model of the dynamic game between petroleum producers is that it models the strategic nature of the decisions of petroleum-producing firms. Petroleum producers consider not only future market conditions but also their competitors' investment and production activities when making their current decisions. Since the production decisions of other firms affect the prices of oil and natural gas, and therefore affect a firm's current payoff from production, and since the investment and production decisions of other firms affect future values of state variables which affect a firm's future payoff from producing and investing, petroleum-producing firms must anticipate the production and investment strategies of other firms in order to make a dynamically optimal decision. As a consequence, there are strategic interactions between petroleum-producing firms.

A third advantage of our structural model is that it enables us to estimate the effect of each state variable on the expected payoffs from exploration, development, production, merger, and acquisition decisions, and therefore enables us to estimate parameters that have direct economic interpretations. Our dynamic model accounts for the continuation value, which is the expected value of the value function in next period. With the structural model we are able to estimate parameters in the payoffs from exploration, development, production, merger, and acquisition, since we are able to structurally model how the continuation values relate to the payoffs from each of these decisions.

A fourth advantage of our structural model is that we are able to model the interdependence of petroleum-producing firms' value functions. When one firm merges with or acquires another firm, the value of the other firm with which it merges or which it acquires is given by that other firm's value function, which is the present discounted value of the entire stream of per-period payoffs of that other firm, and which accounts for the options that that other firm has to explore, develop, produce, merge, and acquire. Thus, a firm's value function depends on the expected value of other firms with which it has the option to merge or acquire. Therefore, the firms' value functions are interdependent.

A fifth advantage of our structural model is that we can use the parameter estimates from our structural model to simulate various counterfactual scenarios. We use our estimates to simulate counterfactual scenarios to analyze the effects of changes in OPEC membership, the privatization of state-owned oil companies, a ban on mergers, and demand shocks on the petroleum industry.

We build on the literature on structural econometric models of dynamic games. In Lin [2013], we develop and estimate a structural model of the multi-stage investment timing game in offshore petroleum production. When individual petroleum-producing firms make their exploration and development investment timing decisions, positive information externalities and negative extraction externalities may lead them to interact strategically with their neighbors. If they do occur, strategic interactions in petroleum production would lead to a loss in both firm profit and government royalty revenue. The possibility of strategic interactions thus poses a concern to policy makers and affects the optimal government policy. In Lin [2013], we examine whether these inefficient strategic interactions take place on U.S. federal lands in the Gulf of Mexico. In particular, we analyze whether one firm's production decisions and profits depend on the decisions of firms owning neighboring tracts of land. The empirical approach is to estimate a structural econometric model of the firms' multi-stage investment timing game.

In our model of the dynamic game among petroleum-producing firms in the world petroleum market in Kheiravar *et al.* [2019], a firm's decisions may depend on the decisions of other firms through several channels. First, aggregate output of oil and natural gas affect the prices of oil and natural gas faced by each firm; as a consequence, owing to market power, each firm's production decisions affect the prices faced by all firms. Second, aggregate output, aggregate reserves, and aggregate capital expenditures affect each firm's policy functions. Thus, each firm's decisions depend on the aggregate output and capital expenditure of all other firms, and on the aggregate reserves of all other firms. Third, aggregate output affects the transition densities for the global state variables. Thus, production decisions of each firm affect future values of the state variables, which then affect the payoffs and decisions of all firms.

There are several sources of uncertainty in our model of a dynamic game in Kheiravar *et al.* [2019]. First, future values of the state variables are stochastic. Second, each player receives private information shocks. Third, there are shocks to oil demand and regional natural gas demand. Fourth, merger and acquisition costs are private information to each firm, and are not observed by either other firms or the econometrician.

We assume that each firm optimizes its behavior conditional on the current state variables, other firms' strategies and its own private information stocks, which results in a Markov perfect equilibrium (MPE). In a Markov perfect equilibrium, the optimal strategy for each firm should therefore yield an expected present discounted value of the entire stream of per-period payoffs at least as high as the expected present discounted value of the entire stream of per-period payoffs from any alternative strategy.

We estimate the structural econometric model in two steps. In the first step, we characterize the equilibrium policy functions for the firms' decisions regarding exploration, development, production, merger, and acquisition as functions of state variables by using reduced-form regressions correlating actions to states. We also estimate the transition density for the state variables. We then calculate value functions using forward simulation following methods in Hotz *et al.* [1994] and Bajari *et al.* [2007].

In the second step, using the condition for a Markov perfect equilibrium, we find the parameters that minimize any profitable deviations from the optimal policy as given by the policy functions estimated in the first step.

An innovation we make in our econometric method arises since a firm's own value function depends on the expected value of the value function of other firms that the firm may acquire or with which the firm may merge. We address the endogeneity of value functions using a fixed point algorithm.

We use the structural econometric model to analyze the effects of changes in OPEC membership, the privatization of state-owned oil companies, a ban on mergers, and demand shocks on the petroleum industry.

The results of our research in Kheiravar *et al.* [2019] will be of interest to academics, policy makers, entrepreneurs, and business practitioners, including oil companies, alike. Our modeling outcomes can be used to help inform decision-making and policy design. This model will also help petroleum firms better respond to government policies, and will help policy makers better design sustainable energy policies.

6. Conclusion

The decisions made by petroleum producers in the world oil market are both dynamic and strategic, and are thus best modeled as a dynamic game. In this chapter, we review the literature on the world oil market and discuss our research on econometric modeling of the world oil market as a dynamic game.

Our results show that dynamic behavior and strategic interactions are important aspects of the world oil market that must be accounted for in empirical analyses of the world oil market.

In ongoing and future work, we hope to use our structural econometric model to better understand how government policies, changing geopolitical landscapes, and disruptive technologies, such as shale oil and gas, and new batteries for electric vehicles, impact future business models, the competition of fuels, and the composition of future energy demand. We would also like to use our structural econometric model to analyze how industry will respond to regulatory and/or societal demands for reduced greenhouse gas emissions and improved environmental quality; to examine how the oil industry might transition to more sustainable fuels; and to better understand what is required for early alternative fuel transitions to succeed.

In future work, we hope to use our structural econometric model outcomes to help inform decision-making and policy design. In particular, we hope to help petroleum firms better respond to government policies, and to help policy makers better design sustainable energy policies.

The results of our research will be of interest to academics, policy makers, entrepreneurs, and business practitioners, including oil companies, alike.

References

Adelman, M. A. (1962). Natural gas and the world petroleum market. *Journal of Industrial Economics* **10**, 76–112.

Alhajji, A. and Huettner, D. (2000a). OPEC and other commodity cartels: A comparison. *Energy Policy* **28**, 1151–1164.

Alhajji, A. and Huettner, D. (2000b). OPEC and world crude oil markets from 1973 to 1994: Cartel, oligopoly or competitive? *Energy Journal* **21** (3), 31–60.

Almansour, A. and Insley, M. (2016). The impact of stochastic extraction cost on the value of an exhaustible resource: An application to Alberta oil sands. *Energy Journal* **37** (2), 61–88.

Almoguera, P., Douglas, C. and Herrera, A. (2011). Testing for the cartel in OPEC: Noncooperative collusion or just noncooperative? *Oxford Review of Economic Policy* **27**, 144–168.

Al-Qahtani, A., Balistreri, E. and Dahl, C. (2008). Literature review on oil market modeling and OPEC's behavior. Working paper, Colorado School of Mines.

Anderson, S. T., Kellogg, R. and Salant, S. W. (forthcoming). Hotelling under pressure. *Journal of Political Economy*.

Asker, J., Collard-Wexler, A. and De Loecker, J. (2017). Market power, production (mis)allocation and OPEC. NBER Working Paper No. 23801.

Bajari, P., Benkard, C. L. and Levin, J. (2007). Estimating dynamic models of imperfect competition. *Econometrica* **75** (5), 1331–1370.

Baumeister, C. and Kilian, L. (2017). Understanding the decline in the price of oil since June 2014. *Journal of the Association of Environmental and Resource Economists* **3** (1), 131–158.

Chapman, D. (1993). World oil: Hotelling depletion or accelerating use? *Natural Resources Research* **2** (4), 331–339.

Chapman, D. and Khanna, N. (2000). World oil: The growing case for international policy. *Contemporary Economic Policy* **18** (1) 1–13.

Crémer, J. and Salehi-Isfahani, D. (1991). *Models of the Oil Market*. (Harwood Academic Publishers, New York).

Crémer, J. and Weitzman, M. L. (1976). OPEC and the monopoly price of world oil. *European Economic Review* **8**, 155–164.

Dahl, C. A. (2015). *International Energy Markets: Understanding Pricing, Policies, and Profits*, 2nd edn. (Pennwell Press, USA).

Dixit, A. K. and Pindyck, R. S. (1994). *Investment Under Uncertainty*. (Princeton University Press, Princeton).

Espinasa, R., ter Horst, E., Guerra Reyes, S., Manzano, O., Molina, G. and Rigobon, R. (2017). A micro-based model for world oil market. *Energy Economics* **66**, 431–449.

Farzin, Y. H. (1985). Competition and Substitutes in the Market for an Exhaustible Resource. JAI Press, Greenwich, CT.

Farzin, Y. H. (1992). The time path of scarcity rent in the theory of exhaustible resources. *Economic Journal* **102**, 841–851.

Farzin, Y. H. (1995). Technological change and the dynamics of resource scarcity measures. *Journal of Environmental Economics and Management* **29**, 105–120.

Gately, D. (1984). A ten-year retrospective: OPEC and the world oil market. *Journal of Economic Literature* **22**, 1100–1114.

Gaudet, G. (2007). Natural resource economics under the rule of Hotelling. *Canadian Journal of Economics* **40**, 1033–1059.

Genc, T. S. (2017). OPEC and demand response to crude oil prices. *Energy Economics* **66**, 238–246.

Ghandi, A. and Lin, C.-Y. C. (2012). Do Iran's buy-back service contracts lead to optimal production? The case of Soroosh and Nowrooz. *Energy Policy* **42**, 181–190.

Ghandi, A. and Lin Lawell, C.-Y. C. (2019). On the economic efficiency of oil production contracts: A dynamic model of the Rumaila oil field in Iraq. Working paper, Cornell University.

Ghoddusi, H., Nili, M. and Rastad, M. (2017). On quota violations of OPEC members. *Energy Economics* **68**, 410–422.

Golombek, R., Irarrazabal, A. A. and Ma, L. (2014). OPEC's market power: An empirical dominant firm model for the oil market. CESifo Working Paper Series 4512, CESifo Group Munich.

Griffin, J. M. (1985). OPEC behavior: A test of alternative hypotheses. *American Economic Review* **75**, 954–963.

Gulen, S. G. (1996). Is OPEC a cartel?: Evidence from cointegration and causality tests. *Energy Journal* **17**, 43–57.

Hanson, D. A. (1980). Increasing extraction costs and resource prices: Some further results. *Bell Journal of Economics* **11** (1), 335–342.

Hnyilicza, E. and Pindyck, R. S. (1976). Pricing policies for a two-part exhaustible resource cartel: The case of OPEC. *European Economic Review* **8**, 139–154.

Hochman, G. and Zilberman, D. (2015). The political economy of OPEC. *Energy Economics* **48**, 203–216.

Hoel, M. (1978). Resource extraction, uncertainty, and learning. *Bell Journal of Economics* **9** (2), 642–645.

Hotelling, H. (1931). The economics of exhaustible resources. *Journal of Political Economy* **39** (2), 137–175.

Hotz, V. J., Miller, R. A., Sanders, S. and Smith, J. (1994). A simulation estimator for dynamic models of discrete choice. *Review of Economic Studies* **61**, 265–289.

Kaufmann, R. K., Dees, S., Karadeloglou, P. and Sánchez, M. (2004). Does OPEC matter?: An econometric analysis of oil prices. *Energy Journal* **24** (4), 67–90.

Kennedy, M. (1974). An economic model of the world oil market. *Bell Journal of Economics and Management Science* **5**, 540–577.

Khalatbari, F. (1977). Market imperfections and the optimum rate of depletion of natural resources. *Economica* **44** (176), 409–414.

Kheiravar, K. H., Lin Lawell, C.-Y. C. and Jaffe, A. M. (2019). A structural econometric model of the dynamic game between petroleum producers in the world petroleum market. Working paper, Cornell University.

Leighty, W. and C.-Y. C. Lin. (2012). Tax policy can change the production path: A model of optimal oil extraction in Alaska. *Energy Policy* **41**, 759–774.

Lin, C.-Y. C. (2009). Insights from a simple Hotelling model of the world oil market. *Natural Resources Research* **18** (1), 19–28.

Lin, C.-Y. C. (2011). Estimating supply and demand in the world oil market. *Journal of Energy and Development* **34** (1), 1–32.

Lin, C.-Y. C. (2013). Strategic decision-making with information and extraction externalities: A structural model of the multi-stage investment timing game in offshore petroleum production. *Review of Economics and Statistics* **95** (5), 1601–1621.

Lin, C.-Y. C., Meng, H., Ngai, T. Y., Oscherov, V. and Zhu, Y. H. (2009). Hotelling revisited: Oil prices and endogenous technological progress. *Natural Resources Research* **18** (1), 29–38.

Lin, C.-Y. C. and Wagner, G. (2007). Steady-state growth in a Hotelling model of resource extraction. *Journal of Environmental Economics and Management* **54** (1), 68–83.

Lin Lawell, C.-Y. C. (2019). Market power in the world oil market: Evidence for an OPEC cartel and an oligopolistic non-OPEC fringe. Working paper, Cornell University.

Matutes, C. (1988). The center of OPEC: An econometric analysis. Working paper, University of California at Berkeley.

Nordhaus, W. (1980). Oil and economic performance in industrial countries. *Brookings Papers on Economic Activity* **11**, 341–400.

Okullo, S. J. and Reynès, F. (2016). Imperfect cartelization in OPEC. *Energy Economics* **60**, 333–344.

Organization of Petroleum Exporting Countries [OPEC]. (2017). Our Mission. URL: http://www.opec.org/opec_web/en/about_us/23.htm

Pesaran, M. H. (1990). An econometric analysis of exploration and extraction of oil in the U.K. Continental Shelf. *Economic Journal* **100** (401), 367–390.

Pindyck, R. S. (1976). Gains to producers from the cartelization of exhaustible resources. MIT Energy Lab working paper (No. MIT-EL 76-012WP).

Pindyck, R. S. (1978). The optimal exploration and production of nonrenewable resources. *Journal of Political Economy* **86** (5), 841–861.

Pindyck, R. S. (1980). Uncertainty and exhaustible resource markets. *Journal of Political Economy* **88** (6), 1203–1225.

Salant, S. W. (1976). Exhaustible resources and industrial structure: A Nash-Cournot approach to the world oil market. *Journal of Political Economy* **84** (5), 1079–1094.

Solow, R. M. and Wan, F. Y. (1976). Extraction costs in the theory of exhaustible resources. *Bell Journal of Economics* **7** (2), 359–370.

Stiglitz, J. E. (1976). Monopoly and the rate of extraction of exhaustible resources. *American Economic Review* **66** (4), 655–661.

Sweeney, J. L. (1977). Economics of depletable resources: Market forces and intertemporal bias. *Review of Economic Studies* **44** (1), 124–141.

Ulph, A. M. and Folie, G. M. (1980). Exhaustible resources and cartels: An intertemporal Nash-Cournot model. *Canadian Journal of Economics* **13** (4), 645–658.

Young, D. and Ryan, D. L. (1996). Empirical testing of a risk-adjusted Hotelling model. *Resource and Energy Economics* **18**, 265–289.

Chapter 3

Forecasting the Return Volatility of Energy Prices: A GARCH-MIDAS Approach

Afees A. Salisu*,‡ and Raymond Swaray†,§

*Centre for Econometric & Allied Research, University of Ibadan, Nigeria
†Economics Subject Group, University of Hull Business, University of Hull, Cottingham Road, UK
‡adebare1@yahoo.com; aa.salisu@cear.org.ng
§r.swaray@hull.ac.uk

This chapter offers an extension to the literature on energy prices by forecasting the return volatility of these prices using the GARCH-MIDAS approach. In addition to the realized volatility, it also evaluates the predictability of relevant macroeconomic information such as industrial growth and consumer prices (with and without energy components) in the predictive model for the return volatility of energy prices. The analyses are distinctly conducted for full sample, pre-GFC and post-GFC periods. On average, the findings support the inclusion of these macroeconomic information, particularly output growth and realized volatility, as they yield good in-sample and out-of-sample predictability results for the return volatility. However, the study finds contrasting evidence between the pre-GFC and post-GFC periods.

Keywords: GARCH-MIDAS; energy prices; return volatility; realized volatility; industrial production; inflation.

1. Introduction

The traditional and common approach of modeling and forecasting in econometrics involves the use of data sampled at the same frequency. The choice of variables in the forecast model in this case is often restricted to those that meet this condition which may affect forecast performance (see [Ghysels *et al.*, 2015]). However, with the emergence of the Mixed Data Sampling (MIDAS) regression and its variants, allowing for macroeconomic (low frequency) variables when forecasting (high frequency) financial series such as stock price, bond price, exchange rate and interest rate, for example, is realizable (see [Ghysels *et al.*, 2006; Clements and Galvão, 2008; and Ghysels *et al.*, 2015], for a review). The computational advantages of using the MIDAS regressions are well documented in Andreou *et al.* [2013].

In this chapter, we employ the univariate GARCH-MIDAS approach proposed by Engle *et al.* [2013] to forecast the return volatility of energy prices. Other variants of the MIDAS regressions are the MIDAS-ADL (MIDAS Autoregressive Distributed Lag) regression, MIDAS Quantile regression, and DCC-MIDAS (the multivariate extension to the GARCH-MIDAS model with dynamic conditional correlations (DCC)). However, we favour the GARCH-MIDAS over other univariate variants of the MIDAS regressions as the former accounts for conditional heteroscedasticity which is a prominent feature of most energy prices (see [Narayan and Liu, 2015]). Information about the volatility of energy prices is crucial for the valuation of cost of production. In other words, as long as energy continues to serve as input to production, producers of goods and services, and by implication final consumers, will be constantly exposed to risk as changes in the volatility of energy prices persist.

Also, there is a strong positive link between energy prices and inflation; higher energy prices drive a higher rate of inflation (see [Salisu *et al.*, 2017]). Similarly, there is a high correlation between energy prices and agricultural commodity prices; a rise in energy prices increases the price of agricultural commodity (see [Koirala *et al.*, 2015]). Thus, information on the extent of volatility in energy prices is useful for commodity derivatives valuation as well as hedging decisions. In addition, a number of studies examining the link between energy consumption and growth have demonstrated different forms of causality (growth hypothesis, conservation hypothesis and feedback hypothesis) between the two variables and therefore unfavourable trends in energy prices may adversely impact on energy consumption and by extension exert a drag on economic growth (see [Omri, 2014]). Overall, understanding the extent of changes in volatility of energy prices is important for effective investment and policy decisions.

We utilize daily spot prices of seven US energy commodities, namely crude oil, gasoline, heating oil, diesel, jet fuel, propane and natural gas. We also consider monthly data on industrial production index and inflation as proxies for real economic activities and macroeconomic uncertainty, respectively; in addition to using the realized monthly volatility of the return series of energy prices. The inclusion of these exogenous factors in the model somewhat follows the Arbitrage Pricing Theory which assumes that asset returns are driven by macroeconomic risks such as output volatility and inflation uncertainty, among others.

To the best of our knowledge, this is the first study to examine the return volatility in the selected energy prices using the GARCH-MIDAS approach with exogenous variables whose inclusion is theoretically motivated. A closely related study to ours is the Valadkhani and Smyth [2017]; however, we differ both in terms of the direction of relationship and methodology. In their study, the objective was to examine the impact of the movements in high frequency (daily) oil prices on low frequency output variables while the reverse is the case in this chapter. We evaluate how low frequency predictors including output can affect the high frequency energy prices including oil price. As the dependent variable is susceptible to conditional heteroscedasticity, the GARCH variant of the MIDAS framework becomes inevitable in our case. This partly explains why the Autoregressive Distributed Lag (ADL) variant of the MIDAS regression, which ignores conditional heteroscedasticity, is employed in the Valadkhani and Smyth [2017] study. The ADL-MIDAS may be valid in the latter case since the dependent variable is of low frequency which is less likely to exhibit conditional heteroscedasticity.

In addition, our analyses capture prominently consumed energy commodities in the US including oil price and, therefore, we are able to offer some meaningful generalizations about the predictability of the selected macroeconomic indices in forecasting the return volatility of energy prices. Thus, the consideration of energy prices in the practical application of GARCH-MIDAS for forecasting constitutes the main contribution of this chapter to the literature on energy modeling.

Foreshadowing our results, we find evidence in support of the inclusion of these macroeconomic information, particularly output growth and realized volatility, as they yield good in-sample and out-of-sample predictability results for the return volatility. Nonetheless, the study finds contrasting evidence between the pre-GFC and post-GFC periods.

The remaining part of this chapter is structured as follows: Section 2 provides a brief review of the literature; Section 3 provides the model set up including estimation procedure and data issues; Section 4 deals with the discussion of preliminary and main results including in-sample and out-of-sample forecast results; and Section 5 concludes the chapter.

2. A Review of the Literature on Forecasting with Energy Prices

Contemporary empirical literature on forecasting the energy price volatilities have taken various dimensions. A strand of the literature approaches this issue by investigating the forecast of energy price volatilities with other macroeconomic fundamentals (see [Kristjanpoller and Minutolo, 2016; Degiannakis and Filis, 2017;

Pan *et al.*, 2017]). Most of these studies, however, focus on oil price volatilities in isolation of other prominent energy prices. Nonetheless, they differ in terms of the methodological approaches adopted. While Degiannakis and Filis, [2017] employ the heterogeneous autoregressive (HAR) model, others adopt multivariate GARCH models such as Artificial Neural Network (ANN)-GARCH model (see [Kristjanpoller and Minutolo, 2016]) and a regime switching GARCH-MIDAS model (see [Pan *et al.*, 2017]).

Although these studies highlight the importance of macroeconomic variables in predicting future oil return volatility, they examine different macroeconomic fundamentals. For instance, Degiannakis and Filis [2017] confirm that information from four asset classes (that is, stocks, foreign exchange, commodities and bonds) enhance the predictive accuracy of oil price realized volatility at all forecast horizons. Also, Kristjanpoller and Minutolo [2016] show that financial variables such as the Euro/Dollar and Yen/Dollar exchange rates, and the DJIA and FTSE stock market indexes are important to the volatility of oil spot and futures prices. Meanwhile, Pan *et al.* [2017] find that both level and volatility of oil supply and demand have significant impacts on oil price volatility.

Another strand of the current empirical literature seeks to tie variations in agricultural commodity prices to volatility in energy prices (see [Koirala *et al.*, 2015; Cabrera and Schulz, 2016]). These studies investigate the nature of linkages between different energy futures prices and agricultural commodities futures prices, albeit in different countries. One is a study on Germany using the Dynamic Conditional Correlation (DCC)-GARCH model (see [Cabrera and Schulz, 2016]) while the other focuses on the US and adopts the copula modeling technique (see [Koirala *et al.*, 2015]).

Results from these studies are mixed. Findings from Cabrera and Schulz [2016] establish that the concern that biofuel is the cause of high and volatile food prices is unfounded. On the other hand, Koirala *et al.* [2015] conclude that increases in the energy prices of natural gas, crude oil, motor gasoline, diesel, and biodiesel would increase agricultural future prices of corn, soybean, and cattle. This indicates that higher energy prices lead to higher costs of production for agricultural commodities.

Another focal point of the recent empirical literature in this line of inquiry is the study of the interdependencies among energy prices (see [Koto, 2015; Ziel *et al.*, 2015; Manera *et al.*, 2016; Baruník and Krehlík, 2016; Serletis and Xu, 2016; Xian *et al.*, 2017; Apergis *et al.*, 2017]). These studies, however, approach the issue from different perspectives, adopting varying methodologies and evaluating different classes of energy prices. For instance, Koto [2015] considers the prices of gasoline, ethanol, natural gas, and crude oil prices with Threshold Autoregressive

(TAR) models; Manera *et al.* [2016] focus on crude oil, heating oil, gasoline and natural gas markets, adopting a plethora of GARCH models; Baruník and Krehlík [2016] analyse crude oil, heating oil, and natural gas and compare the HAR and ARFIMA models against the ANN model; Serletis and Xu [2016] accommodate oil, natural gas, and coal into a trivariate BEKK model; and Ziel *et al.* [2015], Xian *et al.* [2017], and Apergis *et al.* [2017] adopt various GARCH models and divide energy market into renewable and non-renewable energy sources.

In terms of empirical evidence, these studies yield results in support of interactions and spillover effects among the energy prices and their volatilities (see [Ziel *et al.*, 2015; Manera *et al.*, 2016; Baruník and Krehlík, 2016; Serletis and Xu, 2016; Apergis *et al.*, 2017]). Results from the other side of the divide, however, do not reveal evidence in support of energy price volatility interdependencies (see [Koto, 2015; Xian *et al.*, 2017]).

In passing, the debilitating effects of the volatility of energy markets have been linked to uncertainties and distrust among energy companies, investors, consumers, regulators, and legislators (see [Baruník and Krehlík, 2016]). This has driven researches aimed at modeling and forecasting energy price volatility to aid hedging, derivatives trading and policy decisions. The interdependencies of energy prices volatilities suggesting spillover effects have been explored, but with restricted classes of energy fuels compared with the present study. Also, attempts at forecasting energy prices volatilities with macroeconomic information have largely been limited to oil, excluding other biofuels. Further, findings from these studies have remained inconclusive. The foregoing, therefore, represents the gap in the literature which this study attempts to fill.

3. Methodology

3.1. *The model*

Following the works of Engle *et al.* [2013] and Asgharian *et al.* [2013], we specify the GARCH-MIDAS framework used to forecast the return volatility of energy prices as follows:

$$r_{it} = \mu + \sqrt{\tau_t g_{it} \varepsilon_{it}}, \tag{1}$$

$$g_{it} = (1 - \alpha - \beta) + \alpha \frac{(r_{i-1,t} - \mu)^2}{\tau_t} + \beta g_{i-1,t}, \tag{2}$$

$$\tau_t = m + \theta \sum_{k=1}^{K} \psi_k(\omega) \mathrm{V}_{t-k}, \tag{3}$$

$$V_t = \sum_{i=1}^{N} r_{it}^2, \tag{4a}$$

$$V_t = \frac{1}{N}\sum_{i=1}^{N} x_{it}, \tag{4b}$$

$$\psi_k(\omega)\mu\left(1 - \frac{k}{K}\right)^{w-1}, \tag{5a}$$

$$\psi_k(\omega)\mu\left(1 - \frac{k}{K}\right)^{w_1-1}\left(\frac{k}{K}\right)^{w_2-1}, \tag{5b}$$

where r_{it} denotes return series computed as log difference of energy price i in month t. The conditional variance is partitioned into the short-run component (g_{it}) (see Eq. (2)) and the long-run component (see Eq. (3)). Note that the short-run component has GARCH (1, 1)-like while the long-run component is determined by the realized volatility of the macroeconomic series. The variable V_t in Eq. (4a) is the realized volatility of the month while the V_t in Eq. (4b) represents the monthly average of an exogenous variable (such as a monthly industrial growth or inflation whose value x_{it} is fixed for $i = 1, \ldots, N$). As previously mentioned, the macroeconomic series of interest are industrial production index, a proxy for real economic activities and inflation, a proxy for macroeconomic uncertainty. A long history of V_{t-1}, V_{t-2}, $V_{t-3}, \ldots, V_{t-K}$ weighted by Beta polynomials (see Eq. (5a) or (5b)) captures the long-run volatility.

3.2. *Estimation procedure*

The analyses are partitioned into Full Sample and Sub-Samples. The latter involves the Pre-GFC[1] and the Post-GFC. Indeed, the US energy sector has witnessed significant structural changes since the global financial crisis (see [EIA, 2009]). As shown in Figs. 1–7, all the energy prices were moderately stable until the period of global financial crisis beyond which the trends became more unsteady and appear to follow irregular patterns. Thus, we further verify whether the chosen predictors matter for forecasting the return volatility of the US energy prices even in the presence of structural shifts (i.e. regardless of the sub-periods).

For each of the data samples, we singly include the Realized Volatility, Industrial Production Index and Inflation as predictors of the return volatility of US energy

[1]GFC denotes Global Financial Crisis.

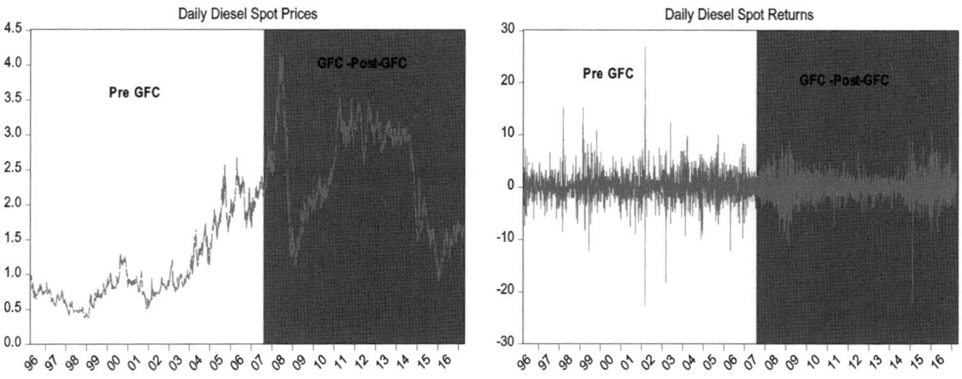

(a) (b)

Fig. 1. Trends in US diesel spot prices and returns.

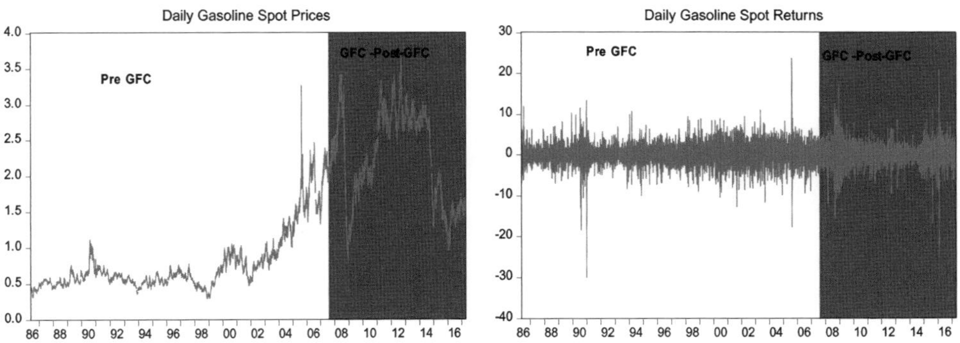

(a) (b)

Fig. 2. Trends in US gasoline spot prices and returns.

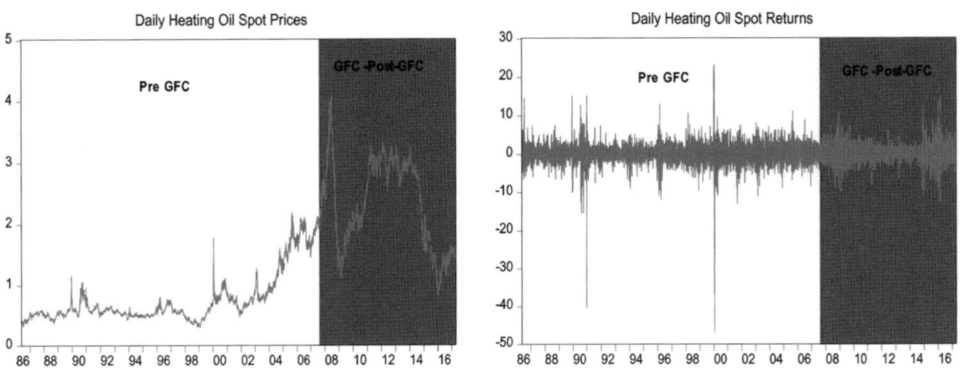

(a) (b)

Fig. 3. Trends in US heating oil spot prices and returns.

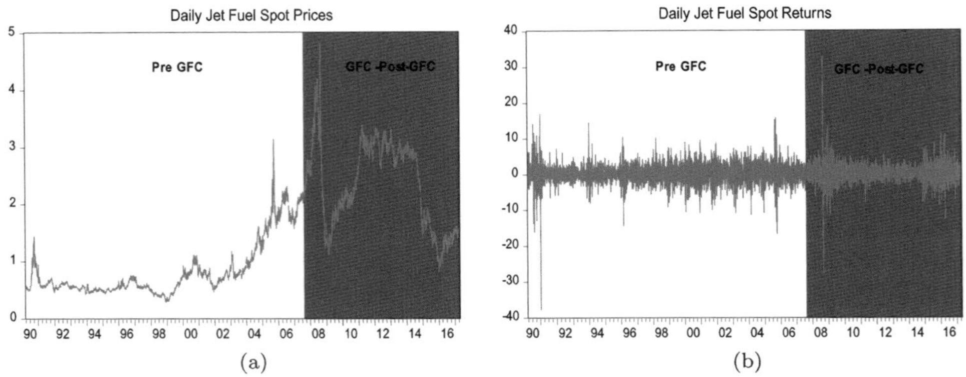

Fig. 4. Trends in US jet fuel spot prices and returns.

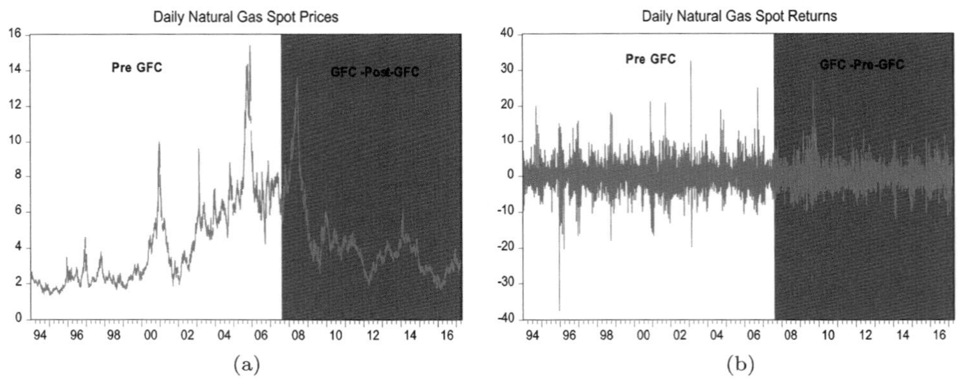

Fig. 5. Trends in US natural gas spot prices and returns.

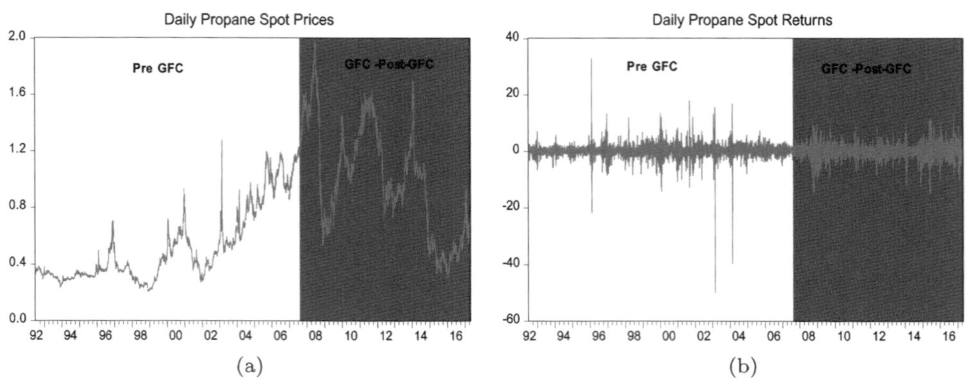

Fig. 6. Trends in US propone spot prices and returns.

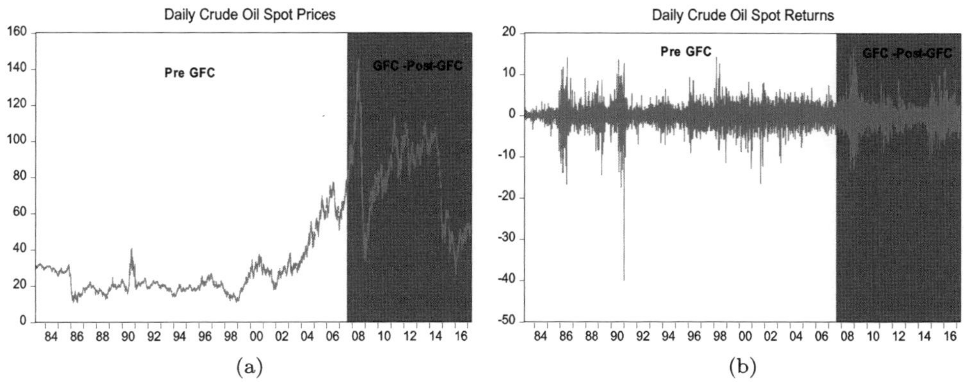

Fig. 7. Trends in WTI crude oil spot prices and returns.

prices. The predictability of each of the predictors under the different data scenarios is evaluated based on the significance of the corresponding coefficient in the conditional variance equation. Thereafter, we evaluate their in-sample and out-of-sample forecast performance. We use 50% of the observations (see [Narayan and Gupta, 2014]) and the balance forms the scope for the out-of-sample forecast. The rolling window approach, in which the long-run component varies every period, is used to generate the forecast results. This is particularly useful when forecasting series that are susceptible to structural changes such as the energy prices.

For the in-sample analyses, our focus is to essentially test the null hypothesis of no predictability for each of the considered predictors and we further complement this outcome by assessing the in-sample forecast accuracy of the predictive models. In other words, the in-sample forecast evaluation involves testing how the predictive models are able to reproduce the actual data. Nonetheless, the out-of-sample forecast evaluation is also required to ascertain the ability of the model to produce accurate forecasts beyond the estimation period.

3.3. *Data issues*

We consider daily spot prices of seven US energy commodities, namely Crude Oil (West Texas Intermediate), New York Harbor Conventional Gasoline Regular, New York Harbor Heating Oil, Ultra-Low Sulfur Diesel, Gulf Coast Kerosene-Type Jet Fuel, Texas Propane and Natural Gas. The unit of measurement for all the prices is in US Dollar per Barrel with the exception of Natural Gas price that is quoted in US Dollar per Million Btu. The US Energy Information Administration is the main source of all the energy prices considered. Table 1 shows the distribution of the data in terms of start date and end date. It can be seen from the table that all the series

Table 1. Distribution of US energy price data.

Energy series	Start date	End date	No. of observations
Diesel	4/17/1996	4/28/2017	5289
Gasoline	6/02/1986	4/28/2017	7781
Heating Oil	6/02/1986	4/28/2017	7777
Jet Fuel	4/02/1990	4/28/2017	6812
Natural Gas	1/13/1994	4/28/2017	5835
Propane	7/09/1992	4/28/2017	6227
WTI	4/04/1983	4/28/2017	8546

have different start dates but a common end date. This is exactly the way the data are structured in the US EIA database.[2]

As demonstrated under the estimation procedure, the GARCH-MIDAS allows for the inclusion of macroeconomic series usually collected at a low frequency in the modeling and forecasting of high frequency series like the energy prices. The monthly data for the macroeconomic series considered in this study, which are industrial production index and inflation, are available from as far back as 1950. However, for the purpose of estimation, the sample data are restricted to the scope of each of the energy prices. For robustness check, we utilize both headline inflation and core inflation in the predictive model for the return volatility. The core inflation excludes the volatile components of the headline inflation such as food and energy and, therefore, it does make sense to ascertain whether the effect of macroeconomic uncertainty (where inflation serves as a proxy) on the return volatility of energy price is not due to the volatile components. Data for the macroeconomic series are obtained from the Bloomberg terminal.

4. Results

4.1. *Preliminary analyses*

In this section, we assess the descriptive properties of the energy return series with statistics such as the mean, skewness, kurtosis and standard deviation to comment on the nature of the distribution of the series. We structure the data into full sample, pre-GFC, and post-GFC. The descriptive statistics are reported in Table 2 while Table 3 presents the results for the serial correlation and heteroscedasticity tests.

[2]The same data samples were used in the paper of Narayan and Liu [2015] to illustrate the relevance of using the GARCH-based unit root test when dealing with high frequency and trending time series. However, we have further updated the datasets to account for current realities.

Table 2. Descriptive statistics of the return series.

Statistics	Energy type	Full sample	Pre-GFC	Post-GFC
Mean	Diesel	0.00969	0.03075	−0.01444
	Gasoline	0.01401	0.04021	−0.01411
	Heating Oil	0.01635	0.04028	−0.01529
	Jet Fuel	0.01397	0.04490	−0.01676
	Natural Gas	0.00687	0.02986	−0.02233
	Propane	0.01042	0.04409	−0.02871
	WTI	0.00604	0.03865	−0.01731
Standard deviation	Diesel	2.36035	2.49375	2.19411
	Gasoline	2.61428	2.87655	2.55570
	Heating Oil	2.51587	2.83568	2.17507
	Jet Fuel	2.55930	2.66741	2.38182
	Natural Gas	3.57324	3.85387	3.08599
	Propane	2.47457	2.61791	2.49171
	WTI	2.39213	2.33502	2.51284
Skewness	Diesel	0.10132	0.32436	−0.29508
	Gasoline	−0.23063	0.09842	−0.34511
	Heating Oil	−1.43258	−1.75531	0.04726
	Jet Fuel	−0.47435	−0.21612	0.31120
	Natural Gas	0.22785	0.37590	0.63787
	Propane	−1.74312	−3.35292	−0.47661
	WTI	−0.71157	−0.27165	0.16746
Kurtosis	Diesel	13.6474	15.37147	9.61252
	Gasoline	10.7110	6.54933	12.2855
	Heating Oil	38.3354	44.5307	7.29701
	Jet Fuel	19.5834	6.23350	28.1943
	Natural Gas	9.88985	7.81420	7.25183
	Propane	50.9006	72.4551	8.15323
	WTI	17.3329	6.10518	7.48704

The descriptive analyses reveal similar mean values for diesel, natural gas and crude oil on one hand and gasoline, heating oil, jet fuel and propane on the other hand for full sample. We do not, however, obtain the same pattern for the pre-GFC sample period as all the return series have similar average values. For the post-GFC era, the mean energy return values are close, except for natural gas and propane that are slightly different. A point that is worthy of note here is that the mean returns are all positive values in full sample and pre GFC while they are all negative in post-GFC era.

Further descriptive analyses from the skewness statistics reveal that majority of the daily energy return series (gasoline, heating oil, jet fuel, propane, and crude oil) are negatively skewed while only diesel and natural gas are positively skewed over

Table 3. Serial correlation and heteroscedasticity tests.

Lag structure	Energy type	Full sample	Pre-GFC	Post-GFC
ARCH LM Test				
(5)	Diesel	154.539***	117.043***	23.7243***
	Gasoline	174.473***	133.663***	76.0801***
	Heating Oil	248.403***	156.361***	54.0616***
	Jet Fuel	125.614***	69.9640***	122.491***
	Natural Gas	56.440***	24.5140***	17.8240***
	Propane	39.091***	15.2570***	56.7071***
	WTI	106.683***	13.1695***	91.1643***
(10)	Diesel	77.568***	58.3455***	15.9979***
	Gasoline	89.150***	67.4703***	40.6088***
	Heating Oil	136.359***	99.9119***	30.9380***
	Jet Fuel	69.916***	41.9138***	80.4388***
	Natural Gas	30.757***	14.38139***	12.3658***
	Propane	19.630***	7.63607***	31.0950***
	WTI	61.200***	6.74113***	55.0213***
(20)	Diesel	39.585***	29.7945***	11.1356***
	Gasoline	45.943***	34.2455***	22.6261***
	Heating Oil	75.811***	62.4467***	18.7926***
	Jet Fuel	35.930***	27.9428***	41.3318***
	Natural Gas	20.587***	9.28462***	8.99689***
	Propane	10.289***	4.06279***	17.42901***
	WTI	32.965***	3.99354***	33.5791***
Serial Correlation (Q Stat) Test				
(5)	Diesel	37.021***	35.505***	15.588***
	Gasoline	27.386***	24.921***	20.317***
	Heating Oil	38.164***	50.931***	9.3015*
	Jet Fuel	14.921**	5.8335	11.224**
	Natural Gas	23.221***	7.6319	29.403***
	Propane	28.358***	27.268***	46.607***
	WTI	44.164***	8.0289	17.489***
(10)	Diesel	39.051***	39.736***	19.636*
	Gasoline	53.783***	34.096***	32.477***
	Heating Oil	52.271***	65.266***	12.066
	Jet Fuel	30.190***	14.137	22.694**
	Natural Gas	37.166***	12.283	39.506***
	Propane	36.624***	36.310***	50.535***
	WTI	57.021***	15.549	18.304***
(20)	Diesel	55.082***	51.070***	33.472*
	Gasoline	85.193***	41.801***	53.842***
	Heating Oil	67.821***	84.477***	28.108
	Jet Fuel	57.931***	48.303***	33.225**

(Continued)

Table 3. (*Continued*)

Lag structure	Energy type	Full sample	Pre-GFC	Post-GFC
	Natural Gas	51.722***	28.500*	54.364***
	Propane	63.495***	57.605***	83.286***
	WTI	69.984***	29.166*	38.265***
Serial Correlation (Q^2 Stat) Test				
(5)	Diesel	1014.4***	725.25***	160.84***
	Gasoline	1084.1***	832.25***	383.49***
	Heating Oil	1791.0***	1078.1***	316.97***
	Jet Fuel	782.80***	514.72***	645.58***
	Natural Gas	374.41***	160.71***	114.33***
	Propane	254.20***	92.180***	454.51***
	WTI	730.76***	78.261***	764.27***
(10)	Diesel	1041.9***	727.20***	278.56***
	Gasoline	1192.1***	844.73***	443.97***
	Heating Oil	1975.8***	1168.2***	452.96***
	Jet Fuel	888.67***	820.72***	659.57***
	Natural Gas	472.91***	222.21***	205.17***
	Propane	265.09***	94.354***	647.66***
	WTI	995.27***	86.931***	1401.9***
(20)	Diesel	1078.7***	728.96***	278.56***
	Gasoline	1358.6***	869.67***	443.97***
	Heating Oil	2160.3***	1261.4***	783.35***
	Jet Fuel	1044.5***	1383.7***	690.84***
	Natural Gas	746.79***	329.64***	370.12***
	Propane	287.39***	101.88***	896.22***
	WTI	1378.4***	107.93***	2501.5***

Note: ***, **, * represent significance at 1%, 5%; and 10%, respectively.

full sample. However, during pre-GFC, all except heating oil, propane, and crude oil are positively skewed. In the post-GFC era, however, only diesel, gasoline and propane returns are negatively skewed. An inspection of the kurtosis values indicates uniformity in the behavior of the series as all of them have their kurtosis values greater than three; and hence, exhibit leptokurtic distribution across full sample, pre- and post-GFC. The foregoing, therefore, provides convincing evidence that the energy returns are not normally distributed.

Having evaluated the distribution of the energy return series, we analyze the standard deviation values to comment on the return volatility of the energy prices. Although the standard deviation values seem to suggest clustering of the volatility, diesel and crude oil are the least volatile while natural gas price seems to be most volatile. In between are propane, heating oil, jet fuel and gasoline for the full sample and pre-GFC periods. For the post-GFC period, however, heating oil and diesel returns are the least volatile while natural gas is still the most volatile energy fuel. The movements in both the level and return series of energy prices are also rendered graphically (see Figs. 1–7). It is evident that there is a notable shift in the level of energy prices which coincides with the period of the global financial crisis and that explains why it may be necessary to partition analyses involving such trends into pre- and post-GFC periods.

We proceed to test for the presence of heteroscedascitity and serial correlation in the data in order to formally justify the suitability of a GARCH-based approach for modeling energy returns (see Table 3). We employ the ARCH-LM test for heteroscedasticity and the Q- and Q^2-Statistics for serial correlation. We run both tests using 5, 10 and 20 lag lengths across the full sample, pre-GFC and post-GFC data samples. The results of the ARCH-LM test reject the null hypothesis of no ARCH effects in the energy price returns at the 1 per cent significance level, regardless of the lag order.

We complement the ARCH-LM test with the serial correlation test and the results are also reported in Table 3. The results also largely suggest the presence of statistically significant serial correlations regardless of the sample period. This further reinforces the suitability of a GARCH-based framework for modeling and forecasting the return volatility of energy prices.

4.2. *Predictability test results*

4.2.1. *Full sample*

Given the motivation of this study, we obtain information from realized volatility and two prominent macroeconomic variables, namely growth in industrial production and inflation, to test whether these variables can help predict the return volatility of energy prices. Although the realized volatility is used to measure macroeconomic volatility in the GARCH-MIDAS framework, the additional exogenous variables included become necessary as the former could be a noisy proxy (see [Engle *et al.*, 2013]). We also test whether the return volatility is sensitive to the choice of measure for inflation. In other words, we consider both headline inflation and core inflation and, thereafter, we test the significance of the two measures in predicting energy prices. The tests are conducted for the full sample as well as for the pre-GFC and post-GFC sub-periods. The predictability performance results are contained in Table 4. These are evaluated based on the significance or otherwise of the respective coefficients of each of the predictors.

Our results are mixed for the three time periods studied. For the full sample (see Table 4), our results reveal that virtually all the macroeconomic information

Table 4. In-sample predictability performance results.

	Full sample				Sub-sample							
					Pre-GFC				Post-GFC			
			π_t				π_t				π_t	
Energy	V_t	y_t	**CPI**	**CPIC**	V_t	y_t	**CPI**	**CPIC**	V_t	y_t	**CPI**	**CPIC**
Diesel	−0.00305***	−0.05237***	−0.2372***	0.0732**	0.01856***	0.02010**	−0.4638***	−0.40439**	0.01021***	−0.03364***	−0.06264**	−0.007567
	(0.00057)	(0.01000)	(0.05568)	(0.03266)	(0.004850)	(0.008349)	(0.05496)	(0.20177)	(0.003277)	(0.01073)	(0.02817)	(0.04213)
Gasoline	0.03087***	0.10003***	0.05527	0.02677	0.01714***	0.08803***	0.11375**	0.09224**	0.03564***	−0.04204***	−0.0861**	−0.05548
	(0.003477)	(0.031926)	(0.03422)	(0.02297)	(0.006173)	(0.03394)	(0.05052)	(0.03963)	(0.00498)	(0.01162)	(0.04088)	(0.1211)
Heating Oil	−0.0012025***	−0.05157**	0.06843	−0.0746	0.03015***	−0.01352	0.14369***	0.04683***	0.04032***	−0.03346***	0.00809	−0.1250**
	(0.00018163)	(0.02124)	(0.05089)	(0.04556)	(0.003556)	(0.010788)	(0.04462)	(0.01445)	(0.00399)	(0.01202)	(0.03288)	(0.0585)
Jet Fuel	0.033492***	−0.01165*	0.02775*	−0.2952***	0.00515	0.082766**	−0.45319**	0.02753**	0.05067***	−0.06033***	−0.2416*	1.9334*
	(0.0027475)	(0.006143)	(0.01455)	(0.05973)	(0.005818)	(0.03808)	(0.21985)	(0.01305)	(0.00414)	(0.009236)	(0.1264)	(1.0376)
Natural Gas	0.032009***	−0.20835***	−0.4660***	−1.6943***	0.03040***	−0.73158	−0.66013*	−2.5808***	0.02550**	−0.02326**	−0.0759**	−0.14552**
	(0.0028233)	(0.05172)	(0.1738)	(0.36769)	(0.003956)	(0.67392)	(0.37557)	(0.73202)	(0.01207)	(0.01100)	(0.03052)	(0.06106)
Propane	−0.003961***	0.09997***	−0.6423***	0.19637***	−0.00396***	−0.22277***	0.18651***	0.19264***	0.04071***	−0.47608***	0.05916**	0.1118**
	(0.0009048)	(0.00107)	(0.1184)	(0.03573)	(0.0009048)	(0.04743)	(0.03490)	(0.03061)	(0.00651)	(0.16047)	(0.02986)	(0.05291)
WTI	0.052445***	0.31545*	−0.17792**	−0.31202***	0.05608***	0.04217	0.002186	−0.5054***	0.03589***	−0.44146***	0.09665**	0.11822***
	(0.002221)	(0.16875)	(0.08125)	(0.10488)	(0.003740)	(0.03769)	(0.01872)	(0.17002)	(0.00567)	(0.12021)	(0.04474)	(0.04507)

Note: The variables V_t, y_t and π_t are the realized volatility, output and inflation, respectively, while CPIC and CPI denote the core and headline CPI, respectively. For brevity, we report only the results for the predictors in the predictive regression model. Thus, the parameter of interest in the GARCH-MIDAS regression is the θ in Eq. 3. Values in parentheses – () denote standard errors, while ***, ** and ** imply significance at 1%, 5% and 10%, respectively.

considered: realized volatility, output, headline, and core inflation, appear as consistent potential predictors of diesel, jet fuel, natural gas, propane and crude oil returns volatility. This evidence is not unexpected since increased productive activities imply a higher consumption of energy products that are used in the production process such as those that are found to respond significantly to the movements in industrial output. Similarly, the comovement between inflation (both headline and core) and energy prices captures the demand side of the energy, in which case increased demands for goods and services may cause the demand for energy products to increase (and by extension energy prices) in order to increase supply to meet such demands.

The nexus between CPI-inflation and energy prices in our study, particularly for crude oil and diesel prices, is consistent with findings from Koirala *et al.* [2015]; Cabrera and Schulz [2016]; and Al-Madid *et al.* [2017]. Koirala *et al.* [2015] adopt copula modeling approach; Cabrera and Schulz [2016] employ the DCC-GARCH model; while Al-Madid *et al.* [2017] apply the VAR-GARCH framework to establish the significant linkages between volatilities in energy and other prices (i.e. food & agricultural prices). These studies are, however, less encompassing compared to our study, given that we assess return volatilities in energy prices and thereafter evaluate the forecast performance of relevant predictors for a broader number of energy commodities.

In addition, the significance of both realized volatility and industrial growth seems to be in tandem with the results from contemporary researches such as Antonakakis *et al.* [2014]; Karali and Ramirez [2014]; Degiannakis and Filis [2017] and Pan *et al.* [2017]. These studies highlight the importance of realized volatility, production and the level of global economic activities in providing information for predicting energy volatility. However, a major drawback in comparing our study with these previous works is that they restricted their analysis to oil price volatility excluding other energy prices.

4.2.2. *Pre-GFC versus post-GFC*

Results obtained in the pre-GFC sample period stand in contrast with those of the full sample (see Table 4). For the pre-GFC sample, all the four variables appear as potential predictors of diesel, gasoline and propane return volatilities. Realized volatility, headline and core inflation are the likely predictors of heating oil and natural gas return volatilities. While our results show output, headline and core inflation as potential predictors of jet fuel, only endogenous shocks (realized volatility) and core inflation could likely predict crude oil return volatility in the period before the global financial crisis. Core inflation is the only consistent potential predictor of all the energy returns in this period. This implies that the return volatility of energy prices responds more prominently to volatility in non-energy consumer prices during the pre-GFC period (see also [Koirala *et al.*, 2015; Cabrera and Schulz, 2016; and Al-Madid *et al.*, 2017]).

Contrary to the pre-GFC but in unison with the full sample results, realized volatility and output emerge as consistent potential predictors of all the seven energy returns in the post-GFC. We can therefore safely infer that the findings of Antonakakis *et al.* [2014]; Karali and Ramirez [2014]; Pan *et al.* [2017] and Degiannakis and Filis [2017] are relevant in the post-GFC era. Further in this period, headline inflation (which contains information about energy prices) is shown as a more consistent potential predictor of energy returns than core inflation. This finding also indicates that the submissions of Koirala *et al.* [2015]; Cabrera and Schulz [2016]; and Al-Madid *et al.* [2017] are valid for the post-GFC period.

In sum, three major conclusions are distinct from the in-sample predictability results. First, on average, the realized volatility and output offer more useful information for predicting energy return volatility than inflation. Second, the impact of these predictors tends to be more pronounced in the post-GFC period than the pre-GFC period. Third, the information about energy prices contained in headline inflation enhances its predictability of energy returns.

4.3. *In-sample forecast evaluation*

4.3.1. *Full sample*

The predictability test results have shown that, on average, realized volatility and output can consistently predict at least five of the energy prices while headline and core inflation play a marginal role. To validate these results, we explore the forecast performance using a simple forecast measure involving the Root Mean Square Error (hereafter, RMSE).[3] The conventional value of the RMSE is zero and, as such, the closer the RMSE value due to a particular predictor is to zero, the better the forecasting accuracy of such a predictor. The in-sample forecast results of the GARCH-MIDAS for the data samples are presented in Table 5.

The in-sample performance evaluation of the full sample period reveals that the predictors provide more accurate in-sample forecasts for gasoline return volatility and least accurate in-sample forecasts for propane return volatility. Based on this,

[3]We do acknowledge other prominent measures of evaluating forecast performance measures such as the Diebold and Mariano [1995] and Campbell-Thomson [2008], among others. However, all these measures are suppressed in this chapter since our mean square errors are consistently found to be very small for all the considered energy prices.

Table 5. In-sample forecast evaluation of GARCH-MIDAS sample using root mean square error.

					Sub-sample							
	Full sample				**Pre-GFC**				**Post-GFC**			
			π_{it}				π_{it}				π_{it}	
Energy	V_t	y_{it}	**CPI**	**CPIC**	V_t	y_{it}	**CPI**	**CPIC**	V_t	y_t	**CPI**	**CPIC**
Diesel	2.294e-03	2.313e-03	2.311e-03	2.321e-03	1.454e-03	1.464e-03	1.469e-03	1.463e-03	1.129e-03	1.032e-03	1.038e-03	1.036e-03
Gasoline	1.943e-03	1.931e-03	1.933e-03	1.928e-03	2.172e-03	2.159e-03	2.155e-03	2.156e-03	1.672e-03	1.671e-03	1.683e-03	1.674e-03
Heating Oil	5.011e-03	5.115e-03	5.113e-03	5.116e-03	3.582e-03	3.488e-03	3.492e-03	3.482e-03	8.896e-04	8.861e-04	9.552e-04	9.769e-04
Jet Fuel	2.866e-03	2.861e-03	2.861e-03	2.864e-03	3.430e-03	3.433e-03	3.432e-03	3.428e-03	3.910e-03	3.882e-03	4.749e-03	4.751e-03
Natural Gas	4.599e-03	4.599e-03	4.598e-03	4.602e-03	4.622e-03	1.379e-02	4.607e-03	4.613e-03	2.957e-03	2.957e-03	2.957e-03	2.974e-03
Propane	5.932e-03	5.885e-03	6.023e-03	6.057e-03	5.932e-03	6.095e-03	6.032e-03	6.041e-03	1.421e-03	1.839e-03	1.503e-03	1.501e-03
WTI	2.915e-03	2.971e-03	2.890e-03	2.888e-03	3.437e-03	3.375e-03	3.357e-03	3.364e-03	1.793e-03	2.071e-03	2.021e-03	2.016e-03

Note: The variables V_t, y_t and π_t are the realized volatility, output and inflation, respectively, while CPIC and CPI denote the core and headline CPI, respectively.

the predictors are less accurate in predictive abilities for forecasting heating oil and natural gas. In this light, after gasoline, the predictors provide good in-sample forecast accuracy for diesel, jet fuel and crude oil return volatility, in that order. Our finding that the forecast performance of the macroeconomic information is relatively lower for heating oil and natural gas returns compared to other energy price returns has been previously established by Karali and Ramirez [2014]. Further, the evidence in support of good in-sample forecast accuracy for gasoline, diesel, jet fuel and crude oil return volatility is partly corroborated by Pan *et al.* [2017] who model WTI and Brent oil return volatility with a regime switching GARCH-MIDAS model. The study finds good in-sample of macroeconomic variables in volatility forecasting. Other studies that find that the inclusion of macroeconomic information improve in-sample of energy returns are Kristjanpoller and Minutolo [2016]; Manera *et al.* [2016]; and Degiannakis and Filis [2017]. These studies, however, include macroeconomic information different from the present study, like financial speculation, exchange rate, stock market indices, and commodity prices, to predict return volatility in energy prices.

4.3.2. *Pre-GFC versus post-GFC*

In the pre-GFC sample period, the predictors record the highest forecast performance for diesel return volatility while the least for natural and propane return volatilities. In between are gasoline, heating oil, jet fuel and crude oil returns with the predictors providing better in-sample forecasts for gasoline after diesel return volatility. These results differ for the post-GFC sample period. Based on the RMSE values, the predictors have more accurate in-sample predictive ability for forecasting heating oil returns followed by diesel, propane, gasoline and crude oil return volatilities, in that order.

In comparison, the predictors offer a lower forecast performance for natural gas and jet fuel return volatilities in the post-GFC compared with the pre-GFC. This stands in contrast with Barunik and Krehlik [2016] who establish in-sample predictability for natural gas in the post-GFC. However, the difference between Barunik and Krehlik [2016] and the present study is that the former adopts a different methodology — the Artificial Neural Networks (ANN) approach — and include only realized volatility in the forecasting model. Nonetheless, our predictors give better in-sample forecast results on the energy return volatility for the post-GFC period compared with the pre-GFC period.

4.4. *Out-of-sample forecast performance evaluation*

4.4.1. *Full sample*

The fact that good in-sample forecast results do not necessarily translate to quality out-of-sample forecast performance has been established. On this note, we consider the out-of-sample forecast performance of the GARCH-MIDAS energy returns predictive model. We report the 30-day and the 60-day periods ahead forecast horizons. Consequently, we evaluate the accuracy of each of the predictors for the out-of-sample forecast. The results are reported in Tables 6 and 7, respectively, for 30-day and 60-day forecast horizons.

Our out-of-sample forecast evaluation result for full sample is consistent with in-sample forecast performance results. These predictors give relatively more accurate out-of-sample forecast for jet fuel and crude oil, and this is consistent for 30-day and 60-day forecast horizons. They are also consistently less-accurate in out-of-sample forecast of natural gas and heating oil in the 30-day and 60-day forecast horizons. In tandem with Haugom *et al.* [2014] and Pan *et al.* [2017], who also adopt the GARCH-MIDAS approach; and Barunik and Krehlik [2016] who adopt the ANN modeling framework, we establish that macroeconomic variables offer useful information that can be exploited in order to enhance the out-of-sample predictability of return volatility of energy prices.

4.4.2. *Pre-GFC versus post-GFC*

The in-sample forecast evaluation results reveal that the predictors produce least RMSE values for gasoline and diesel and relatively higher RMSE values for natural gas and propane in the pre-GFC. Conversely, in the post-GFC era, the predictors provide more accurate in-sample forecasts for all the energy returns except natural gas and jet fuel. Like the in-sample case, our results are also slightly different for the out-of-sample predictability evaluation between the pre-GFC and post-GFC era. The predictors are shown to offer good out-of-sample forecasts predictability for gasoline, heating oil and crude oil consistently for 30-day and 60-day forecast horizons in the pre-GFC. However, in the post-GFC period, the predictors consistently offer good out-of-sample forecast predictability for all the energy returns except natural gas. Notwithstanding the mixed results for pre-GFC and post-GFC periods, the predictors have the least out-of-sample forecast predictability for natural gas returns. This further confirms the findings of Manera *et al.* [2016]; Kristjanpoller and Minutolo [2016]; and Degiannakis and Filis [2017] and equally corroborates our in-sample predictability evaluation results that find

Table 6. Out-of-sample forecast evaluation of GARCH-MIDAS with h = 30.

	Full sample				Sub-sample							
					Pre-GFC				Post-GFC			
			π_{it}				π_{it}				π_{it}	
Energy	V_t	y_{it}	**CPI**	**CPIC**	V_t	y_{it}	**CPI**	**CPIC**	V_t	y_t	**CPI**	**CPIC**
Diesel	1.030e-03	1.004e-03	1.018e-03	1.015e-03	1.586e-03	1.564e-03	1.516e-03	1.566e-03	3.215e-04	3.346e-04	3.350e-04	3.377e-04
Gasoline	1.906e-03	1.928e-03	1.927e-03	1.924e-03	4.007e-04	4.021e-04	3.979e-04	3.955e-04	3.361e-04	3.630e-04	3.510e-04	3.628e-04
Heating Oil	2.050e-03	2.050e-03	2.051e-03	2.050e-03	3.683e-04	3.680e-04	3.780e-04	3.751e-04	3.161e-04	3.189e-04	3.172e-04	3.129e-04
Jet Fuel	7.582e-04	7.595e-04	7.574e-04	7.612e-04	2.105e-03	2.104e-03	2.086e-03	2.103e-03	2.970e-04	3.493e-04	2.765e-04	2.751e-04
Natural Gas	3.844e-03	3.829e-03	3.864e-03	3.806e-03	9.268e-03	9.094e-03	9.157e-03	9.100e-03	1.720e-03	1.714e-03	1.710e-03	1.711e-03
Propane	1.748e-03	1.742e-03	6.023e-03	1.753e-03	1.748e-03	1.763e-03	1.755e-03	1.780e-03	7.233e-04	7.134e-04	7.049e-04	7.006e-04
WTI	9.774e-04	9.707e-04	9.703e-04	9.692e-04	2.883e-04	2.879e-04	2.847e-04	2.877e-04	5.982e-04	5.937e-04	5.392e-04	5.407e-04

Note: The variables V_t, y_t and π_t are the realized volatility, output and inflation, respectively, while CPIC and CPI denote the core and headline CPI, respectively.

Table 7. Out-of-sample forecast evaluation of GARCH-MIDAS with h = 60.

					Sub-sample							
	Full sample				Pre-GFC				Post-GFC			
			π_{it}				π_{it}				π_{it}	
Energy	V_t	y_{it}	CPI	CPIC	V_t	y_{it}	CPI	CPIC	V_t	y_t	CPI	CPIC
Diesel	2.082e-03	2.083e-03	2.083e-03	2.088e-03	1.114e-02	1.153e-02	1.196e-02	1.155e-02	3.691e-04	3.830e-04	3.790e-04	3.828e-04
Gasoline	1.697e-03	1.705e-03	1.710e-03	1.708e-03	3.968e-04	4.062e-04	3.963e-04	3.986e-04	6.152e-04	6.102e-04	6.118e-04	6.129e-04
Heating Oil	1.622e-03	1.622e-03	1.622e-03	1.622e-03	3.888e-04	3.881e-04	3.923e-04	3.901e-04	2.743e-04	2.776e-04	2.729e-04	2.624e-04
Jet Fuel	1.083e-03	1.075e-03	1.070e-03	1.070e-03	1.842e-03	1.840e-03	1.829e-03	1.837e-03	2.623e-04	3.268e-04	2.454e-04	2.456e-04
Natural Gas	3.028e-03	3.017e-03	3.045e-03	2.993e-03	8.163e-03	8.148e-03	8.126e-03	8.111e-03	1.355e-03	1.362e-03	1.348e-03	1.355e-03
Propane	1.748e-03	1.291e-03	1.262e-03	2.315e-05	1.229e-03	1.238e-03	1.263e-03	1.256e-03	8.725e-04	8.726e-04	8.721e-04	8.709e-04
WTI	1.144e-03	1.126e-03	1.122e-03	1.122e-03	3.036e-04	3.009e-04	2.963e-04	2.996e-04	4.679e-04	5.781e-04	4.299e-04	4.315e-04

Note: The variables V_t, y_t and π_t are the realized volatility, output and inflation, respectively, while CPIC and CPI denote the core and headline CPI, respectively.

relatively lower predictability performance for natural gas returns when compared with the forecast performance of other return volatilities.

5. Conclusion

Several studies in the literature have focused on energy prices to study the volatility and factors responsible for such. Even so, there are still several issues of concern. One of these is that most of the studies that seek to forecast energy prices are limited to oil returns excluding other classes of energy fuels. More so, findings from these studies are not unanimous. Further, many of those that consider various energy prices majorly explore the interdependencies of spillover effects among the energy prices volatilities while the role of macroeconomic factors in such spillovers is not analyzed from a forecasting perspective. This study offers evidence on the modeling of different classes of energy prices in the periods before and after the global financial crisis, given the likely impact of the financial crisis on the macroeconomic predictors of energy prices.

We examine the predictive power of such macroeconomic predictors, as realized volatility, output, headline inflation and core inflation, and adopt the GARCH-MIDAS modeling framework to model and forecast return volatilities in diesel, gasoline, jet fuel, heating oil, natural gas, propane and crude oil. We conduct relevant descriptive statistics and pre-test on the series to reveal the volatilities, serial correlation and autoregressive conditional heteroscedasticity in the energy returns. We conduct the predictability performance tests, the in-sample and out-of-sample forecast performance evaluations for the full-sample, pre-GFC and post-GFC time bounds.

Our findings show that the macroeconomic information considered in the model are good predictors of energy return volatilities and these predictors have more reliable in-sample and out-of-sample forecast performances especially in the post-GFC period. In all, this study reveals that realized volatility and output offer more useful information for predicting energy return volatility than inflation.

References

Al-Madid, A., Caporale, G. M., Spagnolo, F. and Spagnolo, N. (2017). Spillovers between food and energy prices and structural breaks. *International Economics* **150**, 1–18.

Andreou, E., Ghysels, E. and Kourtellos, A. (2013). Should macroeconomic forecasters look at daily financial data? *Journal of Business and Economic Statistics* **31**, 240–251.

Antonakakis, N., Chatziantoniou, I. and Filis, G. (2014). Dynamic spillovers of oil price shocks and economic policy uncertainty. *Energy Economics* **44**, 433–447.

Apergis, N., Barunık, J. and Lau, M. C. (2017). Good volatility, bad volatility: What drives the asymmetric connectedness of Australian electricity markets? *Energy Economics* **66**, 108–115.

Asgharian, H., Hou, A. J. and Javed, F. (2013). The importance of the macroeconomic variables in forecasting stock return variance: A Garch-Midas approach. *Journal of Forecasting* **32** (7), 600–612.

Baruník, J. and Krehlík, T. (2016). Combining high frequency data with non-linear models for forecasting energy market volatility. *Expert Systems with Applications* **55**, 222–242.

Cabrera, B. L. and Schulz, F. (2016). Volatility linkages between energy and agricultural commodity prices. *Energy Economics* **54**, 190–203.

Campbell, J. Y. and Thompson, S. B. (2008). Predicting excess stock returns out of sample: Can anything beat the historical average? *Review of Financial Studies* **21**, 1509–1531.

Clements, M. P. and Galvão, A. B. (2008). Macroeconomic forecasting with mixed-frequency data: Forecasting output growth in the United States. *Journal of Business & Economic Statistics* **26** (4), 546–554.

Degiannakis, S. and Filis, G. (2017). Forecasting oil price realized volatility using information channels from other asset classes. *Journal of International Money and Finance* **76**, 28–49.

Diebold, F. X. and Mariano, R. S. (1995). Comparing predictive accuracy. *Journal of Business & Economic Statistics* **13**, 253–263.

Engle, R. F., Ghysels, E. and Sohn, B. (2013). Stock market volatility and macroeconomic fundamentals. *Review of Economics and Statistics* **95** (3), 776–797.

Ghysels, E., Kvedaras, V. and Zemlys, V. (2015). Mixed Frequency Data Sampling Regression Models: The R Package midasr. R user guide for MIDAS regressions: http://github.com/mpiktas/midasr-user-guide.

Ghysels, E., Santa-Clara, P. and Valkanov, R. (2006). Predicting volatility: Getting the most out of return data sampled at different frequencies. *Journal of Econometrics* **131** (1), 59–95.

Haugom, E., Langeland, H., Molnar, P. and Westgaard, S. (2014). Forecasting volatility of the US oil market. *Journal of Banking & Finance* **47**, 1–14.

Karali, B. and Ramirez, O. A. (2014). Macro determinants of volatility and volatility spillover in energy markets. *Energy Economics* **46**, 413–421.

Koirala, K. H., Mishra, A. K., D'Antoni, J. M. and Mehlhorn, J. E. (2015). Energy prices and agricultural commodity prices: Testing correlation using copulas method. *Energy* **81**, 430–436.

Koto, P. S. (2015). Are retail prices of ethanol, gasoline and natural gas in the Midwest cointegrated? An asymmetric threshold cointegration analysis. *Journal of Economics and Business* **77**, 79–93.

Kristjanpoller, W. and Minutolo, M. C. (2016). Forecasting volatility of oil price using an artificial neural network-GARCH model. *Expert Systems with Applications* **65**, 233–241.

Manera, M., Nicolini, M. and Vignati, I. (2016). Modelling futures price volatility in energy markets: Is there a role for financial speculation? *Energy Economics* **53**, 220–229.

Narayan, P. K. and Gupta, R. (2014). Has oil price predicted stock returns for over a century? *Energy Economics* **48**, 18–23.

Narayan, P. K. and Liu, R. (2015). A unit root model for trending time-series energy variables. *Energy Economics* **50**, 391–402.

Omri, A. (2014). An international literature survey on energy-economic growth nexus: Evidence from country-specific studies. *Renewable and Sustainable Energy Reviews* **38**, 951–959.

Pan, Z., Wang, Y., Wu, C. and Yin, L. (2017). Oil price volatility and macroeconomic fundamentals: A regime switching GARCH-MIDAS model. *Journal of Empirical Finance* **43**, 130–142.

Salisu, A. A., Isah, K. O., Oyewole, O. J. and Akanni, L. O. (2017). Modelling oil price — inflation nexus: The role of asymmetries. *Energy* **125**, 97–106.

Serletis, A. and Xu, L. (2016). Volatility and a century of energy markets dynamics. *Energy Economics* **55**, 1–9.

Valadkhani, A. and Smyth, R. (2017). How do daily changes in oil prices affect US monthly industrial output? *Energy Economics* **67**, 83–90, doi: 10.1016/j.eneco.2017.08.009.

Xian, H., Colson, G., Karali, B. and Wetzstein, M. (2017). Do nonrenewable-energy prices affect renewable-energy volatility? The case of wood pellets. *Journal of Forest Economics* **28**, 42–48.

Ziel, F., Steinert, R. and Husmann, S. (2015). Efficient modeling and forecasting of electricity spot prices. *Energy Economics* **47**, 98–111.

Chapter 4

Bayesian Approach to Energy Load Forecast with Neural Networks

Luca Di Persio* and Oleksandr Honchar†
Department of Informatics, University of Verona, Italy
**luca.dipersio@univr.it*
†rachnogstyle@gmail.com

Short- and long-term forecasts have become increasingly important since the rise of highly competitive electricity markets. The latter point is particularly evident within recently liberalized frameworks, as it has happened, e.g. in some European countries like Germany, and it is going to happen in Italy.

Lately, forecasting of possible future loads turned out to be fundamental to build efficient energy management strategies as well as to avoid energy wastage. Such type of challenges are difficult to tackle both from a theoretical and applied point of view. In fact, latter tasks require sophisticated methods to manage multidimensional time series related to stochastic phenomena which are often highly interconnected.

During last years, the most promising results related to energy-based time series and their forecasting were obtained using machine learning algorithms, particularly with respect to the realization of ad hoc developed, deep neural networks (NNs) approaches. It is worth to mention that deep NNs architectures as, e.g. convolutional NNs and recurrent NNs have shown their power in handling complex temporal data. Nevertheless, mostly because of the large number of parameters these models are based on, such NNs are often hard to regularize, difficult to manage for out-of-sample data as well as outliers, and, moreover, they often suffer from lack of meaning.

In what follows, we propose a novel approach to energy load time series forecasting, which is based on tailored realized combination of deep learning NNs techniques and probabilistic programming. Properly merging such approaches, we can include uncertainty components both in predictions and representations. This leads to efficient regularization procedures, with priors, also allowing for a more powerful way to build complex NNs for forecasting data of interest.

Keywords: Neural networks; Bayesian neural networks; deep learning; energy load forecasting; time series forecasting; automatic differentiation variational inference; feed-forward predictors; data mining; NNs classification; multilayers ANNs.

1. Introduction

As witnessed by the large literature devoted to the topic, forecasting problems, and their financial counterparts, have received an exponentially growing attention during the last few years, see, e.g. [Martínez-álvarez *et al.*, 2015; Smyth and Narayan, 2015; Sudheer and Suseelatha, 2015; Nguyen and Le, 2014; Wan *et al.*, 2014; Wang *et al.*, 2015]. The main difficulties related to efficient treatment of such, particular, type of historical data, are related to the heterogeneous character of the sources, which span from renewable ones to fossil-based, to the high variance of productions, which is even more erratic when environment aspects have to be taken into account, as well to factors related to the specific type of infrastructures from which the energy loads depend. These reasons push both people coming from industries and academia to develop techniques that are focused on specific targets. Moreover, such specialization has been even more emphasized by the high amount of money that characterized those markets where financial instruments based on, roughly speaking, energy products, their loads and consumptions have assumed space in terms of exchange rates and related quantities. This is why classical forecasting methods based on statistical approaches have been accompanied by an increasing number of techniques that are related to the so-called machine learning ambit.

Among the most promising results are those obtained exploiting machine learning approaches, see, e.g. [Lago *et al.*, 2018; Li *et al.*, 2017; López *et al.*, 2012] and references therein, in general and those associated with *deep neural networks* (DNNs) architectures, in particular, which have shown their power in handling complex temporal data.

A peculiar issue one has to consider when applying standard NNs architectures is the large amount of parameters needed to describe realistic models, also as a function of the huge amount of data that must be taken into account. As to make an example, this is one of the most relevant obstacle in deriving reliable forecasting results when dealing with weather-based time series as in the case of renewable energy-based quantities, see, e.g. [Herbert *et al.*, 2007], both from the production (implants output), consumption (energy loads), and financial (derivatives exchange) point of view, see also [Boomsma *et al.*, 2012; Gazheli and van den Bergh, 2018]. A typical *case study* being the management of latter aspects within the wind energy sector, where the wind mills performances are subjected to a high number of meteo factors, and the financialization of the produced energy could be very structured, see, e.g. [Gersema and Wozabal, 2017; Pircalabu and Jung, 2017].

This is why, in what follows, we propose a novel approach to energy load time series forecasting based on combination of neural networks (NNs) and probabilistic programming. This original merge is both computationally feasible and, at the same time, gives us the opportunity to enrich the models by considering uncertainty sources. In fact, we are able to consider random noises both in predictions and representations, also allowing for a powerful regularization, rather general, method with priors. This leads to a highly efficient way to build complex neural network architectures for forecasting in abstract settings, hence not only those associated with energy-based frameworks.

Probabilistic programming is a tool that allows for highly customizable as well as efficient random models, and it is used to get insights from given data, see, e.g. [Ben-Tal *et al.*, 2009; Muggleton and de Raedt, 1994; Weinberger and Saul, 2009], and references therein. Moreover, such an approach permits to build NNs whose learning performances often beat those reached by mean of classical, possibly multivariate, techniques. The main idea is to follow the Bayesian approach, see, e.g. [Bergstra and Bengio, 2012; Krishnapuram *et al.*, 2004; Wan, 1990], which implies to specify priors to setup the (information plus constraints) machine learning models, then getting uncertainty estimation in the form of a posterior distribution. A second step is based on Markov Chain Monte Carlo (MCMC) sampling algorithms used to draw samples, from the above mentioned posteriors, to estimate these models. That is why, more recently, variational inference algorithms, see, e.g. [Themelis *et al.*, 2014; Wainwright and Jordan, 2008], have been developed, obtaining solutions that are almost as robust as MCMC, but much faster. In fact, instead of drawing samples from the posterior, they allow to fit a given probability distribution, e.g. Gaussian, Poisson, etc., directly to the posterior, turning a sampling problem into an optimization one. Recent innovations in variational inference allow probabilistic programming to scale model complexity as well as data size, hence allowing, see below, to apply these techniques to multilayer DNNs, see, e.g. [Zheng *et al.*, 2017], and references therein. Having conducted a large set of *experiments* using real data and by mean of different machine learning algorithms, particularly by mean of Random forest regressors, multilayer NNs and similar approaches, we decided to focus our attention on the use of NNs as the main general framework to develop efficient learning algorithms.

In what follows, we first start describing the whole process of data preparation and feature selection. Then, we perform a statistical analysis of our time series, also discussing stationarity as well as other typical properties characterizing them. This preliminary analysis allows us to choose correct data normalization factors. The next step consists in the definition of the *right* forecasting model. In particular, we first select the proper validation subsets for the given data, also performing related hyper-parameters optimization which allows us to obtain the optimal number of layers and kernel sizes for the particular NNs architecture we later develop. Subsequently, we consider the training phase and the validation task for the numerical results obtained along with their visualization. As a final step, we apply the *Automatic Differentiation Variational Inference* (ADVI), see [Kucukelbir *et al.*, 2017] and references therein, to regularize the model even better. In this spirit, the obtained priors will act as *regularizers* aiming at minimizing the ANNs weights. We also show such a procedure is mathematically equivalent to consider an L^2 loss term that penalizes large weights into the objective function, with the difference that, acting as written before, we learn this regularization directly from the data. Last but not least, we explicitly show how to obtain model uncertainty, while forecasting, and we compare basic and Bayesian ANNs performances, focusing the analysis on strengths and weaknesses of both models.

2. How to Train Neural Networks: Different Approaches

Before entering into a detailed description of possible NNs architectures, let us start with the definition of a computationally modelled neuron. Essentially, it is a network of interconnected functional elements each of which has several inputs, but only one output. We can formalize it as follows:

$$y(x_1, \dots, x_n) = f(w_1 x_1 + w_2 x_2 + \dots + w_n x_n), \tag{1}$$

where w_i are parameters, f is the activation function, that is usually assumed to be nonlinear, e.g. a sigmoid, or as a rectified linear unit (ReLU). In this setting a relevant role is played by the *single-layer perceptron* architecture, characterized by n inputs and one output, and formally defined as follows:

$$y(x_1, \dots, x_n) = f(w_1 x_1 + \dots + w_n x_n). \tag{2}$$

To gain flexibility in learning the decision hyperplane, we add a bias term w_0 to the product sum: $y(x_1, \dots, x_n) = f(w_0 + w_1 x_1 + \dots + w_n x_n)$, which implies the implementation of a simple algorithm mainly inspired by biological neural system. It is worth to mention that the latter can learn some functions, but still has limited capabilities. A *multilayer perceptron* is then defined by connecting the output of a *basic perceptron* to the input of another one.

The hidden layer maps inputs to the feature space and to the classification space. The latter allows to simplify the output layer procedure scheme. In fact, each hidden unit computes a separation of the input space so that their combination can carve a polytope in the input space allowing output units to distinguish polytope membership. Basically, stacking the layers in neural network, we achieve a superposition of functions $f_1, \ldots, f_n$, where n is the number of layers, as follows:

$$y(x_1, \ldots, x_n) = f_n(\ldots f_1(w_0 + w_1 x_1 + \cdots + w_n x_n)). \tag{3}$$

2.1. *Backpropagation*

The backpropagation approach is a common method to *train* ANNs. It is usually used in combination with some numerical optimization techniques, e.g. the gradient descent method, in order to reduce computational efforts. The basic algorithm repeats a two phase cycle: the propagation cycle and the weights updating. After having a new input into a neural network, it is propagated (e.g. by multiplying each input by weights, then a nonlinearity is applied before passing the result to the next layer) forward through the network. The latter scheme is repeated *layer by layer*, until it reaches the output one. The output of the network is then compared to the desired output, using a loss function, that is measuring the result of our problem. The error values are then propagated backwards, starting from the output, until each neuron has an associated error value which roughly represents its contribution to the original output. Backpropagation uses these error values to calculate the gradient of the loss function with respect to the weights in the network. In the second phase, this gradient is fed to the optimization method, which in turn uses it to update the weights, in an attempt to minimize the loss function. Technically, backpropagation is an algorithm to calculate derivatives in the computational graph, optimization process can be discussed as a separate part of the method. The network is trained for several iterations, usually, having the whole training dataset as input for several times — it's called an epoch. After the training, the neurons in the intermediate layers organize themselves such that every neuron is supposed to learn a different feature of the input space. If several neurons are learning relationships between the same features it will lead to overfitting of the model. After training, when an arbitrary input pattern is present which contains noise or is incomplete, neurons in the hidden layer of the network will respond with an active output if the new input contains a pattern that resembles a feature that the individual neurons have learned to recognize during their training.

2.2. *Genetic algorithms*

Genetic algorithm is a variant of the well-known *global random search algorithm*. It is very often used for a rather large set of optimization problems, and as far as training a neural network is an optimization process (choosing the weights in order to minimize the loss function), we can apply the *genetic approach* to our problem as well. The main advantage of genetic algorithms is that they do not use gradients for optimization. This implies a dramatic reduction of the probability of being confined in local minima. Nevertheless, it is worth to mention that, when dealing with concrete situation about training NNs, it is a rare case in which we are interested in finding an exact global minima. In fact, even if training NNs, see, e.g. [Montana and Lawrence, 1989], is a procedure that can be reduced to a particular type of optimization problem, with own metric, the real task is also to take into account overfitting. The latter means that in concrete cases, we have to find local minima that do not overfit neither the training scheme nor the test set. Basically, genetic algorithms perform operations on what are called *chromosomes*, which could be defined as a set of features. Continuing the biological analogy, a *population* consists of many chromosomes. In this setting, it becomes essential to establish a proper measurement of fitness. In fact, the optimization scheme is essentially based on the latter to set the right optimization direction. It is worth to mention that all genetic algorithms are characterized by a standard set of basic operations, including

- random initialization of the preliminary population;
- in-loop evaluation of every chromosome by measuring its fitness;
- comparison with the minimal desired fitness;
- selection of the fittest subset of chromosomes;
- *crossing-over* operation, namely a features exchange from the selected subset of chromosome;
- *mutations* introduction, which are random changes applied to randomly chosen features of the chromosomes;
- return to the 2nd point.

Because of their general structure, genetic algorithms can be used in almost any optimization problem, spanning from ANNs training to the definition of best performing structure. During training, every chromosome of the genetic algorithm describes a particular set of ANN's weights. When searching for best structure of ANNs in the network, chromosomes possess information mostly about number of layers and neurons in each layer.

2.3. *Bayesian approach*

To adopt a Bayesian treatment of NNs, we assume a prior distribution $p(W)$ over the weights. It is common to assume that the weights are a priori independent, i.e. $p(W)$ factorizes into a product of elements each of which refers to an individual weight. Typical choices for the prior distribution are zero-mean Gaussian, or Laplace, distributions. Nevertheless, also scale-mixture priors have shown to be effective. Moreover, the output of an NN can be interpreted as a likelihood function $p(D|W)$. The prior, together with the likelihood induces a posterior distribution $p(W|D)$ over the weights. However, $p(W|D)$ is typically intractable. The aim of variational inference is therefore to approximate $p(W|D)$ with a simpler variational distribution $q(W|\nu)$ and then perform inference-based on $q(W|\nu)$, where ν denotes the set of variational parameters that are optimized. Then $q(W|\nu)$ is as close as possible to the posterior $p(W|D)$, provided the adoption of an appropriate metric. In variational inference, see, e.g. [Fox and Roberts, 2012], it is common to minimize $\mathrm{KL}(q(W|\nu)||p(W|D))$. We adopt the common mean-field approximation with an approximate posterior $q(W|\nu)$, that factorizes into a product of factors $q(w|\nu w)$, for each weight $w \in W$. We select the variational distribution $q(w|\nu w)$ to be Gaussian, with mean and variance parameters $\nu m = (\mu w, \sigma m)$. This doubles the total amount of parameters to optimize, while adding useful uncertainty estimates to the weights.

3. Automatic Differentiation Variational Inference

The main purpose of variational inference is to turn the task of computing a posterior into an optimization problem. We set a parametrized family of distributions $q(W) \in Q$, aiming to find a distribution from this family that minimizes the Kullback–Leibler (KL) divergence to the exact posterior. Traditionally, the concrete implementation of a variational inference algorithm (VIA), implies a lot of difficulties with optimization algorithm setting as, e.g. specifying a correct variational family, selecting and computing corresponding loss function, calculating derivatives, and running an iterative gradient-based optimization method. The Automatic Differentiation VIA (ADVI) aims to solve these issues automatically. The user has to just specify the model, expressed as a program, and ADVI, see, e.g. [Kucukelbir *et al.*, 2017], automatically generates a corresponding variational algorithm. The idea is to first automatically transform the inference problem into a common space and then to solve the associated variational optimization. Solving the problem in this common space allows to resolve variational inference for a large set of models. In more detail, ADVI can be split into the following steps.

- ADVI transforms the model into a model that has unconstrained real-valued latent variables. In particular, it transforms $p(x, W)$ to $p(x, \zeta)$, where the mapping from W to ζ is built into the joint distribution. After this, we do not have constraints on variable W anymore; ADVI then sets the corresponding variational problem on the transformed variables, that is, to minimize KL $q(\zeta)||p(\zeta|x)$ as described before. With this transformation, all latent variables are defined on the same space. ADVI can now use a single variational family for all models;
- ADVI recasts the gradient of the variational objective function as an expectation over q. This involves the gradient of the log joint distribution with respect to the latent variables $\nabla W \log p(x, W)$. Having the gradient as expectation allows to use Monte Carlo methods;
- ADVI reparametrizes the gradient in terms of a standard Gaussian. To do this, it uses another transformation, this time within the variational family. This second transformation enables ADVI to efficiently compute Monte Carlo approximations;
- ADVI uses noisy gradients to optimize the variational distribution with adaptively tuned step-size.

4. Data Preparation

In Fig. 1, there is a sample time series from the dataset. It is easy to see that it looks periodic, and, which is the most important feature, stationary. Hence, it is easy to analyze its data as well as to provide related forecasts. We check this hypothesis with Augmented Dickey–Fuller test first (basically testing from mean reverting, which can be considered as equal test). This process refers to a time series that displays a tendency to revert to its historical mean value.

Mathematically, such a (continuous) time series is associated to an Ornstein–Uhlenbeck process. This is in contrast with the Brownian motion case (a symmetric random walk, provided suitable rescaling, from the discrete point of view), since the latter memoryless, being a martingale. We are obtaining rejection of non-stationarity hypothesis with 5% of confidence on the whole dataset, moreover, we also check it calculating Hurst exponent. The goal of the Hurst exponent is to provide a scalar value that will help to identify whether a series is mean reverting, is close to a random walk behaviour, or has a trend component, of course up to a given level of statistical significance. For the sake of completeness, let us recall that a general time series can then be characterized in the following manner:

- $H \leq 0.5$ — the time series is mean reverting;
- $H = 0.5$ — the time series can be seen as geometric Brownian motion realization;
- $H \geq 0.5$ — the time series has a trend component.

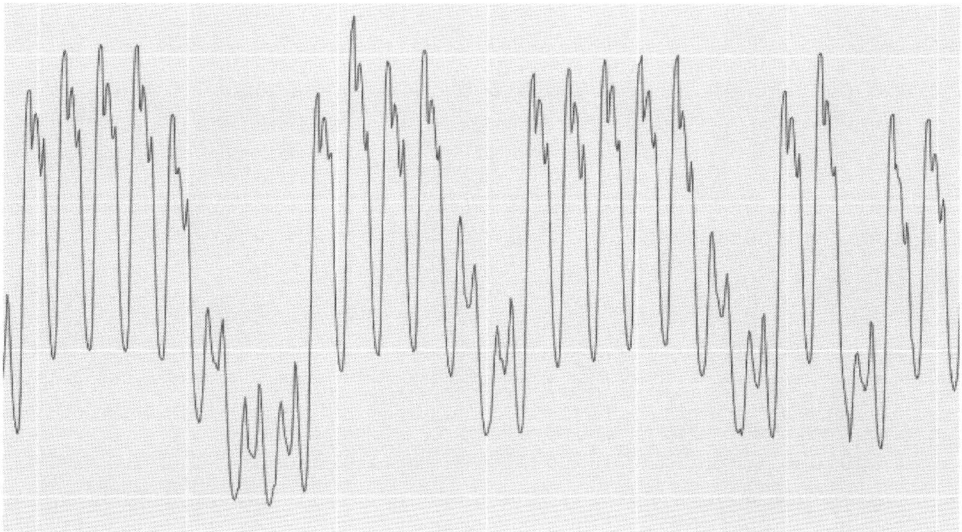

Fig. 1. Energy load hourly time series sample.

Analyzing our dataset, we find a Hurt Exponent that equals 0.130744832753, hence the considered data form a stationary time series. Having stationary time series is very useful because it is possible to normalize their data using statistical parameters from dataset, as, e.g. mean, standard deviation, minimal or maximal value, etc. The data normalization procedures lead to better performance of machine learning models. For normalizing our data we chose the *z-score* normalization, subtracting the mean of time window and then dividing by the standard deviation of the window. Our dataset is then splitted in the *training component* and in the *test component*, as follows: we take 80% of first historical values as train set and check performance on the last 20%, avoiding mixing values from the past and the future. Every training example consists of a pair (X_i, y_i), where X_i is a time window of length 24, for a single day of measurements, while y_i is a value in the next hour. Our training set consists of 31604 examples, while the test set is composed by 12291 examples.

5. Neural Network Architecture

In what follows, we are going to consider a basic model which will be exploited to implement a *two-layer perceptron* NN. In such a scheme, the first layer consists of 64 neurons whose task is to learn a representation of an 24-dimensional input, while the second layer consists of 16 neurons to *squeeze* the representation. The latter step is crucial because it allows us to reduce the set of features which, in principle, are responsible for the dataset characteristics, aiming at picking up just the more representative between them. We would like to underline that, from a more classical point of view in multivariate statistics, such technique is similar to the ones commonly grouped under the *Principal Component Analysis* (PCA) label. As nonlinear function, we have chosen a rectified linear unit (ReLU) component which is considered as a benchmark in most novel NNs, particularly because it has proved to learn faster, while maintaining a high robustness versus overfitting effects. As the last step, we exploit a single neuron, without nonlinear term, to obtain real value of prediction. In order to apply Bayesian approach to our NN-model, we also have to set prior distributions on the model's weights. Therefore, accordingly with the *state of the art* literature, we consider our weights to be Gaussian distributed, with *varying*, according to analysed data, parameters (Fig. 2).

In particular, we start setting the mean of the Gaussian distributions to zero for all the *transision matrices*, namely from the input to the first layer, from this to the second layer, as well as from the second layer to the output. Instead, three different

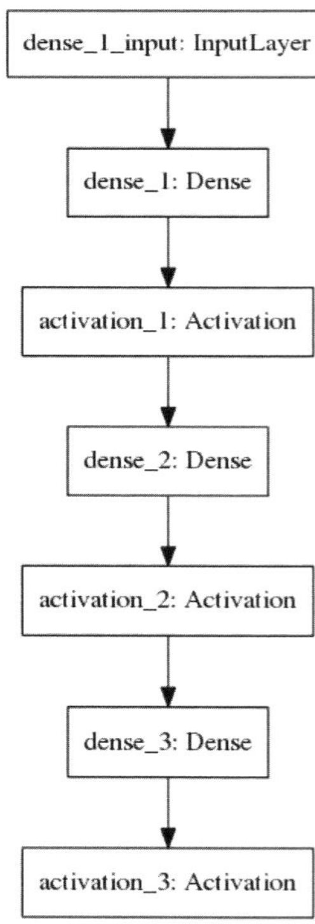

Fig. 2. Neural network's architecture.

half Gaussian distributions have been considered to describe standard deviations. For the sake of completeness, let us recall that a half Gaussian is chosen to avoid negative values occurring with $\mathbb{P}(X \leq \mu) = 1/2$, when considering $X \sim N(\mu, \sigma)$.

Such parameters values essentially play the role of model regularizers, being learned directly from the data. Analogously, we consider model output as normally distributed with unknown parameters. The latter will be a distribution from where predictions will be sampled.

By implementing the backpropagation approach, we train our model on 100 epochs, setting a step value of 0.002, and following [Kingma and Ba, 2015]. The goal is to minimize the mean squared error characterizing the *dataset train phase* and, therefore, the test.

Concerning the variational inference scheme, we first implement 5000 steps of ADVI, where the variational posterior distribution is assumed to be spherical Gaussian, without correlation of parameters, and then we fit it to the true posterior distribution.

The means and standard deviations of the variational posterior are referred to as variational parameters. In such a framework the chosen optimizer is the Adagrad algorithm. After obtaining variational posterior we can draw samples from it to generate the trace of them. The latter has been provided taking a length of 5,000 for both the confidence and the inspection phases of associated parameters. As the last step, we generate data then exploited to provide suitable predictions on the hold-out set in our case, by implementing a posterior predictive check with 100 samples. The extrapolated mean of these samples is considered as a prediction for the next hour and, analogously, related standard deviation is taken as the uncertainty level of the model. In particular, higher uncertainty values mean that our model *is not sure* about sampled data nature. Namely, from a statistical point of view, the confidence interval has to be taken rather large, so large that the statistical inference has not a concrete sense. The resulting message is then very clear: *do not rely on the produced forecast*. We would like to underline that such type of *negative* suggestions are, contrary to what can be thought, very useful for real investors, pushing them to take more prudential positions in the market. On the other hand, an agent particularly inclined to for a concrete case study where different NNs have been implemented and compared in results, as an effective model to stock price predictions.

The backpropagation training has been implemented in the *Keras' framework*, see [Chollet and Roberts, 2015], since it allows for fast prototypization, with the additional advantage of having as built-in features, all the essential functions we need. Concerning the Bayesian approach, we have defined the network by both *Theano* and *NumPy* primitives, while, for ADVI as well as fo the PyMC3 sampling, we refer to [Patil *et al.*, 2016]. In the following section, results obtained by means of the backpropagation approach are compared to those derived by using the variational inference one, in accord with the metrics: mean absolute error on the test set, robustness to overfitting, smoothness of parameter learning process, hence MSE loss for backpropagation and evidence lower bound for ADVI. Moreover, within the Bayesian framework, we also reported criticism as well as a detailed analysis about how the proposed model can estimate uncertainty of its prediction.

6. Results

6.1. *Bayesian approach*

After 5,000 iterations of ADVI method, we see in Fig. 3 the representation of evidence lower bound (ELBO), which clearly shows that it converges to the value $1.0529e + 07$. It is interesting to consider posteriors of the weights and regularization parameters in the figure. The first matrix of weights lies in the range $[-6, 6]$, while the second ones is in the range $[-4, 4]$. Therefore, we have a smaller range for the second matrix's weights, a result which depends on standard deviations that are also treated as random variables. Moreover, regularizer in the first weight matrix has a value of 1.5, while in the second it

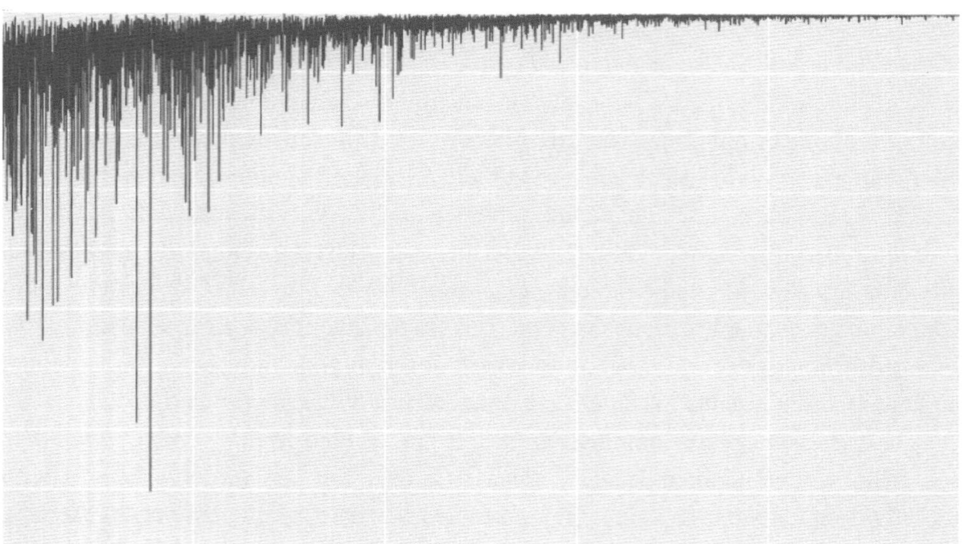

Fig. 3. ELBO evolution over iterations of training.

equals 1.3, and in the third is around 0.4. Such differences suggest that it makes sense to change the amount of regularization to be applied at each layer of the network.

The figure is a sample plot of real points from the test set and predictions on it. The mean absolute error (MAE) is 3234. Moreover, we have also reported a plot of standard deviations, as an indicator of uncertainty estimation.

6.2. *Backpropagation*

After running 100 epochs of backpropagation, we obtain a MSE $= 0.0133$ on the normalized data. In the figure we can see the plot of a decreasing, regular, loss function, which, besides, does not show any overfitting effects. We have also provided a sample plot of real points from the test set and predictions on it, here the MAE equals 313.69, while a graphic comparison of results main metrics is as follows:

MSE/ELBO	**MAE**	**Time for train(s)**	**Time for prediction(s)**
0.0433	1010.75	100	0.2
1.0529e+07	3234.55	8000	2500

Note: Comparison of main metrics of results.

7. Discussion

As we can see from the last section, regular deterministic NN trained with backpropagation shows much better (up to ten times) results in accuracy of forecasting due mainly to the MAE. To check the impact of Bayesian regularization on results we have applied popular regularization technique called Dropout, see, e.g. [Gal and Ghahramani, 2016] to the NN previously trained with backpropagation. Figure 4 shows posterior distributions for the weights of the trained neural network. The illustration explains clearly why the forecasts are less accurate than with the NNs trained via gradient descent: all distributions are "mixed" together which means that each weight is not specialized for specific feature, but rather flattened over all the weights. While applying this regularization, we have randomly set some weights to zero, therefore training a rich ensemble of different architectures, while avoiding neurons coadaptation. It is worth mentioning that we have shown that the Dropout technique acts as a Bayesian regularization. The latter allows us to inspect, better

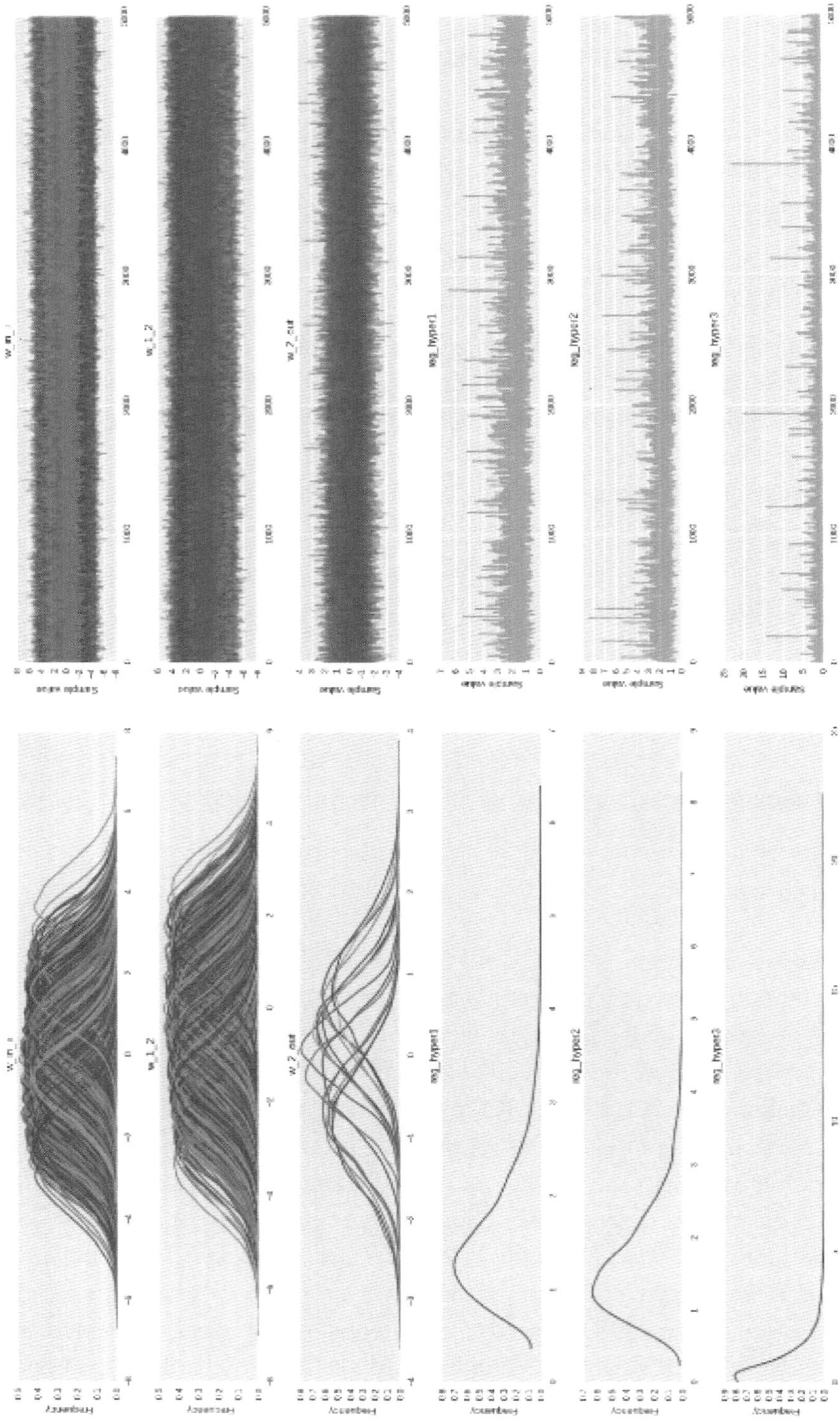

Fig. 4. Details of variational inference.

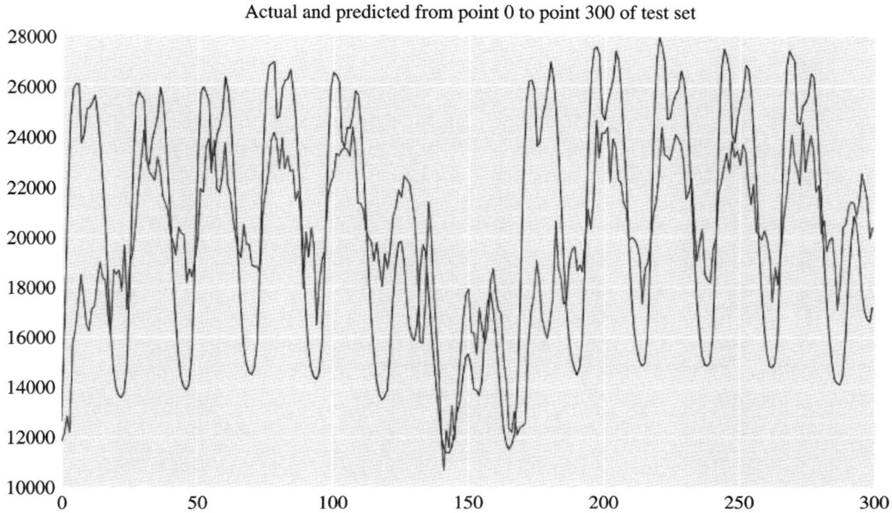

Fig. 5. Bayesian approach forecasting results.

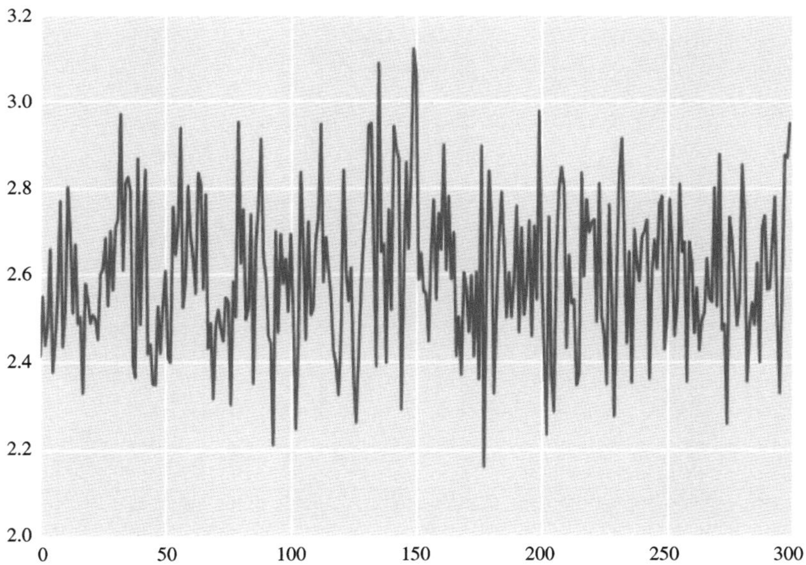

Fig. 6. Uncertainty estimation example.

infer, its dynamics as well as provided results. Let us recall that we have applied the Dropout scheme with *drop rate* $= 0.5$ between the first two layers. Figures 5 and 6 show performance of the NN trained via Bayesian inference: On the Figs. 7–10 one can see performance of the deterministic and dropout NN alongside with their

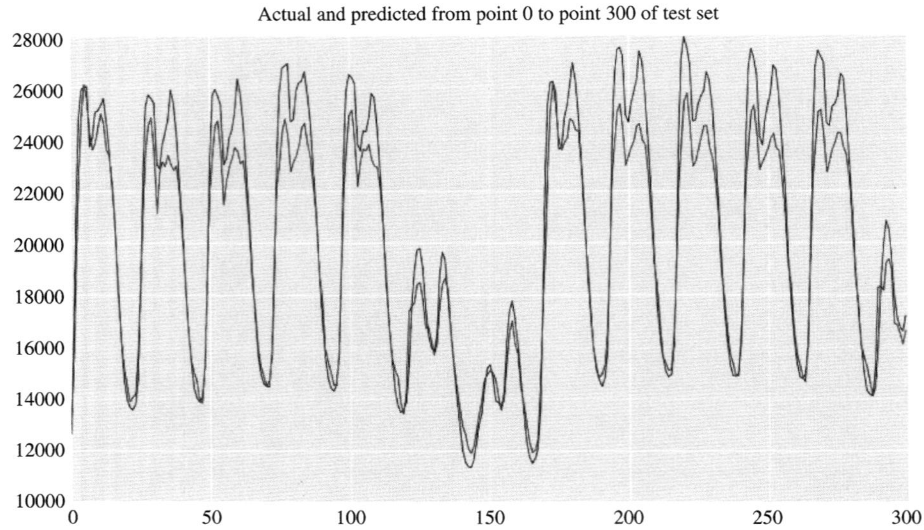

Fig. 7. Determenistic NN forecasting results.

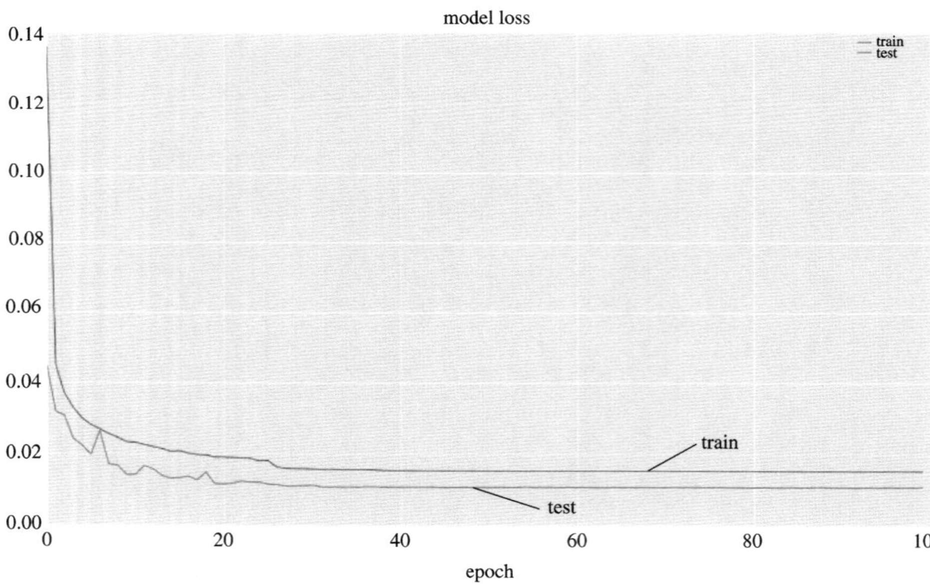

Fig. 8. Train and test set loss evolution for deterministic NN.

loss function evolution over time respectively that show no sign of overfitting. This suggests to stop earlier the training phase, namely before the loss starts to grow

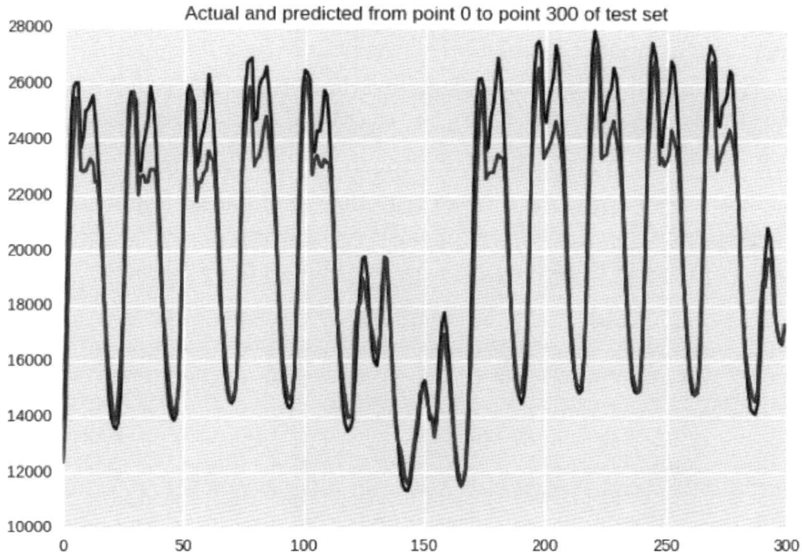

Fig. 9. Dropout model forecasting results.

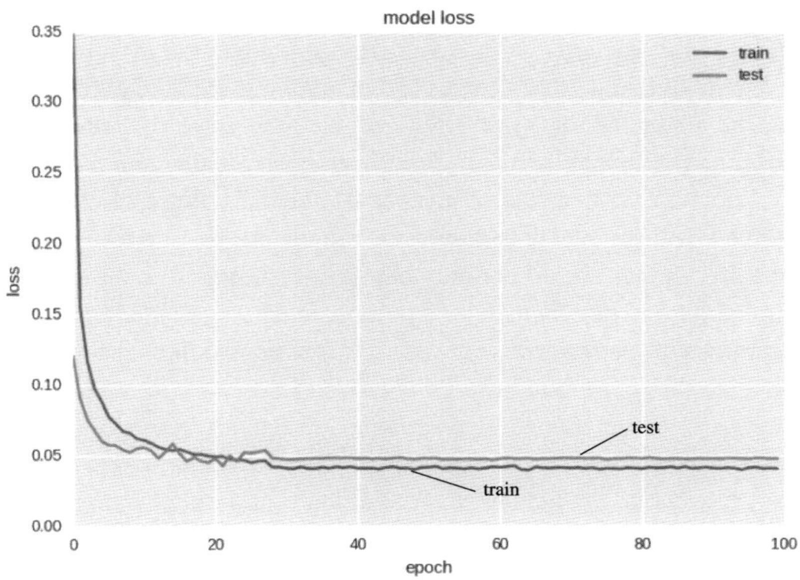

Fig. 10. Train and test set loss evolution for dropout NN.

again. In the Figure 10, we can see that the forecasting results with MAE reach a lower level if compared with the one without Dropout, when MAE = 978.3.

Provided results allow for more accurate predictions, also suggesting that it is better to rely on the model trained with backpropagation with deterministic weights. Moreover, such results also show evident improvements when regularization, within the Bayesian approach, is taken into account. Nevertheless, it is important to recall that the latter approach needs much more deep work on setting the priors, since the initial choice of considering Gaussian distributions is not an invariant one, being used just as trigger point. In particular, during the Bayesian scheme life, other distributions have to be considered to improve forecasting, resulting in a huge computational time growth.

8. Conclusion

The present contribution provides a concrete analysis of energy load time series forecasting using the mean of different NNs architectures and approaches. In particular, after a self-contained introduction to the general methodology that can be used to effectively study forecasting tasks within energy markets, we have provided a self-consistent treatment of the whole *pipeline* which is followed as a standard by both practitioners and data analysts involved in the subject. Therefore, starting from real time series of interest (data set preparation in our treatment) to forecasts details (training NNs' models and obtaining associated outputs), we have considered predictor feed-forward NNs, and we have shown its strength in time series forecasting with high accuracy. Moreover, we have also improved our model by setting priors on the weights, setting robust generalization and clearly identify the role played by the model uncertainty. Our approach allows for huge advantages in practical use. In fact, we do not only prevent overfitting to training set, but also estimate reliability of our forecast in any moment. It is essential to note that the latter feature cannot be reached with deterministic approach to machine learning. Meanwhile, we show that deterministic approach leads to better numerical results, but the generative model trained with variational inference, provided modifications we proposed, can show uncertainty in our prediction. So, we suggest to use both models to get accurate predictions and understand the level of convenience about them. Ways to increase accuracy of our models have been also proposed and tested.

References

Bergstra, J. and Bengio, Y. (2012). Random search for hyper-parameter optimization. *Journal of Machine Learning Research* **13**, pp. 281–305.

Ben-Tal, A., Ghaoui, L. and Nemirovski, A. (2009). *Robust Optimization*. (Princeton University Press, Princeton) p. 542.

Boomsma, T. K., Meade, N. and Fleten, S.-E. (2012). Renewable energy investments under different support schemes: A real options approach. *European Journal of Operational Research* **220** (1), 225–237.

Di Persio, L. and Honchar, O. (2016). Artificial neural networks architectures for stock price prediction: Comparisons and applications. *International Journal of Circuits, Systems and Signal Processing* **10**, 403–413.

Gazheli, A. and van den Bergh, J. (2018). Real options analysis of investment in solar vs. wind energy: Diversification strategies under uncertain prices and costs. *Renewable and Sustainable Energy Reviews* **82**, 2693–2704.

Kucukelbir, A. *et al.* (2016). Automatic differentiation variational inference. *Journal of Machine Learning Research X* **18**, 1–45.

Montana, D. J. and Lawrence, D. (1989). Training feedforward neural networks using genetic algorithms. *BBN Systems and Technologies Corp.*

Fox, C. and Roberts, S. (2012). A tutorial on variational bayes. *Artificial Intelligence Review* **38**, 1–11.

Gersema, G. and Wozabal, D. (2017). An equilibrium pricing model for wind power futures. *Energy Economics* **65**, 64–74.

Herbert, G. M. Iniyan, S., Sreevalsan, E. and Rajapandian, S. (2007). A review of wind energy technologies. *Renewable and Sustainable Energy Reviews* **11** (6), 1117–1145.

Kucukelbir, A., Blei, D. M., Gelman, A., Ranganath, R. and Tran, D. (2017). Automatic differentiation variational inference. *Journal of Machine Learning Research* **18**, 1–45.

Krishnapuram, B., Hartemink, A. J. Carin, L. and Figueiredo, M. A. T. (2004). A Bayesian approach to joint feature selection and classifier design. *IEEE Transactions on Pattern Analysis and Machine Intelligence* **26** (9), 1105–1111.

Kingma, D. and Ba, J. (2015). Adam: A method for stochastic optimization, *arXiv:1412.6980.*

Lago, J., De Ridder, F., Vrancx, P. and De Schutter, B. (2018). Forecasting day-ahead electricity prices in Europe: The importance of considering market integration. *Applied Energy* **211**, 890–903.

Li, P., Arci, F., Reilly, J., Curran, K., Belatreche, A. and Shynkevich, Y. (2017). Predicting short-term wholesale prices on the Irish single electricity market with artificial neural networks. *2017–28th Irish Signals and Systems Conference, ISSC.*

López, M., Valero, S., Senabre, C., Aparicio, J. and Gabaldon, A. (2012). Application of SOM neural networks to short-term load forecasting: The Spanish electricity market case study. *Electric Power Systems Research* **91**, 18–27.

Chollet, F. and Roberts, S. (2015). Keras, *Github, https://github.com/fchollet/keras.*

Martínez-álvarez, F., Troncoso, A., Asencio-Cortés, G. and Riquelme, J. C. (2015). A survey on data mining techniques applied to electricity-related time series forecasting. *Energies* **8** (11), 13162–13193.

Muggleton, S. and de Raedt, R. (1994). Inductive logic programming: Theory and methods. *The Journal of Logic Programming* **19–20** (SUPPL. 1), 629–679.

Nguyen, D. T. and Le, L. B. (2014). Optimal bidding strategy for microgrids considering renewable energy and building thermal dynamics. *IEEE Transactions on Smart Grid* **5** (4), 1608–1620, 6839078.

Patil, A., Huard, D. and Fonnesbeck, C. J. (2016). PyMC: Bayesian stochastic modelling in python. *Journal of Statistical Software* **35** (4), 1–81.

Pircalabu, A. and Jung, J. (2017). A mixed C-vine copula model for hedging price and volumetric risk in wind power trading. *Quantitative Finance* **17** (10), 1583–1600.

Smyth, R. and Narayan, P. K. (2015). Applied econometrics and implications for energy economics research. *Energy Economics* **50**, 351–358.

Sudheer, G. and Suseelatha, A. (2015). Short term load forecasting using wavelet transform combined with Holt-Winters and weighted nearest neighbor models. *International Journal of Electrical Power and Energy Systems* **64**, 340–346.

Themelis, K. E., Rontogiannis, A. A. and Koutroumbas, K. D. (2014). A variational Bayes framework for sparse adaptive estimation. *IEEE Transactions on Signal Processing* **62** (18), 4723–4736, 6853356.

Gal, Y. and Ghahramani, Z. (2016). Dropout as a Bayesian approximation: Representing model uncertainty in deep learning. *University of Cambridge.*

Wan, C., Xu, Z., Wang, Y., Dong, Z. Y. and Wong, K. P. (2014). A hybrid approach for probabilistic forecasting of electricity price. *IEEE Transactions on Smart Grid* **5** (1), 463–470, 6596510.

Wan, E. A. (1990). Neural network classification: A Bayesian interpretation. *IEEE Transactions on Neural Networks* **1** (4), 303–305.

Wainwright, M. J. and Jordan, M. I. (2008). Graphical models, exponential families, and variational inference. *Foundations and Trends in Machine Learning* **1** (1–2), 1–305.

Wang, Q., Zhang, C., Ding, Y., Xydis, G., Wang, J. and Ostergaard, J. (2015). Review of real-time electricity markets for integrating distributed energy resources and demand response. *Applied Energy* **138**, 695–706.

Weinberger, K. Q. and Saul, L. K. (2009). Distance metric learning for large margin nearest neighbor classification. *Journal of Machine Learning Research* **10**, 207–244.

Zheng, Y., Wen, L., Wang, J., Yan, J. and Ji, L. (2017). Sequence modeling with hierarchical Deep Generative Models with dual memory. *International Conference on Information and Knowledge Management, Proceedings*, Part F131841, pp. 1369–1378.

Chapter 5

Electricity Market Coupling in Europe: Status Quo and Future Challenges

Roland Füss[*,‡], Steffen Mahringer[*,§] and Marcel Prokopczuk[†,¶]

[*]*Swiss Institute of Banking and Finance (s/bf), University of St. Gallen, Unterer Graben 21, 9000 St.Gallen, Switzerland*

[†]*School of Economics and Management, Leibniz University Hannover, Koenigsworther Platz 1, 30167 Hannover, Germany*

[‡]*roland.fuess@unisg.ch*

[§]*steffen.mahringer@t-online.de*

[¶]*prokopczuk@fmt.uni-hannover.de*

In electricity markets globally, market participants and policymakers increasingly focus on integrating adjacent, yet separate market areas via cross-border trade in electricity. Based on a discussion of the institutional framework for organizing cross-border trade, this chapter analyzes how spot and futures prices for wholesale electricity are affected by different degrees of market integration. We first contrast the two main mechanisms to allocate transmission capacity between neighboring markets: explicit and implicit auctions. Subsequently, we study the impact of these allocation schemes on the empirical price dynamics of major electricity markets in Europe. Our empirical analysis thereby confirms that under market coupling, economically inefficient cross-border flows in the wrong direction can be avoided. From a policy point of view, however, we show that further market integration can be hindered by individual energy market regulation on a national level, which may be opposed to supra-national frameworks such as market coupling.

Keywords: Energy market coupling; electricity market reforms; explicit and implicit auction; price convergence.

1. Introduction

In the aftermath of market liberalization, energy markets in the US and Europe have been undergoing a number of significant structural developments and institutional changes that strongly affect the interplay of supply and demand and, hence, the general price formation process in these markets. In the case of electricity markets, the rise of exchange-based trading along with regulatory developments (such as the introduction of emissions trading schemes), and also other aspects of market design (such as power exchanges admitting negative prices) have had a marked and long-lasting impact on the price dynamics of spot and derivative contracts. However, the most significant structural change that both US and European electricity markets have seen recently is caused by a general, continued shift toward generation from renewable energy sources.

However, it is not only the volatile nature and general intermittency of renewable generation that makes network integration a demanding task for transmission system operators (TSOs). It is also a problem that, especially for "green" electricity, the location of generation sites may be far away from the actual centers of demand: for instance, with rising numbers of solar panels in Arizona or European wind farms in the North Sea, new ways must be found in order to efficiently direct these electricity flows to high-demand areas which may be thousands of miles away. Hence, increasing *interconnectivity* — i.e. transmission capacity — between electricity wholesale markets is a crucial prerequisite for a successful integration of renewable generation across both Europe and the US.

Within the European Union (EU), reaching this aim coincides with the intended establishment of the "Internal Electricity Market" (IEM),[1] an initiative to support further integration of European electricity markets, with the ultimate goal not only to realize uncongested transfer of "green" energy but also to achieve full electricity price convergence across member states.[2] Fostering integration between national markets, in turn, requires substantial investments in transmission infrastructure both *within* and *across* national markets. Already in March 2002, the Barcelona European Council agreed on a minimum level of interconnectivity between member states of 10% of installed generation capacities within the respective markets. In this context, the European Network of Transmission System Operators for Electricity (ENTSO-E) estimates that for investment projects of "pan-European significance," a total capital expenditure of approximately EUR 104 billion will be required until 2022 [ENTSO-E, 2012].

However, to fulfill the aim of creating a single electricity market across Europe, a well-defined and functioning market model of how to provide access to cross-border

---

[1]See Article 194 of the Lisbon Treaty (*Treaty on the Functioning of the European Union*) that stipulates to further (...) *promote the interconnection of energy networks.*

[2]See, e.g. Article 60(2) of Directive 2009/72/EC: (...) *leading, in the long term, to price convergence.*

transmission capacity is at least as important as further investment into transmission infrastructure. Generally, only few interconnectors in Europe are uncongested,[3] and over time a variety of different congestion management methods have been developed to govern access to scarce transmission capacity for cross-border trade in electricity. In the past, these allocation mechanisms primarily relied on explicit *ex-ante* schemes, where traders *first* have to acquire transmission capacity in order to *then* trade in two interconnected, yet institutionally separated, electricity markets. In Europe, in their most widespread form, explicit schemes are usually implemented as (sealed-bid) auction processes where capacity is allocated for different timeframes.[4] While explicit *ex-ante* auctions of transmission capacity meet the requirement by the EU that access be provided based on "non-discriminatory market-based solutions,"[5] they nevertheless lead to an inefficient market design. Among a number of deficiencies, it is primarily the timing sequence of capacity and electricity spot markets that forces traders to acquire cross-border transmission capacity for a given direction *before* the spread in electricity spot prices between the two respective markets is actually determined. Hence, a trader's decision about both the direction and the amount of transmission capacity to be requested can only be based on an expectation of the price differential between these markets, and in view of generally high levels of volatility in electricity spot markets, this noisy signal may often cause the trader to acquire capacity for the wrong direction.

Since these inefficiencies conflict with the objective of (day-ahead) price convergence within a single pan-European electricity market, the more efficient alternative of implicitly allocating cross-border capacity rights via market coupling is increasingly rolled out across European markets nowadays. Here, markets for transmission capacity and spot electricity are integrated and, hence, clear simultaneously, which allows for an optimal allocation of capacities and results in economically efficient cross-border flows. However, although the previous explicit *ex-ante* design has already been replaced by an implicit mechanism for a number of

[3]For instance, this is the case between Germany and Austria, where transmission capacity is sufficient and no auctioning of rights for interconnector use is required.

[4]Prior to the implementation of market coupling, explicit auction schemes prevailed throughout Europe and were (or still are) used to allocate capacity for exchange between, e.g. England–France, France–Spain, France–Belgium, Belgium–the Netherlands, or the Netherlands–Germany.

[5]See Regulations No. 1228/2003/EC and its follow-up No. 714/2009/EC. Note that this rules out the use of other cross-border congestion management methods, such as rationing or allocation on a "first-come, first-served" basis, given their lack of an inherent market-based mechanism.

interconnectors, it will continue to play a dominant role wherever the harmonization efforts required for market coupling are too high or just infeasible.[6]

In the US, market architecture for most regions is fundamentally different from the uniform (zonal) pricing approach that is prevalent in Europe: instead, nodal pricing (or locational marginal pricing [LMP]) has become the standard pricing approach.[7] In an LMP-based market, the market area is subdivided into numerous pricing points, or nodes, for each of which an individual marginal electricity price is calculated. For instance, in the day-ahead market, participants submit bids and offers for specified point-to-point transactions which are then aggregated and matched by the central market administrator that clears the market. Thus, both day-ahead prices and corresponding flows are determined simultaneously, and in the case of no congestion, marginal prices will be equal at each node.[8] However, it is important to note that this approach optimally addresses transmission constraints *within* markets only, whereas the above-mentioned problems in efficiently setting up cross-border transactions in Europe also apply for transactions *between* markets in the US. For instance, if a trader wants to trade in the PJM and NYISO markets, this transaction still needs to be based on an expectation of the price spread, i.e. the price differential between the two markets. As a consequence, market participants are facing similar problems in organizing efficient cross-border trade as in Europe, making less-than-optimal or even adverse interconnector flows a common problem on both sides of the Atlantic.

In the future, interconnectivity within the still-fragmented US electricity grid is generally expected to further increase — e.g. through projects such as the planned "Tres Amigas Superstation," a bundle of three 5-gigawatt (GW) transmission lines that are supposed to unite the three regional grids in the US into a single national grid.[9] While the market design for this emerging huge trading hub is still being

[6]Also see, e.g. McInerney and Bunn [2013] on this argument. Moreover, should the market coupling algorithm (that determines the optimal cross-border flows) not be available due to technical problems, the explicit *ex-ante* scheme will be used as the default option to allocate capacity.

[7]See, e.g. Bohn *et al.* [1984], Schweppe *et al.* [1988], and Hogan [1992] for an overview. Nodal pricing (in different forms) has been implemented, e.g. in California (CAISO), Texas (ERCOT), in the Midwest (MISO), New York (NYISO) and New England (ISO-NE) markets, in the PJM Interconnection, and in the Southwest Power Pool (SPP).

[8]Exact price convergence, however, will only be reached if transmission losses are not taken into account or are deemed negligible. Otherwise, even in case of no congestion, prices will still not be equal.

[9]Note that a grid or interconnection is defined as comprising several markets (such as PJM, NYISO, ISO-NE, etc., for the Eastern Interconnection) that are electrically tied together and operate at a synchronized frequency. Currently, the three regional grids — the Eastern Interconnection, the Western Electricity Coordinating Council (WECC), and the Electric Reliability Council of Texas (ERCOT) —

worked out, a solution based on implicit allocation, i.e. market coupling, may likely be expected.[10]

Historically, the literature has looked at the question of how to organize cross-border trading mostly form a theoretical point of view. Bohn *et al.* [1984], Schweppe *et al.* [1988] and Hogan [1992] develop a theory of electricity pricing in networks that accounts for the physical properties of electricity. Chao and Peck [1996] extend this analysis and investigate how competition may affect optimal market design. Several studies have shown that market coupling under implicit auctioning leads to a reduction in producers' market power and a reallocation of rents from producers to consumers [Gilbert *et al.* 2004; Parisio and Bosco, 2008; Ehrenmann and Neuhoff, 2009], but there also exist studies that show that consumers might be hurt by increasing prices due to market coupling [Hobbs *et al.*, 2005]. More recently, there have also been some empirical studies. Meeus [2011b] and Parisio and Pelagatti [2014] discuss and analyze the interconnection between Denmark–Germany and Italy–Slovenia, respectively. Finally, Creti *et al.* [2010] provide some evidence from Italy.

In this chapter, we provide a detailed account of the current status of market coupling as a promising and efficient framework to organize the cross-border trade in electricity between adjacent, yet institutionally separated market areas. As such, we contribute to the literature in the following ways. First, we give a comprehensive overview of the various institutional frameworks currently in place for cross-border trade between electricity markets. Given that these organizational settings are ultimately of high significance for electricity volumes to be exchanged in the economically efficient direction, we explicitly focus on microstructure effects, such as the timing sequence of traders' decisions when setting up a trade.

Second, we provide substantial empirical evidence of how electricity prices are impacted by the different ways of organizing cross-border exchange between electricity markets. Based on both interconnector flows and corresponding electricity prices in adjacent markets, we contrast explicit and implicit allocation schemes and examine how the workings of either mechanism are reflected in empirical spot price dynamics. For the period under review, our empirical analysis clearly confirms the well-known inefficiencies of explicit allocation schemes (resulting

are only loosely tied together, which impedes, e.g. the transfer of "green" energy generated from wind in Texas or sun in Arizona to centers of high demand within the Eastern Interconnection.

[10]In 2012, Tres Amigas LLC and EPEX Spot announced a joint cooperation agreement in order to *share mutual expertise in the development and coupling of their respective markets* [EPEX-Spot, 2012]. EPEX Spot operates, among others, the coupled electricity spot markets in Germany and France.

from traders having to acquire transmission capacity before the price differential between the respective market areas has actually been determined), which can effectively be avoided under a market coupling scenario. In addition, however, we broaden the scope of our analysis by also discussing the behavior of futures prices under market coupling, which has so far not been in the focus of extant research.

Third, we assess the current achievements (and drawbacks) of the recent market coupling initiative in Europe from a broader policy perspective. Taking price rigidities in the French market as an example, it becomes obvious that individual electricity market regulation on a national level may easily conflict with a supranational framework such as market coupling. To our knowledge, this aspect has not been discussed in the literature thus far — and may well warrant further analysis in the future.

The remainder of this chapter is structured as follows: Section 2 outlines the workings of the explicit and implicit schemes in more detail and provides further institutional background for the cross-border trading of electricity. Section 3 continues the discussion of the two allocation regimes from an empirical point of view by examining in more detail the price dynamics of coupled and non-coupled electricity markets in Europe. Section 4 discusses from a policy perspective how the merits and effectiveness of market coupling find their boundaries in individual national policies that clearly oppose the idea of the Internal Electricity Market. Section 5 concludes.

2. Institutional Background

In a first step, we qualitatively discuss and compare the two existing allocation schemes in the remainder of this section. This is important since, by its nature, cross-border electricity trade is characterized by a variety of institutional specificities and operational complexities, each of which has significant impact on the topic under consideration. Thereby, several different electricity markets serve as examples for this discussion. We then move on to conduct a detailed empirical analysis of the German–French electricity market where both explicit and implicit allocation schemes have been (or still are) in place. We hence carefully analyze the effect of market coupling by studying price convergence of spot and futures prices in the German–French market before and after the introduction of market coupling. Finally, in a last step, we discuss the issue of policy challenges arising from differences in individual national market designs by using a case-study approach. Here, taking the French electricity market as an example again, we discuss how classic policy intervention can hinder the efficiency of a cross-border trading scheme such as market coupling.

2.1. *Explicit allocation schemes*

The generally widespread implementation of explicit allocation mechanisms is mainly due to the fact that they can quickly be set up without requiring a particularly high level of institutional harmonization between adjacent electricity markets. Importantly, as is characteristic of explicit schemes, physical transmission capacity markets and electricity (spot) markets are separated from each other, with the former usually clearing ahead of the latter. Hence, enabling cross-border trade in this way only requires a low degree of integration and joint coordination between both TSOs and power exchanges in adjacent markets. This avoids the necessity for a common trading platform and uniform exchange rules, including a simultaneous closing of day-ahead auctions for (spot) electricity across markets. However, given that day-ahead prices in both markets are not yet known by the time that traders have to submit their bids for transmission capacity, it generally leads to an inefficient market design.[11] These inefficiencies manifest in such interconnectors frequently not being used up to their thermal capacity limits or in adverse physical flows, where electricity is directed from a more expensive market to a cheaper connected market. In such a situation, cross-border traders have failed to correctly anticipate the price spread *ex-ante*, and hence end up having acquired transmission capacity for the "wrong" direction.

From an operational point of view, for most interconnectors, explicitly allocated transmission rights are physical in nature and are assigned for a pre-specified direction of flow (e.g. F $\rightarrow$ GER) and for different timeframes. For instance, prior to the introduction of market coupling at the French–German border, physical transmission rights (PTRs) could be acquired via explicit annual, monthly and daily auctions. Depending on the timeframe, allocated transmission rights would hence entitle a trader to nominate and physically exchange electricity in a given direction from one market to the other during any hour of the year (month or day, respectively). Figure 1 illustrates in more detail the relevant steps to set up such a cross-border transaction, taking as example the explicit *ex-ante* auction scheme at

[11] This is a well-documented fact in the literature. Inefficient cross-border trade across various European markets has been analyzed by, e.g. Turvey [2006], Kristiansen [2007], Marckhoff and Muck [2009], Bunn and Zachmann [2010], Bunn and Martoccia [2010], and McInerney and Bunn [2013].

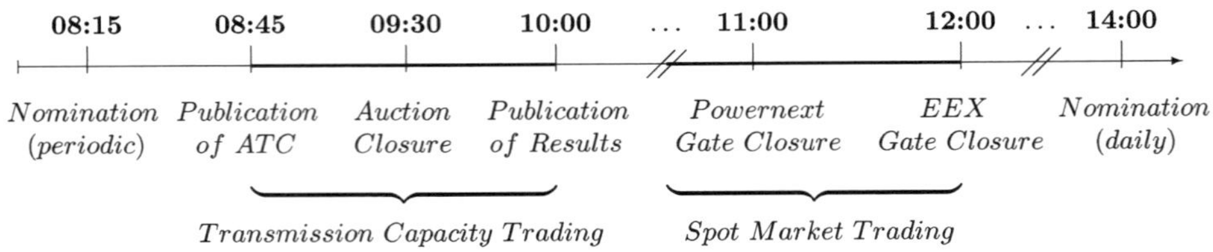

Fig. 1. Timeline for the explicit *ex-ante* auction scheme.

Notes: This figure illustrates the timing sequence of the market for cross-border transmission capacity between France and Germany as well as of the day-ahead electricity markets in these two countries. Note that the nomination procedure, the set-up of the capacity auction and the gate closure times of the power exchanges relate to the explicit *ex-ante* auction scheme which was in place prior to the implementation of the CWE (Central Western Europe) market coupling as per 9 November 2010. See RTE [2009a] and RTE [2009b] for further information.

the French–German border before it was replaced by market coupling in 2010.[12] When the holder of a periodic (i.e. monthly or yearly) transmission right wanted to engage in a cross-border transaction on day t, the TSO had to be notified by 08:15 am on day $t - 1$ and provided with a schedule detailing the respective capacities to be nominated during every hour on day t.[13] In case these capacity holders did not want to trade, their non-nominated capacities originally "earmarked" for periodic transactions were implicitly transferred and added to those capacities to be allocated in the daily market. In that case, according to the "use it or sell it" (UIOSI) principle, traders with monthly or yearly rights received as financial compensation for every megawatt (MW) of non-nominated capacity the price as determined during the daily auction for the corresponding hour.[14] Based on the nominations received by the holders of monthly and yearly transmission rights, the TSO then published an update of the available transmission capacity (ATC) that was to be offered on the daily market by 08:45 am on day $t - 1$; bids for the daily auction then had to be submitted by 09:30 am at the latest, and results were released half an hour later.[15] As already mentioned, this is well ahead of the close of electricity

[12]Although auction rules may differ across markets, the overall structure and timeline of the allocation procedure described here can generally be seen as representative of other explicit *ex-ante* schemes.

[13]See RTE [2009a, p. 17] for transactions between Germany and France.

[14]See RTE [2009b, p. 20].

[15]For further information on the functioning of the capacity daily market under explicit auction schemes, see, e.g. Marckhoff and Muck [2009] who describe the auction design that used to prevail in the capacity daily market at the Dutch–German border: *Investors bid price/volume combinations were several bids per investor are allowed. In case the requested volume is lower than the available capacity, the PTR price is zero. Otherwise, all investors pay the price of the lowest successful bid.*

spot (i.e. day-ahead) markets at around noon: 11:00 am for the French exchange Powernext and 12:00 noon for its German counterpart EEX at that time. Finally, having been awarded a transmission right in the daily market, traders had to notify the TSO by 02:00 pm whether they were going to use it and set up a cross-border transaction on the following day t. As opposed to the UIOSI principle, for holders of daily transmission rights, however, the "use it or lose it" (UIOLI) principle applied instead. In the case of non-nomination, this implied that there was no financial compensation; these unused rights were then, in turn, transferred to the intraday market.

With regard to the electricity markets in the US, the institutional design for cross-border (i.e. market-to-market) transactions is less harmonized than in Europe and a variety of different allocation methods coexist, sometimes even at the same border. While a detailed description of these arrangements is beyond the scope of this chapter, we focus on the following key issues. In view of the nodal pricing system in the US, combining paths of fixed point-to-point transactions would generally allow a trader to ship electricity across states with corresponding path reservations being allocated on a "first-come, first-serve" basis. Given the inherent inefficiency of these fixed allocations, many markets have replaced the physical reservations with a financial transmission rights framework and offer-based export/import scheduling [Spees and Pfeifenberger, 2012]. Alternatively, several *merchant* lines have also been awarded transmission rights which are then re-allocated via long-term contracts or shorter-term auctions.[16] Nevertheless, irrespective of the precise institutional setting, bid selection and pricing by the independent system operator (ISO) and the physical scheduling of a market-to-market transaction are still two clearly distinct procedures for most electricity markets in the US. Hence, whereas other non-auction-based allocation mechanisms may be more common in the US, these mechanisms share a crucial feature of explicit schemes, i.e. of requiring traders to schedule their transactions *ex-ante*. Even though there are increasing efforts to move the physical scheduling process closer to real-time,[17] traders still need to rely on an expectation

---

If there is more volume requested at the lowest successful bid, the allocation for those bids is partitioned relative to the requested volume.

[16]Examples include the Hudson and Linden Variable Frequency Transformer (VFT) interconnectors at the PJM–NYISO border.

[17]For instance, the PJM and NYISO markets have recently proposed "Coordinated Transaction Scheduling" (CTS) where traders have the option to submit a price spread at which they are willing to set up a market-to-market transaction rather than placing individual bids in each market. While this is supposed to enhance economically efficient interconnector use, transactions still need to be scheduled based on an expectation of the spread.

of the price spread between markets, which is — roughly speaking — comparable to the explicit allocation schemes used in Europe.

2.2. *Implicit allocation schemes*

By contrast, the concept of market coupling avoids the above timing problem for cross-border traders by clearing capacity and electricity markets simultaneously, i.e. by implicitly allocating transmission rights within the spot auction of electricity in each market. Conceptually, a pricing mechanism that is closely related to market coupling has already been implemented in the Nordic market, Nord Pool, the common electricity market for Norway, Denmark, Sweden, Finland, Estonia, Latvia and Lithuania. Here, in a first step, the market clearing system price is determined by equating total demand and supply, as aggregated across each national market, thereby ignoring any potential constraints in transmission capacity between bidding areas.[18] Hence, in the case of no congestion, there is a single price for all bidding areas. Otherwise, depending on the location of the transmission bottleneck(s), the market is "split" into several pricing zones that are assigned different area prices and that comprise one or more bidding areas.

The results of the "market splitting" mechanism are in general similar to what is achieved by the variant of market coupling that is currently being implemented between major Western European markets, and that is examined in this study. Yet, in contrast to Nord Pool, it is not a single power exchange that determines (in a "top-down" way) whether to subdivide or retain a single pricing zone across markets. Instead, market coupling is characterized by a more de-centralized ("bottom-up") approach where the joint coordination effort between all involved national TSOs and power exchanges determines which national markets are "coupled" with each other to form a single pricing zone.

Specifically, for every day and each interconnector, TSOs determine the amount of ATC for which the corresponding transmission rights are no longer allocated explicitly but instead assigned to the respective power exchanges in the adjacent markets. In order to achieve spot price convergence, a joint optimization algorithm considers the net import/export positions of each participating exchange for a given clearing price and thus determines the optimal cross-border flows. As such, a buy-order in a higher-priced market can be matched with a sell-order in a cheaper

[18]In the Nordic market, national markets are further subdivided into one or more *bidding areas*, reflecting transmission bottlenecks both within and across national markets. For instance, the Danish market is subdivided into two bidding areas (Western and Eastern Denmark) which are linked by a 600 MW interconnector that is frequently congested.

adjacent market, thus mitigating the price differential, with any resulting cross-border flows implicitly covered by the transferred capacity rights. As shown by Meeus *et al.* [2009] or Weber *et al.* [2010], the underlying optimization problem can be re-formulated as maximizing overall welfare, constrained by interconnector capacities and other real-time limitations. If one of these constraints is binding — e.g. if the flows necessary to equalize prices exceed the ATC — then prices cannot fully converge and the resulting congestion rent is collected by the owner of the interconnector.

The previously outlined explicit setup at the French–German border was modified when Germany joined the already existing market coupling between France, the Netherlands and Belgium (the so-called "Trilateral Coupling") on 9 November 2010, marking the starting point for the Central Western Europe (CWE) day-ahead market coupling. As a major change to the pre-existing setting, an explicit allocation of transmission rights for interconnector access is henceforth only held for monthly and yearly contracts, whereas on a day-ahead stage, all cross-border transmission capacities are available to cover the market coupling flows.[19] Following the harmonization of day-ahead gate closure times (12:00 noon) at all involved power exchanges, the market coupling algorithm then starts to determine the optimal cross-border flows at around 12:05 pm. Finally, the resulting day-ahead prices are published by the CWE power exchanges by 12:55 pm.[20]

3. Empirical Analysis

3.1. *Ex-ante scheduled transactions in Europe*

The general economic inefficiency of explicit *ex-ante* schemes is analyzed in Fig. 2, where the graph plots the spread between German and French day-ahead power prices against corresponding net transit nominations as a percentage of available interconnector capacity (sample period from 26 October 2006 to 9 November 2010, i.e. pre-market coupling). Clearly, not only are interconnector capacities often left (partially) unused, although a non-zero price spread in an efficient market

[19]Note that the transmission capacity of an interconnector is usually "sliced" and allocated for different timescales. Thus, off-exchange transactions, such as customized OTC cross-border trades, can still be executed by traders acquiring monthly or yearly transmission rights, whereas all remaining interconnector capacity can be used by power exchanges for market coupling purposes. Importantly, as pointed out by Meeus [2011a], retaining such a split helps to avoid a potential monopolization of the entire organization of cross-border trade of electricity by the power exchanges participating in market coupling.

[20]See http://www.marketcoupling.com/about-emcc/daily-operations.

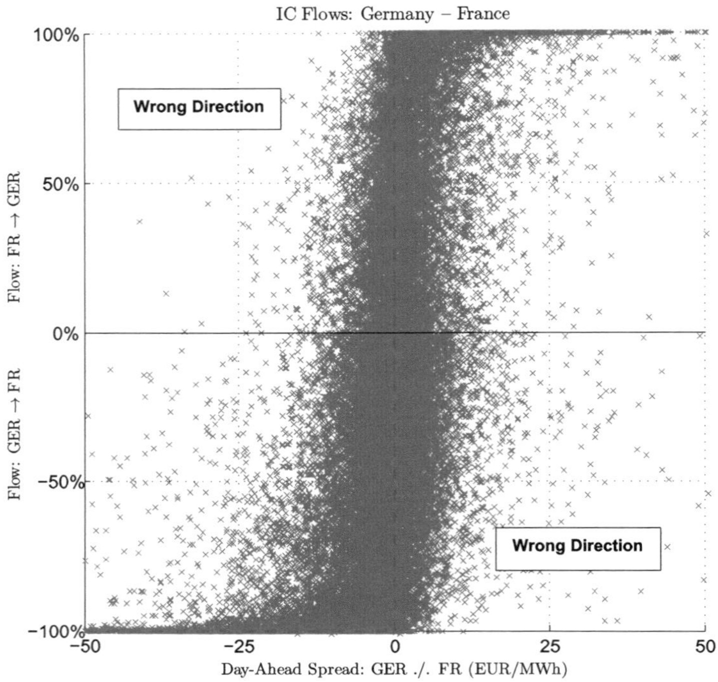

Fig. 2. Interconnector flows: Germany–France.

Notes: This figure illustrates inefficient interconnector use by plotting the day-ahead price spread between the German and French electricity markets versus net transit nominations (as a percentage of interconnector capacity) for the same hours. Data shown for the period from 26 October 2006 to 9 November 2010. The dashed line indicates economically efficient flows (as would have occurred under market coupling) such that there is no flow in the wrong direction, nor less-than-optimal flow in the right direction.

Source: RTE (http://clients.rte-france.com) and Bloomberg.

setting would call for additional cross-border flow until the price spread was fully exploited or the maximum interconnector capacity was reached, even worse, out of all nominations, approximately 32% led to flows in the wrong direction altogether.

On a more detailed level, the data also reveal that during both peak and off-peak hours, French day-ahead power prices exceed German prices more frequently than vice versa — or, more precisely, during approximately 58% of all hourly periods.[21] This pattern, in turn, also seems to impact the nomination behavior by cross-border

[21] Also note that the French–German interconnection, as a series of multiple alternating current (AC) links, has a higher capacity for GER→F than for F→GER.

traders: conditional on the spread being negative. In other words, for French day-ahead prices exceeding German prices, net interconnector flows in the economically correct direction (i.e. to the higher-priced market) can be observed during approximately 82% of all hourly peak and off-peak periods.[22] By contrast, given a positive day-ahead spread (i.e. German prices exceed their French counterparts), the share of net interconnector flows in the right direction is disproportionately lower and correct flows can only be observed during approximately 49% of all hours. Hence, market participants tend to bet on a negative spread, with a positive spread not only being less frequently observed but apparently also harder to predict correctly.

This diverse picture also manifests itself as regards the degree of *net* capacity utilization. On an overall basis, interconnectors are used at slightly less than 50% of their thermal capacity when French power prices exceed German power prices. For the opposite case, average *net* capacity utilization even gets driven down to less than 10% since, as mentioned above, adverse flows are observed more frequently. Disaggregating further, we can observe that for a price spread of up to 5 EUR/MWh (in either direction) and excluding all adverse flows,[23] French–German interconnectors are still used at only slightly more than 40% of their thermal capacity. For the complementary case where only price spreads larger than 5 EUR/MWh are considered, "gross" capacity utilization for flows in the economically correct direction increases to 69%. Clearly, a comparably lower (absolute-level) spread between day-ahead prices increases the likelihood of traders having predicted it wrongly during the capacity auction and of hence having to engage in an unprofitable trade, which ultimately reduces both gross and net capacity utilization.

A general *caveat* is in order here: We generally acknowledge that "inefficient" flows from high- to low-priced markets may in the end be caused by loop flows, as they typically occur within highly meshed grids such as in Europe. As such, the above analysis may likely have been subject to related distortions. While it is impossible to mitigate this issue in practice, we point out to a specific pair of markets where loop flows could be excluded from the research design: the British–French interconnection. Bunn and Zachmann [2010] investigate the efficiency of interconnector flows between these two markets and, although avoiding

---

[22]Note that in practice, traders may schedule more flows for those hours where they can be sure to properly anticipate the price differential between the markets. Hence, on a volume-weighted basis and conditional on a negative spread, even 93% of all exchanged MWs have flowed in the correct direction.

[23]By contrast, the previous two examples related to *net* capacity utilization including adverse flows. In the theoretical case of an interconnector being used up to its full thermal capacity in both directions, the resulting net capacity utilization would then accordingly be 0%.

distortions from loop flows, still find that there are evident inefficiencies from related interconnector flows in the "wrong" direction.[24]

3.2. *Spot and futures prices under the CWE market coupling*

The start of the CWE market coupling has fundamentally changed the dynamics of the day-ahead price spreads between Germany–France and Germany–Netherlands, respectively. Figure 3 illustrates this for hours 9 and 18 of the day. For both hourly periods, with few exceptions at mid-November 2010, the spreads are mainly negative or zero, providing clear evidence of interconnector flows henceforth taking economically correct directions — i.e. from the then mainly lower-priced German market to the higher-priced Dutch and French day-ahead markets. The data show that until year-end 2010, *exact* price convergence was reached in 81% of all hourly periods for the German–Dutch day-ahead spread and in approximately 52% of all

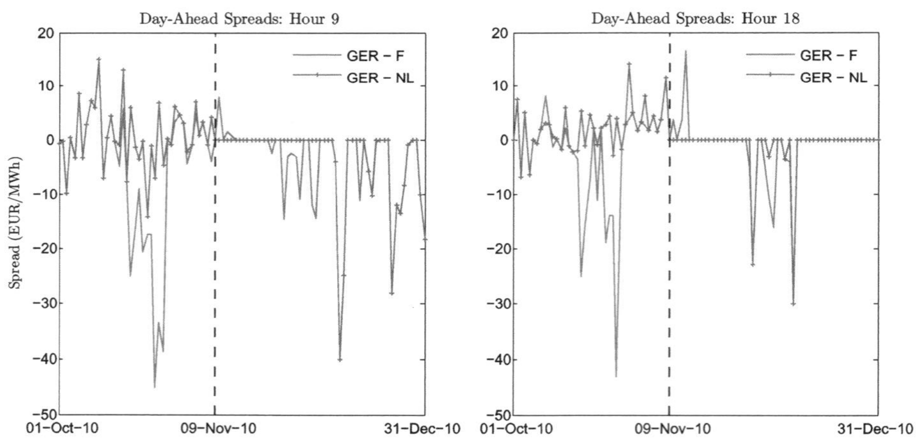

Fig. 3. Spread in day-ahead prices: GER–F and GER–NL.

Notes: This figure shows the spread in day-ahead electricity prices between Germany and France as well as Germany and the Netherlands. The LHS graph displays day-ahead prices for hour 9 of the day (8:00–9:00 am), whereas the RHS graph relates to hour 18 (5:00–6:00 pm). The vertical dashed line marks the start of the CWE (Central Western Europe) market coupling between Germany, France, the Netherlands and Belgium as per 9 November 2010.

Source: All data is sourced from Bloomberg.

[24]In the meantime, the English–French interconnection is no longer the only link between Britain and the Continent. Additional interconnection capacity has been made available, such as BritNed between England and the Netherlands, yet had not been commissioned by the time when Bunn and Zachmann [2010] undertook their study.

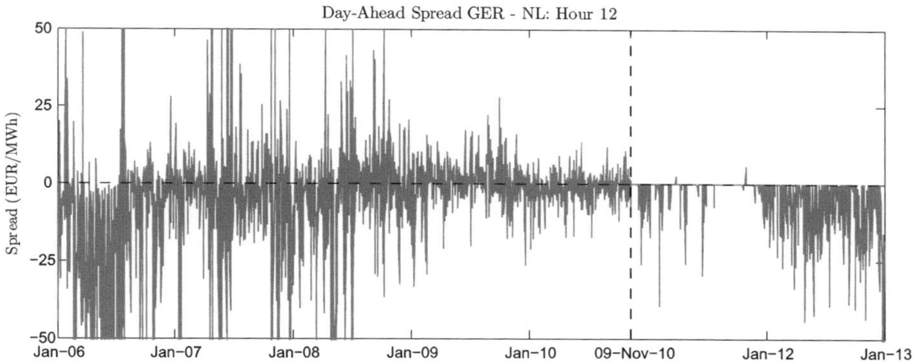

Fig. 4. Spread in day-ahead prices: Germany–Netherlands.

Notes: This figure shows the spread in day-ahead electricity prices between Germany and the Netherlands during the period from 01 January 2006 to 31 December 2012. The underlying day-ahead prices relate to hour 12 of the day (11:00 am–12:00 pm). The vertical dashed line marks the start of the CWE (Central Western Europe) market coupling between Germany, France, the Netherlands and Belgium as per 9 November 2010.

Source: All data are sourced from Bloomberg.

hours for the German–French spread. Note, however, that for specific hours of the day, these percentages can vary significantly. For instance, for the German–French spread over the same period, German day-ahead prices during hour 24 of the day tend to clearly fall below French prices, so that price convergence could only be reached during less than 23% of all hours. By contrast, for hour 17 (18), a zero price spread was observed during 80% (74%) of all periods.

These patterns also manifest themselves when analyzing the *long-term* behavior of the day-ahead spread between the German and the Dutch electricity markets, as illustrated in Fig. 4. For the spread between the prices of electricity to be delivered in both markets during hour 12 (11:00 am–12:00 noon) on the next day, Fig. 4 shows that since the introduction of the CWE market coupling, positive price spreads were no longer observed at all — with very few, notable exceptions. On 27 March 2011, after the close of the day-ahead auction for the following day, the market coupling optimization algorithm could not be run due to a bug in the system which was ultimately caused by the change to daylight-saving time on that day. Consequently, as a fallback mechanism in the case of such a de-coupling, *explicit* ("shadow") auctions had to be organized in order to allocate the available daily transmission capacity.[25] For the remaining days, however, the spread was either zero or negative,

[25]See, e.g. EPEX-Spot [2011] or CREG [2011]. A positive spread could also be observed on 29 October 2011, which, interestingly again coincides with the clock change back to winter time.

implying that whenever available transmission capacity is insufficient in order to reach price convergence between the two markets, this applies to flows for the direction GER→NL, but not vice versa. More recently, negative spreads have been slightly more prevalent, thus driving down the rate of price convergence, which can be attributed to the steadily growing renewables feed-in in Germany, combined with continued strong levels of natural gas prices affecting the gas-based Dutch electricity market.[26]

Table 1 summarizes the above qualitative observations by providing descriptive statistics for the German–Dutch day-ahead spread during selected hours of the day and for the corresponding baseload spread, i.e. the average of all 24 hourly spreads. The key characteristic of market coupling, i.e. price convergence driving down the spread to zero, is reflected in several of the statistics. For instance, note that a zero baseload spread could be observed for approximately. 30% of all days since 9 November 2010, implying that price convergence was not only reached for several hours, but even for all 24 hours on these days. On a more detailed level, we also see that conditional on the spread being negative, both mean and standard deviation tend to be lower. Consequently, since the introduction of market coupling, not only can negative spreads $s^i < 0$ be observed less frequently, their spikiness is also reduced in terms of absolute size and variation. This change in the dynamics of the spread and, hence of its individual components, can be explained by the fact that under market coupling, supply and demand shocks occurring in the interconnected markets can be mitigated more easily — to the extent that these shocks are non-synchronous. The coordination of cross-border flows between coupled markets always helps to reduce the economic scarcity (abundance) of *net* supplies that is signaled by electricity prices in one market spiking upward (downward).[27]

While the results in Table 1 merely confirm the general working of the basic market coupling idea, i.e. fostering price convergence by achieving economically efficient cross-border trade, these empirical findings — in hindsight — could not have been expected from the outset: Keppler *et al.* [2014], for example, report a significant deterioration in convergence rates for German and French electricity spot prices for the years post-2012, thereby essentially reversing the increases in welfare

[26]The role of natural gas as marginal fuel in the Dutch market has been further strengthened due to additional exports to Great Britain since the commissioning of the BritNed subsea cable (linking the Dutch with the British market).

[27]See De Jonghe *et al.* [2008] and Huisman and Kiliç [2013] for an analysis of such volatility reduction potential in the context of the Trilateral Market Coupling between France, Belgium and the Netherlands.

Table 1. Descriptive statistics: GER–NL day-ahead spread.

Hour of day	6	9	12	15	18	21	Base
Pre-market coupling							
n	3234	3234	3225	3229	3205	3234	3234
$s^i < 0$	33.6%	52.3%	69.2%	73.1%	65.5%	61.9%	68.6%
$s^i = 0$	0.4%	0.1%	0.2%	0.2%	0.1%	0.3%	0.0%
Mean	2.01	−2.45	−15.09	−9.10	−12.07	−4.44	−4.84
Mean$^+$	5.34	6.58	7.89	5.64	6.29	3.83	3.30
Mean$^-$	−4.50	−10.66	−25.31	−14.51	−21.75	−9.51	−8.57
Median	1.81	−0.32	−3.90	−3.02	−2.00	−1.55	−1.83
Min	−129.47	−464.17	−481.07	−477.09	−480.13	−376.49	−154.98
Max	43.11	256.84	345.05	430.09	412.31	70.14	74.63
Std. Dev.	7.13	21.97	46.34	33.84	47.07	15.31	13.47
Std. Dev.$^+$	4.94	13.45	19.82	18.96	19.79	4.92	6.10
Std. Dev.$^-$	6.25	24.83	50.90	36.43	53.93	17.21	14.27
Skewness	−2.03	−6.83	−4.58	−6.15	−4.97	−8.08	−4.17
Kurtosis	39.29	141.51	35.15	79.64	40.01	138.19	32.41
Post-market coupling							
n	784	784	784	784	784	784	784
$s^i < 0$	14.7%	15.1%	35.1%	38.5%	24.9%	24.1%	60.5%
$s^i = 0$	83.0%	82.7%	64.5%	61.4%	73.5%	74.4%	30.2%
Mean	−1.77	−1.17	−4.22	−4.92	−3.00	−2.70	−3.11
Mean$^+$	2.38	12.15	2.92	0.75	9.10	5.07	0.77
Mean$^-$	−12.47	−9.64	−12.05	−12.78	−12.67	−11.53	−5.25
Median	0.00	0.00	0.00	0.00	0.00	0.00	−0.50
Min	−217.23	−40.15	−76.90	−139.76	−57.39	−57.04	−89.43
Max	7.02	30.01	5.41	0.75	28.58	9.86	8.23
Std. Dev.	11.58	5.47	8.39	9.63	7.82	6.88	6.67
Std. Dev.$^+$	2.03	10.30	2.25	n.a.	7.26	3.33	1.38
Std. Dev.$^-$	28.01	8.80	10.31	11.85	10.63	9.57	7.85
Skewness	−15.45	−2.17	−2.92	−4.83	−2.89	−3.16	−6.43
Kurtosis	273.80	17.34	12.17	50.54	11.09	12.47	69.76

Note: This table reports summary statistics for the spread s^i between day-ahead electricity prices in Germany and the Netherlands for selected hours of the day ($i = \{6, 9, 12, 15, 18, 21\}$). The baseload spread ($s^{\text{base}}$; "Base") is defined as the (unweighted) arithmetic average of all 24 hourly spreads on a given day. The "Pre-Market Coupling" sample covers the period from 1 January 2002 until 8 November 2009. The "Post-Market Coupling" sample covers the period thereafter until 31 December 2012. Mean$^+$ and Std. Dev.$^+$ are defined as $\mu^+ = \mathbb{E}[s^i | s^i > 0]$ and $\sigma^+ = \sqrt{\mathbb{E}[(s^i - \mu^+)^2 \mid s^i > 0]}$, respectively. Note that spreads beyond a threshold of 500 EUR/MWh were excluded from the samples in order to avoid distortions.
Source: All data are sourced from Bloomberg.

that the market coupling mechanism initially had achieved during the years 2011 and 2012.[28] Taking the German–Dutch border as another example, Platts [2014b] briefly summarizes what can already be seen in Fig. 4: A clear deterioration in convergence at this border, too, ultimately driven by *the Netherlands importing Germany's national energy policy in the shape of massive, fluctuating volumes of subsidized green power.* As such, the initial performance of the market coupling mechanism right after the beginning of the CWE coupling in end-2010 appears remarkable; yet, the drop in convergence rates thereafter raises doubts about its ability in the long term to mitigate adverse fundamentals underlying each individual market, as evidenced by the massive challenges that the ever-increasing inflow from renewable generation in Germany has put on the entire system.

Finally, as regards the impact of market coupling on futures prices, both empirical findings and theoretical arguments provide a mixed picture thus far. On the one hand, as is well known, it is the non-storability of electricity that causes the classic cost-of-carry relationship between spot and futures prices to break down, which has led to the common perception that electricity has a "split personality" with respect to spot and futures prices [Pilipovic, 1998]. As such, the argument that futures prices under market coupling need to converge solely "because spot prices do" does not hold. On the other hand, and regardless of the above, the well-known interpretation of futures prices as expected spot prices at maturity under a suitably chosen (possibly non-unique) pricing measure [Cox and Ross, 1976; Harrison and Kreps, 1979] still holds — also for electricity. Therefore, the fact that the 1-year-ahead German–Dutch futures spread in Fig. 5 qualitatively tracks the flat and, later on, widening trajectory of the corresponding spot spread during the years 2011 and 2012 in Fig. 4, may be seen to be in line with this reasoning.[29] Empirically, the average spread between 1-year-ahead German and Dutch futures contracts (from 1 January 2006 until the start of market coupling) amounts to –4.49 EUR/MWh, whereas the average post-coupling spread has reduced to –1.23 EUR/MWh (0.05 EUR/MWh in 2011 and –2.61 EUR/MWh in 2012). Yet, these results remain slightly inconclusive — especially in view of a generally highly non-constant supply side in each of the two

---

[28] Keppler *et al.* [2014], for instance, estimate that the annual consumer surplus in the French electricity market increased by EUR 1.5 billion in 2012.

[29] This simplified argument assumes any potential risk premia to be constant and sets expected spot spreads equal to realized spreads. Further, note that although movements in the German–Dutch spot and futures spreads may coincide as displayed in the two figures, Fig. 4 only displays the day-ahead spread for hour 12 of the day and not an average baseload spread.

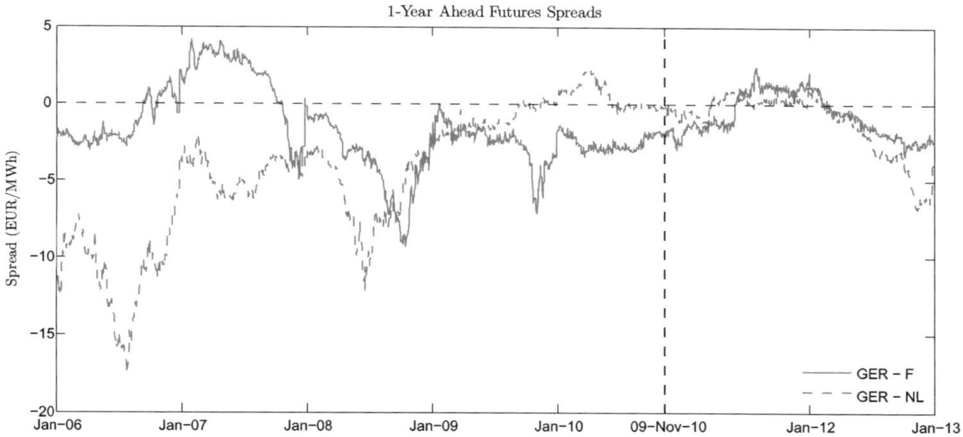

Fig. 5. Spread in 1-year ahead futures prices: GER–F and GER–NL.

Notes: This figure shows the spread in (generic) 1-year-ahead futures contracts between Germany and France as well as Germany and the Netherlands during the period from 1 January 2006 to 31 December 2012. The vertical dashed line marks the start of the CWE (Central Western Europe) market coupling between Germany, France, the Netherlands and Belgium as per 9 November 2010.

Source: All data are sourced from Bloomberg.

markets.[30] By contrast, the widening of the German–French futures spread since 2012 is not primarily attributable to market-endogenous, fundamental factors, but to an external policy factor, as will further be outlined in Section 4.

4. Future Policy Challenges

With the institutional framework for market coupling now fully laid out, we shall focus on the policy challenges that arise when a supra-nationally organized framework, such as market coupling, meets the "market realities" in each of the markets that have joined the coupling mechanism. For although the previous analyses have found promising indications that price convergence in European markets may be realized, there are still considerable obstacles to market coupling becoming an actual "success story." First of all, these obstacles have to be seen in the continued scarcity of interconnector capacity — a situation that is characteristic

[30] For instance, structural changes such as the German nuclear phase-out or a further continued increase in German renewable generation capacity (that outpaces their European neighbors) may well have been anticipated and reflected in futures prices at that time already, but not in spot prices.

for European cross-border trade in electricity and that is furthermore aggravated by massive increases in intermittent (renewable) generation causing congestion on interconnectors even more frequently: Germany's renewable energy policy serves as a prime example here, and we refer to Keppler *et al.* [2014] as one of the first studies that investigates the potential link between increasing, volatile wind and solar feed-in and decreasing price convergence rates within the CWE market coupling. Yet, while restrictions in available interconnector capacity (that could help improve convergence rates again) and their inherent "drain" on the performance of the market coupling mechanism have to be seen as a given, we want to primarily focus on the policy challenges that a market coupling setting, once fully established and in place, may still face, i.e. irrespective of how interconnector capacities or other market fundamentals are supporting or hindering the functioning of the mechanism: We envisage these challenges primarily emanating from *individual electricity market policies on a national level* that will inevitably see market coupling run into headwinds to the extent they may even help to preserve price *divergence* rather than convergence. This section focuses on a prominent example for national electricity market regulation not in accordance with the EU-wide target of promoting the Internal Electricity Market and highlights from a policy point of view both the reasons and the implications thereof.

The French electricity wholesale market has been integrated into a market coupling framework since 2006, the start of the Trilateral Market Coupling between Belgium, France and the Netherlands.[31] Given the strong position of (quasi-) integrated utility Electricité de France (EDF) in both the generation and retail markets, enhancing further competition, especially on the retail side, had been a top priority for policymakers since the liberalization of the French market.[32] In order to foster retail market entry and enable new suppliers to participate in the cost advantages that EDF enjoyed thanks to its strong nuclear generation position in the

[31]The Trilateral Market Coupling was later extended when the German electricity wholesale market joined the existing arrangement to form the CWE market coupling.

[32]In fact, since the early 2000s, there have been several attempts by the European Commission (EC) to promote further competition on the French retail market. In 2006, it sent out a reasoned opinion to the French Government, complaining about yet incomplete implementation of the Electricity Market Directives. Among a number of issues, the Commission also criticized the *persistence of regulated supply tariffs for eligible clients, which blocks the arrival of newcomers and prevents the free choice of supplier* [EC, 2006]. In fact, lower price levels for electricity in the retail market than in the wholesale market back at that time had helped to keep the barriers to entry high for potential alternative electricity suppliers. In 2007, the EC also launched a formal State Aid investigation on French retail electricity tariffs for large and medium-sized companies [EC, 2007]. For further information on the French retail electricity market, see, e.g. Creti *et al.* [2013].

wholesale segment, other electricity suppliers were to be supported via a fixed tariff at which they could purchase electricity from EDF. As stipulated by the "NOME"[33] Law passed by the French Government in 2010, EDF is currently required to make available up to 25% of its nuclear electricity generation to suppliers at a fixed tariff known as ARENH.[34] The level of this regulated wholesale price is intended to reflect the full cost of nuclear-generated electricity, i.e. essentially EDF's costs for operating and maintaining its nuclear plants as well as reactor life extensions and future upgrades. Hence, by allocating ARENH volumes at such a fixed price to alternative suppliers, their sourcing costs should decrease, thus finally supporting their cost structures to become more competitive *vis-à-vis* a fully integrated utility such as EDF.

When the ARENH mechanism finally came into effect in July 2011, the tariff had initially been set to 40.00 EUR/MWh until 1 January 2012 and was subsequently increased to today's level of 42.00 EUR/MWh. In early 2014, the tariff and its method of calculation were under review, facing several delays as well as a strong political and public debate around the question of what the "proper" costs for EDF's nuclear-generated electricity should be.[35]

From a contractual point of view, ARENH electricity volumes are allocated to retail suppliers on a yearly basis,[36] so that ARENH's products are most comparable to electricity *futures* contracts (as opposed to *spot* contracts). Consequently, practitioners have frequently pointed to the importance of the ARENH tariff as a reference price for the electricity futures market, notably 1-year-ahead futures contracts. When futures prices for wholesale electricity rise (far) above the tariff, alternative suppliers will source their volumes at the cheaper rate as offered by the ARENH mechanism, thus reducing demand and liquidity at the OTC- and exchange-based forward and futures markets. For the opposite case of wholesale prices falling below the tariff, previously ARENH-sourced volumes have been observed to add to

[33]Nouvelle Organisation du Marché de l'Electricité — New Organization of the Electricity Market.

[34]Accès Régulé à l'Electricité Nucléaire Historique — regulated access to historic nuclear energy. Note, however, that the amount of generation to be provided by EDF via the ARENH mechanism is capped at 100 terrawatt hours (TWh).

[35]In this context, also see, e.g. Solier [2010]: *Se pose alors la question de l'asymétrie d'information entre le régulateur et l'opérateur historique pour la détermination des coûts supportés par ce dernier.*

[36]See, e.g. Commission Decision 2012/C 398/05: The first period of delivery of regulated access to existing nuclear power started on 1 July 2011. Thirty-two suppliers signed a framework agreement with EDF and 61,3 TWh of regulated access to existing nuclear power were to be delivered between 1 July 2011 and 30 June 2012.

overall wholesale demand, thus driving traded futures prices up to the tariff again.[37] According to Heren [2014], and following the mechanics described in CRE [2013], some market participants even consider the tariff both as a floor and a cap on futures prices at the same time, which, however, would only be a valid assumption for the theoretical case that the volumes made available under the mechanism were never fully exhausted. In fact, in order to get a sense of the volumes in question, CRE [2013] mentions that *EDF has delivered about* 30 *TWh to alternative suppliers under ARENH every six months since the mechanism was implemented.*[38] At the same time, volumes traded in calendar products ("Y+1 products") in the French market in the first half of 2013 amounted to 57.8 TWh.[39]

The availability of such an alternative sourcing channel (albeit smaller compared to total demand) is even more important when considering the rather limited liquidity of the French electricity wholesale market in general, which has continued to deteriorate also throughout the years covered by our analysis, and especially for yearly products, among others. To support this argument, CRE [2013] notes: *Net volumes sold on the wholesale markets were down* 30.1 *TWh compared to the first half of* 2011 *mainly due to sales to ARENH in the first half of* 2012 (30.2 TWh). Against this background, the effect of suppliers shifting from one sourcing channel (i.e. market/exchange) to the other (i.e. ARENH) feeds through on wholesale price dynamics more directly.[40] Moreover, also note that switching between volumes sourced via the ARENH mechanism or via the wholesale market is possible until ARENH volumes communicated to EDF are fixed and binding. In combination, this set-up allows for an obvious arbitrage situation that can lead to remarkable de-coupling of futures prices between Germany and France, as described below.

The impact of the ARENH tariff on price dynamics in the French electricity market became particularly obvious in mid-2013 when French futures prices — previously aligned with German futures prices in a general downward movement — kept oscillating around the currently prevailing ARENH threshold, as shown in Fig. 6. CRE [2013] accordingly notes: (...) *Therefore, for supply for* 2014, *this mechanism provides alternative suppliers with trade-off opportunities until*

[37] See CRE [2013, p. 63]. *When the baseload calendar product market price is over* 42 *EUR/MWh, ARENH supply substitutes wholesale market purchases for alternative suppliers. However, when the wholesale price is at* 42 *EUR/MWh or lower, subscribing to ARENH is called into question by more favourable market conditions.* Also see, e.g. Platts [2014a].

[38] See CRE [2013, p. 43].

[39] See CRE [2013, p. 30].

[40] See, e.g. de Regulation de l'Energie CRE [2014, p. 81]. *Le faible niveau de liquidité a amplifiè le phénomène.*

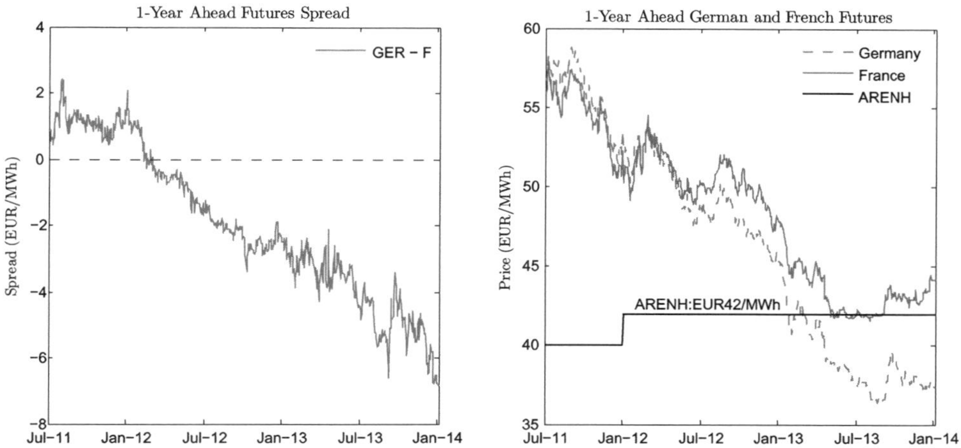

Fig. 6. 1-year-ahead futures and futures spreads: Germany–France.

Notes: The RHS graph shows the development of French and German 1-year-ahead baseload futures prices between July 2011 and January 2014. The LHS graph shows the corresponding spread between the two contracts, defined as German–French electricity price differential.

15 *November* 2013 *when alternative suppliers must define the firm quantities they wish to purchase under the ARENH. (…) The stabilisation of French prices at* 42 *EUR/MWh in May and June* 2013 *reflects actions on the market by participants involved in the ARENH mechanism. This mechanism explains the polarisation of transaction around* 42 *EUR/MWh.* As can be imagined, the oscillating behavior of the French futures price at that time was supported by arbitrage trades of market participants that switch between the two sourcing channels (e.g. selling contracted volumes initially agreed at prices below the ARENH level of 42 EUR/MWh once the wholesale price would jump above the threshold and vice versa). In addition, suppliers with access to ARENH are effectively assigned a long position in electricity with the strike price of the call option set at the ARENH level of 42 EUR/MWh. Most likely, suppliers therefore have contributed to the above-mentioned oscillating price behavior by writing call options, as supposed by de Regulation de l'Energie CRE [2014]. Consequently, with French prices at least temporarily supported by the tariff and with German prices continuing their downturn, the futures spread between the two countries has widened significantly in the course of 2013, even exceeding the 6 EUR/MWh threshold in absolute terms.

Clearly, the existence of a fixed-price mechanism, such as the ARENH regime, cannot be in accordance with the aims of the EU to establish a common electricity market across European borders. Although market coupling, from a technical point of view, only targets *spot* price convergence and does not directly interfere with forward and futures markets, the classic perception of futures prices as expected spot prices nevertheless establishes a link between these markets. Furthermore, although there are various effects on the futures spread when switching to a coupling-based cross-border allocation mechanism, a decoupling of futures prices as displayed in Fig. 6 is, of course, not in line with the theory of interconnected electricity markets. From a more general point of view, despite the "split personality" of electricity prices (see Section 3), the Internal Electricity Market, as envisaged by the EU, should also seek to eliminate differentials in futures prices between coupled markets — especially given that trade in futures contracts still surpasses traded spot volumes by a factor of 5–7.[41]

More generally, this case is a prime example of a market structure deficiency that is caused by the sequential evolution of electricity markets from national isolation toward pan-European integration: While the ARENH mechanism may indeed be instrumental in fostering competition at the retail level, subsequently overlaying such price *rigidity* with a market coupling framework that essentially relies on wholesale prices adjusting *freely*, may only yield a suboptimal market design. As such, whereas the implementation of market coupling has also helped to harmonize wholesale spot markets and related institutions across Europe, the generally holistic pan-European focus of the coupling initiative conflicts with non-market-based allocation procedures in individual member states.

In view of the planned further roll-out of market coupling initiatives across Europe, much of the discussion, thus far, has focused on the technical feasibility of this project. With more and more markets joining the coupling, this will require even more powerful mathematical algorithms to solve the optimization problem posed by the coupling process.[42] However, as highlighted in this example, whenever extending a coupling mechanism by new member states/markets, "soft" criteria such as (i) vertical integration of market participants and (ii) competitiveness in upstream/downstream markets will need to be focused on more strongly than in the past. Otherwise, the idea of a common market zone across multiple countries will only extend to certain market segments of similar structure across borders and, thus, will necessarily remain incomplete.

[41]Based on data provided by CRE [2013] for the French market.

[42]The CWE market coupling is accompanied by other regional coupling initiatives throughout Europe, such as the South-Western Europe (SWE) coupling between France, Spain and Portugal, or the North-Western Europe (NWE) coupling between CWE and the Scandinavian/Baltic countries. Within the "Price Coupling of Regions" (PCR) initiative, these different coupling projects are planned to be integrated in order to finally reach the EU policy goal of a single Internal Electricity Market.

5. Conclusion

Creating a common electricity market, one of the top priorities on the energy policy agenda of the EU, is a complex and multifaceted task. Establishing a framework for cross-border trading to exchange surplus generation between adjacent markets generally opens up the possibility for prices across markets to converge under certain conditions and, importantly, for the well-known efficiency gains of free trade to be realized. However, as shown in this chapter, the merits of cross-border trading *per se* can vary dramatically depending not only on market fundamentals but, likewise, on the actual mechanics and institutional design governing the exchange of electricity across markets.

Market coupling schemes have proven very successful as a way to achieve cross-border flows in an economically efficient direction from low-price to high-price markets, thereby avoiding the classic "defect" of explicit allocation schemes which are especially prone to cause inefficient flows in the wrong direction. However, these efficiency enhancements, as reflected in more frequent spot price convergence across markets, do not necessarily translate into converging prices in other segments of the electricity market such as the futures market. As we have seen, individual energy market policies on a national level can act as severe obstacles, albeit temporarily, to the benefits of market coupling being fully realized.

However, the history of electricity markets in Europe shows that individual national (and formerly even isolated) markets had been established well before the idea of creating a single market was put forward by the EU. As such, apart from the technical effort to harmonize an increasing number of markets with different trading platforms, gate closure times and other specificities, market coupling also faces the difficulty of linking historically developed markets that strongly differ in terms of competitiveness along the energy value chain. While not a case for the German or UK retail electricity markets, competition in the French retail market suffers from a highly concentrated market structure where alternative suppliers are granted access to cheaper nuclear generation volumes at a reduced fixed price via the ARENH mechanism. Yet, such a tariff represents a classic example of how price rigidities in a single market not only take away liquidity from wholesale spot and futures markets, but also help to maintain the very price differences that market coupling actually seeks to eliminate.

In the future, it remains to be seen how the success of market coupling can be preserved despite the increasing number of individual national energy market regulations it will have to accommodate during its further roll-out. Further challenges ahead include, e.g. the reformation of renewables support schemes in countries like

Germany, and, moreover, the potential introduction of capacity mechanisms in a number of European markets. As a point in case, the new electricity market design in the UK was among the first to introduce a capacity remuneration mechanism, thus posing a new threat to the efficiencies and welfare gains expected from the pan-European coupling roll-out: under market coupling, how will energy-only markets interact with those markets where capacity payments are in place? New problems are bound to arise given that cross-border flows will no longer be determined by the underlying fundamentals in each respective market, but also by the way available capacity is remunerated on both sides of the interconnector.[43] For the US, in a similar manner, ongoing efforts to promote market integration will likely continue to be hindered by regulatory disconnects between different market areas (see, e.g. Section 2). Given this outlook, a common energy market policy among EU member states (or across the US) must not only focus on price convergence as key benchmark for the realization of a single electricity market; as a prerequisite to start with, a more holistic approach will instead be required to also focus on the frequently diverging sets of regulations as well as on their idiosyncracies that, at least in the past, have been overlooked too often.

References

Baker, P. and Gottstein, M. (2013). Capacity markets and european market coupling — can they co-exist? Working Paper.

Bohn, R. E., Caramanis, M. C. and Schweppe, F. C. (1984). Optimal pricing in electrical networks over space and time. *RAND Journal of Economics* **15** (3), 360–376.

Bunn, D. W. and Martoccia, M. (2010). The Efficiency of Network Transmission Rights as Derivatives on Energy Supply Chains. *Journal of Derivatives* **18** (2), 46–57.

Bunn, D. W. and Zachmann, G. (2010). Inefficient arbitrage in inter-regional electricity transmission. *Journal of Regulatory Economics* **37** (3), 243–265.

Chao, H.-P. and Peck, S. (1996). A market mechanism for electric power transmission. *Journal of Regulatory Economics* **10**, 25–59.

Commission de Régulation de l'Energie CRE. (2013). Wholesale electricity, CO_2, and gas market functioning. 2012–2013 Report.

Commission de Régulation de l'Electricité et du Gaz; CREG. (2011). The price spike on Belpex DAM for 28-03-11. URL http://www.creg.info/pdf/Etudes/F1099EN.pdf.

Commission de Regulation de l'Energie CRE. (2014). Wholesale electricity, CO_2, and gas market functioning. 2013–2014 Report.

Cox, J. C. and Ross, S. A. (1976). The valuation of options for alternative stochastic processes. *Journal of Financial Economics* **3** (1–2), 145–166.

Creti, A., Fumagalli, E. and Fumagalli, E. (2010). Integration of electricity markets in europe: Relevant issues for Italy. *Energy Policy*, **38**, 6966–6976.

[43]See, e.g. Baker and Gottstein [2013] for more information on the problem of "double payments" if an energy-only market is coupled with a market where a capacity remuneration mechanism has been installed.

Creti, A., Pouyet, J. and Sanin, M. E. (2013). The NOME law: Implications for the French electricity market. *Journal of Regulatory Economics* **43** (2), 196–213.

De Jonghe, C., Meeus, L. and Belmans, R. (2008). Power Exchange Price Volatility Analysis After One Year of Trilateral Market Coupling. Working Paper, Katholieke Universiteit Leuven.

EC. (2006). The Commission takes action against Member States which have still not properly opened up their energy markets. Press Release (IP/06/1768).

EC. (2007). State aid: Commission opens investigation into regulated electricity tariffs in France. Press Release (IP/07/815).

Ehrenmann, A. and Neuhoff, K. (2009). A comparison of electricity market designs in networks. *Operations Research*, **57**, 274–286.

ENTSO-E. (2012). Ten-Year Network Development Plan. URL https://www.entsoe.eu/major-projects/ten-year-network-development-plan/tyndp-2012.

EPEX-Spot. (2011). 27 March 2011 CWE Incident – Public message to the market parties. URL http://static.epexspot.com/document/12668/CWE_MC_SC_1107-04d_Communication_to_market_parties_final.pdf.

EPEX-Spot. (2012). Joint Cooperation Agreement Executed Between EPEX Spot And Tres Amigas. URL http://static.epexspot.com/document/17470/2012-01-10_Tres%20Amigas_EPEXSPOT.pdf.

Gilbert, R., Neuhoff, K. and Newbery, D. (2004). Allocating transmission to mitigate market power in electricity networks. *RAND Journal of Economics* **35**, 691–709.

Harrison, J. M. and Kreps, D. M. (1979). Martingales and arbitrage in multiperiod securities markets. *Journal of Economic Theory*, **20** (3), 381–408.

ICIS Heren. (2014) New French ARENH electricity tariff calculation delayed. Market Commentary for 27 February 2014.

Hobbs, B. F. Rijkers, A. M. and Boots, M. G. (2005). The more cooperation, the more competition? A cournot analysis of the benefits of electric market coupling. *The Energy Journal* **26** (4), 69–97.

Hogan, W. W. (1992). Contract Networks for Electric Power Transmission. *Journal of Regulatory Economics* **4** (3), 211–242.

Huisman, R. and Kiliç, M. (2013). A history of European electricity day-ahead prices. *Applied Economics* **45** (18), 2683–2693.

Keppler, J. H., Phan, S. Le Pen, Y. and Boureau, C. (2014). The impact of intermittent renewable production and market coupling on the convergence of french and german electricity prices. CEEM Working Paper 2014–07.

Kristiansen. T. (2007). An assessment of the German-Danish cross-border auctions. *Energy Policy*, **35** (6), 3369–3382.

Marckhoff, J. and Muck, M. (2009). Jump risk premia in short-term spread options: Evidence from the german electricity market. Working Paper, University of Bamberg.

McInerney, C. and Bunn, D. W. (2013). Valuation anomalies for interconnector transmission rights. *Energy Policy* **55**, 565–578.

Meeus, L. (2011a). Why (and how) to regulate power exchanges in the EU market integration context? *Energy Policy* **39** (3), 1470–1475.

Meeus, L. (2011b). Implicit auctioning on the Kontek Cable: Third time lucky? *Energy Economics* **33** (3), 413–418.

Meeus, L. Vandezande, L. Cole, S. and Belmans, R. (2009). Market coupling and the importance of price coordination between power exchanges. *Energy* **34** (3), 228–234.

Parisio, L. and Bosco, B. (2008). Electricity prices and cross-border trade: Volume and strategy effects. *Energy Economics* **30**, 1760–1775.

Parisio, L. and Pelagatti, M. (2014). Market coupling between electricity markets: theory and empirical evidence for the Italian-Slovenian interconnection. *11th Int. Conf. European Energy Market*, Krakow.

Pilipovic, D. (1998). *Energy Risk: Valuing and Managing Energy Derivatives*. (McGraw-Hill, New York).

Platts. (2014a). French prompt stronger as reactor delayed. Market Commentary for 2 April 2014.

Platts. (2014b). CWE convergence down despite coupling. European Power Daily.

RTE. (2009a). Access Rules for Imports and Exports on the French Public Power Transmission System. URL: http://clients.rte-france.com/lang/an/clients_traders_fournisseurs/services_clients/inter_contrats.jsp.

RTE. (2009b). Rules for Capacity Allocation by Explicit Auctions within Central West Europe Region (CWE Auction Rules). URL: http://clients.rte-france.com/lang/an/clients_traders_fournisseurs/services_clients/initiatives_regionales.jsp.

Schweppe, F. C., Caramanis, M. C., Tabors, R. D. and Bohn, R. E. (1988). *Spot Pricing of Electricity*. (Kluwer Academic Publishers, Boston, MA).

Solier, B. (2010). La Réforme du Marché de l'Electricité Français: Quels Impacts pour la Tarification et la Concurrence? Les Cahiers du PREC, 4. Paris: Série Information et débats.

Spees, K. and Pfeifenberger, J. (2012). Seams Inefficiencies — Problems and Solutions at Energy Market Borders. Presentation by The Brattle Group.

Turvey, R. (2006). Interconnector economics. *Energy Policy* **34** (13), 1457–1472.

Weber, A. Graeber, D. and Semmig, A. (2010). Market coupling and the CWE project. *Zeitschrift für Energiewirtschaft* **34** (4), 303–309.

Chapter 6

Spatial Econometrics in Electricity Markets Research

Rita De Siano and Alessandro Sapio

Department of Business and Economic Studies,
Parthenope University of Naples, via Generale Parisi 13,
80132 Naples, Italy

This chapter outlines the theoretical foundations and empirical applications of spatial econometrics in energy markets research. Spatial econometrics addresses spatial autocorrelation and spatial heterogeneity, two key issues of energy finance that have emerged during the low carbon transition. Indeed, with congested grids and a high penetration of geographically heterogeneous intermittent renewables, electricity markets can be more accurately modeled and forecasted by considering spatial effects. After illustrating the main spatial aspects of electricity pricing, production, and consumption, the chapter summarizes the theory of spatial econometrics and highlights its advantages over alternative estimation methods. Existing applications of spatial econometrics to electricity markets are thus reviewed (e.g. forecasting electricity demand and wholesale electricity prices and assessing the diffusion of photovoltaics). Methodological implications and on-going issues are discussed in the final section.

Keywords: Spatial econometrics; electricity prices; electricity demand; photo-voltaics; estimation; forecasting; spatial weight matrix; spatial autoregressive model; spatial error model; spatial Durbin model.

1. Introduction

The spatial organization of the electricity industry is a key issue in the current energy policy debate in many parts of the world, with its relevance being fostered by policy goals of decarbonization and of integration between physically separated markets. Balta-Ozkan *et al.* [2015a] review the literature on interdependencies between decarbonization and local economic development, showing that five trends motivate the study of the electricity industry through tools of spatial analysis.

First, potentials for renewable energy generation are spatially uneven due to geographical differences in average insolation rates, wind speeds, and geothermal and hydrological endowments, which reflect local climatic and orographic conditions. Second, and as implied by the first trend, the deployment of green energy technologies is spatially concentrated. Spatial patterns of statistical dependence are incorporated into models and forecasts of wind power generation and notably to make inferences on the distribution of wind speeds in new sites for which time series data are lacking or scarcely available. A third trend involves the geographical fragmentation in the governance of liberalized electricity markets. In this new governance setting, relationships between electricity users and producers unfold in space through both physical and social connections. Prosumers using distributed generation facilities are linked by social ties (which may help disseminate information on new technology vintages) and their physical interlinkages are primarily "local", as they are mediated through a (short-distance and low-voltage) distribution grid rather than through a (long-distance and high-voltage) transmission grid. Relatedly, geographical differences in urbanization rates influence the diffusion of distributed generation technologies, marking a fourth trend.

Finally, there are interactions between agglomeration economies and transmission constraints as a specific instance of efficiency gains derived from spatial integration between energy markets. Promoting regional integration indeed is based on the presumption that increased cross-border trade fosters productive efficiency by expanding the reach of the most efficient plants, and it improves allocative efficiency by inducing competition among producers who are geographically separate [Borenstein, 2000; Wolak, 2015].[1] The integration of electricity markets across regional areas has played a significant role in the development of electricity markets in the United States as testified by the Pennsylvania-New Jersey-Maryland (PJM) Interconnection, and it lies at the heart of the European Union's energy policy goal of creating an internal market for energy [Glachant, 2004; Meeus *et al.*, 2005].[2] Reconciling the goal of regional integration with decarbonization targets is

[1]While some simulation analyses corroborate the theoretical expectation of efficiency gains [Wolak, 2015; Valeri, 2009; Boffa *et al.*, 2010; De Nooij, 2011], evidence of collusive behaviors dates from the California electricity crisis [Cicchetti *et al.*, 2004] to more recent examples of inefficient arbitrage across interconnectors [Bunn and Zachmann, 2010; McInerney and Bunn, 2013]. See also Boffa and Sapio [2015].

[2]The EU is also part and parcel of large-scale inter-connection projects such as those envisioned through the Mediterranean Solar Plan [Jablonski, *et al.*, 2012; Escribano, 2010] within the broader

however a difficult challenge [Glachant and Ruester, 2014] as demonstrated by recent evidence of market integration being spoiled by burgeoning growth in renewables, which calls the traditional electricity-fuel nexus into question [De Menezes *et al.*, 2016; Gianfreda *et al.*, 2016].

As a bottom line, both decarbonization and market integration policies are significantly conditioned by the spatial organization of the electricity industry. This is true at the policy-making level and from the perspectives of private production and investment decisions. However, besides spatial interpolation tools such as kriging estimators used to assist wind investment decision-making developed by Haslett and Raftery [1989], Lenzi *et al.* [2016] and others, space has been incorporated into forecasting analyses only through time series. For instance, in Gneiting *et al.* [2006], Hering and Genton [2010] and follow-up studies the mean of the wind speed distribution at one site linearly depends on lagged wind speeds of other locations, resembling a vector autoregressive or a distributed lag model. Similarly, energy econometrics relies primarily upon time series models in regard to understanding and forecasting electricity prices and consumption, which are extremely relevant for policy-making and for shaping the expectations of private actors. Spatial econometric methods have not yet gained comparable status in applied research work, despite the result established by Giacomini and Granger [2004] that in predicting the aggregate of spatially correlated variables, forecasting is inaccurate when spatial effects are overlooked.

Against this background, this chapter outlines the theoretical foundations and the main empirical applications of spatial econometrics in energy markets research. Spatial econometrics uses an array of models, estimation methods and tests in addressing data samples potentially characterized by spatial dependence [Anselin, 1988]. Spatial dependence arises when the value assumed by a variable for a given location is correlated with the value that the same variable assumes for another place or for a set of other places. More specifically, heterogeneity (heteroscedasticity) and autocorrelation (dependence) are the main issues posed by the treatment of data series related to geographical entities. According to Anselin and Bera [1998], spatial autocorrelation occurs when high or low values for a random variable tend to cluster in space (positive spatial autocorrelation) or when locations tend to be surrounded by neighbors with very dissimilar values (negative spatial autocorrelation). The idea that "space matters" was stated by Tobler [1970] with his First Law of Geography: *Everything is related to everything else, but near things are more related than*

goal of building electricity highways running from the North Sea to northern Africa [Sanchis, *et al.*, 2015; Trieb and Müller-Steinhagen, 2007].

distant things. Problems posed by spatially organized data characterized by spatial autocorrelation require distinct treatment, and prohibit the use of approaches based on a one-way direction relationship between different geographical units.

The reviewed evidence sheds light on the value-added of spatial econometric models in our understanding of price setting, demand, and technological diffusion dynamics in the electricity industry and in forecasting electricity prices over time horizons that are relevant to the industry's policy goals of efficiency and reliability. We thereby expand the reach of recent literature reviews on the statistical forecasting of electricity prices [Weron, 2014; Nowotarski and Weron, 2017] and demand [Hong, 2014; Weron, 2007 chapter 3].

After illustrating the main spatial aspects related to the functioning of the electricity industry (Section 2), the chapter summarizes the modelling, estimation, and testing methodologies of spatial econometrics (Section 3). Existing applications of spatial econometrics to electricity markets are thus reviewed in Section 4 (e.g. modelling and forecasting electricity demand and wholesale electricity prices and assessing the diffusion of photovoltaic panels). The works reviewed here show that explicitly considering spatial correlations improves the forecasting performance and understanding of electricity market dynamics. Section 5 presents conclusions while offering a discussion of on-going issues and an outlook on future research.

2. Spatial Aspects of Electricity Markets

As this chapter will show, energy econometrics has only recently recognized the value-added of estimating spatial dependence patterns. In fact, it is remarkable how the importance of spatial networks in affecting the decisions of agents producing and consuming electricity has been neglected for such a long time even in theoretical work. One notable exception is a study conducted by Nijkamp [1983], who explored the nexus between energy policy goals, urban planning, and the spatial distribution of economic activities (as influenced by industrial policy), stressing its strategic relevance for policy makers.

Such neglect can be traced to the history of the electricity industry, which has been gravitating between two opposite configurations [Granovetter and McGuire, 1998]. In the early days, in the US, self-producers were prevailing at a time when long-range interconnections had yet to be sufficiently developed. In the subsequent configuration that took over from approximately 1920 onward, the industry came to be dominated by centralized technical control under vertically integrated (regulated) monopolists when electricity was produced by plants exploiting economies of scale, and this could be considered (within each country) a spatially homogeneous and standardized service. Investments in new generation, transmission, and distribution infrastructures were centrally coordinated. Dispatching, planning, and investment decisions were conditioned by implicit "transport costs" between nodes, but associated issues were addressed within vertically integrated organizations.

From the late 1970s and the 1980s, a growing sensitivity to environmental issues, progress in information and communication technologies, and the fall of the minimum efficient scale following the introduction of combined-cycle gas turbines have been powerful drivers behind the transition to a decentralized and deregulated regime in which facilities along the power supply chain have been unbundled [Pollitt, 2008]. Drawing on the seminal work of Dosi [1988], Künneke [2008] has interpreted the increasingly distributed technical control of electricity systems as a transition between technological paradigms (from centralized to decentralized). Technological paradigms of the power supply chain differ in terms of spatial patterns of energy generation, transmission and distribution, with respect to cost structures and the involvement and reactiveness of energy users. The emergence of prosumers in the decentralized paradigm is a point in case (see Schleicher-Tappeser [2012] among others).

In light of the outlined turns in technological paradigms, economic thinking, policy-making goals and practices, the time is ripe for the explicit incorporation of spatial correlations into the statistical modeling and forecasting of electricity industry variables. It is worth providing a few more details on the theoretical roots of spatial effects on wholesale electricity prices and on corresponding demand and supply determinants.

When applying a structural approach to electricity price modeling, the electricity price at a certain time and location is a function of its "fundamentals", namely, of electricity demand, fuel prices, transmission constraints, parameters of strategic reaction functions (associated with dispatchable energy sources), supply components that are non-strategic within the given bidding horizon (i.e. renewable energy sources and derivative contracts), and unobservable determinants, i.e. the error term of an econometric model (see Carmona and Coulon [2014] for a survey). Such determinants can exercise their effects across time and space, and hence they should be included in econometric models with time and spatial lags. In such structural models, spatial dependence between electricity prices for different locations is due to spatial dependence in electricity price fundamentals and/or in unobservables. More frequently though, econometric models of electricity prices are reduced-form models wherein time and spatial correlations are modeled directly.

As a matter of fact, one key force motivating the use of spatial econometrics in modeling electricity prices can be traced to the seminal work by Bohn *et al.* [1984] on nodal pricing. Nodal prices are computed as the solution of a system cost-minimization programme subject to various constraints. Optimal nodal prices have been shown to vary stochastically across time and locations, and specifically price differences between two nodes may emerge depending on the nature of events occurring throughout the transmission grid. This occurs because whenever an additional power generator injects electricity into the system, thermal constraints may become binding due to congestion, thereby shifting nodal prices away from marginal costs. Even when transmission lines are congested, price differentials reflect the relative scarcity of electricity in neighboring locations such that, following Bushnell and Stoft [1996], the optimal nodal price in one location reflects average nodal prices in neighbouring locations.

In applying such a reduced-form approach to modeling electricity prices, tests of market integration are well suited to illustrate the potentially informative role of spatial econometrics. Indeed, time series tests performed in the literature offer information on spatial linkages between electricity prices, but only implicitly. Under perfect market integration, i.e. whenever congestion does not arise, the set of locational (or zonal) prices is typically represented by means of a univariate time series process. When congestion occurs, a multivariate time series model such as a vector autoregressive (VAR) or vector error correction (VEC) model is assumed instead. In the former case, prices are equalized across zones, whereas in the latter case correlations among prices are expected to be positive albeit imperfect due to common drivers (e.g. fuel prices or weather conditions) and due to relative scarcity in neighboring locations as noted above.

Market integration has been assessed using various approaches (e.g. by testing time dynamics of correlations between price pairs (Pereira and Soares [2008] on European power exchanges) or by testing unit roots of price differentials [Zachmann, 2008]. Granger causality has been used to identify leader-follower relationships between markets or market zones as in Dempster *et al.* [2008] and Bunn and Gianfreda [2010]. When unit roots are found in time series of electricity prices (DeVany and Walls [1999] being among the few) or in fuel prices [Bunn and Gianfreda, 2010; Bosco *et al.*, 2010; Gianfreda *et al.*, 2016; De Menezes *et al.*, 2016], the literature has resorted to the use of cointegration tests. Under the null hypothesis of cointegration, the price differential between two locations is mean-stationary with a zero mean, and there is no intercept in the long-term relationship between prices. In other words, electricity prices in two locations only differ by a random disturbance (conditional on exogenous covariates such as fuel prices and deterministic terms).

Thus, in testing market integration, previous works have only implicitly recognized that price information from one location is useful for understanding and forecasting prices of other locations. The extent of such spatial effects cannot however be easily inferred from existing multivariate time series estimates on electricity prices. This is partly true because all locations in a VAR/VEC model are treated equally, regardless of physical or "socio-economic" distances, which in spatial econometrics are addressed via spatially weighted matrices as is shown in Section 3. Another issue concerns the fact that time is unidirectional and linear whereas space has no obvious beginning or direction, and any location can have more than one neighbor in a higher-dimensional network.

As noted above, when applying a structural model perspective, spatial dependence between prices is ultimately attributable to spatial dependence between price fundamentals. The main electricity price fundamental, electricity demand, is in theory expected to be spatially dependent. Spatial spillovers and spatial clusters can arise when proximate regions are characterized by socio-economic linkages. Similar lifestyles and imitative behaviors made easier by spatial proximity and information conveyed through migration flows can help form a spatial correlation between regional electricity demand levels. Spatial interdependencies may notably arise whenever the effects of regional energy policies "leak" through regional borders as, for example, consumers may arbitrage away price differentials induced by location-specific tariffs, or environmental externalities may affect electricity consumption behaviors observed within the geographical reach of external effects.

Another key instance of spatial dependence is found in the case of wind power generation levels and wind speeds. Wind turbines are typically clustered in wind farms or parks, as wind resources tend to be spatially concentrated. When two turbines are arranged in a row, according to the respective wind direction, the power produced by a turbine that is downwind is reduced by *wake-induced turbulence effects* generated by the upwind turbine [Ye *et al.*, 2017]. Wake effects intensify with decreasing distance between turbines, and thus it is essential to account for spatial correlations between wind speeds or wind power generation from different turbines in a wind farm. As underlying conditions may differ dramatically from site to site, focusing strictly on the time dimension would not allow to extrapolate predictions to sites that have not yet been monitored and that are being considered for a new investment. Moreover, failing to consider spatial correlations means that forecasting errors made at a given time and for a given site are correlated with the forecast errors of neighboring sites for the following period [Tastu *et al.*, 2011].

It must be noted that spatial correlations also matter when one considers a coarser spatial resolution, as is the case for works using the aggregate power generated from a wind farm as a unit of analysis. Evidence reported, e.g. in the literature reviews such as Lei *et al.* [2009], shows that outputs of wind farms spaced less than roughly 100 km apart are highly correlated, but that such a correlation vanishes when the distance exceeds 200 km. On these grounds, one can envisage a geographical distribution of wind farms that minimizes aggregate wind power volatility via the so-called *smoothing effect*. This is a relevant issue from a policy-making perspective, as lower variability in wind outputs mitigates the volatility of wholesale electricity prices and reliance on ancillary services.

In a longer term perspective, space also matters in decisions to invest in renewable energy generation facilities. In addition to the use of geographically dependent insolation rates, the diffusion of photovoltaic panels can be fostered by urbanization, which is expected to facilitate the transmission of information between photovoltaic (PV) adopters and their peers, while also creating agglomeration economies through a stronger presence of skilled workers in the PV sector, which reduces costs of maintenance and related services. At the same time, in urbanized areas a scarcity of space may deter PV installation.

3. Spatial Econometric Models

3.1. *Introduction to spatial analysis*

The last several decades have been characterized by a considerable increase of research that incorporates spatial dimensions into applied economic modeling. Spatial analyses were first conducted in the fields of regional economics and economic geography in line with the notion that "space matters" as stated more precisely by Tobler [1970] with the First Law of Geography.

Accounting for the presence of spatial linkages is extremely important and especially when examining the implications of policies implemented in any place to detect problems in a specific geographical unit. The effects of these policies may spread beyond geographical boundaries and may also affect the conditions of neighboring regions. Spatial econometrics, therefore, represents the set of alternative estimation approaches that can be used when examining spatial data samples [Anselin, 1988]. In particular, heterogeneity (heteroscedasticity) and autocorrelation (dependence) are the main issues posed by the treatment of data series related to geographical entities. These problems, which are common to any econometric application, in the case of spatial data may require distinct treatment. Spatial heterogeneity violates the Gauss–Markov assumption that a single linear relationship exists across sample data observations. When the relationship varies as we use different spatial units, alternative estimation procedures must be applied to model this form of variation (random coefficients, error component models, etc.). Similarly, spatial dependence arising when the value assumed by a variable for a given location is correlated with the value that the same variable assumes for another place or for a set of other places prevents the use of traditional approaches based on a one-way direction relationship between different geographical units. According to Anselin and Bera [1998], spatial autocorrelation occurs when high or low values for a random variable tend to cluster in space (positive spatial autocorrelation) or when locations tend to be surrounded by neighbors with very dissimilar values (negative spatial autocorrelation).

Recently, spatial analysis has been applied to energy economics modeling, as the resources, consumption, and production of energy are defined over time and space and therefore have time and spatial dimensions. In this regard, there are several applications that should involve the use of spatial models (e.g. patterns of energy use across space, spatial externalities of energy production in terms of environmental effects, spatial clustering in exhaustible natural resource exploration activities, spatial structuring of electricity prices, etc.).

3.2. *Modeling space*

Modeling spatial dependence involves making an appropriate representation of relative spatial positions. When considering a sample of R spatial units, the solution is given by a *spatial neighbors matrix* (**W**), which is a square symmetric R x R matrix with an $(i; j)$ element equal to 1 when spatial units i and j are neighbors (or more generally, are spatially related) and zero otherwise. By convention, diagonal elements of this "spatial neighbors" matrix are set to zero. In its simplest form, the element w_{ij} denotes spatial proximity based on the concept of binary contiguity. When two spatial units have a common border, they are considered contiguous and have a value of 1. Conversely, when they are not contiguous, their coupling will have a value of 0.

$$W = \begin{bmatrix} 0 & 1 & 1 & 0 \\ 1 & 0 & 1 & 0 \\ 1 & 1 & 0 & 1 \\ 0 & 0 & 1 & 0 \end{bmatrix}.$$

However, the simple contiguity measure has limits: (a) it does not account for non-reciprocal interactions due to its symmetrical nature; (b) it does not account for other kinds of interactions than those of geographical proximity; and (c) it does not distinguish between different types of neighboring regions with regards to the distance or morphology of a border area (a mountain, hill, or plain) or to the length of a border actually shared. To overcome the latter problem, contiguity matrices of a higher order than the first can be used.[3] It is possible to associate the contiguity matrix with a matrix of distances or with other matrices that combine distance measurements with border lengths. As such, one can use the inverse of the distance between the centres (geographical, but also political or administrative) of spatial units and the distance can either be expressed in terms of linear and road distance or in terms of time distance in relation to travel times. A matrix obtained in this way assigns to each pair of spatial units a different value that decreases with distance to account for the stronger influence closer spatial units may have on one another.

$$W = \begin{bmatrix} 0 & \frac{1}{d_{1,2}} & \frac{1}{d_{1,3}} & \frac{1}{d_{1,4}} \\ \frac{1}{d_{2,1}} & 0 & \frac{1}{d_{2,3}} & \frac{1}{d_{2,4}} \\ \frac{1}{d_{3,1}} & \frac{1}{d_{3,2}} & 0 & \frac{1}{d_{3,4}} \\ \frac{1}{d_{4,1}} & \frac{1}{d_{4,2}} & \frac{1}{d_{4,3}} & 0 \end{bmatrix}.$$

The first and second limitations typically overcome by introducing measures of "economic contiguity" between spatial units like trade volumes (which also identify non-reciprocal relationships) or the degree of similarity in productive specialization. Finally, proximity may also account for other types of distances such as cultural, linguistic or administrative distances.

A spatial neighbors matrix is best used by taking into account research goals and by ensuring that measures of proximity included in a matrix are strongly exogenous with respect to the variable object of study.

Spatial neighbors matrices are usually transformed into "spatial weight" matrices following the most common approach of "row-standardization," which involves dividing each row element by the sum of all elements in a row.

$$w_{ij}^{*} = \frac{w_{ij}}{\sum w_{ij}}.$$

The row-standardized spatial weights matrix is particularly attractive because its elements can be interpreted as the fraction of total spatial effects on unit i attributable to unit j, and when weights are based on the inverse distances, they decrease with increasing distance. In spite of its popularity, row-normalized weighting has

[3]For example, a second-order matrix identifies areas that are contiguous to regions showing a value of 1 in the first-order matrix.

drawbacks. In particular, row-normalization alters the internal weighting structure of a matrix such that comparisons drawn between rows become somewhat problematic. In view of this limitation, an alternative transformation entails simple *scalar normalization* that involves multiplying each element of the neighbors matrix by a single number ($\alpha \cdot W$). This procedure removes any measure-unit effects but preserves relations between all rows of W.

3.3. *Exploratory spatial data analysis for testing spatial dependence*

It is important to test for spatial autocorrelations when using regional level data because in the presence of spatial dependence a regression analysis of spatially distributed variables can generate incorrect statistical inferences when proper corrections for spatial effects are not incorporated into model specifications [Voss *et al.*, 2006].

Following Anselin [2005], an exploratory spatial data analysis (ESDA) involves the application of a useful set of instruments to test for the presence of spatial dependence. ESDA entails the use of a collection of techniques designed to describe and visualize spatial distributions; to identify atypical locations or spatial outliers; to discover patterns of spatial association, clusters or hot spots; and to suggest spatial regimes or other forms of spatial heterogeneity. Central to this conceptualization is the notion of spatial autocorrelation or spatial association, i.e. the phenomenon whereby locational similarity (observations of spatial proximity) is matched by value similarity (attribute correlation). Spatial clustering is said to occur in conjunction with positive spatial autocorrelation [Anselin *et al.*, 2000]. For spatial units for which no correlation exists between a variable's values and its locations, the spatial pattern is considered to exhibit no spatial autocorrelations [Holt, 2007].

Several tests have been used to verify the presence of spatial autocorrelations in the literature.

The most common test for the presence of global spatial autocorrelation was developed by Patrick Moran [1948] and it is typically referred to as Moran's-I statistic:

$$I = \frac{\sum_{ij}^{R} w_{ij}(x_i - \mu)(x_j - \mu)}{\sum_{i}^{R}(x_i - \mu)^2},$$

where x_i represents the variable describing the phenomenon under study in region i, where μ is the sample mean and where w_{ij} is the weight of a row-standardized spatial matrix. The expected value of the Moran index (E(I)) is equal to $-1/(R-1)$. For a sufficiently large R value, the standardized I is normally distributed and therefore a rejection of the null hypothesis of an absence of spatial autocorrelation implies the presence of spatial dependence. Values of I that exceed the expected value denote the existence of a positive spatial autocorrelation, meaning that regions presenting high (low) values tend to be located close to other regions with high (low) levels. Values of I that are less than the expected value denote the presence of a negative association and hence a tendency for dissimilar values to appear in nearby regions.

Local indicators of spatial clustering analysis consider the relationship between each region and its neighbors, identifying hot spots (high-value clusters) and cold spots (low-value clusters). Among such tools are the Getis–Ord statistic [Getis and Ord, 1992; Getis and Ord, 1995; Sokal *et al.*, 1998], the Moran scatterplot [Anselin, 1996] and the Local Indicator of Spatial Association (LISA) [Anselin, 1995].

The Getis–Ord test refers to the concentration of values of a variable of interest in the neighborhood of region i. The original statistic is as follows:

$$G_i = \frac{\sum_{j=1}^{R} w_{ij} x_j}{\sum_{j=1}^{R} x_j}, \quad \text{with } j \neq i,$$

where w_{ij} is the corresponding element of a non-standardized symmetric binary weights matrix that applies a value of 1 to neighboring regions and a value of 0 to the other regions and to the pivot region. Once standardized, positive values of G_i denote a spatial clustering of high values around region i, while negative values denote the presence of a cluster of regions showing low values.

The Moran scatterplot is given by a graph centered on the mean value of the variable of interest x for a number of spatial units. The horizontal axis returns standardized values of the variable (Z), while the vertical one returns the spatially lagged value of the standardized variable (WZ) [Anselin, 2005; Anselin *et al.*, 2000]. The slope of the linear regression line that runs through the scatter plot is the Moran's-I coefficient [Anselin *et al.*, 2000]. When points are equally dispersed across the four quadrants, this will indicate an absence of correlations (the slope is zero). When however there is a clear relationship, the Moran scatterplot can be used to identify different forms of spatial autocorrelations depending on the quadrant considered. High-high (upper right) and low-low (lower left) denote positive spatial autocorrelations (spatial clusters) and low-high and high-low denote negative spatial autocorrelations (spatial outliers) [Anselin, 2005; Anselin *et al.*, 2000].

As Moran scatterplots do not assess the statistical significance of spatial associations, it is useful to associate this global indicator and its graphical representation with a local autocorrelation indicator that can measure interdependence in each of the regions concerned (Fig. 1). The LISA effectively allows each spatial unit to associate a measure of the spatial association level with its surroundings and to

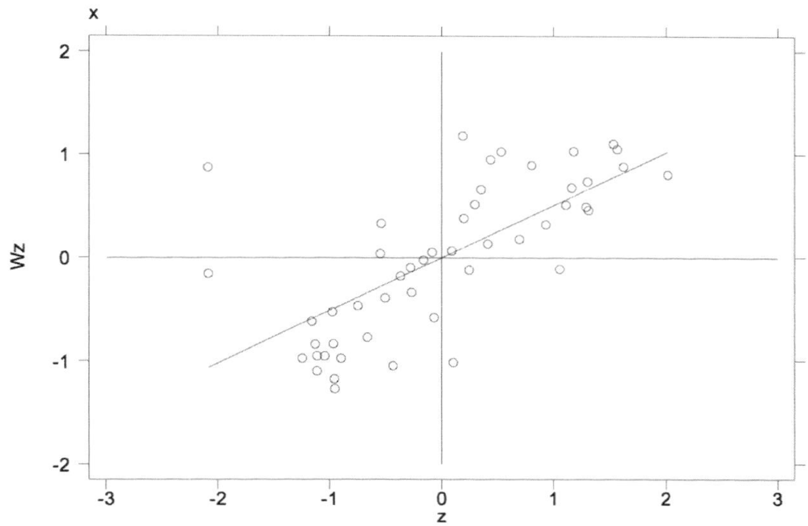

Fig. 1. Moran scatterplot example based on (Moran's $I = 0.511$).

assess its statistical significance. The indicator commonly used for LISA is the local version of Moran's I statistic for each spatial unit i as follows:

$$I_i = \frac{(x_i - \mu)}{m_0} \sum_j^R w_{ij}(x_j - \mu), \quad \text{with } m_0 = \sum_i^R (x_i - \mu)^2 / R.$$

A positive value for I_i denotes a spatial clustering of similar values (high or low), whereas a negative value denotes a spatial clustering of dissimilar values between region $i$and its neighbors.

3.4. *Spatial econometrics models: A taxonomy*

The spatial econometrics literature identifies different ways of modeling spatial interactions [Anselin, 1988]. Depending on types of interactions occurring between observations of neighboring units, estimations may involve the use of different approaches. In what follows, we present some model specifications applied for a cross-section data context.[4]

- Spatial Autoregressive Models (SARs) are used when levels of the dependent variable y depend on levels of y for neighboring regions (spatial lag dependence).

[4]For panel dataset specifications, please refer to Elhorst [2010a, 2011].

In this case, the formal model is

$$y = \lambda \boldsymbol{Wy} + \boldsymbol{X}\beta + \varepsilon,$$

where λ is the spatial autoregression parameter, which must typically be estimated from the data, $\boldsymbol{W}$ is a predefined R by R spatial weighting matrix, $\boldsymbol{X}$ is a vector of explanatory variables and ε is an independently and identically distributed error term for region i with a zero mean and with a variance of σ^2. $\boldsymbol{Wy}$ denotes spatially lagged values of the dependent variable accounting for spatial spillovers occurring in nearby regions. The significance of λ denotes the presence of spatial autocorrelation.

For an individual observation, the basic spatial lagged autoregression equation is simply written as

$$y_i = \lambda \sum_j w_{ij} y_j + X_i \beta + \varepsilon_i.$$

- Spatial Error Models (SEM) are used when error terms are correlated across space (spatial error dependence). This can occur when some determinants of the dependent variable omitted from the model are spatially autocorrelated or when unobserved shocks follow a spatial pattern. The resulting model is written as follows:

$$\boldsymbol{y} = \boldsymbol{X}\beta + \varepsilon,$$
$$\varepsilon = \rho \boldsymbol{W}\varepsilon + \upsilon,$$

where υ is assumed to be normal with a zero mean and a variance of σ^2 I.
- Spatial Durbin Models (SDM) contain a spatially lagged dependent variable and spatially lagged independent variables.

$$\boldsymbol{y} = \lambda \boldsymbol{Wy} + \boldsymbol{X}\beta + \boldsymbol{WX}\theta + \varepsilon.$$

To verify whether a spatial model is more appropriate in describing data than a model without spatial interdependencies, the suggestion is to run a Lagrange multiplier test on a spatially lagged dependent variable (LMlag) and on the spatial error autocorrelation (LMerr) using a baseline non-spatial model [Anselin *et al.*, 2008; LeSage and Pace, 2009, 2010]. The null hypothesis for these tests is an absence of spatial dependence. Alternative hypotheses, respectively, involve the presence of a spatial lag and spatial error dependence. Robust Lagrange multiplier tests can also be performed to test for the existence of one form of spatial dependence conditional on another. Finally, the likelihood ratio (LR) and Wald tests can be used to verify whether the SDM can be simplified to the spatial lag model or to the spatial error model [Elhorst, 2010a, 2010b, 2011].

Regarding these estimation procedures, it is important to remember that the spatially lagged dependent variable (Wy) is correlated with errors, even when they are identical and independently distributed. In other words, the spatial lag of the dependent variable should always be considered endogenous. This means that the OLS estimation approach becomes inadequate by producing biased and inconsistent estimators (typically those resulting from simultaneity problems). Among alternative methodologies used to overcome such drawbacks, the most widely used is the Maximum Likelihood (ML) estimation technique. Indeed, under specific conditions,[5] all classic properties of its estimator (non-distortion, efficiency, and asymptotic normality) remain valid when applying spatially lagged dependent variables.

4. Reviewing the Spatial Econometric Literature on Electricity Markets

The statistical modeling and forecasting of restructured and liberalized electricity industries involves the use of various variables depending on the goals of the interested parties. Wholesale market clearing prices, fuel prices, wholesale demand levels, wholesale generation from intermittent non-dispatchable renewables (e.g. wind and photovoltaic), and the diffusion trajectories of renewable energy sources have attracted scholarly, business, and policy interest. Recently, literature reviews on the forecasting of electricity prices using statistical methods have been conducted by Weron [2014] and Nowotarski and Weron [2017], whereas the statistical forecasting of electricity demand is the topic of a survey presented in Hong [2014] and of chapter 3 of Weron [2007].

This section reviews the main existing applications of spatial econometrics with a focus on electricity prices, electricity demand, and residential PV uptake. Fuel price and wind power forecasting are not considered in this case. While fuel prices are determined in international markets and thus induce common dynamics between zonal markets in the same country, the literature on forecasting wind speeds and power has disregarded spatial econometric models although it has

[5]Conditions concerns the differentiability of the function, the existence of partial derivatives, and the existence of a positive and non-singular covariance matrix.

long made use of spatial information as noted in the Introduction. In the kriging estimators used by Haslett and Raftery [1989], Lenzi *et al.* [2016] and others, non-diagonal entries of the covariance matrix of the error term decline exponentially with distance between wind turbine sites. In Gneiting *et al.* [2006] and Hering and Genton [2010], the location and scale of the predictive distribution of wind speeds in one site are assumed to also depend on wind speeds observed in other sites.

Statistical modeling and variable forecasting reviewed in this study involve methodological dilemmas that we will briefly illustrate in each subsection before providing information on existing applications and results. Issues to be addressed by the econometric design include issues related to measurements, spatial granularity levels, and spatially weighted matrix selection.

As a general note, electricity market forecasting is performed over various time horizons, from real-time and day-ahead units to longer forward contracts and monthly or annual averages in regard to demand and supply variables. In this context, the short-term usually refers to a period ranging from few minutes up to few days ahead, while medium-term extends from a weekly horizon to longer-term monthly, quarterly or annual periods. Short-term forecasting is specifically useful to transmission system operators in ensuring reliability, while also being essential for power generating companies in shaping their bidding strategies for shorter-term wholesale market segments. Long-term forecasting helps facilitate investment and planning decisions and the allocation of resources to long-term contracts on the supply or demand side. While short- and medium-term forecasting relies on econometric models, long-term forecasting is based on a detailed modeling of the system at hand whether economic (oligopoly or auction models in the case of prices) or physical/meteorological (in the case of wind and solar power) and is exposed to modeling risks related to the challenge of predicting regulatory and technological change.

Demand forecasting is a relatively mature paradigm; instead, accurate short-term predictions of electricity prices are still rather challenging in spite of striking progress documented in comprehensive methodological surveys such as that by Weron [2014]. Wholesale electricity prices involve seasonality (annual, weekly, and daily), volatility clustering, skewness, jumps, spikes, and excess kurtosis. Uncertainties associated with forecasting wind power, solar power, and electricity demand only contribute to difficulties associated with predicting wholesale electricity prices.

4.1. *Electricity demand*

4.1.1. *Roots and issues*

Electric power consumption measured in kWh per capita is strictly linked to a country's development level. The World Development Indicators [World Bank, 2017] reveal a considerable difference in per capita electricity consumption levels between upper and lower middle income countries that in 1971 were, respectively, 305.33 and 89.95 kWh and that in 2014 rose to 3533.37 and 769.5 kWh. In the same period, higher-income countries raised their consumption levels by an average annual rate of 2.6% while less developed countries showed an increase of 17.16%.

Since the seminal work of Houthakker [1951], which analyzed electricity consumption in Great Britain, several empirical studies have been conducted to identify the main determinants of electricity demand. Income levels and electricity prices, demographic features, climatic patterns, industrialization trends, and the availability of alternative energy resources together with standards of living have been identified as the main factors that drive electricity demand in developed countries [Fisher and Kaysen, 1962; Silk and Joutz, 1997; Alberini and Filippini, 2011; Filippini and Pachauri, 2004; Flaig, 1990; Houthakker, 1980]. For developing countries, the degree of urbanization is an additional covariate that captures further characteristics of economic development affecting residential electricity consumption [Holtedahl and Joutz, 2004].

Factors determining electricity demand can have short- and long-term effects. Elasticities, which are typically calculated by means of dynamic models, show that electricity may be generally treated as a normal good with long-term price-elasticity values being larger than short-term ones [Atalla *et al.*, 2018]. Some exceptions are found in the case of cross-prices for substitute goods such as natural gas [Fullerton *et al.*, 2015] due to difficulties associated with switching from one power source to another for many types of appliances.

At first, econometric analyses on electricity demand were mostly performed at the country level. However, in the 1960s several governments started to promote regional development to reduce existing disparities within countries, and great efforts were made to support local energy provisions. This shift in energy policies implied a broader concern for regional analyses designed to evaluate the effectiveness of regional measures and to identify the main channels that influence local consumption and the provision of electricity.

The early studies on regional demand for electricity followed two contrasting hypotheses: On the one hand, regions characterized by different socio-economic and climatic conditions were assumed to have different electrical energy requirements in the private (households and firms) and public sectors [Bernstein and Griffin, 2006; Contreras *et al.*, 2009]. The assumption was that model specification and estimation results can strongly differ across regions of the same country. Hence, studies on electricity demand have often referred to individual regions. In this vein, Fullerton *et al.* [2012, 2015] provide evidence for specific states of the US. On the other hand, some studies conducted on aggregate regional panel datasets show that price and income elasticities of electricity demand do not vary across regions [Alberini and Filippini, 2011; Houthakker, 1980; Hsing, 1994; Maddala *et al.*, 1997 and Paul *et al.*, 2009].

The presence of a spatial correlation between the consumption of electric energy in different geographical locations has been long neglected. However, recently, as mentioned in the introduction of this chapter, empirical studies on energy economics have recognized the importance of including the spatial dimension in analyses on resources, consumption, and the production of energy. Extending these analyses to the spatial component reveals motivations of spatial spillovers and spatial clusters of electricity consumption that may arise when proximate regions are characterized by socio-economic linkages. In fact, common lifestyles, imitative behaviors or the presence of migration flows may form spatial autocorrelations between regional electricity demands. Finally, spatial interdependencies may also be driven by regional energy policies that affect nearby regions. In all such cases, disregarding the presence of spatial interdependence would lead to the formation of biased and inefficient estimates [Anselin, 2010; Anselin *et al.*, 2008; LeSage and Pace, 2010] of determinants of local demand for electricity.

The presence of a spatial interaction between nearby regions and the need to account for these influences requires the use of spatial econometric procedures that unlike the standard OLS or fixed effects approaches enable to separate direct effects of an independent variable on regional demand for electricity from those resulting from spatial spillovers. Spatial interactions can refer to the spatially lagged dependent variables (i.e. the value of a dependent variable for a neighboring region), to spatially lagged omitted variables (affecting the error term) or to spatially lagged independent variables (see Section 3).

4.1.2. *Literature review*

A few empirical studies on regional electricity demand have recognized the role of spatial interactions. Among them, Yaylaci *et al.* [2011] use ESDA tools to verify the presence of spatial autocorrelations of electricity consumption between Turkish provinces in 2006. The results of their analysis, which considers adjacent provinces as neighbours, reveal the presence of a positive spatial autocorrelation based on both global and local spatial indicators (Moran's-I and Gi*(d) statistics). Provinces belonging to hot spots are characterized by a high degree of industrial activity and by high levels of population density.

An attempt to test the presence of a spatial autocorrelation following a spatial econometric approach, without considering other factors of electricity demand, was made by Ohtsuka *et al.* [2010] and Ohtsuka and Kakamu [2011] who examined regional electricity consumption across Japanese regions in the period 1992–2003. The authors used a spatial autoregressive moving average model (SAR-ARMA) to improve the forecasting of electricity demand in Japan. However, again spatial proximity considered in these studies is based on the concept of binary contiguity between regions, and spatial weight elements are obtained using a row-standardization procedure.

Among studies that test the presence of spatial effects of residential electricity demand using more complex models, i.e. including the main determinants identified by the energy economics literature, Yu *et al.* [2012] find that the SAR model specification outperforms the SEM. The authors control for gross regional domestic production, population and energy prices and find a statistically significant spatial correlation in energy consumption levels between Chinese provinces for 2007–2009. In particular, they apply the Gibbs sampling method based on the Markov Chain Monte Carlo (MCMC) model and construct a Bayesian spatial econometric model to address potential problems of heteroscedasticity driven by geographic, economic, societal, scientific, technological, population, and cultural differences that characterize Chinese provinces.

Blazquez Gomez *et al.* [2013], in employing a spatial autoregressive model with spatial autoregressive errors (SARAR), estimate income and price elasticities of electricity demand while also testing for the presence of spatial effects. They control for socio-economic factors such as income levels, population and the number of households, own electricity prices, substitute power source prices (i.e. natural gas) and climatic conditions. The analysis refers to 46 Spanish provinces observed in the period 2001–2010. Lagrange multiplier tests suggest that the SARAR model is an appropriate specification, as spatial effects, spatial lags and spatial errors are found to exist. In addition, the authors analyzed the impact of the 2009 crisis on electricity demand by testing the effects of substantial changes in disposable income. The results provide evidence of the crucial role that spatial effects have had in determining differences in provincial responses to the economic crisis, providing insights that can facilitate regional energy policy-making and aid electricity companies in planning investments via intense forecasting.

The last (with respect to dates of publication) is a recent study conducted by Akarsu [2017] that uses a dynamic spatial lag panel model to test for the presence of spatial effects on local electricity demand in Turkey. The author bases this analysis on various datasets that differ in length and geographical disaggregation levels (provinces and regions) and that control for gross domestic product, real electricity prices, urbanization ratios, heating and cooling degree-days and province/region fixed effects. The study results highlight the presence of spatial spillovers and, like other studies (Diabi [1998] on Saudi Arabia and Erdogdu [2007] on Turkey), finds both price and income short- and long-term inelasticity.

4.2. *Wholesale electricity prices*

The literature on forecasting wholesale electricity prices, since Park *et al.* [2006], Dempster *et al.* [2008] and Higgs [2009], makes it increasingly clear that taking care of spatial correlations can improve forecasting accuracy, as spatial effects are firmly rooted in how the market and the technologies work and can partly tame the challenges posed by the peculiar statistical features of electricity prices. In what follows, we first discuss issues to be tackled in the econometric design, including the spatial granularity of the data, the choice of the spatially-weighted matrix, the modelling strategy and the estimator choice; then we present an overview of the existing applications of spatial econometrics to wholesale electricity prices.

4.2.1. *Building blocks*

As argued by Green [2007], economists know how to compute optimal nodal prices but, for various reasons, these are seldom applied in practice. In most markets, such as in Italy, in Germany and in the NordPool, the zonal resolution is the finest available, whereas the PJM is one noteworthy case of nodal pricing. Even in that case, for privacy reasons the market only publishes zonal averages of nodal prices. Building spatially-weighted matrices is simplified by zonal aggregations, at the cost of losing the information in the high geographical resolution guaranteed by the nodal granularity. This cost is minimized if price differentials within zones are small and "well behaved" [Walton and Tabors, 1996]. Averaging nodal prices, as done with PJM-provided zonal prices, can partly hide the estimated spatial dependencies. In a zone of given size, if the spatial dependence in nodal prices dies "fast" enough within a zone, one should not expect any spatial dependence. Hence, a relatively good performance of spatial econometric models requires that spatial dependencies across nodal prices go beyond the zonal boundaries. Aggregating further, e.g. studying the spatial correlation between average national prices in different countries, would only magnify this issue. Indeed, it is worth noting that country differentials in electricity prices are at times due to chronic internal congestion issues, such as with Sicily [Sapio, 2015], or with wind-driven congestion in the German grid [Kunz, 2013].

The choice of spatial granularity bears implications for the choice of the spatially-weighted matrix. As customary in spatial econometrics, there is no univocal way of defining the spatially-weighted matrix. In applications to the electricity prices, it must be noted that geographical adjacency (i.e. the existence of a border between regions or countries), as such, is neither necessary nor sufficient to expect a spatial effect, because two localities can be interconnected without sharing a physical border (e.g. an island with the mainland), whereas borders do not guarantee the existence of a transmission link (e.g. the case of Israel discussed in Yasner [2012], or Baltic States which are insufficiently connected with their EU partners).

The most basic choice for the spatially-weighted matrix consists of a simple adjacency matrix, whose entries are equal to 1 if the localities are interconnected, 0 otherwise. However, dummies treat all interconnections as the same, whereas a larger interconnection supposedly implies a tighter correlation between prices in the zones being linked. Hence, one could use the capacity of the transmission lines linking the zones instead of simple dummies. To account for the fact that a transmission line can be congested, one can set to 0 the entries corresponding to congested lines, if the time granularity of the data is hourly, or the fraction of hours without congestion, if instead the model is specified on average daily prices. Alternatively, one can use the actually available capacity, which however could suffer from endogeneity issues. These more sophisticated choices imply time-varying spatially-weighted matrices. These alternatives can be conceived as robustness checks, while according to LeSage and Pace [2010], there is little theoretical basis to expect that results would change significantly.

In terms of modeling strategy, even though the spatial Durbin model encompasses both the SEM and the SAR, there is still lack of consensus on the most appropriate modeling strategy when it comes to electricity prices. In fact, there are sound reasons for employing either. One may argue that prices at different localities are directly correlated because traders arbitrage away price differentials, supporting SAR. Just as meaningfully, unobservables such as weather conditions or events involving the grid may drive price dynamics in neighboring localities, motivating the use of a SEM model. The SDM, though, remains the most flexible choice, letting the data speak about the nature of the spatial effects — unobservable or mediated by neighboring prices. One interesting feature of the SDM is that it allows to decompose the price impacts into direct and indirect effects, in such a way that one can appraise how price effects transmit to neighboring locations and decline with distance. Notice also that biases and inconsistency result if one ignores spatial dependence in the dependent variables and/or in exogenous regressors (see LeSage and Pace [2009, 2010], Yesilyurt and Elhorst [2014]).

Concerning the estimation method, even after applying filters to remove outliers, wholesale electricity prices depart from Gaussianity in most datasets [Weron, 2007, 2014]. In this respect, the generalized method of moments (GMM) estimation approach appears to be most appropriate as it is distribution free, whereas quasi-maximum likelihood estimation applies to prices that are normally distributed.

4.2.2. *Literature review*

The earliest known application of spatial econometrics to wholesale electricity prices is contained in an unpublished paper by Popova [2004]. The sample included real-time and day-ahead prices from PJM market zones between 1 April 2002 and 31 December 2003. The author estimated a SEM using a maximum likelihood estimator, and the spatially-weighted matrix assigned a value equal to 1 to couples of zones sharing a common border. The choice of running a SEM was corroborated by tests, and estimates revealed the existence of a significant and positive coefficient of spatial correlation in errors. The paper did not include any forecasting exercise.

In a follow-up work, Douglas and Popova [2011] analyzed data on 12 PJM market zones in a more extended period (April 2002–May 2006), again in a SEM framework, but this time using maximum transmission capacities as entries of the spatially-weighted matrix and a GMM-FGLS estimator to deal with departures from a Gaussian error distribution. Spot prices were regressed on forward prices (which proxied for seasonalities and trends) and on temperatures. Interestingly, network configurations were taken into account by stratifying the sample according to transmission system contingencies. The authors found a significant and positive spatial correlation coefficient, with a magnitude between 0.64 and 0.86, depending on the subsample (higher in subsamples with less frequent congestion). It was also shown that while their spatial model outperformed alternatives (OLS, random effects estimator) in terms of in-sample forecasts, no appreciable advantage was detected out of sample.

Subsequent works in this domain have challenged the SEM approach employed in the aforementioned papers, opting for more flexible models. Abate and Haldrup [2017] provide an application to a sample of prices from NordPool's 13 bidding areas between 1 January 2012 and 31 August 2014. The authors focus on daily average day-ahead prices, include temperature data as explanatory variables and allow parameters to be time-varying. Moreover, they experiment with different spatially-weighted matrices, including alternatively geographical contiguity dummies, maximum transmission capacities, and the fraction of non-congested hours. The spatial model is shown to outperform non-spatial alternatives for 7 and 30 days ahead forecasts. As a further interesting result, in the model with time-varying parameters the estimates imply that the spatial correlation in the NordPool has increased over time, supposedly due to intensified market integration.

The analysis in Burnett and Zhao [2017] deals with panel data from 18 PJM bidding zones between 1 January 2012 and 31 October 2013. Forecasts of the real-time system marginal prices are obtained through between-effects SAR, SEM, and spatial dynamic panel data (SDPD) models, and compared to non-spatial alternatives (pooled ordinary least squares, between-effects, and dynamic between-effects estimators). The spatially-weighted matrix is a simple adjacency matrix, and control variables include day-ahead forward prices, zone-specific and time-specific fixed effects. In order to estimate the SDPD model, a quasi-ML strategy is adopted, which forces the authors to assume Gaussian error terms, a difficulty which is circumvented by focusing on forecasting only. This is consistent with findings in Weron and Misiorek [2007], according to whom the forecasting performance improvement of estimating heavy-tailed models is offset by their relatively high computational burden. The forecasting metrics indicate the SDPD model as the best performing, suggesting that serial correlation in electricity prices cannot be ignored even after considering spatial correlation patterns. While no attempt is made to tease out spatially causal relationships, it is still worth noting that pooled OLS estimates of the coefficient of day-ahead forward prices are about 90% lower than those of SAR and SDPD models, and that underestimation of the coefficient is partly due to neglecting serial correlation (as from the comparison between SAR and SDPD).

Forecasting improvements over non-spatial models are also obtained by Maciejowska and Weron [2015], albeit through a rather different modeling approach. Goal of the authors is to predict a relatively aggregate variable — daily average day-ahead prices — through more disaggregate variables such as hourly prices in the day-ahead market segment. Moreover, in order to avoid overfitting problems, they use a factor model: they estimate the factors by means of principal components organizing the data as a panel, with dimensions given by locations and hours. The factors in turn are modeled through a VAR.

Focusing on hourly day-ahead prices from 20 PJM zones in the period 1 January 2008 — 17 December 2013, the authors show that accounting for the inter-zone correlations of electricity prices, in addition to the usual time structure, enables to achieve better price predictions than alternatives (a "restricted" VAR and other factor models) both in the short term and on longer-time horizons, such as 15 days or more.

4.3. *Uptake of residential photovoltaic systems*

4.3.1. *Geographical clustering in residential photovoltaic panel diffusion*

Recent decades have been characterized by a global deployment of renewable energy that has been mainly driven by concerns over the security of energy supplies, implications of climate change and uncertainties related to price variability in the liberalized energy market. Addressing such issues requires a deep reform of global and national energy policies and intense teamwork between institutions, producers and consumers of energy. To this end, the role played by households may be crucial. With adequate legislative and financial support, households may change their habits by undertaking more efficient actions in terms of energy consumption. They may even contribute to promoting technological innovation by becoming self-producers of the energy that they need while mitigating the environmental impacts of their consumption activities.

In this vein, the European Union by means of different Directives (Electricity Production from Renewable Energy Sources 2001/77/EC and Renewable Energy Directive 2009/28/EC) has promoted a strong reduction of carbon dioxide emissions to be reached by the middle of the current century, establishing that 20% of the energy consumed by all member states should derive from renewable resources. To achieve this goal, several governments have introduced market-pull policies favouring decarbonization via the use of renewable energies. Among the typologies available, PV panels represent valid systems that can be installed by households for domestic needs.

The empirical literature on the uptake of PV panels highlights the importance of market-pull policies and feed-in-tariff schemes promoted by national and/or local governments. These have proved fundamental in initially triggering the diffusion of PV systems characterized by high installation costs for domestic applications above all.

Several studies have examined channels and factors favouring PV deployment in the domestic segment, i.e. families' decisions to install cells on their roofs, while less has been done on the other two segments of this market, namely, the non-domestic rooftop and ground-mounted segments. The latter typically contributes to the higher voltage distribution network while both domestic- and non-domestic-rooftops are mainly connected to consumers' premises, directly providing them with the required levels of electricity.

The empirical evidence on small-scale PV systems, namely, on residential uptake and market-pull policies [Cherrington *et al.*, 2013], also focuses on socio-economic, technical and geographical factors related to energy economics [Westacott and Candelise, 2016; Schaffer and Brun, 2015; Gooding *et al.*, 2013; Richter, 2013; Kwan, 2012]. Among economic factors, energy cost savings influenced by feed-in tariffs, self-consumption and lower installation costs make it particularly profitable to use PV panels. Moreover, household disposable income levels, levels of education and environmental concerns seem to positively influence the turnaround to PV. There is evidence that PV diffusion also depends on degrees of urbanization, with denser urban areas facilitating information transmission between PV adopters and their peers [Lutzenhiser, 1993; Wallace and Wang, 2006; Rode and Weber, 2016; Bollinger and Gillingham, 2012] or ensuring a greater presence of skilled workers employed in the PV system itself [Schaffer and Brun, 2015]. By contrast, some studies [Müller and Rode, 2013; Snape and Rynikiewicz, 2012; Snape, 2016] find that the likelihood of installing PV is greater in less densely populated areas positioned away from large conurbations. Eshchanov *et al.* [2013] show that residents of urban areas have few opportunities to install PV panels because of the unavailability of sufficient space both on their rooftops and in urban neighborhoods. This uneven distribution of installation patterns would not have been the expected result if households' choices were mainly the result of market-pull policies (feed-in-tariff) and returns on investment.

This evidence highlights the importance of geographical factors. In particular, geography plays a key role in solar exposition and corresponding average annual solar radiation detected in a region, which both affect the efficiency and profitability of PV installation [Schaffer and Brun, 2015].

4.3.2. *Literature review*

Most related empirical analyses conducted at regional or more disaggregated levels (provinces or counties) shed light on the presence of spatial clustering in residential PV system deployment, confirming the importance of geographical proximity. This is above all true for socio-technical factors such as peer effects and clusters of skills together with solar radiation exposition. Peer effects in particular can be either active, when individuals persuade someone else to use the same energy power system, or passive when a decision is made after simply observing what one's neighbors do. While these effects are highly localized, they tend to spread across adjacent regions, spurring spatial spillovers. Consequently, disregarding the presence of spatial dependence in residential decisions to install PV panels may lead to inconsistent results. As a result, several recent studies on PV deployment at the local level have been based on spatial analysis methodologies.

Dharshing [2017] finds strong peer effects and neighboring spillovers in investigating household solar panel installation as an example of dynamics of technology adoption in the domestic segment of the market. The author considers a panel dataset that includes almost one million PV systems of 402 German counties for 2000–2013. County-level spatial proximity is taken into account by applying a row standardized rook binary contiguity matrix. The presence of spatial dependence between neighboring counties is confirmed by the Moran's-*I* global indicator. An econometric analysis is then performed using a spatial autoregressive and a spatial error model revealing the presence of strong spatial dependence that extends beyond pure socio-economic and demographic factors and settlement structures. Similar results for Germany have been found by Schaffer and Brun [2015] who by means of a SAR panel model show that patterns of PV diffusion vary between counties due to different solar radiation expositions and neighborhood effects resulting from an uneven diffusion of specified craft skills and/or intermediary agents.

The UK context has been widely analyzed as well. Richter [2013] in investigating social learning determinants of PV installation found that passive peers, i.e. the observation of local installations, strongly influence dynamics of further installation at a post-code area level of geographical disaggregation. The author also stresses the need to account for the presence of spatial spillovers between adjacent areas. On this view, Snape [2016] checked for the presence of spatial effects by applying a mixed strategy based on quantitative data on PV adoption and on qualitative information on energy policies applied in 2010–2015. The use of a global spatial indicator (Moran's-*I* index) reveals the presence of a positive spatial autocorrelation at the post-code district level. Local indicators (LISAs) describing the geographical positioning and strength of clusters reveal clusters of high intensity capacity in southwestern England and highlight the emergence of a positive spatial autocorrelation in eastern England. The analysis confirms the presence of low-low clusters around large cities like London, Birmingham, Manchester and Liverpool.

Finally, the spatial autocorrelation of PV installation appears to increase over time after the introduction of feed-in-tariffs. Balta-Ozkan *et al.* [2015b] employ a spatial econometric model to perform a comprehensive analysis of determinants of domestic PV deployment in British regions. Their analysis considers a large number of explanatory variables accounting for financial constraints (per capita income), density levels (population and house density), environmental conditions (share of domestic and industrial emissions of total emissions), electricity demand and solar irradiation levels. The presence of positive spatial dependence between neighbors is confirmed by a Moran's-*I* test. The authors use an inverse distance weight matrix while assuming that spatial dependence is inversely related to distances between regions. According to spatial autocorrelation tests, they apply a general-to-specific approach [Elhorst, 2010a, 2010b] to identify the most appropriate spatial model specification. Lagrange multiplier test results show that the SDM may be used to illustrate PV deployment in British regions and to show that significant spatial spillovers extend through the dependent variable (PV uptake) and the explanatory variables. To account for potential endogeneity biases, a generalized spatial two-stage least-squares procedure (GS-2SLS) is applied while using spatially lagged explanatory variables as instruments. The results show that the SDM and GS-2SLS are similar, denoting the presence of spillovers between neighboring regions. This result is obtained by running spatial correlation tests based on Lagrange multiplier statistics as suggested by Anselin [1988] and LeSage and Pace [2009].

5. Conclusions and On-Going Issues

In spite of the inherently spatial nature of most activities in the electricity industry, which have stimulated the interest of policy makers and private decision-makers alike, the econometric literature has thus far relied almost exclusively on a time series approach to estimation and forecasting. This chapter restores the role that spatial dependence plays as a fruitful interpretive concept for electricity market studies. As shown by the reviewed evidence, spatial econometric models can ameliorate economic understanding of price-setting, demand, and technological diffusion dynamics in the electricity industry while improving the forecasting performance of pricing models over time horizons that are relevant in ensuring the reliability of electricity transmission and the efficiency of bidding strategies. The chapter has also explored practical issues that applied researchers can face in developing econometric designs such as measurement issues, the spatial granularity of data, criteria for spatially-weighted matrix selection, and the setup and interpretation of statistical tests essential to evaluating the presence of spatial dependence in the data under analysis and to discriminating between different spatial model specifications.

As for any field occupying a growth stage, spatial energy econometrics must still address a number of methodological issues. A theme, thus far underplayed in the empirical literature on wholesale electricity prices concerns the simultaneous inclusion of serial and spatial correlation terms in the same model. Douglas and Popova [2011] implicitly accomplished this by using the day-ahead price as a proxy for information available prior to spot price quotation while the approach applied by Maciejowska and Weron [2015] is more effective, as their estimated factors capture common drivers between observation units in the space and time dimensions. Yet other patterns of serial correlations may have to be used as in Burnett and Zhao [2017].

Notably, specifying a serial correlation structure alongside spatial correlation terms could allow one to examine the issue of leader–follower relationships between power generating companies or locations. Leader–follower dynamics are epitomized by the role that the German electricity market may be playing in mittel-Europa and by companies that possess informational advantages over import/export balances by running assets on both sides of a transmission link (e.g. Electricité de France in the plant-level VAR analysis performed by Bunn *et al.* [2015]). Identifying leading companies or locations at a fine spatial resolution would prove very useful, as it would provide information on which nodes in the network are more critical for the competitive functioning of the electricity market.

Leader–follower relationships are typically explored with the aid of VAR models. As is well known, recovering structural VAR coefficients from reduced VAR estimates involves applying restrictions on the causal chain between variables. Unlike those of macroeconomics, theoretical models of nodal electricity pricing under perfect competition are unable to suggest an expected causal chain as a consequence of Kirchhoff's law. In the same vein, the well-known theoretical results of Bushnell and Stoft [1996] showing that optimal nodal prices reflect average nodal prices of neighboring locations serve as yet another indication of the reflection problem highlighted by Manski [1993]. Theoretical models explicitly assuming the presence of leader–follower dynamics, such as the Stackelberg model, while seldom used [Chen *et al.*, 2006; Lee, 2014] have not been specified at the nodal scale as they are essentially framed for a longer-term assessment of electricity planning and competition policies (see Neuhoff *et al.* [2005] and the review in Ventosa *et al.* [2005]). The identification of a likely leader is then left to the inspection of business and regulatory documents in a qualitative fashion that must be reinforced by sound quantitative testing. In this respect, graph-based causality identification methods recently introduced could prove helpful. In Moneta *et al.* [2013], higher-order moments of non-Gaussian VAR residuals are exploited to obtain restrictions needed to compute structural VAR coefficients from reduced-VAR ones without need to apply priori theoretical restrictions. Extensions of this methodology that allow for spatial autocorrelations would be extremely valuable in this respect.

Another critical point concerns endogeneity resulting from simultaneity, omitted variables or measurement errors, which are considered among the main sources of inconsistency in econometric estimations. The progress of spatial econometrics offers different strategies for overcoming such problems. To obtain consistent results from spatial lag models with additional endogenous variables, it has been demonstrated that it is possible to run a two-stage least-squares test that considers lower orders of the spatial lags of exogenous variables [Anselin and Lozano-Gracia, 2008; Dall'Erba and Le Gallo, 2008]. Kelejian and Prucha [2007] consider a general spatial regression model that allows for endogenous regressors, their spatial lags and other exogenous regressors. Their model represents one of the equations of a simultaneous system, but they show that it can also be used to address general problems of endogeneity. Fingleton and Le Gallo [2010] recommend the use of an augmented spatial Durbin model to estimate 2-stage least-square (2SLS) and a spatial heteroskedasticity and autocorrelation consistent (SHAC) procedure to account for endogeneity resulting from omitted variables in a model that presents spatial dependence in error terms.

Finally, it is worth suggesting that spatial econometrics could find valuable applications in further areas of interest for energy economics and policy. Novel estimates of spatial econometric models have been recently published by Sunak and Madlener [2016, 2017] on the impacts of wind farm positioning and visibility on housing prices in Germany; by Lv *et al.* [2017] on energy efficiency levels for a sample of Chinese regions with the goal of assessing spatial spillovers; by Liu *et al.* [2017] on neighbor effects on the adoption of hybrid-electric vehicles in the USA; and by Bowen and Lacombe [2017] who take spatial autocorrelation into account in assessing the impacts of renewable portfolio standards on renewable generation at the state level in the USA. Orea *et al.* [2018] study the cost functions of Norwegian electricity distribution companies, revealing another field of application. In the latter, in particular spatial correlation allows to solve an omitted variable problem caused by a lack of data on weather conditions that shape the operation of the distribution grid and in turn costs of providing such services. One remarkable gap in the spatial econometric literature concerns wind and solar power modeling and prediction. Existing studies reviewed by Kusiak *et al.* [2009] face limitations of time series econometrics in dealing with space. Namely, they impose directionality (past/future) on VAR logic that space does not have whereas forecasting in Ye *et al.* [2017] relies on a physical model. To the best of our knowledge, the only application of spatial econometrics to wind power has been published by Croonenbroeck and Ambach [2015].

References

Abate, G. D. and Haldrup, N. (2017). Space-time modeling of electricity spot prices. *Energy Journal* **38** (5), 175–197.

Akarsu, G. (2017). Analysis of regional electricity demand for Turkey. *Regional Studies, Regional Science* **4** (1), 32–41.

Alberini, A. and Filippini, M. (2011). Response of residential electricity demand to price: The effect of measurement error. *Energy Economics* **33** (5), 889–895.

Anselin, L. (1988). *Spatial Econometrics: Methods and Models*. (Kluwer Academic Publishers, Dordrecht, The Netherlands).

Anselin, L. (1995). Local indicators of spatial association – LISA. *Geographical Analysis* **27**, 93–115.

Anselin, L. (1996). The Moran scatterplot as an ESDA tool to assess local instability in spatial association. In M. M. Fisher, H. J. Scholten and D. Unwin (eds.), *Spatial Analytical Perspectives on GIS* (Taylor&Francis, London, UK).

Anselin, L. (2005) *Exploring Spatial Data with GeoDa: A Workbook*, available at http://geodacenter.asu.edu/system/files/geodaworkbook.pdf.

Anselin, L. (2010). Thirty years of spatial econometrics. *Papers in Regional Science* **89** (1), 3–25.

Anselin, L. and Bera, A. (1998). Spatial dependence in linear regression models with an introduction to spatial econometrics. In A. Ullah and D. Giles (eds.), *Handbook of Applied Economic Statistics* (Marcel Dekker, New York), pp. 237–289.

Anselin, L., Cohen, J., Cook, D., Gorr, W. and Tita, G. (2000). Spatial analysis of crime. *Criminal Justice* **4**, 213–262.

Anselin, L., Le Gallo, J. and Javet, H. (2008). Spatial panel econometrics. In L. Matyas, P. Semester (eds.), *The Econometrics of Panel Data–Fundamentals and Recent Developments in the Theory and Practice* (Kluwer, Dordrecht), pp. 625–660.

Anselin, L. and Lozano-Gracia, N. (2008). Errors in variables and spatial effects in hedonic house price models of ambient air quality. *Empirical Economics* **34** (1), 5–34.

Atalla, T., Bigerna, S. and Bollino, C. A. (2018). Energy demand elasticities and weather worldwide. *Economia Politica* **35**(1), 207–237.

Balta-Ozkan, N., Watson, T. and Mocca, E. (2015a). Spatially uneven development and low carbon transitions: Insights from urban and regional planning. *Energy Policy* **85**, 500–510.

Balta-Ozkan, N., Yildirim, J. and Connor, P. M. (2015b). Regional distribution of photovoltaic deployment in the UK and its determinants: A spatial econometric approach. *Energy Economics* **51**, 417–429.

Bernstein, M. A. and Griffin, J. (2006). *Regional Differences in the Price-elasticity of Demand for Energy*. (National Renewable Energy Laboratory, Golden, CO).

Blázquez Gomez, L. M., Filippini, M. and Heimsch, F. (2013). Regional impact of changes in disposable income on Spanish electricity demand: A spatial econometric analysis. *Energy Economics* **40** (Suppl. 1), S58–S66.

Boffa, F., Viswanath, P. and Davide, V. (2010). Increasing market interconnection: An analysis of the Italian electricity spot market. *International Journal of Industrial Organization* **28** (3), 311–322.

Boffa, F. and Sapio, A. (2015). Introduction to the special issue "The regional integration of energy markets". *Energy Policy* **85**, 421–425.

Bohn, R. E., Caramanis, M. C. and Schweppe, F. C. (1984). Optimal pricing in electrical networks over space and time. *Rand Journal of Economics* **15** (3), 360–376.

Bollinger, B. and Gillingham, K. (2012). Peer effects in the diffusion of solar photovoltaic panels. *Marketing Science* **31** (6), 900–912.

Borenstein, S. (2000). Understanding competitive pricing and market power in wholesale electricity markets. *The Electricity Journal* **13** (6), 49–57.

Bosco, B., Parisio, L., Pelagatti, M. and Baldi, F. (2010). Long-run relations in European electricity prices. *Journal of Applied Econometries* **25** (5), 805–832.

Bowen, E. and Lacombe, D. J. (2017). Spatial dependence in State renewable policy: Effects of renewable portfolio standards on renewable generationwithin NERC regions. *Energy Journal* **38** (3), 177–193.

Bunn, D. and Gianfreda, A. (2010). Integration and shock transmissions across European electricity forward markets. *Energy Econonics* **32** (2), 278–291.

Bunn, D., Koc, V. and Sapio, A. (2015). Resource externalities and the persistence of heterogeneous pricing behavior in an energy commodity market. *Energy Economics* **48**, 265–275.

Bunn, D. and Zachmann, G. (2010). Inefficient arbitrage in inter-regional electricity transmission. *Journal of Regulatory Economics* **37** (3), 243–265.

Burnett, J. W. and Zhao, X. (2017). Spatially explicit prediction of wholesale electricity prices. *International Regional Science Review* **40** (2), 99–140.

Bushnell, J. B. and Stoft, S. E. (1996). Electric grid investment under a contract network regime. *Journal Regulatory Economics* **10** (1), 61–79.

Carmona, R. and Coulon, M. (2014). A survey of commodity markets and structural models for electricity prices. In F. Benth, V. Kholodnyi, and P. Laurence (eds.), *Quantitative Energy Finance*. (Springer, New York), pp. 41–48.

Chen, Y., Hobbs, B. F., Leyffer, S. and Munson, T. S. (2006). Leader-follower equilibria for electric power and NOx allowances markets. *Computational Management Science* **3** (4), 307–330.

Cherrington, R., Goodship, V., Longfield, A. and Kirwan, K. (2013). The feed-in tariff in the UK: A case study focus on domestic photovoltaic systems. *Renewable Energy* **50**, 421–426.

Cicchetti, C. J., Dubin, J. and Long, C. M. (2004). *The California Electricity Crisis: What, Why, and What's Next.* (Springer Science & Business Media, New York).

Contreras, S., Smith, W. D., Roth, T. P. and Fullerton, T. M., Jr. (2009). Regional evidence regarding US residential electricity consumption. *Empirical Economics Letters* **8** (9), 827–832.

Croonenbroeck, C. and Ambach, D. (2015). Censored spatial wind power prediction with random effects. *Renewable and Sustainable Energy Review* **51**, 613–622.

Dall'Erba, S. and Le Gallo, J. (2008). Regional convergence and the impact of European structural funds over 1989–1999: A spatial econometric analysis. *Papers in Regional Science* **87** (2), 219–244.

de Menezes, L. M., Houllier, M. A. and Tamvakis, M. (2016). Time-varying convergence in European electricity spot markets and their association with carbon and fuel prices. *Energy Policy* **88**, 613–627.

Dempster, G., Isaacs, J. and Smith, N. (2008). Price discovery in restructured electricity markets. *Resource and Energy Economics* **30** (2), 250–259.

De Nooij, M. (2011). Social cost-benefit analysis of electricity interconnector investment: A critical appraisal. *Energy Policy* **39** (6), 3096–3105.

De Vany, A. S. and Walls, W. D. (1999). Cointegration analysis of spot electricity prices: Insights on transmission efficiency in the western US. *Energy Economics* **21** (5), 435–448.

Dharshing, S. (2017). Household dynamics of technology adoption: A spatial econometric analysis of residential solar photovoltaic (PV) systems in Germany. *Energy Researchs Social Science* **23**, 113–124.

Diabi, A. (1998). The demand for electric energy in Saudi Arabia: An empirical investigation. *OPEC Review* **22**, 13–29.

Dosi, G. (1988). Sources, procedures, and microeconomic effects of innovation. *Journal of Economic Literature* **26** (3), 1120–1171.

Douglas, S. M. and Popova, J. N. (2011). Econometric estimation of spatial patterns in electricity prices. *The Energy Journal* **32** (2), 81–105.

Elhorst, J. P. (2010a). Spatial panel data models. In M. M. Fischer and A. Getis (eds.), *Handbook of Applied Spatial Analysis*. (Springer, Berlin).

Elhorst, J. P. (2010b). Applied spatial econometrics: Raising the bar. *Spatial Economic Analysis* **5**, 9–28.

Elhorst, J. P. (2011). Matlab software for spatial panels. *International Regional Science Review* **37** (3), pp. 389–405. http://www.regroningen.nl/elhorst/doc/Matlab-paper.pdf.

Erdogdu, E. (2007). Electricity demand analysis using cointegration and ARIMA modeling: A case study of Turkey. *Energy Policy* **35**, 1129–1146.

Escribano, G. (2010). Convergence towards differentiation: The case of Mediterranean energy corridors. *Mediterranears Politics* **15** (2), 211–229.

Eshchanov, B. R., Stultjes, G. P. M., Eshchanov, R. A. and Salaev, S. K. (2013). Prospects of renewable energy penetration in Uzbekistan — perception of the Khorezmian people. *Renewable and Sustainable Energy Reviews* **21** (7), 89–97.

Filippini, M. and Pachauri, S. (2004). Elasticities of electricity demand in urban Indian households. *Energy Policy* **32** (3), 429–436.

Fingleton, B. and Le Gallo, J. (2010). Endogeneity in a spatial context: Properties of estimators. In A. Páez, J. Gallo, R. Buliung, S. Dall'Erba (eds.). *Progress in Spatial Analysis: Methods and Applications*. (Springer Berlin Heidelberg), pp. 59–73.

Fisher, F. M. and Kaysen, C. (1962). *A Study in Econometrics: The Demand for Electricity in the United States*. (North-Holland Publishing Company, Amsterdam, NE).

Flaig, G. (1990). Household production and the short- and long-run demand for electricity. *Energy Economics* **12** (2), 116–1211.

Fullerton, T. M., Jr., Juarez, D. A. and Walke, A. G. (2012). Residential electricity consumption in Seattle. *Energy Economics* **34** (5), 1693–1699.

Fullerton, T. M., Resendez, I. M. and Walke, A. G. (2015). Upward sloping demand for a normal good? Residential electricity in Arkansas. *International Journal of Energy Economics and Policy* **5** (4), 1065–1072.

Getis, A. and Ord, J. K. (1992). The analysis of spatial association by use of distance statistics. *Geographical Analysis* **24**, 189–206.

Getis, A. and Ord, J. K. (1995).Local spatial autocorrelation statistics: Distributional issues and an application. *Geographical Analysis* **27** (4), 286–306.

Gianfreda, A., Parisio, L. and Pelagatti, M. (2016). Revisiting long-run relations in power markets with high RES penetration. *Energy Policy* **94**, 432–445.

Giacomini, R. and Granger, C. W. J. (2004). Aggregation of space-time processes. *Journal of Econometrics* **118** (1), 7–26.

Glachant, J.-M. (2004). European electricity markets: variety and integration. In D. Fino, A. Midttun (eds.), *Reshaping European Gas and Electricity Industries: Regulation, Markets and Business Strategies*. (Elsevier) pp. 139–182.

Glachant, J.-M. and Ruester. (2014). The EU internal electricity market: Done forever? *Utilities Policy* **31**, 221–228.

Gneiting, T., Larson, K., Westrick, K., Genton, M. G. and Aldrich, E. (2006). Calibrated probabilistic forecasting at the stateline wind energy center: The regime-switching space–time method. *Journal of American Statistical Association* **101** (475), 968–979.

Gooding, J., Edwards, H., Giesekam, J. and Crook, R. (2013). Solar city indicator: A methodology to predict city level PV installed capacity by combining physical capacity and socio-economic factors. *Solar Energy* **95**, 325–335.

Granovetter, M. and McGuire, P. (1998). The making of an industry: Electricity in the United States. *The Sociological Review* **46** (S1), 147–173.

Green, R. (2007). Nodal pricing of electricity: How much does it cost to get it wrong? *Journal of Regulatory Economics* **31** (2), 125–149.

Haslett, J. and Raftery, A. R. (1989). Space-time modelling with long-memory dependence: Assessing Ireland's wind power resource. *Journal of the Royal Statistical Society Series C* **38** (1), 1–50.

Hering, A. S. and Genton, M. G. (2010). Powering up with space-time wind forecasting. *Journal of the American Statistical Journal* **105** (489), 92–104.

Higgs, H. (2009). Modelling price and volatility inter-relationships in the Australian wholesale spot electricity markets. *Energy Economics* **31** (5), 748–756.

Holt, J. B. (2007). The topography of poverty in the United States: A spatial analysis using county-level data from the community health status indicators project. *Preventing Chronic Disease* **4** (4), 1–9.

Holtedahl, P. and Joutz, F. L. (2004). Residential electricity demand in Taiwan. *Energy Economics* **26**, 201–224.

Hong, T. (2014). Energy forecasting: Past, present, and future. *Foresight: The International Journal of Applied Forecasting* **32**, 43–48.

Houthakker, H. S. (1951). Some calculations on electricity consumption in Great Britain. *Journal of the Royal Statistical Society* **114** (3), 359–371.

Houthakker, H. S. (1980). Residential electricity revisited. *The Energy Journal* **1**, 29–41.

Hsing, Y. (1994). Estimation of residential demand for electricity with the cross-sectionally correlated and time-wise autoregressive model. *Resource and Energy Economics* **16** (3), 255–263.

Jablonski, S., Tarhini, M., Touati, M., Garcia, D. G. and Alario, J. (2012). The Mediterranean Solar Plan: Project proposals for renewable energy in the Mediterranean Partner Countries region. *Energy Policy* **44**, 291–300.

Kelejian, H. H. and Prucha, I. R. (2007). HAC estimation in a spatial framework. *Journal of Econometrics* **140** (1), 131–154.

Künneke, R. W. (2008). Institutional reform and technological practice: The case of electricity. *Industrial and Corporate Change* **17** (2), 233–265.

Kunz, F. (2013). Improving congestion management: How to facilitate the integration of renewable generation in Germany. *The Energy Journal* **34** (4), 55–79.

Kusiak, A., Zheng, H. and Song, Z. (2009). Short-term prediction of wind farm power: A data mining approach. *IEEE Transactions on Energy Conversion* **24** (1), 125–136.

Kwan, C. L. (2012). Influence of local environmental, social, economic and political variables on the spatial distribution of residential solar PV arrays across the United States. *Energy Policy* **47**, 332–344.

Lee, K. H. (2014). Strategy equilibrium in Stackelberg model with transmission congestion in electricity market. *Journal of Electrical Engineering and Technology* **9** (1), 90–97.

Lei, M., Shiyan, L., Chuanwen, J., Hongling, L. and Yan, Z. (2009). A review on the forecasting of wind speed and generated power. *Renewable and Sustainable Energy Review* **13** (4), 915–920.

Lenzi, A., Pinson, P., Clemmensen, L. H. and Guillot, G. (2016). Spatial models for probabilistic prediction of wind power with application to annual-average and high temporal resolution data. *Stochastic Environmental Research and Risk Assessment* **31** (7), 1615–1631.

LeSage, J. P. and Pace, R. K. (2009). *Introduction to Spatial Econometrics*. (CRC Press, New York).

LeSage, J. P. and Pace, R. K. (2010). Spatial econometric models. *Handbook of Applied Spatial Analysis* 355–376.

Liu, X., Roberts, M. C. and Sioshansi, R. (2017). Spatial effects on hybrid electric vehicle adoption. *Transportation Research Part D: Transport and Environment* **52**, 85–97.

Lutzenhiser, L. (1993). Social and behavioral aspects of energy use. *Annual Review of Energy and Environment* **18** (1), 247–289.

Lv, K., Yu, A. and Bian, Y. (2017). Regional energy efficiency and its determinants in China during 2001–2010: A slacks-based measure and spatial econometric analysis. *Journal of Productivity Analysis* **47** (1), 65–81.

Maciejowska, K. and Weron, R. (2015). Forecasting of daily electricity prices with factor models: Utilizing intra-day and inter-zone relationships. *Computational Statistics* **30** (3), 805–819.

Maddala, G. S., Trost, R. P., Li, H. and Joutz, F. (1997). Estimation of short-run and long-run elasticities of energy demand from panel data using shrinkage estimators. *Journal of Business & Economic Statistics* **15**, 90–100.

Manski, C. F. (1993). Identification of endogenous social effects: The reflection problem. *The Review of Economic Studies* **60** (3), 531–542.

McInerney, C. and Bunn, D. (2013). Valuation anomalies for interconnector transmission rights. *Energy Policy* **55**, 565–578.

Meeus, L., Purchala, K. and Belmans, R. (2005). Development of the internal electricity market in Europe. *The Electricity Journal* **18** (6), 25–35.

Moneta, A., Entner, D., Hoyer, P. O. and Coad, A. (2013). Causal inference by independent component analysis: Theory and applications. *Oxford Bulletin of Economics and Statistics* **75** (5), 705–730.

Moran, P. (1948). The interpretation of statistical maps. *Journal of the Royal Statistical Society Series B* **10**, 243–251.

Müller, S. and Rode, J. (2013). The adoption of photovoltaic systems in Wiesbaden, Germany. *Economics of Innovation and New Technology* **22** (5), 1–17.

Neuhoff, K., Barquin, J., Boots, M. G., Ehrenmann, A., Hobbs, B. F., Rijkers, F. A. and Vazquez, M. (2005). Network-constrained Cournot models of liberalized electricity markets: The devil is in the details. *Energy Economics* **27** (3), 495–525.

Nijkamp, P. (1983). Regional dimensions of energy scarcity. *Environment and Planning C: Government & Policy* **1** (2), 179–192.

Nowotarski, J. and Weron, R. (2017). Recent advances in electricity price forecasting: A review of probabilistic forecasting. *Renewable and Sustainable Energy Reviews* **81**, 1548–1568.

Ohtsuka, Y. and Kakamu, K. (2011). Space-Time model versus VAR model: Forecasting electricity demand in Japan. *Journal of Forecasting* **32**, 75–85.

Ohtsuka, Y., Oga, T. and Kakamu, K. (2010). Forecasting electricity demand in Japan: A Bayesian spatial autoregressive ARMA approach. *Computational Statistics & Data Analysis* **54**, 2721–2735.

Orea, L., Álvarez, I. C. and Jamasb, T. (2018). A spatial stochastic frontier model with omitted variables: electricity distribution in Norway. *Energy Journal* **39**(3).

Park, H., Mjelde, J. W. and Bessler, D. A. (2006). Price dynamics among US electricity spot markets. *Energy Economics* **28** (1), 81–101.

Paul, A., Myers, E. and Palmer, K. (2009). A Partial Adjustment Model of U.S. Electricity Demand by Region, Season, and Sector. Resources for the Future Discussion Papers 08-50 (Washington, D.C., April).

Pereira da Silva, P. and Soares, I. (2008). EU spot prices and industry structure: Assessing electricity market integration. *International Journal of Energy Sector Management* **2** (3), 340–350.

Pollitt, M. (2008). Foreword: Liberalization and Regulation in Electricity Systems-How can We get the Balance Right? In F. P. Sioshansi (ed.), *Competitive Electricity Markets: Design, Implementation, Performance* (Elsevier).

Popova, J. (2004). Spatial pattern in modeling electricity prices: Evidence from the PJM market. *Proc. of 24th USAEE and IAEE North American Conference, July 8*. Vol. 10.

Richter, L. L. (2013). *Social Effects in the Diffusion of Solar Photovoltaic Technology in the UK.* (University of Cambridge, Cambridge, UK).

Rode, J. and Weber, A. (2016). Does localized imitation drive technology adoption? A case study on rooftop photovoltaic systems in Germany. *Journal of Environmental Economics and Management* **78**, 38–48.

Sanchis, G., Betraoui, B., Anderski, T., Peirano, E., Pestana, R., De Clercq, B. and Paun, M. (2015). The Corridors of Power: A Pan-European "Electricity Highway" System for 2050. *IEEE Power and Energy Magazine* **13** (1), 38–51.

Sapio, A. (2015). The effects of renewables in space and time: A regime switching model of the Italian power price. *Energy Policy* **85**, 487–499.

Schaffer, A. J. and Brun, S. (2015). Beyond the sun — Socioeconomic drivers of the adoption of small-scale photovoltaic installations in Germany. *Energy Research & Social Science* **10**, 220–227.

Schleicher-Tappeser, R. (2012), How renewables will change electricity markets in the next five years. *Energy Policy* **48**, 64–75.

Silk, J. I. and Joutz, F. L. (1997). Short and long-run elasticities in US residential demand: A co-integration approach. *Energy Economics* **19**, 493–513.

Snape, J. R. (2016). Spatial and temporal characteristics of PV adoption in the UK and their implications for the smart grid. *Energies* **9** (3), 210.

Snape, J. R. and Rynikiewicz, C. (2012). Peer effect and social learning in micro-generation adoption and urban smarter grids development? *Network Industries Quarterty* **14**, 24–27.

Sokal, R. R., Oden, N. L. and Thomson, B. A. (1998). Local spatial autocorrelation in a biological model. *Geographical Analysis* **30**, 331–54.

Sunak, Y. and Madlener, R. (2016). The impact of wind farm visibility on property values: A spatial difference-in-differences analysis. *Energy Economics* **55**, 79–91.

Sunak, Y. and Madlener, R. (2017). The impact of wind farms on property values: A locally weighted hedonic pricing model. *Papers in Regional Science* **96**(2), 423–444.

Tastu, J., Pinson, P., Kotwa, E., Madsen, H. and Nielsen, H. A. (2011). Spatio-temporal analysis and modeling of short-term wind power forecast errors. *Wind Energy* **14** (1), 43–60.

Tobler, W. (1970). A computer movie simulating urban growth in the Detroit region. *Economic Geography* **46** (2), 234–240.

Trieb, F. and Müller-Steinhagen, H. (2007). Europe–Middle East–North Africa cooperation for sustainable electricity and water. *Sustainability Science* **2** (2), 205–219.

Valeri, L. M. (2009). Welfare and competition effects of electricity interconnection between Ireland and Great Britain. *Energy Policy* **37** (11), 4679–4688.

Ventosa, M., Baillo, A., Ramos, A. and Rivier, M. (2005). Electricity market modeling trends. *Energy Policy* **33** (7), 897–913.

Voss, P. R., Long, D. D. and Hammer, R. B. (2006). County child poverty rates in the U.S.: A spatial regression approach. *Population Research and Policy Review* **25**, 369–391.

Wallace, W. and Wang, Z. (2006). Solar energy in China: Development trends for solar water heaters and photovoltaics in the urban environment. *Bulletin of Science, Technology & Society* **26** (2), 135–140.

Walton, S. and Tabors, R. D. (1996). Zonal transmission pricing: Methodology and preliminary results from the WSCC. *The Electricity Journal* **9** (9), 34–41.

Weron, R. (2007). *Modeling and Forecasting Electricity Loads and Prices: A Statistical Approach*. Vol. 403. (John Wiley & Sons).

Weron, R. (2014). Electricity price forecasting: A review of the state-of-the-art with a look into the future. *International Journal of Forecasting* **30** (4), 1030–1081.

Weron, R. and Misiorek, A. (2007). Heavy tails and electricity prices: Do time series models with non-Gaussian noise forecast better than their Gaussian counterparts? MPRA Paper 2292, pp. 472–480.

Westacott, P. and Candelise, C. (2016). A novel geographical information systems framework to characterize photovoltaic deployment in the UK: Initial evidence. *Energies* **9** (1), 26.

Wolak, F. A. (2015). Measuring the competitiveness benefits of a transmission investment policy: The case of the Alberta electricity market. *Energy Policy* **85**, 426–444.

World Bank (2017). *World Development Indicators*. Electric power consumption (kWh per capita).

Yasner, R. A. (2012). Maximizing Renewable Electricity in Israel: Energy Security, Environmental Impact, and Economic Development, Carnegie Mellon University working paper.

Yaylaci, E. D., Ismaila, A. B., Uşkay, O. and Düzgün, Ş. (2011). Spatial analyses of electricity supply and consumption in Turkey for effective energy management and policy-making. In M. Schmidt, V. Onyango and D. Palekhov (eds.), *Implementing Environmental and Resource Management* (Springer, Berlin-Heidelberg) pp. 153–168.

Ye, L., Zhao, Y., Zeng, C. and Zhang, C. (2017). Short-term wind power prediction based on spatial model. *Renewable Energy* **101**, 1067–1074.

Yesilyurt, F. and Elhorst, J. P. (2014). A regional analysis of inflation dynamics in Turkey. *The Annals of Regional Science* **52** (1), 1–17.

Yu, Y., Li, X., Qian, Z., Yang, M., Li, Z., Guo, P., Liu, L. and Zhu, X. (2012). A study on China's energy consumption by Bayesian spatial econometric model. *Energy Procedia* **16**, 1332–1340.

Zachmann, G. (2008). Electricity wholesale market prices in Europe: Convergence? *Energy Economics* **30** (4), 1659–1671.

Chapter 7

An Investigation into Dynamics, Elasticity and Asymmetry for Residential Natural Gas Markets

Kelly Burns* and Tom Houghton†

School of Economics, Finance and Property,
Curtin University, Perth, Australia
**kelly.burns@curtin.edu.au*
†thomas.houghton@curtin.edu.au

The role of price in determining the level of demand for conventional forms of energy, and how this impacts the development of renewable energy markets, has been widely debated in the literature. In this chapter, we explore these issues using an econometric model of energy demand to investigate short-run dynamics and long-run cointegrating relationships, as well as evidence of price and income asymmetry, for the US residential natural gas energy market. We use this same model to produce estimates of long-run price and income elasticity of demand.

It is well established that energy demand estimation must allow for the dynamic behavior and decisions of energy consumers. Dynamics are important to understanding demand behavior because the long-run response of consumers to price changes is likely to differ from the short-run response. Specifically, long-run elasticities of demand are expected to be larger than short-run elasticities, which is unsurprising given that long-run adjustment of energy demand involves changes in long life assets such as cars and buildings. The lower short-run elasticities of demand makes sense because of the lack of available substitutes in the short-run.

In this chapter, we show the reader one approach to estimating price and income elasticity, and how to test for short-run dynamics, long-run cointegrating relationships and evidence of price and income asymmetry. The information presented here is a valuable resource for market participants, market analysts and policy makers.

Keywords: Price elasticity; cross price elasticity; income elasticity; natural gas price; electricity price; cointegration; dynamic behavior; US domestic demand.

1. Introduction

1.1. *Importance of understanding demand elasticities*

In this chapter, we set out to examine the importance of elasticities of demand in the energy sector and their relationship to market development. In order to do this, we determine the price and income elasticities of demand for natural gas (NG) in the residential sector in the United States. We show the reader one approach to estimating price and income elasticity of demand and how to test for short-run dynamics, long-run cointegrating relationships and evidence of price and income asymmetry. We hope that the information presented here will provide a valuable resource for market participants, market analysts and policy makers.

Burke and Yang [2016] highlight the importance of understanding price and income elasticities of demand in the energy sector, citing several key reasons. First, it is necessary for parametrizing energy-economy models. Second, it aids understanding of the effects of adjustments to tax settings for energy. Relatedly, we argue that quantifying the price elasticities would also be relevant to the setting of carbon pricing, as discussed by Alberini *et al.* [2011]. Third, it influences local consumption effects as a result of opening energy markets to international trade, a highly pertinent issue in Australia, for example. Fourth, it is relevant to forecasting the implications of energy price reform for domestic consumption. An examination of price and income elasticity for natural gas demand, in particular, is important because natural gas accounts for a growing share of the world's energy mix [IEA, 2016]. The dynamics of the natural gas market in the context of the broader energy sector is discussed in more detail in the next section.

The principle contribution of this analysis to the literature on price and income elasticities of demand for natural gas is to apply a vector error correction model in order to test both short- and long-term dynamic behavior. In addition, we explore the cross-price elasticity of demand between natural gas and electricity demand.

We find that natural gas consumption is price and income inelastic and is more responsive to changes in income than price. Natural gas has become increasingly responsive to changes in income in recent times. We show that there is no short-run dynamic relationship between natural gas consumption at the residential level, natural gas price and income, likely reflecting the lack of substitutes. By contrast, there is a long-run cointegrating relationship between consumption and both price and income.

There is no evidence that natural gas consumption is asymmetrically responsive to changes in either price or income. The cross-price elasticity of demand for natural gas is negative with respect to electricity, a rather surprising result given that we would expect these to be substitutes at the residential level.

The remaining sections of the chapter are organized as follows: In Section 2, we discuss some relevant aspects of economic theory before going on to set out what the existing literature tells us about price and income elasticities of demand for NG in Section 3. In Sections 4 and 5, we set out the approach taken to the new analysis reported in this chapter and the preliminary results of that study. Finally, in Sections 6 and 7, we discuss the empirical results in more detail and provide some insights and conclusions.

2. Developments in the Natural Gas Markets

Natural gas contributes a growing share of the world's energy mix, particularly in OECD countries, where natural gas accounted for 20% of final energy consumption in 2014, up from 18% in 1973 [IEA, 2016]. Worldwide, natural gas contributed 15% of total final energy consumption in 2014, slightly up from 14% in 1973 [IEA, 2016]. Burke [2013] highlights that there are large variations in the importance of natural gas between countries, and high-income countries and those rich in natural gas deposits are generally more reliant on this energy source. The International Energy Agency (IEA) predicts the coming of the "golden age" of natural gas, anticipating strong growth in natural gas consumption over the coming decades to around 24% of final energy demand by 2040 [IEA, 2015]. The recent boom in shale and coal seam gas are considered to be a driving force in the growing share of natural gas consumption [Burke and Yang, 2016], not least in the US where the availability of unconventional gas has led to a resurgence in natural gas fired power generation [EIA, 2017].

Consumption of natural gas globally by the residential, agricultural and commercial/public services has also increased over the past 40 years with the majority of natural gas in 2014 being consumed by these sectors (43.2%), followed by industry (39%), non-energy use (11%) and transport (7%) [IEA, 2016]. This is in contrast to 1973, when industry was the largest consumer (55%) followed by agriculture, commercial and public services and residential (40%), non-energy use (3%) and transport (3%) [IEA, 2016].

Turning to the US, the main focus of this study, absolute primary energy consumption has increased by a modest amount since 1973 but has declined from the peak reached in 2007 (see Fig. 1).

Natural gas as a proportion of total primary energy consumption has remained stable over the period while oil and coal consumption have declined and primary electricity increased, as shown in Fig. 2.

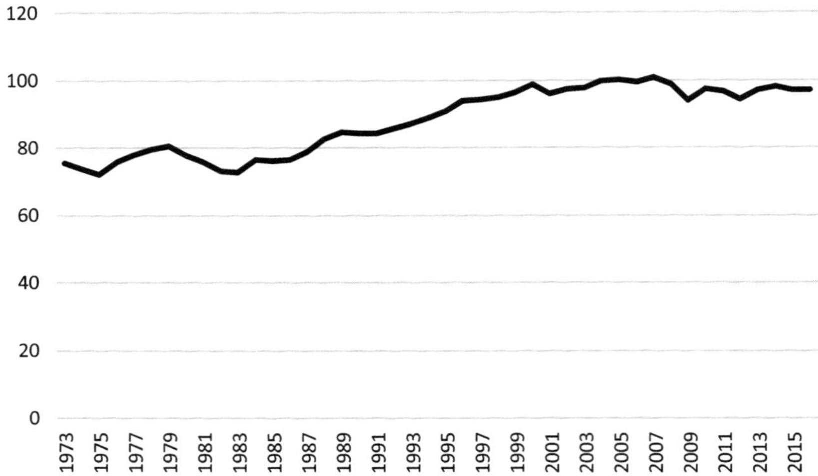

Fig. 1. US Annual primary energy consumption 1973 to 2015 (quadrillion (10^{15}) Btu). *Source*: EIA, 2017 Table 1.1 Primary energy overview.

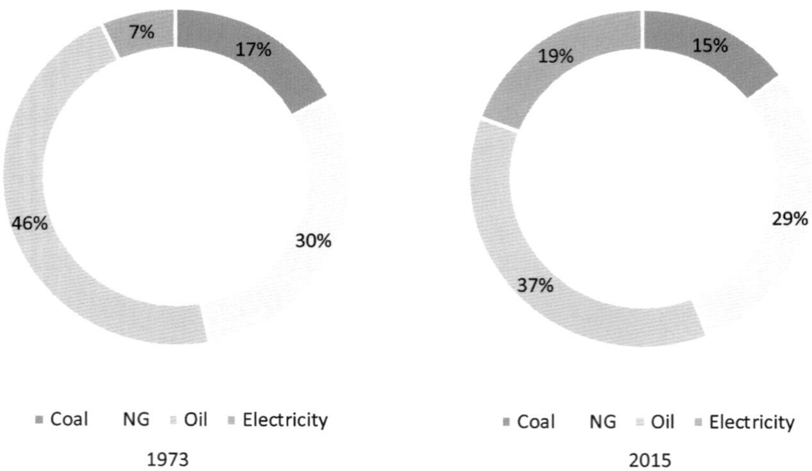

Fig. 2. Proportion of US primary energy consumption by fuel source 1973 and 2015 (%). *Source*: EIA, 2017 Table 1.3 Primary energy overview.

Residential demand has remained a stable proportion of total final energy demand while industrial demand has declined and commercial and transportation increased, as shown in Fig. 3.

As alluded to previously, absolute NG demand in the power sector has shown a quite dramatic rise in the last 10 years, having been more or less stable up to that

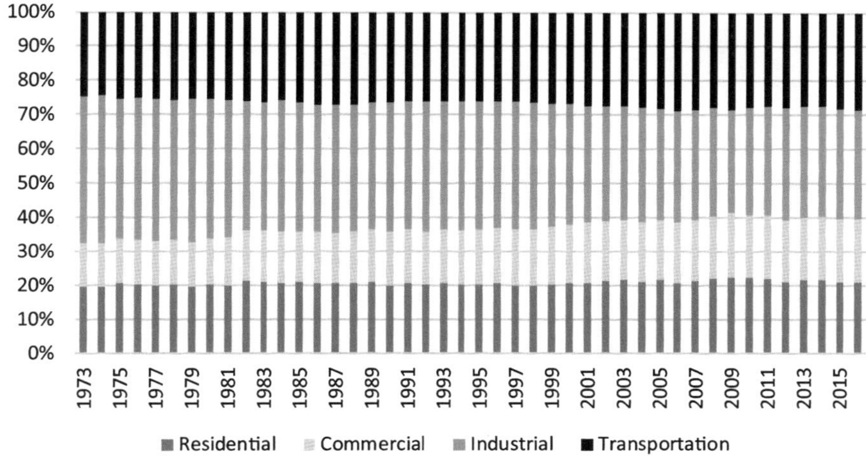

Fig. 3. Proportion of US energy demand by sector of activity (%).
Source: EIA, 2017 Table 2.1 Primary energy overview.

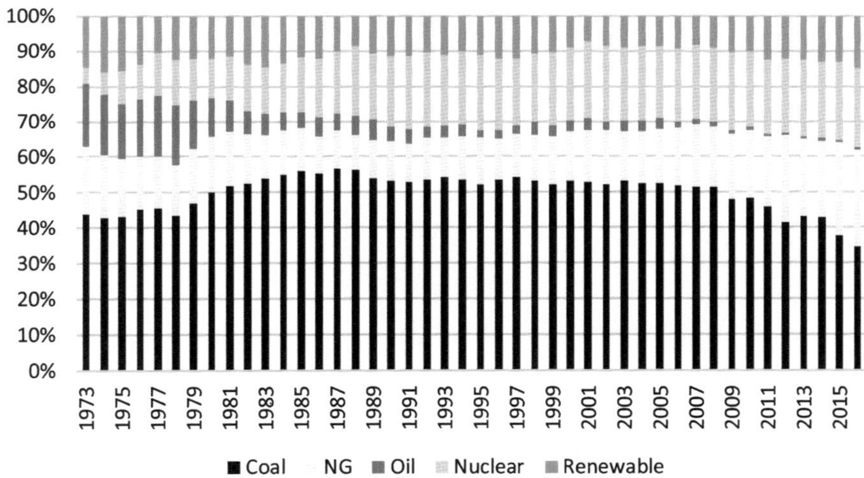

Fig. 4. Proportion of US power generation by fuel source (%).
Source: EIA, 2017 Table 2.2 Final energy demand by fuel.

point. This has been mostly at the expense of coal which had grown significantly to a peak around 2007 but has since declined (Fig. 4). This growth in NG demand is partly a result of greater availability and more moderate wholesale gas prices.

Residential demand for NG has declined both in absolute terms and proportionally while electricity demand has increased dramatically (Fig. 5).

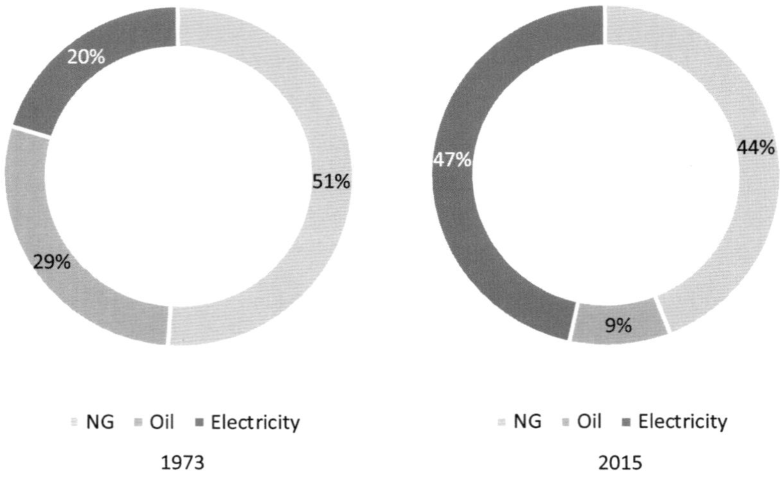

Fig. 5. Proportion of US residential energy demand by fuel source (%).
Source: EIA, 2017 Table 2.1 Primary energy overview.

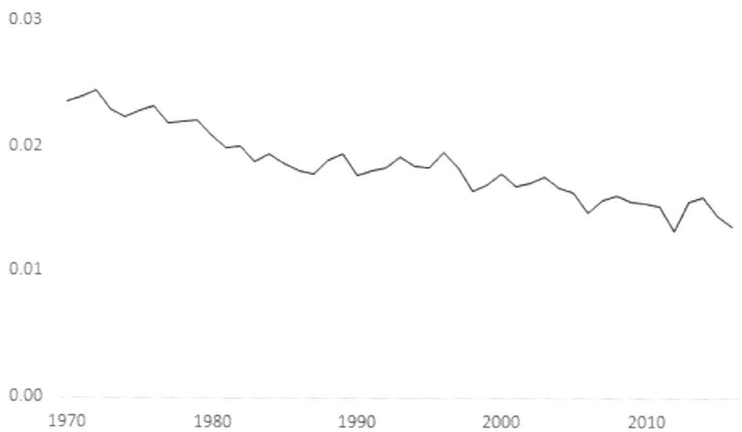

Fig. 6. Annual US natural gas residential consumption per capita 1970 to 2016 (million cubic feet).
Source: US Energy Information Administration (E.I.A), World Bank, author calculations.

This decline is confirmed by IEA data on NG residential consumption per capita (Fig. 6) and may reflect changing preferences but also greater energy efficiency in households.

Turning to pricing, Fig. 7 shows the average retail price of gas delivered to residential consumers in the US in US$/thousand cubic feet. This clearly demonstrates the falling real prices evident since 2010, reflecting cheaper wholesale prices and abundant domestic gas.

Fig. 7. Annual US price of natural gas delivered to residential consumers 1970 to 2016 (Dollars per Thousand Cubic Feet, 2010 constant prices).

Source: US Energy Information Administration (E.I.A), World Bank, author calculations.

The dynamics observed in the NG market in the US have been partially driven by changes to the policy environment, which include:

- Evolution of the regulatory environment with respect to hydraulic fracturing which has facilitated growth in the unconventional gas sector; this, in turn, has been enabled by technological developments;
- Lifting of restrictions on export of hydrocarbons has resulted in export-led demand for conventional and unconventional gas in the US and the building of liquefaction plant for the first time; and
- Climate change and air quality policy measures have meant gas being favored over coal in power generation leading to a surge in gas demand as a primary fuel in the power sector.

In short, we see a complex set of factors including technological advances, policy changes, environmental concerns and consumer preferences all affecting demand for natural gas in the US and globally.

3. Relevant Economic Theory[1]

In the context of a handbook on energy finance, it is worth recapping a number of concepts relevant to demand elasticities in order to frame the results presented in this chapter.

[1]For further reading on these theories and concepts, we recommend Stiglitz *et al.* [2015] and Studenmund [2010].

Demand elasticity provides a measure of how readily the quantity consumed of a product or service varies in response to changes in other variables, notably price and income. It is defined as the percentage change in quantity demanded divided by the percentage change in the dependent variable (e.g. price or income); price elasticity of demand is shown mathematically in the following equation:

$$e_p = \frac{\Delta Q/_Q}{\Delta P/_P}. \tag{1}$$

Products or services for which the quantity demanded varies little in response to a change in price (or income) are said to be price (income) inelastic ($e_p < |1|$); by contrast, a product for which demand varies significantly in response to price (income) is said to be price (income) elastic ($e_p > |1|$).

In this chapter, we consider three principal demand elasticities, own-price elasticity, cross-price elasticity and income elasticity which are defined as follows:

- Own-price elasticity: Response of demand for a product or service to changes in its own price which effectively defines the slope and shape of the demand curve;
- Cross-price elasticity: Extent of variation in demand resulting from changes to the price of a related product or service, e.g. a substitute or complementary good;
- Income elasticity: Magnitude of changes in demand resulting from changes in a consumer's income.

For so-called "normal" goods and services, own price elasticity of demand is negative; that is demand increases as price falls since we would expect the quantity consumed to increase if the price is lower. By contrast, the income elasticity of a normal good is positive since we would normally expect that as incomes rise, consumers will consume more of most goods. Similarly, the cross-price elasticity with respect to substitutes is also positive since demand would be expected to fall if the price of competing products falls; the cross-price elasticity of demand for a complementary good, on the other hand, would be negative.

There are exceptions to these basic principles. For example, so-called "inferior" goods which, as will be seen, are relevant to the discussion here, are products which show an inverse relationship between income and price. As households become wealthier, they switch away from these inferior goods and spend more on higher priced alternatives or, to put it another way, lower income households spend a higher proportion of their income on inferior goods. Conversely, demand for "luxury" goods increases disproportionately more with income than a normal good.

Demand elasticities may vary over time (short-run versus long-run elasticities) and demand may respond differently to rises and falls in prices or income (asymmetry). In general, long-run price elasticities of demand are expected to be greater than the short-run, reflecting aspects such as the challenges inherent in changing behaviors and the cost of abandoning investments.

Price elasticity of demand for energy is generally considered to be low (inelastic) in the short-run reflecting the fact that energy is a necessity and the amount consumed cannot easily be varied. Substitution of one energy source with another is not straightforward since it requires either changes in behaviors or changes in appliances/means of production which may represent significant capital investment. These changes may be effected more readily over the long-run and hence, price elasticities of demand are likely to increase over the longer term.

4. Existing Literature on Energy Demand Elasticities

There exists a significant body of research that estimates price and income elasticities of energy demand in general, and residential natural gas demand in particular. In Table 1, we provide a summary of a selection of empirical studies that estimate price and/or income elasticity for US residential natural gas demand.

Common themes in the empirical literature on price and income elasticities can be summarized as follows:

- Residential natural gas demand is relatively price inelastic and recent estimates of US price elasticities of residential natural gas demand are generally consistent.

Table 1. Summary of recent estimates of US residential gas price and income elasticities of demand.

	Price elasticity		**Income elasticity**	
Author	**Short run**	**Long run**	**Short run**	**Long run**
Aurora [2014]	−0.11 and −0.13	−0.24		
Bernstein and Madlener [2011]	−0.04	−0.16		
Joutz *et al.* [2009]	−0.09	−0.18		
Waheed and Martin [2013]		−0.20		−0.62
Maddala *et al.* [1997]	−0.09 to −0.18	0.24 to −1.36		
Garcia-Cerrutti [2000]		−0.11		
Metcalf and Hassett [1999]	−0.48 to −0.71			
Lavin *et al.* [2011]	−0.11 to −0.41		0.03	
Baker *et al.* [1989]	−0.311		0.115	
Alberini *et al.* [2011]	−0.565 to −0.693		0.00285 to −0.00357	
Max	*−0.040*	*−0.110*	*0.030*	*−0.62*
Min	*−0.710*	*−1.360*	*0.115*	*−0.62*
Mean	*−0.301*	*−0.375*	*0.073*	*−0.62*
Median	*−0.180*	*−0.190*	*0.073*	*−0.62*

- Those studies that distinguish between short-run and long-run price elasticities, in general conclude that the long-run elasticity is larger than the short-run elasticity, meaning natural gas demand is more responsive to income and price in the long-run.
- Income elasticity of demand is relatively inelastic and positive in the short-run (normal good), but in the long-run at least one study shows demand to be more elastic and negative (inferior good).
- Global and country level estimates of income and price elasticity can vary and local level differences may be important.

In contrast to this, Alberini *et al.* [2011] find rather higher values for price elasticity and lower values for income elasticity. One reason for the different results may be that they have used a significantly more disaggregated set of data, down to the level of individual property type and household make-up, etc. (although it should be noted that this is not the only study to have taken a disaggregated approach). Alberini *et al.* [2011] also consider the cross-price elasticity of demand for gas with respect to the price of electricity and find this to be in the range −0.0334 to 0.461 suggesting that NG and electricity are substitutes.[2]

Some recent estimates of price and income elasticity of residential natural gas demand may seem counterintuitive to our expectations based on the theory of demand for normal goods. For instance, while Waheed and Martin [2013] find that residential natural gas demand in Louisiana is price inelastic (estimated to be −0.20), they estimate income elasticity to be −0.62. They explain the counterintuitive sign of income elasticity as reflecting that natural gas was an "inferior good for these consumers over this time period". We argue that it may relate to the concept of the Environmental Kuznets Curve (EKC).

The Kuznets Curve, so called because the theory was first advanced by economist Simon Kuznets, relates the level of inequality in a country and its level of economic development; it is hypothesized that there are two phases of evolution, the first where inequality increases, and a second where it decreases. In a similar way, the Environmental Kuznets Curve [Grossmann and Krueger, 1991] hypothesizes the relationship between environmental degradation (owing to economic activity) and the stage of economic development. This is pictured in Fig. 8.

This suggests that as incomes increase, consumers become more susceptible to concerns about the environment and will seek to find products and services which are more environmentally friendly. In the case of energy, this might mean switching

[2] Although the lower bound is negative it is rather close to zero.

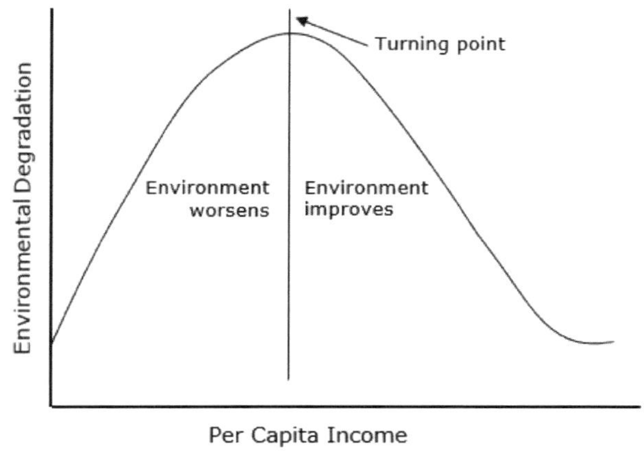

Fig. 8. Illustration of the environmental Kuznets curve.
Source: By Govinddelhi – https://en.wikipedia.org/w/index.php?curid=47019360.

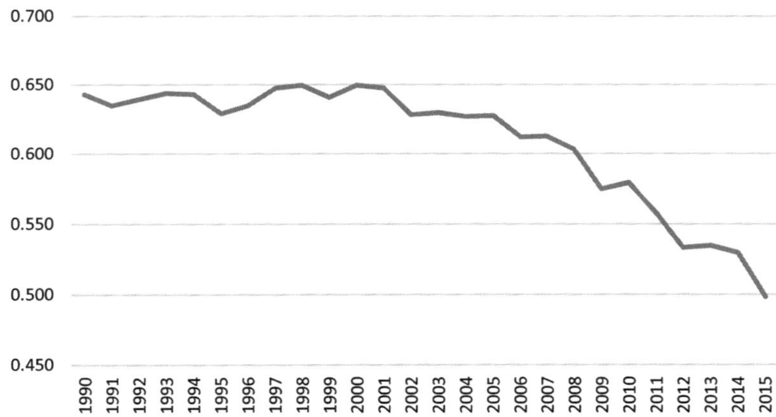

Fig. 9. CO_2 emissions from US electricity production (kg per kWh output).
Source: EIA.

away from natural gas and towards electricity, say, assuming that electricity comes from low carbon sources. In fact, the average carbon intensity of electricity produced in the US was 498 kg/MWh in 2015, (similar to NG power generation from combined cycle plants) but since much new generation being added is low carbon, the marginal intensity may be closer to zero, supporting the view that consumers switch away from NG as incomes rise in order to reduce their impact on the environment. Figure 9 confirms the general decline in emissions per kWh from electricity consumption over time.

Table 2. Summary of recent estimates of non-U.S residential gas price and income elasticities of demand.

	Price elasticity		Income elasticity	
Author	**Short run**	**Long run**	**Short run**	**Long run**
Burke and Yang [2016]		−1.43		
Meier and Rehdanz [2010] – UK	−0.34 to −0.56			
Rehdanz [2007]	−0.63 to −0.44			
Max	*−0.63*	*−1.43*		
Min	*−0.34*	*−1.43*		
Mean	*−0.4925*	*−1.43*		

Table 2 presents the results of two reported studies outside the US which are roughly in line with the findings for the US in direction and magnitude. Many studies that estimate natural gas demand focus on a specific sector or country, the reason being that there may be substantial cross-country variation in natural gas prices and per capita natural gas consumption [Burke and Yang, 2016]. Burke and Yang [2016] studied 44 countries and found that long-run price elasticity of natural gas demand has been stable over time and were unable to reject the null hypothesis that price elasticity equals −1. Income elasticity was also estimated and they were unable to reject the null hypothesis that natural gas demand has unitary income elasticity. At the household level, they found that household natural gas demand is inelastic to price in the short-run (not significantly different to zero) and that income elasticity is greater than one "reflecting strong growth in household natural gas use as income rises" [Burke and Yang, 2016].

Furthermore, variations also exist between consumption sectors, i.e. industry, residential, etc., reflecting different behavioural or investment dynamics. Madlener *et al.* [2011] argue that using data at a lower level of aggregation (for instance, between residential and industry) is necessary because higher aggregation across these heterogeneous sectors is likely to result in incorrect inferences about economic relationships and consumer behavior. As mentioned previously, a number of studies [Alberini *et al.*, 2011; Reiss and White, 2005; Baker *et al.*, 1989] examine demand elasticity at yet smaller units of analysis, recognizing that there are numerous heterogeneous factors affecting individual household demand.

In Table 3, we present results from studies into the own price elasticity of demand for electricity together with the cross-price elasticity of electricity with respect to NG and income elasticity in the US. Table 4 meanwhile, provides the same data for studies outside the US.

Table 3. Summary of recent estimates of US residential electricity price, cross price and income elasticities of demand.

	Price elasticity		Cross-price elasticity with NG	Income elasticity
Author	**Short run**	**Long run**	**Short run**	**Short run**
Dersgiades and Tsoufildis [2008]	−0.386	−1.06		
Kamerschen and Porter [2004]		−0.85 to −0.94		
Alberini and Filippini [2011]	−0.08 to −0.15	−0.44 to −0.78		
Bernstein and Griffin [2005]	−0.243	−0.32		
Paul *et al.* [2009]	−0.13	−0.36		
Maddala *et al.* [1997]	−0.19 to −0.21	−0.56 to −1.03		
Garcia-Cerrutti [2000]		−0.17		
Fell *et al.* [2010]	−0.82 to −1.02			
Metcalfe and Hassett [1999]	−0.78 to −1.11			
Reiss and White [2005]	−0.85 to −1.02			
Alberini *et al.* [2011]	−0.667 to −0.860		0.102 to 0.139	0.007 to −0.025
Lavin *et al.* [2011]	−0.2845		0.03	0.1402
Dubin and McFadden [1984]	−0.26		0.39	0.02
Min	*−0.080*	*−0.170*	*0.030*	*−0.025*
Max	*−1.110*	*−1.060*	*0.390*	*0.140*
Mean	*−0.557*	*−0.651*	*0.153*	*0.029*
Median	*−0.667*	*−0.670*	*0.128*	*0.014*

The own-price elasticity of demand for electricity is rather higher than for NG and, once again, long-run price elasticity, where reported, is higher than in the short-run. The cross-price elasticity with natural gas is positive underlining the previous finding that the two energies are substitutes. As with NG, the income elasticity of demand varies between positive and negative and relatively inelastic.

5. Approach Taken in this Analysis

In this section, we set out the approach taken in the reported study to estimating price and income elasticities of demand.

Table 4. Summary of recent estimates of non-US residential electricity price, cross price and income elasticities demand.

Author	Price elasticity		Cross-price elasticity with NG		Income elasticity	
	Short run	Long run	Short run	Long run	Short run	Long run
Bernard *et al.* [2010]	−0.51	−1.32				
Nesbakken [1999]	−0.33	−0.66				
Shi *et al.* [2012]	−1.091 to −3.735				0.023 to −0.063	
Yoo *et al.* [2007]	−0.2463				0.0593	
Filippini and Pachauri [2004]	−0.29 to −0.51				0.6 to 0.64	
Nesbakken [2001]	−0.55				0.13	
Baker *et al.* [1989]	−0.758		0.185		0.131	
Bernard *et al.* [2010]	−0.51 to −1.32		0.12 to 0.31		0.08 to 0.2	
Min	*−0.246*	−0.660	*0.120*		*−0.063*	
Max	*−3.735*	−1.320	*0.310*		*0.640*	
Mean	*−0.895*	−0.990	*0.205*		*0.200*	
Median	*−0.510*	−0.990	*0.185*		*0.130*	

5.1. *Preliminary steps*

Initially, nominal price data must be deflated to remove inflationary effects. Nominal price data is deflated to yield real price data using the following formula:

$$\text{real price} = \left(\frac{\text{nominal price}}{\text{price index}}\right) \times 100. \tag{2}$$

We use the simple correlation coefficient to examine the level of association between movements in natural gas consumption, natural gas prices and income levels. The correlation coefficient is a measure of the strength and direction of any association between movements in the two variables.[3]

Granger causality testing is then applied to determine if natural gas consumption is "Granger caused" by natural gas price, and income. However, Granger causality tests may produce spurious results in the presence of a cointegrating relationship. Put simply, cointegration refers to the property of a long-run causal relationship as well as a short-run dynamic relationship between the dependant and explanatory

[3]For further reading on these theories and concepts, we recommend Stiglitz *et al.* [2015] and Studenmund [2010].

variables. Where evidence of cointegration is found, an error correction model (ECM) should be used. An ECM combines short-run dynamics and the adjustment to deviations from the long-run equilibrium condition. The presence of a cointegrating relationship confirms the existence of Granger causality between the variables in either or both directions.

In this study, we apply the Engle and Granger two stage approach to cointegration.[4] As pointed out by Madlener *et al.* (2011), "As most economic time series contain stochastic trends, the application of simple regression techniques will likely lead to spurious results. Hence, the application of cointegration analysis, which takes the non-stationarity of the data explicitly into account, is required." We test the data for stationarity to determine the presence of unit roots using conventional methodologies. Specifically, we perform unit root testing using the Augmented Dickey–Fuller (ADF) test. If the explanatory and dependant variables are integrated of the same order, and the residuals are stationary, we conclude that there is evidence of cointegration.

To confirm the validity of our results, we also undertake a series of robustness tests. Specifically, we reestimate the static model over three alternative sample periods. We also estimate an alternative model specification using available data. We compare and contrast these to our main results to demonstrate the validity of our main findings.

5.2. *Model specification*

Our model of residential natural gas demand is expressed in logs to enable long-run elasticities to be estimated. We model US residential gas consumption as follows:

$$\ln G_t = \alpha + \beta_1 \ln P_t + \beta_2 \ln Y_t + \varepsilon_t, \tag{3}$$

where G is natural gas consumption per capita, P is the average price of residential natural gas (real), and Y is GDP per capita (real).

We hypothesize the estimated coefficients as follows: β_1 (short-run price elasticity of demand) to be negative, β_2 (the short-run income elasticity of demand) to be positive. We use conventional t-tests to test the value of long-run price and income elasticity.

[4]Cointegration was first introduced by Engle and Granger [1987]. Since then, a variety of different approaches to cointegration have evolved. However, evidence suggests that the various techniques produce substantively similar results. See, for example, the study by Madlener *et al.* [2011] which employs three different approaches of cointegration analysis and find that the results are substantively the same.

We first estimate a conventional ECM to ascertain whether there is a long-run cointegrating relationship and evidence of Granger causality. The ECM is specified as follows:

$$\Delta \ln G_t = \gamma + \beta_1 \Delta \ln G_{t-1} + \sum_{j=0}^{\lambda} \beta_2 \Delta \ln P_{t-j} + \sum_{j=0}^{\lambda} \beta_3 \Delta \ln Y_{t-j} + \beta_4 \varepsilon_{t-1} + \theta_t, \quad (4)$$

where ε_t are the residuals extracted from Eq. (3).

We use the Akaike information criterion (AIC) to determine the appropriate lag order (λ) and the t-test to test whether the estimated coefficients are statistically significant. For β_2 and β_3, this amounts to testing for a short-run dynamic relationship between demand and price and income, respectively. For β_4, this is a further test of whether a long-run cointegrating relationship exists.

We then test for asymmetric impacts in the long-run cointegration relationship by incorporating asymmetry in the error correction term as follows:

$$\Delta \ln G_t = \gamma + \beta_1 \Delta \ln G_{t-1} + \sum_{j=0}^{\lambda} \beta_2 \Delta \ln P_{t-j} + \sum_{j=0}^{\lambda} \beta_3 \Delta \ln Y_{t-j} + \beta_4 \varepsilon_{t-1}^{+} + \beta_5 \varepsilon_{t-1}^{-} + \theta_t, \quad (5)$$

where

$$\varepsilon_t^{+} = \begin{cases} \varepsilon_t, & \varepsilon_t > 0 \\ 0, & \varepsilon_t < 0 \end{cases} \quad \text{and} \quad \varepsilon_t^{-} = \begin{cases} 0, & \varepsilon_t > 0 \\ \varepsilon_t, & \varepsilon_t < 0 \end{cases}.$$

We are also interested in whether the responsiveness of natural gas consumption to changes in price and income in the short-run is asymmetric. We therefore estimate the following asymmetric ECM:

$$\Delta \ln G_t = \gamma + \beta_1 \Delta \ln G_{t-1} + \sum_{j=0}^{\lambda} \beta_2 \Delta \ln P_{t-j}^{+} + \sum_{j=0}^{\lambda} \beta_3 \Delta \ln P_{t-j}^{-} + \sum_{j=0}^{\lambda} \beta_4 \Delta \ln Y_{t-j}^{+} + \sum_{j=0}^{\lambda} \beta_5 \Delta \ln Y_{t-j}^{-} + \beta_6 \varepsilon_{t-1} + \theta_t, \quad (6)$$

where

$$P_t^{+} = \begin{cases} P_t, & \Delta \ln P_t > 0 \\ 0, & \Delta \ln P_t < 0 \end{cases} \quad \text{and} \quad P_t^{-} = \begin{cases} 0, & \Delta \ln P_t > 0 \\ P_t, & \Delta \ln P_t < 0 \end{cases}$$

and

$$Y_t^+ = \begin{cases} Y_t, & \Delta \ln Y_t > 0 \\ 0, & \Delta \ln Y_t < 0 \end{cases} \quad \text{and} \quad Y_t^- = \begin{cases} 0, & \Delta \ln Y_t > 0 \\ Y_t, & \Delta \ln Y_t < 0 \end{cases}.$$

Data constraints prevent us from controlling for the price of all energy substitutes. In addition, the availability of price data for possible natural gas substitutes is limited. For instance, electricity would be an obvious substitute for natural gas for residential consumers. However, residential electricity price data is only available from 1990 onwards and estimating an ECM over this shorter time period may not capture the true long-run effects. However, to address the possibility of spurious results as a result of the price of substitutes being omitted from the estimated equations, we estimate the following equation over the period 1990 to 2016:

$$\ln G_t = \alpha + \beta_1 \ln P_t + \beta_2 \ln Y_t + \beta_3 \ln E_t + \varepsilon_t, \tag{7}$$

where E is the average real price of residential electricity. We hypothesize β_3, the cross-price elasticity, to be positive due to the substitution effect.

We acknowledge that one limitation of using electricity prices is that natural gas is both an input to electricity generation (accounting for 22% of electricity generation in 2014, up from 12% in 1973 [IEA, 2016]), and an end-use substitution for natural gas. It is also the case that primary electricity (for instance, renewable and nuclear energy) supply is also a substitute for natural gas in power generation. The data we use on final natural gas demand includes direct consumption by end users, but does not include demand from other forms of energy (such as electricity) that are generated using natural gas.

Table 5. Description of data sources used in analysis.

Variable	Source	Description
Natural gas consumption	E.I.A US Natural Gas Consumption by End Use	US Natural Gas Residential Consumption (MMcf)
Natural gas price	E.I.A US Natural Gas Prices	US Price of Natural Gas Delivered to Residential Consumers (Dollars per Thousand Cubic Feet)
GDP deflator	World Bank World Development Indicators	GDP deflator (2010 base year)
GDP per capita	World Bank World Development Indicators	GDP per capita (constant 2010 US$)
Population	World Bank World Development Indicators	US total population

5.3. *Data sources*

We use annual data from 1970 to 2016 and the data sources are defined in Table 5.

6. Preliminary Analysis

Table 6 reports the simple correlation coefficient between natural gas consumption and natural gas price, and natural gas consumption and income. The results find that US residential natural gas consumption per capita is more strongly associated with income rather than price. Further, the negative sign of the correlation coefficient in both cases indicates that an increase in one variable is associated with a decline in the other. For price, this is in line with conventional theory of demand — an increase in price results in a reduction in consumption, consistent with the law of demand. In the case of income, we find that higher levels of income are associated with lower levels of natural gas consumption. This may indicate that natural gas is an inferior good, or may be related to theories underpinning the EKC.

We now proceed to test for Granger causality (refer Table 7). The results find that natural gas prices Granger cause natural gas consumption, and that income per capita also Granger causes natural gas consumption.

Table 6. Correlation coefficients between NG demand, NG prices and incomes.

	Correlation coefficient
Natural gas consumption per capita & natural gas price (real)	−0.782
Natural gas consumption per capita & income per capita (real)	−0.930

Table 7. Granger causality test results.

Null hypothesis	***F*-statistic**	**Prob.**
Natural gas price does not Granger Cause Natural gas consumption	4.49**	0.017
Natural gas consumption does not Granger Cause Natural gas price	2.39	0.104
Income does not Granger Cause Natural gas consumption	7.33***	0.002
Natural gas consumption does not Granger Cause Income	0.33	0.721

Notes: The ** and *** indicates statistical significance at the 5% and 1% level, respectively.

Table 8. Unit root test results.

Variable	Levels	First difference
Natural gas consumption	−1.06 (0.724)	−8.73*** (0.000)
Natural gas price	−2.20 (0.209)	−5.73*** (0.000)
GDP per capita	−1.74 (0.404)	−4.92*** (0.000)

Notes: P-values are reported in parenthesis. The *** indicates statistical significance at the 1% level.

Table 8 reports the unit root test results. The unit root test results indicate that the dependant and explanatory variables are non-stationary and integrated of order 1 (that is, all variables are $I(1)$).

7. Empirical Results

We now proceed to estimate Eq. (3) and the results are reported in Table 9. The estimation of Eq. (3) provides the long-run estimates. The results find that long-run own-price elasticity of natural gas demand is −0.09, and long-run income elasticity is −0.49. These estimates are statistically significant at the 5% and 1% level, respectively. Both estimates are statistically different to one, meaning that there is neither unity elasticity for price or income in the long-run. Rather, we find that natural gas consumption is both price and income inelastic in the long-run. Interestingly, income elasticity is around five times larger than price elasticity and is also negatively signed.

Model diagnostics applied to the long-run static model (Eq. (3)) provide support for the model specification. The estimated long-run equation provides a good fit of the data, explaining almost 90% of the variation in natural gas demand ($\bar{R}^2 = 0.88$). In addition, unit root testing reports that the residuals are stationary (refer Table 10). As the residuals are found to be stationary ($I(0)$), we conclude that there is a long-run cointegrating relationship between these variables.

Turning now to the estimation of the cointegrating model (Eq. 4), we find no evidence of short-run dynamics (refer Table 11). The reason is that the estimated coefficient on the short-run dynamic variables are all statistically insignificant. However, the coefficient on the estimated error correction term is statistically significant, providing further evidence of the existence of a long-run cointegrating relationship between natural gas consumption, price and income. The speed of adjustment back to long-run equilibrium is relatively strong at around two-thirds per annum.

Table 9. Equation (3) estimation results.

Variable	Coefficient	P-values
α	1.36*** (0.442)	0.004
$\ln P_t$	−0.09** (0.043)	0.042
$\ln Y_t$	−0.49*** (0.049)	0.000

Note: Standard errors are reported in parenthesis. The ** and *** indicates statistical significance at the 5% and 1% level, respectively.

Table 10. ADF Unit root test results (residuals equation 3).

		t-statistic	P-value
Test statistic		−4.55***	0.001
Test critical values:	1% level	−3.58	
	5% level	−2.93	
	10% level	−2.60	

Note: The ***indicates statistical significance at the 1% level.

Table 11. Equation (4) estimation results.

Variable	Coefficient		Prob.
α	−0.01	(0.011)	0.443
$\Delta \ln G_{t-1}$	0.06	(0.170)	0.722
$\Delta \ln P_t$	0.08	(0.094)	0.414
$\Delta \ln P_{t-1}$	−0.08	(0.101)	0.440
$\Delta \ln Y_t$	−0.10	(0.393)	0.808
$\Delta \ln Y_{t-1}$	0.05	(0.392)	0.904
ε_{t-1}	−0.68***	(0.205)	0.002

Notes: Standard errors are reported in parenthesis. The ***indicates statistical significance at the 1% level.

To test for long-run asymmetric effects, we present the estimation results for Eq. (5) (refer Table 12). The results indicate that there are no asymmetric long-run impacts. The reason is that although the estimated coefficients on the asymmetric error correction terms are both statistically significant, they are not statistically different to each other. In line with the results presented above, there is no evidence of short-run dynamics and the estimated coefficient on the error correction term is identical in sign and magnitude.

To test for short-run asymmetric effects, we present the estimation results for Eq. (6) (refer Table 13). The estimated coefficients on the asymmetric variables are statistically insignificant in every instance. This provides evidence that neither natural gas prices nor income have asymmetric or short-run impacts on natural gas

Table 12. Equation (5) estimation results.

Variable	**Coefficient**	**Prob.**
α	−0.01 (0.014)	0.562
$\Delta \ln G_{t-1}$	0.06 (0.175)	0.730
$\Delta \ln P_t$	0.08 (0.095)	0.421
$\Delta \ln P_{t-1}$	−0.08 (0.104)	0.451
$\Delta \ln Y_t$	−0.10 (0.400)	0.811
$\Delta \ln Y_{t-1}$	0.05 (0.399)	0.905
ε^+_{t-1}	−0.68* (0.348)	0.058
ε^-_{t-1}	−0.68** (0.313)	0.037

Notes: Standard errors are reported in parenthesis. The ** indicates statistical significance at the 5% level.

Table 13. Equation (6) estimation results.

Variable	**Coefficient**	**Prob.**
α	−0.02 (0.025)	0.479
$\Delta \ln G_{t-1}$	0.05 (0.181)	0.764
$\Delta \ln P^+_t$	0.24 (0.209)	0.262
$\Delta \ln P^+_{t-1}$	−0.12 (0.230)	0.614
$\Delta \ln P^-_t$	−0.11 (0.240)	0.642
$\Delta \ln P^-_{t-1}$	−0.13 (0.231)	0.580
$\Delta \ln Y^+_t$	0.63 (0.705)	0.377
$\Delta \ln Y^+_{t-1}$	−0.61 (0.731)	0.407
$\Delta \ln Y^-_t$	−0.78 (1.185)	0.517
$\Delta \ln Y^-_{t-1}$	1.70 (1.170)	0.155
ε_{t-1}	−0.69*** (0.219)	0.003

Notes: standard errors are reported in parenthesis. The *** indicates statistical significance at the 1% level.

consumption. In addition, the estimated speed of adjustment is almost the same value as that estimated by the symmetric model. This provides evidence of the robustness of the results presented above.

7.1. *Robustness testing*

We now proceed with robustness testing by reestimating Eq. (3) across alternative time periods. These results are presented below in Table 14. Interestingly, natural gas demand is found to be unresponsive to natural gas prices over each of these shorter sample periods. That is, the estimated coefficients on the price of natural gas are not statistically different to zero in any instance. However, we find that natural gas demand is responsive to changes in income and is generally inelastic. That is, the estimated coefficient on the income variable is statistically different

Table 14. Equation (3) estimation results with alternative sample periods.

Sample	Variable	Coefficient	Prob.
1980–2016	$\ln P_t$	−0.06 (0.064)	0.369
	$\ln Y_t$	−0.47*** (0.055)	0.000
1990–2016	$\ln P_t$	0.08 (0.083)	0.335
	$\ln Y_t$	−0.75*** (0.124)	0.000
2000–2016	$\ln P_t$	0.07 (0.089)	0.442
	$\ln Y_t$	−1.38*** (0.306)	0.001

Notes: Standard errors are reported in parenthesis. The *** indicates statistical significance at the 1% level.

Table 15. Equation (7) estimation results.

Variable	Coefficient	Prob.
α	5.39*** (1.177)	0.000
$\ln P_t$	0.06 (0.072)	0.389
$\ln Y_t$	−0.78*** (0.107)	0.000
$\ln E_t$	−0.55*** (0.182)	0.006

Notes: Standard errors are reported in parenthesis. The *** indicates statistical significance at the 1% level.

to zero in each instance. In fact, we find that natural gas demand is becoming increasingly responsive to changes in income in recent times. Furthermore, the results indicate that natural gas demand is in fact negatively related to changes in income.

As a further robustness test, we estimate Eq. (7) over a shorter time period (1990–2016) during which the price of electricity to residential consumers is available as a proxy for the price of substitutes. These results are presented in Table 15. The results demonstrate the robustness of the preceding analysis. First, natural gas consumption is not responsive to changes in price over the long-run. Second, the income elasticity of natural gas demand is negative, statistically different to zero and inelastic. Further, the estimated income elasticity of natural gas demand is in line with that presented earlier. Interestingly, we find that the cross-price elasticity of substitutes (in this case, electricity) is negative, statistically different to zero and inelastic. Theoretically, we would expect a rise in the price of substitutes to increase demand for natural gas. However, it may be the case that as the cost of electricity rises and due to the lack of substitutability in the short-run, energy consumption overall is reduced at the residential level.

8. Discussion/Policy/Industry Relevance

In this chapter, we have presented a picture of the existing thinking with respect to price and income elasticities of demand for natural gas and electricity at the residential level in the US and internationally. The analysis has led us to identify the following common themes:

- Residential natural gas demand is relatively price inelastic and recent estimates of US price elasticities of residential natural gas demand are generally consistent.
- Those studies that distinguish between short-run and long-run price elasticities, in general conclude that the long-run elasticity is larger than the short-run elasticity, meaning natural gas demand is more responsive to income and price in the long-run.
- Demand is relatively inelastic to income in the short-run and positive (normal good), but in the long-run at least one study shows demand to be more elastic and negative (inferior good).
- Global and country level estimates of income and price elasticity can vary and local level differences may be important.

We go on to describe a new analysis carried out to examine the short- and long-run static and dynamic relationship between natural gas prices, income and electricity prices. We apply cointegration techniques in addition to simple correlation coefficients in order to establish the own price and income elasticities of demand for NG in addition to the cross-price elasticity of demand with respect to electricity. The key findings of these analyses can be summarized as follows:

- There is no short-run dynamic relationship between natural gas consumption at the residential level, natural gas price and income. This is likely to reflect the lack of substitutes for natural gas consumption at the residential level.
- There is a long-run cointegrating relationship between residential natural gas consumption, natural gas price and income.
- There is no evidence that natural gas consumption is asymmetrically responsive to changes in either price or income.
- Natural gas consumption is price and income inelastic.
- Natural gas consumption is more responsive to changes in income than price.
- Natural gas responds negatively to increases in both price and income.
- Natural gas has become increasingly responsive to changes in income in recent times.
- The cross-price elasticity of demand for natural gas is negative, a rather surprising result given that we would expect these to be substitutes at the residential level.

Demand elasticities of energy are an important input to energy-economy models and aid in understanding the effects of adjustments to tax settings and carbon pricing as well as international trade and energy price reform. Making accurate estimates of price and income elasticities is therefore of critical importance as is gaining an understanding of both static and dynamic effects. The methodology for estimating price and income elasticity of demand, and how to test for short-run dynamics, long-run cointegrating relationships and evidence of price and income asymmetry could, therefore, be a useful tool to policy-reformers and market designers.

References

Alberini, A. and Filippini, M. (2011). Response of residential electricity demand to price: The effect of measurement error. *Energy Economics* **33** (5), 889–895. doi: 10.1016/j.eneco.2011.03.009.

Alberini, A., Gans, W. and Velez-Lopez, D. (2011). Residential consumption of gas and electricity in the US.: The role of prices and income. *Energy Economics* **33** (5), 870–881. doi: 10.1016/j.eneco.2011.01.015.

Aurora, V. (2014). Estimates of the price elasticities of natural gas supply and demand in the United States. Munich personal RePEc Archive, No. 54232. Available at: http://mpra.ub.uni-muenchen.de/54232/.

Baker, P., Blundell, R. and Micklewright, J. (1989). Modelling household energy expenditures using micro-data. *The Economic Journal* **99** (397), 720–738. doi: 10.2307/2233767.

Bernard, J.-T., Bolduc, D. and Yameogo, N.-D. (2010). A pseudo-panel data model of household electricity demand. *Resource and Energy Economics* **33** (1), 315–325.

Bernstein, M. A. and Griffin, J. (2005). Regional differences in price-elasticity of demand for energy. The Rand Corporation Technical Report.

Bernstein, R. and Madlener, R. (2011). Residential Natural Gas Demand Elasticities in OECD Countries: An ARDL Bounds Testing Approach. Working Paper 15/2011, FCN 2011.

Burke, P. (2013). The national-level energy ladder and its carbon implications. *Environmental and Development Economics* **18** (4), 484–503.

Burke, P. and Yang, H. (2016). The price and income elasticities of natural gas demand: International evidence. *Energy Economics* **59**, 466–474.

Dergiades, T. and Tsoulfidis, L. (2008). Estimating residential demand for electricity in the United States, 1965–2006. *Energy Economics* **30**, 2722–2730.

Dubin, J. and McFadden, D. (1984). An econometric analysis of residential electric appliance holdings and consumption. *Econometrica* **52** (2), 345–362.

EIA (2017). *Monthly Energy Review*. USA, Energy Information Administration. Available at https://www.eia.gov/totalenergy/data/monthly/#summary accessed on 24 September 2017.

Fell, H., Li, S. and Paul, A. (2010). A new look at residential electricity demand using household expenditure data. Resources for the Future Discussion paper 10–57, Washington, DC, November.

Filippini, M. and Pachauri, S. (2004). Elasticities of electricity demand in urban Indian households. *Energy Policy* **32**, 429–436.

Garcia-Cerrutti, L. M. (2000). Estimating elasticities of residential energy demand from panel county data using dynamic random variables models with heteroskedastic and correlated error terms. *Resource and Energy Economics* **22**, 355–366.

Grossman, G. M. and Krueger, A. B. (1991). Environmental Impacts of a North American Free Trade Agreement. National Bureau of Economic Research Working Paper 3914, NBER, Cambridge, MA.

IEA (2016). *Key World Energy Statistics*. (International Energy Agency, Paris, France).

IEA (2015). *World Energy Outlook 2015*. (International Energy Agency, Paris, France).

Joutz, F., McDowell, B., Shin, D. and Trost, R. (2009). Estimating Regional Short-Run and Long-Run Price Elasticities of Residential Natural Gas Demand in the U.S. Working Paper 09-021, USAEE 2009.

Lavín, F., Dale, L., Hanemann, M. and Moezzi, M. (2011). The impact of price on residential demand for electricity and natural gas. *Climatic Change* **109** (Supplement 1), 171–189. doi: 10.1007/s10584-011-0297-0.

Maddala, G. S., Trost, R. P., Li, H. and Joutz, F. (1997). Estimation of short-run and long-run elasticities of energy demand from panel data using shrinkage estimators. *Journal of Business & Economic Statistics* **15** (1), 90–100.

Madlener, R., Bernstein, R. and Gonzalez, M. (2011). Econometric estimation of energy demand elasticities. *E.ON Energy Research Center Series* **3** (8).

Meier, H. and Rehdanz, K. (2010). Determinants of residential space heating expenditures in Great Britain. *Energy Economics* **32**, 949–959.

Metcalf, G. and Hassett, K. A. (1999). Measuring the energy savings from home improvement investments: Evidence from monthly billing data. *The Review of Economics and Statistics* **81** (3), 516–528.

Nesbakken, R. (1999). Price sensitivity of residential energy consumption in Norway. *Energy Economics* **21**, 493–515.

Nesbakken, R. (2001). Energy consumption for space heating: A discrete–continuous approach. *The Scandinvaian Journal of Economics* **103** (1), 165–184.

Rehdanz, K. (2007). Determinants of residential space heating expenditures in Germany. *Energy Economics* **29**, 267–182.

Reiss, P. C. and White, M. W. (2005). Household electricity demand, revisited. *Review of Economic Studies* **72**, 853–858.

Shi, G., Zheng, X. and Song, F. (2012). Estimating elasticity for residential electricity demand in China. *The Scientific World Journal* 395629.

Stiglitz, J., Walsh, C., Gow, J., Guest, R., Richmond, B. and Tani, M. (2015). *Principles of Economics*, 2nd Australian Edn. (Wiley, New Jersey).

Studenmund, A. (2010). *Using Econometrics: A Practical Guide*, 6th Edn. (Pearson).

Waheed, A. and Martin, F. (2013). Estimating the demand elasticities of residential natural gas in Louisiana. *The Global Journal of Finance and Economics* **10** (2), 183–189.

Yoo, S.-H., Lee, J. and Kwak, S.-J. (2007). Estimation of residential electricity demand function in Seoul by correction for sample selection bias. *Energy Policy* **35** (11), 5702–5707.

PART II

Volatility and Jump Modeling

Chapter 8

Applied Models of Heavy Tails and Skewness in Energy Prices with an Application to Electricity Price Risk

W. D. Walls[*,‡] and Wei Zhang[†]

[*]Department of Economics, University of Calgary, Calgary, Alberta, Canada T2N 1N4

[†]Senior Corporate Economist, City of Calgary, Calgary, Alberta, Canada

[‡]wdwalls@ucalgary.ca

Energy prices are characterized by distributions that are asymmetric and that have heavier than Gaussian tails. Yet, many researchers continue to employ statistical methods that do not explicitly account for heavy tails and skewness in energy prices. In this chapter, we explicitly account for heavy tails and skewness with an application to electricity price risk using the Generalized Pareto Distribution and the Generalized Extreme Value Distribution. Specifically, we model value-at-risk (VaR) which is a widely-used measure of the maximum potential change in value of a portfolio of financial assets with a given probability over a given time horizon. VaR has become a standard measure of market risk and a common practice is to compute VaR by assuming that changes in value of the portfolio are conditionally normally distributed. However, assets returns usually come from heavy-tailed distributions, so computing VaR under the assumption of conditional normality can be an important source of error. We illustrate in our application to electric power, that VaR estimates based on extreme value theory models — in particular the generalized Pareto distribution — are more accurate than those produced by alternative models such as normality or historical simulation.

Keywords: Heavy tails and skewness; extreme value theory; value-at-risk; generalized Pareto distribution; generalized extreme value distribution.

1. Introduction

The goal of this chapter is to provide a rigorous introduction to risk analysis that explicitly accounts for the heavy tails and skewness that characterize energy prices. Standard models of risk analysis are typically formalized using statistical models that assume a Gaussian ("Normal") distribution. Yet, in the physical sciences and in the mathematics of insurance markets, it is common to apply alternative statistical distributions that explicitly account for extreme events that are improbably small to occur in Normal models. This chapter integrates the statistical models of extreme events together with a formal risk assessment model, providing a set of practical tools for applied energy economists.

This chapter specifically evaluates extreme value theory and value-at-risk (VaR) analysis as a unified tool for managing price risk in energy markets with an application to restructured electricity markets. Researchers in the physical sciences have long recognized that natural processes lead to outcome distributions that deviate substantially from Gaussian or even heavy-tailed symmetric distributions. The use of heavy-tailed and asymmetric distributions is beginning to penetrate applied finance and become a practical tool [Rocco, 2014]. Most prior research on price distributions in electricity markets has focused on either pure time series models or unit root econometrics, with Paraschiv *et al.* [2016] a notable exception. Our contribution is to unify the statistics of extremes and risk analysis in an exposition that is accessible to applied energy economists.

In the next section of this chapter, we set out the details of statistical distributions that account for extreme events and how these can be incorporated into a quantitative risk analysis framework. In Section 3, we estimate the distribution of Alberta electricity prices and demonstrate a practical application of risk analysis. The relative performance of alternative risk models is quantified in Section 4. Conclusions are made in Section 5.

2. Risk Analysis Using Extreme Value Theory

VaR is the maximum expected loss over a given horizon at a given level of confidence. Summarizing the overall market risks faced by a company in a single quantity number, VaR has become a practical way to quantify market risks. Our focus is on the extreme value theory (EVT) estimation method, including the general Pareto distribution (GPD) model and the generalized extreme value distribution (GEV) model. To see the overall advantages of EVT estimation method, other traditional estimation methods, namely the Normal distribution model and historical simulation (HS), are used as benchmarks.

Risk is the mapping of unforeseen future states of the world into values representing gains and losses. The potential values of a risk have a probability distribution never observed exactly, although past losses are available. Extreme events occur when a risk takes values from the tail of its distribution. VaR summarizes the measuring of a risk with a number. VaR is a high quantile of the distribution of losses, typically above 95th percentile. It provides a kind of upper bound for a loss only exceeded on a small proportion of occasions.

Let $X_1, X_2, \ldots, X_n$ be identically distributed random variables with an unknown underlying distribution function $F(x) = P\{X_i \leq x\}$. There is no assumption of an independent distribution of the random variable here, since the assumption of independence is unnecessary and unrealistic in financial time series [Embrechts *et al.*, 1997]. Measures of extreme risks are defined in terms of the underlying distribution $F(x)$ at high percentiles. Let $0.95 < q \leq 1$, value at risk (VaR) is the qth quantile of the distribution F: $\mathrm{VaR}_q = F^{-1}(q)$, where F^{-1} is the inverse of $F(x)$, and we have $F(\mathrm{VaR}_q) = P\{X_i \leq \mathrm{VaR}_q\} = q$.

Although VaR gives us a single number about the loss at a particular point, it tells us nothing about the potential size of the loss that exceeds it. Artzer *et al.* [1997] propose the use of expected shortfall (ES) or tail conditional expectation instead of VaR. Given a high percentile q, the tail conditional expectation is the expected size of a loss that exceeds VaR: $\mathrm{ES}_q = E[X|X > \mathrm{VaR}_q]$. The ES is related to VaR by $\mathrm{ES}_q = \mathrm{VaR}_q + E[X - \mathrm{VaR}_q|X > \mathrm{VaR}_q]$. The second term is the mean of the excess distribution $F^{[u]}(X - u|X > u)$ over the threshold $u = \mathrm{VaR}_q$.

The ES is an alternative risk measurement that provides some information about the size of the potential losses given that a loss bigger than VaR has occurred. Therefore, this risk measure is expected to be particularly sensitive with respect to the choice of the model for the tail of the return.

2.1. *Block maximum models and the general extreme value distribution*

Instead of focusing on fluctuations of sample averages, block maximum models focus on fluctuations of sample block maxima, $M_1, \ldots, M_n$, which are defined as $M_1 = X_1, M_n = \max(X_1, X_2, \ldots, X_n)$, $n \geq 2$, where $X_1, X_2, \ldots, X_n$ are identically distributed random variables with an unknown underlying distribution function $F(x) = P\{X_i \leq x\}$ [Embrechts *et al.*, 1997, 115]. Only maxima need to be analyzed since the corresponding results for minima can be obtained from $\min(X_1, X_2, \ldots, X_n) = -\max(X_1, X_2, \ldots, X_n)$. The distribution function of the maximum M_n is $P(M_n \leq x) = P(X_1 \leq x, \ldots, X_n \leq x) = F^n(x)$, for $x \in R$, $n \in N$. Extremes happen near the upper end of the underlying distribution, so the asymptotic behavior of M_n must relate to the underlying distribution function $F(x)$ in its right tail near the right endpoint. If x_F is denoted as the right endpoint of $F(x)$, then $P(M_n \leq x) = F^n(x) \to 0$, $n \to \infty$, for all $x < x_F$. In the case $x_F < \infty$, $P(M_n \leq x) = F^n(x) = 1$, for $x \geq x_F$. M_n converges in probability to x_F $M_n \stackrel{p}{\to} x_F$, as n $\to \infty$.

Since the sequence (M_n) is non-decreasing in n, it converges as sure to the right endpoint of $F(x) M_n \stackrel{a.s}{\to} x_F$, as n $\to \infty$. Since the above fact does not provide a lot of information, one needs to have more insight into the weak convergence results for the centered and normalized maxima, which is one of the major topics in classical EVT. The first fundamental theorem is the Fisher–Tippett theorem [Embrechts *et al.*, 1997, 121].

The Fisher–Tippett Theorem (Limit Laws for Maxima): Let $X_1, X_2, \ldots$ be a sequence of iid random variables from an unknown distribution F, and $M_n = \max(X_1, X_2, \ldots, X_n)$ has the distribution function F^n. If there exist normalizing constants $c_n > 0$ and $d_n \in R$, and some non-degenerate distribution function H as $n \to \infty$, such that the sequence of normalized maxima $(M_n - d_n)/c_n$ convergences in distribution to H, then $P\{(M_n - d_n)/c_n \leq x\} = F^n(c_n x + d_n) \to H(x)$, *as* $n \to \infty$. This family of distribution H can be subsumed under a single distribution function, the GEV. The GEV is the natural limit distribution for the normalized maxima. The definition of the distribution of the standard GEV is

$$H_\xi(x) = \begin{cases} \exp\{-(1+\xi x)^{-1/\xi}\}, & \xi \neq 0; \\ \exp\{-e^{-x}\}, & \xi = 0, \end{cases} \tag{1}$$

where x is such that $1 + \xi x > 0$ and ξ is the single parameter. There are three cases of distributions: if $\xi > 0$, there is the Frechet distribution with shape parameter $\alpha = 1/\xi$; if $\xi < 0$, there is the Weibull distribution with shape $\alpha = -1/\xi$; if $\xi = 0$, by applying the well-known formula $(1 + \xi x)^{1/\xi} \to \exp(x)$ as $\xi \to 0$, there is the Gumbel distribution. Here, the interest is on Frechet distributions since they are fat-tailed distributions.

Note that if a random variable X has the distribution function $F(x) = P\{X_i \leq x\}$, then $(\mu + \sigma X)$ has the distribution function $F(\mu + \sigma X_i) = P\{\mu + \sigma X_i \leq x\}$, which is $F_{\mu,\sigma}(x) = F((x - \mu)/\sigma)$ [Reiss and Thomas, 1997, 16]. By introducing location and scale parameters μ and $\sigma > 0$, respectively, the family of distributions H can be extended to three-parameter models. The definition of the general extreme value distribution $H_{\xi,\mu,\sigma}(x)$ to be $H_\xi((x - \mu)/\sigma)$ and $H_{\xi,\mu,\sigma}$ is said to be of the type H_ξ.

$$H_{\xi,\mu,\sigma}(x) = H_\xi\left(\frac{x-\mu}{\sigma}\right) = \begin{cases} \exp\left\{-\left[1+\frac{\xi}{\sigma}(x-\mu)\right]\right\}^{-\frac{1}{\xi}}, & \xi = 0; \\ \exp\left\{-e^{-\frac{x-\mu}{\sigma}}\right\}, & \xi \neq 0. \end{cases} \tag{2}$$

Similar to the central limit theorem, where the stable distributions are the only possible non-degenerate limit laws, the Fisher–Tippett theorem says that the family of distribution H is the only possible limiting distribution for the normalized block maxima.

There are two important concepts for further understanding of the Fisher–Tippett theorem: One is the max-stable distribution, and the other is maximum domain of attraction.

Definition (Max-stable Distribution). A non-degenerate random variable X is called max-stable if it satisfies $F^n(c_n X + d_n) = F(x)$, $d_n \in R$ for a suitable choice of constants $c_n > 0$ and $d_n \in R$ and every $n \geq 2$ [Reiss and Thomas, 1997, 19].

The standardized maximum $F^n(c_n X + d_n)$ is distributed according to the extreme value distribution H: $F(x) = F^n(c_n X + d_n) \to H(x), as\ n \to \infty$.

Definition (Maximum Domain of Attraction). The random variables $X_1, X_2, \ldots$ from an unknown distribution F are said to belong to the maximum domain of attraction of the extreme value distribution H, if there exist constants $c_n > 0$ and $d_n \in R$. We write $X \in \text{MDA}(H)$ or $F \in \text{MDA}(H)$ [Embrechts *et al.*, 1997, 128].

The Fisher–Tippett theorem says conversely that if F is in the MDA of a non-degenerate extreme value distribution H, then we have the normalizing constants $c_n > 0$ and $d_n \in R$. Reiss and Thomas [1997, 19] provide some examples of relative constant c_n and d_n given H is Gumble, Frechet, or Weibull distribution.

- Gumble: $d_n = \log n, \quad c_n = 1$;
- Frechet: $d_n = 0, \quad c_n = n^{1/\alpha}$;
- Weibull: $d_n = 0, \quad c_n = n^{1/\alpha}$.

From the Fisher–Tippett theorem and the definition of relative VaR, one can easily calculate the VaR from the original underlying distribution $F(x)$: $\text{VaR}_q = H^{-1}(q)$, where H is derived by estimated parameters ξ, μ and σ. The explicit expression of *estimated* H is $\hat{H}(x) = H_{\hat{\xi}}((x-\hat{\mu})/\hat{\sigma})$.

The explicit *estimated* VaR expression can be derived as follows:

From

$$H_{\hat{\xi},\hat{\mu},\hat{\sigma}}(x) = \exp\left\{-\left[1+\frac{\hat{\xi}}{\hat{\sigma}}(x-\hat{\mu})\right]^{-\hat{\xi}}\right\}, \tag{3}$$

there is

$$\ln \hat{H} = -\left[1+\frac{\hat{\xi}}{\hat{\sigma}}(x-\hat{\mu})\right]^{-1/\hat{\xi}} \tag{4}$$

$$1+\frac{\hat{\xi}}{\hat{\sigma}}(x-\hat{\mu}) = (-\ln H) - \hat{\xi} \tag{5}$$

$$x-\hat{\mu} = \frac{\hat{\sigma}}{\hat{\xi}}[(-\ln H)^{-\hat{\xi}} - 1]. \tag{6}$$

Substituting $\hat{\text{VaR}} = x$ and $p = \hat{H}(x)$ above, we obtain is

$$\hat{\text{VaR}} = \hat{\mu} + \frac{\hat{\sigma}}{\hat{\xi}}[(-\ln p)^{-\hat{\xi}} - 1]. \tag{7}$$

Recall the ES_q expression, $\text{ES}_q = \text{VaR}_q + E[X - \text{VaR}_q | X > \text{VaR}_q]$. To calculate ES value, one needs to know the exact excess distribution of the model, which is unknown in GEV. Thus, there is no explicit expression equation for ES estimation as there is for VaR estimation.

The difficulty of implementing VaR estimation based on GEV is that a lot of data are required. A sufficiently large block size is needed so that the limiting result of Fisher–Tippett theorem may be taken as approximately exact. On the other hand, a large block size also decreases the number of maximum observations from the raw dataset. There should be a balance between choosing a large block size, and yet keeping enough maxima data for the VaR estimations.

2.2. *Peak-over-threshold* (*POT*) *models and the general Pareto distribution* (*GPD*)

The GPD is usually expressed as a two-parameter distribution function as follows:

$$G_{\xi,\beta}(x) = \begin{cases} 1-(1+\xi x/\beta)^{-1/\xi}, & \xi \neq 0; \\ 1-\exp(x/\beta), & \xi = 0; \end{cases} \tag{8}$$

where

$$\begin{aligned} &\beta > 0, && \\ &x \geq 0, && \text{if } \xi \geq 0, \\ &0 \leq x \leq -\beta/\xi, && \text{if } \xi < 0. \end{aligned}$$

There are three sub-models for GPD functions: The case $\xi > 0$ corresponds to the fat-tailed distributions with the tails that decay like power functions, such as the Pareto, Student-t, Cauchy, Burr, Loggamma and Frechet distributions. The case $\xi = 0$ corresponds to normal, exponential, gamma and lognormal distributions with tails that decay exponentially. The case $\xi < 0$ corresponds to distributions with a finite right endpoint, such as uniform and beta distributions.

The GPD family can be expanded to three-parameter models by adding a location parameter μ. The GPD $G_{\xi,\mu,\beta}(x)$ is defined to be $G_{\xi,\beta}(x-\mu)$

$$G_{\xi,\mu,\beta}(x) = G_{\xi,\beta}(x-\mu) = \begin{cases} 1 - \left[1 + \frac{\xi}{\beta}(x-\mu)\right]^{-\frac{1}{\xi}}, & \xi \neq 0; \\ 1 - \exp\left(\frac{x-\mu}{\beta}\right), & \xi = 0. \end{cases} \tag{9}$$

The ordinary Pareto distribution is the most relevant distribution for risk management purposes since GPD is fat-tailed when $\xi > 0$. Whereas the normal distribution has moments of all orders, a fat-tailed distribution does not possess a complete set of moments. In the case of the GPD with $\xi > 0$, the kth moment of the distribution, $E[X^k]$, is infinite for $k \geq 1/\xi$. When $\xi = ½$, the GPD has infinite variance; when $\xi = ¼$, the GPD has an infinite fourth moment. In the risk analysis, the assumption is that the underlying distribution F has an infinite right endpoint, i.e. it allows the possibility of arbitrarily large losses.

GPD functions $G_{\xi,\mu,\beta}(x)$ are the adequate parametric distribution functions for exceedances. GEV distributions are precisely the distributions with excess distributions converging to a GPD limit. The relationship between GPD distribution functions $G(x)$ and GEV distribution functions $H(x)$ is $G(x) = 1 + \ln H(x)$, if $\ln H(x) > -1$, where $H(x)$ is the GEV distribution [Reiss and Thomas, 2001, 23].

The excess (or exceedance) distribution function, distribution of excess losses over a high threshold u, is defined as $F^{[u]}(y) = P(X - u \leq y | X > u)$, for $0 \leq y < x_F - u$, and where $x_F \leq \infty$ is the right endpoint of $F(x)$. The excess distribution represents the probability that a loss exceeds the threshold u by at most an amount y, given the information that it exceeds the threshold. The exceedance distribution can also be written in terms of the underlying distribution F as $F^{[u]}(y) = [F(y+u) - F(u)]/[1 - F(u)]$.

The parametric modeling of exceedance distribution functions $F^{[u]}$ by the GPD is based on a limit theorem, the Pickands–Balkema–de Haan Theorem (see [Balkema and de Haan, 1974; Pickands, 1975; MeNeil, 1997]). The theorem shows that under MDA conditions, GPD is the limiting distribution for the distribution of the excesses, as the threshold tends to the right endpoint. This is a key result in EVT, which explains the importance of the GPD.

Pickands–Balkema–de Haan Theorem For a large class of underlying distribution, one can find a function $\beta(u)$ such that

$$\lim_{u\to x_F} \sup_{0\le y\le x_F-u} |F^{[u]}(y) - G_{\xi,\beta(u)}(y)| = 0, \tag{10}$$

that is, for a large class of underlying distributions F, as the threshold u is progressively raised, the excess distribution $F^{[u]}$ converges to a generalized Pareto distribution.

In the sense of the Pickands–Balkema–de Haan Theorem, GPD is the natural model for the unknown excess distribution above sufficiently high thresholds. Suppose the tail of the underlying distribution $F(x)$ begins at the threshold u, our model for a risk X_i from this underlying distribution assumes that the excess distribution above the threshold may be taken as exactly GPD for some ξ and β: $F^{[u]}(x-u) = G_{\xi,\beta(u)}(x-u)$. Again, the choice of thresholds is a compromise between choosing a sufficiently high one, which ensures the asymptotic exact of the Pickands–Balkema–de Haan Theorem, and choosing a sufficiently low one, which gives enough exceedances for the estimation of the GPD parameters. From the result of the Pickands–Balkema–de Haan Theorem, it is easy to calculate the tail estimation of underlying distribution.

By setting $x = u+y$, one can rewrite the excesses distribution function as $F(x) = [1-F(u)]F^{[u]}(y) + F(u)$ and this can be written as $F(x) = [1-F(u)]G_{\xi,\beta(u)}(x-u) + F(u)$, for $x > u$. This formula interprets the model in terms of the tail estimation of the underlying distribution $F(x)$ for $x > u$ given the estimation of $F(u)$. One suggestion is to use the HS estimator $F(u) = \frac{n-n_u}{n}$, where n is the sample size and g_{nu} is the number of exceedances over a threshold u. Putting HS estimate of $F(u)$ and the maximum likelihood estimates of the parameters of the GPD together, one can derive the tail estimator as follows:

$$\hat{F}(x) = \left(1 - \frac{n-n_u}{n}\right) G_{\hat{\xi},\hat{\beta},u}(x-u) + \frac{n-n_u}{n} = \frac{n_u}{n}$$

$$G_{\hat{\xi},\hat{\beta},u}(x-u) + \frac{n-n_u}{n} = 1 + \frac{n_u}{n}(G_{\hat{\xi},\hat{\beta},u}(x-u) - 1).$$

Given

$$G_{\xi,\mu,\beta}(x) = 1 - \left[1 + \xi\left(\frac{x-\mu}{\beta}\right)\right]^{-\frac{1}{\xi}},$$

plugging in the equation above, one has

$$\hat{F}(x) = 1 - \frac{n_u}{n}\left(1 + \hat{\xi}\frac{x-u}{\hat{\beta}}\right)^{-\frac{1}{\hat{\xi}}} \frac{n_u}{n}\left(1 + \hat{\xi}\frac{x-u}{\hat{\beta}}\right)^{-\frac{1}{\hat{\xi}}} = 1 - \hat{F}(x) = 1 - q,$$

where q is the high probability above $F(u)$. Let $\alpha = 1 - q$, one has

$$\left(1 + \hat{\xi}\frac{x-u}{\hat{\beta}}\right)^{-\frac{1}{\hat{\xi}}} = \frac{n_u}{n}\alpha\, \hat{\xi}\frac{x-u}{\hat{\beta}} = \left(\frac{n_u}{n}\alpha\right)^{-\hat{\xi}} - 1.$$

For a given probability $q > F(u)$, the VaR estimate x, is calculated by

$$x = \hat{\text{VaR}}_q(1-q) = u + \frac{\hat{\beta}}{\hat{\xi}}\left[\frac{n}{n_n}(1-q)^{-\hat{\xi}} - 1\right]. \tag{11}$$

The GPD model for the excess distribution above the threshold u has a nice stability property. If one takes any higher threshold, such as $u' = \text{VaR}_q$ for $q > F(u)$, the excess distribution $F^{[u']}(y)$ above the higher threshold u' is also a GPD model with the same shape parameter ξ, but a different scale parameter β [McNeil, 1999]. A consequence of the model $F^{[u]}(y) = G_{\xi,\beta(u)}(y)$ is that $F^{[u']}(x-u') = G_{\xi,\beta(u')}(x-u')$ and $F^{[u']}(x - \text{VaR}_q) = G_{\xi,\beta(u')}(x - \text{VaR}_q)$. This results in a simple explicit model for the excess losses above the VaR. With this model, one can calculate many characteristics of the losses beyond VaR. By noting that (providing $\xi < 1$) the mean of the distribution is

$$E[x - \text{VaR}_q] = (\beta + \xi(\text{VaR}_q - u))/(1-\xi), \tag{12}$$

and one can calculate the expected shortfall. The result is $\text{ES}_q = \text{VaR}_q + \frac{1}{1-\xi}[\beta + \xi(\text{VaR}_q - u]$ and $\text{ES}_q = \frac{\text{VaR}_q}{1-\xi} + \frac{\beta-\xi u}{1-\xi}$. The ES is estimated by substituting data-based estimates for everything that is unknown to obtain $\hat{\text{ES}}_q = \frac{\hat{\text{VaR}}_q}{1-\hat{\xi}} + \frac{\hat{\beta}-\hat{\xi}u}{1-\hat{\xi}}$.

2.3. *Variance–covariance method with normal distribution*

The variance–covariance approach is to interpret risks in terms of the standard deviation of the return. The variance–covariance approach is the simplest approach among the various models for the VaR estimation. A most straightforward assumption of the underlying distribution is the normal distribution [Dowd, 1998, 42]. Suppose X is identically distributed random variables with an underlying normal distribution function $N(x) = P\{X_i \leq x\}$. The confidence level can be described in terms of a single parameter, α, which tells how far away the cut-off values of the two tails are from the mean, μ, in terms of units of the standard deviation, σ. In studying extreme high values above X^* in the right tail of the distribution, one considers the probability function $\text{Prob}\{X \geq X^*\} = \text{Prob}\{Z \geq (X^* - \mu)/\sigma\} = c$, where Z is the standard normal variate with $\mu = 0$ and $\sigma = 1$, and c represents the probability of a right-tail event (such as $c = 95\%$ confidence level). In general, one has $X^* = \mu + \alpha\sigma$ where α reflects the selected confidence level. From the standard normal tables, one can read off the implied value of $\alpha = (X^* - \mu)/\sigma$.

The relative VaR of normal distribution is expressed as $\text{VaR}_q = N^{-1}(q)\sigma$, where $N^{-1}(q)$ is the qth quantile value of the normal distribution. The estimate of μ and σ can be obtained from the sample mean and the sample variance by

$$\hat{\mu} = \frac{1}{n}\sum_{i=1}^{n} x_i \text{ and } \hat{\sigma}^2 = \frac{1}{n-1}\sum_{i=1}^{n}(x_i - \hat{\mu})^2.$$

The normal distribution assumption in variance–covariance methods is simple to use. But it does not account for asymmetry. In addition, it has an exponential decay at its tails, characterized as thin-tailedness. As a result, the normal distribution estimation tends to underestimate the risks for high quantiles in the right tail (or lower quantiles in the left tail), given the fact that empirical distributions often have asymmetric fat tails.

2.4. *Historical simulation method*

Based on Dowd [1998], the basic assumption of HS is that the distribution of prices is unknown, and that future risks are much like past risks. Thus, the VaR estimates by HS method are from high quantiles of the empirical distribution obtained from the historical data of the realized observations. HS does not rely on assumptions about the underlying stochastic structure of the distribution. The advantage of a HS is that it accounts for fat tailedness and does not suffer from model specific errors. In this sense, it is better than the variance–covariance method with normal distribution assumption in risk scenario. A disadvantage of HS is its assumption that future risks are much like past risks. When observations are not enough in the historical data, some extreme values not seen in the past situation will not be predicted in the future. As such, the HS is a poor method in the tail of the distribution where data become sparse.

3. Value at Risk and Expected Shortfall Estimations

In this section, we estimate the parameters of the distribution of Alberta electricity prices for the GEV and GDP models. Prior to estimation, a number of diagnostics are carried out on the raw price data. The exposition of the analysis is set out so that practitioners can apply these tools in their own applications.

3.1. *Descriptive statistics on Alberta electricity prices*

The raw data of hourly electricity prices in this chapter are Alberta Power Pool prices from January 2001 to December 2003. Data is obtained from the Alberta Electric System Operator (AESO)'s website, www.aeso.ca. The descriptive statistics of the data are shown on Table 1. It is clear that the two sets of data both disperse largely from their means. Their skewness statistics are both positive, which means that the underlying distributions are asymmetric with the upper tails thicker than their lower tails. Their kurtosis statistics are both much larger than 3, which means that the tails of the underlying distribution are thicker than that of normal distributions, in other words they are fat tails.

3.2. *Diagnostic plots of the distributions of electricity prices*

With the descriptive statistics above, one gets some basic ideas about the shape of the distribution of electricity prices. Further details can be described by diagnostic plots. For studying the tail behavior, I will use Histogram, QQ-plot, and ME-plot. The following description of the plot concepts is based on McNeil [1997], Reiss & Thomas [1997], and Embrechts *et al.* [1997].

Given a set of data to be analyzed, one usually starts with a histogram. A histogram is usually plotted with observation values against their frequency numbers of the data. A histogram shows the wide range of the data. The histograms of Albert's data are shown in Fig. 1.

Table 1. Descriptive statistics.

Data	n	μ	σ	S	K	Min	Max
Winter	7290	80.62	79.5492	4.2643	30.1544	9.81	1000
Non-winter	3660	67.67	78.0555	6.3822	59.9780	6.29	999

Notes: Winter = October to May from 2001 to 2003 peak hourly prices (from 11:00 am to 20:00 pm); Non-winter = June to September from 2001 to 2003 peak hourly prices (from 11:00 am to 20:00 pm); n = sample size; μ = sample mean; σ = sample standard deviation; S = Skewness; K = Kurtosis; Min = Minimum observed price; Max = Maximum observed price.

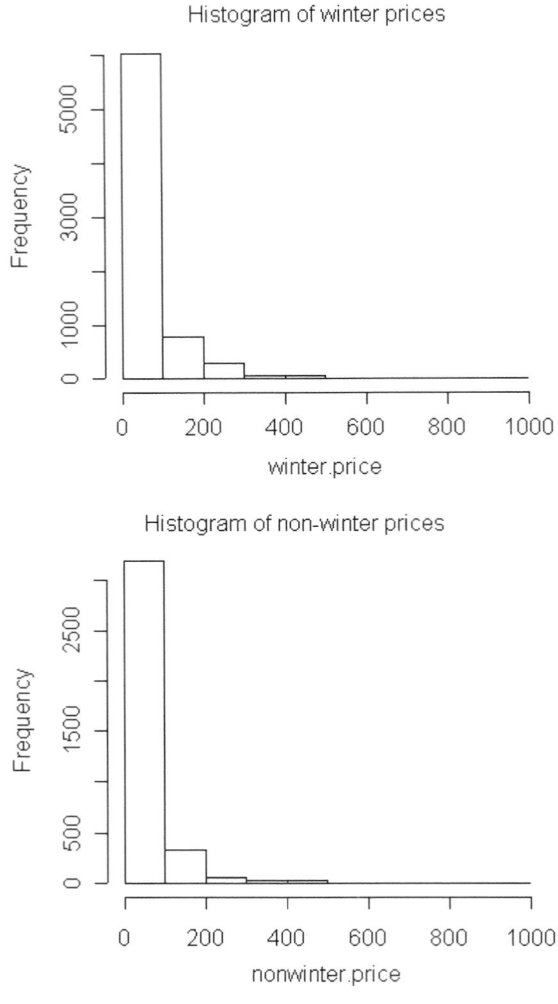

Fig. 1. Histogram of winter and non-winter prices.

A quantile plot, QQ-plot, is the plot of the sample quantiles against the quantiles of an assumed underlying (or tail) distribution. An assumed tail distribution can be any one of the GPD, such as exponential, student t, or beta distributions. Since an underlying distribution has the same shape parameter with its related tail distribution, an exponential tail distribution has an underlying Gumbel distribution. To find the evidence of fat-tailed distribution, the exponential distribution is used as assumed distribution. The relative QQ-plot is plotted with the quantiles of the empirical distribution on the x-axis against the quantiles of the exponential distribution on the

y-axis. That is,

$$\left\{\left(X_{kn}, G_{0,1}^{-1}\left(\frac{n-k+1}{n+1}\right)\right), \quad k=1,\ldots,n\right\},$$

where X_{kn} denotes the kth order statistic, and $G_{0,1}^{-1}$ is the inverse of the distribution function of the exponential distribution. If the points lie approximately along a straight line, the data are an iid sample from an exponential distribution. A concave shape of the points shows a fat-tailed distribution, whereas a convex shape shows a thin-tailed distribution.

The QQ-plots of Alberta's data are shown in Fig. 2, where the empirical quantiles of electricity prices are plotted against exponential quantiles. One can see the concave shapes of the graphs and conclude that the two sets of electricity prices are from fat-tailed distributions with their shape parameter $\xi > 0$.

Another useful graphical tool, in particular for distinguishing different tails, is a sample mean excess plot consisting of the mean excess function. A mean excess function (ME) is the sum of the excesses over the threshold u divided by the number of data that exceed the threshold u, which is expressed by $e(u) = E(X - u|X > u), 0 \leq u < x_F$ where x_F is the right endpoint of the underlying distribution.

A sample mean excess function (sample ME) is an empirical estimate of the ME, which is expressed as

$$e_n(u) = \frac{\sum_{i=1}^{n}(x_i - u)^+}{\sum_{i=1}^{n} I_{\{x_i > u\}}},$$

where I is an indicator function equal to one when $x_i > u$, and equal to zero when $x_i \leq u$. A sample mean excess plot (ME-plot) is the plot of sample mean excess function, which is $\{(u, e_n(u)), X_{n,n} < u < X_{1,n}\}$, where $X_{1,n}$ and $X_{n,n}$ are the 1st- and nth-order statistics and $e_n(u)$ is the sample mean excess function.

A ME-plot is used mainly for distinguishing short-tailed distributions from fat-tailed distributions. If the points in a sample ME-plot show an upward trend, then it is considered an evidence of fat-tailed distribution. An approximately horizontal line of the points relates to an exponential distribution, whereas a downward trend of points relates to a thin-tailed distribution. In particular, if the empirical plot follows a straight line with positive slope above a certain value of u, then the data follow a generalized Pareto distribution (GPD) in the tail above threshold u [McNeil, 1997].

From Fig. 3, we can see the sample ME-plots of our data have upward trends of points, which mean that the electricity prices of Alberta Power Pool are from fat-tailed underlying distributions.

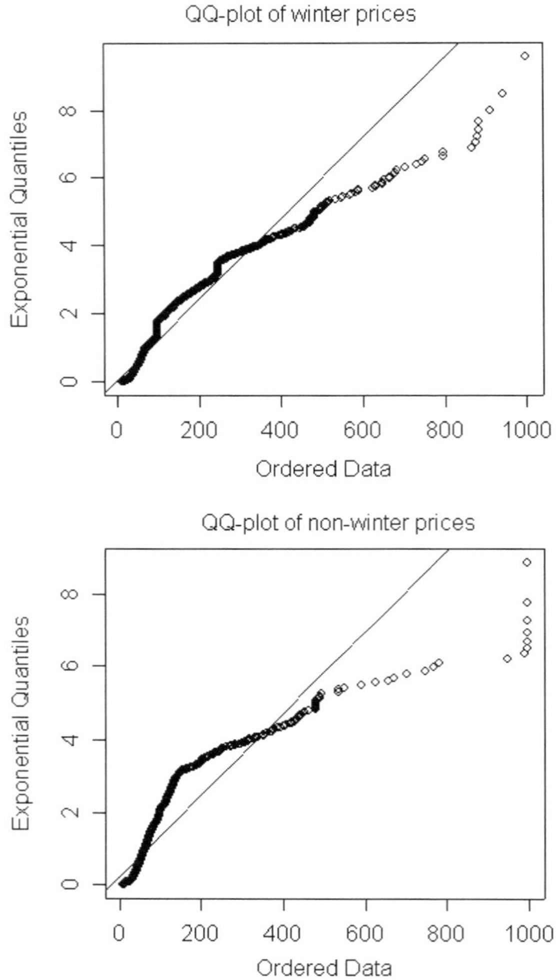

Fig. 2. Exponential QQ-plot of winter and non-winter prices.

3.3. *Maximum likelihood estimation of GEV model*

The key issue of fitting the GEV model for an empirical data is to decide a block size n of maxima for estimating the relative parameters. Recall from the limit law for maxima (the Fisher–Tippett Theorem), the condition holds only if block size $n \to \infty$. Thus, the larger the block size n, the better the fit of GEV model for the data. The problem is that given a set of raw data, the larger the block size n, the less the resulted maxima observations. If one chooses too large a block size n, one will have sparse data for the estimations and gets large standard deviations of estimated parameters.

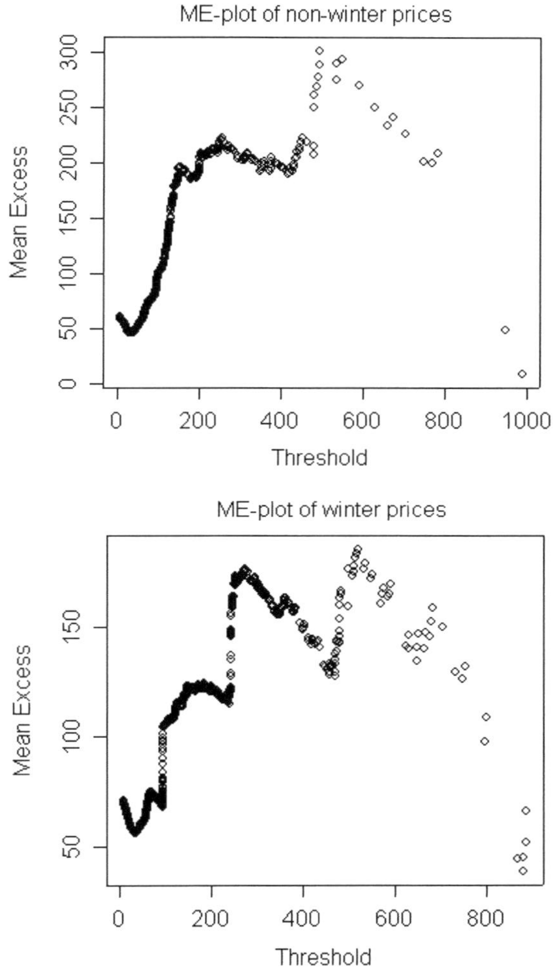

Fig. 3. Sample ME-plot of winter and non-winter data.

In my analysis, since the raw data of prices are ten hourly prices of peak hours, I choose maxima block size from 10, 30, 50, 70, 80, 90, to 110 which is related to 1 day, 3 days, …, to 11 days of peak hours data. The estimation results of parameters and VaR are listed in Tables 2 and 3.

From Table 2, one can see that the estimated value of shape parameter ξ decreases as block size increases. From Fisher–Tippett Theorem, we say that the estimates from large size blocks should be considered correct. As a result, it seems that the estimates from small block sizes tend to exaggerate a fat-tailedness fact and give much larger estimates of ξ values. A small increase in block sizes results in fewer

Table 2. Parameter estimates of GEV model.

Raw data	Block size	Maxima	Estimated parameters & standard deviations					
N	n	m	ξ	s.e. (ξ)	σ	s.e. (σ)	μ	s.e. (μ)
Winter	10	729	0.5712	0.0346	52.3642	2.2207	77.5455	2.1682
$N = 7290$	30	243	0.5870	0.0938	90.0274	7.2798	121.921	7.3232
	50	144	0.4231	0.1120	121.871	11.5224	164.66	12.6746
	70	105	0.2629	0.1322	153.564	16.1165	210.788	19.1002
	80	92	0.1782	0.1312	167.989	17.8041	236.346	21.8923
	90	81	0.1213	0.1248	178.495	18.9851	254.244	24.0494
Non-winter	10	366	0.5267	0.0466	43.6281	2.5015	60.9599	2.5362
$N = 3660$	30	122	0.5990	0.0964	78.9698	8.4532	98.1616	8.1948
	50	74	0.5957	0.1570	102.94	14.8089	133.1727	14.7122
	70	53	0.5262	0.1963	130.142	21.7604	168.7567	22.6411
	80	46	0.4623	0.1872	136.339	22.9293	184.571	24.6125
	110	33	0.2056	0.2038	190.207	32.6987	247.574	40.0149

Table 3. VaR estimates of GEV models.

Raw data	Block size n	Maxima k	Estimated Ξ	VaR(q) estimates $q=0.97$	$q=0.99$	$q=0.999$
Winter	10	729	0.5712	634.21	1229.53	4700.19
$N = 7290$	30	243	0.5870	1127.56	2220.04	8784.13
	50	144	0.4231	1095.77	1851.27	5189.18
	70	105	0.2629	1032.14	1527.22	3160.44
	80	92	0.1782	981.508	1365.18	2453.4
	90	81	0.1213	954.564	1278.23	2108.94
Non-winter	10	366	0.5267	481.857	895.226	3111.09
$N = 3660$	30	122	0.5990	1041.49	2020.92	8206.89
	50	74	0.5957	1313.24	2607.64	10514.18
	70	53	0.5262	1435.71	2665.93	9253.52
	80	46	0.4623	1323	2315.23	7029.84
	110	33	0.2056	1161.75	1647.52	3094.14

observations in maxima datasets. According to asymptotic distribution theory, there is less accuracy in estimation from small samples than from large samples. This is confirmed by the large standard deviations of our parameter estimates.

Substituting estimated parameters into VaR estimation equation VaR $= \mu + \frac{\sigma}{\xi}[(-\ln p)^{-\xi} - 1]$ results in the VaR estimates in Table 3. When block size $n > 10$, a larger estimated shape parameter ξ always relates to a higher estimate value of VaR.

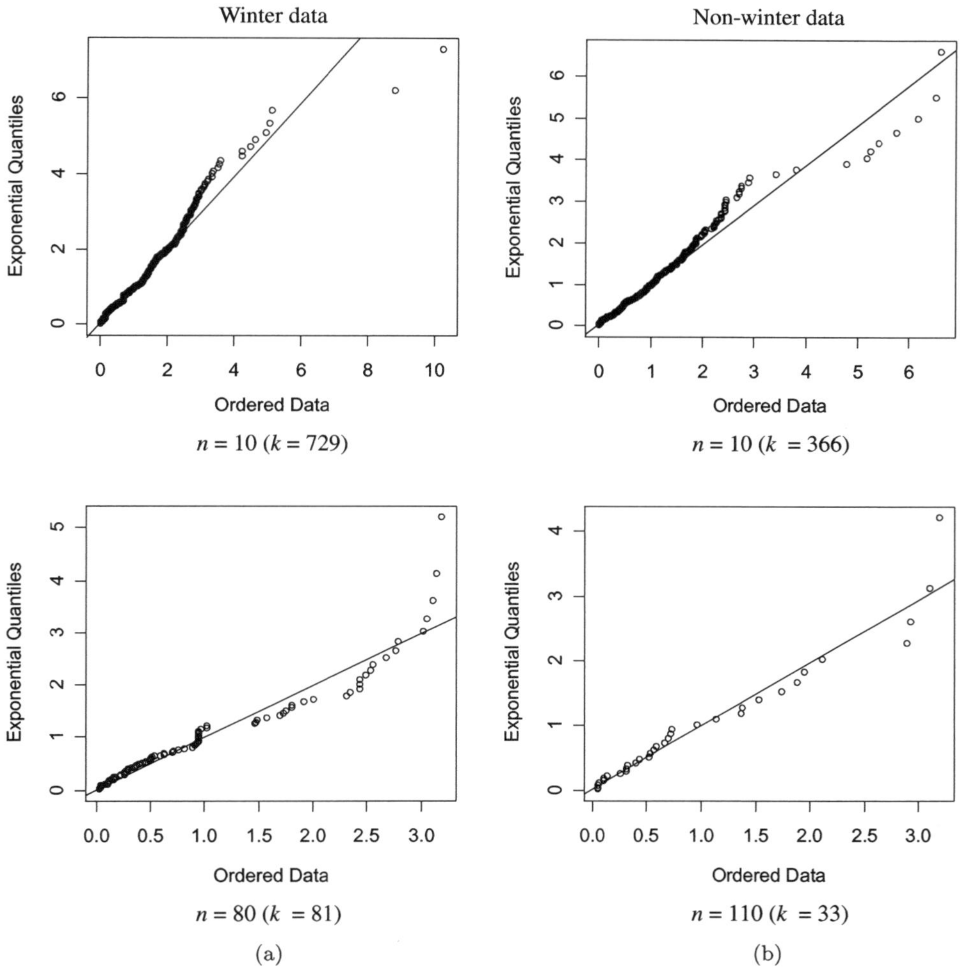

Fig. 4. QQ-plot of residuals.

After estimating parameters by choosing different block sizes, one can check the fitness of the GEV models to the data by residual plots, where the residual is defined as

$$\text{res} = \begin{cases} \left[1 + \frac{\xi}{\sigma}(x - \mu)\right]^{-\frac{1}{\xi}}, & \xi = 0; \\ \exp\left[-\exp\left(-\frac{x-\mu}{\sigma}\right)\right], & \xi \neq 0 \end{cases} \tag{13}$$

The data are converted to unit exponentially distributed residuals under null hypothesis that GEV fits. Figure 4 shows the QQ-plot of residuals with different block sizes for Albert's data. When the block size is $n = 10$, the residual quantiles are not approximately exponential distributions, represented by points not on the straight lines. When $n \geq 80$, the residual quantiles are approximately exponentially distributed with most points on the straight lines, which means that GEV model fits the data well.

3.4. *Maximum likelihood estimations of GPD model*

A similar essential problem of GPD estimation is to choose a suitable value of threshold u, which shows the beginning of a tail distribution converging to GPD. Based on the Pickands–Balkema–de Haan Theorem, a high enough threshold u should be chosen so that the conditional tail distribution fits a GPD model. The dilemma is that a high threshold u ensures a tail distribution as GPD, but leads to less data of exceedances and related high standard errors.

A tool used in threshold determination is the Hill-plot. Hill, B. M proposed an estimator of ξ when $\xi > 0$ [Gencay and Selcuk, 2004]. By ordering the sample data $X_1, \ldots, X_n$ with respect to their values as $X_{1,n} \geq X_{2,n} \geq \cdots \geq X_{n,n}$, the Hill estimator of the shape parameter ξ is

$$\hat{\xi} = \frac{1}{k} \sum_{i=j}^{k} \ln X_{j,n} - \ln X_{k,n}, \tag{14}$$

where $k \to \infty$ is upper-order statistics (the number of exceedances), n is the sample size. Roughly speaking, the higher the value of ξ, the heavier the tail and, thus, the larger the quantile estimates we derive.

In practice, there are two kinds of Hill-plots. A basic Hill-plot is plotted according to the Hill estimator function by fitting GPD models with different thresholds to obtain maximum likelihood estimates of ξ. The estimated shape parameter ξ is plotted on the y-axis. The number of data points exceeding the threshold is plotted on the lower x-axis, and that within the thresholds is plotted on the upper x-axis. This Hill-plot shows a 95% asymptotic confidence interval of the estimation. In general, a threshold is chosen from a part of the plot where the values of shape parameter are stable. Another option of Hill-plot is to use the estimated quantiles as y-axis values, showing different thresholds related to different quantile estimates. Figures 3–6 show the two kinds of the Hill-plots for Alberta's data. The Hill-plots of ξ estimates suggest that for winter data, a threshold is chosen between values around $u = 100$ and $u = 250$, where the estimated ξ is relatively by stable. For non-winter data, the Hill-plot suggests a high threshold from $u = 100$ to $u = 160$.

The Hill-plots of quantile estimates show a stable estimate of quantile (at $p = 0.97$) between $u = 100$ and $u = 250$ for winter data, and between $u = 100$

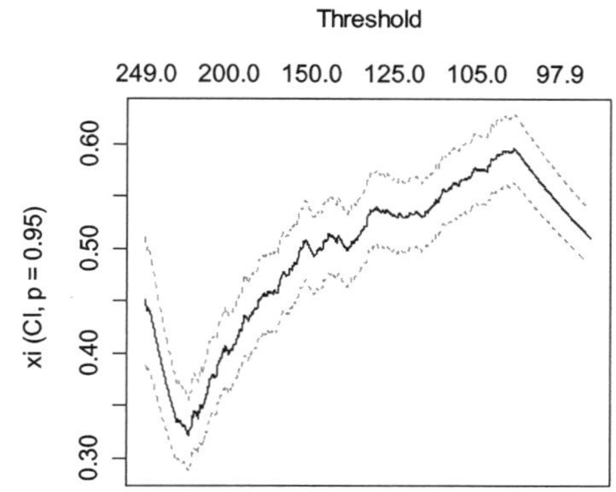

Hill-plot of xi estimates (CI = 0.95)

(a)

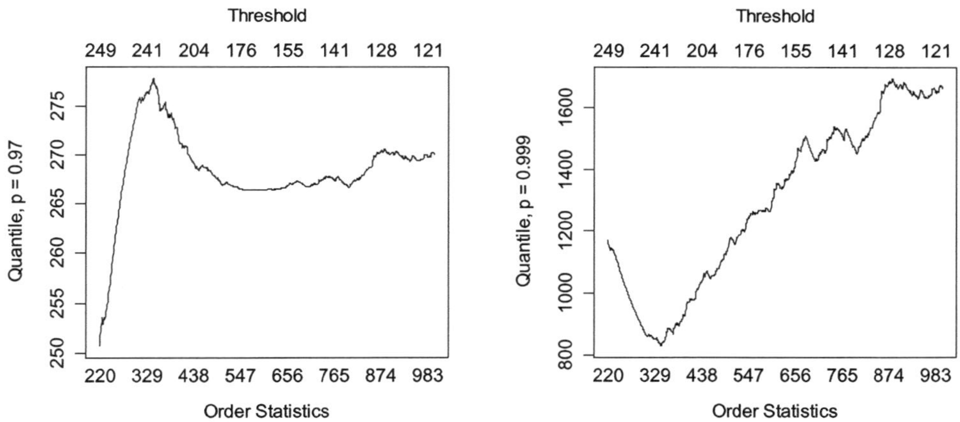

quantile ($p = 0.97$) quantile ($p = 0.999$)

Hill-plot of quantile estimates

(b)

Fig. 5. Hill-plots (winter data).

and $u = 160$ for non-winter data, whereas among the same threshold period, the estimates of quantile (at $p = 0.999$) are not stable, showing more volatility in extreme estimations.

The empirical ML estimates of GPD parameters and relative estimates of VaR and ES for Alberta's data are shown on Tables 4 and 5. One can see from Table 4 that the standard deviations of estimated parameters increase as the threshold quantiles

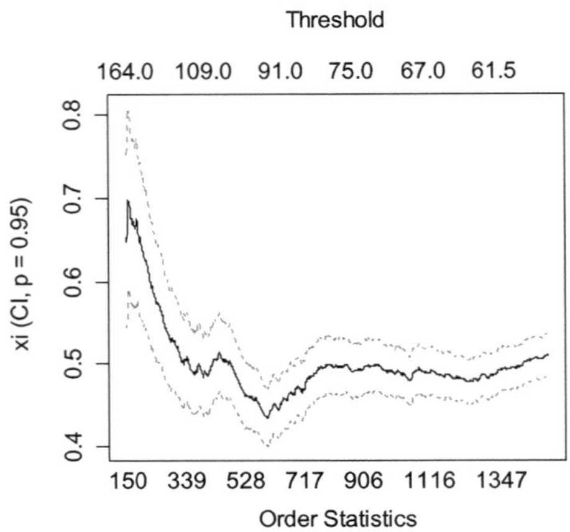

Hill-plot of xi estimates (CI = 0.95)

(a)

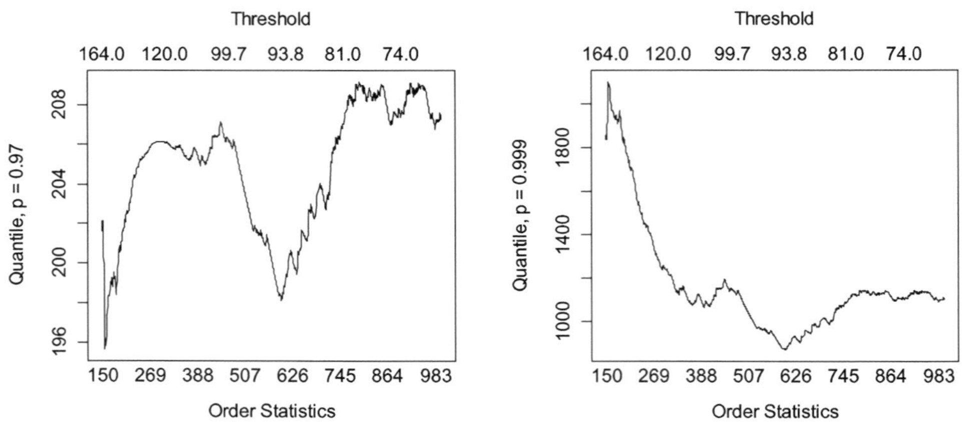

quantile ($p = 0.97$) quantile ($p = 0.999$)

Hill-plot of quantile estimates

(b)

Fig. 6. Hill-plots (non-winter data).

increase. The confidence intervals of VaR and ES estimates in Table 5 are asymmetric with generally a higher upper bound than a lower one.

To see the fitness of a GPD model to empirical data, one can use a plot of excess distribution and QQ-plot of residuals relative to a certain threshold value u. For Alberta's data, the threshold u is chosen at percentile $p = 0.95$ for GPD modeling. Figure 7 shows the plot of excess distribution and the QQ-plot of residuals.

Table 4. Parameter estimates of GPD model.

Raw data		Winter ($N=7290$)			Non-winter ($N=3660$)		
Threshold	p	0.85	0.9	0.95	0.85	0.9	0.95
	u	111.33	145.73	230.16	96	114.02	141.38
Extremes	n	1094	729	365	547	366	183
GPD	ξ	0.1870	0.1377	0.5170	0.7857	0.9322	0.1589
estimates	s.e (ξ)	0.0376	0.0434	0.1202	0.0804	0.1113	0.0997
	β	87.5106	102.3862	66.3815	31.4364	34.5744	150.6797
	s.e. (β)	4.1956	5.8184	7.4150	2.6613	3.9673	18.6269

Table 5. VaR and ES estimates of GPD model.

Raw data			Winter ($N=7290$)			Non-winter ($N=3660$)		
Threshold	p		0.85	0.9	0.95	0.85	0.9	0.95
	u		111.33	145.73	230.16	96	114.02	141.38
Extremes	n		1094	729	365	547	366	183
VaR(q)	$q=0.97$	VaR (q)	275.7236	279.82	269.0882	197.2799	190.8727	221.5587
estimates	CI	upper CI	287.8089	291.9639	275.258	213.8676	206.0949	239.5646
		lower CI	265.2524	270.5211	268.2153	183.7441	178.5305	206.2151
	$q=0.99$	VaR (q)	419.9495	423.1652	397.0555	390.9467	394.2254	417.7387
	CI	upper CI	448.3454	449.2374	425.2012	476.5997	492.8279	468.4331
		lower CI	397.9516	401.0185	373.888	335.2481	334.1847	375.9047
	$q=0.999$	VaR (q)	837.9023	804.1351	1072.995	2100.994	2791.405	958.8986
	CI	upper CI	984.6927	937.067	1499.985	1498.5	NA	1339.638
		lower CI	738.1378	715.2786	835.967	1343.593	NA	785.5563
ES(q)	$q=0.97$	VaR (q)	421.1823	419.9812	448.2352	715.3161	1758.095	415.8845
estimates	CI	upper CI	455.939	450.8721	579.9811	1498.5	1498.5	484.935
		lower CI	397.9516	396.2474	402.7008	456.909	532.315	373.9978
	$q=0.99$	VaR (q)	598.5864	586.2254	713.2293	1619.055	4758.533	649.1536
	CI	upper CI	676.3254	655.1367	1106.787	1498.5	1498.5	834.3869
		lower CI	544.3207	538.8517	582.5228	875.9285	1110.773	561.6198
	$q=0.999$	VaR (q)	1112.686	1028.054	2112.963	NA	NA	1292.623
	CI	upper CI	1406.857	1287.898	1499.985	NA	NA	1498.5
		lower CI	928.799	870.6765	1260.385	NA	NA	965.6855

The plots in Fig. 7 show relatively good fit of GPD models for both winter and non-winter data. As a result, it is prudent to set the high threshold at $p = 0.95$ level. The quantile of the chosen threshold u at high percentile $q = 0.95$ is 230.16 for winter data, and 141.38 for non-winter data. The VaR estimates above the chosen threshold at percentiles $p = 0.97, 0.99, 0.999$ are 269.0882, 397.0555, and 1072.9953 for winter data, and 221.5587, 417.7387, and 958.8986 for non-winter data, respectively. The ES estimates above the chosen threshold at percentiles $p = 0.97, 0.99, 0.999$ are 448.2352, 713.2293, and 2112.963 for winter data,

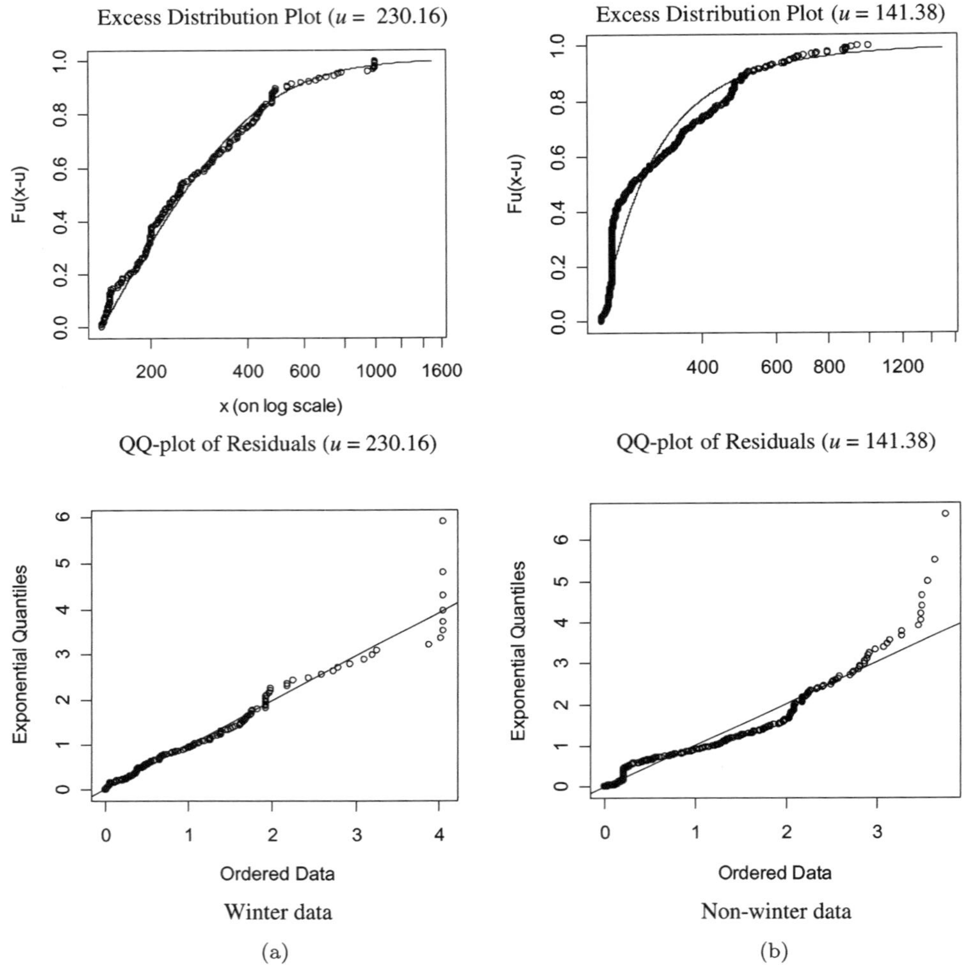

Fig. 7. Plots of GPD model fitness.

and 415.8845, 649.1536, and 1292.6231 for non-winter data, respectively. The confidence intervals of these estimates are displayed in Table 5.

4. Relative Performance of Alternative VaR Models

In this section, we use the estimates from the GEV and GDP models to calculate risk metrics and compare them to those obtained from the standard Normal and HS methods.

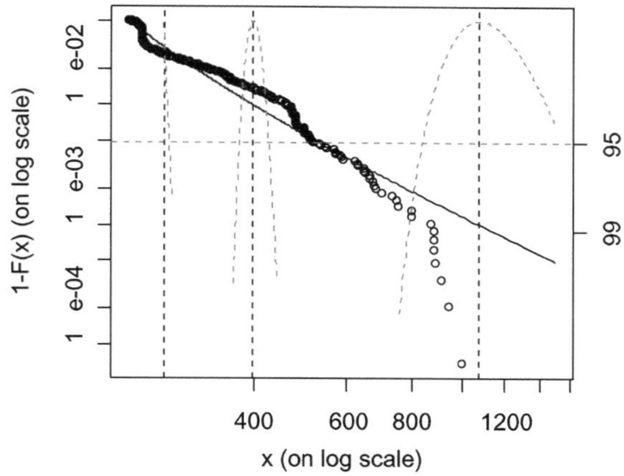

VaR estimates at quantile 0.97, 0.99, and 0.999

(a)

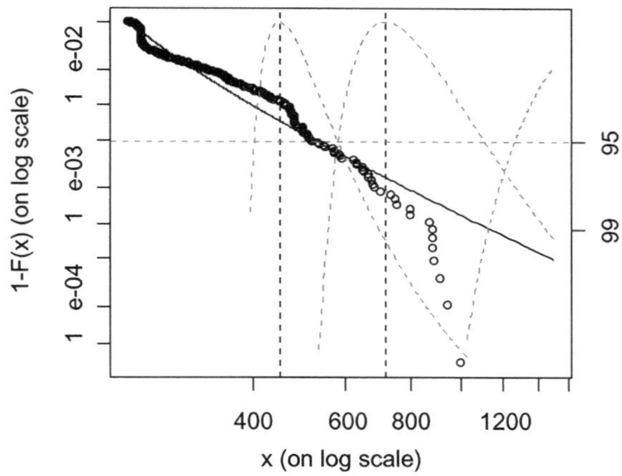

ES estimates at quantile 0.97, 0.99, and 0.999

(b)

Fig. 8. VaR estimate and ES estimate of GPD model (winter data with threshold $u = 230.16$).

4.1. *VaR estimates from different models*

Table 6 shows the estimates of VaR from four different models at high percentiles $q = 0.97, 0.99, 0.999$. The chosen block size of GEV estimation of parameters and VaR is $n = 90$ for winter data, $n = 110$ for non-winter data. The chosen threshold for GPD estimation of parameters and VaR is $q = 0.95$ for both winter and non-winter data. Figures 8–9 plot the VaR and ES estimates for the winter and non-winter data, respectively. In Normal distribution model, there are no parameter estimations, and VaR is calculated from the symmetric distribution with sample mean and standard

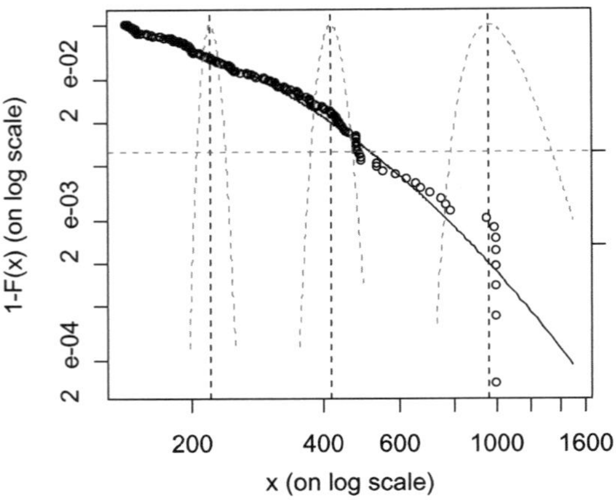

VaR estimates at quantile 0.97, 0.99, and 0.999

(a)

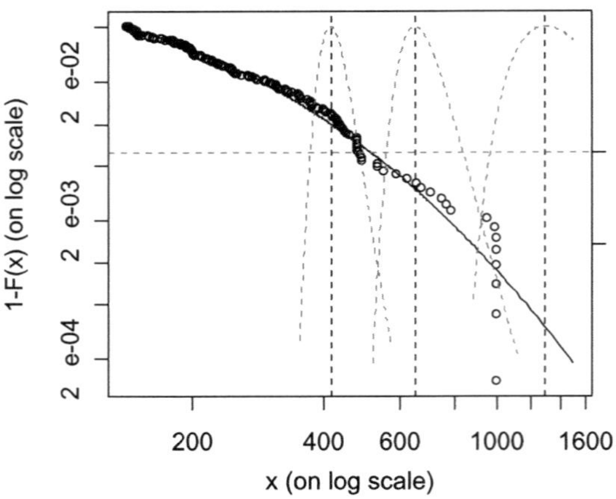

ES estimates at quantile 0.97, 0.99, and 0.999

(b)

Fig. 9. VaR estimate and ES estimate of GPD model (Non-winter data with threshold $u = 141.37$).

deviation. In HS method, with no distribution assumptions and thus no parameter estimations, VaR is simulated from the realized historical data.

It is obvious that different methods give different estimation results. Table 6 shows that the VaR estimates from GEV model are much larger than VaR estimates from other models. When choosing large block size ($n = 80$ for winter data, $n = 110$ for non-winter data) to fit GEV to the standardized maximum distribution, there is a big loss of observations in the dataset. As a result, although the residual plots show good fitness of GEV for the maxima, with few observations of maxima ($k = 81$ for

Table 6. VaR Estimates of Different Models.

Raw data	Model	Block-size n	Maxi k	Thres $q(u)$	Shape ξ	VaR(q) estimates $q=0.97$	$q=0.99$	$q=0.999$
Winter	GEV	90	81		0.12139	954.564	1278.23	2108.94
$N = 7290$	GPD			0.95	0.51709	269.0882	397.0555	1072.995
	Nor					230.2404	256.684	326.4507
	HS					250	457.7096	847.8198
Non-winter	GEV	110	33		0.2057	1161.75	1647.52	3094.14
$N = 3660$	GPD			0.95	0.159	221.5587	417.7387	958.8986
	Nor					214.4083	249.2583	308.8837
	HS					211.925	434.9273	998.9341

winter data, $k = 33$ for non-winter data) the VaR estimates from GEV have large confidence intervals. The EVT estimation method is compared with other traditional methods by GPD model.

Comparing VaR estimates from GPD model and those from Normal distribution model in Table 6, it is clear that at each high percentile $q = 0.97, 0.99, 0.999$, VaR estimates from GPD are larger than from Normal distribution. Comparing VaR estimates from GPD model and those from HS, at $q = 0.97, 0.999$ GPD estimates of VaR are larger than historical estimates, whereas at $q = 0.99$, the historical estimates are larger than GPD estimates. If one believes that the estimates from GPD are closest to the true values, it is said that estimates from Normal distribution model always, and estimates from HS method some times, underestimate the risks of high quantiles, which means underestimating the probability of realization of high quantile values in the right tail.

4.2. *Backtesting process and comparison of models*

Suppose there is a historical series with N observations. To backtest the estimates from risk measurement models, one chooses a subset data size m, where $m \ll N$. The sub dataset is called as a time window of m observations. If one places the first window between the 1st and the mth sub dataset, one can estimate the $(m+1)$th VaR(q) at a high quantile q by this m sub dataset modeling and compare the estimates with the real $(m+1)$th observation value. When moving the window one period ahead from the 2nd to the $(m+2)$th sub dataset, it is called sliding a window. The estimate of the $(m+2)$th VaR(q) is from another m sub dataset modeling and thus has a different result. This time, the comparison is between the estimated $(m+2)$th VaR(q) and the realized $(m+2)$th observation value. Repeating the above steps, one can slide a time window of m observations in a set of historical data with N observations, getting $(N - m)$ estimates of VaR from the backtesting process.

The performance of a risk measurement model is summarized by a violation value (violation number or violation ratio). A violation happens when the realized observation value is greater than the relative estimated VaR (q). By summing all the real violations among $(N - m)$ times of estimations, one gets the violation number of a backtesting process. A violation ratio is the ratio of a violation number divided by the total number of estimations $(N - m)$ during a backtesting process.

To evaluate the performance of a model, a critical value is the "expected violation value" (expected violation number or expected violation ratio). When estimating a VaR at a certain high percentile q, one expects that the realized observation values will have $(1 - q)N$ times or $(1 - q)$ percent of the times higher value than the VaR if the model is correct. In other words, the expected violation number is $(1 - q)N$ and the expected violation ratio is $(1 - q)$. For an example of the violation ratio, if one chooses percentile $q = 0.97, 0.99, 0.999$ for VaR estimations, the expected violation ratios are $(1 - q) = 0.03, 0.01, 0.001$.

The performance of a model is evaluated by comparing the realized violation value with the expected violation value at a given high percentile. If the realized violation number (or ratio) is larger than the expected one, it means that the model consistently underestimates the VaR in the right tail of the underlying distribution. If the realized violation number (or ratio) is less than the expected one, it means that the model consistently overestimates the VaR in the right tail of the underlying distribution. As a result, if all models underestimate the VaR, the model with least underestimation is the most accurate one. If all models overestimation the VaR, the model with least overestimation is the most accurate one. If some models overestimate the VaR and other models underestimate the VaR, one compares the absolute level of the overestimations and underestimations and the model with least overestimation (or underestimation) is the most accurate one.

4.3. *Comparisons of the backtesting results*

In the backtesting process, two different sizes of sliding windows are chosen for both winter and non-winter datasets. One window size is 1,000, which means using a dataset with 100 days' peak hour prices to predict the 1,001th peak hour's price. The other window size is 1,500, which means using a dataset with 150 days' peak hour prices to predict the 1,501th peak hour's price.

These window sizes are chosen not to be too small, such that a high percentile estimate of VaR can be tested. For example, when estimating VaR at percentile $q = 0.97, 0.99, 0.999$ with window size 1,000 and 1,500, the expected violation

Table 7. Violation numbers from different models.

		October–May (winter)				June–September (non-winter)			
Season			**Error**		**Error**		**Error**		**Error**
Data	N	7290		7290		3660		3660	
Window	m	1000		1500		1000		1500	
Estimations	$(N-m)$	6290		5790		2660		2160	
$p=0.97$	Exp	189	0	174	0	80	0	65	0
	GPD	191	2	180	6	99	19	76	11
	Nor	221	32	210	36	99	19	73	8
	HS	198	9	190	16	102	22	82	17
$p=0.99$	Exp	63	0	58	0	27	0	22	0
	GPD	83	20	66	8	50	23	12	−10
	Nor	179	116	165	107	87	60	55	33
	HS	76	13	65	7	50	23	11	−11
$p=0.999$	Exp	6.3	0	5.8	0	2.7	0	2.2	0
	GPD	8	1.7	9	3.2	4	1.3	1	−1.2
	Nor	129	122.7	123	117.2	64	61.3	39	36.8
	HS	15	8.7	11	5.2	7	4.3	0	−2.2

number is 30, 10, and 1, respectively, for window size 1,000, and 45, 15, and 1 (or 2), respectively, for window size 1,500. To test the estimation results at high percentile $q = 0.999$, a window size of least 1,000 is necessary.

On the other hand, the window size is chosen not to be too large, such that enough times of estimation are included in a backtesting process. For example, for the non-winter dataset with 3,660 observations, when choosing window size 1,000 and 1,500, one will backtest the estimation 2,660, 2,160 times, respectively, during the testing process.

The backtesting results for GPD model, Normal distribution model and HS method are shown in Tables 7 and 8 by violation numbers and violation ratios, respectively. From Table 7, at percentile $q = 0.97$, all the differences between real and expected violation numbers from three different models are positive, which means that all models consistently underestimate the risks. At percentile $q = 0.99$, two of the differences of real and expected violation numbers from GPD model and HS are negative in the backtesting process for non-winter data with window size 1,500, which means that these two models consistently overestimate the risks. At percentile $q = 0.999$, backtesting process for non-winter data with window size 1,500 also show the overestimations of VaR from GPD and historical models. Despite the above exceptions, all the other testing processes at quantile 0.99 and 0.999 show positive differences of real and expected violations.

Table 8. Violation ratios.

		October–May (winter)				June–September (non-winter)			
Season			**Error**		**Error**		**Error**		**Error**
Data	N	7290		7290		3660		3660	
Window	m	1000		1500		1000		1500	
Estimates	n	6290		5790		2660		2160	
$p = 0.97$	Exp	0.0300	0	0.0300	0	0.0300	0	0.0300	0
	GPD	0.0304	0.0004	0.0311	0.0011	0.0372	0.0072	0.0352	0.0052
	Nor	0.0351	0.0051	0.0363	0.0063	0.0372	0.0072	0.0338	0.0038
	HS	0.0315	0.0015	0.0328	0.0028	0.0383	0.0083	0.0380	0.0080
$p = 0.99$	Exp	0.0100	0.0000	0.0100	0.0000	0.0100	0.0000	0.0100	0.0000
	GPD	0.0132	0.0032	0.0114	0.0014	0.0188	0.0088	0.0056	−0.0044
	Nor	0.0285	0.0185	0.0285	0.0185	0.0327	0.0227	0.0255	0.0155
	HS	0.0121	0.0021	0.0112	0.0012	0.0188	0.0088	0.0051	−0.0049
$p = 0.999$	Exp	0.0010	0.0000	0.0010	0.0000	0.0010	0.0000	0.0010	0.0000
	GPD	0.0013	0.0003	0.0016	0.0006	0.0015	0.0005	0.0005	−0.0005
	Nor	0.0205	0.0195	0.0212	0.0202	0.0241	0.0231	0.0181	0.0171
	HS	0.0024	0.0014	0.0019	0.0009	0.0026	0.0016	0.0000	−0.0010

In Table 7, the expected violation number for winter data at window size 1,000 test is 189, while the real violation number from GPD estimation is 191, from Normal distribution estimation is 221, and from HS estimation is 198. The least difference between the real violation number and the expected one is 2 from GPD estimation. Thus the conclusion from this backtesting process is that GPD is the most accurate model for VaR estimation at high percentile $p = 0.97$. The same conclusion can be derived from winter data with test window size 1,500 and from non-winter data with test window size 1,000. The exception at $p = 0.97$ estimation is from non-winter data with test window size 1,500. Here, the least violation number 8 is from normal distribution model. In summary, for VaR estimations at high percentile $p = 0.97$, four backtesting processes show that two most accurate results come from GPD model, one from Normal distribution model, and one from both GPD and Normal distribution models.

Similarly, for VaR estimations at percentile $q = 0.99$, four backtesting processes show one of the most accurate results is from the GPD model, two from the HS, and one from both the GPD model and the HS models. For VaR estimations at quantile $q = 0.999$, four backtesting processes show that all the most accurate results are from the GPD models.

The overall conclusion from Table 8 is that compared with other two models, GPD is the most accurate model for extreme value estimations, such as VaRs at extreme high percentile $q = 0.999$. The relative performance of Normal distribution is poor at any high percentile level in the tail of underlying distributions (in our analysis a tail begins from $q = 0.95$). The relative performance of HS is better than that of the Normal distribution, and sometimes even better than GPD model at a modest high quantile ($q = 0.99$). This is reasonable since a Normal distribution is not suitable for asymmetric and fat-tailed distributions, and a HS captures modest high values but not extreme values, and a GPD model fits the tail parts of any underlying distribution.

5. Conclusion

This chapter has applied statistical models that explicitly account for the heavy tails and asymmetries present in energy prices. In the specific context, we have applied and evaluated EVT and VaR analysis as tools to manage electricity price risk in a deregulated market. The empirical application to the Alberta power market has shown that EVT — in particular the generalized Pareto distribution — can provide more accurate estimates of the probability of an extreme price deviation and VaR than the alternative methods based on HS and the Normal distribution. EVT, combined with VaR analysis, appears to be a useful tool that can be implemented in practice to manage electricity price risk. Hazards await the applied statistician who fails to account for heavy tails and skewness in energy prices.

References

Artzer, P., Delbaen, F., Eber, J. M. and Heath, D. (1997). Coherent measure of risk. *Mathematical Finance* **3**, 203–228.

Balkema, A. A. and de Haan, L. (1974). Residual lifetime at a great age. *Annals of Probability* **2**, 792–804.

Dowd, K. (1998). *Beyond Value at Risk: The New Science of Risk Management*. (Wiley Series in Financial Engineering, New York).

Embrechts, P., Kluppelberg, C. and Mikosch, T. (1997). *Modeling Extremal Events*. (Springer-Verlag, Berlin).

Gencay, R. and Selcuk, F. (2004). Extreme value theory and value-at-risk: Relative performance in emerging markets. *International Journal of Forecasting* **20**, 287–303.

McNeil, A. (1997). Estimating the tails of loss severity distributions using extreme value theory. *ASTIN Bulletin* **27**, 117–137.

Paraschiv, F., Hadzi-Mishev, R. and Keles, D. (2016). Extreme value theory for heavy tails in electricity prices. *Journal of Energy Markets* **9** (2), 21–50.

Pickands, J. (1975). Statistical inference using extreme order statistics. *Annals of Statistics* **3**, 119–131.

Reiss, R. D. and Thomas, M. (1997). *Statistical Analysis of Extreme Values*. (Birkhauser, Berlin).

Rocco, M. (2014). Extreme value theory in finance: A survey. *Journal of Economic Surveys* **28** (1), 82–108.

Chapter 9

Jumps in Energy Commodity Markets

Neil A. Wilmot*,‡ and Charles F. Mason†,§

**Department of Economics, University of Minnesota Duluth, 1318 Kirby Drive, Duluth MN 55812, USA*

†H.A. True Chair in Petroleum and Natural Gas Economics, Department of Economics, and Associate Dean, College of Business, University of Wyoming, 1000 E. University Ave., Laramie, WY 82071, USA

‡nwilmot@d.umn.edu

§bambuzlr@uwyo.edu

This chapter is concerned with the statistical behavior of energy commodity prices. A particularly salient feature of many commodity markets is the unexpectedly rapid changes — or jumps — that result from the arrival of new information. Such a process would contradict the view that energy commodity prices follow a geometric Brownian motion (GBM) process (i.e. log returns are normally distributed). That is, assuming a GBM process for the data-generating mechanism would be insufficient to capture the true dynamics of energy commodity markets. The discontinuous arrival of information necessitates a stochastic process that incorporates this feature, and as such, Jump processes have become an important tool in the analysis of energy markets. While such models allow for multiple jumps in a period, the jump intensity is assumed to be constant over time — a questionable assumption given the dynamics of such energy markets. The autoregressive conditional jump intensity (ARJI) model of Chan and Maheu [2002], which allows for a time-varying jump intensity, is applied to important energy commodity markets. The results indicate the importance of incorporating time-varying jump intensities in energy markets.

Keywords: Energy commodity prices; jump diffusion; ARJI; GARCH.

1. Introduction

A central characteristic of many energy commodity prices is the intrinsic stochastic element driving the pricing process. While understanding this underlying stochastic process is of clear importance in any commodity market, it has particular heft for energy commodities, due to their essential role in the world economy. As the literature on modeling energy markets developed, it was commonly assumed prices follow a continuous stochastic process [Schwartz, 1997; Baker *et al.*, 1998; Pindyck, 1999; Sadorsky, 1999; Schwartz and Smith, 2000]. Additionally, several authors have suggested the inclusion of a mean-reverting element in the stochastic process [Pindyck, 1999; Abadie and Chamorro, 2009]. While the assumption of a continuous process was convenient — it provided researchers with tractable models that facilitated closed form solutions — the models typically precluded the fat tails that are often observed in price returns distributions. This is a worrisome implication, as financial data often exhibits fat tails; it also precludes discontinuous movements in prices [Cont and Tankov, 2004]. This latter feature is of particular potential importance for energy markets as they are frequently hit with unexpected news. Examples include natural disasters (hurricanes, earthquakes), geopolitical developments (nationalization, strikes) strategic actions (OPEC), and other unforeseen events (spills, pipeline disruptions). These sorts of effects can lead to unexpectedly large changes in oil prices, either upwards or downwards.

Recent research has examined the relevance of discontinuities for modeling oil prices with conflicting results. Broadly speaking, this emerging literature recognizes that the arrival of new information can lead to unexpectedly rapid changes, also known as "jumps", in spot prices [Askari and Krichene, 2008; Benth *et al.*, 2008; Carmona and Ludvoski, 2010; Chen and Forsyth, 2007; Lee *et al.*, 2010; Mason and Wilmot, 2014; Postali and Picchetti, 2006; Thompson *et al.*, 2009; Wilmot and Mason, 2013; Wilmot, 2016]. Alternatively, one might argue that GBM reasonably describes crude oil and natural gas markets [Postali and Picchetti, 2006; Geman, 2005]. Either way, the implication is that the presumption of normally distributed log-returns may be suspected. In particular, the prospect for abnormally fat tails becomes important.

In this chapter, we discuss the econometric modeling of three dominant US energy commodity markets — crude oil, natural gas and coal. We propose modeling the dynamics of these energy futures markets using an autoregressive conditional jump intensity diffusion processes, which incorporates time-varying volatility through a generalized conditional heteroscedastic autoregressive processes. Because the fat-tailed result we alluded to above may be driven by the sort of volatility clustering associated with the time-varying volatility in commodity prices [Pindyck, 2004], a continuous model utilizing the GARCH framework is investigated. By allowing for the potential interaction of the GARCH and jump diffusion models, we then have three potential processes: continuous diffusion with GARCH, constant jump diffusion with GARCH and time-varying jump diffusion with GARCH. Maximum likelihood methods are used to estimate the models, which allow for direct tests among the nested models. In general, our findings indicate that allowing for jumps yields a statistically important improvement in explanatory power. But allowing for both time-varying jump intensity and variance (ARJI) improves the fit for futures prices.

2. Existing Literature

Initially research on the incorporation of jumps into a model of returns was conducted by Press [1967] and Merton [1976]. The empirical importance of jumps has been documented for oil [Askari and Krichene, 2008; Postali and Picchetti, 2006; Wilmot and Mason, 2013], spot prices of carbon permits in the European Union trading market [Chevallier and Sévi, 2014], and electricity markets [Benth *et al.*, 2008; Huisman and Mahieu, 2003]. Indeed, Huisman and Mahieu [2003] argue that daily jumps in electricity prices on the order of 30% are not uncommon. There have, however, been relatively few such analyses of natural gas prices.

Much existing work analyzing natural gas markets focuses on mean reversion or volatility concerns. For example, Mu [2007] analyzes the dual roles of weather and storage in a model of natural gas prices, explicitly allowing for a GARCH process. He includes weather via a seasonal dummy variable, and incorporates weekly storage data. Pindyck [2004] specifically studies volatility in natural gas and crude oil price returns. Using daily data, he models these price returns with a GARCH process. Shaffie and Topal [2010] review price modeling techniques that include both GBM and mean reversion, while utilizing a binary method of introducing discontinuities (jump and dips) into the process; they conclude that empirical models should include a diffusion component, mean reversion and a jump diffusion component. Asche *et al.* [2006] and Panagiotidis and Rutledge [2007] analyze UK natural gas prices, specifically investigating the link to European crude prices, and the role played by the introduction of a pipeline in 1998 that connects the UK and European gas markets. While this introduction led to a dramatic increase in UK gas prices, Panagiotidis and Rutledge [2007] argue that it did not alter the underlying time series relation between oil and gas prices.

Some recent empirical analyses of natural gas prices allow for jumps [Benth *et al.*, 2008; Thompson *et al.*, 2009]. Benth *et al.* [2008] apply a model including Lévy jumps to daily price data between 2 February 2001 and 24 October 2006. Confronted with some missing observations, they use synthetic data to fill these gaps. Their approach to modeling jumps requires an *ex-ante* definition of a jump; they arbitrarily define a jump as an observation that falls outside of two standard deviations from the mean. After identifying these outliers, they extract them from the data, estimate the mean process over the remaining data, and then reinsert the outliers. Thompson *et al.* [2009] investigate price jumps in Henry Hub natural gas prices using a Poisson process, over the periods 1995–1999 and 2000–2006. They observe "high price spikes far outside normal seasonal equilibrium levels" (p. 227), and argue that some price spikes are "enormous" (p. 229). Similarly, Chen and Forsyth [2010, p. 359] note it "is not uncommon to see spot gas price jumps" and that "spot prices can jump by as much as 20% in a single day." These authors model price jumps using a Poisson process. In light of the evolution of natural gas markets in the latter part of the 20th century, owing to the emerging deregulated markets, the data from the 1990s is unlikely to be the representative of trends that have emerged in this century. In particular, Brown and Yücel [2008, p. 48] argue that there has been a fundamental change in the relationship between oil and gas prices after 2000. And while the data from 2000–2006 is reflective of emerging technological trends, it predates the major burst in gas production that followed the widespread application of fracking. The importance of allowing for jumps has been documented in models that investigate the incentives to hold stockpiles [Chen and Forsyth, 2007, 2010; Thompson *et al.*, 2009]. These papers include storage levels as a state variable in numerical analyses of stochastic control problems. An alternative approach to allowing for large discrete changes in prices is to use a regime switching model. Papers that have adopted such a framework typically use a Markov switching model, wherein there are small finite number of states (often two), and where the probability of moving from one state to another becomes a focus of the investigation. Chen and Forsyth [2010] use a regime switching model in their investigation of optimal storage, and Chen and Forsyth [2007] employ such an approach to analyze Henry Hub NYMEX futures prices between February 2003 and July 2007. Their results indicate 22 switches during this period, and exhibit long periods of non-switching. While these authors provide a thorough analysis of the switching model, they also note that "[a]n obvious improvement would be to include price jumps within each regime" (p. 174).

Like Thompson *et al.* [2009], we approach the empirical exercise by letting the data determine what is a jump, and we use a Poisson process to model jumps. We also investigate more recent data, considering a time period that includes the widespread adoption of fracking in the US.

3. Jump Model for Energy Commodity Returns

To allow for the discontinuous nature of energy commodity returns, a model of conditional jump dynamics is introduced. The method of Chan and Maheu [2002] allows the jump intensity to follow an endogenous autoregressive process. Additionally, the inclusion of a generalized autoregressive conditional heteroskedastic (GARCH) model is assumed for the volatility of energy commodity returns. GARCH models have been used to capture the well-documented time-varying volatility observed in resource markets for many years [Pindyck, 2004].

Consider the following jump model for energy commodity returns:

$$r_t = \mu + \sum_{i=1}^{l} \phi_i r_{t-i} + \sqrt{h_t} z_t + \sum_{k=1}^{n_t} Y_{t,k}, \tag{1}$$

where $z_t \sim NID(0, 1)$ and h_t follows a GARCH(p, q) process [Bollerslev, 1986], that is

$$h_t = \omega + \sum_{i=1}^{q} \alpha_i \epsilon_{t-i}^2 + \sum_{i=1}^{p} \beta_i h_{t-i}. \tag{2}$$

As Chan and Maheu [2002] note the specification of $\epsilon_t = r_t - \mu - \sum_{j=1}^{1} \phi_i r_t$ allows the jump to propagate, affecting future volatility through the GARCH process. The information set is defined as $\Phi_{t-1} = \{r_{t-1}, \ldots, r_1\}$, while the conditional jump size, $Y_{t,k}$ in (1) is assumed to be independent and normally distributed with mean θ and variance δ^2.

A discrete counting process, n_t describes the number of jumps that arrive between $t - 1$ and t, which follows the Poisson distribution with parameter $\lambda_t > 0$, and the density

$$P(n_t = j|\Phi_{t-1}) = \frac{\exp(-\lambda_t)\lambda_t^j}{j!} \quad \text{and} \quad j = 0, 1, 2, \ldots. \tag{3}$$

Specifically, we note the fact that the jump-intensity, λ_t is time-varying in the ARJI model. By imposing the restriction ($\lambda_t = \lambda$) the model nests several mixed jump models that have been applied in energy commodity research [Wilmot and Mason, 2013; Mason and Wilmot, 2014; Askari and Krichene, 2008]. In this current framework of the time-varying jump-intensity model, λ_t is assumed to follow an autoregressive process

$$\lambda_t = \lambda_0 + \sum_{i=1}^{\nu} \rho_i \lambda_{t-i} + \sum_{i=1}^{\kappa} \gamma_i \xi_{t-i}. \quad (4)$$

The conditional jump intensity is forecasted by past lags of the conditional jump intensity and past lags of ξ_t. Here, ξ_{t-i} measures the shock to the jump intensity parameter from the unexpected number of jumps in the preceding κ periods. This shock ξ_t is calculated as

$$\begin{aligned}\xi_{t-1} &\equiv E[n_{t-1}|\Phi_{t-i}] - \lambda_{t-i} \\ &= \sum_{j=0}^{\infty} jP[n_{t-1} = j|\Phi_{t-i}] - \lambda_{t-i}.\end{aligned} \quad (5)$$

Given that j jumps occur, $f(r_t|n_t = j)$ denotes the conditional density of returns. After observing r_t and using Bayes rule, the *ex-post* probability of the occurrence of j jumps at time t can be written as

$$P(n_t = j|\Phi_t) = \frac{f(r_t|n_t = j, \Phi_{t-1})P(n_t = j|\Phi_{t-1})}{P(r_t|\Phi_{t-1})}, \quad (6)$$

where $j = 0, 1, 2, \ldots$ and $P(n_t = j|\Phi_t)$ is specified in Eq. (2). The probability of jump occurrence plays an important role in the volatility model, entering in Eq. (5) and can be used for inference purposes. The filter (6) can be used to assess the probability that at least one jump occurred, $1 - P(n_t = 0|\Phi_t)$.

By integrating out the discrete-valued variable n_t and governing the number of jumps, the conditional density of returns (r_t) is

$$P(r_t|\Phi_{t-1}) = \sum_{j=0}^{\infty} f(r_t|n_t = j, \Phi_{t-1})P(n_t = j|\Phi_{t-1}). \quad (7)$$

The distribution of returns, conditional on j jumps is

$$f(r_t|n_t = j, \Phi_{t-1}) = \frac{e^{-\left[(r_t - \mu - \sum_{i=1}^{j} \phi_i r_{t-i} - \delta_t j)^2)/(2(h_t + j\delta_t^2)\right]}}{\sqrt{2\pi(h_t + j\delta_t^2)}}. \quad (8)$$

While Eq. (7) involves an infinite sum over the possible number of jumps n_t, in practice the maximum number of jumps is truncated to a large value τ such that the probability of τ or more jumps is zero. Given the sample size, T, the log-likelihood function is a sum of the conditional densities:

$$L(\psi) = \sum_{t=1}^{T} \ln f(r_t|\Phi_{t-1}; \psi), \tag{9}$$

where ψ represents the set of all parameters to be estimated.

Different models will be compared within this framework using the log-likelihood statistic $\mathrm{LR} = 2\ln[L(\psi^*; r) - L(\hat{\psi}; r)]$, where ψ^* represents the unrestricted parameter vector estimate and $\hat{\psi}$ represents the estimated parameter vector under a particular list of m restrictions. If the parameter vector is invalid, LR will be distributed as a Chi-squared random variable with m degrees of freedom.

4. Data

The data consist of daily energy commodity futures prices obtained from the Energy Information Administration (EIA). Three energy commodity series are examined: crude oil (West Texas Intermediate), natural gas (Henry Hub), and coal (Eastern Rail).[1] For each of these time series, the price returns are calculated as

$$r_t = 100[\ln(P_t/P_{t-1})], \tag{10}$$

where P_t is the closing price on day t. The time period studied and summary statistics for the relative price returns of each of the time series are given in Table 1; in particular we list the first four moments (mean, variance, skewness and kurtosis). While each series begins at different points of time, there is significant overlap since 2009. In Fig. 1, we plot the log returns for the three major energy resources — oil, natural gas and coal — for the period, January 2005 to January 2017.

Each series displays a substantial amount of variation; there is also evidence of asymmetry in the distribution, as displayed by the presence of skewness. Each series also displays evidence of leptokurtosis or "fat tails" by the large value for kurtosis. We also report the Anderson–Darling test, which measures the departure from normality. For all three returns series, the test rejects the null hypothesis of a normally distributed random variable. These features are corroborated by Fig. 2, which shows the "quantile–quantile" plots for the three series. Such plots compare the quantiles of the empirical distribution (measured on the y-axis) against the quantiles of a theoretical distribution (measured on the x-axis). If the empirical distribution is close to a normal distribution, the relation will be well described by

[1] Eastern rail coal was chosen rather than Appalachian since the latter NYMEX series has since ended.

Table 1. Summary statistics, daily energy commodity price returns.

	Crude oil	**Natural gas**	**Coal**
A. Sample Range			
Start	05 April 1983	14 January 1994	01 July 2009
End	08 August 2017	07 August 2017	07 August 2017
B. Summary Statistics			
Mean	0.006	0.004	0.007
Median	0.036	−0.016	0.000
Min	−40.048	−37.575	−18.516
Max	16.410	32.435	17.869
Std. Deviation	2.388	3.558	1.390
Variance	5.703	12.661	1.931
Coeff. of Variation	401.1	834.7	193.8
Skewness	−0.713	0.230	0.594
Kurtosis[a]	14.326	6.95	58.19
Anderson–Darling test	117.2	44.2	240.1
p-value	<0.005	<0.005	<0.005
Observations	8615	5905	2040
C. Unit Root test			
DF-GLS test[b]	−9.010	−4.586	−7.824

[a]The measure of kurtosis presented is commonly referred to as excess kurtosis.
[b]The 1% critical value = −3.480.

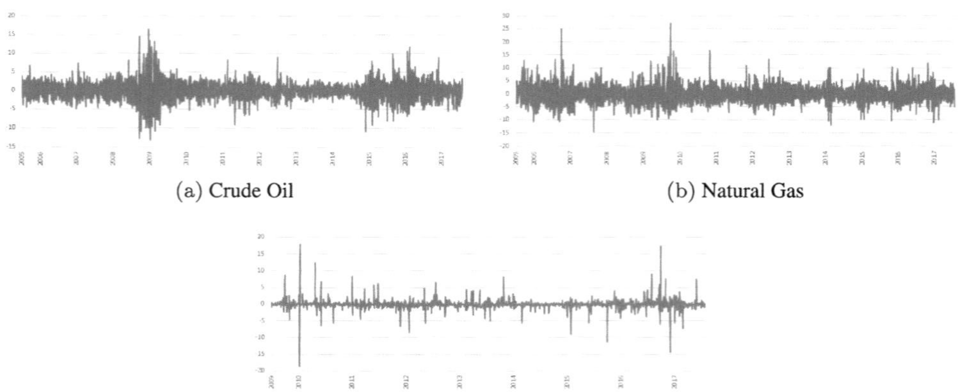

(a) Crude Oil (b) Natural Gas

(c) Coal

Fig. 1. Log price returns for three key energy resources.

a straight line. Alternatively, if — as in this case — there are significant departures from a linear relation, then the data is not well described by a normal distribution. In particular, we note the departures from a linear relation in the tails indicate significant leptokurtosis.

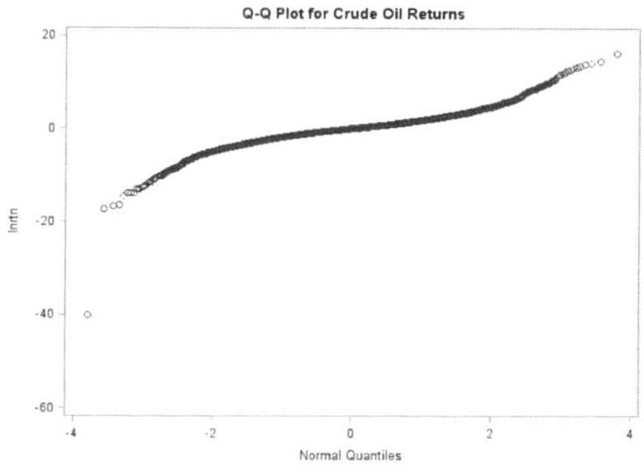

(a) Crude Oil

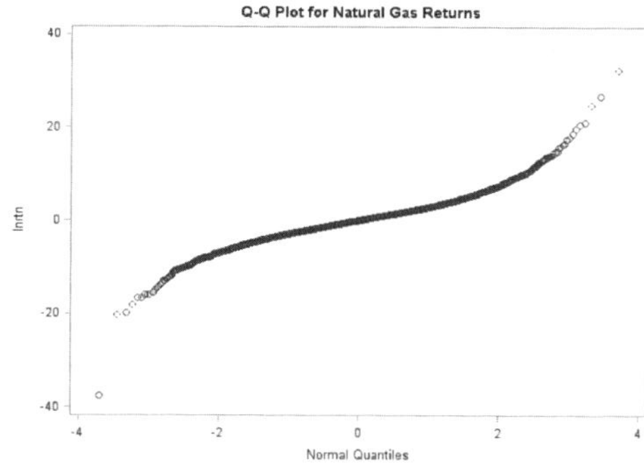

(b) Natural Gas

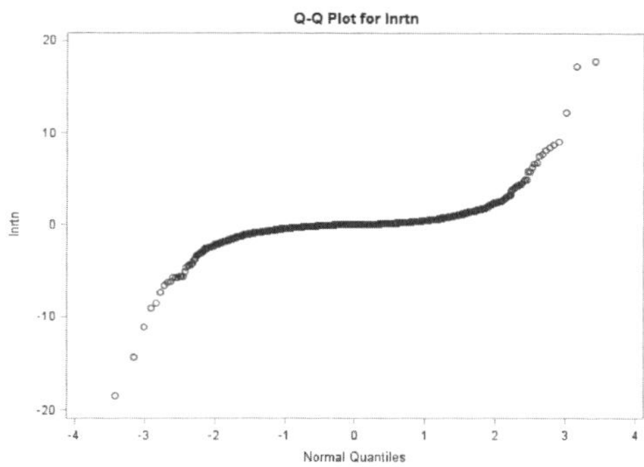

(c) Coal

Fig. 2. QQ plot of returns.

The final section, Part C, in Table 1 displays the results of the DF-GLS test developed by Elliot *et al.* [1996]. The results indicate that all three energy commodity price return series are stationary.[2]

5. Estimation Results

5.1. *Maximum likelihood estimation*

Estimation of the model was undertaken using the full sample for each energy commodity. For all models, $\tau = 20$ was selected as the truncation point for the distribution determining the number of jumps. For expositional simplicity, we assume a GARCH(1,1) process, while the number of lagged returns included in

[2]Results of the DF-GLS unit root test on the energy commodity prices (or levels) indicate the series are non-stationary, as one would expect. Results are excluded for brevity.

Table 2. Jump Model Estimation, Daily Futures Price Returns.

	Crude oil			Natural gas			Coal		
	GARCH	Constant	ARJI	GARCH	Constant	ARJI	GARCH	Constant	ARJI
μ	0.009	0.025	0.025	0.034	−0.066*	−0.056	−0.042	−0.003	−0.003
ω	0.014***	0.004**	0.005**	0.235***	0.190***	0.214***	0.533***	0.024***	0.025***
α	0.084***	0.061***	0.052***	0.090***	0.060***	0.014***	0.204***	0.267***	0.238***
β	0.920***	0.928***	0.936***	0.895***	0.906***	0.934***	0.564***	0.038*	0.031*
ζ_0	—	3.995***	3.759***	—	6.602***	3.742***	—	1.903***	1.843***
η_0	—	−0.541**	−0.450**	—	2.263***	1.84	—	0.028	0.026
λ_0	—	0.059***	0.030***	—	0.049***	0.011***	—	0.292***	0.004**
ρ	—	—	0.624***	—	—	0.976***	—	—	0.987***
γ	—	—	0.359***	—	—	0.345***	—	—	0.026***
Q^2	—	20.97	15.64	—	31.73	42.46	—	34.73	30.49
		[0.138]	[.406]	—	[.007]	[0.000]	—	[.002]	[.010]
Q_{ξ_t}	—	21.58	11.78	—	50.72	033.43		51.57	30.34
		[0.119]	[0.700]		[0.000]	[0.004]		[0.000]	[0.010]
LLF	−18084	−17942	−15343	−17928	−15175	−15151	−3397	−1958	−1946

Note: * Represents statistical significance at the 10% level, ** at the 5% level and *** at the 1% level. The p-values are presented in the brackets.

Eq. (1) is assumed to be zero, $\phi_i = 0, \forall\, i$. Table 2 presents the results of three models: a GARCH(1,1) model without jumps, a GARCH-constant jump intensity model and the autoregressive conditional jump intensity (ARJI) model. The GARCH(1,1) model provides variance parameter estimates (α, β) that are statistically significant. When examining the crude oil returns, we note the sum $\alpha + \beta$ is greater than one, suggesting a stationary GARCH model may not be appropriate. As the addition of jumps to the model causes the sum to be less than one, we perceive this to be evidence of the inadequacy of a GARCH model, especially when combined with the LR test results below. Estimates for the constant jump intensity model, $\lambda_t = \lambda$, provide evidence of the existence of jumps. Across all three energy commodity price series, the jump intensity parameter is statistically significant; the results for coal ($\lambda = 0.292$) is markedly larger than for either crude oil ($\lambda = 0.059$) or natural gas ($\lambda = 0.049$). The mean jump size θ is negative and significant for crude oil, while it is positive and significant for natural gas returns. Similarly, the variance of the jump distributions δ is consistently significant, with natural gas demonstrating the largest variance among the series. Finally, we note the reductions in the estimated GARCH coefficients, particularly notable in the coal series.

An examination of the ARJI results presented in Table 2, reveals the estimate of λ_0 remains significant across the three series, though is notably reduced. The estimate of ρ is a measure of persistence in the conditional jump intensity. The statistically significant estimates are quite high for natural gas (0.976) and coal (0.987) relative to the crude oil market (0.624). The unconditional jump intensity,

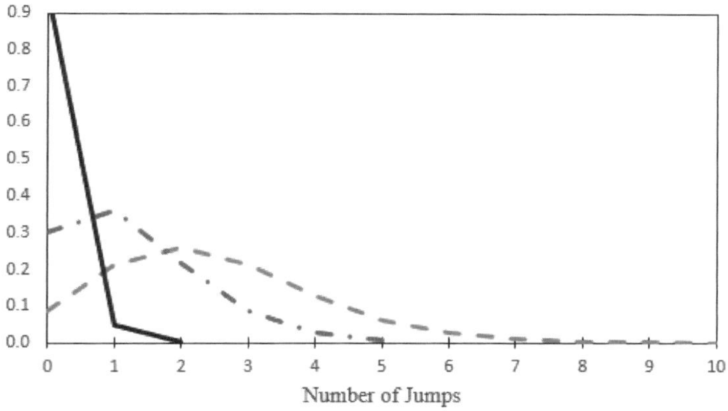

Fig. 3. $P(\eta_t = j|\Phi_{t-1})$ for constant intensity model ($\lambda = 0.06$); the *ARJI* model: 2 December 2008 $\lambda_t = 1.20$, 4 January 1996 $\lambda_t = 2.45$.

λ_t can be obtained from

$$E[\lambda_t] = \frac{\lambda_0}{1-\rho}.$$

Of note, the unconditional jump intensities tend to be larger than those reported in the constant intensity models. The impact of the previous shock on the jump intensity λ_t is measured by γ. The results indicate that the impact of such shocks (ξ_t) is quite mild, resulting in a damping effect on λ_t.

Figure 3 provides an illustration to assess the impact of allowing for a time-varying jump intensity. The Poisson distribution governed by λ_t, for natural gas returns, for two dates is contrasted with the constant jump intensity estimate. The figure illustrates the impact that changes in λ_t can have on the Poisson distribution. Under the assumption of a constant jump intensity, the probability of more than two jumps occurring is effectively zero. A time-varying jump-intensity (ARJI) model, allows for periods in which the probability of observing multiple jumps is significantly larger. Misspecification tests based on the modified LB statistics for autocorrelation in the squared standard residuals (Q^2) and the jump intensity residuals (Q_{ξ_t}), for 15 lags, are presented in Table 2. In a correctly specified model, ξ_t should not display any systematic behavior. We note that the ξ_t statistic rejects the constant intensity assumption for both natural gas and coal. While crude oil is not rejected at the traditional statistical level, we note the p-value of 0.119 means that it is marginally outside the 10% level.

Table 3. Likelihood ratio test results.

	$\mathbf{LR}_{\lambda=0,\lambda_0}$	$\mathbf{LR}_{\lambda_0,\lambda_t}$
Crude oil returns	284	5198
	(0.00)	(0.00)
Natural gas returns	5506	48
	(0.00)	(0.00)
Coal returns	2878	24
	(0.00)	(0.00)

Note: Values in parentheses are p-values for the test statistics, i.e. the probability the null is preferred to the alternative.

5.2. *Likelihood ratio test results*

The results of the pairwise Likelihood ratio (*LR*) tests are presented in Table 3. Each entry in the table is a test statistic of the form $\text{LR}_{x,y}$, where the null hypothesis is that the appropriate stochastic process describing the data is x and the alternative hypothesis is that the appropriate stochastic process describing the data is y. The parenthetical values below each test statistic give the p-value associated with each test statistic. The results in the second column indicate that allowing for jumps yields a statistically important increase in predictive power over the GARCH(1,1) model. The results in the final column indicate that the restrictions imposed by the constant-jump model, namely $\rho = 0$ and $\gamma = 0$ is rejected in favor of the autoregressive jump intensity model, where $\rho \neq 0$ and $\gamma \neq 0$. The consistency of the results across energy commodity reinforces the importance of incorporating a time-varying jump intensity in energy commodity markets.

6. Conclusions

Our results demonstrate the importance of incorporating a time-varying jump-intensity model when examining the jump dynamics of energy commodity markets. The results of the crude oil returns are similar to those of Gronwald [2012], who applies the ARJI model to nominal oil price deflated by the U.S. producer price index, across different time frequencies. There is a large improvement relative to a continuous time process; simply stated, jumps can not be ignored. The time-varying jump-intensity models demonstrate a high degree of persistence in the jump intensity. This suggests that a high probability of many jumps in one period tends to be followed by a high probability of many jumps in the next period. Notably, the GARCH effects remain an important feature of returns even after accounting for discontinuities.

Increasing the accuracy and understanding of the process governing the price dynamics of energy futures market should be beneficial for a number of reasons. It is well known in financial economics that the price of an option is an increasing function of the volatility of the underlying asset. Indeed, Merton [1976] demonstrated that an increase in the probability of a jump will increase the value of the option. The inclusion of jumps and specifically time-varying jump intensity, would impact the pricing of energy derivative contracts, and thus influence hedging strategies. In addition, large scale (irreversible) investment decisions are influenced by the behavior of prices observed in energy markets. As noted in Dixit and Pindyck [1993, p. 153], "investment is highly sensitive to volatility in project values". In the case of real options, the flexibility obtained from holding the option is more valuable in an uncertain environment. Such a finding is consistent with the apparent sluggishness of investment into expanded pipeline export capacity out of the Marcellus shale play, for example, or the reticence of electric utilities to replace old coal-burning plants with newer gas burning facilities in the near future.

While the ARJI is well suited to capture the large discrete changes found in energy commodity returns, one can imagine a number of extensions to the model presented here. First, the base assumption regarding the absence of lagged returns in the mean equation, i.e. $\phi = 0$ could be relaxed. Indeed, it would be straightforward to extend our model by incorporating lagged values of the dependent variables. Second, the analysis could be extended beyond the GARCH(1,1) model used herein. For example, the EGARCH model has been coupled with the ARJI process to study the impact of oil price shocks on China's commodity markets [Zhang and Chen, 2014]. Third, as Chan and Maheu [2002] discuss, the assumption of a Gaussian distribution over jumps may be restrictive. It is possible that alternative distributions could be imposed. Finally, our analysis assumed a constant jump size distribution. The jump size distribution could be extended to incorporate time-varying mean and variance parameters, which could be based on the past values of returns. We leave these extensions for future work.

References

Abadie, L. M. and Chamorro, J. M. (2009). Monte Carlo valuation of natural gas investment. *Review of Financial Economics* **18**, 10–22.

Asche, F., Oglend, A. and Sandsmark, M. (2006). The UK market for natural gas, oil and electricity: Are the prices decoupled? *The Energy Journal* **27**, 27–40.

Askari, H. and Krichene, N. (2008). Oil price dynamics (2002–2006). *Energy Economics* **30** (5), 2134–2153.

Baker, M. P., Mayfield, E. S. and Parsons, J. E. (1998). Alternative models of uncertain commodity prices for use with modern asset pricing methods. *The Energy Journal* **19**, 115–148.

Benth, E. F., Benth, J. and Koekbakker, S. (2008). *Stochastic Modelling of Electricity and Related Markets*. (World Scientific, River Edge, NJ).

Bollerslev, T. (1986). Generalized autoregressive conditional heteroskedasticity. *Journal of Econometrics* **31**, 307–327.

Brown, S. P. A. and Yücel, M. K. (2008). What drives natural gas prices? *The Energy Journal* **29**, 45–60.

Carmona, R. and Ludvoski, M. (2010). Valuation of energy storage: An optimal switching approach. *Quantitative Finance* **10**, 359–374.

Chan, W. H. and Maheu, J. M. (2002). Conditional jump dynamics in stock market returns. *Journal of Business and Economic Statistics* **20** (3), 377–389.

Chen, Z. and Forsyth, P. A. (2007). A semi-lagrangean approach for natural gas storage valuation and optimal operation. *SIAM Journal of Scientific Computing* **30**, 339–368.

Chen, Z. and Forsyth, P. A. (2010). Implications of a regime-switching model on natural gas storage valuation and optimal operation. *Quantitative Finance* **10**, 159–176.

Chevallier, J. and Sévi, B. (2014). On the stochastic properties of carbon futures prices. *Environmental and Resource Economics* **58**, 127–153.

Cont, R. and Tankov, P. (2004). *Financial Modeling with Jump Processes*. (Chapman - Hall, Boca Raton, FL).

Dixit, A. K. and Pindyck, R. S. (1993). *Investment Under Uncertainty*. (Princeton University Press, Princeton, NJ).

Elliot, G., Rothenberg, T. and Stock, J. (1996). Efficient tests for an autoregressive unit root. *Econometrica* **64**, 813–836.

Geman, H. (2005). Energy commodity prices: Is mean-reversion dead? *Journal of Alternative Investments* **8**, 31–45.

Gronwald, M. (2012). A characterization of oil price behavior — evidence from jump models. *Energy Economics* **34**, 1310–1317.

Huisman, R. and Mahieu, R. (2003). Regime jumps in electricity prices. *Energy Economics* **25**, 425–434.

Lee, Y. H., Hu, H. and Chiou, J. (2010). Jump dynamics with structural breaks for crude oil prices. *Energy Economics* **32**, 343–350.

Mason, C. F. and Wilmot, N. A. (2014). Jumps in natural gas prices: Implications for infrastructure. *Energy Economics* **46**, S69–S79.

Merton, R. C. (1976). Option pricing when the underlying stock returns are discontinuous. *Journal of Financial Economics* **3** (1), 125–144.

Mu, X. (2007). Weather, storage and natural gas price dynamics: Fundamentals and volatility. *Energy Economics* **29**, 49–63.

Panagiotidis, T. and Rutledge, E. (2007). Oil and gas markets in the U.K.: Evidence from a co-integrating approach. *Energy Economics* **29**, 329–347.

Pindyck, R. S. (1999). The long-run evolution of energy prices. *The Energy Journal* **20** (2), 1–27.

Pindyck, R. S. (2004). Volatility in natural gas and oil markets. *The Journal of Energy and Development* **30** (1), 1–19.

Postali, F. A. S. and Picchetti, P. (2006). Geometric Brownian motion and structural breaks in oil prices: A quantitative analysis. *Energy Economics* **28** (4), 506–522.

Press, S. J. (1967). A compound events model for security prices. *Journal of Business* **40** (3), 317–335.

Sadorsky, P. (1999). Oil price shocks and stock market activity. *Energy Economics* **21** (5), 449–469.

Schwartz, E. S. (1997). The stochastic behavior of commodity prices: Implication for valuation and hedging. *Journal of Finance* **52**, 923–973.

Schwartz, E. S. and Smith, J. E. (2000). Short-term variations and long-term dynamics in commodity prices. *Management Science* **47**, 893–911.

Shaffie, S. and Topal, E. (2010). A long-term view of worldwide fossil fuel prices. *Applied Energy* **87**, 988–1000.

Thompson, M., Davidson, M. and Rasmussen, H. (2009). Natural gas storage valuation and optimization: A real options application. *Naval Research Logistics (NRL)* **56**, 226–238.

Wilmot, N. A. (2016). Discontinuities in the coal market. *Applied Economics Letters* **23** (11), 790–794.

Wilmot, N. A. and Mason, C. F. (2013). Jump processes in the market for crude oil. *The Energy Journal* **34** (1), 33–48.

Zhang, C. and Chen, X. (2014). The impact of global oil price shocks on china's bulk commodity markets and fundamental industries. *Energy Policy* **66**, 32–41.

Chapter 10

What is the Probability of an Electricity Price Spike? Evidence from the UK Power Market

Paweł Maryniak*,†,‡ and Rafał Weron*,§

**Department of Operations Research, Wrocław University of Science and Technology, 50-370 Wrocław, Poland*

†Department of Financial Investments and Risk Management, Wrocław University of Economics, 53-345 Wrocław, Poland

‡pmaryniak@gmail.com

§rafal.weron@pwr.edu.pl

We study the forward-looking information concerning nation-wide electricity demand and generation that is available to all participants in the UK market and measure its predictive power with respect to forecasting the occurrence of price spikes for horizons ranging from 2 days to 2 weeks. Considering a 14-year period (19 January 2003–31 December 2016), we find that — irrespective of the spike identification algorithm and except for the first 3 years of data — the probability of observing a spike is approximately an exponentially increasing function of the demand-to-capacity ratio. This is in contrast to an earlier study on the UK power market which reported that ca. 85% of spikes occurred when the demand-to-capacity ratio was in the range [0.908, 0.960].

Keywords: Electricity price; price spike; spike identification; spike occurrence; probability of spike occurrence; capacity constraints; indicated demand; indicated generation; demand-to-capacity ratio; forecasting.

1. Introduction

Treated as a stochastic process, electricity prices possess two unique characteristics that make them more difficult to model and predict than most other financial time series: (i) seasonality on the daily, weekly and annual level and (ii) abrupt, short-lived and to a large extent unanticipated price spikes [Weron and Ziel, 2019]. Seasonality of time series is a well-known and investigated phenomenon in econometrics (see e.g. [Hyndman and Athanasopoulos, 2013]). Recently, it has been thoroughly discussed also in the context of modeling and forecasting electricity spot prices [Janczura *et al.*, 2013; Lisi and Nan, 2014; Nowotarski *et al.*, 2013; Weron and Zator, 2015]. Here, we focus on the second, less studied phenomenon.

Electricity price spikes are visible for *intra-day* or *day-ahead* prices on a half-hourly, hourly or daily time grid, but not for forward prices (settled in a more distant future and over a longer delivery period). Their occurrence is generally attributed to the non-storability of electricity on the one hand and unexpected increases in demand, shortfalls in generation, transmission grid congestion and failures of the infrastructure on the other [Christensen *et al.*, 2012; Eydeland and Wolyniec, 2003; Harris, 2006; Weron, 2014]. Their severity, however, cannot be explained only by the dispatch of units with a high marginal cost of production; to a large extent it is driven by gaming or speculation (see e.g. [Weron, 2006]).

Modeling the occurrence of electricity price spikes is not a trivial task. They are an outcome of many, potentially interacting factors. However, a low reserve margin is probably one of the most important [Anderson and Davison, 2008; Boogert and Dupont, 2008; Cartea *et al.*, 2009; Davison *et al.*, 2002; Handika *et al.*, 2014; Maryniak, 2013; Mount *et al.*, 2006; Weron, 2014; Zareipour *et al.*, 2006, 2011]. Recall, that the *reserve margin*, also called *surplus generation*, relates the available capacity (generation, supply), C_t, and the demand (load), D_t, at a given moment in time t. The traditional engineering notion of the reserve margin defines it as the difference of the two, i.e. $\mathrm{RM}_t = C_t - D_t$ [Eydeland and Wolyniec, 2003; Harris, 2006]. However, most authors prefer to work with dimensionless ratios:

- the *demand-to-capacity ratio*, $\rho_t = \frac{D_t}{C_t}$, see e.g. Anderson and Davison [2008], Cartea *et al.* [2009], Davison *et al.* [2002], Maryniak [2013] and Weron [2014],
- the *capacity utilization*, $\mathrm{CU}_t = 1 - \frac{D_t}{C_t} (\equiv \frac{\mathrm{RM}_t}{C_t} \equiv 1 - \rho_t)$, see e.g. Boogert and Dupont [2008],
- the *relative reserve margin* (also called the "reserve margin"), $R_t = \frac{C_t}{D_t} - 1 (\equiv \frac{\mathrm{RM}_t}{D_t} \equiv \frac{1}{\rho_t} - 1)$, see e.g. Handika *et al.* [2014], Mount *et al.* [2006], Zareipour *et al.* [2006] and Zareipour *et al.* [2011]. Note that in the latter two papers, the demand in the formula for R_t is modified to include the so-called *operating reserve requirement* component, i.e. $D_t = \mathrm{demand}_t + \mathrm{ORR}_t$.

In this study, we follow the footsteps of Cartea *et al.* [2009], who provided an original study of the dependence between reserve margin levels and spike occurrence. Like Cartea *et al.* [2009], we focus on publicly available information that measures the extent to which the capacity of the UK generation park will be constrained over the next 2 weeks, with the aim of identifying days when price spikes are more likely to occur. To our best knowledge, the UK market is the only one for which such high quality forward-looking reserve margin data is freely available to all market participants.

Studying the British market in the period June 2003–March 2006, Cartea *et al.* [2009] found that ca. 85% of spikes occurred when the demand-to-capacity ratio was in the interval [0.908, 0.960]. This is surprising, given that much higher values of the ratio have been observed in this period: up to 1.097 for 2 days-ahead, 1.069 for week-ahead and 1.031 for 2 weeks-ahead forecasts. As if beyond a certain very high level of the demand-to-capacity ratio, the supply and perhaps the generation side of the market do everything they can to prevent spikes, while for high but not extremely high values of this ratio they are not very concerned with the situation and do not struggle to prevent them.

Here, we consider a much longer, nearly 14-year time period from 19 January 2003 to 31 December 2016, and try to answer the question if there is indeed a critical range of values of the demand-to-capacity ratio where price spikes are much more likely to occur. To identify the spikes, we use four different techniques, as the choice of the spike identification technique may significantly influence the outcome of the analysis. We find that — irrespective of the spike identification algorithm and except for the first 3 years of data — the probability of observing a spike is approximately an exponentially increasing function of the demand-to-capacity ratio, which is in stark contrast to the results of Cartea *et al.* [2009].

The remainder of the chapter is structured as follows: In Section 2, we review the literature and then in Section 3 the spike identification techniques. In Section 4, we briefly describe the APX and Exelon databases used in this chapter. Next, in Section 5, we conduct the empirical study. Finally, in Section 6 we wrap up the results and conclude.

2. Literature Review

The literature on the use of reserve margin data for forecasting or explaining spike occurrence is not very rich. Yet, there are a few positions worth mentioning. For instance, Anderson and Davison [2008] and Davison *et al.* [2002] propose a functional form for the relation between the reserve margin and the probability of a spike based on the curvature of the hyperbolic tangent:

$$f(\rho_t) = \frac{1}{2}\tanh\left[\{c(\rho_t - 0.85)\}\right] + \frac{1}{2}, \quad (1)$$

where $c = 22$ or 20 is a constant dependent on the studied dataset. They motivate this function by the empirical observation that for $\rho_t < 0.85$ high prices are rarely observed, while for $\rho_t > 0.85$ the probability of obtaining a high price increases rapidly. They further argue that the details of the "thresholding function" are not very important as long as it monotonically increases from zero to one, with a rapid increase, for $\rho_t > 0.85$. Their model is tested and validated using PJM market data and is shown to be able to reproduce the observed price dynamics.

Burger *et al.* [2004] incorporate a function of the demand-to-capacity ratio (called "relative availability of power plants") into their day-ahead price model to obtain a better fit to historical data from the European Energy Exchange. Lu *et al.* [2005] explore the reasons for price spikes based on the measurement of a proposed composite supply–demand balance index (SDI) and relative demand index (RDI). These indexes are able to reflect the relationship among electricity demand, electricity supply and electricity reserve capacity. Bayesian classification and similarity searching techniques are used to mine the database (comprising market clearing price, trading hour, electricity demand, electricity supply and reserve) to find out the internal relationships between electricity price spikes and the remaining data. The forecasting performance of the resulting model is tested successfully using Queensland (Australia) half hourly prices, however, only during a very short period in the early stage of the market (July 2003–September 2003).

Zareipour *et al.* [2006] evaluate the usefulness of publicly available electricity market information in forecasting the hourly Ontario energy price (HOEP) via ARIMA and transfer function models and find that the reserve margin is a useful indicator. Mount *et al.* [2006] propose MRS models where the switching probabilities and the conditional mean of the PJM day-ahead price in each regime vary with time and with the relative reserve margin (R_t). They define the transition probabilities via a logit transformation of the reserve margin (and the system load). Mount *et al.* [2006] conclude that their MRS models can capture the type of volatile price behavior observed in the PJM market. Boogert and Dupont [2008] assume that the spot price is a function of capacity utilization (which they call "reserve margin") and estimate its empirical form within a non-parametric framework for Dutch electricity prices in the period 1 October 2004–17 June 2006.

Zareipour *et al.* [2011] focus on threshold forecasting, which may be treated as a generalization of predicting spike occurrences where the number of states (regimes) is more than two. The rationale for threshold forecasting comes from the fact that applications like demand-side management do not require exact values of future spot prices but rather use specific price thresholds as the basis for making scheduling decisions [Weron, 2014]. Zareipour *et al.* [2011] use two Support Vector Machine (SVM)-based models to classify future electricity prices in the Ontario and Alberta markets with respect to prespecified price thresholds. Historical price, load and reserve margin (only available for Ontario) information are considered in the initial set of features. For both markets the prices are classified into three groups: from the price floor to the average price in the year 2008, from the average price to twice the average price, and from twice the average price to the price cap. The authors find that the proposed models provide more accurate results compared to three autoregressive time series models (ARIMA, ARX, ARMAX), a mixed similar-day and an artificial neural network (ANN) predictor and the pre-dispatch price forecasts published by the Independent System Operator (ISO; available for Ontario only).

Finally, Handika *et al.* [2014] examine the impact of explanatory variables such as load, weather and capacity constraints on the occurrence and magnitude of price spikes in four regional electricity markets in Australia. They apply the so-called Heckman correction, a two-stage estimation procedure that allows to investigate the impact of the considered variables on extreme price observations only, while correcting for a selection bias due to non-random sampling in the analysis. They find that load, relative air temperature and reserve margins are significant variables for the occurrence of price spikes, while electricity loads and relative air temperature are significant variables for the severity of spikes.

3. Identification of Spikes

Price spikes are commonly defined as prices that surpass a specified threshold for a brief period of time. However, it is difficult to gain any consensus on what that threshold or time interval should be [Weron, 2006]. The identification methods (or filters) suggested in the energy economics literature so far include a number of more or less sophisticated approaches that have been grouped by Janczura *et al.* [2013] into nine classes. In this study we use four carefully selected techniques from three classes:

- The CF filter used by Cartea *et al.* [2009] belongs to the class of *variable price change thresholds*, more commonly known as *recursive filters*. Prices corresponding to the returns (or price increments in some variants of the filter) exceeding three standard deviations of all returns (or a different threshold) are removed one by one in an iterative procedure. This is a pretty popular technique, for sample applications see e.g. Cartea and Figueroa [2005] and Weron [2008].
- The *variable price threshold* (denoted here by VPT) is a simple filter where a certain percentage (here 2.5%) of the highest deseasonalized prices (here, using the S_6 wavelet approximation which roughly corresponds to bimonthly smoothing; for details see [Janczura *et al.*, 2013; Weron and Zator, 2015]) is

classified as spikes. In some variants of this filter, a certain percentage of the highest and the same percentage of the lowest prices is classified as outliers [Trück *et al.*, 2007]. The VPT filter is similar to the popular fixed price threshold filter [Boogert and Dupont, 2008; Christensen *et al.*, 2012], but instead of classifying as spikes all prices exceeding some fixed level (e.g. 100 AUD/MWh), it uses a quantile-based threshold.

- The *recursive filter on prices* (denoted here by RFP) also belongs to the class of variable price thresholds. It classifies as spikes, all prices exceeding the mean price level of deseasonalized prices (again using the S_6 wavelet smoother) by three standard deviations, with the outlying observations removed one by one in a "recursive filter" fashion, see Janczura *et al.* [2013] for details.
- The *regime-switching classification* (denoted here by RSC) is a byproduct of calibrating a Markov regime-switching (MRS) model to deseasonalized prices (here using the S_6 wavelet smoother). During the calibration process we obtain the conditional probabilities for the prices being in a certain regime at a given time [Bierbrauer *et al.*, 2007; Huisman, 2008; Janczura and Weron, 2010]. All prices with probabilities of being in an extreme regime exceeding a certain threshold (here 50%) are classified as spikes. In this study, we use a 2-state MRS with an independent lognormal spike regime, heteroskedastic mean-reverting base regime dynamics (i.e. with any γ) and spike cutoff $q_2 = 95\%$; for model and calibration details see Janczura and Weron [2012] or Weron [2014].

While Janczura *et al.* [2013] do not identify a single best method for spike detection, they conclude that the RFP filter leads to the most accurate identification of the seasonal component of electricity prices, while the VPT and RSC filters to the most accurate estimation of the stochastic component. All three are recommended for general use. The fourth filter — CF — is chosen to allow for a direct comparison of our results with those of Cartea *et al.* [2009].

4. UK Market Data

4.1. *Electricity prices*

The APX power exchange (www.apxgroup.com; formerly UKPX) provides detailed information about the intra-day structure of the British power market, including volume-weighted prices for every half-hour (volume-weighting is performed over three types of contracts: half-hourly, two hour block and four hour block contracts). The baseload, i.e. average daily, electricity prices used in this study span the nearly 14-year period from 19 January 2003 to 31 December 2016, see Fig. 1. They were

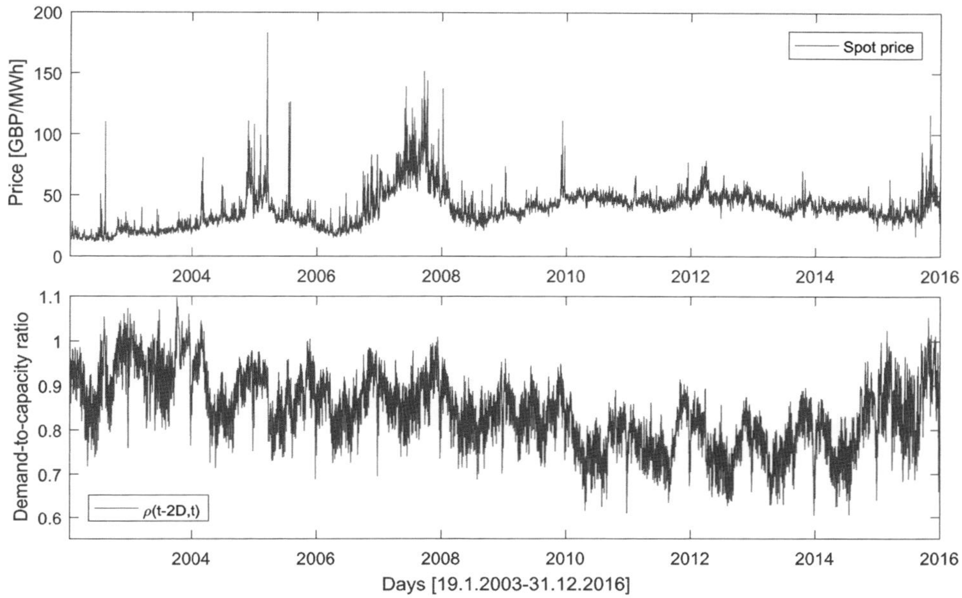

Fig. 1. The APX-UK baseload price (*upper panel*) and the demand-to-capacity ratio 2 days before delivery (*lower panel*; i.e. $\rho(t-2D, t)$, see text for details) in the period 19 January 2003–31 December 2016.

obtained as the arithmetic average of the 48 volume-weighted half-hourly prices for each day.

As can be seen in Figs. 1–3, spike clustering is visible not only on the hourly, but also on the daily time scale [for more empirical evidence see e.g. Christensen *et al.*, 2009]. Naturally, not all prices classified as spikes by one method are classified as spikes by another method. The CF filter is the least sensitive of the four techniques (84 identified spikes in the period 19 January 2003–31 December 2016), while the RFP and RSC filters are the most sensitive (respectively, 235 and 234 spikes). The VPT filter (127 spikes) is ranked in between.

4.2. *Reserve margin forecasts*

Elexon (www.elexon.co.uk), a company that runs the British balancing market, regularly publishes National Demand Forecasts (also referred to as *Indicated Demand*) and surplus (i.e. reserve margin) forecasts. National Demand Forecasts are published daily for 2–14 days-ahead horizons and once a week for 2–52 weeks-ahead. Surplus forecasts, being a difference between *Indicated Generation* (or generation forecasts) and *Indicated Demand*, are published on weekdays for 2–14 days-ahead horizons and once a week for 2–52 weeks-ahead. In this study, we

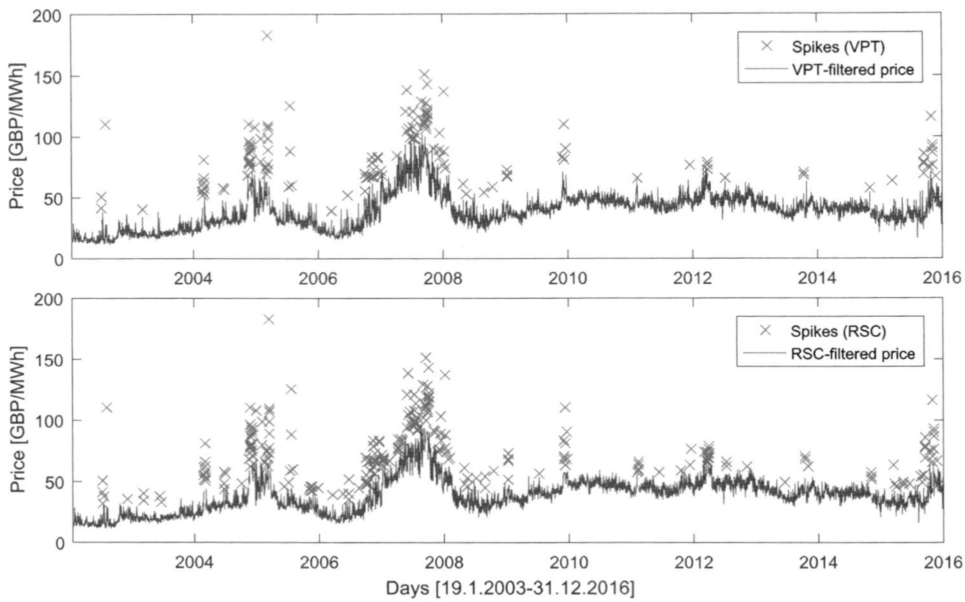

Fig. 2. Spikes identified using the 2.5% variable price threshold method (VPT; *upper panel*) or the regime-switching classification (RSC; *lower panel*) and the resulting spike-filtered prices. Note that the RSC approach is nearly twice more sensitive and yields 234 spikes in the period 19 January 2003–31 December 2016, compared to 127 for VPT.

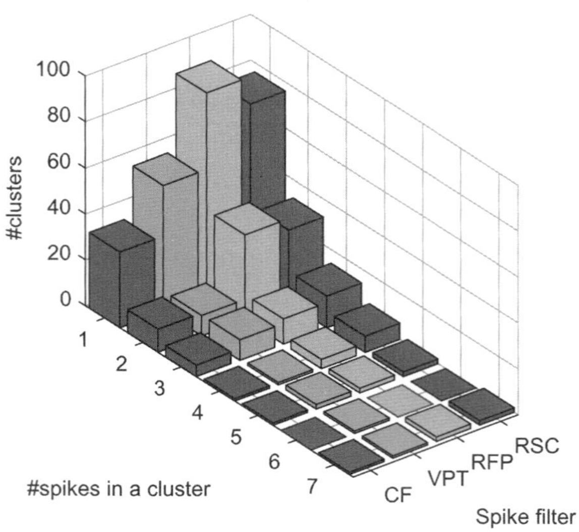

Fig. 3. Histogram of the size of spike clusters for four spike filtering methods — the CF filter of Cartea and Figueroa [2005] and Cartea *et al.* [2009], the 2.5% variable price threshold (VPT), the recursive filter on prices (RFP) and the regime-switching classification (RSC) — in the period 19 January 2003–31 December 2016.

focus on shorter-term forecasting horizons of 2, 3, 7 and 14 days-ahead, respectively denoted by 2D, 3D, 1W and 2W. Since surplus forecasts are not available on a daily basis, we use the most recent available value as a proxy for that day's forecast. The UK market is the only one we are aware of, for which such high quality forward-looking reserve margin data is freely available to all market participants.

5. Price Spikes and Forward-Looking Capacity Constraints

5.1. *Estimating the probability of spike occurrence*

While it is beyond doubt that the reserve margin is a valuable explanatory variable, it remains an open question what the actual functional form of this relationship is and if it does change with the forecasting horizon. To answer these questions, we follow the approach taken by Cartea *et al.* [2009], Maryniak [2013] and Weron [2014] and consider a variant of the demand-to-capacity ratio for the UK power market:

$$\rho(t_1, t_2) = \frac{D(t_1, t_2)}{C(t_1, t_2)}, \tag{2}$$

where $D(t_1, t_2)$ is the *Indicated Demand* and $C(t_1, t_2)$ is the *Indicated Generation*; for data description see Section 4. Both are calculated at time t_1 (e.g. today) for an upcoming period t_2, which may be a day or a week and the forecast horizon (i.e. $\tau = t_2 - t_1$) ranges from 2 days to 52 weeks. Although unlikely, $\rho(t_1, t_2)$ may take values higher than unity because it is based on forecasts, not actual values. Such situations have indeed occurred in the British market between June 2003 and March 2006, i.e. in the period analyzed by Cartea *et al.* [2009]. Analyzing forecasts for week t available 1 week earlier, i.e. $\rho(t - 1W, t)$, they found that ca. 85% of all spikes appeared when $\rho \in [0.908, 0.960]$, see the left panel in Fig. 4. This is surprising, given that values of the ratio as high as 1.069 have been observed in this period for 1 week-ahead forecasts.

If we plot the number of spikes against $\rho(t - \tau, t)$, for τ = 2D, 3D, 1W and 2W, then we can observe that most spikes cluster near $\rho = 0.93$, which coincides with the results of Cartea *et al.* [2009]. The time period considered is the same, but the number of spikes (i.e. 22) is larger than in Fig. 2 and Table 2 of the latter article (i.e. 13), despite the fact that we use the same spike-filtering technique of Cartea and Figueroa [2005]. The reason is that Cartea *et al.* [2009] identify as "spikes" only those prices which correspond to the "peaks" of the multiday spikes (or spike clusters), while we consider all spikes.

Following Maryniak [2013] and Weron [2014], let us now define the *probability of spike occurrence*, denoted by $P(\text{spike}_f|\rho)$, as the conditional probability of

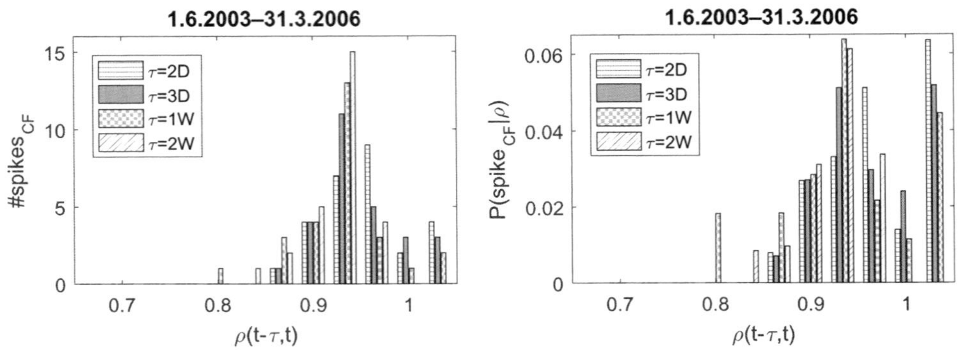

Fig. 4. *Left panel*: The number of spikes against the demand-to-capacity ratio, i.e. $\rho(t-\tau, t)$, for $\tau = 2\text{D}$, 3D, 1W and 2W in the period 1 June 2003–31 March 2006. Note that for $\tau = 3\text{D}$, 1W and 2W, most of the spikes are observed near $\rho = 0.93$, as reported by Cartea *et al.* [2009]. The spikes are identified using the CF filter of Cartea and Figueroa [2005] and Cartea *et al.* [2009]. *Right panel*: The probability of observing a spike $P(\text{spike}_{\text{CF}}|\rho)$, for a given ρ in the same period.

observing a spike, identified using filter f (= CF, VPT, RFP, RSC), given a certain value of the demand-to-capacity ratio. For each of the four forecast horizons considered ($\tau = 2\text{D}$, 3D, 1W and 2W), we construct

(A) a histogram with bars centered at points $\rho = 0.600, 0.63(3), \ldots, 1.06(6)$ of the demand-to-capacity ratios $\rho(t-\tau, t)$ corresponding to spikes identified using filter f and

(B) a histogram with bars centered at the same points of the demand-to-capacity ratios $\rho(t-\tau, t)$ corresponding to all observed prices.

The fraction **(A)**/**(B)** yields an empirical estimate of $P(\text{spike}_f|\rho)$, for each $\rho = 0.600, 0.63(3), \ldots, 1.06(6)$. Note that the grid of ρ's is chosen in such a way as to span the entire range of historically observed demand-to-capacity ratios.

Now, if we plot $P(\text{spike}_{\text{CF}}|\rho)$ for data in the period considered by Cartea *et al.* [2009], then $\rho \approx 0.93$ does not dominate the other values as much as before, especially for $\tau = 2\text{D}$, but also for $\tau = 3\text{D}$ and 1W; see the right panel in Fig. 4 and compare with the left one. In fact, for values of the demand-to-capacity ratio in excess of 1, spike occurrence is roughly as likely as for $\rho \approx 0.93$.

As of today, much more data is available to us than back in 2007 when Cartea *et al.* conducted their analysis. Moreover, the changes that took place in 2005 have had a substantial impact on the structure and behavior of the British power market. In April 2005, the NETA system was replaced by BETTA, which covered not only England and Wales, but also Scotland. As a result of investment in generation, in the following years the supply side has seen further increase of capacity, leading

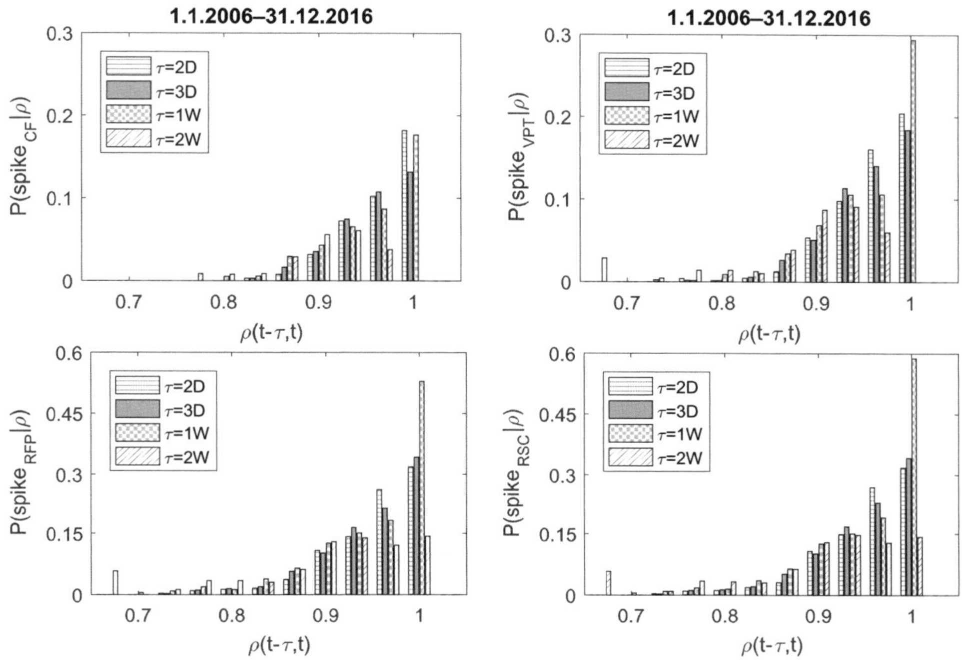

Fig. 5. The probability of observing a spike $P(\text{spike}|\rho)$, for a given ρ in the period 1 January 2006–31 December 2016. The spikes are identified using four different methods: the Cartea and Figueroa [2005] filter (CF; *upper left*), the 2.5% variable price threshold (VPT; *upper right*), the recursive filter on prices (RFP; *lower left*) and the regime-switching classification (RSC; *lower right*).

to a larger reserve margin and fewer spikes. Hence, in what follows, we limit the analysis to an 11-year period from 1 January 2006 to 31 December 2016. This will also allow us to check whether the conclusions formulated by Cartea *et al.* [2009] for the years 2003–2006 hold over a longer and a more recent time period.

In Fig. 5, we plot the empirical probabilities of observing spikes in the period 1 January 2006–31 December 2016, for four different spike-filtering techniques described in Section 3. Clearly, irrespective of the spike identification method, the probability of a spike increases with increasing demand-to-capacity ratio, at least for $\tau < 2W$. It seems that for the 2 weeks-ahead forecasts, there is still ample time to take appropriate countermeasures in case of very high ρ's (close to one) and significantly reduce the probability of a spike.

Interestingly, the obtained results are in line with the "industrial standard" of 85% for the demand-to-capacity ratio warranting a safe functioning of the power system, as mentioned by Anderson and Davison [2008]. For all spike identification methods, the probabilities of spikes for the 2 days-ahead horizon is below 3% for

$\rho < 85\%$, see Fig. 5. On the other hand, it is substantially higher for ρ's above this threshold.

5.2. *Functional form of the probability of spike occurrence*

Now, to assess the functional form of $P(\text{spike}|\rho)$ in Fig. 6 we plot the results for two forecasting horizons (τ = 2D and 1W) and all four spike-filtering techniques. Superimposed on the bars are fits of an exponential function of the form: $f_{\text{exp}}(\rho) = \alpha \cdot \exp(\beta \cdot \rho)$, where α is responsible for the level and β for the curvature. In all four panels, the exponential function yields good fits to the light bars corresponding to CF-identified spikes (left panels) and RFP-identified spikes (right panels). The R^2 values range from 0.93 for the CF filter to 0.97 for the RFP filter. The remaining two filters yield similarly good fits with $R^2 > 0.9$. For the shorter forecasting horizon of 2D, the slope of the exponential function has a higher curvature (is "steeper"; β is larger — ca. 25 versus 18 for the CF filter and ca. 18 versus ca. 15 for the RFP filter)

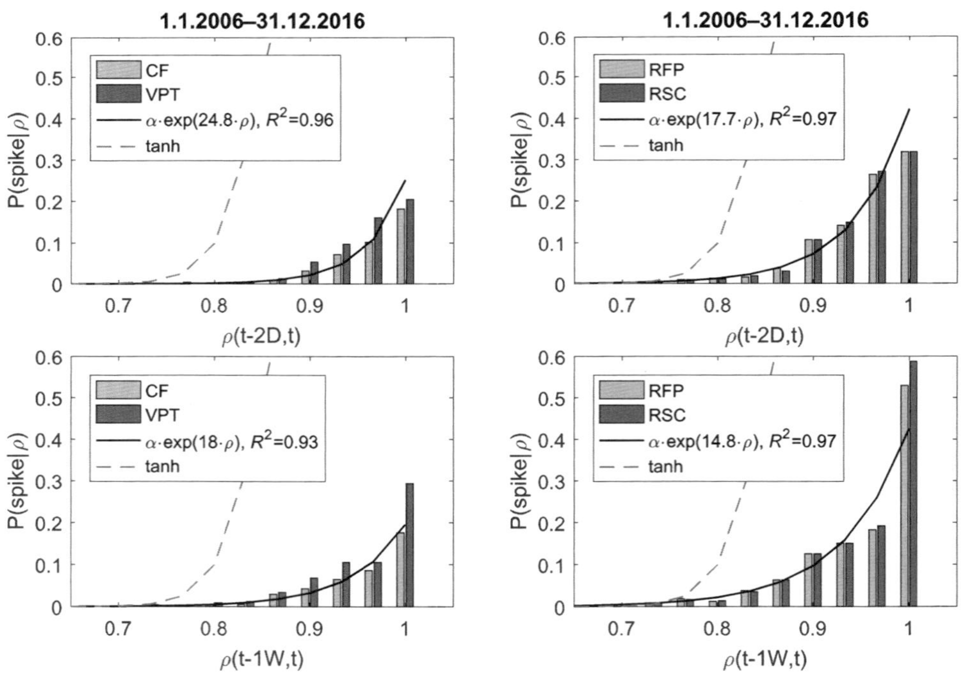

Fig. 6. The probability of observing a spike $P(\text{spike}|\rho)$ for $\rho(t-2D, t)$ in the *top panels* and $\rho(t-1W, t)$ in the *bottom panels*. The spikes are identified using the same four methods and the same data as in Fig. 5. Additionally (i) exponential fits to the light bars (CF in the *left panels* and RFP in the *right panels*) and (ii) the hyperbolic tangent function proposed by Anderson and Davison [2008] are plotted.

than for the 1W forecasting horizon. The second parameter, α, only adjusts the level of the curve, but does not affect its shape. Hence, we do not report its values.

Irrespective of the spike identification algorithm, the probability of observing a spike is roughly an exponentially increasing function of the demand-to-capacity ratio. The probability is close to zero for $\rho < 0.85$, then rapidly increases to ca. 0.2 (for the less sensitive to spikes CF filter) and to ca. 0.3–0.5 (for the more sensitive RFP filter). This is in contrast to Cartea *et al.* [2009] who report that ca. 85% of spikes occur when $\rho \in [0.908, 0.960]$. This is also in contrast to Anderson and Davison [2008] and Davison *et al.* [2002] who assume a functional form of this probability based on the hyperbolic tangent with $P(\text{spike}|\rho) = 1$, for $\rho = 1$, see Eq. (1). Clearly, the hyperbolic tangent (in Fig. 6 plotted for $c = 22$, as in Anderson and Davison [2008]) significantly overestimates the probability of spike occurrence.

6. Conclusions

Studying the forward-looking information that is available to all participants in the UK power market, we empirically evaluate its predictive value with respect to forecasting the occurrence of electricity price spikes. Considering an 11-year period from 1 January 2006 – 31 December 2016, we find that irrespective of the spike identification algorithm, the probability of observing a spike is approximately an exponentially increasing function of the demand-to-capacity ratio. Interestingly, the curvature increases with a decrease in the forecasting horizon. These findings contradict the conjecture made by Anderson and Davison [2008] and Davison *et al.* [2002] regarding the functional form of the probability of spike occurrence and the results of Cartea *et al.* [2009], who reported a non-monotonic relation between the reserve margin and the probability of observing an electricity price spike.

Our empirical study clearly indicates that the reserve margin has a huge potential for explaining the spike probability. Its rare application in electricity spike forecasting can be only justified by the difficulty with obtaining good quality reserve margin data. Given that nowadays more and more system operators are disclosing such information, reserve margin data should play a significant role in electricity price forecasting in the near future.

Acknowledgments

This work was partially supported by the Ministry of Science and Higher Education (MNiSW, Poland) through grant no. 0178/DIA/2012/41 (to PM) and the National Science Center (NCN, Poland) through grant no. 2015/17/B/HS4/00334 (to RW).

References

Anderson, C. L. and Davison, M. (2008). A hybrid system-econometric model for electricity spot prices: Considering spike sensitivity to forced outage distributions. *IEEE Transactions on Power Systems* **23** (3), 927–937.

Bierbrauer, M., Menn, C., Rachev, S. T. and Trück, S. (2007). Spot and derivative pricing in the EEX power market. *Journal of Banking & Finance* **31**, 3462–3485.

Boogert, A. and Dupont, D. (2008). When supply meets demand: The case of hourly spot electricity prices. *IEEE Transactions on Power Systems* **23** (2), 389–398.

Burger, M., Klar, B., Müller, A. and Schindlmayr, G. (2004). A spot market model for pricing derivatives in electricity markets. *Quantitative Finance* **4** (1), 109–122.

Cartea, A. and Figueroa, M. (2005). Pricing in electricity markets: A mean reverting jump diffusion model with seasonality. *Applied Mathematical Finance* **12** (4), 313–335.

Cartea, A., Figueroa, M. and Geman, H. (2009). Modelling electricity prices with forward looking capacity constraints. *Applied Mathematical Finance* **16** (2), 103–122.

Christensen, T. M., Hurn, A. S. and Lindsay, K. A. (2009). It never rains but it pours: Modeling the persistence of spikes in electricity prices. *The Energy Journal* **30** (1), 25–48.

Christensen, T. M., Hurn, A. S. and Lindsay, K. A. (2012). Forecasting spikes in electricity prices. *International Journal of Forecasting* **28** (2), 400–411.

Davison, M., Anderson, C. L., Marcus, B. and Anderson, K. (2002). Development of a hybrid model for electrical power spot prices. *IEEE Transactions on Power Systems* **17** (2), 257–264.

Eydeland, A. and Wolyniec, K. (2003). *Energy and Power Risk Management: New Developments in Modeling, Pricing, and Hedging*. (John Wiley & Sons, Hoboken, NJ).

Handika, R., Truong, C., Trück, S. and Weron, R. (2014). Modelling price spikes in electricity markets — the impact of load, weather and capacity. In M. Prokopczuk. (ed.), *Energy Pricing Models: Recent Advances, Methods, and Tools*. (Palgrave Macmillan), pp. 195–221.

Harris, C. (2006). *Electricity Markets: Pricing, Structures and Economics*. (John Wiley & Sons, Chichester).

Huisman, R. (2008). The influence of temperature on spike probability in day-ahead power prices. *Energy Economics* **30**, 2697–2704.

Hyndman, R. and Athanasopoulos, G. (2013). *Forecasting: Principles and Practice*, Online at http://otexts.org/fpp/.

Janczura, J., Trück, S., Weron, R. and Wolff, R. (2013). Identifying spikes and seasonal components in electricity spot price data: A guide to robust modeling. *Energy Economics* **38**, 96–110.

Janczura, J. and Weron, R. (2010). An empirical comparison of alternate regime-switching models for electricity spot prices. *Energy Economics* **32** (5), 1059–1073.

Janczura, J. and Weron, R. (2012). Efficient estimation of markov regime-switching models: An application to electricity spot prices. *AStA — Advances in Statistical Analysis* **96** (3), 385–407.

Lisi, F. and Nan, F. (2014). Component estimation for electricity prices: Procedures and comparisons. *Energy Economics* **44**, 143–159.

Lu, X., Dong, Z. Y. and Li, X. (2005). Electricity market price spike forecast with data mining techniques. *Electric Power Systems Research* **73**, 19–29.

Maryniak, P. (2013). Using indicated demand and generation data to predict price spikes in the UK power market, MSc Thesis, Wrocław University of Technology.

Mount, T. D., Ning, Y. and Cai, X. (2006). Predicting price spikes in electricity markets using a regime-switching model with time-varying parameters. *Energy Economics* **28**, 62–80.

Nowotarski, J., Tomczyk, J. and Weron, R. (2013). Robust estimation and forecasting of the long-term seasonal component of electricity spot prices. *Energy Economics* **39**, 13–27.

Trück, S., Weron, R. and Wolff, R. (2007). Outlier treatment and robust approaches for modeling electricity spot prices. *Bulletin of the International Statistical Institute* **62**, 1524, available at MPRA: http://mpra.ub.uni-muenchen.de/4711/.

Weron, R. (2006). *Modeling and Forecasting Electricity Loads and Prices: A Statistical Approach.* (John Wiley & Sons, Chichester).

Weron, R. (2008). Market price of risk implied by Asian-style electricity options and futures. *Energy Economics* **30**, 1098–1115.

Weron, R. (2014). Electricity price forecasting: A review of the state-of-the-art with a look into the future. *International Journal of Forecasting* **30** (4), 1030–1081.

Weron, R. and Zator, M. (2015). A note on using the Hodrick-Prescott filter in electricity markets. *Energy Economics* **48**, 1–6.

Weron, R. and Ziel, F. (2019). Electricity price forecasting. In U. Soytas and R. Sari (eds.), Handbook of Energy Economics. (Routledge, forthcoming).

Zareipour, H., Canizares, C. A., Bhattacharya, K. and Thomson, J. (2006). Application of public-domain market information to forecast Ontario's wholesale electricity prices. *IEEE Transactions on Power Systems* **21** (4), 1707–1717.

Zareipour, H., Janjani, A., Leung, H., Motamedi, A. and Schellenberg, A. (2011). Classification of future electricity market prices. *IEEE Transactions on Power Systems* **26** (1), 165–173.

Chapter 11

Stochastic Modeling and Pricing of Energy Markets' Contracts with Local Stochastic Delayed and Jumped Volatilities

Anatoliy Swishchuk

Department of Mathematics and Statistics,
University of Calgary,
2500 University Drive NW,
Calgary, Alberta T2N 1N4, Canada

In this Chapter, we concentrate on stochastic modeling and pricing of energy markets' contracts for stochastic volatilities with delay and jumps. Our model of stochastic volatility exhibits jumps and also past-dependence: the behavior of a stock price right after a given time t not only depends on the situation at t, but also on the whole past (history) of the process $S(t)$ up to time t. The spot price process $S(t)$ is modeled by the Ornstein–Uhlenbeck (OU) process driven by independent increments process. The basic products in these markets are spot, futures and forward contracts and options written on these. We study forwards and swaps. A numerical example is presented for stochastic volatility with delay using the Henry Hub daily natural gas data (1997–2011).

Keywords: Energy markets; stochastic volatility with delay and jumps; independent increments processes (IIP); geometric model for spot price; arithmetic model for spot price; energy contracts; pricing forwards and swaps; OU process; Esscher transform; Henry Hub daily natural gas data (1997–2011).

1. Introduction

Since the early 1990s, the markets for electricity and related products have been liberalized worldwide. It all started off with the Nordic market NordPool and the England&Wales market at around 1992, and over the last two decades trade in electricity and related products on all continents in the world has been liberalized.

In 1999, the Chicago Mercantile Exchange organized a market for temperature derivatives that has gained momentum in recent years.

Exchange-based markets for gas have emerged and are now actively traded at the New York Mercantile Exchange and the Intercontinental Exchange in London.

The basic products in the energy markets, including electricity, gas and temperature markets, are spot, futures and forward contracts and options on these. With organized markets comes the need to have consistent *stochastic models* describing the price evolution of the products.

Energy-related spot prices have several typical characteristics, with the most prominent one being *mean reversion* towards a *seasonally* varying mean level, and frequently occurring *spikes* resulting from an imbalance between supply and demand.

Further, since the energy commodities are driven by the balance between demand and production, the prices tend to mean-revert. A natural class of stochastic models to describe such dynamics is the Ornstein–Uhlenbeck (OU) processes. We use these mean-reverting stochastic processes as our modeling tool.

In the paper [Burger *et al.*, 2004], the authors analyzed the evolution of prices in deregulated electricity markets. They presented a general model that simultaneously takes into account the following features: seasonal patterns, price spikes, mean reversion, price dependent volatilities and long term non-stationarity. In the paper [Benth *et al.*, 2007] a mean-reverting model was proposed for the spot price dynamics of electricity, which includes seasonality of the prices and spikes. The dynamics is a sum of non-Gaussian OU processes with jump processes giving the normal variations and spike behavior of the prices. The pricing of European call and put options written on electricity forward contracts is also discussed. In the paper [Klueppelberg *et al.*, 2010] the authors considered sums of Lévy-driven OU processes for modeling electricity spot price data, and presented a new estimation method with particular emphasis on capturing the high peaks, which is one of the stylized features of such data.

We would like to mention Benth *et al.*'s [2008] book. This is a nice book not only from mathematical point of view — first application of IIPs — but also from practical point of view: this book contains many applications to electricity, gas and temperature markets. This book was also one of the motives to develop the present research.

In this chapter, we concentrate on stochastic modeling and pricing of energy markets' contracts for stochastic volatilities with delay and jumps. Our model of stochastic volatility exhibits jumps and also past-dependence: the behavior of a stock price right after a given time t not only depends on the situation at t, but also on the whole past (history) of the process $S(t)$ up to time t. The basic products in these markets are spot, futures and forward contracts and options written on these. Here, we study forwards and swaps pricing. We would like to mention that the idea to use these stochastic volatility model with delay and jumps was proposed for the first time in [Swishchuk, 2010].

Stock price with delayed stochastic volatility was first introduced in [Kazmerchuk *et al.*, 2005]:

$$dS(t) = \mu S(t)dt + \sigma(t, S_t)S(t)dB(t), \quad t > 0,$$

where $\mu \in R$ is the mean rate of return, the volatility term $\sigma > 0$ is a continuous and bounded function and $B(t)$ is a Brownian motion on a probability space $(\Omega, \mathcal{F}, P)$ with a filtration $\mathcal{F}_t$. We denote $S_t = S(t+\theta), \quad \theta \in [-\tau, 0]$ and the initial data of $S(t)$ is defined by $S(t) = \varphi(t)$, where $\varphi(t)$ is a deterministic function with $t \in [-\tau, 0], \quad \tau > 0$.

We consider the following stochastic volatility with delay and jumps (see [Swishchuk and Xu, 2011]):

$$\frac{d\sigma^2(t, S_t)}{dt} = \gamma V + \frac{\alpha}{\tau}\left[\int_{t-\tau}^{t} \sigma(u, S_u)dB(u) + \int_{t-\tau}^{t} \sigma(u, S_u)d\tilde{N}(u)\right]^2 - (\alpha+\gamma)\sigma^2(t, S_t),$$

where $\tilde{N}(t) := N(t) - \lambda t$, $N(t)$ is a Poisson process with intensity $\lambda > 0$, independent of $B(t)$.

Motivation: Why Delay? Our model of stochastic volatility exhibits jumps and also past-dependence: the behavior of a stock price right after a given time t not only depends on the situation at t, but also on the whole past (history) of the process $S(t)$ up to time t. This draws some similarities with fractional Brownian motion models considered in [Mandelbrot, 1997] due to a long-range dependence property. Another advantage of this model is mean-reversion. It is also well known that time-delay models in economics (see, e.g. [Frisch and Holmes, 1935]) are more realistic than the models without time-delay. Discrete-time stochastic volatility models (see, e.g. [Bollerslev, 1986]) were developed in economics as well. This model is also a continuous-time version of GARCH (1,1) model considered in [Bollerslev, 1986] with jumps (one of the motivations for delay). Another advantage of our stochastic volatility model with delay and jumps is mean-reversion: the volatility is allowed to mean revert. Such models have also shown some success in modeling interest rate (see [Ait-Sahalia, 1996]).

Motivation: Why Jumps? There is currently fairly compelling evidence for jumps in the level of financial and energy prices. The most convincing evidence comes from recent non-parametric work using high-frequency data as mentioned in [Barndorff-Nielsen and Shephard, 2007] and in [Ait-Sahalia and Jacod, 2014] among others.

Also, the paper [Todorov and Tauchen, 2011] conducts a non-parametric analysis of the market volatility dynamics using high-frequency data on the VIX index compiled by the CBOE and the $S\&P500$ index. Many papers in energy markets also indicate the existence of jumps in the energy spot prices, such as, e.g. natural gas daily prices (see [Otunuga and Ladde, 2014]).

Our models and results definitely have practical applications. One of them is described in Section 7 for Henry Hub natural gas daily spot prices using the model for stochastic volatility from [Kazmerchuk *et al.*, 2005] and some numerical results from [Otunuga and Ladde, 2014]. Other practical applications are associated with pricing forwards and swaps in energy markets with our models that contain past-dependent history of the data (or delay), jumps in the spot prices and mean-reverting behavior. One of the other practical applications of our results is the so-called *delayed Samuelson effect* (see Section 6.1) associated with the behavior of forward volatility that converges to the volatility of the underlying spot when time to delivery approaches zero.

The rest of the chapter is organized as follows: Section 2 is devoted to the independent increment processes. In Section 3, we present our main model for the spot price in the form of OU process driven by independent increments process and with stochastic volatility with delay and jumps. We consider geometric and arithmetic models. Section 4 contains risk-neutral forward and swap price modeling. Section 5 deals with risk-neutral probabilities and the Esscher transform. Section 6 prices forwards and swaps under stochastic volatility with delay and jumps. A numerical example using Henry Hub natural gas daily spot prices (1997–2011) is presented in Section 7. Finally, Section 8 concludes the paper and presents the future work.

2. Independent Increments Processes (IIP): Definition and Examples

Let $(\Omega, \mathcal{F}, \mathcal{F}_t, P)$ be complete filtered probability space, $X(t) \equiv X(t, \omega)$ — stochastic process (a family of random variables parametrized over the time t), $X(t)$ is $\mathcal{F}_t$-adapted, (every $X(t)$ is measurable wrt $\mathcal{F}_t$) and $X(t)$ is RCLL, i.e. its paths $t \rightarrow X(t, \omega)$ are right-continuous and has left-limits a.s.

Definition of IIP (see [Skorokhod, 1991; Benth *et al.*, 2008]). An adapted RCLL stochastic process $I(t)$ starting at zero is an IIP (*Independent Increment process*) if it satisfies the following two conditions:

(1) The increments $I(t_0), I(t_1) - I(t_0), \ldots, I(t_n) - I(t_{n-1})$ are independent r.v. for any partition $0 \leq t_0 < t_1 < \cdots < t_n$, and $n \geq 1$.

(2) It is continuous in probability, that is, for every $t \geq 0$ and $\epsilon > 0$,

$$\lim_{s \to t} P(|I(s) - I(t)| > \epsilon) = 0.$$

If we add the condition that increments are stationary, then $I(t)$ is called a *Lévy process* (see [Sato, 1999; Schoutens, 2003]). If the increments of Lévy process are normally distributed, then we have a *Brownian motion.* Lévy processes which are increasing, that is, having only positive jumps, are often called *subordinators*.

Sometimes the IIP are called *additive processes* (see [Sato, 1999]).

The characteristic function of the IIP $I(t)$ is

$$E[\exp(i\theta(I(s) - I(t)))] = \exp(\psi(s, t; \theta)), \quad 0 \leq s < t, \theta \in R$$

and

$$\psi(s, t; \theta) = i\theta(\gamma(t) - \gamma(s)) - \frac{1}{2}\theta^2(C(t) - C(s)) + \int_s^t \int_R (e^{i\theta z} - 1 - i\theta z \mathbf{1}_{|z| \leq 1}) l(dz, du).$$

The function $\psi(s, t; \theta)$ is called *the cumulant function* of the process $I(t)$, and the generating triplet of the IIP is $(\gamma(t), C(t), l)$, with the properties

(1) $\gamma : R \to R$ is a continuous function with $\gamma(0) = 0$,
(2) $C : R \to R$ is non-decreasing and continuous, with $C(0) = 0$,
(3) l is a σ-finite measure on the Boreal σ-algebra of $(0, +\infty) \times R$, with the property

$$l(A \times \{0\}) = 0, \quad l(\{t\} \times R) = 0, \quad t \geq 0, A \in \mathcal{B}(R_+)$$

and

$$\int_0^t \int_R \min(1, z^2) l(ds, dz) < +\infty.$$

If

$$l(ds, dz) = ds\tilde{l}(dz), \quad \gamma(t) = \gamma t, \quad C(t) = ct$$

for constants γ and $c \geq 0$, we have $\psi(t, s, ; \theta) = (t - s)\tilde{\psi}(\theta)$ with

$$\tilde{\psi}(\theta) = i\theta\gamma - \frac{1}{2}\theta^2 c + \int_R (e^{i\theta z - 1 - i\theta z \mathbf{1}_{|z| \leq 1}}) \tilde{l}(dz).$$

The function $\tilde{\psi}$ is called *the cumulant of a Lévy process L*.

The *Lévy–Khintchine decomposition* for IIP $I(t)$ is:

$$I(t) = \gamma(t) + M(t) + \int_0^t \int_{|z|<1} z\tilde{N}(ds, dz) + \int_0^t \int_{|z|\geq 1} zN(ds, dz),$$

where $M(t)$ is a local square integrable continuous martingale.

An adapted RCLL stochastic process $S(t)$ is a *semimartingale* (see [Jacod and Shiryaev, 2003]) if it has the representation

$$S(t) = S(0) + A(t) + M(t) + \int_0^t \int_{R\setminus\{0\}} X_1(s, z)\tilde{N}(ds, dz) + \int_0^t \int_{R\setminus\{0\}} X_2(s, z)N(ds, dz),$$

where $A(t)$ is an adapted continuous stochastic process.

In general, an IIP is not a semimartingale. An IIP $I(t)$ may be represented as the sum of a deterministic RCLL function and a semimartingale (see [Jacod and Shiryaev, 2003]).

Examples of IIP include Brownian motion, compound Poisson process, time inhomogeneous compound Poisson process, normal inverse Gaussian (NIG) and CGMY Lévy processes.

3. Stochastic Volatilities with Delay and Jumps

In this chapter we concentrate on stochastic modeling and pricing of energy markets' contracts for stochastic volatilities with delay and jumps. The basic products in these markets are spot, futures and forward contracts and options written on these. We shall study forwards and swaps.

We study different types of stochastic processes for modeling energy spot dynamics.

3.1. *The Schwartz stochastic model for the energy spot price dynamics*

The classical stochastic process for the spot dynamics of commodity prices is given by the so-called Schwartz' model (see [Schwartz, 1997]).

It is defined as the exponential of an OU process, and has become the standard model for energy prices possessing mean-reverting features. We present in this talk spot price models based on a sum of non-Gaussian OU processes with stochastic delayed and jumped volatility. We will consider geometric models of the kind proposed by Schwartz [1997], but also arithmetic models which may be more analytically tractable in markets where the forward contracts have a delivery period. The starting point for the models is the Schwartz one-factor model from his 1997 paper [Schwartz, 1997]:

$$S(t) = S(0)\exp[X(t)],$$

with

$$dX(t) = \kappa(\alpha - X(t))dt + \sigma dW(t).$$

3.2. *Spot price modeling with OU processes driven by IIP*

Let $I(t)$ be an IIP with a Lévy–Kintchine representation

$$\begin{aligned}\psi(t,s;\theta) &= i\theta(\gamma(s)-\gamma(t)) - \tfrac{1}{2}\theta^2(C(s)-C(t)) \\ &\quad + \int_t^s\int_R \{e^{iz\theta} - 1 - iz\theta\mathbf{1}_{|z|<1}\} l(dz,du),\end{aligned}$$

where γ is of finite variation.

An RCLL process $X(s)$ $(t \le s \le T)$ is an OU process driven by IIP, if it is the unique strong solution to

$$dX(s) = (\mu(s) - \alpha(s)X(s))ds + \sigma(s)dI(s), \quad X(t) = x.$$

The unique solution of the above equation can be written as follows:

$$X(s) = x\,e^{-\int_t^s \alpha(v)dv} + \int_t^s \mu(u)e^{-\int_u^s \alpha(v)dv}du + \int_t^s \sigma(u)e^{-\int_u^s \alpha(v)dv}dI(u).$$

We can calculate expected value and other moments, because we know the characteristic function of $X(t)$.

3.3. *Our stochastic models for pricing energy derivatives with local stochastic delayed and jumped volatilities*

3.3.1. *Geometric models with local stochastic delayed and jumped volatility*

We introduce n pure jump semimartingale II processes $I_j(t)$, $j = 1, \ldots, n$, where I_j and I_k are independent of each other, for all $j \neq k$. We can represent each process via its associated random jump measure $N_j(dt, dz)$ by the Lévy–Itô representation:

$$I_j(t) = \gamma_j(t) + \int_0^t\int_{|z|<1} z\tilde{N}_j(du,dz) + \int_0^t\int_{|z|\ge 1} z\tilde{N}_j(du,dz).$$

Here, $\gamma_j(t)$ has bounded variation and the compensator measure for $N_j(dt, dz)$ is denoted by $l_j(dt, dz)$. Assume, that B is Brownian motion independent of $N_j(dt, dz)$.

Let the stochastic process $S(t)$ be denoted as

$$\ln S(t) = \ln \Lambda(t) + \sum_{i=1}^{m} X_i(t) + \sum_{j=1}^{n} Y_j(t),$$

where for $i = 1, \ldots, m$

$$dX_i(t) = (\mu_i(t) - \alpha_i(t)X_i(t))dt + \sigma_i(t, X_i(t+\theta))dB(t),$$

and for $j = 1, \ldots, n$

$$dY_j(t) = (\delta_j(t) - \beta_j(t)Y_j(t))dt + \eta_j(t, Y_j(t+\theta))dI_j(t).$$

Here, $\theta \in [-\tau, 0]$, $\tau > 0$, is the delay, and on the interval $[-\tau, 0]$, $X_i(t) = \phi_i(t)$ and $Y_j(t) = \psi_j(t)$, where $\phi_i(t)$ and $\psi_j(t)$ are deterministic functions, $i = 1, \ldots, m$ and $j = 1, \ldots, n$. We remark that two factors $X_i(t), i = 1, \ldots, m$, and $Y_j(t)$, $j = 1, \ldots, n$, represent the long- and short-term fluctuations of the spot dynamics which may be correlated. We suppose that jumps components I_j are independent, which is an obvious restriction of generality.

The deterministic seasonal price level is modeled by the function $\Lambda(t)$, (seasonal function) which is assumed to be continuously differentiable. The coefficients $\mu_i, \alpha_i, \delta_j \beta_j$ are all continuous functions. We suppose that volatilities $\sigma_{ik}(t)$ and $\eta_j(t)$ are stochastic volatilities with delay and jumps. We consider the following two cases in this situation:

$$\begin{aligned}\frac{d\sigma_i^2(t, X_i(t+\theta))}{dt} &= \gamma_i^1 V_i + \frac{\alpha}{\tau}\left[\int_{t-\tau}^{t} \sigma_i(u, X_i(u+\theta)dB(u)\right.\\ &\quad \left. + \int_{t-\tau}^{t} \sigma_i(u, X_i(u+\theta)d\tilde{N}_1(t)\right]^2\\ &\quad - (a_i + b_i)\sigma_i^2(t, X_i(t+\theta))\end{aligned}$$

and

$$\begin{aligned}\frac{d\eta_j^2(t, Y_j(t+\theta))}{dt} &= \gamma_j^2 W_i + \frac{\alpha}{\tau}\left[\int_{t-\tau}^{t} \eta_j(u, X_j(u+\theta)dB_1(u)\right.\\ &\quad \left. + \int_{t-\tau}^{t} \sigma_i(u, X_i(u+\theta)d\tilde{N}_2(t)\right]^2\\ &\quad - (c_j + d_j)\eta_j^2(t, X_i(t+\theta)\end{aligned}$$

Here, $B(t)$ and $B_1(t)$ are two independent Brownian motions and $\tilde{N}_1(t)$ and $\tilde{N}_2(t)$ are two independent compensated Poisson processes with intensities λ_1 and λ_2, independent of $B(t)$ and $B_1(t)$.

We note, that in Benth *et al.* [2008] it was considered only deterministic $\sigma_i(t)$ and $\eta_j(t)$.

We study the pricing of forwards, futures, swaps and options for the above-mentioned model with delayed and jumped volatilities.

3.3.2. *Arithmetic models with local stochastic delayed and jumped volatility*

Let the stochastic process $S(t)$ be defined as

$$S(t) = \Lambda(t) + \sum_{i=1}^{m} X_i(t) + \sum_{j=1}^{n} Y_j(t),$$

where $X_i(t), i = 1, \ldots, m$, and $Y_j(t), j = 1, \ldots, n$, are defined for the geometric models above and the seasonality function $\Lambda(t)$ is the same.

We suppose that for this model the volatilites $\sigma_i^2(t, X_i(t+\theta))$ and $\eta_j^2(t, Y_j(t+\theta))$ satisfied the same equations as for the case of geometric models.

We study the pricing of forwards and swaps for the above-mentioned model with delayed and jumped volatilities.

4. Risk-Neutral Forward and Swap Price Modeling

4.1. *Forward pricing*

When entering the forward contract, one agrees on a future delivery time and the price to be paid for receiving the underlying. Suppose that the delivery time is τ, with $0 \leq t \leq T < +\infty$, and that the agreed price to pay upon delivery is $f(t, T)$. At time T, we will effectively receive a (possibly negative) payment

$$S(T) - f(t, T).$$

It is costless to enter such contracts, which gives us a relation where we can extract the forward price:

$$e^{-r(T-t)} E_Q[S(T) - f(t, T)|\mathcal{F}_t] = 0.$$
$$f(t, T) = E_Q[S(T)|\mathcal{F}_t]-$$

fundamental pricing relation between the spot and forward price. Since the energy markets are incomplete, the choice of martingale measure Q is open.

4.2. *Swap pricing*

Let us consider swaps, using the electricity market as the typical example. The buyer of an electricity futures receives power during a settlement period (physically or financially), against paying a fixed price per MWh. The time t value of the payoff from the continuous flow electricity is given as

$$\int_{\tau_1}^{\tau_2} e^{-r(u-t)}(S(u) - F(t, \tau_1, \tau_2))du,$$

where $F(t, \tau_1, \tau_2)$ is the electricity futures price at time t for the delivery period $[\tau_1, \tau_2]$ with $\tau_1 \leq \tau_2$.

Since it is costless to enter an electricity futures contract, the risk-neutral price is defined by the equation

$$e^{-rt} E_Q\left[\int_{\tau_1}^{\tau_2} e^{-r(u-t)}(S(u) - F(t, \tau_1, \tau_2))du|\mathcal{F}_t\right] = 0.$$

As long as F is adapted, we have

$$F(t, \tau_1, \tau_2) = E_Q\left[\int_{\tau_1}^{\tau_2} \frac{re^{-ru}}{e^{-r\tau_1} - e^{-r\tau_2}} S(u)du|\mathcal{F}_t\right].$$

One may have that the settlement takes place financially at the end of the delivery period τ_2. The payoff from the contract at time τ_2 is then

$$e^{-r\tau_2} E_Q\left[\int_{\tau_1}^{\tau_2} (S(u) - F(t, \tau_1, \tau_2))du|\mathcal{F}_t\right] = 0,$$

which yields an electricity futures price

$$F(t, \tau_1, \tau_2) = E_Q\left[\int_{\tau_1}^{\tau_2} \frac{1}{\tau_2 - \tau_1} S(u)du|\mathcal{F}_t\right].$$

The same considerations could be done for gas futures contracts, and in the following we refer to $F(t, \tau_1, \tau_2)$ simply as the *swap price.*

Let us introduce a weight function $\hat{w}(u)$, being equal to one if the swap is settled at the end of the delivery period, or $\hat{w}(u) = \exp(-ru)$ if the contract is settled continuously over the delivery period. Defining the function

$$w(u, s, t) = \frac{\hat{w}(u)}{\int_s^t \hat{w}(v)dv},$$

where $0 \leq u \leq s \leq t$. Observe that $w = 1/(t-s)$, when $\hat{w} = 1$, while we have

$$w(u, s, t) = \frac{re^{-ru}}{e^{-rs} - e^{-rt}},$$

for the case when $\hat{w} = \exp(-ru)$. We note that $\int_s^t w du = 1$.

In general, we can write the link between a swap contract and the underlying spot as

$$F(t, \tau_1, \tau_2) = E_Q\left[\int_{\tau_1}^{\tau_2} w(u, \tau_1, \tau_2) S(u) du | \mathcal{F}_t\right].$$

Proposition 4.1 (See [Benth *et al.*, 2008]). *Suppose* $E_Q[\int_{\tau_1}^{\tau_2} |w(u, \tau_1, \tau_2) S(u)| du] < +\infty$. *It holds that*

$$F(t, \tau_1, \tau_2) = E_Q\left[\int_{\tau_1}^{\tau_2} w(u, \tau_1, \tau_2) f(t, u) du\right].$$

This means that holding a swap contract can be considered as holding a (weighted) continuous stream of forwards.

5. Risk-Neutral Probabilities and the Esscher Transform

The Esscher transform is a generalization of the Girsanov transform of Brownian motion to jump processes.

The Esscher transform is preserving the distributional properties of the jump process in the sense of transforming the cumulant function by a linear change of the argument.

Effectively, the Esscher transform yields an explicit change of measure, where we have access to the characteristics of the jump processes I_j also under the new risk-neutral measure.

It was introduced by Esscher [1932] to study risk theory and used by Gerber and Siu [1994] for derivatives pricing. Suppose we have f probability density and θ is a real number, then, as long as $\int_R e^{\theta y} f(y) dy < +\infty$, we can define a new probability density

$$f(x; \theta) = \frac{e^{\theta x} f(x)}{\int_R e^{\theta y} f(y) dy}.$$

Let now $\theta(t)$ be a $(p+n)$-dimensional vector of real-valued continuous functions on $[0, T]$

$$\theta(t) = (\hat{\theta}_1(t), \ldots, \hat{\theta}_p(t), \tilde{\theta}_1(t), \ldots, \tilde{\theta}_n(t)).$$

Defining for $0 \le t \le \tau$ the stochastic exponential

$$Z^{\theta}(t) = \prod_{k=1}^{p} \hat{Z}_k^{\theta}(t) \times \prod_{j=1}^{n} \tilde{Z}_j^{\theta}(t),$$

where

$$\hat{Z}_k^{\theta}(t) = \exp\left(\int_0^t \hat{\theta}_k(s) dB_k(s) - \frac{1}{2}\int_0^t \hat{\theta}_k^2(s) ds\right), \quad k = 1, 2, \ldots, p,$$

and

$$\tilde{Z}_j^{\theta}(t) = \exp\left(\int_0^t \tilde{\theta}_j(s) dI_j(s) - \phi_j(0, t; \tilde{\theta}_j(\cdot))\right), \quad j = 1, 2, \ldots, n.$$

We note that $\hat{Z}_k^{\theta}(t)$ and $\tilde{Z}_j^{\theta}(t)$ are a positive local martingales with expectation equals to one. Hence, we can define an equivalent probability measure Q^{θ}, such that Z^{theta} is the density process of the Radon–Nikodym derivative dQ^{θ}/dP, that is

$$\frac{dQ^{\theta}}{dP}|_{\mathcal{F}_t} = Z^{\theta}(t).$$

The expectation operator wrt the probability Q^{θ} is denoted by $E_{\theta}[\,\cdot\,]$. We observe that the Radon–Nikodym derivative dQ^{θ}/dP can be factorized as

$$\frac{dQ^{\theta}}{dP}|_{\mathcal{F}_t} = \prod_{k=1}^{p} \hat{Z}_k^{\theta}(t) \times \prod_{j=1}^{n} \tilde{Z}_j^{\theta}(t).$$

Hence, we associate a price of risk to each random source, given by the Brownian motion B_k and the jump factors I_j, $k = 1, 2, \ldots, p$, $j = 1, 2, \ldots, n$ in the model of spot price.

Let us study how the characteristics of B and I are changing when we apply the Esscher transform.

Proposition 5.1 (see [Benth *et al.*, 2008]). *Under measure Q^{θ} the processes*

$$B_k^{\theta}(t) = B_k(t) - \int_0^t \hat{\theta}_k(s) ds$$

are Brownian motions, $k = 1, 2, \ldots, p$. Furthermore, for each $j = 1, 2, \ldots, n$, $I_j(t)$ is an II process with drift

$$\gamma_j(t) + \int_0^t \int_{|z|<1} z(e^{\tilde{\theta}_j(u)z} - 1) l_j(dz, du),$$

and compensator measure $e^{\tilde{\theta}_j(t)z} l_j(dz, dt)$. We denote the new random jump measure by N_j^{θ} and its compensator by $\tilde{N}_j^{\theta}$.

We note that $N_j^\theta = N_j$. However, $\tilde{N}_j^\theta$ is not coinciding with $\tilde{N}_j$:

$$\begin{aligned}\tilde{N}_j^\theta &= N_j^\theta - e^{\tilde{\theta}_j(t)z} l_j(dz, dt)\\ &= N_j - l_j - (e^{\tilde{\theta}_j(t)z} - 1)l_j\\ &= \tilde{N} - (e^{\tilde{\theta}_j(t)z} - 1)l_j.\end{aligned}$$

Hence, $\tilde{N}_j$ translates to $\tilde{N}_j^\theta$ by subtraction of a drift, exactly as the Girsanov transform of B_k to B_k^θ.

5.1. *Esscher transform for some specific models: Time inhomogeneous compound Poisson process*

Compensator $l(dz, dt) = \lambda(t)F_X(dz)dt$, where F_X is the distribution of the jump size r.v. X and $\lambda(t)$ is the time-dependent jump intensity. The compensator measure onder Q^θ is (Proposition 5.1.):

$$l^\theta(dt, dz) = \lambda(t)e^{\tilde{\theta}_z} F_X(dz)dt.$$

A common choice of jump size is the exponential distribution with expectation μ_J. Then, we find the compensator measure under Q^θ to be

$$l^\theta(dt, dz) = \frac{\lambda(t)}{\mu_J} \exp\left(-\left(\frac{1}{\mu_J} - \tilde{\theta}\right) z\right) dzdt.$$

Hence, with $\tilde{\theta} < 1/\mu_J$, $I(t)$ will remain a compound Poisson process under Q^θ, with expectation $1/(1/\mu_J - \tilde{\theta})$ and intensity $\lambda(t)/(1 - \mu_J\tilde{\theta})$.

6. Pricing Forwards and Swaps under Stochastic Volatility with Delay and Jumps

6.1. *Pricing forwards: The geometric case*

Let us assume a geometric spot price model:

$$S(t) = \Lambda(t) \exp\left(\sum_{i=1}^{m} X_i(t) + \sum_{j=1}^{n} Y_j(t)\right) \quad (\textit{geometric} \quad \textit{case})$$

The forward price at time $t \geq 0$ for contracts with settlement at $T \geq t$ is explicitly given in the following Proposition.

Proposition 6.1. *Suppose that*

$$\sup_{0\le t\le T} |\eta_j(t, Y_j(t+\theta))e^{-\int_t^\tau \beta_j(v)dv} + \tilde{\theta}_j(t)| \le c_j, \quad a.s., \quad \theta \in [-\tau, 0].$$

The dynamics of $t \to f(t, T)$ *wrt* Q^θ *is*

$$\frac{df(t,T)}{f(t,T)} = \left\{\sum_{i=1}^m \sigma_i(t, X_i(t+\theta)) \exp\left(-\int_t^T \alpha_i(u)du\right)\right\} dB^\theta(t)$$
$$+ \sum_{j=1}^n \left\{\int_R \exp(z\eta_j(t, Y_j(t+\theta))e^{-\int_t^\tau \beta_j(u)du}) - 1\right\} \tilde{N}_j^\theta(dt, dz).$$

We see that the forward price dynamics becomes a geometric model, and in the case when we do not have any jumps terms Y_i, we are back to a geometric Brownian motion with time-dependent local stochastic volatility with delay and jumps

$$\frac{df(t,T)}{f(t,T)} = \left\{\sum_{i=1}^m \sigma_i(t, X_i(t+\theta)) \exp(-\int_t^T \alpha_i(u)du)\right\} dB^\theta(t).$$

Hence, we find that the volatilities of the forward contract are decreasing with time to delivery, being smaller than the spot volatility.

When time to delivery approaches zero, however, the forward volatility converges to the volatilities of the underlying spot $\sigma_i(t, \cdot)$.

This is known as the *Samuelson effect* (see [Samuelson, 1965]) and is a direct result of the mean-reverting spot price dynamics.

In our case, we have delay and, thus, *delayed Samuelson effect.*

We observe a similar Samuelson effect when including jumps in the spot dynamics, where the so-called "jump volatility" is expressed through the integrands

$$\exp(z\eta_j(t, Y_j(t+\theta))e^{-\int_t^T \beta_j(u)du}) - 1.$$

Suppose that $\eta_j(tY_j(t+\theta)) > 0$. When $t \to T$, the integrands are converging to $\exp(z\eta_j(t)) - 1$, which is identical to the corresponding terms of the spot price dynamics.

However, when $t < T$, we find for $z \ge 0$

$$0 \le \{\exp(z\eta_j(t, Y_j(t+\theta))e^{-\int_t^T \beta_j(u)du}) - 1\} \le \exp(z\eta_j(t, Y_j(t+\theta))) - 1,$$

meaning that the positive jumps in the spot price dynamics are scaled down in the forward price dynamics, and the downscaling is exponential wrt the mean reversion.

For the negative jumps (z < 0), we find

$$0 \geq \{\exp(z\eta_j(t, Y_j(t+\theta))e^{-\int_t^T \beta_j(u)du}) - 1\} \geq \exp(z\eta_j(t, Y_j(t+\theta))) - 1.$$

Thus, also the negative jumps in the spot are scaled down in the forward.

Thus, the "jump volatility" of the forward dynamics is a downscaling of the jump volatility of the spot, in line with the observations we made for the Brownian motion terms.

The downscaling of the jump volatility is dependent on time to maturity. The farther away from maturity, the less influence the jump volatility gets from the spot. The influence is "discounted" by the speed of mean reversion. The stronger the speed of mean reversion, the faster jumps in the spot price are whipped out along the term structure.

It is in general not possible to state an explicit formula for the swap price $F(t, \tau_1, \tau_2)$ of contracts with settlement over the period $[\tau_1, \tau_2]$ when we choose to work with a geometric model of the spot price dynamics. We now elaborate on the approximation of the swap price.

Recalling the relation between forward and swaps

$$F(t, \tau_1, \tau_2) = \int_{\tau_1}^{\tau_2} w(u, \tau_1, \tau_2) f(t, u) du.$$

There exist a few cases where we can derive explicit forward prices for contracts with delivery over a period in the geometric case.

Let's restrict our attention to a non-stationary dynamics of the spot price represented by setting the mean reversion coefficients α_i and β_j equal to zero. Hence, the spot price becomes a geometric Brownian motion in the case of no jumps.

$$S(t) = \Lambda(t) \exp\left(\sum_{i=1}^{m} X_i(t) + \sum_{j=1}^{n} Y_j(t)\right) \quad (\textit{geometric} \quad \textit{case})$$

We find the following risk-neutral dynamics of $F(t, \tau_1, \tau_2)$.

Proposition 6.2. *Suppose that the mean reversion coefficients α_i and β_j are set equal to zero, for $j = 1, 2, \ldots, n$ and $i = 1, 2, \ldots, m$. The risk-neutral dynamics of the forward price $F(t, \tau_1, \tau_2)$ is given by*

$$\frac{dF(t, \tau_1, \tau_2)}{F(t-, \tau_1, \tau_2)} = \sum_{i=1}^{m} \sigma_i(t, X_i(t+\theta)) dB^\theta(t) + \sum_{j=1}^{n} \int_R (e^{\eta_j(t, Y_j(t+\theta))z} - 1) \tilde{N}_j^\theta(dz, dt).$$

However, having zero speed of mean reversion creates a market which does not have the right properties for modeling the riskless of forward, and henceforth swaps.

6.2. *Pricing of swaps: The arithmetic case*

Suppose we have the spot price process that is modeled as the arithmetic dynamics:

$$S(t) = \Lambda(t) + \sum_{i=1}^{m} X_i(t) + \sum_{j=1}^{n} Y_j(t) \quad \text{(arithmetic case)}$$

The Asymptotic of the Swap Prices

Letting $\tau_1 \to +\infty$ and the length of the delivery period $\tau_1 - \tau_2$ be fixed, we obtain

$$F(t, \tau_1, \tau_2) - \int_{\tau_1}^{\tau_2} w(u, \tau_1, \tau_2)\Lambda(u)du - \Theta(t, \tau_1, \tau_2; \theta(\cdot)) \to_{\tau_1 \to +\infty} 0.$$

Hence, the swap price behaves asymptotically as the weighted average seasonal function $\Lambda(u)$ and risk-adjustment function Θ. This is in line with the asymptotic of forwards.

Proposition 6.3. *The risk-neutral dynamics of the stochastic process $F(t, \tau_1, \tau_2)$ is given by*

$$\begin{aligned} dF(t, \tau_1, \tau_2) &= \sum_{i=1}^{m} \sigma_i(t, X_i(t+\theta)) \int_{\tau_1}^{\tau_2} w(u, \tau_1, \tau_2)e^{-\int_v^u \alpha_i(s)ds} du dB^{\theta}(t) \\ &\quad + \sum_{j=1}^{n} \int_R z\eta_j(t, Y_j(t+\theta)) \\ &\quad \times \int_{\tau_1}^{\tau_2} w(u, \tau_1, \tau_2)e^{-\int_v^u \beta_j(s)ds} du \tilde{N}_j^{\theta}(dt, dz). \end{aligned}$$

The volatility in the dynamics of $F(t, \tau_1, \tau_2)$ has an average delayed Samuelson effect. For constant α_i and β_j, we have

$$\begin{aligned} \sigma_i(t, X_i(t+\theta)) \int_{\tau_1}^{\tau_2} w(u, \tau_1, \tau_2)e^{-\int_v^u \alpha_i(s)ds} du &= \frac{\sigma_i(t, X_i(t+\theta))}{\alpha_i(\tau_2 - \tau_1)} \\ &\quad \times (e^{-\alpha_i(\tau_1 - t)} - e^{-\alpha_i(\tau_2 - t)}). \end{aligned}$$

The same argument holds true for the jump volatility.

7. Numerical Example: Henry Hub Natural Gas Daily Spot Prices (1997–2011)

This numerical example and figures are borrowed from [Otunuga and Ladde, 2014]. In this paper, the authors used the model for spot price with delayed stochastic volatility from the paper [Kazmerchuk *et al.*, 2005], and applied it to the Henry Hub daily natural gas data set for the period 1 February 2001–30 September 2004. The data was collected from the United State Energy Information Administration website (www.eia.gov).

From Fig. 1, we can see the properties of the gas daily spot prices: randomly driven, non-negative, mean reversion, jumps (spikes), unpredictability of spot price volatility.

Table 1 gives descriptive statistics of Henry Hub Daily Natural Gas spot prices (1997–2011):

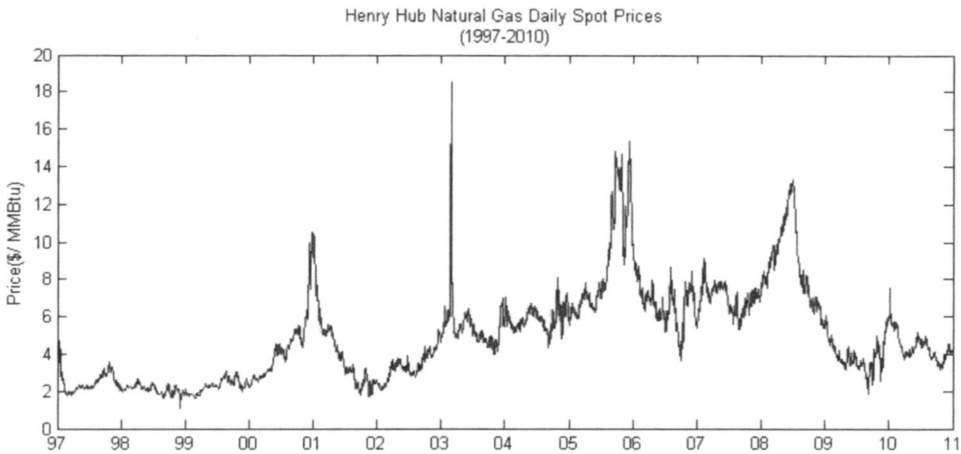

Fig. 1. Plot of Henry Hub daily natural gas spot prices (1997–2011) (Courtesy — [Otunuga and Ladde, 2014]).

Table 1. Descriptive statistics of Henry Hub daily natural gas spot prices (1997–2011) (Courtesy — [Otunuga and Ladde, 2014]).

	Mean	Variance	Skewness	Kurtosis	Minimum	Maximum
S_t	4.9519	2.4966	1.0391	4.3491	1.05	18.48
$S_{t+1} - S_t$	−0.0001142	3.3189	−0.7735	191.8911	−8.01	6.50
$\ln(S_t)$	1.4754	0.5048	−0.0465	2.1540	0.0488	2.9167
$\ln[S_{t+1}/S_t]$	2.8485*e*-5	0.0473	0.4814	22.0473	−0.56	0.5657

As we can see from Table 1, the logarithmic price is better than the raw price data because the variance for log is the smallest.

The following simple model for the log-spot price is considered:

$$\ln S(t) = X(t),$$

where

$$dX(t) = \gamma(k - X(t))dt + \sigma(t, X(t))dB(t),$$

and

$$\frac{\sigma^2(t, X(t))}{dt} = \left[\alpha + \beta \int_{t-\tau}^{t} \sigma(s, X(s))dB(s)\right]^2 + c\sigma^2(t, X(t)).$$

Here, τ is the delay parameter.

The model for $\sigma^2(t, X(t))$ above is the same as the model for stochastic volatility with delay that we considered in [Kazmerchuk *et al.*, 2005].

Discrete scheme is implemented: $l = 2 = [\frac{\tau}{\Delta}]$, where Δ is the size of the mesh of the discrete-time grid, [,] is the floor function.

Estimated Parameters are (Courtesy — [Otunuga and Ladde, 2014]):

γ	k	τ	α	β	c
1.8943	1.5627	0.008	0.433	−0.07	−1.5

8. Conclusion and Future Work

In this chapter, we studied stochastic modeling and pricing of energy markets' contracts for stochastic volatilities with delay and jumps. Our model of stochastic volatility exhibits jumps and also past-dependence: the behavior of a stock price right after a given time t not only depends on the situation at t, but also on the whole past (history) of the process $S(t)$ up to time t. The spot price process is modeled as the OU process driven by independent increments process. The basic products in these markets are spot, futures and forward contracts and options written on these. We studied forwards and swaps. A numerical example was presented for stochastic volatility with delay using the Henry Hub daily natural gas data (1997–2011).

The future work will be associated with implementing of the obtained results, pricing of forwards and swaps with stochastic volatility with delay and jumps using the Henry Hub daily natural gas data (1997–2011), data from electricity and oil markets.

Acknowledgments

The author thanks Professor Gangaram Ladde (University of South Florida) very much for his permission to use the numerical example in Section 7 from their paper [Otunuga and Ladde, 2014]. The author also wishes to thank NSERC for continuing support.

References

Ait-Sahalia, Y. and Jacod, J. (2014). *High-frequency Financial Econometrics*. (Princeton University Press, USA).

Ait-Sahalia, Y. (1996). Testing continuous-time models of the spot interest rate. *Review of Financial Studies* **9**, 385–426.

Barndorff-Nielsen, O. and Shephard, N. (2007). *Financial Volatility: Stochastic Volatility and Lévy Based Models*. (Cambridge University Press, UK).

Benth, F., Kallsen, J. and Meyer-Brandis, T. (2007). A non-gaussian Ornstein–Uhlenbeck process for electricity spot price modelling and derivatives pricing. *Applied Mathematics Finance* **14** (2), 153–169.

Benth, F., Benth, J. and Koekebakker, S. (2008). *Stochastic Modelling of Electricity and Related Markets*. (World Scientific, Singapore).

Bollerslev, T. (1986). Generalized autoregressive conditional heteroscedasticity. *Journal of Econometrics* **31**, 307–327.

Burger, M., Klar, B., Mueller, A. and Schindlmayr, G. (2004). A spot market model for pricing derivatives in electricity markets. *Quantitative Finance* **4** (1), 109–122.

Esscher, F. (1932). On the probability function in the collective theory of risk. *Skandinavisk Aktuarietidskrift* **15**, 175–195.

Frisch, R. and Holmes, H. (1935). The characteristic solutions of a mixed difference and differential equation occurring in economic dynamics. *Econometrica* **3**, 225–239.

Gerber, H. and Shiu, E. (1994). Option pricing by Esscher transforms. *Transactions of Society of Actuaries* **46**, 99–191.

Jacod, J. and Shiryaev, A. (2003). *Limit Theorems for Stochastic Processes*. (Springer, Berlin).

Kazmerchuk, Y., Swishchuk, A. and Wu, J.-H. (2005). A continuous-time GARCH model for stochastic volatility with delay. *Canadian Applied Mathematics Quarterly* **13** (2), 123–150.

Klueppelberg, C., Meyer-Brandis, T. and Schmidt, A. (2010). Electricity spot price modelling with a view towards extreme spike risk. *Quantitative Finance* **10** (9), 963–974.

Mandelbrot, B. (1997). *Fractals and Scaling in Finance: Discontinuity, Concentration, Risk*. (Springer, Berlin).

Otunuga, O. and Ladde, G. (2014). Stochastic modeling of energy commodity spot price processes with delay in volatility. *American International Joronal of Contemporary Research* **4** (5), 1–20.

Samuelson, P. (1965). Proof that properly anticipated prices fluctuate randomly. *Industrial Management Review* **6**, 41–44.

Sato, K.-I. (1999). *Lévy Processes and Infinitely Divisible Distributions*. (Cambridge University Press, UK).

Schoutens, W. (2003). *Lévy Processes in Finance*. (Wiley, USA).

Schwartz, E. (1997). The stochastic behavior of commodity prices: Implications for valuation and hedging. *The Journal of Finance* **52** (3), 923–973.

Skorohod, A. (1991). *Random Processes with Independent Increments*. (Springer, Netherlands).

Swishchuk, A. (2010). Stochastic Modelling and Pricing of Energy Markets Contracts with Local Stochastic Delayed and Jumped Volatilities. *Abstract of SSC 2010 Annual Meeting*, Université Laval, Québec City, QC, Canada, May 24.

Swishchuk, A. and Li, X. (2011). Pricing of variance and volatility swaps for stochastic volatilities with delay and jumps. *International Journal of Stochastic Analysis* **2011** (2011), Article ID 435145, 27 pages.

Todorov, V. and Tauchen, G. (2011). Volatility jumps. *Journal of Business and Economic Statistics* **29** (3), 356–371.

Chapter 12

Volatility Spillover Effects in the Oil and Financial Market: Cross-Hedging in the US Oil Market and the Energy Pipeline Sector

Jingze Jiang*,‡ and Thomas L. Marsh†,§

**Department of Business and Economics, School of Business, Edinboro University, Edinboro, PA, USA*
†School of Economic Sciences, Washington State University, WA, USA
‡jjiang@edinboro.edu
§tl_marsh@wsu.edu

This chapter will provide important insights into the linkages between the oil and financial markets and explore a new cross-hedging strategy to manage risk in the pipeline and energy sector market. Specifically, it will focus on examining the mean and volatility spillover effects between the US oil market, US stock market and the US Energy Pipeline Sector Index. Of particular interest is the impact of the recent liquidity crisis in the financial markets on volatility spillovers. Results demonstrate that both the US oil and stock markets have statistically significant volatility spillover effects on the US Energy Pipeline Sector. In addition, the volatility transmission from the US oil market and stock market to the US energy pipeline market increased after the 2007–2008 financial crisis. Furthermore, decreasing liquidity in the US financial market is associated with a statistically significant increase in volatility transmission between the markets. The analysis of the hedging strategy effectiveness shows that both in-sample and out-of-sample performance of the new cross-hedging strategy introduced in this chapter enhance the oil-stock hedging strategies proposed in previous studies [Basher and Sadorsky, 2016; Salisu and Oloko, 2015].

Keywords: Stock market; US energy pipeline; oil market; volatility spillover effect; cross-hedge; liquidity spread; financial crisis; DJUSPL; SP500; DJIA.

1. Introduction

The energy pipeline industry plays an important role in the growth and stabilization of the US economy, which depends heavily on oil [Elyasiani *et al.*, 2011]. Energy pipeline companies defined by S&P Dow Jones Indices [2015] operate pipelines carrying oil, gas or other forms of fuel for distribution instead of direct sales to end users that are not solely focused on production. The US energy pipelines assist the distribution of energy to support the operation of other industries, such as oil and natural gas to fuel the manufacturing section. Expansion of the US energy pipeline has been justified to reduce the impact of oil price hikes caused by peak demand or the unstable international energy market. Expansion diversifies supply sources and modes of transport, thus improving the efficiency of energy supplies along with energy independence and security [Bielecki, 2002].

Accordingly, changes in the oil market and US economy may impact the energy pipeline industry, drawing investors to subsector index investing related to the pipeline industry. Investors seeking to replicate the performance of a certain index, such as an equity or fixed-income index, invest in index funds or exchange-traded funds by closely tracking the performance of a certain index. Compared with investing in individual stocks, index investing considers an entire specific market and reduces trading frequency, decreasing trading cost, managerial fees, diversifying risk and deferring payment of taxes [Malik and Hassan, 2004; Sharpe, 2002]. In addition, subsector index investing meets investors' needs to allocate assets to the sector, such as the pipeline sector, that they believe are experiencing strong growth.

Although the Dow Jones US Pipeline Index (DJUSPL) was established in 2000, there is limited economic research on the investment value for the DJUSPL [Mohanty and Nandha, 2011]. The current analysis fills an important gap in the research literature to examine the mean and volatility spillover effects between the US oil and stock markets and the DJUSPL. We are particularly interested in the impact of the liquidity crisis in the financial market on the volatility spillovers. Furthermore, we examine a new cross-hedging strategy to manage the risk on the US oil market by including the DJUSPL.

The current research has three main contributions to the literature. First, although numerous studies have examined the stock and oil markets [Arouri *et al.*, 2011a, 2011b; Basher and Sadorsky, 2016; Cifarelli and Paladino, 2010; Hammoudeh *et al.*, 2004; Kollias *et al.*, 2013; Mollick and Assefa, 2013; Nazlioglu *et al.*, 2015; Salisu and Oloko, 2015; Schaeffer *et al.*, 2012; Souček and Todorova, 2013], studies on the US energy pipeline and US oil companies are limited in number. Edwards *et al.* [2000] and Norton [1993] focus on analyzing the operation strategy applying to individual companies. They suggest that US oil companies should integrate the US energy pipeline operation into US crude oil production, since integration can increase company ratings and reduce risks in the stock market. The integration is likely to increase linkages between oil market and energy pipeline sector, but there is scant empirical evidence published on such linkages. The current research empirically pioneers a study of the linkages between the US oil market and energy pipeline sector.

Second, with the level of the liquidity in the financial market changing over time, we test whether spillover effects are time-varying. Therefore, we developed the time-varying spillover model to study the impact of the liquidity changes in the financial market on the spillover effect between the oil and stock markets. This model improves the previous models with structural breaks [Mollick and Assefa, 2013] to study the impact of the shocks in the financial market on the relationship between oil and stock markets over time. Third, a new cross-hedging strategy for managing the oil price risk is proposed and examined in our study.

We follow Bekaert and Harvey [1997], Ng [2000], Salisu and Oloko [2015] and Jiang *et al.* [2015] to develop a bivariate VAR(2)-BEKK-AGARCH(1,1) model for US oil returns and US stock returns, and incorporate oil and stock return shocks into to the AR(2)-AGARCH (1,1) model for the return of the US energy pipeline index. This specification allows for past US oil and stock returns in the mean equation of the DJUSPL and for current return shocks of the US oil and stock returns in the unexpected return of the DJUSPL. We also introduce three parameterizations for the mean and volatility spillover parameters, namely constant, event-dummy and time-varying spillover parameters. Findings indicate that both US oil and stock markets have statistically significant volatility-spillover effect on DJUSPL. In addition, the increasing liquidity spread and interbank liquidity spread, which implies the raising illiquidity in the financial market, is associated with the statistically significant increase in the volatility transmission from the US oil and stock markets to the DJUSPL. Finally, the performance of a new cross-hedging strategy proposed in this chapter enhances the oil-stock hedging strategies proposed in previous studies [Basher and Sadorsky, 2016; Salisu and Oloko, 2015]. Our results will assist policy makers and investors on planning energy, diversifying portfolio and managing energy risk.

The reminder of this chapter is organized as follows: Section 2 identifies an empirical model for the US oil and stock markets. Section 3 specifies a model for the DJUSPL. Section 4 introduces three types of parameterization for spillover effects. Section 5 presents a model to measure the hedging effectiveness. Section 6 presents the data and discusses the empirical results. Section 7 concludes this chapter.

2. Specification for the US Oil and Stock Markets

We test both the daily Dow Jones Industrial Average Index (DJIA), $P_{\text{DJIA},t}$ and S&P 500 stock index (SP500), $P_{\text{SP500},t}$, as proxies for the US stock (points) on the New York Stock Exchange (NYSE). We denote ST = {DJIA, SP500} to represent a proxy for the US stock market in the remainder of the chapter.[1] The average price of the highest and lowest price of West Texas Intermediate (WTI), $P_{\text{WTI},t}$ is used as a proxy for the US oil price (dollar/barrel) on the New York Mercantile Exchange (NYMEX). We use WTI due in part to its popularity in past studies in North American markets. Many hedging financial instruments, such as oil futures, oil forwards, are based on WTI [Boyer and Filion, 2007; Mohanty and Nandha, 2011]. The daily DJUSPL, $P_{\text{DJUSPL},t}$, is used as a proxy for the US energy pipeline sector (points) on the Frankfurt Stock Exchange. Lower-case $p_{\text{ST},t}$, $p_{\text{WTI},t}$ and $p_{\text{DJUSPL},t}$ are used to denote the logarithmic series for ST, WTI and DJUSPL, respectively. In addition, we define $r_{i,t}$, to denote the "returns" of the series i, which is computed as the first difference of the logarithmic series i, i = ST, WTI, DJUSPL. In other words, $r_{i,t}$[2] is satisfied in Eq. (1).

$$r_{i,t} = (p_{i,t} - p_{i,t-1}) * 100, \quad \text{where } i = \text{ST, WTI, DJUSPL}. \tag{1}$$

We follow Bekaert and Harvey [1997], Ng [2000], Salisu and Oloko [2015] and Jiang *et al.* [2015] to setup a two-step GARCH model. A bivariate VAR-BEKK-AGARCH model is estimated for the returns of the US stock market index and the US oil spot returns. The number of the lags, n, in VAR process is determined by Schwarz Criterion (SBC) value. The US oil and stock markets are specified as Eq. (2):

$$R_t = \Theta_0 + \sum_{m=1}^{n} \Theta'_m R_{t-m} + \varepsilon_t, \tag{2}$$

where $R_t = \begin{bmatrix} r_{\text{WTI},t} \\ r_{\text{ST},t} \end{bmatrix}$ and $\Theta_0 = \begin{bmatrix} \theta_{\text{WTI},0} \\ \theta_{\text{ST},0} \end{bmatrix}$, which is the vector of constant terms in the conditional mean of the returns for the US stock market indices and WTI. The mean spillover effects are captured in $\Theta_m = \begin{bmatrix} \theta_{\text{WTI},m} & \theta_{\text{WTI}-\text{ST},m} \\ \theta_{\text{ST}-\text{WTI},m} & \theta_{\text{ST},m} \end{bmatrix}$, where $\theta_{\text{WTI}-\text{ST},m}$ is the mean spillover parameter of WTI that measures the mean spillover effects from the returns of WTI to the US stock market index, and $\theta_{\text{ST}-\text{WTI},m}$ is the mean spillover parameter of the ST. Here, $\varepsilon_t = \begin{bmatrix} \varepsilon_{\text{WTI},t} \\ \varepsilon_{\text{ST},t} \end{bmatrix}$ is a vector of idiosyncratic shocks

[1]To be clear, throughout the remainder of the chapter ST represents either DJIA or SP500. In the empirical section of the chapter, we compare and contrast the results for both the DJIA and SP500.
[2]The value is scaled up by 100 to a more manageable magnitude.

in the US oil and stock markets. Given the information available at time $t-1$, which is denoted as I_{t-1}, ε_t follows the normal distribution with mean zero and conditional variance, $H_t = \{h_{i-j,t}\}_{i,j=\text{WTI,ST}}$, following the BEKK-AGARCH (1,1), or $\varepsilon_t | I_{t-1} \sim N(0, H_t)$, in Eq. (3):

$$H_t = CC' + A'\varepsilon_{t-1}\varepsilon'_{t-1}A + B'H_{t-1}B + D'v_{t-1}v'_{t-1}D, \tag{3}$$

where $C = \begin{bmatrix} c_{\text{WTI}} & 0 \\ c_{\text{ST-WTI}} & c_{\text{ST}} \end{bmatrix}$ is a lower triangular matrix of constant terms in the conditional variance. The coefficients of ARCH term consist of $A = \begin{bmatrix} a_{\text{WTI}} & a_{\text{WTI-ST}} \\ a_{\text{ST-WTI}} & a_{\text{ST}} \end{bmatrix}$, where coefficients on the diagonal shows the effect of shock in the own market in the short term and the off-diagonal coefficients a_{i-j} measures the short-term volatility spillover from market i to market j, for $i, j =$ WTI, ST [Apergis and Rezitis, 2003; Salisu and Oloko, 2015]. The matrix $B = \begin{bmatrix} b_{\text{WTI}} & b_{\text{WTI-ST}} \\ b_{\text{ST-WTI}} & b_{\text{ST}} \end{bmatrix}$ includes the coefficients of the GARCH term, which implies long-term persistence volatility. Coefficients b_{i-j} measure the volatility spillover from market i to market j, for $i, j =$ WTI, ST in the long term. The vector $v_t = [v_{\text{WTI},t}, v_{\text{ST},t}]'$ represents the vector of negative return shocks, where $v_{i,t} = \min\{0, \varepsilon_{i,t}\}$, $i, j =$ WTI, ST. Introducing v_t into the conditional variance helps capture the characteristics on the financial market that stock/indices volatility tends to rise more in response to negative shocks (bad news) than to positive shocks (good news) [Campbell and Hentschel, 1992; Cappiello *et al.*, 2006]. The matrix $D = \begin{bmatrix} d_{\text{WTI}} & d_{\text{WTI-ST}} \\ d_{\text{ST-WTI}} & d_{\text{ST}} \end{bmatrix}$ shows the asymmetric effect coefficients, where the off-diagonal coefficients measure the effect between WTI and ST.

3. Specification for the US Energy Pipeline Market

To assure that the idiosyncratic shocks from the stock and the oil spot markets to DJUSPL are independent, we orthogonalize the idiosyncratic shocks in the stock market and oil market by assuming that the shock in ST is driven by a purely idiosyncratic shock, $e_{\text{ST},t}$, and by the return shock from the WTI, $e_{\text{WTI},t}$. In other words, ε_t is defined in Eq. (4),

$$\varepsilon_t = \begin{bmatrix} \varepsilon_{\text{WTI},t} \\ \varepsilon_{\text{ST},t} \end{bmatrix} = \begin{bmatrix} 1 & 0 \\ f_{t-1} & 1 \end{bmatrix} \begin{bmatrix} e_{\text{WTI},t} \\ e_{\text{ST},t} \end{bmatrix} = F_{t-1}e_t. \tag{4}$$

The conditional $e_t | I_{t-1}$ follows the normal distribution with mean equal to 0 and variance $\Sigma_t = \begin{bmatrix} \sigma^2_{\text{WTI}} & 0 \\ 0 & \sigma^2_{\text{ST}} \end{bmatrix}$. The Cholesky decomposition [Tsay, 2005] allows us to solve the F_{t-1} matrix and the conditional variance σ^2_{WTI}, σ^2_{ST}, given $H_t = F_{t-1}\Sigma_t F'_{t-1}$. After obtaining the independent $e_{\text{WTI},t}$ and $e_{\text{ST},t}$, we model the mean spillover effects from both ST and WIT to DJUSPL as Eq. (5) and risk transmission as Eq. (6):

$$r_{\text{DJUSPL},t} = \theta_{\text{DJUSPL},0} + \sum_{m=1}^{n} \theta_{\text{DJUSPL},m} r_{\text{DJUSPL},m} + \delta_{\text{DJUSPL},t-1} r_{\text{WTI},t-1} + \gamma_{\text{DJUSPL},t-1} r_{\text{ST},t-1} + \varepsilon_{\text{DJUSPL},t} \quad (5)$$

$$\varepsilon_{\text{DJUSPL},t} = e_{\text{DJUSPL},t} + \psi_{\text{DJUSPL},t-1} e_{\text{WTI},t} + \phi_{\text{DJUSPL},t-1} e_{\text{ST},t}. \quad (6)$$

The impact of the return of the US oil spot and stock markets on the return of the US energy pipeline market is presented by the lagged returns of WTI and ST, $r_{\text{WTI},t-1}$ and $r_{\text{ST},t-1}$, respectively. The mean spillover coefficients are denoted as $\delta_{\text{DJUSPL},t-1}$ and $\gamma_{\text{DJUSPL},t-1}$ in Eq. (5). This implies that the past information on the US oil spot and stock markets will consistently affect returns on the US energy pipeline market.

Above $\varepsilon_{\text{DJUSPL},t}$ denotes the unexpected return for the US energy pipeline market, which is explained by the purely idiosyncratic shock at the US energy pipeline market, the current shocks at the US oil spot and stock markets. The purely idiosyncratic shock at the US energy pipeline market, $e_{\text{DJUSPL},t}$, is assumed to be uncorrelated with the return shock on the US oil spot market and the US stock market, $e_{\text{WTI},t}$ and $e_{\text{ST},t}$. The modified shocks from the US oil and stock markets, $e_{\text{WTI},t}$ and $e_{\text{ST},t}$, are unrelated, and they introduce volatility spillover effects from the US oil spot and stock markets to the US energy pipeline market. The volatility spillover coefficients are denoted as $\psi_{\text{DJUSPL},t-1}$ and $\phi_{\text{DJUSPL},t-1}$, in Eq. (6). $e_{\text{DJUSPL},t}$, is the idiosyncratic shock in DJUSPL, which has mean 0 and the variance $\sigma^2_{\text{DJUSPL},t}$, or $e_{\text{DJUSPL},t}|I_{t-1} \sim N(0, \sigma^2_{\text{DJUSPL},t})$. In Eq. (7), $\sigma^2_{\text{DJUSPL},t}$ is assumed to follow an asymmetric GARCH (1,1):

$$\sigma^2_{\text{DJUSPL},t} = c_{\text{DJUSPL}} + a_{\text{DJUSPL}} e^2_{\text{DJUSPL},t-1} + b_{\text{DJUSPL}} \sigma^2_{\text{DJUSPL},t-1} + d_{\text{DJUSPL}} \upsilon_{\text{DJUSPL},t-1} \quad (7)$$

Here, a_{DJUSPL} is the ARCH coefficient and b_{DJUSPL} is the GARCH coefficient. $\upsilon_{\text{DJUSPL},t-1} = \min\{0, e_{\text{DJUSPL},t}\}$, which implies that investors will be more responsive to negative shock than positive shock on the US energy pipeline market. d_{DJUSPL} is the asymmetric effect coefficient.

4. Characterization of the Spillover Effects

The model specification implies that based on the information available at time $t-1$, the conditional variance of the unexpected return for the US energy pipeline market is given as follows:

$$h_{\text{DJUSPL},t} = E(\varepsilon^2_{\text{DJUSPL},t} \mid I_{t-1}) = \sigma^2_{\text{DJUSPL},t} + \psi^2_{\text{DJUSPL},t-1}\sigma^2_{\text{WTI},t} + \phi^2_{\text{DJUSPL},t-1}\sigma^2_{\text{ST},t} \quad (8)$$

Therefore, the volatility spillover ratios from the US oil spot and stock markets to the US energy pipeline market are denoted as $VR_{\text{WTI},t}$ and $VR_{\text{ST},t}$, respectively and defined as follows:

$$VR_{\text{WTI}} = \frac{\psi^2_{\text{DJUSPL},t-1}\sigma^2_{\text{WTI},t}}{h_{\text{DJUSPL},t}}, \quad (9)$$

$$VR_{\text{ST}} = \frac{\phi^2_{\text{DJUSPL},t-1}\sigma^2_{\text{ST},t}}{h_{\text{DJUSPL},t}}. \quad (10)$$

We further specify the mean and volatility spillover coefficients into three models: the constant spillover model, event-dummy model and time-varying model. We first assume that during the sample period, there is no change on the volatility spillover effects. Therefore, the spillover coefficients are all constant over time, where

$$\begin{aligned} \delta_{\text{DJUSPL},t} &= \delta_{\text{DJUSPL}}, \\ \gamma_{\text{DJUSPL},t} &= \gamma_{\text{DJUSPL}}, \\ \psi_{\text{DJUSPL},t} &= \psi_{\text{DJUSPL}}, \\ \phi_{\text{DJUSPL},t} &= \phi_{\text{DJUSPL}}. \end{aligned} \quad (11)$$

Several studies have examined the impact of the 2007–2008 financial crisis on the spillover effects between the US stock market and the oil market, and reported that the spillover effects differ before and after the crisis. For instance, Mollick and Assefa [2013] conclude that there is the statistically significant volatility transmission between the two markets after the 2007–2008 financial crisis, which was not significant before the crisis. However, the constant volatility model does not allow one to consider the potential impact of the 2007–2008 financial crisis on the spillover effects. We further develop the event-dummy model to include the impact of the crisis. Previous studies recognize 9 August 2007, when Banque Nationale de Paris (BNP) and Paribas froze three funds exposed to the stumbling US subprime mortgage market as the starting point of the 2007–2008 financial crisis [Dumontaux and Pop, 2013; Griffiths *et al.*, 2011; Shin, 2009]. Therefore, we create the dummy variable D_t, which is equal to 0 before 9 August 2007 and equal to 1 otherwise, to capture the potential changes related to the 2007–2008 financial crisis. The event-dummy spillover coefficients are defined as

$$\begin{aligned}
\delta_{\text{DJUSPL},t} &= \delta_{\text{DJUSPL},0} + \delta_{\text{DJUSPL},1} D_t, \\
\gamma_{\text{DJUSPL},t} &= \gamma_{\text{DJUSPL},0} + \gamma_{\text{DJUSPL},1} D_t, \\
\psi_{\text{DJUSPL},t} &= \psi_{\text{DJUSPL},0} + \psi_{\text{DJUSPL},1} D_t, \\
\phi_{\text{DJUSPL},t} &= \phi_{\text{DJUSPL},0} + \phi_{\text{DJUSPL},1} D_t.
\end{aligned} \tag{12}$$

Next, we further relax the assumption on the spillover coefficients to consider the time-varying factors. Previous studies find evidence of time-varying correlations between stock markets and oil market [Creti *et al.*, 2013; Sadorsky 2012]. It is a more appropriate way to examine the spillover effects by allowing spillover parameters to vary over time with certain underlying factors identifying financial stress and economic activity. Large decreases in the liquidity on the financial market foreshadow the crisis on the financial market. The 2007–2008 financial crisis is highly related the illiquidity in the financial market, in turn generated wider impact on the US economy [Cornett *et al.*, 2011; Garcia-Appendini and Montoriol-Garriga, 2013; Shin, 2009; Williamson, 2012]. We might expect oil and stock markets to become more connected as the liquidity decreases over time. Therefore, we consider the time-varying liquidity on the US financial market to construct time-varying spillover parameters.

Since the 2007–2008 financial crisis, the US government has searched for tools to monitor the condition of broad financial sectors. The Cleveland Financial Stress Index (CFSI) is one of the important tools developed by Federal Reserve Bank of Cleveland [2012]. The daily CFSI includes two important indicators: the *interbank liquidity spread*[3] and *the liquidity spread*,[4] used to measure liquidity on the US funding market and the credit market, respectively. They capture the characteristics of liquidity at the US financial markets. Therefore, we use the *interbank liquidity spread* denoted as x_{BANK} and *the liquidity spread* labeled as x_{LIQ}, as proxies to the liquidity on the US financial market. Given the vector $X_t = [x_{\text{BANK}}\ x_{\text{LIQ}}]'$, the third

[3]Interbank liquidity spread is measured as the difference between the 3-Month LIBOR and the 3-Month US Treasury Yield. The spread reflects the perception of counterparty risk in interbank lending by measuring the risk premium associated with lending to commercial banks. The spread increases when either market liquidity is scarce or when counterparty default risk increases, both of which are associated with increasing financial stress.

[4]Liquidity spread measures changes in the short-term differences in the bid and ask prices on 3-Month US Treasuries, which reflects liquidity in financial markets. A widening spread signals illiquidity in the market, which is associated with growing stress.

parameterization for the spillover coefficients is represented as:

$$\begin{aligned}\delta_{\mathrm{DJUSPL},t} &= \delta_{\mathrm{DJUSPL},0} + \delta_{\mathrm{DJUSPL},1} X_t,\\ \gamma_{\mathrm{DJUSPL},t} &= \gamma_{\mathrm{DJUSPL},0} + \gamma_{\mathrm{DJUSPL},1} X_t,\\ \psi_{\mathrm{DJUSPL},t} &= \psi_{\mathrm{DJUSPL},0} + \psi_{\mathrm{DJUSPL},1} X_t,\\ \phi_{\mathrm{DJUSPL},t} &= \phi_{\mathrm{DJUSPL},0} + \phi_{\mathrm{DJUSPL},1} X_t.\end{aligned} \tag{13}$$

The interbank liquidity spread reflects the liquidity and default risk in the US banking system which is an important component of the US financial market. The liquidity spread indicates the US baseline liquidity in the US financial market. Between 2 January 2002 and 31 December 2014, the average daily value for interbank liquidity is 1.14, but the maximum value is 3.51 during the period since the financial crisis started, and the minimum value is 0.00. The liquidity spread is from 1.48 to 4.38 and the average value is 2.70. The maximum liquidity spread is presented in the period after the financial crisis started. A widening spread signals illiquidity in the US financial market. Figure 1 shows the time series of these two

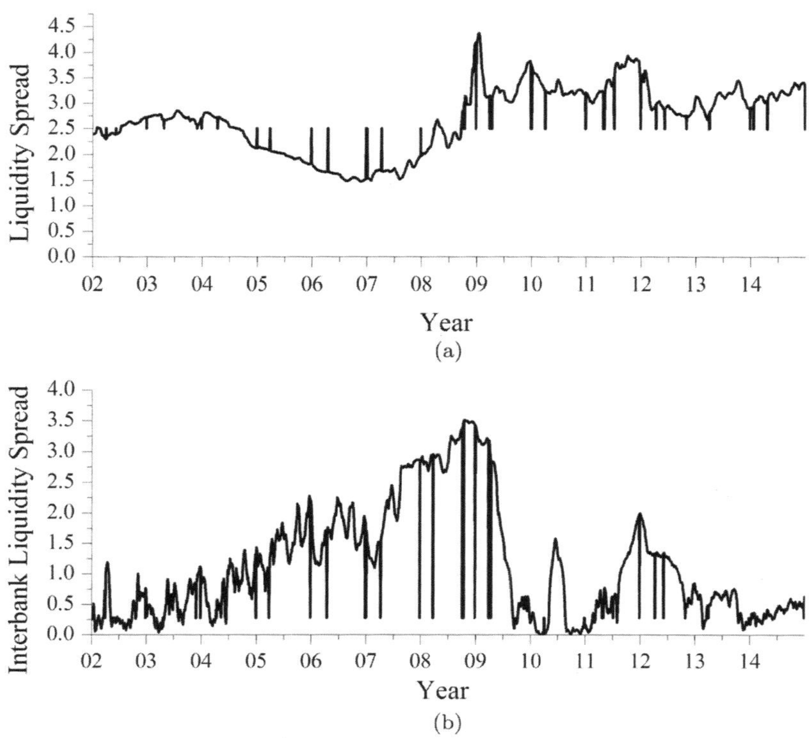

Fig. 1. Financial market liquidity indicators, 2 January 2002–31 December 2014.

indicators, which shows the clear changes in these two indicators after the financial crisis started. The interbank liquidity spread remains at a relatively high value from mid-2007 to mid-2009, but the liquidity spread maintained a relatively high level since the start of 2009.

5. Hedging Strategy Effectiveness Analysis

Based on the strong linkage between the US oil market, the US stock market and the US energy pipeline market, we examine a new cross-hedging strategy for managing US oil price risk.

Following Myers [1991] and Wu *et al.* [2011], we use a one-period portfolio selection framework, where $t-1$ denotes the beginning of the period, and the end of the period is labeled as t. We assume a risk-averse investor holding one-unit oil cash since the beginning of the period, $t-1$. The risk of holding the long position at the oil cash market can be hedged by holding a short position in the US stock market. The investor maximizes the expected utility, $U(\cdot)$ gained from the returns of the portfolio, π_t, at time t:

$$\max_{\{a_{t-1},b_{t-1}\}} E[U(\pi_t)|I_{t-1}], \tag{14}$$

$$s.t.\ \pi_t = r_{\text{WTI},t} + r_{\text{ST},t}a_{t-1} + r_{\text{DJUSPL},t}b_{t-1}. \tag{15}$$

Portfolio returns, π_t, are contributed by holding one unit of WTI, while purchasing a_{t-1} units of ST and b_{t-1} units of DJUSPL (sold if negative). Applying the optimal maximum rules, we obtain the optimal hedge ratio of the cross hedge as:[5]

$$-a_{t-1} = \frac{m_{\text{WTI,ST}}m_{\text{DJUSPL,DJUSPL}} - m_{\text{WTI,DJUSPL}}m_{\text{ST,DJUSPL}}}{m_{\text{DJUSPL,DJUSPL}}m_{\text{ST,ST}} - m_{\text{DJUSPL,ST}}m_{\text{ST,DJUSPL}}}, \tag{16}$$

$$-b_{t-1} = \frac{m_{\text{WTI,DJUSPL}}m_{\text{ST,ST}} - m_{\text{ST,DJUSPL}}m_{\text{ST,WTI}}}{m_{\text{DJUSPL,DJUSPL}}m_{\text{ST,ST}} - m_{\text{DJUSPL,ST}}m_{\text{ST,DJUSPL}}}, \tag{17}$$

where m_{ij} is the conditional variance and covariance between WTI, ST and DJUSPL. $m_{\text{DJUSPL,DJUSPL}}$ is defined in Eq. (8). $m_{\text{WTI,ST}}$ and $m_{\text{ST,ST}}$ is the $H_{\text{WTI,ST}}$ and $H_{\text{ST,ST}}$ in Eq. (3), respectively. The remaining elements are identified as follows:

$$m_{\text{ST,DJUSPL}} = E(\varepsilon_{\text{DJUSPL},t}e_{\text{ST},t}|I_{t-1}) = \phi_{\text{DJUSPL},t-1}\sigma^2_{\text{ST},t} \tag{18}$$

$$m_{\text{WTI,DJUSPL}} = E(e_{\text{WTI},t}\varepsilon_{\text{DJUSPL},t}|I_{t-1}) = \psi_{\text{DJUSPL},t-1}\sigma^2_{\text{WTI},t} \tag{19}$$

[5] The proof is available upon request to authors.

To examine the effectiveness of this new cross-hedging strategy, we separate the full sample into two parts: in-sample and out-of-sample. We apply rolling analysis to compute the out-of-sample time-varying hedge ratios. In other words, we reestimate the parameters of each model, adding one more observation to the estimation data each time. We forecast the target variable and then recalculate the optimal hedge ratio. Analysis of the performance of the out-of-sample hedge ratio allows investors to evaluate the future performance of our proposed strategy. We compare the performance of the optimal hedge ratios with the other two scenarios: no hedge and the cross-hedging ratios, β_{ST}, proposed by Salisu and Oloko [2015], which only considers the US stock market, ST. Then, we compute β_{ST} with Eq. (20):

$$\beta_{\text{ST}} = \frac{H_{\text{ST,WTI}}}{H_{\text{ST}}}. \tag{20}$$

Following Ku *et al.* [2007], we evaluate the effectiveness of hedging strategies in terms of the portfolio's variance reduction across constructed portfolios with Eq. (21)

$$HE = \frac{\text{Var}_{\text{unhedged}} - \text{Var}_{\text{hedged}}}{\text{Var}_{\text{unhedged}}} * 100\%, \tag{21}$$

where $\text{Var}_{\text{unhedged}}$ is the variance of the return of only holding the oil cash. In Eq. (21), the $\text{Var}_{\text{hedged}}$ is the variance of the return on the oil-stock or oil-stock-pipeline portfolio. A higher HE ratio implies a greater hedging effectiveness and a better hedging strategy.

6. Empirical Analysis

In this section, we analyze models specified in the previous sections using daily data from 2 January 2002 to 31 December 2014 for a total of 3,390 observations. Initially, we estimate the US oil and US stock markets, and then we estimate the mean and volatility spillover models for the US energy pipeline market with three different specifications of volatility spillover parameters. To complete the analysis, we will discuss the results of the hedging strategy comparison.

6.1. *Data and descriptive statistics*

Each data series is divided by its own mean or $\frac{P_{i,t}}{\sum P_{i,t}/T^6}$, i = DJIA, SP500, WTI, DJUSPL (shown in Fig. 2), allowing the price series measured by different units to be shown in the same scale.

[6] T is the total number of weeks in this study.

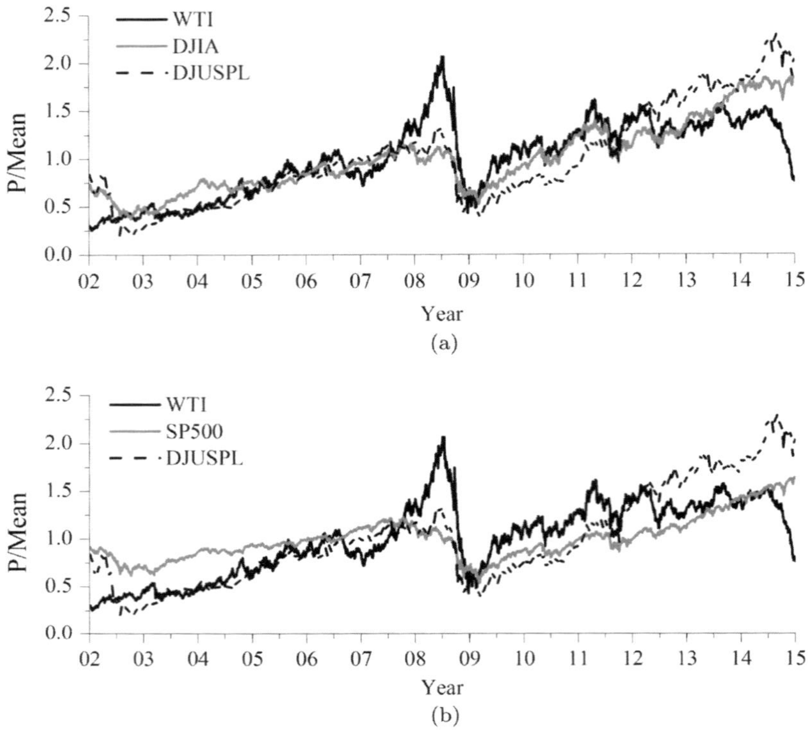

Fig. 2. US daily WTI prices, DJIA, S&P500 and DJUSPL indices divided by their respective means, 2 January 2002–31 December 2014.

Figure 2 shows that the pattern of the movement for the DJIA, SP500, WTI and DJUSPL are somewhat similar from January 2002 to December 2014. However, comparing Fig. 1(a) with Fig. 1(b), we find that the movement pattern of DJIA appears closer to the movement pattern of WTI than does the SP500, especially after the end of 2007.

Furthermore, by examining the returns of the DJIA, SP500, DJUSPL and WTI (Fig. 3), additional connections among the series are exhibited. All four series appear to fluctuate around a constant level, but also exhibit that the amplitude of the returns varies, or exhibits volatility clustering, around the same time periods. For instance, from 2002 to mid-2003, DJIA, SP500 and DJUSPL show large changes in returns that clustered together. Furthermore, from the end of 2008 to the end of 2009 and at the end of 2011, all four series show volatility clustering. Volatility clustering implies conditional heteroscedasticity, while linkages between the volatility clustering of different series indicate potential volatility spillovers.

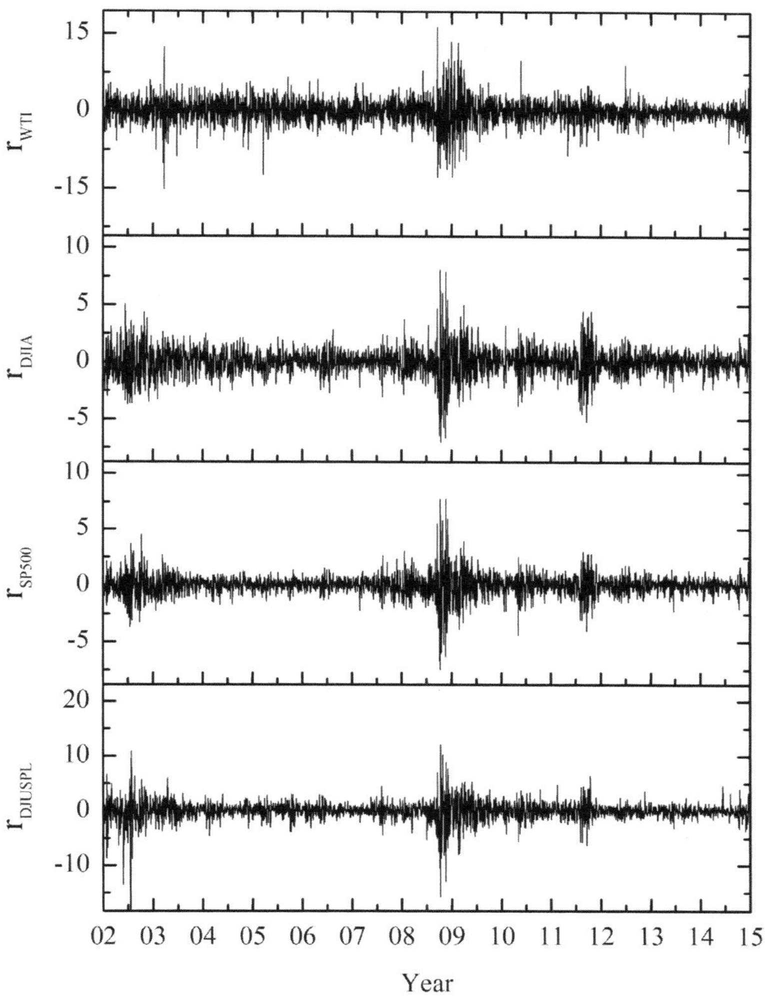

Fig. 3. US Daily WTI crude oil spot prices, DJIA, S&P500 and DJUSPL indices returns, 2 January 2002–31 December 2014.

Table 1 displays results from descriptive statistics. The mean returns for all series are positive and close to each other (either 0.03% or 0.02%). However, the variability of returns fluctuates. The oil market has the highest variability (2.26%), followed by DJUSPL (1.74%) and stock-price weighted DJIA (1.34%). The capitalization-weighted SP500 has the lowest variability (0.92%).

Skewness and kurtosis imply the shape of the distribution for each series and the returns. Returns show that all returns are negatively skewed, implying that the returns for each series tend to have an extreme negative value. Except for the logarithmic series for the return of SP500, the logarithmic series are also negatively

Table 1. Descriptive statistics and diagnostics results.

	WTI		DJIA		SP500		DJUSPL	
	$p_{\mathrm{WTI},t}$	$r_{\mathrm{WTI},t}$	$p_{\mathrm{DJIA},t}$	$r_{\mathrm{DJIA},t}$	$p_{\mathrm{SP500},t}$	$r_{\mathrm{SP500},t}$	$p_{\mathrm{DJUSPL},t}$	$r_{\mathrm{DJUSPL},t}$
Mean	4.16	0.03	5.28	0.03	7.13	0.02	6.05	0.03
Median	4.28	0.09	5.30	0.06	7.13	0.05	6.06	0.11
Std. Dev.	0.21	2.26	0.37	1.34	0.22	0.92	0.28	1.74
Min	2.89	−15.19	4.59	−7.02	6.53	−7.50	4.36	−21.39
Max	4.98	16.41	7.01	8.07	7.64	7.77	5.96	12.09
Skewness	−0.72	−0.16	−0.10	−0.10	0.17	−0.21	−0.30	−1.76
Kurtosis	−0.55	5.35	−0.57	4.16	−0.17	9.97	−0.46	20.59
P-J-B	0.00	0.00	0.00	0.00	0.00	0.00	0.00	0.00
P-LB-Q (30)	0.00	0.00	0.00	0.00	0.00	0.00	0.00	0.00
P-ML (30)	0.00	0.00	0.00	0.00	0.00	0.00	0.00	0.00

Notes: P-J-B is the p-value for the Jarque–Bera test with null hypothesis: normality.
P-Q (n) is the p-value for the Ljung–Box Q statistic for testing autocorrelation with null hypothesis: The data are independently distributed.
P-ML (n) is the p-value for the McLeod–Li statistic for autocorrelation in the variance with the null hypothesis: There is no ARCH effect.

Table 2. Augmented Dickey–Fuller tests.

i	p_i	r_i
WTI	−2.44	−32.08***
DJIA	−0.48	−31.79***
SP500	−0.51	−32.36***
DJUSPL	−0.77	−30.53***

Notes: Lags are selected by choosing the smallest Schwarz Criterion (SBC) value.
***Significant at the one percent level.

skewed. Kurtosis coefficients for returns of four series are leptokurtic compared with the normal distribution with a higher chance of huge deviations for the returns. Furthermore, the Jarque–Bera [Jarque and Bera, 1980] test statistics indicate non-normality, and the Ljung–Box [Ljung and Box, 1978] Q statistic implies the serial correlation and the McLeod–Li [McLeod and Li, 1983] statistic shows the serial correlation in the variance strongly supporting an AR-ARCH-type model for returns of all series [Elyasiani *et al.*, 2011].

We test the stationarity of all four logarithmic series with the augmented Dickey–Fuller (ADF) test [Dickey and Fuller, 1981], as shown in Table 2. Results suggest that all three logarithmic price series are non-stationary, although they are stationary at the first difference. Furthermore, the Granger-causality test find that the returns of the DJIA, SP500 and WTI Granger result in the returns of the DJUSPL (Table 3).

Table 3. Granger-causality Wald test.

Group 1	Group 2	χ^2
$r_{WTI,t}$	$r_{DJIA,t}$ and $r_{DJUSPL,t}$	12.98
$r_{DJIA,t}$	$r_{WTI,t}$ and $r_{DJUSPL,t}$	5.95
$r_{DJUSPL,t}$	$r_{WTI,t}$ and $r_{DJIA,t}$	19.79***
$r_{WTI,t}$	$r_{SP500,t}$ and $r_{DJUSPL,t}$	11.40
$r_{SP500,t}$	$r_{WTI,t}$ and $r_{DJUSPL,t}$	9.21
$r_{DJUSPL,t}$	$r_{WTI,t}$ and $r_{SP500,t}$	14.57***

*** Significant at the one percent level.
Null hypothesis is that group 1 is significantly affected by itself, and not by group 2.

Table 4. Correlation analysis.

	Full sample			Pre-crisis			During-and post-crisis		
	$r_{WTI,t}$	$r_{DJIA,t}$	$r_{SP\ 500,t}$	$r_{WTI,t}$	$r_{DJIA,t}$	$r_{SP\ 500,t}$	$r_{WTI,t}$	$r_{DJIA,t}$	$r_{SP\ 500,t}$
$r_{DJUSPL,t}$	0.34	0.62	0.70	0.15	0.47	0.56	0.47	0.73	0.79

We also perform correlation analysis and compare the correlation coefficients for the returns during the pre-crisis period (before 9 August 2007) for the period after the crisis began.

Results in Table 4 indicate that the returns of DJUSPL are most correlated with the returns of SP500. This is followed by the correlation between the returns of DJUSPL and DJIA, and then by the correlation between the returns of DJUSPL and WTI. Most importantly, there is an apparent distinction between correlation coefficients for the returns during the pre-crisis period and those during the period since the crisis started. This implies that the connections between the returns of series are stronger after the start of the financial crisis.

6.2. *Bivariate model for the US oil and stock markets*

It is important to correctly identify the relationship between the US oil market and the US stock market before studying the spillover effects from these two markets onto the US energy pipeline market. One reason is that an incorrect specification of the US oil and US stock markets carries the distortion into the spillover models for the US energy pipeline market. Another reason is that spillover effects between the US oil market and the US stock market must be considered in order to avoid underestimating or overestimating spillover effects from the US oil or the stock market to the US energy pipeline market. In other words, the information introduced to the US energy pipeline model from the US oil market should be separated from the data for the US stock market. Given the sample period, we find that the optimal number of lags, n, in Eq. (2) is two. In other words, the VAR (2) process is the best fit for the conditional mean of the returns for the ST and WTI, which is estimable and has the smallest Schwarz Criterion (SBC) value.[7]

The conditional mean spillover parameters, $\theta_{\text{WTI}-\text{ST},1}$ and $\theta_{\text{WTI}-\text{ST},2}$, in Table 5 imply that there are no statistically significant mean spillover effects from the return of WTI to DJIA or to SP500 at the 1% level. We also cannot find the statistically significant mean spillover effects from the return of DJIA or SP500 to the WTI, since both $\theta_{\text{ST}-\text{WTI},1}$ and $\theta_{\text{ST}-\text{WTI},2}$ are not significant at the 1% level. This indicates that there are no statistically mean spillover effects between the US stock market and the US oil market.

However, volatility spillover effects exist between these two markets. When we use DJIA as a proxy to the stock market, the volatility spillover parameters $b_{\text{ST}-\text{WTI}}$ is statistically significant at the 1% level, indicating long-term persistence volatility spillover effects from the US stock market to the US oil market. We also find that any bad news released from WTI or DJIA will significantly increase the volatility transmission to both WTI and DJIA, since both $d_{\text{WTI}-\text{ST}}$ and $d_{\text{ST}-\text{WTI}}$ are statistically significant at least the 5% level. When we use the SP500 as a proxy to the US stock market, we observe short-term volatility spillover effects at the US oil and stock market at both directions $[a_{\text{ST}-\text{WTI}}, a_{\text{WTI}-\text{ST}}]$. Furthermore, the significant $d_{\text{ST}-\text{WTI}}$ implies that when the US stock market produces bad news, the US oil market will increase with more volatility than the good news released from the stock market. Our findings show the statistically significant volatility spillover effects between the US oil market and the US stock market, aligning with past findings [Cifarelli and Paladino, 2010; Hammoudeh *et al.*, 2004; Kilian, 2008; Tokic, 2012].

The analysis implies that certain common news drives both the oil and stock markets, thus creating a problem in differentiating the influence between the US oil market and the US stock market on the US energy pipeline market. However, by applying Eq. (4), we are able to obtain orthogonalized innovations at the US oil and stock markets used to identify the mean and volatility spillover effects at the US energy pipeline market. Results are discussed in the following sections.

[7]The SBC for VAR (2) is 7.45 for WTI and DJIA, and the SBC for VAR(2) is 6.99 for WTI and SP500. Choosing lag 2 gives us the smallest SBC for US oil and stock markets.

Table 5. Model for the US oil and stock markets.

	$r_{WTI,t}$ & $r_{DJIA,t}$		$r_{WTI,t}$ & $r_{SP500,t}$	
Coefficients	**Estimate**	**Std.**	**Estimate**	**Std.**
Conditional Mean (WTI)				
$\theta_{WTI,0}$	0.02	0.03	0.01	0.03
$\theta_{WTI,1}$	−0.04**	0.02	−0.05**	0.02
$\theta_{WTI,2}$	0.02	0.02	0.03	0.02
$\theta_{ST-WTI,1}$	0.02	0.03	0.06	0.05
$\theta_{ST-WTI,2}$	−0.01	0.03	**−0.07***	0.04
Conditional Mean (DJIA or SP500)				
$\theta_{ST,0}$	0.03**	0.01	0.02**	0.01
$\theta_{WTI-ST,1}$	−0.00	0.01	−0.00	0.00
$\theta_{WTI-ST,2}$	0.00	0.01	0.01	0.00
$\theta_{ST,1}$	0.33***	0.02	0.30***	0.01
$\theta_{ST,1}$	−0.10***	0.02	−0.09***	0.01
Conditional Variance				
c_{WTI}	0.15***	0.04	0.14***	0.03
c_{ST-WTI}	0.05**	0.02	0.03*	0.02
c_{ST}	0.08***	0.01	0.07***	0.01
a_{WTI}	0.17***	0.03	0.15***	0.03
a_{WTI-ST}	−0.02	0.01	**−0.02****	0.01
a_{ST-WTI}	−0.06	0.04	**−0.20*****	0.06
a_{ST}	0.10***	0.02	0.08***	0.03
b_{WTI}	0.97***	0.01	0.98***	0.01
b_{WTI-ST}	−0.00	0.00	−0.00	0.00
b_{ST-WTI}	**−0.02*****	0.01	−0.02	0.01
b_{ST}	0.96***	0.00	0.95***	0.01
d_{WTI}	0.17***	0.03	0.18***	0.03
d_{WTI-ST}	**0.02****	0.01	0.01	0.01
d_{ST-WTI}	**0.15*****	0.04	**0.17*****	0.06
d_{ST}	0.31***	0.02	0.39***	0.02
Model Diagnostics				
SBC	6.81		6.13	
P-M-Q (30]	0.77		0.92	
P-M-ARCH (30]	0.06		0.13	

Notes: *,** ,*** Significant at the ten, five and one percent level, respectively.
P-M-Q (n) is the P-value for the multivariate generalizations of Ljung-Box Q statistic for testing autocorrelation with null hypothesis: The data are independently distributed.
P-M-ARCH (n) is the P-value for the test for multivariate ARCH with null hypothesis: There is no ARCH effect.

6.3. *Constant spillover model for the energy pipeline market*

The first model constrains volatility spillover effects from the US oil and stock markets to the US energy pipeline market to be constant over time. Results are presented in Table 6.

Table 6. Constant spillover model for the pipeline market.

	DJUSPL, WTI & DJIA		DJUSPL, WTI & SP500	
Spillover coefficients	**Estimate**	**Std.**	**Estimate**	**Std.**
Mean				
δ_{DJUSPL}	0.04***	0.01	0.03***	0.01
γ_{DJUSPL}	−0.03	0.02	−0.01	0.03
Variance				
ψ_{DJUSPL}	0.14***	0.01	0.12***	0.01
ϕ_{DJUSPL}	0.62***	0.02	1.02***	0.03
Diagnostics				
SBC	2.79		2.64	
P-LB-Q(30)	0.1		0.25	
P-ML(30)	0.60		0.64	
$a_{\text{DJUSPL}} + b_{\text{DJUSPL}}$	0.95		0.97	
Wald(WTI)	139.35***		119.38***	
Wald(ST)	528.37***		832.34***	

Notes: *,** ,*** Significant at the ten, five and one percent level, respectively.
P-LB-Q (n) is the P-value for the Ljung–Box Q statistic for testing autocorrelation with null hypothesis: The data are independently distributed.
P-ML(n) is the P-value for the McLeod–Li statistic for autocorrelation in the variance with null hypothesis: There is no ARCH effect.

$$
\begin{aligned}
r_{\text{DJUSPL},t} &= \theta_{\text{DJUSPL},0} + \textstyle\sum_{m=1}^{2} \theta_{\text{DJUSPL},m} r_{\text{DJUSPL},m} + \delta_{\text{DJUSPL}} r_{\text{WTI},t-1} \\
&\quad + \gamma_{\text{DJUSPL}} r_{\text{ST},t-1} + \varepsilon_{\text{DJUSPL},t}, \\
\varepsilon_{\text{DJUSPL},t} &= e_{\text{DJUSPL},t} + \psi_{\text{DJUSPL}} e_{\text{WTI},t} + \phi_{\text{DJUSPL}} e_{\text{ST},t}, \\
&\quad e_{\text{DJUSPL},t} | I_{t-1} \sim N(0, \sigma^2_{\text{DJUSPL},t}), \\
\sigma^2_{\text{DJUSPL},t} &= c_{\text{DJUSPL}} + a_{\text{DJUSPL}} e^2_{\text{DJUSPL},t-1} + b_{\text{DJUSPL}} \sigma^2_{\text{DJUSPL},t-1} \\
&\quad + d_{\text{DJUSPL}} v_{\text{DJUSPL},t-1}.
\end{aligned}
$$

We find statistically significant spillover effects from both the US oil and the stock market to the DJUSPL. A robust Wald (WTI) test rejects the hypothesis that there is no spillover from the WTI to DJUSPL, or $\delta_{\text{DJUSPL}} = \psi_{\text{DJUSPL}} = 0$, at the 1% level. The robust Wald (ST) test rejects the hypothesis that there is no spillover effect from the US stock market to the US energy pipeline markets, or $\gamma_{\text{DJUSPL}} = \phi_{\text{DJUSPL}} = 0$, at 1% level. In addition, ψ_{DJUSPL} is smaller than ϕ_{DJUSPL}, which implies that the US stock market has more influence on the volatility of the DJUSPL than the US oil market. Given that DJUSPL is part of the stock market, it is not surprising that the US stock market has a greater effect on the risk of DJUSPL. Furthermore, the US oil market has a significant positive impact on the return of DJUSPL, since $\delta_{\text{DJUSPL}^{\text{L}}} > 0$ is statistically significant at the 1% level.

We further estimate the series of the volatility spillover ratios based on Eqs. (9) and (10), as shown in Figs. 4–5. The summary statistics of the volatility ratios are

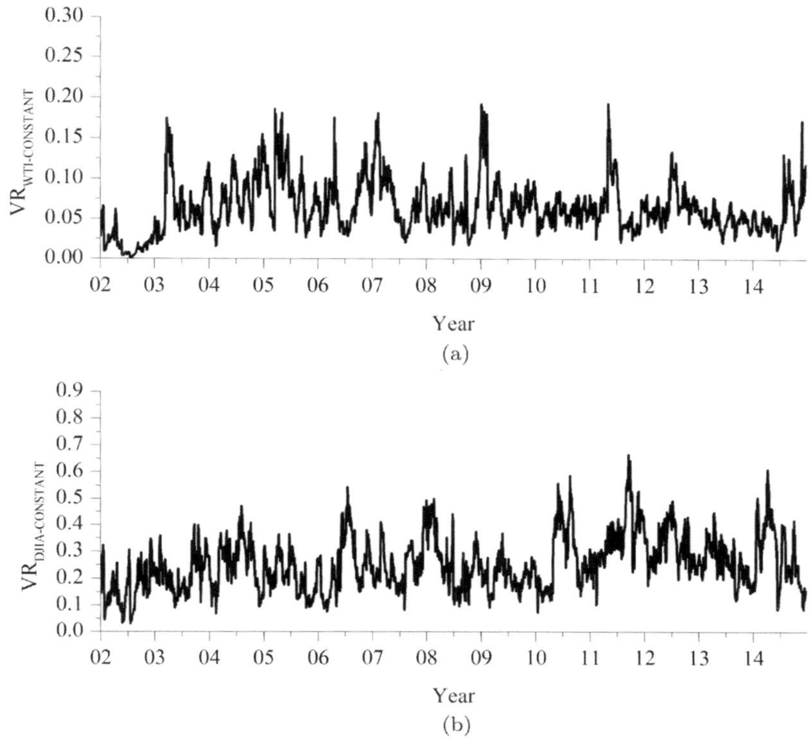

Fig. 4. Volatility spillover ratios for DJUSPL in the constant spillover model, DJIA as proxy to the US Stock market, 2 January 2002 – 31 December 2014.

shown in Table 7. Considering DJIA as the proxy to the US stock market during the sample period, we find that the average of the US oil volatility spillover ratios is 6%, but it can reach a maximum of 19%. However, the larger portion of the volatility is transmitted from the US stock market. On average, the DJIA volatility spillover ratio is 25%, and the maximum value is 67%. Fig. 4 depicts the time series of the volatility spillover ratios, when we use DJIA as a proxy to the US stock market. Compared with the period after the late 2007, US oil volatility spillover ratios are more volatile, but the average level of the spillover ratio is relatively smaller before the end of 2007 (Fig. 4(a)). A similar pattern can be observed for the US stock volatility spillover ratios (Fig. 4(b)).

Comparing with DJIA, when using SP500 as the proxy to the stock market, we find that the US oil volatility spillover ratio decreases to 5% on average, but the mean of the US stock volatility spillover ratio increases to 36%. However, we still observe that the US oil volatility spillover ratio and the SP500 volatility spillover ratio are more volatile after the end of 2007 (Fig. 5).

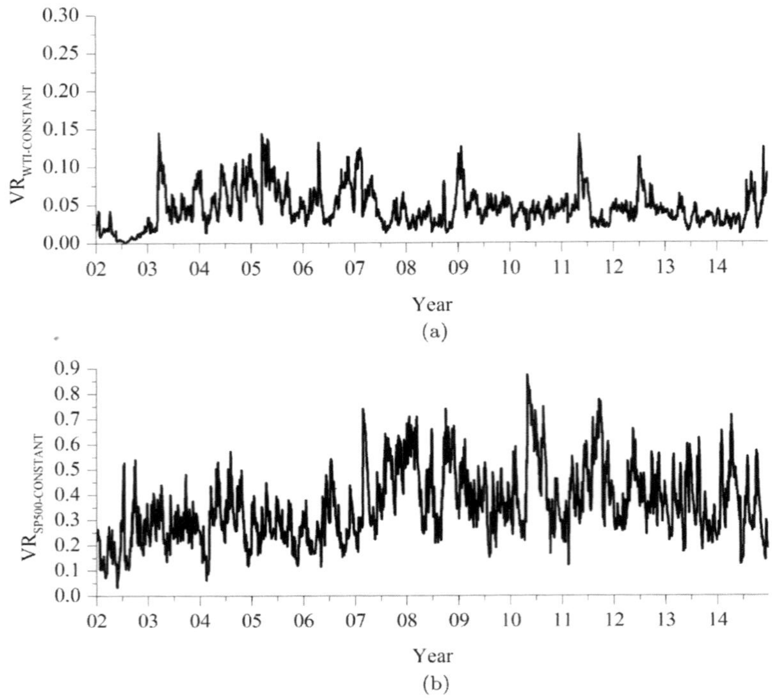

Fig. 5. Volatility spillover ratios for DJUSPL in the constant spillover model, SP500 as proxy to the US stock market, 2 January 2002–31 December 2014.

Table 7. Statistics summary for volatility spillover ratio-constant spillover model.

	WTI & DJIA		**WTI & SP500**	
	WTI	**DJIA**	**WTI**	**SP500**
Mean	0.06	0.25	0.05	0.36
Median	0.06	0.24	0.04	0.33
Std.	0.03	0.10	0.03	0.14
Min	0.00	0.03	0.00	0.03
Max	0.19	0.67	0.14	0.87

6.4. *Event-dummy spillover model for the energy pipeline market*

Both the correlation analysis and the volatility spillover ratio in the constant model imply a potential structural break related to the 2007–2008 financial crisis. Therefore, the event-dummy spillover model is developed to consider the impact of the 2007–2008 financial crisis. Results are presented in Table 8.

Table 8. Statistics summary for volatility spillover ratio-constant spillover model.

	WTI & DJIA		WTI & SP500	
	WTI	**DJIA**	**WTI**	**SP500**
Mean	0.06	0.25	0.05	0.36
Median	0.06	0.24	0.04	0.33
Std.	0.03	0.10	0.03	0.14
Min	0.00	0.03	0.00	0.03
Max	0.19	0.67	0.14	0.87

For the conditional mean, spillovers from the US oil market and the US stock market to the US energy pipeline market differ. We find that the increasing returns of the US oil spot price will significantly raise the return of DJUSPL, since the US oil mean spillover parameter, $\delta_{\mathrm{DJUSPL},0}$, is positive and significant at the 1% level. However, the insignificant $\delta_{\mathrm{DJUSPL},1}$ implies that since the financial crisis began in 9 August 2007, the mean spillover effect from the US oil market does not change significantly. The finding further confirms the stable connection between the oil market and the energy pipeline market in the United States. For the mean spillover effects from the US stock markets, we find that the increasing returns in the stock market reduce returns of DJUSPL significantly since 9 August 2007.

The even-dummy spillover model reveals more information about the volatility spillover effects. The volatility spillover from DJIA and WTI to DJUSPL has significantly increased after the start of the financial crisis. This suggests that the financial crisis may increase the correlation between the risk of DJUSPL and the risk of DJIA and WTI. However, there is no significant change before and after the financial crisis, when SP500 is considered as the proxy to stock market. The above findings point to the importance of choosing the proxy to the US stock market, since this may result in different impacts of the financial crisis on the volatility spillovers. The difference may be related to the characteristics of the index. The DJIA is a price-weighted index consisting of the 30 largest companies. Therefore, if the price of a high-priced company changes, the index will change greatly. However, the SP500 is compromised by the 500 largest companies and uses the value of each stock as weights. Therefore, the DJIA will be more volatile than SP500 and more responsive to the sudden changes in the financial market during the financial crisis. More responsiveness may allow the DJIA to carry more information about the risk and transmit to DJUSPL during the financial crisis. The difference may be also caused by liquidity changes related to the financial crisis, and the responses of the DJIA and SP500 are likely to differ, as discussed below.

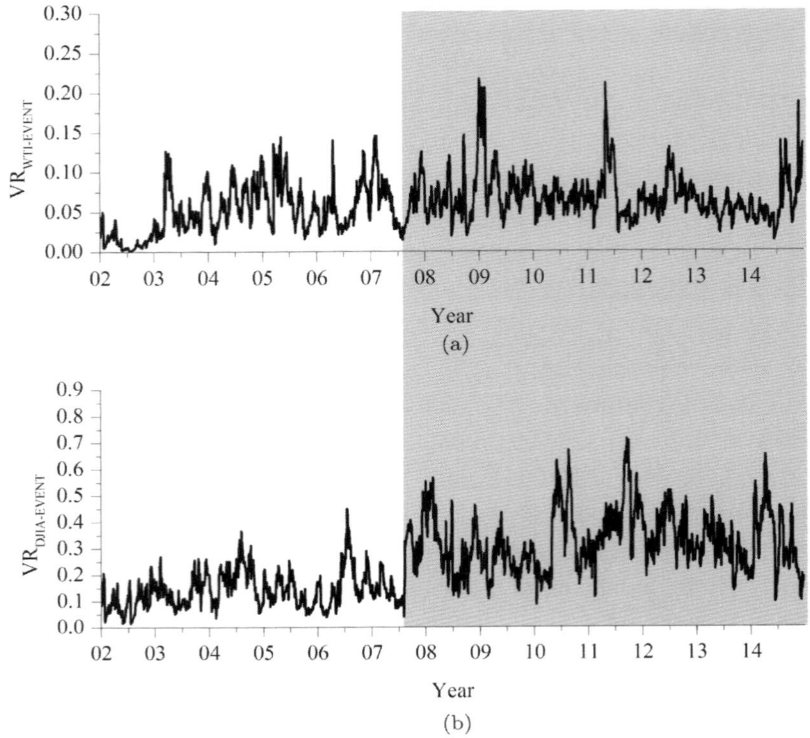

Fig. 6. Volatility spillover ratios in the event-dummy spillover model, DJIA as proxy to the US stock market, 2 January 2002–31 December 2014.

We also calculate the volatility spillover ratios of DJIA and WTI to DJUSPL. The time series of the spillover ratios are represented and shown in Fig. 6, where the shaded area represents the period since the 2007 financial crisis began. The summary of the statistics for the volatility spillover ratios is represented in Table 9. Figure 6(b) clearly shows dramatic changes in the DJIA spillover ratio after the financial crisis started and the shaded areas imply the periods after 9 August 2007. Table 9 shows that the stock market still plays a more important role in DJUSPL movement than the oil market. Most importantly, the summary also reveals large increases in the volatility spillover ratios after the financial crisis began. On average, the WTI counts 5% and DJIA counts 14% of the total risk in DJUSPL before the crisis started, but the ratios increase to 7% for WTI and 32% for DJIA since the crisis started. Before the crisis, the maximum risk contributes from the WTI and DJIA was 15% and 45%, respectively. After the beginning of the crisis, the risk contribution to DJUSPL can be as large as 22% from WTI and 71% from DJIA.

Table 9. Event-dummy spillover model for the pipeline market.

	DJUSPL,WTI & DJIA		**DJUSPL,WTI & SP500**	
Spillover coefficients	**Estimate**	**Std. error**	**Estimate**	**Std. error**
Mean				
$\delta_{\text{DJUSPL},0}$	0.04***	0.01	0.04***	0.01
$\delta_{\text{DJUSPL},1}$	−0.02	0.02	−0.02	0.02
$\gamma_{\text{DJUSPL},0}$	0.04	0.03	0.13***	0.04
$\gamma_{\text{DJUSPL},1}$	−0.10***	0.04	−0.18***	0.05
Variance				
$\psi_{\text{DJUSPL},0}$	0.11***	0.01	0.12***	0.01
$\psi_{\text{DJUSPL},1}$	0.04**	0.02	0.00	0.02
$\phi_{\text{DJUSPL},0}$	0.46***	0.03	1.00***	0.5
$\phi_{\text{DJUSPL},1}$	0.23***	0.04	0.03	0.05
Diagnostics				
SBC	2.76		2.65	
P-LB-Q(30)	0.13		0.32	
P-ML(30)	0.67		0.75	
$a_{\text{DJUSPL}} + b_{\text{DJUSPL}}$	0.95		0.96	
Wald(WTI)	68.23***		63.73***	
Wald(ST)	297.62***		457.71***	

Notes: *,** ,*** Significant at the ten, five and one percent level, respectively.
P-LB-Q (n) is the P-value for the Ljung–Box Q statistic for testing autocorrelation with null hypothesis: The data are independently distributed.
P-ML (n) is the P-value for the McLeod–Li statistic for autocorrelation in the variance with null hypothesis: There is no ARCH effect.

$$\begin{aligned} r_{\text{DJUSPL},t} &= \theta_{\text{DJUSPL},0} + \textstyle\sum_{m=1}^{2} \theta_{\text{DJUSPL},m} r_{\text{DJUSPL},m} + \delta_{\text{DJUSPL}} r_{\text{WTI},t-1} \\ &\quad + \gamma_{\text{DJUSPL}} r_{\text{ST},t-1} + \varepsilon_{\text{DJUSPL},t}, \\ \varepsilon_{\text{DJUSPL},t} &= e_{\text{DJUSPL},t} + \psi_{\text{DJUSPL}} e_{\text{WTI},t} + \phi_{\text{DJUSPL}} e_{\text{ST},t}, \\ &\quad e_{\text{DJUSPL},t} | I_{t-1} \sim N(0, \sigma^2_{\text{DJUSPL},t}), \\ \sigma^2_{\text{DJUSPL},t} &= c_{\text{DJUSPL}} + a_{\text{DJUSPL}} e^2_{\text{DJUSPL},t-1} + b_{\text{DJUSPL}} \sigma^2_{\text{DJUSPL},t-1} \\ &\quad + d_{\text{DJUSPL}} v_{\text{DJUSPL},t-1}. \end{aligned}$$

$$\text{where } \begin{cases} \delta_{\text{DJUSPL},t} = \delta_{\text{DJUSPL},0} + \delta_{\text{DJUSPL},1} D_t \\ \gamma_{\text{DJUSPL},t} = \gamma_{\text{DJUSPL},0} + \gamma_{\text{DJUSPL},1} D_t \\ \psi_{\text{DJUSPL},t} = \psi_{\text{DJUSPL},0} + \psi_{\text{DJUSPL},1} D_t \\ \phi_{\text{DJUSPL},t} = \phi_{\text{DJUSPL},0} + \phi_{\text{DJUSPL},1} D_t. \end{cases}$$

In summary, the volatility spillover effects from the US oil and stock markets to the US energy pipeline market are significant, and the effects have increased since the 2007–2008 financial crisis began. In addition, the DJIA accounts for a relatively large proportion of total volatility in DJUSPL than the WTI does for the DJUSPL. However, we also see that the even-dummy volatility model may overlook some information. For instance, Fig. 6(a) also shows that during the end of 2007 to the middle of 2011, the ratios are relatively larger than for

Table 10. Statistics summary for volatility spillover ratio-event-dummy spillover model.

	Pre-crisis		During- and post-crisis	
	WTI	**DJIA**	**WTI**	**DJIA**
Mean	0.05	0.14	0.07	0.32
Median	0.05	0.13	0.06	0.31
Std.	0.03	0.07	0.03	0.11
Min	0.00	0.02	0.01	0.09
Max	0.15	0.45	0.22	0.71

other times over the entire sample period. Importantly, the models do not capture the possibilities that the spillover effects from the US oil and stock markets are likely to change over time. Therefore, we further developed the time-varying spillover model to study the spillover effects over time for the US energy pipeline market.

6.5. *Time-varying spillover model for the energy pipeline market*

In this section, we discuss how we allow the spillover effects to change over time by introducing the impact of the *interbank liquidity spread* and the *liquidity spread* on the mean and volatility spillover parameters. The time-varying spillover model provides insight on how the liquidity changes in the US financial market affects the changes in spillover effects. Results are presented in Table 10.

The estimation result implies that the size of the volatility spillover depends on the magnitude of the liquidity indicators at the US financial market. Considering the time-varying interbank liquidity spread, we find that $\psi_{\mathrm{DJUSPL},1}$ are positive and statistically significant at the 1% level, indicating that the increasing interbank spread will significantly increase the volatility spillover effects from the US oil market to the US energy pipeline market. However, the interbank liquidity spread has a different impact on the volatility spillovers from the US stock market. For instance, the spillover effects from DJIA to DJUSPL is not significantly associated with the interbank liquidity, since $\phi_{\mathrm{DJUSPL},1}$ is not statistically significant. If the SP500 is considered, $\phi_{\mathrm{DJUSPL},1}$ is negative and statistically significant, implying that the increasing interbank liquidity spread will significantly reduce the volatility transmission from the US stock market.

Considering the time-varying liquidity spread, the estimation shows that $\phi_{\mathrm{DJUSPL},1}$ are also positive and statistically significant at the 1% level, so the rising liquidity spread also will significantly increase the volatility spillover effects from the US stock market to the US energy pipeline market. The impact of the liquidity spread on the volatility spillover from the oil market to the US energy pipeline market depends on the proxy to the stock market. When DJIA is considered, we find that $\psi_{\text{DJUSPL},1}$ is not statistically significant, so the liquidity spread will have little impact on the volatility spillover from the US oil market to the energy pipeline market. However, when SP500 is used, $\psi_{\text{DJUSPL},1}$ is statistically significant and it is negative. Therefore, the increasing liquidity spread will significantly decrease the volatility spillover from the US oil market to the US energy pipeline market.

Following Eqs. (9) and (10), we compute the volatility spillover ratios that are significantly affected by the liquidity indicators as shown in Table 11. The time series of the ratios are presented in Figs. 7–9, and the shaded areas imply the illiquid periods when either the interbank liquidity spread or the liquidity spread indicates the relative illiquid US financial market.[8] The summary of statistics of the ratios is shown in Table 11. When we use the DJIA as the proxy to the US stock market, Fig. 7(a) shows a clear increase in the volatility spillover ratio of the WTI to the DJUSPL during the illiquid periods, indicated by the interbank liquidity spread. The average spillover ratio of the WTI is 6% during the entire sample period, but it is 67.7% higher during the illiquid period from 10 April 2007 to 30 June 2009. The increasing volatility spillover ratio of the DJIA during the illiquid period indicated by the liquidity spread is identified in Fig. 7(b). The mean of the spillover ratios is 33% during the illiquid period, which is 7% above the mean value over the entire sample period. The difference in size of the spillover ratios during the illiquid period and the entire sample period is also implied when we use the SP500 as the proxy to the stock market. Figure 8 shows that the volatility spillover ratio of the WTI has increased, but the increase in the volatility spillover ratio of the SP500 is not obvious during the illiquid period as measured by the *interbank liquidity spread*. Results shown in Table 11 confirm this finding; the mean of the volatility spillover ratio of the WTI increases by 40%, but volatility spillover ratios of the SP500 do not change during illiquid period. In terms of the impact of the *liquidity spread*, the volatility spillover ratio of the SP500 increases significantly, while that of the WTI decreases during the illiquid period (Fig. 9). The spillover ratio of the SP500 has increased 25%, but the spillover ratio of the WTI decreases 50% during the illiquid period.

[8]When the interbank liquidity spread is larger than two or the liquidity spread is larger than three, we considered the market as relatively illiquid (two and three are the thresholds for the interbank liquidity spread and liquidity spread, respectively. The illiquidity period requires that the interbank liquidity spread is larger than two or the liquidity spread is larger than three on least 14 continuous days. During the illiquid period, we allowed at most 7 continuous days that did not meet the thresholds.

Table 11. Time-varying spillover model for the pipeline market.

$$
\begin{aligned}
r_{\text{DJUSPL},t} &= \theta_{\text{DJUSPL},0} + \textstyle\sum_{m=1}^{2} \theta_{\text{DJUSPL},m} r_{\text{DJUSPL},m} + \delta_{\text{DJUSPL}} r_{\text{WTI},t-1} \\
&\quad + \gamma_{\text{DJUSPL}} r_{ST,t-1} + \varepsilon_{\text{DJUSPL},t}, \\
\varepsilon_{\text{DJUSPL},t} &= e_{\text{DJUSPL},t} + \psi_{\text{DJUSPL}} e_{\text{WTI},t} + \phi_{\text{DJUSPL}} e_{\text{ST},t}, \\
&\quad e_{\text{DJUSPL},t} | I_{t-1} \sim N(0, \sigma^2_{\text{DJUSPL},t}), \\
\sigma^2_{\text{DJUSPL},t} &= c_{\text{DJUSPL}} + a_{\text{DJUSPL}} e^2_{\text{DJUSPL},t-1} + b_{\text{DJUSPL}} \sigma^2_{\text{DJUSPL},t-1} \\
&\quad + d_{\text{DJUSPL}} \upsilon_{\text{DJUSPL},t-1}
\end{aligned}
$$

	DJUSPL,WTI & DJIA				DJUSPL,WTI & SP500			
	Interbank liquidity spread		Liquidity spread		Interbank liquidity spread		Liquidity spread	
Spillover coefficients	**Estimate**	**Std.**	**Estimate**	**Std.**	**Estimate**	**Std.**	**Estimate**	**Std.**
Mean								
$\delta_{\text{DJUSPL},0}$	0.03***	0.01	0.04	0.03	0.02	0.01	0.05***	0.03.
$\delta_{\text{DJUSPL},1}$	0.00	0.01	−0.01	0.01	0.01	0.01	−0.01	0.01
$\gamma_{\text{DJUSPL},0}$	−0.03	0.03	0.07	0.07	−0.03	0.04	0.16*	0.09
$\gamma_{\text{DJUSPL},1}$	0.01	0.02	−0.04*	0.02	0.01	0.02	−0.06*	0.03
Variance								
$\psi_{\text{DJUSPL},0}$	0.11***	0.01	0.15***	0.02	0.09***	0.01	0.20***	0.03
$\psi_{\text{DJUSPL},1}$	0.02***	0.01	−0.00	0.01	0.02***	0.01	−0.03***	0.01
$\phi_{\text{DJUSPL},0}$	0.63***	0.03	0.24***	0.08	1.11***	0.04	0.62***	0.10
$\phi_{\text{DJUSPL},1}$	−0.00	0.02	0.14***	0.03	−0.07***	0.02	0.15***	0.04
Diagnostics								
SBC	2.80		2.80		2.65		2.64	
P-LB-Q(30)	0.08		0.10		0.23		0.31	
P-ML(30)	0.60		0.62		0.63		0.75	
$a_{\text{DJUSPL}} + b_{\text{DJUSPL}}$	0.95		0.95		0.97		0.97	
Wald(WTI)	87.49***		72.69***		60.74***		52.20***	
Wald(ST)	270.16***		293.95***		482.75***		446.78***	

Note:*,**,*** Significant at the ten, five and one percent level, respectively.
P-LB-Q (n) is the P-value for the Ljung–Box Q statistic for testing autocorrelation with null hypothesis: The data are independently distributed.
P-ML (n) is the P-value for the McLeod–Li statistic for autocorrelation in the variance with null hypothesis: There is no ARCH effect.

In summary, the volatility spillover effects from the US oil market and the US stock market to the US energy pipeline market are significantly affected by the liquidity at the financial market. Using the interbank liquidity spread to measure the liquidity, we find that as liquidity decreases, the US oil market significantly increases the volatility transmission to the US energy pipeline market. Results from this analysis also suggest that DJIA is a preferred proxy to the stock market than the SP500 to help capture changes in risk spillover from the US oil market to the US

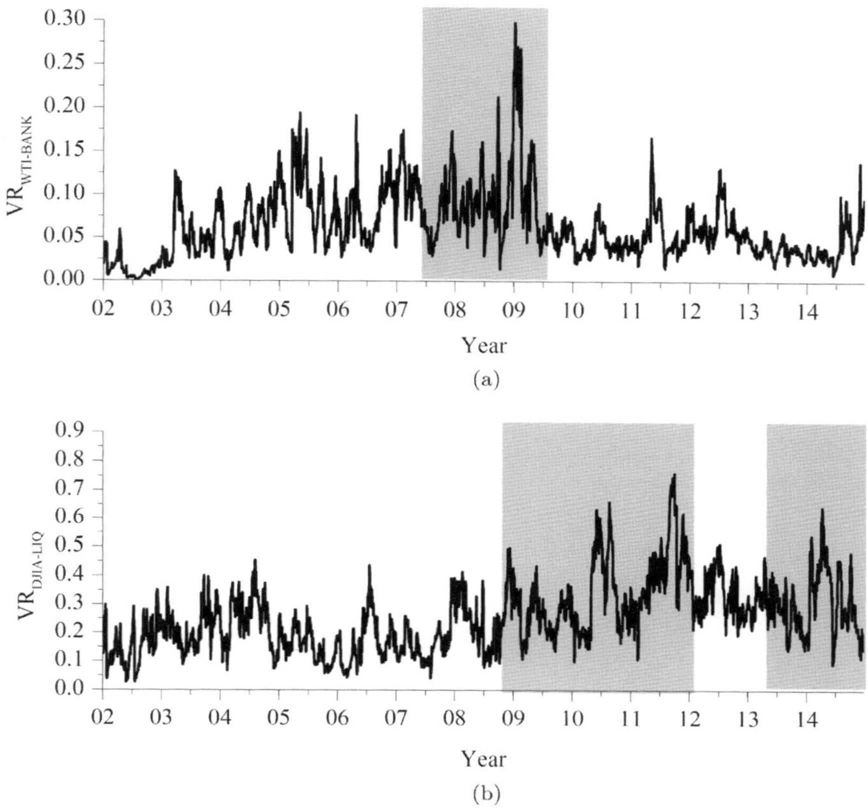

Fig. 7. Volatility spillover ratios in the time-varying spillover model, DJIA as the proxy to the US stock market, 2 January 2002–31 December 2014.

energy pipeline market. Results also highlight the limitations of constant and event-dummy specifications. Findings will have many implications. For instance, when the investor observes liquidity in the US financial market decreasing, the increasing linkages between the oil and DJUSPL allow the investor to use DJUSPL, hedging the risk in US oil market. In addition, facing the decreasing liquidity in the US financial market, the US energy pipeline sector stakeholders will need to consider the potential increase in the risk spillover from the US oil market.

6.6. *Hedging strategy comparison*

To examine the effectiveness of the new cross-hedging strategy, we separate the full sample into two parts: the first part contains the first 1,801 observations, which is used for in-sample evaluation, and the remaining 1,590 observations from 26 November 2008 to 31 December 2014 are used for the out-of-sample evaluation.

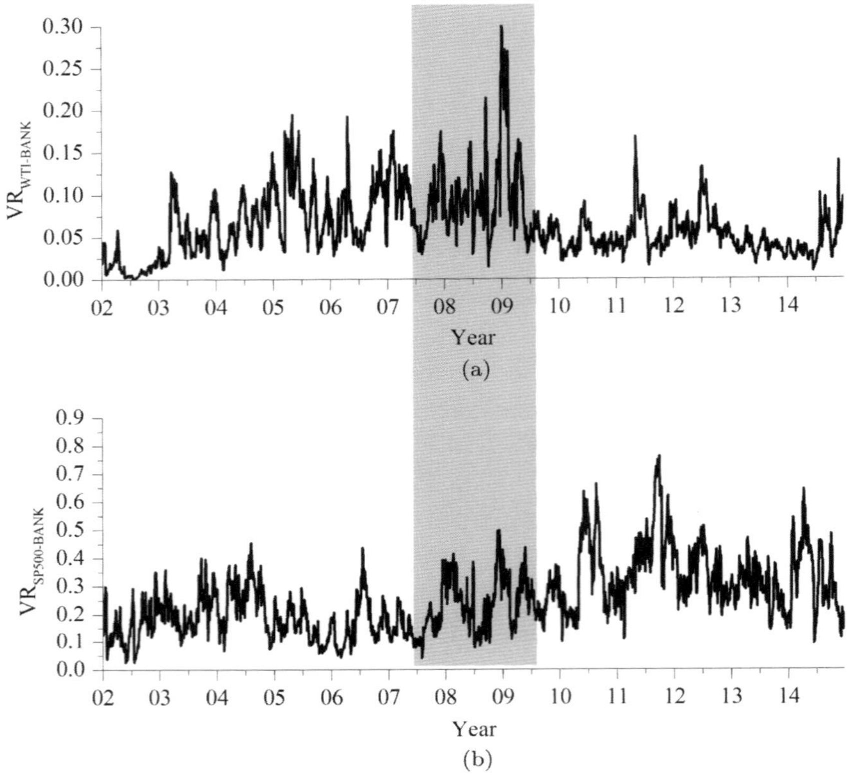

Fig. 8. Volatility spillover ratios in the interbank liquidity spread affected time-varying spillover model, SP500 as proxy to the US stock market, 2 January 2002–31 December 2014.

Results in Table 12 show that the new cross-hedging strategy considering US oil, stock and US pipeline indices can reduce portfolio risk considerably. Based on the cross-hedging strategy proposed by Salisu and Oloko [2015], the in-sample HE is 0.1% using DJIA as the proxy and 0.04% using SP500 as the proxy to the US stock market. For the out-of-sample evaluation, the HE increases to 3.80% (using DJIA) and 4.41% (using SP500). However, if we introduce the DJUSPL into the hedging strategy, the in-sample HE increases to 7.31% (using DJIA) and 7.40% (using SP500), and the out-of-sample HE raises to 13.93% (using DJIA) and 10.81% (using SP500). In addition, for the investors concerning with the future performance of our cross-hedging strategy, we find that the hedge strategy is more effective, when using DJIA as proxy to the US stock rather than SP500.

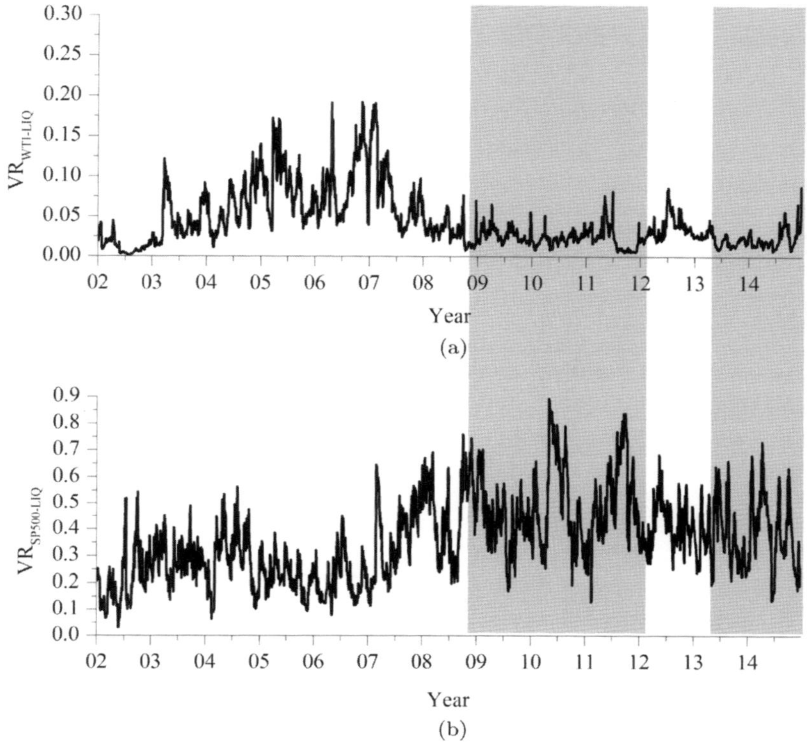

Fig. 9. Volatility spillover ratios in the liquidity spread affected time-varying spillover model, SP500 as proxy to the US stock market, 2 January 2002–31 December 2014.

7. Summary and Conclusions

This chapter follows Bekaert and Harvey [1997], Ng [2000], Salisu and Oloko [2015] and Jiang *et al.* [2015] to develop a bivariate VAR(2)-BEKK-AGARCH(1,1) model, which we apply to examine the mean and volatility spillover effects between US oil and stock markets and the US energy pipeline market. We are particularly interested in the impact of the liquidity crisis in the financial market on volatility spillovers, as well as assessing new hedging strategies.

This study yields three main contributions to the literature: First, the research empirically pioneers the linkages between the US oil market and the US energy pipeline sector. Second, we develop the time-varying spillover model to study the impact of liquidity changes in the US financial market on the spillover effect between the US oil and stock markets. This model improves the previous models with structural breaks [Mollick and Assefa, 2013] to study the impact of the shocks in the US financial market on the relationship between the US oil market and the US stock

Table 12. Statistics summary for volatility spillover ratio-time-varying spillover model.

	WTI & DJIA				WTI & SP500			
	Interbank liquidity spread		**Liquidity spread**		**Interbank liquidity spread**		**Liquidity spread**	
	WTI	**DJIA**	**WTI**	**DJIA**	**WTI**	**SP500**	**WTI**	**SP500**
Full Sample								
Mean	0.06	0.26	0.06	0.26	0.05	0.36	0.04	0.36
Median	0.05	0.24	0.05	0.24	0.04	0.34	0.03	0.34
Std.	0.04	0.10	0.00	0.02	0.03	0.14	0.04	0.16
Min	0.00	0.03	0.00	0.03	0.00	0.04	0.00	0.03
Max	0.30	0.66	0.19	0.76	0.21	0.89	0.19	0.90
10 April 2007–30 June 2009[a]								
Mean	0.10				0.07	0.36		
Median	0.09				0.06	0.34		
Std.	0.05				0.04	0.12		
Min	0.01				0.01	0.19		
Max	0.30				0.21	0.68		
20 November 2008–24 February 2012 and 29 April 2013–31 December 2014[b]								
Mean				0.33			0.02	0.45
Median				0.31			0.02	0.43
Std.				0.13			0.01	0.15
Min				0.09			0.01	0.13
Max				0.76			0.09	0.90

Note: [a]The period is indicated by the interbank liquidity spread as illiquidity, when the indicator is larger than 2 for at least 14 days. We allow indicators smaller than 2 for no more than 7 days during the illiquid period.
[b]The period is indicated by the liquidity spread as illiquidity, when the indicator is larger than 3 for at least 14 days. We allow indicators smaller than 3 for no more than 7 days during the illiquid period.

markets over time. Third, we propose a new cross-hedging strategy for managing the US oil price risk by including the DJUSPL, which improves the performance of the hedging strategies proposed by Basher and Sadorsky [2016] and Salisu and Oloko [2015].

Results indicate that both the US oil market and the US stock market have a statistically significant volatility-spillover effect on the DJUSPL. We find that volatility transmission from the US oil and stock markets to the DJUSPL increases after the 2007–2008 financial crisis started. The time-varying model indicates that the increasing *liquidity spread* and *interbank liquidity spread* is associated with a statistically significant increase in the volatility transmission from the US oil and stock markets to the US energy pipeline market. Therefore, when the investor observes liquidity in the US financial market decreasing, the increasing linkages

Table 13. Hedging effectiveness.

	In-sample		Out-of-sample	
	Var	HE(%)	Var	HE(%)
DJIA				
Unhedged	5.42		4.70	
Oil-stock hedged	5.42	0.10	4.52	3.80
Oil-stock-pipeline hedged	5.03	7.31	4.05	13.94
SP500				
Unhedged	5.43		4.70	
Oil-stock hedged	5.43	0.04	4.50	4.41
Oil-stock-pipeline hedged	5.03	7.40	4.19	10.81

between the oil and DJUSPL allow the investor to use DJUSPL, hedging the risk in the US oil market. In addition, facing the decreasing liquidity in the US financial market, the US energy pipeline sector stakeholders will need to consider the potential increase in the risk spillover from the US oil market. Findings from our study can be used to inform policy makers and investors in planning energy, diversifying portfolios and managing energy risk.

References

Apergis, N. and Rezitis, A. (2003). An examination of Okun's law: Evidence from regional areas in Greece. *Applied Economics* **35**, 1147–1151.

Arouri, M. E. H., Jouini, J. and Nguyen, D. K. (2011a). Volatility spillovers between oil prices and stock sector returns: Implications for portfolio management. *Journal of International Money and Finance* **30**, 1387–1405.

Arouri, M. E. H., Lahiani, A. and Nguyen, D. K. (2011b). Return and volatility transmission between world oil prices and stock markets of the GCC countries. *Economic Modelling* **28**, 1815–1825.

Basher, S. A. and Sadorsky, P. (2016). Hedging emerging market stock prices with oil, gold, VIX, and bonds: A comparison between DCC, ADCC and GO-GARCH. *Energy Economics* **54**, 235–247.

Bekaert, G. and Harvey, C. R. (1997). Emerging equity market volatility. *Journal of Financial Economics* **43**, 29–77.

Bielecki, J. (2002). Energy security: Is the wolf at the door? *The Quarterly Review of Economics and Finance* **42**, 235–250.

Campbell, J. Y. and Hentschel, L. (1992). No news is good news: An asymmetric model of changing volatility in stock returns. *Journal of Financial Economics* **31**, 281–318.

Cappiello, L., Engle, R. F. and Sheppard, K. (2006). Asymmetric dynamics in the correlations of global equity and bond returns. *Journal of Financial econometrics* **4**, 537–572.

Cifarelli, G. and Paladino, G. (2010). Oil price dynamics and speculation: A multivariate financial approach. *Energy Economics* **32**, 363–372.

Cornett, M. M. *et al.* (2011). Liquidity risk management and credit supply in the financial crisis. *Journal of Financial Economics* **101**, 297–312.

Creti, A., Joëts, M. and Mignon, V. (2013). On the links between stock and commodity markets' volatility. *Energy Economics* **37**, 16–28.

Dickey, D. A. and Fuller, W. A. (1981). Likelihood ratio statistics for autoregressive time series with a unit root. *Econometrica: Journal of the Econometric Society* **49**, 1057–1072.

Dumontaux, N. and Pop, A. (2013). Understanding the market reaction to shockwaves: Evidence from the failure of Lehman Brothers. *Journal of Financial Stability* **9**, 269–286.

Edwards, K., Jackson, J. D. and Thompson, H. L. (2000). A note on vertical integration and stock ratings of oil companies in the U.S. *Energy Journal* **21**, 145–151.

Elyasiani, E., Mansur, I. and Odusami, B. (2011). Oil price shocks and industry stock returns. *Energy Economics* **33**, 966–974.

Engle, R. F. (1982). Autoregressive conditional heteroscedasticity with estimates of the variance of United Kingdom inflation. *Econometrica: Journal of the Econometric Society* **50**, 987–1007.

Federal Reserve Bank of Cleveland (2012). The Cleveland Financial Stress Index: A Tool for Monitoring Financial Stability. Available at https://www.clevelandfed.org/newsroom-and-events/publications/economic-commentary/2012-economic-commentaries/ec-201204-the-cleveland-financial-stress-index-a-tool-for-monitoring-financial-stability.aspx. Accessed October 22, 2015.

Garcia-Appendini, E. and Montoriol-Garriga, J. (2013). Firms as liquidity providers: Evidence from the 2007–2008 financial crisis. *Journal of Financial Economics* **109**, 272–291.

Hammoudeh, S., Dibooglu, S. and Aleisa, E. (2004). Relationships among US oil prices and oil industry equity indices. *International Review of Economics & Finance* **13**, 427–453.

Jarque, C. M. and Bera, A. K. (1980). Efficient tests for normality, homoscedasticity and serial independence of regression residuals. *Economics Letters* **6**, 255–259.

Jiang, J., Marsh, T. L. and Tozer, P. R. (2015). Policy induced price volatility transmission: Linking the US crude oil, corn and plastics markets. *Energy Economics* **52**, 217–227.

Kilian, L. (2008). Exogenous oil supply shocks: How big are they and how much do they matter for the US economy? *The Review of Economics and Statistics* **90**, 216–240.

Kollias, C., Kyrtsou, C. and Papadamou, S. (2013). The effects of terrorism and war on the oil price–stock index relationship. *Energy Economics* **40**, 743–752.

Ku, Y.-H. H., Chen, H.-C. and Chen, K.-H. (2007). On the application of the dynamic conditional correlation model in estimating optimal time-varying hedge ratios. *Applied Economics Letters* **14**, 503–509.

Ljung, G. M. and Box, G. E. (1978). On a measure of lack of fit in time series models. *Biometrika* **65**, 297–303.

Malik, F. and Hassan, S. A. (2004). Modeling volatility in sector index returns with GARCH models using an iterated algorithm. *Journal of Economics and Finance* **28**, 211–225.

McLeod, A. I. and Li, W. K. (1983). Diagnostic checking ARMA time series models using squared-residual autocorrelations. *Journal of Time Series Analysis* **4**, 269–273.

Mohanty, S. K. and Nandha, M. (2011). Oil risk exposure: The case of the US oil and gas sector. *Financial review* **46**, 165–191.

Mollick, A. V. and Assefa, T. A. (2013). US stock returns and oil prices: The tale from daily data and the 2008–2009 financial crisis. *Energy Economics* **36**, 1–18.

Myers, R. J. (1991). Estimating time-varying optimal hedge ratios on futures markets. *Journal of Futures Markets* **11**, 39–53.

Nazlioglu, S., Soytas, U. and Gupta, R. (2015). Oil prices and financial stress: A volatility spillover analysis. *Energy Policy* **82**, 278–288.

Ng, A. (2000). Volatility spillover effects from Japan and the US to the Pacific–Basin. *Journal of International Money and Finance* **19**, 207–233.

Norton, S. W. (1993). Vertical integration and systematic risk: Oil refining revisited. *Journal of Institutional and Theoretical Economics* **149**, 656–669.

S&P Dow Jones Indices (2015). Sector Classification Structure Definitions.pdf. Available at https://www.djindexes.com/mdsidx/downloads/Sector_Classification_Structure_Definitions.pdf. Accessed October 22, 2015.

Sadorsky, P. (2012). Correlations and volatility spillovers between oil prices and the stock prices of clean energy and technology companies. *Energy Economics* **34**, 248–255.

Salisu, A. A. and Oloko, T. F. (2015). Modeling oil price–US stock nexus: A VARMA–BEKK–AGARCH approach. *Energy Economics* **50**, 1–12.

Schaeffer, R. *et al.* (2012). Dow Jones sustainability index transmission to oil stock market returns: A GARCH approach. *Energy* **45**, 933–943.

Sharpe, W. F. (2002). Indexed investing: A prosaic way to beat the average investor. In *Spring President's Forum, Monterey Institute of International Studies.* Available at https://web.stanford.edu/~wfsharpe/art/talks/indexed_investing.htm. Accessed October 22, 2015.

Shin, H. S. (2009). Reflections on Northern Rock: The bank run that heralded the global financial crisis. *The Journal of Economic Perspectives* **23**, 101–120.

Souček, M. and Todorova, N. (2013). Realized volatility transmission between crude oil and equity futures markets: A multivariate HAR approach. *Energy Economics* **40**, 586–597.

Tokic, D. (2012). Speculation and the 2008 oil bubble: The DCOT Report analysis. *Energy Policy* **45**, 541–550.

Tsay, R. S. (2005). *Analysis of Financial Time Series*. (John Wiley & Sons, Hoboken, New Jersey).

Williamson, S. D. (2012). Liquidity, monetary policy, and the financial crisis: A new monetarist approach. *The American Economic Review* **102**, 2570–2605.

Wu, F., Guan, Z. and Myers, R. J. (2011). Volatility spillover effects and cross hedging in corn and crude oil futures. *Journal of Futures Markets* **31**, 1052–1075.

Chapter 13

Analysis of NCG Prices Under Different Shapes of Oil Price Recovery with a Worldwide Gas Market Model

Maik Günther*,‡ and Mostafa Fallahnejad†,§
*Stadtwerke München GmbH, 80287 Munich, Germany
†Technische Universität Wien, 1040 Vienna, Austria
‡guenther.maik@swm.de
§fallahnejad@eeg.tuwien.ac.at

Natural gas plays an important role in Europe. During the last 10 years, the European gas market has undergone significant changes. While the share of oil-indexed gas in markets has declined, gas-on-gas competition has grown significantly. This chapter investigates gas prices at the trading hub NetConnect Germany (NCG) under various oil price scenarios in the period 2017 to 2023. This is done by performing sensitivity analyses using the worldwide gas market model WEGA. The results reveal that the NCG prices are very sensitive to the changes of oil prices throughout this period. However, NCG prices are smoothed and delayed due to the price formula of oil-indexed contracts as well as the decline of the share of oil-indexed gas.

Keywords: Natural Gas; NCG; oil-indexation; oil price recovery; Brent; long-term contracts; gas market model; WEGA; SWM; linear programming.

1. Introduction

Natural gas plays an important role in Europe. During the last 10 years, the European gas market has undergone significant changes, particularly with the introduction of the Third Energy Package of the European Union in 2009, which aims at the liberalization of the European energy markets. Natural gas is consumed in space and water heating, power generation and industrial processes. It is the fastest growing fossil fuel. According to British Petroleum (BP), worldwide, the demand for natural gas will grow by 1.6% p.a. until 2035 [BP, 2017]. With the increase of the gas demand, the forecast of gas prices and their drivers becomes more important.

The prices of oil or oil products are an important driver for gas prices [Nick and Thoenes, 2014]. In November 2014, the Organization of the Petroleum Exporting Countries (OPEC) decided not to restrain the production level of oil. As a result, the oil market had to find its equilibrium by itself. In January 2016, oil prices slumped to its lowest in the last decade due to a still oversupplied market. The slump of the oil prices affects future production through decreased investment in exploration and development of new fields. With the actual oil prices, the development costs for new fields (especially offshore, deep sea and arctic) are often too high and establishment of new projects is not profitable [Dale, 2015]. It is expected that in the future, due to the increase of the demand and the decline in production of current projects, oil prices will rise again and stimulate investments in new projects. However, the question is when and how the oil price recovery will occur.

Worldwide, the share of oil-indexation in gas imports declined from 63% in 2005 to 49% in 2016. Europe experienced the most significant decline. In 2016, only 36% of gas imports were linked to the oil-indexation [IGU, 2017]. Nevertheless, oil prices are still an important driver of gas prices and maintain their impact in the following years [Mitrova, 2015]. The gas supply in Europe involves long-term contracts (LTCs). Due to the oil-indexation in LTCs, e.g. in LTCs with Russia, European hub prices for natural gas are influenced by oil prices [European Parliament, 2014].

In the literature, only time series models and historical data have been used to analyze the cointegration of oil and gas prices. These time series models are not suitable for the long-term forecast of gas prices. In this chapter, the gap in the literature about the long-term impact of changes of oil prices on natural gas prices with the consideration of LTCs is filled. To study the cointegration of oil and gas prices until 2023, relevant data about the worldwide oil and gas markets was collected through an analysis of public and commercial literature and databases. Thanks to this comprehensive dataset, all relevant components and characteristics of the worldwide gas markets as well as oil-indexation in LTCs were modeled in the worldwide gas market model WEGA.

In this chapter, we introduce four possible oil price scenarios in the period 2017 to 2023. To see the impact of introduced oil price scenarios, gas prices at the trading point NetConnect Germany (NCG) are calculated with WEGA. The results of the study show that NCG prices are very sensitive to the changes of oil prices. Nevertheless, the effect is smoothed and delayed due to the formulas in LTCs and the relatively low share of oil-indexation. Thus, extremely high oil prices do not necessarily lead to extremely high gas prices. However, high oil-indexed gas prices besides low hub prices will probably motivate renegotiations of oil-indexed LTCs. The experiments in this chapter show that buyers will use the available volume flexibility of their LTCs whenever oil-indexed gas becomes cheaper or more expensive. This leads to the shift of the oil-indexed gas from the middle to the left or right of the merit order diagram. If it moves, for example to the left, buyers order as much gas as possible. This will push the most expensive sources out of the merit order and hub prices will decline.

The outline of this study is as follows: In Section 2, related works from the literature are discussed and their strengths and weaknesses are enumerated. In Section 3, the worldwide gas market model WEGA, its concept and its components are described. In Section 4, LTCs for natural gas in WEGA as well as their perspective in European gas markets are explained. In Section 5, oil price scenarios and the assumptions behind them are introduced. These oil price scenarios are input parameters for WEGA. In Section 6, the results of sensitivity analyses on NCG prices are presented and discussed. Finally, this chapter is concluded in Section 7 with a summary of the obtained results.

2. Related Work

Several authors searched in historic data for the cointegration of oil and gas prices, often with a focus on the North American market. Serletis and Herbert [1999] analyzed the cointegration of the Henry Hub (HH) gas prices and residual fuel oil prices. Five years later, Serletis and Rangel-Ruiz [2004] evaluated the cointegration of the HH prices and West Texas Intermediate (WTI) crude oil prices. Villar and Joutz [2006] added factors such as storage levels, transitory shocks and seasonality for the analysis of the HH and WTI prices. Brown and Yücel [2008] included factors such as weather, storage levels, seasonality and production cut in the study of the drivers of the natural gas prices. In the same year, Hartley *et al.* [2008] followed the approaches of Villar and Joutz [2006] and Brown and Yücel [2008]. Ramberg and Parsons [2012] extended the work of Brown and Yücel [2008] and concluded that the cointegration relationship between the HH and the WTI prices does not remain stable over time.

Statistical analyses for the cointegration of the HH and WTI prices, as well as the cointegration of the National Balancing Point (NBP) and Brent prices were made by IEA *et al.* [2011]. The cointegration of UK wholesale gas prices and Brent prices was studied by Panagiotidisa and Rutledgeb [2007]. Similarly, the cointegration of NBP prices and Brent prices was analyzed by Asche *et al.* [2012]. A vector autoregressive model for the NCG prices was developed by Petrovich [2014]. In their study, they included the impacts from the Brent prices, LNG imports to the EU, the coal price and the heating degree days.

Within the above mentioned studies, only historic data was analyzed. The developed time series models only allow the short-term forecast of gas prices, based on the knowledge of oil prices and other factors [Hassan and Nassar, 2013] and are not suitable for the long-term forecasts. Sensitivity analyses of gas prices for a longer period of time under different oil prices using market models are rare in the literature. Barden *et al.* [2009] calculated the impact of changes of oil prices on gas prices using INGM model. However, their gas market model had a focus on oil and gas competition in a few demand sectors only. Furthermore, oil-indexation in LTCs was not implemented in INGM. Thus, the calculated impact on gas prices was too small and did not reflect the reality. Chyong [2015] formulated an equilibrium problem in the form of a mixed complementary problem to analyze the effect of three different oil price scenarios on gas prices. Although the difference between hub prices and contract prices was presented with time intervals of 5 years till 2040, the European hub prices were not published. Thus, there is no analysis available in the literature about the long-term impact of changes of oil prices on hub prices.

3. Gas Market Model WEGA

WEGA is a worldwide gas market model used by Stadtwerke München GmbH (SWM) since 2013. It is a Linear Programming (LP) model which was developed under FICO Xpress Optimization Suite. The source code and the graphical user interface of WEGA are based on the commercial gas market model Pegasus, which was developed by Pöyry Management Consulting (UK) Ltd. [Davies and Sarsfield-Hall, 2014]. SWM also purchased the dataset from Pöyry. This dataset was changed by SWM. Thus, all scenarios and results from WEGA in this chapter are the view of SWM. SWM has its assumptions and forecasts of parameters, for example, about oil prices, exchange rates, costs of gas storages, production costs of gas fields, gas demand of power sector and non-power sectors. These data come from researches conducted by SWM and from a SWM fundamental power model [Schaber *et al.*, 2014]. The dataset is constantly updated using public sources as well as commercial data services from PIRA Energy Group, Wood Mackenzie, IHS Markit and Bloomberg New Energy Finance. For plausibility checks, NCG, NBP and Title Transfer Facility (TTF) future prices are frequently calculated and results are discussed with experts from SWM and other companies.

WEGA dispatches sources through a perfect competition under various constraints. Market power of producers as well as investment decisions are fixed.

However, these values can be modified through the introduction of scenarios. A scenario, for example, can be a situation in which the pipeline Nord Stream 2 is constructed and Russia uses its market power to add overcapacity in pipeline imports and hinders entry of other players to the European gas market. WEGA calculates a scenario in a daily resolution within 25 minutes.

The worldwide gas market in WEGA is modeled as a network consisting of a set of nodes and edges. Nodes are sometimes aggregated to reduce the CPU-time for the optimization. WEGA distinguishes the following types of nodes:

- **Demand zones:** These are countries, regions or trading hubs. NCG, TTF and NBP are three examples of trading hubs in WEGA. The gas demand of each demand zone exist in a daily resolution for the forecasting horizon [Fallahnejad *et al.*, 2017].
- **Gas fields in a demand zone:** These gas fields represent indigenous production of a demand zone. Available parameters are minimum and maximum production capacities, production costs and annual production profiles (e.g. at the gas field Groningen). It is possible to set these parameters in annual, monthly or daily resolution within the forecasting horizon.
- **Gas fields outside demand zones:** These are gas fields with a pipeline connection and/or with a connection to LNG export facilities. An example is the gas field Yamal in Russia. For these nodes, the same parameters as for gas fields in demand zones are available. Therefore, an expansion path for worldwide LNG export capacity can be given with this type of nodes.
- **Delivery points for pipelines:** Gas fields with a pipeline connection need a pipeline delivery point in a demand zone. An example is the delivery point in Lubmin in Germany for the pipeline Nord Stream.
- **Delivery points for LNG:** These nodes are LNG regasification terminals. All worldwide terminals are modeled in WEGA. Also, data about the expansion path for the regasification capacity till 2040 is stored in WEGA.
- **Gas storage facilities:** All gas storage facilities in Europe are modeled individually. Storage facilities in North America or in China are aggregated into groups. Each storage facility or each aggregation of storage facilities has a storage volume, an injection and a withdrawal capacity, short-run marginal costs and long-run marginal costs. Parameters of the worldwide expansion path of the storage capacity and parameters of the closing of storage facilities are available till 2040.
- **Flexibility options:** Each demand zone can have flexibility options such as price levels for the coal-to-gas switches or for the interruptible customers. Also demand shedding is possible to always guarantee a feasible solution. If demand shedding occurs, it is a sign that the dataset of WEGA is not well calibrated and has to be adjusted.

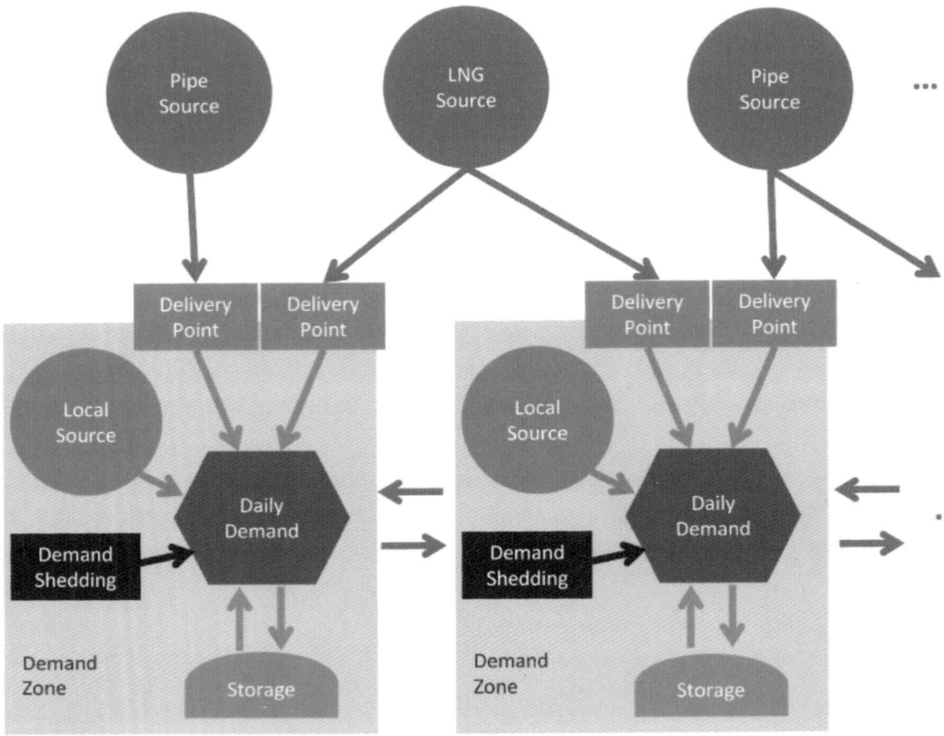

Fig. 1. Example of two demand zones.

Edges are used to represent the possibility of transporting gas between nodes. Each edge is a connection of two nodes. There are different types of edges including shipping routes of LNG, transmission pipelines and interconnections. An interconnection is an edge between two demand zones. It has a daily capacity in one direction and utilization costs. To model gas flows in both directions between two nodes, two edges are needed. Figure 1 demonstrates two demand zones. It can be seen that a liquefaction terminal can be connected to more than one regasification terminals. Furthermore, a gas field with pipeline connection can be connected to several pipeline delivery points. For example, gas from Norway can flow to Germany and UK.

The model also contains a database of worldwide LTCs with minimum and maximum contracted quantities, weekly, monthly and annual flexibility regulations, take or pay clauses, contract durations and price formulas. The price formulas take account of the oil-indexation or hub-indexation or a mixture of both. Contracts can be changed from 1 year to another in order to model renegotiations. The share of the oil-indexation is declining in WEGA and the share of the hub-indexation is increasing till 2040.

WEGA optimizes each gas year separately in a daily resolution. A hard constraint is to cover the demand $Demand_{z,d}$ of each demand zone $z \in Z$ at each day $d \in D$ (see Eq. (1)). This is achieved by using different types of gas flows *In* and *Out* of demand zones. The gas flow types include flows to and from pipelines $PipeIn_{z,d}$ and $PipeOut_{z,d}$, flows from LNG regasification terminals $LNGIn_{z,d}$ or to LNG liquefaction terminals $LNGOut_{z,d}$, flows between demand zones $InterconIn_{z,d}$ and $InterconOut_{z,d}$, flows in and out of storage facilities $StorageIn_{z,d}$ and $StorageOut_{z,d}$, flexibility options $FlexIn_{z,d}$ and $FlexOut_{z,d}$ and flows from indigenous production $IndigenousIn_{z,d}$.

$$\begin{aligned} Demand_{z,d} = {} & PipeIn_{z,d} - PipeOut_{z,d} \\ & + LNGIn_{z,d} - LNGOut_{z,d} \\ & + InterconIn_{z,d} - InterconOut_{z,d} \\ & + StorageIn_{z,d} - StorageOut_{z,d} \\ & + FlexIn_{z,d} - FlexOut_{z,d} \\ & + IndigenousIn_{z,d} \end{aligned} \quad \forall z \in Z; d \in D. \tag{1}$$

Other constraints correspond to the properties of edges, nodes and contracts. For instance, it is not allowed to exceed the maximum capacity of a pipeline or a LNG regasification terminal. It is also not allowed to exceed the contracted quantities or to change the contracted route of gas flows.

The goal of the optimization is the minimization of overall annual costs C to cover the demand $Demand_{z,d}$ of each demand zone in daily resolution (see Eq. (2)). Overall costs consist of daily production costs $CProd_d$, transportation costs $CTransp_d$, storage costs $CStorage_d$ and flexibility costs $CFlex_d$.

$$Min\ C = \sum_{d=1}^{D} (CProd_d + CTransp_d + CStorage_d + CFlex_d). \tag{2}$$

For the visualization purpose of the parameters and results, the business intelligence software Tableau is integrated into WEGA (see Fig. 2). Additional information about WEGA can be found in [Günther, 2017].

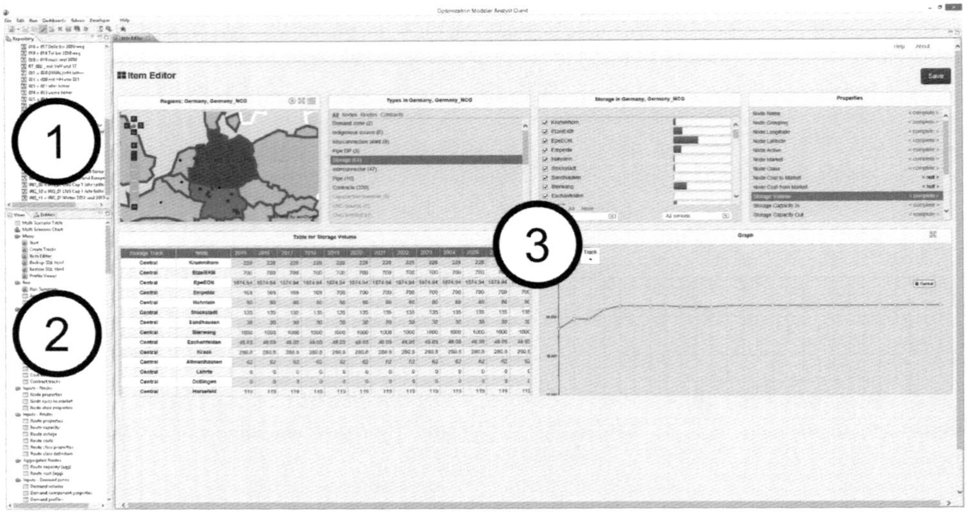

Fig. 2. Screenshot of WEGA (with data about gas storage facilities in Germany).
Notes: In the frame “1”, new scenarios can be created or the existing scenarios can be cloned. In the frame “2”, the predefined views and tables can be chosen for displaying in the frame “3”.

4. Long-Term Contracts in WEGA

As mentioned in Section 1, the share of oil-indexation in worldwide gas imports declined from 63% in 2005 to 49% in 2016. There is no sign for the termination of this transformation even with extremely low oil prices [Stern and Rogers, 2014]. Thus, in the dataset of WEGA, the indexation to oil or oil products is set to diminish gradually from year to year. Moreover, expired contracts are set only in few cases to be renewed; however, with lower volumes and shorter contract durations. Thus, gas-on-gas competition will play a more important role than today. At the trading hubs, the prices will be set by the principles of supply and demand. This trend of more gas-on-gas competition is important because historically, hub prices in Northwest Europe are strongly correlated to the Brent prices.

Gazprom is facing with a transforming European gas market and new price mechanisms. While Gazprom prefers traditional oil-indexation in their LTCs [Komolev and Gnatyuk, 2015], the company is flexible in its pricing strategy of LTCs [Mitrova, 2015]. Some examples are retroactive payments, price discounts, reduced take or pay levels or implementation of spot price components [Rogers, 2015]. However, in the event of a glut on LNG in Europe, which would possibly result in NCG prices of below 15 EUR/MWh (in 2015 real terms), the dataset of WEGA includes an assumption in which Gazprom would not be able to influence prices to a level that compensates for lower pipeline exports to Europe till the beginning of the 20s. Thus, they do not make a price protection strategy in medium term; rather, they compete for the market share. Also their export volumes to Europe remain in the range of 160–170 bcm. For analysis of possible strategies of Gazprom reference is made to [Chyong, 2015; Henderson and Mitrova, 2015; Mitrova, 2015; Rogers, 2015].

5. Oil Price Scenarios

In this section, a short overview of the oil market is given. Afterward, oil price scenarios, which are input parameters for WEGA, are explained. It has to be noted that the presented Brent and NCG prices are exemplary. Due to the internal restrictions, the main scenarios and calculated prices by SWM cannot be published.

Despite the increase of energy efficiency and the growth in the share of renewable energies and electric mobility, the worldwide liquids demand (oil, biofuels and other liquids) is expected to grow in the long term [BP, 2017; IEA, 2017; OPEC, 2017]. According to Wood Mackenzie [2016], over 20 million barrels per day (bbl/d) will be needed from new developments by 2025 to meet the demand. Less than half of this volume can be covered by reserve growth and new discoveries. The rest should be covered by the pipeline of pre-FID projects and future drilling activities in the US Lower 48. Figure 3 depicts the cumulative production in 2025 by breakeven of these pre-FID projects and future drilling activities in the US Lower 48. The sources in Fig. 3 provide nearly 13 million bbl/d of which only 9 million bbl/d are commercial at US$60 per bbl. In that sense, deepwater and ultra-deepwater projects have the highest costs and the greatest risk of delay. On the other hand, onshore projects as well as tight oil and shallow water projects have the most robust economics. It can be concluded that in order to meet the demand in the long run, the oil prices are expected to rise to over US$70 per bbl.

Indeed, the way oil prices will recover is unknown. To perform the sensitivity analyses on NCG prices using the global gas market model WEGA, the following oil price scenarios are created.

- **L-shaped:** This scenario shows constant prices of US$42.54 per bbl Brent from 2016 till 2023. With such low prices, it is not possible to cover the future demand. This price scenario is only possible if the liquids demand decreases significantly and if new technology improvements result in increased well productivity and in sharply reduced production costs of new fields. However, this is not likely to happen. With such low oil prices there is also a risk of renegotiations of existing LTCs [Chyong, 2015].

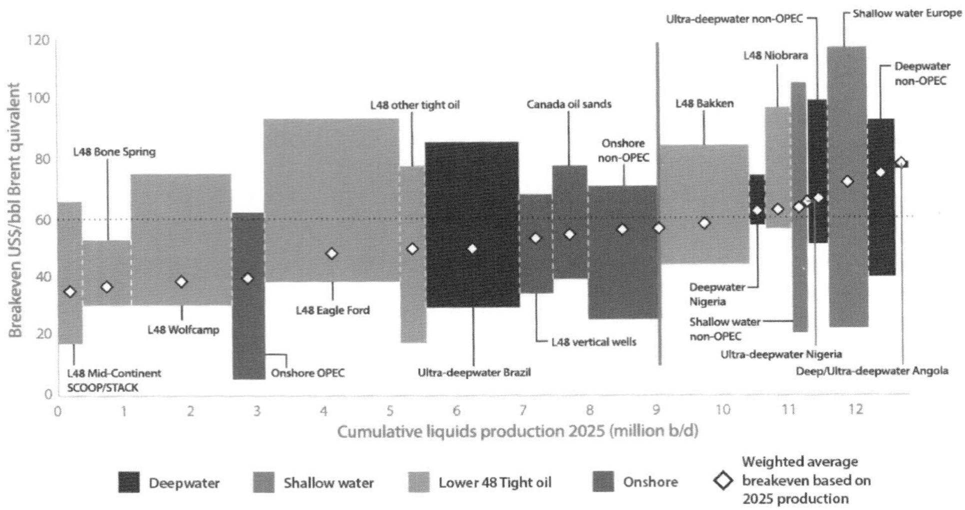

Fig. 3. Cumulative production from pre-FID projects and the US Lower 48 future drilling by breakeven in 2025 [Wood Mackenzie, 2016].

Notes: To meet the oil demand in the long run, the prices of Brent are expected to rise to over US$70 per bbl in the long term. Onshore and offshore assets are calculated at a nominal discount rate of 10% and 15%, respectively. This reflects a higher risk for offshore projects. All breakeven levels are shown in Brent equivalent.

- **U-shaped:** A modified version of the L-shaped scenario is the U-shaped scenario. It has the same profile as the L-shaped scenario until 2017; however, it jumps to US$75.00 per bbl Brent in 2018 and remains constant for the rest of the span.
- **J-shaped:** Here, an extreme surge in prices is assumed due to an undersupply of the market at the end of this decade, driven mainly by extremely low investments in oil production. At such high prices, shale oil production in North America will increase dramatically. As a result, the market will be once more oversupplied at the beginning of the 20s and a second collapse in oil prices will occur. This scenario looks like a "J" if the time span from 2015 to 2018 is taken into account. This is an extreme scenario to show the effect of very volatile oil prices on gas prices.
- **W-shaped:** A slow recovery of oil prices is expected at the W-shaped scenario. It is assumed that the market needs time to find its equilibrium by itself. OPEC would not be willing and able to do this. In addition, abundance of oil in storages lead to a pressure on Brent prices.

Figure 4 depicts the four scenarios. To see the effect of the inflation rate, oil price scenarios in real terms for the basis year 2015 are also presented in Table 1. It can be seen that oil prices in 2015 real terms are diminished in the U-shaped

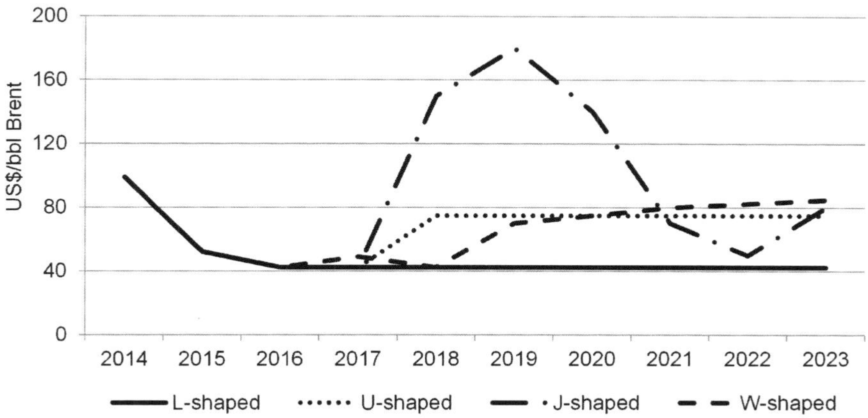

Fig. 4. Brent prices in nominal terms under the four shapes of oil price development.

Table 1. Brent prices under four scenarios of oil price development ("L", 'U", 'J" and "W" shape scenarios) in nominal terms and in real terms for the basis year 2015.

	US$/bbl brent nominal				US$/bbl brent real$_{2015}$			
Shape	**L**	**U**	**J**	**W**	**L**	**U**	**J**	**W**
2014	98.98	98.98	98.98	98.98	99.28	99.28	99.28	99.28
2015	52.32	52.32	52.32	52.32	52.32	52.32	52.32	52.32
2016	42.54	42.54	42.54	42.54	41.91	41.91	41.91	41.91
2017	42.54	42.54	42.54	49.20	41.29	41.29	41.29	47.76
2018	42.54	75.00	150.00	42.54	40.68	71.72	143.45	40.68
2019	42.54	75.00	180.00	70.00	40.08	70.66	169.59	65.95
2020	42.54	75.00	140.00	75.00	39.49	69.62	129.96	69.62
2021	42.54	75.00	70.00	80.00	38.90	68.59	64.02	73.16
2022	42.54	75.00	50.00	82.40	38.33	67.58	45.05	74.24
2023	42.54	75.00	80.00	84.87	37.76	66.58	71.02	75.34

and the L-shaped scenarios due to the constant prices in nominal terms. The prices corresponding to 2014 and 2015 are the historic Brent prices. These values are just informative and are not used for the calculation of NCG prices since within LTCs the prices of oil or oil products are averaged over 6–9 months.

6. Experiments and Results

NCG prices are highly correlated to TTF and NBP prices under normal conditions [Petrovich, 2014]. The results of WEGA for the NCG prices are also close to

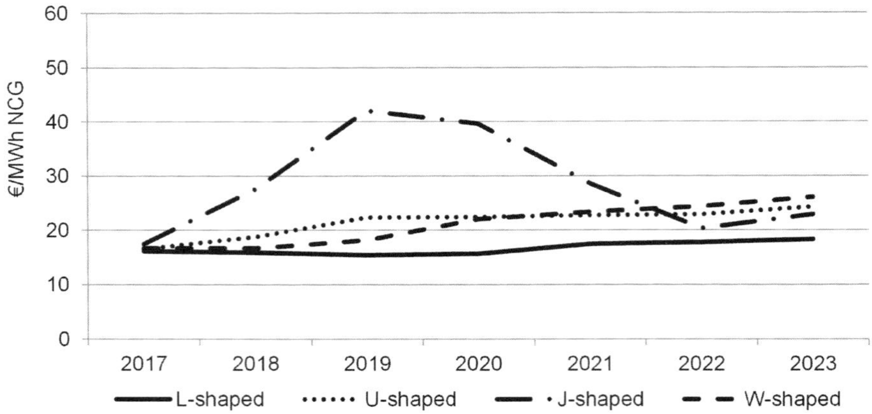

Fig. 5. Calculated NCG prices in nominal terms under four shapes of oil price development as a result of the gas market model WEGA.

the TTF or NBP prices. In this section, only the results for NCG prices are published to avoid overloaded diagrams.

Figure 5 depicts NCG prices in nominal terms under the different oil price shapes. The NCG prices in nominal and 2015 real terms can also be seen in Table 2. The structures of the gas prices for the J-shaped and W-shaped scenarios are similar to their corresponding oil price scenarios. Nevertheless, their gradients are smoothed. The J-shaped scenario illustrates a good example. In this scenario, oil prices increase by 253% from 2017 to 2018 while the NCG prices experience an increase of 58%. From 2018 to 2019, on the other hand, oil prices rise by 20% while the NCG prices in the J-shaped scenario rise by 52%. This effect is based on the price formula of the oil-indexed contracts. Prices of oil or oil products are averaged over 6–9 months with a 3–6-month time lag. The second reason is that not all the gas volumes are oil-indexed. Moreover, considering the high oil prices of the J-shaped scenario, whenever the gas prices from oil-indexed contracts are above the NCG price, the importers will use the volume flexibility of their LTCs and order as less oil-indexed gas as possible.

Oil-indexed gas is relatively cheap at the L-shaped scenario due to very low Brent prices. When oil-indexed gas becomes cheap, it moves to the left in the merit order diagram. Subsequently, it is beneficial for an importer to use all the volume flexibility of his LTCs to order as much oil-indexed gas as possible. As a result, the oil-indexed gas moves not only to the left of the merit order diagram, but also its volume expands and the most expensive sources are pushed out of the merit order diagram.

Although oil prices at the L-shaped and U-shaped scenarios are fixed, their corresponding gas prices slightly increase. There are several reasons for this

Table 2. Calculated NCG prices under four scenarios of oil price development ("L", "U", "J", and "W" shape scenarios) in nominal terms and in real terms for the basis year 2015.

	EUR/MWh NCG nominal				EUR/MWh NCG real$_{2015}$			
Shape	**L**	**U**	**J**	**W**	**L**	**U**	**J**	**W**
2017	16.13	16.50	17.40	16.70	15.66	16.02	16.89	16.21
2018	15.92	18.79	27.57	16.64	15.22	17.97	26.37	15.91
2019	15.40	22.32	42.03	18.15	14.51	21.03	39.60	17.10
2020	15.64	22.44	39.63	22.01	14.52	20.83	36.79	20.43
2021	17.44	22.70	28.55	23.38	15.95	20.76	26.11	21.38
2022	17.76	22.91	20.31	24.36	16.00	20.64	18.30	21.95
2023	18.26	24.29	22.91	26.04	16.21	21.56	20.34	23.12

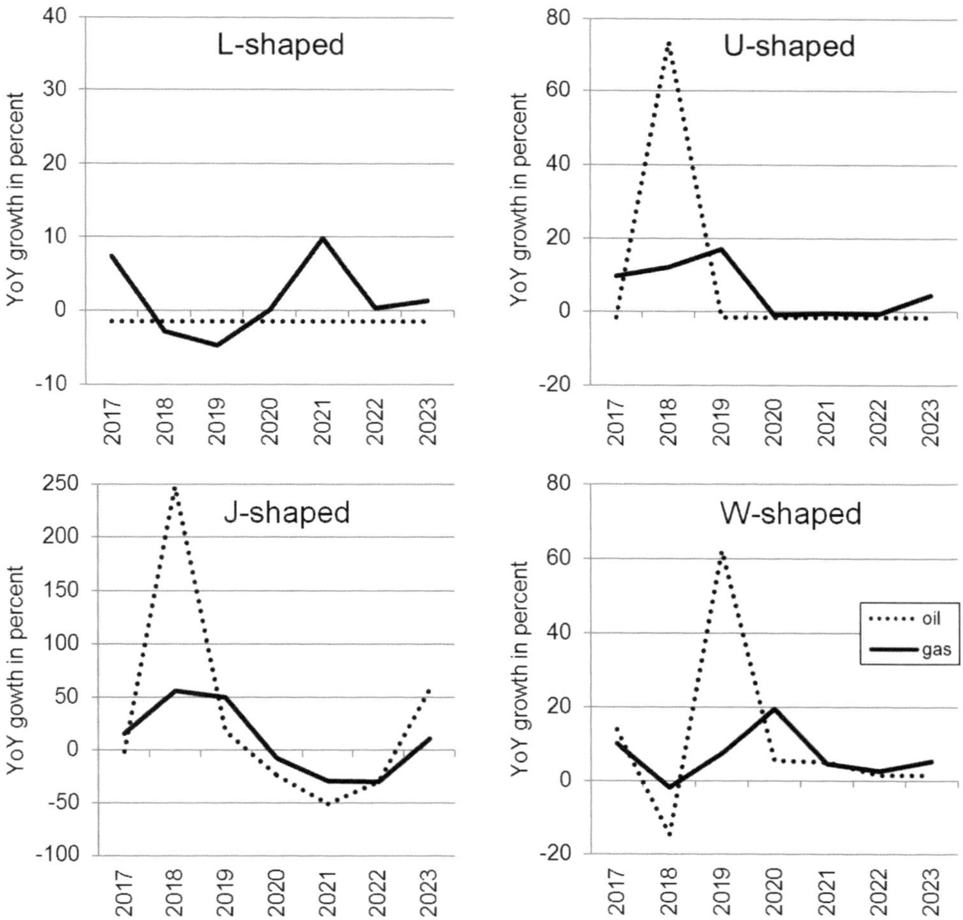

Fig. 6. Year-on-year (YoY) growth of 2015 real term oil and gas prices in percentage.

phenomenon: First of all, not all the gas volumes are oil-indexed and secondly, an ongoing drift in contracts to a hub-indexed pricing has been implemented in WEGA. The drift intensity is not identical for different producing countries (e.g. Russia versus Norway). Thus, low oil prices are not a guarantee for low NCG prices. This is especially important in the 2030s when the following trends have a stronger effect on the NCG prices: Indigenous production in Europe will be continuously diminishing in the future and Europe becomes more and more dependent on imports. In addition, with more gas-on-gas competition a major supplier like Gazprom would be able to manipulate hub prices [Mitrova, 2015]. This should not be analyzed here, because the 2030s are not within the scope of this chapter.

Figure 6 depicts the year-on-year growth in the percentage of Brent and NCG prices in 2015 real terms. Real terms are used to exclude the effect of the inflation rate. The smoothed and delayed NCG prices are evident as well. Considering the L-shaped scenario, the NCG prices in 2015 real terms increase on average while the Brent prices in 2015 real terms decline. It can also be seen in the L-shaped and U-shaped scenarios that the percentage increase of gas prices is higher than the percentage increase of oil prices after 2019. This is due to the drift to the hub-indexation, the expiration of LTCs and slight increase in long-run marginal costs of new gas fields.

7. Conclusion

In this chapter, a short overview of the oil market has been explained. Due to the decline of production from current projects and the increase of the demand, it is expected that oil prices will rise in coming years. However, the question is when and how the oil price recovery will occur. This question was addressed by introduction of four oil price recovery scenarios. The probability of reaching very low (L-shaped scenario) or very high (J-shaped scenario) oil prices is relatively low. According to the actual fundamental data, the W-shaped scenario seems to be the most realistic case. Higher oil prices will push oil-indexed gas prices upward. In contrast, the glut on LNG with a peak in the mid-20s pushes the hub prices downward. Consequently, natural gas prices in Europe will not always follow the oil prices. Moreover, high oil-indexed gas prices besides low hub prices will probably motivate renegotiations of oil-indexed LTCs and will lead to a further drift to the hub-indexation of LTCs.

To analyze the effect of the four oil price scenarios on NCG prices until 2023, the worldwide gas market model WEGA was used. The sensitivity analyses reveal that NCG prices are very sensitive to the changes of oil prices. However, the effect is smoothed and delayed. It was also demonstrated that extremely high oil prices of the J-shaped scenario do not result in extremely high NCG prices.

In addition, the impact of oil prices on the natural gas merit order was described in this chapter. Buyers will benefit from available volume flexibility of their LTCs when the oil-indexed gas moves to the left or right in the merit order diagram. As an example, if the oil-indexed gas moves from the middle to the left in the merit order diagram, buyers order as much gas as possible and use their maximum volume flexibility. This will push the most expensive sources out of the merit order diagram and as a result, hub prices will decline.

The gas-on-gas competition does not solely guarantee low gas prices on European trading hubs. This comes particularly into effect in the long term. Because of declining indigenous production in Europe, Gazprom can use its market power to enforce higher prices. Other policies such as a stronger indigenous production, a faster transition to renewable energies and effective regulations will help to decrease the market power of oligopolies.

References

Asche, F., Osmundsen, P. and Sandsmark, M. (2012). The UK market for natural gas, oil and electricity: Are the prices decoupled? *The Energy Journal* **27** (2), 27–40.

Barden, J., Pepper, W. and Aggarwal, V. (2009). The impact of high oil prices on global and regional natural gas and LNG markets. *The Energy Journal* **30**, (Special Issue: World Natural Gas Markets and Trade: A Multi-Modeling Perspective), pp. 55–71.

BP (2017). *BP Energy Outlook.* 2017 edn.

Brown, S. P. A. and Yücel, M. K. (2008). What drives natural gas prices? *The Energy Journal* **29** (2), 43–57.

Chyong, C.-K. (2015). Markets and long-term contracts: The case of Russian gas supplies to Europe. Working Paper 1524 (EPRG).

Dale, S. (2015). New Economics of Oil. *SBE Annual Conference*, Vancouver.

Davies, G. and Sarsfield-Hall, R. (2014). Gas SCR — Cost benefit analysis for a demand-side response mechanism. A report to Ofgem (Pöyry).

European Parliament. (2014). *The Impact of the Oil Price on EU Energy Prices.*

Fallahnejad, M., Eberl, B. and Günther, M. (2017). Long-Term Forecast of Residential & Commercial Gas Demand in Germany. In *Book of Abstracts of VSS 2017*, pp. 108–109.

Günther, M. (2017). Practical Application of a Worldwide Gasmarket Model at Stadtwerke München, in *Proc. of OR 2015*, pp. 715–721.

Hartley, P. R., Medlock, K. B. and Rosthal, J. E. (2008). The relationship between crude oil and natural gas prices. *The Energy Journal* **29** (3), 47–66.

Hassan, M. and Nassar, R. (2013). Empirical investigation and modeling of the relationship between gas price and crude oil and electricity prices. *Journal of Economics and Economic Education Research* **14** (3), 119–129.

Henderson, J. and Mitrova, T. (2015). *The Political and Commercial Dynamics of Russia's Gas Export Strategy*, NG 102 (OIES).

IEA (2017). *World Energy Outlook 2017.*

IEA, IEF, IMF and OPEC (2011). *Extending the G20 Work on Oil Price Volatility to Coal and Gas.*

IGU (2017). *Wholesale Gas Price Survey - 2017 Edition. A Global Review of Price Formation Mechanisms 2005–2016.*

Komolev, S. and Gnatyuk, A. (2015). Pipeline LTCs in the 'New World' of European Natural Gas. *17th Meeting of the EU-Russia GAC's Work Stream on Internal Market.*
Mitrova, T. (2015). Changing Gas Price Mechanisms in Europe and Russia's Gas Pricing Policy, in *Book of Abstracts of 38th IAEE International Conference*, pp. 39–40.
Nick, S. and Thoenes, S. (2014). What drives natural gas prices? — A structural VAR approach. *Energy Economics* **45**, 517–527.
OPEC (2017). *2017 World Oil Outlook.*
Panagiotidisa, T. and Rutledgeb, E. (2007). Oil and gas markets in the UK: Evidence from a cointegrating approach. *Energy Economics* **27** (2), 329–347.
Petrovich, B. (2014). *European Gas Hub Price Correlation: Barriers to Converge?*, NG 91 (OIES).
Ramberg, D. J. and Parsons, J. E. (2012). The weak tie between natural gas and oil prices. *The Energy Journal* **33** (2), 13–35.
Rogers, H. V. (2015). *The Impact of Lower Gas and Oil Prices on Global Gas and LNG Markets*, NG 99 (OIES).
Schaber, K., Roth, H. and Fallahnejad, M. (2014). Can the Gas Sector Provide the Flexibility to the Power Sector for the Integration of Renewables? In *13th WIW*, pp. 46–51.
Serletis, A. and Herbert, J. (1999). The message in North America energy prices. *Energy Economics* **21**, 471–483.
Serletis, A. and Rangel-Ruiz, R. (2004). Testing for common features in North American energy markets. *Energy Economics* **26**, 401–414.
Stern, J. and Rogers, H. V. (2014). *The Dynamics of a Liberalised European Gas Market: Key Determinants of Hub Prices, and Roles and Risks of Major Players*, NG 94 (OIES).
Villar, J. A. and Joutz, F. L. (2006). *The Relationship Between Crude Oil and Natural Gas Prices* (EIA, Office of Oil and Gas).
Wood Mackenzie (2016). *Pre-FID Oil Projects: Global Breakeven Analysis and Cost Curves*, www.woodmac.com/analysis/preFID-oil-projects.

PART III

Regulation, Risk Management and Network System

Chapter 14

Energy Risk Management in Practice

Wieger Johan Hinderks, Andreas Wagner* and Prilly Oktoviany
Department for Financial Mathematics,
Fraunhofer Institute for Industrial Mathematics ITWM,
Fraunhofer-Platz 1, 67663 Kaiserslautern, Germany
**andreas.wagner@itwm.fraunhofer.de*

An overview of risk measurement techniques for typical energy utilities is given. Most common calculated risk measures are explained among the often simple calculation methods used in practice. For a more sophisticated risk analysis, the various model classes proposed in the literature are reviewed. A three-factor model is explained in mathematical detail and its application to the practical modeling of energy prices is shown. This includes spot and futures prices in different time resolutions as well as the calibration of such models.

Keywords: Electricity market; electricity price modeling; energy trading; risk management; market risk; price forward curve; risk indicators; factor models; reduced-form models; structural models.

1. Introduction

Since the deregulation started in the 1980s, energy markets have developed and matured as financial markets. This gave rise to purely financial derivatives on energy contracts, such as financially settled futures. Due to the deregulation and financialization of the energy markets, they are prone to the financial risks just like the stock market is. Market participants are therefore striving to hedge their positions and manage their risks. The more effectively an energy utility manages this, the more capital can be invested in the development of the company.

Over the past decades, many thorough studies on risk management in energy markets have appeared, e.g. [Pilipovic, 1997; Eydeland and Wolyniec, 2003; Burger *et al.*, 2014; Swindle, 2014]. Due to the volatility of market prices — especially for electricity — market risk is of great importance for the risk management in energy finance. To properly hedge and manage this risk, energy prices need to be modeled. An overview of the methods for electricity price forecasting can be found in [Weron, 2014]. Market price forecasts or models can then be used to assess the risk of fluctuating market prices.

In this chapter, we try to combine an up-to-date overview of both risk and market price modeling. We present an overview of all typical practices in energy risk management. We will focus on market risk and provide a link between classical risk measurement and more complex market models. For example, we show how the classical risk figure Value-at-Risk (VaR) can be transferred to and computed with a stochastic model. Furthermore, we give an example of a factor model, which could be the fundamental of a risk management framework for a medium-sized energy utility. This model provides a good economic interpretation of all its components and offers potential for extensions, such as simulating correlated prices of different commodities and pricing of options on futures.

This chapter consists of three sections: In Section 2, we introduce six different types of risk and several analytical approaches to calculate risk figures for these types of risk. Focusing on market risk, which is the most prominent type of risk, we introduce different modelling approaches for commodity prices in Section 3. Finally, in Section 4 we go into detail about an advanced multifactor model.

2. Overview of Typical Risk Indicators Used in the Industry

In this section, we will discuss several different sources of risk, some of which also appear in other financial markets. The main risk types we consider are

- Market risk,
- Liquidity risk,
- Credit risk,
- Operational risk,
- Volume risk, and
- Model risk.

For each of these risk types we will explain the typical *risk figures* or *risk measures*, i.e. methods to reduce a complex risk source to a simple number. By calculating multiple risk figures, the risk management department determines which positions are vulnerable and if there are any measures that need to be taken, such as hedging or liquidation of the position.

Throughout the rest of this chapter we use the studies of Pilipovic [1997]; Eydeland and Wolyniec [2003]; Burger *et al.* [2014] and Swindle [2014] as supporting literature and we refer the interested reader to these textbooks for more information on the subject of energy risk management.

2.1. *Market risk*

As in stock markets, market risk is the most dominating type of risk in energy markets. Although its exact definition changes slightly from author to author, the idea is that changing market prices cause fluctuations in the value of a portfolio. Therefore, we define market risk as the risk that *arises from changes in the market price and its volatility.*

Mark-to-Market. A mark-to-market (MTM) valuation includes the most recent market information (both exchange-traded and OTC[1]) in its computation. This method generates benchmark results for risk evaluation, since it tries "[..] to arrive at true market value as opposed to a trader's 'view' or opinion of value" [Pilipovic, 1997]. It is good practice to mark a portfolio (or book) to market every trading day after the market closes to keep track of the portfolio value. In an electricity market context, marking to market could be done after the day-ahead spot auction has been held.

From its very definition, it is clear that all contracts bought and sold can be valued by their corresponding market prices. However, in energy it is often the case that the portfolio possesses a plan (or a profile) of spot and futures positions that will be bought or sold at some future time. These planned positions are often unknown in advance and are therefore predicted. Taking these predictions into account while marking a portfolio to market is beneficial since these variable positions often cannot be neglected and need to be hedged in real-time. For example, an energy utility has to meet the variable demand of its customers and make sure their positions are balanced.

The question that arises is how to value these planned positions. All positions in futures contracts can be valued by the futures prices. The residual spot positions, however, do not (yet) have a known market price. The solution is to use the price

[1] Over-the-counter (OTC) contracts are bilateral contracts not traded through a centralized exchange.

forward curve (PFC) as a prediction for the future spot prices.[2] Since the PFC is assumed to be arbitrage-free,[3] the whole load at time t_0 can be valued with the PFC, i.e.

$$\mathrm{MTM}_{\mathrm{load}} := \sum_{T \in \mathcal{T}} Q(t_0, T) \cdot f(t_0, T), \tag{1}$$

where $Q(t_0, T)$ denotes the (at t_0 estimated) load at time T of the portfolio (positive for long and negative for short positions), $f(t_0, T)$ the value of the PFC at time T, and $\mathcal{T}$ is the set of all delivery times under consideration.

The MTM value of the portfolio is then given by the sum of $\mathrm{MTM}_{\mathrm{load}}$ and the MTM values of all other contracts. Computing the MTM for different partitions of the considered time horizon (also including different delivery profiles such as base, peak or off-peak) could yield information on the hours/days during which risk is accumulating.

Value-at-Risk. VaR is a well-known risk indicator for market risk, which became widely known after the publication of *RiskMetrics*, see [J.P. Morgan/Reuters, 1996]. It is also explained in detail in the textbooks cited above. The VaR is a quantile of the profit-and-loss distribution (P&L) of a portfolio. For example, the 1-day 95% VaR is a loss which the portfolio does not exceed over the course of one day of trading with probability of 5% (i.e. on average the portfolio loses more than the VaR every 20th day). It is also common to calculate the 10-day 99% VaR. The time frame over which the VaR is computed is usually called the *holding period*, whereas the probability for which the VaR-statement holds is called the *confidence level*.

The easiest approach to calculate a VaR is a *historical simulation* and relies on constructing the empirical P&L distribution from historical returns in the market price and then taking the quantile of this distribution. Although this method is easy to compute, it usually does not estimate the risk correctly, since historical market prices in general do not have any predictive power.

The classical (analytical) approach of the $\alpha\%$ VaR, or VaR_α with holding period of n days, is described in J.P. Morgan/Reuters [1996, Section 1.2] and is given by the difference

$$\mathrm{VaR}_\alpha := |(1 - e^{\hat{r}})\,\mathrm{MTM}| \approx |\hat{r}\,\mathrm{MTM}|, \tag{2}$$

---

[2] Another non-analytical solution would be to use a Monte Carlo method and simulate spot prices with some stochastic model. We will discuss such models in the remaining two sections.

[3] A PFC is arbitrage-free, if for any existing futures contract the average value of the PFC within its delivery time yields its current market price.

where $\hat{r}$ is the $(1-\alpha)$-quantile of n-day portfolio's log return distribution. The approximation in (2) only holds for small $\hat{r}$. Moreover, the portfolio's log returns are often assumed to be normally distributed, yielding

$$\hat{r} := \sqrt{n} \cdot \sigma \cdot \Phi^{-1}(1-\alpha), \tag{3}$$

where σ is the volatility of the portfolio's daily log returns and $\Phi^{-1}(x)$ is the inverse of the cumulative distribution function of the standard normal distribution. This classical method is sometimes called the *delta-normal method* and, as suggested by its naming, it only takes the portfolio's delta into account. Therefore, this method could lead to an incorrect risk estimation if the portfolio contains nonlinear positions such as options. To better evaluate the risk from nonlinear positions, Burger *et al.* [2014] suggest the *delta-gamma approach*. This is similar to the *estimated variance-covariance method* given by Pilipovic [1997].

The analytical methods are easy to understand and compute, but they might not capture the risk properly, e.g. when the market prices are not log-normally distributed. An alternative to the analytical methods is computing the VaR with the help of Monte Carlo simulation. This allows for more complicated price dynamics, for example, by using the multi-factor model discussed in Section 4.

Profit-at-Risk. The Profit-at-Risk (PaR) is a risk measure similar to VaR, but focusses on the spot risk. The estimated load is hedged using futures contracts. Later we introduce several methods to calculate such a hedge. The remaining spot position after hedging is now the load under consideration. The PaR is defined as the difference between the current value of the residual spot load and its value in a risk scenario. From this definition, it is clear that the PaR depends solely on the choice of hedge method and risk scenario. In this paragraph, we will consider different methods for risk scenarios, whereas the next paragraph will focus on several hedge methods, cf. [Burger *et al.*, 2014].

The easiest analytical approach is to stress the PFC with a constant factor. This can be done by stressing the PFC globally, thus changing the whole forward curve with the same relative factor, or point-wise depending on the sign of the load (i.e. long or short). Let $0 < \alpha < 1$ be a constant relative factor. If we stress the whole forward curve, then

$$\mathrm{PaR}_\alpha := |\alpha \cdot \mathrm{MTM}| \tag{4}$$

$$= \begin{cases} \mathrm{MTM} - (1-\alpha)\,\mathrm{MTM}, & \mathrm{MTM} > 0 \\ \mathrm{MTM} - (1+\alpha)\,\mathrm{MTM}, & \mathrm{MTM} < 0 \end{cases}, \tag{5}$$

where MTM is the mark-to-market value of the residual spot positions of the utility's portfolio. As it can be seen from the formula, the PFC is decreased if the portfolio is long and increased if the portfolio is short. The choice of α can be determined either by expert judgement or by an empirical analysis of historical spot price volatilities. The point-wise stressing technique is much more conservative and can be computed as follows:

$$\mathrm{PaR}_\alpha := \sum_{T \in \mathcal{T}} |\alpha \cdot Q^h(t_0, T) \cdot f(t_0, T)|, \tag{6}$$

where $Q^h(t_0, T)$ is the remaining spot position after hedge defined in (9). In this setting, each time point of the portfolio is stressed, cf. Eq. (1).

Of course, one could also apply Monte Carlo simulation to evaluate the PaR. For this purpose, we simulate N spot price paths and determine the portfolio value for every path i

$$V_i := \sum_{T \in \mathcal{T}} Q^h(t_0, T) \cdot S_i(T), \tag{7}$$

where $S_i(T)$ denotes the simulated spot price at time T. With the N simulated values of V_i, the portfolio's empirical distribution can be determined and used to find the $(1 - \alpha)$-quantile. The PaR is then computed by taking the difference between the MTM value and the empirical $(1 - \alpha)$-quantile.

Hedging. There are several approaches to hedge a position, depending on the utility and the availability of sophisticated models. Hedging in general has the aim to buy or sell forward contracts on the market such that, for a certain position, the financial risk from a change in market prices is reduced. As the delivery obligations of a typical utility do not match the delivery profile of standardized futures contracts (i.e. baseload or peakload contracts for electricity), the risk cannot be hedged completely. We discuss two approaches, which are commonly used in German energy utilities and show how to improve them if suitable models are available.

Like before, we denote the load profile (i.e. the open position of the portfolio) by $Q(T) = Q(t_0, T)$. So, for the case of electricity or gas, $Q(T)$ denotes the difference between the long and short positions of the utility at delivery time T in MWh. We assume that there is a futures contract with price F that delivers at all time points $\mathcal{T} = \{T_1, T_2, \ldots, T_N\}$ of our load profile Q. If this is not the case, we can partition the load profile in delivery intervals of tradable futures contracts. Our goal is to determine an amount h of the futures contract F (in MWh), which we should buy in order to hedge the load profile during the delivery timespan $\mathcal{T}$. Furthermore, we assume that for $T_i \in \mathcal{T}$ the PFC can be expressed as $f(t_0, T_i) = v_i \cdot F$ with constant weights $\upsilon_i \in \mathbb{R}$ satisfying

$$\frac{1}{N}\sum_{i=1}^{N} \upsilon_i = 1, \tag{8}$$

where N is the number of hours/days in the delivery time interval $\mathcal{T}$. We further denote the MTM value of the load profile Q as given by Eq. (1) by $V(F)$, using the PFC based on the current futures price F. The remaining position $Q^h(T_i)$ after hedging at each point in time $T_i \in \mathcal{T}$ is determined by

$$Q^h(T_i) := Q(T_i) - h. \tag{9}$$

This is the remaining spot risk which can be assessed using the PaR outlined above.

Delta-Hedge (Value-Hedge). The Delta-Hedge is set up such that the hedge position compensates the change in the MTM value V driven by a small movement of market prices. The position in futures can be calculated as $V(F+1) - V(F)$, i.e. the difference in the value of $Q(T)$ under the current price level F and a shifted price level $F+1$. Using the form of the PFC given by the weights υ_i this can also be rewritten as

$$h_\Delta = \frac{V(F+1) - V(F)}{N} = \frac{V(F)}{N \cdot F} = \frac{1}{N}\sum_{i=1}^{N} \upsilon_i \cdot Q(T_i), \tag{10}$$

i.e. the required position h_Δ is the ratio between the MTM value and the current price of the futures F.

Quantity-Hedge. In a quantity hedge, the hedge position h is determined such that the open position of the portfolio is offset optimally by the amount of energy delivered from the futures contract. Assuming the futures delivers exactly one MWh of energy, we get

$$h_{\text{quantity}} = \frac{1}{N}\sum_{i=1}^{N} Q(T_i). \tag{11}$$

This corresponds to a delta-hedge if we assume all hourly weights to be equal.

For electricity, peak and baseload futures contracts are available in many markets. Therefore, the utility can take positions in two contracts (with the same time period), which adds another degree of freedom for hedging. One way of utilizing this is to separate the load profile Q in peak and offpeak and setting up separate hedges for each (so-called peak/offpeak-hedge). As an alternative, one can hedge such that the Delta-Hedge and the Quantity-Hedge are fulfilled, the so-called *Delta/Quantity-Hedge*. If the utility has an advanced spot-price model at hand, see the next sections on common models and approaches, it is possible to also implement a *Variance Minimizing Hedge*. The idea is to delta-hedge the position and to minimize the variance of the remaining spot-position using peakload and baseload contracts. We refer to Burger *et al.* [2014], for example.

2.2. *Liquidity risk*

Liquidity risk arises usually due to the insufficient *market liquidity* or insufficient *available funds* [Burger *et al.*, 2014, Section 3.5]. These are two different types of liquidity risk, which we will discuss in this section.

This type of risk is (supposed to be) bound by regulators, e.g. the international regulatory framework for banks *Basel III*. However, despite existing regulations there are still events where a lot of firms defaulted due to liquidity risk (among other reasons), such as the credit crunch in 2008.

Market Liquidity Risk. The expression liquidity risk usually refers to market liquidity risk. This is the risk of failing to hedge positions adequately due to market conditions. Eydeland and Wolyniec [2003, p. 29] summarize market liquidity risk as the "[...] inability to hedge at the right time, at the right price, at the right size." Basically, this type of risk arises *when closing a position is exceeding the markets liquidity*.

If the market is not liquid, it might happen that some positions cannot be closed as wished. However, this type of risk can also occur in a liquid market when the size of the position is large relative to the circulation, because then it might also take a long time to close this position at an economic price.

Liquidity-Adjusted Value-at-Risk. The Liquidity-Adjusted Value-at-Risk (LVaR) is a risk indicator extending the VaR to estimate the market liquidity risk in addition to the market risk [Burger *et al.*, 2014, Section 3.2.6]. It extends the VaR approach for futures contracts by limiting the amount of contracts that can be bought or sold daily and thus includes the fact that closing the positions stretches over several days after the holding period elapses, inducing more (market) risk.

Funding Liquidity Risk. The second type is the risk in liquidity of funding. This type of risk occurs when liabilities cannot be fulfilled due to lack of funds. As remarked by Burger *et al.* [2014], there exist several ratios defined by regulators for the financial industry, which can be used to measure funding liquidity risk of energy utilities, too.

Due to clearing, funding liquidity risk is closely related to credit risk (see Section 2.3). For example, in the European energy markets there is a central clearing through the European Commodity Clearing (ECC). It reduces credit risk by inducing margining. All market participants have their own margin account, in which they have to store an amount of capital, which depends on their position and is determined by the ECC. On the one hand, the ECC can use the margin account of a market participant to fulfill her contracts to other market participants in case of her default, thus reducing credit risk for all participants. On the other hand, this increases funding liquidity risk due to the fact that part of the capital of a firm is stuck in the margin account or that engaging in a position might cause a margin call[4] which is greater than the amount of available capital. Therefore, to avoid default, the size of future margin calls have to be estimated. This can be done by computing the same margins as the regulators induce. For example, the margin rules of the ECC can be found online in their margining documentation [ECC, 2017].

2.3. *Credit risk*

Credit or counterparty risk is the risk that a contractual partner is unable to fulfill the contract for whatever reason. In the 1990s, this type of risk was often not considered by energy utilities [Pilipovic, 1997]. Nowadays, however, this risk type is treated with special care as pointed out in Swindle [2014]. Compared to stock markets, credit risk in energy markets is an even more delicate matter, where high volatility of the market prices requires hedging credit risk more often with products from a more illiquid market. As mentioned in the previous section on liquidity risk, exchanges are often cleared by an independent firm, limiting credit risk for all parties. This is why credit risk is of high importance for over-the-counter (OTC) traded contracts.

A crucial step to quantify credit risk is to determine the probability of default of a counterparty. In practice, the easiest way is the use of external rating systems, which represent an estimated classification of probabilities of default. Merton [1974] proposed a model where the default of a firm can be deduced by the relationship between its equities and debts, both representing the firm's asset value. At the debt's maturity date, the value of the firm's equity can be modeled as a call option on its assets. Using the Black–Scholes option pricing formula, this provides a closed-form solution for the calculation of the firm's probability of default. Other credit risk models are based on the Merton model, see [Lütkebohmert, 2009].

[4]The moment, when the position of a market player changes and the minimum margin on her margin account increases, is called a *margin call*. The market player has to add the extra capital to her margin account, which is often referred to as *to post margin*.

Settlement Risk. Settlement risk is the risk that the counterparty of a contract cannot fulfill its payment of delivered goods or services. For example, in the case of bankruptcy of a client of an electricity supplier the settlement risk is the value of the delivered load between the last payment and the deactivation of supply to this bankrupt client. When trading commodities in shipments such as oil or coal, the commodity is often first delivered and then paid a few days or weeks later [Swindle, 2014]. During this time, the seller has a settlement risk called *delivered-not-paid* (DNP), which is a short-term credit exposure, but often of high value.

Replacement Risk. Replacement risk is the risk of the contractual partner being unable to fulfill the contract and the need of replacing the original contract with a new contract with another counterparty. The replacement contract has to be entered at a future time and market conditions might have changed for the worse upon entering the replacement contract, inferring a loss on the switch of contractual partner. It is clear that this type of risk depends on the unknown market prices at that point in time.

2.4. *Other risk types*

Besides market risk, liquidity risk and credit risk there are further types of risk, many of which are discussed in the works of Pilipovic [1997], Eydeland and Wolyniec [2003], Burger *et al.* [2014] and Swindle [2014]. In this section, we will briefly describe the three most important remaining risk types: operational risk, volume risk and model risk.

Operational Risk. In general, operational risk is the risk of potential losses caused due to failure of internal processes and systems, errors in people's action or external events. Operational risk is different from the other types of risk since "[..] market risk is typically exploited by traders and fund managers and credit risk is exploited by lending institutions to create a profit [..]" [Burger *et al.*, 2014], but operational risk is always minimized. However, operational risk is hard to quantify by risk indicators or other mathematical methods. Therefore, there are more management approaches involving interviews with technical experts and observation of work processes [James, 2012, Chapter 15].

Volume Risk. All flexible energy contracts generate volume risk. For example, electricity suppliers that serve the retail market do not know in advance how much electricity will be consumed by their served households. The risk that is induced by this contract volume flexibility is called volume risk. Volume risk is often assessed in a scenario analysis.

Model Risk. For all risk indicators using assumptions on the development of market prices model risk is involved. Model risk includes the chance of choosing a wrong model or of choosing the wrong parametrization. Pilipovic [1997] suggests that management should insist on regular verification of the mathematical models. Model risk can also be assessed by using more complex *convex risk measures*, see [Föllmer and Schied, 2002], since this type of risk measure can be expressed as the worst case value among a set of possible models.

3. Overview of Modern Market Price Models

The limitations of the analytically traceable approaches shown in the previous section motivate the choice of more realistic, but more complicated and mathematically more demanding price models. In this section, we give an overview of existing modeling approaches for electricity spot prices. We discuss the most popular models within each approach and their pros and cons. The variety of approaches is a result of the history of energy price modeling as scientists with different backgrounds left their footprints. Traditionally, driven by engineering and energy economists, optimization approaches and time series models were developed. The main goal was to understand long-term development of the market by evaluating different scenarios, but also to create short-term forecasts of demand and other fundamental factors. Later, in particular after the deregulation of the market and the creation of exchanges also (financial) mathematicians applied their tools to the electricity markets. This development mainly brought up reduced-form and structural models which focus on risk management and the valuation of derivatives.

In this section, we focus on models for the electricity spot price, which in many cases can be simplified and applied to other energy commodities like gas prices. We also limit the discussion to continuous models, which are commonly used in financial modeling. Many of the models in the following sections may also be used for forward price modeling, even though the models usually have their strengths on one side, so either spot or forward. In the next section, we will introduce a factor model, which is from our point of view a good balance between spot and forward modeling and can be used for an integrated and consistent pricing of derivatives (on either spot or forward). In the remainder of the section, we consider three categories of models: *fundamental models*, *reduced-form models* and *structural models*. For each of them we explain the general idea, give the main references for further reading and assess the appropriateness for risk-management.

3.1. *Fundamental models*

Fundamental market models map the whole electricity system and also consider physical laws and limitations as close as possible. The essential components of a fundamental model are:

- Supply model: Power plants (with a description of their technical peculiarities like efficiency, start-up times and costs, ramping rates, availabilities), primary fuel markets, a hydro storage model, renewables, etc.
- Demand model: Calendar effects, weather, industry production, etc.
- Network model: Interconnections, price zones, etc.

Based on a scenario for all input factors, an optimization algorithm minimizes the system costs, i.e. the total cost of electricity production needed to satisfy demand for each point in time (usually hourly). The optimization also takes interdependencies between different times into account. A typical example for such an interdependency is the ramp-up of a power plant. Defining the scenarios is a demanding task which is usually done by experts like energy analysts. The difficulty lies in the definition of realistic assumptions, e.g. on primary fuel prices, and the consistency between the different input factors.

In practice, the value of such a model comes mainly from the underlying database, which contains details on power plants, a detailed network model and many other data on the electricity market. Therefore, there are a few commercial models and databases in the market next to some universities, which run their own models mainly for a scientific analysis of market effects, particularly relevant for the regulator.

Fundamental models are computationally expensive. They are not used to generate a high number of paths in day-to-day business, e.g. in order to calculate a VaR. For the purpose of short- to medium-term (few years ahead) risk management, these models are not practicable. They are rather the tool of choice for a thorough scenario analysis with respect to the long-term development of prices, an analysis of network flows, and others. However, these models can give valuable insights when a long-term analysis is needed, e.g. for the valuation of a new power plant. For a more detailed description of fundamental models, we refer to [Burger *et al.*, 2014].

3.2. *Reduced-form models*

Reduced-form models represent the other extreme. They originate from existing approaches already proposed for other financial markets like stocks or interest rates. The physical relationships in electricity are more or less ignored and the price for electricity S_t at time t is viewed as a time series and modeled as some stochastic process. A feature of those models is that derivative prices and volatilities, risk figures and other results of interest may be calculated through analytic formulae, which is desirable in some applications. However, it strongly depends on the structure of the model and the fact that closed-form solutions are available or not.

Nowadays, it is important to distinguish between arithmetic and geometric modeling approaches. In the first set-up, the price itself is modeled as a stochastic process, whereas in the latter, the logarithm of the price process S_t, i.e. $\log(S_t)$, is the modeled quantity. The decision depends on the market and its properties. Many analytical models allow for negative prices and therefore are a good choice for electricity markets. For gas, oil, coal, or other storable commodities, geometric models without the possibility of negative prices may perform better. Most models outlined in the following can be used in an arithmetic or geometric[5] way, even though the latter approach is used in traditional literature (simply because negative prices were not imaginable[6] at the time the models had been developed). Reduced form models may further be classified as (jump-)diffusion models, regime-switching models and factor models.

Diffusion Models. Diffusion models consist of a combination of stochastic processes with some economical motivation. The most traditional diffusion model is by Black and Scholes [1973]. It uses a geometric Brownian motion (GBM) to capture the dynamics of the stock price, and Eydeland and Wolyniec [2003] discuss the use of a GBM in the context of energy markets. In its simplest form, the GBM has the following stochastic differential equation:

$$dS_t = \mu S_t dt + \sigma S_t dW_t, \quad \sigma > 0, \tag{12}$$

where μ denotes the drift parameter, σ the volatility and W_t denotes a standard Brownian motion. For a heuristic interpretation of a stochastic differential equation, one interprets dS_t as the change in S_t between two (close) points in time, dt as the corresponding difference in time and dW_t as a normally distributed random variable (with mean zero and a volatility depending on the time difference). Even though the GBM-dynamic is not suitable for modeling the dynamics of commodity spot prices, the Black-model [Black, 1976], which corresponds to the GBM with $\mu = 0$, is the standard model for forward prices and also applicable to electricity forwards. For commodity spot-prices, the models rely on the Ornstein–Uhlenbeck (OU) process,

[5] By arithmetic we mean that the spot price itself is directly modeled, whereas geometric indicates that its logarithm is used.

[6] Models for the interest rate markets had similar issues after the financial crisis when interest rates became negative for the first time.

which has the form

$$dS_t = \kappa(\mu - S_t)dt + \sigma dW_t, \quad \kappa > 0, \sigma > 0, \tag{13}$$

and is one of the approaches suggested by Schwartz [1997]. The popularity of the OU model in commodities is explained by its mean-reverting behavior, which most commodities exhibit due to the interactions of supply and demand. The mean reversion property is contained in the drift term $\kappa(\mu - S_t)$, which pulls the process to its long-term mean μ with speed κ.

These models have been extended by using more than one Brownian motion, i.e. multiple stochastic drivers. Those multi-factor mean-reverting models have been proposed early as they are capable of separating the long- and short-term dynamics in commodities. The long-term dynamics are mean-reverting, supported by economical arguments on supply and demand balance, whereas a lot more volatility may be generated from short-term supply or demand shocks. A very popular approach based on those arguments is the two-factor model proposed in Schwartz and Smith [2000], where the spot price S_t is assumed to satisfy $\ln(S_t) = X_t + Y_t$ (i.e. formulated as a geometric model) with X_t an OU-process with mean reversion level zero and Y_t a Brownian motion with drift, i.e.

$$dY_t = \mu dt + \sigma dW_t. \tag{14}$$

The Brownian motions driving X and Y may also be correlated. Lucia and Schwartz [2002] compare different one- and two-factor models, and also apply the model above to electricity markets by adding a deterministic seasonality function $f(t)$, i.e. $\ln(S_t) = f(t) + X_t + Y_t$. In fact, all reduced-form electricity price models have some seasonality component capturing the deterministic movements in the spot price, which is generated by the seasonality (daylight, temperature) in electricity demand. In academic literature (see also e.g. [Lucia and Schwartz, 2002]), some effort is taken to find a function which properly captures historical seasonality. However, in practice each utility has a price-forward curve (usually denoted as hourly price forward curve, HPFC) at hand, which can be used as a seasonality function in the reduced-form model. For storable commodities, a popular approach is to use a stochastic convenience yield as in Gibson and Schwartz [1990]. More complicated models use jump-processes instead of Brownian motions in order to generate more realistic dynamics as, for example, the model in Cartea and Figueroa [2005] or the model we propose in the next section.

Regime-Switching Models. Motivated by the structure of electricity production units, regime-switching models also gained popularity. They consist of a set of diffusion models, each describing a different state (regime) of the system, with an additional transition matrix modeling the switch between the states. Popular approaches in the literature are by Weron *et al.* [2004] and Huisman and Mahieu [2003]. From an economic point of view, the different regimes may be interpreted as electricity production from different technologies (with different characteristics of price level and volatility). In practice, regime-switching models often suffer from calibration issues as the state of the market is usually hidden (not observable in prices) and needs to be estimated. For more details, we refer to the comparison of different regime-switching models in Bierbrauer *et al.* [2004] and Janczura and Weron [2010].

Factor Models. Factor models are closely related to the jump-diffusion approach. Usually, factor models consist of a sum of different factors, at first sight often without an economic interpretation. As with regime-switching models, a lot of work has to be invested into the calibration of such models. A comprehensive presentation of factor models and their application in commodity markets is given in Benth *et al.* [2008a]. In the following section, we will introduce a factor model which has been proven suitable to model the German electricity market in practice. Therefore, we refer the reader to the following section for more details on factor models.

3.3. *Structural (hybrid) models*

Hybrid, or structural, models integrate the physical ideas of fundamental models with the stochastic processes from diffusion models. The idea is to model the price-driving factors of electricity (primary fuel prices, demand, ...) with reduced-form models and suitably combine them into one model for the electricity price. Therefore, structural models always consists of a supply-side (also known as merit order curve) and a demand-side model. The intersection of both models at a given point in time delivers the simulated market prices, as shown in Fig. 1. They are particularly suitable for pricing derivatives with correlation to price drivers like temperature, renewable production, demand, primary fuel and others. The first one to follow this approach was Barlow [2002]. He essentially showed that the complicated dynamics of observed electricity prices can be modeled using the structural approach with standard stochastic processes for demand and a simple supply-function. In the past few years, there was a lot of literature on structural models and it is not in the scope of this chapter to list all of them. However, we will shortly discuss the different approaches in the literature.

Building up on the results of Barlow, Wagner [2014] proposed a structural model which explicitly takes renewable energy production from wind and solar into account

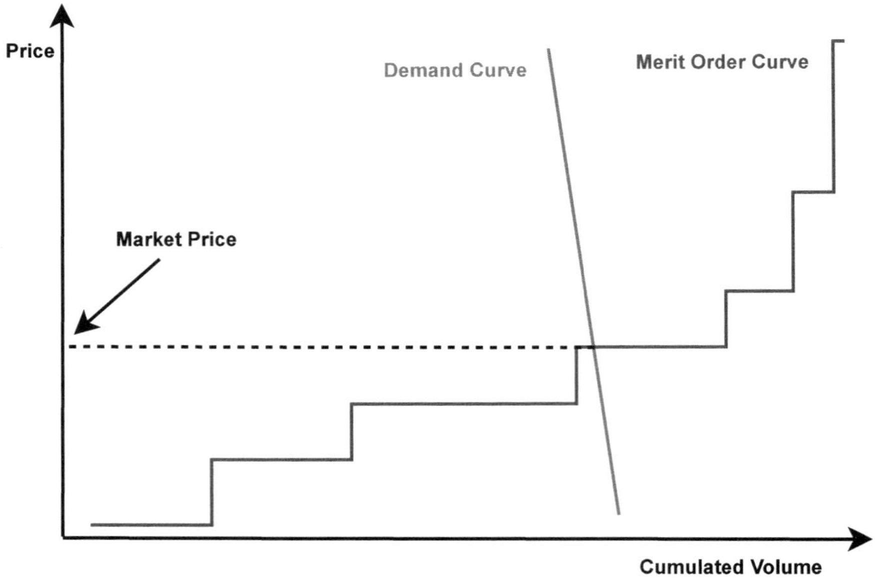

Fig. 1. Structural models are based on the price fixing methodology in electricity markets.

by using a sophisticated demand-side model. Burger *et al.* [2004] introduce a spot-market structural model using an empirical supply function and add a stochastic short-term variation, a demand model with a stochastic component, and a stochastic availability factor. The model requires a demand forecast, which has to be generated by a separate model (which may already be at hand in an energy utility). Coulon and Howison [2009] introduce the stochastic bid-stack model, where the supply function is derived from a sophisticated analysis of market bids. An improved version of the model is Carmona *et al.* [2013], which we recommend as a starting point for a practical application of the model. Further approaches to modeling the supply side are taken in Aïd *et al.* [2009, 2012]. Using diffusion models for primary fuel prices, stochastic demand and stochastic availability, they derive analytic formulae for forward prices. From our experience, the model is hard to apply in practice and requires a lot of effort to calibrate.

For more details on structural models for pricing or risk-management purposes, we refer the interested reader to [Carmona and Coulon, 2014].

4. A Multifactor Model in Practice

As described in the previous section, multifactor models are capable of modeling complex spot and futures price characteristics. Especially with generalized

Ornstein–Uhlenbeck (generalized OU) processes[7] spot prices can exhibit spikes, mean reversion, heavy-tailed returns, and — in the arithmetic case — negative prices.

4.1. *Model description*

For practical purposes, we restrict ourselves to one specific factor model: we consider a three-factor model of arithmetic type as described by Benth *et al.* [2008a]. In our model, the spot price $S(t)$ is given by

$$S(t) = \Lambda(t)X_1(t) + X_2(t) + X_3(t), \tag{15}$$

where Λ is a deterministic function modeling the seasonal and cyclic behavior and X_1 to X_3 are stochastic processes called *factors*. These factors have the following economic interpretation:

- X_1 is a long-term mean level, slowly changing over time due to long-term expectations,
- X_2 contributes the day-to-day fluctuations, which can be interpreted as caused by changes in the weather or demand, for example,
- X_3 models the severe imbalances of the system, causing spikes.

These are modeled as stochastic processes which correspond to each interpretation mentioned above.

The process X_1 is assumed to follow a geometric Brownian motion (GBM) without drift, i.e.

$$dX_1(t) = \sigma_1 X_1(t) dW_1(t), \quad X_1(0) = 1. \tag{16}$$

We chose a GBM without drift, since we assume that the seasonality function Λ captures the (current) trend of the spot prices.

The second factor X_2 is a classical Brownian motion-driven OU process with constant mean reversion speed $\alpha_2 > 0$ and volatility $\sigma_2 > 0$, yielding the following stochastic differential equation (SDE):

$$dX_2(t) = -\alpha_2 X_2(t) dt + \sigma_2 dW_2(t), \quad X_2(0) = 0, \tag{17}$$

where we assume that W_2 is independent of W_1.

---

[7]Generalized OU processes are OU processes that are driven by an independent increment process instead of a Brownian motion.

The final factor X_3 is a generalized OU process driven by an independent increment process. In particular, we choose a compound Poisson process with normally distributed jump sizes. Let $D_1, D_2, \ldots$ be a sequence of i.i.d. $\mathcal{N}(\mu_3, \sigma_3^2)$-distributed random variables. Let $N(t)$ be a homogenous Poisson process of rate $\lambda_3 > 0$, then the sum

$$L_3(t) := \sum_{n=1}^{N(t)} D_n, \tag{18}$$

defines an independent increment process[8] and the dynamics of X_3 are given as for X_2, cf. Eq. (17), but with mean reversion speed $\alpha_3 > 0$ and L_3 as driving factor instead of $\sigma_2\, dW_2(t)$.

4.2. *Risk-neutral pricing and forward premia*

As is common practice, we assume that derivatives of the spot price are priced under a risk-neutral measure $\mathbb{Q}$, which is assumed to be an equivalent martingale measure. As discussed in many other works, e.g. [Benth *et al.*, 2008a; Cartea and Villaplana, 2008], due to the lack of *buy-and-hold* trading strategies of electricity spot contracts, and therefore replication strategies, the electricity market is incomplete and a *unique* equivalent martingale measure $\mathbb{Q}$ does not exist like in the Black–Scholes model for stock prices.

To restrict the possibilities for the equivalent martingale measure it is often assumed that $\mathbb{Q}$ is given by the class of measures induced by the Esscher transform. This forms a convenient class, since it preserves the distributional properties of the driving factors. Computing the value of forward contracts is then done under the risk-neutral measure $\mathbb{Q}$, i.e.

$$f(t, T) := \mathbb{E}^{\mathbb{Q}}[S(T)|\mathcal{F}_t] \tag{19}$$

is the value of a contract sold at time $t > 0$ and deliver at $T > t$.

In the literature, the risk premium or forward premium is often studied, e.g. see [Benth *et al.*, 2008b] or [Cartea and Villaplana, 2008]. This premium is the

[8]The process L_3 is, in fact, even a Lévy process, which is a subclass of the independent increment processes.

difference between the forward price and the expected spot price, i.e.

$$p(t, T) := f(t, T) - \mathbb{E}[S(T) \mid \mathcal{F}_t] = \mathbb{E}^{\mathbb{Q}}[S(T) \mid \mathcal{F}_t] - \mathbb{E}[S(T) \mid \mathcal{F}_t]. \tag{20}$$

This premium is usually assumed to be negative for energy markets due to the fact that early hedging is more beneficial to the supply side than it is to the demand side [Benth *et al.*, 2008b]. However, assuming that $f(t, T)$ is known, it is not clear what the expected spot price is. Furthermore, by the simple fact that (day-ahead) spot contracts are auctioned a day before delivery, they could be seen as forward contracts themselves. This would induce a risk premium of zero.

Moreover, if we are able to generate an hourly price forward curve (HPFC), one could argue that the expected spot price should equal the value given by the PFC. We combine this with the arguments of Lyle and Elliott [2009] to take $\mathbb{P} = \mathbb{Q}$. This allows us to use the the real-world measure $\mathbb{P}$ to price derivatives. As a consequence, the risk premium $p(t, T)$ equals zero. Furthermore, we use the PFC as the basis for the seasonal level Λ.

4.3. *Futures valuation*

Due to Eq. (19) and our discussion in the previous section, the (instantaneous) forward price in our model introduced in Section 4.1 at time $t > 0$ and delivering at time $T > t$ is given by

$$f(t, T) = \Lambda(T)\, X_1(t) + e^{-\alpha_2(T-t)} X_2(t) + e^{-\alpha_3(T-t)} X_3(t) \tag{21}$$

$$+ \frac{\lambda_3\, \mu_3}{\alpha_3}(1 - e^{-\alpha_3(T-t)}). \tag{22}$$

The futures price at time $t > 0$ delivering from $T_1 > t$ to $T_2 > T_1$ is then given by

$$F(t; T_1, T_2) = \frac{1}{T_2 - T_1} \int_{T_1}^{T_2} f(t, s)\, ds \tag{23}$$

$$= \overline{\Lambda}(T_1, T_2)\, X_1(t) + A_2(t, T_1, T_2)\, X_2(t) \tag{24}$$

$$+ A_3(t, T_1, T_2)\, X_3(t) + \frac{\lambda_3\, \mu_3}{\alpha_3}(1 - A_3(t, T_1, T_2)), \tag{25}$$

where

$$\overline{\Lambda}(T_1, T_2) := \frac{1}{T_2 - T_1} \int_{T_1}^{T_2} \Lambda(s)\, ds \tag{26}$$

and for $i = 2, 3$

$$A_i(t, T_1, T_2) := \frac{e^{-\alpha_i(T_1-t)} - e^{-\alpha_i(T_2-t)}}{\alpha_i(T_2 - T_1)} \tag{27}$$

are deterministic functions.

Remark 1. In practice, the found mean reversion speeds α_2 and α_3 are so fast that on larger time scales the influence of X_2 and X_3 disappears in $F(t; T_1, T_2)$. This is easily seen from the fact that $A_i(t, T_1, T_2) \approx 0$ for $i = 2, 3$. This reduces the futures price approximately to

$$F(t; T_1, T_2) \approx \overline{\Lambda}(T_1, T_2)\, X_1(t) + \frac{\lambda_3\, \mu_3}{\alpha_3}, \tag{28}$$

which could even be exploited to (approximately) price other derivatives. For example, options on futures could be priced by the Black–Scholes formula for options, see [Black and Scholes, 1973].

4.4. *Calibration*

Calibration of the model is done using the historical spot and futures prices and involves the technique to filter jumps as described by Meyer-Brandis and Tankov [2008]. The spot price is deseasonalized by seasonal dummy variables[9] and from the autocorrelation function the mean reversion speeds are estimated.

For simulation, we use the PFC as the daily seasonal level, as discussed in Section 4.2. The stochastic factors are also simulated daily. However, to include simulated hourly spot prices without increasing the computational complexity too much, we introduced a random sampling method to simulate hourly spot price profiles from historical ones.

5. Conclusion

This chapter gives an introduction to the typical risks a medium-sized energy utility faces. It shows the classical way of calculating corresponding risk figures and shows, in detail, how market risk can be captured using more realistic modeling approaches. The factor model introduced in the final section turned out to be very useful in

[9]The seasonal dummy variables correspond to the years, months and days of the week/holidays. This method is chosen to simulate a PFC structure.

practice. It provides enough flexibility while maintaining a good interpretation of all model components. This model may also serve as a starting point for a sophisticated risk management framework.

Usually, each energy utility is also exposed to additional and more specific types of risk. Energy producers, for example, may face a long list of operational risks, but also additional market risks in primary fuel and emissions. From a modeling perspective, the challenge in this case is to address the dynamics of the *spread* between primary fuel, emissions and electricity (*clean spark spread* and *clean dark spread*). In the case of hydro power plants, uncertainty in precipitation, inflow and snow-melt is a big issue, whereas wind-farms and photovoltaic-plants need to understand the stochastics in wind speed and solar radiation, respectively. In the near future, volume and structural risk on the demand side will also be increasingly important. Electric cars are expected to act not only as consumers of power, but also as a provider of storage, which will change the traditional and well-understood demand profiles of households and small utilities. Sector coupling introduces additional dependencies, e.g. nowadays there are already restrictions from heat requirements in a CHP (combined heat and power plant).

Apart from managing those specific risks, which usually require their own models (e.g. solar radiation, inflow, ...) or at least adapted models (e.g. spread modeling), market evolution leads to a need for continuous revision of existing approaches. Market integration, i.e. the coupling of formerly separated market zones, leads to a high dependency in spot prices, which has to be accounted for, in particular when a company holds positions in both market zones. This is a demanding issue and highly depends on the markets under consideration, as they often have very different characteristics. In case of electricity markets, the structural approach is often suitable as it provides enough flexibility. In addition to that, trading activity (liquidity) increasingly shifts from long-term (futures) to short-term (intra-day) markets.

From our point of view, current research is in need of models for integrated markets in a multi-commodity setting and the manageable integration of fundamentals (in particular weather) in stochastic price models. Moreover, the short-term markets, in particular the continuous intra-day market, should be taken into account in a consistent manner. In order to develop real-time risk-management, pricing algorithms need to be revisited. The stochastic optimization should be examined as an alternative to pure Monte Carlo simulation for the pricing of complex derivatives like take-or-pay contracts that are common in the gas business.

References

Aïd, R., Campi, L., Huu, A. N. and Touzi, N. (2009). A structural risk-neutral model of electricity prices. *International Journal of Theoretical and Applied Finance* **12** (7), 925–947.

Aïd, R., Campi, L. and Langrené, N. (2012). A structural risk-neutral model for pricing and hedging power derivatives. *Mathematical Finance* **23** (3), 387–438, doi:10.1111/j.1467-9965.2011.00507.x.

Barlow, M. T. (2002). A diffusion model for electricity prices. *Mathematical Finance* **12** (4), 287–298, doi:10.1111/j.1467-9965.2002.tb00125.x.

Benth, F. E., Benth, J. Š. and Koekebakker, S. (2008a). *Stochastic Modeling of Electricity and Related Markets*, Vol. 11 (World Scientific), doi:10.1142/6811.

Benth, F. E., Cartea, Á. and Kiesel, R. (2008b). Pricing forward contracts in power markets by the certainty equivalence principle: Explaining the sign of the market risk premium. *Journal of Banking & Finance* **32** (10), 2006–2021, doi:10.1016/j.jbankfin.2007.12.022.

Bierbrauer, M., Trück, S. and Weron, R. (2004). *Modeling Electricity Prices with Regime Switching Models* (Springer Berlin Heidelberg, Berlin, Heidelberg), ISBN 978-3-540-25944-2, pp. 859–867, doi:10.1007/978-3-540-25944-2_111, https://doi.org/10.1007/978-3-540-25944-2_111.

Black, F. and Scholes, M. (1973). The pricing of options and corporate liabilities. *The Journal of Political Economy* **81** (3), 637–654.

Black, F. (1976). The pricing of commodity contracts. *Journal of Financial Economics* **3**, 167–179.

Burger, M., Graeber, B. and Schindlmayr, G. (2014). *Managing Energy Risk: A Practical Guide for Risk Management in Power, Gas and Other Energy Markets*, 2nd edn. (John Wiley & Sons, Ltd).

Burger, M., Klar, B., Müller, A. and Schindlmayr, G. (2004). A spot market model for pricing derivatives in electricity markets. *Quantitative Finance* **4** (1), 109–122.

Carmona, R., Coulon, M. and Schwarz, D. (2013). Electricity price modeling and asset valuation: A multi-fuel structural approach. *Mathematics and Financial Economics* **7** (2), 167–202.

Carmona, R. and Coulon, M. (2014). *A Survey of Commodity Markets and Structural Models for Electricity Prices* (Springer New York), pp. 41–83.

Cartea, A. and Figueroa, M. (2005). Pricing in electricity markets: A mean reverting jump diffusion model with seasonality. *Applied Mathematical Finance* **12** (4), 313–335.

Cartea, A. and Villaplana, P. (2008). Spot price modeling and the valuation of electricity forward contracts: The role of demand and capacity. *Journal of Banking & Finance* **32**, 2502–2519.

Coulon, M. and Howison, S. (2009). Stochastic behaviour of the electricity bid stack: From fundamental drivers to power prices. *The Journal of Energy Markets* **2** (1), 29–69.

ECC (2017). *ECC Margining*, 1st edn., http://www.ecc.de/blob/15092/a7041c1f5ab79cb9fef1d8dc5a0b004c/margining-data.pdf.

Eydeland, A. and Wolyniec, K. (2003). *Energy and Power Risk Management* (Wiley).

Föllmer, H. and Schied, A. (2002). Convex measures of risk and trading constraints. *Finance and Stochastics* **6** (4), 429–447, doi:10.1007/s007800200072.

Gibson, R. and Schwartz, E. S. (1990). Stochastic convenience yield and the pricing of oil contingent claims. *The Journal of Finance* **45** (3), 959–976, doi:10.1111/j.1540-6261.1990.tb05114.x.

Huisman, R. and Mahieu, R. (2003). Regime jumps in electricity prices. *Energy Economics* **25** (5), 425–434.

James, T. (2012). *Energy Markets: Price Risk Management and Trading*, Wiley Finance (Wiley).

Janczura, J. and Weron, R. (2010). An empirical comparison of alternate regime-switching models for electricity spot prices. *Energy economics* **32** (5), 1059–1073.

J. P. Morgan/Reuters. (1996). *RiskMetrics Technical Document*, 4th edn., https://www.msci.com/documents/10199/5915b101-4206-4ba0-aee2-3449d5c7e95a.

Lucia, J. J. and Schwartz, E. S. (2002). Electricity prices and power derivatives: Evidence from the nordic power exchange. *Review of Derivatives Research* **5** (1), 5–50, doi:10.1023/a:1013846631785.

Lütkebohmert, E. (2009). *Concentration Risk in Credit Portfolios* (Springer Berlin Heidelberg), doi:10.1007/978-3-540-70870-4.

Lyle, M. R. and Elliott, R. J. (2009). A 'simple' hybrid model for power derivatives. *Energy Economics* **31** (5), 757–767, doi:10.1016/j.eneco.2009.05.007, http://www.sciencedirect.com/science/article/pii/S0140988309000802.

Merton, R. C. (1974). On the pricing of corporate debt: The risk structure of interest rates. *The Journal of Finance* **29** (2), 449–470, doi:10.1111/j.1540-6261.1974.tb03058.x.

Meyer-Brandis, T. and Tankov, P. (2008). Multi-factor jump-diffusion models of electricity prices. *International Journal of Theoretical and Applied Finance* **11** (5), 503–528, doi:10.1142/s0219024908004907.

Pilipovic, D. (1997). *Energy Risk: Valuing and Managing Energy Derivatives* (McGraw-Hill).

Schwartz, E. S. (1997). The stochastic behavior of commodity prices: Implications for valuation and hedging. *The Journal of Finance* **52** (3), 923–973, doi:10.1111/j.1540-6261.1997.tb02721.x.

Schwartz, E. S. and Smith, J. E. (2000). Short-term variations and long-term dynamics in commodity prices. *Management Science* **46** (7), 893–911.

Swindle, G. (2014). *Valuation and Risk Management in Energy Markets* (Cambridge University Press), doi:10.1017/cbo9781139568302.

Wagner, A. (2014). Residual demand modeling and application to electricity pricing. *The Energy Journal* **35**, 45–73.

Weron, R., Bierbrauer, M. and Trück, S. (2004). Modeling electricity prices: Jump diffusion and regime switching. *Physica A: Statistical Mechanics and its Applications* **336** (1–2), 39–48, doi:10.1016/j.physa.2004.01.008.

Weron, R. (2014). Electricity price forecasting: A review of the state-of-the-art with a look into the future. *International Journal of Forecasting* **30** (4), 1030–1081, doi:10.1016/j.ijforecast.2014.08.008.

Chapter 15

Optimal Design of Energy Distribution Network using Power Flow Controller

Takayuki Shiina

Department of Industrial and Management Systems Engineering,
School of Creative Science and Engineering, Waseda University
3-4-1 Okubo, Shinjuku-ku, Tokyo 169-8555, Japan
tshiina@waseda.jp

In power delivery systems, the use of dispersed generation and security control to improve network utilization requires the optimal use of system control devices. The installation of loop controller allows the distribution system to operate in a loop configuration, achieving effective management of voltage and power flow. In the investment planning process, it is important to identify the optimal location and installed capacity of the equipment such that all operational constraints are satisfied. This chapter presents a method for identifying the optimal location and capacity with the minimum installation cost. Our novel approach uses an economic model that considers the fixed costs. A slope scaling procedure is presented, and its efficiency is demonstrated using numerical experiments.

Keywords: Optimization; linear approximation; stochastic programming; power system; optimal power flow; loop controller.

1. Introduction

In the electric power industry, many issues are dealt with as mathematical programming problems. Representative integer programming and combinatorial optimization problems include the unit commitment problem [Shiina and Birge, 2004; Shiina and Watanabe, 2004] and the power generation planning problem [Shiina and Birge, 2003]. Discussions of the application of stochastic programming methods to the electricity industry can be found in works by Ruszczyński and Shapiro [2003] and Shapiro *et al.* [2009]. For these problems, the branch-and-bound methods are used in which discrete variables are enumerated. Solution methods using a discrete structure for the problem are most commonly used. Until recently, it has been extremely difficult to solve large-scale combinatorial optimization problems, but the development of mathematical programming methods has provided techniques that allow approximate solutions to be found effectively. These approximation methods are referred to collectively as metaheuristics. If the local search method is to function effectively, then it is important that the set of feasible solutions be identified quickly.

In contrast, the basic economic power dispatch problem is a nonlinear programming problem. In the case of convex nonlinear programming problems, solution methods that solve large-scale problems effectively have been demonstrated [Bazaraa *et al.*, 2003]. Shiina [1999] addressed a convex programming problem that considered the uncertainty in demand in a power supply. However, the problem becomes very challenging when convex programming cannot be applied. In calculating the optimal power flow (OPF) [Wood and Wollenberg, 1996; Zhu, 2015], because the flow equation is described as a nonlinear equality constraint, the problem becomes one of nonlinear optimization with a feasible set that is not convex. In this case, a feasible solution may not be obtainable. In recent years, solutions based on the semidefinite programming have been studied [Bai *et al.*, 2008; Molzahn *et al.*, 2013]. However, implementation using these solution methods is not always easy to introduce. A simple method using software that is easy to obtain is desired.

The problem considered in the present chapter is one of optimization under combinatorial conditions that represent the location of the equipment and the installation of a loop controller (LPC) to control the power flow, in addition to the calculation of the OPF. The installation of equipment is formulated as an integer programming problem or a combinatorial optimization problem, but because the calculation of flow is a non-convex nonlinear programming problem, it is difficult to find a solution. This problem takes the power demand as an input condition and determines the installation that minimizes costs under the operational constraints of the network. The network operational constraints to be considered here are the voltage operating range and the line thermal capacity. However, when optimizing large-scale systems or considering flow constraints in multiple scenarios, the number of variables and constraints in the optimization problem becomes huge, and a more efficient optimization technique is required. A conventional technique uses a two-stage approach that mixes combinatorial optimization and nonlinear optimization, in which the search for a location and the determination of the capacity of the equipment are treated separately. When this technique is applied, there are many cases in a local search for the installation location in which no feasible flow exists, which makes it difficult for an efficient search to be conducted. In this study, we investigated a new technique in which the installation cost is linearly approximated, without relying on a local search. This linear approximation method is called the dynamic slope scaling procedure [Kim and Pardalos, 1999, 2000a, 2000b], and has the advantage that a feasible power flow can always be obtained. Since this method approximates an objective function that includes a fixed cost, it does not include a 0–1 variable representing the installation, and so always retrieves a feasible value for the location and power flow.

The rest of the chapter is organized as follows: In Section 2, the problem is formulated. In Section 3, the technique based on local search is discussed and the principle for designing a solution for the optimal installation is described. A novel algorithm based on linear approximation is then demonstrated. In Section 4, the technique is applied to the optimization of a full-scale system model. Both single scenario and multiple scenario optimizations are considered, and the effectiveness of our novel technique is demonstrated. We summarize our results in Section 5.

2. Formulation of the Optimal Installation Problem

The power system to be considered is represented by a network $N = (V, E)$, where V is a node set and E is the arc set, consisting of node pairs $(i, j) \in E$ such that there exists an arc between each pair with nodes i, j as its ends. In the power system, a piece of electrical equipment referred to as a bus corresponds to a node on the network, and factors such as the transformer and transmission lines correspond to the arcs. The power flow through each piece of equipment in the network is called the flow, and the OPF defines the optimal mode of operation of the system that satisfies the flow equation for the network.

In this chapter, we consider the problem of calculating an OPF that takes into account the installation of the equipment. In order to maintain the voltage in the system at a suitable level, it is necessary to determine the location of the installation and its capacity. The collection of nodes (i, j) at which the equipment can be installed, is the set A of (i, j) $(i, j \in V)$, and is given as follows:

$$A = \{(i, j) | \text{ the equipment can be installed between nodes } i \text{ and } j\} \tag{1}$$

Here, in relation to set A, we assume that $A \cap E = \emptyset$. In other words, the equipment is not installed on the existing arcs in the network, rather we define A as the collection of node pairs that are candidate locations. As we must take into account both the power flowing out of the LPC and that flowing in, the direction of $(i, j) \in A$ must be considered. When power flows from node i into the equipment, we call i the start node in the collection of installation nodes (i, j), and when the power flows out from the equipment to node j, we call node j the end node. The sets of start nodes and end nodes in the collection of installation nodes are designated V^+ and V^-, respectively, and defined as follows:

$$\begin{aligned} V^+ = \{i \in V | \exists (i, j) \in A, \\ \text{power flows from node } i \text{ into the equipment}\}, \end{aligned} \tag{2}$$

$$\begin{aligned} V^- = \{j \in V | \exists (i, j) \in A, \\ \text{power flows from the equipment into node } j\}. \end{aligned} \tag{3}$$

If we remove from set V the collection of nodes belonging to the set of start nodes V^+ and the set of end nodes V^- belonging to set A, the remaining set of nodes is $\bar{V}$ and we define $\bar{V} = V \setminus \{V^+ \cup V^-\}$. There is no intersection between the LPC and the nodes belonging to set $\bar{V}$. The values of the current flowing in and out of each bus, and the active and reactive power, can be calculated using the value of the voltage variable. In exceptional cases, $\bar{V}$ includes one slack bus, $N_0 \in \bar{V}$; in the slack bus, the voltage value is given and the active and reactive power values are treated as variables.

The binary variables relating to the installation location are determined as follows. If the equipment is installed at pair $(i, j) \in A$, then $x_{ij} = 1$; if no equipment is installed, then $x_{ij} = 0$. The capacity of the equipment to be installed at pair $(i, j) \in A$ is defined as variable y_{ij}. The objective function is the installation cost, α_{ij} represents the fixed costs for installation at node pair (i, j), and β_{ij} represents the variable costs per unit capacity of the equipment. The objective function is given as follows:

$$\min \sum_{(i,j)\in A} (\alpha_{ij} x_{ij} + \beta_{ij} y_{ij}). \tag{4}$$

Next, we present the constraints on the optimal installation problem. Here, j is the imaginary unit. The active and reactive power of bus $i \in V$ are defined as variables P_i and Q_i, respectively. The active and reactive power generated at bus i are given by PG_i and QG_i, and the load active and reactive power are given by PL_i and QL_i, respectively. In this case, we exclude any slack buses, and for each bus $i \in \bar{V} \setminus \{N_0\}$ at which the LPC is not installed, the following constraint (5) must be satisfied:

$$P_i + \mathrm{j}Q_i = PG_i - PL_i + \mathrm{j}(QG_i - QL_i), i \in \bar{V} \setminus \{N_0\} \tag{5}$$

At the slack bus $N_0 \in \bar{V}$, no load exists and the following constraint (6) must be satisfied:

$$P_{N_0} + \mathrm{j}Q_{N_0} = PG_{N_0} + \mathrm{j}QG_{N_0}. \tag{6}$$

At the slack bus, the values of P_{N_0}, Q_{N_0} are given and in their place PG_{N_0}, QG_{N_0} are defined as variables. If a pair $(i, j) \in A$ is a candidate for the installation location, the active power and reactive power flowing into the equipment are represented by variables P_i^{LPC} and Q_i^{LPC}, and the active power and reactive power flowing from the equipment into bus j are represented by variables P_j^{LPC} and Q_j^{LPC}. At the start node $i \in V^+$ in the collection of pairs $(i, j) \in A$ that are candidates for the installation, the constraint (7) must be satisfied.

$$\begin{aligned} P_i + \mathrm{j}Q_i = PG_i - PL_i + \mathrm{j}(QG_i - QL_i) - x_{ij}(P_i^{LPC} + \mathrm{j}Q_i^{LPC}), \\ i \in V^+, (i, j) \in A. \end{aligned} \tag{7}$$

At the end node $i \in V^-$ in the collection of pairs $(i, j) \in A$ that are candidates for the installation, the constraint (8) must be satisfied.

$$\begin{aligned} P_i + \mathrm{j}Q_i = PG_i - PL_i + \mathrm{j}(QG_i - QL_i) + x_{ij}(P_i^{LPC} + \mathrm{j}Q_i^{LPC}), \\ i \in V^-, (i, j) \in A. \end{aligned} \tag{8}$$

Here, the values of the active power flowing into the equipment and the active power flowing out from the equipment must be equal.

$$P_i^{LPC} = P_j^{LPC}, \quad (i, j) \in A \tag{9}$$

Care should be taken to ensure that there are no constraints on the reactive power flowing into and out of the LPC.

Next, we represent the variable V_i that indicates the voltage at bus i in Cartesian coordinates as $V_i = e_i + \mathrm{j}f_i$, where e_i and f_i are variables corresponding to the real and imaginary parts of the voltage, respectively. The admittance of arc (i, j), namely $G_{ij} + \mathrm{j}B_{ij}$ is given. The current I_i flowing into the network from bus i can be represented by (10).

$$I_i = \sum_{k=1}^{N}(G_{ik} + \mathrm{j}B_{ik})(e_i + \mathrm{j}f_i). \tag{10}$$

From this, we can represent the relation between the voltage at each bus $i \in \bar{V}$ and the active and reactive power P_i, Q_i by (11), where $\bar{I_i}$ represents the complex conjugate of I_i.

$$P_i + \mathrm{j}Q_i = V_i\bar{I_i}. \tag{11}$$

By taking the real and complex components of Eq. (11), we obtain the following relations:

$$P_i = e_i\sum_{k=1}^{N}(G_{ik}e_k - B_{ik}f_k) + f_i\sum_{k=1}^{N}(B_{ik}e_k + G_{ik}f_k), \tag{12}$$

$$Q_i = -e_i\sum_{k=1}^{N}(B_{ik}e_k + G_{ik}f_k) + f_i\sum_{k=1}^{N}(G_{ik}e_k - B_{ik}f_k). \tag{13}$$

Using relations (12) and (13), we can represent (5) by (14) and (15) for $i \in \bar{V}\setminus N_0$.

$$e_i\sum_{k=1}^{N}(G_{ik}e_k - B_{ik}f_k) + f_i\sum_{k=1}^{N}(B_{ik}e_k + G_{ik}f_k) - PG_i + PL_i = 0 \tag{14}$$

$$-e_i\sum_{k=1}^{N}(B_{ik}e_k + G_{ik}f_k) + f_i\sum_{k=1}^{N}(G_{ik}e_k - B_{ik}f_k) - QG_i + QL_i = 0 \tag{15}$$

In the same way, using relations (12) and (13), we can represent (6) by (16) and (17), where e_{N_0} and f_{N_0} at the slack bus are given as constants, whereas PG_{N_0} and QG_{N_0} are defined as variables.

$$e_{N_0}\sum_{k=1}^{N}(G_{N_0k}e_k - B_{N_0k}f_k) + f_{N_0}\sum_{k=1}^{N}(B_{N_0k}e_k + G_{N_0k}f_k) - PG_{N_0} = 0, \tag{16}$$

$$-e_{N_0}\sum_{k=1}^{N}(B_{N_0k}e_k + G_{N_0k}f_k) + f_{N_0}\sum_{k=1}^{N}(G_{N_0k}e_k - B_{N_0k}f_k) - QG_{N_0} = 0. \tag{17}$$

At the start node in the collection of pairs $(i, j) \in A$ that are candidates for the installation location, using relations (12) and (13), we can represent (7) by (18) and

(19) for $i \in V^{+}$, $(i, j) \in A$.

$$e_i \sum_{k=1}^{N} (G_{ik} e_k - B_{ik} f_k) + f_i \sum_{k=1}^{N} (B_{ik} e_k + G_{ik} f_k)$$
$$- PG_i + PL_i + x_{ij} P_i^{LPC} = 0, \tag{18}$$
$$- e_i \sum_{k=1}^{N} (B_{ik} e_k + G_{ik} f_k) + f_i \sum_{k=1}^{N} (G_{ik} e_k - B_{ik} f_k)$$
$$- QG_i + QL_i + x_{ij} Q_i^{LPC} = 0. \tag{19}$$

At the end node in the collection of pairs $(i, j) \in A$ that are candidates for the installation location, using relations (12) and (13), we can represent (8) by (20) and (21) for $i \in V^{-}$, $(i, j) \in A$.

$$e_j \sum_{k=1}^{N} (G_{jk} e_k - B_{jk} f_k) + f_j \sum_{k=1}^{N} (B_{jk} e_k + G_{jk} f_k)$$
$$- PG_j + PL_j - x_{ij} P_j^{LPC} = 0, \tag{20}$$
$$- e_j \sum_{k=1}^{N} (B_{jk} e_k + G_{jk} f_k) + f_j \sum_{k=1}^{N} (G_{jk} e_k - B_{jk} f_k)$$
$$- QG_j + QL_j - x_{ij} Q_j^{LPC} = 0. \tag{21}$$

The above constraints are concerned with power flow. The voltage of each bus i must also satisfy inequality (22), where $V_{\max}$, $V_{\min}$ are given constants.

$$V_{\min} \le \sqrt{e_i^2 + f_i^2} \le V_{\max}, \quad i \in V. \tag{22}$$

For the current flowing through each arc $(i, j) \in E$, an upper bound is given as (23), where $I_{\max}$ is a given constant.

$$\{G_{ij}(e_i - e_j) - B_{ij}(f_i - f_j)\}^2 + \{G_{ij}(f_i - f_j) + B_{ij}(e_i - e_j)\}^2$$
$$\le (I_{\max})^2. \tag{23}$$

On the pairs of nodes that are candidate installation locations, the capacity y_{ij} must be determined such that inequalities (24) and (25) are satisfied.

$$y_{ij}^2 \ge (P_i^{LPC})^2 + (Q_i^{LPC})^2, \quad (i, j) \in A. \tag{24}$$
$$y_{ij}^2 \ge (P_j^{LPC})^2 + (Q_j^{LPC})^2, \quad (i, j) \in A. \tag{25}$$

Putting these together, we can formulate the mathematical programming problem as a large-scale non-convex mixed 0–1 integer programming problem, shown here as (LPC-installation).

$$
\begin{aligned}
\text{(LPC-installation):}\min\ & \textstyle\sum_{(i,j)\in A}(\alpha_{ij}x_{ij}+\beta_{ij}y_{ij}) \\
\text{subject to}\quad & (14), (15), \quad i\in \bar{V}\setminus\{N_0\} \\
& (16), (17) \\
& (9), (i,j)\in A \\
& (18), (19), i\in V^+, (i,j)\in A \\
& (20), (21), i\in V^-, (i,j)\in A \\
& (22), i\in V \\
& (23), (i,j), \in E \\
& (24), (25), (i,j)\in A \\
& x_{ij}\in\{0,1\}, (i,j)\in A \\
& y_{ij}\geq 0, (i,j)\in A.
\end{aligned}
$$

The present model can be used to analyze multiple scenario constraints by introducing variables for each scenario. Defining all variables except x and y as stochastic makes this problem a stochastic programming problem.

3. Solution Algorithm

In this section, we demonstrate a solution using linear approximation. For a network flow problem with fixed costs, Kim and Pardalos [1999] presented a linear approximation of the objective function, called slope scaling. This method, restricts the range that the variables can take, and adjustments are made at each each iteration [Kim and Pardalos, 2000a, 2000b]. We applied a similar linear approximation method to the optimal installation problem.

First, we outline of the linear approximation method. We consider the design problem of a network with fixed costs. The network N is represented as $N = (V, E)$. Sets V and E represent the nodes on the network and the arc set, respectively. The demand at each node $i \in V$ in set V is b_i and the column vector in which the ith element is b_i is $b \in \Re^{|V|}$. The upper bound on the flow at arc $(i, j) \in E, i, j \in V$ is u_{ij}. The incidence matrix for the network is $A \in \Re^{|V|\times|E|}$. The variables are the flow on arc (i, j), $v_{ij} \geq 0$ and $x_{ij} \in \{0, 1\}$, which represent whether there is a flow on arc (i, j). The objective function is the sum of the costs in relation to the flow in each arc and the fixed costs when the flow is positive. For the case in which the fixed cost f_{ij} is applied when the flow v_{ij} is a positive value, and the cost per flow in arc (i, j) is c_{ij}, the following problem (FCNFP) can be formulated:

$$
\left|\begin{array}{l}
\text{(FCNFP): min } cv + fx \\
\qquad \text{subject to } Av = b \\
\qquad\qquad 0 \leq v_{ij} \leq u_{ij}x_{ij}, (i, j) \in E \\
\qquad\qquad x_{ij} \in \{0, 1\}, (i, j) \in E.
\end{array}\right.
$$

This is a mixed 0–1 integer programming problem. If the 0–1 variables were not present, the problem would be one of the the minimum cost flow problems, and a solution could be determined effectively. The linear approximation method solves the approximate linear programming problems obtained by adjusting the cost of the original mixed integer programming problem with fixed costs. The integer program involving variables v and x of (FCNFP) is replaced by an approximate problem involving only variable v (FCNFP-LP). If a feasible solution $(\bar{v}, \bar{x})$ to the problem (FCNFP) is given, then the objective function value in the feasible solution, $\bar{v}$ of the approximate linear programming problem (FCNFP-LP), matches the objective function value of the original problem. First, when the number of iterations is $k = 0$, and taking $c^k = c$, we solve (FCNFP-LP) as follows:

$$
\left|\begin{array}{l}
\text{(FCNFP-LP): min } c^k v \\
\qquad \text{subject to } Av = b \\
\qquad\qquad 0 \leq v_{ij} \leq u_{ij}, (i, j) \in E.
\end{array}\right.
$$

In the optimal solution v^k of (FCNFP-LP), if for (i, j) such that $v_{ij}^k > 0$ we take $x_{ij}^k = 1$, and for (i, j) such that $v_{ij}^k = 0$ we take $x_{ij}^k = 0$, then (v^k, x^k) is the feasible solution for (FCNFP). To make the objective function value at $v = v^k$ for problem (FCNFP-LP) match the objective function value at $(v, x) = (v^k, x^k)$ in problem (FCNFP), we set c_{ij}^{k+1} as follows, where k is the current number of iterations.

$$
c_{ij}^{k+1} = \begin{cases} c_{ij} + f_{ij}/v_{ij}^k & \text{if } v_{ij}^k > 0 \\ c_{ij}^k & \text{if } v_{ij}^k = 0. \end{cases} \tag{26}
$$

In this case, it can be seen from the following equations that the objective function value at solution $v = v^k$ for (FCNFP-LP) matches the objective function value at

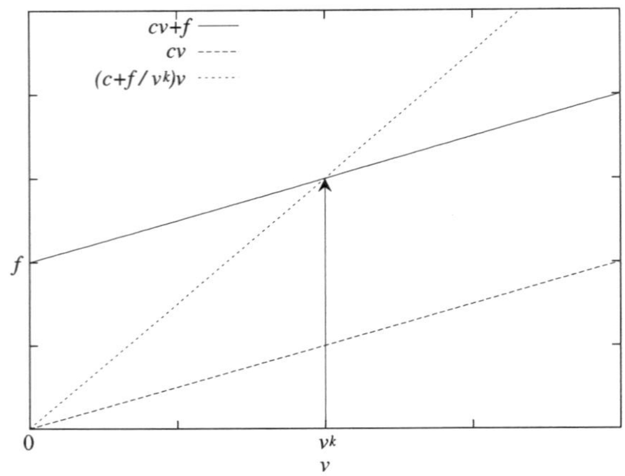

Fig. 1. Slope scaling.

solution $(v, x) = (v^k, x^k)$ in (FCNFP), as shown in Fig. 1.

$$\begin{aligned}\sum_{(i,j)\in E} c_{ij}^{k+1} v_{ij}^k &= \sum_{(i,j)\in E, v_{ij}>0} c_{ij}^{k+1} v_{ij}^k \\ &= \sum_{(i,j)\in E, v_{ij}>0} (c_{ij} + f_{ij}/v_{ij}^k) v_{ij}^k \\ &= \sum_{(i,j)\in E, v_{ij}>0} (c_{ij} v_{ij}^k + f_{ij}). \end{aligned} \tag{27}$$

The linear approximation method is applied to solve (LPC-installation). Here, we fix all $x_{ij} = 1, (i, j) \in A$, and solve the next problem (LPC-installation-slope) in which the cost in the objective function is adjusted.

$$\begin{aligned} &\text{(LPC-installation-slope):} \min \textstyle\sum_{(i,j)\in A} \beta_{ij}^k y_{ij} \\ &\text{subject to} \quad (14), (15), i \in \bar{V} \setminus \{N_0\} \\ &\qquad (16), (17) \\ &\qquad (18), (19), i \in V^+, (i, j) \in A \\ &\qquad (20), (21), i \in V^-, (i, j) \in A \\ &\qquad (9), (i, j) \in A \\ &\qquad (22), i \in V \\ &\qquad (23), (i, j), \in E \\ &\qquad (24), (25), (i, j) \in A \\ &\qquad x_{ij} = 1, y_{ij} \geq 0, (i, j) \in A. \end{aligned}$$

- **Step 0. (Initial setting):** We take the number of iterations $k = 0$, $\beta^k = \beta$. $\epsilon > 0$ is given.
- **Step 1. (Final decision condition):** If $k \geq 1$, then we halt when $\sum_{(i,j)\in\mathcal{A}}(y_{ij}^k - y_{ij}^{k-1}) < \epsilon$. The solution y_{ij}^k finally obtained, is the LPC capacity, when $y_{ij}^k > 0$, $x_{ij} = 1$ and in all other cases $x_{ij} = 0$, the solution for (LPC-installation) is obtained.
- **Step 2. (Calculation of (FCNFP-LP)):** Problem (LPC-installation-slope) is solved, the solution $y = y^k$ is obtained.
- **Step 3. (Update costs):**

$$\beta_{ij}^{k+1} = \begin{cases} \beta_{ij} + \alpha_{ij}/y_{ij}^k & \text{if } y_{ij}^k > 0 \\ \beta_{ij}^k & \text{if } y_{ij}^k = 0 \end{cases}$$

- **Step 4. (Update number of iterations):** Let $k = k + 1$ and return to Step 1.

Fig. 2. Algorithm for LPC installation.

Figure 2 shows the method by which LPC installation problem is solved. The advantage of this method is that a feasible solution is always obtained. As there is no variable representing the installation location, a search for the location is not conducted. By approximating the cost function dynamically, the same cost as the conventional location cost is obtained.

4. Numerical Example Using a Full-Scale Model System

4.1. *Comparison between local search and the linear approximation method*

We used a full-system-scale model of a power distribution system to demonstrate the applicability of this method to the optimization of the installation location and capacity. Figure 3 shows the model used, representing a 6.6 kV system supplying power from distribution substations at seven locations, for a standard demand scale of 250 MW per single secondary substation (154/66 kV). We assumed an urban neighborhood with an approximate area of 15 km × 15 km, based on the impedance value set at each feeder. The following conditions are used to model the 6.6 kV feeder structure and load:

- One distribution substation has a three-bank (20MVA*3) structure, with four feeders coming from each transformer bank.
- There is no supply from the same transformer bank into adjacent feeders.

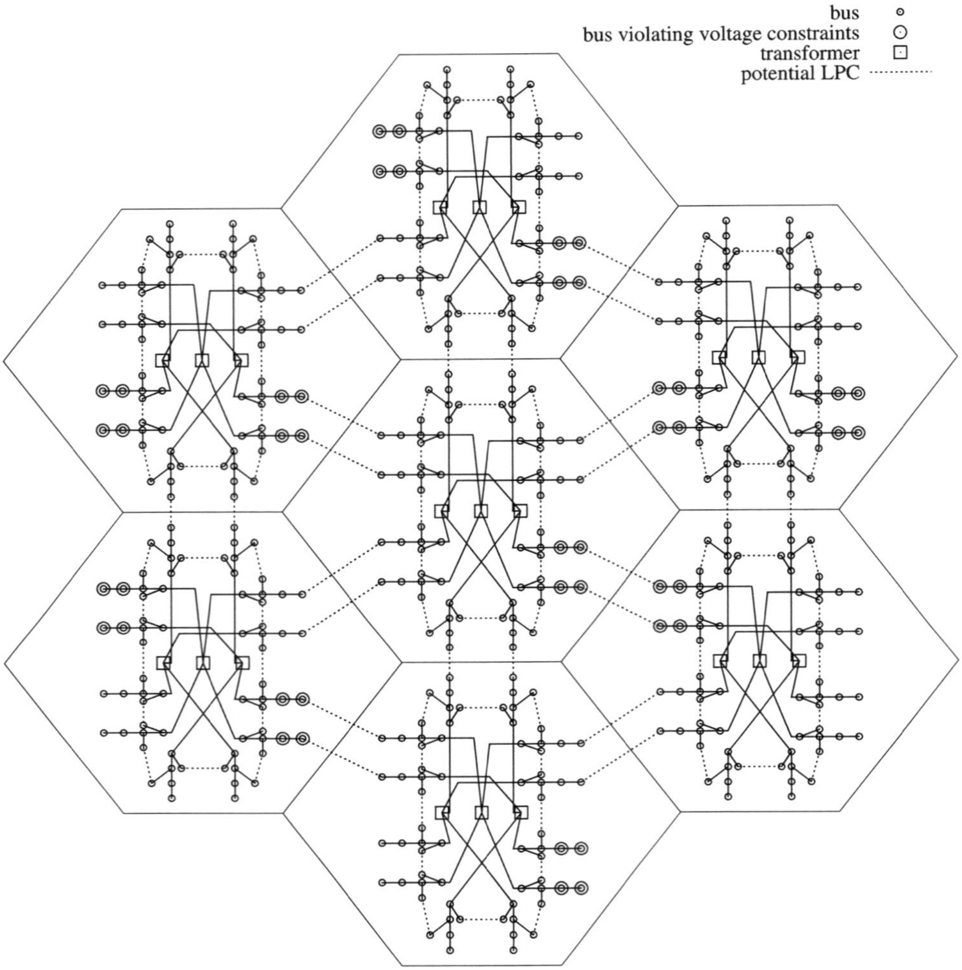

Fig. 3. Power distribution system.

- One feeder is represented as a six-node circuit with two arcs branching off. The distribution line inductance is 1.2 mH/km.
- It is possible to loop the end nodes of each feeder (three nodes per feeder) with the adjacent feeder.
- The above feeder structure is common to all seven distribution substations.

In the calculation, the initial condition was a violation of the operational constraints arising simultaneously in multiple nodes at the ends of the feeders due to a voltage increase (number of nodes where violation occurred: 44), because of the interconnection of the distributed power sources. This initial condition was used

Table 1. Calculation results (local search).

Iterations	Number of LPCs	Cost	Number of times OPF solved
0	15	17.78	2
1	14	16.92	20
2	13	15.99	20
3	12	15.13	12
4	11	13.75	16
5	11	13.75	14
Total number of times OPF solved			84
Calculation time			15070 (sec)

Table 2. Calculation results (linear approximation).

Iterations	Number of LPCs	Cost	Number of times OPF solved
1	16	18.48	1
2	15	17.71	1
3	13	15.71	1
4	11	13.75	1
5	11	13.75	1
Total number of times OPF solved			5
Calculation time			1402 (sec)

to determine the optimal installation location and capacity of the LPC. Simulations were then carried out using the numerical optimizer NUOPT on a 2.00 GHz Xeon E5507 with two processors and 12.0 GB memory. Examples of modern portfolio optimization problems were given by Scherer and Martin [2005].

It was shown that the minimum-cost solution in resolving all voltage violations using linear approximation had a calculation time 1/10 that of the previously developed local search method. The results of these calculations are shown in Tables 1 and 2. As can be seen from these tables, our linear approximation approach required OPF to be solved only 5 times, in contrast to the 84 times required when local search was used.

This reduction in searching is because there is no requirement to search the 0–1 variable relating to the installation when using the linear approximation method. Linear approximation is a technique that lacks global convergence, and it is not necessary to converge on an optimal solution. In our simulation, the same solution was obtained when using local search and linear approximation, in both cases a

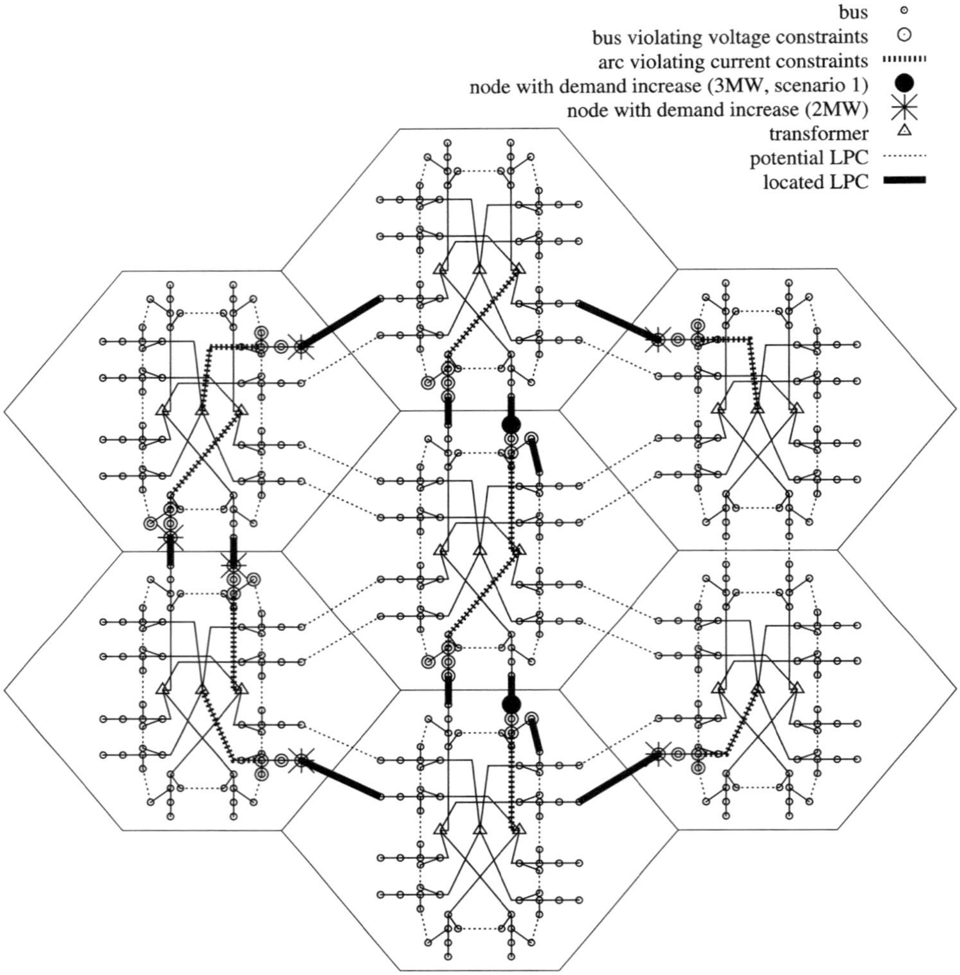

Fig. 4. Optimal location (scenario 1).

suitable solution was obtained for the positional relation with constraint violations in the system.

Although the efficiency of the local search method can be improved by using a set in which the variables representing the installation decision are fixed, the calculation time remains much longer than that of the linear approximation method.

4.2. *Investigation of multi-scenario optimization*

We next investigated multi-scenario optimization by performing a simulation that simultaneously took into consideration two scenarios with different demand

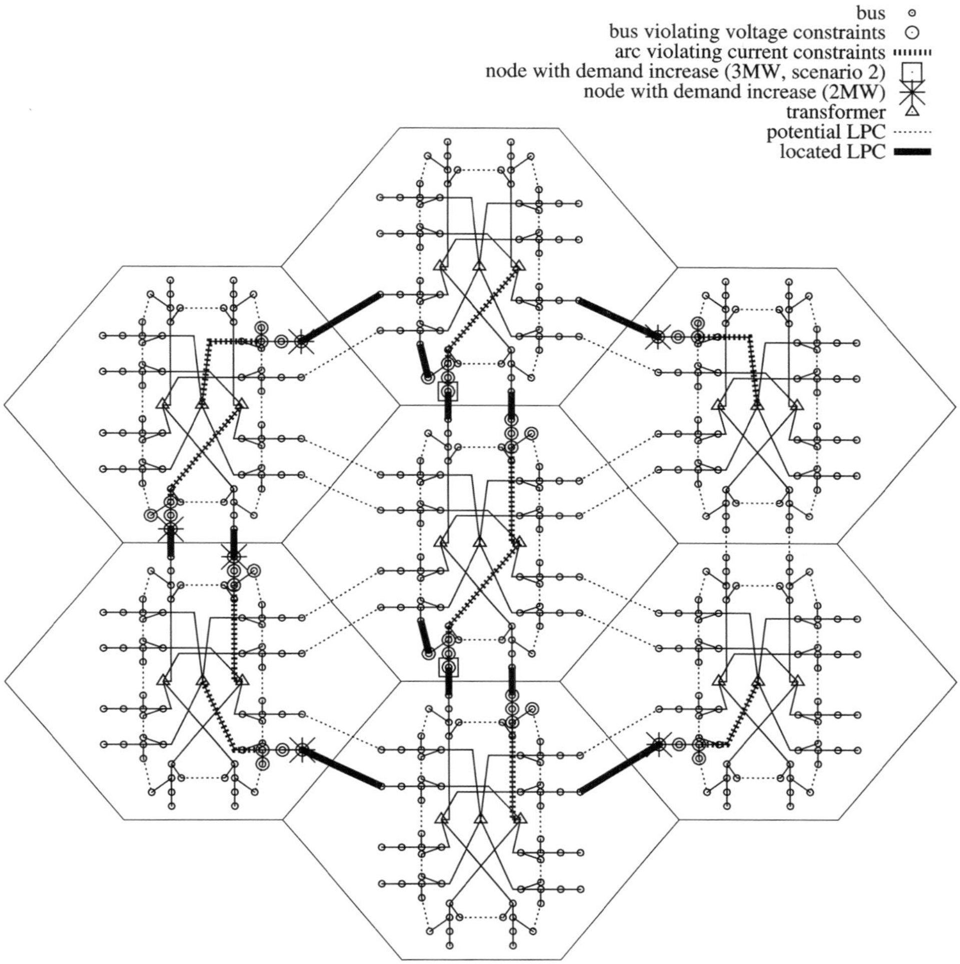

Fig. 5. Optimal location (scenario 2).

patterns, using the same model. In the two scenarios, demand increased on a total of eight buses. In both scenarios, six buses had a demand increase of 2 MW, but the locations of buses with a demand increase of 3 MW were different. This is shown in Figs. 4–6. No account was taken of distributed power sources, and the optimal installation location and capacity of the LPC was determined from an initial condition of voltage constraint violations arising in multiple nodes at the ends of feeders (number of nodes where violation occurred: 40). This was due to an increase in demand, with violations of the line thermal capacity constraint arising concurrently in 10 lines.

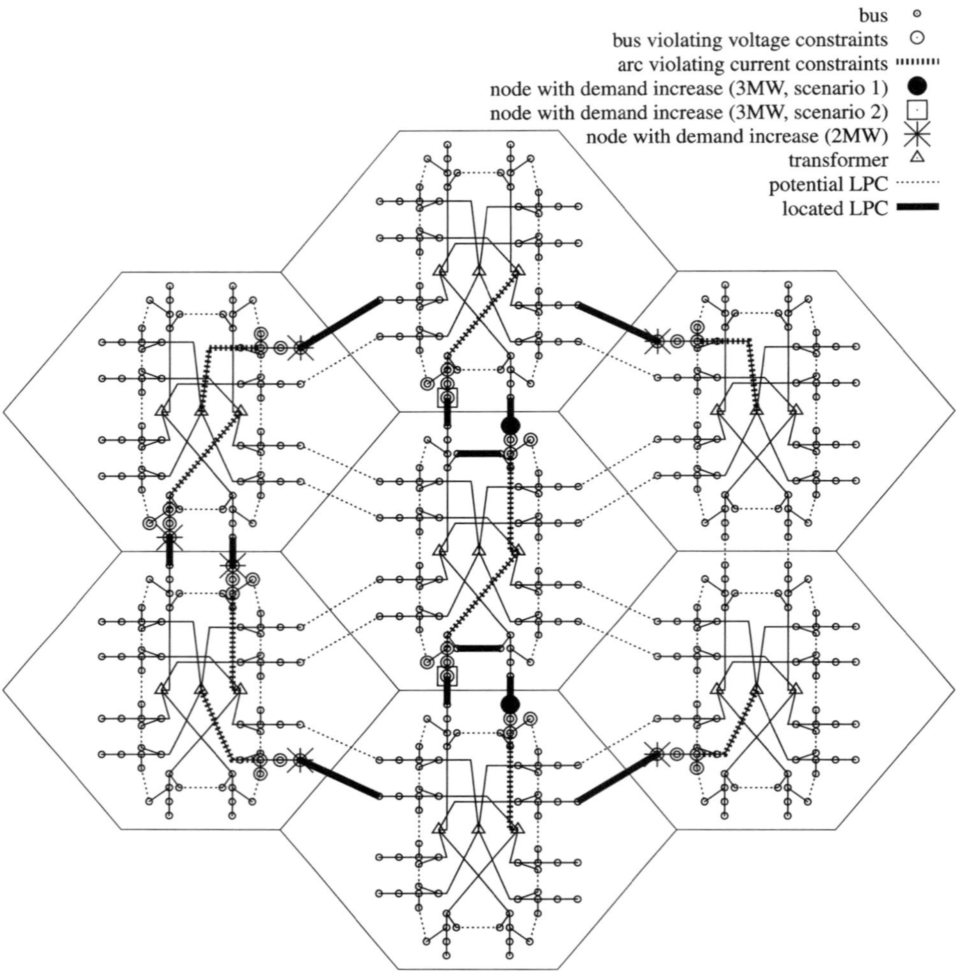

Fig. 6. Optimal location (multi-scenario).

First, we determined the optimal location for the LPC in each individual scenario.

As can be seen from Table 3, the calculation time when using the linear approximation method was much shorter than that of the local search method. The optimal solutions obtained are shown in Figs. 4–5.

Next, we consider a model that takes multiple scenarios simultaneously into account. In this model, the variables x and y are defined as deterministic variables and the variables e and f are defined as stochastic variables representing voltage values. The variables e and f have the subscript s for the scenario s, and it can vary for

Table 3. Calculation results (per scenario).

Scenario	**Solution method**	**Calculation Time(s)**	**Number of times OPF solved**
1	Local search	4997	48
1	Linear approximation	391	4
2	Local search	3667	70
2	Linear approximation	385	4

Table 4. Calculation results with multiple scenarios (local search).

Iterations	**Number of LPCs**	**Cost**	**Number of times OPF solved**
0	24	35.78	2
1	22	33.79	2
2	21	32.86	4
3	20	31.94	2
4	16	27.39	4
5	16	27.38	4
6	16	27.26	4
7	14	25.25	4
8	13	24.25	6
9	13	24.23	6
10	13	24.22	6
11	12	23.27	6
12	12	23.27	24
Total number of times OPF solved			74
Calculation time			9530 (sec)

each scenario. The stochastic multi-scenario problem we consider is an extension problem of the original problem (LPC-installation), and it is defined so that the constraints are satisfied for all scenarios. Figure 6 shows the optimal locations when both scenarios were considered.

When the single scenarios were resolved separately, 14 LPC units were installed, whereas when multiple scenarios are considered simultaneously, the number fell to 12 units. As shown in Fig. 6, when the scenarios produce different installation patterns, it is possible to reduce the number of units by considering multiple scenarios simultaneously. The calculation results are given in Tables 4 and 5. It can be seen that the LPC installation locations can be determined quickly using the linear approximation method.

Table 5. Calculation results with multiple scenarios (slope scaling).

Iterations	Number of LPCs	Cost	Number of times OPF solved
1	24	35.70	1
2	20	31.79	1
3	16	27.37	1
4	13	24.30	1
5	13	24.27	1
6	12	23.27	1
Total number of times OPF solved			6
Calculation time			886 (sec)

5. Conclusions

When addressing the LPC optimal installation problem, conventional methods require repeated calculations to be performed both when searching for an installation location and for calculating the OPF. These approaches require long time to produce a solution and make it difficult to perform optimization under multi-scenario constraints. In the present study, we developed a more efficient approach for solving practical problems. Using a technique that linearly approximates the installation cost, it becomes possible to obtain solutions through nonlinear optimization of the minimum conditions. This increases the speed of the process. We investigated the effectiveness of our novel technique using a full-scale system model, and demonstrated its capacity to minimize the cost of resolving all voltage violations efficiently, and with a shorter calculation time than conventional techniques based on local searches.

Our technique was also applied to a problem with multi-scenario flow constraints. When the demand patterns were different in each scenario, our optimization approach was able to resolve the multiple scenarios simultaneously. This new technique has potential applications across a wide range of optimization problems in the electric power filed.

References

Bai, X., Wei, H., Fujisawa, K. and Wang, Y. (2008). Semidefinite programming for optimal power flow problems. *Electrical Power and Energy Systems* **30**, 383–392.

Bazaraa, M. S., Sherali, H. F. and Shetty, C. M. (1993). *Nonlinear Programming-Theory and Algorithm*, 2nd edn. (John Wiley & Sons, New York).

Kim, D. and Pardalos, P. M. (1999). A solution approach to the fixed charge network flow problem using a dynamic slope scaling procedure. *Operations Research Letters* **24**, 195–203.

Kim, D. and Pardalos, P. M. (2000a). Dynamic slope scaling and trust interval techniques for solving concave piecewise linear network flow problems. *Networks* **35**, 216–222.

Kim, D. and Pardalos, P. M. (2000b). A dynamic domain contraction algorithm for nonconvex piecewise linear network flow problems. *Journal of Global Optimization* **17**, 225–234.

Molzahn, D. K., Holzer, J. T., Lesieutre, B. C. and DeMarco, C. L. (2013). Implementation of a large-scale optimal power flow solver based on semidefinite programming. *IEEE Transactions on Power Systems* **28**, 3987–3998.

Ruszczyński, A. and Shapiro, A. (2003). Stochastic programming. In J. R. Brige and V. Linetsky (eds.), *Handbooks in Operations Research and Management Science*, Vol. 10 (Elsevier).

Scherer, B. and Martin, D. (2005). *Modern Portfolio Optimization with NUOPT™, S-PLUS®, and S+Bayes™* (Springer).

Shapiro, A., Dentcheva, D. and Ruszczyński, A. (2009). *Lectures on Stochastic Programming: Modeling and Theory*. (SIAM).

Shiina, T. (1999). Numerical solution technique for joint chance-constrained programming problem — An application to electric power capacity expansion. *Journal of the Operations Research Society of Japan* **42**, 128–140.

Shiina, T. and Birge, J. R. (2003). Multistage stochastic programming model for electric power capacity expansion problem. *Japan Journal of Industrial and Applied Mathematics* **20**, 379–397.

Shiina, T. and Birge, J. R. (2004). Stochastic unit commitment problem. *International Transactions in Operational Research* **11**, 19–32.

Shiina, T. and Watanabe, I. (2004). Lagrangian relaxation method for price-based unit commitment problem. *Engineering Optimization* **36**, 705–719.

Wood, A. J. and Wollenberg, B. J. (1996). *Power Generation, Operation and Control* (John Wiley & Sons, New York).

Zhu, J. (2015). *Optimization of Power System Operation* (Wiley).

Chapter 16

The Troubled Path Toward Greater Transparency as a Means to Foster Good Corporate Governance and Fight Against Corruption in the Energy Sector

Costantino Grasso

Department of Business Management and Law,
University of East London, London, UK
c.grasso@uel.ac.uk

Corruption has traditionally been wildly rampant in the energy sector and its effects have proved to be extremely dramatic. For decades energy companies have perpetrated corrupt practices with impunity to obtain from the local governments the green light to construct intrusive energy infrastructures, which have the potential of causing serious damages to a country's environment and social fabric. This illicit way of carrying out business activities has been *de facto* tolerated by governments for a long time. It affected particular developing nations, causing the so-called "resource curse". Then, almost unpredictably, over the course of last two decades, significant and increasingly determined efforts have been devoted to fighting against such a criminal phenomenon. It is well established that the role that transparency plays within such a grim scenario is fundamental. This chapter will examine the intimate relationship between the lack of corporate transparency and corruption, and analyze the most important legal instruments that have been developed to encourage a transparent way of conducting business activities in the energy sector at the international, regional and domestic level. Then, will also focus on the recent Trump's administration decision to nullify the US transparency rules for the extractive industries analyzing the scope of its potentially dramatic consequences.

Keywords: Transparency; corruption; resource curse; corporate lobbying; EITI; extractive industry; energy sector; oil and gas.

> *Hence the major effect of the Panopticon: To induce in the inmate a state of conscious and permanent visibility that assures the automatic functioning of power*
> (Michel Foucault, Discipline and Punish: The Birth of the Prison, 1975)

1. Introduction

In recent years, the concept of transparency has become a fundamental organizing and administrative principle. It is opposed to the notion of secrecy, which is currently considered as corrosive and antithetical to democratic values. As Stiglitz [1999] observed, secrecy gives those in command exclusive control over certain areas of knowledge, and thereby increases their power, making it difficult to verify if that power is abused. As a result, transparency has gradually risen as the crucial element of any system of decision-making that tries to temper the vast concentration of power, which typically characterizes multinational corporations. In the corporate world, the need for enhanced transparency regimes is particularly felt within companies operating in the energy sector, where the great ambition is to implement more open ways of conducting business operations in order to curb the pandemic plague of corruption that afflicts the extractive industry. The call for transparency has been intensified by phenomena such as globalization and free trade, which press for the creation of universal forms of administration and governance, and entail making transnational business operations legible and clear [Garsten and Lindh de Montoya, 2008].

The position of this chapter compared to the existent academic literature can be defined as entailing at the same time both a specialist and innovative perspective. It is a specialist piece of work because it focuses on the role of corporate transparency in the energy sector, which is characterized by several unique features. It is innovative because it offers an analysis of the most innovative measures that have been developed in this sector over the course of the latest years as well as of the most relevant political issues that are currently affecting the achievement of corporate transparency in the energy sector.

This chapter argues that a growth of transparency in the business operations of energy companies represents a crucial element of the fight against corruption in resource-rich countries, which become too often victims of the so-called "resource curse." In setting out this proposition, this chapter proceeds in seven parts which include this introduction, Section 1. Then, Section 2, "Conceptualizing transparency," deals with the difficulty in articulating what transparency is and why it is important, which threatens to make corporate transparency measures ineffective and blind to the larger purposes for which they must serve. Section 3, "Transparency and corruption, the plague of the energy industry," examines the intimate connection between the lack of transparency and corruption, and its relevance for the energy companies. Section 4, "The international regime for transparency in the energy sector," offers an analysis of the most relevant initiatives that have been taken at the international level to improve corporate transparency in the energy sector.

Before the conclusion, two parts of the chapter (i.e. Section 5, "Corporate America and the never-ending battle against transparency," and Section 6, "The European Union's efforts to foster corporate transparency") examine the legal instruments developed respectively in the US and in the EU to foster corporate transparency in the extractive industry. As a matter of fact, over the course of the last decade, significant efforts have been made on both sides of the Atlantic to develop instruments of "hard law" consisting in imposing legal obligations on energy companies to disclose information related to payments made to foreign governments. The higher degree of effectiveness and pervasiveness that characterizes the domestic legal instruments in comparison to the international ones imposes the need for their analysis. Although other countries, such as Canada and Norway, have recently adopted similar transparency regimes for the energy sector, a comprehensive examination of all those sets of rules falls beyond the scope of this chapter; whereas the decision to focus on the US and the EU experiences is based on the circumstance that several of the most relevant energy companies have been incorporated within those jurisdictions.

2. Conceptualizing Transparency

The Oxford English Dictionary (1989) defines the term "transparency" as "the quality or condition of being transparent; perviousness to light; diaphaneity; pellucidity." In turn, the adjective "transparent" is defined as "having the property of transmitting light, so as to render bodies lying beyond completely visible; that can be seen through; diaphanous." Although the common use of the word primarily refers to a physical property, it can also be used in a figurative sense, which is "easily seen through, recognized, understood or detected." The Oxford English Dictionary records many early uses of the term in its figurative meaning. For instance, in the following statement that appeared in the work "The Religion of Protestants," which William Chillingworth wrote in 1638, it is possible to find one of the uses of the word in such a sense: "Your Argument against us, is a transparent fallacy." Then, the word "transparency" has become increasingly used metaphorically to indicate a procedural or administrative process that is open and available for examination and scrutiny [Scauer, 2011]. In particular, although in its ordinary use transparency has a generic connotation, in the legal world the term has lost its neutral stance and acquired a deeper and more precise meaning, which is related to financial disclosures and organizational policies and practices. In this regard, the Black's Law Dictionary (2014) defines transparency as "openness; clarity; unobstructed access, especially to business and governmental records; lack of guile and of any attempt to hide

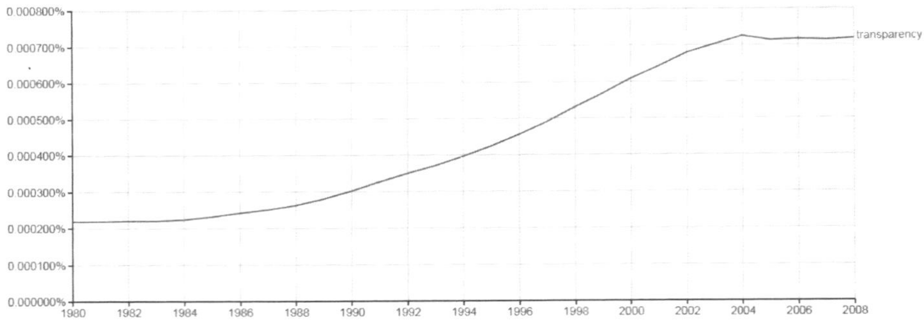

Fig. 1. Google Ngram Viewer — Statistical data on the use of the use of the term "transparency" (1980–2008).

damaging information." The exponential growth in the use of the term over the last two decades (see Fig. 1) makes every attempt to define or classify the legal notion of transparency extremely difficult.

This is because, as clearly expressed by Möslein & Reinsehuber [2012], the concept of transparency is currently related to several different dimensions, has ambiguous meanings and is used differently, if not contradictorily, in different contexts:

> "From the perspective of information recipients, markets are regarded as transparent when the information that is available is as comprehensive as possible. For the one holding the information, in contrast, transparency does not necessarily imply disclosure, but requires in the first instance refraining from deceit with regard to certain facts and 'not dissimulating.' As far as information is provided transparency concerns a clear and comprehensible form of presentation, i.e. primarily 'how,' not 'if' information is disclosed. For the rule-maker, transparency stands for the potential regulatory objective of see-through markets [. . .]"

Such a recent evolution of the use and meaning of the word "transparency" appears to be closely connected with the activities that have been carried out by non-governmental organizations (NGOs), supranational organizations and national governments [Ball, 2009]. In particular, the establishment of "Transparency International,"[1] which is an NGO that aims at fighting the criminal phenomenon of corruption at the global level, has surely contributed to the spread of the word within the academic world and the broader public. The term "transparency" has also been adopted by many international and regional organizations, which have included it as a key element of their policies. For instance, the World Bank has

[1] www.transparency.org/about/.

defined transparency as "citizen access to publicly available information about the actions of those in government and the consequences of these actions," highlighting how it can play a crucial role in development by nourishing political engagement.[2] Transparency has also become a top priority in the World Bank's Public-Private Partnerships project,[3] which aims at eliminating extreme poverty and boosting shared prosperity by enhancing the reach and quality of the delivery of basic infrastructure services.[4] The term has also been widely used by the Organization for Economic Cooperation and Development (OECD), which has developed the concept of transnational tax transparency as an essential component of its plan to fight globally against tax evasion.[5] Another glaring example is represented by the International Monetary Fund, which fosters the adoption of greater transparency within its member countries on the ground that it would encourage more widespread public discussion and examination of policies, enhance the accountability of policy makers, and facilitate the efficient and orderly functioning of financial markets.[6] At the domestic level, the word "transparency" has been progressively more used as a significant element of governmental policies. The statement made by Barak Obama [2009] in the Freedom of Information Act Memorandum is illustrative of such an approach: "In our democracy, the Freedom of Information Act (FOIA), which encourages accountability through transparency, is the most prominent expression of a profound national commitment to ensuring an open Government." Similarly, the following passages from a speech delivered by Obama [2006] during the Lobbying Reform Summit at the National Press Club in Washington, D.C. is emblematic of the importance that transparency has acquired in the contemporary political debate:

> "The American people are tired of a Washington that's only open to those with the most cash and the right connections [...] When big oil companies are invited into the White House for secret energy meetings, it's no wonder they end up with billions in tax breaks while Americans still struggle to fill up their gas tanks and heat their homes [...] Real reform means making sure that Members of Congress and the Administration tell us when they're negotiating for jobs with industries they're responsible for regulating [...] Real reform means giving the public access to now-secret conference committee meetings and posting all bills on the Internet 24 hours before they're voted on, so the public can scrutinize what's in them

[2]www.worldbank.org/en/research/publication/making-politics-work-for-development.

[3]http://blogs.worldbank.org/governance/public-private-partnerships-transparency-and-accountability-where-my-data.

[4]www.worldbank.org/en/topic/publicprivatepartnerships/overview#1.

[5]www.oecd.org/tax/transparency/.

[6]www.imf.org/en/About/Factsheets/Sheets/2016/07/27/15/35/Transparency-at-the-IMF

[...] Finally, I think that real reform must include real oversight and accountability."

According to such recent developments, transparency can be defined as the dissemination of timely and reliable economic, social and political information, which is accessible to all relevant stakeholders [Bellver and Kaufmann, 2005]. Also, a good readability of the information has to be assured. It is illustrative that, in its handbook to create clear disclosure documents, the US Securities and Exchange Commission (SEC) has highlighted several factors that should be avoided to make a document more readable: Long sentences; passive voice; weak verbs; superfluous words; legal and financial jargon; numerous defined terms; abstract words; unnecessary details; unreadable design and layout [Securities and Exchange Commission, 1998].

Such a new concept of transparency is characterized by an inherent positive connotation; moreover, the adoption of transparency initiatives is ordinarily considered as a general enhancement of the way of administrating public and private organizations. However, as it has been argued by some scholars, the adoption of higher levels of transparency is not free from controversial aspects in that it might cause several problems of corporate governance. Specifically, in relation to corporations, greater transparency may carry a political cost consisting in allowing stakeholders as well as the general public to use disclosed information to demand active political interventions that, aiming at limiting executives' discretion, may end up curbing their legitimate attempt to maximize the firm's value [Bahar, 2007]. The tension between transparency and governance is not a novelty, for years ethicists have wondered if governance without secrecy is even possible [Bremmer, 2017]. Such an issue has proved to be particularly critical within democratic systems where the dissemination of information may directly affect the government through the process of voting. It is not surprising that the Panama Papers scandal,[7] which revealed illicit financial dealings of some of the world's most powerful insiders, produced more harmful effects within democracies than in less-accountable authoritarian systems. The latter might adopt dictatorial or totalitarian instruments to prevent ordinary people from accessing such kind of information. For instance, on that occasion Chinese authorities imposed a strict censorship of websites, ordering all content related to the Panama Papers to be removed as new revelations emerged of how relatives of some of the country's top leaders had used secretive offshore companies to hide their wealth [Phillips, 2016]. Other experts have asserted that in recent years transparency seems to have become an end in itself and have criticized the

[7]https://panamapapers.icij.org/.

global tendency to pursue it no matter the consequences [Messik, 2015]. Even if the above-mentioned criticisms of the implementation of unrestricted openness within complex organizations may contain elements of truth, the intimate connection that exists between lack of transparency and spread of corrupt practices constitutes a compelling argument supporting the necessity for establishing greater levels of corporate transparency. Although the concept of transparency has become extremely popular, its role in reducing corruption and its importance in countering the resource curse that afflicts many developing countries are still poorly understood [Kolstad, 2009].

3. Transparency and Corruption: The Plague of the Energy Industry

The concept of transparency has acquired a particular importance in connection with the activities carried out by commercial organizations that are increasingly under pressure to show a higher level of receptiveness to the wider environment in which they operate. It is well known that entrepreneurial activity traditionally makes use of elements of secrecy and confidentiality. Corporate executives pay particular attention to the ways in which the information related to their companies is disseminated, and they are naturally cautious about providing access to commercially sensitive information fearing that it may help competitors. It is not surprising that corporations are extremely reluctant to disclose information about their business arrangements, production costs and payments made to partners and suppliers. However, such a tendency often ends up generating a veil of mystery that, surrounding their business operations, facilitates the perpetration of corporate misconducts and, specifically, of corrupt practices. Moreover, serious problems of monitoring corporate activities commonly afflict supervisory authorities where key information asymmetries are present [Khan, 1999]. Corruption is notoriously difficult to track and discover, and it is widely acknowledged that where the decision-making process is shrouded in mystery, corrupt practices can hardly be detected [Bac, 2001]. This inherent risk of corruption has become one of the most relevant factors that demand greater transparency in the business world. In particular, such a compelling need is strongly felt within the energy sector where corrupt practices are especially rampant and produce dramatic consequences on the social texture and environment of the countries whose natural resources are exploited. Energy companies that carry out extractive operations have a responsibility to address this impact, and the public has a legitimate interest in being informed about it. This is particularly true where their business activities are conducted in developing countries, which are rich in natural resources but, at the same time, very vulnerable to corruption.

Corrupt practices perpetrated by energy companies in developing countries have traditionally been an extremely serious problem. Several key reasons appear to lie behind the pervasiveness of corruption in the energy sector. The first reason is the crucial geopolitical importance that energy resources have always had due to the asymmetric distribution of reserves, production and consumption of natural resources around the globe [Leal-Arcas *et al.*, 2016]. Another reason is represented by the enormous amount of money usually involved in energy transactions. Energy companies tend to become huge and enormously rich corporations, which in many cases are also backed by governments. Such immense corporate wealth allows these firms to obtain an unfair advantage in the political marketplace. Thanks to their wealth, power and political connections it is easy for them to arrange complex schemes to deceive the public and the prosecuting authorities about their unlawful activities. Consequently, on many occasions, they could easily avoid accountability, making use of the vast number of skilled lawyers and accountants at their disposal [Grasso, 2017]. Another determining factor is the inherent intrusiveness of the vast majority of energy investments with respect to a country's environment and social fabric. The health and environmental risks increase dramatically in developing countries, without considering that local populations are often subject to practices of forced land dispossession to ensure the commercial exploitation of their natural resources [Gilbert, 2016]. As a result, in order to obtain the green light from host governments to construct such intrusive and damaging energy infrastructures, the powerful energy corporations have methodically used corruption as an effective means of obtaining political support or controlling local rulers [Grasso, 2017]. Finally, the vast majority of countries that are rich in terms of energy resources appear also more vulnerable to corruption. In particular, in developing countries, corruption has proved to be a pervasive and persistent criminal phenomenon also because the exponents of the dominant class, instead of seeking to curb corruption, commonly use illicit activities to maintain themselves in power, often at the expense of the poor and their nation's development [Klitgaard, 1991]. Due to a weak rule of law and a malfunctioning bureaucracy, those countries tend to rent their natural resources stimulating corruption among bureaucrats and politicians [Mehlum *et al.*, 2006]. As a matter of fact, the dominant class commonly adopts a model of clientelism under which the domestic natural riches are overexploited and the related revenues are inefficiently and unfairly redistributed by politicians to manipulate the national public sector and influence elections. [Robinson *et al.*, 2006].

Within such a grim scenario, a growth of transparency in business operations is one of the factors that can help combat corruption. Experts agree that a higher degree of transparency may be effective in curbing corruption on the ground that, where a transparent decision-making process is adopted, decisions can easily be verified, there is no secrecy concerning the rules and the identities of decision makers, and large payments to governmental officials are traceable and cannot be hidden. Consequently, under a highly transparent regime, corporations cannot abuse the connections established with local rulers and politicians [Bac, 2001]. For that reason, the recent trend of fostering the adoption of more incisive instruments of corporate transparency is to be warmly welcomed.

The process of democratization has been an important transparency promoter. Over the course of the last 30 years, the civil society has become more mature and its level of general awareness has grown. It is not surprising that the past decades have witnessed an increase in the pressure exerted on governments to implement more stringent transparency rules both for the public and private sector [Halter *et al.*, 2009]. Globalization and free trade have also exerted a profound influence upon this process gradually transforming transparency from a generic attitude into a crucial business rule. The globalized economy created an extremely competitive market environment that has progressively led to a special attention to the risks, costs and consequences of bribery, graft and other forms of corruption in international business. Such a globalized market, where only the fittest survive, inherently requires a trading system characterized by honesty, transparency and fair dealing [Grasso, 2017].

In any case, the way in which transparency is implemented within the corporate sector is also important. This is because more transparency does not necessarily imply less corruption. As some scholars observed, the perpetration of corrupt practices may be facilitated by local improvements in transparency. The problem lies in that where information about the identities of key decision makers and the amount of payments made to them is disclosed; this can potentially represent an incentive to build illicit connections, which are the basic prerequisite of corruption. In other words, potential corruptors may receive better information about with whom they should connect through the information disclosed by their more transparent competitors [Bac, 2001]. The validity of such an argument is strictly connected with the close relationship that should exist between transparency and accountability, which stand side by side, are complementary and require each other.

While some countries have adopted adequate legislative instruments to criminalize bribery of foreign public officials, such as the US Foreign Corrupt Practice Act and the UK Bribery Act, many others have not yet developed them or are not willing to enforce the existing rules in an effective way. Moreover, in many developing countries where corruption takes place, bribed public officials are rarely prosecuted being the governing authorities often enmeshed in corruption. A recent example is represented by the fact that, although in the UK an investigation led to a deferred prosecution agreement between ICBC Standard Bank Plc and the Serious Fraud Office for a case of transnational bribery perpetrated in Tanzania, no prosecution was initiated for the same illicit activity in the African country [Grasso, 2016]. Another glaring example is given by the events in which a former president of Zambia, Frederick Chiluba, was involved. In 2002, after his departure from the presidency, Chiluba was indicted on 100 charges of corruption by siphoning public money into private bank accounts in London. His trial dragged on for 6 years but, although an English civil court found he plundered around £30m from state coffers to help fund extravagant spending on designer clothes and shoes, when the presidency passed to one of his closest friends he was eventually acquitted [Brittain, 2011]. Not surprisingly, the Mo Ibrahim Prize, which was established in 2006 by the Sudanese billionaire Mo Ibrahim and aims at celebrating excellence in African leadership, has only conferred the prestigious award four times over the course of the last decade [Eniola, 2017]. Consequently, it may be theoretically possible that the implementation of greater transparency regimes can be exploited by unscrupulous competitors thanks to such discrepancies in the global fight against bribery and corruption. However, if this argument can be validly used to support the international efforts that aim at leveling the playing field through the adoption of more stringent and homogeneous standards of criminalization of corrupt practices, it cannot be sensibly used to slow down the process of enhancing corporate transparency. Transparency represents a key factor in reducing corruption and other dysfunctions especially in relation to business operations carried out by multinational corporations in natural resource-rich countries.

4. The International Regime for Transparency in the Energy Sector

Traditionally, the international legal framework appears fragmentary and dominated by legal instruments falling into the category of soft law, which is most commonly defined as including hortatory, rather than legally binding, obligations. As a matter of fact, the typical international legal instrument consists in a non-binding agreement with limited possibilities, if any, of enforcement. It is not surprising that, because of those characteristics, some scholars have questioned, on the one hand, the very existence of the international legal order and, on the other, the legal nature of these measures [Guzman, 2010].

Notwithstanding such inherent limits, the adoption of initiatives aimed at enhancing corporate transparency at the international level appears to be an indispensable element of business development. As it has been observed above, the asymmetry existent between the transnational nature of energy companies' business operations and the discrepancies in the way in which at the domestic level corporate transparency and anti-corruption measures are implemented is one of the main reasons behind the inefficacy of the attempts to restrain corporate misconducts.

Among the programs introduced at the international level to foster transparency, it is possible to mention the Global Transparency Initiative. It is a network of civil society organizations which aims at promoting openness at the international financial institutions, such as the World Bank, the International Monetary Fund, the European Investment Bank and the other regional development banks. Through the projects they finance, such institutions exert significant power over people's lives, especially in developing countries that represent their primary borrowers. However, these institutions constantly face a substantial corruption risk as the United States General Accounting Office clearly underlined in its Report to Congressional Committees of 2000: "Many borrowers lack well-functioning public management systems; accountable organizations; and a strong legal framework to prevent, detect, and redress corruption" [Report to Congressional Committees, 2000]. Consequently, the adoption of greater transparency within their operations will help to reduce corruption, avoid adverse social and environmental influences, and increase participation, engagement and ownership over projects.

Another relevant international project is the Guide on Resource Revenue Transparency[8] published by the International Monetary Fund, which offers detailed transparency guidelines for countries rich in natural resources aiming at addressing the special issues arising from the technical complexity and volatility of resource revenue flows and from the sheer magnitude of the related transactions.

However, in relation to the energy sector, the international project that has recently acquired the greatest relevance is the Extractive Industries Transparency Initiative (EITI),[9] which specifically aims at establishing principles of greater transparency and accountability in the oil, gas and mining sectors. It has been promoted since 2003 as a scheme that can assist mineral-rich participating nations in fighting against corruption. The project is also supported by the World Bank through the Multi-Donor Trust Fund that provides countries with economic resources to implement it. The EITI is based on 12 founding principles, which include, *inter alia*, the necessity to manage domestic natural resource wealth for the benefit of the home country's citizens and in the interests of their national development.

In particular, such an aim is pursued through the voluntary disclosure, in a publicly accessible, comprehensive and comprehensible way, of all material oil, gas

[8]www.imf.org/external/np/fad/trans/guide.htm.
[9]https://eiti.org/.

and mining payments made by corporations to governments and all material revenues received by governments from these companies. More importantly, participating in the EITI implies to be subject to a validation process, which serves to assess performance and safeguard the integrity of the project. This audit procedure, which is carried out by independent valuators appointed by the EITI Board, is intended to provide all stakeholders with an impartial assessment of whether EITI implementation in a country is consistent with the provisions of its standards. The EITI project is based on the adoption of a simple but effective mechanism. It persuades governments to disclose the revenues they earn from renting their natural resources so that the companies, which conduct extractive operations in a participating country, have to unveil what they pay to them. Any discrepancies between the figures given by governments and corporations would need to be reconciled before an EITI report could be published, because such inconsistencies may have originated by the payment of bribes [David-Barrett and Okamura, 2016]. This is one of the main strengths of the initiative: While it is voluntary for countries to take part in the project, the participating governments undertake to oblige all energy companies, which carry out extractive operations within their borders, to submit their data for the scheme. Therefore, at the domestic level, where a country implements the EITI, it becomes mandatory for energy companies to participate in it [Eigen, 2007]. The involvement of all energy companies operating in a given member country represents a turning point in that it allows to avoid collective action problems such as the one that BP faced in Angola when, in 2001, it unilaterally decided to publish information related to its business operations. On that occasion, not only no other major corporation followed BP's example but also the Angolan government, which was highly displeased by the transparency approach adopted unilaterally by BP, even threatened to expel the company from the country [Frynas, 2010].

In February 2016, the EITI Board adopted a new set of standards. Among other things, the 2016 EITI Standard, following the trail of other supranational legal instruments like the EU 4th Anti-Money Laundering Directive, entails beneficial ownership reporting. Specifically, as of 1 January 2020, it is required that implementing countries request, and companies disclose, beneficial ownership information for inclusion in the EITI Report. This applies to corporate entities that bid for, operate or invest in extractive assets and should include the identities of their beneficial owners, the level of ownership and details about how ownership or control is exerted.

Although the EITI is a meritorious project, it presents serious limitations. It does not cover in a sufficient way discretionary social expenditures by companies, which are often used as a vehicle for bribes. The 2016 EITI Standard provides only that "where reconciliation of key transactions is not possible, e.g. where company payments are in kind or to a non-governmental third party," the system relies on voluntary unilateral approach for disclosures. Moreover, it only recommends the disclosure of information on revenue management and expenditures (i.e. the way in which the revenues that come from the extractive sector are used). Consequently, the project does not necessarily help to increase the accountability of government spending. This issue is particularly relevant taking into consideration that the countries that historically were more successful in addressing the "resource curse," such as Chile and Indonesia, were the ones that demonstrated prudence in spending extractive revenues and directed them towards productive activities [Stevens, 2005]. Although at the beginning the rate of progress of implementing the EITI principles was somewhat disappointing [Kolstad and Wiig, 2009], the project has grown to include 52 countries at various stages of implementation. However, as of 2017, only nine of them have done satisfactory progress in order to meet the newly implemented 2016 EITI Standard, whereas the vast majority, including the US and the UK, are still candidates or have not been assessed yet. Moreover, extremely relevant countries both in terms of natural resources and political and economic clout, like Russia and China, have decided not to participate in the initiative. Finally, the absence of an effective sanctions system to be applied in case of non-compliance represents at the moment one of the most relevant limitations.

Notwithstanding these serious deficiencies, on the positive side it has to be recognized that the EITI has sealed the emergence of a norm of transparency at the international level, which is capable of generating a virtuous circle based on the following dynamics: Governments seek to obtain advantages through the creation of a reputation for transparency while international actors encourage transparency reforms [David-Barrett and Okamura, 2016]. Furthermore, although the impact of EITI membership on corruption in mineral-rich countries appears still obscure also because the relatively short life of the initiative prevents from appreciating changes in corruption over long time periods, a recent empirical study has suggested that participation in the scheme can offset to a large extent the tendency of mineral rents to fuel corruption [Papyrakis *et al.*, 2017].

To illustrate how this international initiative has been concretely adopted by national states, it follows a brief analysis of the Nigerian experience. The decision to focus on Nigeria is based, on the one hand, on the crucial geopolitical importance that such a country has acquired in its continent and, on the other, on the serious problems of corruption connected with the exploitation of its natural resources that it has historically faced.

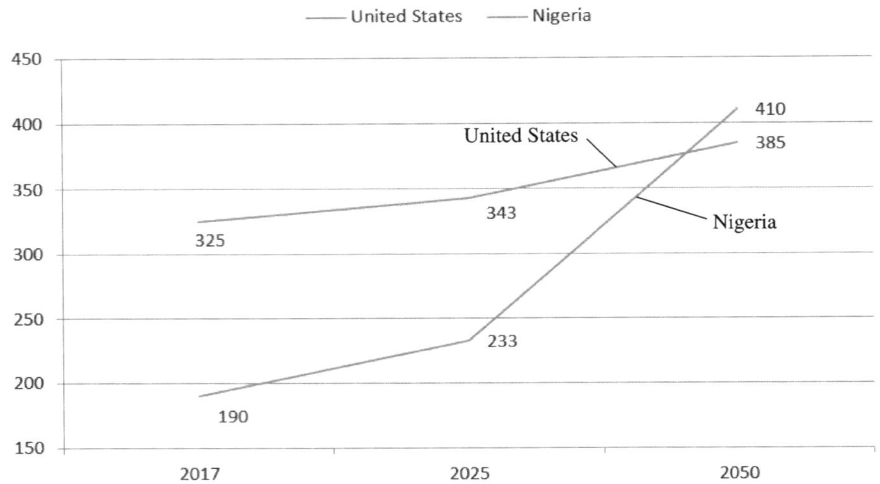

Fig. 2. US and Nigeria World Bank population estimates 2017–2050 (in millions).

Although the Nigerian economy was hit hard by the decline in oil prices that began in 2014, which caused an outright contraction in 2016 [Ibrahim *et al.*, 2017], Nigeria is among the biggest African economies together with South Africa and Egypt. The oil and gas sector continues to play a significant role in the economy of the country and accounts 77% of total revenue to the government. With more than 190 million inhabitants, it is also an extremely populous country, which accounts for almost 50% of West Africa's population, and has one of the largest populations of youth in the world.[10] According to the World Bank estimates (see Fig. 2), in 2050 the overall population of Nigeria will surpass that of United States.

Moreover, in Nigeria, corruption has always represented the main tool for allowing foreign companies like Shell to access the country's oil and gas resources [Frynas *et al.*, 2000]. The perpetration of corrupt practices has, in turn, generated substantial health and environmental risks in the country. Suffice here to mention the tremendous amount of crude oil spilled from oil pipelines in the Niger delta and the related tragic effects produced on the soil and the local population [Ordinioha and Brisibe, 2013].

Although Nigeria has always represented the quintessence of the countries plagued by the resource curse, it became with Azerbaijan one of the early adopters of the EITI in 2003. The main reason behind the decision to implement the EITI in Nigeria, which was taken by the then finance minister Ngozi Okonjo-Iweala

[10] www.worldbank.org/en/country/nigeria/overview.

with the full support of the then President Obasanjo, was to build an international reputation for reforming governance and fighting corruption in order to gain concrete rewards from the international community of donors, lenders and peers [David-Barrett and Okamura, 2016]. The following excerpts from a sensitive US document of 27 October 2003, whose official publication had been prevented by the authorities until it was unveiled by WikiLeaks, are emblematic of such an approach:

> "Okonjo-Iweala is still prickly about what she considered U.S. hesitation about her reform plans [...] While acknowledging that the foreign skepticism is born of experience with Nigeria, she said that the U.S. would be of great assistance if it would provide some concrete political support. The technical assistance the U.S. and others can provide is useful, she said, but what she really needs is for the U.S. and others to promise certain concrete responses in return for concrete Nigerian reform steps. [...] Okonjo-Iweala said that EITI is only one step, of many, toward full GON [Government of Nigeria] transparency. She stressed that the GON was not signing up to a British plan any more than it was signing up to a U.S. plan [...] She and the new economic team represent the best chance that Nigeria has had for years for some real movement forward. The question is whether the necessary political backing is there for her to realize essential parts of her program [...] Providing rhetorical support is good, but that will not go too far with the very direct and down-to-earth Okonjo-Iweala. Better and more effective will be whatever can be identified in the way of concrete USG support for measurable GON progress in the area of transparency and other reforms."[11]

This demonstrates what kind of leverage the adoption of international projects may exert at both the international and internal level, as well as the critical importance of developing these legal instruments in triggering a virtuous circle of reform despite their voluntary nature. The program, which was formally launched in February 2004, received from the beginning support from an impressive group of stakeholders and was also backed by the Nigerian legislature through the 2007 EITI Act. In this way Nigeria has gone beyond the basic implementation of the project, requiring the open publication of not only aggregated payments from all companies to government, but also the breakdown by individual company, production field and category of payment [Eigen, 2007]. Such approach to EITI has to be welcomed because, as the experience gained in other participating countries has demonstrated, in the absence of supporting national legislation EITI by itself might not be sufficient to compel all companies to report.

[11] https://wikileaks.org/plusd/cables/03ABUJA1853_a.html.

According to the reports issued by the EITI board, it appears that the country has embarked on the road of reforms seriously. Nigeria has so far published EITI Reports covering 15 fiscal years in oil and gas, and 7 fiscal years in solid minerals, which have led to recovery of more than USD 2.4 billion for the Federal Government. Finally, on 11 January 2017, the EITI Board included Nigeria among the few countries that have made meaningful progress in implementing the 2016 EITI Standard to date. As it emerges from the Validation Report of 11 October 2016,[12] although the country is yet to conform many of its procedures to the EITI Standard, it has an impressive history of over a decade of implementation, contributing to a national debate regarding governance of extractive industries, greater public understanding of the extractives sector and a culture of transparency and accountability in the area. In particular, according to the independent validator, the sectors in which the Nigerian Government has obtained the best results include *inter alia* Government Engagement, Monitoring Production — Exploration Data, Distribution of Extractive Industry Revenues, and Outcomes and Impact — Public Debate; whereas the areas of Policy on Contract Disclosure and Revenue Collection — Transportation Revenues have been classified as inadequate.

5. Corporate America and the Never-ending Battle Against Transparency

In America, everything started with the Watergate scandals, which unexpectedly brought into the public domain the circumstance that some of the major American corporations, like Gulf Oil, Exxon and Lockheed, had paid bribes to foreign public officials and politicians on a massive scale. The public condemnation that followed the scandals resulted in the enactment of the Foreign Corrupt Practices Act (FCPA), whose adoption has constituted a point of no return permanently changing the rule of the global trade game [Grasso, 2017]. Although the FCPA severely punishes the perpetration of corrupt practices abroad, it does not include any mandatory requirement of disclosing the payments made by corporations to foreign governments. Such a gap became evident only after several years with the occurrence of the financial crisis of 2008, which was triggered the previous year when the collapse of the US housing prices unveiled the rotten US mortgage-backed securities (subprime) that had been widely sold to and insured throughout the world's major financial institutions [Dignam, 2013]. This dramatic event, which

---

[12] https://eiti.org/nigeria#validation.

is widely considered as one of the worst economic crisis of all times, not only exposed the weaknesses of the financial system but also demonstrated that the regulatory system was incapable of monitoring the risks generated by the extremely complex business operations that characterize the global trade [Kelleher, 2016]. In 2010, the US government responded through the enactment of the Dodd–Frank Wall Street Reform and Consumer Protection Act (hereinafter "Dodd–Frank Act"), whose express purpose is "to promote the financial stability of the United States by improving accountability and transparency in the financial system." The act, which can be considered as the most comprehensive reform of the country's financial laws since the Great Depression, aims at minimizing the probability that the financial sector might incur distress through the establishment of specific regulatory and market arrangements and the promotion of a higher level of transparency. In particular, among the new rules introduced by the act, Section 1504, which is entitled "Disclosure Of Payments By Resource Extraction Issuers," expressly provides that companies in the extractive industries (oil, gas and mining) have to publicly disclose the amounts that they pay to foreign governments in connection with projects abroad. The act specifies that: "To the extent practicable, the rules [...] shall support the commitment of the Federal Government to international transparency promotion efforts relating to the commercial development of oil, natural gas, or minerals." However, the Dodd–Frank Act essentially being a framework law, its Section 1504 lacks direct applicability. The same provision establishes that "not later than 270 days after the date of enactment" of the act the Securities and Exchange Commission (SEC) "shall issue final rules that require each resource extraction issuer to include in an annual report [...] information relating to any payment made [...] to a foreign government." Notwithstanding such an express provision, Section 1504 has not been implemented yet. In truth, although the SEC made several attempts to finalize the rule mandated by the act, its efforts have always been frustrated by the energy firms, which have spared no expense in financing a relentless war to annihilate the financial reform. Like what the big Wall Street firms have done in relation to other parts of the Dodd–Frank Act, at every stage of the rule-making process, the energy companies through their lobbyists and political allies have aggressively opposed the implementation of the act carrying out actions consisting in: lobbying the regulatory agency as the implementing rules were being considered, proposed and finalized; filing lawsuits challenging the rules promulgated by the agency when they did not come out the way they desired; filing bills and amendments to annihilate the implementing rules [Kelleher, 2016].

In particular, when the implementing rule was initially adopted by the SEC on 22 August 2012, the American Petroleum Institute, which is the main lobbying organization for the oil and gas industry, together with the US Chamber of Commerce and two other industry groups challenged it in court. On 2 July 2013, the US District Court for the District of Columbia considered the rule invalid and vacated it.

To fulfill its duties, the SEC had structured the rule in such a way that it compelled the public disclosure of corporate reports and did not grant any exemption in the event that the business operation was carried out in countries that prohibit disclosure of payments. Such a decision was met with resistance and criticism by energy companies that, on the one hand, wanted to file their reports confidentially with the Commission and, on the other, were concerned about potential losses of many billions of dollars in countries like Angola, Cameroon, China and Qatar, which prohibit disclosure of payment information.

It is interesting to analyze the reasons why the court considered such rules, which clearly represented positive steps to assure that the spirit of the law was respected, as invalid. As regards the decision to include the public disclosure requirement, the court asserted that it was invalid because neither the dictionary definition nor the ordinary meaning of the word "report" contained such an obligation, and that, although the SEC could have taken such a decision exercising its administrative discretion, it emerged that the Commission intended to adopt it on the unjustified assumption that it was Congress' judgment that such a regulation was desirable or required. Concerning the choice not to grant any exemption for when disclosure is prohibited by foreign governments, it was deemed by the court as "arbitrary and capricious."[13]

The SEC amended and issued the rule again only in 2016.[14] In the new rule, the Commission reaffirmed its decision to require the public disclosure of corporate reports. On this occasion, the independent agency specified it believed that requiring public disclosure would best accomplish the purpose of the statute and that it was exercising its discretion "to adopt final rules that require issuers to disclose the full payment information publicly, including the identity of the issuer." Concerning the exemption issue, the Commission reconsidered its original choice so to mitigate any potential competitive harm that issuers might experience where their business operations were conducted in countries not allowing disclosure of payment information. However, from the SEC perspective, the adoption of a blanket exemption was inopportune because it could lead foreign governments

---

[13]*American Petroleum Institute et al v. Securities And Exchange Commission*, Civil Action No. 12-1668 (JDB), filed on 2 July 2013, www.sec.gov/rules/final/2013/34-67717-court-decision-vacatin g-rule.pdf.

[14]www.sec.gov/rules/final/2016/34-78167.pdf.

to introduce anti-disclosure laws to prevent the disclosures. On the contrary, the Commission opted for a case-by-case approach to exemptive relief, which would permit it to tailor the exemptions to the particular facts and circumstances presented by the company and allow the development of alternative forms of disclosure that might comply with the foreign country's laws or the phasing out of the exemption over an appropriate period of time. Such a decision was wise and balanced, also because the scenario depicted by the independent agency is far from hypothetical. History teaches us that less developed countries often compete against each other through the so-called "race to the bottom," also known as "race of laxity," which is characterized by "the progressive movement of capital and technology from countries with relatively high levels of wages, taxation and regulation to countries with relatively lower levels" [Spar and Yoffie, 1999]. In other words, according to the logic of unregulated globalization, on the one hand, developing countries try to attract foreign investments by depressing their regulations and, on the other, multinational corporations, guided by a social irresponsible profit-making logic, predictably move their business operations to nations that adopt laxer regulatory standards, fomenting in this way such a perverse phenomenon. To avoid competitive harm, the Commission also introduced an exemption, consisting in a 1-year delay in reporting of payments to foreign governments so to prevent the disclosure of commercially sensitive information in connection with exploratory activities conducted prior to the beginning of the extractive operations.

However, also this new rule, which was planned to be effective as of 25 September 2016, met with determined opposition from the energy companies lobby, which on this occasion received the support of their Republican allies in the Congress shortly after Donald John Trump was elected president of the United States. As a matter of fact, on 3 February 2017, with a resolution sponsored by 34 Republican Representatives,[15] the US Congress nullified the rules that the SEC issued in 2016 to implement Section 1504 of the Dodd–Frank Act. The circumstance that Rex Tillerson, Trump's new secretary of state, personally lobbied against those transparency rules when he was Exxon's top executive as well as the following statement made by James Inhofe, senator from Oklahoma and member of the Republican Party who once displayed a snowball in Congress to demonstrate that global warming wasn't happening [Bump, 2015], are emblematic of the situation described so far:

[15]See US Congress Joint Resolution H.J.Res.41 of 3 February 2017.

> "Section 1504 of the Dodd–Frank bill requires the Securities and Exchange Commission to develop a rule that requires companies to report payments made to a foreign government or the U.S. Federal Government relating to the commercial development of oil, natural gas, and minerals [. . .] While that may not sound all that significant, it strikes at the heart of American competitiveness. It makes public the information of our very best companies on how to win oil and gas deals. It requires companies to disclose and make public highly confidential and commercially sensitive information, and this is information that foreign competitors don't have to provide. Under this regulation, we would be required to provide it. That means that American companies would have to disclose all of the background and sensitive information that companies develop in competing for contracts of some kind having to do with oil and gasoline. It could be with another country, like Iran. It could be with individuals over there who are not friendly to the United States. Countries that don't wish to disclose the details of their commercial deals would now have a strong incentive to go with companies in countries that don't have that burdensome requirement. That is only natural."[16]

Moreover, under the new Trump's administration, even the American participation in the Extractive Industries Transparency Initiative (EITI) appears to be questioned. Although a spokesperson for Interior Secretary said afterwards that the US remain "committed to the principles and goals of EITI including transparency and good governance of the extractive sectors...," in April 2017 the US Department of the Interior announced its intention to halt the work on implementing the global transparency initiative [Milin, 2017].

The American experience represents a tough lesson to learn. The sad reality is that, although in response to the financial crisis the Dodd–Frank Act was presented to Americans as the cure for the deep-rooted unfairness of the economic system, after almost a decade many of its key provisions have not been implemented yet. This shows that, where strong economic interests are at stake, even the most developed societies face almost insurmountable obstacles in their efforts to foster transparency and eradicate corruption. This is in part due to corporate lobbying by which a disproportionate amount of money is spent for safeguarding a narrow range of private interests. As some scholars have highlighted, in the US over the last decades large donors have contributed a disproportionate amount of campaign money, and these small elite groups have overwhelmingly favored Republicans [Tomain, 2017]. This is particularly true in the energy sector where the corporations have the means and power to oppose any attempt to introduce rules that are uncongenial for them,

[16] Congressional Record, 30 January 2017, 115th Congress, 1st Session, Vol. 163, No. 15.

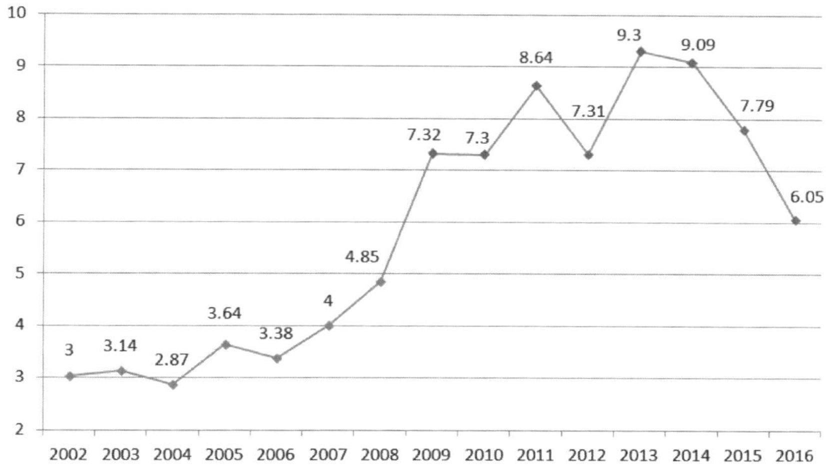

Fig. 3. OpenSecrets — Annual lobbying expenditure by American Petroleum Institute, 2002–2017 (in millions of US dollars). www.opensecrets.org/lobby/clientsum.php?id=D000031493&year=2013.

and may relentlessly lobby for protecting their economic interests irrespective of the circumstance that such an activity might generate significant human and social costs. On the basis of these premises, it is not surprising that the Republicans have sided firmly with the energy firms in the above-mentioned battle and have decided to protect the competitiveness of US energy companies even if this might entail giving the green light to secret and potentially corrupt deals abroad. Such an argument also sheds light on the considerable increase that has been recorded in the American Petroleum Institute's lobbying activity from 2009 to 2016, i.e. the period from the occurrence of the financial crisis, which sparked off the regulatory debate on transparency, to the advent of the Trump's administration, which represents the end of the threat for the American energy companies (see Fig. 3). In 2013, such a spending reached the highest peak of $9,300,000.

The American experience implicitly demonstrates also that the payment of bribes and the perpetration of other corrupt practices are still a common way of conducting business, especially in less developed countries. Such a discouraging scenario has sent a troubling message about the US government's changing stance on anti-corruption, and challenged the so far unquestioned leadership the US have historically assumed on these issues at the global level.

6. The European Union's Efforts to Foster Corporate Transparency

The global nature of the financial crisis of 2008 raised the awareness about the need for profound changes in market regulation also among the European governments.

Such a necessity was felt as well at the Europe Union level, where it was recognized that major reforms, which often paralleled the ones introduced in the US through the Dodd–Frank Act, were to be put in place.

In particular, as regards the energy sector, the European Parliament and Council of the European Union adopted two directives that included payment disclosure rules: The EU Accounting Directive 2013[17] and the EU Transparency Directive 2013.[18] As directives do not normally have direct effect and have to be transposed into domestic law, these two legal instruments did not include immediately applicable rules. As a matter of fact, directives, which are binding as to the result to be achieved upon the Member States, leave to the national authorities the choice of form and methods of implementation within a timeframe set out in the directives themselves [Becker and Campbell, 2007]. Specifically, the EU Accounting Directive established that Member States had to bring into force its provisions by 20 July 2015, whereas the EU Transparency Directive granted the Member States a period of 24 months, which expired at the end of November 2015.

The two directives closely resemble each other in that they determine the applicability and scope of the disclosure requirements. However, while the EU Accounting Directive aims at imposing disclosure requirements on corporations incorporated under the laws of an EU Member State or those of a European Economic Area (EEA) country, the provisions of the EU Transparency Directive have to be applied by every company listed on EU-regulated markets even if not registered in the EEA or incorporated in other countries.

Recitals 44 and 45 of the EU Accounting Directive explain in clear terms the background to and the aims of the European legislation. They also highlight the interconnections between those measures and the international efforts to foster corporate transparency in the energy sector:

> "In order to provide for enhanced transparency of payments made to governments, large undertakings and public-interest entities which are active in the extractive industry or logging of primary forests should

[17] Directive 2013/34/EU of the European Parliament and of the Council of 26 June 2013 on the annual financial statements, consolidated financial statements and related reports of certain types of undertakings, amending Directive 2006/43/EC of the European Parliament and of the Council and repealing Council Directives 78/660/EEC and 83/349/EEC.

[18] Directive 2013/50/EU of the European Parliament and of the Council of 22 October 2013 amending Directive 2004/109/EC of the European Parliament and of the Council on the harmonization of transparency requirements in relation to information about issuers whose securities are admitted to trading on a regulated market, Directive 2003/71/EC of the European Parliament and of the Council on the prospectus to be published when securities are offered to the public or admitted to trading and Commission Directive 2007/14/EC laying down detailed rules for the implementation of certain provisions of Directive 2004/109/EC.

> disclose material payments made to governments in the countries in which they operate in a separate report, on an annual basis. Such undertakings are active in countries rich in natural resources, in particular minerals, oil, natural gas and primary forests. The report should include types of payments comparable to those disclosed by an undertaking participating in the Extractive Industries Transparency Initiative (EITI) [...] The report should serve to help governments of resource-rich countries to implement the EITI principles and criteria and account to their citizens for payments such governments receive from undertakings active in the extractive industry or loggers of primary forests operating within their jurisdiction."
> "In order to provide for enhanced transparency of payments made to governments, large undertakings and public-interest entities which are active in the extractive industry or logging of primary forests should disclose material payments made to governments in the countries in which they operate in a separate report, on an annual basis. Such undertakings are active in countries rich in natural resources, in particular minerals, oil, natural gas and primary forests. The report should include types of payments comparable to those disclosed by an undertaking participating in the Extractive Industries Transparency Initiative (EITI) [...] The report should serve to help governments of resource-rich countries to implement the EITI principles and criteria and account to their citizens for payments such governments receive from undertakings active in the extractive industry or loggers of primary forests operating within their jurisdiction."

As regards their content, under the EU Accounting Directive the term "payment" has to be interpreted as any amount paid, whether in money or in kind, for activities involving the exploration, prospection, discovery, development and extraction of minerals, oil, natural gas deposits and similar resources.[19] The directive sets a threshold of EUR 100,000, whether made as a single payment or as a series of related payments within a given financial year, for determining the relevance of any payment to the disclosure regime. It is interesting to notice that such a threshold closely resembles the rule proposed in 2016 by the US Securities and Exchange Commission, under which only payments that equal or exceed $100,000 during the most recent fiscal year were considered *not de minimis*. Disclosure of payments is made on a per project and per government basis. Under the directive the report shall disclose, in respect of any relevant financial year, the total amount of payments made to each government and specify where those payments have been attributed to a specific project. The directive also requires the Member States to impose the

[19] See EU Accounting Directive 2013, Chapter 10, Article 41.

disclosure of payments made to foreign governments on an annual basis and in a public way.[20]

The European Union's efforts that led to the adoption of the Accounting Directive and Transparency Directive in 2013 have to be praised. However, the effectiveness of these measures in curbing corporate corruption in resource-rich countries appears doubtful. It is possible to identify a serious deficiency in the way in which the recipients of the payments have been defined. The directives consider relevant only payments made to foreign governments, which in turn are defined as "any national, regional or local authority of a Member State or of a third country. It includes a department, agency or undertaking controlled by that authority."[21] As it is structured the rule does not require the disclosure of payments made to private entities such as agents, intermediaries and local partners. The European legislature seems to have ignored that the most popular method of hiding the payment of bribes consists in simulating apparently legitimate expenses, corresponding to invoices submitted by third parties for totally or partially sham services [Dell'Osso, 2014]. Those third parties, which act on behalf of the company and have relevant contacts with key governmental authorities, are often used as the vehicle for paying bribes. To interrupt the connecting link between the corporation and the government, different methods may be used such as paying the unjustified fees in cash so to prevent the further traceability of the movement of money. This emerged, for instance, during the investigations carried out in the UK by the Serious Fraud Office in relation to a case of transnational bribery perpetrated in Tanzania, which consisted in the payment of a large fee by Standard Bank to a third party company, Enterprise Growth Market Advisors (EGMA), in order to obtain the green light for a US $600 million private placement on behalf of the local government. Specifically, a fee of US $6 million was withdrawn in cash and paid to EGMA even if: there was no evidence that the payment to EGMA represented reasonable consideration for services rendered on the financial transaction; no evidence was found to suggest that EGMA won a tender to provide the alleged advisory services on the deal; EGMA's chairman was a serving member of the Government of Tanzania throughout the currency of this transaction as Commissioner of the Tanzania Revenue Authority and one of its three shareholders and directors was the former Chief Executive Officer of the Tanzanian Capital Markets and Securities Authority [Grasso, 2016]. As a result, in order to make it more effective the corporate transparency rules, it was necessary to make it compulsory for energy companies to disclose also the payments made to private

[20] See EU Accounting Directive 2013, Chapter 10, Articles 43 and 45.
[21] See EU Accounting Directive 2013, Chapter 10, Article 41(3).

agents, intermediaries and other third parties where those payments were attributed to a specific project falling within the relevant categories.

To illustrate how the European initiative has been concretely adopted by national states, it follows a brief analysis of the way in which the directives have been implemented in the UK, which has been the first country to transpose the new rules into national law in December 2014. Then, the Italian implementing law will be examined from a comparative perspective. The decision to focus on these two countries is based on the circumstance that they are the home countries of giant energy companies like British Petroleum and ENI that have historically been enmeshed in corruption.

In the UK, the implementing rules were adopted by the Financial Conduct Authority (FCA), which is a financial regulatory body that is financed by charging fees to members of the financial services industry and operates independently of the government. It is the conduct regulator for some 56,000 financial services companies.[22]

Section 89A of the Financial Services and Markets Act 2000 has empowered the FCA to make rules for the purposes of the transparency obligations directive. Consequently, the Authority included them in its Disclosure Guidance and Transparency Rules (DTRs) sourcebook.[23] The measures came into force on 26 November 2015. In particular, part 4.3A of the DTRs, which is entitled "Reports on payments to governments," is applicable to any issuer: (1) active in the extractive or logging of primary forest industries; (2) whose transferable securities are admitted to trading; and (3) whose Home State is the United Kingdom.[24] The rules provide that such issuers must prepare a report annually on payments made to governments for each financial year,[25] that the reports must be filed with the FCA[26] and made public at the latest 6 months after the end of each financial year.[27] It is also provided that the issuers must ensure that the reports remain publicly available for at least 10 years.[28] As regards the content of the documents, the rules refer simply and effectively to the EU Directive stating that "the report on payments to governments must be prepared in accordance with Chapter 10 of the Accounting Directive,"[29] and that

[22] www.fca.org.uk/about/the-fca.

[23] www.handbook.fca.org.uk/handbook/DTR.pdf.

[24] See The FCA's Disclosure Guidance and Transparency Rules, s. 4.3A1.

[25] ibid, s. 4.3A.4.

[26] ibid, s. 4.3A.10(1).

[27] ibid, s. 4.3A.5.

[28] ibid, s. 4.3A.6.

[29] ibid, s. 4.3A.7(1).

"Payments to governments must be reported at consolidated level."[30] In case of violations the issuers are subject to the sanctioning power of the FCA as provided by Section 1.5.3 of the DTRs, which establishes that: "If the FCA considers that an issuer [. . .] has breached any of the disclosure requirements it may [. . .] impose on that person a financial penalty or publish a statement censuring that person." Such a provision implements the parts of the EU directives that expressly mandate the adoption of "effective, proportionate and dissuasive" sanctioning regimes in the Member States.[31]

To understand how these rules are currently working in practice, it is possible to examine the Report on payments to governments issued by British Petroleum (BP) and published according to the above-mentioned rules. Specifically, BP has published two reports so far: the first one related to the fiscal year ended 31 December 2015,[32] and the second one related to the fiscal year ended 31 December 2016.[33] The reports, which are about 30 pages long, seem to fall also within the context of the corporate social responsibility (CSR) activities carried out by the company in that they also include the following statement of principle: "[BP] supports the concept of transparency in revenue flows from oil and gas activities in resource-rich countries. It helps citizens of affected countries access the information they need to hold governments to account for the way they use funds received through taxes and other agreements." According to the reports, BP paid to foreign governments an overall amount of US $15,198 in 2015 and US $12,930.4 in 2016, half of which were directed solely to Azerbaijan (respectively, US $8,258.8 and US $6,290.4). The reports also include a breakdown by country, which identifies the specific local authority that received the money.

In Italy, the implementing rules were adopted through the enactment of Legislative Decree no. 139 of 18 August 2015.[34] Although in the Italian statute the provisions of the directives have been transposed in full, the final result appears to be the same. In particular, also under the Italian law the reports on payments to governments have to be not only submitted to the national business register but also published so to remain in the public domain for at least 10 years.[35] The most relevant

---

30 ibid, s. 4.3A.7(2).

31 See EU Accounting Directive 2013, Article 51 and EU Transparency Directive 2013, Article 28.

32 www.bp.com/content/dam/bp/pdf/sustainability/group-reports/bp-report-on-payments-to-governments-2015.pdf.

33 www.bp.com/content/dam/bp/en/corporate/pdf/sustainability-report/group-reports/bp-report-on-payments-to-governments-2016.pdf.

34 www.gazzettaufficiale.it/eli/id/2015/09/04/15G00153/sg.

35 See Legislative Decree no. 139 of 18 August 2015, Article 5(1).

points of difference between the UK and Italian regulations are related to the adopted sanctioning system. As a matter of fact, under the Italian law, the responsibility of submitting and publishing lies with the corporate executives. Article 5(2) of the Legislative Decree provides that where the reports are not submitted, are submitted more than 60 days after the deadline of 6 months from the end of each fiscal year, or include false information, the involved corporate executives shall on conviction be liable to imprisonment for a term not exceeding 1 year and to a fine not exceeding EUR 120,000.[36] As a result, the Italian government instead of opting for corporate liability has decided to criminalize the corporate executives' misconducts. Such a choice raises some doubts as to the effectiveness, proportionality and dissuasiveness of the sanction. Even though criminal sanctions are generally considered as more serious than the administrative ones, the Italian authorities have resorted to a minor offense, which is comparable to a misdemeanor. Consequently, short statutes of limitations are applicable, the imprisonment can be easily avoided and the fine hardly seems to create a real deterrent effect where it is applied to top executives of huge corporations. This, especially taking into consideration that any intentional violation of the disclosure requirements would be logically justified by the necessity of putting a veil of secrecy over a business operation of strategic importance and/or hiding serious cases of transnational corruption. From a positive point of view, it is possible to observe that, under the Italian law, for such kind of minor offenses prosecutors do not have the daunting task of proving intent because to constitute the crime is sufficient the least level of culpability of negligence. A more adequate sanctioning system would have combined individual and corporate liability by means of the inclusion of the above-mentioned offense in the list of the predicate offenses for which corporations can be deemed liable under Legislative Decree no. 231 of 2001, which introduced in the Italian legal system the liability regime for corporations involved in criminal conducts.

Another element that emerges from a comparative analysis of the British and Italian rules is the lack of consistency in the way in which the reports are drafted. While BP has published its reports in English expressing all the figures in US dollars, ENI has published it in Italian expressing all the figures in euros. Such inconsistency might represent an issue frustrating the efforts of conducting a comparative analysis among the European countries. Without prejudice to the possibility of publishing the reports in the official language of each country, the directives should have mandated the obligation of publishing them in English expressing all the figures in US dollars,

[36]ibid, Article 5(3).

which are respectively, the language and the currency used in the vast majority of international transactions.

In any case, although the efforts to ensure higher levels of corporate transparency in the energy sector are still at the beginning stages, the implementation of the above-mentioned transparency rules in the European Union appears a good start. This not only because the publication of the reports may trigger a virtuous circle of declining corruption at the global level but also because such level of transparency allows international experts and scholars to conduct research activities that were earlier impossible. As a mere example, it is now possible to investigate the potential link between the significant amount of money that Azerbaijan has received by energy companies in the latest years and its sudden decision of leaving the Extractive Industries Transparency Initiative (EITI) after that on 10 March 2017 its membership was suspended due to concerns about limits on civic freedoms in the South Caucasus country.[37]

7. Conclusion

This work has shown that, although significant positive developments have been recently recorded, the path to establishing an adequate level of corporate transparency and eradicating corruption in the energy sector is still long and strewn with obstacles at every turn. The critical discrepancies in the global fight against corruption, the weak rule of law and malfunctioning bureaucracy that characterize many resource-rich developing countries and the stubborn resistance to change from the corporate world, have been all identified as the most serious problems that have to be confronted.

The enabling environment for promoting transparent business transactions in the energy sector requires a multifaceted and multileveled approach, which combines the action of the international organizations with a collective response by businesses, governments and non-governmental organizations at both the international and domestic level. The awareness of adopting a worldwide approach to these issues has increased over the years as the statement included in recital 53 of the EU Accounting Directive 2013 illustrates: "In line with the conclusions of the G8 Summit in Deauville in May 2011 and in order to promote a level international playing field, the Commission should continue to encourage all the international partners to introduce similar requirements concerning reporting on payments to

[37] https://eiti.org/azerbaijan.

governments. Continued work on the relevant international accounting standard is particularly important in this context." However, the protectionist and isolationistic tendencies recently adopted by some national governments pose a major threat to the positive results that have been achieved so far. In particular, the complete change in the United States' anti-corruption strategy under the Trump's administration entails the risk of triggering a domino effect that could let the world slip back to the old days where multinational corporations corrupted with impunity to secure profitable contracts. It is hard to believe that the other virtuous countries will continue to impose on their companies transparency rules that are more stringent than the ones applicable to the firms of the world's biggest economy.

In particular, as regards the corporate world, although it is reasonable that the energy companies need to protect commercially sensitive information, such a necessity cannot justify an approach that foments the perpetration of corrupt practices and all the adverse consequences related to them. There is a need for a profound cultural change in the corporate world, without which effective results will be difficult to be achieved. As the American experience has taught, multinational corporations are key players in our societies and, thanks to the immense power and wealth that is concentrated in their hands, they can effectively resist to any attempt to regulate their business activities. Consequently, it is necessary to convince them of the importance of adopting a responsible way of acting. An initial step to address this issue could be implementing voluntary and/or mandatory corporate social responsibility measures aiming at achieving a more conscientious use of corporate lobbying. For instance, it could be imposed on corporations an obligation to disclose and publish if they or their partners employ, even as external consultants, ex-politicians or public officials or their relatives or close friends. Another solution could consist in requiring firms to publicly disclose and motivate the specific aims of their lobbying activities. In any case, due to their novelty, it will be necessary to wait in order to appreciate the effects of the transparency measures that have been undertaken so far at both the international and domestic level. Such a necessity and the circumstance that no comprehensive empirical study has focused exclusively on the effects of transparency initiatives on corruption within the energy industry will surely lead experts to pursue a rich and rigorous research agenda in the near future.

References

Bac, M. (2001). Corruption, connections and transparency: Does a better screen imply a better scene? *Public Choice* **107** (1), 87–96.

Bahar, R. (2007). Transparency as a Problem. In L. Thévenoz and R. Bahar. (eds.) *Conflicts of Interest: Corporate Governance and Financial Markets*. (Kluwer Law International, The Netherlands).

Ball, C. (2009). What is transparency? *Public Integrity* **11** (4), 293–308.

Becker, F. and Campbell, A. (2007). The direct effect of European directives: Towards the final act. *Columbia Journal of European Law* **13** (2), 401–426.
Bellver, A. and Kaufmann, D. (2005). "Transparenting Transparency" Initial Empirics and Policy Applications. *World Bank Policy Research*, Working Paper, 1–73.
Bremmer, I. (2017). The Real Cost of "Forced Transparency." *Time* **189** (11), 14.
Brittain, V. (2011). Frederick Chiluba obituary. *The Guardian*. www.theguardian.com/world/2011/jun/19/frederick-chiluba-obituary.
Bump, P. (2015). Jim Inhofe's snowball has disproven climate change once and for all. *The Washington Post*. www.washingtonpost.com/news/the-fix/wp/2015/02/26/jim-inhofes-snowball-has-disproven-climate-change-once-and-for-all/?utm_term=.58f79d5eca20.
David-Barrett, E. and Okamura, K. (2016). Norm diffusion and reputation: The rise of the extractive industries transparency initiative. *Governance* **29** (2), 227–246.
Dell'Osso, V. (2014). Empirical Features of International Bribery Practices: Evidence from Foreign Corrupt Practice Act Enforcement Actions. In S. Manacorda, F. Centonze and G. Forti, (eds.) *Preventing Corporate Corruption* (Springer, Switzerland).
Dignam, A. J. (2013). The future of shareholder democracy in the shadow of the financial crisis. *Seattle University Law Review* **36**, 639–694.
Eigen, P. (2007). Fighting corruption in a global economy: Transparency initiatives in the oil and gas industry. *Houston Journal of International Law* **29**, 327–354.
Eniola, D. (2017). No winner emerged in 2016 Mo Ibrahim Foundation's leadership Prize. *The Guardian — Nigeria*, https://guardian.ng/news/no-winner-emerged-in-2016-mo-ibrahim-foundations-leadership-prize/.
Frynas, J. G., Beck M. P. and Mellahi K. (2000). Maintaining corporate dominance after decolonization: The "first Mover advantage" of Shell-BP in Nigeria. *Review of African Political Economy* **27** (85), 407–425.
Frynas, J. G. (2010). Corporate social responsibility and societal governance: Lessons from transparency in the oil and gas sector. *Journal of Business Ethics* **93**, 163–179.
Garsten, C. and Lindth de Montoya, M. (2008) Introduction: Examining the politics of transparency. In C. Garsten, and M. Lindth de Montoya, (eds.), *Transparency in a New Global Order* (Edward Elgar, United Kingdom).
Gilbert, J. (2016). Land grabbing, investors, and indigenous peoples: New legal strategies for an old practice? *Community Development Journal* **51** (3), 350–366.
Grasso, C. (2016). Peaks and troughs of the English deferred prosecution agreement: The lesson learned from the DPA between the SFO and ICBC SB PLC. *Journal of Business Law* **5**, 388–408.
Grasso, C. (2017). The dark side of power: corruption and bribery within the energy industry. In R. Leal-Arcas, and J. Wouters, (eds.), *Research Handbook on EU Energy Law and Policy* (Edward Elgar, London).
Guzman, A. T. and Meyer, T. L. (2010). International soft law. *Journal of Legal Analysis* **2** (1), 171–225.
Ibrahim, M., Saito, M., Tamene, M., Tapsoba S. J. and Swiston, A. (2017). Nigeria: Selected Issues. *International Monetary Fund*, IMF Country Report No. 17/81, pp. 1–56.
Kelleher, D. M., Hall, S. W. and Medina, F. (2016). The Dodd–Frank act is working and will protect the American people if it is not killed before fully implemented. *North Cardina Banking Institute* **20**, 127–144.
Khan, H. A. (1999). Corporate Governance of Family Businesses in Asia: What's Right and What's Wrong? Asian Development Bank, ADBI Research Papers, https://www.adb.org/sites/default/files/publication/157212/adbi-rp3.pdf.
Klitgaard, R. (1991). *Controlling Corruption* (University of California Press, Los Angeles).
Kolstad, I. and Wiig, A. (2009). Is transparency the key to reducing corruption in resource-rich countries? *World Development* **37** (3), 521–532.

Leal-Arcas, R., Grasso, C. and Alemany Ríos, J. (2016). *Energy Security, Trade and the EU: Regional and International Perspectives* (Edward Elgar, London).

Mehlum, H., Moene, K. and Torvik, R. (2006). Institutions and the resource curse. *The Economic Journal* **116**, 1–20.

Messik, R. (2015). The Case of the Disappearing Transparency Report. *GAB*. https://globalanticorruptionblog.com/2015/11/04/the-case-of-the-disappearing-transparency-report.

Milin, Z. (2017). US Govt. signals it may reverse domestic steps on extractive industry revenue transparency — move is counter to global trend. *Business and Human Rights Resource Centre*. https://business-humanrights.org/en/us-govt-signals-it-may-reverse-domestic-steps-on-extractive-industry-revenue-transparency-move-is-counter-to-global-trend.

Möslein, F. and Reinsehuber, K. (2012). Transparency. In Basedow, J. *et al.* (eds.), *The Max Plank Encyclopaedia of European Private Law* (Oxford University Press, Oxford).

Obama, B. (2006). Does the legislative transparency and accountability act provide for sufficient reforms? *Congressional Digest* **85** (5), 138–140.

Obama, B. (2009). Memorandum — Freedom of Information Act. *Federal Register* **74** (15), 4683–4684.

Ordinioha, B. and Brisibe, S. (2013). The human health implications of crude oil spills in the Niger delta, Nigeria: An interpretation of published studies. *Nigerian Medical Journal*, **54** (1), 10–16.

Papyrakis, E., Rieger, M. and Gilberthorpe, E. (2017). Corruption and the extractive industries transparency initiative. *The Journal of Development Studies* **53** (2), 295–309.

Phillips, T. (2016). China steps up Panama Papers censorship after leaders' relatives named *The Guardian*. www.theguardian.com/world/2016/apr/07/china-ramps-up-panama-papers-censorship-after-leaders-relatives-named.

Report to Congressional Committees (2000). World Bank — Management Controls Stronger, but Challenges in Fighting Corruption Remain. United States General Accounting Office. www.gao.gov/new.items/ns00073.pdf.

Robinson, J. A., Torvik, R. and Verdier T. (2006). Political foundations of the resource curse. *Journal of Development Economics* **79**, 447–468.

Scauer, F. (2011). Transparency in three dimensions, *University of Illinois Law Review 2011*, 1339–1357.

Securities and Exchange Commission. (1998). *A Plain English Handbook: How to create clear SEC disclosure documents*. www.sec.gov/pdf/handbook.pdf.

Spar, D. L. and Yoffie, D. B. (1999). Multinational enterprises and the prospects for justice. *Journal of International Affairs* **52** (2), 557–581.

Stevens, P. (2005). "Resource curse" and how to avoid it. *The Journal of Energy and Development* **31** (1), 1–20.

Stiglitz, J. E. (1999). On Liberty, the Right to Know, and Public Discourse: The Role of Transparency in Public Life. *Oxford Amnesty Lecture*. www.internationalbudget.org/wp-content/uploads/On-Liberty-the-Right-to-Know-and-Public-Discourse-The-Role-of-Transparency-in-Public-Life.pdf.

Tomain, J. P. (2017). Gridlock, lobbying, and democracy. *Wake Forest Journal of Law Policy* **7** (1), 87–140.

Chapter 17

The Hidden Role of Civil Liability in the Electronuclear Industry: Accident Costs, Insurance and Industrial Organization

Gérard Mondello

Université Côte d'Azur, GREDEG, UMR 7321, CNRS,
250, rue Albert Einstein, 06560 Valbonne, Sophia Antipolis, France
gerard.mondello@gredeg.cnrs.fr

This chapter mainly deals with the internalization process of accidents and pollution risk of nuclear energy through the setting of the nuclear third-party liability. The international treaties governing this liability regime favor a capped strict liability exclusively "channeled" through the operator. This responsibility increasingly concerns private companies. Indeed, since the end of the last century, the electronuclear energy has undergone full or partial privatization process. The underlying question bears on the compliance of the liberalization tendency with safety and care. Through a literature review, this chapter's main concern is about the research on a specific industrial organization that would optimize the safety level of electronuclear parks.

Keywords: Strict liability; capped strict liability; electronuclear energy; nuclear plants; major nuclear accident; industrial organization; monopoly; electricity markets; competition; insurance.

1. Introduction

Nowadays, the choice for civilian nuclear energy seems paradoxical. Indeed, new nuclear plants require heavy investments and generate sunk costs, while, simultaneously, the future of nuclear power is becoming fundamentally uncertain because of two major data. Indeed, this energy's survival highly depends, first, on any potential highly catastrophic accident [von Hippel, 2010, Chap. 6; Halligan *et al.*, 2017] and second, its rising building costs face continuous decrease in costs and prices of renewable energies [REN21, 2017]. As a result, nuclear power deeply divides public opinions between pro and contra [Shogren, 2011, p. 522]. Electronuclear economics is a multifaceted field. Economists deal with different matters that give the feeling of a non-unified area. For instance, studies may compare the efficiency and markets of different power sources [MIT, 2009; Bickel and Rainer, 2005; Vithayasrichareon, 2017] or, still, its operating conditions underprice uncertainty [Gollier *et al.*, 2005; Linares and Conchado, 2009]. Economic studies focused also on the plants decommissioning and the reprocessing of nuclear waste [NEA/IAEA, 2017b]. Recent works studied the evolution of building costs of nuclear plants with severe controversies about their trend ([Yip and Nordhaus, 2016; Koomey *et al.*, 2017; Grubler, 2014] among others). Lévêque [2014] aims at studying the different sources of uncertainties that affect the electronuclear sector. He establishes that looking for the effective costs of nuclear power depends on too many random factors that make their determination impossible. Quite near from the present chapter's approach, are the debates about the impact of the nuclear tort liability on the price of electricity. Most of these contributions [Dubin and Rothwell, 1990; Heyes and Heyes, 1998, 2000a, 2000b; Faure and Borre, 2008; Faure and Fiore, 2009; Rothwell, 2001] show that establishing a ceiling on damage leaves unpaid the potential external costs and, implicitly, subsidizes this industry.

Undoubtedly, the above debates nourish the present chapter's argument although the latter's primary concern is understanding how important third-party liability is in the nuclear sector industrial organization. Recall that, legally, civil liability obliges the person who caused the damage to repair it. Furthermore, an effective liability rule must encourage potential troublemakers to take significant measures to prevent accidents. Consequently, the civil nuclear liability's characteristics make conditional either its expansion or its ending.

Nowadays, international treaties governing nuclear civil liability favor a capped strict liability exclusively "channeled" through the operator (i.e. the person or the company in charge of the nuclear plant management). Without this institutional convenience for smoothing the legal consequences, this energy would not have expanded. The present study aims at finding out how the nuclear specific liability regime influences its industrial organization by regulating the radical or Knightian uncertainty that this energy creates [Knight, 1920]. Indeed, the nuclear field falls within the *Low probability, high consequences* paradigm because a nuclear station presents evolutionary risks depending on the imperfectly known combination of factors that may impact the reactors' working [Wen and Ellingwood, 2005; Kameda, 2012]. For example, the fragility factors concern physical characters as the aging of materials, changes in climate, meteorology, human factors, etc.

This chapter's first section assesses the electronuclear future in the medium and the long term. The second one analyzes the plants' building costs and the reasons for their increasing trend. The explanation is that, in this sector, dissociating security and plant building costs is awkward. This fact is crucial to understand nuclear liability. A third section analyzes the economic implications of liability regimes in terms of industrial organization in particular and in relation to other challenging energies. A fourth section questions the nuclear industrial organization itself through the third-party liability.

2. Nuclear Energy: A Challenging Future

Is nuclear energy liable to disappear in the near future? Nuclear civilian programs emerged in the 1950s and quickly grew from the 1970s to the 1990s. This concerned mainly, first, the United States, then simultaneously, Europe, Japan and the former USSR. On 31 December 2016, the World counted 448 reactors with an installed capacity of 391,116 GW(e) (Electric Giga Watt) (see [IAEA, 2017]). The Occidental Countries share almost the whole of the installed nuclear capacity: European Union (114 reactors), the United States (99), the former USSR (including Ukraine) (50), China (36), Japan (42) and Korea (42). However, the lifetime of power stations is limited (30–40 years) and, nowadays, aging parks are calling for mass plants dismantling. Furthermore, in the European Union, some countries are planning to definitively exit from nuclear power (Austria since the late 1970s, Germany in 2022), while others either do not forecast new plants (Sweden) or contemplate limiting their plants number (France). The Occidental public opinion's reaction after the successive accidents at Three Miles Island in 1979, Chernobyl in 1986 and Fukushima in 2011 explains this disaffection. Japan closed most of its plants after Fukushima and if its installed capacity shutdown in 2010 from 280.25 TW/h (Terawatt/hour), (44 reactors) to 4.35 TW/h in 2015 from two reactors, then the 42 others are operational but temporarily at a standstill. Consequently, the nuclear industry development is at stake. Indeed, the examination of new projects reveals a contrasting situation. On a global scale, the number of plants under construction was 61 in 2016 [IAEA, 2017]. However, note a "China effect" insofar as this country aims at implementing 21 new reactors leaving the remaining 40 other ones spread over 14 countries. Furthermore, the power stations connections to the grid show a marked slowdown. Indeed, there were 102 connections between 1981 and 1985, but, between 2011 and 2016 [IAEA, 2017, p. 21], this number limits to 38. Once again, a "China effect" appears because of its 23 connections out of the 38 mentioned.

However, the whole World connection to grid shows a slowdown in the use of nuclear energy.

Considering these data, it is difficult to make predictions. Indeed, except some emerging countries such as India, China or Russia, most of the Western "pioneer" countries are slowing down their nuclear implementation. Consequently, it clearly appears that new Occidental projects do not compensate the planned plants' closure. In December 2016, there were 91 shutting down (including 28 in Germany) and scheduled ones were around 70 (including 22 in Russia). The Energy Transition Act of 2015[1,2] induces France to decrease its power stations number to achieve a 50% nuclear energy mix in spite of some strong political opposition.

The nuclear energy survival could come from its low carbon emissions in the fight against global warming. Indeed, nuclear energy produces less carbon than fossil energies. Following the December 2015 governmental agreements (COP21) and the International Energy Agency [IAEA, 2015] requests, it becomes imperative to limit the temperature increase to below 2°C (rather targeting to 1.5°C). In the past, by their nuclear program development, France and Sweden reached this objective: their CO_2/GDP ratio decrease was about 5.5% per year between 1978 and 1988 in France and 6.2% in Sweden. In addition, as Kidd [2015] points out, nuclear energy consumes fewer natural resources in the facilities' implementation compared to other energies, including renewable energies. In conclusion, although nuclear energy seems to be declining, the constraint of global warming and the need to conserve natural resources could help this energy revival in the medium term. This is in spite of the fact that renewables extend more rapidly than nuclear. Indeed, according to Schneider *et al.* [2017], as nuclear power grew by 1.4% (up to 35 TW/h) in 2016, wind power increased by 16% (132 TW/h), and solar by 30% (77 TW/h).

3. The Entanglement of Internal and External Costs

More than any other industry or energy, nuclear power is sensitive to hazards, obsolescence or wear and tear of materials. Further, it is a hard task distinguishing the safety costs from the other costs (building, operation, waste disposal, management costs, etc.). To enlighten this factor, we study the building costs of power plants.

[1]In "Loi No. 2015-992 du 17 août 2015 relative à la transition énergétique pour la croissance verte" Art. L104-1. al.

[2]Following the World Nuclear Association, France disposes of 58 nuclear reactors, all operated by Electricité de France (EDF). Its capacity is around 63.2 GW(e) that supplies 436 TW/h in 2014.

To address this issue, as a simplification, we stick to D'Haeseleer [2013]'s analysis as did the European Commission [EU Commission, 2016]. D'Haeseleer [2013, p. 13] considers two fundamental costs elements. On the one hand, nuclear cost comprises all private or internal costs needed in a reactor construction and operation and, on the other hand, the external costs, i.e. the costs generated by its potential negative externalities (radioactive pollution and major accidents) or its positive one [NEA–OECD, 2003].[3]

Internal costs correspond to overnight costs: Civil and structural costs, mechanical equipment and their installation, electrical and control instrumentation, indirect project costs, study and development costs. To these, add the financing costs: capital cost of the building process, interest on debt and dividends. The latter increase with delays accumulation and with interest rates variations. For example, the European Commission [EU Commission, 2016, p.12] example that shows the evolution of construction costs according to the interest cost and construction time (see Table 1).

Thus, the higher the reactor's construction time, the higher its costs, even if learning effects may limit their expansion [Berthélemy and Escobar-Rangel, 2013]. However, new safety requirements increase construction times as shown by the EPR reactors that EDF build simultaneously in France (Flamanville) and Finland (Olkiluoto). Both accumulate significant delays (respectively, +6 years and +8 years) and corresponding rise in costs (respectively, €3.5 billion in 2005 and 2007 at the start to more than €10 billion in 2017).

Including financial costs in assessing the reactor construction costs is fundamental as shown in the severe dispute between Lovering *et al.* [2016] and Koomey *et al.* [2017]. The former estimate the overnight costs of the whole set of reactors in seven countries between 1954 and 2015, corresponding to 58% of the World

Table 1. Illustration of financing costs as a % of overnight construction costs.

	Interest rates				
Construction time	**4 (%)**	**5 (%)**	**7 (%)**	**10 (%)**	**13 (%)**
5 years	8	10	14	21	28
7 years	11	14	20	29	39
10 years	19	25	37	57	80

Source: EU Commission [2016, p. 12].

[3]External costs correspond to the risks of irradiation, accidents, dissemination, treatment of waste, etc. Each of these two types of costs is subject to considerable uncertainty.

reactors. This complete oversight leads them to criticize previous approaches that exclusively focused on France and United States. Lovering *et al.* [2016]'s results contradict previous works that asserted that construction costs tend to grow over time. In their opinion, focusing on overnight costs adjusted with exchange rates and year's correction put into question the construction costs growth. This validates the idea that, in the nuclear sector, learning effects apply and accumulate knowledge. However, Thomas [1988], MacKerron [1992], Koomey and Hultman [2007], Grubler [2014] and Escobar-Rangel and Lévêque [2015] highlight that building costs tend to increase because of negative learning-by-doing process.

This countercurrent vision prompted a keen response from Koomey, Hultman and Grubler [2017] who criticized Lovering *et al.* [2016]'s methodology. Furthermore, the authors raise doubts about the quality of Lovering's data, particularly the French ones that come from the French Court of Auditors of 2012 on *The costs of the nuclear power sector* [Cour des Comptes, 2012]. Indeed, Grubler [2014] shows that the latter systematically undervalued nuclear costs to an order of 30%. Koomey *et al.* [2017] underlines that the financial costs that result from longer delivery times cannot be ignored. All the requirements about safety issues increase on longer building delays, and it becomes impossible to separate internal costs from the internalizing externalities costs as Von Hippel, [2010, p. 1] summarizes it:

> Safety requires redundant cooling and control systems, massive leak-tight containment structures, very conservative seismic design and extremely stringent quality control.

Indeed, in 2015, ASN[4] identified anomalies in the steel of the vessel and the cover composition of the Flamanville EPR tank (carbon in excess). To justify the adequacy of the mechanical properties of these components, AREVA (the French building reactor company) proposed implementing a test program by the end of 2016. In June 2017, the ASN and the Radiation Protection Institute and Nuclear Safety (IRSN) allowed, but under conditions, the EPR construction continuation and among them, the possible lid change (i.e. its masterpiece) in the short term. This does put under question the EPR's viability because AREVA forecasts it until a 60 years lifetime.

In conclusion, the exclusive "overnight" cost approach is not realistic. Indeed, the financial costs of delays are an important part of the costs. Consequently, separating building costs from safety costs is impossible.

[4]The French nuclear regulatory agency: Agence de la Sûreté Nucléaire.

4. Nuclear Liability and Industrial Organization

The above section shows that investments in safety measures limit the consequences of nuclear negative externalities. Indeed, positive or negative externalities appear as sway on a given agent's utility function by other agents' actions without the former being able to limit or control its effects. Negative externalities (i.e. detrimental consequences) call for compensation or reparation (or internalization) that must restore the victim's initial utility level. When this is not possible (or only partially possible), the internalization process is missing (or partial). This means that the tortfeasor escapes to his (her) repair duty (totally or partially), while the victims or the community bear the remaining damage cost. Electronuclear energy generates two kinds of negative externalities: the first are the radioactive emissions during uranium mining, fuel processing, reprocessing and storage of nuclear waste, while the second consist in the reactor melting risks and the release of radioactive materials into the atmosphere. The "fuel" resulting from the production of nuclear energy consists of 97% uranium and 3% other isotopes that create the fission process.[5] Nuclear accidents are likely to produce harmful radioactive emissions similar to those associated with storage or reprocessing. Then, for this reason, both aspects fall under civil liability regimes. Now, these regimes do not distinguish major accidents from massive radiation. Indeed, the 2004 OECD Protocol radically changes nuclear accident concept by including not only facts of accidental origin ("damage"), but also structural externalities (gradual, repetitive), with common origin to several nuclear facilities ("nuclear damage"). This means damages to persons and their property, to the environment, intangible damage (any loss of profit), the cost of the safeguard and repair measures and any other associated loss or damage.

Since the mid-1950s and the beginning of civilian nuclear energy use, the concerned nations rapidly became aware of its danger. In response, they drew up conventions that take account of the possible transboundary effects of fissile material dispersal. At the international level, several international conventions based on Third-Party Liability ruled electronuclear energy. The object was both providing victims with rapid redress means and encouraging operators to take internationally recognized safety measures. However, the latter raises many questions related to the compensation effectiveness, its fairness and the efficacy of the reparations "threat" that should induce operators to take effective precautionary measures.

[5]These isotopes include cesium-137, iodine-129, cesium-137 and platinum-239.5. Some of them are still half-active after millions of years, such as iodine-129, which has a half-life of 17 million years. Plutonium-239 has a half-life of 24,360 years and the release of constituents into the biosphere (ingestion, respiration) and also near storage sites expose populations.

Furthermore, the need to preserve nuclear energy development counterbalances the repair necessity for nuclear damage as shown in the introduction of the 1960 Paris Convention. On the one hand, nuclear civil liability has to promote the development of the nuclear industry and, on the other hand, it must achieve sufficient coverage for the repair of damage. Are both purposes companionable? It is the question we attempt to answer in what follows.

4.1. *Nuclear liability: An impossible unification?*

Because no nuclear convention was signed, the Soviet Union escaped its repair duty after the Chernobyl catastrophe in 1986 (see [IAEA, 2005]). Consequently, to avoid any detrimental repetition, the International Atomic Energy Agency (IAEA) in Vienna and the Nuclear Energy Agency (NEA) amended the international conventions on Nuclear weapons. So, the 1988 Joint Protocol linked the IAEA, Vienna Convention on Civil Liability for Nuclear Damage of 1963 and the OECD Paris Convention on Civil Liability of 1960 and included nuclear nations that escaped civil liability [Schwartz, 2006]. On 12 February 2004 in Paris (see [NEA-OECD, 2016]), protocols amended the Paris Convention and the Brussels Convention. Finally, the Fukushima-Daiichi accident reinforced a desire to unify nuclear liability regimes.[6]

Apart from the United States, India and Austria,[7] all nuclear countries tend to agree on a number of basic principles, but there still remain significant differences between the regimes. Some countries are parties to some conventions, but not others, so that harmonization of nuclear liability is a complex process. To expose this principle in a comprehensive way, we follow the Pelzer [2016] methodology:

- First Principle: The nuclear installation operator is the sole person responsible for an accident.[8]
- Second Principle: Strict liability rules the operator's responsibility. Consequently, the mere relationship between nuclear accidents and nuclear damage entails the operator's responsibility under the applicable agreement terms. "Force majeure"

[6]These conventions and protocols are the following: (1) the Paris Conventions of 1960/2004 (PC) on civil liability in the field of nuclear energy, (2) the Brussels Conventions of 1963/2004 (BC) supplementary to the Paris Convention, (3) the Vienna Conventions of 1963/1997 (VC) on civil liability for nuclear damage, (4) the attached Protocol of 1988 relating to the Application of the Vienna Convention and the Paris (JP) Convention and (5) the 1997 Convention on Supplementary Compensation for damage nuclear (CSC annex).

[7]We study below the respective cases of India United States.

[8]Articles 1 1960 and 2004 PCs, I 1963 and 1997 VCs, I CSC and 1 CSC Annex.

(as wars, insurrections, various hostilities) exonerate from any responsibility except terrorism acts.

- Third Principle: All civil liability is channeled on the operator. This position refers to the fundamental principles of strict liability and allows prompt compensation to victims by avoiding seeking other responsible and costly procedures. However, the operator's insolvency is at risk, [Ameye, 2010] for instance, recall that TEPCO in Japan has been nationalized after the Fukushima accident.
- Fourth Principle: The amount of repairs is limited. Then, the 2004 Paris Protocol amends the Paris and Brussels Conventions of 2004. It sets maximum compensation levels up to €1.5 billion, whereas (currently 2017), this amount is €350 million.[9] This is a threshold not a limit [Pelzer, 2016].[10]
- Fifth Principle: Operators must take out private insurance or a guarantee fund. This ensures that the compensation amount is available.
- Sixth Principle: The duration of liability is limited in time. The Paris Convention of 2004 and Vienna 2007 increased the time period to 30 years for all bodily injuries and 10 years for other types of damages. However, for insurance, the period is 10 years. This measure is doubtless cosmetic because, as Pelzer points out, this in the long term prevents establishing a certain causal relationship between the appearance of the damage and its effective real cause.

4.2. *The special situation of the United States: The Price–Anderson Act*

The Price–Anderson Act, adopted in 1957, is the United States nuclear liability regime. It limits the amount of accident repairs attributable to civil nuclear power stations. Over time, the "repair limit" for a nuclear accident has increased and a specialized insurance pool has to eventually repair up to $12 billion. Insurance premiums owed by operators amounted to $375 million (2014) in private insurance for off-site liability coverage for each plant (not per reactor). Then, a second level supplements this primary insurance. In the event that a nuclear incident results in damages in excess of $375 million, each licensee will make a pro-rata share of the excess up to $12.255 million per reactor. The insurance pool comprises 104 reactors

[9]Four countries, Austria, Germany, Japan and Switzerland, place unlimited liability on the operator, while others like the Russian Federation remain ambiguous. As mentioned in Section 4.2, the United States' nuclear is ruled by the Price–Anderson Act since 1957.

[10]The compensation ceilings comprise three parts:

(a) A mandatory insurance policy or a financial guarantee that insures a substantial part of its repair share (Fifth principle).

(b) The State is responsible for the nuclear plants located in its territory.

(c) All Contracting States share responsibility.

and the level of secondary insurance amounts to \$12.6 billion. If 15% of these funds are committed, the Federal District Court determines the allocation of funds. Beyond that, it is up to the Congress to define the priorities. Then, the average annual premium for a reactor is approximately \$1.1 million. The premium for a second or a third reactor on the same site is bounded. The Energy Policy Act of 2005 extended the Price–Anderson Act to 31 December 2025. Furthermore, although not required by the insurance companies, NRC regulations require operators to maintain \$ 1.06 billion for each reactor on site. The objective is to cover on-site repairs so that the operators fulfill their obligations of stabilization and decontamination of the reactor and the site after an accident. Only the "Nuclear Electric Insurance Limited" Company provides this insurance for the operators.

4.3. *Reconciling nuclear compensation and nuclear promotion: An impossible equation?*

The successive accidents of Three Miles Island, Chernobyl and Fukushima show a mismatch between the damage value and the amount of repairs. For instance, in 2013, the French Institute of Radiation Protection and Nuclear Safety (IRSN) issued a prospective study that quantifies the possible cost of a nuclear accident in France [IRSN, 2013]. It considers scenarios according to their seriousness. Accident includes not only the core melting, but also, the diffusion of radioactivity into the atmosphere and lands. Thus, this study defines scenarios with their costs and social impact according to the accident's intensity. Two main scenarios are at stake: first, a serious accident and, second, a major accident. Their difference lies in the release of fissile material into the atmosphere. The economic cost assessment is specific to the French economy. They relate to the impact on the residential sector (population displacements), agricultural costs (domestic demand and export production), tourism, reduction of electricity production and switching to other energy sources (such as after Fukushima Daiichi in Japan). The estimated cost of the serious accident is €120 billion and €450 billion for the major accident. This study echoes similar studies that estimate the Chernobyl accident costs and served as a model for the IRSN 2013's study (see [IEAE, 2005]). These amounts are not commensurate with the sums of the reparation of the various civil liability schemes that do not exceed €1.5 billion after ratification of the 2004 Protocol. There, the operator must mobilize €700 million from its funds and insurance, the other 800 million are guaranteed by the State and the signatory States. This limitation of the amount of reparations would, as mentioned in the introduction of the Paris Protocol, aim not to discourage nuclear activity. As a result, many authors consider that the low level of repairs constitutes a disguised subsidy to this industry. This is the point we are studying now.

4.3.1. *Civil liability as a weapon of international competition*

To give an image of how liability regimes influence the competition model, we refer to India's 2010 Nuclear Liability Act. India's rapid economic growth generates increasing energy needs that its obsolete infrastructure cannot satisfy. As a result, the Indian government decided to set up an ambitious nuclear program that aims at increasing India's capacity from 4,120 MW€ to 10,000 MW€ by 2020. However, until 2010, in India a standard regime of no-fault liability governed all the ultra-hazardous activities including the nuclear sector and it was in the unique position of not having either national legislation on nuclear liability or adherence to international conventions. The Indian nuclear program requires international cooperation with advanced nuclear countries such as the Russian Federation, France and the US. However, these countries have different laws covering foreign investment by their domestic firms. For example, France and Russia tend to favor their companies by offering free insurance (or insurance guaranteed by the State), in other words, States guarantee their respective national companies. However, it is compulsory for US operators to insure their nuclear power reactors. In the United States, the Price–Anderson Nuclear Industries Indemnity Act requires operators to jointly constitute a fund and pay up to $10 billion. As a result, after a nuclear disaster, the plant insurer pays the first $375 million. Therefore, reestablishing fair competitive conditions required changes to the Indian civil liability law. After tumultuous debates, the Indian Parliament finally passed the 2010 Nuclear Liability Act, which imposes strict liability on the operator, with a ceiling on reparations.[11] Then, this institutional change opened the door to competition for US companies (see [Heffron *et al.*, 2016], for a finer analysis of the Indian case).

4.3.2. *Nuclear liability: A disguised but common subsidy in the field of energy*

In this section, we examine the issue of civil nuclear liability in the economic literature as a disguised subsidy [Froggatt *et al.*, 2006]. Pelzer [2016, p. 381] perfectly summarizes the situation:

> The failure to develop a proper regime that would ensure full restitution and compensation for the harm resulting from nuclear facilities constitutes a continuing subsidy to the nuclear industry and distorts decisions regarding energy choices.

Implicit subventions involve underestimating the market price of kW/h for the consumer. Let us specify the meaning of this notion.

---

[11] Civil Liability for Nuclear Damage Act 2010 http://dae.nic.in/sites/default/files/civilnucliab.pdf accessed August 2017.

(a) *Nuclear liability: A hidden subsidy*

In the past, many contributions supported this view. For instance, Dubin and Rothwell [1990] and Rothwell [2001] estimated the amount of the US operators' subsidies from the Price–Anderson Act. Further, Heyes and Liston-Heyes [1998] applied their methodology to Canada and Fiore [2007, 2008] and Fiore and Faure [2009] to the French situation. These enquiries issued on similar results regardless of the Country. Dubin and Rothwell [1990] start from the insurance premiums required for the first $160 million coverage and the Nuclear Regulatory Commission's estimate of the probability of the worst loss and they model the damage distribution with a Log-logistic density function. This function assumes that the higher the expected damage, the lower the major accident probability. They conclude that the value of the Price–Anderson Act subsidy was $60 million per year per reactor before 1982, but after the 1988 amendments, this one dropped to $22 million per reactor per year. One finds similar conclusions in the methodologies of Heyes and Liston-Heyes [1998] for Canada and Fiore and Faure [2009] for the French situation. Fiore [2008] considers increasing damage depending on the accident intensity in accordance with whether the core melts with or without radiation emission. This distinction makes introducing conditional probabilities of spreading thresholds of radioactive release possible. Her analysis is therefore finer than the previous ones. She compares EDF's current situation, excluding, first, the ratification of the 2004 Paris Protocol, then, with this protocol application. As in the previous studies, increasing the coverage of repairs leads to a reduction in the implicit subsidy represented by the cap on repairs. All these authors emphasize that these subsidies distort competition by the low level of internalization of potential externalities. They attempt translating the impact of this subsidy on the price of a kW/h. A full integration of accident-related externalities dramatically increases the global cost and hence the kW/h cost. However, as Fiore and Faure [2005] point out, this dimension must also incorporate the additional prevention costs.

(b) *The hidden subsidies of the fossil industries*

If nuclear power enjoys the advantage of implicit subvention, this is also the case for other energies. Indeed, fossil fuels benefit from direct subsidies linked to their exploitation and, also, from implicit subsidies. Indeed, fossil energies' operators are totally exempt from the need to internalize environmental damage such as global warming or damage to biodiversity, or urban air pollution. For example, Bast *et al.* [2015] point out that between 2013 and 2014, the G20 countries directly subsidized up to $444 billion fossil energies. Production subsidies include domestic subsidies, which correspond to direct expenditures or tax reductions for $70 billion, investments made by nationalized enterprises are about $286 billion and public funding from banks and nationalized institutions for $88 billion.

Concerning the costs of externalities generated by fossil fuels, HEAL's report supported by the European Union assesses the impact of fossil energies subsidies on Health [HEAL-Report, 2017]. It highlights the costs induced by fossil fuels and estimates the subsidies amount paid by governments to the coal, oil and gas sectors, particularly in the G20 countries. The report contrasts the $444 billion of subsidies granted by these countries to fossil fuels in 2014 with $2,760 billion of health costs induced by carbon-based pollution. It seems difficult to know how much a kW/h produced by fossil fuels would cost without subsidy. As with the nuclear industry sector, it is necessary to know the cost of negative externalities. The HEAL report [2017] focused only on health aspects without considering the global cost on the whole environment (pollution, GH).

In conclusion, implicit subsidies to nuclear industry impact competition. However, every energy source is subsidized including green energies. No doubt that ending subsidies to polluting and/or dangerous energies would *ipso-facto* benefit low externalities energies. But this point far exceeds the dimensions of our study.

5. The Industrial Organization of the Electronuclear Sector: Safety versus Profitability?

5.1. *The electronuclear industrial organization*

In the beginning of the nuclear adventure, the States closely controlled the nuclear power sector that was integrated both vertically as well as by the military. However, the emergence of civilian nuclear power led to distinguish two organization types: The first one retains the centralized organization with a strong State involvement. This applies both to the electricity generation and distribution achieved by a monopoly and a company that manufactures the reactors as, for example, EDF and AREVA in France. The second one is market-based. This means that private actors organize the reactor building, power generation and distribution in several countries (as in the US) (see [Joskow, 2008] for an appraisal of the privatization in the power energy sector).

An examination of the European situation shows that, here, both organizations prevail. It is important to note that the organization type is independent from the country size or the reactors number. Thus, in Western Europe (including Switzerland and Ukraine) considering 16 countries produce nuclear electricity, the number of operators is about 28. Among them, 17 operate either a single reactor (six operators) or two. Then, nine operators manage from three to seven reactors. Conversely, EDF is responsible for both the French and United Kingdom parks entirely, with, respectively, 58 reactors in France and 15 in Britain. Most of the other nuclear countries share their fleets between four and five operators (such as Sweden and Germany, respectively, that own seven and ten reactors), while only one operator is present in France, Belgium, Bulgaria, the Czech Republic, Romania, Slovakia, Slovenia, Ukraine and the United Kingdom. However, considering the European level as a single market, it is the oligopolistic situation that prevails (see Table A.1).

As a result, the sector is internally subject to competition in terms of takeovers and mergers. For example, in 2003, CERNA's study [Codognet *et al.*, 2003] points out that the electricity sector knew 135 mergers and acquisitions between 1998 and 2002. For example, in the 2000s, EDF launched an aggressive policy towards nuclear operators and, gradually took over the entire UK nuclear power fleet that, previously, was a monopoly. This policy began in the late 1990s and came to an end in 2009 when EDF (owned up to 85% by the French State) took control of British Energy with eight Advanced Gas-cooled (AGR) reactors. Finally, EDF plans to build two EPRs at Hinkley Point C with a capacity of 3,200 MW (e) (project approved by the EDF Board and the UK government in 2015). Consequently, now, EDF-UK controls the whole of the British nuclear fleet and concentrates the supply of electricity from nuclear power. As a conclusion, even if theoretically the European nuclear market is competitive, it remains in an asymmetric situation, torn between giant operators like EDF and smaller companies.

In the United States, 23 operators manage the 99 nuclear reactors, but each carries a different weight (see [NEI, 2017]). Originally, the energy sector was vertically integrated, with power stations owned by states or municipalities. However, since the 1980s, between 1990 and 2000, the Federal Energy Regulatory Commission (FERC) prescribed the opening to competition of the whole electricity public networks. Since then, the power sector has known numerous takeovers and participations. Lucas and Wolfram show that deregulation in the United States induced productivity improvement with an increase in electricity production [Lucas and Wolfram, 2012].

In the Russian Federation, only one operator (Rosenergoatom) enjoys a monopoly position. Created in 1992, the Russian government transformed Rosenergoatom into a holding company in 2006–2007. This one brings together the entire Russian civil nuclear industry and works both as an operator and a producer. It operates 10 nuclear power plants with 33 reactors. The company plans to build new reactors and increase the number of reactors to 59 by 2030. The activities related to the supply of fuel are entrusted to a specific company, TVEL, and the construction of nuclear equipment, to Atomstroyexport.

In China, state control is as important as in France, India or the Russian Federation. However, the organization scheme differs: regional operators control the regional nuclear fleet, but under the aegis of two major state-owned companies, China National Nuclear Corporation (CNNC) and China General Nuclear Power Group (CGN). So the Liaoning Hongyanhe Nuclear Power Co. Ltd. has five reactors, Daya Bay Nuclear Power Operations and Management Co, Ltd. has six reactors, Guangxi Fangchenggang Nuclear Power Company Ltd. has two reactors, Fujian Fujing Nuclear Power Co., Ltd., Liaoning Hongyanhe Nuclear Power Co. Ltd. (LHNPC) has two reactors, etc.

The question that arises is whether a typical industrial organization could emerge that would ensure both the highest efficiency and safety levels. Policy makers face the need to increasingly integrate the accident risk following their knowledge of the past major accidents (for instance Three Miles Island (1979), Chernobyl (1986) and Fukushima-Daïchi (2016)). Economists and engineers regularly try assessing the likelihood of such accidents taking into account the world's nuclear fleet based on past major accidents. Each new accident questions this risk evaluation and modifies the probability distributions related to this accident [Escobar-Rangel and Lévêque, 2014 and 2015]. The majority of the estimates focus mainly on the probability of a major accident occurrence. It considers the entire nuclear fleet in a given geographical area and the list of past accidents. This reference helps in defining prior accident probability in order to infer the present probability assessment for future events. These approaches consider the global nuclear fleet lifetime and show that the population should expect probable large-scale accidents inside it. However, although some studies conclude that, on a 30 year period, their probability accident could be quite high, this knowledge does not jeopardize some states' choices for electronuclear programs. By extrapolating the methodology of these studies, one may apply it to individual operators for understanding their potential default risk. And these could raise the question about the better number of reactors that a single operator should handle by balancing risk accident and profitability.

5.2. *What is the meaning of studies on the probabilities of a major nuclear accident?*

Each new disaster leads to drastic changes characterized by a temporary or a definitive nuclear program shut down. For example, the Three Miles Island accident contributed to slowing down the US nuclear program. Then, Chernobyl disaster in 1986 encouraged the nuclear States to permanently review the responsibility rules and the safety of power stations. Finally, Fukushima-Daiichi favored the halt of certain programs (Japan, Germany in particular) and the revision of the beliefs concerning major accidents [NEA-OECD, 2017a].

5.2.1. *Some contributions on the issue of nuclear accident probabilities*

The reader may find an updated bibliography in the papers by Ha Duong and Journe [2014] and Wheatley *et al.* [2016] about the "probability" of a major nuclear accident question. The stakes are by no means negligible. Indeed, obviously several convergent studies showing a high plausibility level of a major nuclear accident may lead to public opinion requiring the shutting down of nuclear programs by authorities. Most studies are based on the probability assessment of nuclear reactor core melting. These are built from sophisticated decision trees (Probability Risk Assessment, or PRA) that take into account the chain of events that can lead to major accidents. Depending on the type of reactor, these probabilities differ. We present here two reasonable approaches: the Ha Duong and Journe [2014] and Wheatley *et al.* [2016] ones. Ha Duong and Journe [2014] synthesize the NEA-OECD [2012]'s report by conceiving an exhaustible table that presents a major nuclear accident risk by considering the probability ε of an accident per reactor per year as it results from PRA studies. Depending on the nature of the reactors, the scale of probabilities ranges from 10^{-4} to 10^{-6} from the older (less effective) to the supposed most efficient ones (EPR). By the end of 2012, 437 reactors were in operation worldwide. They assess up to 15,080 the cumulative number of reactors/year in operation (from the European Nuclear Society in 2013). They consider up to four major accidents for the whole "nuclear" period, i.e. from 1950 to 2013, counting two reactors for the Fukushima accident. In the Table 2, the numbers of accidents that appear in this column are theoretical and are lower, respectively (0.015, 0.15, 1.5, 15) than

Table 2. Four viewpoints on accident probability.

Accident probability per reactor per year ε	**Expected number of accidents since 1950 15080 *ε**	**Probability of at least one accident in 5 years $1-(1-\varepsilon)$^ (437*5) (%)**	**Probability of at least one accident in 30 years $1-(1-\varepsilon)$^ (437*30) (%)**
10^{-6}	0.015	0.22	1.30
10^{-5}	0.15	2.16	12.29
10^{-4}	1.5	19.63	73.05
10^{-3}	15	88.76	99.998

Source: Ha-Duong and Journe [2014].

the reality (i.e.), the number of 15 comes from a probability level of 10^{-3} which is too high to allow implementing any nuclear program. The other columns give the probability of an accident for two periods: 5 and 30 years, depending on the probability of an accident per reactor.

Table 2 summarizes the forward-looking calculations that implicitly assume that the global fleet consists of homogeneous reactors (here, each line corresponds to a risk level). It is obvious that these calculations should take into account the fleet heterogeneity, the aging of plants and materials. The study of Ha-Duong and Journe considers accidents of level 4 to 7 listed on the INES scale.[12] They refine the results above and show that for a 5-year random sample, the probability of a major accident (INES scale 7) is 14.3%, and for two accidents of this nature it is 1.0%. In the same random time interval (5 years) the probability of an accident (<4–6 on the INES scale) is 66.6%. Over a random period of 30 years, the risk of a major accident is around 63.2%.

Wheatley *et al.* [2016] built a database by listing all incidents and accidents, according to the INES scale accessible by costing them from 1952 to the present. They show that since the 1970s (the date of the great expansion of nuclear power in the world) nuclear energy has become safer with a reduction in accidents. The current rate of occurrence would be 0.003 per year per reactor (considering the world park) and would have decreased compared to the 1970s. This result is from better feedback and knowledge after the major disasters like the accident of Three Miles Island seems to have been decisive for the improvement of the safety of the installations. However, catastrophic accidents are characterized by greater damage.

5.2.2. *Methodological reflections on the issue of major accident hazards*

Responding to a controversy born in French media [Ghys, 2011; Dessus and Laponche, 2011; Gautheron, 2017], Schwartz [2011] recalled that the probabilistic studies that try to evaluate the risks of accident are carried out under very strong hypotheses. Her argument joins Lochbaum *et al.* [2014]. She assumes:

(1) Reactors do not wear out and their safety does not improve (the probability of an accident does not depend on time);

---

[12]INES: International Nuclear and Radiological Event Scale. This scale was created by the IAEA in 1990 to ensure universal communication on nuclear risks. The events are classified according to a logarithmic scale of one to seven depending on the severity of the events. From one to four these are considered minor and are called incidents, whereas from four to seven they become accidents, where level seven is a major accident (smelting of reactors and release of radioactive material into the environment) atmosphere.

(2) The possibility of several severe accidents occurring in the same reactor is excluded;
(3) Accidents occur independently (excluding chain accidents or a cause such as a tsunami that would produce several major accidents);
(4) All reactors are identical in terms of major accident probability and their number does not vary in the chosen time window.

Concerning the assumptions 1 and 4 above, as regularly reported by nuclear regulatory authorities like ASN in France, the lifetime of a plant depends on several factors such as the reactor vessel quality. Indeed, irradiation may alter it and may modify the mechanical properties of its steel. Periodic checks are then necessary [ASN, 2009]. This remark weakens Hypotheses 1 and 4 above. In this way, this joins the comments of Lochbaum [2014] that show that comparing nuclear reactors is impossible. Of course, there are many other risk factors. For example, in France, the ASN in its 2016 report [ASN, 2017, pp. 68–69] distinguishes internal failures (the loss of power supplies or cooling means, ejection of a control cluster, rupture of piping of the primary or secondary circuit of a nuclear reactor, failure of reactor emergency shutdown), internal aggressions and external aggressions (Earthquakes, floods, terrorism, etc.). Most of the time, reactors do not work in isolation, as in France where they are built in pairs or in Japan (Fukushima with four reactors), the independence assumption does not hold either. We may maintain Hypothesis 2 because a serious accident at a reactor causes its shutdown either definitively by or over a long period. The accident may impact its future viability. Sometimes, the latter may increase because of technical repairs and maintenance.

Finally, these approaches exclude human failure. However, the latter appears as being a fundamental factor in the occurrence of the three major nuclear disasters as recalled it the IAEA [2014]'s report on the role of the human factor in the prevention of accidents.

In conclusion, studies that aim at assessing the likelihood of a major nuclear accident are based on strong assumptions of the "caeteris paribus" type, regarding the immovability of the installation quality, as if they were perfect dice. In addition, projections are made on the basis of past accidents and incidents. All of these studies show relatively high probabilities of accidents when considering the worldwide fleet. In fact, these projections have little impact on public decision-making and resemble Cassandra's predictions. A more interesting route is then individually pondering the operators, as firms that incur default risk. This approach presupposes a global vision of optimizing the industrial sector organization by emphasizing safety rather than profitability.

5.3. *Acquisition and merger: Security or profitability?*

Since some States have liberalized their electricity sector, in the 1980s, mergers and acquisitions have been numerous. The question that can arise is whether the restructuring of nuclear power stations impacts their safety, or whether, the contrary, it is neutral.

5.3.1. *The operators' failure risk*

We are inspired here by the global Schwartz [2011]'s methodology and apply it to individual operators. To do that, consider the worldwide 448 reactors and the inter-accident durations between Three Miles Island, Chernobyl and Fukushima (i.e. 7 years, from 1979 to 1986) and 25 years (from 1986 to 2011). Thus, under the assumption that a reactor does not wear out and does not improve, it is equivalent to saying that its duration of operation without a major accident follows an exponential parameter law $1/\mu$ with a $1/\mu$ Exp $[-\frac{x}{\mu}]$ density (where μ is the expected working free of failure). A strong but necessary hypothesis assumes that the reactors are identical and the accidents are independent from each other. It follows that the law of operating time without a major accident considering a system composed of n reactors is an exponential parameter law n/μ with n/μ Exp $[-\frac{nx}{\mu}]$ as density and μ/n its expectation. The probability of the number of accidents during a given period τ follows a Poisson's law with $n\tau/\mu$ as parameter. I identify each period, i.e. 7 and 25 years, then, starting from these I calculate the corresponding values $\mu_1$and μ_2 consistent for the whole park to a working without failure. It follows that as, $7 = \mu_1/448$, then $\mu_1 = 3136$ years and as $25 = \mu_2/448$, then $\mu_2 = 11200$ years. It is implicitly assumed that, theoretically, a reactor will receive continuous regular maintenance. Then, we see that, either $\mu_1 = 3150$ years or $\mu_2 = 1125$ years is the time that a reactor works without failure. Then, let X be the random value that corresponds to an accident occurrence, then $p\,(X \geq 1, k)$ is the probability for at least one accident occurrence in a park of k reactors on a given period τ, then:

$$p\,(X \geq 1, k) = 1 - \text{Exp}\left[-k \cdot \frac{\tau}{\mu_i}\right], \quad i = 1, 2.$$

We can build the following Table 3.

These figures prove to be quite close to the figures of Fiore [2007] who determines the likelihood of a major accident by another way. Her method is based on the log-logistic model of Heyes and Liston-Heyes [1998, 2000], adding the reactor's melting risk and the risk of diffusion of fissile material into the atmosphere. The log-logistic model assumes that the accident probabilities are related to the damage extent: The

Table 3. Major accident probability using the Poisson law (Schwartz [2011]'s methodology).

	$1 - \text{Exp}\left[-k.\frac{\tau}{\mu_i}\right]$	$\mu_1 = 3150$ (7 years without accident)	$\mu_2 = 11200$ (25 years without accident)	$E(\mu) = 7168$ (average of μ_1 and μ_2)
$k = 1$ $\tau = 1$	Accident Probability	0.0003188	0.0000892	0.0001394

Table 4. Accident Probability on a given nuclear reactor (following [Fiore, 2007, p. 212]).

Damage (million euros)	$P_1 = 10^{-4}$ ($p = 0.19$)	$P_2 = 10^{-6}$ ($p = 0.19$)	$P_3 = 10^{-6}$ ($p = 0.19$)
$D_1 = 10000$	0.00018	0.00039	0.00076
$D_2 = 40000$	0.00012	0.00024	0.00026
$D_3 = 70000$	0.0001	0.00019	0.00024
$D_4 = 100000$	0.00009	0.00018	0.0002

greater the assumed damage, the lower the likelihood of an accident occurrence. Concerning the accident risks, Fiore [2007] distinguishes three types of reactors according to their safety degree. Thus, current reactors have a fusion probability of the order of $P_2 = 10^{-5}$, whereas for future generations of EPR reactors, this probability is about of $P_3 = 10^{-6}$. The melting of a reactor is not necessarily a sign of a major accident, which requires a contingency match that corresponds to a probability quantified by Fiore [2007] at $p = 0.19$. The application of the log-logistic model leads to Table 4 which corresponds to the definition of the probabilities of major accidents, according to the nature of the reactors on the one hand and the extent of the damage.

Then, using Poisson's law gives an approximation of the risk of failure given a set of reactors. As noted above, the authors generally focus on the risk of a nuclear accident in general or in a given geographical area. However, this kind of analysis can be extended to single operators. This means that we assess not the accident risk, but also its default risk. Thus, if one considers, the French operator EDF that manages 58 reactors in France, the probability of suffering a major accident over 30 years is then for μ_1, (case of an accident after 7 years):

$$p(X \geq 1, k = 58, \mu_1) = 1 - \text{Exp}\left[-58 \cdot \frac{30}{3136}\right] = 0.42584,$$

and for 25 years without accident:

$$p\,(X \geq 1, k = 58, \mu_2) = 1 - \text{Exp}\left[-58 \cdot \frac{30}{11\,200}\right] = 0.143891.$$

Thus, the more the reactors the operators possess, the greater the likelihood that they will experience a major accident in a given time interval. This fact is mechanical and it mathematically deduces from the model's data.

Beyond the 58 reactors on the French territory, EDF also possesses 15 reactors in the United Kingdom. Consequently, for a given year ($\tau = 1$), I assess the level of risk of accident for this operator, considering first the French territory (58 reactors) and then both France and United Kingdom (73 reactors), we may compare the following three situations: ($\mu_1 \mu_2 \overline{\mu}$) in Table 5.

Then, in Table 6 we compare with a lag of 30 years.

Before analyzing this situation, it is legitimate to raise the question of this projection relevancy. The answer requires looking at an accident occurrence in a 30 year interval, this for the worldwide nuclear park. Thus, here, an accident probability is about 69.8% when the interval without accident is 25 years (μ_2). This means that, during this time-lag, the technology expertise is better than in the 7 years-lag without an accident (μ_1). This probability is close to that determined by Huong and Journe [2014] as shown in Table 7.

Here, N_i is the number of major accidents in 30 years. When $N_i = 0$, the probability is 36.8%, this means that an accident occurrence probability is

Table 5. Comparison of the risk of a major accident on 1 year ($\tau = 1$) depending on the number of detained reactors k.

		$k = 1$	**$k = 58$**	**$k = 73$**	**$k = 448$**
$\tau = 1$	μ_1	0.0003	0.018	0.023	0.13
	μ_2	0.00009	0.005	0.006	0.04
	$\overline{\mu}$	0.00014	0.008	0.0101	0.06

Table 6. Comparison of the risk of a major accident in 30 years ($\tau = 30$) depending on the number of reactors held k.

		$k = 1$	**$k = 58$**	**$k = 73$**	**$k = 448$**
$\tau = 30$	μ_1	0.0095	0.426	0.5	0.986
	μ_2	0.0026	0.14	0.18	0.698
	$\overline{\mu}$	0.0041	0.215	0.263	0.847

Table 7. Probability of nuclear accident or major accident worldwide in 30-years.

	Probability of a given number of accidents				
Severity of events	$P(\text{Ni} = 0)$	$P(\text{Ni} = 1)$	$P(\text{Ni} = 2)$	$P(\text{Ni} = 3)$	$P(\text{Ni} \geq 4)$
Accident (INES = 7)	36.8%	37.4%	18.4%	5.8%	1.6%

Source: Ha-Duong and Journé, 2014, p. 16, Table 5b.

$100 - 36.8 = 63.2\%$. In our representation, calculating μ_a (that represents 30 years without an accident), then, in a 30-year interval where $\mu_a = 448 \times 30 = 13440$, then

$$p\,(X \geq 1, k = 448, \mu_a) = 1 - \text{Exp}\left[-448 \cdot \frac{30}{448.30}\right] = 63.21\%.$$

Consequently, the Poisson's law that we use seems to present good nuclear accident likelihood. It follows that, a monopoly as EDF presents an important risk of major accident, for the present (0.5% by year for 58 reactors or 0.6% by year for 73 reactors).

In the present case, the question is whether, in the European context, EDF does not weigh too heavily on European nuclear power. From an insurance point of view, it is difficult to compare the situation of EDF with a simple operator that owns only three or four reactors.

The probability of a major accident is calculated assuming that the operator owns a number of identical reactors. Regarding EDF, its fleet consists of reactors of different generations. In France, 30 out of its 58 reactors were commissioned at the end of 1984, 20 between 1985 and the end of 1989, and 8 between 1990 and 2002. In other words, the most recent ones are between 15 and 17 years old (for four of them). Thus, 54 reactors are between 20 and 40 years of service. The obsolescence of the park implies a weakening of the materials and installations which increases the probability of an accident. In the United Kingdom, the EDF's fleet also is a longstanding one. Indeed, most of its commissioning phase began between 1977 and 1989, indicating that, at best, the most recent power stations are 30 years old.

The operator's fragility comes from either technical reason (their reactors' number, their age, their wear and tear, the plants location, etc.) or from its economic and financial health. The latter are fundamental because they condition the operator's ability to provide funds for repairs. However, these are linked to the institutional guidelines for civil liability. If it evolves to become as, in Germany or Japan, unlimited liability, or simply if the ceiling increases, then confidence in the operator disappears when its economic prospects are degraded.

At present, major nuclear building companies are experiencing major difficulties of various kinds. Both Toshiba-Westinghouse and AREVA, are waning. The first one became bankrupt in March 2017, and the second is in a state of near bankruptcy. This is due to, in the case of Toshiba-Westinghouse, to unwarranted investments and delays and additional costs in reactor construction (V.C. Summer and Vogtle reactors in the US for Toshiba-Westinghouse). For AREVA, the causes are years of bad management, unsuccessful investments in uranium mines, the failure of its suppliers and delays in ongoing projects. Furthermore, the major nuclear operators Centrica (UK), EDF, Engie (France), E.ON and RWE (Germany) have seen their financial situation deteriorate with a dramatic loss of 10-year market capitalization: RWE −82%, E. ON −87%, EDF −89%, Engie −75%. This has led to rating agencies degrading their rating [Schneider *et al.*, 2017].

5.3.2. *An industrial organization of nuclear power based on safety*

Can a regulation of the industrial organization of nuclear energy lead to improvement of its safety? Numerous studies estimate the energy market liberalization consequences from the 1980s onwards [Green and Newbery, 1992]. Electricity was initially a natural monopoly that is subdivided into four main sectors: generation, transport, distribution and retail. Joskow [2008] stresses the importance of opening power generation to competition, this to facilitate access to competition on wholesale markets. These studies test the impact on profitability for companies and the improvement of social welfare [Newbery and Pollitt, 1997] by the falling price of kW/h and increasing supply of electricity. The studies in this field left out security considerations and only studied the impact of nuclear plant restructuring on economic performance [Zhang, 2007] for the period 1992–1998 and [Lucas and Wolfram, 2012] nowadays.

5.4. *Theoretical approaches to the relationship between industrial organization and civil liability*

In short, is the electronuclear parks' restructuring concerned with improved safety? This topic received little input. In France, for example, the questions about the nuclear fleet privatization are limited to general considerations. For instance, for Berte and Naudet [2004] the question is still prospective insofar as the liberalization of production could help encourage operators to reduce their costs, but safety is less considered in tandem with the electronuclear organization scheme. For some, privatization could increase the authorities' supervision and lead to an improvement of both safety and production (see [Bertel and Naudet, 2004, pp. 328–329]). Sajarroff *et al.* [2002, p. 382] summarize this opinion:

> However, a safety management system can erode due to indifferent attitudes at corporate level when nuclear safety or nuclear activities in general are seen as a political problem or a cost rather than a strategic objective and a resource.

Mondello [2015] focuses on the relationship between safety and concentration and decentralization in the operating of nuclear plants. The question, then, is: which organization (either monopolist or decentralized) may insure the highest care level? The model introduces civil liability basis (see [Shavell, 1987]) and contestable markets framework [Baumol *et al.*, 1982] and compares the performances of *operators* when they choose to furnish power on centralized, or on a decentralized basis. The most efficient ownership structure is the one that minimizes the accident costs: $y + p(y)(c - Q)$, where y, $y \geq 0$ are the prevention costs plus the expected repairs cost understood as the product of the major accident probability $p(y)$ by the amount of repairs $(c - Q)$, where c is the ceiling of repairs and Q the level of repairs that insurance companies refund (insurance and reinsurance corporations). The model assumes the non-independence of accident probabilities: an accident at a reactor involves either a shutdown or an activity reduction, increased control that issues in the absence of additional accidents. Furthermore, an accident at a reactor involves a cost $(e, e > 0)$ linked to the temporary or total program suspension. Then, the program resolution shows that the choice of one of the two structures depends closely on the relationships between the three values: (c, e, Q). A centralized organization (monopoly) ensures a higher level of prevention and higher prevention costs than a decentralized structure when $\frac{c-Q}{e} > 1$. on the contrary, when $\frac{c-Q}{e} < 1$ [Mondello, 2015, propositions 4, 5 and 6], a decentralized structure would be preferable. Then, it may be interesting to study the nature of this ratio, rewritten as: $c - Q < e$. In this case, the opportunity costs e are higher than the ratio of the repairs owed by the operator after deducting the insurance cover. In other words, once the compulsory insurance Q increases, without increasing the amount of the institutional cap c, then the organizational structure has to be decentralized. Given the complexity of the universe of nuclear power, concrete situations must flesh this theoretical approach.

5.5. *The qualitative constraints of the relationship between industrial organization and civil liability*

Nuclear parks are composite and different types and generations of reactors may coexist in such a way that the probabilities of accidents are specific to a given operator and difficult to appreciate. Similarly, liability regimes differ from one country to another and legislation on institutional prevention, insurance and coverage is changing. Then, the relationships between regulatory agencies, the States, the operator and its suppliers and the public are complex processes.

5.5.1. *Moral hazard between the operator and its suppliers*

A good knowledge of the operators is fundamental to assess their fleet's actual risk. Thus, for example, the operator EDF owns pressurized water reactors, designed in the 1960s by Westinghouse Corporation. Despite different capacities (900, 1,300 and 1,450 MW(e)), this design ensures homogeneity, scale economies in the pooling of resources and great feedback from experience. However, this standard implies that an incident on a given nuclear unit may also occur elsewhere. This standardization can pose moral hazard problems when suppliers or subcontractors are likely to fail in the materials design. For instance, since 2016, EDF is faced with a major structural crisis concerning the tank structure of several former reactors. Indeed, after it discovered the defecting Flamanville EPRs tank and cover, the ASN extended its controls on all the French nuclear plants. There, a very high carbon concentration appeared, particularly on the primary vessels manufactured by Japan Casting & the Forging Corporation (JCFC), a Japanese blacksmith, subcontractor of AREVA. Then, 12 French reactors are considered [ASN, 2016]. It turns out that the whole set of steam generators with a too high carbon degree were forged at LeCreusot (France). In total, several reactors are weakened in such a way that without further inspection, their long-term impact can be assessed.

5.5.2. *Moral hazard between supervisory authorities, operators and insurance companies*

In the nuclear sector, an insurance company cannot fully cover the potential losses that follow a major accident. So, after, the Three Miles Island accident in 1979, insurance companies created an organized insurance and reinsurance system [Picard, 2011] to prevent any bankruptcy that could occur in the event of a major accident. More recently, for ensuring a better coverage, operators self-insured themselves by creating self-insuring subsidiaries (or captive) (Nuclear Electric Insurance Limited (NEIL) in the US, and, European Mutual Association for Nuclear Insurance (EMANI) in Europe). [Culp, 2002; Picard, 2011]. In the insurance field, the competitive game is strong because captives are challenging the traditional insurance companies.

National laws are free to increase the liability limits set by these international regimes. Spaeter and Schmitt [2007] study the impact of a change in the amount of liability of the nuclear operator on its accident prevention policy and on its solvency. It follows that an increase in the operator's liability beyond the ceiling leads to a reduction in its prevention activities, contrary to what is expected. Indeed, the cost of prevention increases linearly or more than proportionally, while the improvement in risk distribution is decreasing. Moreover, the impact of prevention activities on the financial constraint of the operator depends on the sensitivity of the risk distribution to the evolution of the level of prevention. Schmitt and Spaeter's article poses the question of the optimal fleet size given the insurance and prevention constraints.

The 2004 Paris Convention definitively makes compulsory insuring a part of the first reparation tranche by the operator. Moral hazards may arise if insurance companies cannot access all information concerning the nature of the risks of the facilities and the treatment of nuclear fuel. For Heal and Kunreuther [2010, p. 246], the Price–Anderson Act does not induce the operators to achieve an optimal level of prevention because insurance premiums are too low [Faure and Borre, 2008; Faure and Fiore, 2009]. It follows fewer involvements in prevention from the operators. Furthermore, the insurance premium levels do not reflect the performance and risk associated with nuclear power plant operations. Indeed, accidents or incidents on a given reactor do not lead to upward adjusting of the insurance premiums to reflect the risk increase. If, whatever the circumstances, insurance premiums remain constant, the interdependence of risks is undervalued. Thus, the financial vulnerability of a nuclear power plant depends not only on its prevention policy but also on the other stakeholders' actions. Then, a plant's failure may financially involve all similar plants.

This may be illustrated by the Mukhopadhyay *et al.* [2016]'s study about the causes of the five major nuclear accidents: Chernobyl in 1986 (INES degree 7); Fukushima-Daiichi in 2011 (INES degree 7); Three Mile Island in 1979 (INES degree 5); Chalk River in Canada in 1952 (INES degree 4); and SL-1 USA, 1961 (INES degree 4). Despite their own specificity, these accidents share the common feature of human errors due to the staff's station, and involve moral hazard situations.

6. Conclusion

The future of nuclear power is uncertain. It seems to be increasingly linked to three factors: The first concerns the commitment of countries to global warming. This energy is less CO_2-emitting than fossil energies. The second one, associated to the first one, is the expansion of renewable energies and the evolution of their prices, as well as energy-saving policies. A third factor is the possible occurrence of a large-scale accident that put into question the nuclear power policies. In all cases, the industrial organization of the nuclear sector will undergo major changes with an increasingly rapid penetration of the private sector in its management. Consequently, redefining the frontiers of civil liability is essential in this sector.

Nuclear energy is specific because it presents a range of particularly important and poorly understood risks and uncertainties, from the cradle of uranium mining to the grave of wastes that always remain an uncertain issue. The industrial organization theory of such a complex sector remains to be written. The question of defining the optimal size of a nuclear fleet in order to ensure the highest level of safety must be deepened. Restructuring this sector cannot be dominated by the sole search for profitability, leaving questions of safety and risk prevention in the background. The type of industry organization is an important risk factor that depends on the chosen civil liability, insurance constraints and governance decisions. The remaining questions concern the modalities of nuclear risk control. Mergers and acquisitions decisions in this sector are not insignificant and must be guided by the search for ever higher security. This chapter focused on the issue of civil liability and accident prevention as a driving force in the industrial organization of this sector. The issues of dismantling old power plants and reprocessing high-level radioactive waste must be incorporated into this thinking.

Appendix

Table A.1. European operators by country.

N° Operators	N° Countries	Countries	Operators	Nr Reactors
1	1	Belgium	*Electrabel*	7
2	2	Bulgaria	*KOZNPP*	2
3	3	Czech Rep.	*ČEZ Group*	6
4	4	France	*EDF*	58
5	5	Finland	*TVO*	2
6	5		FORTUMPH	2
7	6	Germany	*E.ON Kernkraft*	2
8	6		*EnKK*	2
9	6		*KGG*	2
10	6		*KLE*	1
11	6		*KWG*	1
12	7	Hungary	*PAKS*	4
13	8	Netherlands	*EPZ*	2
14	8		DELTA	2
13	9	Romania	SNN	2

(*Continued*)

Table A.1. (Continued)

N° Operators	N° Countries	Countries	Operators	Nr Reactors
14	10	Slovakia	*Slovenske Elektrarne*	4
15	11	Slovenia	NEK	1
16	12	Spain	CNAT	3
18	12		*Iberdrola*	1
19	12		ANAV	3
20	13	Sweden	*OKG*	3
21	13		*FKA*	3
22	13		RAB	4
23	14	Switzerland	KKL	1
24	14		AXPO	2
25	14		KKG	1
26	14		BKW	1
27	15	U. Kingdom	EDF-UK	15
28	16	Ukraine	NNEGC	15

Source: IAEA [2017].

References

ASN. (2017). Rapport de l'année 2016. https://www.asn.fr/Informer/Publications/Rapports-de-l-ASN/La-surete-nucleaire-et-la-radioprotection-en-France-en-2016.

Ameye, E. (2010). *Channelling of Nuclear Third Party Liability Towards the Operator: Is it Sustainable in a Developing Nuclear World or is There a Need for Liability of Nuclear Architects and Engineers*? In: INLA/AIDN (ed) Nuclear Inter Jura 2009 Proceedings/Actes du Congrès, Toronto, pp. 339–379; European Energy Environment Law Review 19, 33–58.

Bast, E., Doukas, A., Sam, P., van der Burg, L. and Whitley, S. (2015). Empty promises: G20 subsidies to oil, gas and coal production Research reports and studies, November. Overseas Development Institute (ODI). https://www.odi.org/publications/10058-empty-promises-g20-subsidies-oil-gas-and-coal-production.

Baumol, W. J., Panzar, J. C. and Willig, R. D. (1982). *Contestable Markets and the Theory of Industry Structure*. (Harcourt Brace Jovanovich, Inc, New York).

Bertel, É. and Naudet, G. (2004). *L'économie de l'Energie Nucléaire*. (EDP Sciences, Paris).

Berthélemy, M. and Escobar-Rangel, L. (2013). Nuclear reactors' construction costs: The role of lead-time, standardization and technological progress. CERNA. Paris, Working Paper 14-ME-01.

Bickel, P. and Friedrich, R. (eds.) (2005). ExternE Methodology, Update, European Commission, http://ec.europa.eu/research/energy/pdf/kina_en.pdf.

Carroll, S. and Froggatt, A. (2007). *Nuclear Third Party Insurance The Nuclear Sector's "Silent" Subsidy State of Play and Opportunities in Europe*, Conference Discussion Paper for The Future of Nuclear Energy in A Carbon Constrained World, November 5th 2007 New York. http://www.npolicy.org/files/DRAFT-20071105-Froggatt-NuclearThirdPartyInsurancePaper.pdf.

Codognet, M.-K., Glachant, J.-M., Hiroux, C., Mollard, M., Lévêque, F. and Plagnet, M.-A. (2003). *Mergers and Acquisitions in the European Electricity Sector Cases and Patterns*. CERNA, Paris, pp. 1–166 http://www.iaea.org/inis/collection/NCLCollectionStore/_Public/34/035/34035642.pdf.

Cour des Comptes. (2012). *Les Coûts de la Filière Électronucléaire*. (*Cour des Comptes*, Paris). http://www.ccomptes.fr/Publications/Publications/Les-couts-de-la-filiere-electro-nucleaire.

Culp, C. (2001). *The art (Alternative Risk Transfer) of risk management*. (Wiley Finance ed., New York).

D'Haeseleer, W. D. (2013). Synthesis on the Economics of Nuclear Energy. European Commission. https://www.mech.kuleuven.be/en/tme/research/energy_environment/Pdf/wpen2013-14.pdf.

Dessus, B. and Laponche, B. (2011). " *Accident nucleaire: une certitude statistique*". Liberation, 3 June, 2011. http://www.liberation.fr/politiques/01012341150-accident-nucleaire-une-certitudestatistique3june2011.

Dubin, J. A. and Rothwell, G. S. (1990). Subsidy to nuclear power through Price–Anderson liability limit. *Contemporary, Policy Issues* p 3, 7 (1990).

EU, Commission. (2016). Nuclear Illustrative Programme presented under Article 40 of the Euratom Treaty for the opinion of the European Economic and Social Committee COM(2016) 177 final.

Escobar-Rangel, L. and Leveque, F. (2014). How Fukushima Dai-ichi core meltdown changed the probability of nuclear accidents? *Safety Science* **64**, 90–98.

Escobar-Rangel, L. and Lévêque, F. (2015). Revisiting the cost escalation curse of nuclear power New lessons from the French experience. *Economic Energy and Environnement Policy* **4**(2), 103–126.

Faure, M. G., Fiore, K. (2009). An economic analysis of the nuclear liability subsidy school of law". *Pace Environmental Law Review* **26**, 419–448.

Faure, M. G. and Borre, T. V. (2008). Compensating nuclear damage: A comparative economic analysis of the US and international liability schemes. *Environmental Law & Policy Review* **33**, 219–286.

Fiore, K. (2007). Industrie nucléaire et gestion du risque d'accident en Europe: du défaut d'internalisation à l'organisation de la couverture, PhD, Aix-Marseille.

Fiore, K. (2008). The Nuclear Liability Limit in the OECD Conventions: An Implicit Subsidy. Mimeo, Centre d'Analyse Economique, Aix-en-Provence. https://ssrn.com/abstract=1086290 or http://dx.doi.org/10.2139/ssrn.1086290

Gautheron, L. (2017). Détermination empirique de la probabilité d'un accident nucléaire "majeur". Mediapart, May, https://blogs.mediapart.fr/lucas-gautheron/blog/180517/determination-empirique-de-la-probabilite-dun-accident-nucleaire-majeur

Ghys, E. (2011). "Accident nucléaire : une certitude statistique ". Libération, 5 juin, 2011.

Gollier, C., Proult, D., Thais, F. and Walgenwitz, G. (2005). Choice of nuclear power investments under price uncertainty: Valuing modularity, *Energy Economics* **27** (4), 667–685.

Grubler, A. (2014). The French pressurized water reactor programme. In A. Grubler and C. Wilson (eds.), *Energy Technology Innovation, Learning from Historical Successes and Failures* (Cambridge University Press, Cambridge, UK), pp. 146–161.

HEAL-Report. (2017). Hidden price tags — How ending fossil fuel subsidies would benefit our health. Health and Environment Alliance. http://env-health.org/IMG/pdf/healthandenvironmentalliance_hidden_price_tags_report.pdf.

Ha-Duong, M. and Journe, V. (2014). Calculating nuclear accident probabilities from empirical frequencies. *Environmental System Decision* **34** (2), 96–100.

Halligan, J., Mukhopadhyay, S. and Hastak, M. (2016). Assessment of major causes: Nuclear power plant disasters since 1950. *International Journal of Disaster Resilience in the Built Environment* **7** (5), 521–543, http://dx.doi.org/10.1108/IJDRBE-11-2015-0056.

Heal, G. and Kunreuther, H. (2010). Environment and energy: Catastrophic liabilities from nuclear power plants. In D. Lucas (ed.) *Measuring and Managing Federal Financial Risk* (University of Chicago Press), pp. 235–257. http://www.nber.org/chapters/c3037.

Heffron, R. J., Ashley, S. F. and Nuttall, W. J. (2016). The global nuclear liability regime post Fukushima Daiichi. *Progress in Nuclear Energy* **90**, 1–10.

Heyes, A. and Liston-Heyes, C. (2000a). An empirical analysis of the nuclear liability act (1970) in Canada. *Resource and Energy Economics* **22** (1), 91–101.

Heyes, A. and Liston-Heyes, C. (2000b). Capping environmental liability: The case of North American nuclear power. *The Geneva Papers* **25** (2), 196–202.

Heyes, A. and Liston-Heyes, C. (1998). Subsidy for nuclear power through the Price–Anderson liability limit. *Contemporary Economic Policy* **16** (1) 122–124.

IAEA. (2005). *Chernobyl's Legacy: Health, Environmental and Socio-Economic Impacts*. IAEA Division of Public Information: D. Kinley III (Editor). https://www.iaea.org/sites/default/files/chernobyl.pdf.

IAEA. (2014). IAEA Report on Human and Organizational Factors in Nuclear Safety in the Light of the Accident at The Fukushima Daiichi Nuclear Power Plant. International Experts Meeting Vienna, 21–24 MAY 2013. https://www.iaea.org/sites/default/files/humanfactors0914.pdf.

IAEA. (2015). *Climate Change and Nuclear Power.* International Energy Agency edition.

IAEA. (2017). *Nuclear Power Reactors in The World*. International Atomic Energy Agency, 2017 Edition. http://www-pub.iaea.org/MTCD/Publications/PDF/RDS_2-37_web.pdf.

IRSN. (2013). " Méthodologie appliquée par l'IRSN pour l'estimation des coûts d'accidents nucléaires en France ", PRP-CRI/SESUC/2013-00261, 68 pages. http://www.irsn.fr/FR/expertise/rapports_expertise/Documents/surete/IRSN-PRP-CRI-SESUC-2013-00261_methodologie-cout-accident.pdf.

Joskow, P. L. (2008). Lessons learned from electricity market liberalization. *The Energy Journal* **29** (Special Issue 2), 9–42.

Kameda, H. (2012). Engineering agenda on nuclear safety from the 2011 Tohoku-Pacific earthquake. In *Proceedings of International Symposium Engineering Lessons Learned from the 2011 Great East Japan*. Earthquake, March 1–4, 2012, Tokyo, Japan, pp. 102–121. http://www.neimagazine.com/opinion/opinionis-climate-change-the-worst-argument-for-nuclear-4493537/.

Kidd, S. (2015). Is climate change the worst argument for nuclear? *Nuclear Engineering International,* 21 January 2015.

Knight, F. H. (1921). *Risk, Uncertainty and Profit* (University of Chicago Press, Chicago) reprinted.

Koomey, J. G. and Hultman, N. E. (2007). A reactor-level analysis of busbar cost for US nuclear plants, 1970–2005. *Energy Policy* **35** (11), 5630–5642. http://dx.doi.org/10.1016/j.enpol.2007.06.005.

Koomey, J. G., Hultman, N. and Grubler, A. (2017). A reply to "Historical construction costs of global nuclear power reactors". *Energy Policy* **102**, 640–643.

Lévêque, F. (2014). *The Economics and Uncertainties of Nuclear Power* (Cambridge University Press, Cambridge).

Lochbaum, D. (2000). Nuclear Plant Risk Studies, Failing the Grade. Union of Concerned Scientists, UCS Publications.

Lochbaum, D., Lyman, E., Stranahan, S. Q. and Scientists, T. U. O. C. (2014). *Fukushima: The Story of a Nuclear Disaster*. (New Press, New York, NY).

Lovering, J. R., Yip, A. and Nordhaus, T. (2016). Historical construction costs of global nuclear power reactors. *Energy Policy* **91** (4), 371–382. http://www.sciencedirect.com/science/article/pii/S0301421516300106.

Lucas, W. D. and Wolfram, C. (2012). Deregulation, Consolidation, and Efficiency: Evidence from US Nuclear Power: Dataset. *American Economic Journal*: *Applied Economics* **4** (4), 194–225. http://dx.doi.org/10.1257/app.4.4.194.

MIT. (2009). Update on the cost of nuclear power. An Interdisciplinary MIT Study. http://web.mit.edu/nuclearpower/pdf/nuclearpower-update2009.pdf.

MacKerron, G. (1992). Nuclear costs: why do they keep rising? *Energy Policy*, **20** (7), 641–652. http://dx.doi.org/10.1016/0301-4215(92)90006-N.

Mondello, G. (2015). Splitting nuclear parks or not? The third party liability role. *Energy Economics* **51**, 553–559.

NEI (Nuclear Energy Institute). (2017). US Nuclear Power Plants General U.S. Nuclear Info. https://www.nei.org/Knowledge-Center/Nuclear-Statistics/US-Nuclear-Power-Plants.

Newbery, D. and Pollitt, M. (1997). The restructuring and privatization of Britain's CEGB – Was it worth it? *Journal of Industrial Economics* **45** (3), 269–303.

Nuclear Energy Agency (NEA). (2017a). Impacts of the Fukushima Daiichi Accident on Nuclear Development Policies. English, p. 68, #7212published: 04/06/17 http://www.oecd-nea.org/ndd/pubs/2017/7212-impacts-fukushima-policies.pdf.

Nuclear Energy Agency (NEA). (2017b). Addressing Uncertainties in Cost Estimates for Decommissioning Nuclear Facilities, OECD Publishing, Paris. http://dx.doi.org/10.1787/9789264284289-en.

Nuclear Energy Agency (NEA–OECD). (2003). Nuclear Electricity Generation: What are the External Costs? OECD, Paris.

Nuclear Energy Agency (NEA–OECD). (2012). Use and Development of Probabilistic Safety Assessment, An Overview of the Situation at the end of 2010. December 2012.

Nuclear Energy Agency (NEA-OECD). (2016). Protocol to Amend the Convention on Third Party Liability in the Field of Nuclear Energy of 29 July 1960, as amended by the Additional Protocol of 28 January 1964 and by the Protocol of 16 November 1982. IAEA. In https://www.oecd-nea.org/law/joint-protocol-fr.html.

Pelzer, N. (2016). Nuclear Accidents: Models for Reparation in Nuclear Non-Proliferation in International Law — Volume III. *Legal Aspects of the Use of Nuclear Energy for Peaceful Purposes*, L. Jonathan Black-Branch, Dieter Fleck (eds.), (T.M.C. ASSER PRESS, Springer).

Picard, P. (2011). The insurability of Nuclear Risk, HEC, Ecole Polytechnique. www.hec.fr/heccontent/download/7818/175862/file/Picard.pdf.

REN21. (2017). Renewables 2017 Global Status Report. http://www.ren21.net/wp-content/uploads/2017/06/178399_GSR_2017_Full_Report_0621_Opt.pdf.

Rothwell, G. (2001). Further Comments on Subsidy to Nuclear Power through the Price–Anderson Liability Limit. mimeo, August 2001.

Sajarroff, P. M., Lederman, L., Lepecki, W., Medina Vaillard, M. and Obadia, I. (2002). Organizational Factors and the Safety of Nuclear Power Plants: A Challenge to the Nuclear Industry and Regulatory Authorities: "Simposiom de la LANS/ANS. Río de Janeiro, Brasil, 17-19 June 2002. http://www.foroiberam.org/documents/193375/199920/Organizational+factors+and+the+safety+of+nuclear+power+plants.+A+challenge+to+the+nuclear+industry+and+regulatory+authorities/0f56e7d0-6454-434a-9b2d-ffd7bd27832b;version=1.0&previewFileIndex=1.

Schmitt, A. and Spaeter, S. (2007). Risque nucléaire civil et responsabilité optimale de l'exploitant. *Revue économique* **58**, 1331–1351.

Schneider, M., Froggatt, A., Hazemann, J., Tadahiro, K., Ramana, M. V., Rodriguez, J. C., Rudinger, A. and Stienne, A. (2017). The World Nuclear Industry Status Report, A Mycle Schneider Consulting Project, Paris, London, Tokyo, Sept. 2017 https://www.worldnuclearreport.org/-2017-.htm.

Schwartz, C. (2011). A propos d'une probabilité supérieure à 1d'avoir un accident nucléaire majeur. Statistix, June, pp.1–4. http://www.statistix.fr/spip.php?article87

Schwartz, J. A. (2006). International Nuclear Third Party Liability Law: The Response to Chernobyl. http://www.npec-web.org/files/DRAFT-20071105-Froggatt-NuclearThirdPartyInsurancePaper.pdf.

Shavell, S. (1987). *Economic Analysis of Accident Law*. (Harvard University Press, Cambridge, MA).

Shogren, E. (2011). Are nuclear plants safe? Environmentalists are split, NPR: Special Series — Rebuilding Japan. www.npr.org/2011/03/28/134863507/are-nuclear-plantssafe-environmentalists-are-split.

Thomas, S. (1988). *The Realities of Nuclear Power: International Economic and Regulatory Experience.* (Cambridge University Press, Cambridge, UK).

Vithayasrichareon, P., Riesz, J. and MacGill, I. (2015). Using renewables to hedge against future electricity industry uncertainties — An Australian case study. *Energy Policy*, **76**, pp. 43–56.

von Hippel, F. (ed.), Bunn, M., Diakov, A., Ding, M., Katsuta, T., McCombie, C., Ram Mana, M. V. Suzuki, T., Voss, S. and Yu, S. (2010). *The Uncertain Future of Nuclear Energy*. (Report for International Panel on Fissile Materials, Princeton, NJ).

Wen, Y.-K. and Ellingwood, B. R. (2005). Risk-benefit-based design decisions for low-probability/high consequence earthquake events in Mid-America. *Progress in Structural Engineering and Materials* **7** (2), 56–70.

Wheatley, S., Sovacool, B. and Sornette, D. (2016). Reassessing the safety of nuclear power. *Energy Research & Social Science* **15**, 96–100.

Zhang, F. (2007). Does electricity restructuring work? Evidence from the U.S. nuclear energy industry. *Journal of Industrial Economics* **55**(3), 397–418.

Chapter 18

Estimation of the Hotelling Rule for Oil under Stochastic Investment Opportunities

Johnson Kakeu*,‡ and Mohammed Bouaddi†,§

*Department of Economics, University of Prince Edward Island, Canada

†Department of Economics, The American University in Cairo, Egypt

‡jkakeu@upei.ca

§m.bouaddi@aucegypt.edu

This empirical work uses market capitalization of oil companies and proved reserves to investigate the role of in-ground oil stocks in risk diversification. It builds on the theoretical model of Gaudet and Khadr [1991], who use an intertemporal capital asset pricing approach to derive the stochastic version of the Hotelling rule which forms the basis for the estimations done in this chapter. The proxy used for the scarcity rent of oil is the difference between the growth rate of market capitalization of oil firms and that of oil proved reserves. In estimating the Gaudet and Khadr's stochastic Hotelling rule, we rely on an econometric approach that combines both the Nowman [1997] method for estimating diffusion processes and the Delta method. The empirical results suggest that holding oil reserves as assets can constitute a form of insurance against adverse long-run market fluctuations.

Keywords: Oil reserves; market capitalization; oil companies; stochastic Hotelling rule; risk diversification; long-run; beta; CKLS model; CRSP database; delta method.

1. Introduction

What role do *in situ* oil resource stocks play in a context of risk diversification in the long run? This chapter provides an empirical insight on this issue by building on the theoretical model of Gaudet and Khadr [1991], which combines insights from the finance and energy economics literature to develop a stochastic version of the Hotelling rule. The Gaudet and Khadr's stochastic Hotelling rule provides a useful theoretical framework to understand the evolution of the return on holding an oil stock in a context of risk diversification.

This chapter contributes to the small but growing literature that looks at the problem of hedging against uncertainty shocks to consumption derived from holding in-ground energy resources stocks in portfolio choices. Our analysis shows that the *long-run* beta for oil resources stocks, over the sample period (1959–2006), is negative, suggesting that holding *in situ* oil resource stocks may be used as a long-run hedging strategy against adverse shocks to consumption. In other words, over the long run, including oil resource stocks in portfolio choice could be a good choice for risk mitigation and value investing. In estimating the Gaudet and Khadr's stochastic Hotelling rule, we use an econometric approach that combines both the Nowman [1997] method for diffusion processes and the Delta method (see [Ver Hoef, 2012] for a review on the Delta Method). The proxy used for the scarcity rent of oil is the difference between the growth rate of market capitalization of oil firms and that of oil proved reserves.

From an empirical point of view, very few works have looked at the holding of in-ground stocks of non-renewable resources from the perspective of risk diversification [Gaudet, 2007]. The work by Slade and Thille [1997] is one of them. They modified the framework of Gaudet and Khadr [1991] and specified an econometric static approach that has the inconvenience of not taking into account the effects of time-varying investment opportunities in resource exploitation. They found a negative beta related to the riskiness of holding *in situ* resource stocks of copper, which suggests that copper stocks can be used to hedge against market risk. They proxy the *in situ* value of copper as the difference between price and the marginal extraction costs estimated by Young [1992].

In an empirical study on risk diversification and natural resources, Young and Ryan [1996] use a Generalized Method of Moments (GMM) estimation approach with the Epstein and Zin [1989] recursive utility to analyze lead, zinc, copper and silver. They proxy the value of a unit of the resource stock by using the difference between the Canadian price of the metal and the average operating costs. They found that attitudes toward the temporal resolution of uncertainty matter to understand the management of natural resources were under uncertainty. For a review of the empirical literature on exhaustible resources, see for instance Slade and Thille [2009] and Livernois [2009].

More recently, Kakeu and Nguimkeu [2017] have analyzed the oil prices implications of habit formation in consumption using a GMM estimation approach. They found that long-run future prospects related to habit formation constitute a forward-looking risk factor to be taken into account in explaining the dynamics of energy prices under uncertainty. Along the same lines, Kakeu and Bouaddi [2017] have used an econometric method that incorporates a dynamic latent factor analysis [Bouaddi and Taamouti, 2013; Ludvigson and Ng, 2009] to show that news about future prospects of the economy matter for explaining the pricing of oil resource stocks.

This chapter provides empirical evidence of how risk stemming from uncertainty shocks to consumption changes can be hedged, over the long run, through the holding of oil resource stocks in the portfolio choice. This suggests that long-term investors such as hedge funds and insurance companies should pay particular attention to energy resource assets when building their long-term development strategy for their clients.

The proxy used for the scarcity rent in this chapter is the difference between the growth rate of market capitalization of mining firms and that of proved reserves. To justify this choice, we derive a formal relationship between the return on a unit of the resource in the ground and the stock market return of a mining company. We then use the market capitalization of mining companies and proved reserves in the empirical investigation of Gaudet and Khadr's stochastic Hotelling rule.

The chapter is organized as follows: Section 2 presents Gaudet and Khadr's stochastic Hotelling rule. Section 3 describes the econometric approach. Section 4 relates a firm's market capitalization to the return on its *in situ* stock of the natural resource. Section 5 presents the data, while Section 6 presents the results of the econometric estimation of the Gaudet and Khadr's stochastic Hotelling rule. The final section offers conclusion of this chapter.

2. Gaudet and Khadr's Stochastic Hotelling Rule

In this section, we synthesize the main features and results of the Gaudet and Khadr [1991] model, which is the foundation for our empirical work. They assume two good economies: one of which is a non-renewable natural resource, whose stock at date t, $S(t)$, is irreversibly reduced by extraction and the other is a reproducible composite good, that can be either consumed or accumulated. If accumulated, it can be either in the form of physical capital, whose accumulated stock is denoted $K(t)$, or of a "bond". The accumulated stock of bonds is assumed to reproduce itself at an exogenously given risk free rate $r(t)$, which represents the force of interest.

Both the production of the composite good and the extraction of the natural resource are assumed to be stochastic.[1]

[1]The productivity indices are assumed to evolve over time according to Itô processes.

The representative consumer derives utility $U(c(t))$ from consuming the flow $c(t)$ of the composite good and is the ultimate owner of the stock of composite good and the stock of the natural resource. He chooses for each date his consumption and the allocation of his wealth between the resource stock and the accumulated composite good so as to maximize his discounted flow of future utility subject to his stochastic wealth constraint. His consumption and portfolio decisions generate consumption and asset demands, through which he sends price signals to the resource firms and the firms producing the composite good.

Gaudet and Khadr show that, in equilibrium,

$$\mu_S(t) - r(t) = \beta(t)[\mu_M(t) - r(t)], \tag{1}$$

where $\beta(t)$ is the so-called "beta coefficient" associated to the resource stock as an asset, $\lambda(t)$ the price of a unit of resource *in situ* and $\mu_S(t) = \frac{1}{\lambda(t)}\frac{1}{dt}E_t(d\lambda(t))$ is the expected instantaneous rate of return on the resource stock being held in the ground, $\mu_M(t)$ is the expected rate of return on any market portfolio whose observed return has a non-zero covariance with changes in consumption.

Thus, depending on whether $\beta(t)$ is positive or negative, the expected excess return on holding the resource will be positive or negative, meaning that the expected rate of change in the *in situ* price of the resource will be greater or smaller than the rate of interest. This is the formulation of the Hotelling rule which is retained for the empirical investigation that follows.

3. An Econometric Specification of the Stochastic Hotelling Rule

In what follows, we borrow from recent financial econometrics methods to estimate the above stochastic Hotelling rule.

We want to estimate the time-varying coefficient $\beta(t)$, which is a measure of the sensitivity of the return on the resource stock to the return on the chosen "market" portfolio. It will be an indicator of that part of the variance on the return on the resource stock that cannot be diversified away by investing in the chosen portfolio of assets.

If the values of $\mu_S(t)$ and $\mu_M(t)$ were known, then, given $r(t)$, the value of $\beta(t)$ could be easily computed by noting that:

$$\beta(t) = \frac{\mu_S(t) - r(t)}{\mu_M(t) - r(t)}. \tag{2}$$

Thus, estimated values $\mu_S(t)$ and $\mu_M(t)$ will provide us with estimated values of $\beta(t)$.

The rate of return on holding a stock of the resource in the ground is given by the rate of change in its *in situ* price, $d\lambda/\lambda$. It is shown in Gaudet and Khadr [1991] that it will in equilibrium follow an Itô process of the form:

$$\frac{d\lambda(t)}{\lambda(t)} = \mu_S dt + \sigma_S \xi_S \sqrt{dt}, \tag{3}$$

where μ_S and σ_S are equilibrium values, and $\xi_S \sim N(0, 1)$.

In order to specify an estimable form, it is useful to reformulate Eq. (3) in terms of the cumulative return on the *in situ* resource stock, $R^S(t) = \int_0^t d\lambda(s)/\lambda(s)$. We can use its infinitesimal variation $dR^S(t) = d\lambda(t)/\lambda(t)$ to rewrite Eq. (3) as

$$dR^S(t) = \mu_S(t, R^S(t))dt + \sigma_S(t, R^S(t))d\zeta_S(t), \tag{4}$$

where the drift and the variance coefficients are now expressed explicitly in terms of time and of $R^S(t)$ and where $d\zeta_S(t) = \xi_S(t)\sqrt{t}$, with $\xi_S \sim N(0, 1)$.

Similarly, the stochastic process for the cumulative return on the market portfolio, $R^M(t)$, is given by:

$$dR^M(t) = \mu_M(t, R^M(t))dt + \sigma_M(t, R^M(t))d\zeta_M(t). \tag{5}$$

The commonly used strategy to estimate this stochastic process consists first in specifying a functional form for both the drift and the diffusion coefficients and, second, in discretizing the stochastic process in order to estimate the parameters from observed data, which are typically recorded discretely over a certain time interval $[0, T]$.

Consequently, we consider a specific class of continuous time diffusion processes known as the CKLS model (see [Chan *et al.*, 1992]) and defined as follows:

$$dR(t) = (\alpha_1 + \alpha_2 R(t))dt + \sigma R(t)^{\alpha_3} d\zeta(t). \tag{6}$$

This model therefore adopts a linear function of time for the drift and a power function for the volatility. Equation (6) allows the conditional mean and variance to depend on the level of $R(t)$, which is the cumulative return on the stock of the resource. The parameters α_1 and α_2 are the unknown drift and mean reversion structural parameters, σ is the volatility parameter and α_3 is the proportional conditional volatility exponent.

The general CKLS specification in Eq. (6) facilitates the construction of a discrete time version. The discrete approximation of the continuous time diffusion process developed by Nowman [1997] and based on some results found in Bergstrom [1983] is given by:

$$R_t = e^{\alpha_2} R_{t-1} + \frac{\alpha_1}{\alpha_2}(e^{\alpha_2} - 1) + \eta_t, \tag{7}$$

where the error term η_t satisfies:

$$E(\eta_s \eta_t) = \begin{cases} 0 & \text{if } s \neq t \\ \frac{\sigma^2}{2\alpha_2}(e^{2\alpha_2} - 1) R_{t-1}^{2\alpha_3} & \text{if } s = t. \end{cases}$$

Define $L(\alpha_1, \alpha_2, \alpha_3, \sigma)$ as the logarithm of the likelihood function of the model:

$$L(\alpha_1, \alpha_2, \alpha_3, \sigma) = \sum_{t=1}^{T} \left[\log E(\eta_t^2) + \frac{(R_t - e^{\alpha_2} R_{t-1} - \frac{\alpha_1}{\alpha_2}(e^{\alpha_2} - 1))^2}{E(\eta_t^2)} \right] + \textit{constant term},$$

with $E(\eta_t^2)$ as defined above. Maximum Likelihood Estimation consists in solving for

$$(\widehat{\alpha_1}, \widehat{\alpha_2}, \widehat{\alpha_3}, \widehat{\sigma}) = \underset{\alpha_1, \alpha_2, \alpha_3, \sigma}{\arg\max}\, L(\alpha_1, \alpha_2, \alpha_3, \sigma)$$

to get estimates of the unknown parameters in the drift and diffusion coefficients. The method is a sort of quasi-maximum method since Eq. (7) is not the true discrete model corresponding to Eq. (6), but is merely a conditional Gaussian approximation. In doing so, this method replaces a non-Gaussian process by an approximate Gaussian one.

The estimated drift of the return on the natural resource stock is then given by

$$\widehat{\mu_S(t)} = \widehat{\alpha_1^S} + \widehat{\alpha_2^S} R^S(t),$$

while that on the return on the market portfolio is given by

$$\widehat{\mu_M(t)} = \widehat{\alpha_1^M} + \widehat{\alpha_2^M} R^M(t).$$

The estimated *short-run* beta can then be computed as:

$$\widehat{\beta(t)} = \frac{\widehat{\mu_S(t)} - r(t)}{\widehat{\mu_M(t)} - r(t)}, \tag{8}$$

where $r(t)$ is the risk free rate.

We define a *long-run* beta over the period [0,T] as:

$$\overline{\beta} = \frac{\left[\frac{\sum_{t=1}^{T}(\mu_S(t)-r(t))}{T}\right]}{\left[\frac{\sum_{t=1}^{T}(\mu_M(t)-r(t))}{T}\right]}. \tag{9}$$

Notice that if we substitute for $\mu_S(t) - r(t)$ from Eq. (1), the *long-run* beta, $\overline{\beta}$, can be rewritten in the following way:

$$\bar{\beta} = \frac{\sum_{t=1}^{T} \beta_t[\mu_M(t) - r(t)]}{\sum_{t=1}^{T} [\mu_M(t) - r(t)]}, \tag{10}$$

which is a weighted average of the betas over the interval $[0, T]$, with the weights given by $[\mu_M(t) - r(t)]/\sum_{t=1}^{T} [\mu_M(t) - r(t)]$.

A point estimate of the *long-run* beta (10) is then given by

$$\widehat{\bar{\beta}} = \frac{\sum_{t=1}^{T} \widehat{\beta(t)}\ [\widehat{\mu_M}(t) - r(t)]}{\sum_{t=1}^{T} [\widehat{\mu_M}(t) - r(t)]}. \tag{11}$$

A negative value of *long-run* beta would mean that holding natural resource stocks can constitute a form of insurance against long-run market uncertainty.

In what follows, we adopt an approach similar to that of Lucas [1978], Breeden [1979], Hansen and Singleton [1983] and Mankiw and Shapiro [1986], who use the consumption growth risk (or consumption beta) to measure the riskiness of an asset. The betas will be measured relative to consumption growth rather than the market portfolio index. This is analogous to the Eqs. (1), (8) and (9) with the expected return on the market portfolio μ_M replaced by the expected rate of growth in consumption μ_C. In this case, the beta is the conditional covariance between the return on the resource asset and the consumption growth. A non-renewable resource asset is more risky if it pays less when consumption is low. For sake of clarity, it should be noted that using real or nominal monetary variables will lead to the same value of beta. This is because the point estimate of the *long-run* beta, $\widehat{\bar{\beta}}$, can be rewritten as the ratio of real monetary values by dividing the nominal interest rate, the nominal market return, the nominal return on the resource by the price level.

4. Market Capitalization and the Rate of Return on the *in situ* Resource Stocks

One way for individual investors to invest in non-renewable reserves (such as oil) is to buy stocks in the companies that hold those reserves. However, at any moment of time, the stock market value of those companies will reflect their holdings not only of *in situ* stocks of the non-renewable resource, but also of some reproducible assets. Let $K(t)$ represent the stock of capital held at date t in the form of those other assets. If we denote by $\nu(t)$ the value of a unit of that capital, then, if the company owns reserves in the quantity $S(t)$, valued at $\lambda(t)$, the company's market capitalization can be written as follows:

$$\Pi(t) = \lambda(t)S(t) + \nu(t)K(t) \tag{12}$$

$$= [\lambda(t) + \gamma(t)\nu(t)]S(t), \tag{13}$$

where $\gamma(t) = K(t)/S(t)$ is the ratio of fixed capital to reserves.

In the absence of reasonable measures of the evolution over time of $\gamma(t)$ and $\nu(t)$ we will assume them to be constant. It follows that:

$$E_t\left[\frac{d\Pi(t)}{\Pi(t)}\right] = E_t\left[\frac{d\lambda(t)}{\lambda(t)}\left[\frac{\lambda(t)}{\lambda(t)+\gamma\nu}\right] + \frac{dS(t)}{S(t)}\right]. \tag{14}$$

Since the evolution of reserves are assumed to deterministic, it follows that:

$$E_t[dR^S(t)] = E_t\left[\frac{d\lambda(t)}{\lambda(t)}\right] = \left(1 + \frac{\gamma\nu}{\lambda(t)}\right)\left(E_t\left[\frac{d\Pi(t)}{\Pi(t)} - \frac{dS(t)}{S(t)}\right]\right). \tag{15}$$

The return on the resource stock is therefore proportional to the difference between the rate of change in the company's capitalization and the rate of change in its reserves. The factor of proportionality $(1 + (\gamma\nu)/\lambda(t))$ is a decreasing function of $\lambda(t)$, but is always positive. In the absence of observations on $\lambda(t)$, it therefore seems reasonable to use

$$E_t\left[\frac{d\Pi(t)}{\Pi(t)} - \frac{dS(t)}{S(t)}\right] \tag{16}$$

as a proxy for the return on the resource stock for estimation purposes, since they both must move in the same direction. This is what will be done in the estimations that follow.[2] Let us mention that the idea of using the market capitalization of oil firms to investigate the Hotelling rule was pioneered by Miller and Upon [1985a, 1985b].

[2]It is also worth mentioning that the use of the proxy (16) will introduce measurement error that are difficult to quantify accurately.

5. The Data

5.1. *Oil*

The data used to compute the proxy (16) for oil are presented in this section. We need data on market capitalization of oil companies and on oil reserves. Data are obtained from different sources for the period 1959(2) to 2006(12).[3] The data on market capitalizations of oil companies comes from the Center for Research in Security Prices (CRSP) database. The CRSP (http://www.crsp.com) provides a comprehensive database on NYSE, AMEX and NASDAQ stock markets. The CRSP database provides firms' characteristics including: name, industry sector and market capitalizations. The selection of oil and gas firms is based on the availability of data on market capitalization. The selection is composed of 56 oil and gas firms in the CRSP database that are quoted on US stock exchanges for at least 5 years. All of the 56 companies are classified under US Department of Labor SIC number 1311 (Crude petroleum and natural gas). The 56 oil companies which were at one time or another a part of the sample are listed in Table A.1. It is worth noting that 39 companies in the sample obtained from the CRSP database are ranked by Energy Intelligence (2006) in the top 100 largest operators that account for more than 85% of world's oil proven reserves. The 61 other companies in the top 100 were not listed on the US stock exchange, which is a prerequisite for being retained in our sample. The data on world reserves comes from the BP Statistics web site, on a yearly basis for the period 1959–2006.[4] A temporal disaggregation technique will be used to generate monthly equivalent proven reserves over the period 1959(2) to 2006(12).

The proxy (16) for the change in the cumulative return of the oil reserves at date t can be computed in discrete time as follows:

$$\Delta R_\tau^{\text{oil}} = \left[\frac{\sum_{n=1}^{N_\tau} X_{n,\tau}^{\text{oil}}}{\sum_{n=1}^{N_{\tau-1}} X_{n,\tau-1}^{\text{oil}}} - 1\right] - \left[\frac{S_\tau}{S_{\tau-1}} - 1\right], \tag{17}$$

where $\tau \in \{1959(2), \ldots, 2006(12)\}$, $X_{n,\tau}^{\text{oil}}$ is the market capitalization of oil company n at date τ and N_τ the total number of companies at that date. The number N_τ changes over time as the number of companies present on the stock exchange changes. A change in the number of companies can be because of the split of an existing company, the entry of a new company, the merger of two existing companies or the exit of an existing company. Taking into account all of those changes assures

[3]The data ends in 2006, due to our limited access to the database CRSP.

[4]See www.bp.com.

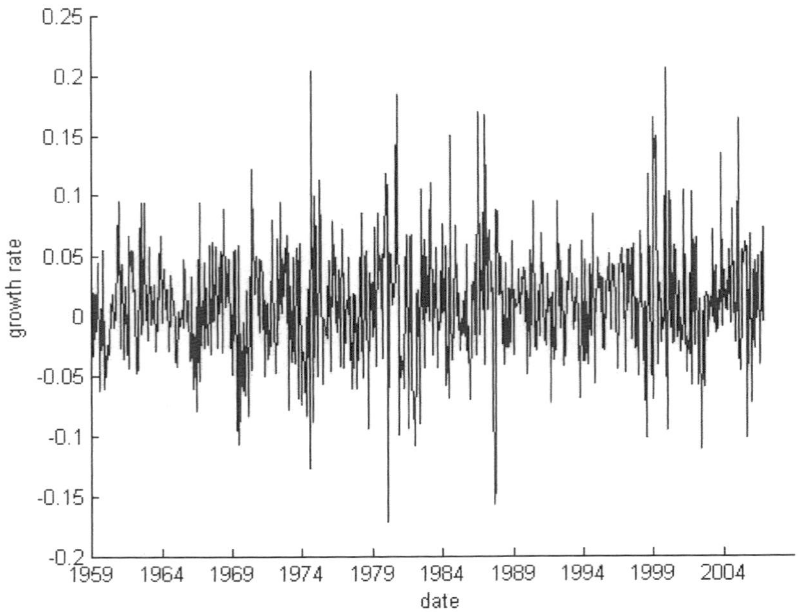

Fig. 1. Growth rate of the market capitalization of oil companies.

the coherence of the index over time. The number of companies in the sample retained for this study varies between 5 and 56 over the period of observation. S_τ is the level of world proven oil reserves at date τ. The first term of this formula reflects the rate of change in the market capitalization of the oil sector and the second term reflects the change in the proven oil reserve.

Figure 1 shows the evolution of the first term of Eq. (17), which is the monthly growth rate in the index of market capitalization of the oil companies.

Due to the unavailability of data on oil reserves held by the companies in the sample over a sufficiently long period of time, we use data on world's oil proven reserves as its proxy.[5]

[5]It is only in 1978 that the US Securities and Exchange Commission's oil and gas reserves reporting requirements were adopted (Rule 4-10 of Regulation S-X). The original disclosure requirements have not kept up with current practices, and therefore are of limited value. Indeed, the oil and gas industry and markets have seen significant changes, including technological advances. These developments, and others, caused the SEC's reporting requirements to increasingly lag behind the capabilities of the petroleum industry. On 31 December 2008, the US Securities and Exchange Commission released new rules amending oil and gas reporting requirements.

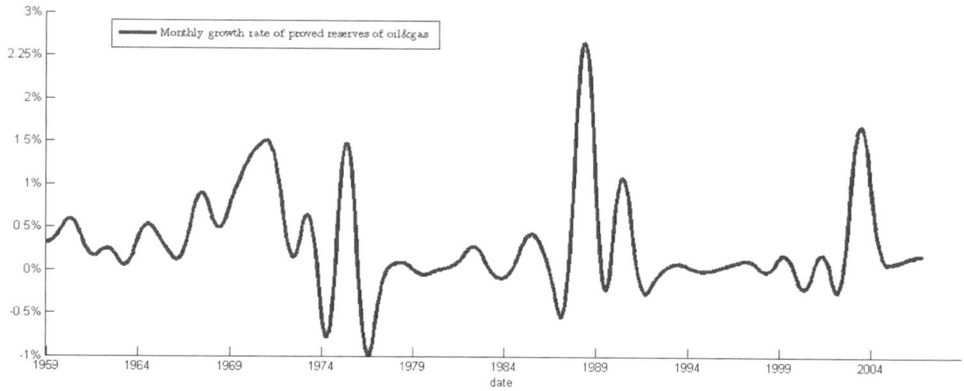

Fig. 2. Growth rate of the oil world proved reserves.

The data on world proven oil reserves are from the web site of BP Statistics. Since it is annual in frequency and the market capitalization data is monthly, we need to compute the monthly equivalent of the annual proven reserves. To do this we use an interpolation technique for deriving a monthly series from annual data (see Lisman and Sandee [1964]; Boot *et al.* [1967]). The method generates estimated monthly reserves that are consistent with the annual series on proven reserves. It generates the estimated monthly reserves series by solving the following constrained quadratic minimization problem:

$$\min \sum_{i=2}^{12k} (s_i - s_{i-1})^2$$

$$s.t. \quad \sum_{i=12t-11}^{12t} s_i = S_t, \; (t = 1, 2, .., k), \tag{18}$$

where k is the number of annual observations, S is the annual proven reserve and s is the estimated monthly proven reserve. The result is shown in Fig. 2.

The proxy for the cumulative return on the reserves can then be calculated as:

$$R_t^{\text{oil}} = \sum_{\tau=0}^{t} \Delta R_\tau^{\text{oil}} + R_0^{\text{oil}}, \tag{19}$$

where $\Delta R_\tau^{\text{oil}}$ is given by Eq. (17). Figure 3 plots the evolution over time of this proxy for the cumulative return on oil reserves.

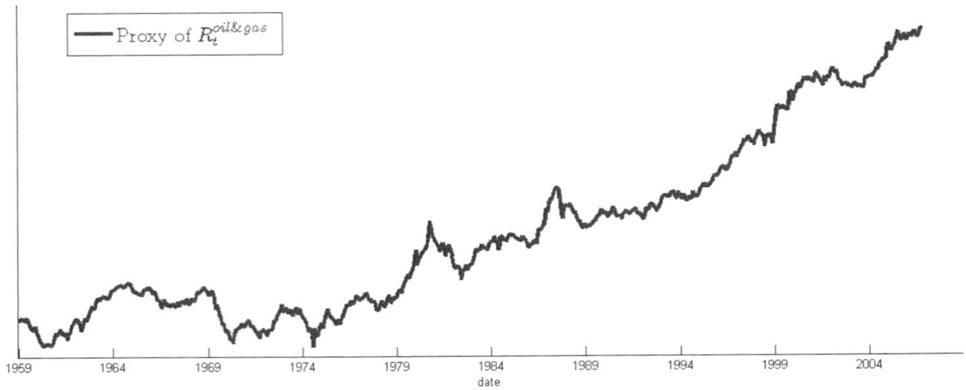

Fig. 3. Proxy of the cumulative returns of the oil in the ground (R_t^{oil}).

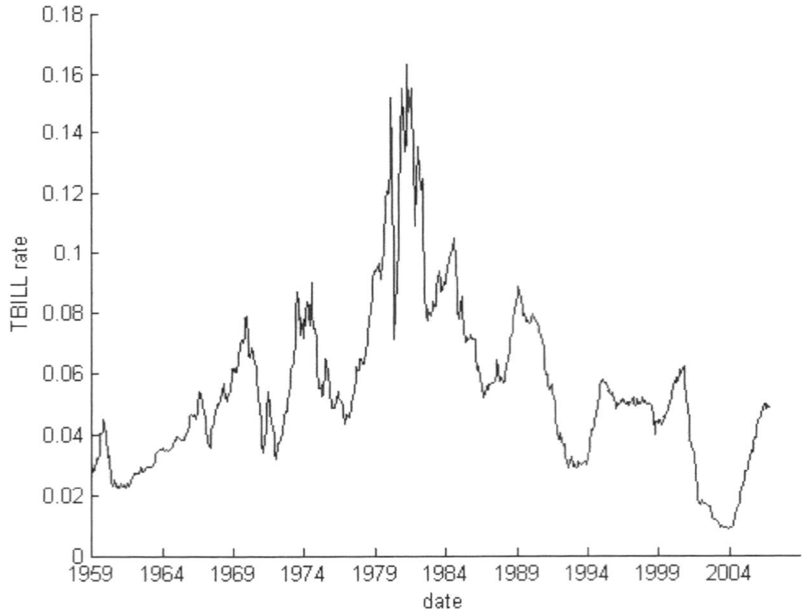

Fig. 4. 1-month US Treasury bill.
Source: CRSP database

5.2. *The risk-free rate*

For the risk-free rate of interest, we use the monthly equivalent of the annual rate on the 1-month US Treasury bill, taken from the CRSP database. The data ranges from February 1959 to December 2006.

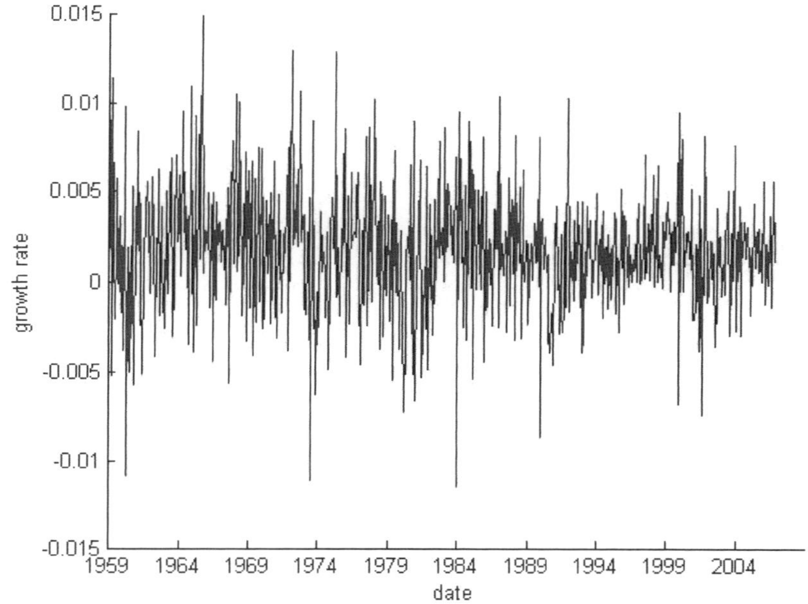

Fig. 5. Growth rate of per-capita consumption.
Source: St. Louis Federal Reserve Bank

5.2.1. *US consumption data*

Data on US consumption are from the St. Louis Federal Reserve Bank and cover the period February 1959 to December 2006.[6] We used monthly per capita consumption of services and non-durable goods.

6. Estimating the Gaudet and Khadr's Stochastic Hotelling Rule

6.1. *The short-run betas and the long-run beta for the in situ oil asset*

The estimation of the stochastic process for the returns on the *in situ* oil asset was conducted using the CKLS model given by

$$dR^{\text{oil}}(t) = (\alpha_1 + \alpha_2 R^{\text{oil}}(t))dt + \sigma R^{\text{oil}}(t)^{\alpha_3} d\zeta(t). \tag{20}$$

[6]We focus on US consumption date since the proxy for the scarcity rent is built using oil and gas companies that are listed on the US Stock Exchange. Furthermore, the interest rate on the US Treasury bill is commonly used as a proxy for the risk-free rate.

Table 1. Maximum likelihood estimates of the CKLS model (20) for the returns on oil.

$\widehat{\alpha_1^{oil}}$	$\widehat{\alpha_2^{oil}}$	$\widehat{\alpha_3^{oil}}$	$\widehat{\sigma^{oil}}$
−0.0008	0.0082	0.9847	0.0536
(−0.7646)	(1.7634)	(19.1920)	(18.0914)

Note: Estimated t-values are shown in parentheses.

Table 2. Maximum likelihood estimates of the CKLS model (21) for consumption.

$\widehat{\alpha_1^c}$	$\widehat{\alpha_2^c}$	$\widehat{\alpha_3^c}$	$\widehat{\sigma^c}$
−0.0002	0.0020	0.2678	0.0013
(0.7646)	(2.6012)	(0.6454)	(1.7054)

Note: Estimated t-values are shown in parentheses.

The parameters are estimated from 48 years of monthly data (575 observations). The estimations of the diffusion parameters of the oil returns in Eq. (20) are presented in Table 1.

The results of the parameters estimated for oil returns using the model of maximum likelihood show that all the estimators, besides $\widehat{\alpha_1^{\text{oil}}}$, are statistically significant at the 10% level.

We estimated the stochastic process for the rate of growth of consumption using the CKLS model given by

$$dR^c(t) = (\alpha_1 + \alpha_2 R^c(t))dt + \sigma R^c(t)^{\alpha_3} d\zeta(t). \tag{21}$$

The parameters are estimated from 48 years of monthly data (575 observations). The results of the estimation of the diffusion parameters of the rate of growth of consumption in Eq. (21) are reported in Table 2.

The results of the parameters estimated for consumption using the model of maximum likelihood show that all the estimators, besides $\widehat{\alpha_1^c}$ and $\widehat{\alpha_3^c}$, are statistically significant at the 10% level.

The estimated beta coefficients are given by:

$$\widehat{\beta}^{\text{oil},C}(t) = \frac{\widehat{\alpha_1^{\text{oil}}} + \widehat{\alpha_2^{\text{oil}}}\, R^{oil}(t) - r(t)}{\widehat{\alpha_1^c} + \widehat{\alpha_2^c}\, R^c(t) - r(t)}. \tag{22}$$

From the expressions (11) and (22), it follows that the estimated value of the *long-run* beta is

$$\widehat{\overline{\beta}}_{\text{oil}} = \frac{\sum_{t=1}^{T} \widehat{\beta}^{\text{oil},C}(t)\,[\widehat{\alpha_1^c} + \widehat{\alpha_2^c}\,R^c(t) - r(t)]}{\sum_{t=1}^{T} [\widehat{\alpha_1^c} + \widehat{\alpha_2^c}\,R^c(t) - r(t)]} = -3.99 < 0. \tag{23}$$

The negative value of the point estimate of the *long-run* beta seems to suggest that oil in the ground can be used to hedge against risk in the long run. An investor wanting to make a long-term strategy of hedging against consumption risk may include oil assets in his portfolio.

We need to compute a confidence interval for the long-run beta (10), which is a ratio parameter. Building a confidence interval for a parameter ratio is not easy due to the problem of the overdiversification of the model. The denominator can be equal to zero, for example, causing the interval to be unbounded. We follow the Bolduc *et al.* [2007] approach to build the confidence interval for long-run beta. They use a procedure which combines the parametric bootstrap, the Fieller method and the Delta Method. See Appendix B for more details on this procedure. Using this procedure, it follows that the 95% Bootstrap Fieller confidence interval for the *long-run* beta $\widehat{\overline{\beta}}_{\text{oil}}$ is $FC = [-\infty, +\infty]$. It appears the Fieller confidence interval which is unbounded is less informative than the 95% Bootstrap Delta confidence interval for the *long-run* beta $\widehat{\overline{\beta}}_{\text{oil}}$ which is

$$DC = [-4.5293; -3.3454]. \tag{24}$$

The Bootstrap Delta confidence interval suggests that in-ground oil stock is an asset providing insurance against fluctuations in consumption in the long run. Investing in oil in the ground is a good hedge against the market risk in the long run.

Finally, let us mention that, over the last three decades, the emergence of sovereign wealth funds in several countries has been an important development in global finance and energy economics [van den Bremer *et al.*, 2016]. Our empirical results may also point to the idea that global investors and sovereign wealth funds owning below-ground oil assets may play an important role in strengthening countries' long-run hedging strategy against market uncertainty.

7. Conclusion

Building on the financial resource economics model of Gaudet and Khadr [1991], this chapter has empirically investigated the role of non-renewable natural resource stocks in a context of risk diversification. In doing so, we have used the market capitalization of mining companies and the world proved reserves in the construction of a proxy for the return on holding in-ground energy resources stocks. We have estimated a stochastic version of the Hotelling rule of exhaustible resource exploitation and used it to infer on the riskiness of investment in oil reserves. The empirical results indicate that investing in oil reserves is a good hedge against risk in the long run. The negative *long-run* beta coefficient means that the return on holding in-ground oil resource stocks as assets tends to vary inversely with changes in the market, as captured by the relative change in consumption. In that sense, in-ground oil resource stocks are shown to be playing a long-term insurance role against the consumption risk in capital markets. This suggests that long-term investors such as hedge funds and insurance companies should pay particular attention to energy resource assets when building long-term development strategies for their clients.

In recent decades, the emergence of sovereign wealth funds in several countries has been an important development in global finance and energy economics [van den Bremer *et al.*, 2016]. Our empirical results may also point to the idea that global investors and sovereign wealth funds owning below-ground oil assets can play an important role in strengthening countries' long-run hedging strategy against market uncertainty. While holding large amount of oil reserves in the portfolio can serve as an instrument to hedge against consumption risk in the long run for resource-rich countries, awareness to issues such as political stability, governance capacity and environmental sustainability should not be overlooked [Monga, 2017; Hooper, 2016; Carney, 2016; Kakeu, 2017].

Acknowledgements

We would like to thank the editors for their comments and feedback that substantially improved this chapter. We thank Gérard Gaudet and Benoit Perron for insightful discussions and comments. We also thank workshop participants of the 2010 World Congress of Environmental and Resource Economists, the Montréal Natural Resources and Environmental Economics Workshop and the Canadian Resource and Environmental Economics Study Group.

Appendix

A. *List of oil companies*

Table A.1. Sample of oil companies.

Companies	Beginning[a]	End
UNITED STATES STEEL CORP	1959(02)	2006(12)
STANDARD OIL CO CALIFORNIA	1959(02)	2006(12)
PHILLIPS PETROLEUM CO	1959(02)	2006(12)
STANDARD OIL CO N J / EXXON MOBIL CORP	1959(02)	2006(12)
UNOCAL CORP	1959(02)	2005(12)
BRITISH PETROLEUM LTD	1962(07)	2006(12)
KERR MCGEE CORP	1956(03)	2006(12)
CANADA SOUTHERN PETROLEUM LTD	1962(08)	2006(12)
JEFFERSON LAKE PETROCHEMICALS	1962(08)	2006(12)
IMPERIAL OIL LTD	1962(08)	2006(12)
OCCIDENTAL PETROLEUM CORP	1962(08)	2006(12)
BRITALTA PETROLEUMS LTD / WILSHIRE OIL CO TX	1962(08)	2006(12)
MURPHY CORP	1962(02)	2006(12)
APACHE CORP	1963(08)	2006(12)
BARNWELL INDUSTRIES INC	1965(08)	2006(12)
BROWN TOM INC	1972(12)	2004(04)
FOREST OIL CORP	1972(12)	2006(12)
PATRICK PETROLEUM CO	1972(12)	2006(12)
NOBLE AFFILIATES INC	1972(12)	2006(12)
TIPPERARY LAND & EXPLORATION	1972(12)	2005(09)
WISER OIL CO DE	1972(12)	2004(06)
K R M PETROLEUM CORP	1974(07)	2006(12)
MAYNARD OIL CO	1975(08)	2002(06)
GEORESOURCES INC	1976(04)	2006(12)
PYRAMID OIL CO	1976(08)	2006(12)
CREDO PETROLEUM CORP	1979(03)	2006(12)
HARKEN OIL & GAS INC	1979(12)	2006(12)
DOUBLE EAGLE PETE & MNG CO	1980(01)	2006(12)
BELLWETHER EXPLORATION CO	1980(12)	2005(06)
CENTRAL PACIFIC MINERALS N L	1981(03)	2002(02)
PARALLEL PETROLEUM CORP DE	1981(01)	2006(12)
SANTOS LIMITED	1981(03)	2006(12)
MAGELLAN PETROLEUM CORP	1982(11)	2006(12)
SASOL LTD	1982(05)	2006(12)
ENSERCH EXPLORATION PARTNERS LTD	1985(04)	2002(12)
WALKER ENERGY PARTNERS	1985 (11)	2006(12)
ANADARKO PETROLEUM CORP	1986(10)	2006(12)
NORSK HYDRO A S	1986(07)	2006(12)

(Continued)

Table A.1. (***Continued***)

Companies	**Beginning**[a]	**End**
PARKER & PARSLEY DEVELOPMENT PAR	1987(12)	2006(12)
REPSOL S A	1989(05)	2006(12)
ENRON OIL & GAS CO	1989(10)	2006(12)
VINTAGE PETROLEUM INC	1990(09)	2005(12)
TOTAL S A	1991(11)	2006(12)
NEWFIELD EXPLORATION CO	1993(12)	2006(12)
SUNCOR INC	1994(01)	2006(12)
CROSS TIMBERS OIL CO	1993(06)	2006(12)
PETRO CANADA	1995(11)	2006(12)
LEVIATHAN GAS PIPELINE PTNERS LP	1998(09)	2004(09)
DEVON ENERGY CORP NEW	1988(10)	2006(12)
PETROLEO BRASILEIRO SA PETROBRAS	2000(09)	2006(12)
PANCANADIAN ENERGY CORP	2001(11)	2006(12)
STATOIL A S A	2001(07)	2006(12)
INTEROIL CORP	2004(10)	2006(12)
BILL BARRETT CORP	2005(01)	2006(12)
ROYAL DUTCH SHELL PLC	2005(07)	2006(12)

[a] In the CRSP, the data on market capitalizations of some companies such as UNITED STATES STEEL CORP begin in 1925, but due to the unavailability of data on monthly consumption at this period, we were constrained to begin in 1959.

B. *The confidence interval for the long-run beta*

Assume that the ratio parameter is

$$\bar{\beta} = \frac{\kappa_1}{\kappa_2}, \tag{B.1}$$

where $\kappa_1 = \sum_{t=1}^{T} \beta_t[\mu_M(t) - r_t]$ and $\kappa_2 = \sum_{t=1}^{T} [\mu_M(t) - r_t]$.

A point estimation of the long-run beta is given by

$$\widehat{\bar{\beta}} = \frac{\widehat{\kappa_1}}{\widehat{\kappa_2}}, \tag{B.2}$$

where $\widehat{\kappa_1} = \sum_{t=1}^{T} \widehat{\beta_t}[\widehat{\mu_M}(t) - r_t]$ and $\widehat{\kappa_2} = \sum_{t=1}^{T} [\widehat{\mu_M}(t) - r_t]$.

Let $\widehat{\Sigma_{12}} = \begin{bmatrix} \widehat{\upsilon_1} & \widehat{\upsilon_{12}} \\ \widehat{\upsilon_{12}} & \widehat{\upsilon_2} \end{bmatrix}$ denotes the covariance matrix that corresponds to $(\widehat{\kappa_1}, \widehat{\kappa_2})$.

B.1. *Bootstrap Fieller confidence interval*

The t-test statistic is as follows:

$$t(\overline{\beta}) = \frac{\widehat{\kappa_1} - \overline{\beta}\widehat{\kappa_2}}{(\overline{\beta}^2 \widehat{\upsilon_2} - 2\widehat{\upsilon_{12}} + \widehat{\upsilon_1})^{\frac{1}{2}}} \rightsquigarrow_{asymp} N(0, 1).$$

The Fieller method provides the $(1-\alpha)\%$ confidence interval by inverting the t-test statistic. This corresponds to the values of $\overline{\beta}$ such that $|t(\overline{\beta})| \leq z_{\alpha/2}$.

Let $A = \widehat{\kappa_2}^2 - z_{\frac{\alpha}{2}}^2 \widehat{\upsilon_2}$, $B = \widehat{\kappa_1}\widehat{\kappa_2} + z_{\frac{\alpha}{2}}^2 \widehat{\upsilon_{12}}$, $C = \widehat{\kappa_1}^2 - z_{\frac{\alpha}{2}}^2 \widehat{\upsilon_1}$, $\Delta = B^2 - AC$.

The $(1-\alpha)\%$ Fieller confidence interval depends on the sign of $\Delta = B^2 - AC$.

If $\Delta < 0$,

$$FC(\alpha) = [-\infty, +\infty]. \tag{B.3}$$

If $\Delta \geq 0$,

$$FC(\alpha) = \begin{cases} \left[\frac{-B-\sqrt{\Delta}}{A}, \frac{-B+\sqrt{\Delta}}{A}\right] & \text{if } A > 0, \\ \left]-\infty, \frac{-B-\sqrt{\Delta}}{A}\right] \cup \left[\frac{-B+\sqrt{\Delta}}{A}, +\infty\right[& \text{if } A < 0. \end{cases} \tag{B.4}$$

B.2. *Bootstrap delta confidence interval*

$$DC(\alpha) = \left[\frac{\widehat{\kappa_1}}{\widehat{\kappa_2}} - z_{\frac{\alpha}{2}}\widehat{L}^{\frac{1}{2}}, \frac{\widehat{\kappa_1}}{\widehat{\kappa_2}} + z_{\frac{\alpha}{2}}\widehat{L}^{\frac{1}{2}}\right], \tag{B.5}$$

where $\widehat{L}^{\frac{1}{2}} = \begin{bmatrix} \frac{1}{\widehat{\kappa_1}} & -\frac{\widehat{\kappa_1}}{\widehat{\kappa_2}^2} \end{bmatrix} \begin{bmatrix} \widehat{\upsilon_1} & \widehat{\upsilon_{12}} \\ \widehat{\upsilon_{12}} & \widehat{\upsilon_2} \end{bmatrix} \begin{bmatrix} \frac{1}{\widehat{\kappa_1}} \\ -\frac{\widehat{\kappa_1}}{\widehat{\kappa_2}^2} \end{bmatrix}$.

The parametric bootstrap procedure by Efron [1979] is used to compute the covariance matrix that corresponds to $(\widehat{\kappa_1}, \widehat{\kappa_2})$ as follows.

Let $(\widehat{\alpha_1}^{(0)}, \widehat{\alpha_2}^{(0)}, \widehat{\alpha_3}^{(0)}, \widehat{\sigma}^{(0)})$ an estimate of $(\alpha_1, \alpha_2, \alpha_3, \sigma)$ obtained from the original sample path denoted by $R_t^{(0)}$. The parametric bootstrap procedure consists of the following steps:

Step 1. Generate a bootstrap sample path $R_t^{(b)}$ from

$$R_t^{(b)} = e^{\widehat{\alpha_2}^{(b-1)}} R_{t-1}^{(b)} + \frac{\widehat{\alpha_1}^{(b-1)}}{\widehat{\alpha_2}^{(b-1)}}(e^{\widehat{\alpha_2}^{(b-1)}} - 1) + \eta_t^{(b)}, \tag{B.6}$$

where we have simulated the random variable $\widehat{\eta_t}^{(b)}$ such that

$$E(\eta_s^{(b)}\eta_t^{(b)}) = \begin{cases} 0 & \text{if } s \neq t, \\ \frac{\widehat{\sigma^2}^{(b-1)}}{2\widehat{\alpha_2}^{(b-1)}}(e^{\widehat{\alpha_2}^{(b-1)}} - 1) R_{t-1}^{2\widehat{\alpha_3}^{(b-1)}} & \text{if } s = t. \end{cases}$$

Step 2. Obtain a new maximum likelihood estimator from the bootstrap sample path by applying the same estimation procedure.

Step 3. Repeat Steps 1 and 2 D number of times and obtain a set of bootstrap estimates.
We can compute $b = 1, \ldots, D$ bootstraps sample by using the estimated parameters the discrete model and the initial values of the variable.

Step 4. From the original sample, we generate sample $b = 1$ by using with estimates parameters of the original sample in the discrete specification and by simulating random numbers representing the error term $\eta_t^{(b)}$.

Step 5. So we use the parametric bootstrap sample $b - 1$ to estimate the new parameters $\widehat{\alpha_1}^{(b-1)}, \widehat{\alpha_2}^{(b-1)}, \widehat{\alpha_3}^{(b-1)}, \widehat{\sigma^2}^{(b-1)}$ and there we plug in the discrete specification and simulate $\eta_t^{(b)}$ to obtain the sample b.

From $R^S(t)$, we use this parametric bootstrap method to obtain the bootstrap replications of the drift $\widehat{\kappa_1^b} = \frac{\sum_{t=1}^{T}(\mu_S^{(b)}(t)-r_t)}{T}$ for the samples $b = 1, \ldots, D$.

Once we have estimated distribution for $\widehat{\kappa_1}$, we use it to estimate the standard error for $\widehat{\kappa_1}$. This estimate is given by $\widehat{\upsilon_1} = \frac{1}{B}\sum_{b=1}^{B}(\kappa_1^b - \overline{\widehat{\kappa_1}})^2$, where $\overline{\widehat{\kappa_1}} = \frac{1}{B}\sum_{b=1}^{B}\widehat{\kappa_1}^b$.

From the consumption $R^C(t)$, we use this parametric bootstrap method to obtain the bootstrap replications of the drift $\widehat{\kappa_2^b} = \frac{\sum_{t=1}^{T}(\mu_M^{(b)}(t)-r_t)}{T}$ for the samples $b = 1, \ldots, D$.

Using simulated distribution of the estimators $\left(\widehat{\kappa_1^b}, \widehat{\kappa_1^b}\right)_{b=1,\ldots,D}$, we can compute $\widehat{\upsilon_{12}}$ which is the estimate of the covariance between $\widehat{\kappa_1}$ and $\widehat{\kappa_1}$.

References

Bergstrom, A. (1983). Gaussian estimation of structural parameters in higher-order continuous time dynamic models. *Econometrica* **51**, 117–152.

Bolduc, D., Khalaf, L. and Yelou, C. (2007). Identification robust confidence set methods for inference on parameter ratios with application to discrete choice models. *Journal of Econometrics* **157**, 317–327.

Boot, J., Feibes, W. and Lisman, J. (1967). Further methods of derivation of quarterly figures from annual data. *Applied Statistics* **16**, 65–75.

Bouaddi, M. and Taamouti, A. (2013). Portfolio selection in a data-rich environment. *Journal of Economic Dynamics and Control* **37**, 2943–2962.

Breeden, D. (1979). An intertemporal asset pricing model with stochastic consumption and investment opportunities. *Journal of Financial Economics* **7** (3), 265–296.

Carney, M. (2016). Resolving the climate paradox. Arthur Burns Memorial Lecture, Berlin.

Chan, K., Longstaff, F. A. and Sanders, A. B. (1992). An empirical comparison of alternative models of the short-term interest rate. *Journal of Finance* **47**, 1209–1228.

Efron, B. (1979). Bootstrap methods: Another look at the jackknife. *Annals of statistics* **7**, 1–26.

Epstein, L. and Zin. S. (1989). Substitution, risk aversion and the temporal behavior of consumption and asset returns: A theoretical framework. *Econometrica* **57**, 937–969.

Gaudet, G. (2007). Natural resource economics under the rule of hotelling. *Canadian Journal of Economics* **40**, 1033–1059.

Gaudet, G. and Khadr, A. (1991). The evolution of natural-resource prices under stochastic investment opportunities: An intertemporal asset-pricing approach. *International Economic Review* **32**, 441–455.

Hansen, L. and Singleton, K. (1983). Stochastic consumption, risk aversion, and the temporal behavior of asset returns. *The Journal of Political Economy* **91** (2), 249–265.

Hooper, E. (2016). Oil and gas, which is the belle of the ball? The impact of oil and gas reserves on sovereign risk. Working Papers halshs-01211506, Aix-Marseille University.

Kakeu, J. (2017). Environmentally conscious investors and portfolio choice decisions. *Journal of Sustainable Finance & Investment* **7**, 360–378.

Kakeu, J. and Bouaddi, M. (2017). Empirical evidence of news about future prospects in the risk-pricing of oil assets. *Energy Economics* **64**, 458–468.

Kakeu, J. and Nguimkeu, P. (2017). Habit formation and exhaustible resource risk-pricing. *Energy Economics* **64**, 1–12.

Lisman, J. and Sandee, J. (1964). Derivation of quaterly figures from annual data. *Applied Statistics* **13**, 87–90.

Livernois, J. (2009). On the empirical significance of the Hotelling rule. *Review of Environmental Economics and Policy* **3**, 22–41.

Lucas, R. (1978). Asset prices in an exchange economy. *Econometrica* **46** (6), 1429–1445.

Ludvigson, S. and Ng, S. (2009). Macro factors in bond risk premia. *Review of Financial Studies* **22**, 5027–5067.

Mankiw, N. and Shapiro, M. (1986). Risk and return: Consumption beta versus market beta. *The Review of Economics and Statistics* **68**, 452–459.

Miller, M. and Upton, H. (1985a). A test of the Hotelling valuation principle. *Journal of Political Economy* **93**, 1–25.

Miller, M. and Upton, H. (1985b). The pricing of oil and gas: Some further results. *Journal of Finance* **40**, 1009–1018.

Monga, C. (2017). Truth is the safest lie: A reassessment of development economics. *Africa Economic Brief* **8**, 1–8.

Nowman, K. (1997). Gaussian estimation of single-factor continuous time models of the term structure of interest rates. *The Journal of Finance* **52**, 1695–1706.

Slade, M. and Thille, H. (1997). Hotelling confronts CAPM: A test of the theory of exhaustible resources. *Canadian Journal of Economics* **30**, 685–708.

Slade, M. and Thille, H. (2009). Whither Hotelling: Tests of the theory of exhaustible resources. *Annual Review of Resource Economics* **1**, 239–260.

van den Bremer, T., van der Ploeg, F. and Wills, S. (2016). The elephant in the ground: Managing oil and sovereign wealth. *European Economic Review* **82**, 113–131.

Ver Hoef, J. (2012). Who invented the delta method? *The American Statistician* **66**, 124–127.

Young, D. (1992). Cost specification and firm behaviour in a Hotelling model of resource extraction. *Canadian Journal of Economics* **25**, 41–59.

Young, D. and Ryan, D. (1996). Empirical Testing of a Risk-Adjusted Hotelling Model. *Resources Energy Economics* **18**, 265–289.

PART IV

Environmental, Green and Renewable Energy

Chapter 19

Financing the Reduction of Greenhouse Gas Emissions: A New Allocation System for Dependent Risks

Lorena Remuzgo, Carmen Trueba and José María Sarabia

Department of Economics, University of Cantabria, Spain

The allocation of fixed resources among multiple dimensions is a usual challenge faced by natural resource managers. In this chapter, we propose a capital allocation framework for assigning financial resources among multiple environmental dependent risks. This approach relies on the use of the multivariate gamma distribution as a formal model for the estimation of different capital allocation principles, given its properties of dependence and positive skewness. The presented methodology is applied to the CO_2, CH_4 and N_2O emissions of the EU-28 in 2013 in order to determine the incomes we should use for financing the reduction of the risks related to each gas. Our results indicate that CO_2 is the riskiest pollutant, and then more capital is allocated to it. Finally, using simulation techniques, we study the sensitivity of our results.

Keywords: Climate change risks; risk management measures; climate change adaptation; multivariate gamma distribution; resource allocation framework; capital allocation principles; greenhouse gas emissions; emissions trading system; European union allowances; simulation process.

1. Introduction

Regarding the environmental area, the joint effect of the current concentration of CO_2, CH_4 and N_2O in the atmosphere is very likely to have been the dominant cause of global warming since the mid-20th century [IPCC, 2013]. One alternative to deal with climate change has been the stabilization of greenhouse gas (GHG) concentration in the atmosphere, which is the ultimate goal of the United Nations Framework Convention on Climate Change [UNFCCC, 1992]. However, such stabilization target does not deal with the implicit risks which are present in climate change [Obersteiner *et al.*, 2001].

Risks associated with climate change — floods, droughts and cyclones, between others — have always been present in the course of history [Lamb, 1995]. Environmental risks may cause catastrophic damages and result in substantial costs [Shafiee, 2015]. Global environmental risks are increasing its importance because they are threatening a stable development pathway. Moreover, the path dependency between climate change risks provokes that shocks which occur in one country could have even a major impact in other parts of the world [Kleindorfer, 2009]. In this sense, the UNFCCC also advocates the use of risk management measures:

> The parties should take precautionary measures to anticipate, prevent or minimize the causes of climate change and mitigate its adverse effects. Where there are threats of serious or irreversible damage, lack of scientific certainty should not be used as a reason for postponing such measures, taking into account that policies and measures to deal with climate change should be cost effective so as to ensure global benefits at the lowest possible cost... [UNFCCC, 1992, Article 3.3].

Climate risk management tries to incorporate the knowledge of the financial risk management to reduce potential losses associated with climate-related events. Thus, while mitigation measures reduce GHG emissions concentration at the source, adaptation measures have the potential to make less the adverse effects of climate change. Therefore, the aim of adaptation strategies should be to apply management to address climate change, enhance the adaptability of species and ecosystems and reduce vulnerability due to climate variability [Hulme, 2005]. Although risk approaches appeared in climate research a couple of decades ago [Yohe, 2009], they are still rare in climate change adaptation (CCA) analysis. In this sense, Jones and Preston [2010] conclude that "risk management stands as the most appropriate overarching framework for assessing CCA". The increasing economic losses related to such risks have led to a stronger insistence on the need for CCA and how it can benefit from the background in risk management [IPCC, 2012]. Assessment of the vulnerability to climate change is necessary to promote relevant adaptation policies [Jun *et al.*, 2013], being essential find ways of supporting CCA [Stern, 2006].

In this context, a resource allocation framework is necessary for determining what percentage of the total budget we must use to cover CCA measures for reducing the risks coming from the different GHG emissions. Thus, a *constant allocation* means distributing the total capital by the number of gases; a *proportional allocation* gives more importance to the gases that represent a greater hazard, and an *optimal allocation* considers the dependence between the different GHG emissions.

One of the most daunting challenges faced by natural resource managers is how to allocate a fixed resource, for example, money, among multiple dimensions [Hajkowicz, 2009]. Such dilemma has received much attention in the field of water resources allocation [Mianabadi *et al.*, 2014; Read *et al.*, 2014; Hillman *et al.*, 2012]. Given that the EU has planned to use a share of the revenues from the auctioning of EU Emissions Trading System (ETS) allowances for climate and energy related purposes [European Commission, 2014], we develop a resource allocation system for determining the incomes we should use for financing the reduction of the risks related to each GHG, measured in terms of number of EU ETS allowances. In particular, we consider the CO_2, CH_4 and N_2O emissions of the EU-28 in 2013 and calculate the number of EU ETS allowances we should intend to reduce the impact of each gas emissions. Note that we do not establish how to determine the total capital that must be allocated but we assume it as given. It is noted that different allocation principles had been applied in the context of operational risks within a firm [Urbina and Guillén, 2014] or automobile insurance [Ai *et al.*, 2013; Artis *et al.*, 1999, 2002; Viaene *et al.*, 2004].

The strong evidence suggesting that climate change is linked with an increase in GHGs is something that we cannot ignore. Assuming independence between GHG emissions seems to be unrealistic given the dependence of the radiative forcing[1] of a gas on its concentration and the concentration of other gases [IPCC, 1990, 2007]. In this sense, Fig. 1 shows how to deal with dependence risks from a three-dimensional perspective of GHG emissions.

It should be highlighted that the methodological contribution of this chapter lies in the use of the multivariate gamma distribution as a formal model for the estimation of capital allocation principles, given its properties of dependence and positive skewness. In addition, despite the fact that the abatement of the risks related to the GHGs build-up in the atmosphere lie at the heart of the climate debate, this is the first attempt to employ different allocation principles in the environmental area.

Our results indicate that CO_2 is the riskiest gas and therefore more capital is allocated to it. While the Haircut allocation principle assigns fewer allowances than the other principles to the risks related to CO_2 emissions, the covariance principle is the one that allocates a greater number of allowances to the emissions of this pollutant. Finally, using a simulation process to study the behavior of the different capital principles to changes in emissions, we can conclude that the Overbeck type

[1] Radiative forcing is defined as the change in the balance between radiation coming into and going out of the atmosphere as a result of internal changes in the composition of the atmosphere. Thus, a positive radiative forcing tends to warm the Earth's surface.

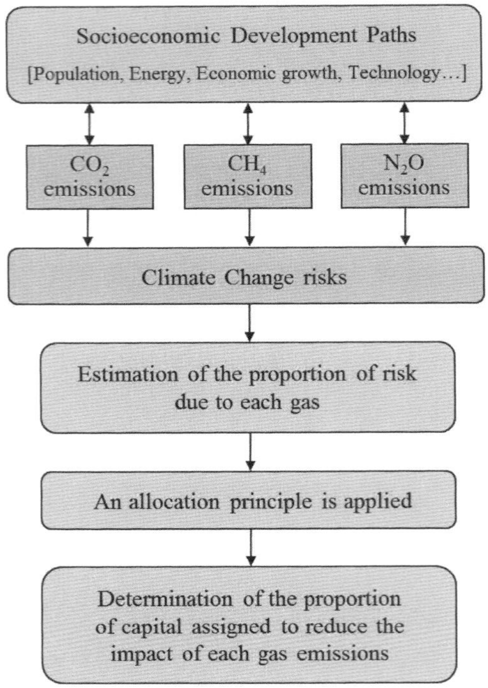

Fig. 1. Climate change risk assessment system with three GHG emissions.

I principle is the most convenient to use in this framework as it presents the lowest variability throughout the simulated period.

This chapter is organized as follows: In Section 2, the multivariate gamma distribution is proposed as a model when there is dependence between risks. Considering the previous distribution, the expressions of different capital allocation principles are specified in Section 3. An application to GHG emissions is addressed in Section 4. Conclusions and future research lines are presented in the last section.

2. The Multivariate Gamma Distribution

The uncertainty around climate change consequences makes necessary the use of probability distribution functions which allow a better approach to consider a range of possible outcomes rather than a single most likely one [IPCC, 2004]. In order to calculate different capital allocation principles, we choose the multivariate gamma distribution because it admits the existence of dependence between risks and it can be applied to positively skewed distributions. The class of gamma distributions is widely used in theoretical and applied actuarial statistics [Furman and Landsman,

2005]. In particular, we consider the multivariate gamma distribution which was introduced by Cheriyan [1941] and Ramabhadran [1951] and generalized by Mathai and Moschopoulus [1991].

A random variable X is said to be distributed according to a gamma distribution if its probability density function is given by:

$$f(x) = \frac{\alpha^{\gamma} x^{\gamma-1} e^{-\alpha x}}{\Gamma(\gamma)}, \tag{1}$$

if $x > 0$ with $\alpha, \gamma > 0$. We will represent $X \sim \text{Ga}(\gamma, \alpha)$.

Let $Y_0, Y_1, \ldots, Y_m$ be mutually independent gamma random variables $Y_i \sim \text{Ga}(\gamma_i, \alpha_i)$, where $\gamma_i, \alpha_i > 0, i = 0, 1, 2, \ldots, m$ are the shape and scale parameters, respectively, and let:

$$X_i = \frac{\alpha_0}{\alpha_i} Y_0 + Y_i, \quad i = 1, 2, \ldots, m. \tag{2}$$

Then, the joint distribution of the random vector $\mathbf{X} = (X_1, X_2, \ldots, X_m)^T$, whose components are defined in (2), is a multivariate gamma distribution, where the marginal distributions are standard gamma distributions but correlated. The moment generating function of $\mathbf{X}$ is given by:

$$\begin{aligned} M_{\underline{X}}(t) &= E\left[\exp\left(Y_0 \sum_{i=1}^{m} \frac{\alpha_0}{\alpha_i} t_i\right)\right] \prod_{i=1}^{m} E\left[e^{t_i Y_i}\right] \\ &= \left(1 - \sum_{i=1}^{m} \frac{t_i}{\alpha_i}\right)^{-\gamma_0} \prod_{i=1}^{m} \left(1 - \frac{t_i}{\alpha_i}\right)^{-\gamma_i}. \end{aligned} \tag{3}$$

Some relevant properties of the multivariate gamma are the following:

- Marginal distributions:

$$X_i \sim \text{Ga}(\gamma_0 + \gamma_1, \alpha_i), \quad i = 1, 2, \ldots, m. \tag{4}$$

- The components of the mean vector are:

$$E(X_i) = \frac{\gamma_0 + \gamma_i}{\alpha_i}, \quad i = 1, 2, \ldots, m. \tag{5}$$

- The variances are:

$$\mathrm{Var}(X_i) = \frac{\gamma_0 + \gamma_i}{\alpha_i^2}, \quad i = 1,\ 2, \ldots,\ m. \tag{6}$$

- The covariances and the linear correlation coefficients are, respectively:

$$\mathrm{Cov}(X_i, X_j) = \frac{\gamma_0}{\alpha_i \alpha_j}, \quad i \neq j \tag{7}$$

and

$$\rho(X_i, X_j) = \frac{\gamma_0}{\sqrt{(\gamma_0 + \gamma_i)(\gamma_0 + \gamma_j)}}, \quad i \neq j. \tag{8}$$

2.1. *Estimation of the multivariate gamma distribution*

In this section, we propose a simple estimation methodology for the multivariate gamma distribution when losses exhibit a dependence structure in the case $m = 3$. We proceed in two steps. In the first step, we estimate the parameters $\alpha_i, i = 1, 2, 3$ using (5) and (6). If we solve for α_i, we obtain

$$\hat{\alpha}_i = \frac{E(X_i)}{\mathrm{Var}(X_i)}, \quad i = 1,\ 2,\ 3. \tag{9}$$

For estimating the rest of the parameters we use previous estimates (9), Eqs. (2.5) and (2.6) and the generalized variance, which is the determinant of the covariance matrix. We have

$$\left|\sum\right| = \frac{\gamma_0(\gamma_1\gamma_2 + \gamma_1\gamma_3 + \gamma_2\gamma_3) + \gamma_1\gamma_2\gamma_3}{\alpha_1^2\alpha_2^2\alpha_3^2} \tag{10}$$

and

$$\gamma_0 + \gamma_i = \frac{[E(X_i)]^2}{\mathrm{Var}(X_i)}, \quad i = 1,\ 2,\ 3, \tag{11}$$

where $\alpha_i, i = 1, 2, 3$ are estimated using previous equations. Finally, the estimates of γ_i are obtained solving (10) and (11) for $\gamma_i, i = 1, 2, 3$.

Previous model (2) contains the independence case. When $\gamma_0 \to 0$, $X_i \sim \mathrm{Ga}(\gamma_i, \alpha_i)$, the random vector $\mathbf{X}$ consists of m independent gamma random variables. Subsequently, the joint distribution of $\mathbf{X}$ is a multivariate independent gamma distribution. In consequence, $E(X_i) = \gamma_i/\alpha_i$, $\mathrm{Var}(X_i) = \gamma_i/\alpha_i^2, i = 1, 2, \ldots, m$

and we can obtain the simple estimators for γ_i and α_i given by:

$$\hat{\gamma}_i = \frac{\bar{x}_i^2}{S_i^2}, \quad i = 1,\ 2, \ldots,\ m, \tag{12}$$

$$\hat{\alpha}_i = \frac{\bar{x}_i}{S_i^2}, \quad i = 1,\ 2, \ldots,\ m. \tag{13}$$

3. Capital Allocation Principles Using the Multivariate Gamma Distribution

In this section, we provide an exact functional form for each capital allocation principle assuming that the random vector of losses $\mathbf{X} = (X_1, X_2, \ldots, X_m)^{\mathrm{T}}$ is a multivariate gamma distribution.

Let $X_1, X_2, \ldots, X_m$ be m random losses arising from different risks which are materializing at a fixed future date T. Assume that each loss X_i has a finite mean and denote the cumulative distribution function (cdf) of X_i by $F_{Xi}(x)$. The aggregate loss is defined by:

$$S = \sum_{i=1}^{m} X_i, \quad i = 1,\ 2, \ldots,\ m. \tag{14}$$

Given an exogenous capital K to cover S, capital allocation seeks the distribution of K across the different risks, that is, to determine non-negative real numbers $(K_1, K_2, \ldots, K_m)$ satisfying the full allocation requirement:

$$\sum_{i=1}^{m} K_i = K. \tag{15}$$

Allocation principles are methods conceived to establish K_i considering different risk measures and assumptions. Thus, a *constant allocation* means dividing the total capital by the number of gases regardless of the contribution each gas emissions makes to global climate change risk. Meanwhile, a *proportional allocation* gives more importance to the gases that represent a greater risk. Finally, an *optimal allocation* takes into account the contribution of each gas considering the dependence between the different emissions within the climate system [Dhaene *et al.*, 2012].

We refer to Table 1 for a summary of different capital allocation principles. Based on the VaR measure, the Haircut allocation principle is defined as the inverse of the distribution function of X, for a given fixed probability level p. In the standard deviation principle, the amount of capital is related to the variability of the loss [Bühlmann, 1970; Hardy, 2006]. A dynamic version of the standard

Table 1. Capital allocation principles.

Name	$K_i \quad i = 1, 2, \ldots, m$
Proportional capital allocation principles	
Haircut	$\frac{K}{\sum_{i=1}^{m} F_{X_i}^{-1}(p)} F_{X_i}^{-1}(p)$
Optimal capital allocation principles. Business driven capital allocation[a]	
Standard deviation principle	$\frac{K}{E[S]+a\sum_{i=1}^{m}\sigma X_i}\left[E[X_i]+a\sigma X_i\right], \quad a \geq 0$
Esscher principle	$\frac{K}{\sum_{i=1}^{m} E\left[\frac{X_i e^{aX_i}}{E(e^{aX_i})}\right]} E\left[\frac{X_i e^{aX_i}}{E(e^{aX_i})}\right], \quad a > 0$
Optimal capital allocation principles. Aggregate portfolio driven capital allocation[b]	
Covariance principle	$\frac{K}{Var[S]} Cov(X_i, S)$
Overbeck type I	$\frac{K}{E[S]+a\sum_{i=1}^{m}\sigma X_i}\left[E[X_i]+\frac{a}{\sum_{i=1}^{m}\sigma X_i} Cov(X_i, S)\right], \quad a \geq 0$

[a]Under business driven capital allocation, heavier weights are attributed to deviations that correspond to states that involve larger losses.
[b]Under aggregate portfolio driven capital allocation, heavier weights are attributed to deviations that correspond to states that involve a larger aggregate loss.

deviation principle in an economic environment is studied by Schweizer [2001] and Møller [2001]. The Esscher principle [Bülhmann, 1980; Gerber, 1981] has a formal similarity to the Esscher transform. The covariance allocation principle assigns a larger amount of capital to the losses that are more correlated with the aggregate loss (S), in comparison to those that are less correlated. Overbeck [2000] presents and analyzes a capital allocation rule based on the marginal contributions to the expected shortfall risk measure. The constant a in the standard deviation, Esscher and Overbeck type I principles measure the risk aversion (also named as Arrow–Pratt measure) so, the higher it is, the more risk averse. Figure 2 shows which allocation method are or not influenced by the dependence structure between the different losses, X_i.

If the losses follow a multivariate gamma distribution, the expressions of the previous capital allocation principles are as specified in Table 1 but the Esscher principle which is provided by the following formula:

$$K_i[K, a; \gamma_0, \gamma_i, \alpha_i] = \frac{K}{\sum_{i=1}^{m} \frac{\gamma_0+\gamma_i}{\alpha_i - a}} \left(\frac{\gamma_0 + \gamma_i}{\alpha_i - a}\right), \quad a > 0, \tag{16}$$

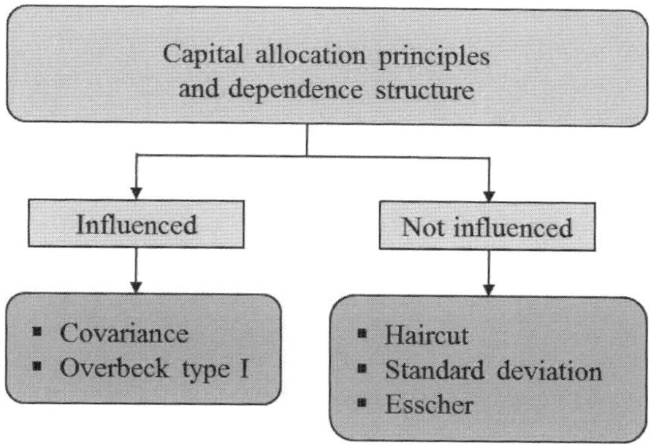

Fig. 2. Dependence structure and capital allocation principles.

where γ_0, γ_i and α_i are the dependence, shape and scale parameters of the multivariate gamma distribution, respectively.

4. Application to the Main GHG Emissions

The EU has planned to use a share of the revenues from the auctioning of EU ETS allowances for climate and energy related purposes [European Commission, 2014]. In this section, we determine the incomes we should use for financing the reduction of the risks related to each GHG. The incomes are given in terms of the total quantity of allowances to be auctioned in 2013 which was established by Commission Decision 2013/448/UE of 5 September 2013 in 2084301856 allowances.[2] Note that we do not establish how to determine the total number of allowances that must be allocated but we assume it as given.

In particular, we apply the allocation principles estimated in the previous section to per capita CO_2, CH_4 and N_2O emissions in the EU-28 (see Fig. 3) in 2013 in order to calculate what share of the revenues from the auctioning of EU ETS allowances we should intend for reducing the impact of each gas. Such emissions, measured in tonnes of CO_2-eq, have been taken from the estimates compiled by the European Environment Agency in the approximated EU GHG inventory for 2013.

We choose the multivariate gamma distribution in order to calculate the different capital allocation principles because it admits the existence of dependence between risks and it can be applied to positively skewed distributions. In this context, the

[2]One allowance gives the holder the right to emit one tonne of CO_2-eq.

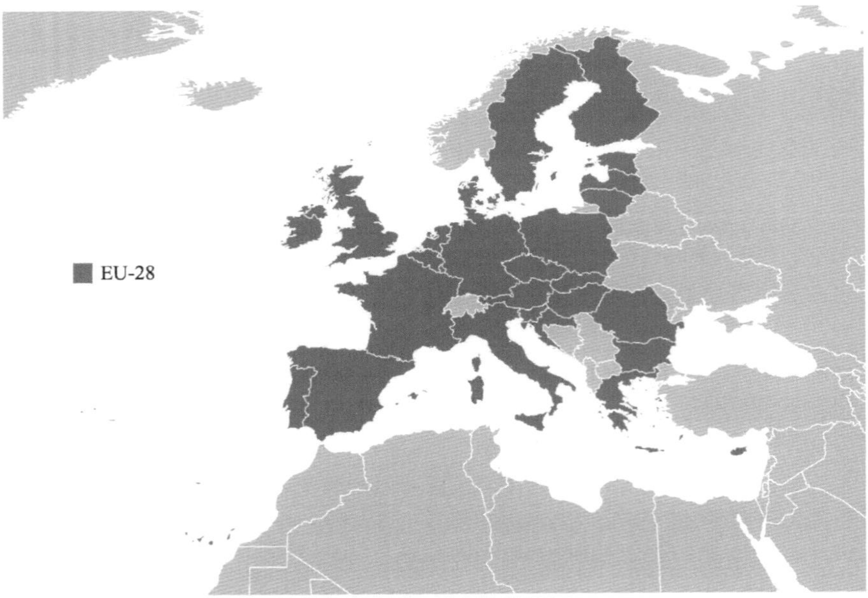

Fig. 3. Countries selected for this study.

use of the multivariate gamma distribution is appropriate given the existence of dependence between GHG emissions and the positive skew of per capita GHG emissions (see Table 2).

We determine the number of EU ETS allowances, and therefore the revenues, we should intend for reducing the risks related to CO_2 (K_1), CH_4 (K_2) and N_2O (K_3) emissions under different capital allocation principles: Haircut, standard deviation, Esscher, covariance and Overbeck type I. We have computed these principles using the formulation contained in Table 1, formula (16) and the estimation methodology described in Section 2.1, and Eqs. (9)–(12), (13) for the dependence and independence case, respectively. To study if the dependence can or cannot be ignored in this context, we compare two case studies: in the first one, we consider the relation of dependence exhibited by the different GHG emissions, while in the second one, we assume a structure of independence between them.

Tables 3 and 4 show the distribution of EU ETS allowances among the three gases based on different capital allocation principles under the assumption of dependence and independence structure, respectively.

Assuming dependence among gases, CO_2 is the riskiest gas and so more capital is allocated to it. While the Haircut allocation principle allocates fewer allowances than the other principles to the risks related to CO_2 emissions, the covariance principle

Table 2. Descriptive statistics of the CO_2, CH_4 and N_2O emissions.

	CO_2	CH_4	N_2O
Number of observations	28	28	28
Minimum	1406.5488	0.1058	0.0000
Maximum	8130.0939	2.5406	0.2456
Mean	3097.6095	0.9406	0.0911
Median	3049.7734	0.7342	0.0889
Sum	86733.0669	26.3362	2.5498
Standard deviation	1439.3858	0.6016	0.0552
Skewness	1.7425	1.0522	1.2053
Kurtosis	3.6054	0.4667	1.6273

Units: Kg of CO_2-eq.

Table 3. Capital allocation principles: Dependence structure.

Name	K_1	K_2	K_3
Haircut	2083509451	723991	68414
Standard deviation principle	2083559537	677577	64762
Esscher principle	2083608155	632468	61233
Covariance principle	2084099420	149373	53063
Overbeck type I	2083700569	541577	59710

Table 4. Capital allocation principles: Independence structure.

Name	K_1	K_2	K_3
Haircut	2083509451	723991	68414
Standard deviation principle	2083559537	677577	64762
Esscher principle	2083608155	632468	61233
Covariance principle	2084301489	364	3
Overbeck type I	2083738649	513498	49709

assigns a greater number of allowances to the emissions of this pollutant. The standard deviation principle results are very similar to those of the Haircut principle. Meanwhile, the Esscher and Overbeck type I principles present close findings.

Under the independence assumption, the Overbeck type I principle gives similar outcomes to those observed when there is dependence between gases. The Haircut, the standard deviation and the Esscher principles present the same results under both assumptions given that they do not consider the dependence structure between losses. The covariance allocation principle performs worse than the other principles as it assigns more capital than the other principles to the risks related to CO_2 emissions.

Given that the capital allocation principles provide different results, we use a simulation process to determine which principle is the most suitable to apply in this context. We also study the sensitivity of the allocations made under the different criteria.

For this purpose, we consider the CO_2, CH_4 and N_2O emissions reported by the 28 countries of the European Union in the period 2008–2013. Then, we simulate the distribution of allowances in a future scenario, in accordance with the annual reduction in the total quantity of allowances to be issued from 2013 onwards, established by Commission Decision 2010/634/UE of 22 October 2010, for the period 2014–2020. For each year and gas, we construct a random distribution of emissions, whose values are between the minimum and the maximum values of the period 2008–2013 corrected by the expected decrease in emissions, according to the reduction in the total quantity of allowances mentioned previously. Using this new distribution, we distribute the allowances between the three gases obtaining K_1, K_2 and K_3, according to the different principles. In order to ensure data consistency, this operation is repeated 50,000 times. Finally, we study the evolution of the corresponding standard deviation of K_1, K_2 and K_3 associated with each principle along the simulated period (2014–2020).

Based on the simulation carried out, we study the behavior of different capital principles to changes in emissions under multiple scenarios. The principle which presents a lower variability in the assignment of allowances to mitigate the risk associated with CO_2 (K_1), CH_4 (K_2) and N_2O (K_3) emissions, throughout the simulated period, will be the most appropriate to apply in this context (see Fig. 4). On the basis of the foregoing, the Overbeck type I principle is the most convenient to use in this framework. On the contrary, the least desirable would be to use the covariance principle as it has associated the largest standard deviation for K_1, K_2 and K_3.

In addition, the performed simulation allows us to study the sensitivity of allocations based on different principles. Thus, the covariance principle is the most sensitive of all because its standard deviation is more than proportionately reduced to small reductions in emissions. We can also observe that the standard deviation and Overbeck type I principles have the lowest sensitivity which is *a priori* a desirable feature for the principles.

Finally, as illustrated in Fig. 4, all principles show a decrease in variability over time, which is consistent with the emissions reduction simulated. Similarly, the different principles maintain their relative position except Haircut and Esscher, which have an anomaly that is accentuated when the assignment occurs to mitigate the impact of the minority gas in the atmosphere (K_3). The standard deviation and Overbeck type I principles are the most consistent throughout the period.

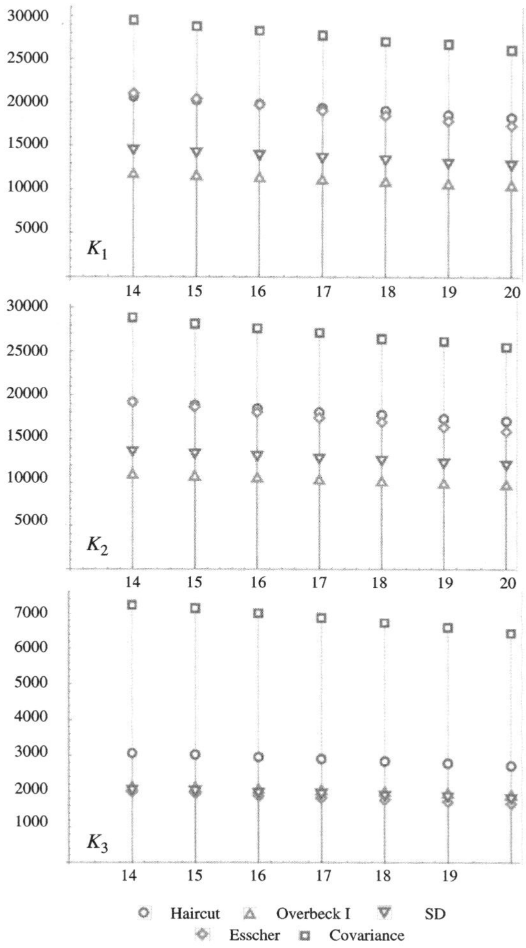

Fig. 4. Evolution of the standard deviation of CO_2 (K_1), CH_4 (K_2) and N_2O (K_3) EU ETS allowances (2014–2020).

5. Conclusions

In this study, we propose a capital allocation framework for assigning financial resources among multiple environmental dependent risks. The methodological contribution of this study lies in the use of the multivariate gamma distribution as a formal model for the estimation of capital allocation principles, given its properties of dependence and positive skewness. We provide an exact functional form for each capital allocation principle, assuming that the random vector of losses follows a multivariate gamma distribution.

We apply this methodology to the CO_2, CH_4 and N_2O emissions of the EU-28 in 2013 in order to determine the incomes we should use for financing the reduction of the risks related to each GHG. To study if the dependence can or cannot be ignored in this context, we compare two case studies: in the first one, we consider the relation of dependence exhibited by the different GHG emissions, while in the second one, we assume a structure of independence between them. Our results indicate that the CO_2 is the riskiest gas and then more capital is allocated to it. The covariance allocation principle performs worse than the other principles as it assigns more capital than the other principles to the risks related to CO_2 emissions. The Haircut, the standard deviation and the Esscher principles present the same results under both assumptions given that they do not consider the dependence structure between losses.

We carried out a simulation process to study the behavior of different capital principles to changes in emissions under multiple scenarios. The Overbeck type I principle is the most convenient to use in this framework because it presents a lower variability in the assignment of allowances to mitigate the risk associated with CO_2 (K_1), CH_4 (K_2) and N_2O (K_3) emissions, throughout the simulated period. We can also observe that the standard deviation and Overbeck type I principles have the lowest sensitivity which is *a priori* a desirable feature for the principles.

The availability of yearly data series in the near future will let investigate the temporal evolution in the assignments of allowances which will be a useful tool to implement policies to reduce the impact of GHG emissions. Future research should be addressed to determine how the revenues from the auctioning of EU ETS allowances should be allocated to the European countries.

Acknowledgments

The authors thank Ministerio de Economía y Competitividad (Project ECO2016-76203-C2-1-PE) for the partial support of this work. In addition, this work is a part of the Research Project APIE 1/2015–17: "New methods for the empirical analysis of financial markets" of the Santander Financial Institute (SANFI) of UCEIF Foundation resolved by the University of Cantabria and funded with sponsorship from Fundación Banco Santander.

References

Ai, J., Brockett, P. L., Golden, L. L. and Guillén, M. (2013). A robust unsupervised method for fraud rate estimation. *Journal of Risk and Insurance* **80**, 121–143.

Artis, M., Ayuso, M. and Guillén, M. (1999). Modelling different types of automobile insurance fraud behaviour in the Spanish market. *Insurance: Mathematics and Economics* **24**, 67–81.

Artis, M., Ayuso, M. and Guillén, M. (2002). Detection of automobile insurance fraud with discrete choice models and misclassified claims. *Journal of Risk and Insurance* **69**, 325–340.

Bühlmann, H. (1970). *Mathematical Methods in Risk Theory*. (Springer-Verlag, Berlin, Heidelberg, New York).

Bühlmann, H. (1980). An economic premium principle. *Astin Bulletin* **11**, 52–60.

Cheriyan, K. (1941). A bivariate correlated gamma–type distribution function. *Journal of the Indian Mathematical Society* **5**, 133–144.

Dhaene, J., Tsanakas, A., Valdez, E. A. and Vanduffel, S. (2012). Optimal capital allocation principles. *Journal of Risk and Insurance* **79**, 1–28.

European Commission. (2014). Report from the Commission to the European Parliament and the Council on Progress Towards Achieving the Kyoto and EU 2020 Objectives.

Furman, E. and Landsman, Z. (2005). Risk capital decomposition for a multivariate dependent gamma portfolio. *Insurance: Mathematics and Economics* **37**, 635–649.

Gerber, H. U. (1981). The Esscher premium principle: A criticism comment. *Astin Bulletin* **12**, 139–140.

Hajkowicz, S. (2009). Cutting the cake: Supporting environmental fund allocation decisions. *Journal of Environmental Management* **90**, 2737–2745.

Hardy, M. (2006). An Introduction to Risk Measures for Actuarial Applications. SOA Syllabus Study Note.

Hillman, B., Douglas, E. M. and Terkla, D. (2012). An analysis of the allocation of Yakima River water in terms of sustainability and economic efficiency. *Journal of Environmental Management* **103**, 102–112.

Hulme, P. E. (2005). Adapting to climate change: Is there scope for ecological management in the face of a global threat? *Journal of Applied Ecology* **42**, 784–794.

IPCC. (1990). *Climate Change 1990: Scientific Assessment of Climate Change*. Contribution of Working Group I to the First Assessment Report of the IPCC. [Houghton, J. T., Jenkins, G. J. and Ephraums, J. J., (eds.)]. (Cambridge University Press, Cambridge, United Kingdom).

IPCC. (2004). *IPCC Workshop on Describing Scientific Uncertainties in Climate Change to Support Analysis of Risk and of Options*. A Special Report of Working Group I of the IPCC [Manning, M., Petit, M., Easterling, D., Murphy, J., Patwardhan, A., Rogner, H. -H., Swart, R. and Yohe, G., (eds.)]. (IPCC, Geneva, Switzerland).

IPCC. (2007). *Climate Change 2007: The Physical Science Basis*. Contribution of Working Group I to the Fourth Assessment Report of the IPCC. [Solomon, S., Qin, D., Manning, M., Chen, Z., Marquis, M., Averyt, K. B., Tignor M. and Miller, H. L., (eds.)]. (Cambridge University Press, Cambridge, United Kingdom and New York, USA).

IPCC. (2012). *Managing the Risks of Extreme Events and Disasters to Advance Climate Change Adaptation*. A Special Report of Working Group I and II of the IPCC [Field, C. B., Barros, V., Stocker, T. F., Qin, D., Dokken, D. J., Ebi, K. L., Mastrandrea, M. D., Mach, K. J., Plattner, G. -K., Allen, S. K., Tignor, M. and Midgley, P. M., (eds.)]. (Cambridge University Press, Cambridge, United Kingdom, and New York, USA) 582 pp.

IPCC. (2013). *Climate Change 2013: The Physical Science Basis*. Contribution of Working Group I to the Fifth Assessment Report of the IPCC [Stocker, T. F., Qin, D., Plattner, G. -K., Tignor, M., Allen, S. K., Boschung, J., Nauels, A., Xia, Y., Bex, V. and Midgley, P.M. (eds.)]. (Cambridge University Press, Cambridge, United Kingdom and New York, USA) 1535 pp.

Jones, R. N. and Preston, B. L. (2010). Adaptation and risk management. Climate Change Working Paper No. 15, Centre for Strategic Economic Studies, Victoria University, Melbourne, 18 pp.

Jun, K-.S., Chung, E-.S., Kim, Y-.G. and Kim, Y. (2013). A fuzzy multi-criteria approach to flood risk vulnerability in South Korea by considering climate change impacts. *Expert Systems with Applications* **40**, 1003–1013.

Kleindorfer, P. R. (2009). Climate Change and Insurance: Integrative Principles and Regulatory Risk. INSEAD Working Paper No. 2009/43/TOM/INSEAD. [Available at SSRRN: http://ssrn.com/abstract=1456862.]

Lamb, H. (1995). *Climate, History and a Modern World*, 2nd edn. (Routledge, USA).

Mathai, A. M. and Moschopoulos, P. G. (1991). On a multivariate gamma. *Journal of Multivariate Analysis* **39**, 135–153.

Mianabadi, H., Mostert, E., Zarghami, M. and van de Giesen, N. (2014). A new bankruptcy method for conflict resolution in water resources allocation. *Journal of Environmental Management* **144**, 152–159.

Møller, T. (2001). On transformations of actuarial valuation principles. *Insurance: Mathematics and Economics* **28**, 281–303.

Obersteiner, M., Azar, C., Kauppi, P. E., Moellersten, K., Moreira, J., Nilsson, S., Read, P., Riahi, K., Schlamadinger, B., Yamagata, Y., Yan, J. and Van Ypersele, J. P. (2001). Managing climate risk. IIASA Interim Report, IR-01-051.

Overbeck, L. (2000). Allocation of economic capital in loan portfolios. In J. Franke, W. Härdle and G. Stahl (eds.). *Measuring Risk in Complex Stochastics Systems*. (Springer, Berlin).

Read, L., Madani, K. and Inanloo, B. (2014). Optimality versus stability in water resources allocation. *Journal of Environmental Management* **133**, 343–354.

Ramabhadran, V. (1951). A multivariate gamma–type distribution. *Journal of Multivariate Analysis* **38**, 213–232.

Shafiee, M. (2015). A fuzzy analytic network process model to mitigate the risks associated with offshare wind farms. *Expert Systems with Applications* **42**, 2143–2152.

Schweizer, M. (2001). From actuarial to financial valuation principles. *Insurance: Mathematics and Economics* **28**, 31–47.

Stern, N. (2006). What is the economics of climate change? *World Economics* **7**, 1–10.

UNFCCC (1992). Report of the Intergovernmental Negotiating Committee for a Framework Convention on Climate Change on the work of the Second Part of Its Fifth Session, celebrated in New York from 30 April to 9 May 1992, United Nations, New York, USA.

Urbina, J. and Guillén, M. (2014). An application of capital allocation principles to operational risks and the cost of fraud. *Expert Systems with Applications* **41**, 7023–7031.

Viaene, S., Van Gheel, D., Ayuso, M. and Guillén, M. (2004). Cost-sensitive design of claim fraud screens. In P. Perner (ed.), *Advances in Data Mining: Applications in Image Mining, Medicine and Biotechnology, Management and Environmental Control, and Telecommunications*. (4th Industrial Conference on Data Mining (ICDM), Leipzig, Germany) July, 04–07, 2004 (pp. 78–87).

Yohe, G. (2009). Toward an integrated framework derived from a risk-management approach to climate change. *Climate Change* **95**, 325–339.

Chapter 20

Efficiency of Source Differentiated Sectoral Energy Demand Accounting for Climate

Saleem Shaik

Department of Agribusiness and Applied Economics,
North Dakota State University,
400F Richard H. Barry Hall, Fargo, ND 58108, USA
Saleem.Shaik@ndsu.edu

The duality of cost minimization is utilized to examine the effects of climate change on US source differentiated sectoral energy demands or cost shares from 1970 to 2015 using a transcendental logarithmic cost function. The sectors include commercial, industrial, residential and transportation, while the sources include coal, electricity, natural gas, petroleum and wood & waste. The first-order conditions of cost function provide source differentiated sectoral compensated demand for energy. Second, the efficiency of source differentiated sectoral energy demand is estimated using a random panel stochastic frontier analysis model. The results suggest a differential impact of mean and variance of upside and downside precipitation and temperature risk on source differentiated energy demand. The efficiency of source differentiated sectoral energy demand ranges from 43% to 98%.

1. Introduction

The energy industry has been evolving and adapting to changing energy consumption by commercial, industrial, residential and transportation sectors as well as the changes in the sources of energy from coal, electricity, natural gas, petroleum and wood & waste. Figure 1 presents the flow chart of source differentiated sectoral energy demand. Energy for commercial and industrial sectors comes from coal, electricity, natural gas, petroleum and wood and waste. However, the sources of

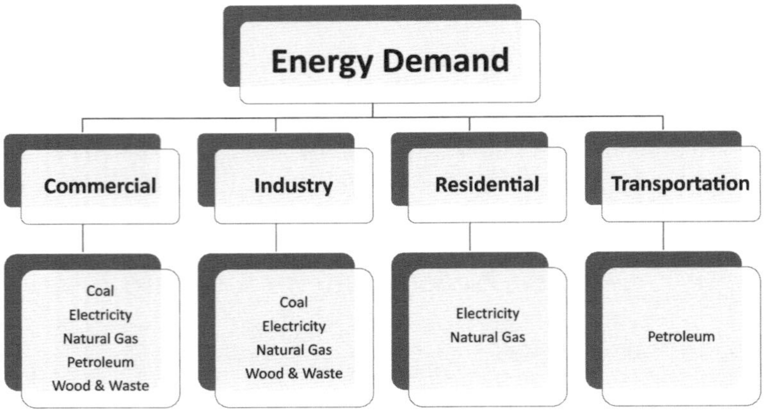

Fig. 1. Sources supplying energy to different sectors.

energy for residential comes from electricity and natural gas, and for transportation, petroleum.

In recent years, a majority of countries including the United States are engaged in evaluating issues associated with sources supplying energy and sectors demanding energy due to regulations, air pollution, cleaner sources and industrial production/operation requirements. Using a system of equations, traditional analyses evaluated changes in the demand or supply due to technological changes and prices [Griffin, 1977; Boustead and Yaros, 1994; Caloghirou *et al.*, 1997; Barnett *et al.*, 1998; Kemfert, 1998; Kuper and Soest, 2003; Thompson, 2005; Koetse *et al.*, 2007]. However, climate defined by temperature and precipitation is an additional factor affecting the evolution and adaptation of the energy demanded by sectors and sources of energy supplied in the United States. Researchers looked at the importance of alternative measures of climate change on the shares of energy consumed [Warren and LeDuc, 1981; Scott *et al.*, 1994; Sailor and Munoz, 1997; Sailor *et al.*, 1998; Barron, 2002; and Sailor, 2001].

Recently, there is increased emphasis on the energy efficiency and associated financial investments to increase energy efficiency supported by the International Energy Agency (IEA). According to IEA, in 2016 global investments in energy efficiency rose to $231 billion with commercial and residential buildings accounting for 58%.[1] Energy intensity (amount of energy used to produce a unit of output) as

[1]Investments in the residential sector are financed by household income, savings and loans, while companies finance investments in transportation, industrial and commercial sector.

an indicator of energy efficiency is published annually in Market Report Series: Energy Efficiency (https://www.iea.org/publications/freepublications/publication/market-report-series-energy-efficiency-2017-.html).

Extending earlier analyses, this study evaluates the importance of prices, technological changes, and downside and upside measures of temperature and precipitation on the efficiency of the source differentiated sectoral energy demand. This is carried out by estimating source differentiated sectoral energy demand functions (first-order conditions of transcendental logarithmic cost function) using a panel stochastic frontier analysis (SFA) model with pure random error (v) and one-side error or inefficiency (u). The objectives of the study are to (a) present source differentiated sectoral energy demand system of equation to include commercial-coal, commercial-electricity, commercial-natural gas, commercial-petroleum, commercial-wood and waste, industrial-coal, industrial-electricity, industrial-natural gas, industrial-petroleum, industrial-wood and waste, residential-electricity, residential-natural gas and transportation-petroleum; (b) estimate efficiency of source differentiated sectoral energy demands; (c) compare the efficiency between sectors with the same energy source. Findings of this study will be relevant in the discussion of the efficient use of energy across source differentiated sectoral energy demands in the US.

This research estimates source differentiated sectoral energy demand accounting for technology and price changes along with changes in climate, i.e. average and variance of temperature and precipitation associated with negative deviations (downside) and positive deviations (upside). The efficiency of source differentiated sectoral energy demand estimated using SFA models is used in pair-wise comparison of efficiency measures between sources within each sector and between sectors by energy source. The trend variable is significant for all sources within the commercial sector except natural gas. It is negative (positive) for coal, electricity and natural gas (wood & waste) within the industrial sector. The trend variable is positive and significant for electricity use by the residential sector, and petroleum use by the transportation sector. It is negative for natural gas usage by the residential sector. Pair-wise efficiency results show coal being the least efficient across sectors. Electricity, natural gas and petroleum seem to be more efficient, but are sensitive to different sectors. The rest of the chapter is organized as follows: Section 2 presents the theory of the source differentiated sectoral energy demand and associated panel SFA models. Collection and computation of the data for the analysis are presented in Section 3. Results of the analysis and its discussions are presented in Section 4 while Section 5 presents the conclusion.

2. Economic Framework

The duality of maximizing utility and cost minimization is utilized to examine the effects of climate on the energy demanded by residential, commercial, transportation and industrial sectors using a transcendental logarithmic cost function. The first-order conditions of a cost function provide sectorial compensated demand for energy and substitution elasticities between different sectors.

2.1. *Cost minimizing framework for energy demand*

Following Deaton and Muellbauer [1994], the utility maximization is a function of energy consumption by residential, commercial, transportation and industrial sectors subject to the constraint that cost equals to the quantity times the price of energy.

$$\begin{aligned} &\text{utility } (u) = \max_{u \geq 0} \{(u) \ \text{ subject to } w \cdot x = \text{cost } (c)\} \\ &\text{(or)} \\ &\text{Maximize utiilty } (u) = v\ (x) \ \text{ subject to } \ w \cdot x = \text{cost } (c)\,. \end{aligned} \tag{1}$$

The dual problem of utility maximization is to minimize cost of energy consumption subject to the constraint that consumption of energy from alternative sources maximize utility and defined as:

$$\begin{aligned} &\text{cost } (c) = \min_{x \geq 0} \{(w * x) \ \text{ subject to } v\ (x) = \text{utility } (u)\} \\ &\text{(or)} \\ &\text{Minimize cost } (c) = (w * x) \ \text{ subject to } v\ (x) = \text{utility } (u)\,. \end{aligned} \tag{2}$$

To examine the effects of climate on the energy demanded Eq. (2) is rewritten to include climate variables as:

$$\text{cost } (c) = \min_{x \geq 0} \{(w * x, z) \ \text{ subject to } v\ (x, z) = \text{utility } (u)\}\,. \tag{3}$$

The transcendental logarithmic cost function with non-Hicks neutral technology is tested and assumed in this study. The non-Hicks neutral transcendental logarithmic cost function for source differentiated sectoral energy demand is presented as:

$$\begin{aligned} \ln C = \alpha_0 + \sum_{i=1}^{I} \sum_{j=1}^{J} \alpha_i \ln w_{i_j} + \sum_{k=1}^{K} \beta_k \ln z_k \\ + \frac{1}{2} \sum_{i=1}^{I} \sum_{h=1}^{I} \sum_{j=1}^{J} \sum_{m=1}^{J} \delta_{i_j, h_m} \ln w_{i_j} \ \ln w_{h_m} \end{aligned}$$

$$+\frac{1}{2}\sum_{k=1}^{K}\sum_{l=1}^{K}\phi_{k,l}\ln z_k\ \ln z_l+\frac{1}{2}\sum_{i=1}^{I}\sum_{j=1}^{J}\sum_{k=1}^{K}\varphi_{i_j,k}\ln w_{i_j}\ \ln z_k$$

$$+\gamma_t\,\mathrm{T}+\frac{1}{2}\gamma_{t,t}\,\mathrm{T}^2+\sum_{i=1}^{I}\lambda_{i,t}\ln w_i * T+\sum_{k=1}^{K}\rho_{k,t}\ln z_k * T+\varepsilon, \qquad (4)$$

where subscripts i and h denote sectors (i, h = $1, \ldots, I$) and j and m denote sources of energy (j, m = $1, \ldots, J$), C is the cost function; w is a vector of energy prices paid by residential, commercial, transportation and industrial sectors, T represents technology change and z represents vector of temperature and precipitation variables, and subscript k ($k = 1, \ldots, K$) denotes four measures for temperature — downside and upside variance for monthly averages and standard deviations, and four measures for precipitation — downside and upside variance for monthly averages and standard deviations.

The cost shares of source differentiated sectoral demand functions defined as the logarithmic first-order conditions of the cost function is represented as:

$$\frac{\partial \ln C}{\partial \ln w_{i_j}}=CS_{i_j}=\alpha_{i_j}+\sum_{i=1}^{4}\delta_{h_m}\ln w_{h_m}+\sum_{k=1}^{6}\varphi_k\ln z_k+\lambda_t\ln T+\varepsilon. \qquad (5)$$

Using the transcendental logarithmic functional form implies that the following homogeneity and symmetry conditions are met in Eq. (5).

$$\sum \alpha_{i_j}=1 \quad \text{and} \quad \delta_{i_j,h_m}=\delta_{h_m,i_j}=0. \qquad (6)$$

Even though price and substitution elasticity could be computed based on Eqs. (5) and (6), the focus is efficiency of source differentiated sectoral energy demand functions. Efficiency evaluates the relationship between endogenous or independent and exogenous or dependent variables. Efficiency is built on the distance function concept introduced by Farrell [1957] and is defined as the distance between the observed output of a farm relative to a theoretical frontier, for a given set of inputs. The theoretical frontier could be cross-sectional units, time series units or both with highest production, i.e. output produced if it were 100% efficient. So efficiency benchmark is the distance function that measures by how much an individual's input use can be reduced to produce the same level of output as the frontier. Efficiency benchmark values range from zero (least efficient) to one (most efficient). Efficiency can be estimated using statistical stochastic frontier analysis (SFA) or programming data envelopment analysis (DEA). The SFA methodology is used not only to estimate efficiency of source differentiated sectoral energy demand functions but also to test if efficiency is different between sources within each sector or between sectors for each source. The traditional SFA model is extended to estimate Eq. (5).

2.2. *Stochastic frontier analysis of source differentiated sectoral energy demand*

SFA was introduced simultaneously by Aigner, Lovell and Schmidt [1977] (normal–half normal and an exponential distribution) and Meeusen and van den Brubeck [1977] (exponential distribution). Jondrow *et al.* [1982] suggested a method to estimate firm specific inefficiency measures. The estimation of a normal-gamma stochastic frontier model via simulated maximum likelihood is proposed by Greene [2003]. A recent survey by Greene [2008] provides extended reviews of these classical stochastic frontier models.[2] Following the SFA framework, the source differentiated sectoral energy demand function is defined as:

$$CS_{i_j} = \alpha_{i_j} + \sum_{i=1}^{I}\sum_{j=1}^{J} \delta_{h_m} \ln w_{h_m} + \sum_{k=1}^{K} \varphi_k \ln z_k + \lambda_t \ln T + \upsilon - u. \qquad (7)$$

3. Data and Variables Used in the Analysis

The US Energy Information Administration (www.eia.gov) publishes the US and state energy production and sectoral use accounts. To estimate the source differentiated sectoral demand equations, the total energy expenditure, expenditure by residential, commercial, transportation and industrial sectors in millions of dollars were obtained for all the 48 states. Further, the source differentiated expenditures by commercial-coal, commercial-electricity, commercial-natural gas, commercial-petroleum, commercial-wood and waste, industrial-coal, industrial-electricity, industrial-natural gas, industrial-petroleum, industrial-wood and waste, residential-electricity, residential-natural gas and transportation-petroleum were obtained from the same source. The source differentiated sectoral demand shares and sectoral demand shares are computed from the total and individual sectoral expenditures. Also, the corresponding prices (dollars/million Btu) paid by source differentiated residential, commercial, transportation and industrial sectors for the same period were obtained.

The climate data on monthly temperature and precipitation is obtained from the National Oceanic and Atmospheric Administration (https://www.ncdc.noaa.gov/).

[2]The stochastic frontier model for primal production function is represented as $y = f(\mathbf{x}; \beta) + \upsilon - u$, where y represents an endogenous dependent variable in logs, $\mathbf{x}$ is a vector of $k = 1, \ldots, 4$ exogenous independent inputs in logs and time trend used in the production function; $beta$ is a vector of coefficients associated with inputs, pure random error υ and negatively skewed one-sided inefficiency u that may be represented by alternative distributions including half normal, exponential or truncated normal.

The data obtained is used in the computation of temperature and precipitation variables. Given the energy context, it is important to capture the variance of downside and upside, and not overall variance.

The downside and upside variance in temperature and precipitation is computed for the monthly average based on a moving window of 25 years. For example, the downside and upside variance measures for the year 2015 is computed based on data from 1991 to 2015. Observations with negative deviations during 1991–2015 are used in the computation of downside variance, while observations with positive deviation during the same period are used in the computation of upside variance. To summarize, the total number of climate variables included in the analysis are four — (1) two measures for temperature — downside and upside variance for monthly averages; and (2) two measures for precipitation — downside and upside variance for monthly averages.

Table 1 summarizes the mean and standard deviation for source differentiated sectoral demand prices and shares across 48 states from 1970 to 2015. Also,

Table 1. Mean and standard deviation of variables.

	Shares		**Prices**	
	Mean (%)	**Std. Dev. (%)**	**Mean**	**Std. Dev.**
Commercial	15.42	4.49		
Commercial-Coal	0.08	0.13	1.519	1.117
Commercial-Electricity	10.95	3.63	20.146	9.632
Commercial-Natural Gas	2.80	1.27	5.848	3.989
Commercial-Petroleum	1.60	1.49	8.949	6.923
Commercial-Wood & Waste	0.02	0.03	4.081	3.257
Industry	20.96	8.11		
Industry-Coal	1.19	1.98	1.817	1.072
Industry-Electricity	8.09	3.37	14.489	8.298
Industry-Natural Gas	3.82	2.47	4.381	3.135
Industry-Petroleum	7.67	5.59	8.146	6.516
Industry-Wood & Waste	0.34	0.50	1.730	0.724
Residential	19.16	4.41		
Residential-Electricity	14.09	3.77	22.756	11.280
Residential-Natural Gas	5.09	2.72	7.034	4.855
Transportation	44.46	7.66		
Transportation-Petroleum	44.46	7.66	11.234	7.497
	Precipitation		**Temperature**	
Average downside risk	0.065	0.045	0.471	0.416
Average upside risk	0.103	0.080	0.544	0.314
Variance downside risk	0.379	0.412	609.111	675.718
Variance upside risk	2.272	3.101	778.915	656.277

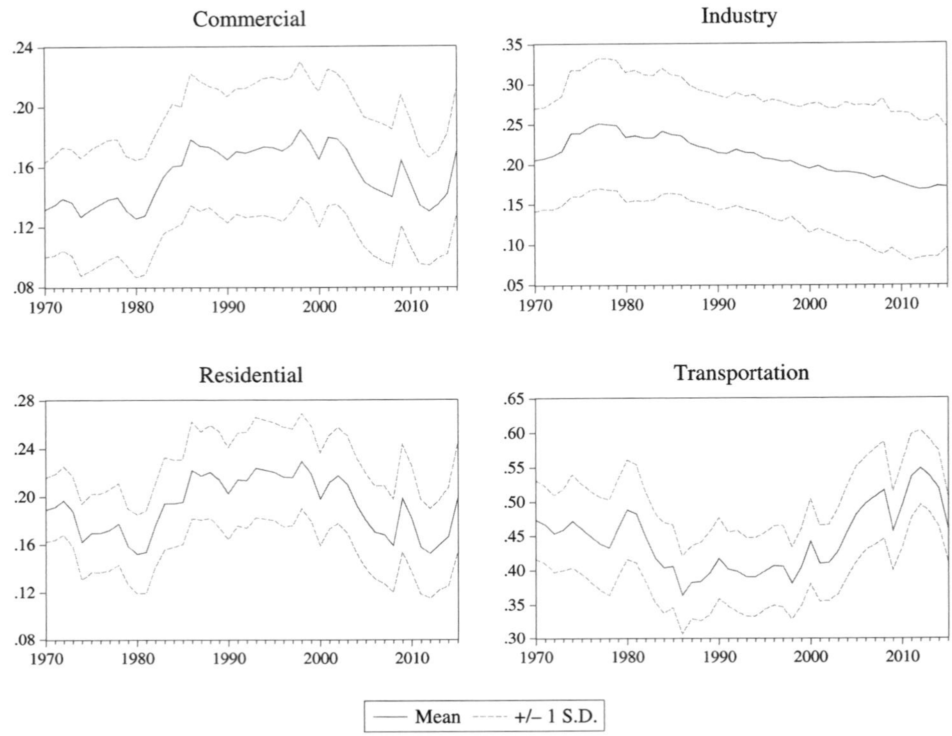

Fig. 2. Average sectoral energy demand shares, 1970–2015.

presented in Table 1 are the mean and standard deviation for four climate variables used in the analysis.

Based on Energy Information Administration (www.eia.gov) data from 1970 to 2015, Fig. 2 presents trends in average shares of energy consumption by commercial, industrial, residential and transportation sectors across the 48 states with one standard deviation. Of the four sectors, the industrial sector is the least variable and has been stable through time compared to the residential, commercial and transportation sectors in that order. The commercial and transportation sectors show an increase in the use of energy from 1970 to 2015. However, the commercial sector use was higher during the late 1980s to 2000, while the transportation sector use of energy was lower during the same time-period. The residential share of energy use declined slight from 1970 to 2015.

Figure 3 presents trends in the average share of source differentiated sectoral energy demand consumption across the 48 states with one standard deviation. The source differentiated commercial sector energy demand is 71% from electricity, 18% from natural gas, 10% from petroleum and less than 1% from coal and wood/waste.

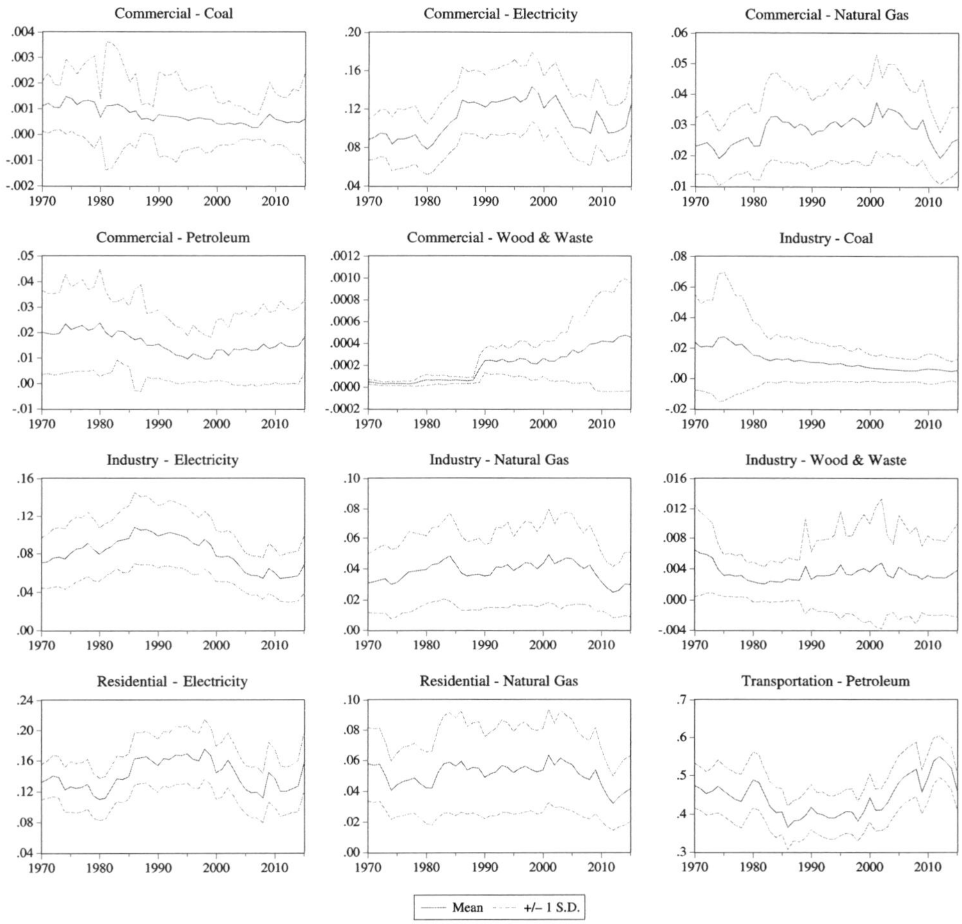

Fig. 3. Average source differentiated sectoral energy demand shares, 1970–2015.

Similarly, the source differentiated industrial sector energy demand is 39% from electricity, 37% from petroleum, 18% from natural gas, 6% from coal and 2% from wood/waste. The source differentiated residential sector energy demand is 74% from electricity and 26% from natural gas, while the source differentiated transportation sector energy demand is 100% from petroleum.

4. Empirical Application and Results

The estimation of the source differentiated sectoral energy demand equations are based on one-way fixed effect stochastic frontier model and implemented in SAS using PROC HPQLIM.

The empirical model for the system of demand share equations is:

$$CS_{i_j,nt} = \alpha_{i_j} + \sum_{i=1}^{I}\sum_{j=1}^{J} \delta_{h_m} \ln w_{h_m,nt} + \sum_{k=1}^{K} \varphi_k \ln z_{k,nt} \\ + \lambda_t \ln T_{i_j,nt} - u_{i_j,nt} + v_{i_j,nt}, \tag{8}$$

where i represents the residential, commercial, transportation and industrial sector for demand share equations and $n = 1, \ldots, N(states)$ and $t = 1, \ldots, T(years)$; u are unobserved state-level effects; and w are the observation-specific random errors. The transportation sector petroleum source price is used to normalize the demand equations and hold the homogeneity.

Equation (8) is estimated for 12 source differentiated sectoral energy demand functions: commercial-coal, commercial-electricity, commercial-natural gas, commercial-petroleum, commercial-wood and waste, industrial-coal, industrial-electricity, industrial-natural gas, industrial-petroleum, industrial-wood and waste, residential-electricity, residential-natural gas and transportation-petroleum using random panel SFA model. The energy demand shares are multiplied by 100. The endogenous energy demand shares, price variables and technology represented by trend variables are in logarithms, while the climate variables are in levels.

Table 2 presents the empirical results for source differentiated commercial sector energy demand functions. This includes commercial-coal, commercial-electricity, commercial-natural gas, commercial-petroleum, commercial-wood and waste. The trend variable is significant for all sources within the commercial sector except natural gas. Thus, a 1% increase in technologies will increase the energy demand for sources electricity (0.013%) and wood & waste (0.056%) and decrease the energy demand for sources coal (−0.066%) and petroleum (−0.026%) in the commercial sector. In contrast, the trend variable in the industrial sector is negative and significant for coal, electricity and natural gas, but positive for wood & waste. The trend variable is positive and significant for electricity use by the residential sector and petroleum use by the transportation sector, while it is negative for natural gas usage by the residential sector.

4.1. *Importance of climate on energy demand*

The climatic variables used in the analysis are the upside and downside deviations of the mean and variance of precipitation and temperature. Within commercial sector energy demands, the downside and upside risk of mean and variance of precipitation and temperature are statistically significant to the source of energy. Results from Table 2 suggest there is an increased (decreased) commercial sector energy demand

Table 2. Stochastic Frontier results of source differentiated commercial sector energy demand.

	Coal		Electricity		Natural Gas		Petroleum		Wood & Waste	
	Estimate	***t* value**	**Estimate**	***t* value**	**Estimate**	***t* value**	**Estimate**	***t* value**	**Estimate**	***t* value**
Commercial-Coal	1.268	8.67	0.156	8.31	−0.016	−0.38	0.321	4.77	−0.368	−2.77
Commercial-Electricity	−0.378	−1.11	0.570	12.48	−0.253	−2.92	−1.017	−7.00	−0.100	−0.35
Commercial-Natural Gas	−0.209	−0.75	0.007	0.20	0.192	2.55	0.386	3.15	−0.377	−1.68
Commercial-Petroleum	−0.285	−1.33	0.004	0.15	0.048	0.93	0.179	1.98	−0.186	−1.21
Commercial-Wood & Waste	−0.012	−0.13	−0.017	−1.40	−0.121	−4.98	0.040	0.99	−0.130	−2.02
Industry-Coal	−0.405	−2.66	−0.194	−9.70	−0.243	−5.54	−0.286	−3.89	−0.337	−2.40
Industry-Electricity	−0.367	−1.96	0.022	0.82	0.184	3.93	0.127	1.52	0.170	1.19
Industry-Natural Gas	0.119	0.85	−0.030	−1.76	0.145	3.95	−0.184	−2.97	−0.086	−0.84
Industry-Petroleum	0.146	0.88	0.020	1.00	0.122	3.07	0.362	5.36	−0.754	−6.79
Industry-Wood & Waste	−0.361	−4.8	−0.031	−3.24	0.075	4.28	0.114	3.67	−0.440	−8.16
Residential-Electricity	0.116	0.35	0.002	0.04	0.086	1.07	0.196	1.31	0.982	3.58
Residential-Natural Gas	0.668	2.33	0.082	2.23	0.187	2.55	−0.207	−1.66	0.088	0.39
Transportation-Petroleum	−0.180	−0.94	−0.028	−1.29	0.090	2.02	0.050	0.62	0.705	4.84
Average prcp. downside risk	−0.036	−0.75	−0.015	−2.25	−0.025	−1.90	0.089	4.18	−0.028	−0.77
Average prcp. upside risk	0.031	0.69	−0.020	−3.04	−0.031	−2.67	−0.014	−0.73	−0.060	−1.67
Variance prcp. downside risk	−0.067	−1.29	0.025	2.89	0.023	1.68	0.055	2.54	0.071	1.99
Variance prcp. upside risk	0.122	4.02	−0.008	−2.11	−0.056	−7.00	0.019	1.37	−0.113	−5.22
Average tmp. downside risk	0.006	0.09	−0.006	−0.73	−0.019	−1.18	−0.150	−5.55	0.051	1.00
Average tmp. upside risk	−0.179	−3.08	0.014	1.91	0.073	4.94	−0.021	−0.84	−0.022	−0.57
Variance tmp. downside risk	0.192	3.66	−0.024	−3.13	−0.079	−5.67	0.019	0.79	0.229	6.20
Variance tmp. upside risk	−0.007	−0.16	0.036	6.58	−0.013	−1.23	0.000	0.02	−0.044	−1.44
Time trend	−0.066	−14.4	0.013	22.77	−0.002	−1.72	−0.026	−13.52	0.056	16.25
Intercept	−2.091	−4.1	1.508	22.55	1.649	13.54	2.048	8.78	−10.150	−28.80
Sigma_u	0.604	15.46	0.101	23.55	0.157	18.16	0.093	1.67	0.273	9.72
Sigma_v	0.503	18.66	0.056	19.57	0.131	23.15	0.307	17.45	0.385	23.17
lambda	1.200	19.46	1.782	278.16	1.194	91.18	0.303	4.17	0.710	16.80

using petroleum (electricity) sources with an increase in the average downside risk of precipitation. In contrast, an increase in the average upside risk of precipitation negatively effects the commercial sector energy demand using electricity and natural gas sources. An increase in the variance of downside precipitation risk increases the commercial sector energy demand using electricity, petroleum and wood & waste sources. In contrast, an increase in the variance of upside precipitation risk decreases commercial sector energy demand using electricity, natural gas and wood & waste sources. An increase in the average downside precipitation risk decreases commercial sector energy demands using petroleum. In contrast, an increase in the average upside precipitation risk negatively (positively) effects commercial sector energy demand using coal (natural gas) sources. An increase in the variance of downside precipitation risk increases (decreases) the commercial sector energy demand using coal and wood & waste (electricity) sources. In contrast, an increase in the variance of upside precipitation risk increases the commercial sector energy demand using an electricity source.

Table 3 results show the differential impact of climate variables on source differentiated industrial sector energy demands. There is an increased (decreased) industrial sector energy demand using electricity and wood & waste (coal and natural gas) sources with an increase in the average downside precipitation risk. An increase in the average upside precipitation risk negatively effects the industrial sector energy demand using electricity, natural gas and wood & waste sources. However, there is an increase in the industrial sector energy demand using coal. An increase in the variance of downside precipitation risk increases industrial sector energy demand using coal, electricity and natural gas sources. In contrast, an increase in the variance of upside precipitation risk increases only industrial sector energy demand using wood & waste sources. An increase in average downside precipitation risk decreases industrial sector energy demand using wood & waste. In contrast, an increase in the average upside precipitation risk negatively (positively) affects the industrial sector energy demand using natural gas (electricity and wood & waste) sources. An increase in the variance of downside precipitation risk increases (decreases) industrial sector energy demand using electricity and natural gas (wood & waste) sources. In contrast, an increase in the variance of upside precipitation risk increases the industrial sector energy demand using wood & waste sources.

Finally, Table 4 presents the results for the residential and transportation sector energy demand equations. An increase in average downside precipitation risk did not have any significant effect on source differentiated energy demands. An increase in the average upside precipitation risk positively (negatively) effects the transportation (residential) sector energy demand using a petroleum (natural gas) source. An

Table 3. Stochastic Frontier results of source differentiated industry sector energy demand.

	Coal		Electricity		Natural Gas		Wood & Waste	
	Estimate	***t* value**	**Estimate**	***t* value**	**Estimate**	***t* value**	**Estimate**	***t* value**
Commercial-Coal	−0.522	−7.11	0.068	2.29	−0.290	−4.41	−0.096	−1.09
Commercial-Electricity	−0.311	−1.82	0.150	3.31	−0.013	−0.10	−0.759	−3.29
Commercial-Natural Gas	0.518	3.46	0.157	2.98	−0.322	−2.90	0.315	1.53
Commercial-Petroleum	0.029	0.27	0.009	0.30	−0.035	−0.42	0.008	0.05
Commercial-Wood & Waste	0.032	0.83	0.037	2.31	−0.053	−1.40	−0.505	−7.55
Industry-Coal	1.259	17.15	−0.087	−2.84	−0.034	−0.49	0.221	2.22
Industry-Electricity	−0.453	−4.42	0.585	19.93	−0.199	−2.81	0.035	0.25
Industry-Natural Gas	−0.110	−1.53	−0.077	−3.62	0.666	12.33	−0.094	−1.01
Industry-Petroleum	−0.168	−2.06	−0.116	−4.35	0.122	1.89	−0.454	−4.04
Industry-Wood & Waste	−0.151	−4.03	−0.197	−15.84	−0.058	−2.02	0.791	15.62
Residential-Electricity	0.839	5.14	−0.036	−0.83	0.285	2.17	0.724	3.31
Residential-Natural Gas	−0.647	−4.42	−0.199	−3.75	0.034	0.30	−0.305	−1.62
Transportation-Petroleum	−0.302	−3.46	−0.078	−2.59	0.004	0.05	0.336	2.74
Average prcp. downside risk	−0.117	−4.2	0.040	4.86	−0.048	−2.42	0.143	4.08
Average prcp. upside risk	0.045	2.08	−0.053	−5.95	−0.039	−2.21	−0.269	−7.68
Variance prcp. downside risk	0.136	6.1	0.023	3.23	0.048	2.40	0.041	1.10
Variance prcp. upside risk	−0.016	−1.04	0.004	0.63	0.012	0.92	0.167	6.03
Average tmp. downside risk	−0.024	−0.86	0.004	0.24	0.015	0.62	−0.198	−4.89
Average tmp. upside risk	−0.016	−0.56	0.077	7.03	−0.045	−2.00	0.162	3.23
Variance tmp. downside risk	−0.045	−1.81	0.083	8.60	0.046	2.06	−0.304	−6.92
Variance tmp. upside risk	−0.026	−1.23	−0.001	−0.21	0.010	0.60	0.081	2.79
Time trend	−0.030	−13.09	−0.005	−5.39	−0.009	−5.01	0.016	5.64
Intercept	0.608	2.53	1.274	12.31	0.590	2.99	−0.092	−0.28
Sigma_u	0.496	23.66	0.165	28.31	0.213	12.97	0.853	30.98
Sigma_v	0.205	13.95	0.062	16.74	0.230	21.49	0.176	10.29
lambda	2.418	74.33	2.676	322.89	0.926	36.10	4.834	123.70

Table 4. Stochastic Frontier results of source differentiated residential and transportation sectors energy demand.

	Residential				Transportation	
	Electricity		Natural Gas		Petroleum	
	Estimate	*t* value	Estimate	*t* value	Estimate	*t* value
Commercial-Coal	0.124	6.60	−0.032	−1.24	−0.023	−2.21
Commercial-Electricity	0.069	2.10	−0.299	−6.00	−0.074	−3.33
Commercial-Natural Gas	−0.037	−1.50	0.104	2.33	−0.059	−3.30
Commercial-Petroleum	−0.088	−4.26	−0.094	−2.63	0.060	4.51
Commercial-Wood & Waste	0.002	0.21	−0.004	−0.33	0.006	1.03
Industry-Coal	−0.112	−5.57	−0.150	−5.44	0.035	3.17
Industry-Electricity	−0.050	−2.57	0.010	0.41	−0.016	−1.34
Industry-Natural Gas	−0.090	−7.17	0.032	1.43	−0.052	−5.77
Industry-Petroleum	0.015	0.92	0.014	0.51	−0.107	−11.60
Industry-Wood & Waste	−0.038	−5.56	0.106	9.28	0.054	11.81
Residential-Electricity	0.460	14.62	0.321	6.41	−0.234	−11.50
Residential-Natural Gas	0.161	6.43	0.315	7.74	−0.034	−1.98
Transportation-Petroleum	−0.003	−0.17	0.127	4.38	0.053	4.68
Average prcp. downside risk	0.005	1.05	0.011	1.34	−0.003	−1.02
Average prcp. upside risk	−0.007	−1.65	−0.014	−2.09	0.015	5.14
Variance prcp. downside risk	0.001	0.29	0.017	2.70	−0.018	−5.78
Variance prcp. upside risk	0.002	0.69	−0.024	−4.82	0.001	0.44
Average tmp. downside risk	−0.011	−1.92	0.057	6.58	0.015	3.64
Average tmp. upside risk	0.003	0.53	0.029	3.17	−0.010	−2.92
Variance tmp. downside risk	−0.016	−3.15	−0.026	−3.10	0.013	3.31
Variance tmp. upside risk	0.024	6.24	−0.008	−1.25	−0.020	−7.67
Time trend	0.007	17.17	−0.004	−5.83	0.001	2.18
Intercept	2.036	44.22	1.495	18.49	4.046	133.34
Sigma_u	0.063	17.24	0.070	9.24	0.036	14.31
Sigma_v	0.049	19.32	0.121	28.74	0.035	20.52
lambda	1.280	222.65	0.582	52.22	1.030	257.99

increase in the variance of downside precipitation risk increases (decreases) residential (transportation) sector energy demand using a natural gas (petroleum) source. In contrast, an increase in the variance of upside precipitation risk decreases residential sector energy demands using a natural gas source. An increase in the average downside precipitation risk increases residential (transportation) sector energy demand using natural gas (petroleum) source. In contrast, an increase in average upside precipitation risk negatively (positively) affects the transportation (residential) sector energy demand using a petroleum (natural gas) source. An increase in the variance of downside precipitation risk increases (decreases) transportation (residential) sector energy demand using petroleum (electricity and natural gas) sources. In contrast, an increase in the variance of upside precipitation risk increases (decreases) residential (transportation) sector energy demand using an electricity (petroleum) source.

Overall, the average and variance of precipitation and temperature upside and downside risk has differential impacts on source differentiated sectoral energy demands.

4.2. *Efficiency of source differentiated energy demand*

The results of the average efficiency measures estimated using a random panel stochastic frontier analysis model are presented in Table 5. While summary statistics are presented in Table 5, Fig. 4 shows the annual efficiency measures.

Table 6 presents the mean difference in efficiency measures between sources of energy by sector. The t-value for the difference between sources of energy by sector

Table 5. Summary statistics of efficiency by source differentiated sector energy demand.

	Mean	**Maximum**	**Minimum**	**Std. Dev.**
Commercial-Coal	0.578	0.922	0.021	0.191
Commercial-Electricity	0.893	0.988	0.237	0.100
Commercial-Natural Gas	0.837	0.974	0.017	0.108
Commercial-Petroleum	0.892	0.963	0.448	0.054
Commercial-Wood & Waste	0.768	0.919	0.185	0.109
Industry-Coal	0.519	1.183	0.000	0.235
Industry-Electricity	0.815	0.988	0.028	0.178
Industry-Natural Gas	0.812	0.969	0.119	0.115
Industry-Wood & Waste	0.434	0.931	0.000	0.283
Residential-Electricity	0.923	0.990	0.433	0.061
Residential-Natural Gas	0.868	0.974	0.374	0.063
Transportation-Petroleum	0.959	0.993	0.650	0.034

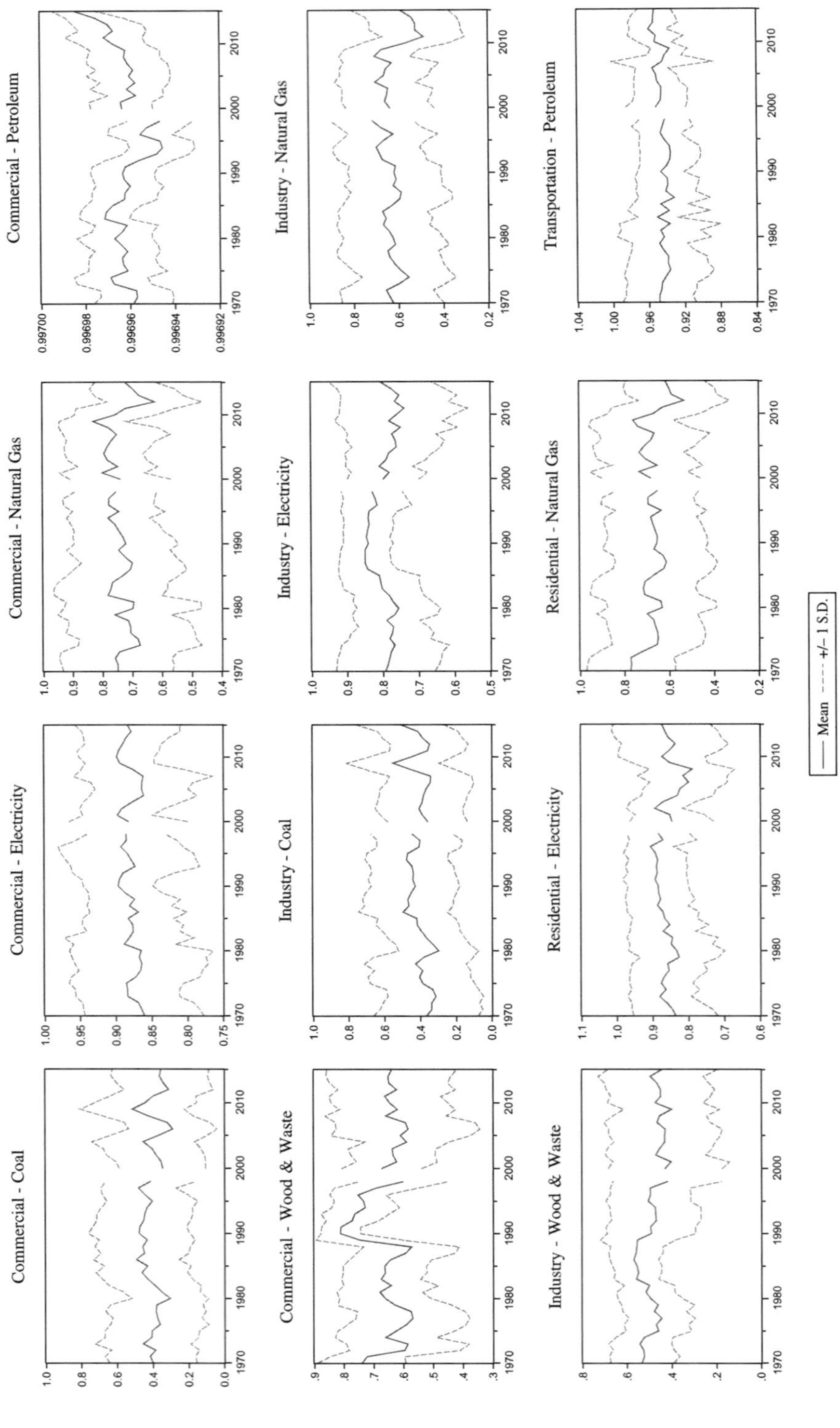

Fig. 4. Annual efficiency measures of source differentiated sectoral energy demand shares, 1970–2015.

Table 6. Mean difference in efficiency between sources by sector.

	N	**Mean**	**Std. Dev.**	**Minimum**	**Maximum**	$t >$ **Value**	**Pr > |t|**
Efficiency difference between sources within commercial sector							
2-8 Coal-Electricity	1517	−0.313	0.209	−0.947	0.400	−58.51	<.0001
Coal-Natural Gas	1516	−0.257	0.224	−0.891	0.602	−44.69	<.0001
Coal-Petroleum	1517	−0.313	0.200	−0.910	0.228	−61.12	<.0001
Coal-Wood & Waste	1263	−0.191	0.216	−0.866	0.450	−31.45	<.0001
Electricity-Natural Gas	1669	0.056	0.141	−0.701	0.837	16.31	<.0001
Electricity-Petroleum	1670	0.001	0.116	−0.685	0.458	0.29	0.7734
Electricity-Wood & Waste	1403	0.129	0.143	−0.601	0.749	33.74	<.0001
Natural Gas-Petroleum	1669	−0.055	0.105	−0.899	0.300	−21.44	<.0001
Natural Gas-Wood & Waste	1403	0.074	0.135	−0.728	0.755	20.73	<.0001
Petroleum-Wood & Waste	1403	0.125	0.122	−0.305	0.750	38.52	<.0001
Efficiency difference between sources within industry sector							
2-8 Coal-Electricity	1656	−0.297	0.262	−0.956	0.681	−46.22	<.0001
Coal-Natural Gas	1656	−0.294	0.247	−0.907	0.614	−48.35	<.0001
Coal-Wood & Waste	1645	0.086	0.352	−0.844	1.117	9.89	<.0001
Electricity-Natural Gas	1670	0.003	0.204	−0.820	0.753	0.6	0.5482
Electricity-Wood & Waste	1659	0.382	0.339	−0.776	0.969	45.83	<.0001
Natural Gas-Wood & Waste	1659	0.378	0.294	−0.745	0.924	52.28	<.0001
Efficiency difference between sources within residential sector							
2-8 Electricity-Natural Gas	1670	0.055	0.085	−0.460	0.596	26.6	<.0001

are also presented. Table 7 presents t-value for the statistical difference along with the mean difference in efficiency measures between sectors by source of energy.

The results from Table 5 show the usage of coal (natural gas) energy source by commercial sector was 57.8% (89.3%), i.e. the least (most) efficient. The petroleum, natural gas and wood & waste sources of energy used by commercial sector were 89.2%, 83.7% and 76.8% efficient, respectively. Within the industrial sector, the wood & waste, coal, natural gas and electricity energy sources were 43.4%, 51.9%, 81.2% and 81.5% efficient, respectively. The residential sector use of electricity and natural gas energy source was 92.3% and 86.8% efficient, respectively. The most (95.9%) efficient was the use of petroleum by the transportation sector. Overall, the usage of wood & waste as an energy source by the industrial sector is the lowest with 43.4% efficiency.

Table 6 presents a pair-wise difference in mean efficiency measures and an associated statistical mean efficiency difference test. All the pair-wise efficiency measures were statistically different with the exception of electricity and petroleum (natural gas) sources of energy in the commercial (industrial) sector. In the commercial sector, coal relative to other sources of energy is least efficient and it is statistically significant. The efficiency of electricity and petroleum energy source is 31.3% higher than coal. The efficiency of natural gas and wood & waste are 25.7% and 19.1%, respectively, higher than coal. The efficiency of electricity relative to natural gas and wood & waste energy source usage by commercial sector is higher by 5.6% and 12.9%, respectively. In contrast, the efficiency of natural gas relative to petroleum (wood & waste) energy source was lower (higher) by 5.5% (12.5%). In the industrial sector, once again coal as source of energy is 29% least efficient relative to electricity and natural gas, but 8.6% higher than wood & waste. Electricity usage by the industrial sector is relatively efficient compared to natural gas and wood & waste by 0.3% and 38.2%, respectively. Compared to wood & waste, natural gas usage by the industrial sector is 37.8% highly efficient.

Within the residential sector, the difference in efficiency between electricity and natural gas is 5.5%. This suggests the residential sector uses the electricity energy source most efficiently.

The mean difference in efficiency measures between sectors by source of energy is presented in Table 7. The efficiency differences in coal, electricity, natural gas and wood & waste sources of energy usage by commercial and industrial sectors are statistically significant. The commercial sector uses energy efficiently compared to the industrial sector by 34.1%, 7.8%, 6.8% and 2.5%, respectively, for wood & waste, electricity, coal and natural gas. Residential use of electricity as the source of energy is relatively higher than commercial and industrial usage of electricity. The

Table 7. Mean difference in efficiency between sectors by source.

	N	**Mean**	**Std. Dev.**	**Minimum**	**Maximum**	***t* > Value**	**Pr > |t|**
Efficiency difference between commercial and industry sector by source							
2-8 Coal	1504	0.068	0.299	−0.820	0.801	8.83	<.0001
Electricity	1670	0.078	0.203	−0.621	0.920	15.68	<.0001
Natural Gas	1669	0.025	0.139	−0.879	0.683	7.28	<.0001
Wood & Waste	1392	0.341	0.300	−0.641	0.881	42.43	<.0001
Efficiency difference between sectors within electricity source							
2-8 Commercial-Residential	1670	−0.031	0.100	−0.698	0.397	−12.45	<.0001
Industry-Residential	1670	−0.108	0.182	−0.896	0.540	−24.29	<.0001
Efficiency difference between sectors within natural gas source							
2-8 Commercial-Residential	1669	−0.031	0.103	−0.870	0.386	−12.45	<.0001
Industry-Residential	1670	−0.056	0.133	−0.813	0.482	−17.29	<.0001
Efficiency difference between sectors within petroleum source							
2-8 Commercial-Transportation	1670	−0.067	0.057	−0.435	0.211	−48.26	<.0001

residential sector use of electricity as energy source is 10.8% and 3.1% higher than the industrial and commercial sectors, respectively. Similarly, a pair-wise comparison between residential and commercial sectors, and the residential and industrial sector use of natural gas presents a similar pattern. Residential sector use of natural gas as an energy source is 5.6% and 3.1% higher than industrial and commercial sectors, respectively. Finally, the use of petroleum as an energy source by commercial and transportation sectors shows that transportation sector uses petroleum with 6.7% higher efficiency.

5. Conclusion

In this chapter, the importance of climate, i.e. average and variance of temperature and precipitation associated with negative deviations (downside) and positive deviations (upside) along with technology and price changes on cost shares or source differentiated sectoral energy demand are examined. More importantly, the efficiency of efficiency of source differentiated sectoral energy demand equations are estimated using random panel stochastic frontier models. Finally, a pair-wise comparison of efficiency measures between sources within each sector and between sectors by energy source gives information to policy makers in decision-making. The source differentiated sectoral energy demand equations included: commercial-coal, commercial-electricity, commercial-natural gas, commercial-petroleum, commercial-wood and waste, industrial-coal, industrial-electricity, industrial-natural gas, industrial-petroleum, industrial-wood and waste, residential-electricity, residential-natural gas and transportation-petroleum.

Based on the results of technology variable, commercial sector saw an increase in the use of energy irrespective of the source of energy except for natural gas. This could be due to increased activity in the commercial sector or a decline in innovation leading to increased use of energy. In contrast, the technology variable in the industrial sector is negative and significant for coal, electricity and natural gas, but positive for wood & waste. Decline in the use of energy could be due to regulation or environmental issues associated with sources of energy or due to innovations in the industrial sector. However, there is an increase in the supply of energy from wood & waste. Technological innovations in electric appliances and cars lead to lower use of energy but due to increase in the number of electric appliances and number of cars on the road the use of energy increased in residential and transportation sectors. Finally, increased movement of natural gas and innovations lead to decline in the use of energy after accounting for changes in temperature and precipitation.

To summarize, technology innovations were positive for sectoral energy demand irrespective of sources of energy.

The efficiency measures suggest commercial, industrial, residential and transportation sectors use of electricity as the source of energy is most efficient with a score of 89.3%, 81.5% and 92.3%, respectively. However, the use of petroleum by transportation sector was most efficient with a score of 95.9%. This could de due to policies and regulations related to high fuel efficiency standards and the relative cost of extraction of petroleum in the US compared to other sources. In commercial and industrial sectors, coal and wood & waste as the source of energy are least efficient suggesting the need for policies to closely look at potential innovations or investment and changes in the rules and regulations in the US.

Pair-wise efficiency results show coal being least efficient across sectors. Electricity, natural gas and petroleum seem to be more efficient, but is sensitive to different sectors.

References

Aigner, D., Lovell, C. A. K. and Schmidt, P. (1977). Formulation and estimation of stochastic frontier production function models. *Journal of Econometrics* **6**, 21–37.

Barnett, A. H., Reutter, K. and Thompson, H. (1998). Electricity substitution: Some local industrial evidence. *Energy Economics* **20** (4), 411–419.

Barron, E. (2002). Potential Consequences of Climate Variability and Change for the Northeastern United States, Climate Change Impacts on the United States: The Potential Consequences of Climate Variability and Change, *National Assessment Synthesis Team*.

Boustead, I. and Yaros, B. R. (1994). Electricity supply in North America. *Resources, Conservation and Recycling* **12** (3–4), 121–134.

Caloghirou, Y. D., Mourelatos, A. G. and Thompson, H. (1997). Industrial energy substitution during the 1980s in the Greek economy. *Energy Economics* **19** (4), 476–491.

Deaton, M. and Muellbauer, J. (1994). *Economics and Consumer Behavior*. (Cambridge University Press).

Farrell, M. J. (1957). The measurement of productive efficiency. *Journal of the Royal Statistical Society Series A* **120**, 253–281.

Greene, W. (2003). Simulated likelihood estimation of the normal-gamma stochastic frontier function. *Journal of Productivity Analysis* **19**, 179–190.

Greene, W. (2008). The Econometric Approach to Efficiency Analysis, In H. O. Fried, C. A. K. Lovell and I. S. Materov (eds.), *The Measurement of Productive Efficiency and Productivity Growth*. (Oxford University Press), pp. 92–250.

Griffin, J. M. (1977). Inter-fuel substitution possibilities: A translog application to inter-country data. *International Economic Review* **18** (3), 755–770.

Jondrow, J., Lovell, C. A. K., Materov, I. S. and Schmidt, P. (1982). On the estimation of technical inefficiency in the stochastic Frontier production function model. *Journal of Econometrics* **19** (2–3), 233–238.

Kemfert, C. (1998). Estimated substitution elasticities of a nested CES production function approach for Germany. *Energy Economics* **20** (3), 249–264.

Koetse, M. J., de Groot H. L. and Florax, R. J. (2008). Capital-energy substitution and shifts in factor demand: A meta-analysis. *Energy Economics* **30** (5), 2236–2251.
Kuper, G. and Soest, D. P. V. (2003). Path-dependency and input substitution: Implications for energy policy modeling. *Energy Economics* **25**, 397–407.
Meeusen, W. and van den Broeck, J. (1977). Efficiency estimation from Cobb-Douglas production function with composed errors. *International Economic Review* **18** (2), 435–444.
Sailor, D. J. (2001). Relating residential and commercial sector electricity loads to climate-evaluating state level sensitivities and vulnerabilities. *Energy* **23** (2), 91–103.
Sailor, D. J. and Munoz, J. R. (1997). Sensitivity of electricity and natural gas consumption to climate in the USA — methodology and results for eight states. *Energy* **23** (10), 987–998.
Sailor, D. J., Rosen, J. N. and Munoz, J. R. (1998). Natural gas consumption and climate: A comprehensive set of predictive state-level models for the United Sates. *Energy* **23** (2), 91–103.
Scott, M. J., Wrench, L. E. and Hadley, D. L. (1994). Effects of climate change on commercial building energy demand. *Energy Sources* **16**, 317–332.
Thompson, H. (2005) The applied theory of energy substitution in production. *Energy Economics* **28** (4), 410–425.
Warren, H. E. and LeDuc, S. K. (1981). Impact of climate on energy sector in economic analysis. *Journal of Applied Meteorology* **20**, 1431–1439.

Chapter 21

Impact of the Global Financial Crisis 2007 on Project Finance in the Renewable Energy Sector

Iris Pfarl*,‡ and Christian Bellak†,§

*University of Applied Sciences BFI Vienna, Vienna, Austria

†WU Vienna University of Economics and Business, Vienna, Austria

‡iris.pfarl@gmail.com

§bellak@wu.ac.at

This study provides descriptive evidence on the adjustment in selected determinants of the credit margin carried out by project participants in the renewable energy sector facing the Global Financial Crisis after 2007. A dataset comprising financing parameters of 950 credit tranches granted in the renewable energy sector in the years 2000–2011 was retrieved from the database Dealogic ProjectWare. We provide descriptive evidence on the impact of the Global Financial Crisis after 2007 on the credit margin. The selection of determinants is based on the existent literature as well as on the realization of 13 case studies of project-financed transactions in the renewable energy sector. Our results show the substantial upward effect on the margins, shorter credit maturities and the need of considerably larger collaterals in order to achieve a Financial Close for projects initiated after the year 2007. A thorough examination of the methods of financing, the structure of project finance, the risk assessment methods and collaterals complement our analysis of the determinants of the credit margin. Overall, an adjustment in certain financing parameters as well as the application of risk-mitigating instruments such as, for example, project bonds, miniperm loans or cofinancing structures allow project finance to remain a proven and stable instrument for energy finance throughout the financial crisis.

Keywords: Renewable energy sector; project finance; credit margin; empirical study; financial crisis.

1. Introduction

Interest in financial aspects of the renewable energy sector inter alia is based on the fact that global goals, like the United Nations Framework Convention on Climate Change,[1] the UN Sustainable Development Goals,[2] the European Commission Europe 2020 Strategy and international agreements like the Paris Agreement[3] may only be approached via huge investments into energy production, innovative network infrastructures etc. Capital-intensive investment projects in the renewable energy sector (in sub-sectors like solar energy, wind, geothermal energy, hydropower, biomass and biofuels) entail complex questions concerning the financing structure and risk-sharing issues. Investment projects, therefore, require a sound financial basis if profitable investment opportunities are to be generated.

On the one hand, tighter capital markets, as for example, during the Global Financial Crisis after 2007, not only raise the cost of capital [Simshauser, 2014] but also raise the awareness of the financial sector in general, and financial institutions in particular, about technical risks, political instabilities and economic uncertainties in the regions/countries affected. For example, Kann [2009, p. 3139] reports that among the main barriers to project finance in Australian wind farms, "limited capital availability resulting from the recent global credit crisis" ranks prominently. As "(p)roject-financed wind-farms became the norm" [Kann 2009, p. 3144 on Australia] in many countries, it is important to note that project finance is also a proven financing instrument to overcome the challenges of tight capital markets.

On the other hand, it is interesting to note that the volume of project finance in the renewable energy sector stayed remarkably stable during and shortly after the Global Financial Crisis after 2007 (cf. Fig. 1).

As the worldwide energy demand is on a steady and considerable rise, the development of the power sector in general has been relatively stable even in times of financial crises. It is reflected in the global project finance volume that project finance is a proven instrument for the financing of power investments. In 2014, the energy sector accounted for 33% of the global project finance volume and was the leading sector with a finance volume of USD 133.7 billion. The renewable energy sector in particular contributes considerably to this upward development. The rise in the volume of windfarm projects on and offshore underpins this trend (cf. Fig. 1).

[1] http://unfccc.int/2860.php.

[2] http://www.un.org/sustainabledevelopment/sustainable-development-goals/ in particular #12: Responsible Production; #13: Climate Action.

[3] http://unfccc.int/paris_agreement/items/9444.php.

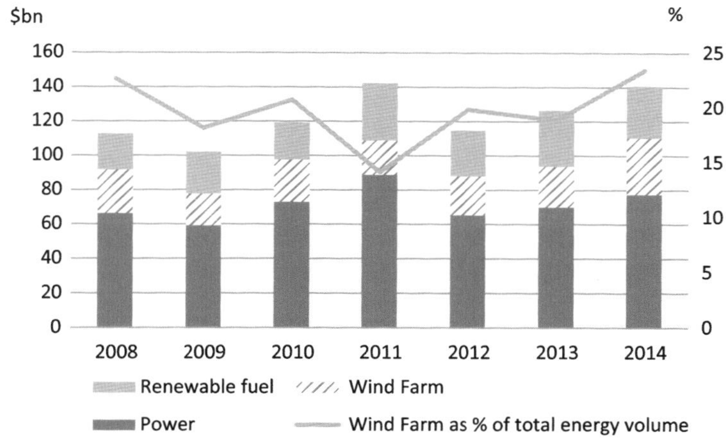

Fig. 1. Energy sector volume breakdown.
Source: Sector analysis/dealogic project finance review/full year 2014.

Yet, would it not be highly implausible to argue that the renewable energy sector was unaffected by the Global Financial Crisis after 2007?

This chapter is motivated by this stylized fact that tight capital markets following the financial crises generally carry the potential of reducing the volumes of project financing, which, however, does not seem to have materialized after the recent Global Financial Crisis after 2007. Plausible arguments point to the capacity of the renewable energy sector to adapt quickly to the new realities.

This chapter therefore seeks to identify adaptations which were introduced in the wake of the Global Financial Crisis after 2007. What are these parameters in the field of project finance? Are they linked to the Global Financial Crisis after 2007 or just mere results of innovations in the financial markets? Which financing parameters and mitigation techniques are relevant? Questions like these are highly relevant, since learning from other sectors and experiences is an important aspect of the sustainability of sectors of the economy. Likewise, lesson-drawing in public policy (e.g. [Rose, 1993]) is particularly relevant concerning highly regulated (and subsidized) and capital-intensive sectors like the renewable energy sector. While the existing literature has of course focused on such questions, they have not been linked to the occurrence of crisis.

Our results show the substantial upward effect on the margins, shorter credit maturities and the need of considerably larger collaterals in order to achieve a Financial Close for projects initiated after the year 2007. Based on the cash-flow and non-recourse financing structure and thanks to diverse creative risk mitigation measures including private and public partners, project finance remains a crisis-resistant means of financing that governments rely on in times of severe capital markets (see e.g. [Della Croce and Gatti, 2014]). The existing literature focusing on the credit margin, a key parameter, is presented in Section 2. Methodological considerations and descriptive evidence are presented in Sections 3 and 4. Section 5 concludes.

2. Extant Literature Survey

The empirical studies of Kleimeier and Megginson [2000, 2001], which have frequently been cited in the relevant literature of the last decade, analyze the project characteristics of about 5,000 project-financed international loans and around 90,000 syndicated loans. In a regression analysis, Kleimeier and Megginson [2000] show the behavior of various project-specific factors using the credit margin as dependent variable: Project-financed loans have higher average maturities, are more likely to be allocated to risk-free countries and are often structured with guarantees from third parties. In addition, fixed-rate credits are more common and — in case of variable-rate credits — they are priced on average with lower margins than comparable non-project-financed loans. According to Kleimeier and Megginson [2001], the credit margin in project financing is positively influenced by the level of political risk in the country of the borrower and the debt/equity ratio in the project. Further, the covenants used in the credit agreement have an influence on the margin. While the existence of third-party guarantees in projects results in a reduction of the credit margin, the size and maturity of the loan do not have a significant impact on the margin (see [Kleimeier and Megginson, 2000, 2001].

Based on a regression analysis, Sorge and Gadanecz [2004] investigate the interest structure of credit margins (dependent variable) of approximately 30,000 observations in the period 1993–2001 on loans and credits in project finance. In line with Kleimeier and Megginson [2001], it is revealed that there is no linear relationship between the credit margin and the credit maturity of project-financed transactions. Sorge and Gadanecz [2004] show that risk factors (such as negative macroeconomic indicators, political and institutional instability, current IMF credit lines, or technical assistance by IFIs in the country) are essential determinants for the setting of the credit margin, especially in emerging markets. This is in line with the findings of Altunbas and Gadanecz [2003] on syndicated loans in developing countries of the period 1993–2001 and with the study of Girardone and Snaith [2011] on project-financed loans of the period 1996–2003. Further, Sorge and Gadanecz [2004] show that the existence of a risk insurance in the form of an ECA guarantee or IFI cofinancing results in reduced credit margins (see [Altunbas and Gadanecz, 2003;

Girardone and Snaith, 2011; Sorge and Gadanecz, 2004]). Blanc-Brude and Strange [2007] empirically investigate a sample of 125 EU-wide Public Private Partnership (PPP)-projects in the road construction sector and a data set consisting of 177 Private Finance Initiative (PFI)-projects across all sectors in the UK in the period 1994–2005. The credit margin is used as the dependent variable. The interdependence of macroeconomic factors (such as the project country, the level of inflation) and risk parameters of project-specific factors (such as the size and duration of the credit lines, the size of the bank consortium, any refinancing of the project, possible splitting into different financing instruments) with the margin is examined. It is shown that the risk assessment of "systematic risks" (for example, the traffic volume in the sample of road construction projects) is relevant for the amount of the credit margin. Other risks on project levels are more likely to be overcome by the contractual structure or the project structure (see [Blanc-Brude and Strange 2007]).

The possibilities of risk management through extensive contractual agreements, so-called "nonfinancial contracts", which are intended to shift risks from the Special Purpose Vehicle (SPV) to other partners involved in the project, are considered by Corielli *et al.* [2010]. Within an analysis of around 1,000 project-financed loans of the period from 1998 to 2003, for which information on the risk-to-equity ratios are available, Corielli *et al.* [2010] confirm their *ex-ante* hypothesis that the absence of nonfinancial contracts leads to higher credit margins at the time of the signing of the credit agreements. Furthermore, they empirically show the positive relationship between the credit margin and the debt-to-equity ratio. As in many other studies on determinants of the credit margin in project financing, Corelli *et al.* [2010] also show that the result of the country risk assessment has a considerable influence on the credit margin.

Nelson *et al.* [2013] further examine the consequences of policy uncertainty (which is comparable to a situation of uncertainty on the financial markets) in the financing environment for renewable energy projects in Australia. A policy of public subsidization, which has been subject to many alterations over the years and which has favored solar energy investments has led to a distortion in the diversification of renewable energy subsectors. Further, as a consequence of this uncertainty in the policy on greenhouse gas emissions the credit margins in project-financed renewable energy projects has increased significantly relative to margins in bonds [Nelson *et al.*, 2013].

Pinto and Alves [2016] examine an extensive sample of around 200,000 credit transactions and their findings suggest that project finance is used for capital-intensive projects with high country risk and long maturities. They state that project finance loans show lower margins than syndicated loans. Examining the influence of the Global Financial Crisis after 2007 on pricing, their findings suggest that credit margins are significantly higher during the crisis and that country risk affects pricing [Pinto and Alves, 2016].

Further, using a sample of almost 6,000 project-financed ventures, Byoun and Xu [2014] examine the influence of country risk on contractual structures of a project-financed transaction. Their findings suggest that projects with a high country risk are less likely to entail statutory concessions or power purchase agreements. Thus, governments of unstable states do not have the potential to influence projects [Byoun and Xu, 2014].

The size of the respective sample in the above studies varies according to differences in regional extent, sectoral size, period of analysis and the chosen type of credit. Some of the studies are international, others are subdivided into groups of countries according to their economic power. For example, a sectoral restriction, selected by Blanc-Brude and Strange [2007], considerably reduces the observation sample compared to studies involving all available sectors. Except for Nelson *et al.* [2013] none of the empirical studies focuses on the analysis of projects in the renewable energy sector. The importance of this sector has grown dramatically in the course of recent years due to the increasing environmental impact of fossil fuels and the resulting diversification efforts of energy sources. The differences in the sample size are also due to the fact that some of the studies combine syndicated and project-financed loans. The majority of the analyses, however, relate exclusively to project-financed loans.

In most cases, the variables included in the analyses such as the number of creditors, the project or tranche value, the regional allocation expressed in ratings or macroeconomic parameters, the sector affiliation and the availability of guarantees show a highly significant influence on the margin. Variables such as the type of borrower, the base rate, the setting of covenants in the credit agreement or credit fees usually have no or only a marginal effect on the dependent variable. The interpretation of the behavior of the variables in the individual studies is not dealt with here, since this only makes sense with respect to the particular sample size chosen.

It should be emphasized that the studies reviewed above aimed to establish a causal link between credit margin and financing parameters, whereas the present empirical analysis presents descriptive evidence.

3. Methodological Considerations

Before presenting the empirical evidence, a word of caution is required as we provide *descriptive evidence* for changes in the characteristics of project finance in the renewable energy sector, which must not be interpreted as causal.

Surveys such as the one by Fritz-Morgenthal *et al.* [2009] may shed light on the optimism or pessimism of key decision makers and managers at a certain point in time, yet must not be interpreted as causal studies, although their titles suggest otherwise. In order to draw causal inferences regarding the impact of the Global Financial Crisis after 2007 on the structure and characteristics of project finance in the renewable energy sector, techniques of event history analysis would have to be employed (see e.g. [Steele, 2005; Khotari and Warner, 2006; Sun and Zhao, 2013]).

Event history analysis is used to analyze the occurrence of distinct events like changes in occupation, political change from democratic to non-democratic regimes, violation of international treaties by governments within observed historical periods for a group of subjects, which may be individuals, governments, or, indeed, projects. The occurrence (and vice versa non-occurrence) of an event is treated as a dichotomous dependent variable. As Steele [2005] points out, "(t)here are two particular features of event history data which must be considered in their analysis. First, the event of interest may not yet have occurred to a proportion of the sample. The duration to event occurrence, the response variable in an event history analysis, is said to be right censored for these individuals. Second, we are usually interested in the effects of explanatory variables on the timing of events, and some of these variables may change value over the course of the observation period; such variables are called time-varying covariates." Hence, it is crucial to note that OLS, the method used here, clearly does not take these features into account. With respect to project finance in the renewable energy sector, for example, one may define the start of the individual project finance as the beginning of the period measuring the duration to event occurrence, and ask whether the occurrence of the Global Financial Crisis after 2007 (financial, political, etc.) has triggered a shift in the number of tranche providers, in the main currency denomination of tranches or indeed, the credit margin. The effect of the independent variables on the duration of the project finance would be estimated before the structure is altered.

4. Descriptive Evidence

4.1. *Data, variables and estimation strategy*

Which factors have impact on the credit margin in project finance in the renewable energy sector? In particular, how is the Global Financial Crisis after 2007 related to the impact of critical determinants on the credit margin.

A dataset comprising financing parameters of 950 credit tranches granted in the renewable energy sector in the years 2000–2011 was retrieved from the database Dealogic ProjectWare. In order to shed light on the questions mentioned above, we provide descriptive evidence using a simple OLS regression model, covering a pooled cross-section of projects during the period 2000–2011. Ideally, time-invariant factors will have to be included into the regression and fixed effects will have to be controlled for. Yet, they cannot be accounted for due to the lack of a panel structure.

The dependent variable (see Table A.2) is the margin of a credit tranche, Tr_Margin, which is defined as the premium added to a baserate (EURIBOR, LIBOR, etc.). The credit margin is the relevant key risk figure in project-financed transactions.

The independent variables used are partly determined by their availability in the single database Dealogic ProjectWare and partly based on a series of case studies of single projects (see [Pfarl and Moser, 2017]), which has further influence on the selection of the variables in our empirical strategy. However, some of the key variables, which have been used by earlier studies (e.g. [Girardone and Snaith, 2011; Sorge and Gadanecz, 2004; Altunbas and Gadanecz, 2003]) could not be used, including information on guarantees (for example, the availability of state export credit guarantees) and on collateral. As these variables have shown a highly significant negative effect on the credit margin, it is likely that our results overstate the effects on the credit margin as our variables partly account for the influence of the variables just mentioned. This again underpins our caveat regarding the limitations of the analysis.

The variables used and their definitions are shown in Table 1.

Table 1. Variables.

Variable name	**Unit**	**Description**
Tr_Margin	Basis points	Credit margin, logged
Tr_Maturity	Months	Duration of credit per tranche
TrancheProviders	Number	Credit providers per tranche
Tranches	Number	Tranches per project
Currency_n	Dummy variable	Currency used in a tranche
ProjectSector_n	Dummy variable	Subsector of the project
Region_n	Dummy variable	Region of the project
YearFinancialClose200_n	Year	Financial close date of the project
Borrower_x	Dummy variable	Borrower is a public or private entity

Note: _n . . . denotes n units.

The following equations have been estimated.[4]

$$\begin{aligned}\text{Tr\_Margin}_i &= \alpha + \beta_1\,\text{Tr\_Maturity}_i + \beta_2\,\text{Tranche Providers}_i \\ &\quad + \beta_3\,\text{Tranches}_i + \beta_4\,\text{Currency}_i \\ &\quad + \beta_5\,\text{Project Sector}_i + \beta_6\,\text{Region}_i \\ &\quad + \beta_7\,\text{Year Financial Close}_i + \beta_8\,\text{Borrower}_i + \varepsilon_i \\ &\quad (i = 1, 2, 3 \ldots) \\ \text{Tr\_Margin}_{i,j} &= \alpha + \beta_1\text{Tr\_Maturity}_{i,j} + \beta_2\,\text{Tranche Providers}_{i,j} \\ &\quad + \beta_3\,\text{Tranches}_{i,j} + \beta_4\,\text{Project Sector}_{i,j} \\ &\quad + \beta_5\,\text{Year Financial Close}_{i,j} + \beta_6\,\text{Borrower}_{i,j} + \varepsilon_{i,j} \\ &\quad (j = 1 \ldots \text{Europe})\end{aligned}$$

4.2. *Results*

Table 2 shows the coefficients for all variables. Note that data have been corrected for outliers and tested for heteroscedasticity and multicollinearity. (Descriptive statistics are shown in Table A.1.) All coefficients carry the expected signs.

Based on this table the following descriptive information can be derived:

- Credit margins as the central risk parameter in bank financing have generally risen during the period 2009–2011. Expectedly, an impact of the Global Financial Crisis after 2007 on the credit margin with respect to the financial close date of the project is clearly discernible: While in the years prior to 2008 credit margins have been significantly lower than in 2008, they were significantly higher in the years after 2008. Already in projects with financial close date 2009, credit margins are 73 base points higher than in 2008 and increase by 94% (90%) in the year 2010 (2011). This increase is even more pronounced for European projects (results, see Table 2, cols. 5–7). Moreover, a simple t-test of the split sample confirms the lagged intensified impact of the Global Financial Crisis after 2007 in the subsequent years.[5] Table A.5 additionally underlines that the credit margin showed a considerable rise: Margins reach an average amount of 233 basis points

[4]The sample was checked for possible multicollinearity and endogeneity. Both turned out not to be relevant.

[5]Define diff = mean(0) − mean(1); H_0: diff = 0 versus. H_1: diff > 0 tested on the 5% level.

Table 2. Descriptive results.

Tr_Margin (log)	International (est. 1)			Europe (est. 2)		
Variable	**Coeff.**	***t***		**Coeff.**	***t***	
Tr_Maturity	0.0021	10.15	***	0.0024	10.89	***
TrancheProviders	−0.0227	4.20	***	−0.0255	4.22	***
Tranches	0.0328	2.49	**	0.0653	4.25	***
Currency2	−0.6409	5.43	***	—	—	
Currency3	−0.5414	5.30	***	—	—	
ProjectSector2	0.0174	0.46		0.0176	0.44	
Region2	−0.1799	1.48		—	—	
Region3	0.4156	3.23	**	—	—	
Region4	−0.1832	1.87	**	—	—	
Region5	0.0036	0.03		—	—	
YearFinancialClose2000	0.1382	1.09		−0.0258	0.19	
YearFinancialClose2001	−0.2119	0.89		−0.1401	0.52	
YearFinancialClose2002	0.0467	0.40		0.0905	0.68	
YearFinancialClose2003	0.0939	1.18		0.0539	0.60	
YearFinancialClose2004	−0.0096	0.13		0.0088	0.11	
YearFinancialClose2005	−0.1866	2.80	**	−0.2362	3.28	**
YearFinancialClose2006	−0.1918	3.11	**	−0.2171	3.30	**
YearFinancialClose2007	−0.2604	4.78	***	−0.3360	5.95	***
YearFinancialClose2009	0.5498	8.81	***	0.5259	7.49	***
YearFinancialClose2010	0.6610	11.07	***	0.6526	9.04	***
YearFinancialClose2011	0.6422	8.60	***	0.8648	7.73	***
Borrower1	0.1790	0.87		0.0749	0.27	
_cons	5.0319	35.61		4.2752	52.20	
Observations	635			447		
R^2	0.5806			0.5223		
Adjusted R^2	0.5656			0.5045		
Breusch–Pagan/Cook–Weisberg test H0: Constant Variance						
χ^2	0.94			0.34		
Prob > χ^2	0.3334			0.5586		

Notes: *, **, and *** indicate significance at 10%, 5%, and 1%, respectively.

in 2009 and show a substantial increase by almost 100 basis points compared to 2008. The upward trend continues with an average of almost 300 basis points in 2011 reaching the peak within the observation period.

This is a clear reflection of the more complex risk situation in the financial markets. Additionally, the number of projects realized per year declined for the years (see Table A.4). Projects have longer lead times, as participants are far more cautious and the risk assessment process is therefore more intensive.

- Tranche maturity is significantly and positively correlated with tranche margin. Therefore, a reduction of the credit maturity serves as a measure to prevent even larger increases in the margin. The use of miniperm loans (see Case Study findings below) with shorter maturities softening the effects of cost explosions in margins further underlines this effect.
- A larger number of tranche providers expectedly reduces the margin. Besides the risk diversification effect, the latter may be due to the fact that some tranche providers profit from lead banks or participating International Financial Institutions that carry the efforts for the risk and feasibility assessment of a project (see [Sheppard, 2012; Gianturco 2001]).
- All tranches financed in currencies other than US$ have significantly lower credit margins (see Table A.2). This may be due to the fact that the crisis had its origin in the US financial market. Due to the problems in the American banking system, banks started to follow a more risk-averse and conservative approach in their lending policy. Switching of currencies can further be used as a means of lightening the effects of margin increase.
- Compared to European projects, credit margins of projects in other regions are significantly higher (South America) or lower (Asia). This is usually a clear reflection of the political risks involved (e.g. [OECD, 2017]). However, the latter points to the fact that some of the projects are development projects supported by International Financial Institutions like development banks involving a grant element or a subsidized interest rate and — in line with other publications (e.g. [UN ESCAP, 2010]) — capital markets in Asia did "... not view significant risks for sovereign debt issued from the region" (see Table A.3).

Coefficients as those shown in Table 2 cannot be compared directly, as the underlying variables are measured in different units. Therefore, *standardized beta coefficients*, which allow for direct comparison of the size of the coefficients, are shown in Table 3 to provide complementary information. The original units of measurement of dependent and independent variables are replaced by standard deviations, which "puts the explanatory variables on equal footing." [Wooldridge, 2002, p. 182] Note that *standardized beta coefficients* cannot meaningfully be interpreted for dichotomous variables (i.e. for the dummy variables in our sample). Hence, no comparison of our key variable reflecting the years prior to and after the Global Financial Crisis after 2007 can be made.

Among the remaining variables, tranche maturity and the number of tranche providers are more important than any other variable, both in the total sample and in the European sample.

Table 3. Beta-coefficients.

Tr_Margin	International (est. 1)		Europe (est. 2)	
Variable	**ß Coeff.**	*t*	**ß Coeff.**	*t*
Tr_ Maturity	0.2773	10.15***	0.3705	10.89***
TrancheProviders	−0.1235	4.20***	−0.15638	4.22***
Tranches	0.0707	2.49**	0.15364	4.25***
Currency2	−0.5123	5.43***	—	—
Currency3	−0.3078	5.30***	—	—
ProjectSector2	0.0141	0.46	0.0163	0.44
Region2	−0.1181	1.48	—	—
Region3	0.1082	3.23**	—	—
Region4	−0.0694	1.87	—	—
Region5	0.0009	0.03	—	—
YearFinancialClose2000	0.0337	1.09	−0.00678	0.19
YearFinancialClose2001	−0.0241	0.89	−0.01749	0.52
YearFinancialClose2002	0.0110	0.40	0.02377	0.68
YearFinancialClose2003	0.0351	1.18	0.02316	0.60
YearFinancialClose2004	−0.0039	0.13	0.00401	0.11
YearFinancialClose2005	−0.0850	2.80**	−0.12609	3.28**
YearFinancialClose2006	−0.0973	3.11**	−0.13124	3.30**
YearFinancialClose2007	−0.1529	4.78***	−0.24321	5.95***
YearFinancialClose2009	0.2731	8.81***	0.28998	7.49***
YearFinancialClose2010	0.3604	11.07***	0.33628	9.04***
YearFinancialClose2011	0.2681	8.60***	0.27175	7.73***
Borrower1	0.0235	0.87	0.00934	0.27
Observations	635		447	
R^2	0.5806		0.5223	
Adjusted R^2	0.5656		0.5045	

Notes: *, **, and *** indicate significance at 10%, 5%, and 1%, respectively.

Summarizing, our results show the substantial upward effect on the margins, shorter credit maturities and the need of considerably larger collaterals in order to achieve a Financial Close for projects initiated after the year 2007.

While this evidence is descriptive in nature, a number of case studies carried out on particular projects in the renewable energy sector concluded before and during the Global Financial Crisis after 2007 suggests that the hints provided by the descriptive analysis may also figure prominently in a causal analysis. To the best of our knowledge, no empirical event history study on this issue is available to date.

The case study analysis confirms the following findings of the quantitative analysis: Compared to investments completed before the Global Financial Crisis after 2007 projects concluded in the years of financial crisis show a clear rise in margins, tend to have shorter maturities and show switches in currencies to absorb an even larger increase of the margin. However, not all of the projects in the case study analysis underpin the effect that a higher number of tranche providers may absorb a rise in the margin of projects throughout a crisis.

The case studies also revealed several financing instruments that proved to be factors of success for the realization of project-financed transactions effected during the financial crisis, like *project bonds*. Project bonds are debt securities which a creditor acquires from a project company issuing the bond. The buyer of the bond, thus grants the project company credit on a long-term basis and receives periodic interest payments as well as the repayment of the capital amount at the end of the agreed maturity of the project bond (see e.g. [Mobius, 2012]).

Another instrument suitable for overcoming difficulties in a severe financing environment are *miniperm loans*, which are usually concluded at the beginning of a project when no or only low income is generated. They serve as an instrument to bridge the construction and start-up phase until banks are willing to provide long-term financing against the background of steady flows. A miniperm loan is usually completely redeemed at the end of the construction period and simultaneously refinanced. After the project has generated income banks normally offer the possibility to refinance the miniperm loan or convert it into a long-term financing model (see [Greve and Hodge, 2013]).

Also, *leasing transactions* may be a suitable instrument to solve financing questions in project-financed transactions during a financial crisis. In project financing for industrial plants often a "sale-and-lease-back" structure is applied where the future lessor acquires the leased object, for example, the project equipment, from the future lessee. The sale of the project, i.e. of the project assets, enables the lessee to repay the liabilities or create liquid funds. In times of a tense economic situation, leasing offers a company the opportunity to directly generate liquidity from existing assets of project investments (see [Kratzer and Kreuzmair, 2002]).

Further, *cofinancing* is a reliable instrument for enabling project finance transactions (cf. [Rajan Annamalai and Jain, 2013]). It refers to the structuring of financing an investment project through the interaction of IFIs, ECAs and private commercial banks as well as investors. The participation of an IFI leads to an improved risk-sharing situation. In addition, from the point of view of private partners and banks this implies a reduction in political risks and project risks. IFIs also have access to information on investment opportunities in the respective target countries and provide in-depth know-how on the regulatory environment in the project country. Their excellent rating allows IFIs to have favorable terms on the capital market. Creditors participating in cofinancing also benefit from a careful project assessment, implementation and monitoring, as well as the privileged creditor status of an IFI (see [Gianturco, 2001; Yescombe, 2002; Merna and Al-Thani, 2001; Sheppard, 2012]).

An *escrow account* solution can be a suitable and common instrument to overcome risk and render projects more attractive. In this scenario, an account is created where the income from energy generation is transferred to the banks and serves as a security for them [Taylor *et al.*, 2008]. Subramanian and Tung [2016] consider project accounts in project finance a suitable means to overcome threats caused by a weak legal framework in the project country.

Also, creditors' willingness to support project-financed investments is positively influenced by the existence of fixed purchase contracts for the corresponding period, for example, in the form of power purchase agreements. Such contracts again significantly reduce the market risk and thus, have a negative effect on the margin [Bonetti, 2010].

To reach financial closing during the crisis, suppliers of equipment were also forced to participate in the project risk. In the case of the Belgian offshore wind farm Bligh Bank closed in 2009, for example, the producer of the turbines had to guarantee a certain amount of operational hours [Euromoney Trading Limited, 2010].

Another possible parameter of adaptation is the *capital structure* (see [Pierru *et al.*, 2013]). For the Spanish solar energy projects Extresol I (concluded in 2007) and Extresol II (concluded in 2009) the equity ratio in the crisis project more than doubled compared to the 2007 financing [Dealogic, 2013].

In general, the existence of diverse securities is a valid means to influence the possibility to reach financial close under severe conditions on the capital market. Surely, the more extensive and substantive securities offered by the project initiators are, the more likely it is to get support from the banking sector.

5. Concluding Comments

The occurrence of more and deeper financial crises over time (cf. the literature discussed in Bjørnskov [2016]) has important implications for market confidence, which is an important enabling factor of project finance [Nelson *et al.*, 2013]. The relatively stable volume of project finance in the wind energy sector after the Global Financial Crisis after 2007, suggests that market confidence has not been deeply distorted by the Global Financial Crisis after 2007. Yet, several adjustment strategies have been introduced as a result of the Global Financial Crisis after 2007.

Firstly, this chapter aimed to discuss such adjustment strategies. Secondly, we provide descriptive evidence on the adjustment of selected determinants of the credit margin carried out by project participants in the renewable energy sector facing the Global Financial Crisis after 2007.

Overall, it seems that the project participants, especially the financing community in the renewable energy sector, reacted quickly and flexibly to the challenges caused by the Global Financial Crisis after 2007. This was a key factor in keeping the volume of financial transactions in this sector relatively stable. We conclude that the extraordinary quick adjustment of some of the key parameters and the financial structure in the market of project finance allowed a considerably steadier development of the volume of financial transactions than in other sectors. Based on the cash-flow and non-recourse financing structure, and thanks to diverse creative risk mitigation measures including private and public partners, project finance remains a crisis-resistant means of financing which governments rely on in times of severe capital markets (see e.g. [Della Croce and Gatti, 2014]).

Appendix

Table A.1. List of variables used in OLS regression.

Variable	Observations	Mean	Std. Dev.	Min	Max
Tr_Margin	657	164.2201	96.10072	25	500
Tr_Maturity	751	128.8296	80.22199	5	300
TrancheProviders	787	3.958069	3.256939	1	18
Tranches	787	3.475222	1.269262	1	7
Currency1	787	0.227446	0.4194495	0	1
Currency2	787	0.6442186	0.4790539	0	1
Currency3	787	0.1283355	0.3346756	0	1
ProjectSector1	787	0.6289708	0.4833875	0	1
ProjectSector2	787	0.3710292	0.4833875	0	1
Region1	787	0.7064803	0.455664	0	1
Region2	787	0.1867853	0.3899869	0	1
Region3	787	0.0317662	0.1754886	0	1
Region4	787	0.0508259	0.2197818	0	1
Region5	787	0.0241423	0.1535885	0	1
Year2000	786	0.019084	0.1369073	0	1
Year2001	786	0.0089059	0.0940095	0	1
Year2002	786	0.0203562	0.1413056	0	1
Year2003	786	0.0496183	0.2172934	0	1
Year2004	786	0.0661578	0.2487159	0	1
Year2005	786	0.0903308	0.2868376	0	1
Year2006	786	0.1017812	0.3025528	0	1
Year2007	786	0.1399491	0.3471551	0	1
Year2008	786	0.2099237	0.4075132	0	1
Year2009	786	0.0890585	0.2850096	0	1
Year2010	786	0.1221374	0.3276529	0	1
Year2011	786	0.0826972	0.2755994	0	1
Borrower1	765	0.0052288	0.072168	0	1
Borrower2	765	0.9947712	0.072168	0	1

Table A.2. Credit margin in bp per currency USD/EUR and baserate LIBOR/EURIBOR.

Tr_Margin	Observations	Mean	Std. Dev.	Min	Max
US Dollar	149	244.54	95.62	45	450
Euro	421	137.22	80.77	30	500
Others	87	157.31	89.75	25	370
LIBOR	169	218.48	94	40	425
EURIBOR	367	135.5	78.06	35	500
Others	21	221.9	98.82	50	370

Table A.3. Credit margin in basis points per currency (other than USD and EUR).

Tr_Margin	Observations	Mean	Std. Dev.	Min	Max
Australian Dollar	15	132.53	64.66	40.00	340.00
Brazilian Real	7	319.29	38.99	280.00	370.00
Canadian Dollar	3	369.40	0.00	369.40	369.40
Czech Koruna	6	273.33	45.02	220.00	320.00
Hungarian Forint	1	95.00	0.00	95.00	95.00
Indian Rupee	2	31.00	8.49	25.00	37.00
Italian Lira	4	92.50	35.00	40.00	110.00
Japanese Yen	4	103.13	66.44	50.00	187.50
New Taiwan Dollar	4	91.00	36.72	50.00	122.00
Polish Zloty	4	180.00	53.39	120.00	250.00
South Korean Won	2	125.00	35.36	100.00	150.00
Spanish Peseta	5	99.34	16.26	81.70	125.00
Sterling	28	130.71	29.70	100.00	250.00
Thai Baht	2	142.20	165.75	25.00	259.40

Table A.4. Number of projects per year.

Year	Frequency	Percent
2000	15	1.91
2001	7	0.89
2002	16	2.04
2003	39	4.96
2004	52	6.62
2005	71	9.03
2006	80	10.18
2007	110	13.99
2008	165	20.99
2009	70	8.91
2010	96	12.21
2011	65	8.27
Total	786	100

Table A.5. Credit margin in bp per year.

Tr_Margin	Observations	Mean	Std. Dev.	Min	Max
2000	14	183.48	125.42	40	400
2001	5	104	37.98	60	145
2002	14	125.88	32.63	75	181
2003	36	139.13	50.43	50	325
2004	43	130.97	62.05	30	425
2005	58	116.33	45.24	35	215
2006	70	103.25	45.15	50	275
2007	95	108.32	58.98	40	370
2008	135	137.2	77.55	25	500
2009	63	233.25	94.85	25	388
2010	80	274.3	64.1	130	450
2011	43	296.49	95.46	37	500

Abbreviations

ECA	Export Credit Agency
IFI	International Financial Institution
IMF	International Monetary Fund
PFI	Private Finance Initiative
PPP	Public Private Partnership
SPV	Special Purpose Vehicle

References

Altunbas, Y. and Gadanecz, B. (2003). Developing country economic structure and the pricing of syndicated credits. BIS Working Papers No. 132. *Journal of Development Studies* **40**(5), 3–17.

Bjørnskov, C. (2016). Economic freedom and economic crises. *European Journal of Political Economy* **45**, 11–23.

Blanc-Brude, F. and Strange, R. (2007). How banks price loans to public-private partnerships: Evidence from the European markets. *Journal of Applied Corporate Finance* **19**, 94–106.

Bonetti, V. *et al.* (2010). Offtaking agreements and how they impact the cost of funding for project finance deals: A clinical case study of the Quezon Power Ltd. Co. *Review of Financial Economics* **19**, 60–71.

Byoun, S. and Xu, Z. (2014). Contracts, governance and country risk in project finance: Theory and evidence. *Journal of Corporate Finance* **26**, 124–144.

Corielli, F. *et al.* (2010). Risk shifting through nonfinancial contracts: Effects on loan spreads and capital structure of project finance deals. *Journal of Money, Credit and Banking* **42**(7), 1295–1320.

Dealogic (2013). ProjectWare Database. Project Data Sheets. Retrieved from www.dealogic.com.

Della Croce, R. and Gatti, S. (2014). Financing infrastructure — International trends. *OECD Journal: Financial Market Trends* **2014**(1), 123–138.

Euromoney Trading Limited (2010). Belwind: Belgian benchmark. *Project Finance and Infrastructure Finance*. Vol. February 2010.

Fritz-Morgenthal, S., Greenwood, Ch., Menzel, C., Mironjuk, M. and Sonntag-O'Brien, V. (2009). *The Global Financial Crisis and its Impact on Renewable Energy Finance*, study was commissioned by UNEP's Division of Technology, Industry and Economics (DTIE) under its Sustainable Energy Finance Initiative: Frankfurt.

Gianturco, D. E. (2001). *Export Credit Agencies: The Unsung Giants of International Trade and Finance*. (Greenwood Publishing Group), pp. 60–65.

Girardone, C. and Snaith, S. (2011). Project finance loan spreads and disaggregated political risk. *Applied Financial Economics* **21**, 1725–1734.

Greve, C. and Hodge, G. (2013). *Rethinking Public-Private Partnerships: Strategies for Turbulent Times*. (Routledge, New York), p. 40.

Kann, S. (2009). Overcoming barriers to wind project finance in Australia. *Energy Policy* **37**, 3139–3148.

Khotari, S. P. and Warner, J. B. (2006). Econometrics of Event Studies. In B. E. Eckbo (ed.), *Handbook of Corporate Finance: Empirical Corporate Finance*, Volume A (Handbooks in Finance Series, Elsevier/North-Holland), Ch. 1.

Kleimeier, S. and Megginson, W. L. (2001). *An Empirical Analysis of Limited Recourse Project Finance*, University of Oklahoma, Michel F. Price College, Business Working Paper Series, SSRN eLibrary, pp. 1–25.

Kleimeier, S. and Megginson, W. L. (2000). Are project finance loans different from other syndicated credits? *Journal of Applied Corporate Finance* **13**, 75–87.

Kratzer, B. and Kreuzmair, J. (2002). *Leasing in Theorie und Praxis*. 2nd edn., (Gabler, Wiesbaden), pp. 15–76.

Merna, T. and Al-Thani, F. F. (2001) *Corporate Risk Management*, 2nd edn. (Wiley, West Sussex), pp. 18–54.

Mobius, M. (2012). *Bonds: An Introduction to the Core Concepts*. (Wiley, Singapore) pp. 2–8.

Nelson, T. *et al.* (2013). An analysis of Australia's large scale renewable energy target: Restoring market confidence. *Energy Policy* **62**, 386–400.

OECD (2017). *Country Risk Classifications of the Participants to the Arrangement on Officially Supported Export Credits*, http://www.oecd.org/trade/xcred/cre-crc-current-english.pdf accessed 15.7.2017.

Pfarl, I. and Moser, R. (2017). Projektfinanzierung als erfolgreiche Finanzierungsform im internationalen Geschäft: Fallstudien im Bereich Erneuerbare Energien: Springer Fachmedien Wiesbaden GmbH.

Pfarl, I. (2014). *Empirische Analysen der Projektfinanzierung 2000–2012 im Sektor Erneuerbare Energie*: Doctoral Thesis, Vienna University of Economics and B.A.

Pierru, A., Roussanaly, S. and Sabathier, J. (2013). Capital structure in LNG infrastructures and gas pipelines projects: Empirical evidences and methodological issues. *Energy Policy* **61**, 285–291.

Pinto, J. M. and Alves, P. P. (2016). *Project Finance in Europe: An Overview and Discussion of Key Drivers*, EIB Working Papers, Luxembourg. 04-2016. pp. 5–10.

Rajan Annamalai, T. and Jain, N. (2013). Project finance and investments in risky environments: Evidence from the infrastructure sector. *Journal of Financial Management of Property and Construction* **18**(3), 251–267.

Rose, R. (1993). *Lesson-Drawing in Public Policy: A Guide to Learning across Time and Space*, (Chatham House, Chatham).

Sheppard, B. (2012). The Role of Multilateral Banks and ECAs. In R. Morrison, (ed.) *The Principles of Project Finance*. (Gower Publishing, Surrey), pp. 81–94.

Simshauser, P. (2014). The cost of capital for power generation in atypical capital market conditions. *Economic Analysis and Policy* **44**, 184–201.

Sorge, M. and Gadanecz, B. (2004). The term structure of credit spreads in project finance, BIS Working Papers No. 159. SSRN eLibrary, pp. 1–18.

Steele, F. (2005). *Event History Analysis*, NCRM Methods Review Papers, NCRM/004, University of Bristol.

Subramanian, K. V. and Tung, F. (2016). Law and project finance. *Journal of Financial Intermediation* **25**, 155–177.

Sun, J. and Zhao, X. (2013). *The Statistical Analysis of Panel Count Data* (Springer: Berlin, Heidelberg, New York).

Taylor, R. P., Govindarajalu, Ch., Levin, J., Meyer, A. and Ward, W. (2008). *Financing Energy Efficiency: Lessons from Brazil, China, India and Beyond*, ESMAP/Energy Sector Management Assistance Program, (World Bank Publication, Washington), pp. 112–113.

UN ESCAP (2010). *The European Debt Crisis: Implications for Asia and the Pacific*, MPDD Policy Briefs, Macroeconomic Policy and Development Division, No. 4, August, http://www.unescap.org/sites/default/files/pb4.pdf, accessed 27.4.2017.

Wooldridge, J. M. (2002). *Introductory Econometrics: A Modern Approach*, 2nd edn., (Itps Thomson Learning, Mason).

Yescombe, E. R. (2002). *Principles of Project Finance* (Academic Press, London und San Diego), pp. 7–15.

Chapter 22

Environmental Concerns and the Cost of Equity in the US Energy Sector

Marcelo Bianconi* and Xue Wang

Department of Economics, Tufts University, 111 Braker Hall Medford, MA 02155, USA

**marcelo.bianconi@tufts.edu*

This chapter studies how a well-defined environmental concerns factor influences the equity performance of US energy firms and whether or not this influence differs for renewable and non-renewable energy firms. We construct the environmental sentiment factor and seven sub-group environment-related risk factors using the Dynamic Factor Model econometric method. Then, we estimate stock abnormal returns from well-established asset pricing models to measure firm equity performance. We use an unbalanced panel of 448 US energy firms at the monthly frequency from January 2004 to October 2016. First, we find that all US energy companies show negative abnormal returns in the sampled period, that is the actual returns were lower than expected. Renewable energy firms had higher company value, since renewable energy stocks had lower abnormal returns. We also find that the abnormal returns of renewable energy stocks mainly come from environment regulation risks, while the abnormal returns of non-renewable energy stocks are more sensitive to the measure of public environmental concerns and extreme weather conditions. Consequently, we find that holding the level of environmental related risks constant, non-renewable energy stocks command relative lower abnormal returns.

Keywords: Environmental sentiment measure; renewable energy firms; non-renewable energy firms; dynamic factor model; asset pricing model; abnormal returns; alpha; extreme weather; regulation; social media.

1. Introduction

Climate change has been a topic of controversial and heated debate around the world, at least in the last 15 years or so. As a result, scientific climate conferences are held, agreements are planned and eventually signed, and green energy and consumption is fully promoted. The public awareness of environmental issues has also increased substantially. The overall increase in environmental awareness sentiment should impact related firms' performance and capabilities. We would expect that risk and uncertainty for firms related to the environment, such as energy firms, should ultimately impact the firms' stock market and valuation performance. Thus, we propose here to examine the more general relationship between the public environmental sentiment and the stock market returns of energy firms. More specifically, we want to tease out how and why the relationship between the public environmental sentiment and the stock market returns of energy firms differ between renewable and non-renewable energy firms.

The research agenda in this area is active. One avenue has been the relationship between external weather conditions, as a proxy for climate change, and stock market performance. Authors such as Lepori [2016], Levy and Yagil [2011], Chang *et al.* [2008] study this topic, using data on an aggregate stock market index and the observed exogenous climate data. The key results are that weather conditions such as pollution, temperature, cloud cover, the amount of sunshine and the length of daylight can influence the capital market performance by altering traders or investors' sentiment, thus further influencing their investment behavior. In those studies, only weather data around stock exchange are used and the time scope of these studies is usually very short, for example, the main focus is on how the stock market performance changes with traders–investors changed emotions due to weather conditions.

In another avenue of research, economists inquire about how corporations' environmental performance (CEP) relates to the corporations' financial performance (CFP). Usually, researchers compare the financial performance of corporations with measure of good and bad environmental performance. Most studies show that different measures of financial performance and environmental performance give different results. The traditional view is that corporations with superior environmental performance get less financial returns, since the additional costs trade-off economic returns as a sacrifice for social/environmental goals. Authors such as Elshahat *et al.* [2015] used reduced factors to measure CEP and found that the relationship between CEP and stock market returns is negative, while its relationship with accounting returns is positive. Chava [2014] got similar results using the implied cost of capital (ICC) as a measure of financial performance. On the same avenue, Hamilton *et al.* [1993] studied the abnormal returns of mutual funds categorized as either socially responsible or not socially responsible. They found that social responsibility factors have no effect on mutual funds' abnormal returns and thus concluded that these factors are not efficiently priced by the stock market. Ng and Zheng [2016] also found that green and non-green firms have comparable firm values, thus concluding that investors of non-green portfolios would not be punished with lower returns.

Other empirical studies also get a positive relationship between CEP and other forms of firm performance. Authors such as Herremans *et al.* (1993) show that superior corporate environmental performance (CEP) can reduce the total corporate risks. Saeidi *et al.* [2015] show that CEP improves a firm reputation and therefore, gives firms significantly positive returns. On the other hand, significant negative returns would act as supplement punishments for inferior CEP, e.g. Laplante *et al.* [1998]; Klassen and McLaughlin [1996]; Heinkel *et al.* (2001); and Khairollahi *et al.* [2016].

Basically, studies of weather conditions and stock market performance focus on external variance — the climate condition. The external variance influences stock market performance via traders/ investors emotional changes. Studies of CEP and CFP focus on inner variance — the characteristics of the corporation. Our contribution in this chapter is to combine those two approaches by focusing on how a specific measure of public environmental sentiment influences stock performance in the energy sector, thus examining how capital markets price a specific measure of environmental sentiment. In addition, we ask whether or not environmental sentiment impacts differently the stock market performance of renewable and non-renewable energy firms.

Our contribution here is several fold. First, we focus on a measure of the environmental sentiment of the public, not only that of investors or traders. Second, the climate–weather data we use are not limited to the stock exchange sites but are for the whole of US. Third, our study's key objective is not the performance of the whole capital market, but the performance of individual securities in the US energy sector. Fourth, we provide a detailed empirical analysis of the relationship between environmental sentiment and stock returns in the US energy sector, with an extensive construction of the abstract concept of environmental sentiment.

Our empirical evidence indicates that when weather conditions become more extreme or when the measure of public environmental concern increases, investors would favor renewable energy equities over non-renewable energy ones. Our result follows from the uncovered empirical evidence that, holding environmental risk factors constant, renewable energy equities give higher abnormal returns, which adds more attractiveness to renewable energy firms' stocks. Of course, the consequence is that the cost of equity should be higher in the renewable energy sector.

The rest of the chapter is as follows: Section 2 gives a detailed description of the construction of the environmental sentiment factor, including a specific literature review, the construction methods, the data and the results. Section 3 provides a detailed description of the measure of firm's financial performance, including the model, data and regression results. Section 4 analyzes the main results for the relationship between environmental sentiment and stock abnormal returns. Section 5 concludes.

2. The Construction of the Environmental Sentiment Factor

2.1. *Possible sentiment measures*

One of the main contributions of this chapter is construction of a proper environmental sentiment measure. Based on a wide literature review, we found three basic methods that can be used: survey method, social media method and the econometric method. We present a review of each of them and ultimately chose to use the econometric method here.

2.1.1. *Environmental sentiment via survey method*

The survey method is the most traditional one, whereby researchers construct sentiment factors using the data collected by surveys. The New Environmental Paradigm (NEP) Scale, e.g. Dunlap [1978] and Dunlap *et al.* [2000] measures the public pro-environmental orientation based on a survey asking respondents their intensity of strength of agreement or disagreement with fifteen basic statements. Although the NEP Scale has been widely used, its shortcomings and validity have been extensively discussed by Amburgey and Thoman [2012]. Alternatively, the annually released environmental survey by Gallup is another application of the survey method. Issues regarding the specific timeline and the general difficulty to access survey data are some of the main drawbacks of this method.

2.1.2. *Environmental sentiment via social media*

Social media is a newly developed method to access environmental sentiment. The explosion of cyber information and the availability of big data makes this a widely used form. Many have started to take advantage of the trend in big data to measure public attitude and to predict public behavior.

Search engine data and new media data from Twitter and Facebook have been used to predict the spread of influenza-like illness, job searching activities, the unemployment rate and employment policy effects [Ginsberg *et al.* 2009; Askitas and Zimmermann, 2009; D'Amuri and Marcucci, 2010; Baker and Fradkin, 2011]. The social media method has been used in capital markets research for prediction of investor sentiment. Those include analyzing words in main financial newspapers or analyzing related internet search queries to indicate investor sentiment [Tetlock, 2007; Garcia, 2013; Da *et al.* 2011; Bianconi *et al.* 2015; Dimpfl and Jank, 2016]. O'Connor *et al.* [2010] have examined the potential for social media data to perform either as a substitute or as a supplement for more traditional forms of polling.

However, few studies have used social media data in measuring environmental sentiment. Kahn and Kotchen [2010] used query data of the term "global warming" in *Google Insights for Search* to measure public environmental concerns and examined its relationship with business cycles. When compared with the more traditional survey method, the social media method can provide more real-time and easy-to-access data. Therefore, social media could be a potential useful method for the construction of an environmental concerns factor.

2.1.3. *Environmental sentiment via the econometric method*

The econometric method is based on statistics, computational capability, and availability of rich datasets. In this chapter, we use the econometric Dynamic Factor Model (DFM) to construct an environmental sentiment factor. The DFM was initially proposed by Sargent and Sims [1977] and Geweke [1977] applied it to the study of macro fluctuations in economic activity, e.g. Stock and Watson [1989, 1998]. The model is appropriate when the number of time series aggregated exceeds the number of time series observations. The general econometric expression of a typical DFM is as follows:

$$X_t = Pf_t + e_t, \tag{1}$$

$$f_t = Rw_t + A_1 f_{t-1} + A_2 f_{t-2} + \cdots + A_{t-p} f_{t-p} + \eta_t, \tag{2}$$

$$e_t = C_1 e_{t-1} + C_2 e_{t-2} + \cdots + C_{t-q} e_{t-q} + \varepsilon_t. \tag{3}$$

In the above equations, X_t is the observed informational dependent variable, f_t is the unobserved coincident variable, and e_t is the exogenous variable. Suppose there are N observable time series, X_t and e_t would be $N \times 1$ vectors. It is assumed that the vector of time series (X_t) has two parts: a common component driven by some latent common factors (f_t) and an idiosyncratic component driven by idiosyncratic factors (e_t). The model allows autoregressive processes for the unobserved factor [as in Eq. (2)] and for the error term [as in Eq. (3)] thus capturing dynamic effects. As seen in (1)–(3), the fundamental assumption of the DFM approach is that each economic variable can be decomposed into a common factor component and an idiosyncratic component.

Although DFMs have been widely used in studying macroeconomic issues, such as obtaining real-time estimates of Hong Kong's real economy state [Gerlach and Yiu, 2005] or detecting monetary policy effects on the economy [Bernanke *et al.* 2005]; to our knowledge, no applications have been implemented in constructing an environmental sentiment index. Our contribution here is to construct an environmental sentiment factor via DFMs.

2.2. *Data used in the dynamic factor models*

According to Eq. (1), the first step to obtain the coincident factor f_t is to have the $N \times 1$ vector X_t of observable time series. We assemble a set of time series that have potential relationship with or could reflect public environmental sentiment. Then, we apply DFMs to those series to obtain a representative reduced single factor. Following this procedure, we divide the set of time series into five categories according to the literature: Google search queries, macroeconomic status, environmental conditions, energy consumption and environmental regulation stringency. All data are limited to the US.

2.2.1. *Google search queries*

Google search queries is a part of the social media method. We focus on search frequency data of query terms *pollution, climate change*, *global warming* and *renewable energy* using Google Trends. All data are monthly from January 2004 to October 2016, throughout the US Google Trends data are such that each data point is divided by the total searches of the geography and time range it represents. Thus, the resulting numbers are then scaled on a range from 0 to 100 based on a topic's proportion to all searches on all topics. Figure 1 presents each of the series associated with each term while Table 1 presents the summary statistics of the sampled data.

2.2.2. *Macroeconomic status*

The aggregate macroeconomic status is reflected in an individual behavior through several channels and income is very important in this dimension. In a bad income aggregate state, individuals may be less concerned about other factors such as the environment, while in good income aggregate states individuals may be more

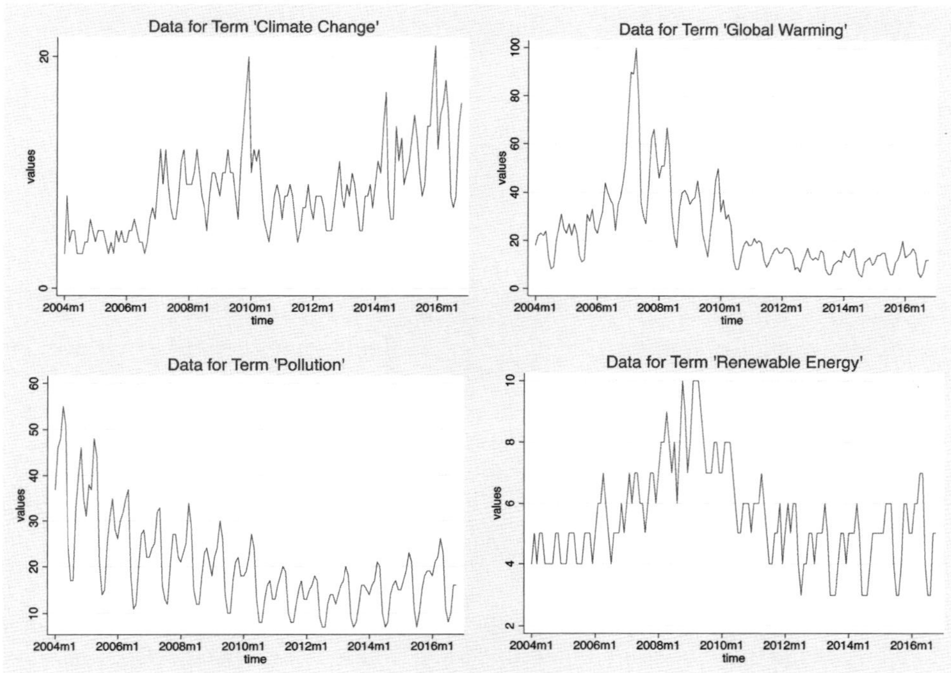

Fig. 1. Data for google search queries.

Source: Google Trend

Table 1. Summary statistics for google search queries.

Variable	Observations	Mean	Std. Dev.	Min	Max
Climate change	154	8.39	3.72	3	21
Global warming	154	24.23	17.65	5	100
Pollution	154	20.17	9.74	7	55
Renewable energy	154	5.56	1.58	3	10

open to other factors. Liere and Dunlap [1980] first connected income levels to an individual environmental concern. For example, when a family's income is low due to high unemployment rates, their interest would turn to their financial problems and thus pay less attention to the environment, e.g. Soretz and Ott [2015]; Kahn and Kotchen [2010]. Here, we conjecture that environmental concerns should be lower during recessions. The data we use are the monthly US CPI rate of inflation, the

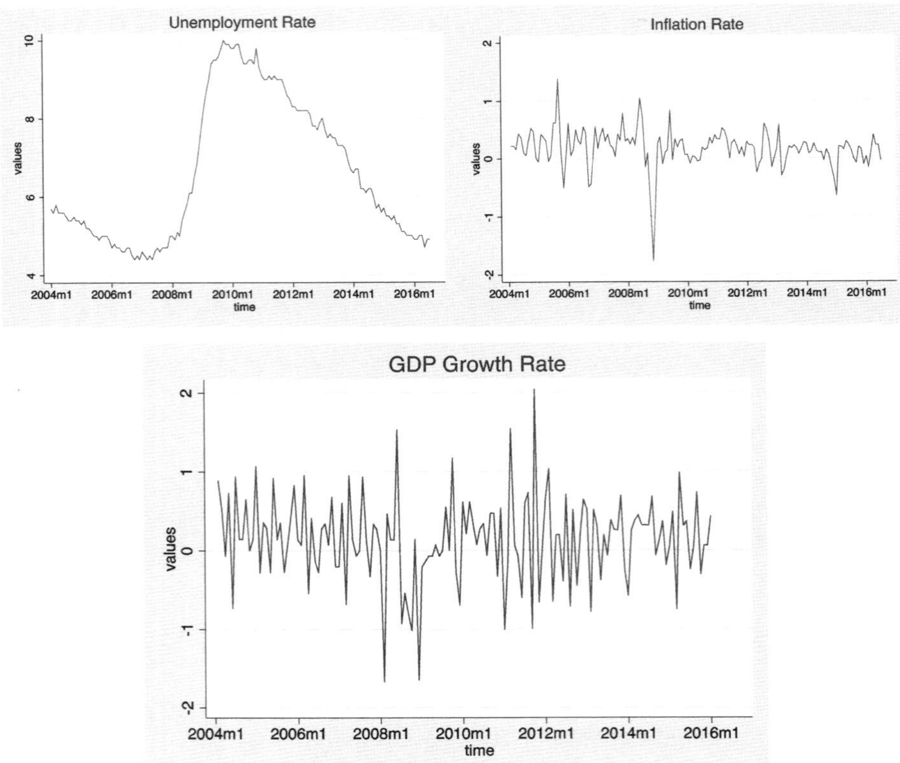

Fig. 2. Macroeconomic status.

Sources: U.S. Bureau of Labor Statistics; FRED.

Table 2. Statistic summary table for economic status data (%).

Variable	**Observations**	**Mean**	**Standard deviation**	**Min**	**Max**
Unemployment rate	145	6.61	1.82	4.40	10.00
Growth of GDP	144	0.14	0.57	−1.68	2.05
Inflation	145	0.17	0.34	−1.77	1.38

Source: FRED.

unemployment rate and the growth rate of real GDP, all from January 2004 to January 2016 as part of the vector X_t. Figure 2 presents each of the series associated with each macro variable, while Table 2 presents the summary statistics of the sampled data.

2.2.3. *Environmental conditions*

Current environmental conditions are an obvious determinant of the public environmental sentiment and concern. Liere and Dunlap [1980] proposed the "residence hypothesis" when examining potential determinants of environmental concerns. The idea is that individuals in urban areas who are exposed to higher levels of pollution and other types of environmental deteriorations care more about the environment. Soretz and Ott [2015] used the same hypothesis to study the relationship between green attitudes and economic growth. Here, in order to capture environmental conditions in the US, we use two basic series: The US data of carbon dioxide (CO_2) emissions; and the data on climate extremes of the National Oceanic and Atmospheric Administration (NOAA).

The CO_2 emissions data is taken directly from the US Energy Information Administration (EIA). The Climate Extremes Index (CEI) is an index used as a framework for quantifying observed changes in climate within the US. It was first introduced in early 1996 with the goal of describing and presenting a complex set of multivariate and multidimensional climate changes in the United States.[1] More specifically, the US CEI is the arithmetic average of several components including extreme temperatures (maximum/minimum temperature much above/below normal), severe drought, degree and frequency of precipitation, and tropical storm/hurricane wind. Higher CEI indicates worse environmental conditions.

Figures 3–4 present each of the series associated with each variable while Table 3 presents the summary statistics of the sampled data.

2.2.4. *Energy consumption*

Concerns with climate change may induce households to look for new forms of energy saving. For example, shifting from fossil fuels to renewable energy can potentially mitigate climate change or at least be perceived this way by concerned households. We may conjecture that public environmental concern is positively correlated to renewable energy consumption and negatively correlated with non-renewable energy consumption. Therefore, changes in renewable and non-renewable energy consumption could reflect public environmental sentiment.

We consider US EIA data on coal, natural gas, petroleum, solar, wind and biomass energy consumption. Table 4 presents the summary statistics of the sampled data.

[1] https://www.ncdc.noaa.gov/extremes/cei/introduction.

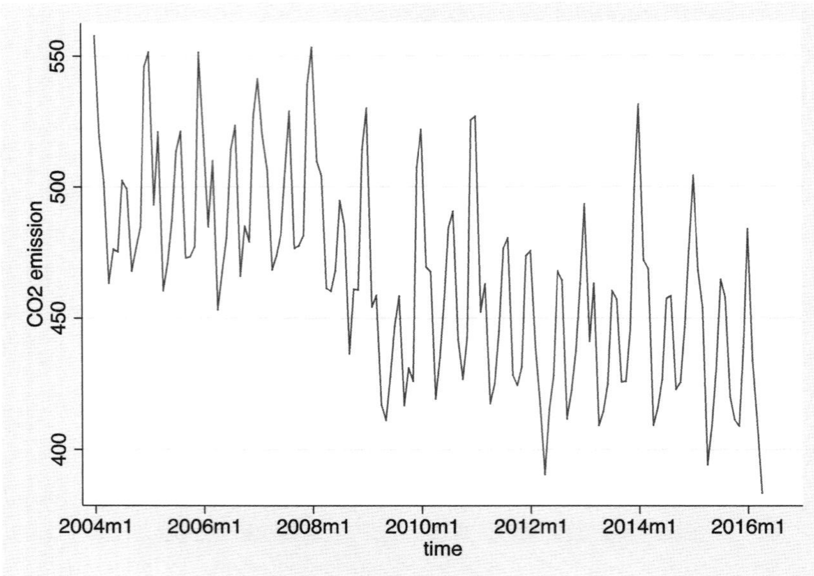

Fig. 3. CO_2 emissions (monthly): from 2004m1 to 2016m4 (Millions of Metric Tons).

Source: U.S. Energy Information Administration (EIA).

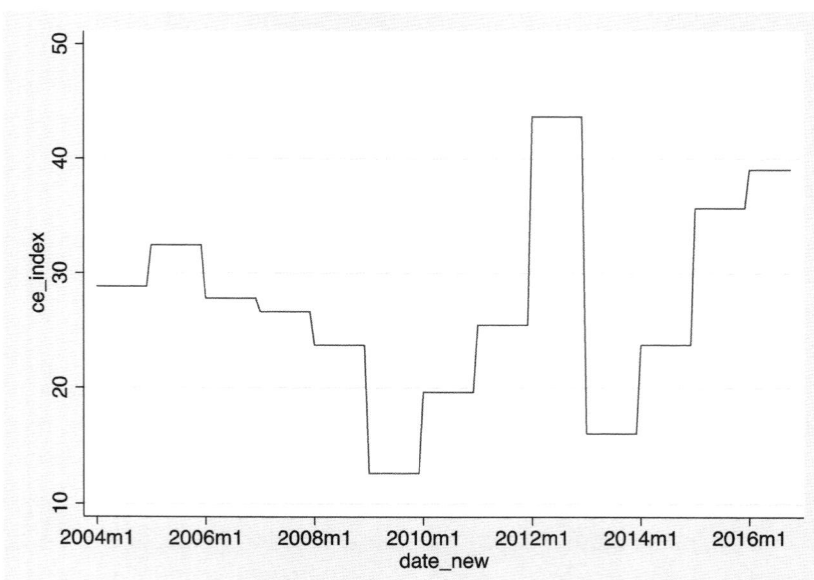

Fig. 4. The US climate extreme index (monthly): from 2004m1 to 2016m10.

Data source: National Oceanic and Atmospheric Administration (NOAA).

Table 3. Summary statistics for environmental conditions data.

Variable	Observations	Mean	Std. Dev.	Min	Max
CO_2 Emissions	148	466.70	39.03	383.50	557.72
CEI	154	27.19	8.46	12.63	43.67

Table 4. Summary statistics for energy consumption in log levels: 2004m1–2016m6.

Variable	Observations	Mean	Std. Dev.	Min	Max
Coal	150	0.49	0.18	−0.17	0.76
Natural Gas	150	0.71	0.20	0.38	1.20
Petroleum	150	1.11	0.07	0.96	1.27
Nuclear energy	150	−0.37	0.08	−0.56	−0.25
Solar Energy	150	−4.67	0.77	−5.84	−2.88
Wind Energy	150	−2.87	0.90	−4.67	−1.58
Biomass Energy	150	−1.11	0.17	−1.43	−0.86

Source: US Energy Information Administration (EIA).

2.2.5. *Environmental regulation stringency*

A vast literature shows that people can attribute the responsibility of protecting the environment to the government [Chyong *et al.* 2006] and that public opinions are influential on public policies [Burnstein, 2003; Shove, 2010]. We conjecture that environmental regulation stringency in the US is related to the public environmental concern. When the public is more concerned about the environment, they put more pressure on government regulation policy, thus tightening the environmental regulation stringency.

Brunel and Levinson [2016] summarized five traditional measures of regulatory stringency by reviewing the related literature: One widely used natural experiment relies on the US Clean Air Act. Another is to use a specific regulation as an indicator of the overall environmental regulatory stringency. A third one is to use composite indexes that come from surveys of government officials, business managers or counts of regulation. The fourth one is to use emissions, pollution or energy use data as an indicator of regulation stringency; and the last measure is to use the public sector expenditures or enforcement cases in the regulatory capacity.

Here, we consider the latter by counting the number of US Environmental Protection Agency's (EPA) yearly enforcement cases on civil cleanup, Clean Air Act (CAA) and Clean Water Act (CWA). Figure 5 present each of the series associated

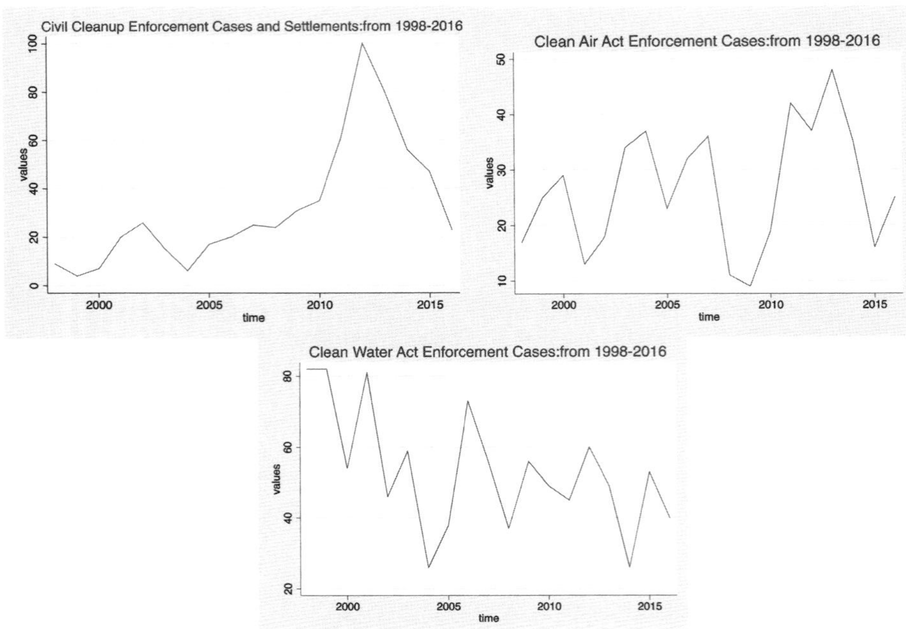

Fig. 5. Regulation stringency indicators (yearly): from 1998 to 2016.
Source: United States Environmental Protection Agency (EPA).

Table 5. Summary statistics for environment regulation stringency from 1998 to 2016.

Variable	Observations	Mean	Std. Dev.	Min	Max
Civil cleanup	19	31.89474	26.06167	4	100
Clean air act	19	26.63158	11.18635	9	48
Clean water act	19	53.26316	17.03213	26	82

with each variable while Table 5 presents the summary statistics of the sampled data.

2.3. *Dynamic factor models*

We performed unit-root tests in all series sampled in Section 2.2, and applied first-differencing when appropriate. A Johansen test indicated no cointegration at the 5% significance level for all non-stationary series. We applied the DFM in two steps in order to gain insight into the alternative categories sampled. In the first step, we applied DFM to the stationary series in all five categories to get a set of seven sub-group factors: Google search factor, macroeconomic factor, weather factor, pollution

Table 6. Components of constructed factors.

Sub-group factors	Included in environmental sentiment factor?	Component series	Categories
Google search factor	Yes	"pollution" "climate change" "global warming" "renewable energy"	Google search queries
Macroeconomic factor	No	inflation CPI log of GDP unemployment rate	macroeconomic status
Weather factor	Yes	CEI	environment condition
Pollution factor	Yes	CO_2 emission	
Non-renewable energy consumption factor	Yes	Coal consumption Natural gas consumption Petroleum consumption	
Renewable energy consumption factor	Yes	nuclear energy consumption solar energy consumption wind energy consumption biomass energy consumption	energy consumption
Regulation factor	Yes	civil cleanup enforcement clean air act enforcement clean water act enforcement	environment regulation stringency

factor (CO_2 emission), non-renewable energy consumption factor, renewable energy consumption factor and regulation factor.

In the second step, we obtained a single common factor by applying DFM to six or all seven sub-group factors. In the six sub-groups case, we excluded the macroeconomic factor because it is an important separate source of potential cause and control for the effect of environmental concerns on asset prices and returns. Table 6 presents a summary of each series included in each factor.

In both steps, we applied the DFM general model (1)–(3) in the following form:

$$X_{it} = p_i f_t + e_{it}, \quad i = 1, 2, 3 \ldots 6 \tag{4}$$

$$f_t = a f_{t-1} + \eta_t, \tag{5}$$

$$e_{it} = c_i e_{i,t-1} + \varepsilon_{it}, \tag{6}$$

where we allowed an AR(1) process for the unobserved factor f_t and for the idiosyncratic component e_{it}. We are interested here in the first principal component and extract a single factor only. We estimate the models via maximum likelihood by writing the model in state-space form and using the Kalman filter.

Table 7 presents the estimates of the coefficient a in the AR(1) process of the unknown factor f_t; of the coefficient c_i in the AR(1) process of the exogenous part e_{it}; and p_i and the variance of the disturbances e_i in the DFM for the cases without and with the macroeconomic factor. The subscript numbers 1,2...7 indicate: Google Search factor, nonrenewable energy consumption factor, renewable energy consumption factor, weather factor, regulation factor, pollution factor (CO_2 emission) and macroeconomic factor, respectively. For column (1) without the macroeconomic factor included, the estimated autoregressive coefficient of f_t

Table 7. DFM results: Maximum likelihood estimation.

	(1) Without macroeconomic factor[a]		(2) With macroeconomic factor[b]	
Parameters	**Estimates**	**z-values**	**Estimates**	**z-values**
a	0.6712***	7.97	0.6563***	6.89
c_1	0.9538***	32.08	0.9511***	28.85
c_2	0.1777	0.37	0.1358	0.16
c_3	−0.5002***	−6.03	−0.5084	−5.98
c_4	−0.0026	−0.5	−0.0026	−0.49
c_5	0.9066***	40.66	0.9174***	39.76
c_6	0.4792***	6.27	0.4874***	6.95
c_7			−0.1374	−1.42
p_1	−0.6521***	−7.72	0.6395***	6.09
p_2	0.4875***	7.31	−0.4821***	−5.18
p_3	−0.0055	−0.28	0.0054	0.27
p_4	−0.0915	−0.91	0.0961	0.81
p_5	−0.0312	−0.62	0.0401	0.91
p_6	1.0963***	3.63	−0.9928***	−3.29
p_7			0.0404	0.87
Var(e_1)	0.2052**	2.38	0.2156*	1.93
Var(e_2)	0.0458	0.97	0.0414	0.6
Var(e_3)	0.2636***	6.45	0.2613***	6.14
Var(e_4)	10.594*	1.83	10.8893*	1.83
Var(e_5)	0.5742**	2.78	0.5284*	2.54
Var(e_6)	7.9063***	7.4	7.8299**	7.21
Var(e_7)			0.6569***	8.06
Log-likelihood	−1263.4987		−1395.1001	

+0.1; *0.05; **0.01; ***0.001.

[a](1) Stands for the case when f_t is constructed without macroeconomic factor.

[b](2) Stands for the case when f_t is constructed with macroeconomic factor.

is 0.6712, which indicates a sizable persistence in the coincident factor. The coefficients for the renewable energy consumption factor (p_3), the weather factor (p_4) and the regulation factor (p_5) are not statistically significant, suggesting that the unobserved factor (f_t) is not a statistically significant predictor for them; however, the coefficients for the Google Search factor (p_1), the nonrenewable energy consumption factor (p_2) and the pollution factor (p_6) are statistically significant and the signs for p_2 and p_6 are positive, while the sign for p_1 is negative. Thus, our estimates show that the unobserved factor (f_t) is a statistically significant predictor for the nonrenewable energy consumption factor and the pollution factor (CO_2 emission), and it is also a statistically significant predictor of the Google Search factor, but with opposite sign.

Column (2) includes the macroeconomic factor when constructing the coincident factor. The results are mostly consistent with column (1) in terms of high persistence; and the statistical significance of the coefficients p_1 *to* p_6. The key difference is that the statistically significant coefficients (p_1, p_2 and p_6) changed their signs when compared to the results in column (1) without the macroeconomic factor.

The importance of the macroeconomic factor as a separate series is that the coincident factor behaves much differently when the macroeconomic factor is

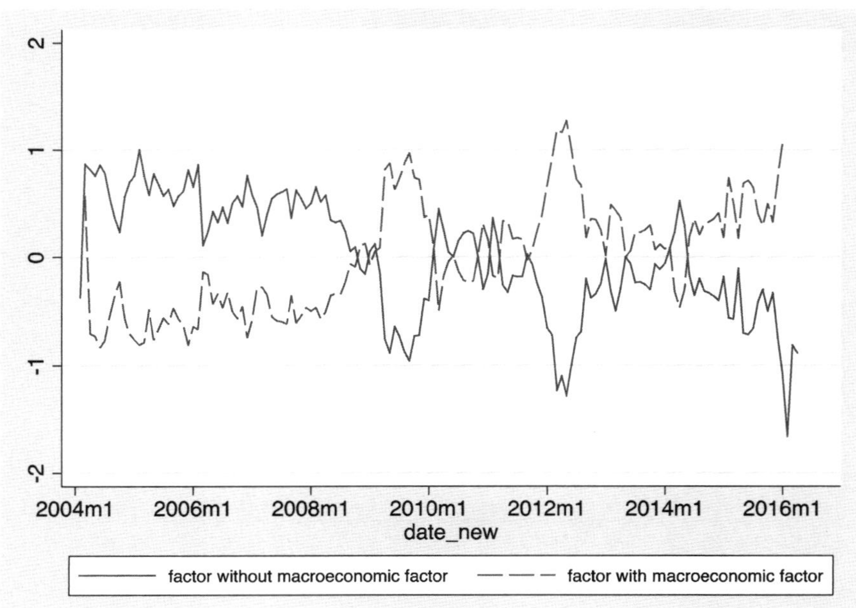

Fig. 6. Constructed environmental sentiment factor: With and without macroeconomic factor.

Note: The two constructed environmental sentiment factors are all deseasonalized.

included or not (see Table 7). Figure 6 shows the two coincident factors estimated without and with the macroeconomic factor and we note a visible negative correlation between them.

Several of the factors and the environmental sentiment factor obtained via (4)–(6) did show seasonality patterns. We correct for seasonal patterns using a simple regression of the form:

$$f_t = \gamma_t + \theta_t \, \text{Month} + e_t, \tag{7}$$

where *Month* is a set of time dummies; f_t is the factor suffering from seasonality; and e_t is the deseasonalized factor. Figure 7 presents the deseasonalized environmental sentiment factor, Fig. 8 presents the deseasonalized macroeconomic factor and Fig. 9 presents the six sub-group deseasonalized factors.

2.4. *The environmental sentiment factor and its economic implications*

Dynamic factor models provide a reduction framework where the coincident factor measures comovement among the included variables. While the estimated parameters may be helpful in understanding the implications of the model, they

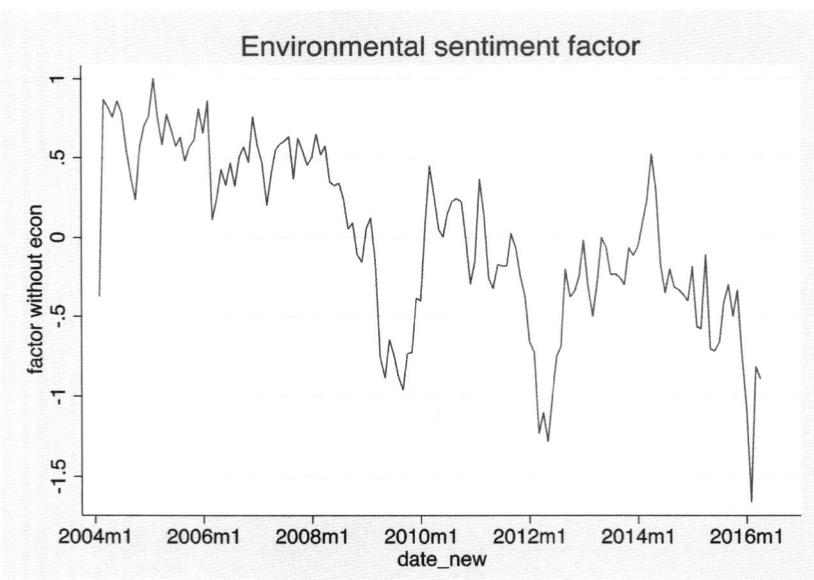

Fig. 7. Deseasonalized environmental sentiment factor (f).

Note: The deseasonalized environmental sentiment factor above is constructed without macroeconomic factor.

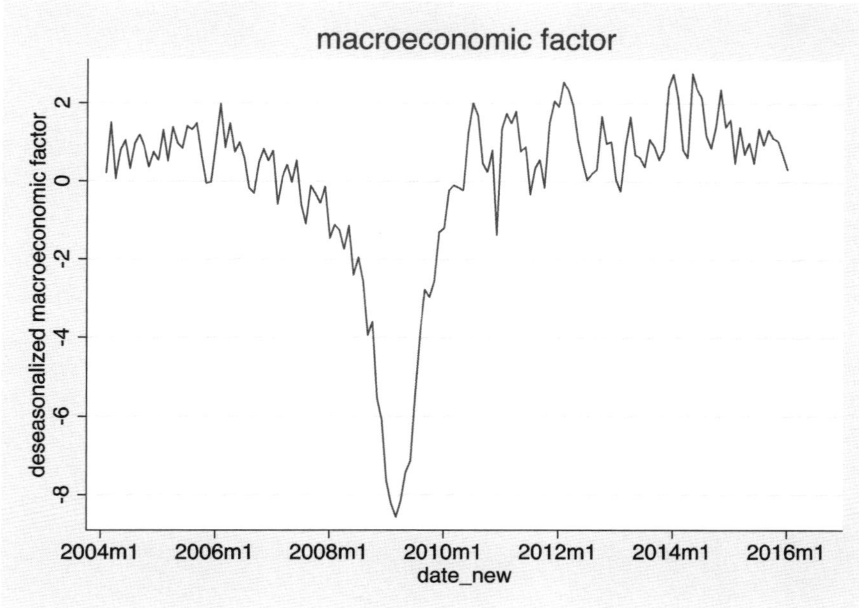

Fig. 8. Deseasonalized macroeconomic factor.

can be difficult to interpret. One reason for this difficulty is the identification issues between the factor loadings and the unobserved factors. One way to see the identification issue is the sign of the loadings and the factors. The estimated coincident factor without and with the macroeconomic factor have reversed signs on factor loadings.

Table 8 presents the contemporaneous correlations between the coincident factor without the macroeconomic factor and the sub-group factors. We expected the coincident factor to be positively correlated with the weather factor, regulation factor, Google Search factor, renewable energy consumption factor and macroeconomic factor; while it should be negatively related with the nonrenewable energy consumption factor. But we observe the reverse signs, hence we conclude that this coincident factors refer to environmental relief as opposed to concern. That is, a decrease (increase) in the coincident factor f indicates an increase (decrease) in environmental concerns. We note, for example, that in Fig. 6, around October 2006 when the Stern Review on the Economics of Climate Change came out, the factor without the macroeconomic factor declines sharply, while with the macroeconomic factor increases sharply. The same pattern is observed in the final months of 2011 and 2012 when the Paris agreement starts to take shape through the Durban Platform. Thus, we find coherence interpreting the coincident factors as described.

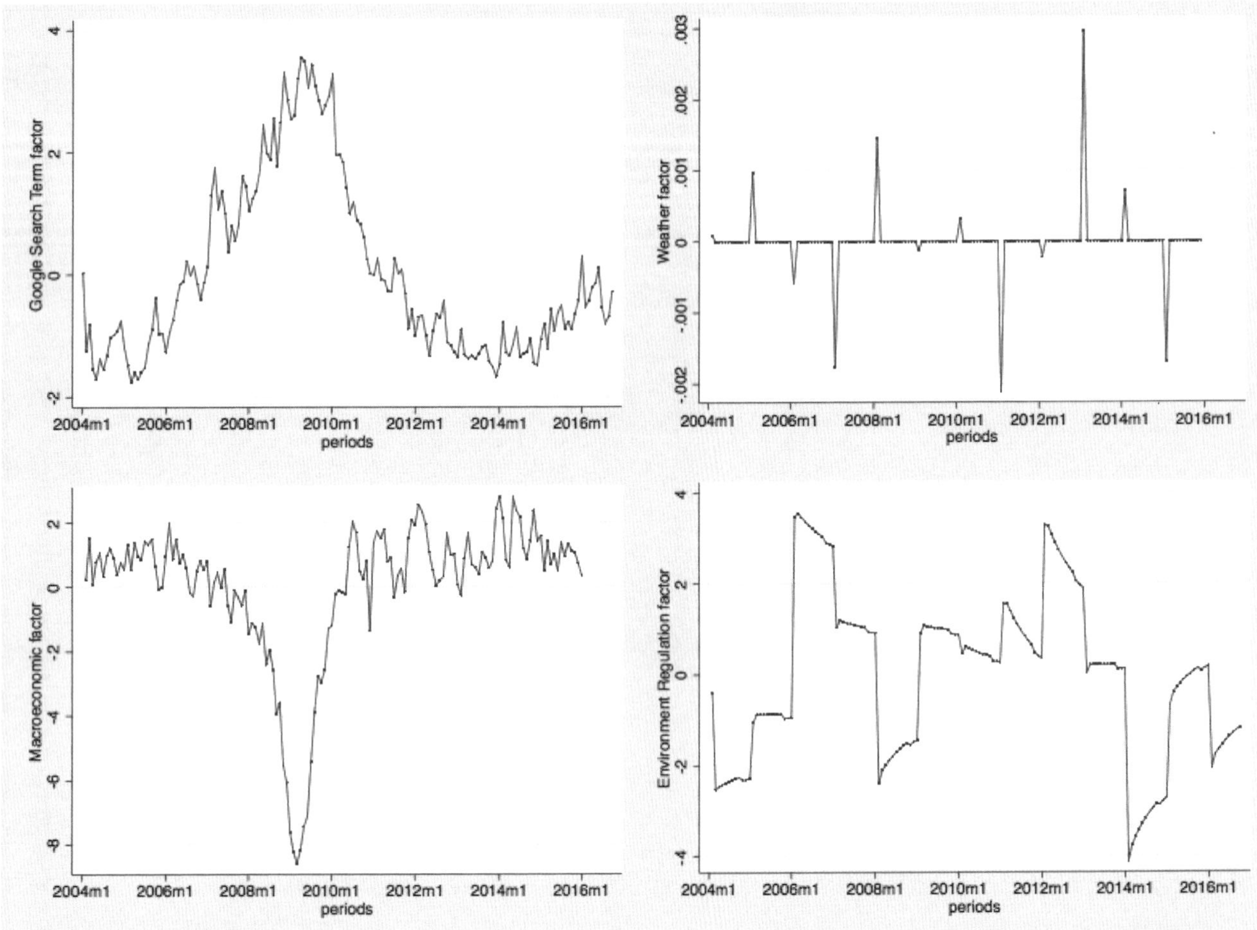

Fig. 9. Deseasonalized sub-group factors: DFM.

Note: The subgroup factors are: Google Search term factor, weather factor, macroeconomic factor and environment regulation factor.

Table 8. Correlation matrix for environmental sentiment factor f and sub-group factors.

	Environmental sentiment factor (f)	**Weather factor**	**Google search factor**	**Nonrenewable energy consumption factor**
Environmental sentiment factor (f)	1			
Weather Factor	−0.0937	1		
Google search factor	−0.0901	−0.016	1	
Non-renewable energy consumption factor	0.8477*	−0.0441	−0.053	1
Renewable energy consumption	−0.0682	−0.135	−0.0802	−0.0209
Regulation Factor	−0.1853*	−0.0716	0.1725*	−0.1502
Pollution factor (CO_2 emission)	0.7961*	−0.0292	0.0553	0.8309*
Macroeconomic factor	0.126	0.1499	−0.7874*	0.1083

	Renewable energy consumption	**Regulation factor**	**Pollution factor (CO_2 emission)**	**Macro factor**
Renewable energy consumption	1			
Regulation Factor	−0.0255	1		
Pollution factor (CO_2 emission)	−0.0099	−0.0502	1	
Macroeconomic factor	0.0295	−0.0231	−0.0102	1

Notes: (i) * 0.05 significance level. (ii) The pollution factor and nonrenewable energy consumption factor show high correlation which exceeds 0.8.

3. Asset Pricing and Abnormal Returns

3.1. *Asset pricing models*

In the simple capital asset pricing model of Sharpe [1964], Lintner [1965] and Mossin [1966] the premium of equity is proportional to the market premium. Empirically, using *ex-post* data, the linear model is estimated with a constant term, α, which denotes an abnormal return that should vanish under efficient markets. In other words, the abnormal return is the difference between actual returns and expected returns calculated by the asset pricing model. An abnormal return α, is a potential measure of a stock performance when studying the effects of risk factors that are not included in asset pricing models [Herremans *et al.* 1993; Lorraine *et al.* 2004). It is also used to implement event studies, or analyzing how stock returns would react when new information is released [Flammer, 2015]. In this chapter, we use the firm potential abnormal return as a measure of stock performance and examine its relationship with the developed environmental sentiment factors.

We obtain abnormal returns using three well-recognized asset pricing models: the traditional CAPM model, the Fama and French [1993] three-factor model and the more recent Fama and French [2015] five-factor model. The general form of the linear asset pricing models is written as

$$R_{it} - R_{Ft} = \alpha_{it} + \beta_1(R_{mt} - R_{Ft}) + \beta_2 SMB_t + \beta_3 HML_t + \beta_4 RMW_t + \beta_5 CMA_t, \tag{8}$$

where R_{it} is the stock return of firm i in period t, R_{Ft} is the risk-free rate of interest for period t and R_{mt} is the market rate of return in period t. We call $R_{it} - R_{Ft}$ the company excess return, which measures and investor payoffs for her assumed risk; and $R_{mt} - R_{Ft}$ is the market premium. The factors SMB_t,[2] HML_t,[3] RMW_t[4] and CMA_t[5] are size factor, value factor, profitability factor and investment factor for each period t; and α_{it} is the abnormal return. In Eq. (8), for the traditional CAPM model (one-factor model), we impose the restrictions

$$\beta_2 = \beta_3 = \beta_4 = \beta_5 = \alpha_{it} = 0; \tag{9a}$$

for the Fama-French three-factor model, we impose

$$\beta_4 = \beta_5 = \alpha_{it} = 0; \tag{9b}$$

and for the Fama-French five-factor model, we impose

$$\alpha_{it} = 0. \tag{9c}$$

[2]SMB is size factor that describes the difference between the returns on a portfolio of small market capitalization (the bottom 50%) stocks and the returns on a portfolio of large market capitalization (the top 50%) stocks.

[3]HML is value factor that describes the difference between the return on portfolio of high (the top 30%) book-to-market stocks and the return on a portfolio of low (the bottom 30%) book-to-market.

[4]RMW is Profitability factor that describes the difference between the returns on diversified portfolios of stocks with robust and weak profitability.

[5]CMA is Investment factor that measures the difference between the returns on diversified portfolios of stocks with low and high investment firms, which we call conservative and aggressive.

3.2. *Methodology for abnormal returns*

The basic econometric model for expression (8) is written as, η_{it} is the error term:

$$R_{it} - R_{Ft} = \alpha + \beta_1(R_{mt} - R_{Ft}) + \beta_2 SMB_t + \beta_3 HML_t + \beta_4 RMW_t + \beta_5 CMA_t + \eta_{it}, \tag{10}$$

where η_{it} is the error term. In Eq. (10), α is the average of all constant terms in the panel regression; and the error term η_{it} indicates random returns for specific risk factors of each individual firm, with $E[\eta_{it}] = 0$. Thus, the abnormal return is

$$\alpha_{it} = \alpha + \eta_{it}, \tag{11a}$$

$$E[\alpha_{it}] = E[(\alpha + \eta_{it})] = E[\alpha]. \tag{11b}$$

In (11a–b), α has non-zero expected value, giving an additional return for investors beyond the justified by the factors. η_{it} is the random return related to individual firm characteristics and it has a zero expected value, hence reflects unsystematic risk.

We obtain the abnormal return for each firm using a panel dataset and estimating the three asset pricing models thus obtaining estimated values for α_{it}. More specifically, we obtain

$$\hat{\alpha}_{it} = \text{actual(company premium)} - \text{expected(company premium)} \tag{12}$$

as the actual company premium minus the expected company premium.

We proceed in the second stage by estimating regressions for determinants of the predicted abnormal returns. More specifically, we estimate models of the form

$$\hat{\alpha}_{it} = \gamma_0 + \gamma_1 D_i + \gamma_2 f_t + \gamma_3 f_t * D_i + \gamma_4 m_t + \gamma_5 m_t * D_i + u_i' + v_t' + \eta_{it}', \tag{13}$$

where $D_i = 1$ for renewable energy firms, $D_i = 0$ for nonrenewable energy firms; f_t is the obtained environmental sentiment factor or its component sub-group factors; $f_t * D_i$ is the interaction terms intended to capture whether or not environment-related factors influence renewable and non-renewable energy firms differently; m_t is the macroeconomic factor; $m_t \times D_i$ is the interaction term of renewables and macroeconomic factor; u_i' is a firm fixed effect; v_t' is a time fixed effect; and η_{it}' is error term.[6]

[6]We chose to use the two-stage approach with the understanding that there may be some loss in efficiency, however, at the benefit of reducing the potential bias due to the large number of regressors.

3.3. *Equity data information*

The equity panel dataset includes 448 US energy publicly traded companies, with 53 renewable energy firms and 395 non-renewable energy firms. All stock price data are monthly, from January 2004 to October 2016. Table 9 describes the equity data in terms of sectors and sub-sectors.[7]

The realized stock returns were calculated using the formula $R_{it} = \log(p_{i,t}) - \log(p_{i,t-1})$, where $p_{i,t}$ is the dividend-adjusted close price each month for each stock. We used monthly data of the US S&P500 index return as the market return R_{mt} and the monthly yield of the 3-month US T-bill as the risk-free rate R_{Ft}. The monthly data of R_{mt} and R_{Ft} are both from FRED, running from January 2004 to October 2016. The monthly data for SMB_t, HML_t, RMW_t *and* CMA_t are from the website[8] of Kenneth R. French.

3.4. *Regression results for the asset pricing models*

First, Fig. 10 plots the obtained average abnormal returns for all firms, and for non-renewables and renewables separately. We note more variability in the abnormal returns for renewable companies on average.

Table 10 shows the estimated asset pricing models that generate the abnormal returns described in Section 3.2. The table shows results for each of the asset pricing

Table 9. Equity information.

Sector	**Sub-sector**	**Number of equities**	**Total number of firms**
Renewable energy industry	Biofuels	20	
	Renewable Energy Equipment	24	53
	Renewable Energy Project Development	9	
Non-renewable energy industry	Coal Operations	1	
	Exploration & Production	223	
	Integrated Oils	2	
	Integrated Utilities	1	395
	Midstream — Oil & Gas	69	
	Oil & Gas Services & Equip	80	
	Refining & Marketing	19	

Source: Bloomberg.

[7] A list of the companies included in this study is available from the authors upon request.
[8] http://mba.tuck.dartmouth.edu/pages/faculty/ken.french/data_library.html.

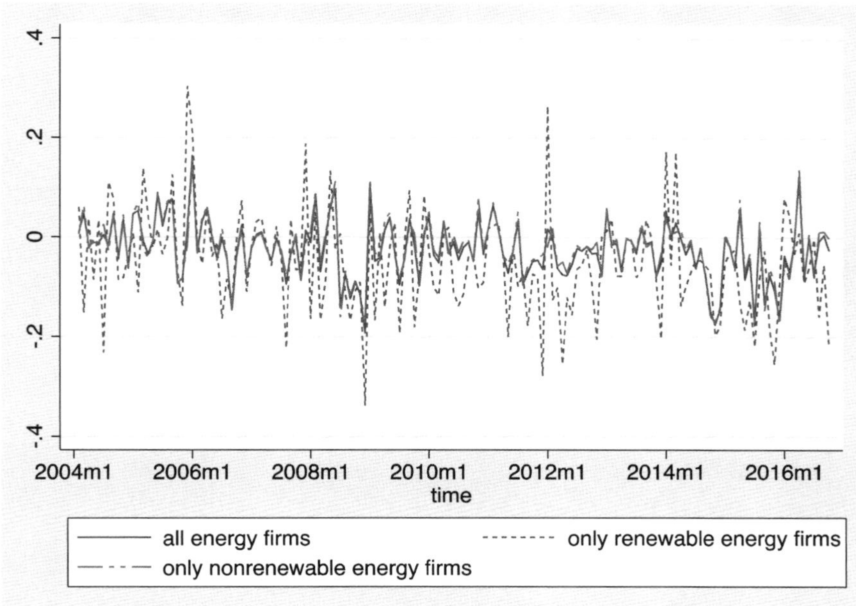

Fig. 10. Abnormal returns for US energy firms: 2004m1 to 2016m10.

models, and in each case, we have alternative panel samples: the full panel; only the renewable energy firms panel; and only the non-renewable energy firms panel. The estimated market betas indicate the sensitivity of asset's returns to market returns. The market beta is a measure of systematic risks, and the higher (lower) the market beta the higher (lower) the systematic risks. We note that renewable energy firms tend to have a higher point estimate of the market beta than non-renewable energy firms, except for the case under Fama–French five-factor model. However, we tested the differences in the coefficients in Table 11 and note that the difference is not statistically significant, thus renewable and non-renewable energy firms have similar market risks.

The constant term α in Table 10 remains significantly negative under all asset pricing models in all different panels. The negative signs for the constant term α indicate that investors in the energy sector get lower returns than predicted by the CAPM. Besides, we found that the abnormal returns for renewable energy firms are about 3.5% lower than that for non-renewable energy firms and this difference is statistically significant as shown in Table 10. Hence, the evidence suggests that the actual returns of renewable energy firms are lower than that of nonrenewable energy firms. Hamilton *et al.* [1993] also obtain similar results and suggest that the market efficiently priced the green character of renewable energy

Table 10. Regression results for asset pricing model.

Dependent variable: Company premium			
One-factor model	**All energy firms**	**Renewables**	**Non-renewables**
Market premium	1.13599	1.19268	1.12777
	(0.04451)***	(0.14291)***	(0.04672)***
Constant	−0.02771	−0.05877	−0.02378
	(0.00191)***	(0.00748)***	(0.00182)***
R^2	0.01707	0.01155	0.01843
N	47,607	5,344	42,263
Three-factor model	**All energy firms**	**Renewables**	**Non-renewables**
Market premium	1.01546	1.04754	1.01125
	(0.04707)***	(0.16075)***	(0.04901)***
SMB	0.51287	0.85664	0.46986
	(0.07594)***	(0.22215)***	(0.08067)***
HML	0.1201	−0.11475	0.14772
	(0.07060)*	(0.28)	(0.07090)**
Constant	−0.02772	−0.05902	−0.02377
	(0.00191)***	(0.00753)***	(0.00181)***
R^2	0.0182	0.01313	0.01955
N	47,607	5,344	42,263
Five-factor model	**All energy firms**	**Renewables**	**Non-renewables**
Market premium	0.97387	0.96183	0.97577
	(0.05000)***	(0.17785)***	(0.05165)***
SMB	0.49393	0.78519	0.4578
	(0.08168)***	(0.23952)***	(0.08678)***
HML	0.28602	0.06447	0.30826
	(0.08556)***	(0.31219)	(0.08790)***
RMW	−0.07497	−0.36521	−0.03928
	(0.11893)	(0.4052)	(0.12348)
CMA	−0.61353	−0.69345	−0.59144
	(0.13810)***	(0.59841)	(0.13593)***
Constant	−0.02721	−0.0573	−0.02341
	(0.00187)***	(0.00762)***	(0.00177)***
R^2	0.01863	0.01358	0.01998
N	47,607	5,344	42,263

+ 0.1; *0.05; **0.01; ***0.001

firms, as the value of renewable energy firms increased the expected returns are lower.

We proceed examining the determinants of abnormal returns including the constructed environmental sentiments measure.

Table 11. Analysis of differences in coefficients.

	CAPM model			
	Renewable	**Non-renewable**	**Difference**	**z-score**
Market beta	1.19268	1.12777	0.0649	0.4317
	(0.1429)	(0.04672)		
Abnormal returns	−0.05877	−0.02378	−0.0350	−4.5452
	(0.00748)	(0.00182)		
	Three-factor model			
	Renewable	**Non-renewable**	**Difference**	**z-score**
Market beta	1.04754	1.01125	0.0363	0.2159
	(0.16075)	(0.04901)		
Abnormal returns	−0.05902	−0.02377	−0.0353	−4.5516
	(0.00753)	(0.00181)		
	Five-factor model			
	Renewable	**Non-renewable**	**Difference**	**z-score**
Market beta	0.96183	0.97577	−0.0139	−0.0753
	(0.17785)	(0.05165)		
Abnormal returns	−0.0573	−0.02341	−0.0339	−4.3322
	(0.00187)	(0.00177)		

Note: z-score defined as $z = \frac{\beta_1 - \beta_2}{\sqrt{se_1^2 + se_2^2}}$.

4. Environmental Sentiment and Abnormal Returns

We estimate expression (12) to calculate the predicted abnormal returns $\hat{\alpha}_{it}$. Then, we merge the panel data of security information with time series data of various factors and regress to the estimated abnormal returns on those according to expression (13). We separate models to gain more insight into how renewable and non-renewable energy firms differ when their abnormal returns are explained.

4.1. *With 3 component sub-group factors*

In this section, for Tables 12–14, we only used three out of the six component sub-group factors, e.g. Tables 12–14. The excluded factors are the renewable energy consumption factor, the non-renewable energy consumption factor and the pollution factor (CO_2 emission), since the energy consumption factors and the pollution factor (CO_2 emission) seem to be relatively endogenous compared with the other three.

Table 12. Regression results for abnormal returns ($\hat{\alpha}_{it}$) and environmental sentiment factor (f).

	Abnormal returns for one-factor model		
Dependent variable	**Benchmark**	**(1)**	**(2)**
Renewable		−0.348	−0.352
Environmental sentiment factor (f)		0.0470***	
f*renewable		0.0146	
Google Search factor	−0.0148***		−0.003
Weather factor			−0.00235***
Macroeconomic factor		0.00693***	0.00815***
Regulation factor			−0.0155***
Google Search factor*renewable			−0.00186
Weather factor*renewable			0.00527*
Macroeconomic factor*renewable		0.00167	−0.000277
Regulation factor*renewable			−0.00329
Constant	0.161***	0.0593*	0.0249
Company fixed effect controlled	Yes	Yes	Yes
Time fixed effect controlled	Yes	Yes	Yes
N	47607	44059	44059
F	3.523	3.835	5.358
	Abnormal returns for three-factor model		
Dependent variable	**Benchmark**	**(3)**	**(4)**
Renewable		−0.348	−0.351
Environmental sentiment factor (f)		0.0460***	
f*renewable		0.0146	
Google search factor	−0.0137***		−0.00278
Weather factor			−0.00249***
Macroeconomic factor		0.00700***	0.00832***
Regulation factor			−0.0156***
Google Search factor*renewable			−0.00192
Weather factor*renewable			0.00524*
Macroeconomic factor*renewable		0.00169	−0.000286
Regulation factor*renewable			−0.00332
Constant	0.167***	0.0684**	0.0352
Company fixed effect controlled	Yes	Yes	Yes
Time fixed effect controlled	Yes	Yes	Yes
N	47607	44059	44059
F	3.473	3.745	5.057

(*Continued*)

Table 12. (*Continued*)

	Abnormal returns for five-factor model		
Dependent variable	**Benchmark**	**(5)**	**(6)**
Renewable		−0.348	−0.351
Environmental sentiment factor (f)		0.0443***	
f*renewable		0.0146	
Google Search factor	−0.0137***		−0.00301
Weather factor			−0.00288***
Macroeconomic factor		0.00714***	0.00858***
Regulation factor			−0.0155***
Google Search factor*renewable			−0.00189
Weather factor*renewable			0.00522*
Macroeconomic factor*renewable		0.00168	−0.000274
Regulation factor*renewable			−0.00334
Constant	0.157***	0.0799**	0.0494+
Company fixed effect controlled	Yes	Yes	Yes
Time fixed effect controlled	Yes	Yes	Yes
N	47607	44059	44059
F	3.423	3.766	4.689

+0.1; *0.05; **0.01; ***0.001

Notes: (i) The regressions in all columns controlled both company fixed effects and time fixed effects. To control for company fixed effects, we included 447 company dummies (448 equities in total); to control for time fixed effects, we included 11 month dummies and 12 year dummies (13 years in total). Their estimates are omitted in the above table.

(ii) Theoretically, if properly constructed, the results in Table 12 should be the consolidation of Tables 13 and 14. Here, we did not interact the renewable dummy with firm and time dummies when using the full dataset which makes the results different and allows us to emphasize the results of separate datasets. (iii) The benchmark factor Google Search is a relatively direct measure of environmental concerns. Comparing the benchmark factor and the environmental sentiment factor, we can conclude that the economic implication of environmental sentiment factor is environmental relief, not environmental concerns. Hence, the decrease in the environmental sentiment factor f means an increase in environmental concerns. The economic implication of the environmental sentiment factor always holds for all regressions.

We apply the Newey–West estimation procedure and control for company and time fixed effects.

Tables 12–14 are divided into three sections based on the different asset pricing models used to predict abnormal returns. In Tables 12–14, columns (1), (3) and (5) are regression results for the environmental sentiment factor (f) while controlling for the macroeconomic factor, together with the dummy variable "renewable" and the interaction terms. Columns (2), (4) and (6) are regression results for the three component sub-group factors, the Google Search factor, the Weather factor and

Table 13. Regression results for abnormal returns ($\hat{\alpha}_{it}$) and environmental sentiment factor (f): Renewables.

	Abnormal returns for one-factor model	
Dependent variable	**(1)**	**(2)**
Environmental sentiment factor (f)	0.0390$^+$	
Google Search factor		0.0123
Weather factor		0.00265
Macroeconomic factor	0.0108*	0.0122*
Regulation factor		−0.0206*
Constant	−0.208*	−0.171
Company fixed effect controlled	Yes	Yes
Time fixed effect controlled	Yes	Yes
N	4967	4967
F	3.953	2.739
	Abnormal returns for three-factor model	
Dependent variable	**(3)**	**(4)**
Environmental sentiment factor (f)	0.0379	
Google Search factor		0.0123
Weather factor		0.00246
Macroeconomic factor	0.0109*	0.0124*
Regulation factor		−0.0212*
Constant	−0.207*	−0.175
Company fixed effect controlled	Yes	Yes
Time fixed effect controlled	Yes	Yes
N	4967	4967
F	4.124	2.741
	Abnormal returns for five-factor model	
Dependent variable	**(5)**	**(6)**
Environmental sentiment factor (f)	0.0357	
Google Search factor		0.0123
Weather factor		0.00204
Macroeconomic factor	0.0110*	0.0127*
Regulation factor		−0.0212*
Constant	−0.210*	−0.174
Company fixed effect controlled	Yes	Yes
Time fixed effect controlled	Yes	Yes
N	4967	4967
F	4.118	2.658

$^+$0.1; *0.05; ** 0.01; *** 0.001

Note: The regressions in all columns control for both company fixed effects and time fixed effects. To control company fixed effects, we included 52 renewable energy company dummies (53 renewable energy equities in total); to control time fixed effects, we included 11 month dummies and 12 year dummies (13 years in total).

Table 14. Regression results for abnormal returns ($\hat{\alpha}_{it}$) and environmental sentiment factor (f): Nonrenewables.

	Abnormal returns for one-factor model	
Dependent variable	**(1)**	**(2)**
Environmental sentiment factor (f)	0.0497***	
Google search factor		−0.00514
Weather factor		−0.00233***
Macroeconomic factor	0.00663***	0.00760***
Regulation factor		−0.0153***
Constant	−0.0353	−0.0791**
Company fixed effect controlled	Yes	Yes
Time fixed effect controlled	Yes	Yes
N	39092	39092
F	3.682	3.8
	Abnormal returns for three-factor model	
Dependent variable	**(3)**	**(4)**
Environmental sentiment factor (f)	0.0488***	
Google search factor		−0.0049
Weather factor		−0.00247***
Macroeconomic factor	0.00670***	0.00776***
Regulation factor		−0.0154***
Constant	−0.0311	−0.0735*
Company fixed effect controlled	Yes	Yes
Time fixed effect controlled	Yes	Yes
N	39092	39092
F	3.540	3.637
	Abnormal returns for five-factor model	
Dependent variable	**(5)**	**(6)**
Environmental sentiment factor (f)	0.0471***	
Google Search factor		−0.00516
Weather factor		−0.00286***
Macroeconomic factor	0.00683***	0.00802***
Regulation factor		−0.0152***
Constant	−0.0176	−0.0570+
Company fixed effect controlled	Yes	Yes
Time fixed effect controlled	Yes	Yes
N	39092	39092
F	3.575	3.594

+0.1; *0.05; **0.01; ***0.001.

Note: The regressions in all columns controlled both company fixed effects and time fixed effects. To control company fixed effects, I included 394 non-renewable energy company dummies (395 non-renewable energy equities in total); to control time fixed effects, I included 11 month dummies and 12 year dummies (13 years in total).

the Regulation factor, also including the "renewable" dummy and interaction terms while also controlling for the macroeconomic factor.

In Table 12, we included a benchmark column in each section. This column is the result of regressing abnormal returns on a single factor, the Google Search factor. The benchmark column is used to provide evidence on the economic implications of the environmental sentiment factor f, since the Google Search factor is a relatively direct social media measure of the public environmental concern. An increase (decrease) in the Google Search factor can be understood as an increase (decrease) in the public environmental concern. The estimated coefficient of the benchmark factor is negative while the estimated coefficient of the environmental sentiment factor is positive. Together with the factor's correlation matrix (see Section 2.4) and the DFM estimation results (see Section 2.3), we confirm that the obtained environmental sentiment factor f has an economic meaning of environmental relief. Therefore, a decrease (increase) in the environmental sentiment factor implies a decrease (increase) in environmental relief and an increase (decrease) in the public environmental concern.

Another important point when explaining the regression results is that the dependent variable in this section is $\hat{\alpha}_{it}$, which includes two parts α *and* η_{it}. The usual risk-return tradeoff is not applicable here when explaining abnormal returns, $\hat{\alpha}_{it}$. Unlike the case of expected returns, we do not expect to obtain positive covariance between risk and abnormal return.

In columns (1), (3) and (5) of Table 12, when using full panel dataset, the environmental sentiment factor and the macroeconomic factor appear to have significantly positive effects on abnormal returns under each section, while the renewable dummy and the interaction terms are not statistically significant. The evidence suggests that better economic status improves the market's prospects of the whole energy industry, which leads to higher abnormal returns for energy firms. On the other hand, higher environmental concerns (lower f) would make investors less confident about the energy industry's future performance, thus covarying negatively with the energy industry's abnormal returns. With the full panel, we do not observe differences in these effects between renewable and non-renewable energy firms.

Columns (2), (4) and (6) of Table 12 refer to the component sub-group factors of the environmental sentiment factor separately. We find that the weather factor and the regulation factor have statistically significant negative impact on abnormal returns, while the macro factor continues to be significantly positive. No interaction terms are statistically significant except for the weather factor-renewable which is positive. These results are intuitively reasonable results. When the environmental regulation becomes stricter, there should be more stringency for energy firms and there would be higher possibility for energy firms to violate the regulations, which may cause additional costs and impair the energy companies' financial performance. This effect does not differ between renewables and non-renewables which indicates that the market believes renewables won't do better under the same regulatory status. For the weather factor, it has different effects on abnormal returns for renewable and non-renewable energy firms. For non-renewables, when the climate change becomes more severe (higher weather factor), there are lower abnormal returns since the market expects a worse future for non-renewable energy firms. For renewables, the effect of the weather factor on abnormal returns is positive, which means worse weather conditions would give renewable energy firms more future profit opportunities, thus increasing its abnormal returns. This suggests that investors expect renewable and non-renewable firms to perform differently given extreme weather and the data show that renewables performed better during the sampled period of January 2004 to October 2016.

Tables 13 and 14 help us better understand the results so far. In the case of nonrenewable energy firms shown in Table 14, the results are similar to Table 12. However, the results for the renewable energy firms (Table 13) are different. First, the coefficient of the environmental sentiment factor is only statistically significant in column (1); second, the coefficients of the weather factor are not statistically significant under columns (2), (4) and (6). Third, for the statistically significant coefficients in Table 13, the signs are consistent with Table 12. Hence, the evidence points to neither the environmental sentiment factor nor the weather factor, significantly influencing the renewable energy firms' abnormal returns; their abnormal returns are significantly affected by the environment regulation factor and the macroeconomic factor.[9]

4.2. *With 5 and 6 component sub-group factors*

In this section, we include the renewable energy consumption factor, non-renewable energy consumption factor and pollution factor. In Tables 15–17, columns (1), (4) and (7) are regression results for the environmental sentiment factor, the macroeconomic factor, the renewable dummy and interaction terms; while columns (2), (5) and (8) are regression results for the five component sub-group factors,

[9]We should note that the environmental sentiment factor is not a simple average of the component sub-group factors. It is plausible for the environmental sentiment factor coefficient to be insignificant while the coefficient of some of the sub-group factors are significant due to the existence of the idiosyncratic factors mentioned in Section 2.

Table 15. Regression results for abnormal returns ($\hat{\alpha}_{it}$) and environmental sentiment factor (f).

	Abnormal returns for one-factor model			
Dependent variable	**Benchmark**	**(1)**	**(2)**	**(3)**
Renewable		−0.348	−0.347***	−0.354
Environmental sentiment factor (f)		0.0470***		
f*renewable		0.0146		
Google Search factor	−0.0148***		−0.0044	−0.00162
Weather factor			−0.00259***	−0.00282***
Macroeconomic factor		0.00693***	0.00800***	0.00824***
Regulation factor			−0.0141***	−0.0156***
Renewable energy consumption factor			−0.0186**	−0.0212**
Nonrenewable energy consumption factor			0.0268***	0.0156+
pollution factor				0.00562**
Google Search factor*renewable			−0.00383	−0.00419
Weather factor*renewable			0.00591**	0.00587**
Macroeconomic factor*renewable		0.00167	−0.00185	−0.00169
Regulation factor*renewable			−0.00161	−0.00192
Renewable energy consumption factor* renewable			0.0215	0.0205
Nonrenewable energy consumption factor*renewable			0.0281+	0.0143
pollution factor*renewable				0.00276
Constant	0.161***	0.0593*	0.0496+	0.0609
Company fixed effect controlled	Yes	Yes	Yes	Yes
Time fixed effect controlled	Yes	Yes	Yes	Yes
N	47607	44059	44059	44059
F	3.523	3.835	4.134	3.82

	Abnormal returns for three-factor model			
Dependent variable	**Benchmark**	**(4)**	**(5)**	**(6)**
Renewable		−0.348	−0.347***	−0.356
Environmental sentiment factor (f)			0.0460***	
f*renewable			0.0146	
Google Search factor	−0.0137***		−0.00432	−0.000933
Weather factor			−0.00272***	−0.00300***
Macroeconomic factor		0.00700***	0.00815***	0.00845***
Regulation factor			−0.0140***	−0.0158***
Renewable energy consumption factor			−0.0182**	−0.0213**

(*Continued*)

Table 15. (*Continued*)

	Abnormal returns for three-factor model			
Dependent variable	**Benchmark**	**(4)**	**(5)**	**(6)**
Nonrenewable energy consumption factor			0.0301***	0.0160+
pollution factor		0.00694***		
Google search factor*renewable			−0.00389	−0.00424
Weather factor*renewable			0.00589**	0.00586**
Macroeconomic factor*renewable		0.00169	−0.00187	−0.00172
Regulation factor*renewable			−0.00162	−0.00193
Renewable energy consumption factor* renewable			0.022	0.021
Nonrenewable energy consumption factor*renewable			0.0283+	0.0147
pollution factor*renewable				0.00272
Constant	0.167***	0.0684**	0.0591*	0.0729
Company fixed effect controlled	Yes	Yes	Yes	Yes
Time fixed effect controlled	Yes	Yes	Yes	Yes
N	47607	44059	44059	44059
F	3.473	3.745	4.03	3.673

	Abnormal returns for five-factor model			
Dependent variable	**Benchmark**	**(7)**	**(8)**	**(9)**
Renewable		−0.348	−0.347***	−0.356
Environmental sentiment factor (f)			0.0443***	
f*renewable			0.0146	
Google Search factor	−0.0137***		−0.00448	−0.00105
Weather factor			−0.00317***	−0.00346***
Macroeconomic factor		0.00714***	0.00840***	0.00870***
Regulation factor			−0.0142***	−0.0161***
Renewable energy consumption factor			−0.0214**	−0.0247***
Nonrenewable energy consumption factor			0.0269***	0.0126
pollution factor		0.00705***		
Google Search factor*renewable			−0.00386	−0.0042
Weather factor*renewable			0.00587**	0.00584**
Macroeconomic factor*renewable		0.00168	−0.00186	−0.00171
Regulation factor*renewable			−0.00165	−0.00195
Renewable energy consumption factor* renewable			0.0221	0.0211

(*Continued*)

Table 15. (*Continued*)

Dependent variable	Abnormal returns for five-factor model Benchmark	(7)	(8)	(9)
Nonrenewable energy consumption factor*renewable			0.0283+	0.0149
pollution factor*renewable				0.00268
Constant	0.157***	0.0799**	0.0695*	0.0835
Company fixed effect controlled	Yes	Yes	Yes	Yes
Time fixed effect controlled	Yes	Yes	Yes	Yes
N	47607	44059	44059	44059
F	3.423	3.766	4.008	3.622

+0.1; *0.05; **0.01; ***0.001.

Notes: (i) The regressions in all columns controlled both company fixed effects and time fixed effects. To control company fixed effects, we included 447 company dummies (448 equities in total); to control time fixed effects, we included 11 month dummies and 12 year dummies (13 years in total). Their estimates are omitted in the above table.

(ii) Theoretically, if properly constructed, the results in Table 15 should be the consolidation of Tables 16 and 17. Here, we did not interact the renewable dummy with firm and time dummies when using the full dataset which makes the results different and allows us to emphasize the results of separate datasets.

Table 16. Regression results for abnormal returns ($\hat{\alpha}_{it}$) and environmental sentiment factor (f): Renewables.

Dependent variable	Abnormal returns for one-factor model (1)	(2)	(3)
Environmental sentiment factor (f)	0.0390+		
Google search factor		0.0105	0.0117
Weather factor		0.00292	0.00283
Macroeconomic factor	0.0108*	0.0119*	0.0120*
Regulation factor		−0.0170+	−0.0176+
Renewable energy consumption factor		0.00511	0.00390
non-renewable energy consumption factor		0.0485+	0.0431
pollution factor			0.00250
Constant	−0.208*	−0.275**	−0.281**
Company fixed effect controlled	Yes	Yes	Yes
Time fixed effect controlled	Yes	Yes	Yes
N	4967	4967	4967
F	3.953	3.836	3.86

(*Continued*)

Table 16. (*Continued*)

	Abnormal returns for three-factor model		
Dependent variable	**(4)**	**(5)**	**(6)**
Environmental sentiment factor (f)	0.0379		
Google search factor		0.0104	0.0122
Weather factor		0.00275	0.00262
Macroeconomic factor	0.0109*	0.0121*	0.0122*
Regulation factor		−0.0173+	−0.0182+
Renewable energy consumption factor		0.00575	0.00396
nonrenewable energy consumption factor		0.0520+	0.0439
pollution factor			0.00374
Constant	−0.207*	−0.279**	−0.288**
Company fixed effect controlled	Yes	Yes	Yes
Time fixed effect controlled	Yes	Yes	Yes
N	4967	4967	4967
F	4.124	4.066	4.156
	Abnormal returns for five-factor model		
Dependent variable	**(7)**	**(8)**	**(9)**
Environmental sentiment factor (f)	0.0357		
Google search factor		0.0105	0.0123
Weather factor		0.00227	0.00214
Macroeconomic factor	0.0110*	0.0124*	0.0125*
Regulation factor		−0.0176+	−0.0185+
Renewable energy consumption factor		0.00261	0.000798
non-renewable energy consumption factor		0.0487+	0.0406
pollution factor			0.00377
Constant	−0.210*	−0.285**	−0.294**
Company fixed effect controlled	Yes	Yes	Yes
Time fixed effect controlled	Yes	Yes	Yes
N	4967	4967	4967
F	4.118	4.087	4.199

+0.1; *0.05; **0.01; ***0.001.

Note: The regressions in all columns controlled both company fixed effects and time fixed effects. To control company fixed effects, I included 52 renewable energy company dummies (53 renewable energy equities in total); to control time fixed effects, I included 11 month dummies and 12 year dummies (13 years in total).

the Google Search factor, the Weather factor, the Regulation factor, the Renewable energy consumption factor and the Non-renewable energy consumption factor, the renewable dummy and interaction terms while controlling for the macroeconomic factor; columns (3), (6) and (9) are regression results for the

Table 17. Regression results for abnormal returns ($\hat{\alpha}_{it}$) and environmental sentiment factor (f): Non-renewables.

	Abnormal returns for one-factor model		
Dependent variable	**(1)**	**(2)**	**(3)**
Environmental sentiment factor (f)	0.0497***		
Google search factor		−0.00672	−0.00381
Weather factor		−0.00256***	−0.00282***
Macroeconomic factor	0.00663***	0.00725***	0.00753***
Regulation factor		−0.0140***	−0.0157***
Renewable energy consumption factor		−0.0190**	−0.0218**
non-renewable energy consumption factor		0.0274***	0.0137
pollution factor			0.00639***
Constant	−0.0353	−0.0394	−0.0352
Company fixed effect controlled	Yes	Yes	Yes
Time fixed effect controlled	Yes	Yes	Yes
N	39092	39092	39092
F	3.682	5.107	3.973
	Abnormal returns for three-factor model		
Dependent variable	**(4)**	**(5)**	**(6)**
Environmental sentiment factor (f)	0.0488***		
Google search factor		−0.00662	−0.0031
Weather factor		−0.00268***	−0.00300***
Macroeconomic factor	0.00670***	0.00739***	0.00773***
Regulation factor		−0.0138***	−0.0159***
Renewable energy consumption factor		−0.0186**	−0.0220***
nonrenewable energy consumption factor		0.0307***	0.0141
pollution factor			0.00771***
Constant	−0.0311	−0.0293	−0.0241
Company fixed effect controlled	Yes	Yes	Yes
Time fixed effect controlled	Yes	Yes	Yes
N	39092	39092	39092
F	3.540	4.742	3.995
	Abnormal returns for five-factor model		
Dependent variable	**(7)**	**(8)**	**(9)**
Environmental sentiment factor (f)	0.0471***		
Google Search factor			
Weather factor		−0.00680+	−0.00324
Macroeconomic factor	−0.00313***	−0.00345***	0.00798***
Regulation factor		−0.0140***	−0.0161***

(*Continued*)

Table 17. (*Continued*)

	Abnormal returns for five-factor model		
Dependent variable	**(7)**	**(8)**	**(9)**
Renewable energy consumption factor		−0.0218***	−0.0253***
non-renewable energy consumption factor		0.0307***	0.0106
pollution factor			0.00782***
Constant	−0.0176	−0.0172	−0.0119
Company fixed effect controlled	Yes	Yes	Yes
Time fixed effect controlled	Yes	Yes	Yes
N	39092	39092	39092
F	3.575	4.487	4.074

+0.1; *0.05; **0.01; ***0.0

Note: The regressions in all columns controlled both company fixed effects and time fixed effects. To control company fixed effects, I included 394 non-renewable energy company dummies (395 non-renewable energy equities in total); to control time fixed effects, I included 11 month dummies and 12 year dummies (13 years in total).

overall six component sub-group factors including the pollution factor (CO_2 emission).

Table 15 shows that the regression results for the sub-group factors are quite robust, since adding more sub-group factors in the regression model didn't dramatically change the coefficients for most of the sub-group factors. The exceptions are the pollution factor and the non-renewable energy consumption factor. When the pollution factor was included, the non-renewable energy consumption factor became statistically insignificant in column (9). An *F*-test rejected the null hypothesis that the coefficients of non-renewable energy consumption factor and pollution factor are jointly zero, thus we might just be capturing some multicolinearity.[10] Hence, we focus on the non-renewable energy consumption factor.

The renewable energy consumption factor has a statistically significant negative effect on abnormal returns for non-renewable energy firms (as shown in Table 17), while the effect for renewable energy firms is not statistically significant. The non-renewable energy consumption factor has a statistically significant positive effect on abnormal returns for both non-renewable and renewable energy firms. To sum, we obtain a positive relationship between non-renewable energy consumption and energy firms' abnormal returns, but a negative relationship between renewable

[10]The correlation between the non-renewable energy consumption factor and the pollution factor is over 0.8 as noted in Table 8.

energy consumption and energy firms' abnormal returns. These results are consistent with the premise that when environmental concerns increase, non-renewable energy consumption would decrease and renewable energy consumption would increase.

From Tables 15–17, we can conclude that after including more factors, the abnormal returns for renewable energy firms are still only significantly influenced by the macroeconomic factor, the environment regulation factor; while the weather factor, the energy consumption factor and the environmental sentiment factor do not seem to be as influential as for nonrenewable energy firms.

4.3. *Summary of the results*

A brief summary of our results is as follows:

a. In our sample, all energy firms have negative abnormal returns from January 2004 to October 2016; renewable energy firms show even lower abnormal returns (α) relative to non-renewable energy firms, indicating higher company value for renewable energy firms.
b. The environmental sentiment factor has a significant positive impact on abnormal returns for non-renewable energy firms, while for the renewable energy firms the impact is only marginally significant under the CAPM model. A decrease in the environmental sentiment factor indicates an increase in the public environmental concern.
c. The macroeconomic factor always has a statistically significant positive impact on abnormal returns for both renewable and non-renewable energy firms, and the impact is not statistically different for renewable and non-renewable firms, regardless of the panel used.
d. For renewable energy firms, only the environment regulation factor has statistically significant negative effects on abnormal returns.
e. For non-renewable energy firms, except for the Google Search factor, all other component sub-group factors have statistically significant effects on abnormal returns. The environmental regulation factor (negative coefficient), the weather factor (negative coefficient), the renewable energy consumption factor (negative coefficient), the non-renewable energy consumption (positive coefficient) are all found to be statistically significant.

Although renewable and non-renewable energy firms have comparable and statistically indistinguishable market betas, renewable energy firms provide lower stock returns and have higher company value than non-renewable firms. For renewable energy firms, the total predicted abnormal returns $\hat{\alpha}_{it}$ are mainly impacted by the environmental regulation factor; while for non-renewable energy firms, the predicted abnormal returns $\hat{\alpha}_{it}$ are mainly impacted by the environmental sentiment factor, the weather factor, the environment regulation factor and the energy consumption factors. Our findings suggest that when holding all other risk factors constant, facing with same level of environment-related risks, renewable energy firms have higher total abnormal returns than non-renewable energy firms.

5. Conclusions

We provide an empirical analysis of the relationship between environmental sentiment and stock performance in the energy sector, with particular focus on renewables versus non-renewables. We constructed an environmental sentiment factor and seven sub-group factors using the Dynamic Factor Model and calculated the predicted abnormal returns $\hat{\alpha}_{it}$ using well-established asset pricing models. We then estimated Newey–West regressions to explain the variation of the predicted abnormal returns. Our sample includes an unbalanced panel dataset of 448 US energy equities with monthly observations from January 2004 to October 2016. Our evidence suggests that all energy firms received lower actual returns than expected; renewable energy firms had higher company values due to the lower abnormal returns; and the predicted abnormal returns for non-renewable energy firms were more sensitive to environmental sentiment and weather conditions, while the predicted abnormal returns for renewable energy firms are more closely related to environment regulation. Of course, in both cases, other potential risks omitted in the regression could influence firms' abnormal returns.

Our evidence indicates that when extreme weather conditions become worse or when the public environmental concern becomes higher, investors would favor renewable energy equities over non-renewable energy ones. This is because, under the same environmental risk factors, renewable energy equities give higher abnormal returns, which adds more attractiveness for renewable energy firms' stocks. Of course, the consequence is that the cost of equity should be higher in the renewable energy sector.

Further research on the total cost of capital in this framework would be fruitful, mostly to understand the leverage and cost of debt aspects of renewable and non-renewable firms under conditions of environmental concerns.

Acknowledgment

We thank Dan Richards, Jeff Zabel, the participants of the Sungkyunkwan University and Tufts University Economics Research Conference, and participants of several

Tufts economics research workshops for their comments and suggestions. We thank the Tufts University department of economics for their financial support and Xue Wang thanks the Tufts Henken scholarship fund. Any errors are our own.

References

Askitas, N. and Zimmermann, K. F. (2009). Google econometrics and unemployment forecasting. *Applied Economics Quarterly* **55** (2), 107–120.

Amburgey, J. W. and Thoman, D. B. (2012). Dimensionality of the new ecological paradigm: Issues of factor structure and measurement. *Environment and Behavior* **44** (2), 235–256.

Baker, S. and Fradkin, A. (2011). What drives job search? Evidence from Google search data. Discussion Papers: 10-020.

Bernanke, B. S., Boivin, J. and Eliasz, P. (2005). Measuring the effects of monetary policy: A factor-augmented vector autoregressive (FAVAR) approach. *The Quarterly Journal of Economics* **120** (1), 387–422.

Bianconi, M., Hua, X. and Tan, C. M. (2015). Determinants of systemic risk and information dissemination. *International Review of Economics and Finance* **38**, 352–368.

Brunel, C. and Levinson, A. (2016). Measuring the stringency of environmental regulations. *Review of Environmental Economics and Policy* **10** (1), 47–67.

Burstein, P. (2003). The iImpact of public opinion on public policy: A review and an agenda. *Political Research Quarterly* **56** (1), 29–40.

Chang, S.-C., Chen, S.-S., Chou, R. K. and Lin. Y.-H. (2008). Weather and intraday patterns in stock returns and trading Activity. *Journal of Banking & Finance* **32** (9), 1754–66.

Chava, S. (2014). Environmental externalities and cost of capital. *Management Science* **60** (9), 2223–2247.

Da, Z., Engelberg, J. and Gao, P. (2011). In search of attention. *The Journal of Finance* **66** (5), 1461–1499.

D'Amuri, F. and Marcucci, J. (2010). Google It! Forecasting the US Unemployment Rate with A Google Job Search Index. SSRN Scholarly Paper ID 1594132. Rochester, NY: Social Science Research Network.

Dimpfl, T. and Jank, S. (2016). Can Internet Search Queries Help to Predict Stock Market Volatility? SSRN Scholarly Paper ID 2740779. Rochester, NY: Social Science Research Network.

Dunlap, R. E., Van Liere, K. D., Mertig, A. G. and Jones, R. E. (2000). New trends in measuring environmental attitudes: Measuring endorsement of the new ecological paradigm: A revised NEP Scale. *Journal of Social Issues* **56** (3), 425–42.

Dunlap, R. E. and Van Liere, K. D. (1978). The new environmental paradigm. *The Journal of Environmental Education* **9** (4), 10–19.

Elshahat, I., Freedman, M. and Elshahat, A. (2015). Are index measures better than individual measures in assessing the association between environmental and financial performance? A multivariate analysis study. *International Journal of Critical Accounting* **7** (2), 191–212.

Flammer, C. (2015). Does corporate social responsibility lead to superior financial performance? A regression discontinuity approach. *Management Science* **61** (11), 2549–2568.

Fama, E. F. and French, K. R. (1993). Common risk factors in the returns on stocks and bonds. *Journal of Financial Economics* **33** (1), 3–56.

Fama, E. F. and French, K. R. (2007). Disagreement, tastes, and asset prices. *Journal of Financial Economics* **83** (3), 667–689.

Fama, E. F. and French, K. R. (2015). A five-factor asset pricing model. *Journal of Financial Economics* **116** (1), 1–22.

García, D. (2013). Sentiment during recessions. *The Journal of Finance* **68** (3), 1267–1300.

Gerlach, S. and Yiu, M. S. (2005). A dynamic factor model of economic activity in Hong Kong. SSRN Scholarly Paper ID 735830. Rochester, NY: Social Science Research Network.

Geweke, J. (1978). The dynamic factor analysis of economic time series models. Social Systems Research Institute, University of Wisconsin-Madison.

Ginsberg, J., Mohebbi, M. H., Patel, R. S., Brammer, L., Smolinski, M. S. and Brilliant, L. (2009). Detecting influenza epidemics using search engine query data. *Nature* **457** (7232), 1012–1014.

Hamilton, S., Jo, H. and Statman, M. (1993). Doing well while doing good? The investment performance of socially responsible mutual funds. *Financial Analysts Journal* **49** (6), 62–66.

Herremans, I. M., Akathaporn, P. and McInnes, M. (1993). An investigation of corporate social responsibility reputation and economic performance. *Accounting, Organizations and Society* **18** (7): 587–604.

Heinkel, R., Kraus, A. and Zechner, J. (2001). The effect of green investment on corporate behavior. *Journal of Financial and Quantitative Analysis* **36** (4), 431–449.

Kahn, M. E. and Kotchen, M. J. (2010). Environmental concern and the business cycle: The chilling effect of recession. Working Paper 16241. National Bureau of Economic Research, Cambridge, MA.

Khairollahi, F., Shahveisi, F., Vafaei, A. and Alipour, M. (2016). From Iran: Does improvement in corporate environmental performance affect corporate risk taking? *Environmental Quality Management* **25** (4), 17–33.

Klassen, R. D. and McLaughlin, C. P. (1996). The impact of environmental management on firm performance. *Management Science* **42** (8), 1199–1214.

Laplante, B., Dasgupta, S. and Mamingi, N. (1998). Capital market responses to environmental performance in developing cCountries. SSRN Scholarly Paper ID 604915. Rochester, NY: Social Science Research Network. https://papers.ssrn.com/abstract$=$604915.

Lepori, G. M. (2016). Air pollution and stock returns: Evidence from a natural experiment. *Journal of Empirical Finance* **35** (January), 25–42.

Levy, T. and Yagil, J. (2011). Air pollution and stock returns in the US. *Journal of Economic Psychology* **32** (3), 374–383.

Liere, K. D. Van and Dunlap, R. E. (1980). The social bases of environmental concern: A review of hypotheses, explanations and empirical evidence. *Public Opinion Quarterly* **44** (2), 181–197.

Lintner, J. (1965). The valuation of risk assets and the selection of risk investments in stock portfolios and capital budgets. *Review of Economics and Statistics* **47**, 13–37.

Lorraine, N. H. J., Collison, D. J. and Power, D. M. (2004). An analysis of the stock market impact of environmental performance information. *Accounting Forum* **28** (1), 7–26.

Mossin, J. (1966). Equilibrium in a capital asset market. *Econometrica* **35**, 768–783.

Ng, A. and Zheng, D. (2016). The investment performance of green energy firms. Working paper, Department of Accounting and Finance, School of Business and Economics, Thompson Rivers University, Canada.

O'Connor, B., Balasubramanyan, R., Routledge, B. R. and Smith, N. A. (2010). From tweets to polls: Linking text sentiment to public opinion time series. *ICWSM* **11** (122–129), 1–2.

Saeidi, S. P., Sofian, S., Saeidi, P., Saeidi, S. P. and Saaeidi, S. A. (2015). How does corporate social responsibility contribute to firm financial performance? The mediating role of competitive advantage, reputation, and customer satisfaction. *Journal of Business Research* **68** (2), 341–50.

Sargent, T. J. and Sims, C. A. (1977). Business cycle modeling without pretending to have too much a priori economic theory, In A. S. Christopher (ed.), *New Methods in Business Research* (Federal Reserve Bank of Minneapolis, Minneapolis.)

Sharpe, W. F. (1964). Capital asset prices: A theory of market equilibrium under conditions of risk, *Journal of Finance* **19**, 425–442.

Soretz, S. and Ott, I. (2015). Green attitude and economic growth. In ZBW - Deutsche Zentralbibliothek für Wirtschaftswissenschaften, Leibniz-Informationszentrum Wirtschaft. https://www.econstor.eu/handle/10419/113208.

Stock, J. H. and Watson, M. W. (1989). New indexes of coincident and leading economic indicators. *NBER Macroeconomics Annual* **4** (January), 351–394.

Stock, J. H. and Watson, M. W. (1998). A comparison of linear and nonlinear univariate models for forecasting macroeconomic time series. Working Paper 6607. National Bureau of Economic Research.

Shove, E. (2010). Beyond the ABC: Climate change policy and theories of social change. *Environment and Planning A* **42** (6), 1273–1285.

Tetlock, P. C. (2007). Giving content to investor sentiment: The role of media in the stock market. *The Journal of Finance* **62** (3), 1139–1168.

Tsen, C., Phang, G., Hasan, H. and Buncha, M. R. (2006). Going green: A study of consumers' willingness to pay for green products in Kota Kinabalu. *International Journal of Business and Society* **7** (2), 40–54.

PART V

Pricing and Hedging

Chapter 23

German Natural Gas Seasonal Effects on Futures Hedging

Beatriz Martinez[*,x], Hipòlit Torró[†,¶] and Vanesa Garcia[‡,‖]

[*]*Department of Business Finance, University of Valencia, Spain*
[†]*Department of Financial and Actuarial Economics, University of Valencia, Spain*
[‡]*BBVA Bank*
[x]*Beatriz.Martinez-Martinez@uv.es*
[¶]*hipolit.torro@uv.es*
[‖]*seli_1991@hotmail.com*

In energy markets, changes in the spot price due to the influence of weather and seasonal demand conditions are partially predictable. In this work, we examine the German GASPOOL and NetConnect Germany natural gas markets using the Ederington and Salas [2008] framework that considers the predictive power of the base (futures price minus spot price) in the estimation of minimum variance hedge ratios. A considerable improvement in risk reduction and hedging effectiveness can be obtained by considering the partial predictability of changes in spot prices. We find that long hedges perform better than short hedges and there is no benefit to be gained by using more complex hedging estimations (BEKK) over the simpler OLS model. Seasonality is also found in hedging ratios.

Keywords: Natural gas market; futures; hedging ratio; natural gas price risk.

1. Introduction

Following the path set in other European countries, Germany began the liberalization of its natural gas markets in the beginning of the 2000s. However, progress was very disappointing and the culmination produced many difficulties, as stated by the EU Commission in one of its reports at the beginning of 2004 [Lohmann, 2006].

The first German natural gas hub to develop was GASPOOL (GPL) in July 2009. It is the result of merging two gas zones in the north of Germany and is owned by six transmission system operators (TSOs). According to Heather [2012], GASPOOL is a "physical hub" because it is mainly used by traders to adjust their storage portfolios in relation to NetConnect Germany (NCG). GASPOOL's trading activity is very small when compared to NCG.

NCG was formed on October 2009 following the merger of two zones in southern Germany and like GASPOOL has six TSO shareholders. As Heather [2012] states, in contrast to GASPOOL, NCG is a "virtual hub" because it is a virtual trading point within the pipelines of five network companies. It is the largest gas market area in Germany with both physical and financial activities.

Both NCG and GASPOOL can be traded on the European Energy Exchange (EEX) electronic clearing platform (and from where we collected the data). Since January 2011, the EEX has published an All-German Gas Index (EGIX). The index is calculated as the arithmetic mean of the daily volume weighted average prices of all the NCG and GASPOOL trades conducted on its exchange. Although traded volumes have risen substantially in recent years in German hubs, especially in NCG, they are still far from the liquidity levels of the most important European hubs (TTF in the Netherlands and NBP in Britain) [Heather, 2015]. In July 2017, a law was enacted establishing a plan to merge the two German gas markets of NCG and GASPOOL by 2022 with the aim of increasing liquidity and transparency, and so ensuring Germany's position as a key European hub (ICIS white paper).

A common feature of energy prices is that spot price changes are partially predictable due to seasonal weather and demand. Moreover, natural gas volatilities are also seasonal, because low storage levels in winter complicate the task of managing unexpected changes in demand, unlike summer, when storage levels are high [Mu, 2007; Suenaga *et al.* 2008; Alterman, 2012; Henaff *et al.* 2013; Efimova and Serletis, 2014].

Ederington and Salas [2008] adapted the standard minimum variance hedge ratio approach [Ederington, 1979] to the case where spot price changes are partially predictable. Taking into account this predictability, more efficient estimates of the hedge ratios are obtained. They propose using the basis (futures price minus spot price) at the beginning of the hedge as the information variable to approximate the expected spot price change. As Fama and French [1987] affirm, if futures prices are unbiased predictors of futures spot prices, the basis will be a measure of the expected change in the spot price before maturity. As spot natural gas price changes are partially predictable due to seasonal demand and storage levels, this approach perfectly fits the purpose of this research. The Ederington and Salas [2008] framework is also considered both in the hedging ratio computation and in the measurement of hedging effectiveness.

In the literature on risk management in energy markets, the influence of seasonality in energy prices for hedging purposes has been discussed in several papers. Suenaga *et al.* [2010] find that seasonal hedging is quite discretional under strong price seasonality. The existence of seasonal patterns in price and volatility has also been analyzed in Arismendi *et al.* [2016] for option valuation. Furthermore, the number of published papers modeling conditional covariance in energy markets has increased significantly in recent years, see Chang *et al.* [2011], Efimova and Serletis [2014], Ji and Fan [2011], Wang and Wu [2012] and Alexander *et al.* [2013]. In the estimation of the hedging ratios, we follow the BEKK specification proposed in Engle and Kroner [1995]. This model requires the estimation of fewer parameters than some alternatives, enables changing correlations and ensures a positive definite covariance matrix (which also facilitates its estimation).

The main objective of this work is to analyze German natural gas seasonal effects on futures hedging and to compare different hedging strategies in order to choose the optimal strategy. Moreover, we study if hedge ratios and their effectiveness have a significant seasonal pattern. We are going to apply the new approach developed in Ederington and Salas [2008] to the German natural gas hubs: NCG and GASPOOL. This chapter could be seen as an extension of the study developed by Martinez and Torró [2015] to the German natural gas market. We use four strategies: naive; "ordinary least squares (OLS) without basis", i.e. standard approach [Ederington, 1979]; "OLS with basis", i.e. the [Ederington and Salas, 2008] (E&S, 2008) approach; and BEKK (see [Engle and Kroner, 1995]). We then compare the risk reduction achieved by each hedging strategy. We analyze risk reduction attained for 1 week and 1 month hedges and we detect a positive duration effect in the hedging effectiveness. We find that the standard approach tends to underestimate the risk reduction — and overestimate the riskiness of unhedged position when changes in the spot prices are partially predictable. Finally, we can affirm that our results are similar to those obtained by Martinez and Torró [2015] for other European markets.

Results can be summarized in the following points: (i) hedging performance improves as hedging duration increases. That is, 1-month hedges perform better than 1-week hedges; (ii) minimum variance hedge ratios are unconditionally estimated with the Ederington and Salas [2008] approach for all hedge periods, and conditionally estimated with the multivariate GARCH model proposed by Engle and Kroner [1995] for weekly hedging periods. The greatest risk reduction for weekly hedges is obtained by the BEKK specification in GASPOOL, and the Ederington and Salas [2008] approach in NCG. For monthly hedges, no model beats the others. (iii) the basis has a clear seasonal pattern with positive on-peak values in winter and negative off-peak values in summer. (iv) we find a seasonal pattern in both spot and futures returns volatility, but we detect no significant seasonal pattern on futures hedge ratios. (v) very large risk reductions are achievable using the approach proposed in Ederington and Salas [2008].

This work is organised as follows: In the following section, we review the existing literature. Sections 3 and 4 describe the estimation methodology and the data, respectively. Section 5 presents the empirical results. Section 6 contains a brief conclusion.

2. Literature Review

The literature modeling time-varying volatility has become abundant since the development of ARCH by Engle [1982] and GARCH by Bollerslev [1986]. Bekaert and Wu [2000] introduce asymmetries in GARCH and conclude that "negative shocks increase conditional covariances substantially, whereas positive shocks have a mixed impact on conditional covariances." Other authors who model time-varying volatility are Efimova and Selertis [2014] and Hendry and Sharma [1999].

The literature modeling conditional covariance is less extensive. Bollerslev *et al.* [1988] proposed the VECH model in which the univariate GARCH is extended to the vectorized conditional-variance matrix. Bollerslev [1990] propose a multivariate time series with time-varying conditional variances and covariances but constant conditional correlation, that is to say, the constant correlation model (CCORR). Engle and Kroner [1995] propose a class of MGARCH (the BEKK) that practically ensures the covariance matrix is positive definite. These three models are the most used for modeling conditional variance.

The literature comparing risk management models is also quite extensive. Yang [2001] analyzes the traditional model, as well as the VAR model, VECM and DVEC multivariate GARCH, and finds that the GARCH time-varying hedge ratios provide the greatest portfolio risk reduction. Bonga-Bonga and Umoetok [2016] estimate the hedging ratio in an emerging equity market and conclude that the most effective method for daily hedging periods is the traditional model estimated by OLS; however, the VECM and multivariate GARCH models are more effective for weekly and monthly hedges. Cotter and Hanly [2012] find that the OLS model is the most effective for hedging and suggest that "there is little economic benefit to be gained by the use of more complex hedging estimation models over the simple OLS model irrespective of the characteristics of the return distribution."

Natural gas prices have a clear seasonal pattern. Mu [2007] estimates a GARCH model from the American natural gas market using deviation of temperature as a proxy for demand shocks. He concludes that this proxy has a significant effect on the conditional volatility of natural gas prices. Nick and Thoenes [2014] show that "natural gas price is affected by temperature, storage and supply shortfalls in the short term, whereas the long-term development is closely tied to both crude oil and coal prices." Henaff *et al.* [2013] take into account the seasonal pattern and the existence of spikes, and incorporate seasonality in the futures curve of their futures model and spikes in their spot model. Efimova and Selertis [2014] introduce a seasonal dummy variable in the mean equation and find higher volatility in winter and summer than in the transition seasons.

Fama and French [1987] analyze the basis through two alternative theories: firstly, the theory of storage; and secondly, the basis as the sum of an expected premium and an expected change in the spot price. They conclude that the basis has reliable information about the future change in the spot price for most maturities.

Ederington and Salas [2008] extend the Ederington [1979] approach to the case when changes in the spot are partially predictable. They propose using the basis (futures-spot spread) as the information variable to approximate the expected spot price change. They conclude that "incorporating measures of the expected change in the spot price into the regression results in substantially lower estimates of the riskiness of hedged and unhedged positions, and substantially higher estimates of the risk reduction achievable through hedging." Therefore, when spot price returns can be partially forecasted, his approach produces the more efficient estimates.

Martinez and Torró [2015] apply this new approach to the European gas market. Significant improvements for hedging strategies are obtained and unexpected shocks in spot prices can be partially anticipated using the information contained in the basis (between 10%–30%). Martinez and Torró conclude that hedging effectiveness improves as the duration of the hedge increases. They find a strong seasonal pattern in the volatility of spot and futures price returns, which have been significantly higher in winter than in summer. Martinez and Torró [2015] also use the BEKK with the asymmetrical extension, but their results show that the better statistical performance of the GARCH models does not imply a better hedging strategy performance.

3. Methodology

We are going to implement three models to check the hedging effectiveness each model produces in terms of variance risk reduction. The models analyzed are: the traditional model (or the standard minimum variance hedge ratio); an alternative model (implementing the innovative approach developed in Ederington and Salas [2008]); and a GARCH model (specifically the BEKK model). We will then analyze the hedging effectiveness of each model to make a comparison between them.

3.1. *Traditional model*

Following Martinez and Torro [2015], we define the conventional minimum variance hedge ratio in a one-period model for an individual committed to a given position in the spot market at the beginning of the period, or 't'. To reduce the risk exposure, the individual may choose to hedge at time 't' in the futures market with the same underlying asset. At the end of the period, say, "$t+1$," the hedger's result per unit of spot is calculated as follows:

$$x_{t+1} = \Delta S(t) - b_t \Delta F(t, T), \tag{1}$$

where x_{t+1} is the value variation between t and $t+1$, $\Delta S(t) = (S(t+1) - S(t))$ is the spot value variation, $\Delta F(t, T) = (F(t+1, T) - F(t, T))$ the futures value variation of a futures contract maturing at T and b_t is the hedging ratio. If b_t is positive (negative), short (long) positions are taken in futures. The hedger will choose b_t to minimize the risk associated with the random result x_{t+1}. As in Alexander *et al.* [2013], we use realised returns instead of log returns (because they are more appropriate for assets with prices that can jump).

We use the variance conditional on the available information, ψ_t, to measure risk. The risk of a hedge strategy is calculated as the variance of x_{t+1},

$$\mathrm{VAR}[x_{t+1} | \psi_t] = \mathrm{VAR}[\Delta S(t) - b_t \Delta F(t, T) | \psi_t]. \tag{2}$$

The optimal hedge ratio has been defined as the amount of futures position per unit spot position such that the hedged portfolio variance is minimized and can be obtained by minimizing Eq. (2).

$$b_t = \frac{\mathrm{cov}(\Delta S(t), \Delta F(t, T) | \psi_t)}{\mathrm{var}(\Delta F(t, T) | \psi_t)}. \tag{3}$$

Equation (3) can be estimated from a linear relationship between spot and futures returns if we use an unconditional probability distribution. Thus, by estimating the linear relationship appearing in Eq. (1) by ordinary least squares (OLS henceforth) but adding an intercept and white noise, we obtain

$$\Delta S(t) = a + b \Delta F(t, T) + \varepsilon(t), \tag{4}$$

where b is the unconditional definition of the optimal hedge ratio of Eq. (3) [Ederington, 1979] estimated with OLS.

3.2. *Alternative model*

Ederington and Salas [2008] adapted this previous approach to the case where spot price changes are partially predictable and futures prices are unbiased estimators of future spot prices. In this context, Ederington and Salas [2008] show that the riskiness of the spot position is overestimated, while the achievable risk reduction is underestimated. If we consider this approach, the unexpected result of the hedge in Eq. (1) can be reformulated as

$$x_{t+1} = (\Delta S(t) - E[\Delta S(t)|\,\psi_t]) - b'_t \Delta F(t, T). \tag{5}$$

The risk of the hedge strategy in Eq. (2) is reformulated as

$$\mathrm{VAR}[x_{t+1}|\psi_t] = \mathrm{VAR}[(\Delta S(t) - E[\Delta S(t)|\psi_t]) - b'_t \Delta F(t, T)|\psi_t], \tag{6}$$

and the minimum variance hedge ratio obtained after minimizing Eq. (6) is

$$b'_t = \frac{\mathrm{cov}((\Delta S(t) - E[\Delta S(t)|\psi_t]), \Delta F(t, T)|\psi_t)}{\mathrm{var}(\Delta F(t, T)|\psi_t)}. \tag{7}$$

Fama and French [1987] argue that if futures prices are unbiased predictors of futures spot price, the basis will be a measure of the expected change in the spot price until maturity. Ederington and Salas [2008] adapted the above approach proposed to use the basis at the beginning of the hedge as the information variable to approximate the expected spot price change. An unconditional estimate of the hedge ratio in Eq. (7) can be obtained by estimating the following linear regression using OLS:

$$\Delta S(t) = a' + b' \Delta F(t, T) + \lambda(F(t, T) - S(t)) + \varepsilon'(t), \tag{8}$$

where $\lambda(F(t, T) - S(t))$ is used to estimate $E[\Delta S(t)|\psi_t]$. Ederington and Salas [2008] show that this unconditional minimum variance hedge ratio estimator (b') produces more efficient estimates than that obtained by using Eq. (4), providing that the basis at the beginning of the hedge perfectly approximates the expected change in the spot price.

3.3. *GARCH model: BEKK*

The asymmetric version of the BEKK is estimated to obtain conditional estimates of the second moments. The input to the BEKK are the residuals obtained after estimating a model in means. Firstly, we propose the same vector error correction as Martinez and Torro [2015], by introducing the lagged value of the basis in the model as follows (this can be seen as an error correction term when spot and futures prices are cointegrated, see Lien [1996]):

$$\begin{aligned}\Delta^k S(t) &= \gamma_1 + \gamma_{10}(F(t,T_k) - S(t)) + \sum_{\tau=1}^{p} \gamma_{11\tau}\Delta^k S(t-\tau) \\ &\quad + \sum_{\tau=1}^{p} \gamma_{12\tau}\Delta^k F(t-\tau, T_i) + \varepsilon_{1,t+k}; \\ \Delta^k F(t,T_i) &= \gamma_2 + \gamma_{20}(F(t,T_k) - S(t)) + \sum_{\tau=1}^{p} \gamma_{21\tau}\Delta^k S(t-\tau) \\ &\quad + \sum_{\tau=1}^{p} \gamma_{22\tau}\Delta^k F(t-\tau, T_i) + \varepsilon_{2,t+k},\end{aligned} \tag{9}$$

where $\Delta^k S(t)$ and $\Delta^k F(t, T_i)$ are computed as shown in Table 1; the gammas are parameters to estimate; p is the lag of the VAR and is chosen by minimizing the Hannan and Quinn [1979] information criteria with the objective of eliminating any autocorrelation pattern. The vector of residuals $\varepsilon_{t+k} = (\varepsilon_{1t+k}, \varepsilon_{2t+k})'$, obtained by estimating the VAR by OLS,[1] is saved and used as observable data to estimate the multivariate GARCH. The number of parameters to estimate in the second part is reduced with this procedure,[2] the estimation error is reduced and a faster convergence in the estimation procedure is also enabled.

Engle and Kroner [1995] proposed a class of MGARCH model called the BEKK, we estimate this model by introducing asymmetries following the Glosten *et al.* [1993] approach. The two-dimensional asymmetric BEKK model can be written in its compacted form as

$$H_t = C'C + B'H_{t-1}B + A'\varepsilon_{t-1}\varepsilon'_{t-1}A + G'\eta_{t-1}\eta'_{t-1}G, \tag{10}$$

where C, A, B are 2×2 matrices of parameters; H_t is the 2×2 conditional covariance matrix, the diagonal elements of H_t are variance terms, and elements outside the diagonal are covariances; and ε_t and η_t are 2×1 vectors containing the shocks and

[1]Least squares standard errors will be consistent estimates of the true standard errors [Engle and Granger, 1987].

[2]Estimates of the unexpected returns at time t (ε_t) are treated as a collective measure of news at time t, and then, used as observable data in the ARCH and GARCH models estimation as in Engle and Ng [1993]. Kroner and Ng [1998] follow a similar procedure, and estimate four multivariate GARCH models (BEKK; FARCH; VECH and CCORR) in two steps: firstly, estimating the mean equation to obtain the residuals; and secondly, estimating the conditional covariance matrix parameters using the maximum likelihood method.

threshold terms series. The unfolded covariance model is written as follows:

$$\begin{aligned}\begin{bmatrix} h_{11t} & h_{12t} \\ . & h_{22t} \end{bmatrix} &= \begin{bmatrix} c_{11} & c_{12} \\ 0 & c_{22} \end{bmatrix}' \begin{bmatrix} c_{11} & c_{12} \\ 0 & c_{22} \end{bmatrix} + \begin{bmatrix} b_{11} & b_{12} \\ b_{21} & b_{22} \end{bmatrix}' \begin{bmatrix} h_{11t-1} & h_{12t-1} \\ . & h_{22t-1} \end{bmatrix} \begin{bmatrix} b_{11} & b_{12} \\ b_{21} & b_{22} \end{bmatrix} \\ &+ \begin{bmatrix} a_{11} & a_{12} \\ a_{21} & a_{22} \end{bmatrix}' \begin{bmatrix} \varepsilon_{1t-1}^2 & \varepsilon_{1t-1}\varepsilon_{2t-1} \\ . & \varepsilon_{2t-1}^2 \end{bmatrix} \begin{bmatrix} a_{11} & a_{12} \\ a_{21} & a_{22} \end{bmatrix} \\ &+ \begin{bmatrix} g_{11} & g_{12} \\ g_{21} & g_{22} \end{bmatrix}' \begin{bmatrix} \eta_{1t-1}^2 & \eta_{1t-1}\eta_{2t-1} \\ . & \eta_{2t-1}^2 \end{bmatrix} \begin{bmatrix} g_{11} & g_{12} \\ g_{21} & g_{22} \end{bmatrix}, \end{aligned} \tag{11}$$

where h_{ijt} for all $i, j = 1, 2$ are the conditional second moment series; c_{ij}, b_{ij}, a_{ij} and g_{ij}, for all $i, j = 1, 2$ are parameters; ε_{1t} and ε_{2t} are the unexpected shock series obtained from Eq. (10); and $\eta_{1t} = \max[0, -\varepsilon_{1t}]$ and $\eta_{2t} = \max[0, -\varepsilon_{2t}]$ are the Glosten *et al.* [1993] dummy series capturing negative asymmetries from the shocks.

The parameters of the BEKK model are estimated by maximizing the conditional log-likelihood function:

$$L(\theta) = -\frac{TN}{2}\ln(2\pi) - \frac{1}{2}\sum_{t=1}^{T}(\ln|H_t(\theta)| + \varepsilon_t' H_t^{-1}(\theta)\varepsilon_t), \tag{12}$$

where θ denotes the vector of all the parameters to be estimated; T is the number of observations; and N is the number of equations in the system. The log-likelihood function is estimated using the BFGS algorithm via quasi-maximum likelihood estimation (QMLE).

3.4. *Hedging effectiveness*

Hedging effectiveness is measured by the percentage reduction in variance of the hedged position relative to the unhedged position ($b = 0$), given as

$$\frac{\text{var}(U) - \text{var}(H)}{\text{var}(U)} = 1 - \frac{\text{var}(H)}{\text{var}(U)}, \tag{13}$$

where var(U) is the variance of the unhedged position and var(H) is the variance of the hedged position. The risk reduction is calculated to compare the hedging effectiveness of each of the following hedging strategies:

- Naive strategy: a hedge where futures positions have the opposite sign to the position held in the spot market but the same size ($b_t = 1$ for all t).
- OLS without basis: obtained after estimating Eq. (4).
- OLS with basis: obtained after estimating Eq. (8).
- BEKK: obtained after estimating the BEKK model in Eqs. (9)–(12).

Furthermore, *ex-post* and *ex-ante* results are distinguished by splitting the data sample into two parts: In the first part, the hedging strategies are compared *ex-post*, whereas in the second part, an *ex-ante* approach is used. That is, in the *ex-ante* study, strategies are compared using forecasted hedge ratios, and models are estimated when a new observation is considered. The variance of the unhedged position is computed following the standard and Ederington and Salas [2008] approaches, respectively,

$$\mathrm{VAR}[\Delta^k S(t)] \tag{14}$$

$$\mathrm{VAR}[\Delta^k S(t) - \hat{\lambda}(F(t, T_k) - S(t))]. \tag{15}$$

The variance of hedged positions is computed with the same procedure used to compute the variance of the unhedged positions, that is to say, with the standard and Ederington and Salas [2008] approaches, respectively,

$$\mathrm{VAR}[\Delta^k S(t) - \hat{b}_t \Delta^k F(t, T_i)] \tag{16}$$

$$\mathrm{VAR}[\Delta^k S(t) - \hat{b}_t \Delta^k F(t, T_i) - \hat{\lambda}(F(t, T_k) - S(t))]. \tag{17}$$

We apply the study to futures with different maturities: 1 week and 1 month are considered to hedge the spot price variation. Table 1 shows the four types of hedges carried out in this chapter, one per row.

4. Data and Preliminary Analysis

The spot and futures natural gas prices used are from EEX. In the study of weekly frequency data, the prices are taken on Wednesday, or the previous trading day if not tradable. For monthly frequency data, the rollovers taken are the last Wednesday of the month, or the previous trading day if Wednesday is the last trading day of the month. We use realized returns calculated as in Table 1. The basis used to approximate the expected spot price appears in the last column.

Figure 1 exhibits the time series for the spot and first to 'delivery' future prices. We can observe a clear seasonal pattern, both in spot and future prices, with higher

Table 1. Types of hedges.

Duration k	**Spot variation $\Delta^k S(t)$**	**Futures variation $\Delta^k F(t,T_i)$**	**Basis approximating $E[\Delta^k S(t)\|_t]$**
1 week	$\Delta^{\mathrm{w}} S(t) = S(t+1 \text{ week}) - S(t)$	$\Delta^{\mathrm{w}} F(t, T_1) = F(t+1 \text{ week}, T_1) - F(t, T_1))$	$F(t, T_1) - S(t)$
1 month	$\Delta^{\mathrm{m}} S(t) = S(t+1 \text{ month}) - S(t)$	$\Delta^{\mathrm{m}} F(t, T_1) = F(t+1 \text{ month}, T_1) - F(t, T_1))$	$F(t, T_1) - S(t)$

Notes: This table displays the types of hedges and helps clarify the notation. Spot returns are computed as $\Delta^k S(t) = S(t+k) - S(t)$ with $k = 1$ week and 1 month; and represent the spot price variation for the k period. Note that prices are taken on Wednesday (previous trading day is used if not tradable) and futures rollovers are taken for the last Wednesday of the month (or previous trading day if the last trading day of the month is a Wednesday). The "Duration" column reports the hedging period. The final column reports the basis used to approximate the expected spot price change in Eq. (8).

prices in winter and lower prices in summer. The highest prices are in December 2008, January 2009, February 2012 and March 2013, and these are explained by the combination of several factors: the dispute between Russia and Ukraine about gas prices and transit conditions, and tight supply and storage conditions due to an unexpected increase in demand caused by colder than expected weather.

Table 2 displays the basic statistics of weekly and monthly spot and future price returns. Spot mean values are negative but not significantly different from zero, except for the GASPOOL weekly returns. Futures mean return values are negatives and significantly different from zero (ranging between −0.11 and −0.47 for weekly and monthly returns, respectively). As we see, a declining pattern in futures prices (futures prices above expected spot prices) we would assume that the futures market is in contango. Using the Kruskal–Wallis test, we contrast the null hypothesis of median equality between futures and spot time series. At a 5% significance level, the null hypothesis is rejected for the weekly frequency data — but not for the monthly data from both hubs. We also test equality of variance with the Levene test. In this case, the null hypothesis of variance equality is rejected for weekly returns — but cannot be rejected for monthly returns in both hubs. As expected, standard deviation is always higher in spot returns. All the time series analysed have significant excess of Kurtosis, but significant skewness is only found in spot returns for the NCG hub. Following the Jarque–Bera test, we can clearly reject the normality of the distribution in all the series. The Ljung–Box test with 20 lags detects significant autocorrelation and heteroscedasticity (except for monthly spot returns in NCG hub).

Table 3 displays the correlation between spot and futures returns for both hubs. They present quite high values, between 0.69 and 0.98. For both hubs, the highest

Fig. 1. European spot and futures natural gas markets. (a) NCG spot and first to 'delivery' futures contract. (b) GASPOOL spot and first to 'delivery' futures contract.

Notes: Spot price (——) and the first to 'delivery' futures price (- - -).

Table 2. Summary statistics of spot and futures prices returns.

	NCG		GASPOOL	
	$\Delta^{w}S(t)$	$\Delta^{w}F(t,T_1)$	$\Delta^{w}S(t)$	$\Delta^{w}F(t,T_1)$
Panel (A): 1 week variations				
Mean	−0.0038 [0.95]	−0.1318 [0.00]	0.0035 [0.95]	−0.11 [0.00]
Median	−0.0540	−0.13	0.0000	−0.10
Kruskal–Wallis		4.11 [0.04]		4.457 [0.03]
S. D.	1.2676	0.9251	1.3259	0.9280
Levene		16.72 [0.00]		15.00 [0.00]
Skewness	−0.0151 [0.89]	−0.2766 [0.01]	−0.403 [0.00]	−0.275 [0.01]
Kurtosis	7.3578 [0.00]	5.7774 [0.00]	9.0573 [0.00]	6.3898 [0.00]
Jarque–Bera	391.70 [0.00]	165.41 [0.00]	776.41 [0.00]	245.20 [0.00]
Maximum	6.40	3.51	6.03	3.92
Minimum	−6.25	−4.45	−7.85	−4.55
$Q(20)$	116.80 [0.00]	139.79 [0.00]	121.03 [0.00]	146.33 [0.00]
$Q^2(20)$	133.95 [0.00]	247.69 [0.00]	181.16 [0.00]	223.87 [0.00]
Panel (B): 1 month variations				
Mean	−0.0376 [0.86]	−0.5602 [0.00]	−0.009 [0.97]	−0.477 [0.01]
Median	−0.01	−0.346	−0.031	−0.25
Kruskal–Wallis		3.1545 [0.07]		2.6476[0.10]
S. D.	2.3202	1.957	2.418	1.982
Levene		2.328 [0.12]		1.958 [0.16]
Skewness	−0.497 [0.03]	−1.31 [0.00]	−0.533 [0.01]	−1.363 [0.00]
Kurtosis	5.26 [0.00]	6.692 [0.00]	6.428 [0.00]	6.898 [0.00]
Jarque–Bera	29.13 [0.00]	97.36 [0.00]	61.78 [0.00]	108.47 [0.00]
Maximum	6.64	2.95	8.70	3.03
Minimum	−9.45	−8.64	−9.75	−8.56
$Q(20)$	55.53 [0.00]	61.86 [0.00]	54.87 [0.00]	59.83 [0.00]
$Q^2(20)$	5.905 [0.99]	37.007 [0.01]	6.99 [0.99]	47.78 [0.00]

Notes: The variables appearing in the heading of each column are described in Table 1. The *Kruskal–Wallis* and *Levene* statistics test median and variance equality, respectively, between $\Delta^k S(t)$ and $\Delta^k F(t, T_i)$. *Skewness* means the skewness coefficient and has the asymptotic distribution N(0,6/T) under normality, where T is the sample size. The null hypothesis tests whether the skewness coefficient is equal to zero. *Kurtosis* means the excess kurtosis coefficient and it has an asymptotic distribution of N(0,24/T) under normality. The hypothesis tests whether the kurtosis coefficient is equal to zero. The *Jarque–Bera* statistic tests for the normal distribution hypothesis. The Jarque–Bera statistic is calculated as T[*Skewness*^{2}/6+(*Kurtosis*)^2/24]. The Jarque–Bera statistic has an asymptotic $\chi^2(2)$ distribution under the normal distribution hypothesis. $Q(20)$ and $Q^2(20)$ are Ljung–Box tests for 20th-order serial correlation in the differentiated and squared series, respectively. Marginal significance levels of the statistical tests are displayed as [.].

correlation is obtained by spot and futures for monthly returns. As we will see later, hedging effectiveness increases as the hedging period increases, as does the correlation coefficient.

Throughout the year, natural gas prices undergo changes due to the weather and temperature variations that cause a strong seasonal pattern. The same behavior

Table 3. Correlation matrix of the spot and futures prices log variations.

		NCG		GASPOOL	
		$\Delta^{1m}S(t)$	$\Delta^{1m}F(t,T_1)$	$\Delta^{1m}S(t)$	$\Delta^{1m}F(t,T_1)$
Panel (A). 1-week					
NCG	$\Delta^{1m}S(t)$	1.0			
	$\Delta^{1m}F(t,T_1)$	0.71*	1.0		
GASPOOL	$\Delta^{1m}S(t)$	0.91*	0.69*	1.0	
	$\Delta^{1m}F(t,T_1)$	0.70*	0.97*	0.69*	1.0
Panel (B). 1-month					
NCG	$\Delta^{1m}S(t)$	1.0			
	$\Delta^{1m}F(t,T_1)$	0.74*	1.0		
GASPOOL	$\Delta^{1m}S(t)$	0.98*	0.73*	1.0	
	$\Delta^{1m}F(t,T_1)$	0.74*	0.98*	0.75*	1.0

Notes: The variables appearing in the heading of each row and column are described in Table 1. For a sample size of T observations, the asymptotic distribution of the $\sqrt{T}$ times the correlation coefficient is a zero-one normal distribution. *indicates significance at the 1% significance level.

presents the convenience yield and the basis. In winter, demand is great and so storage levels decrease and storage costs increase (positive convenience yield), producing a positive basis. In the warmth of summer, demand for natural gas is lower and storage prices decrease while storage levels increase (negative convenience yield), and the combination of these effects results in a negative basis [Martinez and Torró, 2015]. We study this seasonality through basis and price volatility. In Figs. 2 and 3, we have plotted the basis and returns volatility, respectively. We observe high values in winter and lower values in summer — and both show a clear seasonal pattern. All in all, the basis itself could depict the information contained in the demand, convenience yield, weather, storage levels and risk premiums.

To test the predictive power of the basis, we regress spot and futures returns on the basis in Table 4. The basis presents better predictability power with spot returns than with futures for both hubs and varies between 6.62% and 14.74%. These results coincide with the Martinez and Torró [2015] and Ederington and Salas [2008] approaches in which spot price changes are partially predictable. For the futures prices, the martingale hypothesis is applicable.

To analyze the seasonal effects, in Table 5 we divided the year in two seasons for weekly spot and futures returns: winter from October to March and summer from April to September (as in the EEX). We can see that mean equality between basis, spot and futures returns cannot be rejected. On the other hand, winter volatility is significantly higher than summer volatility in all cases.

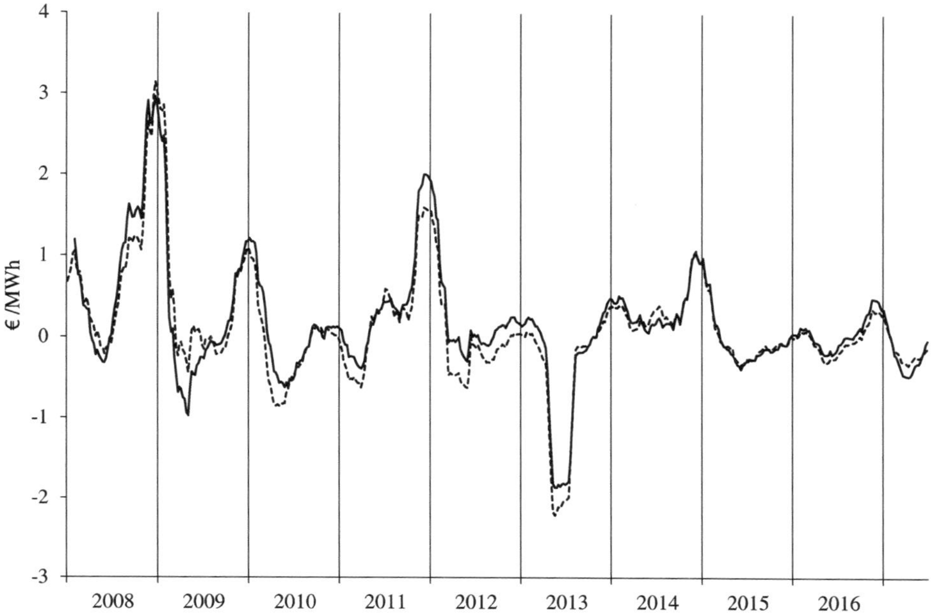

Fig. 2. Seasonal basis.

Notes: This figure shows seasonal basis. 13-week moving average basis approximating at NCG (——) and GPL (--------).

5. Results

In this section, we analyze the results of the estimation for the models for BEKK, the traditional minimum variance hedging ratio [Ederington, 1979] and the innovative approach by Ederington and Salas [2008]. The sample is divided into two periods: an in-sample estimation (*ex-post* period) and an out-of-sample estimation (*ex-ante* period) in which the models are reestimated by a moving window of 4 years when a new observation is added.

Figures 4–5 exhibit the estimated conditional second moment of the BEKK estimation and hedging ratios, respectively.

We can see a clear seasonal pattern in Fig. 4, very alike the volatility of raw data in Fig. 3: an increasing volatility in winter and a decreasing tendency in summer. The model also captures the highly volatile period observed for the raw data in the winter 2008–2009. The BEKK model also reflects the highest spot price volatility, which is about twice the futures volatility. As happened in Martinez and Torro [2015], the strength of the seasonal pattern appears to soften towards the end of the sample period.

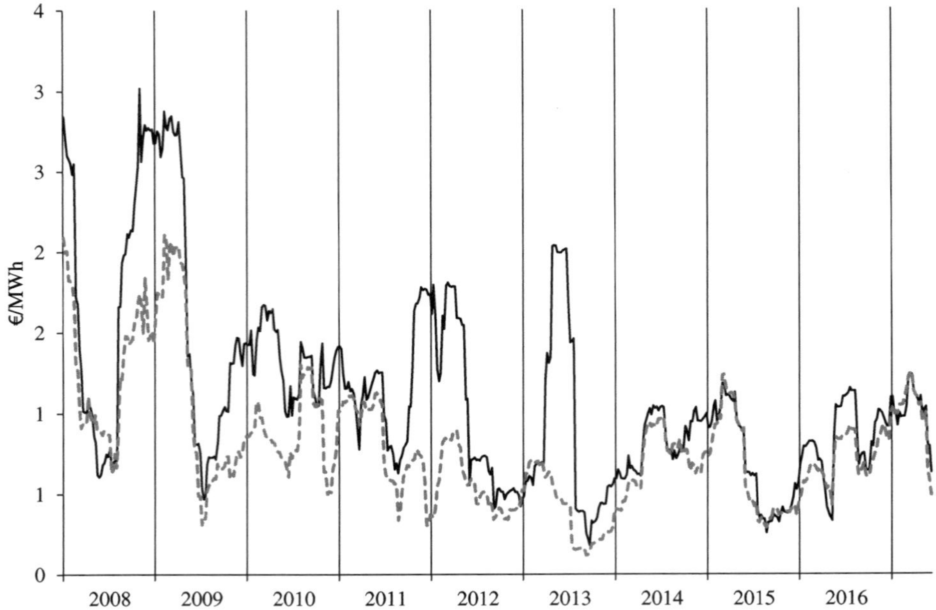

(a)

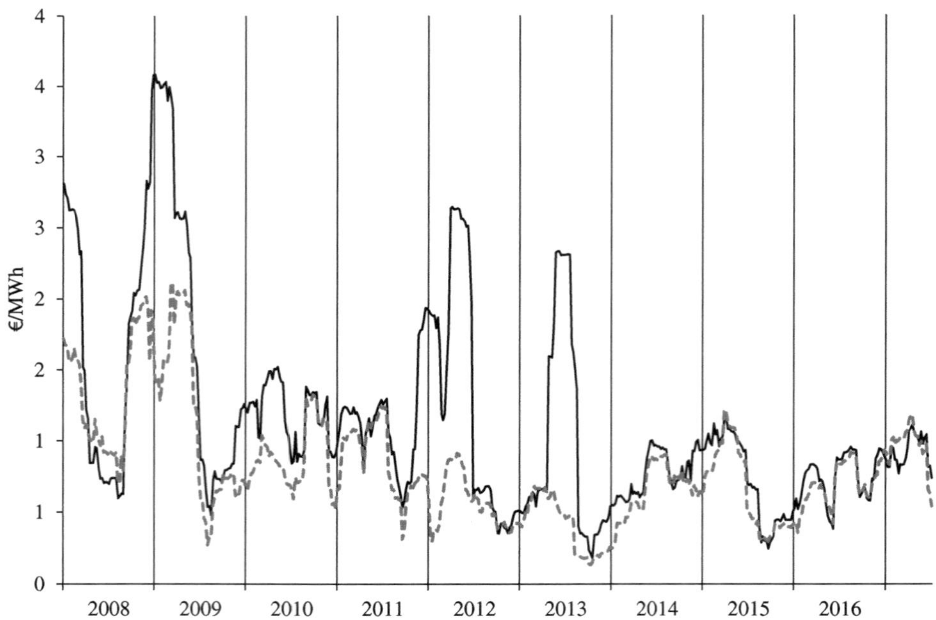

(b)

Fig. 3. Seasonal volatility.

Notes: Spot volatility (——) and its front monthly futures volatility (- - -) are reported. Standard deviation of 13-week moving window returns are reported. (a) NCG (b) GASPOOL.

Table 4. The basis as a predictor of change in spot and futures prices.

	Dependent variable	Basis	Intercept	Basis coefficient	Adjusted R^2 (%)
Panel (A). Week returns					
NCG	$\Delta^{w} S(t)$	$F(t, T_1)-S(t)$	−0.06 (−1.13)	0.30 (3.10)*	7.72
	$\Delta^{w} F(t, T_1)$	$F(t, T_1)-S(t)$	−0.11 (−2.56)*	−0.10 (−2.35)*	1.56
GSP	$\Delta^{w} S(t)$	$F(t, T_1)-S(t)$	−0.03 (−0.54)	0.28 (2.97)*	6.62
	$\Delta^{w} F(t, T_1)$	$F(t, T_1)-S(t)$	−0.09 (−2.32)**	−0.13 (−3.87)*	2.57
Panel (B). 1-month returns					
NCG	$\Delta^{1m} S(t)$	$F(t, T_1)-S(t)$	−0.15 (−0.75)	1.10 (5.61)*	14.74
	$\Delta^{1m} F(t, T_1)$	$F(t, T_1)-S(t)$	−0.54 (0.02)**	−0.15 (−0.80)	0.38
GSP	$\Delta^{1m} S(t)$	$F(t, T_1)-S(t)$	−0.05 (−0.22)	0.98 (4.91)*	12.80
	$\Delta^{1m} F(t, T_1)$	$F(t, T_1)-S(t)$	−0.47 (−2.13)**	−0.21 (−1.31)	0.85

Notes: This table displays the results of the regression between spot and futures returns appearing in the second column on the basis. The t-statistic values computed with Newey–West standard errors are reported between brackets. Significant coefficients at the 1%, 5% and 10% significance levels are highlighted with one (*), two (**) and three (***) asterisks, respectively.

Table 5. Summer and winter mean and volatility.

	Summer mean	Winter mean	Equality test	Summer volatility	Winter volatility	Equality test
$F(t, T_1) - S(t)$						
NCG	0.20	0.19	0.41	0.80	1.43	0.00
GSP	0.11	0.13	0.81	0.75	1.52	0.00
$\Delta^{w} S(t)$						
NCG	0.009	−0.02	0.54	0.98	1.48	0.00
GSP	0.02	−0.01	0.67	0.97	1.59	0.00
$\Delta^{w} F(t, T_1)$						
NCG	−0.07	−0.19	0.13	0.75	1.06	0.00
GSP	−0.06	−0.16	0.15	0.81	1.02	0.00

Notes: This table reports the weekly mean and volatility (standard deviation) of basis, spot and futures returns in winter (October to March) and summer (April to September). The *p-values* of the *Kruskal–Wallis* and *Levene* statistics test for median and variance equality, respectively, are reported.

In Figs. 5 (a) and (b), the hedging ratios estimated with the new Ederington and Salas [2008] approach are shown above the standard hedging approach for both hubs and for the whole period. We can also highlight that conditional BEKK hedging ratios in Fig. 5 (c) are similar to the values of linear regression-based ratios. The GASPOOL conditional hedging ratios are above the NCG ratios in most of the period considered.

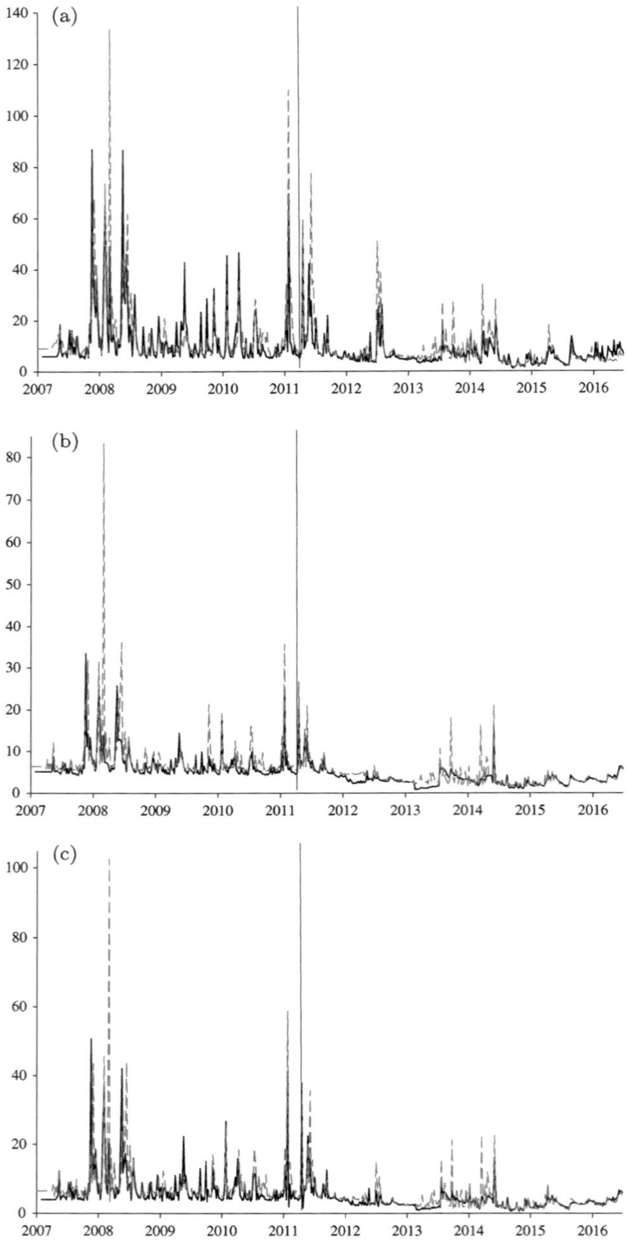

Fig. 4. Annualized conditional volatilities. (a) Spot annualized volatility. (b) First to 'delivery' annualized volatility. (c) Annualized covariance between spot and futures.

Notes: In each graph, the solid line (——) and the dashed line (- - -) correspond to the annualised conditional volatility of the BEKK model for the NCG and GASPOOL hubs, respectively. The displayed conditional volatilities are estimated in the "1-week" hedging period models. The vertical line separates the *ex-post* and *ex-ante* (4-year moving window) hedging periods.

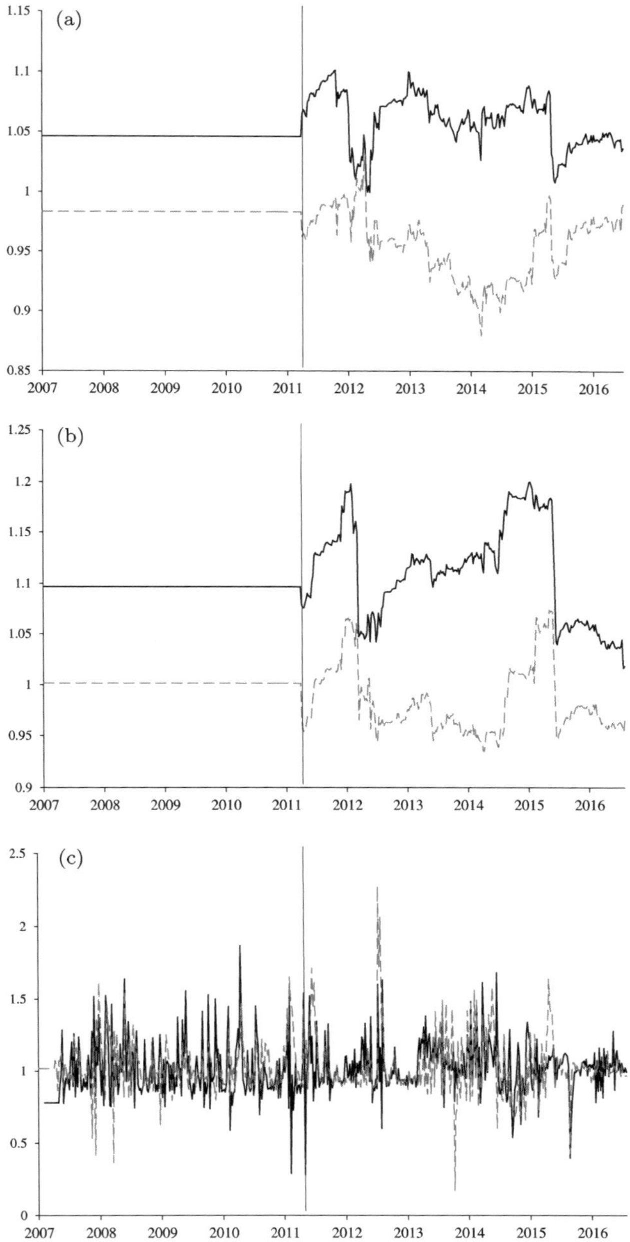

Fig. 5. Hedging ratios (a) NCG (b) GASPOOL (c) BEKK hedging ratios for NCG and GASPOOL.

Notes: Figures (a) and (b) correspond to OLS hedging ratios, represented with continuous lines (——). those estimated with Eq. (8) and with dashed lines (- - -), those estimated using Eq. (4). BEKK hedging ratios are represented with continuous lines (——) for the NCG hub and with dashed lines (- - -) for the GASPOOL hub. A vertical line separates the *ex-post* and *ex-ante* (4-year moving window) hedging periods.

It is interesting to test if hedging ratios differ in summer and winter. In the *ex-post* period, the BEKK hedging ratio means are lower in summer than in winter for both hubs. In Table 6, we tested if these differences are statistically significant for the *ex-ante* period — and as Table 6 shows, they are significant, and therefore, we cannot accept equality in means for summer and winter at a 5% significance level (except for the hedging ratios obtained with the traditional methodology in both hubs). Regarding equality in volatility, equality in variance cannot be rejected at a 5% significance level for the BEKK, and the traditional model for NCG, and the E&S (2008) approach for GASPOOL. Apparently, although there are differences in summer and winter in terms of hedging, similar results (not reported here to save space) are obtained for those in Table 6 for monthly hedges. Therefore, we have obtained statistical evidence that optimal hedging ratios are usually higher and more volatile in winter.

In Tables 7 and 8, the variance reduction in the various hedging methods analyzed are displayed. The risk reduction for weekly hedges in NCG and GASPOOL are displayed in panels A and B of Table 7, respectively. The first important result to highlight is that the Ederington and Salas [2008] approach always produces greater risk reduction than the standard approach. The attained risk reduction for all the hedging strategies and for both hubs are always similar in the Ederington and Salas [2008] approach. For the NCG hub, the worst performing strategy, both for *ex-ante* and *ex-post* periods, is the BEKK hedge. Just the opposite happens with GASPOOL, where the greatest risk reductions are achieved with the BEKK hedging strategy for

Table 6. Seasonal hedging ratios.

	Summer mean	**Winter mean**	**Equality test**	**Summer volatility**	**Winter volatility**	**Equality test**
NCG						
BEKK	0.99	1.07	0.00	0.17	0.18	0.27
OLS with basis	1.06	1.05	0.00	0.01	0.02	0.01
OLS without basis	0.95	0.96	0.31	0.02	0.03	0.24
GASPOOL						
BEKK	0.98	1.08	0.00	0.21	0.23	0.03
OLS with basis	1.12	1.10	0.02	0.05	0.04	0.85
OLS without basis	0.99	0.98	0.46	0.03	0.04	0.03

Notes: This table reports the weekly mean and volatility (standard deviation) of weekly hedging ratios estimated using OLS with basis OLS without basis and BEKK in winter (October to March) and summer (April to September) for the *ex-ante* period. The *p-values* of the *Anova* and *Levene* statistics test for mean and variance equality, respectively, are reported.

Table 7. Hedging effectiveness in weekly hedges.

	In the sample		**Out of the sample**	
	Standard approach	**E&S(2008) approach**	**Standard approach**	**E&S(2008) approach**
	Panel (A). Hedging 1-week spot risk in NCG			
Period	Oct., 2007–Dec., 2011		Jan., 2012–Apr. 2017	
Spot variance (no hedged)	2.57	2.33	0.84	0.85
Hedging strategy	**Risk reduction (%)**		**Risk reduction (%)**	
Naive (b =1)	49.84	62.11	54.56	62.62
OLS w/o basis	49.86	62.00	54.52	62.08
OLS with basis	49.65	62.23*	54.25	62.75*
BEKK	47.33	61.98	50.53	60.71
	Panel (B). Hedging 1-week spot risk in GASPOOL			
Period	Sep., 2007–Dec., 2011		Jan., 2012–Apr. 2017	
Spot variance (no hedged)	2.68	2.54	1.02	1.01
Hedging strategy	**Risk reduction (%)**		**Risk reduction (%)**	
Naive (b =1)	51.01	64.16	45.97	54.30
OLS w/o basis	51.02	64.18	45.94	53.83
OLS with basis	50.55	64.66	45.48	54.58
BEKK	51.41	65.82*	43.31	56.49*

Notes: This table displays the risk reduction achieved by each hedging strategy: naive, OLS without basis (see Eq. (4)), OLS with basis (see Eq. (8)), and BEKK (see Eq. (11)). The in-sample results are computed using the first 4 years of data and then, a moving window of 4 years is used to compute the out-of-sample results. In the second row of each panel, the unhedged spot position variance is reported and constitutes the base to calculate the risk reduction achieved with each hedging strategy. This variance is computed as $VAR[\Delta^k S(t)]$ and $VAR[\Delta^k S(t) - \hat{\lambda}(F(t, T_k) - S(t))]$ in the 'standard' and Ederington and Salas (2008) approaches, respectively. Variance of each hedging strategy is computed as $VAR[\Delta^k S(t) - \hat{b}_t \Delta^k F(t, T_i)]$ and $VAR[\Delta^k S(t) - \hat{b}_t \Delta^k F(t, T_i) - \hat{\lambda}(F(t, T_k) - S(t))]$ in the standard and "E&S(2008)" approaches, respectively. Spot and futures variations are defined as in Table 1 and b_t represents the hedging ratio. *Ex-ante* hedging ratios are forecasted values in t–1, and each time the moving window sample moves ahead, the model is estimated again. Those strategies with the largest risk reduction in each panel are indicated with an asterisk (*).

both *ex-ante* and *ex-post* periods (56.49% and 65.82%, respectively). For NCG, the largest risk reduction is obtained with the OLS with basis strategy, 62.23% and 62.75% for the *ex-post* and *ex-ante* periods, respectively. For GASPOOL, the OLS without basis produces the poorest result for the out-of-sample period, 45.94%, for the in-sample period, the worst strategy is the naive, 64.16%, followed very closely by the OLS without basis strategy at 64.18%. In any case, the *ex-ante* period is the most suitable way to compare risk reductions because hedge strategies are compared using forecasted hedge ratios, and models are estimated every time a new observation is considered. We can observe that risk reduction for the standard

Table 8. Hedging effectiveness in long-time hedges.

	In the sample		Out of the sample	
	Standard approach	**E&S(2008) approach**	**Standard approach**	**E&S(2008) approach**
	Panel (A). Hedging 1 month spot risk in NCG			
Period	Oct., 2007–Dec., 2011		Jan., 2012–Apr. 2017	
Spot variance (not hedged)	7.46	6.63	3.85	3.03
Hedging strategy	**Risk reduction(%)**		**Risk reduction (%)**	
Naive (b =1)	50.29	65.13	60.84	74.29*
OLS w/o basis	54.44	67.95	56.09	68.45
OLS with basis	54.28	68.13*	57.47	70.09
	Panel (B). Hedging 1 month spot risk in GSP			
Period	Sep., 2007–Dec., 2011		Jan., 2012–Apr. 2017	
Spot variance (not hedged)	7.88	7.54	4.52	3.53
Hedging strategy	**Risk reduction (%)**		**Risk reduction (%)**	
Naive (b =1)	64.34	72.99	47.25	68.00*
OLS w/o basis	66.26	74.16	45.38	64.33
OLS with basis	66.18	74.25*	46.52	66.04

Notes: This table is similar to Table 7, but uses monthly data frequency and only linear regression and naive hedges because of a data sample restriction. The in-sample results are computed from the beginning of each time series until December 2011 for both NCG and GASPOOL. In the out-of-sample period, OLS hedging ratios b_t (see Eqs. (4) and (8)) are forecasted values and each time a new observation is added, the model is estimated again.

approach is around 50% for NCG and below 50% for GASPOOL. According to Carter [1999, Section 3.2], this is quite common for commodity hedging with futures when using the standard approach.

Table 8 displays the results for the monthly hedging period. The standard approach also produces worse results than the Ederington and Sala [2008] approach in this case. For the in-sample period, the greatest risk reduction is the "OLS with basis" for both hubs (68.13% in NCG and 74.25% in GASPOOL). The lowest risk reduction is obtained with the naive strategy. In the out-of-sample period, the naive strategy beats the others — and for both hubs (74.29% in NCG and 68.00% in GASPOOL). The worst performance in this *ex-ante* case is for the "OLS w/o basis" for both hubs.

Observing both tables, we can conclude there is a positive duration effect in hedging effectiveness. The achieved risk reduction is larger in 1 month than in the 1-week hedging period. Regarding risk reduction with OLS methodology, we cannot conclude that either with or without base is superior to the other. Although in Fig. 5

OLS weekly hedge ratios with basis are above those without basis, the reverse result is obtained for longer hedging periods.

Ederington and Salas [2008] show that when spot price returns are partially predictable, then more efficient estimates can be obtained. Nevertheless, risk reductions are not always higher when hedge ratios are estimated with this more efficient approach.

Finally, when comparing OLS and GARCH hedge ratio performances, results are inconclusive. Lien and Tse [2002, page 367] argue that the performance of GARCH hedge ratios is mixed, conventional hedging strategies perform as well as, or better than, GARCH strategies. Moreover, in some cases the best strategy is the naive strategy.

6. Conclusions

In this chapter, we follow the Martinez and Torro [2015] and Ederington and Salas [2008] framework. They argue that minimum variance hedge ratios can improve significantly when considering the expected change in spot prices, namely, past values of the basis are used to anticipate the seasonal trend of the spot price return. That is, using the information contained in the basis, part of spot shocks can be partially anticipated and substantial risk reduction attained, improving the effectiveness of hedging with regard to the standard approach, as we have seen in the results.

We have detected a positive duration effect in the hedging performance. Results can be considerably improved by increasing hedging duration. Risk reduction reaches values of between 43% and 74%, depending on the hedging duration (1 week or 1 month), and the sub-period considered (in-sample and out-of-sample sub-periods). There is no clear model that outperforms the others and even the naive model is the best in some cases. Moreover, the results are inconclusive when comparing OLS and GARCH hedge ratio performances.

Finally, we found that volatility of spot and futures price returns are significantly higher in winter than in summer — and show a clear and strong seasonal pattern. Seasonality is also found in hedging ratios. In the *ex-ante* period, this difference is statistically significant, being higher in winter than in summer.

Our results are of interest for financial risk managers with natural gas assets in their portfolios and those industries that use natural gas as the main input in the production process, such as electricity producers with gas-fired power plants. Achieving greater variance reduction and better hedging performance is an important issue for these agents in a context of declining prices and narrowing business margins. The chapter is also important for regulators because electricity producers with gas-fired power plants are seen as the least polluting and most flexible of all fossil fuels in providing backup for renewable energy sources.

Acknowledgments

Funding: This work was supported by the Spanish Ministry of Economy and Competitiveness [Grant No: ECO2013-40816-P]. We are particularly grateful for their assistance with data received from the European Energy Exchange (EEX). The preliminary version of this research was Vanesa García Seligrat master's thesis presented in the XIV Workshop in Banking and Quantitative Finance in Madrid, in July 2016.

References

Alexander, C., Prokopczuk, M. and Sumawong, A. (2013). The (de)merits of minimum-variance hedging: Application to crack spread. *Energy Economics* **36**, 698–707.

Alterman, S. (2012). Natural gas price volatility in the UK and North America. Oxford Institute for Energy Studies.

Bekaert, G. and Wu, G. (2000). Asymmetric volatility and risk in equity markets. *The Review of Financial Studies* **13**, 1–42.

Arismendi, J. C., Back, J., Prokopczuk, M., Paschke, R. and Rudolf, M. (2016). Seasonal stochastic volatility: Implications for the pricing of commodity options. *Journal of Banking and Finance* **66**, 53–65.

Bollerslev, T. (1986). Generalized autoregressive conditional heteroskedasticity. *Journal of Econometrics* **31**, 307–327.

Bollerslev, T. (1990). Modeling the coherence in short-run nominal rates: A multivariate generalized ARCH approach. *Review of Economics and Statistics* **72**, 498–505.

Bollerslev, T., Engle R. F. and Wooldrige, J. M. (1988). A capital asset pricing model with time varying covariances. *Journal of Political Economy* **96**, 116–131.

Bonga-Bonga, L. and Umoetok, E. (2016). The effectiveness of index futures hedging in emerging markets during the crisis period of 2008–2010: Evidence from South Africa. *Applied Economics* **48**, 3999–4018.

Carter, C. A. (1999). Commodity futures markets: A survey. *The Australian Journal of Agricultural and Resource Economics* **43**, 209–247.

Chang, C.-L., McAleer, M. and Tansuchat, R. (2011). Crude oil hedging strategies using dynamic multivariate GARCH. *Energy Economics* **33**, 912–923.

Cotter, J. and Hanly, J. (2012). Hedging effectiveness under conditions of asymmetry. *European Journal of Finance* **18** (2), 135–147.

Ederington, L. H. (1979). The hedging performance of the new futures markets. *Journal of Finance* **34**, 157–170.

Ederington, L. H. and Salas, J. M. (2008). Minimum variance hedging when spot price changes are partially predictable. *Journal of Banking and Finance* **32**, 654–663.

Efimova, O. and Serletis, A. (2014). Energy markets volatility modelling using GARCH. *Energy Economics* **43**, 264–273.

Engle, R. F. (1982). Autoregressive conditional heteroscedasticity with estimates of the variance of United Kingdom inflation. *Econometrica* **50** (4), 987–1007.
Engle, R. F. and Granger, C. W. (1987). Cointegration and error correction: Representation, estimation and testing. *Econometrica* **55**, 251–276.
Engle, R. F. and Kroner, K. F. (1995). Multivariate simultaneous generalized ARCH. *Econometric Theory* **11**, 122–150.
Engle, R. F. and Ng, V. K. (1993). Measuring and testing the impact of news on volatilily. *The Journal of Finance* **48**, 1749–1778.
Fama, E. F. and French, K. R. (1987). Commodity futures prices: Some evidence on forecast power, premiums, and the theory of storage. *Journal of Business* **60**, 55–74.
Glosten, L. R., Jagannathan, R. and Runkel, D. E. (1993). On the relation between the expected value and volatility of nominal excess return on stocks. *The Journal of Finance* **48**, 1779–801.
Hannan, E. J. and Quinn, B. G. (1979). The determination of the order of an autoregression. *Journal of the Royal Statistical Society B* **41**, 190–195.
Heather, P. (2012). Continental European Gas Hubs: Are they fit for purpose? Oxford Institute for Energy Studies, NG 63.
Heather, P. (2015). The evolution of European traded gas hubs. Oxford Institute for Energy Studies, NG 104.
Henaff, P., Laachir, I. and Russo, F. (2013). Gas storage valuation and hedging: A quantification of the model risk. Working paper. ArXiv:1312.3789v1[q-fin.PR] 13 Dec 2013.
Hendry, O. L. and Sharma, J. (1999). Asymmetric conditional volatility and firm size: Evidence from Australian equity portfolios. *Australian Economic Papers* **38**, 393–406.
ICIS White Paper (August 2017). German Natural Gas Hub Unification.
Ji, Q. and Fan, Y. (2011). A dynamic hedging approach for refineries in multiproduct oil markets. *Energy* **36**, 881–887.
Kroner, K. F. and Ng, V. K. (1998). Modeling asymmetric comovements of asset returns. *The Review of Financial Studies* **11**, 817–844.
Lien, D. (1996). The effect of the cointegration relationship on futures hedging: A note. *The Journal of Futures Markets* **16**, 773–780.
Lien, D. and Tse, Y. K. (2002). Some recent developments in futures hedging. *Journal of Economic Surveys* **16**, 357–396.
Lohmann, H. (2006). The German Path to Natural Gas liberalisation: Is It a Special Case? The Oxford Institute for Energy Studies, NG 14.
Martinez, B. and Torro, H. (2015). European natural gas seasonal effects on futures hedging. *Energy Economics* **50**, 154–168.
Mu, X. (2007). Weather, storage and natural gas price dynamics: Fundamentals and volatility. *Energy Economics* **29**, 46–63.
Nick, S. and Thoenes, S. (2014). What drives natural gas prices? — A structural VAR approach. *Energy Economics*, **45**, 517–527.
Suenaga, H., Smith, A. and Williams J. (2008). Volatility dynamics of NYMEX natural gas futures prices. *The Journal of Futures Markets* **28**, 438–463.
Viswanath, P. V. (1993). Efficient use of information, convergence adjustments, and regression estimates of hedges ratios. *The Journal of Futures Markets* **13**, 43–53.
Wang, Y. and Wu, C. (2012). Forecasting energy market volatility using GARCH models: Can multivariate models beat univariate models? *Energy Economics* **34**, 2167–2181.
Yang, W. (2001). M-GARCH Hedge Ratios and Hedging Effectiveness in Australian Futures Markets. School of Finance and Business Economics, Edith Cowan University.

Chapter 24

An Alternative Valuation of Energy Options for Atypical Markets

David G. Carmichael[*,‡] and Maria C. A. Balatbat[†,§]

[*] *School of Civil and Environmental Engineering, University of New South Wales, Sydney, NSW 2052, Australia*

[†] *UNSW Business School, University of New South Wales, Sydney, NSW 2052, Australia*

[‡] *D.Carmichael@unsw.edu.au*

[§] *m.balatbat@unsw.edu.au*

Energy has unique features in terms of storage, transportation and consumption, while the energy price in deregulated markets exhibits its own uncertainty, volatility, spikes and seasonality characteristics. Hedging with energy options (energy derivatives) provides one way that players in the market deal with the price uncertainty and associated risk. Common financial option pricing tools, such as modified Black–Scholes and binomial and trinomial lattices, can be used to value the options. However, in atypical markets, including those where something unforeseen happens in energy production or supply, or there are changes in economic conditions or external factors, such pricing tools may not apply. This chapter shows how energy options can be valued in such atypical markets. The approach adopts a probabilistic present worth analysis based on isolating the cash flows, with the approach's strengths being that it is intuitive to understand, straightforward to implement and requires low mathematical sophistication. Different types of energy options are explored — plain call and put options, spark spread options and swing options, and options associated with callable and putable forwards. As background to the approach, the peculiarities of the Australian context on derivatives, trading and energy prices are given, including comment on the differences between the country's various States on practices, sources of energy including renewables and varied climate effects.

Keywords: Energy options; financial options; real options; derivatives; atypical markets; probabilistic present worth; cash flow view; alternative options analysis; intuitive approach; Australian context.

1. Introduction

The liberalization and deregulation of energy markets have occurred and are occurring in a number of countries, in order to introduce competition, to increase efficiency, transparency and accountability, and to transform energy markets from centralized to competitive [Girish and Vijayalakshmi, 2013]. Energy is a unique, traded commodity, in terms of storage, transportation and consumption. This uniqueness, in conjunction with economic and external factors, affects its price causing uncertainty, high volatility, seasonality and price spikes [Huisman and Mahieu, 2003; Geman and Roncoroni, 2006; Bierbrauer *et al.*, 2007]. Such characteristics have undergone considerable study. One way in which parties involved can deal with the risks [Carmichael, 2016b] associated with energy prices, is hedging with financial derivatives, such as energy options. An energy option grants the holder the right to buy and/or sell energy at a pre-agreed price. Common financial option pricing tools, such as modified Black–Scholes and binomial and trinomial lattices, can be used to value the options.

However, in atypical markets, including those where something unforeseen happens in energy production or supply, or there are changes in economic conditions or external factors, such pricing tools may not apply. This chapter shows how energy options can be valued in such atypical markets. The approach adopts a probabilistic present worth analysis based on isolating the cash flows, with the approach's strengths being that it is intuitive to understand, straightforward to implement and requires low mathematical sophistication. It relies on future probabilistic estimates of energy prices, which can be made by any means available to the user, and can incorporate experience, historical performance, knowledge of the market and knowledge of anticipated changes in economies or external factors. It does not rely on any predetermined time series describing the evolution of energy prices over time, though any existing knowledge on time series, trend lines and related forecast thinking can be used to inform these estimates.

In this chapter, the approach is outlined, demonstrated and compared with Black–Scholes. The different types of energy options explored are plain call and put options, spark spread options, swing options and options associated with callable and putable forwards.

The approach is based on discounting all cash flows involved in the option to their probabilistic present worth equivalent, and then interpreting the present worth distribution. For usual option calculations, the results are almost the same as those obtained using methods such as Black–Scholes, but the approach is capable of dealing with situations with far less restrictions than those assumed within Black–Scholes and other financial options analysis methods. Numerical results in Carmichael *et al.* [2011] and Carmichael [2014, 2016a] confirm the similar results. Both the Black–Scholes method and the probabilistic present worth approach can be shown to have structurally similar calculations. However, users are able to incorporate their individual perceptions in addition to any other information, qualitative or quantitative, that is available or can be forecast.

The outline of this chapter is as follows: The Australian context on energy markets is reviewed as background information of energy trading in that country. Energy derivatives are described before outlining this chapter's approach to evaluating options. The chapter's approach relies on establishing future estimates, and some suggested ways in which this might be done are outlined. The chapter then goes on to describe applications in different energy derivatives. A conclusion follows. The chapter will be of interest to anyone involved with derivatives in energy markets.

2. Background — Australian Context

2.1. *Deregulation and energy markets*

Prior to the 20th century, the energy market in Australia was a monopoly and only a single entity produced and distributed energy to the entire population. At the turn of the century, deregulation and restructuring of energy markets caused fundamental changes in the behavior of energy prices [Higgs and Worthington, 2008]. Today, in most States, there are multiple energy producers/providers who are importers and/or generators of energy, and there are also multiple energy retailers who buy energy from producers and sell to energy consumers. Table 1 shows the number of energy players in the Australian energy market post-deregulation.

Full retail contestability (FRC) in electricity and gas applies throughout most of Australia, allowing all energy consumers to enter a market contract with their retailer of choice. There are generally two types of consumer energy contracts: (1) standing contracts which are basic contracts that prescribe terms and conditions that the retailer cannot change, thus providing protection to consumers, and with no fixed term; and (2) market contracts which permit retailers to tailor their energy

Table 1. Deregulation year and number of players in Australia's energy market by State as of January 2017 [AER, 2017].

		Electricity market		Gas market	
State	**Year of deregulation**	**Producers**	**Retailers**	**Producers**	**Retailers**
Victoria	2002	6	23	3	11
New South Wales	2002	4	26	3	8
South Australia	2003	1	21	1	6
Queensland	2007	2	11	1	3
Western Australia	—	1	—	1	3
Tasmania	—	1	3	—	1
ACT	—	1	7	1	3

offers to consumers with more competitive contracts — tariff structures, discounted prices and billing options, among others [AER, 2017].

2.2. *Volatility in energy prices*

Deregulation has allowed energy retailers to interpose between producers and consumers. This has increased trading activity considerably both in the spot and derivative markets. Wholesale energy prices (spot prices) exhibit three particular characteristics: energy prices mean revert toward a level that represents marginal cost; there exists a small random fluctuation of price around the average trend which shows a temporary supply and demand imbalance in the network; and energy prices experience unanticipated price spikes. DPMC [2004] highlights the economic impact of energy price spikes. A supply and demand mismatch [Girish and Vijayalakshmi, 2013], price inelasticity, energy storage concerns and supply transportation difficulties explain the price characteristics of energy in Australia. Demand is very seasonal [Bierbrauer *et al.*, 2007].

Price volatility caused by weather is a bigger issue in Australia than other countries due to the el-Niño and la-Niña climate effects [Douglas *et al.*, 1998]. Temperature variability is a main driving factor in demand forecasting. As temperatures increase, there is a reduced capacity in energy transmission and distribution lines; this is a supply constraint and increases the marginal cost of production, which in turn increases energy prices.

Technology change impacts on the wholesale electricity and gas markets, while network costs are falling and new and innovative products and services are emerging [AER, 2017]. Energy producers occasionally require temporary shutdown for periodic maintenance, and this is usually scheduled at times where demand is anticipated to be low. During this time, producers may fall short in supply, and this contributes further to price fluctuation [Geman and Roncoroni, 2006]. Unexpected generator outages may also occur, and this causes more expensive capacity to be used, thus driving up wholesale prices.

2.3. *Energy sources*

Australia lags behind other developed nations in implementing renewable sources in energy production. Burning fossil fuels, including gas, coal and oil to produce energy, is the most dominant method used in Australia. From 2007 to 2008, fossil fuels accounted for over 90% of Australia's electricity generation [World Nuclear Association, 2012; DIIS, 2015]. Due to the large role fossil fuels hold on Australia's electricity generation, a fluctuating carbon price will contribute to the volatility of electricity.

2.4. *Derivatives market*

Both standardized agreements, which are traded on the Australian Securities Exchange (ASX), and non-standardized agreements, which are traded in over-the-counter (OTC) markets, exist. Standardized agreements are formal agreements and do not require physical contact of both parties. OTC derivatives have their terms negotiated between the parties. Energy derivatives are mainly traded in the OTC markets, and the most popular derivatives are forwards, swaps, plain vanilla options and exotic options such as spark spread options, and swing options [Deng and Oren, 2006].

3. Energy Derivatives

Derivatives are most commonly used for either speculating, or hedging risk, and depend on the underlying price of energy. Within energy markets, derivatives are useful for limiting risk associated with fluctuating prices. For example, a retailer purchasing energy from a producer can purchase forwards, lock-in a specific future energy price, and hedge any associated risk; the hedging enables retailers to protect themselves from high energy prices caused by unfavourable economic factors impacting the market. Options, used as a hedging tool, enable energy retailers to limit their exposure; if energy prices change greatly, retailers can exercise their options and transact at a contracted exercise price, either buying from or selling back to the producer.

The energy options covered below include: plain call and put options; spark spread options; callable and putable forwards; and swing options. These are in the form of contracts between two parties. A European option is exercised on a specified date; an American option can be exercised at any time before or on the specified date. The exercise price of an option is stated in the options contract, and may be negotiated between the buyer and the seller. The concept of options is said to have been utilized in the energy industry for many decades through terms and conditions of trade, however the US and UK restructuring and deregulation in the 1990s has promoted the more recent usage of options [Deng and Oren, 2006].

Options are also a speculative tool. They allow leverage in directional bets with a limit to any loss. This is so because options buyers are not required to exercise those options, and so losses can be limited to the up-front premium. In the energy market, options usually have short to medium maturity times ranging from months to a few years [Deng and Oren, 2006].

4. Option Valuation

The Black–Scholes equation is a commonly accepted method of evaluating European options. In the context of energy options, the underlying asset is the price of energy, and its movement is assumed to follow geometric Brownian motion with a constant volatility over time, while energy prices are assumed to be lognormally distributed; a constant risk-free interest rate is used. Users adjust the standard Black–Scholes' assumptions to suit their applications.

The Black–Scholes equation (call option) can be reinterpreted to provide directly an estimate of the value of an option using familiar present worth analysis and assumptions less-restrictive than that required for Black–Scholes.

The following refers to the exercise price (denoted K) and the price of energy (denoted S) as cash flows. From the buyer's viewpoint, for a call option, the exercise price is a regarded as a negative cash flow, while the energy price is regarded as a positive cash flow. Consider exercising at time T. At time T, energy prices (S_T) greater than K reflect the option value or upside.

Define the option value at time T, OV_T, as the expected value of the net cash flow at T, evaluated on the assumption that the option is only exercised if it is worthwhile (in the money, $S_T > K$). Then,

$$\mathrm{OV}_T = E^*[\text{Net cash flow}_T] = E^*[S_T - K],$$

where $E[\,]$ denotes expected value. To denote that the option is only exercised if it is worthwhile (in the money), the symbol * is used. This can now be discounted to time 0. Using continuous time discounting, in order to compare with Black–Scholes, an estimate of the option value at time 0 with an interest rate r is

$$\begin{aligned} \mathrm{OV} &= e^{-rT}\mathrm{OV}_T = E^*[e^{-rT}S_T - e^{-rT}K], \\ &= \text{Expected * PW of energy price} \\ &\quad - \text{Expected * PW of exercise price.} \end{aligned}$$

OV is evaluated assuming that the option is only exercised if it is worthwhile (in the money). In effect, OV is being calculated as in

$$\mathrm{OV} = e^{-rT}E[\max(S_T - K,\ 0)].$$

For a lognormal assumption on the energy price and a risk-free rate, this leads to Black–Scholes; a proof of this is given, for example, in Hull [2006].

That is, the call option value in Black–Scholes, and OV above are obtained through expressions that are structurally the same. In both cases, the assumption is that the option will only be exercised if it is worthwhile.

A distinction between the exercise price and the energy price was made above in order to make a comparison with Black–Scholes and for no other reason. However, in terms of getting to OV, there is no need to make this distinction; both the energy price and the exercise price are treated as cash flows. Accordingly, assuming that the option is only exercised if it is worthwhile, that is there is no exercising (probability of zero) if the present worth is negative,

$$\begin{aligned} \mathrm{OV} &= E^*[\mathrm{PW}] \\ &= (1-\Phi)\times 0 + \Phi \times M \\ &= \Phi M, \end{aligned} \tag{1}$$

where PW is the present worth of all cash flows at time 0, M is the mean of the present worth upside, and Φ is referred to as feasibility and equals $P[\mathrm{PW} > 0]$, the upside area in Fig. 1 [Carmichael, 2014, 2016a; Carmichael *et al.*, 2011]. The mean of the present worth upside is measured from PW = 0. The situation at time 0 is shown in Fig. 1. The term "upside" is used here to denote positive present worth, and represents a worthwhile deal. Φ and M are perhaps most easily evaluated numerically. Denoting X as present worth and $f_X(x)$ as the present worth distribution,

$$\Phi = \int_0^{\infty} x f_X(x)dx;$$

$$M = \frac{\int_0^{\infty} x f_X(x)dx}{\int_0^{\infty} f_X(x)dx}.$$

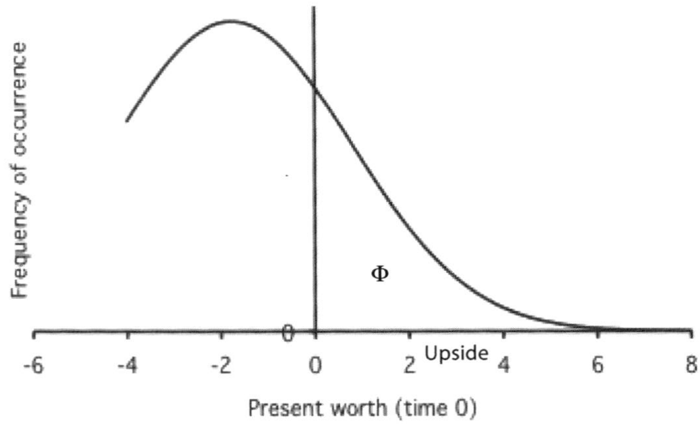

Fig. 1. Example of present worth distribution of $[S_T - K]$ at time 0, showing the upside and feasibility, Φ.

All options can be valued by the single Eq. (1). For example, a put option is treated no differently to a call option. Each option calculation is interpreted from the respective party's viewpoint. Everything which is favorable to a party is regarded as a cash inflow, and everything unfavorable is regarded as a cash outflow; strict accounting conventions need not be used. Any cash flows connected with exercising an option are discounted to give PW, and hence OV from Eq. (1). The discounting of the cash flows, which generally are random variables, can be done using Monte Carlo simulation, or as is done in this chapter, through a second order moment analysis. A second order moment analysis requires no assumptions to be made on the distributions of the cash flows, but rather works in terms of expected values, $E[\,]$, and variances, Var[ ], of the cash flows. Possible ways of estimating the expected values and variances of energy prices are discussed in the next section.

Higher uncertainty in energy prices leads to greater spread in the present worth distribution, and hence higher option values, as in Black–Scholes.

Put-call parity. Put-call parity can be shown to hold [Carmichael, 2014].

American option. For an American option, let the time to exercising the option follow a probability distribution. Let p_t be the probability that the exercise takes place in period t, $t = 0, 1, 2, \ldots, T$, and let $\mathrm{PW}_{(t)}$ be the associated present worth. Then,

$$E[\mathrm{PW}] = \sum_{t=0}^{T} p_t E[\mathrm{PW}_{(t)}],$$

$$\mathrm{Var}[\mathrm{PW}] = E[\mathrm{PW}^2] - \{\mathrm{E}[\mathrm{PW}]\}^2.$$

The choice of distribution for the exercise time is up to the user. Example, possible distributions are uniform where exercising is equally likely at any time up to T; a declining triangular distribution where the value of the option is perceived as decreasing with time; or a rising triangular distribution where exercising is more likely the closer time gets to T. The case $p_T = 1$ and $p_t = 0, t = 0, 1, 2, \ldots, T-1$ is the European option.

Differences with Black–Scholes. There are some differences in the assumptions of the chapter's approach compared with Black–Scholes. The most notable are mentioned here.

The approach does not assume that the underlying follows any particular time series such as geometric Brownian motion. No assumptions are made on the distribution of energy prices at any time; rather, with a second order moment approach, cash flows are characterized by their expected values and variances, and the present worth distribution can be chosen by the user. The exercise price need not be deterministic and a single value; Equation (1) allows for general exercise prices containing uncertainty and not necessarily a single value at one point in time. Uncertainty is incorporated through variance terms of the cash flows, and not through any volatility measure; uncertainty can vary throughout time and is not restricted to an equivalent constant volatility. Interest rates can be chosen to suit the user, can vary throughout time, and can be different for the exercise price and the energy price. Discounting may be either continuous time or discrete time.

Comparison with Black–Scholes. With comparable assumptions, Eq. (1) gives option values almost the same as Black–Scholes. Exact correspondence with Black–Scholes is not anticipated because a direct one-for-one substitution of variables is not possible. The variance in the energy price can be related to the energy price volatility [Hull, 2006]; however, it is sufficient to estimate the variance directly, where volatility may not be able to be established in an atypical market. A numerical example comparing the chapter's approach and Black–Scholes is given at the end of Section 6.

Adjustments. Like other methods such as Black–Scholes, over time users will come to understand the approach's strengths and weaknesses and what fine adjustments need to be made in order to suit particular user requirements.

5. Energy Price Estimates

Estimating is not a precise science, and invariably involves a combination of knowledge of: the market; historical trends; and national and international economies and events. This is coupled with experience, education and "gut feel" (a combination of logic and emotion).

Some suggested approaches are given here in summary form, and these might all be used in various combinations. In applying Eq. (1), users are free to adopt whatever methods they like in order to estimate the characteristics of future energy prices, and so estimating is not dealt with in detail in this chapter. The future price of energy is uncertain.

Time series models. Energy supply and demand data based on trading activities facilitate forecasts [Nogales *et al.*, 2002]. Uncontrollable and unanticipated factors lead to outliers, which may be removed from the data. Other mathematical manipulation of the raw data may occur, including the removal of seasonalities. However, time series models are not so useful in atypical markets, where the past does not carry forward to the future.

Time series models include those with unknown parameters where the "best" values of these parameters are established from the available data. Or approaches such as exponential smoothing and weighted moving average can be used where the past repeats. Trend functions or functions of best fit are similar in intent to time series models, and can be, for example, linear, polynomial, exponential, logarithmic or trigonometric. These might also be established in conjunction with qualitative manipulation, or industry data (e.g. [AEMO, 2017]).

Estimating moments directly. Estimating expected values and variances (moments) of energy prices or other variables directly may also be done in any reasonable way, but in the absence of anything else, the following approaches, among others, might be tried:

- Firstly, optimistic (a), most likely (b) and pessimistic (c) values are estimated as is done in PERT. This, then gives expected value or mean $= (a + 4b + c)/6$ and variance $= [(c - a)/6]^2$ (see e.g. [Carmichael, 2006; Carmichael and Balatbat, 2008]).
- As an example of this, the optimistic estimate might be taken as the value at the upper 5th percentile of the probability distribution. The pessimistic estimate might be taken as the value at the lower 5th percentile, with the most likely estimate taken as the mean of the distribution.
- A proxy approach to estimating variance can be used if the user has previous similar situations.
- Users may prefer to estimate maximum, minimum and most likely values, use a triangular distribution, and calculate an expected value and variance based on this.

- Dandy [1985] estimates a most likely value (M), an upper value (U), and a lower value (L), where the upper and lower values represent 95% confidence limits. Then, mean $= M$ and variance $= [(U - L)/3.92]^2$.
- The estimates might be based on historical data, experience, or subjective probability estimates and adjusted based on current news and forecasts of the future.
- A combination of the above.

Uncertainty in the energy price could be anticipated to increase with time; data will be less well known into the future. Such changes in uncertainty over time can be accommodated by assuming larger variances with time.

6. Plain Call and Put Options

Call and put options appear popular for hedging in the energy markets, with most options traded based on an agreement between the retailer and producer [Deng and Oren, 2006]. Energy retailers holding call options to hedge against a rise in energy prices, appear common. Energy retailers may also be able to sell back energy to the producers, creating a put option that enables the retailers to hedge against price drops when energy is to be returned. The option is only exercised when the energy price drops below the exercise price. These options have maximum losses capped at their premiums. Call and put options are also used for speculative purposes and are traded on a stock exchange.

Plain options enable retailers to meet supply obligations without serious harm to profit margins during periods of price increases, and when unexpected events such as price spikes and generator outages occur. Electricity producers can also hedge against events such as a generator outage through holding options.

History repeating. Assume, firstly, that the future will repeat the past, that is the future fluctuations in energy prices will be the same as the past. Black–Scholes and similar approaches deal with this. Values are required for a risk free interest rate, constant volatility and current energy price in order to establish the call or put option value. Black–Scholes and similar approaches are well established and won't be repeated here.

Atypical market. Where the market is atypical, Black–Scholes and similar approaches would generally not work. This chapter's approach, however, can deal with any market irregularities; it relies on making an informed estimate of the energy price (that at the time of exercizing T), S_T, and its uncertainty. The informed estimate can incorporate knowledge of the market, national and international economies, seasonality, experience, education, historical performance and "gut feel"; it does not have to accord with any pre-conceived time series modeling of energy prices, but would obviously be informed by such modeling. The earlier discussion on estimating energy prices is relevant. With a second order moment analysis in mind, estimates are made of the moments, $E[S_T]$ and $\text{Var}[S_T]$. Here, $E[\ ]$ denotes expected value, and Var[ ] variance. Both S_T and the exercise price, K, are discounted to time 0 to give the present worth, PW. Using a second order moment analysis (alternatively, Monte Carlo simulation could be used):

$$E[\text{PW}] = \frac{E[S_T] - K}{(1+r)^T},$$

$$\text{Var}[\text{PW}] = \frac{\text{Var}[S_T]}{(1+r)^{2T}},$$

where r is the interest rate.

With $E[\text{PW}]$ and Var[PW] in hand, any two-parameter probability distribution of the user's choice can be fitted to PW. The option value, OV, follows from Eq. (1).

Procedure. The following procedure can be adopted:

Estimate $E[S_T]$ and $\text{Var}[S_T]$.
Discount these together with K to give $E[\text{PW}]$ and Var[PW].
Fit any reasonable probability distribution to PW.
Calculate Φ and M, and hence OV.

The put option is obtained by looking at the other tail of the present worth distribution, and is evaluated in the same way as a call option, in both cases looking at the cash flows from the option holder's viewpoint, namely a cash inflow being positively viewed and a cash outflow being negatively viewed, irrespective of any accounting conventions.

Example and comparison with Black–Scholes. A numerical example is used to demonstrate the calculations involved as well as the closeness of the results of the chapter's approach and Black–Scholes.

Assume estimates of the energy price at $T = 1$ year, obtained via estimating optimistic, most likely and pessimistic values, are $E[S_T] = \$11.05$ and $\text{Var}[S_T] = (\$2.81)^2$. Prices are per unit of energy. These are discounted along with the exercise price of \$13.00 to give $E[\text{PW}] = -\$1.77$, and $\text{Var}[\text{PW}] = (\$2.55)^2$, for an interest rate of 0.10 per annum. Using a normal distribution for convenience (but users are free to use any appropriate distribution), OV = \$0.37.

To compare with Black–Scholes, it is first necessary to find the equivalent volatility. Here, the relationship between volatility and variance adopted is that given in Hull [2002]:

$$\sigma = \sqrt{\frac{\ln\left(\frac{\mathrm{Var}[S_T]}{E[S_T]^2} + 1\right)}{T}},$$

where σ is the volatility. This gives $\sigma = 0.25$. Discounting S_T, gives $S_0 = \$10.05$, leading to a Black–Scholes option value of \$0.42, a difference of \$0.05 or 0.4% as a proportion of the exercise price. Assumed PW distributions, other than a normal distribution, could make this difference smaller.

7. Spark Spread Options

Spark spread call options are European non-standardized cross-commodity options which grant the holder the right, but not an obligation, to pay $H \times S_{GT}$ on exercising at T, and in return receive one unit of electricity; H is the fuel heat rate and S_{GT} is the unit price of fuel at T [Hsu, 1998; Deng *et al.*, 2001].

Spark spread calls can be useful for energy producers by allowing them to hedge against unfavorable price movements and uncertainty in energy production inputs [Deng *et al.*, 2001]. The price of electricity is that at the time the spark spread option is exercised. The payoff relates to the difference between the energy price, S_{ET}, and $H \times S_{GT}$. Spark spread put options, which grant the holders the right but not an obligation to pay for one unit of electricity and receive $H \times S_{GT}$ at T, appear less common and more used for speculative purposes [Hsu, 1998].

History repeating. Where future fluctuations in energy prices will be the same as the past, Black–Scholes, with alteration, and similar approaches can deal with this. Such approaches are well established and won't be repeated here.

Atypical market. Where the market is atypical, Black–Scholes and similar approaches would generally not work. This chapter's approach however, as with plain call and put options, can deal with any market irregularities, and also incorporate uncertainty in the heat rate and exercise price.

Using the notation similar to Deng *et al.* [2001], a spark spread call option written on fuel G at a heat rate H, gives the option holder the right but not the obligation to pay H times the unit price of fuel G at T, and receive one unit of electricity.

Let S_{ET} and S_{GT} be the unit prices of electricity and fuel at time T, respectively. This chapter's approach relies on making informed estimates of S_{ET}, H and S_{GT}, and their uncertainty, as outlined earlier. With a second order moment analysis in mind, estimates are made of the moments $E[S_{ET}]$, $\mathrm{Var}[S_{ET}]$, $E[H]$, $\mathrm{Var}[H]$, $E[S_{GT}]$ and $\mathrm{Var}[S_{GT}]$. Let $K = H S_{GT}\, S_{GT}$ be the exercise price. Then, for H and

S_{GT} independent,

$$E[K] = E[H]E[S_{GT}],$$
$$\text{Var}[K] = E^2[H]\text{Var}[S_{GT}] + E^2[S_{GT}]\text{Var}[H] + \text{Var}[H]\text{Var}[S_{GT}];$$

and

$$E[\text{PW}] = \frac{E[S_{ET}] - E[K]}{(1+r)^T},$$
$$\text{Var}[\text{PW}] = \frac{1}{(1+r)^{2T}}\left[\text{Var}[S_{ET}] + \text{Var}[K] - 2\text{Cov}[S_{ET}, K]\right].$$

For any of the above variables being deterministic, then its variance is zero. The option valuation then proceeds as for the plain call option. The put option also proceeds similarly.

8. Forwards

Forwards are contracts between a producer and a retailer, and contain agreed set terms and conditions for trading energy at some point in the future. Forwards are non-standardized derivatives and are thus traded over the counter. This allows negotiation between the producers and retailers. Forwards are valued based on past prices. A forward contract holds no value itself; its value is that of the underlying at the time of maturity. In energy derivatives, forwards may not be used alone, but rather include derivatives [Kamat and Oren, 2002].

A common hedging technique, which combines the use of forwards and options, is callable and putable forwards. A callable forward involves one party to the contract to buy (long) one forward and sell (short) one call option with a predetermined exercise price. The other party holds the opposite position. In putable forwards, one party buys (long) one forward contract and sells (short) a put option. The other party holds the opposite position. The effect of these trades is to hedge the risk associated with price changes [Kamat and Oren, 2002]. Such options can be evaluated as for the plain call and put options developed above.

9. Swing Options

Swing options involve multiple exercise rights before the maturity date, but packaged as one. The volume of energy which is traded lies within a defined range [Jaillet *et al.*, 2004]. The exercise price of the contract is fixed throughout the life of the contract and is set at the beginning of each time period [Deng and Oren, 2006].

Swing options may be bundled with forward contracts. A commonly used method for pricing swing options is via dynamic programming and trinomial trees. The option valuation method outlined in this chapter, rather than say trinomial trees, could be used in conjunction with dynamic programming.

10. Conclusion

Energy prices are uncertain, and energy options provide one way of dealing with the associated risk. In atypical markets, including those where something unforeseen happens in energy production or supply, or there are changes in economic conditions or external factors, conventional option pricing tools may not apply. This chapter showed how energy options can be valued in such atypical markets. It offers a practical way of evaluating such options. The approach adopts a probabilistic present worth analysis based on isolating the cash flows, with the approach's strengths being that it is intuitive to understand, straightforward to implement and requires low mathematical sophistication. It relies on future probabilistic estimates of energy prices, which can be made by any means available to the user, and can incorporate experience, knowledge of the market and knowledge of anticipated changes in economies or external factors. The approach allows flexibility to allow the user to intuitively adjust the value of the option by incorporating any information known to the user. It does not rely on any predetermined time series describing the evolution of energy prices over time, though any existing knowledge on time series, trend lines and related forecast thinking can be used to inform these estimates.

The chapter explored different energy options including plain call and put options, spark spread options, callable and putable forwards and swing options, and demonstrated how these might be valued in atypical markets.

References

AEMO (2017). *Electricity Price and Demand*, Australian Energy Market Operation 2014, http://www.aemo.com.au/Electricity [August 30, 2017].

AER (2017). *State of the Energy Market May 2017*, Australian Energy Regulator, https://www.aer.gov.au/publications/state-of-the-energy-market-reports [August 29, 2017].

Bierbrauer, M., Menn, C., Rachev, S. T. and Truck, S. (2007). Spot and derivative pricing in the EEX power market. *Journal of Banking and Finance* **31** (11), 3462–3485.

Carmichael, D. G. (2006). *Project Planning, and Control*. (Taylor and Francis, London).

Carmichael, D. G. (2014). *Infrastructure Investment: An Engineering Perspective*. (CRC Press, Taylor and Francis, London).

Carmichael, D. G. (2016a). A cash flow view of real options. *The Engineering Economist* **61** (4), 265–288.

Carmichael, D. G. (2016b). Risk — A commentary. *Civil Engineering and Environmental Systems* **33** (3), 177–198.

Carmichael, D. G., Hersh, A. M. and Parasu, P. (2011). Real options estimate using probabilistic present worth analysis. *The Engineering Economist* **56** (4), 295–320.

Carmichael, D. G. and Balatbat, M. C. A. (2008). Probabilistic DCF analysis, and capital budgeting and investment — A survey. *The Engineering Economist* **53** (1), 84–102.

Dandy, G. C. (1985). An approximate method for the analysis of uncertainty in benefit-cost ratios. *Water Resources Research* **21** (3), 267–271.

Deng, S. J., Johnson, B. and Sogomonian, A. (2001). Exotic electricity options and the valuation of electricity generation and transmission assets. *Decision Support Systems* **30** (3), 383–392.

Deng, S. J. and Oren, S. S. (2006). Electricity derivatives and risk management. *Energy* **31** (6–7), 940–953.

DIIS (2015). *Energy in Australia 2015*, Department of Industry, Innovation and Science, Australian Government, www.industry.gov.au/oce [August 29, 2017].

DPMC (2004). *Securing Australia's Energy Future*, Department of the Prime Minister and Cabinet, Australian Government, http://www.pmc.gov.au, http://trove.nla.gov.au/work/17241630?selectedversion=NBD26776162 [August 30, 2017].

Douglas, A., Breipohl, A., Lee, F. and Adapa, R. (1998). The impacts of temperature forecast uncertainty on Bayesian load forecasting. *IEEE Transactions on Power Systems* **13** (4), 1507–1513.

Geman, H. and Roncoroni, A. (2006). Understanding the fine structure of electricity prices. *The Journal of Business* **79** (3), 1225–1261.

Girish, G. and Vijayalakshmi, S. (2013). Determinants of electricity price in competitive power market. *International Journal of Business and Management* **8** (21), 70–75.

Higgs, H. and Worthington, A. (2008). Stochastic price modelling of high volatility, mean-reverting, spike-prone commodities: The Australian wholesale spot electricity market. *Energy Economics* **30** (6), 3172–3185.

Hsu, M. (1998). Spark spread options are hot! *The Electricity Journal* **11** (2), 28–39.

Huisman, R. and Mahieu, R. (2003). Regime jumps in electricity prices. *Energy Economics* **25** (5), 425–434.

Hull, J. C. (2002). *Options, Futures and Other Derivatives*, 5th edn. (Prentice Hall, Upper Saddle River, New Jersey).

Hull, J. C. (2006). *Options, Futures and Other Derivatives*, 6th edn. (Prentice Hall, Upper Saddle River, New Jersey).

Jaillet, P., Ronn, E. I. and Tompaidis, S. (2004). Valuation of commodity-based swing options. *Management Science* **50** (7), 909–921.

Kamat, R. and Oren, S. S. (2002). Exotic options for interruptible electricity supply contracts. *Operations Research* **50** (5), 835–850.

Nogales, F. J., Contreras, J., Conejo, A. J. and Espínola, R. (2002). Forecasting next-day electricity prices by time series models. *IEEE Transactions on Power Systems* **17** (2), 342–348.

World Nuclear Association (2012). Australia's Electricity, http://www.world-nuclear.org/info/Country-Profiles/Countries-A-F/Appendices/Australia-s-Electricity/ [May 22, 2014].

Chapter 25

Non-Financial Firms Hedging Risks in East Asia: The Link Between Financial Derivatives Use, Firm Value and Exposures to Country Risks

Trang Kim* and Quang Nguyen†

*Department of Banking and Finance, Foreign Trade University, 91 Chua Lang ST., Dong Da Dist, Hanoi, Vietnam

†Business School, Middlesex University, London NW4 4BT, UK

Derivatives have been used widely in the world over the last 30 years as an important risk management instrument. Although theoretical researchers suggest that derivatives usage can enhance value of a firm by alleviating costs arising from several market imperfections, the existing evidence is not quite consistent among empirical studies up to date. The purpose of this chapter, therefore, aims to examine determinants of derivatives use, a relationship between derivatives use, firm value and exposures for a sample of 881 non-financial firms in eight East Asian countries in the 2003–2013 period. The analysis is based on a novel and manually collected data.

We find that firms in countries with lower corruption have more incentive to use financial derivatives and use derivatives with greater intensity than those firms located in highly corrupt countries. Better governance induces firms to use derivatives to hedge exposure and mitigate costs. Firms in countries with weak governance use derivatives for speculating and/or selective hedging or self-management purposes. Overall, our findings provide strong evidence of the role of countries' governance quality in driving firms' derivatives-related behaviors. This macro-based effect on derivatives use is independent from firm-specific factors, which are frequently invoked by hedging theories.

Regarding relationship between firm value and derivatives use, using Tobin's Q as a proxy of firm value, we find that low corruption level of home country (host country) induces the use of financial derivatives and rewards domestic firms and domestic MNCs (foreign affiliates) with higher value. Hedging behavior of domestic MNCs outperforms domestic firms and foreign affiliates in terms of firm value. Derivative usage is value-enhancing activity for domestic firms and domestic MNCs, but it does not add value for foreign affiliates.

Finally, we measure exposure to home (host) country risks, and provide novel evidence that financial hedging of domestic firms and domestic MNCs reduces exposure to home country risks by 10.91% and 14.42% per 1% increase in national derivative holdings, respectively, while affiliates of foreign MNCs fail to mitigate exposure to host country risks. Domestic MNCs with derivatives activities reduce exposures of a larger magnitude than do other firms.

Keywords: Derivatives use; hedging behavior; firm value; exposures; country risk exposures; non-financial firms; risk management; domestic MNCs; domestic firms; foreign affiliates.

1. Introduction

This chapter focuses on one of the most talked-about financial instruments among both academics and policy makers: derivatives. A key feature of derivatives is that their prices are dependent upon or derived from one or more underlying financial assets. The most common types of financial derivatives include foreign exchange, interest rate and commodity price derivatives. These instruments aim to protect participants in financial markets from adverse movements in prices of the underlying assets. Following the deregulation of interest rate controls and the adoption of floating exchange rate system in many countries, especially the global financial crisis of 2007–2008, the movements of interest rates and foreign exchange rates have become much more volatile. Facing increasing volatility of financial risks, managers in many companies have been using derivatives as one of the most important hedging strategies.

Derivatives have been used widely in the world, and contributed significantly to the strong growth and innovation of financial markets over the last 30 years. Given the global scale and trading volume of derivative markets, derivatives have become more complicated and interconnected. The Bank for International Settlement reports that at the end of June 2015, and at the end of December 2014, the global OTC derivatives notional amount outstanding contracts are USD 553 trillion, and USD 630 trillion [BIS, 2014, 2015]. These figures indicate that derivatives are one of the main pillars in the global financial system. In addition, globalization and capital liberalization speeding up enormously over the past decades have encouraged firms to increasingly involve themselves in international operations, many firms are no longer uni-national domestic firms but multinational corporations (henceforth MNCs). By going global, firms are increasingly exposed to market and financial risks. Thus, risk management is going hand-in-hand with globalization, and one of the strategies that firms apply is to use financial derivatives. The survey of the International Swaps and Derivatives Association shows that over 94% of the world's top 500 companies actively use financial derivatives to hedge their various exposures [ISDA, 2009].

However, the rationales for hedging have not been well sustained. According to the irrelevance proposition of Modigliani and Miller [1958], in an efficient market, hedging activities should have no impact on a firm's value. Some studies have theoretically shown that hedging can increase firm value by reducing costs arising from several market imperfections such as taxes, agency problems, bankruptcy and financial distress, managerial incentives, information asymmetries, and economies of scale. Nevertheless, many empirical studies do not find evidence supporting those propositions. For example, Graham and Rogers [2002], Charumathi and Kota [2012]. Moreover, Bartram, Brown and Fehle [2009] indicate that traditional theories have little power to explain a firm's decision on using derivatives.

Yung-Ming Shiu [2010] classifies derivatives use studies into two categories: The first is to identify the determinants of decisions on derivatives use. Another strand of research is to examine the effect of derivative use on risk exposure, and firm value. In fact, the extant empirical evidence on this area is still mixed. Some studies find positive relationship between derivatives use and firm value (e.g. [Allayannis and Weston, 2001; Clark and Judge, 2009; Campello *et al.* 2011; Chen and King, 2014]), and negative association between exposures and derivatives usage (see [Nguyen and Faff, 2010; Zhou and Wang, 2013]). However, some researchers find opposite evidence or no evidence (e.g. [Fauver and Naranjo, 2010; Clark and Mefteh, 2011]). Therefore, the incentives for using financial derivatives and the effect of derivatives use on firm value or exposures are still an open question. Judge [2006b] indicates that whichever it is, one thing is certain, existing research has only touched the surface and many unresolved issues remain.

Although there is a wide range of literature on country and international evidence on this area, most empirical studies focus on the derivatives usage of US non-financial firms. Besides, there is a growing literature on derivatives in developed countries, and emerging countries, but the research in East Asian firms is still relatively scarce, even though there has been large increase in using derivatives in these countries. The annual survey of the Future Industry Association in 2015 reveals that trading in Asia-Pacific is around $7.25 billion, accounting for about one-third of global trading volume [FIA, 2015].

The purpose of this chapter, therefore, aims to examine determinants of derivatives use, impacts of derivatives usage on firm value, and a relationship between derivatives use and multifaceted exposures in eight East Asian countries over the period of 2003–2013 by using the unique hand-collected data containing information about derivatives activities of 881 non-financial firms across 34 different industries. Our sample consists of countries with different economic and financial development levels, from the world's third and second largest economies (Japan, China) to newly industrialized countries (Singapore, Hong Kong) and then emerging markets (Thailand, Philippines, Indonesia, Malaysia).

Additionally, these sample countries are also heterogeneous in terms of economic, political and business environments. In particular, governance mechanism varies among East Asian countries. Some countries share the same governance quality as that of the US, and other developed countries. Some are more problematic because of less transparent markets, weaker law enforcement and lower government effectiveness. Such variation provides us a natural laboratory to explore the effect of country governance mechanism on derivatives use. Further, there is huge difference in corruption levels of the sample countries. For example, according to the most recent 2015 survey of the Transparency International, in which a higher score represents less corruption, Philippines and Indonesia are at low scores of 35 and 36 out of 100, respectively, while Singapore scores a high 85 relative to Japan at 75. Likewise, our sample countries have different degrees of country risks, for example Singapore has AA grade while grades of Indonesia and Thailand are B.[1] Such heterogeneity allows us to examine whether differences in firms' behaviors of using derivatives across countries can be explained by differences in institutional environments. Doing so, our study may provide further insights into an emerging literature linking macro and firm-specific factors.

We first investigate the link between incentives to use derivatives of non-financial firms and countries' governance quality. Determining a firm's motivation for using derivatives is vital for at least two reasons: First, it helps managers diagnose what sources enhance firm value, because given a type of market imperfection, benefits of derivatives use differ across different firms. Second, it induces managers to figure out what type of risk(s) should be hedged and identity targets of hedging, so that they can conduct an effective hedging strategy.

Differentiating from prior studies, we focus on the role of country-specific factors, specifically governance quality, in shaping firms' decisions on using derivatives. The reason motivating us to conduct this study is that the sample countries are heterogeneous in terms of economic, political and social environments. The relatively large variation in country-specific characteristics gives us a unique

[1]Euler Hemes. 2015. *Country risk rating March 2015.*

opportunity to explore other determinants than firm's specific factors — which are frequently invoked by hedging theories. Additionally, as a matter of fact that although the literature on derivatives use has been blossoming, most empirical studies focus on US non-financial firms. Meanwhile, research on hedging behavior of East Asian firms is still very limited, even though they have become the world's key derivative users as we presented above. Further, given many of our firms (nearly 45%) are domestic, 48.23% is domestic MNC headquarters, we would expect the role of country's specific characteristics to become more salient in determining derivatives use.

We then explore the value implication of derivatives usage on domestic firms, domestic MNCs, and foreign affiliates conditional on corruption environments in home and host countries. The motivation behind this research comes from the following reasons. First, although the previous studies provide significant insights into the relationship between derivatives use and firm value, drivers of value implication are not limited to the structural characteristics of firm-specific resources and capabilities, as all firms are embedded in institutional environments. As a matter of fact, corruption has become the norm rather than exception worldwide today and firms regularly engage in corrupt practices such as bribery [Beets, 2005]. In East Asian countries, corruption is a serious problem.[2] Thus, without directly taking into account the corruption environment, it would be difficult to determine whether the use of derivatives is a value-enhancing activity.

Second, scholars have neglected what type of firm the value effect of derivatives use is greater (or less), and what factors determine such difference. Undertaking this research need, we shed new light on this gap by examining how value effects of derivatives use vary across domestic firms, domestic MNCs and foreign affiliates. Third, although there are numerous studies on effects of financial crisis on economic area, little has been done to analyze its impacts on derivatives use. Thus, we investigate the dynamic of relationship between derivatives use and firm value when firms face exogenous shocks brought about by the 2007–2008 global financial crisis. Our study does not merely investigate consequences of the global financial crisis on value implication of derivatives usage, but focuses on the role of corruption levels in mitigating adverse effects.

We finally scrutinize the impact of derivatives usage on exposures to country risks, exchange rate and interest rate risks by the following types of firm: Domestic firms, domestic MNCs and foreign affiliates. Our research is inspired by the

[2]According to the Transparency International, in 2013, 64% of these countries scored below 50 in perceived level of public corruption.

following reasons. First, while we have long learned over the last decades about exposures to exchange rate, and sometimes interest rate exposures; to the best of our knowledge, the research linking derivatives use with exposure to country risk is non-existent in the current literature. Thus, our study aims to estimate exposure to home (host) country risks and investigates the relationship between derivatives use and those types of exposure.

Second, whether MNCs are more exposed than domestic firms and other firms are not well understood because most of the prior studies on exposures and derivatives use rule out domestic firms by explicitly focusing on MNCs, while a purely domestic firm still is exposed to market risks. Therefore, we examine the link between derivatives use and exposures on the comparison of domestic firms, domestic MNCs and foreign affiliates. We also consider how this link is moderated by the 2007–2008 global financial crisis.

Third, in recent years many interest rates exhibited volatility as the exchange rates, presenting a comparably important source of risk to firms as exchange rate risks, but up to date little has been done on interest rate exposure of non-financial firms in general, and on link between that exposure and derivatives use in particular. Thus, we aim to present comprehensive analysis of the relationship between derivatives use and interest rate exposure for a large sample of cross-country non-financial firms.

Our main findings can be summarized as follows: We found that firms in countries with lower corruption levels have a greater incentive to use financial derivatives and use derivatives with greater intensity than those firms located in highly corrupt countries. Better governance induces firms to use derivatives to hedge exposure and mitigate costs. Firms in countries with weak governance use derivatives for speculative and/or selective hedging or self-management purposes. Secondly, using Tobin's Q as a proxy for firm value, we find that low corruption levels induce the use of derivatives, and reward domestic firms and domestic MNCs with higher value. The hedging behavior of domestic MNCs outperforms domestic firms and foreign MNC affiliates in terms of firm value. Derivative use is a value-enhancing activity for domestic firms and domestic MNCs, but it has an insignificant effect on foreign MNC affiliates. Finally, we provide novel evidence that financial hedging of domestic firms and domestic MNCs reduces exposure to home country risks by 10.91% and 14.42% per 1% increase in notional derivative holdings, respectively, while affiliates of foreign MNCs fail to mitigate exposure to host country risks. Domestic MNCs with derivatives activities reduce exposures of a larger magnitude than do other firms.

We proceed with the remainder of this chapter as follows: Section 2, reviews the literature on incentives for derivatives use in East Asia, provides the theoretical background, discusses the existing empirical literature on this area and develops hypotheses. Section 3 describes our sample, identifies variables and presents empirical specifications. Section 4 reports and discusses empirical analyses. Section 5 concludes the chapter.

2. Literature Review and Hypothesis Development

2.1. *Literature on derivatives use*

Financial derivatives are defined as financial instruments whose prices are dependent on/derived from the value of other, more basic, underlying variables [Hull, 2012]. An underlying variable is an asset, reference rate, or index from which a derivative inherits its principal source of value [Kolb and Overdahl, 2003]. More specifically, Gupta [2006] states that the underlying assets or instruments can be equity shares, stocks, bonds, debentures, treasury bills, foreign currencies, interest rates, commodity prices, or different market indices such as stock market indices, consumer price indices, etc. Thus, based on diversified underlying variables, a large number of financial derivatives have been used extensively all over the world in the last few decades. However, in the context of this chapter, we focus on the types most widely used by non-financial firms in different countries to manage market risks: foreign currency, interest rate and commodity price derivatives. When the underlying variables are foreign currencies, interest rates and commodity prices, the types of derivatives will be foreign currency, interest rate and commodity price derivatives, respectively.[3]

Modigiliani and Miller's [1958] seminal paper shows that in an efficient market, the financing policies of firms are irrelevant; that is, hedging or derivatives use does not affect firm value. Hence, the incentives of hedging depend on the degree to which the use of derivatives effectively addresses market imperfections, such as corporate taxes (see [Smith and Stulz, 1985; Mayers and Smith, 1990]), financial distress or bankruptcy costs (see [Nance *et al.* 1993; Froot *et al.* 1993]), or agency costs of debts (see [Mayers and Smith, 1982; Bessembinder, 1991]).

[3]Foreign currency, interest rate and commodity price derivatives are settled at a specific future date, and their values are derived from changes in foreign currencies (exchange rates), interest rates and prices of commodities, respectively.

Existing evidence, however, provides mixed support for hedging theories. Judge [2006] finds a strong relationship between financial distress costs and foreign currency hedging decisions, much stronger than that found in many previous studies in the UK. Recently, Chen and King [2014] examined 1,832 US non-financial firms and presented significant evidence consistent with financial distress cost arguments. In contrast, Charumathi and Kota [2012] state that there is no evidence supporting this hypothesis. Supanvanij and Stauss [2010] find that tax loss carried forward is an important factor in determining the use of foreign currency derivatives, while Kumar and Rabinovitch [2013] indicate that foreign tax credits are in the direction hypothesized and firms use derivatives to increase the present value of tax losses. In contrast, Sprcic and Sevic [2012] find that the evidence in favor of the tax hypothesis is very weak, while Gay *et al.* [2011] do not find any evidence in support of the tax incentive to increase debt capacity.

Empirical studies on testing the agency costs of debt theory also provide inconclusive evidence. Chen and King [2014], among others, find evidence to support the agency costs of debt theory. However, Charumathi and Kota [2012] do not find evidence in support of the agency costs of debt hypothesis. This finding is consistent with a recent study by Lievenbruck and Schmid [2014] and earlier studies such as Nance *et al.* [1993].[4]

2.2. *Hypothesis development*

2.2.1. *Linking derivatives use and governance quality*

The institution-based view argues that a network of firms is a coordinated system of value-added activities whose structure is determined by the institutions that control or affect firms' objectives and behaviors [Dunning, 2003]. North [1990, 1994] was among the first to emphasize the importance of institutions. He considers institutions much more than background conditions and defines institutions as "rules of the game", including the formal rules (laws, regulations) and informal constraints (customs, norms, cultures) that organizations face. Institutions shape firm actions by determining transaction costs and transformation costs of production. As such, institutions play a key role in determining the organizational outcomes and effectiveness of organizations [Khanna and Rivkin, 2001] as well as framing their organizational strategic choices [Peng *et al.*, 2005]. In addition, Jiang and Peng [2010] point out that from institution-based standpoint, firms are embedded

[4]Overall, Guay and Kothari [2003] suggest the need to rethink the past empirical research on firms' derivatives use.

in a nexus of formal and informal institutions, while from a resource-based view, multiple blockholders such as governments or financial institutions represent valuable resources which may confine firms' principal-principal conflicts.

Therefore, to better understand the determinants of firms' activities and their effects, it is necessary to consider institutional influences inside the firm and the external environment where firms operate simultaneously. Dunning and Lundan [2008] introduce a theoretical framework in the context of the OLI paradigm [Dunning, 1988] in order to accommodate both firm- and country-specific considerations. The *ownership* advantages (O) in the OLI paradigm now include institutional ownership advantages (Oi), which comprise the firm-specific characteristics and an indentation of the institutional environment (L attributes) [Cantwell *et al.* 2010]. On the other hand, the institutionally related *location* advantages of countries (Li) allow for the interdependence between the firm and national institutions on both the micro and macro levels. Thus, in the chapter we incorporate institutional theory (e.g. [North, 1990, 1994; Dunning, 2003; Peng *et al.* 2005]) and Dunning's OLI paradigm [Dunning, 1988; Dunning and Lundan, 2008] into the analysis of derivative activities. This approach sheds a new light on the hedging theory (e.g. [Smith and Stulz, 1985; Mayers and Smith, 1990; Nance *et al.* 1993; Froot *et al.* 1993]), which concentrates mainly on firm-specific characteristics. Through this research approach, we intend to show whether a firm's decision on using financial derivatives is determined by factors within that firm's boundary and we argue that it is necessary to improve hedging theory as well as the variables to measure determinants of derivatives use.

Within the literature on hedging, although studies on traditional hedging theories are abundant, few empirical studies have investigated the link between differences in cross-country characteristics and firms' use of derivatives. Furthermore, the findings of these studies provide mixed evidence. For example, Lievenbruck and Schmid [2014] together with Lel [2012] obtained a significant association between GDP per capital and the use of derivatives in the predicted directions, although Lievenbruck and Schmid only found supporting evidence in the case of commodity price derivatives use. The effect of financial risk is always statistically significant but inconsistent with the hypothesized prediction (see [Bartram *et al.* 2009]). Likewise, regulatory quality and long-term interest rates are insignificant, while the effect of inflation rate and long-term exchange rate are very weak (see [Bartram *et al.* 2009; Livenbruck and Schmid, 2014]).

Thus, our study explores countries with great variances in terms of economic, political and social environments. Hence, we expect to observe differences in derivatives use due to the differences in governance mechanisms.

Governance mechanisms

Governance quality of a country in general represents attributes of legal systems, institutions, regulations and policies established by its government that help to define that country's business and economic environments, frame for legal and social relations, and condition effectiveness and transparency of the government and political institutions [Knack, 2001]. Kaufmann *et al.* [2005], Oh and Oetzel [2011] show that the quality of a country's governance has significant influence on its government's ability and willingness to respond to economic volatility. In a weakly governed country with high levels of political uncertainty, government's poor organizational capabilities are less effective at responding to unexpected economic events than in a well-governed country [Oh and Oetzel, 2011]. Furthermore, according to Globerman and Shapiro [2003], governance mechanisms consist of institutions and policies targeting economic, legal and social relations. Good governance mechanisms value "independent judiciary and legislation, fair and transparent laws with impartial enforcement, reliable public financial information and high public trust" [Li, 2005, p. 298]. As such, good governance mechanisms are able to reduce transaction, production and R&D costs, leading to reductions in the variability of firms' profitability and high-return, low-risk investments [Ngobo and Fouda, 2012]. They implement policies that favor free and open markets and form effective and non-corrupt institutions [Globerman and Shapiro, 2003]. On the contrary, poor governance mechanisms increase costs and uncertainty [Cuervo-Cazurra, 2008], and they can lead to smaller, more volatile and less liquid stock markets in emerging economies [Lin *et al.* 2008] as well as a lack of transparent financial data and other information on firms and a shortage of specialized financial intermediaries [Khanna *et al.* 2005].

In this study, we investigate two aspects of governance mechanisms: Corruption and quality of governance system, which is measured by regulatory quality, government effectiveness and rule of law. Corruption is the key dimension of governance quality as it reflects the exercise of public power for private gain [Kaufmann *et al.* 2005]. It is said that "illegal payments are generally expected throughout lower levels of government", which are in kinds of "bribes connected with import and export licences, exchange controls, tax assessment, police protection, or loans" [Knack, 2001, p. 327]. Regulatory quality, government effectiveness and rule of law are additional aspects of country governance quality. By these indicators, we refer to the ability of the government in formulating and implementing sound policies and regulations. We also refer to the quality of public and civil services and the degree of its independence from political pressures as well as the credibility of the government's commitment to such policies. While the concept of corruption is widely studied in the economics and international business areas, to our knowledge, there is currently no research linking corruption with derivatives use in the literature. Bardhan [1997], Quazi [2014] and others view corruption as a "grabbing hand" because it increases uncertainty and transaction costs, and one major cause of corruption is bad governance mechanisms [Lambsdorff, 2006]. When it is costly to transact, institutions matter, and when institutions matter, it is costly to transact [North, 1993]. Consequently, corruption gives rise to a shadow economy, which distorts firms' activities in financial markets and reduces the effectiveness of the government. Along this line, a large number of empirical evidence indicates that corruption directly deters economic growth and development, causing business environment to become more uncertain and less favorable for profit making (e.g. [Habib and Zurawicki, 2002; Lee and Hong, 2012]).

In Tufano's [1996] view, the two main streams of incentives to hedge include maximization of shareholder value and maximization of managerial utility. The former may consist of motivations related to market imperfections such as convex tax function, financial distress costs, underinvestment costs and economies of scale. The latter may include market imperfections related to information asymmetry and managerial risk aversion. However, firms in highly corrupt countries may face higher transaction costs due to bribe payments and related expenses [Brouthers *et al.* 2008], due to lower quality of infrastructure services, economic growth and financial stability [Rose-Ackerman, 1978, 1999], which in turn leads to higher hedging costs that may reduce the benefits or even make costs outweigh benefits, and eventually dampen the effectiveness of derivative activities. The existing literature also shows that a higher level of corruption is associated with higher borrowing cost, worse corporate governance and lower stock valuation. In their analyses, Donadelli *et al.* [2014] report that firms operating in highly corrupt countries tend to have relatively low returns. While those firms operating in countries with lower level of corruption can capitalize on the advantages generated by a more favorable institutional context for firms, which in turn has a positive influence on performance and profitability of firms [Levy and Spiller, 1994; Bergara *et al.*, 1998].

Building upon this insight, we propose the following hypothesis:

> **Hypothesis 1**: Firms located in countries with higher corruption levels are less likely to use derivatives.

Considering a globalized macroeconomic environment, we wonder whether corruption influences firms' decisions on derivatives use through firm-specific and country-specific characteristics. Conditional on the levels of corruption, various factors might play a role in explaining a firm's hedging behavior. Petrou [2015] along with Petrou and Thanos [2014] show that corruption often generates additional difficulties rather than opportunities for firms to benefit from non-market environments. In addition, a high level of corruption is associated with a sophisticated bribery system, discouraging firms from using derivatives as a risk management tool. We thus propose the following hypothesis:

> **Hypothesis 1a**: High levels of corruption discourage firms from using derivatives to reduce exposure as stated by hedging theory.

Likewise, we expect a positive relationship between firms' use of derivatives and quality of governance mechanisms. Several studies motivated by La Porta *et al.* [1997, 1998] emphasize that legal institutions (either laws or enforcement) play a significant role in explaining cross-country differences in financial development, decision-making and valuation, because laws and the quality of their enforcement determine the rights and operation of firms participating in financial systems. Beck and Levine [2008] note that finance can be considered a set of contracts. Because derivatives are financial contracts, we expect that legal institutions are likely to influence derivatives use. Finally, Bevan *et al.* [2004] note that an efficient legal infrastructure reduces institutional uncertainty as well as facilitates contract establishment and lowers transaction costs. We therefore propose that better governance mechanisms encourage firms to enter into derivatives contracts given the lower cost of hedging.

> **Hypothesis 2**: Firms located in countries with higher governance quality are more prone to use derivatives.

2.2.2. *Linking derivatives use and firm value by firm types*

We conjecture in the previous section that firms operating in countries with lower levels of corruption are more likely to use derivatives. Derivatives use under the influence of a corrupt environment does not have the same value effect on all types of firms. It is well supported in the international business literature that institutional environments shape firms' behavior and decisions, whether those firms are foreign-owned or domestic-owned, and also contribute to significant variations in the performance of different firm types (see [Henisz, 2000; Feinberg and Gupta, 2006; Eden and Miller, 2004]). Henisz [2000] and Feinberg and Gupta [2006] point out that firms usually shift resources and change investment activities in response to institutional hazards, while Eden and Miller [2004] state that due to institutional distance, MNCs might be at a disadvantage even when operating in the same institutional environments, and bear additional costs of doing business that local counterparts do not encounter. In this study, we investigate a dynamic relationship between derivatives use and firm value on comparison of foreign-owned firms (i.e. foreign MNC affiliates) and domestic-owned firms, the latter of which are categorized into domestic firms and domestic MNCs.

A particularly important distinction between domestic MNCs and foreign MNC affiliates is the assertion that the former's organizational routines and management processes are rooted in local institutional conditions [Bruton *et al.*, 2008], and that they have well-developed access to relevant information and knowledge regarding the local institutional setting that encourages effective running of their operations, including knowledge of the economy, social needs and preferences, norms, cultures and law [Nachum, 2003; Bell *et al.*, 2012]; foreign MNC affiliates, for their part, are embedded in the institutional settings of both their home and host countries, so they often experience "liability of foreignness" [Zaheer, 2015]. On the other hand, in spite of the fact that both domestic MNCs and domestic firms are actively embedded in local institutional settings, the fundamental distinction between them is based on multinationality. Thus, we follow Higón and Antolín [2012] in arguing that comparison of domestic MNCs and domestic firms reveals a multinationality effect, while comparison of domestic MNCs and foreign MNC affiliates reveals the effects of foreignness.

First, IB literature often argues that MNCs, in comparison with domestic firms, possess some firm-specific advantages (FSA)[5] that compensate for the high costs of international operation and enable them to compete successfully. Indeed, following OLI theory [Buckley and Casson, 1976; Dunning, 1977], IB scholars have found that MNCs should be able to exploit cost differentials on a global scale thanks to multinationality [Allen and Pantzalis, 1996; Chung *et al.*, 2010].

Multinationality gives domestic MNCs an ability to diversify the portfolios of firms, making MNCs' cash flows less dependent on domestic market-level cash flows [Krapl, 2015], ultimately decreasing the volatility of a company's cash flows and earnings, and thus improving firm value [Rugman, 1976; Khanna and Yafeh, 2005]. By virtue of multinationality, domestic MNCs themselves are likely to reduce the probability of bankruptcy [Michel and Shaked, 1986], overcome inefficiencies arising from high agency and information costs [Khanna and Yafeh, 2005], and provide shareholders with lower systematic and idiosyncratic risk and superior return opportunities relative to domestic firms [Fatemi, 1984]. Furthermore, domestic MNCs also develop expertise in hedging risks and are more likely to possess superior

[5]FSAs are benefits and strengths specific to a firm as compared to its rivals, such as management and administrative knowledge, know-how, marketing, or innovation [Rugman, 1981].

capability for reducing exposure to market risks such as those related to exchange rates by using financial derivatives (e.g. [Allayannis and Ofek, 2001; Choi and Jiang, 2009]), which leads to lower capital costs. Also, MNCs transfer material and knowledge resources among affiliates, thereby not only reducing the cost of acquisition of those resources for affiliates but also contributing to a hedge against market risks. These advantages may contribute to increasing firm value for MNCs.

Second, in terms of foreign MNC affiliates, Kostova *et al.* [2008] recognize that the liability of foreignness is the key driver behind many missteps and inefficiencies. Foreign MNC affiliates often bear higher costs arising from their foreignness, such as costs and risks related to exchange rate fluctuations, as well as high agency and information costs, which arise from their lack of knowledge about local cultures and networks that could connect them with important actors in a host country's economy — in general, costs arising from their weak links to the institutional setting of their host countries [Hymer, 1976; Zaheer, 2002; Nachum, 2003; Castellani and Zanfei, 2006; Higón and Antolín, 2012].

We follow Higón and Antolín [2012] among others in assuming that the key driver behind foreignness is the institutional distance between home and host country. Specifically, it has long been learned that the physical distance between the headquarter in a different country and foreign affiliates increases the governance, communication and travel costs associated with managing an overseas operation [Hymer, 1976; Zaheer, 2002]. In terms of hedging activities, such physical distance may increase hedging costs, thereby reducing the value effect of financial derivatives use. Khanna and Palepu [1997] also note that foreign affiliates face challenges arising from inconsistencies in decision- and law-making by the regulatory institutions and governments of their host countries. Such inconsistencies add difficulties to the operations of foreign MNC affiliates, thus potentially exposing them to significant financial losses and undermining derivative activities.[6] Similarly, the distance between cultural and social orientations in the home and host countries creates an obstacle limiting foreign MNC affiliates' abilities to gain legitimacy and other favorable economic transactions with local firms and government authorities [Peng and Luo, 2000; Luo, 2001; Makino *et al.* 2004].

Moreover, Kostova *et al.* [2008], as well as Petrou [2014], among others, argue that the idiosyncrasies of a corrupt host country's institutions and regulations create additional issues, including a rise in transaction costs and information asymmetries, which present more challenges to foreign MNC affiliates compared to domestic-owned firms. In particular, in a corrupt country, government officials

[6] Beck and Levine [2008] note that finance can be considered a set of contracts. Because derivatives are financial contracts, it is likely that legal institution influences derivatives use.

in search of bribes can constrain the performance of foreign MNC affiliates by changing the structure of taxation, laws and regulations in order to impede foreign MNC affiliates' participation in local competition and access to local resources [Lecraw, 1984; Contractor, 1990; Javorcik and Wei, 2009]. Hymer [1976] also argues that governments sometimes also generate costs arising from taxation differentials or bureaucratic delays in government approvals and paperwork for foreign MNC affiliates that often put them at a disadvantage relative to local firms. Such unstable institutional environments threaten foreign MNC affiliates, thereby increasing the costs of doing business [Makino *et al.* 2004] and the costs of implementing derivatives activities in a host country. Overall, it is likely that the high costs of foreignness could dampen the value effect of derivatives use for foreign MNC affiliates.

Based on the above logic, we hypothesize the following:

> **Hypothesis 3a**: In light of a corrupt environment, the use of financial derivatives is more valuable to domestic MNCs than to domestic firms.
>
> **Hypothesis 3b**: Under the influence of a corrupt environment, the use of financial derivatives rewards domestic MNCs with higher value than foreign MNC affiliates.

2.2.3. *Linking derivatives use and exposures to country risks by firm types*

Shapiro [1999] defines country risk as a general level of political and economic uncertainty in a country that influences the value of investments in that country. Butler [2008] and Madura [2010] demonstrate that country risk underlines the risk related to an unexpected change in a country's environment and can be partitioned into political risk and financial risk.[7] Allien and Carletti [2013] further indicate that the interaction of institutions and markets determine the country risk that drives firms' activities [Cantwell *et al.* 2010]. Relatedly, Pástor and Veronesi [2012, 2013] stated that policy-related uncertainty cannot be diversified away as uncertainty is made up of a large fraction of risk premiums. Hence, it depresses asset prices by raising the discount rate when the new policy is announced. Additionally, Butler [2008, p. 299] shows that "many political risks can be mitigated through political risk insurance" and "insurance contracts, such as insurance against political risk, are forms of put options", which is one type of derivative contract. Thus, it is reasonable to anticipate

[7] Political risk is the risk that a government will unexpectedly change the rules of games under which firms operate. Financial risks can be defined as unexpected events in a country's financial and economic situation, and it is determined by financial and economic factors, many of which are interrelated with political risk [Butler, 2008, p. 285].

that derivatives use may influence exposure to country risks, which can be defined as the sensitivity of corporate stock returns to changes in a country's environment.

Indeed, based on pecking order theory, Durnev [2011] and Huang *et al.* [2015] argue that if information asymmetry is time-varying and stock prices become less informative during a time of high political uncertainty that is associated with uncertainty about future government policies, then firms' cost of external capital may increase in that period [Glover and Levine, 2015]. In addition, future economic policies make managers less informed and less willing to base their decisions on revealed information [Durnev, 2011], while Labmert *et al.* [2009] find that information precision is a primary determinant of the cost of capital. With regard to foreign affiliates, the influence of a host country's uncertainty will affect production strategies within an MNC network [Lee and Song, 2012].

Although the literature on political and economic uncertainty has been investigated extensively, both economic theories and prior literature have largely been silent on the link between derivatives use and country risk. Bartram *et al.* [2009] state that firms located in countries with greater economic, financial and political risks are more likely to use derivatives. On the other hand, firms based in less risky countries may have lower expected financial distress costs and less need for risk management. Recently, Azad *et al.* [2012] and Kim *et al.* [2017] found evidence that a higher degree of economic, financial and political risks encourages firms to use derivatives more intensively.

On the other hand, the use of financial derivatives does not have the same impact on exposures for different firm types. Institutional literature provides evidence that firms are not equally influenced by market and country risks. That heterogeneity derives from firms' differential resources, capabilities and stock of experience in the same and or similar environment [Holburn and Zelner, 2010; Cuervo-Cazurra, 2011].

Compared with domestic firms, MNCs have far greater opportunities than domestic firms to utilize a combination of organizational and external resources to spread market risks and enhance performance, by means of their multinationality, as suggested by the OLI paradigm [Dunning and Lundan, 2008]. While domestic firms must rely on limited financial instruments to hedge their exposures, MNCs have superior ability to engage in additional hedging tools [Pantzalis *et al.* 2001]. In terms of foreign affiliates, recent IB and international finance studies suggest that foreign affiliates tend to be at a disadvantage, as they often suffer from liability of foreignness, in which they are likely to bear higher cost of capital, lower liquidity and less analyst coverage *vis-à-vis* local firms [Blass and Yafeh, 2001; Bell *et al.* 2012] and suffer from higher risks of having foreign operations [Van de Waeyenberg and Hens, 2012; Lo, 2016]. Foreignness is usually associated with issues such as foreign affiliates' lack of knowledge about local cultures and networks connecting them with important actors in host country's economy and their weak link to local institutional settings [Zaheer, 2002; Bell *et al.* 2012]. Thus, it is reasonable to suggest that foreignness adds more difficulties in implementing derivative activities for MNC affiliates than domestic MNCs.

Overall, taking both the literature on the association between derivatives use and exposures and theoretical and empirical studies on country risks together, and based on the extant research in the realm of domestic MNCs, domestic firms and foreign affiliates, and on the arguments developed above, we hypothesize the following:

> **Hypothesis 4**: There is a negative relationship between the use of financial derivatives and exposure to country risks.
>
> **Hypothesis 5**: Derivatives use by domestic MNCs results in a greater decrease in their exposures compared to both domestic firms and foreign affiliates.

3. Research Design

3.1. *Sample and descriptive statistics*

Our sample consists of 9691 firm-yearly observations; it is a balanced panel dataset of 881 non-financial firms across 34 different industries in eight countries in East Asia, namely, China, Hong Kong, Japan, Singapore, Malaysia, Thailand, Philippines and Indonesia over the period from 2003 to 2013. All data on derivatives contracts were hand-collected. We strived to verify the data accuracy by searching through a subset of firms' annual reports, Morningstar[8] — an independent investment research database — and the stock exchanges of each country.

Our study uses a new hand-collected dataset of derivatives use and provides greater statistical power. This sample was chosen for the following reasons: Firstly, although the literature on derivatives use has been growing, most empirical studies focus on the derivatives usage of US non-financial firms (e.g. [Treanor *et al.* 2014; Hutson and Laing, 2014; Talbot *et al.* 2013; Wei and Starks, 2013; Gay *et al.* 2011; Lee and Jang, 2010; Huffman *et al.* 2010; Choi and Jiang, 2009; Verschoor and Muller, 2007]). Therefore, research on the hedging behavior of East Asian firms is still relatively scarce, even though they have become the world's key derivatives users.[9] Secondly, our sampled firms are located in countries with

[8] http://quote.morningstar.com/stock-filing/Annual-Report/.

[9] According to the annual survey of the Future Industry Association in 2015, the trading volume in Asia-Pacific is $7.25 billion, accounting for about one-third of global trading volume.

great variance in terms of their economic, political and social environments. Such variation and country heterogeneity allow us to focus on the differences in exposures to home and host country risks that our sample firms face, and to explore the link between derivatives use and those exposures. Thirdly, many prior studies investigated derivatives use and exposures over 1 or 2 years, our sample covers the period from 2003 to 2013, and spans beyond the global financial crisis of 2007–2008, which provides us with the unique natural experiment of derivatives use and financial risks, allowing us to provide new insights into firms' hedging activities during that turbulent period. Lastly, in the sample, 389 domestic firms, 427 domestic MNCs and 65 foreign affiliates are identified. This rich dataset gives us a unique opportunity to examine the effects of derivatives use on multifaceted exposures among diverse types of firms.

We used the Corporate Affiliations database to classify firm types. We distinguished between two types of domestic firms: uni-national domestic firms, i.e. firms with no overseas investments, and domestic MNCs which include firms that are part of a domestically owned MNC. Similarly, foreign affiliates belong to incoming MNCs, i.e. with a parent company based elsewhere in the world [Pantzalis, *et al.*, 2001; Castellani and Zanfei, 2006, pp. 122–123 and 189].

As eight countries in our sample have different local currencies with different values, sampling bias may have occurred. Hence, we decided to use a common currency for the amount of derivatives use and all other financial data, and we chose United States dollars (USD). When the reporting currency is not USD, data are converted into USD using exchange rates on the Datastream database. We collected financial data on control variables from the Datastream database, Economist Intelligence Unit and the World Bank. All financial data are yearly and in thousands of USD.

Summary statistics on the use of derivatives by the sample firms is reported in Table 1. Across all countries, approximately 53.5% of our sample observations use at least one type of derivative, while the usage rate in Japan, Philippines and Thailand is 100%, indicating that the use of derivatives is common among non-financial firms in East Asian countries. Firms using foreign currency derivatives account for 42.55%, while 25.81% firms use interest rate derivatives.

Table 1 also shows that there is an obvious change in derivatives use before and after the global financial crisis of 2007–2008. In particular, derivatives usage increases markedly after 2009 in response to the crisis, as shown by 46.08% foreign currency derivatives' users in the post-crisis period compared to 36.71% in the pre-crisis period.

Table 1. Descriptive statistics of derivatives use of sample firms.

	Total	Any derivatives		Foreign currency derivatives		Interest rate derivatives	
Countries	*N*	*N*	%	*N*	%	*N*	%
Panel A: Derivatives use by country							
Indonesia	429	158	36.83	122	28.44	111	25.87
Philippines	352	352	100.00	139	39.49	99	28.12
Singapore	1639	651	39.72	735	44.98	434	26.58
Japan	1661	1661	100.00	1293	78.22	1020	61.71
Hong Kong	1606	382	23.79	350	21.88	265	16.56
Malaysia	1760	669	38.01	661	37.58	219	12.46
China	1111	179	16.11	202	18.20	100	9.01
Thailand	1133	1133	100.00	613	54.10	247	21.84
Total	9691	5185	53.50	4115	42.55	2495	25.81

	Observations	Mean	Std. Dev.
Panel B: Firms' derivatives use information			
Notional value of FCD	8842	245118.4	2121091
Notional value of IRD	9095	328000.5	4793611
Notional value of any derivative	6070	339721.1	4300822

	Total	Any derivatives		Foreign currency derivatives		Interest rate derivatives	
Years	*N*	*N*	%	*N*	%	*N*	%
Panel C: Derivatives use by year							
2003–2006	3524	1752	49.72	1293	36.71	782	22.20
2007–2008	881	477	54.14	387	43.98	225	25.57
2009–2013	4405	2462	55.89	2021	46.06	1261	28.77
Total	9691	5185	53.50	4115	42.55	2495	25.81

Notes: This table shows the number of firms and the percentage of firms that use derivatives. We present derivatives users separately for any derivatives, foreign currency derivatives (FCD) and interest rate derivatives (IRD). Panel A presents derivatives use based on firm-year observations by country. Panel B reports the information about the use of derivatives by derivative users, non-users and notional value of derivatives contracts. Panel C shows the trend of derivatives use over time.

3.2. *Measuring derivatives use*

We collected the information on derivatives use and some explanatory variables from firms' annual reports. Currently, information on the notional principal amount of derivatives instruments is grouped with off-balance sheet items (e.g. [Allayannis and Ofek, 2001; Guay and Kothari, 2003; Judge, 2006; Ameer *et al.* 2011; Lievenbruck and Schmid, 2014]); therefore, there is no database containing data on the derivatives usage of non-financial firms in East Asian countries. Hence, we hand collected these data directly from annual reports. To measure a firm's likelihood of using derivatives, we constructed a binary variable with the value of one or zero depending on whether a firm used derivatives.

We construct derivative intensity by using notional amount of derivatives scaled by firm size. Consistent with the literature, we use the natural logarithm of the book value of total assets to proxy for firm size (e.g. [Allayannis and Ofek, 2001; Guay and Kothari, 2003; Lievenbruck and Schmid, 2014]). When a firm is not considered a derivative user, we set the notional derivative value to zero. This derivative intensity is censored at zero by construction. Further, in this study, we classify derivatives by underlying assets and investigate general derivatives use, including foreign currency, interest rate and commodity price derivatives, and two specific types: foreign currency and interest rate derivatives.

We did not use accounting definitions, because accounting standards differ across countries and accounting classifications do not always reveal a firm's intention in holding a derivative position. We focused on textual descriptions; as such, a firm was classified as a derivatives user if it had any numerical or narrative disclosures of derivatives use in the fiscal year. The binary variable was an effective measure of derivatives usage given the nature of our sample. Applying this measure, we were able to investigate the use of derivatives for a large sample of firms over a long period of time. Consistent with the literature (e.g. [Allayannis and Ofek, 2001; Guay and Kothari, 2003; Lievenbruck and Schmid, 2014]), we then constructed derivatives use to total assets as the dependent variable. This derivatives usage ratio was censored at zero by construction.

3.3. *Measuring firm performance*

In this study, we use the most commonly used method in previous studies (e.g. [Allayannis and Weston, 2001; Bartram *et al.* 2011; Chen and King, 2014]) — Tobin's Q as a proxy for firm value. While there are many variants of Tobin's Q in the existing empirical studies, Tobin's Q is generally defined as the ratio of the market value of a firm to the replacement cost of assets. The measures of Tobin's Q differ broadly depending on whether elaborate algorithms are used to derive the market value of preferred stock and long-term debt as well as the replacement value of capital stock and inventories.

More elaborate algorithms for Tobin's Q do not improve quality of measurement, however, they may lead to a sample-selection bias as a result of data unavailability, as Erickson and Whited [2006] have argued. Therefore, we construct Tobin's Q

by calculating the ratio of a firm's market value of total assets (the book value of total assets minus the book value of equity plus the market value of equity) to the firm's book value of total assets, evaluated at the end of the fiscal year. Fauver and Naranjo [2010], Allayannis *et al.* [2012] and others use this same firm-value measurement to construct Tobin's Q. We compute Tobin's Q for a total of 9,691 firm-year observations (881 firms per year). Similar to Allayannis and Weston [2001], among others, we use the natural logarithms of Tobin's Q in our multivariate tests to control for skewness.

3.4. *Measuring exposures*

We apply the two-stage approach, following most previous studies (e.g. [Allayannis and Ofek, 2001; Clark and Mefteh, 2011; Zhou and Wang, 2013; Berghofer and Lucey, 2014]). The dependent variables are exposures to country risks, exchange rate risk and interest rate risk, i.e. the coefficients estimated by the market model[10] in the first stage.

Stage one: Exposure estimation

We use the total monthly sample from January 2003 to December 2013 to estimate augmented market model (cross-sectional) regressions.[11] For individual firms, we calculate stock returns in USD, the USD returns of the corresponding national stock market index, the percentage change in the nominal exchange rate (in local currency relative to one unit of USD), interest rates and country risks. We use the 1-year Interbank offered rate, which is compounded monthly, in each country obtained from Datastream as a proxy for the interest rate. We use overall country risk rating, which is obtained from the Economist Intelligence Unit to measure country risk. The overall country risk rating is the average scores for sovereign risk, currency risk, banking sector risk and economic structure risk of each country on a scale from 0 (minimum risk) to 100 (maximum risk). In particular, we estimate the following equations for each firm:

$$R_{ijt} = \mu_{0i} + \mu_{1ijt} R_{mjt} + \beta_{2ijt} CR_{jt} + \varepsilon_{ijt} \quad (1)$$

$$R_{ijt} = \alpha_{0i} + \alpha_{1ijt} R_{mjt} + \beta_{3ijt} FX_{jt} + \varepsilon_{ijt} \quad (2)$$

---

[10] The market model is developed by Adler and Dumas [1984] and augmented by Jorion [1990].

[11] Daily and weekly data are noisier and usually afflicted by nonsynchroneity problems [Allayannis and Ofek, 2001].

$$R_{ijt} = \gamma_{0i} + \gamma_{1ijt} R_{mjt} + \beta_{4ijt} IR_{jt} + \varepsilon_{ijt} \quad (3)$$
$$i = 1, \ldots, n; \quad j = 1 - 8, \quad t = 1, \ldots, k$$

where

- R_{ijt}: The rate of return on stock of firm i located in country j in period t
- R_{mjt}: The rate of return on country j's benchmark stock index in period t
- CR_{jt}: The rate of change in country j's overall risk index in period t
- FX_{jt}: The rate of change in nominal exchange rate in country j in period t
- IR_{jt}: The rate of change in Interbank offered rate in country j in period t
- β_{2ijt}: Exposure to country risk of firm i located in country j in period t
- β_{3ijt}: Exchange rate exposure of firm i located in country j in period t
- β_{4ijt}: Interest rate exposure of firm i located in country j in period t
- ε_{itt}: Error term clustered by country.

The coefficients β_{2ijt}, β_{3ijt} and β_{4ijt} represent exposures to country, exchange rate and interest rate risks, respectively. The exposure to exchange rate risk measures the percentage change in the rate of return on a firm's common stock against a 1% change in the exchange rate [Allayannis and Ofek, 2001]. Similar to the exchange rate exposure, the exposures to country risk and to interest rate risk measure the percentage change in the rate of return on a firm's common stock against a 1% country risks and a 1% change in the interest rate, respectively.

Stage two: Model estimated exposures

In the second stage, potential effects of firms' derivatives use on exposure to country risks and the impacts of the use of specific derivative types on equivalent exposures will be investigated. In particular, absolute values of the estimated exposure coefficients in Eqs. (1)–(3) act as dependent variables in multivariate analysis.[12] In testing the above stated hypotheses, our baseline models can be written in condensed forms in Eqs. (4)–(6) as follows:

$$|\hat{\beta}_{2ijt}| = \delta_0 + \delta_1 DER_{ijt} + \sum_{t=1}^{k} \delta_k V_{ijt} + \varepsilon_{ijt} \quad (4)$$

$$|\hat{\beta}_{3ijt}| = \lambda_0 + \lambda_1 FCD_{ijt} + \sum_{t=1}^{k} \lambda_k X_{ijt} + \varepsilon_{ijt} \quad (5)$$

[12]In the multivariate tests, we use absolute rather than actual estimated exposures because the sign of exposures measures only the direction of risk exposures, while the magnitude of exposures are more important [Faff and Marshall, 2005].

$$|\hat{\beta}_{4ijt}| = \varphi_0 + \varphi_1 IRD_{ijt} + \sum_{t=1}^{k} \varphi_k \boldsymbol{Y}_{ijt} + \varepsilon_{ijt} \tag{6}$$

$$i = 1, \ldots, n, \quad j = 1 - 8, \quad t = 2003\text{–}2013$$

where

$|\hat{\beta}_{2ijt}|$, $|\hat{\beta}_{3ijt}|$, $|\hat{\beta}_{4ijt}|$: Absolute values of exposures to country risks, exchange rate risks, and interest rate risks estimated from Eqs. (1)–(3) of firm i located in country j in year t, respectively.
DER_{ijt}, FCD_{ijt}, IRD_{ijt}: General derivative, foreign currency, interest rate derivative intensity of firm i located in country j in year t, measured by notional amount of derivative contracts scaled by total assets, respectively.
V_{ijt}, X_{ijt}, Y_{ijt}: Vector of firm and country-specific variables in year t, including operational hedging, international involvement, firm size, leverage and country-level variables (GDP per capita, financial system deposits to GDP and rule of law).
ε_{ijt}: Error terms clustered by country.

In our initial tests, we use a pooled regression model for Eqs. (4)–(6) with the subsamples of domestic firms, domestic MNCs and foreign affiliates. To control for unobserved time-varying effects and to measure within-country and within-industry differences in the effect of derivatives use on exposures, we use country, industry and year fixed effects. Further, we employ a clustering method developed by Rogers [1993] to adjust for heteroscedasticity and the serial correlation of standard errors. We then assess the robustness of our results by carrying out panel data regressions with random effect specifications. Although the regression results from both fixed effect and random effect specifications are comparable, the Hausman [1978] test shows a preference for the random effect model over the fixed effect model.

3.5. *Country-level governance quality and some main control variables*

Country-level governance quality

We use two sets of proxies for governance mechanisms: corruption and quality of governance. To measure the corruption level, we collected the Corruption Perception Index (CPI) from the TI, ranging from 0 (highly corrupt) to 100 (very clean). Quality of governance mechanisms was constructed using three measures: The first was the rule of law, which is a proxy for the quality of law enforcement. The second was regulatory quality, which measures the governmental ability to formulate and implement sound policies and regulations. The last was government effectiveness, which measures the quality of public and civil services and the credibility of the government's commitment to policies. All these variables were on a scale from −2.5 (weak governance) to 2.5 (strong governance), and they were obtained from the World Bank.

We implemented Pearson correlations for country-specific variables (untabulated). The pair-wise correlations showed that rule of law, regulatory quality and government effectiveness was highly correlated, suggesting that some of these variables should be dropped in the multivariate analysis. Therefore, we only used government effectiveness, which represents the overall legal system, in the following analyses.[13]

Some main control variables

Operational hedging: Empirical research documents that many firms actively manage exposures to market risks though the use of operational hedging (e.g. [Choi and Jiang, 2009; Pantzalis *et al.* 2001; Berghofer and Lucey, 2014]), as Pantzalis *et al.* [2001], so it is necessary to control for operational hedging when trying to understand firms' exposures. We use a diversification dummy that equals one for firms operating in more than one business segment in the SIC industry classification, and zero otherwise.

International involvement: It is well established in the existing literature that foreign sale ratios are important determinants of exposures [Jorion, 1990; Bodnar and Wong, 2000; Allayannis and Ofek, 2001], as they indicate that firms with a large proportion of foreign sales tend to be more exposed to market risks. Following Allayannis and Ofek [2001], we use the ratio of foreign sales to total sales, denoted as FORSALES, to measure a firm's degree of international involvement.

Firm size: Recent studies have identified that smaller firms are more subject to market risk exposures than larger firms [Pantzalis *et al.* 2001; Hutson and Stevenson, 2010], and MNCs are associated with smaller and less significant exchange rate exposures than non-MNCs [Choi and Jiang, 2009]. Thus, we use the natural logarithm of the book value of total assets as a proxy for firm size.

Leverage: The extent to which a firm is exposed to market risks has been shown to depend on leverage [He and Ng, 1998], as the use of derivatives reduces expected financial distress and bankruptcy costs [Smith and Stulz, 1985; Froot *et al.* 1993]. We therefore use the ratio of total debts to total assets as our definition of leverage.

[13]The results are almost the same if we use the other two variables instead of government effectiveness.

Table 2. Definitions of variables.

Variables	Definitions	Sources
Dependent variables and Main independent variables		
USE	Derivative use intensity (notional value of derivatives contracts in thousands of USD/total assets)	Authors' calculation
DER	General derivative intensity (notional value of derivatives contracts in thousand USD/total assets)	Authors' calculation
FCD	Foreign currency derivative intensity (notional value of FC derivatives contracts in thousand USD/total assets)	Authors' calculation
IRD	Interest rate derivative intensity (notional value of IR derivatives contracts in thousand USD/total assets)	Authors' calculation
$\|\hat{\beta}_{2ijt}\|$	Absolute value of exposure to country risks estimated from equation (7.1) of firm i located in country j in year t	Authors' estimation
$\|\hat{\beta}_{3ijt}\|$	Absolute value of exposure exchange rate risks estimated from equation (7.2) of firm i located in country j in year t	Authors' estimation
$\|\hat{\beta}_{4ijt}\|$	Absolute value of exposure to interest rate risks estimated from equation (7.3) of firm i located in country j in year t	Authors' estimation
Corruption index	Corruption Perception Index (CPI): Inverse ranking of country corruption levels on a scale from 100 (very clean) to 0 (highly corrupt) (from Transparency International)	Transparency International
Regulatory quality	Index measuring the governmental ability to formulate and implement sound policies and regulations with values from −2.5 (weak) to 2.5 (strong)	World Bank
Government effectiveness	Index measuring the quality of public and civil services and the degree of its independence from political pressures as well as the credibility of the government's commitment to such policies with values from −2.5 (weak) to 2.5 (strong)	World Bank
Main control variables		
Firm size	Natural logarithm of market value of total assets scaled by Producer price index (PPI)	Datastream
Leverage	Total debt to total assets	Datastream
FORSALES	Foreign sales to total sales	Datastream
Diversification indicator	Dummy variable which equals one for firms operating in more than one business segment in the SIC industry classification, and zero otherwise	Authors' construction
GDP per capita	(Gross domestic products (GDP) / midyear population)	World Bank
Financial system deposits to GDP	The demand, time, saving deposits in deposit money banks and other financial institutions as a share of GDP	World Bank
Rule of law	Index measures the confidence of agents in and abide by the rules of society, the quality of contract enforcement, property rights with −2.5 (weak) to 2.5 (strong)	World Bank

Note: This table defines the dependent and independent variables, and control variables that we examine.

Country-level control variables: We use GDP per capita to proxy for the countries' relative performance and financial system deposits to GDP to proxy for financial market development, an increase in GDP per capita and financial system deposits to GDP indicates growth in the economy and tends to signal a reduction in market risks. Additionally, Hutson and Stevenson [2010] find a significant negative link between exposure and the extent of creditor protection in a country. Thus, we use rule of law to proxy for country-governance quality.

4. Empirical Results and Discussion

4.1. *Linking derivatives use and governance quality*

Following our discussion above, we estimated a series of probit models and Tobit models in general forms as Eqs. (7) and (8):

$$\begin{aligned}&\textit{Probability (Derivatives use}_{it}\textit{)}\\&\quad = f(\textit{firm-specific variables},\ \textit{country-specific variables}) \qquad (7)\end{aligned}$$

$$\begin{aligned}&\textit{Derivatives use}_{it}\\&\quad = f(\textit{firm-specific variables},\ \textit{country-specific variables}) \qquad (8)\end{aligned}$$

where:

- *Probability* (*Derivatives use*) is a binary variable that indicates whether firm i uses derivatives at year t.
- *Derivatives use* is a continuous variable that is measured by the notional amount of derivatives contracts scaled by total assets.
- *Country-specific variables* include proxies for country risk and governance mechanisms.
- *Firm-specific variables* are the aforementioned variables that are used in testing value-creation theories through hedging and control variables for exposure to financial risks.

It is worth noting that in our analysis, we used country random effects to focus on the effects of country-level factors and the variance component structure, as the main explanatory variables were at the country level and time invariant.[14] Our

[14]We also performed the Hausman tests on the random-effects versus the fixed-effects model. The result showed that the random-effects model gave better fit.

approach is in line with Bryan and Jenkins' [2013] insight that the country-random-effects approach is more efficient than the fixed-effects approach, as it "borrows strength" from between-group variation, while the fixed-effects approach uses only within-group variation. We also used industry and year fixed effects to measure the within-industry differences in the effect of country-level factors on firms' derivatives usage and control for unobserved time-varying effects. In addition, following Rogers [1993], we employed a clustering method to adjust for the heteroscedasticity and serial correlation of standard errors.

4.1.1. *Determinants of the decision to use derivatives*

Pooled probit results

In line with Hypothesis 1, we find that corruption is positively and significantly associated with a firm's likelihood of using derivatives. This result may be attributed to a lower transaction cost associated with lower corruption. Put differently, lower corruption enables firms to enter financial derivatives contracts at a lower cost. Likewise, consistent with Hypothesis 2, there exists a significant and positive effect of government effectiveness on a firm's tendency to use derivatives. This result is due to the fact that a well-functioning legal system and high legal enforceability lower the costs of contracting and administrating, thereby facilitating firms' use of derivatives.

Taken together, these findings suggest that good governance increases a firm's inclination to use derivatives. Relatedly, firms in weakly governed countries are likely to use derivatives for purposes other than reducing exposure to financial risks. In particular, when examining the proxies for exposure, we find the coefficient estimates of all other proxies are insignificant; implying that exposure to financial risks does not play an important role in the determinants of a firm's derivatives usage. This finding is similar to that of Allayannis *et al.* [2003], who found that there is no evidence that East Asian firms eliminate their foreign exchange exposure by using derivatives.

Pooled probit results based on corruption levels

In this section, we replicate pooled probit regressions with respect to the corruption level. We group countries into low and high corruption levels based on the scales of the CPI as defined by the TI. The low corruption level group consists of all countries having scores equal to or greater than 75, whereas any country with a CPI score less than 75 is placed in the high corruption level group. In that way, we can identify the factors that might or might not be determinants of derivatives' usage by firms

Table 3. Probit regression estimates of the likelihood of using derivatives.

Explanatory variables	Any derivatives		Foreign currency derivatives		Interest rate derivatives		Commodity price derivatives	
	Model 1	**Model 2**	**Model 1**	**Model 2**	**Model 1**	**Model 2**	**Model 1**	**Model 2**
Country-specific factors								
Corruption	0.105***	0.0939***	0.097***	0.0855***	0.109***	0.0972***	0.0416***	0.0366***
	(3.87)	(4.04)	(3.77)	(3.78)	(7.09)	(9.36)	(3.84)	(2.81)
Government effectiveness	0.651	0.503*	0.644*	0.496*	0.0838	−0.0402	−0.296	−0.246
	(1.02)	(1.76)	(2.09)	(2.03)	(0.24)	(−0.10)	(−1.15)	(−0.81)
Overall risk rating	0.132*	0.111*	0.126*	0.105*	0.105**	0.0923**	0.0367	0.0337
	(1.77)	(1.65)	(1.81)	(1.72)	(2.44)	(2.38)	(1.11)	(0.98)
Firm-specific factors								
Firm size		0.0436***		0.0449***		0.0409*		0.0142
		(3.9)		(4.09)		(1.9)		(0.84)
Leverage		0.0197**		0.0252***		0.0347***		−0.0333
		(2.31)		(4.3)		(2.79)		(−0.22)
Interest coverage		0.0521		0.0295**		−0.007		0.0132
		(1.5)		(2.31)		(−0.96)		(1.39)
Tax rate		−0.0247***		−0.0268**		−0.0537		−0.0213
		(−2.71)		(−2.30)		(−0.46)		(−0.88)
Deferred taxes		−0.0283*		−0.0577***		0.0512***		0.0493***
		(−1.76)		(−3.93)		(2.7)		(6.14)
Market to book value		−0.0106***		−0.0117***		−0.0127*		−0.0961**
		(−3.55)		(−3.03)		(−1.78)		(−2.22)
Current ratio		−0.0737		−0.0762		−0.0667		−0.0129
		(−0.94)		(−0.93)		(−0.77)		(−0.96)
Dividend payout		−0.0694		−0.0953		−0.0222**		0.0485
		(−1.27)		(−0.73)		(−2.55)		(0.25)

Control variables								
FORSALES	0.0757	0.0125	0.0108	0.0174	0.0203*	0.0256**	0.0139	0.0939
	(0.47)	(0.84)	(0.58)	(0.96)	(1.74)	(−2.06)	(0.96)	(0.53)
FORASSETS	−0.0326	−0.0302	−0.028	−0.0248	−0.021	−0.0212	−0.0192	−0.0256
	(−1.39)	(−1.11)	(−1.12)	(−0.91)	(−1.02)	(−0.97)	(−1.27)	(−1.10)
GDP per capita	−0.0616***	−0.0530***	−0.059***	−0.0496***	−0.0530***	−0.0430***	−0.0107	−0.0889
	(−3.30)	(−2.93)	(−3.37)	(−2.90)	(−5.61)	(−5.19)	(−1.57)	(−0.95)
DEPOSITSTOGDP	−1.253	−1.436*	−0.931	−1.066	0.328	−0.755	0.587	0.606
	(−1.57)	(−1.68)	(−1.21)	(−1.21)	(0.34)	(−0.83)	(0.8)	(0.82)
Intercept	−8.927**	−7.627**	−8.561**	−7.271**	−8.984***	−7.962***	−4.520***	−4.225**
	(−2.36)	(−2.22)	(−2.39)	(−2.25)	(−4.01)	(−4.13)	(−2.72)	(−2.31)
Industry dummies	Yes	Yes	Yes	Yes	Yes	Yes	Yes	Yes
Year dummies	Yes	Yes	Yes	Yes	Yes	Yes	Yes	Yes
Observations	3672	2686	3671	2679	3663	2680	3644	2661
Adjusted R^2	0.1356	0.1776	0.1301	0.1675	0.1361	0.1775	0.0551	0.0797

Notes: This table reports the regression for the probability of using any type of derivatives, foreign currency, interest rate and commodity price derivatives. The dependent variable is binary variable, which takes on a value of one if firm use derivative, and zero otherwise. All independent variables definitions are reported in Table 2. The coefficients and significance levels are reported on each model. Standard errors are clustered by country to control for heteroscedasticity and serial correlation. Model 1 investigates the country-specific characteristics only; both firm-specific and country-specific variables are included in Model 2. ***, ** and * indicate significance at the 1%, 5% and 10% level, respectively; t-statistics in parentheses with standard errors clustered by countries.

located in countries with low corruption and the factors most likely to affect firms' decisions when they are influenced by high corruption.

When the corruption level is low, the results show that governance mechanism quality is a significant determinant explaining why firms use derivatives, but traditional hedging theories have very little power to explain why firms use derivatives. In particular, we find mixed supporting evidence for the hypothesis of bankruptcy and financial distress costs: Leverage is positively related with firms' likelihood of using derivatives, while the interest coverage ratio is never different from zero at any significance level. Consistent with Gay *et al.* [2011] and Sprcic and Sevic [2012], we do not find any significant evidence of a link between proxies for corporate tax and firms' probability of using derivatives, as they are statistically significant but counter to the hypothesized sign. In line with Géczy *et al.* [1997] and Allayannis and Ofek [2001], we do not find any link between agency costs of debt and decisions on derivatives use by firms in countries with low corruption.

The significant and positive coefficient estimates of foreign sales to total sales and leverage, however, suggest firms with greater exposure to exchange rate and interest rate risks are more likely to use derivatives. This result indicates that firms in countries with low corruption appear to use derivatives to mitigate exposure to financial risks rather than to speculate, in line with arguments about speculation of prior studies such as Géczy *et al.* [1997] and Júnior [2013].

When we analyze the results by type of derivatives, we find that the driving factors of firms' decisions on using derivatives vary somewhat among the types of derivatives, and there is still a lack of supporting evidence for traditional hedging theories. Specifically, when a firm makes a decision on derivatives usage in the situation of low corruption, leverage is a significant determinant. However, if coefficients on leverage are significant and with the predicted sign in the case of foreign currency and interest rate derivatives use, the negative effects for leverage in the case of commodity price derivatives use are counter to the hypothesis of bankruptcy and financial distress costs. These results indicate that firms use foreign currency and interest rate derivatives more aggressively when the costs of financial distress are higher. Similarly, firm size is an important factor influencing firms' likelihood of using foreign currency derivatives, while it does not affect firms'decisions in the case of interest rate and commodity price derivatives.

When the level of corruption is high, the factors influencing firms' decisions on using derivatives are different. *First*, contrary to Nance *et al.* [1993], the observed negative coefficient estimate on deferred taxes implies that in highly corrupt countries, the more progressive the marginal tax rates are, the less the firms are induced to use derivatives. *Second*, the market-to-book ratio has a highly

Table 4. Probit estimations for determinants of derivative use based on corruption levels.

	Any derivatives		Foreign currency derivatives		Interest rate derivatives		Commodity price derivatives	
Explanatory variables	**Low corruption**	**High corruption**	**Low corruption**	**High corruption**	**Low corruption**	**High corruption**	**Low corruption**	**High corruption**
Country-specific factors								
Government effectiveness	0.598***	0.819***	1.368***	0.525**	0.773***	1.570***	1.329**	0.970**
	(2.76)	(2.74)	(3.32)	(2.07)	(3.23)	(7.86)	(2.19)	(2.19)
Overall risk rating	−0.0638	0.0435	−0.281	0.0557	0.0656	0.0616	0.0556	−0.0173
	(−0.20)	(0.86)	(−0.80)	(1.05)	(0.24)	(0.20)	(0.42)	(−0.37)
Firm-specific factors								
Firm size	0.0327***	0.0297**	0.0414***	0.0283*	0.0500	0.0396	−0.0353	0.0262
	(13.36)	(2.22)	(3.17)	(1.88)	(1.18)	(1.58)	(−0.86)	(1.33)
Leverage	0.0194***	0.0114	0.0274***	0.0167	0.0363***	0.0204	−0.0417***	0.0109
	(2.83)	(0.62)	(4.17)	(1.37)	(4.60)	(1.19)	(−2.81)	(0.78)
Interest coverage	0.0192	0.0438	0.0674*	0.0287	−0.0751***	−0.0116	0.0326***	−0.0225
	(1.54)	(1.26)	(1.67)	(1.06)	(−3.28)	(−0.74)	(9.15)	(−0.86)
Tax rate	−0.0303*	0.0350	−0.0313***	−0.0759	−0.0249	0.0474***	−0.0439***	0.0142
	(−1.72)	(0.24)	(−2.92)	(−0.65)	(−0.91)	(4.92)	(−2.74)	(1.02)
Deferred taxes	0.0063	−0.0358***	0.0216	−0.0594***	0.0209	0.0592***	0.0534***	0.0384***
	(0.10)	(−4.99)	(0.39)	(−4.37)	(1.06)	(3.59)	(4.14)	(4.06)
Market to book value	−0.0863	−0.0842**	−0.0169**	−0.0568	0.0113	−0.0411***	−0.0396	−0.0179
	(−1.08)	(−2.28)	(−2.04)	(−1.27)	(0.36)	(−2.71)	(−1.60)	(−0.75)

(Continued)

Table 4. *(Continued)*

Explanatory variables	Any derivatives		Foreign currency derivatives		Interest rate derivatives		Commodity price derivatives	
	Low corruption	High corruption	Low corruption	High corruption	Low corruption	High corruption	Low corruption	High corruption
Control variables								
FORSALES	0.0117**	0.0474	0.0103***	0.0610	0.0828***	0.0527***	−0.0214*	0.0344
	(2.33)	(1.12)	(11.61)	(1.37)	(3.46)	(3.46)	(−1.71)	(1.28)
FORASSETS	−0.0348	0.0310	−0.0156	0.0240	−0.0297	0.0106	−0.0614***	0.0152
	(−1.26)	(1.41)	(−0.61)	(0.79)	(−0.90)	(1.64)	(−81.82)	(0.37)
GDP per capita	0.0400***	0.0127***	0.0547***	0.0114***	0.0330***	0.0132***	0.0356***	0.0485**
	(7.44)	(5.05)	(6.76)	(3.80)	(4.43)	(7.79)	(2.87)	(2.55)
DEPOSITSTOGDP	−1.349	−2.932***	−1.898	−2.826***	−2.159***	−3.994***	4.257	−0.296
	(−1.05)	(−3.46)	(−0.74)	(−3.72)	(−2.75)	(−3.86)	(1.35)	(−0.51)
Intercept	0.170	−3.502	5.295	−3.869	−2.843	−2.809**	−2.169	−1.389
	(0.02)	(−1.51)	(0.66)	(−1.54)	(−0.42)	(−1.99)	(−0.73)	(−0.67)
Other firm-specific factors	Yes	Yes	Yes	Yes	Yes	Yes	Yes	
Industry dummies	Yes	Yes	Yes	Yes	Yes	Yes	Yes	Yes
Year dummies	Yes	Yes	Yes	Yes	Yes	Yes	Yes	Yes
Observations	927	1757	927	1750	927	1748	822	1733
Adjusted R^2	0.0873	0.1880	0.0933	0.1654	0.0933	0.2001	0.0942	0.0854

Notes: This table presents regressions from pooled probit models of the likelihood of using derivatives on the basis of corruption levels: low corruption and high corruption. We define corruption levels based on corruption index, in which those countries having scores greater than 75 are grouped into low corruption level, and those countries having scores less than 75 are considered to be highly corrupt. The dependent variable is binary variable, which takes on a value of one if firm uses derivative, and zero otherwise. All independent variables definitions are reported in Table 2. The coefficients and significance levels are reported on each model. Standard errors are clustered by country to control for heteroscedasticity and serial correlation. Asterisks ***, ** and * indicate significance at the 1%, 5% and 10% level, respectively.

significant and negative effect on firms' likelihood of using derivatives in highly corrupt countries but an insignificant effect in countries with low corruption. This result suggests that firms in highly corrupt countries do not use derivatives to reduce agency costs of debt. Meanwhile, firms with growth opportunities in countries with low corruption may have greater sufficient funds and/or higher external financing availability and thus have less incentive to use derivatives to deal with the mismatch between domestic costs and foreign revenues, as shown in Géczy *et al.* [1997]. *Third,* the observed insignificant coefficient estimates on all proxies for exposure indicate that firms in highly corrupt countries do not use derivatives to eliminate exposure to financial risks. They use derivatives for other purposes, such as speculation or self-management purposes.

4.1.2. *Determinants of the intensity of derivatives use*

Pooled Tobit estimations

Consistent with Hypothesis 1, the corruption index has a significant and positive impact on the intensity of derivatives use. We also observe a positive effect for government effectiveness. Taken together, these results suggest that good institutions with strong legal enforceability and governance capabilities lower hedging costs, hence facilitating firms' use of derivatives. Meanwhile, firms in countries with high corruption have less motivation to use derivatives because entering into contracts is more costly due to bribes and other administrative payments.

Regarding types of derivatives, we find that besides the similar results to those in the case of any derivatives, the effects of some factors vary across types of derivatives. For interest rate derivatives, we observe that corruption is a significant determinant influencing firms' extent of using derivatives, while we do not find any significant effect of government effectiveness or country risk on firms' level of derivatives use. For commodity price derivatives, we find that there is a strong relation between a country's corruption level and risks and a firms' decision on the extent of derivatives use. This result is different from the findings of previous studies that firms use commodity price derivatives for other reasons arising from industry-specific factors.

Moderating effect of corruption levels

When the corruption level is low, consistent with the findings from probit estimations, Table 6 shows that although some firm-specific factors are statistically significant determinants of firms' level of derivatives use, they do not support any traditional hedging theories, as most of the significant results are counter to predictions. In particular, the results do not support the hypothesis of economies of

Table 5. Tobit estimates for the extent of the corporate use of derivatives.

	Any derivatives		Foreign currency derivatives		Interest rate derivatives		Commodity price derivatives	
Explanatory variables	**Model 1**	**Model 2**	**Model 1**	**Model 2**	**Model 1**	**Model 2**	**Model 1**	**Model 2**
Country-specific factors								
Corruption	0.0267	0.0585*	0.0304*	0.0467*	0.0143**	0.0136**	0.0102**	0.0675**
	(1.16)	(1.93)	(1.74)	(1.72)	(2.17)	(2.01)	(1.97)	(1.98)
Government effectiveness	0.204***	0.0329*	0.0447*	−0.0350	−0.234	−0.223	−0.0598	−0.0699
	(4.22)	(1.96)	(1.84)	(−0.35)	(−1.45)	(−1.16)	(−0.73)	(−0.12)
Overall risk rating	0.0204***	0.0108	0.0864	0.0457	0.0678	0.0195	0.0120*	0.0972
	(2.59)	(1.52)	(1.29)	(0.66)	(0.08)	(0.20)	(1.69)	(1.55)
Control variables								
FORSALES	0.0673	0.0459	0.0545	0.0394	0.0722	0.0465	0.0955	0.0559
	(1.08)	(1.13)	(0.88)	(1.03)	(1.21)	(1.29)	(1.24)	(0.72)
FORASSETS	−0.0117*	−0.0775	−0.0758	−0.0404	−0.0154*	−0.0915	−0.0155	−0.0182
	(−1.87)	(−1.25)	(−1.38)	(−0.77)	(−1.74)	(−1.28)	(−1.48)	(−1.33)
GDP per capita	−0.0363	−0.0301	−0.0223	−0.0191	−0.0196	−0.0198	0.0170	0.0191
	(−0.97)	(−0.89)	(−0.54)	(−0.54)	(−0.46)	(−0.59)	(0.92)	(1.19)
DEPOSITSTOGDP	−0.281*	−0.269*	−0.276*	−0.279*	−0.121	−0.237	0.282	0.254
	(−1.67)	(−1.72)	(−1.79)	(−1.69)	(−0.47)	(−0.80)	(0.62)	(0.72)
Intercept	−0.729	−0.419	−0.428	−0.281	−0.924	−0.738	−2.054**	−1.657**
	(−1.22)	(−0.90)	(−0.71)	(−0.60)	(−1.22)	(−1.33)	(−2.46)	(−2.30)
Firm-specific factors	No	Yes	No	Yes	No	Yes	No	Yes
Industry dummies	Yes	Yes	Yes	Yes	Yes	Yes	Yes	Yes
Year dummies	Yes	Yes	Yes	Yes	Yes	Yes	Yes	Yes
Observations	3471	2540	3676	2691	3422	2486	3595	2627
Adjusted R^2	0.071	0.112	0.091	0.1406	0.073	0.1066	0.0664	0.1291

Notes: This table reports the pooled tobit regressions with censoring at zero and one for the extent of firms' using any type of derivatives, foreign currency, interest rate and commodity price derivatives. The dependent variable is a continuous variable, which is measured as notional amount of derivatives use divided by total assets. Non-derivative users are set to zero. All independent variables definitions are reported in Table 2. The coefficients and significance levels are reported on each model. Standard errors are clustered by country to control for heteroscedasticity and serial correlation. Model 1 investigates the country-specific characteristics only; both firm-specific and country-specific variables are included in the Model 2. Asterisks ***, ** and * indicate significance at the 1%, 5% and 10% level, respectively; *t*-statistics in parentheses with standard errors clustered by countries.

scale, as evidenced by the insignificant coefficient estimate on firm size. We are also unable to find any supporting evidence in favor of the corporate tax hypothesis or the argument of agency costs of debt. On the other hand, even though leverage and interest coverage are statistically significant, they are both opposite to the predicted sign.

We observe that governance mechanism quality is a consistently important factor influencing non-financial firms' level of derivatives use, as government effectiveness is statistically different from zero and positively associated with firms' level of derivatives use in all models. On the other hand, we find the interesting result that non-financial firms in countries with low corruption consider countries' risk levels when they make decisions on the extent of derivatives use. This finding is consistent with our prior finding from the probit model in the previous section.

We note that the factors affecting firms' derivatives use in countries with low corruption and countries with high corruption differ somewhat. First, firm size is a significant determinant of derivatives use by firms located in highly corrupt countries, as evidenced by the negative and significant coefficient estimates. In line with Clark and Judge [2008], we propose a possible explanation that in highly corrupt countries, small firms face greater information asymmetries and higher financing transaction costs, which is likely to make external financing more expensive for smaller firms and thus motivate them to use higher levels of derivatives.

Second, the coefficient estimates on current ratio and convertible debts are statistically different from zero and negatively related to firms' derivatives use decisions, while these variables are insignificant factors for firms located in countries with low corruption. According to Nance *et al.*'s [1993] argument on substitutes for hedging with derivatives, these results suggest that firms in highly corrupt countries possess liquid assets or issue debt instruments to mitigate the probability of financial distress and agency costs of debt with respect to long-term financing, which acts as a substitute to hedging with derivatives. This finding also supports Hypothesis 1 that firms have less incentive to enter into derivatives contracts if they are located in highly corrupt countries. Meanwhile, the countries with low corruption facilitate the use of derivatives, so firms based in these countries are not induced to use liquid assets and debt instruments as substitutes for derivatives.

Third, overall risk rating has a highly significant and positive effect on firms' likelihood of using derivatives, while it is an insignificant determinant of derivatives use by firms located in countries with low corruption. This result suggests that firms in highly corrupt countries use derivatives more aggressively, simply because their countries have higher degrees of economic, financial and political risks.

Table 6. Tobit estimates for the extent of corporate derivative use based on corruption levels.

Explanatory variables	Any derivatives		Foreign currency derivatives		Interest rate derivatives		Commodity price derivatives	
	Low corruption	High corruption	Low corruption	High corruption	Low corruption	High corruption	Low corruption	High corruption
Country-specific factors								
Government effectiveness	18.97***	0.389*	17.34***	0.335	26.29***	0.542***	4.450***	0.0903
	(4.95)	(1.83)	(9.81)	(1.52)	(3.85)	(5.00)	(5.93)	(0.51)
Overall risk rating	0.924	0.0437***	−0.582	0.0409**	0.712	0.0491***	0.321	−0.0842
	(0.69)	(2.73)	(−1.34)	(2.50)	(0.73)	(4.97)	(0.99)	(−0.59)
Firm-specific factors								
Firm size	−0.871	−0.0268***	−0.482	−0.0598***	−0.0780	−0.0963	−0.0583	−0.0226
	(−1.50)	(−13.93)	(−1.49)	(−5.42)	(−0.08)	(−0.11)	(−0.24)	(−0.59)
Leverage	−0.0491**	−0.0454	−0.0464	0.0850	−0.0127	−0.0432	−0.0238	−0.0195
	(−2.17)	(−0.34)	(−0.49)	(0.10)	(−0.17)	(−0.52)	(−1.18)	(−0.81)
Interest coverage	−0.0174***	−0.0129	−0.0138***	0.0991	−0.0597***	−0.0127*	0.0455***	−0.0374
	(−36.18)	(−0.03)	(−25.71)	(0.35)	(−3.68)	(−1.73)	(2.79)	(−0.77)
Tax rate	−0.0101	0.0126**	−0.0600***	0.0851*	−0.0531	0.0226***	−0.0101	0.0582
	(−0.58)	(2.53)	(−5.84)	(1.93)	(−0.69)	(5.14)	(−1.20)	(1.00)
Deferred taxes	0.0640	−0.0235	0.0531	−0.0503	0.0821	0.0353	0.0103	0.0149
	(1.52)	(−0.04)	(1.40)	(−1.01)	(1.33)	(0.59)	(1.07)	(1.01)
Market to book value	−0.121	−0.0917	−0.138***	0.0109	−0.0319	−0.0817**	−0.0622	−0.0198
	(−1.39)	(−0.27)	(−4.77)	(0.04)	(−0.33)	(−2.22)	(−0.99)	(−0.89)
Current ratio	−0.145	−0.0260*	−0.197	−0.0514***	−0.0247	0.0160	−0.299***	0.0303
	(−0.28)	(−1.71)	(−1.12)	(−4.17)	(−0.05)	(0.14)	(−10.63)	(0.03)
Dividend payout	0.0458	−0.0201**	0.0351***	−0.0266***	−0.0656***	−0.0707*	−0.0460	0.0201
	(0.18)	(−2.04)	(8.85)	(−3.32)	(−2.82)	(−1.66)	(−0.45)	(0.45)

Convertible debt	2.176	−6.063***	−7.059	−5.734***	−23.11***	−3.470	−25.27***	−4.444*
	(0.12)	(−3.05)	(−0.60)	(−3.30)	(−4.06)	(−1.25)	(−5.09)	(−1.87)
Control variables								
FORSALES	0.0183	0.0317***	0.0754	0.0278***	0.0105	0.0143***	−0.0125***	0.0126*
	(1.18)	(4.11)	(0.56)	(5.21)	(1.43)	(3.27)	(−2.84)	(1.81)
FORASSETS	−0.0257	0.0181	−0.0171	0.0133	−0.0131	0.0551	−0.0360***	0.0306
	(−0.61)	(0.78)	(−0.86)	(0.69)	(−0.36)	(0.65)	(−5.38)	(0.40)
GDP per capita	−9.342***	0.131***	−6.811***	0.159***	−9.416***	0.0496*	0.890***	0.0326
	(−49.72)	(4.43)	(−15.04)	(5.66)	(−11.73)	(1.67)	(7.37)	(1.41)
DEPOSITSTOGDP	−0.338	−1.951***	3.525	−1.965***	−0.607	−0.972*	12.37	−0.0209
	(−0.50)	(−5.66)	(0.24)	(−4.37)	(−0.13)	(−1.69)	(1.20)	(−0.11)
Intercept	133.9***	−0.369	128.8***	−0.905	142.6***	1.011*	−32.77***	−0.446
	(3.52)	(−0.57)	(17.15)	(−1.36)	(3.99)	(1.94)	(−5.38)	(−1.63)
Industry dummies	Yes	Yes	Yes	Yes	Yes	Yes	Yes	Yes
Year dummies	Yes	Yes	Yes	Yes	Yes	Yes	Yes	Yes
Observations	804	1669	907	1716	848	1578	887	1675
Adjusted R^2	0.0220	0.0411	0.0303	0.0484	0.0132	0.152	0.0953	0.1842

Notes: This table reports the pooled tobit regressions with censoring at zero and one for the extent of firms' using derivatives on the basis of corruption levels: low corruption, and high corruption level. We define corruption levels based on corruption index, in which those countries having scores greater than 75 are grouped into low corruption level, and those countries having scores less than 75 are considered to be highly corrupt. The dependent variable is a continuous variable, which is measured as notional amount of derivatives use divided by total assets. Non-derivative users are set to zero. All independent variables definitions are reported in Table 2. The coefficients and significance levels are reported on each model. Standard errors are clustered by country to control for heteroscedasticity and serial correlation. Asterisks ***, ** and * indicate significance at the 1%, 5% and 10% level, respectively; t-statistics in parentheses.

4.2. *Linking derivatives use and firm value by firm types*

In testing the above-stated Hypotheses 3a and 3b, our baseline models can be written in condensed forms in Eq. (9) as follows:

$$Ln(Tobin\text{'}s\ Q)_{ijt} = \alpha_{use}USE_{ijt} + \alpha_c C_{jt} + \lambda_{use\_c}USE_{ijt}{}^{*}C_{jt} + \alpha_x X_{ijt} + u_{ijt} \quad (9)$$
$$i = 1, \ldots, n; \quad j = 1 - 8; \quad t = 2003\text{–}2013,$$

where:

— $Ln\ (Tobin\text{'}s\ Q)_{ijt}$: Firm value of firm i located in country j in year t, measured by natural logarithm of book value of total assets minus book value of equity plus market value of equity to book value of total assets.
— USE_{ijt}: Derivatives use intensity of firm i located in country j in year t, measured by a notional amount of derivative contracts scaled by total assets.
— C_{jt}: Corruption index of country j in year t, which is an inverse ranking of country corruption levels on a scale from 100 (very clean) to 0 (highly corrupt) (from Transparency International).
— X_{ijt} is a vector of firm- and country-specific variables in year t, including firm size, leverage, ROA, capital expenditures, quick ratio, dividend yield, foreign sales to total sales, financial system deposits to GDP and GDP per capita.
— u_{ijt}: Error terms clustered by country

In our initial tests, we use OLS estimation of Eq. (9) for the subsamples of domestic firms, domestic MNCs and foreign MNC affiliates. We then assess the robustness of our results by carrying out additional investigation. Our sample confirms previous results in the existing literature that the characteristics of firms using derivatives are, on average, quite different from those of firms that do not. These differences are likely to lead to selection bias when one investigates the value effects of derivatives use under corrupt conditions. To control for this self-selection bias, following Bartram *et al.* [2011], and Chen and King [2014], we employ the Heckman treatment effect model.

Value effects of derivatives use under the influence of a corrupt environment

Table 7 presents the results of a pooled OLS estimation for our sample of domestic firms, domestic MNCs and foreign MNC affiliates. We find several interesting results. For domestic firms, we observe that there are positive and significant estimated coefficients on derivatives use and corruption (0.0418, 0.154 and 0.0759, respectively, $p < 0.01$). Due to inverse ranking of corruption levels, these results

Table 7. Firm value and derivatives use under the influence of a corrupt environment.

Variable	**Domestic firms**	**Domestic MNCs**	**Foreign MNC affiliates**
Derivative use	0.0418**	0.049*	−0.070***
	(0.029)	(0.057)	(0.000)
Derivative*corruption	0.076***	0.078**	0.057***
	(0.003)	(0.018)	(0.001)
Corruption index	0.154*	0.059***	0.094
	(0.176)	(0.004)	(0.134)
Firm size	0.945***	0.202***	0.804***
	(0.000)	(0.001)	(0.001)
Leverage	0.072**	0.065*	−0.091
	(0.019)	(0.081)	(0.112)
ROA	−0.055**	−0.036	−0.049
	(0.029)	(0.626)	(0.745)
Capital expenditure	0.031	0.030**	−0.089
	(0.242)	(0.015)	(0.836)
Quick ratio	−0.061	−0.026	−0.012***
	(0.647)	(0.127)	(0.002)
Dividend yield	−0.010	0.031**	0.015
	(0.577)	(0.014)	(0.256)
Forsales	−0.046*	0.035	−0.069
	(0.077)	(0.643)	(0.994)
Geomart	−0.211	0.034	0.091
	(0.166)	(0.570)	(0.776)
Diversification indicator	−0.056	−0.057	−0.835**
	(0.747)	(0.289)	(0.013)
GDP per capita	0.067	−0.617	0.479**
	(0.967)	(0.188)	(0.010)
Financial system deposits to GDP	0.003	−0.004*	0.007
	(0.883)	(0.091)	(0.261)
Intercept	−2.915	3.472	−62.01***
	(0.812)	(0.422)	(0.002)
Country dummies	Yes	Yes	Yes
Industry dummies	Yes	Yes	Yes
Year dummies	Yes	Yes	Yes
Observations	1420	1431	272
R^2	0.413	0.367	0.533

Notes: This table reports the effects of derivatives use on firm value from an OLS estimation, divided into domestic firms, domestic MNCs and foreign MNC affiliates. The dependent variable is Ln (Tobin's Q), which is calculated as the natural logarithm of book value of total assets minus book value of equity plus market value of equity over book value of total assets. Derivatives use is calculated as the notional value of any derivative contract (foreign currency, interest rate and commodity price derivatives) in thousands of USD, scaled by total assets. All other independent variable definitions are reported in Appendix. Standard errors are clustered by country to control for heteroscedasticity and serial correlation. P-values are in parentheses. Asterisks ***, ** and * indicate significance at the 1%, 5% and 10% levels, respectively.

suggest that the effects of derivatives use on the value of domestic firms vary with the corruption levels of the home countries. Specifically, in countries with low corruption,[15] the use of derivatives increases the value of domestic firms between 9.87% and 11.77%, conforming to the findings of Kim *et al.* [2017] that the lower the level of corruption, the higher the likelihood that firms will use derivatives. The hedging premium is slightly higher than the premium of between 4.87% and 6.33% reported by Allayannis and Weston [2001], Nain [2004], Kim *et al.* [2006] and Magee [2008] for samples of US firms, but broadly similar to the 12% found by Clark and Judge [2009] who use a sample of 412 UK firms.

For domestic MNCs, we find results generally consistent with our Hypotheses 2a and 2b. In particular, a lower corruption level (higher CPI) is associated with higher firm values as evidenced by a significant and positive coefficient estimate for corruption ($p < 0.01$). We also find both statistically and economically significant coefficients on derivatives use and derivatives use interacted with corruption (0.0494 and 0.0778, respectively). These results indicate that domestic MNCs are likely to use financial derivatives in countries with low corruption levels, and such a low-corruption environment facilitates the use of derivatives and rewards those firms with higher firm value. Despite this conforming to Hypothesis 3a, however, we note that the difference in the hedging premium of domestic MNCs compared to domestic firms is not striking (4.94% to 12.72% versus 4.18% to 11.77%).

In contrast to the above findings, when we analyze the results for the case of foreign MNC affiliates, we find strong evidence that the use of derivatives decreases firm value, with a hedging discount of 7% ($\beta = -0.07,\ p < 0.01$). This can be partly attributed to the fact that their business operations are more complicated than those of domestic firms [Kim and Pantzalis, 2003], and they endure pressure to comply with the practices of both their parent companies and their host countries [Nell *et al.*, 2015]. Another possible explanation here is the findings of Chan *et al.* [2008] that the performance of foreign MNC affiliates in some emerging countries, such as China, Indonesia and Thailand, is "high risk, low return".

However, we also observe that the coefficient on the interaction term between derivatives use and corruption is highly significant and positive ($\beta = 0.0570$, $p < 0.01$). This supports Hypothesis 3b, and suggests that foreign MNC affiliates residing in a country with a low-corruption environment and engaging in financial derivatives use are significantly more valuable than those affiliates residing in a country with high corruption levels.

[15]We define corruption levels based on the Corruption Perception Index (CPI), in which those countries having scores greater than 75 are considered to be countries with low levels of corruption, and those countries having scores less than 75 are considered to be highly corrupt countries.

When we look at the results of other independent and control variables, although the effects for firm-specific and country-specific factors are broadly similar across subsamples, certain characteristics seem to be important in explaining the different effects of derivatives use on firm types. *First*, we observe that diversification indicators negatively affect the firm value of foreign MNC affiliates, while these do not influence the value of domestic firms and domestic MNCs. This result complies with the assertions of Denis *et al.* [2002], Fauver and Naranjo [2010], and Marami and Dubois [2013], among others, that, on average, industrial diversification is harmful to firm value.

Second, we find that the exchange risk exposure, measured by foreign sales to total sales (FORSALES), is actually significant for domestic firms ($\beta = -0.0466,\ p < 0.1$) but not for domestic MNCs and foreign MNC affiliates. This result supports the findings of Choi and Jiang [2009], and may explain why the value implication of derivatives use does not differ significantly between domestic firms and domestic MNCs, as Géczy *et al.* [1997], and Allayannis and Ofek [2001], state that a firm with a higher ratio of foreign sales to total sales is more likely to use derivatives to hedge exposure, thereby increasing firm value.

Heckman treatment model: Controlling for self-selection bias

In this section, following Chen and King [2014], and Lievenbruck and Schmid [2014], we execute a treatment effects model as found in Heckman [1979] to control for self-selection bias. The corresponding results for second-stage estimations for domestic firms, domestic MNCs and foreign MNC affiliates are reported in Table 8.

The Heckman treatment model confirms our previous findings that the use of derivatives is associated with an increase in firm value for domestic firms and domestic MNCs, with hedging premiums of 4.2% ($p < 0.1$) and 11.1% ($p < 0.1$), respectively. We notice that after controlling for self-selection bias, the magnitude of the value effect of derivatives use is higher than the OLS estimation, and this strongly supports the findings of previous studies that domestic MNCs outperform domestic firms (e.g. [Lin *et al.* 2009]). We also find that firms in countries with low levels of corruption are more valuable than those in highly corrupt countries, but a home country with low levels of corruption favors domestic MNCs more than domestics firms ($\beta_{Domestic\ MNCs} = 0.1186,\ p < 0.01;\ \beta_{domestic\ firms} = 0.0457,\ p < 0.1$). With regard to foreign MNC affiliates, we find that derivatives use decreases firm value by 6.89%, although a lower corruption level in the host country rewards foreign MNC affiliates with higher value ($\beta = 0.0077,\ p < 0.05$). These results are consistent with those findings reported from the OLS estimation in Table 7.

Table 8. Heckman treatment model.

Variable	Domestic firms	Domestic MNCs	Foreign MNC affiliates
Derivative use	0.042*	0.111***	−0.069**
	(0.071)	(0.000)	(0.018)
Derivative*corruption	0.046*	0.119***	0.007**
	(0.054)	(0.000)	(0.023)
Corruption index	0.058	0.016*	−0.092
	(0.798)	(0.072)	(0.614)
Firm size	0.935***	0.142***	0.712***
	(0.000)	(0.000)	(0.000)
Leverage	0.004	0.002*	0.012
	(0.408)	(0.084)	(0.160)
ROA	0.024*	−0.019***	0.037
	(0.064)	(0.000)	(0.235)
Capital expenditure	0.005	−0.007	−0.038*
	(0.169)	(0.731)	(0.078)
Quick ratio	−0.003	−0.074***	0.521***
	(0.916)	(0.000)	(0.002)
Dividend yield	−0.034	0.025***	−0.002
	(0.264)	(0.006)	(0.535)
Forsales	−0.002	−0.001**	−0.004
	(0.472)	(0.048)	(0.512)
Geomart	0.212	−0.032	0.001
	(0.141)	(0.357)	(0.997)
Diversification indicator	−0.162	−0.767	−0.176***
	(0.286)	(0.633)	(0.000)
GDP per capita	−0.006	0.003	−0.076***
	(0.961)	(0.325)	(0.000)
Financial system deposits to GDP	47.700	6.581	−161.1***
	(0.392)	(0.678)	(0.000)
Intercept	−0.335	−0.317**	0.550
	(0.620)	(0.047)	(0.393)
Country dummies	Yes	Yes	Yes
Industry dummies	Yes	Yes	Yes
Year dummies	Yes	Yes	Yes
No of observations	1086	1405	202
Mills ratio	0.422*	0.110***	−0.269**

Notes: This table presents the impacts of derivatives use on firm value from the perspective of a Heckman treatment model, divided into domestic firms, domestic MNCs and foreign MNC affiliates. The dependent variable is Ln (Tobin's Q), which is calculated as the natural logarithm of book value of total assets minus book value of equity plus market value of equity over book value of total assets. Derivatives use is calculated as the notional value of any derivative contract (foreign currency, interest rate and commodity price derivatives) in thousands of USD scaled by total assets. All other independent variable definitions are reported in Appendix. Standard errors are clustered by country to control for heteroscedasticity and serial correlation. P-values are in parentheses. Asterisks ***, ** and * indicate significance at the 1%, 5% and 10% levels, respectively.

4.3. *Linking derivatives use and exposures to country risks by firm types*

A comparison of exposures and derivatives use for domestic firms, domestic MNCs, and foreign affiliates

In terms of exposure to country risks in the panel C, we find some interesting results. For domestic firms, we observe that the derivatives use variable is significant and negatively related to exposure to country risks ($\beta = -0.1091,\ p < 0.1$), which indicates that firms using derivatives reduce exposure by 10.91% for each 1% increase in the notional value of general derivatives. It is also clear that, in the case of domestic MNCs, exposure to country risks decreases when the general notional amount of derivatives increases. Particularly, exposure declines by 14.42% for each 1% increase in notional holdings ($\beta = -0.142,\ p < 0.01$), which is higher than the corresponding figure for domestic firms. However, for foreign affiliates, we cannot find any evidence supporting a relationship between derivatives use and exposures to host country risks, even though derivative usage has a negative effect on exposure ($\beta = -0.094,\ p > 0.1$). In general, the overall results reported in panel C support Hypotheses 4 and 5.

Similar results are found with regard to exchange rate exposure. Panel A indicates that the use of foreign currency derivatives is inversely associated with exchange rate exposure in the case of domestic firms and domestic MNCs ($\beta_{domestic\ firms} = -0.1021,\ p < 0.01$; $\beta_{Domestic\ MNCs} = -0.1247,\ p < 0.05$). We also note that the derivatives use of foreign affiliates has a negative effect on exposure, although it is not significantly different from zero ($\beta = -0.1149,\ p > 0.1$).

With respect to interest rate exposure, we find the negative and significant signs on the use of interest rate derivatives, which shows that derivative usage has a significant impact on mitigating interest rate exposure, irrespective of whether firms are domestic firms, domestic MNCs, or foreign affiliates ($\beta_{domestic\ firms} = -0.1267,\ p < 0.1$; $\beta_{Domestic\ MNCs} = -0.1545,\ p < 0.05$; $\beta_{foreign\ affiliates} = -0.0151,\ p < 0.1$). The estimated coefficients indicate that the use of derivatives decreases interest rate exposure by 12.67%, 15.45% and 1.51% per 1% increase in notional derivative holdings for domestic firms, domestic MNCs and foreign affiliates, respectively.

Random effects model

For domestic firms, the estimated coefficients on foreign currency, interest rate, and general derivative intensities are significantly negative at −0.0695, −0.1188, and −0.1104 ($p < 0.01$, $p < 0.1$ and $p < 0.1$), respectively, indicating that, in all cases, the use of derivatives contributes to a reduction in exposures to exchange rate, interest rate risks and home country risks. For foreign affiliates, we obtain findings very similar to those found in Table 9, in which only the coefficient on interest rate

Table 9. Exposures and derivatives use.

Variables	Domestic firms		Domestic MNCs	Foreign affiliates
Panel A: FX exposures				
FCD	−0.1021*** (0.000)	−0.1247** (0.027)	−0.1149 (0.230)	
Firm size	−0.0101 (0.135)	−0.0203* (0.059)	−0.0104 (0.385)	
Leverage	−0.0023 (0.762)	−0.0416* (0.086)	−0.0126*** (0.001)	
FORSALES	0.0194 (0.760)	0.0326 (0.377)	0.0128 (0.237)	
Diversification indicator	0.0555* (0.068)	−0.0414 (0.146)	−0.0320 (0.541)	
GDP per capita	0.2194*** (0.004)	0.202* (0.070)	−2.212*** (0.003)	
DEPOSITSTOGDP	−0.0613** (0.013)	−0.0462*** (0.009)	0.0215 (0.566)	
Rule of law	−0.0519 (0.773)	0.160 (0.482)	0.379 (0.589)	
Intercept	−3.1646*** (0.003)	−2.645* (0.072)	2.1538*** (0.004)	
Country dummies	Yes	Yes	Yes	
Industry dummies	Yes	Yes	Yes	
Year dummies	Yes	Yes	Yes	
Observations	1053	1250	446	
R^2	0.225	0.290	0.270	
Panel B: IR exposures				
IRD	−0.1267* (0.058)	−0.1545** (0.039)	−0.0151* (0.075)	
Firm size	−0.0196 (0.364)	−0.0832* (0.061)	−0.0347 (0.107)	
Leverage	−0.0254** (0.038)	−0.0143 (0.308)	−0.0327** (0.045)	
FORSALES	0.0528 (0.513)	0.0116 (0.221)	0.0780 (0.846)	
Diversification indicator	0.134 (0.630)	−0.1065 (0.373)	−0.321 (0.290)	
GDP per capita	−0.119 (0.905)	−1.639 (0.234)	−1.729 (0.509)	
DEPOSITSTOGDP	−0.0445* (0.059)	−0.0416** (0.022)	−0.0476* (0.064)	
Rule of law	−0.5790 (0.173)	−0.1654 (0.148)	−0.3139 (0.197)	
Intercept	−5.395 (0.618)	8.8270 (0.358)	21.97 (0.583)	
Country dummies	Yes	Yes	Yes	
Industry dummies	Yes	Yes	Yes	
Year dummies	Yes	Yes	Yes	
Observations	645	2398	430	
R^2	0.326	0.278	0.362	
Panel C: Exposure to country risks				
DER	−0.1091* (0.059)	−0.1442*** (0.001)	−0.094 (0.327)	
Firm size	−0.0940 (0.454)	−0.0747** (0.033)	−0.494 (0.251)	
Leverage	−0.034 (0.477)	−0.0386 (0.686)	0.069 (0.373)	
FORSALES	0.0566 (0.196)	0.0107* (0.073)	0.096** (0.029)	
Diversification indicator	−0.288 (0.359)	−0.0411* (0.071)	−0.820 (0.780)	
GDP per capita	0.568 (0.946)	0.1458 (0.088)	0.629 (0.477)	
DEPOSITSTOGDP	−0.0695*** (0.003)	−0.116 (0.130)	−0.073** (0.025)	
Rule of law	4.911 (0.853)	0.1026 (0.174)	−0.4054** (0.038)	

(*Continued*)

Table 9. (*Continued*)

Intercept Variables	**Domestic firms**	**Domestic MNCs**	**Foreign affiliates**
Intercept	−1.4906 (0.208)	−1.8547 (0.125)	−5.986** (0.012)
Country dummies	Yes	Yes	Yes
Industry dummies	Yes	Yes	Yes
Year dummies	Yes	Yes	Yes
Observations	2007	1272	198
R^2	0.323	0.256	0.404

Notes: This table reports the effects of derivatives use on exposures across domestic firms, domestic MNCs and foreign affiliates from pooled regression models split up with regard to exposure to country risks, exchange rate and interest rate risks. The dependent variable are absolute values of exposures to country risks $|\hat{\beta}_{2ijt}|$ (panel A), exchange rate risks $|\hat{\beta}_{3ijt}|$ (panel B) and interest rate risks $|\hat{\beta}_{4ijt}|$ (panel C). DER is the notional value of any derivative contracts in thousand USD scaled by total assets. FCD is the notional value of foreign currency derivatives in thousand USD scaled by total assets. IRD is the notional value of interest rate derivatives in thousand USD scaled by total assets. All other independent variables definitions are reported in Table 2. Standard errors are clustered by country to control for heteroscedasticity and serial correlation. P-values are in parentheses. Asterisks ***, ** and * indicate significance at the 1%, 5% and 10% levels, respectively.

Table 10. Random effects model.

Variables	**Domestic firms**	**Domestic MNCs**	**Foreign affiliates**
Panel A: FX exposures			
FCD	−0.0695*** (0.001)	−0.1473* (0.093)	−0.1336 (0.758)
Firm size	−0.0317* (0.056)	−0.0212 (0.873)	−0.0108 (0.216)
Leverage	−0.0156 (0.459)	−0.0638* (0.056)	0.0133* (0.044)
FORSALES	0.0335 (0.515)	0.0391 (0.476)	0.0164* (0.069)
Diversification indicator	0.6151 (0.178)	−0.0395 (0.177)	−0.1297 (0.973)
GDP per capita	−0.0125 (0.943)	0.0185** (0.049)	0.0765*** (0.001)
DEPOSITSTOGDP	−0.2156*** (0.006)	−0.0472** (0.020)	−0.1971 (0.409)
Rule of law	−0.0537* (0.078)	0.159 (0.430)	−0.4365 (0.878)
Intercept	0.2460 (0.341)	−2.404 (0.430)	1.494 (0.396)
Country dummies	Yes	Yes	Yes
Industry dummies	Yes	Yes	Yes
Year dummies	Yes	Yes	Yes
Observations	2616	2859	481
Panel B: IR exposures			
IRD	−0.1188* (0.064)	−0.1483** (0.041)	−0.0151* (0.063)
Firm size	−0.0279 (0.937)	−0.0644** (0.047)	−0.0347 (0.637)
Leverage	−0.0142 (0.911)	−0.0209** (0.017)	−0.0406* (0.064)
FORSALES	0.0397** (0.037)	0.0110 (0.571)	0.0388 (0.947)
Diversification indicator	0.1757 (0.860)	−0.107 (0.253)	−0.0287 (0.937)

(*Continued*)

Table 10. (*Continued*)

Variables	**Domestic firms**	**Domestic MNCs**	**Foreign affiliates**
GDP per capita	−0.1370** (0.022)	−0.876 (0.516)	−0.0252 (0.178)
DEPOSITSTOGDP	−0.0606*** (0.000)	−0.0419*** (0.000)	−0.0476** (0.028)
Rule of law	−0.2718*** (0.001)	0.453 (0.258)	−0.3873 (0.212)
Intercept	9.6163* (0.083)	7.3024 (0.479)	6.953 (0.836)
Country dummies	Yes	Yes	Yes
Industry dummies	Yes	Yes	Yes
Year dummies	Yes	Yes	Yes
Observations	2311	2604	464
Panel C: Exposures to country risks			
DER	−0.1104* (0.087)	−0.1430*** (0.007)	0.0417 (0.282)
Firm size	−0.1238 (0.470)	−0.0313 (0.277)	−0.0702* (0.087)
Leverage	−0.0346 (0.401)	0.0449 (0.563)	−0.0360** (0.016)
FORSALES	0.0680* (0.065)	0.0108 (0.536)	0.0698** (0.038)
Diversification indicator	−0.2883 (0.361)	0.0276* (0.033)	−0.0955 (0.768)
GDP per capita	0.568** (0.046)	−0.1033 (0.457)	−0.0395 (0.664)
DEPOSITSTOGDP	−0.819 (0.340)	−0.0984** (0.038)	−0.0639 (0.103)
Rule of law	0.4911 (0.912)	0.1339 (0.536)	−0.0307 (0.167)
Intercept	0.2021 (0.859)	1.6581 (0.360)	0.3372 (0.786)
Country dummies	Yes	Yes	Yes
Industry dummies	Yes	Yes	Yes
Year dummies	Yes	Yes	Yes
Observations	2007	2716	473

Notes: This table presents the impacts of derivatives use on exposures across domestic firms, domestic MNCs and foreign affiliates from random effects models split up with regard to exposure to country risks, exchange rate and interest rate risks. The dependent variable are absolute values of exposures to country risks $|\hat{\beta}_{2ijt}|$ (panel A), exchange rate risks $|\hat{\beta}_{3ijt}|$ (panel B) and interest rate risks $|\hat{\beta}_{4ijt}|$ (panel C). DER is the notional value of any derivative contracts in thousand USD scaled by total assets. FCD is the notional value of foreign currency derivatives in thousand USD scaled by total assets. IRD is the notional value of interest rate derivatives in thousand USD scaled by total assets. All other independent variables definitions are reported in Table 2. Standard errors are clustered by country to control for heteroscedasticity and serial correlation. P-values are in parentheses. Asterisks ***, ** and * indicate significance at the 1%, 5% and 10% levels, respectively.

derivatives is significantly inverse to interest rate exposure ($\beta = -0.0151$, $p < 0.1$), while we fail to find any evidence supporting a negative link between derivatives use and exposures to exchange rate risks, and to home country risks ($\beta_{in\,panel\,A} = -0.1336$, $p > 0.1$; $\beta_{in\,panel\,C} = 0.0417$, $p > 0.1$).

For domestic MNCs, similar findings to those found in Table 9 are observed, as we find that the use of any derivatives, foreign currency derivatives, and interest rate derivatives are separately associated with lower degrees of equivalent types of exposures ($\beta_{in\,panel\,C} = -0.1430$, $p < 0.01$; $\beta_{in\,panel\,A} = -0.1473$, $p < 0.1$; $\beta_{in\,panel\,B} = -0.1483$, $p < 0.05$). We also observe that the estimated coefficients on derivatives use for domestic MNCs are larger in magnitude than domestic firms and foreign affiliates, confirming the findings in the previous section that the negative relation between derivatives use and exposures is strongest for domestic MNCs.

5. Conclusion

5.1. *Theoretical and methodological contributions*

The first theoretical contribution of this study is to incorporate institutional theory (e.g. [North, 1990, 1994; Dunning, 2003; Peng *et al.* 2005]) and Dunning's OLI paradigm [Dunning, 1988; Dunning and Lundan, 2008] into the analysis of derivative activities. This approach sheds a new light to the hedging theory (e.g. [Smith and Stulz, 1985; Mayers and Smith, 1990; Nance *et al.* 1993; Froot *et al.* 1993]), which concentrates mainly on firm-specific characteristics. Through this research approach, we first demonstrate that not only is a firm's decision on using financial derivatives determined by factors within that firm's boundary, but it is also necessary to improve hedging theory as well as variables to measure determinants of derivatives use.

Second, our research contributes to theoretical literature by taking an institution-based view of value effects of derivatives use for different firm types including domestic firms, domestic MNCs and foreign affiliates. It is important to highlight that our study adopts a new approach by applying concepts of institutional theory in international business (IB) to the recently developed conditional analysis of relationship between derivatives use and firm value in finance (e.g. [Fauver and Naranjo, 2010; Allayannis *et al.* 2012]). Doing so, our approach underlines the role as "rule of games" of institutions in general [North, 1990, 1994], and corruption environment in particular, in shaping firm valuation, and argues that without directly taking into account institutional environment in analysis, it will be difficult to determine whether derivatives use is a value-enhancing activity.

Third, we apply the market model [Alder and Dumas, 1984; Jorion, 1990] to estimate exposures to home and host country risks, which is one of the foremost theoretical contributions of this research. The innovation and distinction of our method is to demonstrate clearly how country risk exposures can be measured as a regression coefficient by using well-known linear regression techniques. To our knowledge so far, we are one of the first to measure exposures to country risks, and contribute to the existing literature on this area by providing a quantitative measurement, which will open an access for researchers to exploit further perspectives of country risk exposures. This approach also conforms to interests of policy makers, stockholders, investors and analyst firms as efforts must be made by each firm to approximate and quantify their exposures.

Finally, the fundamental starting point in discussion of conditions under which firms hedge and hedging can add value is Modigliani and Miller (MM) theorem. Modiglian and Miller [1958] find that under a specific set of assumptions about frictionless markets, equal access to market prices, rational investors and equal access to costless information, hedging is irrelevant and cannot contribute to the creation of firm value. This study, therefore, improves upon key assumptions of MM theorem and contributes to methodological literature by building on institutional conditions and heterogeneity of firm types, i.e. domestic firms, domestic MNCs and foreign affiliates. We find that hedging can add value and reward firms with higher value if there are well-governed and good-functioning institutions, and such effect of hedging somewhat depends on heterogeneity of firm types.

5.2. *Empirical contributions*

Our study not only enriches the empirical literature by adding, to our best knowledge, the first East Asian evidence on determinants of derivatives use, value effects of derivatives use, and the association between the use of derivatives and exposures across eight East Asian countries covering from developed countries to emerging economies, and with differences in terms of business, economic and political environments, but also contributes to the extant literature up to date in the following ways:

First, our research provides a comprehensive examination on determinants of derivatives' use with a focus on country-specific factors that have not been thoroughly examined in the existing literature, namely governance mechanism, corruption levels and country risks. Our study strongly finds that countries' governance mechanisms have significant and positive effect on firms' decisions on derivatives' use, and corruption levels play a significant role in explaining the use of derivatives. These findings suggest that country-specific characteristics may explain some of the ambiguity in the existing empirical literature.

Second, to our knowledge so far, this study is one of the first to examine how derivatives' use affects firm value under influence of corrupt environments. Our study evidences that low corruption level of home country rewards domestic firms and domestic MNCs with higher value (hedging premiums are from 9.87% to 11.77%, and 10.78% to 12.72%, respectively), and foreign affiliates are more valuable in host countries where corruption is less severe.

Third, to the best of our knowledge, we are among the first to measure exposures to country risks by using the market model, and focus specifically on answering whether the use of financial derivatives can reduce those exposures. We provide a strong finding that derivatives activities of domestic firms and domestic MNCs significantly reduce exposures to home country risks by 10.91% and 14.42% per 1% increase in notional derivatives holdings, respectively, meanwhile foreign affiliates with derivatives use fail to mitigate exposures to their host country risks.

Fourth, our study is different from the prior studies in the way of comparing value effects of derivatives use for a wide range of firm types including domestic firms, domestic MNCs and foreign affiliates in order to answer important but unexplored questions: what firm type in which value implication of derivatives use is greater; and which corruption level rewards firm with higher value. Our findings consistently notice that domestic MNCs outperform domestic firms and foreign affiliates, and evidence that home country's low corruption levels favor domestic MNCs than domestics firms.

5.3. *Practical implications*

Even though there is vast evidence on derivatives' use by firms in US and European developed firms, these countries have quite similar economic, financial and social environments. Our sample of East Asia countries, in contrast, covers both developed and developing countries with heterogeneity in institutional environments, which enables us to exploit comprehensively multifaceted hedging behaviors of a wide range of firm types. As such, this study provides important practical implications to firm managers, country-level regulators, and policy makers as follows:

First, our research approach and findings propose some avenues for further theoretical and empirical research on institutional environments and firms' hedging activities aimed at elucidating firms' decision on using derivatives. Additionally, the study provides important policy implications emphasizing the role of policy makers in institutional development to facilitate firms to explore benefits of hedging such as enhancing legal systems, and improving government efficiency.

Second, the empirical findings provide useful and practical insights to firms' managers to increase their firm value through derivative activities, and clearly suggest that they should include measures for home/host country's corruption levels when determining hedging policy. Additionally, our findings provide direct implications for firms' managers on decision regarding capital structure. It suggests that firms could influence cost of capital in particular, and capital structure in general by using financial derivatives, thus firm managers better perform the important tasks of strategic capital planning and managing risks.

Third, our findings also have practical and meaningful implications for policy makers and regulators. The study first proposes that regulators or policy makers should be more active in cracking down corruption levels in order to enhance performances of non-financial firms using derivatives. Further, the finding that a firm's exposure to home country risk is mitigated through the use of financial derivatives suggests that effective management of derivative markets is necessary to ensure stability of financial system and economy in general.

Fourth, due to characteristics of our wide range of sample firms including both domestic-owned, and foreign-owned firms, and our sample countries covering both developed and developing countries, the results of this thesis can be easily generalized into any other developing and developed countries in which there are non-financial firms using financial derivatives, as well as where country-level governance and corruption exist. Further, our sample consists of Japan — the world's third largest economy — and China — the second largest economy and a key player in the world economy and markets — thus the results of this thesis can be applicable to various aspects of international business and finance.

Acknowledgment

This chapter is built upon Trang Kim's PhD thesis and three related papers. The first paper is "Multinationals and the impact of corruption on financial derivatives use and firm value: Evidence from East Asia"; the second paper is "Linking country governance quality and derivatives use: Insights from firms' hedging behavior in East Asia"; and the third paper is "Multinational corporations managing risk in East Asia: Empirical analysis of the association between derivatives use and exposures". The authors would like to express our sincerest gratitude to Prof. Marina Papanastassiou, Dr. Xufei Zhang, Dr. Amrit Judege, the internal and external examiners of Trang Kim's thesis. We also would like to thank the editors and referees who have given helpful feedback to improve the materials related to this chapter.

References

Adler, M. and Dumas, B. (1984). Exposure to currency risk: Definition and measurement. *Financial Management* **13** (2), 41–50.

Allayannis, G., Lel, U. and Miller, P. D. (2012). The use of foreign currency derivatives, corporate governance, and firm value around the world. *Journal of International Economics* **87**, 65–79.

Allayannis, G. and Ofek, E. (2001). Exchange rate exposure, hedging, and the use of foreign currency derivatives. *Journal of International Money and Finance* **20**, 273–296.

Allayannis, G. and Weston, P. J. (2001). The use of foreign currency derivatives and firm market value. *Review of Financial Studies* **14** (1), 243–276.

Allen, L. and Pantzalis, C. (1996). Valuation of the operating flexibility of multinational corporations. *Journal of International Business Studies* **27** (4), 633–653.

Ameer, R., Matisa, R. and Abduliah, A. (2011). A survey on usage of derivatives and their effect on cost of equity capital. *Journal of Derivatives* **19** (1), 56–71.

Bartram, S. M., Brown, G. W. and Fehle, F. R. (2009). International evidence on financial derivatives usage. *Financial Management* **38** (1), 185–206.

Bartram, S. M., Brown, W. G. and Conrad, J. (2011). The effects of derivatives on firm risk and value. *Journal of Financial and Quantitative Analysis* **46** (4), 967–999.

Beck, T. and Levine, R. (2008). Legal institutions and financial development. In C. Menard and M. Shirley (eds.), *Handbook of New Institutional Economics*. (Springer, Dordrecht, the Netherlands).

Beets, S. D. (2005). Understanding the demand-side: Issues of international corruption. *Journal of Business Ethics* **57**, 65–81.

Bell, G., Filatotchev, I. and Rasheed, A. (2012). The liability of foreignness in capital markets: Sources and remedies. *Journal of International Business Studies* **43** (2), 107–122.

Bergara, M. E., Henisz, W. J. and Spiller, P. T. (1998). Political institutions and electric utility investment: A cross-nation analysis. *California Management Review* **40** (2), 18–35.

Berghofer, B. and Lucey, B. (2014). Fuel hedging, operational hedging and risk exposure — Evidence from the global airline industry. *International Review of Financial Analysis* **34**, 124–39.

Bessembinder, H. (1991). Forward contracts and firm value: Investment incentive and contracting effects. *Journal of Financial and Quantitative Analysis* **26**, 519–532.

BIS. (2014). *OTC derivatives statistics at the end-December 2014*. Bank for International Settlements.

BIS. (2015). *OTC derivatives statistics at the end-December 2015*. Bank for International Settlements.

Blass, A. and Yafeh, Y. (2001). Vagabond shoes longing to stray: Why foreign firms list in the United States. *Journal of Banking and Finance* **25** (3), 555–572.

Bodnar, G. M. and Wong, M. H. F. (2000). Estimating exchange rate exposures: Some weighty issues. *National Bureau of Economic Research (NBER)* Working paper 7497.

Brouthers, L. E., Gao, Y. and McNicol, J. P. (2008). Corruption and market attractiveness influences on different types of FDI. *Strategic Management Journal* **29** (6), 673–680.

Bruton, G. D., Ahlstrom, D. and Obloj, K. (2008). Entrepreneurship in emerging economies: Where are we today and where should the research go in the future? *Entrepreneurship Theory and Practice* **32** (1), 1–14.

Bryan, M. L. and Jenkins, S. P. (2013). Regression analysis of country effects using multilevel data: Cautionary tale. https://www.iser.essex.ac.uk/research/publications/working-papers/iser/2013-14 [19 August 2013].

Buckley, P. J. and Casson, M. (1976). *The Future of Multinational Enterprise* (McMillan, London).

Butler, C. K. (2008). *Multinational Finance*. 4th edn. (John Wiley & Sons, West Sussex, England).

Campello, M., Lin, C., Ma, Y. and Zou, H. (2011). The real and financial implication of corporate hedging. *Journal of Finance* **66** (5), 1615–1647.

Cantwell, J., Dunning, J. H. and Lundan, S. M. (2010). An evolutionary approach to understanding international business activity: The co-evolution of MNEs and the institutional environment. *Journal of International Business Studies* **41**, 567–586.

Castellani, D. and Zanfei, A. (2006). *Multinational Firms, Innovation and Productivity* (Edward Elgar, Cheltenham).

Charumathi, B. and Kota, H. B. (2012). On the determinants of derivative usage by large Indian non-financial firms. *Global Business Review* **13** (2), 251–267.

Chen, J. and King, T. H. D. (2014). Corporate hedging and the cost of debt. *Journal of Corporate Finance* **29**, 221–245.

Choi, J. J. and Jiang, C. (2009). Does multinationality matter? Implications of operational hedging for the exchange risk exposure. *Journal of Banking and Finance* **33**, 1973–1982.

Chung, C. H., Lee, S. H., Beamish, P. and Isobe, T. (2010). Subsidiary expansion/contraction during times of economic crisis. *Journal of International Business Studies* **41** (3), 500–525.

Clark, E. and Judge, A. (2008). The determinants of foreign currency hedging: Does foreign currency debt induce a bias?*European Financial Management* **14** (3), 445–469.

Clark, E. and Judge, A. (2009). Foreign currency derivatives versus foreign currency debt and the hedging premium. *European Financial Management* **15** (3), 606–642.

Clark, E. and Mefteh, S. (2011). Asymmetric foreign currency exposures and derivatives use: Evidence from france. *Journal of International Financial Management and Accounting* **22** (1), 27–45.

Contractor, F. J. (1990). Ownership patterns of U.S. joint ventures abroad and the liberalization of foreign government regulations in the 1980s: Evidence from the benchmark surveys. *Journal of International Business Studies* **21** (1), 55–73.

Cuervo-Cazurra, A. (2008). Better the devil you don't know: Types of corruption and FDI in transition economies. *Journal of International Management* **14** (1), 12–27.

Cuervo-Cazurra, A. (2011). Global strategy and global business environment: The direct and indirect influences of the home country on a firm's global strategy. *Global Strategy Journal* **1** (3–4), 382–386.

Denis, D. J., Denis, D. K. and Yost, K. (2002). Global diversification, industrial diversification, and firm value. *Journal of Finance* **57**, 1951–1979.

Donadelli, M., Fasan, M. and Magnanelli, B. S. (2014). The agency problem, financial performance and corruption: Country, industry and firm level perspectives. *European Management Review* **11**, 259–272.

Dunning, J. H. and Lundan, S. M. (2008). Institutions and the OLI paradigm of the multinational enterprise. *Asia Pacific Journal of Management* **25**, 573–593.

Dunning, J. H. (1977). Trade, location of economic activity and the MNE: A search for an eclectic approach. In B. Ohlin, P. O. Hesselborn and P. M. Wijkman (eds). *The International Allocation of Economic Activity* (McMillan, London and Basingstoke), 395–418.

Dunning, J. H. (1988). The eclectic paradigm of international production: A restatement and some possible extensions. *Journal of International business studies* **19** (1), 1–31

Dunning, J. H. (2003). Some antecedents of internalization theory. *Journal of International Business Studies* **34** (1), 108–115.

Durnev, A. (2011). The real effects of political uncertainty: Elections, capital allocation, and performance. Working paper, University of Iowa.

Eden, L. and Miller, S. R. (2004). Distance matters: Liability of foreignness, institutional distance, and ownership strategy. *Advances in International Management* **16**, 187–221.

Erickson, T. and Whited, T. (2006). On the accuracy of different measures of q. *Financial Management* **35**, 5–33.

Faff, R. W. and Marshall, A. (2005). International evidence on the determinants of foreign exchange rate exposure of multinational corporations. *Journal of International Business Studies* **36** (5), 539–558.

Froot, K. A., Scharfstein, D. S. and Stein, J. C. (1993). Risk management: Coordinating corporate investment and financing policies. *Journal of Finance* **48** (5), 1629–1658.

Gay, G. D., Lin, C. M. and Smith, S. D. (2011). Corporate derivatives use and the cost of equity. *Journal of Banking and Finance* **35**, 1491–506.

Géczy, C., Minton, B. A. and Schrand, C. (1997). Why firms use currency derivatives. *Journal of Finance* **52** (4), 1323–1354.

Globerman, S. and Shapiro, D. (2003). Governance infrastructure and U.S. foreign direct investment. *Journal of International Business Studies* **34** (1), 19–39.

Glover, B. and Levine, O. (2015). Uncertainty, investment, and managerial incentives. *Journal of Monetary Economics* **69**, 121–37.

Graham, J. R. and Rogers, D. A. (2002). Do firms hedge in response to tax incentives? *Journal of Finance* **57**, 815–839.

Guay, W. and Kothari, S. P. (2003). How much do firms hedge with derivatives? *Journal of Economics and Business* **70**, 423–461.

Gupta, S. L. (2006). *Financial Derivatives: Theory, Concepts, and Problems* (Prentice-Hall, India).

Habib, M. and Zurawicki, L. (2002). Corruption and foreign direct investment. *Journal of International Business Studies* **33** (2), 291–308.

Hausman, J. A. (1978). Specification tests in econometrics. *Econometrica: Journal of the Econometric Society* **46** (6), 1251–1271.

He, J. and Ng, L. K. (1998). The foreign exchange exposure of Japanese multinational Corporations. *Journal of Finance* **53** (2), 733–753.

Heckman, C. R. (1985). A financial model of foreign exchange exposure. *Journal of International Business Studies* **16**, 83–99.

Henisz, W. (2000). The institutional environment for multinational investment. *The Journal of Law, Economics, and Organization* **16** (2), 334–364.

Higón, D. A. and Antolín, M. M. (2012). Multinationality, foreignness and institutional distance in the relation between R&D and productivity. *Research Policy* **41** (3), 592–601.

Holburn, G. L. F. and Zelner, B. A. (2010). Political capabilities, policy risk, and international investment strategy: Evidence from the global electric power generation industry. *Strategic Management Journal* **31** (12), 1290–1315.

Huang, T., Wu, F., Yu, J. and Zhang, B. (2015). Political risk and dividend policy: Evidence from international political crises. *Journal of International Business Studies* **46**, 574–595.

Huffman, S. P., Makar, S. D. and Beyer, S. B. (2010). A three-factor model investigation of foreign exchange rate exposure. *Global Finance Journal* **21**, 1–12.

Hull, J. C. (2012). *Options, Futures, and Other Derivatives* (Pearson, England). ISDA. (2009). Research notes. [Online]. Available from: http://www.isda.org/researchnotes/pdf/ISDA-Research-Notes2.pdf

Hutson, E. and Laing, E. (2014). Foreign exchange exposure and multinationality. *Journal of Banking and Finance* **43**, 97–113.

Hutson, E. and Stevenson, S. (2010). Openness, hedging incentives and foreign exchange exposure: A firm-level multi-country study. *Journal of International Business Studies* **41**, 105–22.

Hymer, S. H. (1976). *The International Operations of National Firms: A Study of Direct Foreign Investment* (MIT Press, Cambridge, MA).

Javorcik, B. S. and Wei, S. J. (2009). Corruption and cross-border investment in emerging markets: Firm-level evidence. *Journal of International Money and Finance* **28**, 605–624.

Jiang, Y. and Peng, M. (2010). Principal-principal conflicts during crisis. *Asia Pacific Journal of Management* **28** (4), 683–695.

Jorion, P. (1990). The exchange rate exposure of US multinationals. *Journal of Business* **63** (3), 331–345.

Judge, A. (2006). Why and how UK firms hedge? *European Financial Management* **12** (3), 407–441.

Júnior, J. L. R. (2013). Hedging, selective hedging, or speculation? Evidence of the use of derivatives by Brazilian firms during the financial crisis. *Journal of Multinational Financial Management* **23**, 415–433.

Kaufmann, D., Kraay, A. and Mastruzzi, M. (2005). Measuring governance using cross-country perception data. MPRA Paper 8219, University Library of Munich, Germany.

Khanna, T. and Palepu, K. (1997). Why focused strategies may be wrong for emerging markets. *Harvard Business Review* **75**, 41–48.

Khanna, T., Palepu, K. G. and Sinha, J. (2005). Strategies that fit emerging markets. *Harvard Business Review* **83**, 6–15.

Khanna, T. and Rivkin, J. W. (2001). Estimating the performance effects of business groups in emerging markets. *Strategic Management Journal* **22** (1), 45–74.

Khanna, T. and Yafeh, Y. (2005). Business groups and risk sharing around the world. *The Journal of Business* **78**, 301–340.

Kim, C. F. and Pantzalis, C. (2003). Global/industrial diversification and analyst herding. *Financial Analysis Journal* **59**, 69–79.

Kim, T., Papanastassiou, M. and Nguyen, Q. (2017). Linking governance quality and derivatives use: Insights from firms' hedging behavior. Working Paper, Middlesex University Business School.

Kim, Y., Mathur, I. and Nam, J. (2006). Is operational hedging a substitute for or a complement to financial hedging? *Journal of Corporate Finance* **12**, 834–853.

Knack, S. (2001). Aid dependence and the quality of governance: Cross-country empirical tests. *Southern Economic Journal* **68** (2), 310–329.

Kolb, R. W. and Overdahl, J. A. (2003). *Financial Derivatives* (John Wiley & Sons, Hoboken, New Jersey).

Kostova, T., Roth, K. and Dacin, M. T. (2008). Institutional theory in the study of multinational corporations: A critique and new directions. *Academy of Management Review* **33** (4), 994–1006.

Krapl, A. A. (2015). Corporate international diversification and risk. *International Review of Financial Analysis* **37**, 1–13.

Kumar, P. and Rabinovitch, R. (2013). CEO entrenchment and corporate hedging: Evidence from the oil and gas industry. *Journal of Financial and Quantitative Analysis* **48** (3), 887–917.

La Porta, R., Lopez-de-Silanes, F., Shleifer, A. and Vishny, R. W. (1997). Legal determinants of external finance. *Journal of Finance* **52**, 1131–1150.

La Porta, R., Lopez-de-Silanes, F., Shleifer, A. and Vishny, R. W. (1998). Law and finance. *Journal of Political Economy* **106**, 1113–1155.

Labmert, R., Leuz, C. and Verrecchia, R. (2009). Information asymmetry, information precision, and the cost of capital. Working paper, University of Chicago.

Lambsdorff, J. G. (2006). Causes and consequences of corruption: what do we know from a cross-section of countries? In S. Rose-Ackerman (ed.), *International Handbook on the Economics of Corruption* (Edward Elgar, Northampton, UK), 3–51.

Lecraw, D. J. (1984). Bargaining power, ownership, and profitability of transnational corporations in developing countries. *Journal of International Business Studies* **15**, 27–43.

Lee, S. H. and Hong, S. J. (2012). Corruption and subsidiary profitability: US MNC subsidiaries in the Asia Pacific region. *Asia Pacific Journal of Management* **29** (4), 949–964.

Lee, S. H. and Song, S. (2012). Host country uncertainty, intra- MNC production shifts, and subsidiary performance. *Strategic Management Journal* **33** (11), 1331–1340.

Lee, S. K. and Jang, S. C. S. (2010). Internationalization and exposure to foreign currency risk: An examination of lodging firms. *International Journal of Hospitality Management* **29**, 701–710.

Lel, U. (2012). Currency hedging and corporate governance: A cross-country analysis. *Journal of Corporate Finance* **18**, 221–237.

Levy, B. and Spiller, P. T. (1994). The institutional foundations of regulatory commitment: A comparative analysis of telecommunications regulation. *Journal of Law, Economics, & Organization* **10**, 201–246.

Lievenbruck, M. and Schmid, T. (2014). Why do firms (not) hedge? — Novel evidence on cultural influence. *Journal of Corporate Finance* **25**, 92–106.

Lin, J. B., Pantzalis, C. and Park, J. C. (2009). Derivatives use, information asymmetry, and MNC post-acquisition performance. *Financial Management Autumn* **2009**, 631–661.

Lin, Z., Peng, M. W., Yang, H. and Sun, S. L. (2008). What drives M&As in China and America? Networks, learning, and institutions. Working paper, University of Texas: Dallas.

Luo, Y. D. (2001). Toward a cooperative view of MNC–host government relations: Building blocks and performance implications. *Journal of International Business Studies* **32** (3), 401–419.

Madura, J. (2010). *International Financial Management* (South-Western Cengage Learning, USA).

Magee, S. (2008). Foreign currency hedging and firm value: A dynamic panel approach. Working paper.

Makino, S., Isobe, T. and Chan, C. M. (2004). Does country matter? *Strategic Management Journal* **25** (10), 1027–1043.

Marami, A. and Dubois, M. (2013). Interest rate derivatives and firm value: Evidence from mandatory versus voluntary hedging. *Risk Management eJournal* **82** (82), 1–47.

Mayers, D. and Smith, C. W. (1982). On the corporate demand for insurance. *Journal of Business* **55** (2), 281–296.

Mayers, D. and Smith, C. W. (1990). On the corporate demand for insurance: Evidence from the reinsurance market. *Journal of Business* **63**, 19–40.

Michel, A. and Shaked, I. (1986). Multinational corporations vs. domestic corporations: Financial performance and characteristics. *Journal of International Business Studies* **17**, 89–100.

Modigliani, F. and Miller, M. H. (1958). The cost of capital, corporation finance and the theory of investment. *American Economic Review* **48**, 261–297.

Nachum, L. (2003). Liability of foreignness in global competition? Financial service affiliates in the city of London. *Strategic Management Journal* **24**, 1187–1208.

Nain, A. (2004). The strategic motives for corporate risk management. University of Michigan. Working paper.

Nance, D. R., Smith, C. W. and Smithson, C. W. (1993). On the determinants of corporate hedging. *Journal of Finance* **48** (1), 267–284.

Nell, P. C., Puck, J. and Heidenreich, S. (2015). Strictly limited choice or agency? Institutional duality, legitimacy and subsidiaries' political strategies. *Journal of World Business* **50**, 302–311.

Ngobo, P. V. and Fouda, M. (2012). Is "good" governance good for business? A cross-national analysis of firms in African countries. *Journal of World Business* **47**, 435–449.

Nguyen, H. and Faff, R. (2010). Are firms hedging or speculating? the relationship between financial derivatives and firm risk. *Applied Financial Economics* **20**, 827–843.

North, D. C. (1990). *Institutions, Institutional Change and Economic Performance* (Cambridge University Press, Cambridge, UK).

North, D. C. (1993). Economic institutions through time. Nobel Lecture.

North, D. C. (1994). Economic performance through time. *American Economic Review* **84** (3), 359–368.

Oh, C. H. and Oetzel, J. (2011). Multinationals' response to major disasters: How does subsidiary investment vary in response to the type of disaster and the quality of country governance? *Strategic Management Journal* **32**, 658–681.

Pantzalis, C., Simkins, B. J. and Laux, P. A. (2001). Operational hedges and the foreign exchange exposure of U.S multinational corporations. *Journal of International Business Studies* **33**, 793–812.

Pástor, L. and Veronesi, P. (2012). Uncertainty about Government policy and stock prices. *Journal of Finance* **57**, 1219–1264.

Pástor, L. and Veronesi, P. (2013). Political uncertainty and risk premia. *Journal of Financial Economics* **110**, 520–545.

Peng, M. W., Lee, S. H. and Wang, D. Y. L. (2005). What determines the scope of the firm over time? A focus on institutional relatedness. *Academy of Management Review* **30** (3), 622–633.

Peng, M. W. and Luo, Y. D. (2000). Managerial ties and firm performance in a transition economy: The nature of a micro-macro link. *Academy of Management Journal* **43** (3), 486–501.

Petrou, A. P. and Thanos, I. C. (2014). The "grabbing hand" or the "helping hand" view of corruption: Evidence from bank foreign market entries. *Journal of World Business* **49**, 444–454.

Petrou, A. P. (2014). Bank foreign affiliate performance in the face of pervasive and arbitrary corruption. *European Management Review* **11**, 209–221.

Petrou, A. P. (2015). Arbitrariness of corruption and foreign affiliate performance: A resource dependence perspective. *Journal of World Business* **50**, 826–837.

Quazi, R. M. (2014). Corruption and FDI in East Asia and South Asia: An econometric study. *International Journal of Economics and Financial Issues* **4** (2), 231–242.

Rogers, W. H. (1993). sg17: Regression standard errors in clustered samples. *Stata Technical Bulletin* **13**, 19–23. In *Stata Technical Bulletin Reprints* **3**, 88–94, College Station, TX: Stata Press.

Rose-Ackerman, S. (1978). *Corruption: A Study in Political Economy* (Academic Press, New York).

Rose-Ackerman, S. (1999). *Corruption and Government: Causes, Consequences, and Reform* (Cambridge University Press, London).

Rugman, A. M. (1976). Risk reduction by international diversification. *Journal of International Business Studies* **7** (2), 75–80.

Rugman, A. M. (1981). *Inside the Multinationals: The Economics of Internal Markets*. (Columbia Press, New York).

Smith, A. W. and Stulz, R. M. (1985). The determinants of firms' hedging policies. *Journal of Financial and Quantitative Analysis* **20** (4), 391–405.

Sprcic, D. M. and Sevic, Z. (2012). Determinants of corporate hedging decision: Evidence from Croatian and Slovenian companies. *Research in International Business and Finance* **26**, 1–25.

Supanvanij, J. and Strauss, J. (2010). Corporate derivative use and the composition of CEO compensation. *Global Finance Journal* **21**, 170–185.

Talbot, E., Artiach, T. and Faff, R. (2013). What drives the commodity price beta of oil industry stocks? *Energy Economics* **37**, 1–15.

Treanor, S. D., Rogers, D. A., Carter, D. A. and Simkins, B. J. (2014). Exposure, hedging, and value: New evidence from the US airline industry. *International Review of Financial Analysis* **34**, 200–211.

Tufano, P. (1996). Who manages risk? An empirical examination of risk management practices in the gold mining industry. *Journal of Finance* **51** (4), 1097–1137.

Van de Waeyenberg, S. and Hens, L. (2012). Overcoming institutional distance: Expansion to base-of-the pyramid markets. *Journal of Business Research* **65**, 1692–1699.

Verschoor, W. F. C. and Muller, A. (2007). The Asian crisis exchange risk exposure of US multinationals. *Managerial Finance* **33** (9), 710–740.

Wei, K. D. and Starks, L. T. (2013). Foreign exchange exposure elasticity and financial distress. *Financial Management Winter* **2013**, 709–735.

Zaheer, S. (2002). The liability of foreignness, redux: A commentary. *Journal of International Management* **8**, 351–358.

Zaheer, S. (2015). Overcoming the liability of foreignness. In P. Buckley and P. Ghauri (eds.), *International Business Strategy, Theory and Practice* (Routledge, London), pp. 362–380.

Zhou, V. Y. and Wang, P. (2013). Managing foreign exchange risk with derivatives in UK non-financial firms. *International Review of Financial Analysis* **29**, 294–302.

Chapter 26

Risk Management and Hedging Approaches in Energy Markets

Jim Hanly
College of Business, Technological University Dublin, Ireland
James.Hanly@dit.ie

Energy-based assets are showing increased susceptibility to volatility arising out of geo-political, economic, climate and technological events. Given the economic importance of energy products, their market participants need to be able to access efficient strategies to effectively manage their exposures and reduce price risk. This chapter will outline the key futures-based hedging approaches that have been developed for managing energy price risk and evaluate their effectiveness. A key element of this analysis will be the breadth of assets considered. These include Crude and Refined Oil products, Natural Gas and wholesale Electricity markets. We find significant differences in the hedging effectiveness of the different energy markets. A key finding is that, Natural Gas and particularly Electricity futures are relatively ineffective as a risk management tool when compared with other energy assets.

Keywords: Hedging; risk management; energy; futures; oil; natural gas; electricity; volatility; GARCH; VaR.

1. Introduction and Context

The importance of energy markets within the global economic framework cannot be overstated. They underpin and significantly impact all economic activity and are also important as an asset class within the investment context. However, it is also a fact that they are particularly affected by a variety of events such as political change, weather, technological change and of course economic growth. Given their importance, an analysis of the price movements and associated risks of the major energy products is essential as an aid to understanding energy markets. Furthermore, an ability to manage these risks is key if investors and more generally firms are to engage and participate confidently with energy products and markets. This chapter examines the energy market by breaking it down into the key products. We compare the price volatility of these key products as well as their correlation and comovement characteristics. This is done with a view to showing how volatility and associated risk can be managed through the use of futures hedging strategies. We focus on futures given their broad presence and application to energy markets and because for most products they can be effectively applied to reduce risk in an efficient manner. This is true not just for energy markets but for the broader financial markets where effective hedging strategies have been documented. This literature has examined equities [Cotter and Hanly, 2006], various commodities [Conlon *et al.* 2016, Wu, *et al.* 2011], foreign exchange [Caporin *et al.* 2014] and the use of Oil as a hedge for other markets [Bashar and Sadorsky, 2016].

Looking more specifically at the literature on energy market hedging, a number of papers have examined the efficacy of hedges for various products. Crude Oil, Gasoline and Heating have all been examined with many papers finding useful hedging outcomes. For example, Alizadeh *et al.* [2008], Chang *et al.* [2011] and Pan *et al.* [2014] all found that hedging oil or oil products generally yielded risk reductions of the order of 50% or above. While results from the literature indicate very good outcomes with respect to crude oil and its derivatives, the results in terms of other energy assets aren't as strong. For example, Cotter and Hanly [2012] in a comparison between Oil and Natural Gas hedges find that Oil hedges tend to outperform Natural Gas hedges by around 30%–35%. More recently, Hanly [2017] showed that Natural Gas hedges tended to return risk reductions of less than 40% on average. The case for Electricity price risk management using futures is weaker again. Papers that have examined futures-based Electricity hedging include: Tanlapco *et al.* [2002]. Bystrom [2003] and Zanotti *et al.* [2010]. The results from these studies vary widely with hedging effectiveness measuring as low as 2% to a high of 38% depending on the market under study and the methodology employed.

This chapter contributes to the literature by making a broad-based comparison that allows the interested reader to see where futures hedging adds value as a managerial proposition and where the gains are marginal. It accomplishes this by investigating the volatility and hedging characteristics of the various energy markets using some of the most broadly applied methodologies and evaluation metrics. Well-known and applied methods were particularly chosen to allow for our finding to be contextualized against the literature and to emphasize the commonalities and differences between energy markets rather than as a function of different econometric models. We also highlight performance differentials between the different energy product hedges using both statistical and economic criteria.

Our major finding is that while futures hedging is generally effective in reducing risk for Crude Oil and its derivatives, it is significantly less effective in the case of Natural Gas and Electricity in particular. The implication for market participants is that futures hedging efficacy is contingent on the particular market under consideration. The rest of this chapter is organized as follows: We begin by looking at the general characteristics of the different energy products and the correlation dynamics between them before moving on to analyze volatility using a GARCH framework. We then estimate and compare futures hedging efficacy thus facilitating an up-to-date analysis across the major markets and products. For the purposes of our study, we will constrain ourselves to an analysis using a weekly data to reflect a useful time horizon that reflects many energy market participants and that allows for volatility persistence.

2. Energy Products

Energy markets for the most part consist of Oil and its various derivative products, Natural Gas and of course Electricity. For the purposes of this chapter, we initially consider these general markets for which an active futures market exists. These are West Texas Intermediate [WTI] and Brent Oil,[1] Heating Oil, Gasoil [Diesel], Gasoline[Petrol], and Natural Gas. We also examine Electricity for which we proxy by using the Electricity price from the European Nordpool Market. Taken together, these products account for about 84% of total energy consumption in the EU.[2]

2.1. *General characteristics and comparisons*

From Fig. 1, a number of key findings emerge. First, there is a considerable divergence between the prices of Crude Oil and its derivatives on the one hand,

[1]These are two of the global pricing benchmarks. Further contract details on each of the energy products are available as follows: WTI, Brent, https://www.theice.com/global-crudes.
Henry Hub Natural Gas, http://www.cmegroup.com/trading/energy/natural-gas/natural-gas_contract_specifications.html.
Unleaded Gasoline, http://www.cmegroup.com/trading/energy/refined-products/rbob-gasoline.html.
Heating Oil, http://www.cmegroup.com/trading/energy/refined-products/heating-oil_contract_specifications.html.
Gasoil, https://www.theice.com/productguide/ProductSpec.shtml?specId=909.
http://www.nordpoolspot.com/Market-data1/#/nordic/table.

[2]Source. http://ec.europa.eu/eurostat/web/energy.

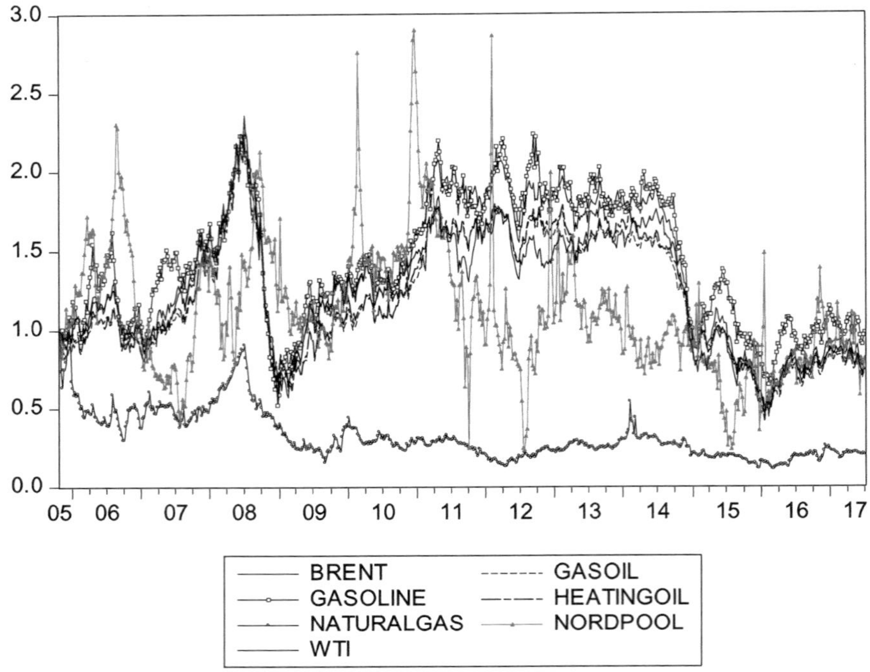

Fig. 1. Energy prices for the period 26 October 2005 to 21 June 2017 are presented based on weekly data. They are rebased for comparison purposes.

and both Natural Gas and Electricity on the other. Secondly, both of the Crude Oils and each of the derivatives, namely Heating Oil, Gasoline and Gasoil, while moving broadly together still show obvious differences in terms of their price behavior.

Table 1 presents price correlations across three different frequencies: daily weekly and monthly, that support this view. Of particular note are the low correlations between the Oil-based assets and both Natural Gas and Electricity. This is useful to highlight as it shows investors that all energy assets are not the same despite their substitutability and similarities. Also worth noting is that price correlations across different time horizons are broadly similar.

Table 2 presents results of stationarity tests. Broadly speaking, each of the price series is non-stationary with the possible exception of Electricity for which there is some small predictability; however, each of the returns series is stationary. Therefore, to further examine the characteristics of each series, we use log returns.

Table 3 presents correlations between the returns of the different assets. A number of findings emerge from Table 3, chief among them is that the correlations for the returns are generally below the correlation between prices. The other findings of

Table 1. Price correlations.

	WTI	Brent	Heating oil	Gasoline	Gasoil	Natural gas	Nordpool
				Daily			
WTI	1.000						
Brent	0.964	1.000					
Heating oil	0.962	0.987	1.000				
Gasoline	0.937	0.977	0.963	1.000			
Gas oil	0.966	0.987	0.996	0.962	1.000		
Natural gas	0.301	0.148	0.213	0.116	0.222	1.000	
Nordpool	0.312	0.248	0.248	0.183	0.253	0.241	1.000
				Weekly			
WTI	1.000						
Brent	0.963	1.000					
Heating oil	0.962	0.987	1.000				
Gasoline	0.938	0.978	0.963	1.000			
Gas oil	0.967	0.987	0.996	0.963	1.000		
Natural gas	0.293	0.137	0.206	0.105	0.214	1.000	
Nordpool	0.327	0.266	0.266	0.200	0.271	0.235	1.000
				Monthly			
WTI	1.000						
Brent	0.962	1.000					
Heating oil	0.961	0.986	1.000				
Gasoline	0.939	0.979	0.963	1.000			
Gas oil	0.966	0.987	0.995	0.963	1.000		
Natural gas	0.278	0.130	0.203	0.106	0.206	1.000	
Nordpool	0.340	0.292	0.291	0.239	0.298	0.196	1.000

Notes: Correlations between the prices of the different energy assets are presented for the period 26 October 2005 to 21 June 2017 for data at Daily, Weekly and Monthly intervals.

note are that again, the oil-based assets are broadly similar whereas both Natural Gas and particularly Electricity show only very small similarities in terms of how they move together. We also note that the correlations are much higher at lower frequencies. This is to be expected as using lower frequency data has a smoothing effect. From our initial analysis, we will next look at volatility before estimating and analyzing some risk management strategies using futures hedging.

Given our initial findings, we propose to narrow down the dataset and exclude those assets that are broadly similar. We will therefore carry out further analysis using Brent Crude Oil, Gasoline, Natural Gas and Nordpool (Electricity). Some detail is now provided on the general methodological approach to volatility and hedging analysis.

Table 2. Stationarity.

	Price	Returns
WTI	−1.77	−9.00**
Brent	−1.59	−8.75**
Heating oil	−1.41	−10.12**
Gasoline	−2.08	−8.96**
Gas oil	−1.52	−9.77**
Natural gas	−2.21	−11.98**
Nordpool	−3.80*	−13.63**
Critical values: 1% = −3.44 5% = −2.86		

Notes: Stationarity is testing using the Augmented Dickey–Fuller test with four lags. *Denotes a stationary series at the 5% level. **Denotes a stationary series at the 1% level.

Table 3. Returns correlations.

	WTI	Brent	Heating oil	Gasoline	Gas oil	Natural gas	Nordpool
Daily							
WTI	1.000						
Brent	0.601	1.000					
Heating oil	0.527	0.418	1.000				
Gasoline	0.607	0.485	0.506	1.000			
Gas oil	0.697	0.653	0.562	0.607	1.000		
Natural gas	0.060	0.131	0.090	0.046	0.111	1.000	
Nordpool	−0.018	0.010	0.027	−0.022	−0.012	0.060	1.000
Weekly							
WTI	1.000						
Brent	0.790	1.000					
Heating oil	0.605	0.651	1.000				
Gasoline	0.665	0.701	0.596	1.000			
Gas oil	0.826	0.855	0.698	0.698	1.000		
Natural gas	0.135	0.177	0.273	0.144	0.187	1.000	
Nordpool	−0.003	0.052	0.108	0.006	0.017	0.018	1.000
Monthly							
WTI	1.000						
Brent	0.962	1.000					
Heating oil	0.961	0.986	1.000				
Gasoline	0.939	0.979	0.963	1.000			
Gas oil	0.966	0.987	0.995	0.963	1.000		
Natural gas	0.278	0.130	0.203	0.106	0.206	1.000	
Nordpool	0.340	0.292	0.291	0.239	0.298	0.196	1.000

Notes: Correlations between log returns of the different energy assets are presented for the period 26 October 2005 to 21 June 2017 for data at Daily, Weekly and Monthly intervals.

3. General Method and Models

For the purposes of this chapter we define the optimal hedge (OHR) as the ratio between the futures and the spot that minimizes the risk of the hedgers' position. Risk is defined as the variance of the hedged portfolio whose returns are given as

$$+r_{st} - \beta r_{ft}, \tag{1}$$

where r_s and r_f are returns on the spot and futures, respectively, and β is the OHR. To estimate the OHR, we use two different models that have been broadly applied across many literatures: The first is a Naïve or 1:1 hedge ratio. The second model we use is the Constant Correlation or CCGARCH model introduced by Bollerslev [1990]. The model is specified as follows:

$$y_t = E\left(y_t \,|F_{t-1}\right) + \varepsilon_t, \varepsilon_t = D_t \eta_t; \tag{2}$$

$$\text{var}\left(\varepsilon_t \,|F_{t-1}\right) = D_t R D_t, \tag{3}$$

where $y_t = (y_{1t} \ldots y_{mt})', \eta_t = (\eta_{1t} \ldots \eta_{mt})'$ is a sequence of independent and identically distributed random vectors, F_t is the information set at time t, $D_t = diag\left(h_1^{1/2}, \ldots h_m^{1/2}\right)$, m is the number of returns and $t = 1 \ldots n$. $R = E\left(\eta_t \eta_t' \,|F_{t-1}\right) = \left(\eta_t \eta_t'\right)$ where $R = \rho_{ij}$ for $i, j = 1, \ldots, m$. $\varepsilon_t \varepsilon_t' = D_t \eta_t \eta_t' D_t D_t = (diag Q_t)^{1/2}$ and $E\left(\varepsilon_t \varepsilon_t' \,|F_{t-1}\right) = Q_t = D_t R D_t$, where Q_t is the conditional covariance matrix. The model assumes that conditional correlations are constant and therefore the conditional covariances are proportional to the product of the corresponding conditional standard deviations. Each of the conditional variances in D_t has a univariate GARCH (1, 1) specification has follows:

$$h_{it} = \omega_i + \sum_{j=1}^{r} \alpha_{ij} \varepsilon_i^2{}_{,t-j} + \sum_{j=1}^{s} \beta_{ij} h_{i,t-j}. \tag{4}$$

These models were chosen as they are broadly used in the literature, have shown good performance in many applications and also because they range in complexity from the very simple Naive hedge to the somewhat more complex CCGARCH model. We have left out many models that are commonly applied such as the OLS model and many different specifications of GARCH models on the basis that both of the models we use cover the spectrum of models and have in many cases shown the best performance. See Alexander and Barbosa [2008] or Hanly [2017] for more detail.

We primarily compare hedging performance using measures based on Variance because it is a standard measure of risk in finance and because of its prominence in the literature. We also use Value at Risk [VaR] to allow for a demonstrated economic or currency-based analysis of hedging efficiency. VaR estimates the expected loss for a given confidence level and a specified time period. The VaR at confidence level α is

$$\text{VaR}_\alpha = q_a, \tag{5}$$

where q_a is the quantile of the loss distribution. We calculate VaR using the 5% confidence level. For both risk metrics, we measure hedging efficiency by measuring the percentage reduction in the metric for a hedged as compared to an unhedged position.

4. Data for Hedging and Volatility Analysis

Our data consist of three of the largest and most important energy products that trade on either CMEGROUP or the Intercontinental Exchange (ICE). These are: Brent crude oil, Unleaded Gasoline and Natural Gas. We also analyze Electricity using Nordpool as our data proxy. These products together have highly liquid spot and futures markets and have a significant pricing history. The total sample period runs from 26 October 2005 to 28 June 2017. The data is analyzed at the weekly interval which comprises one observation per week. The prices used are closing spot prices on a Wednesday. Table 1 provides descriptive statistics of the data for the full sample period. The data exhibit both skewness and kurtosis as is common for most energy assets. Jarque–Bera (J–B) statistics indicate non-normality for each series. Heteroskedasticity is present at the weekly frequency for all assets. This provides a strong case for the use of GARCH models to estimate the conditional variance and covariance. All series are stationary as measured using the Kwiatkowski, Phillips, Schmidt and Shin (KPSS) [1992] tests with the single exception of Nordpool which shows evidence of non-stationarity about a trend. In terms of volatility, the most volatile series as measured by standard deviation is Electricity followed by Natural Gas. This is to be expected given the supply considerations and non-storability of Electricity.

For each of the energy products, we formed hedged portfolios using Eq. (1) with the OHR as estimated from using the Naive and CCGARCH models. The procedure generated 488 t-period hedges in-sample at the weekly frequency for the period October 2005 to February 2015, upon which we based our hedging effectiveness estimates. We also retained a subsample equivalent to two and a half years of data for the period February 2015 to July 2017 for out-of-sample testing. This was done by generating one-step-ahead forecasts of the OHR for use in period $t + 1$. The OHRs

Table 4. Summary statistics.

	Mean (%)	Std. Dev. (%)	Skewness	Kurtosis	JB	LM	KPSS
Brent	−0.04	4.70	−0.009	2.24*	117.2*	546.19*	C 0.184* T 0.055*
Gasoline	0.01	5.06	−0.394*	1.24*	50.25*	75.57*	C 0.123* T 0.039*
Natural gas	0.10	7.61	0.445*	4.12*	414.9*	42.24*	C 0.037* T 0.035*
Electricity	−0.15	17.96	−0.665*	12.95*	3957.5*	60.41*	C 0.014* C 0.717

Notes: Summary statistics are presented for the log returns of each spot series. The mean and standard deviation [Stdev] are in percentages. The total sample period runs from 26 October 2005 until 28 July 2017. Weekly returns are 5-day. Jarque and Bera (J–B) statistic measures normality. LM with four lags is the Lagrange multiplier test for ARCH effects proposed by Engle [1982]; it is distributed as χ^2. Stationarity is tested using the KPSS test, which tests the null of stationarity against the alternative of a unit root. Critical values for the KPSS test at the 1% level are 0.739 and 0.216 for the constant (C) and trend (T) statistics, respectively.

were assumed to follow a random walk process and the one-step-ahead forecasts for the time varying hedges were generated using a rolling window approach.

5. Empirical Analysis

5.1. *Volatility*

Volatility was examined using a univariate GARCH [1, 1] model with results presented in Table 5 and Figs. 3–4. Figures 3–4 illustrates a number of clear findings. Firstly, Electricity and to a lesser extent Natural Gas clearly standout in terms of showing markedly larger volatility than both of the Oil-based series.

A second element is that the volatility spikes are not aligned for the most part between the series. This shows that even similar series such as Crude Oil and Gasoline have different triggers for market volatility. For the most part these can be traced to supply concerns and refinery bottlenecks. Also looking at a comparison of Crude Oil and Gasoline, we can see that volatility is higher for Gasoline.

These findings are supported in Table 5 with unconditional volatility highest for Electricity at 0.914%. The next highest is Natural Gas at 0.101% which is considerably lower as is Gasoline which is 0.067%, and finally Crude Oil, showing just 0.057% — the lowest in our dataset. Also, worth noting is that for volatility persistence the pattern is reversed with the effect of shocks showing highest for Brent at 0.985 followed by Gasoline (0.946), Natural Gas (0.916) and Electricity (0.766) in that order. Across the energy sector, we can see that the effects of shocks can remain in the market for long periods. For energy hedgers,

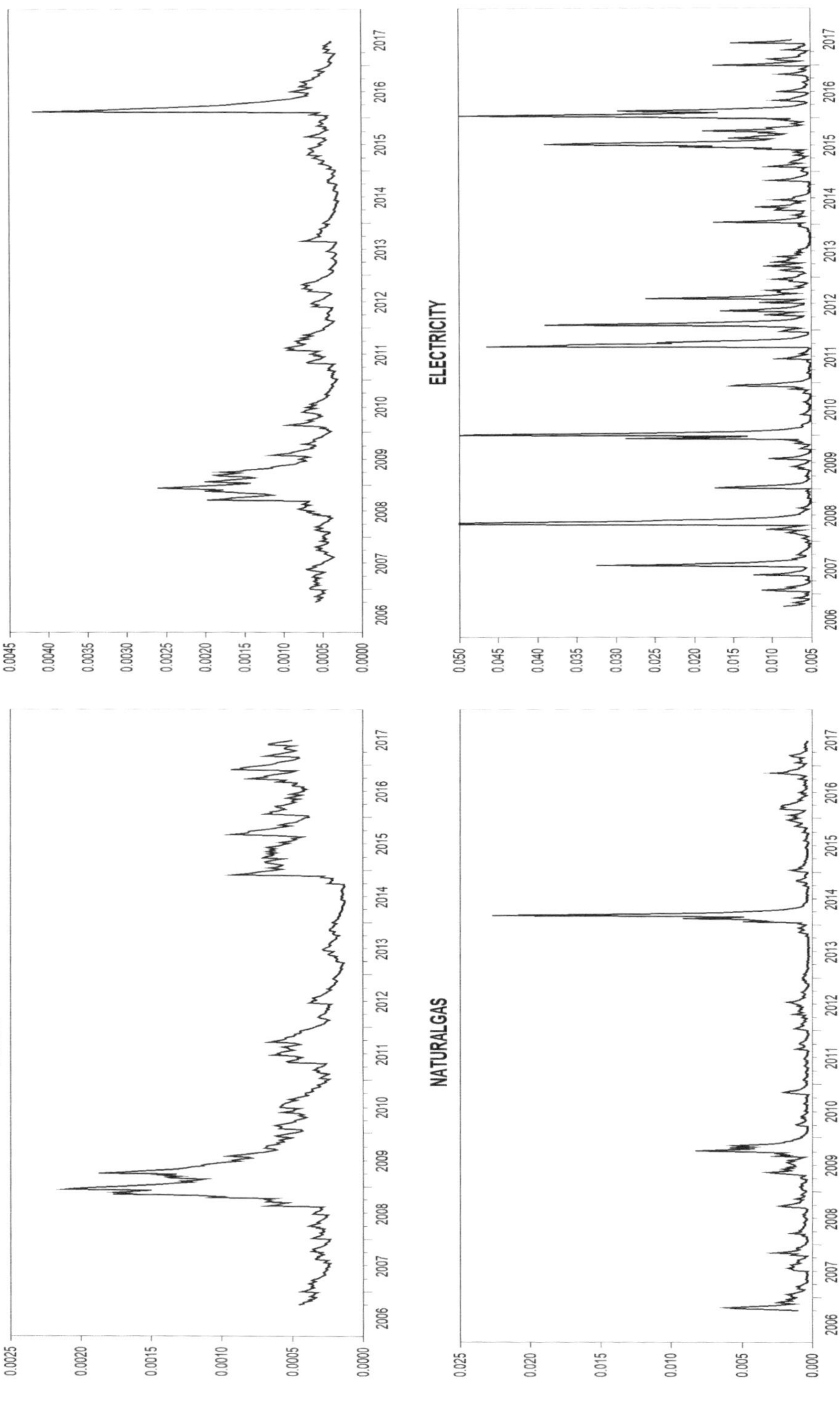

Fig. 2. Energy product volatility is modeled using a GARCH (1, 1) process.

Notes: Illustrates the pattern of each series' volatility.

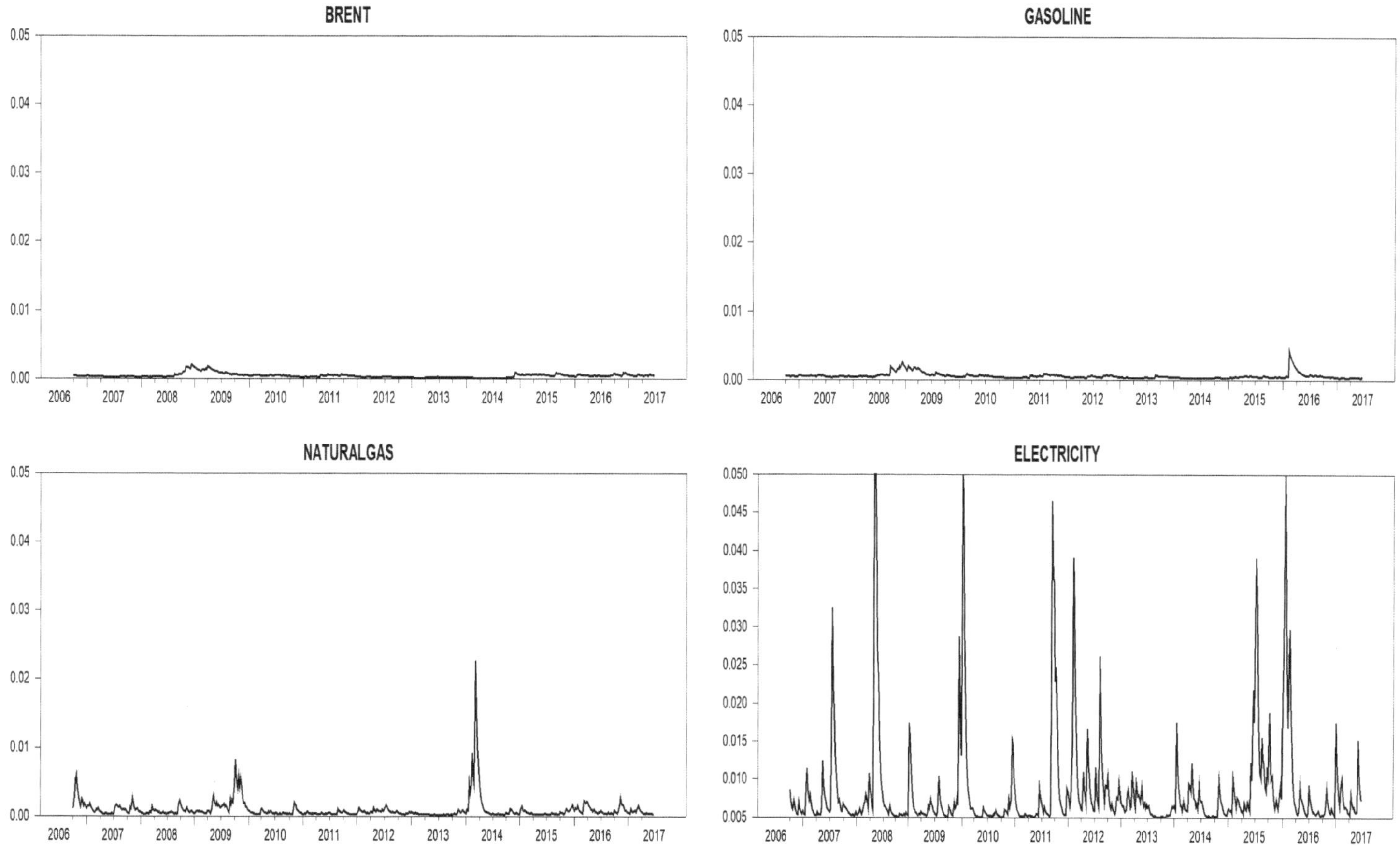

Fig. 3. Energy product volatility (Comparison to Scale).

Notes: Volatility in modeled using a GARCH (1, 1) process. Figure 3 shows each volatility series using the same scale on the *y* axis to illustrate starkly how the volatility of Electricity and to a lesser extent Natural Gas is significantly higher than the other energy products.

Table 5. Volatility of energy products GARCH (1, 1).

	ω	α	β	α C β **volatility persistence**	**Volatility unconditional**
Brent	0.000008	0.077	0.908	0.985	0.057%
Gasoline	0.000036	0.088	0.858	0.946	0.067%
Natural gas	0.000085	0.273	0.643	0.916	0.101%
Electricity	0.002139	0.192	0.574	0.766	0.914%

Notes: Volatility is measured as the unconditional volatility estimated using $\omega_i/1(-\alpha - \beta)$ from a univariate GARCH (1, 1) process as in Eq. (5): $h_{it} = \omega_i + \sum_{j=1}^{r} \alpha_{ij}\varepsilon_i^2,_{t-j} + \sum_{j=1}^{s} \beta_{ij} h_{i,t-j}$. The sum of $\alpha + \beta$ measures volatility persistence.

this illustrates the importance of managing volatility given its persistence in energy markets.

5.2. *Optimal hedging strategies*

Figure 4 presents a comparison of the Time-Varying OHR's for each energy product. We can see that despite the similarity in the price movements between Brent and Gasoline and the high correlation between them (0.701), the optimal hedge strategies are quite different. This reflects the relationship between the spot and futures of the different assets and the fundamentals of futures pricing having an effect. The differences between the optimal hedges for the Oil-based assets and Natural Gas is even starker. The OHRs for the refined oil products for the most part fall within a range of 0.80 to 1.0, whereas the OHRs for Natural Gas tend to a much larger range in the region of 0.50 to 1.50 in the majority of cases. This reflects the higher volatility of Natural Gas. Turning to Electricity, we can see that the fundamental differences in terms of Supply and Demand and the non-storability condition which result in very high volatility carry over in terms of optimal hedge estimation. For example, the Nordpool OHRs are typically in excess of 1.5 and on one occasion exceed 8.0. The interpretation of this would be that for an investor in the Electricity market with a long spot position, they would need to go short the equivalent of eight futures contracts to hedge their exposure. In practical terms, this is not a realistic proposition from a risk management perspective, however, it does serve to highlight that for Electricity Markets, futures used in a conventional way as a hedging tool are not optimal.

5.3. *Hedging efficacy*

The results detailing hedging efficacy are shown in Table 6. Looking first at the In-Sample results, a number of key findings emerge. Firstly, for both of the Oil-based

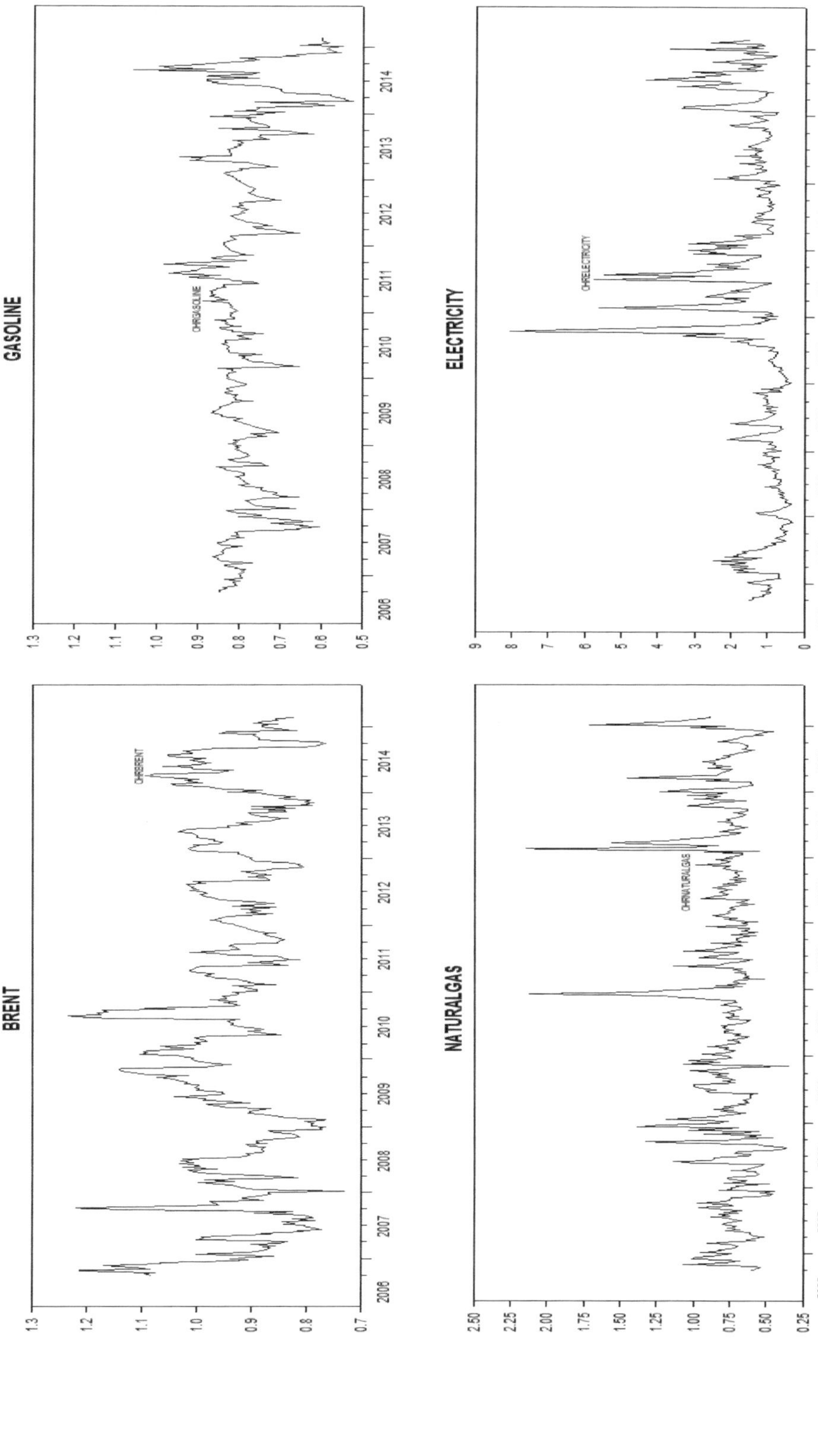

Fig. 4. Optimal time-varying [CCGARCH] hedges are presented for each of the different energy products.

Table 6. Hedging performance.

	In-sample		Out-of-sample	
	Naïve	**CC GARCH**	**Naïve**	**CC GARCH**
Variance				
Brent	76.22	**77.30***	79.67	**80.75***
Gasoline	71.92	**74.14***	**77.51***	76.61
Natural Gas	27.35	**33.10***	35.54	**40.56***
Electricity	**5.28***	4.78	5.62	**5.25***
VaR 5%				
Brent	51.14	**51.91***	55.75	**57.13***
Gasoline	46.69	**49.11***	**52.37***	51.22
Natural Gas	16.87	**19.61***	16.56	**19.42***
Electricity	**2.84***	2.05	3.66	**3.89***

Notes: *denotes the best performing hedging model for a given energy product. Figures are in percentages. For example, hedging Brent with the CCGARCH model yields a 77.3% reduction in the In-sample Variance as compared with a No-Hedge strategy.

energy products, futures-based hedging is a viable method for managing energy price risk. In terms of the Variance risk metric, risk reductions are in excess of 70% and for VaR around the 50% mark. This result is broadly similar to the large literature that has examined hedging efficacy for Oil and Oil derivatives. For Natural Gas, the results are markedly poorer with the best performing model showing just a 33% risk reduction as measured by the variance, and just under 20% for the VaR metric. The poor performance for Natural Gas hedges relates to a variety of factors including volatility and higher associated basis risk. While quite low in relative terms, these numbers are nevertheless reasonable, as they offer investors the hope of mitigating risk by way of futures hedging. For Electricity, however, the results are uniformly poor with the best performing model showing a 5.28% reduction in the variance and 2.84% reduction in the VaR. These findings indicate that Electricity hedges perform very poorly when compared with the broader hedging literature for which hedging efficiency in the range 50%–90% is not uncommon. These numbers are so low that we can safely state that futures when using conventionally as a hedging tool are of little use. Indeed, we could question the existence of a futures market in Electricity markets given this very poor performance when using commonly applied methods for futures markets.

What this means is that for investors, speculators and producers in energy markets, the ability to offset risk is dependent on the underlying asset being hedged. For Oil market participants, the results are useful in that they show that almost three quarters of energy price risk can be offset with the use of futures hedging.

Natural Gas market participants in particular will only be able to offset about one-third of their exposure and for Electricity market participants the figure is around one-twentieth.

5.4. *Hedging model performance*

In this chapter, we applied only two hedging models. The simple Naive model is applied as it is essentially a 1:1 ratio between the spot and the futures. It requires no estimation and is extremely simple conceptually and in terms of its application. Despite its simplicity, it has been advocated as one of the best overall hedging approaches as it delivers good performance and is simple to apply. For this reason, it is a benchmark against which other methods can be compared. We also chose to only apply one of the myriad more complex models (CCGARCH) as this model has compared well to many of the even more complex approaches in the literature (see Hanly [2017] for a discussion). In a sense therefore, we cover both simple and complex in our hedging approaches. From Table 6 we can see that while the CCGARCH model is the better performer overall showing better performance in 75% of cases, the performance differentials are not economically significant, particularly as we haven't included the effects of transactions' costs or estimation and applications' complexity. Our view on this is that while complex models may offer better performance — in most cases this is only theoretical, or paper-based superiority. When the full cost versus benefit of complex hedging approaches are considered, they offer little additional advantage to the energy market participant over the very simple 1:1 hedging approach.

6. Conclusion

We estimate and compare optimal energy hedges using widely applied hedging models and risk measures to capture hedging performance. We carry out an initial analysis on the relationships between six different energy products which together comprise the majority of the energy traded in energy markets. We then model the volatility and hedging characteristics of a sample of four of the key assets, Crude Oil, Gasoline, Natural Gas and Electricity to show investors how energy price risk can be managed using futures contracts. We also estimate the relative efficacy of these approaches. This allows us to make a comprehensive comparison of the relative hedging performance of the some of the most important energy products trading in the markets and to inform the reader of the same. Our findings indicate that there are significant differences between volatility and the hedging characteristics and performance for the different energy products we examine. Of particular note is the relatively poor hedging performance of Natural Gas hedges and the extremely poor ability of conventional futures hedging to yield substantive risk reductions for Electricity markets. The implication of this is that Natural Gas energy and particularly Electricity market participants will struggle to obtain meaningful risk management outcomes from conventional futures-based hedging strategies. Our results also show that hedging is generally effective in reducing risk for Crude Oil and its derivatives. Our results show that energy market hedge strategies should be tailored to the individual energy product being hedged. They also show that for certain assets such as Electricity, managing volatility using futures hedging may only be of little use and alternative approaches should be considered.

References

Alexander, C. and Barbosa, A. (2008). Hedging index exchange traded funds. *Journal of Banking & Finance* **32**, 326–337.

Alizadeh, A., Nomikos, N. and Pouliasis, P. (2008). A Markov regime switching approach for hedging energy commodities. *Journal of Banking & Finance* **32**, 1970–1983.

Basher, S. A. and Sadorsky, P. (2016). Hedging emerging market stock prices with oil, gold, VIX, and bonds: A comparison between DCC, ADCC and GO-GARCH. *Energy Economics* **54**, 235–247.

Bollerslev, T. (1990). Modeling the coherence in short-run nominal exchange rates: A multivariate generalized ARCH model. *Review of Economics and Statistics* **72**, 498–505.

Bystrom, H. N. E. (2003). The hedging performance of electricity futures on the Nordic power exchange. *Applied Economics* **35**, 1–11.

Caporin, M., Jimenez-Martin, J.A. and Gonzalez-Serrano, L. (2014). Currency hedging strategies in strategic benchmarks and the global and Euro sovereign financial crises. *Journal of International Financial Markets, Institutions and Money* **31**, 159–177.

Chang, C., McAleer, M. and Tansuchat, R. (2011). Crude oil hedging strategies using dynamic multivariate GARCH. *Energy Economics* **33**, 912–923.

Conlon, T., Cotter, J. and Gencay, R. (2016). Commodity futures hedging, risk aversion and the hedging horizon. *European Journal of Finance* **22**, 1534–1560.

Cotter, J. and Hanly, J. (2006). Re-examining hedging performance. *Journal of Futures Markets* **26**, 657–676.

Cotter, J. and Hanly, J. (2012). A utility based approach to energy hedging. *Energy Economics* **34**, 817–827.

Engle, R. (2002). Dynamic conditional correlation: A simple class of multivariate generalized autoregressive conditional heteroskedasticity models. *Journal of Business and Economic Statistics* **20**, 339–350.

Hanly, J. (2017). Managing energy price risk using futures contracts: A comparative analysis. *Energy Journal* **38**, 93–112.

Kwiatkowski, D., Phillips, P., Schmidt, P. and Shin, Y. (1992). Testing the null hypothesis of stationarity against the alternative of a unit root: How sure are we that economic time series have a unit root? *Journal of Econometrics* **54**, 159–178.

Pan, Z., Wang, Y. and Yang, L. (2014). Hedging crude oil using refined product: A regime switching asymmetric DCC approach. *Energy Economics* **46**, 472–484.

Tanlapco, E., Lawarrée, J. and Liu, C. (2002). Hedging with Futures Contracts in a Deregulated Electricity Industry. *IEEE Transactions on Power Systems* **17**, 577–582.

Wu, F., Guan, Z. and Myers, R. J. (2011). Volatility spillover effects and cross hedging in corn and crude oil futures. *Journal of Futures Markets* **31**, 1052–1075.

Zanotti, G., Gabbi, G. and Geranio, M. (2010). Hedging with futures: Efficacy of GARCH correlation models to European Electricity markets. *Journal of International Financial Markets, Institutions and Money* **20**, 135–148.

PART VI

Cross-Market Linkages

Chapter 27

Modeling the Dynamics of Implied Carbon Price and its Influence on the Stock Price Variability of Energy Companies in the Australian Electric Utility Sector

Liangxu Zhu* and Tiho Ancev†

School of Economics, The University of Sydney,
Camperdown NSW 2006, Australia
**zhuliangxu@googlemail.com*
†tiho.ancev@sydney.edu.au

In July 2012, the Australian government introduced a Carbon Pricing Mechanism (CPM) to regulate national Greenhouse Gas (GHG) emissions. However, due to political controversies, there were concerns over the fate of this policy throughout its implementation. To determine the effect of carbon pricing policy on major electric utility companies, this chapter extracts an implied carbon price from the Australian electricity derivative market and models its volatility interaction with the utility index in Australian Stock Exchange (ASX). We find that Autoregressive Conditional Heteroscedasticity (ARCH) model can adequately simulate and forecast the dynamics of implied carbon price. As the cost of carbon emissions was fully transparent and passed onto the market, carbon pricing pushed up electricity prices, which subsequently enhanced expected stock returns of electric utility companies. While shocks from implied carbon price caused immediate response in the stock market, transfer of volatility from the latter to electricity derivative market was lagged. The persistent shift of volatility level further demonstrates the effect of carbon pricing and related policy uncertainty on the Australian electric utility sector. Findings from this chapter provide insight into market sentiment on carbon pricing policy and can contribute to financial risk management.

Keywords: Autoregressive conditional heteroscedasticity (ARCH) model; carbon pricing; electricity market; forecasting; impulse response analysis; policy uncertainty; vector autoregressive (VAR) model; volatility.

1. Introduction

In July 2012, the Australian government imposed a carbon price under the framework of Carbon Pricing Mechanism (CPM). According to the Clean Energy Act [2013], the price was applicable to emitters with annual emissions above 25,000 tons carbon dioxide equivalent (tCO_2−e). It started at $23 per tCO_2−e, and was set to increase at a rate of 4% annually until July 2015. Although Garnaut [2011] pointed out that mitigating the climate change effect is in Australia's national interest, concerns over the economic impacts from CPM resulted in a weak public support [Jotzo, 2012]. As a result of political controversies, CPM was scrapped by the newly elected government in July 2014 before its planned transition to the Emission Trading Scheme (ETS) [Rootes, 2014]. Hence, policy uncertainty throughout CPM implementation caused inconsistent outlooks regarding the fate of Australia's climate change policy [Jotzo *et al.* 2012]. This chapter derives market expectation on carbon price and studies its influence on the stock price volatility of Australian electric utility companies.

Despite the uncertainty related to the Australian carbon pricing policy, little attention has been given to its effect on market expectation in the existing literature. Jotzo *et al.* [2012] conducted a survey to gather expert opinion on the outlook of Australia's carbon pricing policy. However, it did not collect information to reflect market valuation of the carbon price. In this light, the present chapter makes use of different mechanisms that were applied to incorporate carbon price in both exchange-traded derivative (ETD) market and over-the-counter (OTC) derivative market. Based on this, we derive an implied carbon price to reveal expectation on the cost of carbon emissions in the Australian electricity derivative market. Its variation over time reflects the influence of policy uncertainty on market anticipation regarding the fate of CPM. Furthermore, by means of econometric modeling, we explore a proper model to simulate dynamics of implied carbon price. The appropriateness of the estimated model is validated by out-of-sample forecasting.

A further contribution of this chapter is that it explores the effect of carbon pricing on the stock price variability of Australian electric utility companies. Existing studies on the European carbon market found that prices of EU Allowance (EUA) and EUA futures tend to respond negatively to the shocks from financial and commodity markets [Chevallier, 2009; 2011a]. Furthermore, there is also evidence showing the volatility comovement between market for carbon permits and stock market [Chevallier, 2011b]. As a result of various political events and growing uncertainties related to international agreements, the price of allowances in the EU ETS exhibited large scale of fluctuation from 2005 to 2008 [Feng *et al.* 2011]. Additionally, uncertainties related to carbon pricing policy have induced price fluctuation in the European carbon markets, which consequently caused price variation in the stock market [Oberndorfer, 2009; Veith *et al.* 2009]. Tian *et al.* [2012] found that volatility transmission between European market for carbon permits and stock market is significant in the short run. Previous studies regarding the correlation between European carbon market and stock market motivate an investigation on such relationship between electricity financial market and stock market in Australia. This chapter closes a broader research gap by exploring whether expectation on carbon price in electricity derivative market influences stock price variability of electric utility companies. To pursue this question, we apply vector autoregressive (VAR) model to detect volatility comovement between implied carbon price and S&P/ASX 200 Utilities (AXUJ) index of the Australian Stock Exchange (ASX), which is a composite index comprised of some leading Australian electric utility companies. In addition, impulse response analysis (IRA) is conducted to reveal the magnitude of volatility spill-over.

Results from the current chapter demonstrates the changing market expectation on cost of carbon due to uncertainty related to Australia's carbon pricing policy. The dynamics of implied carbon price can be captured and forecasted by Autoregressive (AR) model with conditional heteroscedastic error term. Furthermore, policy uncertainty related to carbon pricing affected stock price variability of electric utility companies. Variation of implied carbon price led to immediate and persistent volatility level shift for AXUJ index, which reflected market concerns over the effect of policy uncertainty on electric utility sector. On the other hand, as fixed-rate carbon price made carbon cost predictable, volatility spill-over from stock market to electricity derivative market was lagged and caused little fluctuation to implied carbon price. Overall, magnitude of volatility interaction between both markets was limited and asymmetric.

The remainder of this chapter proceeds as follows: the next section explains the derivation of implied carbon price and develops a specific ARCH model to study its dynamics. The appropriateness of estimated model is validated by out-of-sample forecasting. Furthermore, the third section looks into joint volatility movement between implied carbon price and the AXUJ index. After studying the two-way volatility interaction with IRA, the final section concludes.

2. Dynamics of Implied Carbon Price

2.1. *Implied carbon price*

Prices of electricity derivative contracts can be used to infer market expectation about carbon price. Due to limited generation capacity and rapidly changing demand for electricity, the Australian electricity derivative market has become an important platform to manage future price variation [AER, 2015]. As the country's major greenhouse gas (GHG) emitter, electricity sector was highly exposed to carbon pricing [AER, 2013a]. Therefore, cost of carbon emissions was a major issue influencing electricity derivative market during the CPM implementation [AFMA, 2015]. However, there was a significant difference in the way that carbon price was included in derivative contracts. While ETD electricity derivative contracts incorporated cost of carbon directly into prices, trading parties in the OTC market were allowed to settle carbon cost apart from the contracts at trade maturity [AFMA, 2012].[1]

Given the hypothesis that financial products with same charateristics are supposed to have the same price in an efficient market [Malkiel and Fama, 1970], any observed price difference between the ETD and OTC electricity derivative contracts of the same type and same trade duration can be articulated as an implied carbon price. Hence, it can be used to draw inferences on market expectations about carbon cost. The implied carbon price is empirically derived from the prices of major ETD and OTC contracts that are traded in the Australian electricity derivative market. It is defined as

$$\text{Implied Carbon Price} = \text{Price}^{\text{ETD}}(t, T) - \text{Price}^{\text{OTC}}(t, T), \tag{1}$$

where t indicates trading date and T denotes trade maturity date. The implied carbon price is derived using daily closing prices of Quarterly Baseload Electricity Futures that were procured from the ASX Energy, and Daily Curves of the OTC Quarterly Baseload Electricity Forward that were provided by the AFMA.[2,3] The implied carbon price used in this chapter is of national level, which is the average of implied prices for three major Australian states (New South Wales, Queensland and Victoria) from 3 December 2010 to 3 December 2013.

Figure 1 demonstrates the dynamics of implied carbon price from December 2010 to December 2013. After the Australian government unveiled its plan to impose a price on carbon emissions, speculation in the electricity derivative market quickly amplified the price spread between ETD and OTC derivative contracts since

[1] The Carbon Benchmark Addendum was released by the Australian Financial Market Association (AFMA) to neutralize the carbon price risk on the OTC derivative market. As a financial industry association with more than 130 members. The AFMA collects OTC financial product data independently from contributors on daily basis.

[2] According to statistics of AER [2015], electricity derivative contracts traded for three states make up the majority of trading volume in Australia's ETD electricity derivative market. In 2014–2015, 98% of electricity futures were traded for NSW, QLD and VIC.

[3] The AFMA collects OTC financial product data independently from price contributors on daily basis. The daily average of OTC electricity forward prices are converted to build forward price curve.

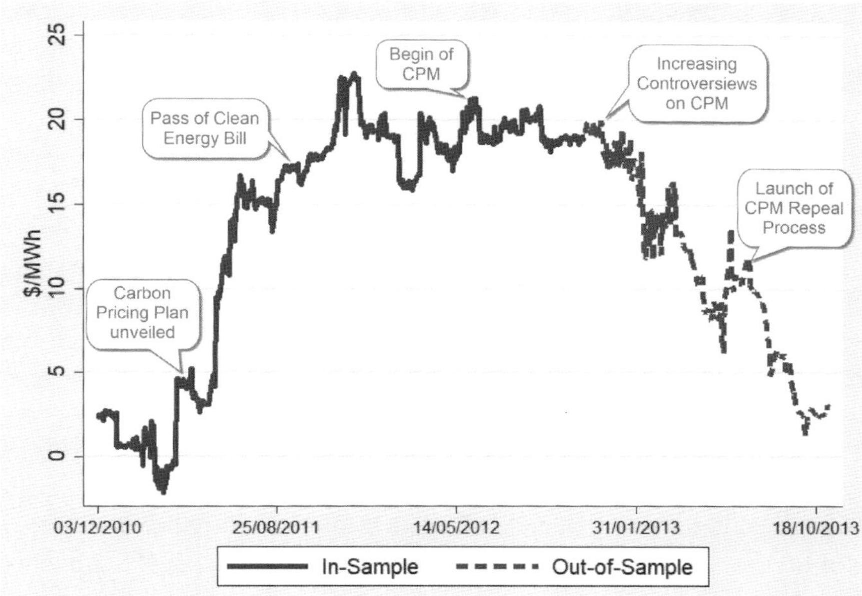

Fig. 1. Dynamic path of implied carbon price reflecting the effect of policy uncertainty (3 December 2010–3 December 2013).

February 2011, which surpassed $15/MWh in July 2011.[4] After the Clean Energy Bill was passed by the Australian Parliament in November 2011, the spread exceeded $20/MWh mark and peaked at $23/MWh. Shortly after that it reverted to $20/MWh and remained relatively stable until early 2013. As political controversies during Australia's federal election campaign in 2013 depressed the market faith over the future existence of CPM, the implied carbon price declined to $15/MWh in February 2013. Despite a rebound in mid-2013, it kept decreasing and hit $5/MWh by the end of the same year [ABC, 2014].

The trajectory of implied carbon price demonstrates dynamic market expectation about carbon price. According to Fig. 1, various political and economic incidents influenced the market outlook on the Australian carbon pricing policy. Due to policy uncertainty, the market continuously adjusted its valuation and anticipation regarding carbon price throughout the observation period. Besides, shocks from oversea markets also affected the confidence in Australia's carbon pricing policy.

[4] In response to proposed Carbon Pollution Reduction Scheme Bill 2009, the AFMA released Carbon Benchmark Addendum in August 2010 [AFMA, 2010]. Although this cap-and-trade scheme failed to pass in the Parliament, the addendum provided market guidance to clarify the way of incorporating carbon cost into OTC electricity derivative contracts.

For instance, the crunch of EU ETS market since late 2012 put a downward pressure on the implied carbon price in Australia. The trend of implied carbon price by the end of 2013 indicated negative market outlook after the newly elected government launched legislative process to repeal the CPM in September.

2.2. *Modeling the dynamics of implied carbon price*

This section reports the empirical study on the dynamics of implied carbon price and the modeling procedure. Due to political controversies, CPM was under pressures throughout its implementation, which caused considerable uncertainty. Despite the repeal of carbon pricing policy, majority of the Australian-based experts still expect that a carbon price will be in place before 2020 [Jotzo *et al.* 2012]. Recent progress achieved at the UNFCC Conference in Paris manifested the global willingness of mitigating climate change through international cooperation. Subsequent commitment announced by the Australian government increased the possibility of a come-back of carbon price as well [Bamsey, 2015]. An empirical study provides insight into characteristics of implied carbon price and effect of policy uncertainty on market expectation. The findings can contribute to the evaluation of Australia's carbon pricing policy and design of future policy framework.

2.2.1. *ARCH model*

Engle [1982] introduced the Autoregressive Conditional Heteroscedasticity (ARCH) model to address heteroscedasticity in the conditional variance of time series. An AR process of order p for y_t is as follows:

$$y_t = a_0 + \sum_{i=1}^{p} a_i y_{t-i} + \mu_t, \tag{2}$$

where a_0 denotes constant term, a_i is autoregressive coefficient and μ_t represents the error term. Conditional variance h_t of error term μ_t is in form of a weighted sum of squared preceding observations:

$$h_t = \alpha_0 + \alpha_1 \varepsilon_{t-1}^2 + \alpha_2 \varepsilon_{t-2}^2 + \alpha_3 \varepsilon_{t-3}^2 + \cdots + \alpha_i \varepsilon_{t-q}^2, \tag{3}$$

where ε_{t-q} are identical independent distributed ($i.i.d.$) variables with zero mean and finite variance. As the conditional variance of error term, h_t is dependent on the realization of ε_{t-i}, which is in an autoregressive form. Hence, in case of positive serial correlation, a large (small) magnitude of ε_{t-i} tends to be followed by large (small) successive values.

As an emerging market-based policy instrument, carbon price often exhibits volatile movement. Hence, conventional econometric models that assume disturbance term with constant variance are not able to capture heteroscedasticity [Feng *et al.* 2011]. Therefore, Daskalakis *et al.* [2009], Benz and Trück [2009] and Paolella and Taschini [2008] applied Generalized Autoregressive Conditional Heteroskedasticity (GARCH) models to study volatile price movement in the European carbon market. As the path of implied carbon price is characterised by volatility clustering (Fig. 1), this chapter applies ARCH-family model to study its dynamics. Notably, electricity is a unique commodity as it cannot be stored in large volumes to generate convenience yield. Hence, derivative contracts for electricity are not likely to exhibit many of the stylized effects that are common for the returns on other traded financial assets. Therefore, ARCH-type models are applicable to simulate the dynamics of implied carbon price, which is derived directly from the prices of electricity derivative contracts.

2.2.2. *In-sample and out-of-sample datasets*

This chapter divides the sample of implied carbon price data into two subsets for the purpose of empirical study: Data from 3 December 2010 to 3 December 2012 are used as training dataset to estimate the proposed model and data for implied carbon price from 4 December 2012 to 3 December 2013 are held out as out-of-sample dataset for model validation purpose (Table 1).[5] Due to the large-scale variation, both datasets depict high standard deviation and kurtosis. According to the augmented Dickey–Fuller (ADF) test statistics, in-sample and out-of-sample datasets are characterized with unit root processes. Therefore, model estimation proceeds with the first-order differenced data, which become non-stationary after transformation (Table 1).

2.2.3. *ARCH modeling and estimation results*

The modeling procedure commences with the selection of an appropriate AR model, which follows the Box–Jenkins approach. Both Autocorrelation Function (ACF) and Partial Autocorrelation Function (PACF) analysis indicate significant autocorrelation in the first two lags. While the Akaike Information Criterion (AIC)

[5] In econometrical time series study, data are usually separated into subsets for different purposes. While in-sample dataset is used to estimate model parameters, out-of-sample dataset is withheld from the model calibration process. It is used to compare with the values forecasted by estimated model, in order to validate model selection and evaluate model's forecasting performance [Brooks, 2014].

Table 1. Summary statistics for implied carbon price — in-sample (3 December 2012–3 December 2012) and cut-of-sample (4 December 2012–3 December 2013) periods.

Period	n	Mean	Std. Dev.	Skewness	Kurtosis	$Z(t)$
03/12/2010–03/12/2012	502	14.19	7.38	−1.01	2.40	−1.50
03/12/2010–03/12/2012 (*First-order Difference*)	501	0.03	0.64	2.22	23.56	−25.71*
04/12/2012–03/12/2013	252	11.05	5.38	−0.06	1.96	−1.31
04/12/2012–03/12/2013 (*First-order Difference*)	251	−0.07	0.91	−0.66	6.52	−18.23*

Notes: The second and fourth rows represent the first-order differenced data. $Z(t)$ indicates augmented Dickey–Fuller test statistic, whose null hypothesis assumes unit root process.
*Augmented Dickey–Fuller test statistic significant at 1% level.

Table 2. AR-ARCH modelling results.

Parameter	AR(1)	AR(2)	AR(3)	AR(1)-ARCH(1)	AR(1)-ARCH(2)	AR(1)-ARCH(3)
a_1	−0.1377	−0.1475	−0.1477	−0.1616	−0.1572	−0.1557
	(0.0370)	(0.0368)	(0.0368)	(0.0711)	(0.0700)	(0.0701)
a_2		−0.0713	−0.0718			
		(0.0591)	(0.0610)			
a_3			−0.0037			
			(0.0425)			
α_1				0.0299	0.0284	0.0287
				(0.0233)	(0.0224)	(0.0224)
α_2					−0.0127	−0.0126
					(0.0060)	(0.0060)
α_3						0.0074
						(0.0152)
AIC	970.2683	969.7100	969.7679	969.6129	968.6227	970.4403
BIC	978.7015	982.3579	990.8509	982.2627	985.4891	991.5234
Ljung–Box	48.7385*			50.3614*		
MAE				0.5489		
MSE				0.8160		
RMSE				0.9033		

Notes: *Ljung–Box static significant at 1% level.
Standard deviation in parentheses.

suggests an AR model of two lags, the AR(1) model is favored according to the Bayesian Information Criterion (BIC) (Table 2). Furthermore, as the estimated constant term is found not significantly different from zero, the more parsimonious AR(1) model without constant term is preferred.

The results of Ljung–Box test indicate no significant autocorrelation in the residuals of estimated AR(1) model (Table 2). However, rejection of the null hypothesis

Table 3. LM test results for ARCH effect examination.

	AR(1)			AR(1)-ARCH(1)		
Lags	χ^2	**df**	$P>\chi^2$	χ^2	**df**	$P>\chi^2$
1	3.836	1	0.0501	0.319	1	0.5724
2	9.897	2	0.0071	0.463	2	0.7935
3	11.764	3	0.0082	0.472	3	0.9250
4	11.777	4	0.0191	0.627	4	0.9600
5	11.932	5	0.0357	0.669	5	0.9846
6	13.972	6	0.0300	0.706	6	0.9944
7	14.997	7	0.0360	0.768	7	0.9978
8	19.727	8	0.0114	0.848	8	0.9990
9	19.706	9	0.0198	1.028	9	0.9994
10	21.668	10	0.0169	1.241	10	0.9995

Notes: The null hypothesis of test assumes no ARCH effect among residuals.

assuming homoscedasticity based on the squared residuals implies remaining non-constant variance. Further investigation with the Lagrange Multiplier-ARCH Effect (LM-ARCH) test detects significant heteroscedasticity in the residuals of AR(1) model (Table 3). Therefore, conditional heteroscedastic error term that follows a normal distribution is integrated into the AR(1) model, in order to eliminate the ARCH effect. Given the constraint of non-negative conditional variance h_t assumed by the ARCH process (Equation (3)) [Enders, 2008], ARCH(2) and ARCH(3) models are abandoned due to negative coefficient on the second lag (Table 2). Hence, AR(1)-ARCH(1) model is selected to simulate the dynamics of implied carbon price.

Estimating the mean and conditional variance equations for AR(1)-ARCH(1) model yields:

$$\begin{aligned} \mathrm{V}y_t &= -0.1616\mathrm{V}y_{t-1} + \mu_t; \\ h_t &= 0.0299\varepsilon_{t-1}^2, \end{aligned} \tag{4}$$

where $\mathrm{V}y_t$ denotes the first-order difference of implied carbon price, μ_t represents the error term and h_t is the conditional variance of error term μ_t, which is in the form of a weighted sum of squared preceding observation ε_t. The AR coefficient of -0.1616 satisfies the stability condition $|a_1| < 1$ for autoregressive process and has a standard error of 0.0711. The ARCH coefficient of 0.0299 implies a stationary process with low amount of persistence, which is associated with a standard error of 0.0233. As the AR coefficient indicates negative correlation in the in-sample dataset of implied carbon price, the upward trend is mostly due to volatility clustering.

Furthermore, the modeling results demonstrate suitability of AR(1)-ARCH(1) to capture the dynamics of implied carbon price. Besides insignificant autocorrelation in residuals according to the Ljung–Box test statistic (Table 2), LM-ARCH Effect test results provided in Table 3 indicate no remaining heteroscedasticity after integrating the ARCH term. In comparison to AR(1) model, the AIC statistic for AR(1)-ARCH(1) model further declines, which implies improved model estimation results (Table 2). However, since the BIC imposes a stronger penalty term for additional parameters [Kuha, 2004], the value of BIC increases as a result of extra parameters in conditional variance equation h_t. Overall, the BIC of AR(1)-ARCH(1) model is still the lowest compared to other models under consideration.

2.2.4. *Out-of-sample forecasting*

In the next step, we conduct forecasting based on the estimated AR(1)-ARCH(1) model for the period from 4 December 2012 to 3 December 2013. A comparison between predicted results and actual prices in the out-of-sample period validate model's ability to simulate the dynamics of implied carbon price. Updating AR(1)-ARCH(1) model by one period yields one-step ahead forecast that is conditioned on the information available at period t:

$$E_t \Delta y_{t+1} = E(\mathrm{V} y_{t+1} | \mathrm{V} y_t, \mathrm{V} y_{t-1}, \mathrm{K}\varepsilon_{t,}\varepsilon_{t-1,}\mathrm{K}), \tag{5}$$

where $E_t \mathrm{V} y_{t+1}$ represents the conditional expectation of $\mathrm{V} y_t$. As estimation of AR(1)-ARCH(1) model is based on the first-order differenced data, the one-step ahead prediction results are converted back to the forecasted implied carbon price:

$$E_t y_{t+1} = y_t + E_t \mathrm{V} y_{t+1}. \tag{6}$$

The forward iterative process, which starts from the final observation of in-sample dataset, generates out-of-sample forecast for implied carbon price (Fig. 2).

Furthermore, we also develop random walk models to conduct one-step ahead predictions. A comparison of forecasting results between the estimated AR(1)-ARCH(1) model and the alternative random walk models validates the robustness of out-of-sample forecasting. The random walk model can be expressed as:

$$E y_{t+1} = y_t + \varepsilon_{t+1} \varepsilon_t : N(0, \sigma^2), \tag{7}$$

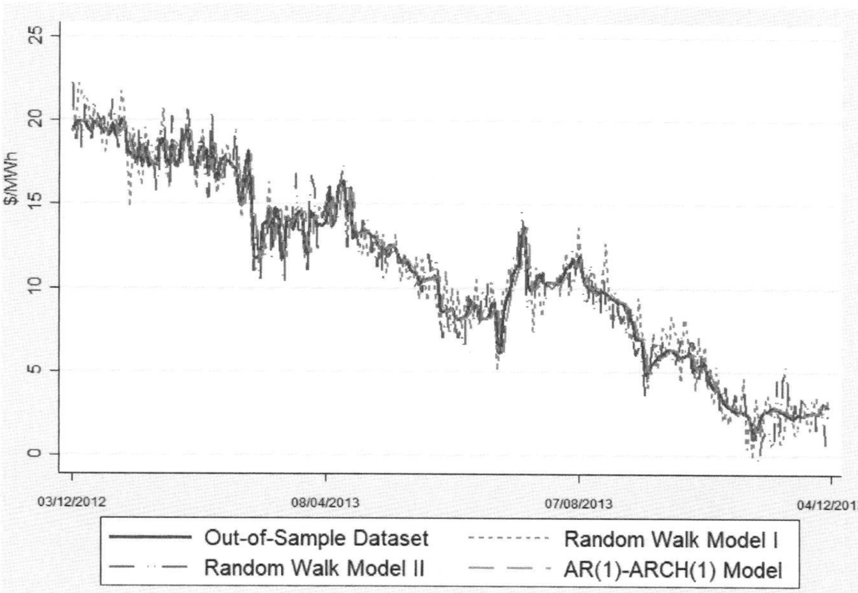

Fig. 2. Results of one-step ahead out-of-sample implied carbon price forecasting ($/MWh).

where $\mathrm{E}y_{t+1}$ denotes one-step ahead forecast of implied carbon price at $t+1$, ε_{t+1} represents the random walk process following i.i.d. normal distribution with zero mean and variance of σ^2. It is assumed that the best estimate of implied carbon price at $t+1$ is the previous price at time t adjusted by a Gaussian drift.

Figure 2 shows that AR(1)-ARCH(1) model is advantageous in forecasting the dynamics of implied carbon price. Visual observation suggests that both AR(1)-ARCH(1) model and random walk model deliver good prediction outcomes. However, it is also obvious that predictions by the random walk models have greater deviations from the actual path of implied carbon price in the out-of-sample period. Furthermore, to articulate quantitative measurement for forecasting performance, the forecast error at time t is computed as:

$$e(t) = E_t y_{t+1} - y_{t+1}, \tag{8}$$

where $e(t)$ is the difference between forecasted value $E_t y_{t+1}$ and actual data y_{t+1}. Subsequently, mean absolute error (MAE) and root mean square error (RMSE) are derived as:

$$\mathrm{MAE} = \left[\frac{1}{n}\sum_{i=1}^{n} |e(t)|\right] \tag{9}$$

Table 4. A comparison of models' forecasting accuracy using MAE and RMSE.

	MAE	RMSE
AR(1)-ARCH(1)	0.5468	0.8997
Random Walk Model I	0.8315	1.0431
Random Walk Model II	0.8513	1.0506

and

$$\text{RMSE} = \left[\frac{1}{n}\sum_{i=1}^{n}|e(t)|^2\right]^{\frac{1}{2}}, \tag{10}$$

which quantitatively evaluate the forecasting performance [Willmott and Matsuura, 2005].

MAE and RMSE in Table 4 show that AR(1)-ARCH(1) model outperforms other models in forecasting the dynamics of implied carbon price. In comparison to the two other random walk simulations, the estimated AR(1)-ARCH(1) model achieves the lowest MAE and RMSE. Considering the range of implied carbon price, which varies between 0 and $20/MWh, MAE indicates that the forecast errors of AR(1)-ARCH(1) model are rather small. However, greater RMSE implies large scale of dispersion in forecasting results, as the indicator is sensitive to outliers in forecast errors [Hyndman and Koehler, 2006]. This can be explained by the statistical properties of out-of-sample dataset and volatility clustering observed in implied carbon price (Table 1 and Fig. 2). The fluctuation also reflects changing market expectation on carbon price due to policy uncertainty. Overall, it can be concluded that AR(1)-ARCH(1) model outwits random walk model in terms of forecasting dynamic of implied carbon price.

3. The Influence of Implied Carbon Price on the Stock Price Variability of Energy Companies in the Electric Utility Sector

Recent studies discovered the effects of carbon pricing on stock market. In Europe, wholesale electricity prices increased as a result of high carbon pass-through rate, which in turn enhanced revenue of electricity companies and their stock prices [Oberndorfer, 2009; Veith *et al.* 2009]. Furthermore, volatility in the European carbon market also affected the short-term stock price variability of electricity companies [Tian *et al.* 2012]. However, little attention has been given to the relationship between carbon pricing and stock price variability of energy companies in Australia. Having established the dynamics of market expectations throughout CPM implementation (Fig. 1), this section further evaluates the influence of implied carbon price on the stock price variability for electric utility companies listed on the ASX.

3.1. *VAR model*

We employ a VAR model to study the volatility co-movement between implied carbon price and stock price of electric utility companies. The VAR model is a popular econometric tool, which is eligible to capture interdependencies between time series. The VAR system contains an equation for each variable, whose evolution is explained by its own lags and lags of other variables. Furthermore, all variables are treated as endogenous. In comparison to other structural models, the VAR model is a theory-free method for detecting economic relationships [Sims, 1986]. This feature has been applied to study interaction between energy and stock markets [Chang *et al.* 2013; Olson *et al.* 2014; Sadorsky, 1999; Shaharudin *et al.* 2009]. Moreover, the VAR model is also a popular tool for exploring the effect of carbon pricing policy on the stock market as well as the wider economy [Chevallier, 2011a; Fezzi and Bunn, 2009; Kumar *et al.* 2012; Oberndorfer, 2009].

The VAR model is a system of equations, in which all variables are treated as endogenous. Consider a bivariate first-order VAR system:

$$\begin{aligned} y_t &= b_{10} + b_{12}z_t + \gamma_{11}y_{t-1} + \gamma_{12}z_{t-1} + \varepsilon_{yt}; \\ z_t &= b_{20} + b_{21}y_t + \gamma_{21}z_{t-1} + \gamma_{22}y_{t-1} + \varepsilon_{zt}, \end{aligned} \tag{11}$$

where y and z are endogenous variables, b_{i0} are $k \times 1$ vectors of constant terms, b_{ij} and γ_{ij} are $k \times 1$ vectors of coefficients, and ε_{yt} and ε_{yt} are $k \times 1$ vectors of uncorrelated white-noise disturbances. In addition, this linear function system incorporates feedback effect between variables. Hence, b_{ij} represents contemporaneous effect from other variables and γ_{ij} is parameter that captures the effects of the past realisations of variable itself. The time path of one variable could be affected by the past and current realizations of other variables. In the case of a non-zero b_{21}, the pure innovation ε_{yt} would have an indirect contemporaneous effect on z_t [Enders, 2008]. The standard form of VAR model of order p can be expressed as

$$Y_t = A_0 + A_1Y_{t-1} + \cdots + A_pY_{t-p} + e_t \quad e_t : N(0, \Omega), \tag{12}$$

where Y_t contains $k \times 1$ variable, Y_{t-i} are lagged dependent variables and e_t represents the error term of the VAR(p) model, which is a composite of shocks of variables ε_t. It is assumed that

$$Ee_t = 0; \quad Ee_t e_{t-i} = 0; \quad Ee_t e_t^{'} = \sum, \tag{13}$$

where $\sum$ is contemporaneous covariance matrix of errors:

$$\sum = \begin{bmatrix} \mathrm{var}(e_{1t}) & \mathrm{cov}(e_{1t}, e_{2t}) \\ \mathrm{cov}(e_{1t,e_{2t}}) & \mathrm{var}(e_{2t}) \end{bmatrix}.$$

3.2. *Volatilities of the S&P/ASX 200 utilities index and the implied carbon price*

S&P/ASX 200 Utilities (AXUJ) index is a composite stock index for Australian energy companies in the electric utility sector. It is comprised of major companies that are involved in electric, gas and multi utility services (Table 5). All constituent companies have businesses related to electricity generation, retail and distribution.[6] In terms of market capitalization, companies that provide electric utility service make up the majority of AXUJ index [S&P Dow Jones Indices, 2016; The Sydney Morning Herald, 2016]. Since these companies were heavily exposed to the carbon pricing policy, the AXUJ index is used as a proxy for the performance of Australian electric utility sector during the CPM implementation. The data collected from the SIRCA covers daily observation of AXUJ index for the period from 3 December 2010 to 3 December 2013 (Fig. 3).[7]

We derive daily variances of implied carbon price and AXUJ index to study their volatility comovement (Fig. 3). Based on half-hourly market data collected from the SIRCA database, daily variance of the AXUJ index is calculated as:

$$\sigma_t = \sqrt{\frac{\sum_{i=1}^{N} w_i (p_i - \overline{p_t})^2}{\frac{N-1}{N} \sum_{i=1}^{N} w_i}}, \quad \text{where } \overline{p_t} = \frac{\sum_{i=1}^{N} w_i p_i}{\sum_{i=1}^{N} w_i}, \tag{14}$$

[6]In March 2016, APA Group acquired the 100% ownership of gas-powered stations in Queensland from AGL Energy Limited [APA Group, 2016]. Therefore, it becomes an electric utility provider in the major Australian state as well.

[7]SIRCA is a research data provider aiming at promoting and enabling financial research and innovation. It is an independent institute constituted by member universities, central banks, regulators and public sector agencies.

Table 5. Composite of S&P/ASX 200 utilities (AXUJ) index in the Australian stock market.

Company name	ASX code	Market capital (million AUD)	Sub industry	Country
AGL Energy Limited	AGL	12657	Multi-Utilities	Australia
APA Group	APA	9817	Gas Utilities	Australia
SP Ausnet	AST	5501	Electric Utilities	Australia
Duet Group	DUE	5670	Multi-Utilities	Australia
Spark Infrastructure Group	SKI	3734	Electric Utilities	Australia

Source: S&P Dow Jones Indices [2016]; The Sydney Morning Herald [2016].

where σ_t denotes the volatility on day t, N represents the number of observation during day t (N equals to 12, as there are 12 observations for trading hours of ASX from 10 am to 16 pm within a business day). P_i denotes the value of the AXUJ index observed within the time interval, which is weighted by w_i (w_i is equal among all observed periods), and $\overline{p}_t$ is a daily average index. According to the ADF test statistics, both datasets are stationary (Table 6). The overall correlation between variances of implied carbon price and AXUJ index is −0.008.

3.3. *Modeling the joint volatility movement between implied carbon price and AXUJ index*

The VAR modeling commences with the determination of appropriate lag for the model. While final prediction error (FPE) and AIC suggests eight lags, Hannan and Quinn information criterion (HQIC) is in favour of two lags (Table 7). The likelihood ratio test developed by Sims [1980] helps to determine the exact lag number. It is expressed as:

$$(T-c)\left(\log\left|\sum_2\right| - \log\left|\sum_8\right|\right), \tag{15}$$

where T denotes the number of usable observations, c is the number of parameters estimated for each equation in the unrestricted system and $\log|\sum_n|$ represents the determinant of $\sum_n$ in form of a natural logarithm. The likelihood ratio test statistics follows an asymptotic χ^2 distribution, whose degrees of freedom are equal to the number of restrictions in the system [Enders, 2008]. The χ^2 statistic of 58.75 leads to a rejection of the restricted VAR(2) model at 1% significance level with six degrees of freedom. Lags that are not significantly different from zero are further excluded from the VAR(8) model. According to the Lagrange multiplier test, there is no remaining autocorrelation among residuals after estimation of VAR model

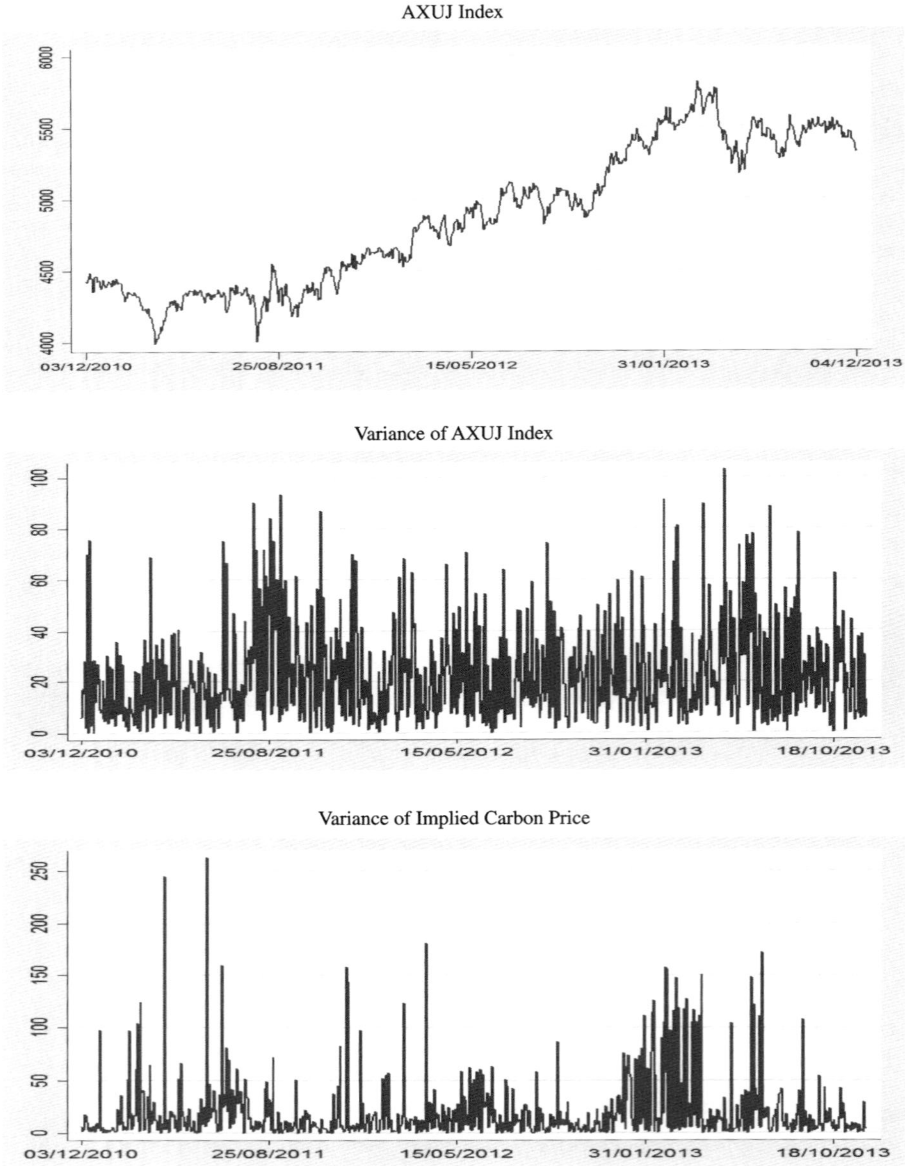

Fig. 3. Variances of implied carbon price and AXUJ index (3 December 2010–4 December 2013).

with the seemingly unrelated regression (SUR). Since all eigenvalues lie inside the unit circle, the VAR modeling results satisfy the stability condition (Fig. 4). It also demonstrates the suitability of VAR model to study the volatility interdependency between implied carbon price and AXUJ index.

Table 6. Summary statistics for variances of implied carbon price and AXUJ index (3 December 2010–3 December 2013).

	n	Mean	Std. Dev.	Skewness	Kurtosis	*Z(t)*
Implied Carbon Price	744	20.36	31.21	3.28	16.75	−24.44*
AXUJ Index	744	23.08	18.87	1.29	4.58	−25.98*

Notes: *Z(t) indicates Dickey–Fuller Test statistic, whose null hypothesis assumes unit root process.
*Augmented Dickey–Fuller test statistic significant at 1% level.

Table 7. Results of VAR lag selection tests.

Lag selection					Wald lag-exclusion statistics					
		Criterion			Equation implied carbon price		Equation AXUJ		Equation all	
Lag	df	FPE	AIC	HQIC	df	$P>\chi^2$	df	$P>\chi^2$	df	$P>\chi^2$
1	4	348468	18.44	18.45	2	0.27	2	0.01	4	0.03
2	4	338018	18.41	<u>18.43</u>	2	0.00	2	0.00	4	0.00
3	4	336834	18.40	18.44	2	0.06	2	0.01	4	0.00
4	4	337294	18.40	18.45	2	0.95	2	0.00	4	0.01
5	4	338128	18.41	18.46	2	0.98	2	0.00	4	0.01
6	4	335159	18.40	18.46	2	0.05	2	0.00	4	0.00
7	4	334191	18.40	18.47	2	0.01	2	0.06	4	0.01
8	4	330563	18.38	18.47	2	0.00	2	0.01	4	0.00

Note: The null hypothesis of Wald Lag-exclusion test assumes that endogenous variables are jointly zero at a given lag.

3.4. *VAR modeling results*

The estimated VAR(8) model detects positive volatility comovement between implied carbon price and AXUJ Index. The Granger-Causality test statistics are significant at 1% level for all estimated equations (Table 8), which implies that volatilities of implied carbon price and the AXUJ index can be used to predict each other. Furthermore, the estimated VAR coefficients indicate positive correlation between both variables (Table 9). The empirical results can be confirmed by findings from other studies, which discovered high carbon pass-through rate in Australia during the CPM implementation [AER, 2013b; Nazifi, 2016]. As a result, costs of carbon were passed to end-users through higher electricity wholesale prices. Electric utility companies achieved greater revenue, which positively affected their stock prices. Moreover, fixed-rate carbon price under the CPM made the compliance costs transparent and predictable for electricity generation. We believe that this may

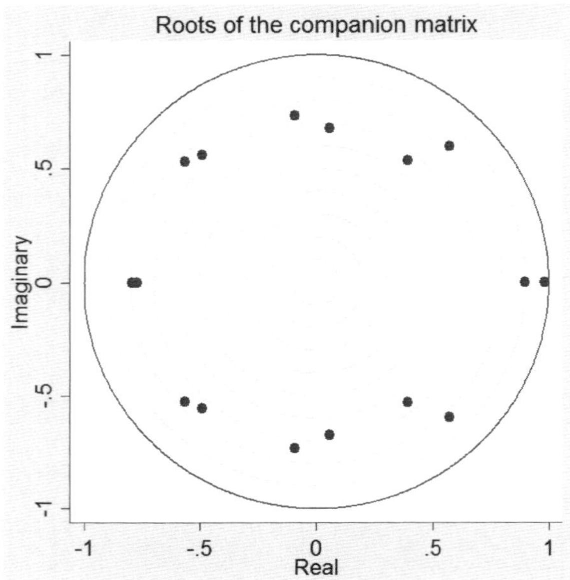

Fig. 4. Eigenvalue check results for VAR modeling stability.

Table 8. Summary of the Granger-causality tests.

Equation	**Excluded**	χ^2	**df**	$P > \chi^2$
Implied Carbon Price	AXUJ	20.00	8	0.01
Implied Carbon Price	ALL	20.00	8	0.01
AXUJ	Implied Carbon Price	20.93	8	0.01
AXUJ	ALL	20.93	8	0.01

Note: The null hypothesis of Granger-Causality test assumes that dependent variable does not Granger cause independent variable.

be one major reason for the positive volatility relationship between implied carbon price and AUXJ Index. According to the estimated VAR model parameters, the magnitude of this comovement is relatively small.

VAR modeling also indicates asymmetric volatility interaction between implied carbon price and AXUJ index. The estimated coefficients for equation of implied carbon price suggest that the variability impact from AXUJ index is only significant at the second lag (Table 9). The possible reason for lagged volatility spill-over from stock market is participant structure in the electricity derivative market. In Australia's electricity derivative market, electricity generators and retailers are major market players [AER, 2015]. Other participants such as financial institutions usually make up approximately 20% of the annual turnover in the OTC electricity derivative

Table 9. VAR modeling results.

Equation: Implied carbon price				
Implied carbon price	**Coefficient**	**Standard error**	**z**	**P > |z|**
Lag 2	0.18	0.04	5.09	0.00
Lag 3	0.11	0.04	3.06	0.00
Lag 6	0.11	0.04	3.06	0.00
Lag 7	0.12	0.03	3.35	0.00
Lag 8	0.17	0.04	4.62	0.00
AXUJ	**Coefficient**	**Standard error**	**z**	**P>|z|**
Lag 2	0.19	0.05	4.13	0
Equation: AXUJ				
Implied carbon price	**Coefficient**	**Standard error**	**z**	**P > |z|**
Lag 1	0.05	0.02	2.09	0.04
Lag 7	0.05	0.02	2.21	0.03
Lag 8	0.05	0.02	2.24	0.03
AXUJ	**Coefficient**	**Standard error**	**z**	**P > |z|**
Lag 1	0.08	0.04	2.22	0.03
Lag 2	0.14	0.04	3.98	0.00
Lag 3	0.11	0.04	3.11	0.00
Lag 4	0.14	0.04	3.78	0.00
Lag 5	0.13	0.04	3.66	0.00
Lag 6	0.13	0.04	3.47	0.00
Lag 8	0.08	0.04	2.2	0.03

market (Fig. 5). As a result, investors have limited market power, and the volatility in the stock market did not significantly impact the electricity derivative market. On the other hand, variability of implied carbon price affected AXUJ index at the first lag. This indicates that fluctuating expectation of carbon price had contemporaneous effect on the stock market. According to the estimated coefficients for AXUJ equation displayed in the second half of Table 9, the variability from implied carbon price still affects AXUJ index at the seventh and eighth lags (Table 9).

3.5. *Impulse response analysis*

An IRA traces out the time path of endogenous variable in the VAR system after a shock induced by another variable. In the context of this chapter, it visually depicts how implied carbon price responded to one unit volatility increase in AXUJ

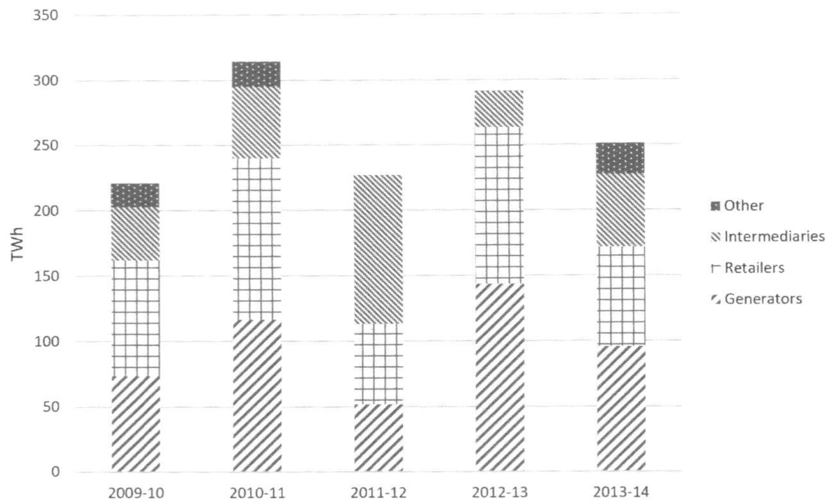

Fig. 5. Australia's OTC electricity derivative market turnover by participants (2009–2014). *Source*: AFMA [2014].

index and vice versa. To conduct IRA, impulse response function (IRF), which is the long-run multiplier derived from vector moving average (VWA) form of the VAR model [Hamilton, 1994; Lütkepohl, 2005], is plotted for 20 business days. The convergence condition of IRF is satisfied, since the estimated VAR model is stable as shown in previous section (Fig. 4). Furthermore, there is no difference in impulse response between different orderings, as Choleski decomposition delivered symmetric IRA outcomes.[8]

The variability of implied carbon price caused immediate and persistent volatility reaction in stock market. One unit shock from implied carbon price induced a rise of volatility by 0.047 units for AXUJ index on the following day (Fig. 6). After reversing to the level close to zero in the second period, it bounced back to 0.02 units on the 3rd day and remained relatively stable until the sixth period. On the 7th day, volatility of the AXUJ index jumped to 0.07 units and stayed unchanged until the day after. It decreased to 0.048 units on the 9th day and kept steady until day 12. From the 13th period till the 15th period, it gradually climbed up to 0.056 units. Changes in subsequent days were very small until the end of forecasting period. The time path of IRF demonstrates changing volatility response in the Australian

[8]The Choleski decomposition is a classical approach to impose restriction on underidentified VAR system, in order to explore the impulse response. By constraining the contemporaneous effect from one variable to the other, the Choleski decomposition enables the IRA to trace out the reaction of the unconstrained variable to the shock caused by other endogenous variables. The ordering refers to the order of the contemporaneous effect constrain applied to the endogenous variables.

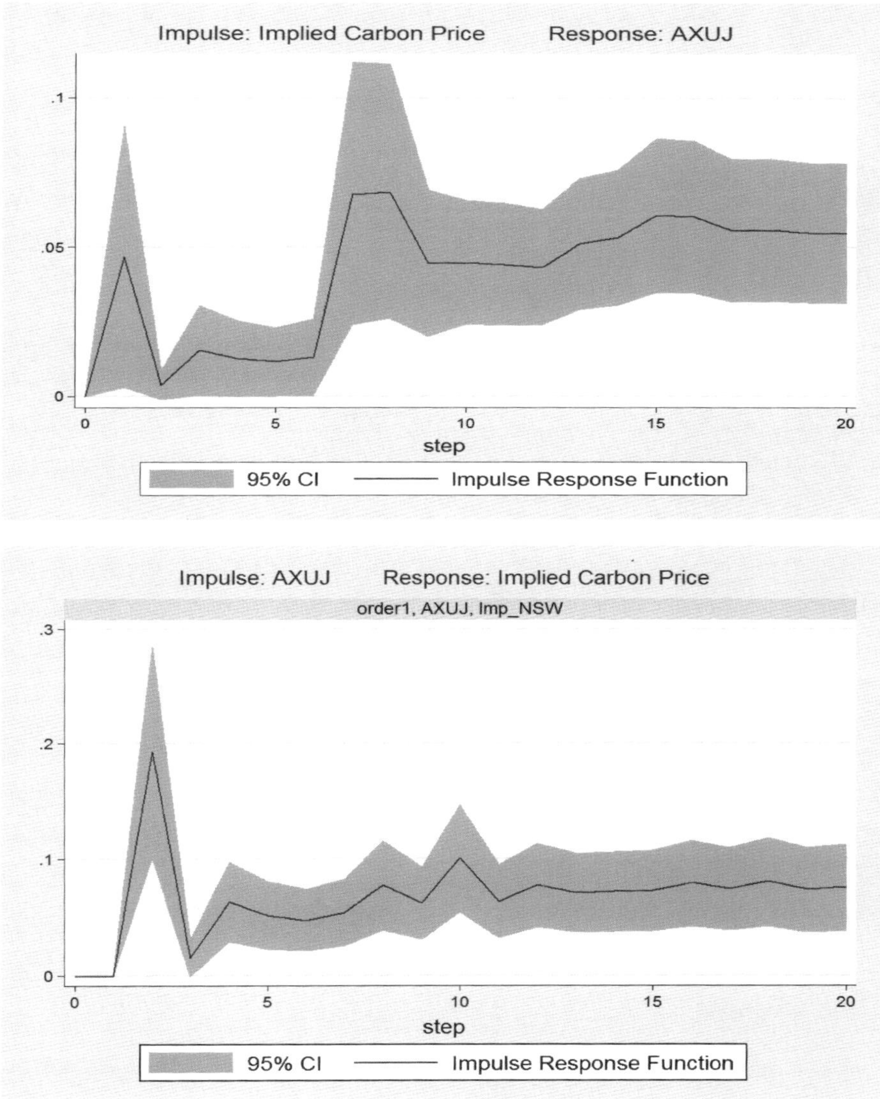

Fig. 6. Time path of impulse response function.

stock market due to the shock from electricity derivative market. This implies that uncertainty related to carbon pricing policy transferred to stock market, which in turn affected the outlook on business performance of major electric utility companies. The persistent volatility level change for AXUJ index reflects market anxiety over the effect of carbon pricing policy uncertainty on the electric utility sector.

On the other hand, volatility shock in the stock market induced rapid and fluctuating reaction in the Australian electricity derivative market. In response to one unit shock in the AXUJ index, volatility of implied carbon price jumped by 0.195 units within 2 days (Fig. 6). Despite a decline on the following day, which brought volatility level to 0.01 units, it rose again on the 3rd day and reached 0.06 units on day 4. Although the volatility of the implied carbon price started to decline slightly until day 6, it was again in an upward trend since day 7 and reached 0.08 units on the 8th day. After a decrease to 0.07 units on day 9, it rose to 0.1 units on day 10. Although a decrease brought the volatility back to 0.07 units on the following day, it bounced back to 0.08 units on day 12. Since then, volatility for implied carbon price remained relative stable until the twentieth forecasting period.

Figure 6 also demonstrates asymmetric volatility comovement between implied carbon price and AXUJ index. According to the path of IRF, the magnitude of volatility response by implied carbon price to a unit shock was four times higher than the AXUJ index in the first 3 days. As the Australian government imposed a carbon price in form of tax, the actual cost of carbon emissions was fully transparent. Hence, the impact of carbon pricing on business performance of electric utility companies was predictable. As a result, volatility shock from implied carbon price had limited effect on variability of AXUJ index. On the other hand, electricity generators and retailers are major players in electricity derivative market (Fig. 5). Due to their limited stock trading activities, a shock from the stock market had relatively low influence on the volatility of implied carbon price in electricity derivative market. However, the effect of shock from the AXUJ index can be exaggerated by financial intermediaries due to their speculative activities in the electricity derivative market. Therefore, implied carbon price tended to responsed to a greater extent to a volatility shock from the stock market in the short run. Overall, the time path of IRF indicates limited magnitude of volatility interaction between both markets in the long run.

4. Conclusion

In July 2012, the Australian government introduced CPM to regulate GHG emissions. Using data from the Australian electricity derivative market, this chapter derives an implied carbon price to demonstrate the market expectations throughout CPM implementation. Furthermore, the chapter develops econometric models to simulate and forecast the dynamics of implied carbon price, which provides insights into its characteristics. In addition, we link implied carbon price with Utility (AXUJ) index of the Australian Stock Exchange, in order to explore their joint volatility movement. The investigation uncovers whether the sentiment of carbon pricing in electricity market influenced stock price variability of electricity companies that are listed on the Australian stock market.

Despite the effect of climate change policy on constraining GHG emissions, concerns over its economic impact resulted in weak public support. As a consequence, doubts about the fate of CPM caused inconsistent market expectations on carbon price. As Australia's major GHG emitter, electricity sector was highly exposed to carbon price. Hence, an implied carbon price is derived as the price spread between electricity derivative contracts of different classes to reveal market expectation on carbon cost. Its dynamics manifests the influence of political and economic events on market sentiment. Moreover, modeling results show that AR model with conditional heteroscedastic error term can capture the volatility clustering induced by policy uncertainty.

Due to the high carbon pass-through rate, carbon pricing enhanced expected return of electric utility companies listed on the Australian stock market. As a result, Granger-Causality test detects positive correlation in price variability between implied carbon price and AXUJ index. While variability of implied carbon price caused immediate and persistent volatility reaction in stock market, volatility spill-over from stock market to electricity derivative market was lagged. The persistent volatility level shift reveals market concerns over the effects of carbon pricing and related policy uncertainty on electric utility sector. However, responses to volatility shock in both markets were asymmetric. Magnitude of short-term response by implied carbon price to volatility shock was four times higher than AXUJ index. This can be explained by factors such as predictable carbon cost, unique participant structure of Australian electricity derivative market and speculative activities. Overall, the long-term volatility spill-over between both markets was limited.

Despite the repeal of CPM, the majority of Australian-based experts still expect a comeback of carbon price in the future [Jotzo *et al.* 2012]. The empirical study outlined in this chapter not only extends knowledge regarding the effect of policy uncertainty on market sentiment, but also develops appropriate models to simulate and forecast the trends of market expectation on carbon price. Furthermore, findings regarding asymmetric volatility interaction between electricity derivative market and stock market could also contribute to financial risk management.

References

ABC. (2014). Carbon tax: A timeline of its tortuous history in Australia. *ABC NEWS*. Retrieved from http://www.abc.net.au/news/2014-07-10/carbon-tax-timeline/5569118.

AER. (2013a). State of the Energy Market 2013. *Chapter 1-National Electricity Markets*, 10, 20, 22–24. Retrieved from http://www.aer.gov.au/system/files/Chapter%201%20-%20National%20electricity%20markets%20A4.pdf.

AER. (2013b). State of the Energy Market 2013, 36. Retrieved from https://www.aer.gov.au/system/files/Complete%20report%20A4.pdf.

AER. (2015). State of the Energy Market 2015. *Chapter 1-National Electricity Markets*, 53–54. Retrieved from https://www.aer.gov.au/system/files/State%20of%20the%20energy%20market%202015%20%28A4%20format%29%20%E2%80%93%20last%20updated%204%20February%202016.pdf.

AFMA. (2010). Australian Carbon Benchmark Addendum. Retrieved from http://www.afma.com.au/afmawr/_assets/main/lib90047/2010%2008%20carbon%20addendum.pdf.

AFMA. (2012). The AFMA Carbon Benchmark Addendum explained 1–3. Retrieved from http://www.afma.com.au/afmawr/_assets/main/lib90047/ca%20website%20note%20v4.pdf.

AFMA. (2015). 2015 Australian Financial Markets Report. Retrieved from http://www.afma.com.au/data/AFMR.

APA Group. (2016). APA moves to 100% ownership of Diamantina and Leichhardt Power Stations. Retrieved from http://www.apa.com.au/investor-centre/news/asxmedia-releases/2016/apa-acquisiton-of-dps-and-lps.aspx.

Bamsey, H. (2015). The Paris Agreement: Suddenly All Seems Possible. Retrieved from http://www.internationalaffairs.org.au/australianoutlook/23421/.

Benz, E. and Trück, S. (2009). Modeling the price dynamics of CO_2 emission allowances. *Energy Economics* **31** (1), 4–15.

Brooks, C. (2014). *Introductory Econometrics for Finance*. (Cambridge University Press).

Chang, C.-L., McAleer, M. and Tansuchat, R. (2013). Conditional correlations and volatility spillovers between crude oil and stock index returns. *The North American Journal of Economics and Finance* **25**, 116–138.

Chevallier, J. (2009). Carbon futures and macroeconomic risk factors: A view from the EU ETS. *Energy Economics* **31** (4), 614–625.

Chevallier, J. (2011a). Macroeconomics, finance, commodities: Interactions with carbon markets in a data-rich model. *Economic Modelling* **28** (1), 557–567.

Chevallier, J. (2011b). Detecting instability in the volatility of carbon prices. *Energy Economics* **33** (1), 99–110.

Clean Energy Act. (2013). §3–4.

Daskalakis, G., Psychoyios, D. and Markellos, R. N. (2009). Modeling CO_2 emission allowance prices and derivatives: Evidence from the European trading scheme. *Journal of Banking & Finance* **33** (7), 1230–1241.

Enders, W. (2008). *Applied Econometric Time Series* 4th edn. (John Wiley & Sons), pp. 126–129, pp. 298–299, pp. 315–317.

Engle, R. F. (1982). Autoregressive conditional heteroscedasticity with estimates of the variance of United Kingdom inflation. *Econometrica: Journal of the Econometric Society* **50** (4), 987–1007.

Feng, Z.-H., Zou, L.-L. and Wei, Y.-M. (2011). Carbon price volatility: Evidence from EU ETS. *Applied Energy* **88** (3), 590–598.

Fezzi, C. and Bunn, D. W. (2009). Structural interactions of European carbon trading and energy prices. *The Journal of Energy Markets* **2** (4), 53–69.

Garnaut, R. (2011). The Garnaut review 2011: Australia in the global response to climate change, ix. Retrieved from http://www.garnautreview.org.au/update-2011/garnaut-review-2011.html

Hamilton, J. D. (1994). *Time Series Analysis*, Vol. 2. (Princeton university press, Princeton), pp. 319–323.

Hyndman, R. J. and Koehler, A. B. (2006). Another look at measures of forecast accuracy. *International Journal of Forecasting* **22** (4), 679–688.

Jotzo, F. (2012). Australia's carbon price. *Nature Climate Change* **2** (7), 475–476.

Jotzo, F., Jordan, T. and Fabian, N. (2012). Policy uncertainty about Australia's carbon price: Expert survey results and implications for investment. *Australian Economic Review* **45** (4), 395–409.

Kuha, J. (2004). AIC and BIC comparisons of assumptions and performance. *Sociological Methods & Research* **33** (2), 188–229.

Kumar, S., Managi, S. and Matsuda, A. (2012). Stock prices of clean energy firms, oil and carbon markets: A vector autoregressive analysis. *Energy Economics* **34** (1), 215–226.

Lütkepohl, H. (2005). *New Introduction to Multiple Time Series Analysis*. (Springer Science & Business Media). pp. 51–55.

Malkiel, B. G. and Fama, E. F. (1970). Efficient capital markets: A review of theory and empirical work. *The journal of Finance* **25** (2), 383–417.

Nazifi, F. (2016). The pass-through rates of carbon costs on to electricity prices within the Australian National Electricity Market. *Environmental Economics and Policy Studies* **18** (1), 41–62.

Oberndorfer, U. (2009). EU emission allowances and the stock market: Evidence from the electricity industry. *Ecological Economics* **68** (4), 1116–1126.

Olson, E., Vivian, A. J. and Wohar, M. E. (2014). The relationship between energy and equity markets: Evidence from volatility impulse response functions. *Energy Economics* **43**, 297–305.

Paolella, M. S. and Taschini, L. (2008). An econometric analysis of emission allowance prices. *Journal of Banking & Finance* **32** (10), 2022–2032.

Rootes, C. (2014). A referendum on the carbon tax? The 2013 Australian election, the Greens, and the environment. *Environmental Politics* **23** (1), 166–173.

S&P Dow Jones Indices. (2016). S&P/ASX 200 Utilities. Retrieved from http://au.spindices.com/indices/equity/sp-asx-200-utilities-sector.

Sadorsky, P. (1999). Oil price shocks and stock market activity. *Energy Economics* **21** (5), 449–469.

Shaharudin, R. S., Samad, F. and Bhat, S. (2009). Performance and volatility of oil and gas stocks: A comparative study on selected O&G companies. *International Business Research* **2** (4), 87.

Sims, C. A. (1980). Macroeconomics and reality. *Econometrica: Journal of the Econometric Society* **48** (1) 1–48.

Sims, C. A. (1986). Are forecasting models usable for policy analysis? *Federal Reserve Bank of Minneapolis Quarterly Review* **10** (1), 2–16.

The Sydney Morning Herald. (2016). BusinessDay. Retrieved from http://www.smh.com.au/business/markets/indices/share-listing/XUJ/sandpasx-200-utilities-sector.

Tian, Y., Akimov, A., Roca, E. and Wong, V. (2012). Does the carbon market help or hurt the stock price of electricity companies? further evidence from the European context. *Journal of Cleaner Production* **112** (2), 1619–1626.

Veith, S., Werner, J. R. and Zimmermann, J. (2009). Capital market response to emission rights returns: Evidence from the European power sector. *Energy Economics* **31** (4), 605–613.

Willmott, C. J. and Matsuura, K. (2005). Advantages of the mean absolute error (MAE) over the root mean square error (RMSE) in assessing average model performance. *Climate research* **30** (1), 79–82.

Chapter 28

Cointegrating Relationship and Granger Causal Analysis in Energy Economics — A Practical Guidance

Zheng Fang*,‡ and Thai-Ha Le†,§

**School of Business, Singapore University of Social Sciences, Singapore*

†School of Business & Management, RMIT University, Vietnam

‡fangzheng@suss.edu.sg

§ha.lethai@rmit.edu.vn

Cointegrating relationship and Granger causal analysis are used widely in empirical macroeconomics, especially in energy economics. This chapter aims to provide a survey of the development of the two widely used econometric methodologies with a practical guidance on issues that should be considered in implementation and software packages that are available for usage. An example which studies the existence of cointegrating and Granger causal relationship between energy consumption and economic growth is given to illustrate how such analysis can be carried out.

Keywords: Cointegration; Granger causality; energy economics; energy-growth nexus; Stata; time series; panel data; nonlinearity; cross-sectional dependence; unit root tests.

1. Introduction

Cointegration and Granger causal analysis are two popular econometric techniques used in empirical macroeconomics, especially in energy economics. Cointegration describes a particular kind of long-run equilibrium relationship between economic variables. In technical terms, if X and Y are two non-stationary time series (i.e. their means and variance are unstable over time or time-dependent) but X and Y

become stationary after first difference (i.e. integrated of order one series, or $I(1)$ series) and some linear combination of X and Y is stationary (aka, $I(0)$), then we say that X and Y are cointegrated. This original definition of cointegration could be extended to multiple time series, with higher orders of integration. Cointegration could be utilized as a form of estimation for describing a long-run equilibrium between variables. The presence of cointegration enables us to estimate the long-run equilibrium as well as do proper forecasting and inference. Furthermore, we can estimate short-run dynamics around the equilibrium to examine how a pair of cointegrated variables will revert back to their long-run relationship.

One can give various real-life examples of cointegrated pairs, such as size of police force and amount of criminal activity, and a video game and its movie adaptation. In economics, well-known cointegrated pairs of variables include short-term and long-term interest rates, income and consumption, money supply and GDP, and so on and so forth. In finance, one of the most popular applications of cointegration is to form the basis of the pairs trading strategy.

In a nutshell, cointegration analysis advises us whether there is an equilibrium relationship between time series that individually are not in equilibrium. Cointegration is kind of in contrast with (Pearson) correlation, which describes a linear relationship between variables. Furthermore, one should not be confused between the notions of cointegration and regression. The reason is that standard regression analysis fails when dealing with non-stationary variables, and yields spurious results that suggest relationships even when there are none. Cointegration is useful because it allows us to incorporate both short-term dynamics (deviations from equilibrium) and long-run expectations (corrections to equilibrium).

We are naturally interested in causal relationships as we seek to intervene in the normal course of events or to change things in an organized and scientific way. Causal relationships advise us how the causes (e.g. policies, programs, treatments) affect the outcomes of interest. Policy makers need to be aware of the consequences of various policy changes that are being considered for implementing. For instance, if they want to increase the amount of money in circulation, how would this action affect other critical macroeconomic variables such as the general price level and output, given their presumed linkages? In this regard, understanding causal relationships enable policy makers to address and eliminate some of the major common concerns. Specifically, if the increased use of primary energy sources causes environmental degradation, policy makers might implement policies to discourage their usage while encouraging the usage of renewable energy sources such as wind and solar power.

Studying causal linkages among variables is a critical but challenging issue in economics, due to its non-experimental nature. Specifically, a (dependent) variable is impacted by a group of other (explanatory) variables simultaneously and we could not control repeated experiments. Two most challenging issues are: (1) correlation does not imply causation; and (2) possibly ignored common causes might affect the causal relationship among variables. While it is probably impossible to give solutions to these two problems, graphical models were proposed to address the second matter. Meanwhile, the first problem was tackled by relying on the unique unidirectional property of time arrow: cause precedes effect. In particular, Granger developed a working definition of causality based on this concept, using the foreseeability as a yardstick. This gives rise to the so-called "Granger causality" — a popular method for causality analysis, especially in time series, thanks to its computational simplicity [Eichler, 2012].

The ability to identify directed functional ("causal") interactions from time series data makes Granger causality analysis a powerful method. It implements a statistical and predictive notion of causality whereby causes precede, and help predict, their effects. Granger causality is "defined in both the time and frequency domains, and allows for the conditioning out of common causal influences" [Seth *et al.* 2015].

However, the original definition of Granger causality has several limitations. First, Granger causality does not necessarily imply true causality. This is because latent confounding effects are not considered. In the Granger causality analysis, only the Humean definition of causality — that is, the cause-effect relations with constant conjunctions — is identified [Maziarz, 2015]. If two variables X and Y are determined by a common third process with different lags, one might still fail to reject the alternative hypothesis of Granger causality that lagged X-values explain the variation in Y. Nevertheless, manipulation of one of the variables would not change the other. In other words, since the Granger causality analysis is originally designed to handle pairs of variables, it may produce misleading results when the true relationship involves three or more variables. Second, instantaneous and nonlinear causal relationships are not captured. There is no guarantee that the relationship between two variables is monotonic. It might be U-shaped, inverted U-shaped or sinusoidal. For instance, the Environmental Kuznets Curve hypothesizes an inverted U-shaped relationship between environmental quality and economic development. That is, various indicators of environmental performance tend to get worse as modern economic growth occurs, until average income reaches a certain point over the course of development. In such a case, it will not be possible to provide a simple characterization of the direction of the causal influence based on the original definition of Granger causality.

Other possible sources of misguiding Granger causality test results are: (1) not frequent enough or too frequent sampling, (2) time series non-stationarity and nonlinearity, and (3) existence of rational expectations [Maziarz, 2015]. Several extensions have been proposed to address these issues [Eichler, 2012]. For instance, a similar test involving more variables can be applied with vector autoregression (VAR) [Maziarz, 2015].

The remainder of the chapter is organized as follows: Section 2 surveys the development of the econometric methods in these two areas and summarizes key stages of development using a specific application in energy economics. Section 3 describes various methods proposed in the literature in detail and points out issues practitioners should pay attention to in the implementation, as well as listing available software packages. Section 4 uses energy and macroeconomic data to illustrate how the methods should be applied to address the existence of cointegrating and Granger causal relationships between energy consumption and economic development. Empirical results are discussed and compared across different model frameworks and econometric methods with reference to the vast energy-growth nexus literature. The last section summarizes the chapter and points out the promising future development of methodologies and applied questions that can be explored.

2. Literature Review

This section presents a brief review of cointegration and Granger causality analysis in the field of energy economics. A time series X is said to Granger-cause another time series Y if the prediction error of current Y decreases by using past values of X in addition to past values of Y. Energy economics has overtime seen the development of econometric procedures carried out to test for Granger causality with advanced time series techniques. Granger causality tests should be conducted on stationary time series (i.e. integrated of order zero), otherwise it can lead to invalid inferences [Granger, 1969; Granger and Newbold, 1974]. As such, unit root tests are often carried out to examine whether the variables are stationary in level or after first-differencing.

In energy economics, Granger causality principle [Granger, 1969] is mostly employed to analyze the energy-GDP nexus. Generally these studies are time series or panel data analysis, conducted for a single country or for a group/panel of countries. A range of econometric techniques and methodologies have been developed and employed to examine the Granger causality between variables. We classify these studies into five main groups, out of which the first three are based on Chontanawat *et al.* [2006]. The first group employs the conventional methodologies by Granger [1969] and Sims [1972], with the majority being conducted for developed countries covering the period from 1947 to 1988. For instance, Kraft and Kraft [1978], Akarca and Long [1979], Eden and Hwang [1984], Abosedra and Baghestani [1989], Stern [1993] and Cheng [1996] study the United States (US), Yu and Choi [1985] examine five developed countries, and Hwang and Gum [1991] investigate Taiwan, among others.

The second group uses cointegration and the error correction model (ECM) [Granger, 1988] to examine developed and some developing countries, mostly covering the period from 1950 to 2002. The standard Granger causality tests were extended by Engle and Granger [1987] to include the possibility that two time series may share a long-run common stochastic trend (i.e. cointegrated). When cointegration is present, Granger causality is tested within the context of an ECM. Granger causality within an ECM may arise from two sources: short-run and long-run causalities. Short-run causality is tested by a partial F-test of the lagged coefficients associated with the first-differences of the respective variables in the model while long-run causality is tested by a t-test of the error correction terms. If there is no cointegration between the respective variables, but each variable is stationary after first differencing (i.e. integrated of order one), standard Granger-causality tests are applied to the variables in first-differences. The Engle–Granger procedure works well in the context of a bivariate framework. However, ordinary least estimation of the cointegrating parameters is sensitive to the choice of normalization of the variables in the model.

The concerns raised by the Engle–Granger approach are addressed in the Johansen [1988] multivariate cointegration procedure since this procedure allows for: (1) all the variables to be viewed as endogenous avoiding the normalization issue, (2) the presence of more than one cointegrating vector, (3) the ability to test restrictions on the cointegrating vector(s), and (4) the simultaneous estimation via maximum likelihood of the short-run dynamics which improves estimation efficiency [Payne, 2010]. The use of the Johansen–Juselius procedure requires the appropriate specification of the intercept and trend terms within the cointegrating vector and ECM [Kennedy, 2003]. The Johansen–Juselius cointegration approach was the most common approach in the examination of the energy-growth nexus. For instance, Nachane *et al.* [1988] studied the nexus using the Johansen cointegraion method for 16 countries, Hoa [1993] for Thailand, Masih and Masih [1996] for six Asian countries, Glasure and Lee [1997] for South Korea and Singapore, Masih and Masih [1997] for two Asian NICs, Asafu-Adjave [2000] for four Asian countries, Stern [2000] for the US, Ghosh [2002] for India, Glasure [2002] for Korea, Soytas and Sari [2003] for G-7 and emerging markets, Oh and Lee [2004b] for South Korea, Yoo [2005] for South Korea, Zhixin and Xin [2011] for China, Alan *et al.* [2012] for

Bangladesh, Alshhry and Belloumi [2015] for Saudi Arabia and Tang *et al.* [2016] for Vietnam.

The third group incorporates the use of the Akaike's [1969] Final Prediction Error (FPE) criteria in the Hsiao's [1981] technique to improve the power of Granger causality analysis. This group includes studies for the US and the developing world in Latin America and Asia, mostly covering the period from 1947 to 2000, such as Hwang and Gum [1992] for Taiwan, Cheng [1996] for the US, Cheng [1997] for three Latin countries, Cheng and Lai [1997] for Taiwan, Altinay and Karagol [2004] for Turkey and Dagher and Yacoubian [2012] for Lebanon.

On the other hand, several studies apply Gregory and Hansen [1996] test of cointegration with endogenously determined structural breaks to find the absence of cointegration once structural breaks are taken into account (for instance, [Solarin and Shahbaz, 2013]).

In the context of the econometric approaches and methodologies discussed so far in this section, the validity of causality testing depends on the pre-testing for unit roots and cointegration. The pre-tests when conducting causality tests, however, may suffer from size distortions and result in variables with different orders of integration [Clark and Mizra, 2006]. The appropriateness of the model when undertaking causality tests could thus be doubted. A number of econometric procedures have been developed to address the potential biases of these pre-tests. Furthermore, these procedures are valid irrespective of whether the time series are integrated of different orders, non-cointegrated, or cointegrated. This gives rise to the fourth and more recent group of studies which employs these procedures including the autoregressive distributed lag (ARDL) model and bounds testing approach set forth by Pesaran and Shin [1999] and Pesaran *et al.* [2001] as well as the Toda–Yamamoto's [1995] and Dolado–Lütkepohl's [1996] adaptations of the Granger method to test for long-run causality.

The ARDL approach to cointegration and error correction modeling performs well in small samples which is often the case in the electricity consumption-growth literature. Moreover, the ARDL allows for the simultaneous estimation of the short-run and long-run components within a vector error correction model (VECM). Examples of energy economics studies employing ARDL include Wang *et al.* [2011] for China, Fuinhas and Marques [2012] for five countries, Shahbaz *et al.* [2013] for China, Ozturk and Acaravci [2013] for Turkey, Solarin and Shahbaz [2013] for Angola, Sebri *et al.* [2014] for BRICS countries.

The Toda–Yamamoto and Dolado–Lütkepohl approaches provide long-run information on causality by using a vector autoregressive model on the levels of the variables. The caveat to the estimation of a vector autoregressive model in levels, as in the case of the Toda–Yamamoto and Dolado–Lütkepohl approaches, is the loss in efficiency and power given that these approaches intentionally overfit the vector autoregressive model. The Toda–Yamamoto and Dolado–Lütkepohl approaches to test for the energy-growth nexus can be found in the studies by Wolde-Rufael [2004] for Shanghai (China), Altinay and Karagol [2005] for Turkey, Wolde-Rufael [2004] for 19 African countries, Bowden and Payne [2009] and Payne [2009] for the US, Soytas and Sari [2009] for Turkey, Tsani [2010] for Greece and Dagher and Yacoubian [2012] for Lebanon.

As a consequence of the relatively short data span in many of the studies on the causal relationship between energy and growth, the power and size properties of conventional unit root and cointegration tests are reduced. The panel cointegration tests advanced by Pedroni [1999, 2004], Larsson *et al.* [2001] and Westerlund [2007] address these concerns by providing additional power in combining cross-section and time series while allowing for heterogeneity across cross-sectional units. The fifth (and most recent) group of studies using these advanced panel cointegration tests includes Lee [2005] for 18 developing countries, Ouedraogo [2013] for 15 countries in West African States, Nasreen and Anwar [2014] for 15 Asian countries, Kasman and Duman [2015] for 15 new EU member and candidate countries, Fang and Chang [2016] for 16 Asia-Pacific countries, and Le [2016] for 15 sub-Saharan African countries. Several studies also employ bootstrap and advanced Granger non-causality tests for their panel data analysis such as Wolde-Rufael [2014] using Konya [2006] test for 15 transition economies, and Fang and Chang [2016] using Emirmahmutoglu and Kose [2011] test for 16 Asia-Pacific countries.

Furthermore, while bivariate models are employed in the majority of studies in the literature to establish the causal linkages between energy consumption and economic growth, multivariate models have seen an increase in use in recent years. In this multivariate model specification, besides GDP and energy usage, additional variables such as capital, labor, trade, finance and pollutant emissions are explicitly included. Bartleet and Gounder [2010] for New Zealand, Wang *et al.* [2011] and Zhixin and Xin [2011] for China, Fang and Chang [2016] for 16 Asia-Pacific countries, and Le [2016] for sub-Saharan African countries among others, are good examples in which the multivariate framework is used by incorporating other critical variables such as physical capital stock, labor force, human capital, trade openness and financial development to examine the direction of causality between energy consumption and economic growth.

As the study of energy-growth nexus is critical for policy makers to design environmental and energy policies that will support sustainable development, a large number of researches have attempted to examine this nexus. Table 1 presents

Table 1. Summary of literature on the energy-growth nexus.

No.	Authors	Countries	Data period (Frequency)	Methodologies	Main variables	Other variables	Findings on the energy-growth Nexus
1	Kraft and Kraft [1978]	US	1947–1974 (annual)	Granger causality	GNP, E		GNP $\to$ E
2	Akarca and Long [1979]	US	1/1973–3/1978 (monthly)	Sim's technique	GNP, E		GNP $\neq$ E
3	Eden and Hwang [1984]	US	1947–1979 (annual)	Sim's technique and Granger causality	GNP, E		GNP $\neq$ E
4	Yu and Choi [1985]	US UK Poland South Korea Philippines	1950–1976 (annual)	Sim's technique and Granger causality	GNP, E		GNP $\neq$ E Gas $\to$ GNP GNP $\neq$ E Liquid fuels $\to$ GNP, GNP $\to$ E E $\to$ GNP
5	Nachane *et al.* [1988]	16 countries (11 LDCs and 5 DCs)	1950–1985	Sim's technique, Granger causality and cointegration	GDP, E		E $\to$ GDP (except Colombia and Venezuela) GDP $\to$ E (except Colombia and Venezuela)
6	Abosedra and Baghestani [1989]	US	1947–1974 1947–1972, 1947–1979, 1947–1987 (annual)	Granger causality	GNP, E		GNP $\to$ E for 1947–1974
7	Hwang and Gum [1992]	Taiwan	N.A.	Hsiao's Granger	GNP, E		GNP $\Leftrightarrow$ E

8	Hoa [1993]	Thailand	1/1966–1/1991 (quarterly)	Cointegration	Oil, GDP	P	GNP $\Leftrightarrow$ Oil
9	Stern [1993]	US	1947–1990 (annual)	Granger causality	E, GDP	K, L	E $\rightarrow$ GDP
10	Cheng [1995]	US	1947–1990 (annual)	Hsiao's Granger	E, GNP	K	GNP $\neq$ E
11	Ebohon [1996]	Tanzania Nigeria	1960–1984 1960–1981 (annual)	Granger causality	E, GDP, GNP		E $\rightarrow$ GNP, GDP and GNP, GDP $\rightarrow$ E for both countries
12	Masih and Masih [1996]	6 Asian Countries: Malaysia Singapore Philippines India Indonesia Pakistan	1955–1990 1960–1990 1955–1991 1955–1990 1960–1990 1955–1990 (annual)	Johansen's multivariate cointegration and VECM based Granger causality	E, GNP		GNP $\neq$ E GNP $\neq$ E GNP $\neq$ E E $\rightarrow$ GNP GNP $\rightarrow$ E E $\Leftrightarrow$ GNP
13	Cheng [1997]	3 Latin Countries: Mexico Venezuela Brazil	1949–1993 1952–1993 1963–1993 (annual)	Hsiao's Granger	E, GDP	K	GDP $\neq$ E GDP $\neq$ E E $\rightarrow$ GDP(−)
14	Cheng and Lai [1997]	Taiwan	1955–1993 (annual)	Hsiao's Granger	E, GDP	Employment	GDP $\rightarrow$ E

(*Continued*)

Table 1. (*Continued*)

No.	Authors	Countries	Data period (Frequency)	Methodologies	Main variables	Other variables	Findings on the energy-growth Nexus
15	Glasure and Lee [1997]	South Korea and Singapore	1961–1990 (annual)	Engle-Granger cointegration and VECM based Granger causality	E, GDP		$E \Leftrightarrow GDP$
16	Masih and Masih [1997]	2 Asian NICS: South Korea Taiwan	1955–1991 1952–1992 (annual)	Johansen's multivariate cointegration and VECM based Granger causality	E, GNP	P	$E \Leftrightarrow GNP$ for both countries
17	Cheng [1998]	Japan	1952–1995 (annual)	Hsiao's Granger	E, GNP	Employment, K	$GNP \rightarrow E$
18	Cheng [1999]	India	1952–1995 (annual)	Johansen cointegration and VECM based Hsiao's Granger	E, GNP	K, L	$GNP \rightarrow E$
19	Asafu-Adjaye [2000]	India Indonesia Thailand Philippines	1973–1995 1973–1995 1971–1995 1971–1995 (annual)	Johansen multivariate cointegration and VECM based Granger causality	E, GDP	P	$E \rightarrow GDP$ (SR) $E \rightarrow GDP$ (SR) $E \Leftrightarrow GDP$ (SR) $E \Leftrightarrow GDP$ (SR)
20	Stern [2000]	US	1948–1994 (annual)	Johansen cointegration	E, GDP	K, L, trade	$E \rightarrow GDP$
21	Ghosh [2002]	India	1950–1997 (annual)	Johansen–Juselius cointegration and Granger causality	Electricity, GDP		$GDP \rightarrow$ Electricity

22	Glasure [2002]	South Korea	1961–1990 (annual)	Johansen cointegration and VECM based Granger causality	E, GDP	Money supply, real oil price, government expenditure	E → GDP (SR) GDP → E (LR)
23	Soytas and Sari [2003]	G-7 and Emerging Markets: Argentina Italy Korea Turkey France German Japan Poland Indonesia	1950–1990 1950–1992 1953–1991 1950–1992 1950–1992 1950–1992 1950–1992 1965–1994 1950–1992 (annual)	Johansen and Johansen–Juselius cointegration and VECM based Granger causality	E, GDP		E ⇔ GDP GDP → E GDP → E E → GDP E → GDP E → GDP E → GDP GDP ≠ E GDP ≠ E
24	Altinay and Karagol [2004]	Turkey	1950–2000 (annual)	Hsiao's Granger	E, GDP		GDP ≠ E
25	Ghali and El-Sakka [2004]	Canada	1961–1997 (annual)	Johansen cointegration and VECM based Granger causality	E, GDP	K, L	E ⇔ GDP
26	Oh and Lee (2004a)	South Korea	1970–1999 (annual)	Johansen–Juselius cointegration and VECM based Granger causality	E, GDP	K, L	E ⇔ GDP

(*Continued*)

Table 1. (*Continued*)

No.	Authors	Countries	Data period (Frequency)	Methodologies	Main variables	Other variables	Findings on the energy-growth Nexus
27	Oh and Lee (2004b)	South Korea	1/1981–4/2000 (quarterly)	Johansen–Juselius cointegration and VECM based Granger causality	E, GDP	K, L	GDP → E
28	Shiu and Lam [2004]	China	1971–2000 (annual)	Johansen cointegration and VECM based Granger causality	Electricity, GDP		Electricity → GDP
29	Wolde-Rufael [2004]	Shanghai (China)	1952–1999 (annual)	Toda and Yamamoto's Granger	Disaggregate E, GDP		Coal → GDP, Coke → GDP, Electricity → GDP, E → GDP
30	Altinay and Karagol [2005]	Turkey	1950–2000 (annual)	Dolado–Lütkepohl/Granger	Electricity, GDP		Electricity → GDP
31	Lee [2005]	18 Developing countries	1975–2001 (annual)	Pedroni panel cointegration and ECM based Granger causality	E, GDP		E → GDP
32	Wolde-Rufael [2005]	19 African countries	1971–2001 (annual)	Toda and Yamamoto's Granger	Electricity, GDP		Algeria, Congo DR, Egypt, Ghana, Ivory, Coast : GDP → Electricity Cameroon, Morocco, Nigeria: Electricity → GDP Gabon, Zambia: Electricity ⇔ GDP Benin, Congo RP, Kenya, Senegal, South Africa, Sudan, Togo, Tunisia, Zimbabwe: GDP ≠ Electricity

33	Yoo [2005]	South Korea	1970–2002 (annual)	Johansen cointegration and VECM-based Granger causality	Electricity, GDP		Electricity ⇔ GDP
34	Chen, Kuo and Chen [2007]	China Hong Kong Indonesia India South Korea Malaysia Philippines Singapore Taiwan Thailand	1971–2001 (annual)	Johansen–Juselius, Pedroni panel cointegration, VECM based Granger causality	Electricity, GDP		Electricity ≠ GDP Electricity ⇔ GDP Electricity → GDP GDP → Electricity GDP → Electricity GDP → Electricity GDP → Electricity GDP → Electricity Electricity ≠ GDP Electricity ≠ GDP Ten country panel: Electricity ⇔ GDP
35	Soytas *et al.* [2007]	US	1960–2004 (annual)	Granger causality	E, GDP	Carbon emissions	E ≠ GDP
36	Zamani [2007]	Iran	1967–2003 (annual)	Johansen and Johansen–Juselius cointegration and VECM based Granger causality	E, GDP		GDP → E
37	Bowden and Payne [2009]	US	1949–2006 (annual)	Toda and Yamamoto's Granger	E, GDP		E → GDP

(*Continued*)

Table 1. *(Continued)*

No.	Authors	Countries	Data period (Frequency)	Methodologies	Main variables	Other variables	Findings on the energy-growth Nexus
38	Payne [2009]	US	1949–2005 (annual)	Toda and Yamamoto's Granger	E, GDP		E $\neq$ GDP
39	Soytas and Sari [2009]	Turkey	1960–2000 (annual)	Toda and Yamamoto's Granger	E, GDP		E $\neq$ GDP
40	Bartleet and Gounder [2010]	New Zealand	1960–2004 (annual)	Granger causality	E, GDP		Y $\rightarrow$ GDP
41	Tsani [2010]	Greece	1960–2006 (annual)	Toda and Yamamoto's Granger	E, GDP		E $\Leftrightarrow$ GDP
42	Wang *et al.* [2011]	China	1972–2006 (annual)	ARDL bounds test to cointegration, VECM based Granger causality	E, GDP		E $\rightarrow$ GDP
43	Zhixin and Xin [2011]	China	1980–2008 (annual)	Johansen cointegration, VECM based Granger causality	E, GDP		E $\Leftrightarrow$ GDP
44	Alam *et al.* [2012]	Bangladesh	1972–2006 (annual)	Johansen cointegration, VECM based Granger causality	E, Electricity, GDP		E $\rightarrow$ GDP (both SR and LR) Electricity $\neq$ GDP (SR) Electricity $\Leftrightarrow$ GDP (LR)
45	Dagher and Yacoubian [2012]	Lebanon	1980–2009 (annual)	Hsiao's Granger causality, Toda and Yamamoto's Granger, VECM based Granger causality	E, GDP		E $\Leftrightarrow$ GDP

46	Fuinhas and Marques [2012]	Portugal, Italy, Greece, Spain, Turkey	1965–2009 (annual)	ARDL bounds test to cointegration	E, GDP		E ⇔ GDP for all countries
47	Ouedraogo [2013]	15 countries in West African States (ECOWAS)	1980–2008 (annual)	Pedroni [1999] panel cointegration, panel Granger causality	E, Electricity, GDP		GDP → E (SR) and E → GDP (LR) Electricity ≠ GDP (SR) and Electricity → GDP (LR)
48	Ozturk and Acaravci [2013]	Turkey	1960–2007 (annual)	ARDL bounds test to cointegration, ECM based Granger causality	E, GDP	Y^2, trade openness, financial development, carbon emissions	E ≠ GDP
49	Shahbaz *et al.* [2013]	China	1971–2011 (annual)	ARDL bounds test to cointegration, Johansen cointegration, ECM based Granger causality	E, GDP	Financial development, capital, exports, imports, international trade	E → GDP
50	Solarin and Shahbaz [2013]	Angola	1971–2009 (annual)	ARDL bounds test to cointegration, Gregory–Hansen structural break cointegration and VECM Granger causality	Electricity, GDP	Urbanization	Electricity → GDP

(*Continued*)

Table 1. (*Continued*)

No.	Authors	Countries	Data period (Frequency)	Methodologies	Main variables	Other variables	Findings on the energy-growth Nexus
51	Nasreen and Anwar [2014]	15 Asian countries	1980–2011 (annual)	Panel cointegration by Pedroni [1999, 2004] and Larsson *et al.* [2001] and Granger causality	E, GDP	Trade openness, energy price	E $\Leftrightarrow$ GDP
52	Sebri *et al.* [2014]	BRICS countries	1971–2010 (annual)	ARDL bounds test to cointegration, and VECM based Granger causality	RE, GDP	Trade openness, carbon dioxide emissions	RE $\Leftrightarrow$ GDP
53	Wolde-Rufael [2014]	15 transition economies	1975–2010 (annual)	Panel Granger non-causality test by Konya [2006]	Electricity, GDP		Belarus, Bulgaria: Electricity $\rightarrow$ GDP Czech Republic, Latvia, Lithuania, Russian Federation: GDP $\rightarrow$ Electricity Ukraine: Electricity $\Leftrightarrow$ GDP Albania, Macedonia, Moldova, Poland, Romania, Serbia, Slovak Republic, Slovenia: Electricity $\neq$ GDP
54	Alshehry and Belloumi [2015]	Saudi Arabia	1971–2010 (annual)	Johansen multivariate cointegration and Granger causality	E, GDP	Carbon emissions, energy price	E $\rightarrow$ GDP (LR) E $\neq$ GDP (SR)
55	Kasman and Duman [2015]	15 new EU member and candidate countries	1992–2010 (annual)	Panel cointegration tests by Kao [1999], Pedroni [1999, 2004], Westerlund [2007] and panel Granger causality	E, GDP	Carbon emissions, trade openness, urbanization	GDP $\rightarrow$ E

56	Caraiani *et al.* [2015]	5 emerging European countries: Hungary, Poland, Turkey, Romania and Bulgaria	1980–2013 (annual)	Causality analysis based on Engle and Granger model	Total E, coal, gas, oil and RE, GDP		At 1% level (SR): Hungary (GDP $\rightarrow$ RE) Poland (GD{$\rightarrow$ gas, coal and E $\rightarrow$ GDP) Turkey (coal $\rightarrow$ GDP) Romania (coal $\rightarrow$ GDP) At 10% level (SR): Hungary (GDP $\rightarrow$ gas and E $\Leftrightarrow$ GDP) Romania (E, gas and oil $\rightarrow$ GDP) Bulgaria (RE $\Leftrightarrow$ GDP)
57	Fang and Chang [2016]	16 Asia-Pacific countries	1970–2011 (annual)	Panel cointegration test by Westerlund [2007] and bootstrap panel Granger non-causality test by Emirmahmutoglu and Kose [2011]	E, GDP	K, L and human capital	India: E $\Leftrightarrow$ GDP Korea, Pakistan, Taiwan: E $\rightarrow$ GDP Australia: GDP $\rightarrow$ E The rest: E $\not\Leftrightarrow$ GDP
58	Fang and Wolski [2016]	China	1965–2014 (annual)	Nonlinear Granger causality by Diks and Wolski [2016]	Disaggregate E, GDP	K, human capital	E, coal, gas $\not\Leftrightarrow$ GDP GDP $\rightarrow$ oil
59	Le [2016]	15 sub-Saharan African countries	1983–2010 (annual)	Panel cointegration test by Westerlund [2007] and panel-based ECM Granger causality	E, GDP	K, trade openness, financial develop-ment	middle-income countries: GDP $\rightarrow$ E low-income countries: E $\rightarrow$ GDP (SR)

(Continued)

Table 1. (*Continued*)

No.	Authors	Countries	Data period (Frequency)	Methodologies	Main variables	Other variables	Findings on the energy-growth Nexus
60	Tang *et al.* [2016]	Vietnam	1971–2011 (annual)	Johansen cointegration, Granger causality	E, GDP	FDI, DI, capital	E $\rightarrow$ GDP
61	Mutascu [2016]	G7 countries	1970–2012 (annual)	Bootstrap and classical panel Granger causality	E, GDP		Canada, Japan, US: E$\Leftrightarrow$GDP France, Germany: GDP $\rightarrow$ E Italy, UK: E $\neq$ GDP
62	Fang *et al.* [2017]	Malaysia, Indonesia, Thailand, Singapore and the Philip-pines	1965–2011 (annual)	Toda and Yamamoto's Granger	E, GDP	K, human capital	Malaysia, Indonesia, Singapore: E $\neq$ GDP The Philippines: GDP $\rightarrow$ E Thailand: E$\Leftrightarrow$GDP
63	Fang and Chen [2017]	Chinese provinces	1995–2014 (annual)	Bootstrap panel Granger non-causality test by Emirmahmutoglu and Kose [2011]	E, disaggre-gate E, GDP	K, human capital	GDP$\rightarrow$Petroleum, electricity GDP$\Leftrightarrow$Coal, coke, gas, E
64	Chen and Fang [2017]	Chinese cities	2003–2012 (annual)	Bootstrap panel Granger non-causality test by Dumitrescu and Hurlin [2012]	Electricity, GDP	K, human capital	Central and western China: GDP $\rightarrow$ Electricity Eastern China: GDP$\Leftrightarrow$Electricity

Notes: E $\rightarrow$ GDP means that the causality runs from energy consumption to growth. GDP $\rightarrow$ E means that the causality runs from growth to energy consumption. E $\Leftrightarrow$ GDP means that bidirectional causality exists between energy consumption and growth. E $\neq$ GDP means that no causality exists between energy consumption and growth. The same explanation applies to Electricity. GDP: gross domestic product, GNP: gross national product, K: capital, L: labor, RE: renewable energy consumption, FDI: foreign direct investment, DI: direct investment, DC: developing countries, LDC: less developing countries, LR: long run, SR: short run.

a summary of the literature covering key studies on energy-growth nexus belonging to the five groups as described above. As shown in the table, the findings indicate variations in empirical results and thus have no clear direction for policy makers. In other words, results from the reviewed studies in this section show that the literature on energy consumption-growth nexus produced inconclusive results and there is no consensus either on the existence or on the direction of causality among energy consumption and economic growth. This is not surprising as it is attributable to the differences in country cases, model specifications, econometric methodologies as well as datasets and periods.

3. Advances in Econometric Methods

3.1. *From bivariate to multivariate*

In earlier studies on the energy-growth nexus, Granger causality tests proposed by Granger [1969] and Sim [1972] are used for a bivariate case. After the concept of cointegration is raised, the cointegration test and the ECM became popular [Engle and Granger, 1987]. In a multivariate case where there can be more than one cointegrating relationship, Johansen cointegration approach by Johansen and Juselius [1990] may be more appropriate. Details are given in Section 3.2.1. For the multivariate Granger causality tests, some researchers use the pairwise Granger causal relationships. A simple extension of the ECM is the VECM model, from which the short-run and long-run Granger causality in the multivariate framework can be identified. The extension from the bivariate to multivariate framework is also seen in the nonlinear Granger causality tests. More discussions on this from a bivariate test to a multivariate test by Diks and Wolski [2016] are given in Section 3.3.

3.2. *From time series to panel*

3.2.1. *Time series cointegration and causality tests*

To test for cointegration, the first step is to examine whether the time series are non-stationary. Augmented Dickey–Fuller (ADF) tests, Dickey–Fuller tests with GLS detrending (DF-GLS), Phillips–Perron (PP) tests and Kwiatkowski–Phillips–Schmidt–Shin (KPSS) tests can be used to test for the presence of unit roots. The first three have the null hypothesis of the presence of unit root, while the KPSS test assumes stationarity of series in the null hypothesis. When there is one structural break, Zivot and Andrews [1992] proposed a method to endogenously determine the break time. When there are two potential structural breaks, Lumsdaine and Papell's [1997] unit root test can be applied. Other unit root tests that have considered structural changes include Perron–Vogelsang tests [Perron and Vogelsang, 1992] and Clemente–Montanes–Reyes tests [Clemente *et al.*, 1998]. When the variables are found to be integrated of the same order, one can proceed to test whether the variables are cointegrated, i.e. whether there is a long-run equilibrium in the variables.

For the cointegration test, there are two widely used methods. One is Engle and Granger's [1987] residual-based two-step approach and the other is the Johansen cointegration test [Johansen, 1991; Johansen and Juselius, 1990]. Engle and Granger's [1987] method is to, first, obtain the residuals from OLS regressions, and second, test the stationarity of the residuals. If the residuals are stationary, it means the series are cointegrated; otherwise, there is no cointegrating relationship among the variables.

Let X_t be a vector of variables; if all the variables in X_t are $I(1)$, according to the Granger representation theorem, the vector X_t has a vector error correction (VEC) representation as follows:

$$\Delta X_t = \Pi X_{t-1} + \sum_{i=1}^{p-1} \Gamma_i \Delta X_{t-i} + \mu + \epsilon_t. \tag{1}$$

Johansen cointegration method is based on the coefficient matrix for the one-period lag variables. If the rank of Π equals the number of variables in the model, the variables are stable in levels and there is no cointegration. If the rank of Π equals zero, the VEC specification is reduced to an unrestricted VAR and none of the linear combinations are stationary. Otherwise, the rank of Π determines the number of cointegrating relationships in the system, and the decomposition of Π gives the cointegrating coefficients and the associated adjustment speeds that measure how soon it takes for the variables to revert to the long-run equilibrium when the data deviates from the equilibrium. Johansen cointegration test has two test statistics: maximum eigenvalue test statistic and trace test statistic, both of which are likelihood ratio tests. In particular, suppose the eigenvalues of the Johansen test are computed and ordered in such a way that $\lambda_1 \geq \lambda_2 \geq \cdots \geq \lambda_n \geq 0$ (note that these eigenvalues are not the same as eigenvalues of the matrix Π, and they are non-negative and real), the maximum eigenvalue test statistic is

$$\mathrm{LR}(r_0, r_0 + 1) = -T \ln(1 - \lambda_{r_0+1}), \tag{2}$$

where $\mathrm{LR}(r_0, r_{0+1})$ is the likelihood ratio test for the null hypothesis $rank(\Pi) = r_0$ versus the alternative hypothesis $rank(\Pi) = r_0 + 1$. The trace test statistic is

$$\mathrm{LR}(r_0, n) = -T \sum_{i=r_0+1}^{n} \ln(1 - \lambda_i), \tag{3}$$

where $\mathrm{LR}(r_0, n)$ is the likelihood ratio test for the null hypothesis $rank(\Pi) = r_0$ versus the alternative hypothesis $r_0 < rank(\Pi) \leq n$. Johansen cointegration method allows for more than one cointegrating relationship. When there are more than two variables in the system, or more than one cointegrating relationship is possible, the Johansen cointegration method may be preferred.

When there are structural breaks, cointegration tests proposed by Gregory and Hansen [1996], Johansen *et al.* [2000] and Carrion-i-Silvestre and Sansó [2006] can be applied. Gregory and Hansen [1996] detect both the regime shift and stable cointegrating relationship. Johansen *et al.* [2000] analyze cointegration in a VAR model with known break points in the broken linear trend. Carrion-i-Silvestre and Sansó [2006] allow for a structural break in both the deterministic and the cointegrating vectors. Unlike Gregory and Hansen [1996], their null hypothesis is the presence of cointegration rather than non-cointegration. When the break point is unknown, the minimization of the sum of the squared residuals leads to a consistent estimator of the break fraction.

However, if one series is stationary and another variable is integrated of order one, the two variables are definitely not cointegrated. How can the long-run relationship between the two variables be estimated? The answer lies in the ARDL bounds test proposed by Pesaran and Shin [1999].[1]

For the Granger causality test, VEC model and Toda and Yamamoto [1995] test method that can be applied when the series are not stationary.

Assume in a bivariate system, each of the two variables is integrated of order one, the VEC model can be expressed as follows:

$$\Delta X_t = \mu_1 + \alpha_1 EC + \sum_{s=1}^{p-1} \beta_{1,s} \Delta X_{t-s} + \sum_{s=1}^{p-1} \gamma_{1,s} \Delta Y_{t-s} + \epsilon_{1,t} \tag{4}$$

$$\Delta Y_t = \mu_2 + \alpha_2 EC + \sum_{s=1}^{p-1} \beta_{2,s} \Delta X_{t-s} + \sum_{s=1}^{p-1} \gamma_{2,s} \Delta Y_{t-s} + \epsilon_{2,t} \tag{5}$$

where EC denotes the error correction term.

First, if $\gamma_{1,s}(s = 1, 2 \ldots p - 1) \neq 0$, it implies that there exists a short-run Granger causal relationship running from variable Y to variable X; similarly, if $\beta_{2,s}(s = 1, 2 \ldots p - 1) \neq 0$, it suggests variable X Granger causing variable Y in the short run. Second, the long-run Granger causality can be tested by examining the

[1]The detailed step-by-step guidance is given in a post by Professor Dave Giles at http://davegiles.blogspot.sg/2013/06/ardl-models-part-ii-bounds-tests.html.

significance of the speed of adjustment coefficients α. Third, one can perform the joint test of the lagged independent variables and the error correction term for strong Granger causality. For instance, if α_1 and $\gamma_{1,s}(s = 1, 2 \ldots p - 1)$ are significantly different from zero, it implies that there exists a strong long-run Granger causality relationship running from Y to X.

Toda and Yamamoto's [1995] Granger causality test method is based on the following equations:

$$X_t = \mu_1 + \sum_{s=1}^{p+m} \beta_{1,s} X_{t-s} + \sum_{s=1}^{p+m} \gamma_{1,s} Y_{t-s} + \epsilon_{1,t}; \tag{6}$$

$$Y_t = \mu_2 + \sum_{s=1}^{p+m} \beta_{2,s} X_{t-s} + \sum_{s=1}^{p+m} \gamma_{2,s} Y_{t-s} + \epsilon_{2,t}, \tag{7}$$

where m is the maximum order of integration of variables in the system and p is the optimal lag length determined in the standard VAR. If $\sum_{s=1}^{p} \gamma_{1,s} = 0$, Y does not Granger cause X; otherwise, there is evidence on Granger causality running from Y to X. Similarly, if $\sum_{s=1}^{p} \beta_{2,s} = 0$, X does not Granger cause Y; otherwise, X is found to Granger cause Y.

Recent development has gone beyond the linear framework, which will be discussed in more detail in Section 3.3.

3.2.2. *Panel cointegration and causality tests*

Similar to time series analysis, we will perform unit root tests, cointegration tests, Granger causality tests in the panel data setting. There are two generations of panel unit root tests. The first generation of panel unit root test does not consider the interdependence of cross-sectional units [Maddala and Wu, 1999; Hadri, 2000; Choi, 2001; Levin *et al.* 2002; Im *et al.* 2003]. Here, we focus on the LLC test [Levin *et al.* 2002] and the IPS test [Im *et al.* 2003]. Consider the following panel-based ADF specification:

$$\Delta y_{it} = \alpha_i + \rho_i y_{i,t-1} + \sum_{k=1}^{p_i} \gamma_k \Delta y_{i,t-k} + \varepsilon_{it}. \tag{8}$$

The LLC test assumes $\rho_i = \rho$ for all units i. The hypotheses of the LLC test are $H_0 : \rho = 0$ versus $H_1 : \rho < 0$. The IPS test relaxes the assumption of a common ρ and allows ρ_i to vary across cross-section units. The hypotheses of the IPS test are $H_0 : \rho_i = 0$ for all i versus $H_1 : \rho_i = 0$ for some i and $\rho_i < 0$ for the other cross-sectional units. The LLC test can be considered as a pooled ADF test and the modified t-statistic is used for the test, while the IPS test is to run the ADF regression for each unit and use a form of the average of the t-statistics for the test statistic. The IPS test statistic has a better performance in the finite sample than the LLC test.

The second generation of panel unit root test assumes that cross-sectional units are dependent [Phillips and Sul, 2003; Bai and Ng, 2004; Moon and Perron, 2004; Pesaran, 2007]. Pesaran's [2007] approach is one of the most widely applied in empirical studies. Specifically, Pesaran [2007] proposed to run the following cross-sectionally augmented Dickey–Fuller (CADF) regression for each unit i:

$$\Delta y_{it} = \alpha_i + \rho_i y_{i,t-1} + d_0 \bar{y}_{t-1} + \sum_{j=0}^{p} d_{j+1} \Delta \bar{y}_{t-j} + \sum_{k=1}^{p} c_k \Delta y_{i,t-k} + \varepsilon_{it}, \quad (9)$$

where $\bar{y}_t$ is the cross-section average at time t. Obtain the t-ratio t_i of the OLS estimate of ρ_i; the cross-sectionally augmented version of the IPS (CIPS) test is then

$$\text{CIPS} = \frac{1}{N} \sum_{i=1}^{N} t_i. \quad (10)$$

Subsequently, panel cointegration tests are needed to examine whether there exists a long-run equilibrium relationship. Pedroni's [1999, 2004] seven statistics are one of the most popular tests in empirical studies. Pedroni's [1999, 2004] tests are in fact an extension of the Engle and Granger's [1987] two-step cointegration test to the panel framework, allowing the intercept and trend to vary across cross-sectional units. The null hypothesis is no cointegration; i.e. ρ_i in the second-step residual regression $\Delta e_{it} = \rho_i e_{it-1} + u_{it}$ equals zero for each unit i. Four of the seven statistics are for the homogenous alternative hypothesis that $\rho_i = \rho < 0$. They are the panel υ-statistic, the panel ρ-statistic, the panel PP-statistic and the panel ADF-statistic. The other three are for the heterogeneous alternative hypothesis that $\rho_i < 0$ for at least one unit. They are the group ρ-statistic, the group PP-statistic and the group ADF-statistic.

Westerlund's [2007] panel cointegration method has recently gained increasing popularity as it allows for the cross-sectional dependence present in panels. Similarly, he proposed two types of statistics: one is panel test statistics which corresponds to the alternative hypothesis that the panel as a whole is cointegrated, and the other is group-mean test statistics which corresponds to the alternative hypothesis that there is at least one cross-sectional unit that is cointegrated. The null hypothesis of the Westerlund's [2007] test is no cointegration, no matter which types of test statistics are considered. Specifically, consider the following VECM:

$$\Delta y_{it} = \delta_i' d_t + \alpha_i \left(y_{i,t-1} - \beta_i' x_{i,t-1} \right) + \sum_{j=1}^{p_i} \alpha_{ij} \Delta y_{i,t-j} + \sum_{-q_i}^{p_i} \gamma_{ij} \Delta x_{i,t-j} + e_{it}, \quad (11)$$

where d_t is the deterministic component, and p_i and q_i are the lag and lead orders for unit i. The proposed panel test statistics are:

$$P_\tau = \frac{\hat{\alpha}}{SE(\hat{\alpha})}, \quad P_\alpha = T\hat{\alpha},$$

where $\hat{\alpha}$ is the estimated common error-correction parameter, and $SE(\hat{\alpha})$ is its standard error. The proposed group-mean tests are:

$$G_\tau = \frac{1}{N} \sum_{i=1}^{N} \frac{\hat{\alpha}_i}{SE(\hat{\alpha}_i)}, \quad G_\alpha = \frac{1}{N} \sum_{i=1}^{N} \frac{T\hat{\alpha}_i}{\hat{\alpha}_i(1)},$$

where $\hat{\alpha}_i(1)$ is the estimated ratio of variance estimators for $\hat{u}_{it} = \sum_{-q_i}^{p_i} \hat{\gamma}_{ij} \Delta x_{i,t-j} + \hat{e}_{it}$ and Δy_{it}, and $SE(\hat{\alpha}_i)$ is the standard error of the estimator $\hat{\alpha}_i$. The results can be generalized to account for cross-sectional dependence using the bootstrap method mentioned in Westerlund [2007]. The technical details are given in Persyn and Westerlund [2008].

As for the panel Granger causality test, the panel-based VECM is widely used in earlier works on energy-growth nexus (e.g. [Lee and Chang, 2008; Noor and Siddiqi, 2010]). The two-variable system is specified as follows:

$$\Delta X_{it} = \mu_{1i} + \phi_{1i}\mathrm{ECT}_{it-1} + \sum_{s=1}^{p} \beta_{1,is} \Delta X_{i,t-s} + \sum_{s=1}^{p} \gamma_{1,is} \Delta Y_{i,t-s} + \epsilon_{1,it}, \quad (12)$$

$$\Delta Y_{it} = \mu_{2i} + \phi_{2i}\mathrm{ECT}_{it-1} + \sum_{s=1}^{p} \beta_{2,is} \Delta X_{i,t-s} + \sum_{s=1}^{p} \gamma_{2,is} \Delta lnY_{i,t-s} + \epsilon_{2,it}. \quad (13)$$

When the coefficients are assumed the same across units and the cross-sections are assumed to be independent, the panel model can be estimated in a similar way as the time series model, and the Granger causality results can be similarly interpreted. Dumitrescu and Hurlin [2012] relax the assumption on the homogeneity of coefficients and allow them to differ across units. To account for cross-sectional dependence, Konya [2006] and Emirmahmutoglu and Kose [2011] propose the bootstrapped methods. Konya [2006] considers the SUR system as follows:

$$y_{i,t} = \alpha_i + \sum_{j=1}^{p_i} \beta_{ij} x_{i,t-j} + \sum_{j=1}^{q_i} \gamma_{ij} y_{i,t-j} + e_{it}. \tag{14}$$

To test whether x non-Granger causes y, the first step is to assume non-Granger causality from x to y and obtain the residuals $\hat{e}_{i,t}$ from the OLS regressions. The second step is to resample residuals in such a way that a full column of the residual matrix $[\hat{e}_{i,t}]_{N\times T}$ is selected every time with replacement. The third step is to generate a bootstrap sample of y using:

$$y^*_{i,t} = \hat{\alpha}_i + \sum_{j=1}^{q_i} \hat{\gamma}_{ij} y^*_{i,t-j} + \tilde{e}^*_{i,t}. \tag{15}$$

The last step is to estimate the equation without imposing any restrictions using $y^*_{i,t}$ as a replacement of $y_{i,t}$, and obtain the Wald test statistic for each cross-sectional unit. The empirical distribution of the Wald test statistics are obtained by repeating steps 2–4 many times.

Emirmahmutoglu and Kose [2011] proposed a similar approach. They considered the level VAR model as follows:

$$x_{i,t} = \alpha_i^X + \sum_{j=1}^{k_i+dmax_i} \beta_{ij}^X x_{i,t-j} + \sum_{j=1}^{k_i+dmax_i} \gamma_{ij}^X y_{i,t-j} + e_{ij}^X; \tag{16}$$

$$y_{i,t} = \alpha_i^Y + \sum_{j=1}^{k_i+dmax_i} \beta_{ij}^Y x_{i,t-j} + \sum_{j=1}^{k_i+dmax_i} \gamma_{ij}^Y y_{i,t-j} + e_{ij}^Y, \tag{17}$$

where $dmax_i$ is the maximal order of integration of variables in the system for unit i. Emirmahmutoglu and Kose [2011] proposed the Fisher test statistic $\lambda = -2\sum_{i=1}^{N} \ln(p_i)$, and a five-step bootstrap procedure for the panel Granger causality test. Focusing on the test to see whether variable x Granger causes variable y, the first step is to determine the maximal order of integration of variables using the conventional time series unit root tests and the lag orders using Schwarz or Akaike information criteria for each cross-sectional unit i. This is not explicitly explained in Konya [2006]. The second step is to assume $\beta_{ij}\,(j = 1, 2, \ldots, k_i)$ in the second equation equals 0 and obtain the residuals $\hat{e}_{i,t}$ from the OLS regressions. The third step is to obtain the bootstrap residuals $\tilde{e}^*_{i,t}$ by first forming the matrix $[\tilde{e}_{i,t}]_{N\times T}$

where:

$$\tilde{e}_{i,t} = \hat{e}_{i,t} - (T - \max(k_i) - \max(dmax_i) - 2)^{-1} \sum_{t=\max(k_i)+\max(dmax_i)+2}^{T} \hat{e}_{i,t} \tag{18}$$

and then selecting columns randomly with replacement so as to keep the cross-sectional structure unchanged. These two steps are similar to Konya [2006] but the residuals are centered in Emirmahmutoglu and Kose [2011] but not in Konya [2006]. The next step is to get the bootstrap sample by:

$$y^*_{i,t} = \hat{\alpha}_i + \sum_{j=k_i+1}^{k_i+dmax_i} \hat{\beta}_{ij} x_{i,t-j} + \sum_{j=1}^{k_i+dmax_i} \hat{\gamma}_{ij} y^*_{i,t-j} + \tilde{e}^*_{i,t}, \tag{19}$$

where $\hat{\alpha}_i$, $\hat{\beta}_{ij}$ and $\hat{\gamma}_{ij}$ are estimated from the second step. This is different from Konya [2006] because the restriction of coefficients being zeros is only added to the first k_i lags in this approach. The last step is to reestimate the second equation by replacing $y_{i,t}$ with $y^*_{i,t}$, and obtain the Wald statistics and the associated p-values for each unit so as to calculate the Fisher test statistic $\lambda = -2\sum_{i=1}^{N} \ln(p_i)$. The critical values for the Fisher test statistics are obtained from the bootstrap empirical distribution by repeating steps 3–5 many times.

Recently there have been more advances in panel econometrics. For example, Banerjee and Carrion-i-Silvestre [2015] allow for both structural breaks and cross-sectional dependence in the test for cointegration in panel data. Panel cointegration tests where strong and weak cross-sectional dependence may be present as discussed in Banerjee and Carrion-i-Silvestre [2017].

3.3. *From linear to nonlinear*

As argued by Hiemstra and Jones [1994], the real world "is almost certainly nonlinear". Nevertheless, traditional Granger causality tests can fail to uncover a nonlinear relationship between the two variables under study. Hiemstra and Jones [1994] thus proposed a test for the nonlinear non-Granger causality using ratios of correlation integrals, a non-parametric estimator of temporal relations within and across series. In the empirical exercise of the stock price-volume relation, they find that the linear Granger causal test results point to the unidirectional relationship from stock returns to trading volume, but the nonlinear Granger causal test results show bidirectional causal relationship between the two. This is a very influential paper, after which there have been many empirical studies in different fields studying the presence of a nonlinear Granger causal relationship [Chiou-Wei *et al.* 2008]. After

Diks and Panchenko [2006] pointed out the over-rejection of the null hypothesis of non-Granger causality using Hiemstra and Jones's [1994] test and proposed a new test statistic, Diks and Panchenko's [2006] test is widely applied by practioners [Bekiros and Diks, 2008]. Specifically, to test whether X Granger causes Y, the null hypothesis of non-Granger causality can be specified as:

$$H_0 : Y_{t+1} \left| \left(X_t^{l_X}, Y_t^{l_Y} \right) \sim Y_{t+1} \right| \left(Y_t^{l_Y} \right), \tag{20}$$

where $X_t^{l_X}$ and $Y_t^{l_Y}$ refer to the lag vectors of X_t and Y_t. That is, the historical values of X do not provide any useful information in the prediction of Y. Let $Z_t = Y_{t+1}$, Diks and Panchenko [2006] propose the T_n statistic as follows:

$$T_n(\varepsilon) = \frac{n-1}{n(n-2)} \sum_i (\hat{f}_{X,Y,Z}(X_i, Y_i, Z_i)\, \hat{f}_Y(Y_i) - \hat{f}_{X,Y,}(X_i, Y_i)\, \hat{f}_{Y,Z}(Y_i, Z_i)), \tag{21}$$

where $\hat{f}_W(W_i)$ is a local density estimator of a d_W-variate vector W at the value W_i which equals $\frac{(2\varepsilon)^{-d_W}}{n-1} \sum_{j,j\neq i} I(\|W_i - W_j\| < \varepsilon)$. They prove that for a sequence of bandwidths $\varepsilon_n = Cn^{-\beta}$ where C is any positive constant and β is between $\frac{1}{4}$ and $\frac{1}{3}$, the test statistic is asymptotically normally distributed.

The restriction is, however, that Diks and Panchenko's [2006] approach is applicable to a bivariate framework. When it is applied to a multivariate framework, it is quite cumbersome and may cause significant information loss. Recently, Diks and Wolski [2016] extended the bivariate nonlinear Granger causality test to the multivariate setting by evaluating the conditional densities at the sharpened dataset, which help reduce the estimation bias in a multivariate setting. To test whether X Granger causes Y taking into consideration additional time series Q, the null hypothesis of non-Granger causality can be specified as:

$$H_0 : Y_{t+1} \left| \left(X_t^{l_X}, Y_t^{l_Y}, Q_t^{l_Q} \right) \sim Y_{t+1} \right| \left(Y_t^{l_Y}, Q_t^{l_Q} \right). \tag{22}$$

Let $\boldsymbol{Y}_t = (Y_t, Q_t)$ and $Z_t = Y_{t+1}$; Diks and Wolski's [2016] sharpened test statistic is as follows:

$$T_n^s(\varepsilon) = \frac{n-1}{n(n-2)} \sum_i (\hat{f}_{X,Y,Z}^s(X_i, Y_i, Z_i)\, \hat{f}_Y^s(Y_i) - \hat{f}_{X,Y}^s(X_i, Y_i)\, \hat{f}_{Y,Z}^s(Y_i, Z_i)), \tag{23}$$

where $\hat{f}_W^s(W_i)$ is a sharpened form of the local density estimator of a d_W-variate vector W, i.e. $\hat{f}_W^s(W_i) = ((n-1)\varepsilon)^{-d_W} \sum_{j,j\neq i} K\left(\frac{W_i - \psi_p(W_j)}{\varepsilon}\right)$ where $K()$ is a density estimation kernel and $\psi_p()$ is a sharpening function. They show that for a sequence of bandwidths $\varepsilon_n = Cn^{-\beta}$, where C is any positive constant and β is between $\frac{1}{2p}$ and $\frac{1}{d}$ (p is the order of bias reduction in $\psi_p()$, and d is the number of variables in the system + 1), the test statistic is asymptotically normally distributed. The technical details can refer to Hiemstra and Jones [1994], Diks and Panchenko [2006] and Diks and Wolski [2016].

4. A Practical Example: Energy-Growth Nexus

There is a large body of literature that has studied the cointegrating and Granger causal relationships between energy consumption and economic growth in different countries for different time periods since the seminal work of Kraft and Kraft [1978]. This is an important topic because economic growth is impossible without consumption of energy. Furthermore, the investigation of the energy-growth nexus can provide useful guidance for policy makers working on energy efficiency and energy conservation policies. There are four hypotheses about the Granger causal relationships between economic growth and energy consumption, as follows:

(1) The growth hypothesis: If energy Granger causes GDP, reducing energy consumption will have deleterious effects on economic growth and employment. The underlying assumption of this hypothesis is that energy is a factor input of production and a complement to capital and labor.
(2) The conservation hypothesis: If GDP is found to Granger cause energy, energy conservation policies can be implemented without causing side effects on the economy.
(3) The feedback hypothesis: If there is a bidirectional relationship between energy and GDP, energy policies will have an impact on growth and at the same time changes in economic growth will likewise affect energy consumption.
(4) The neutrality hypothesis: If there is no causal link between energy and GDP, energy and economic development policies should be considered separately.

In this chapter, we use data from the Penn World Table version 9.0 [Feenstra *et al.* 2015; Fang, 2016] and the British Petroleum's 2016 Statistical Review of World Energy to illustrate step-by-step how the cointegration test and Granger causality analysis can be conducted. Real GDP, physical capital and population are obtained from the Penn World Table; primary energy consumption is retrieved from the British Petroleum's 2016 Statistical Review of World Energy. Taking all data available, we get a sample which contains 48 countries covering a period from 1965 to 2014. These countries account for more than 80% of GDP and primary energy consumption in the world. A list of the countries is provided in the appendix (Table A1). Per capita

Table 2. Descriptive statistics of per capita variables.

	Mean	**S.D.**	**Min**	**Max**
United States				
log_gdp	10.465	0.287	9.937	10.852
log_k	11.618	0.267	11.098	11.984
log_energy	2.038	0.582	1.869	2.130
Sample of 48 countries				
log_gdp	9.577	0.866	6.869	11.344
log_k	10.719	1.093	7.286	12.559
log_energy	0.582	1.093	−2.751	2.841

Note: The GDP and physical capital are in 2011 US dollars, and primary energy consumption is in tones oil equivalent.

variables in natural logarithm are used for the following analysis. The summary statistics for the US and the whole sample are given in Table 2.

4.1. *Time series analysis*

First, we conduct the time series analysis using the United States as an example. Here, we consider only economic growth and energy consumption, a bivariate case.

(1) Unit root tests

Box 1: Stata code for time series unit root test.

```
varsoc log_gdp if country=="US", max(10)
dfuller log_gdp if country=="US", lags(2)
dfuller log_gdp if country=="US", lags(2) trend
pperron log_gdp if country=="US", lags(2)
pperron log_gdp if country=="US", lags(2) trend
kpss log_gdp if country=="US", auto notrend
kpss log_gdp if country=="US", auto trend
zandrews log_gdp if country=="US", maxlags(4) graph
zandrews log_gdp if country=="US", maxlags(4) break(trend) graph
```

Stata codes that can be used for the time series unit root test include the four conventional ones *dfuller*, *dfgls*, *pperron* and *kpss*; and *zandrews* when there is one potential break. The Stata command *varsoc* can be employed to determine the optimal lag length used in the *dfuller* and *pperron* specification. Box 1 shows the

Stata codes to test the stationarity of the series log_gdp in the United States. The optimal lag length for log_gdp is two as determined by the AIC, HQIC and SBIC in the *varsoc* results; therefore, in the *dfuller* and *pperron* line, we use lags(2). *auto* in the *kpss* line indicates that the bandwidth is automatically selected and used to determine *maxlag*. The Zivot and Andrews [1992] unit root test with one potential break is performed by the Stata code *zandrews*. The option *break()* specifies whether the break happens at the intercept, trend or both; the default is intercept. Lastly, *graph* is optional. Unit root tests for other variables can be similarly conducted but the codes are omitted due to space constraint.

Table 3 reports the test results for log_gdp and log_energy at both levels and first-differences. All the four tests confirm that log_gdp is stationary after first difference. For log_energy, KPSS test seems to suggest stationarity, but ZA test suggests the opposite, that it has unit root even after first difference; however, ADF and PP tests confirm the integration of order one. Combining all the results, we conservatively proceed with $I(1)$ for log_energy series. This is not uncommon in empirical studies where different tests generate different conclusions; one of the solutions is to agree with results with the most evidence, and another option is to dig deeper on the

Table 3. Unit root test results.

	Level		**First difference**	
	Intercept	**Intercept and trend**	**Intercept**	**Intercept and trend**
ADF test				
log_gdp	−1.625	−1.225	−4.960***	−5.245***
log_energy	−2.786*	−2.830	−5.222**	−5.424***
PP test				
log_gDP	−1.850	−1.512	−5.579***	−5.673***
log_energy	−3.013**	−2.932	−5.166***	−5.368***
KPSS test				
log_gdp	0.933***	0.156**	0.340	0.117
log_energy	0.0981	0.0962	0.306	0.106
ZA test				
log_gdp	−3.921	−5.543***	−5.979***	−5.475***
log_energy	−3.408	−3.188	−3.760	−3.475

Note: The lag lengths for the variables log_gdp and log_energy in the ADF and PP tests are two and one, respectively; and the lag lengths in the KPSS test are five for both variables. *, **, and *** denote the significance levels of 10%, 5%, and 1%, respectively.

property of the series. Furthermore, the break time identified by the ZA test is 2007 for log_gdp and 1988 for log_energy, which coincides with the global financial crisis and 1980s oil glut.

For the unit root test allowing for two structural breaks proposed by Lumsdaine and Papell [1997], there is LPUNIT procedure available in RATS. For the unit root test proposed by Clemente *et al.* [1998], refer to Stata codes *clemao1* and *clemio1* which allow for one structural break, or *clemao2* and *clemio2* which allow for two structural breaks.

(2) Cointegration tests

Box 2: Stata code for cointegration tests.

```
varsoc log_gdp log_energy if country=="US", maxlag(10)
egranger log_gdp log_energy if country=="US", lags(4)
egranger log_gdp log_energy if country=="US", lags(4) trend
vecrank log_gdp log_energy if country=="US", lags(4) max trend(constant)
levela
vecrank log_gdp log_energy if country=="US", lags(4) max trend(trend) levela
ghansen log_gdp log_energy if country=="US", break(level) lagmethod(aic)
```

Stata codes that can be used for the time series cointegration tests include *egranger*, *vecrank* and *ghansen*. The code *egranger* is to perform the Engle and Granger's [1987] two-step test; *vecrank* is to perform the Johansen and Juselius's [1990] cointegration test and *ghansen* is to conduct the Gregory and Hansen's [1996] cointegration test with regime shifts. The EG cointegration test makes fewer distribution assumptions than the Johansen cointegration test, but it does not allow for the identification of the number of cointegrating vectors. This is not a concern here for a bivariate system, but in the multivariate system, the Johansen cointegration test is more preferred. Besides using for the cointegration test, *egranger* can also estimate an ECM model by specifying *ecm* in the option. Box 2 shows the Stata codes to test the cointegrating relationship between GDP and energy consumption in the United States. *varsoc* is used to determine the optimal lag length in the VAR system. Results from SBIC indicate a lag length of one, but results from AIC and HQIC suggest a lag length of four, so in the following steps, the lag length of four is selected. The option *max* in the *vecrank* line is to ask Stata to report maximum-eigenvalue statistics besides the default trace statistics, the option *levela* asks Stata to report 1% critical values besides the default 5% critical values, and *trend()* can assume five values: *constant*, *rconstant*, *trend*, *rtrend* and *none*, which

Table 4. Cointegration test results.

	Test statistic	1% Critical value	5% Critical value
EG cointegration test			
No trend	−0.851	−4.129	−3.464
Trend	−1.417	−4.658	−3.980
Johensen cointegration test			
No trend			
Trace statistic			
$r = 0$	19.708	20.04	15.41
$r = 1$	3.253	6.65	3.76
Max eigenvalue statistic			
$r = 0$	16.455	18.63	14.07
$r = 1$	3.253	6.65	3.76
Trend			
Trace statistic			
$r = 0$	17.458	23.46	18.17
$r = 1$	0.215	6.40	3.74
Max eigenvalue statistic			
$r = 0$	17.243	21.47	16.87
$r = 1$	0.215	6.40	3.74
Gregory and Hansen [1996] test			
ADF	−2.42	−5.13	−4.61
Zt	−2.65	−5.13	−4.61
Za	−9.71	−50.07	−40.48

correspond to the five model specifications in the Johansen cointegration tests. In the *ghansen* line, *break()* is to specify the break type in the cointegration vector and *lagmethod()* is to specify the algorithm to determine the lag lengths in the ADF test.

The cointegration test results are presented in Table 4. Results from all the three test methods suggest no cointegration at the significance level of 1%, but results are mixed at the significance level of 5%. When there is a cointegrating relationship between two variables, there is definitely Granger causal relationship; one can continue with the VECM to identify the direction of the Granger causality. When there is no cointegrating relationship found among variables, one may use other methods such as Toda and Yamamoto's [1995] causality test to explore whether there is a Granger causal relationship.

For the cointegration test with structural breaks proposed by Johansen *et al.* [2000], R and Eviews program file is available at http://web.uvic.ca/~dgiles/downloads/johansen/index.html. The Gauss code for the cointegration test with structural breaks proposed by Carrion-i-Silvestre and Sansó [2006] is available at http://www.eco.ub.edu/~carrion/Welcome.html.

(3) Granger causality tests

Box 3: Stata code for Granger causality tests.

```
*Engle and Granger [1978] pairwise Granger causality test
varsoc dlog_gdp dlog_energy if country=="US", maxlag(10)
var dlog_gdp dlog_energy if country=="US", lag(1/3) dfk small
vargranger

*Toda and Yamamoto (1995) Granger causality test
var log_gdp log_energy if country=="US", lags(1/4)
varlmar
var log_gdp log_energy if country=="US", lags(1/5)
test [log_gdp]L.log_energy [log_gdp]L2.log_energy [log_gdp]L3.log_energy
[log_gdp]L4.log_energy
test [log_energy]L.log_gdp [log_energy]L2.log_gdp [log_energy]L3.log_gdp
[log_energy]L4.log_gdp
```

Table 5. Granger causality test results.

	Test statistic	***p*-Value**
Engle and Granger [1978] pairwise test		
Log_energy not Granger cause log_gdp	0.1843	0.9965
Log_gdp not Granger cause log_energy	1.3534	0.2712
Toda and Yamamoto [1995]		
Log_energy not Granger cause log_gdp	0.93	0.9200
Log_gdp not Granger cause log_energy	5.49	0.2409

Box 3 shows the Stata codes to test the Granger causal relationship between GDP and energy consumption in the United States using two methods. The Stata code *vargranger* is to perform pairwise Granger causality tests, which is used after *var* or *svar*. In the *var* line, *lag(1/3)* is determined by the results from *varsoc*; *dfk* is used for the small-sample adjustment, together with *small* which specifies small-sample

t and F statistics. Since log_gdp and log_energy are integrated of order one, first difference terms are used in the variable list.

Using Stata to perform the Toda and Yamamoto's [1995] Granger causality test, the first step is to decide the integration order of all variables in the system; as shown in the first step, log_gdp and log_energy are integrated of order one. The second step is to determine the max lag length for the VAR model; and *varsoc* has indicated a lag length of four. The third step is to test whether there is no serial correlation in the appropriate VAR model by specifying the selected lag length; the codes are shown in the *var* and *varlmar* lines. If there is serial correlation, one can increase the lag length in the VAR model until no serial correlation test is passed. In this example, the lag length of four is appropriately determined. So we can proceed to the last step of Granger causality test by following the last three lines in the codes. The lag length specified here should be the sum of maximum integration order and the lag length, which is one plus four in this example. The first *test* line is to test for the null hypothesis that energy does not Granger cause economic growth and the second *test* line is to test for the null hypothesis that economic growth does not Granger cause energy consumption.

Table 5 reports the Granger causality test results from both methods. Within expectation, there is no Granger causality in any direction. If one suspects a nonlinear Granger causal relationship between the variables, the code is available in C at http://research.economics.unsw.edu.au/vpanchenko/software/2006_GC_JEDC_c_and_exe_code.zip. The R package and a nonlinear Granger causality test for the multivariate case are available at http://marcinwolski.org/. This example only serves the purpose of illustrating steps to follow to test for the cointegration and Granger causality in the time series. In the next section, we move on to the panel analysis.

4.2. *Panel analysis*

We illustrate steps to perform the panel cointegration test and panel Granger causality analysis by using the whole sample.

(1) Panel unit root tests

To begin with, we need to examine whether there is cross-sectional dependence in the data. The Stata code for the cross-sectional dependence test is *xtcsd*, which allows three test statistics proposed by Friedman [1937], Frees [1995] and Pesaran [2004]. Stata codes are shown in Box 4 and results are reported in Table 6.

Box 4: Stata code for cross-sectional dependence test for the panel data.

```
xtreg log_gdp log_k log_energy, fe
xtcsd, Frees
xtcsd, Friedman
xtcsd, Pesaran
```

Table 6. Cross-sectional dependence test results.

	Frees' test	**Friedman's test**	**Pesaran's test**
Statistics	12.928	317.310	25.885
p-values	[0.000]	[0.000]	[0.000]

Note: The tests are based on the fixed effect regression of log_GDP against log_K and log_Energy. The null hypothesis for the tests is cross-sectional independence.

As can be seen from Table 6, there is strong evidence of the presence of cross-sectional dependence. This is quite common in the macroeconomic series across countries or regions due to globalization and trade penetration. Ideally, we should use tests that allow for cross-sectional dependence in the following analysis. Here, for demonstration purposes, we will sometimes consider both cases with or without cross-sectional dependence.

For the panel unit root tests, there are many test statistics that can be employed when we assume there is cross-sectional independence. For example, in the Stata code *xtunitroot*, one can specify *llc, ht, breitung, ips, fisher*, and *hadri* for Levin, Lin and Chu [2002], Harris and Tzavalis [1999], Breitung [2001], Im *et al.* [2003], Choi [2001] and Hadri [2000] tests, respectively.

When there is cross-sectional dependence, the popular second-generation panel unit root test is Pesaran's [2007] CIPS test, which can be executed by *xtcips* in Stata.

Box 5: Stata code for panel unit root test assuming cross-sectional dependence.

```
xtcips log_gdp, maxlags(4) bglags(9)
xtcips log_gdp, maxlags(4) bglags(9) trend
...
```

Box 5 shows the Stata codes to test the presence of unit roots in the panel data when there is cross-sectional dependence. Table 7 reports the panel unit root test results from the CIPS approach in the presence of cross-sectional dependence.

Table 7. Panel unit root test results with cross-sectional dependence.

	Level		First difference	
	Intercept	**Intercept and trend**	**Intercept**	**Intercept and trend**
Log_GDP	−1.416	−1.616	−4.285***	−4.594***
Log_K	−1.863	−1.921	−2.502***	−3.130***
Log_Energy	−1.914	−2.401	−5.437***	−5.502***

Note: The maximum lag is set to four. Breusch–Godfrey serial correlation lag order is set to nine. *** denotes the significance level of 1%.

It is evident that all the three variables are not stationary at levels but stationary after first difference. Because they are integrated of the same order, the next step is to examine whether they are cointegrated in the long run.

(2) Panel cointegration tests

Box 6: Stata code for panel cointegration test.

```
*panel cointegration test assuming cross-sectional independence
xtpedroni log_gdp log_k log_energy, lagselect(aic) adflags(4)
xtpedroni log_gdp log_k log_energy, trend lagselect(aic) adflags(4)

* Panel cointegration test assuming cross-sectional dependence
set seed 10010010
xtwest log_gdp log_k log_energy, lags(1 4) leads(0) lrwindow(2) bootstrap(100)
xtwest log_gdp log_k log_energy, lags(1 4) leads(0) lrwindow(2) constant
bootstrap(100)
```

The Stata codes used for the panel cointegration test include *xtpedroni* for the seven statistics proposed by Pedroni [1999, 2004] and *xtwest* for the panel cointegration test proposed by Westerlund [2007]. The options *lagselect()* specifies the criterion used to select the lag length, which is *aic* by default; *adflags()* tells Stata the maximum lag length considered in the lag selection process, which is automatically determined if not specified. Box 6 shows the Stata codes for panel cointegration tests under two scenarios, with and without cross-sectional dependence. Table 8 reports the cointegration test results from the seven statistics; results for the model without trend suggest no cointegration while results for the model with a trend seem to suggest a cointegrating relationship at least at the significance level of 10%. It is common that the seven statistics generate different conclusions on the cointegration; one practice is to conclude based on the majority

Table 8. Panel cointegration test results.

Test	Panel v-statistic	Panel ρ-statistic	Panel PP-statistic	Panel ADF-statistic	Group ρ-statistic	Group PP-statistic	Group ADF-statistic
No trend	1.222	0.977	0.474	−1.407	2.583***	1.485	−1.695*
With trend	−1.069	2.733***	1.955*	0.264	3.933***	2.762***	−0.021

Note: The lag length is determined by the Akaike Information Criterion with the max lag length fixed at four. The model specification includes deterministic trend and intercept. * and *** denote the significance levels of 10% and 1%, respectively.

Table 9. Panel cointegration test results [Westerlund, 2007].

Test	Gt	Ga	Pt	Pa
Without constant	−1.227	−3.912	−6.562	−2.140
	[0.570]	[0.590]	[0.600]	[0.500]
With constant	−2.084	−8.519	−13.275	−7.025
	[0.320]	[0.070]	[0.800]	[0.270]

Note: The variables considered in the system are log_gdp, log_k and log_energy.

of the conclusions, although a thorough analysis of the statistics that best fit the scenario is preferred.

The *xtwest* line in Box 6 performs the panel cointegration test in the presence of cross-sectional dependence through bootstrapping. The critical values are calculated based on 100 repetitions; a larger number is avoided because 100 times' repetition already consumes quite a long computation time. The *set seed* line makes sure that the results can be replicated. Results in Table 9 show that no matter which model is considered, most or all statistics support the conclusion of no cointegration. Through this example, the many cointegrating relationships identified in the empirical literature may not be so common as it might seem to be. The interpretation of the Westerlund [2007] cointegration results needs to be careful. The rejection of the null hypothesis by the Gt and Ga statistics suggest that there is at least a cointegrating relationship for some of the cross-sectional units; the rejection of the null hypothesis by the Pt and Pa statistics suggest that the whole panel is cointegrated. One needs to be mindful of the difference between the two distinct alternative hypotheses.

The recent panel cointegration test that considers both the structural breaks and cross-sectional dependence [Banerjee and Carrion-i-Silvestre, 2015] can be performed in GAUSS and the code is available at http://www.eco.ub.edu/~carrion/Welcome.html.

(3) Panel Granger causality tests

We test the panel Granger causal relationship between economic growth and energy consumption in this subsection. The panel causality tests assuming the homogeneous coefficients and heterogeneous coefficients are available in Eviews (Fig. 1).

The bootstrap panel Granger causality test proposed by Emirmahmutoglu and Kose [2011] can be performed in Matlab and the code is available at http://www.runmycode.org/companion/view/89.

Results in Table 10 show that there is a bidirectional Granger causal relationship between the two variables, GDP and energy consumption. Besides the Granger causal results on the panel of 48 countries, the results report the Granger causality for individual cross-sectional units. Due to space constraint, the results are not reported here.

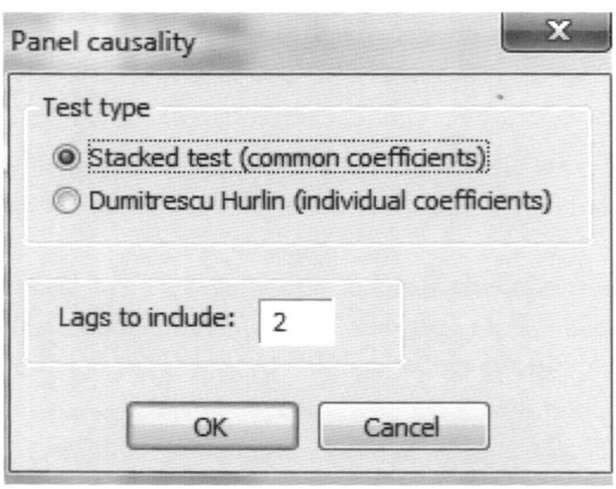

Fig. 1. Eviews screenshot for the panel causality test.

Table 10. Emirmahmutoglu and Kose [2011] panel Granger causality test results.

Hypothesis	**Statistic**	**CV 1%**	**CV 5%**	**CV 10%**
E→GDP	132.692**	149.483	131.819	123.698
GDP→E	163.611***	146.211	134.344	125.783

Note: The null hypothesis of the test is no Granger causal relationship. The lag orders are selected based on the Schwarz information criteria with the max lag length set at four; the bootstrap critical values are generated from 1,000 replications. ** and *** denote the significance levels of 5% and 1%, respectively.

5. Conclusion

This chapter reviews two widely used econometric analyses in energy economics, namely, cointegration and Granger causality, through examples of energy-growth nexus studies. Specifically, these methods are employed to examine the cointegrating and causal relationships between economic growth and four types of energy consumption (total energy consumption, electricity consumption, nuclear consumption and renewable energy consumption). The purpose of such studies is to provide a basis for discussion in order to design and implement effective energy and environmental policies. Cointegration and causality techniques have been developed and extended to applications in several dimensions including from bivariate to multivariate cases, from time series to panel data, and from linear to nonlinear contexts. Apart from their applications in examining the energy-growth nexus as discussed in detail in this chapter, the two techniques can also be used in a large number of macroeconomic studies such as investigating causal relationships between stock prices and exchange rates, stock price and volume, money and income, economic growth and various macroeconomic variables such as international trade, government spending, and environmental quality. The well-examined energy-growth nexus topic, however, seems to be in a bottleneck since the majority of studies in this field use a set of common variables with the usual methodologies, just for different countries or regions or by changing the time periods. Henceforth, there is a need for breakthroughs in data frequency, econometric methodologies or sound theoretical supports.

Appendix

Table A1. Country list.

Algeria	Colombia	Iran	Pakistan	Switzerland
Argentina	Denmark	Ireland	Peru	Taiwan
Australia	Ecuador	Israel	Philippines	Thailand
Austria	Egypt	Italy	Portugal	Trinidad & Tobago
Belgium	Finland	Japan	Romania	Turkey
Brazil	France	Malaysia	Singapore	United Kingdom
Canada	Germany	Mexico	South Africa	United States
Chile	Greece	Netherlands	South Korea	Venezuela
China	India	New Zealand	Spain	
Hong Kong	Indonesia	Norway	Sweden	

References

Abosedra, S. and Baghestani, H. (1989). New evidence on the causal relationship between United States energy consumption and gross national product. *The Journal of Energy and Development* **14** (2), 285–292.

Akaike, H. (1969). Fitting autoregressive models for prediction. *Annals of the Institute of Statistical Mathematics* **21**, 243–247.

Akarca, A. T. and Long, T. V. (1979). Energy and employment: A time-series analysis of the causal relationship. *Resources and Energy* **2** (2–3), 151–162.

Alam, M. J., Begum, I. A., Buysse, J. and Van Huylenbroeck, G. (2012). Energy consumption, carbon emissions and economic growth nexus in Bangladesh: Cointegration and dynamic causality analysis. *Energy Policy* **45**, 217–225.

Alshehry, A. S. and Belloumi, M. (2015). Energy consumption, carbon dioxide emissions and economic growth: The case of Saudi Arabia. *Renewable and Sustainable Energy Reviews* **41**, 237–247.

Altinay, G. and Karagol, E. (2004). Structural break, unit root, and the causality between energy consumption and GDP in Turkey. *Energy Economics* **26** (6), 985–994.

Altinay, G. and Karagol, E. (2005). Electricity consumption and economic growth: Evidence from Turkey. *Energy Economics* **27** (6), 849–856.

Asafu-Adjaye, J. (2000). The relationship between energy consumption, energy prices and economic growth: Time series evidence from Asian developing countries. *Energy Economics* **22** (6), 615–625.

Bai, J. and Ng, S. (2004). A PANIC attack on unit roots and cointegration. *Econometrica* **72** (4), 1127–1178.

Banerjee, A. and Carrion-i-Silvestre, J. L. (2015). Cointegration in panel data with structural breaks and cross-section dependence. *Journal of Applied Econometrics* **30** (1), 1–23.

Banerjee, A. and Carrion-i-Silvestre, J. L. (2017). Testing for panel cointegration using common correlated effects estimators. *Journal of Time Series Analysis* **38** (4), 610–636.

Bartleet, M. and Gounder, R. (2010). Energy consumption and economic growth in New Zealand: Results of trivariate and multivariate models. *Energy Policy* **38** (7), 3508–3517.

Bekiros, S. D. and Diks, C. G. (2008). The relationship between crude oil spot and futures prices: Cointegration, linear and nonlinear causality. *Energy Economics* **30** (5), 2673–2685.

Bowden, N. and Payne, J. E. (2009). The causal relationship between US energy consumption and real output: A disaggregated analysis. *Journal of Policy Modeling* **31** (2), 180–188.

Breitung, J. (2001). The local power of some unit root tests for panel data. In B. H. Baltagi (ed.) *Nonstationary Panels, Panel Cointegration, and Dynamic Panels* (Emerald Group Publishing Limited), pp. 161–177.

Caraiani, C., Lungu, C. I. and Dascălu, C. (2015). Energy consumption and GDP causality: A three-step analysis for emerging European countries. *Renewable and Sustainable Energy Reviews* **44**, 198–210.

Carrion-i-Silvestre, J. L. and Sansó, A. (2006). Testing the null of cointegration with structural breaks. *Oxford Bulletin of Economics and Statistics* **68** (5), 623–646.

Chen, S. T., Kuo, H. I. and Chen, C. C. (2007). The relationship between GDP and electricity consumption in 10 Asian countries. *Energy Policy* **35** (4), 2611–2621.

Chen, Y. and Fang, Z. (2017). Industrial electricity consumption, human capital investment and economic growth in Chinese cities. *Economic Modelling* (forthcoming).

Cheng, B. S. (1995). An investigation of cointegration and causality between energy consumption and economic growth. *The Journal of Energy and Development* **21** (1), 73–84.

Cheng, B. S. (1997). Energy consumption and economic growth in Brazil, Mexico and Venezuela: A time series analysis. *Applied Economics Letters* **4** (11), 671–674.

Cheng, B. S. (1998). Energy consumption, employment and causality in Japan: A multivariate approach. *Indian Economic Review* **33** (1), 19–29.

Cheng, B. S. (1999). Causality between energy consumption and economic growth in India: An application of cointegration and error-correction modeling. *Indian Economic Review* **34** (1), 39–49.

Cheng, B. S. and Lai, T. W. (1997). An investigation of co-integration and causality between energy consumption and economic activity in Taiwan. *Energy Economics* **19** (4), 435–444.

Chiou-Wei, S. Z., Chen, C. F. and Zhu, Z. (2008). Economic growth and energy consumption revisited — Evidence from linear and nonlinear Granger causality. *Energy Economics* **30** (6), 3063–3076.

Choi, I. (2001). Unit root tests for panel data. *Journal of International Money and Finance* **20** (2), 249–272.

Chontanawat, J., Hunt, L. C. and Pierse, R. (2006). Causality between energy consumption and GDP: Evidence from 30 OECD and 78 non-OECD countries (No. 113). Surrey Energy Economics Centre (SEEC), School of Economics, University of Surrey.

Clarke, J. A. and Mirza, S. (2006). A comparison of some common methods for detecting Granger noncausality. *Journal of Statistical Computation and Simulation* **76** (3), 207–231.

Clemente, J., Montanes, A. and Reyes, M. (1998). Testing for a unit root in variables with a double change in the mean. *Economics Letters* **59**, 175–182.

Dagher, L. and Yacoubian, T. (2012). The causal relationship between energy consumption and economic growth in Lebanon. *Energy Policy* **50**, 795–801.

Diks, C. and Panchenko, V. (2006). A new statistic and practical guidelines for nonparametric Granger causality testing. *Journal of Economic Dynamics and Control* **30** (9), 1647–1669.

Diks, C. and Wolski, M. (2016). Nonlinear Granger causality: Guidelines for multivariate analysis. *Journal of Applied Econometrics* **31** (7), 1333–1351.

Dolado, J. J. and Lütkepohl, H. (1996). Making Wald tests work for cointegrated VAR systems. *Econometric Reviews* **15** (4), 369–386.

Dumitrescu, E. I. and Hurlin, C. (2012). Testing for Granger non-causality in heterogeneous panels. *Economic Modelling* **29** (4), 1450–1460.

Ebohon, O. J. (1996). Energy, economic growth and causality in developing countries: A case study of Tanzania and Nigeria. *Energy Policy* **24** (5), 447–453.

Eden, S. H. and Hwang, B. K. (1984). The relationship between energy and GNP: Further results. *Energy Economics* **6** (3), 186–190.

Eichler, M. (2012). Causal inference in time series analysis. In C. Berzuini, P. Dawid and L. Bernardinelli (eds.) *Causality: Statistical Perspectives and Applications*. (John Wiley & Sons), 327–354.

Emirmahmutoglu, F. and Kose, N. (2011). Testing for Granger causality in heterogeneous mixed panels. *Economic Modelling* **28**, 870–876.

Engle, R. F. and Granger, C. W. J. (1987). Cointegration and error correction: Representation, estimation, and testing. *Econometrica* **55**, 251–276.

Fang, Z. (2016). Data on examining the role of human capital in the energy-growth nexus across countries. *Data in Brief* **9**, 540–542.

Fang, Z., Chang, Y. and Hamori, S. (2017). Energy and human capital: A driver or drag for economic growth. *The Singapore Economic Review* (forthcoming).

Fang, Z. and Chang, Y. (2016). Energy, human capital and economic growth in Asia Pacific countries — Evidence from a panel cointegration and causality analysis. *Energy Economics* **56**, 177–184.

Fang, Z. and Chen, Y. (2017). Human capital and energy in economic growth — Evidence from Chinese provincial data. *Energy Economics* **68**, 340–358.

Fang, Z. and Wolski, M. (2016). Human capital, energy and economic growth in China — Evidence from multivariate nonlinear granger causality. *European Investment Bank* **1** (1), 1–25.

Feenstra, R. C., Inklaar, R. and Timmer, M. P. (2015). The next generation of the Penn World Table. *The American Economic Review* **105** (10), 3150–3182.

Frees, E. W. (1995). Assessing cross-sectional correlation in panel data. *Journal of Econometrics* **69**, 393–414.

Friedman, M. (1937). The use of ranks to avoid the assumption of normality implicit in the analysis of variance. *Journal of the American Statistical Association* **32** (200), 675–701.

Fuinhas, J. A. and Marques, A. C. (2012). Energy consumption and economic growth nexus in Portugal, Italy, Greece, Spain and Turkey: An ARDL bounds test approach (1965–2009). *Energy Economics* **34** (2), 511–517.

Ghali, K. H. and El-Sakka, M. I. (2004). Energy use and output growth in Canada: A multivariate cointegration analysis. *Energy Economics* **26** (2), 225–238.

Ghosh, S. (2002). Electricity consumption and economic growth in India. *Energy Policy* **30** (2), 125–129.

Glasure, Y. U. (2002). Energy and national income in Korea: Further evidence on the role of omitted variables. *Energy Economics* **24** (4), 355–365.

Glasure, Y. U. and Lee, A. R. (1997). Cointegration, error-correction, and the relationship between GDP and energy: The case of South Korea and Singapore. *Resource and Energy Economics* **20** (1), 17–25.

Granger, C. W. J. (1969). Investigating causal relations by econometric models and cross-spectral methods. *Econometrica* **36**, 424–438.

Granger, C. W. J. and Newbold, P. (1974). Spurious regressions in econometrics. *Journal of Econometrics* **2**, 111–120.

Granger, C. W. J. (1988). Some recent developments in a concept of causality. *Journal of Econometrics* **39**, 199–211.

Gregory, A. W. and Hansen, B. E. (1996). Residual-based tests for cointegration in models with regime shifts. *Journal of Econometrics* **70** (1), 99–126.

Hadri, K. (2000). Testing for stationarity in heterogeneous panel data. *The Econometrics Journal* **3** (2), 148–161.

Harris, R. D. and Tzavalis, E. (1999). Inference for unit roots in dynamic panels where the time dimension is fixed. *Journal of Econometrics* **91** (2), 201–226.

Hiemstra, C. and Jones, J. D. (1994). Testing for linear and nonlinear Granger causality in the stock price-volume relation. *The Journal of Finance* **49** (5), 1639–1664.

Hoa, T. V. (1993). Effects of oil on output growth and inflation in developing countries: The case of Thailand from January 1966 to January 1991. *International Journal of Energy Research* **17** (1), 29–33.

Hsiao, C. (1981). Autoregressive modelling and money-income causality detection. *Journal of Monetary Economics* **7**, 85–106.

Hwang, D. B. and Gum, B. (1991). The causal relationship between energy and GNP: The case of Taiwan. *The Journal of Energy and Development* **16** (2), 219–226.

Im, K. S., Pesaran, M. H. and Shin, Y. (2003). Testing for unit roots in heterogeneous panels. *Journal of Econometrics* **115** (1), 53–74.

Johansen, S. (1988). Statistical analysis of cointegration vectors. *Journal Economic Dynamics and Control* **12**, 231–254.

Johansen, S. (1991). Estimation and hypothesis testing of cointegration vectors in Gaussian vector autoregressive models. *Econometrica: Journal of the Econometric Society* **59** (6), 1551–1580.

Johansen, S. and Juselius, K. (1990). Maximum likelihood estimation and inference on cointegration — With applications to the demand for money. *Oxford Bulletin of Economics and Statistics* **52** (2), 169–210.

Johansen, S., Mosconi, R. and Nielsen, B. (2000). Cointegration analysis in the presence of structural breaks in the deterministic trend. *Econometrics Journal* **3**, 216–249.

Kao, C. (1999). Spurious regression and residual-based tests for cointegration in panel data. *Journal of Econometrics* **90**, 1–44.

Kasman, A. and Duman, Y. S. (2015). CO_2 emissions, economic growth, energy consumption, trade and urbanization in new EU member and candidate countries: A panel data analysis. *Economic Modelling* **44**, 97–103.

Kennedy, P. (2003). *A Guide to Econometrics*, (5th edn). (MIT Press, Cambridge, MA).

Konya, L. (2006). Exports and growth, Granger causality analysis on OECD countries with a panel data approach. *Economic Modelling* **23**, 978–992.

Kraft, J. and Kraft, A. (1978). On the relationship between energy and GNP. *The Journal of Energy and Development* **3** (2), 401–403.

Larsson, R., Lyahagen, J. and Lothgren, M. (2001). Likelihood-based cointegration tests in heterogeneous panels. *Econometrics Journal* **4**, 109–142.

Le, T. H. (2016). Dynamics between energy, output, openness and financial development in sub-Saharan African countries. *Applied Economics* **48** (10), 914–933.

Lee, C. C. (2005). Energy consumption and GDP in developing countries: A cointegrated panel analysis. *Energy Economics* **27** (3), 415–427.

Lee, C. C. and Chang, C. P. (2008). Energy consumption and economic growth in Asian economies: A more comprehensive analysis using panel data. *Resource and Energy Economics* **30** (1), 50–65.

Levin, A., Lin, C. F. and Chu, C. S. J. (2002). Unit root tests in panel data: Asymptotic and finite-sample properties. *Journal of Econometrics* **108** (1), 1–24.

Lumsdaine, R. and Papell, D. (1997). Multiple trend breaks and the unit-root hypothesis. *The Review of Economics and Statistics* **79** (2), 212–218.

Maddala, G. S. and Wu, S. (1999). A comparative study of unit root tests with panel data and a new simple test. *Oxford Bulletin of Economics and Statistics* **61** (S1), 631–652.

Masih, A. M. and Masih, R. (1996). Energy consumption, real income and temporal causality: Results from a multi-country study based on cointegration and error-correction modelling techniques. *Energy Economics* **18** (3), 165–183.

Masih, A. M. and Masih, R. (1997). On the temporal causal relationship between energy consumption, real income, and prices: Some new evidence from Asian-energy dependent NICs based on a multivariate cointegration/vector error-correction approach. *Journal of Policy Modeling* **19** (4), 417–440.

Maziarz, M. (2015). A review of the Granger-causality fallacy. *The Journal of Philosophical Economics: Reflections on Economic and Social Issues* **8** (2), 86–105.

Moon, H. R. and Perron, B. (2004). Testing for a unit root in panels with dynamic factors. *Journal of Econometrics* **122** (1), 81–126.

Mutascu, M. (2016). A bootstrap panel Granger causality analysis of energy consumption and economic growth in the G7 countries. *Renewable and Sustainable Energy Reviews* **63**, 166–171.

Nachane, D. M., Nadkarni, R. M. and Karnik, A. V. (1988). Co-integration and causality testing of the energy — GDP relationship: A cross-country study. *Applied Economics* **20** (11), 1511–1531.

Nasreen, S. and Anwar, S. (2014). Causal relationship between trade openness, economic growth and energy consumption: A panel data analysis of Asian countries. *Energy Policy* **69**, 82–91.

Noor, S. and Siddiqi, M. W. (2010). Energy consumption and economic growth in South Asian countries: A co-integrated panel analysis. *International Journal of Human and Social Sciences* **5** (14), 921–926.

Oh, W. and Lee, K. (2004a). Causal relationship between energy consumption and GDP revisited: The case of Korea 1970–1999. *Energy Economics* **26** (1), 51–59.

Oh, W. and Lee, K. (2004b). Energy consumption and economic growth in Korea: Testing the causality relation. *Journal of Policy Modeling* **26** (8), 973–981.

Ouedraogo, N. S. (2013). Energy consumption and economic growth: Evidence from the economic community of West African States (ECOWAS). *Energy Economics* **36**, 637–647.

Ozturk, I. (2010). A literature survey on energy-growth nexus. *Energy Policy* **38**, 340–349.
Ozturk, I. and Acaravci, A. (2013). The long-run and causal analysis of energy, growth, openness and financial development on carbon emissions in Turkey. *Energy Economics* **36**, 262–267.
Payne, J. E. (2009). On the dynamics of energy consumption and output in the US. *Applied Energy* **86** (4), 575–577.
Payne, J. E. (2010). A survey of the electricity consumption-growth literature. *Applied energy* **87** (3), 723–731.
Pedroni, P. (1999). Critical values for cointegration tests in heterogeneous panels with multiple regressors. *Oxford Bulletin of Economics and Statistics* **61** (S1), 653–670.
Pedroni, P. (2004). Panel cointegration: Asymptotic and finite samples properties of pooled time series tests with an application to the PPP hypothesis. *Econometric Theory* **20**, 597–625.
Perron, P. and Vogelsang, T. (1992). Nonstationarity and level shifts with an application to purchasing power parity. *Journal of Business and Economic Statistics* **10**, 301–320.
Persyn, D. and Westerlund, J. (2008). Error-correction-based cointegration tests for panel data. *Stata Journal* **8** (2), 232–241.
Pesaran, M. H. (2004). General diagnostic tests for cross section dependence in panels. Cambridge Working Papers in Economics No. 0435.
Pesaran, M. H. (2007). A simple panel unit root test in the presence of cross-section dependence. *Journal of Applied Econometrics* **22**, 265–312.
Pesaran, M. H. and Shin Y. (1999). An autoregressive distributed lag modelling approach to cointegration analysis. In S. Strom (ed.) *Econometrics and Economic Theory in the 20th Century: The Ragnar Frisch Centennial Symposium* (Cambridge University Press, Cambridge, UK).
Pesaran, M. H., Shin Y. and Smith R. (2001). Bounds testing approaches to the analysis of level relationships. *Journal of Applied Econometrics* **16**, 289–326.
Phillips, P. C. and Sul, D. (2003). Dynamic panel estimation and homogeneity testing under cross section dependence. *The Econometrics Journal* **6** (1), 217–259.
Sebri, M. and Ben-Salha, O. (2014). On the causal dynamics between economic growth, renewable energy consumption, CO_2 emissions and trade openness: Fresh evidence from BRICS countries. *Renewable and Sustainable Energy Reviews* **39**, 14–23.
Seth, A. K., Barrett, A. B. and Barnett, L. (2015). Granger causality analysis in neuroscience and neuroimaging. *Journal of Neuroscience* **35** (8), 3293–3297.
Shahbaz, M., Khan, S. and Tahir, M. I. (2013). The dynamic links between energy consumption, economic growth, financial development and trade in China: Fresh evidence from multivariate framework analysis. *Energy Economics* **40**, 8–21.
Shiu, A. and Lam, P. L. (2004). Electricity consumption and economic growth in China. *Energy Policy* **32** (1), 47–54.
Sims, C. A. (1972). Money, income, and causality. *The American Economic Review* **62**, 540–552.
Solarin, S. A. and Shahbaz, M. (2013). Trivariate causality between economic growth, urbanisation and electricity consumption in Angola: Cointegration and causality analysis. *Energy Policy* **60**, 876–884.
Soytas, U. and Sari, R. (2003). Energy consumption and GDP: Causality relationship in G-7 countries and emerging markets. *Energy Economics* **25** (1), 33–37.
Soytas, U., Sari, R. and Ewing, B. T. (2007). Energy consumption, income, and carbon emissions in the United States. *Ecological Economics* **62** (3), 482–489.
Soytas, U. and Sari, R. (2009). Energy consumption, economic growth, and carbon emissions: Challenges faced by an EU candidate member. *Ecological Economics* **68** (6), 1667–1675.
Stern, D. I. (1993). Energy and economic growth in the USA: A multivariate approach. *Energy Economics* **15** (2), 137–150.
Stern, D. I. (2000). A multivariate cointegration analysis of the role of energy in the US macroeconomy. *Energy Economics* **22** (2), 267–283.

Tang, C. F., Tan, B. W. and Ozturk, I. (2016). Energy consumption and economic growth in Vietnam. *Renewable and Sustainable Energy Reviews* **54**, 1506–1514.

Toda, H. Y. and Yamamoto, T. (1995). Statistical inference in vector autoregressions with possibly integrated processes. *Journal of Econometrics* **66** (1), 225–250.

Tsani, S. Z. (2010). Energy consumption and economic growth: A causality analysis for Greece. *Energy Economics* **32** (3), 582–590.

Wang, Y., Wang, Y., Zhou, J., Zhu, X. and Lu, G. (2011). Energy consumption and economic growth in China: A multivariate causality test. *Energy Policy* **39** (7), 4399–4406.

Westerlund, J. (2007). Testing for error correction in panel data. *Oxford Bulletin of Economics and Statistics* **69** (6), 709–748.

Wolde-Rufael, Y. (2004). Disaggregated industrial energy consumption and GDP: The case of Shanghai, 1952–1999. *Energy Economics* **26** (1), 69–75.

Wolde-Rufael, Y. (2005). Energy demand and economic growth: The African experience. *Journal of Policy Modeling* **27** (8), 891–903.

Wolde-Rufael, Y. (2014). Electricity consumption and economic growth in transition countries: A revisit using bootstrap panel Granger causality analysis. *Energy Economics* **44**, 325–330.

Yoo, S. H. (2005). Electricity consumption and economic growth: Evidence from Korea. *Energy Policy* **33** (12), 1627–1632.

Yu, E. S. and Choi, J. Y. (1985). The causal relationship between energy and GNP: An international comparison. *The Journal of Energy and Development* **10** (2), 249–272.

Zamani, M. (2007). Energy consumption and economic activities in Iran. *Energy Economics* **29** (6), 1135–1140.

Zhixin, Z. and Xin, R. (2011). Causal relationships between energy consumption and economic growth. *Energy Procedia* **5**, 2065–2071.

Zivot, E. and Andrews, D. W. K. (1992). Further evidence on the great crash, the oil-price shock, and the unit-root hypothesis. *Journal of Business & Economic Statistics* **20** (1), 25–44.

Chapter 29

The Impact of Unconventional Monetary Policy Shocks on Energy Prices

Panagiota Makrychoriti*,§, Georgios Moratis†,¶ and Spyros Spyrou‡,‖

**Department of Management, Birkbeck University of London, UK Athens University of Economics and Business, Athens, Greece*

†Department of Accounting and Finance Athens University of Economics and Business, Athens, Greece

‡Spyros Spyrou Audencia Business School, Nantes, France Athens University of Economics and Business, Athens, Greece

§p.makrychoriti@bbk.ac.uk

¶g.moratis@yahoo.com

‖sspyrou@aueb.gr

We examine the effect of European Central Bank's (ECB's) unconventional monetary policy measures on energy prices. Our results indicate that the non-standard ECB monetary policies during the recent financial crises had a significant and negative impact on energy prices. For example, we find that these policies accounted for approximately 10% of the price variance for the Light Crude Oil Futures Contract. Impulse Response Functions suggest that an increase in the ECB's propensity to unconventional policy decreases energy prices for all five energy price proxies during the first two months after the monetary shock. Since these policies have now become part of a central bank's arsenal during financial turmoil and may be used in future crises, these results shed light on their potential impact energy prices.

Keywords: Unconventional monetary policy; qual-VAR; panel-VAR; commodity prices; oil prices; energy futures prices; GSCI index; Bloomberg commodity index.

1. Introduction

During the financial crisis in the US (2007–2009) and the financial crisis in the EU (2010–2013) central bank rates, an important conventional (standard) monetary policy tool which has an impact on economic expectations and prices, reached their zero lower bound; thus, becoming ineffective as a policy tool in dealing with the crisis and the financial turmoil. The response of many major central banks was to adopt unconventional (non-standard) monetary policy actions (see, among others, Fawley and Neely [2013]). For instance, the European Central Bank (ECB) initiated procedures where liquidity at the main refinancing rate was provided to euro-area financial institutions via currency swaps, collateral extensions and covered bond purchases, (Supplementary Long-Term Refinancing Operations (SLTROs) and "Very" Long-Term Refinancing Operations (VLTROs)). In addition, between 2010 and 2012 the ECB announced the Securities Markets Programme (SMP), i.e. direct purchases of Greek, Portuguese and Irish government bonds, and the Outright Monetary Transactions (OMTs), i.e. purchases of bonds from countries in adjustment programmes.

In this chapter, we address a gap in the relevant literature, and examine the effect of ECB's unconventional monetary policy measures on energy prices; that is, we examine if, and to what extent, ECB's expansionary unconventional monetary policy shocks affected energy prices. We focus on ECB's policy since recent studies examine Fed's monetary policy effects on energy and commodity prices: Rosa [2014], with an event study methodology, examines the impact of both Fed's standard and non-standard policy measures on energy futures prices and finds that monetary policy surprises have a significant impact on both the level and the volatility of prices trading volume; Basistha and Kurov [2015] find that energy prices exhibit a negative and significant intraday response to Fed funds target changes subsequent to policy announcements. This response, however, becomes insignificant for the days following the announcement and, in addition, using a VAR methodology they find an insignificant effect of monetary policy on oil prices.

Note that many authors have argued that monetary conditions affect commodity prices. For instance, Frankel [1986] demonstrates that there is a theoretical link between interest rates and oil, while Bernanke *et al.* [1997] suggest that monetary policy could be used to eliminate any recessionary consequences of an oil price shock, while Barsky and Kilian [2004] find that oil price increases in the 1970s were also due to monetary policy regime changes and global liquidity, a result consistent with the findings of Taghizadeh and Yoshino [2014]. Frankel [2008] shows that there is a significant and relation between commodity prices and interest rates, while Yoshino and Taghizadeh [2014] find that following the 2007–2009 financial crisis in the US and the quantitative easing policy, the weaker dollar pushed oil prices upwards (see also, Anzuini *et al.* [2010]; among others). Note also that, recently, Lutz [2015] documents a link between monetary policy and investor sentiment.

We propose an alternative way to estimate the effects of unconventional monetary policy on commodity/oil prices, which combines binary information about ECB's announcements with an otherwise standard monetary policy VAR. Although VAR models are widely used by macroeconomists, their inability to handle unconventional monetary policy measures such as SMP, OMT and LTROs actions as endogenous factors constitutes a major disadvantage of conventional VAR modeling. We produce dynamic forecasts and employ a Qual VAR [Dueker, 2005] model that is based on the single-equation dynamic ordered probit model of Eichengreen *et al.* [1985] and Dueker [1999].

The main advantage of the Qual VAR is its capability to handle a binary variable as endogenous, allowing the use of unconventional monetary policy announcements as an endogenous factor of the system, after modeling the interaction with business cycle variables. The continuous latent variable deriving from the model mirrors the propensity to unconventional monetary policy, and results after the estimation of the dynamic probit model through Markov Chain Monte Carlo (MCMC) techniques. The continuous series on monetary policy's propensity to ECB's unconventional measures deriving from the model is then entering a Panel VAR as a regressor with the capability of delivering Forecast Error Variance Decompositions (FEVDs) and Impulse Response Functions (IRFs). This approach allows the combination of traditional VAR procedures with a panel-data approach (see [Love and Zicchino, 2006]).

Our results indicate that the non-standard ECB monetary policies during the recent financial crises had a significant and negative impact on energy prices. For example, we find that these policies accounted for approximately 10% of the price variance for the Light Crude Oil Futures Contract, during the crises. The second more important contribution has been to the Bloomberg Commodity Index where 8.42% of price volatility is explained. In addition, IRFs suggest that an increase in the ECB's propensity to unconventional monetary policy decreases energy prices for all five energy price proxies during the first 2 months after the monetary shock.

These results have implications for monetary policy makers, market participants and investors, since they shed further light on the impact of non-standard monetary policy tools on energy prices, which in turn affect consumer prices, inflation and output. Also, since unconventional monetary policies have now become part of a central bank's arsenal during financial turmoil and crisis, and thus may be used in future crises, these results shed light on the potential impact of these policies on important economic variables, such as energy prices.

The rest of the chapter is organized as follows: Section 2 presents the data and the testing methodologies, Section 3 presents the results, while Section 4 concludes the chapter.

2. Data and Testing Methodology

For the empirical analysis, we employ monthly data on oil prices, macroeconomic aggregates, investor sentiment proxy and financial variables (see, among others, Galariotis *et al.* [2018]), for the period between May 2007 and October 2012. All data are obtained from EIKON and Bloomberg. More specifically, our sample consists of nine Eurozone countries, Germany, France, Netherlands, Belgium, Austria, Spain, Portugal, Italy and Greece. For these countries, we collect data on Industrial Production (IP), Stock Returns (Stock_Ret, main equity indexes), Consumer Prices (HICP) and Economic Sentiment (ESI). As a proxy for energy price developments we use the future prices for Brent (ICE, continuous settlement price – U$/BL) denoted as *ICE_BCO*, the futures prices for Light Crude Oil (NYM, continuous settlement price – U$/BL) denoted as *NYM_LCO*, the futures prices for Natural Gas (ICE, continuous settlement price – SP/TE) denoted as *ICE_NG*, the Standard and Poor's GSCI Index (S&P GSCI) denoted as *GSCI* and the Bloomberg Commodity Index denoted as *BCOM*.

2.1. *Measuring unconventional monetary policy: A Qual VAR approach*

Recent studies that examine the effect of unconventional monetary policies employ a binary variable which takes the value of one in the month of surprise (unexpected) monetary policy announcement and zero otherwise. One way to ensure that the events employed are significant and unexpected is to focus only on events and announcements related to SLTROs, SMP and OMT that appeared in the front page of financial newspapers (e.g. the *Financial Times*) on the day following the announcements. Table A.1 presents a list of the unexpected events related to non-standard policies employed in this study (for more details and a discussion see Fratzscher *et al.* [2013, 2014]). Fratzscher *et al.* [2014] examine the global effect of ECB policies and find that these policies have a positive spill-over effect on global markets (higher equity prices, lower risk aversion, lower risk).

With these announcements, we construct a binary variable, which we then transform to a continuous latent variable with the use of Qual VAR model of Dueker [2005]. This model is based on the single-equation dynamic ordered probit model (see Eichengreen *et al.* [1985] Dueker [1999]). The latent variable that is derived from the Qual VAR model mirrors the propensity to non-standard monetary policy and is obtained following the estimation of a dynamic probit model through MCMC techniques. Thus, we are able to employ non-standard monetary policy announcements as an endogenous factor in a Panel VAR system. This way, all variables constitute the same vector autoregressive system, and the only variable needed to produce multi-step forecasts is the dependent variable's own history (see for more details Meinusch and Tillmann [2016], Assenmacher-Wesche and Dueker [2010]).

To describe the model more formally (see Dueker [2005]; Assenmacher-Wesche and Dueker [2010]) suppose y^* is a latent variable (Eq. (1)) that captures non-standard monetary policies. The binary variable y_t takes the value one if unconventional policy actions occur in period t and zero otherwise. That is, the value of the binary variable y_t takes the form:

$$y_t = \begin{cases} 0 & \text{if } y_t^* \leq 0 \\ 1 & \text{if } y_t^* \geq 0\,. \end{cases} \tag{1}$$

The latent variable is estimated as in Eq. (2):

$$y_t^* = \delta + \sum_{l=1}^{\rho} \varphi_l y_{t-l}^* \sum_{l=1}^{\rho} \beta_l X_{t-l} + e_t, \quad e_t \sim N(0, 1). \tag{2}$$

It is an autoregressive process of order ρ that depends on the constant δ, a set of explanatory variables X_{t-P} (lagged) and own past values. The terms φ and β are coefficient vectors, while e_t is the random error term from a standard normal distribution. Finally, the time index is denoted as $t = 1, \ldots$ T. The second component of the model, is a VAR (ρ) process for the dynamics of k regressors:

$$Y_t = \mu + \sum_{l=1}^{\rho} \Phi^l Y_{t-l} + \nu_t, \quad \nu_t \sim N(0, \Sigma) \tag{3}$$

In (3) there is a $k \times 1$ vector $Y_t = \left(X_t, y_t^*\right)'$.$k - 1$ time series of observed macroeconomic data constitute the X_t while y_t^* complements a vector of the latent variable. The set of VAR coefficients are shown as:

$$\Phi^l = \begin{bmatrix} \Phi_{XX}^{(l)} & \Phi_{Xy^*}^{(l)} \\ \Phi_{y^*X}^{(l)} & \Phi_{y^*y^*}^{(l)} \end{bmatrix}. \tag{4}$$

In (4) μ is a $k \times 1$ vector of constants and ν_t comprises the $k \times 1$ error vector and the covariance matrix of the errors is Σ. The complete Qual VAR system is derived from the linear relation between the regressors and the latent variable.

MCMC techniques (Gibbs Sampling) can be employed to estimate the model. This makes possible the generation of posterior samples by sweeping through each variable and/or block of variables, in order to sample from its conditional distribution, while keeping the remaining variables fixed (see for details, Dueker [2005], Assenmacher-Wesche and Dueker [2010]). Next, Kalman Smoothing techniques allow the derivation of the different states mean and variance, in other words, the latent variable (which is conditional on its own previous and future values and the rest of the variables). In a second stage, from the binary data and the OLS coefficient estimates (given the binary data) initial values are obtained for use in the Smoother, and then a latent variable is drawn from the truncated Normal. In a third stage, the estimation of the VAR model takes place utilizing the sampled time series of the latent variable and OLS estimates for Φ and Σ (denoted by $\hat{\Phi}$ and $\hat{\Sigma}$).

The assumed Jeffrey's prior and the above information conduct a draw for Σ from the inverted Wishart distribution with $T - k$ degrees of freedom. Note that T mirrors the number of observations, k the number of explanatory variables and $(\mathrm{T}\hat{\Sigma})^{-1}$ describes the covariance from OLS:

$$\Sigma \sim IW\left\{\left(\mathrm{T}\hat{\Sigma}\right)^{-1}, T - k\right\}. \tag{5}$$

The latent variable's variance equals unity and thus the appropriate element in Σ is adjusted and a normalization of the rest of the elements in the corresponding column takes place.

We next add the OLS estimates mean to the draw, following a multivariate Normal distribution with a covariance matrix which stands for the Kronecker product, draws for Φ, given Σ, and derive of the draw for Σ and $(Y'Y)^{-1}$:

$$\Phi \sim \mathrm{N}\left\{\hat{\Phi}, \Sigma \otimes (Y'Y)^{-1}\right\}. \tag{6}$$

If a sufficiently large number of iterations takes place (we run 10,000 iterations and discard the first 5,000 for convergence towards the posterior distribution [Dueker, 2005], then the draw from either conditional distribution represents a draw from the joint posterior distribution.

Then the VAR coefficients and variance are derived from the resulting sample. The binary variable enters the model as y_t $\{0, 1\}$ and, along with the remaining variables in the X_t vector, is employed in order to derive the latent propensity to non-standard monetary policy of ECB unconventional monetary policy measures ECB, i.e. y_t^*, (y-star).

As discussed above, the variables that we include in the model proxy for energy prices, the Eurozone business cycle, the financial markets' response on ECB's unconventional monetary policy stance and expectations are OIL, IP, HICP, Stock_Ret, ESI, respectively. We conclude to a six-variable Qual VAR model i.e. OIL, IP, HICP, ystar, Stock_Ret, ESI. We adopt five different Qual VAR models for each one of the countries of our sample, since we investigate the effects of monetary policy on energy prices by using five different proxies, namely the future prices for

Brent, the futures prices for Light Crude Oil, the futures prices for Natural Gas, the Standard and Poor's GSCI Index and the Bloomberg Commodity Index.

The model is estimated in first differences in order for the variables to be stationary and thus consistent with the assumptions in the MCMC estimations, as well as with the concept of the latent variable. To identify monetary policy shocks, we follow Christiano *et al.* [1999]'s recursive ordering. We use a Cholesky decomposition based on the following ordering of variables for the model: *OIL, IP, HICP, ystar, Stock_Ret, ESI.*

We list first in the ordering as the most exogenous variable in the system, the oil prices, since it is a global factor and affects all variables in the system contemporaneously. We considered alternative orderings, but the change in ordering does not affect our analysis and conclusions. As lag selection criteria are not defined for binary data we choose to use three lags in our Qual VAR system, which is appropriate for a short sample according to Meinusch and Tillmann [2016]. We also implement multivariate Q-tests which confirm the absence of serial correlation in the residuals of each estimated model.

In order to study the effects on a regional basis, Eurozone as a whole, we enter the latent variable filtered out of the Qual VAR model in a panel VAR model. In this setting, all variables in the system are treated as endogenous, while allowing for unobserved individual heterogeneity.

With this approach we are now able to apply the panel-data approach based on the PVAR routine written by Love [Love and Zicchino, 2006]. First, a first-order six-variable VAR model is specified:

$$Z_{i,t} = \gamma_o + \gamma_1 Z_{i,t-1} + f_i + u_t \quad i = 1, \ldots, N, \quad t = 1, \ldots T. \tag{7}$$

The time invariant fixed effects in (7) are expressed with $u_t \sim i.i.d.(0, \Sigma)$ and f_i.

We present results from (7) based on IRFs and Variance Decompositions (VDs), and utilize a Cholesky decomposition of the variance-covariance matrix of residuals, i.e. orthogonality is ensured. In order to identify unconventional monetary policy shocks, we adopt the recursive ordering of Christiano *et al.* [1999], i.e. *OIL, IP, HICP, ystar, Stock_Ret, ESI.* We also consider alternative orderings; however, the results remain qualitatively the same.

Since we have five different proxies for energy prices, we estimate five different Panel VAR models one for each proxy: the future prices for Brent, the futures prices for Light Crude Oil, the futures prices for Natural Gas, the Standard and Poor's GSCI Index and the Bloomberg Commodity Index. We allow for individual heterogeneity in levels by introducing fixed effects, however, simple-mean differencing will provide biased estimators, as fixed effects are correlated with the regressors due to lags of the dependent variables. In order to avoid that we follow Love and Zicchino [2006] and introduce the forward mean-differencing procedure of Helmert transformation and estimate coefficients with system GMM.

To analyze the impulse response functions we calculate the standard errors of the impulse-response functions and generate confidence intervals using Monte Carlo simulations with 200 replications. Therefore, whenever the zero line lies outside the confidence bands there is evidence of a statistically significant response to the shock inflicted.

3. Results

In Table 1, Panel A, we present descriptive statistics for the main variables. The panel unit root tests of IPS test suggest that we strongly reject the null hypothesis of a unit root, for all sample variables (available upon request). The next step is the lag selection for the PVAR model. In order to decide on the lag structure, we

Table 1. Descriptive statistics.

Descriptive statistics					
Variable	**Obs**	**Mean**	**Std. dev.**	**Min**	**Max**
ESI	594	−0.3936	2.5906	−10.8	7.2
IP	594	−0.0015	0.0230	−0.0846	0.0894
HICP	594	0.0065	0.4220	−1.6	2.3
STOCK	594	−0.0064	0.0713	−0.2782	0.2192
ICE_BCO	594	0.0071	0.0965	−0.4074	0.2544
NYM_LCO	594	0.0041	0.1039	−0.3948	0.2601
ICE_NG	594	0.0205	0.1505	−0.6190	0.4361
GSCI	594	−0.0029	0.0812	−0.3312	0.1795
BCOM	594	−0.0029	0.0632	−0.2400	0.1221

Notes: Panel A presents descriptive statistics for the following variables: The Stock market returns (denoted as Stock_Ret), the Industrial Production index (denoted as IP), the Harmonized Index of Consumer Prices (denoted as HICP) and the Economic Sentiment Indicator (denoted as ESI), the future prices for Brent (ICE, continuous settlement price – U$/BL), the futures prices for Light Crude Oil (NYM, continuous settlement price – U$/BL), the futures prices for Natural Gas (ICE, continuous settlement price – SP/TE), the Standard and Poor's GSCI Index (S&P GSCI) and the Bloomberg Commodity Index. All-time series are transformed to ensure stationarity; Harmonized Index of Consumer Prices and Economic Sentiment Indicator are used in first differences, Stock market returns, Industrial Production, the future prices for Brent, the futures prices for Light Crude Oil, the futures prices for Natural Gas, the Standard and Poor's GSCI Index and the Bloomberg Commodity Index in log differences. All data are monthly and obtained from EIKON and Bloomberg. The sample covers the period between May 2007 and October 2012.

use Hansen's [1982] J-statistic and corresponding p-value, and moment model selection criteria developed by Andrews and Lu [2001] based on the J-statistic (available upon request).

The results indicate that the optimal lag structure is one lag. Nevertheless, in order to enhance a six–variable VAR model with richer dynamics, we choose a panel VAR model with four lags (the results after using the lags proposed by the model selection criteria remain qualitatively the same).

In Fig. 1, we report evidence on the stability properties of each one of the five estimated PVAR models, which requires the moduli of the eigenvalues of the dynamic matrix to lie within the unit circle, which is the case in our estimated model.

As discussed above, to identify monetary policy shocks, we follow Christiano *et al.* [1999] and use a Cholesky decomposition based on the following ordering

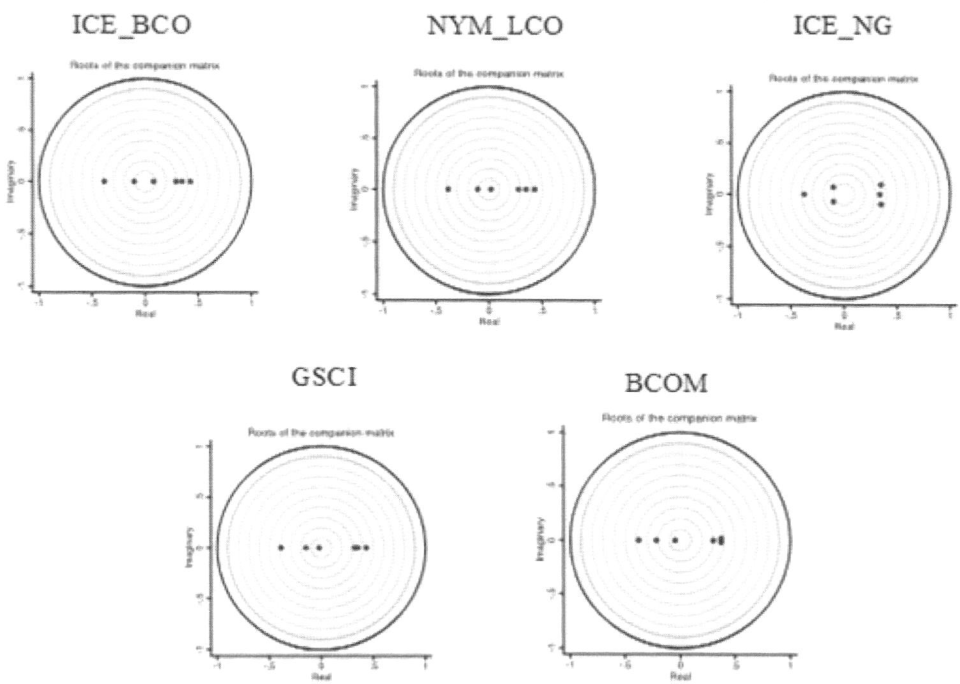

Fig. 1. Roots of companion matrix.

Notes: The stability of the panel VAR requires the moduli of the eigenvalues of the dynamic matrix to lie within the unit circle. Panel VAR for all five models (first, second, third, fourth and fifth model the one including ICE_BCO, NYM_LCO, ICE_NG, GSCI and BCOM prices, respectively) satisfies stability condition as all eigenvalues lie inside the unit circle.

(note that, as Lutkepohl and Poskitt [1991] argue, the ordering of the variables makes little difference when the residual correlation is small) of the variables with oil prices listed first as the most exogenous variable in the system: OIL, IP, HICP, ystar, Stock_Ret, ESI. Note that we also employ alternative orderings and the results (available upon request) remain qualitatively the same. We focus and present results on the underlying moving average (MA) representation of the VAR model, i.e. the IRFs and the associated Forecast Error Variance Decompositions (FEVDs). These two combined convey information on how each variable responds to a surprise change (a shock) to another variable in the system.

As discussed above, we employ the Qual VAR model in order to derive the ECB's latent propensity to unconventional monetary policy measures, (ystar), based on our initial binary variable. We then employ this continuous variable in our Panel VAR model for all variables and for each one of the five different oil prices in a panel data set. Figures 1–6 present this variable for each country for each one of the five different energy proxies, i.e. the estimated latent propensity to unconventional monetary policy measures for each one of the sample countries. During the announcement dates (shaded areas) this series is required to be positive [Meinusch and Tillmann, 2016]. The ECB's latent propensities appear very similar for countries, an expected result since ECB's monetary stance is common. The sharp increases underline their magnitude.

Table 2 presents the FEVD results for the Eurozone countries after running a panel VAR with four lags for each one of the five different proxies employed, that is for the future prices for Brent, the futures prices for Light Crude Oil, the futures prices for Natural Gas, the Standard and Poor's GSCI Index and the Bloomberg Commodity Index (Panel A, B, C, D and E, respectively).

The results indicate that unconventional measures have a significant effect on energy prices, where 6.78%, 10.06%, 7.92%, 6.56% and 8.42% of the total variance of each variable is explained, for the future prices for Brent, the futures prices for Light Crude Oil, the futures prices for Natural Gas, the Standard and Poor's GSCI Index and the Bloomberg Commodity Index, respectively. Unconventional policy shocks account more for the future prices for Light Crude Oil where 10.06% of price volatility is explained. The second more important contribution is to the Bloomberg Commodity Index, where 8.42% of price volatility is explained.

Figure 7 presents orthogonalized IRFs and the 95% error bands generated by Monte Carlo simulation (200 repetitions) obtained with the Panel VAR model on the effect of Unconventional Monetary Policy on energy prices. Note that the response

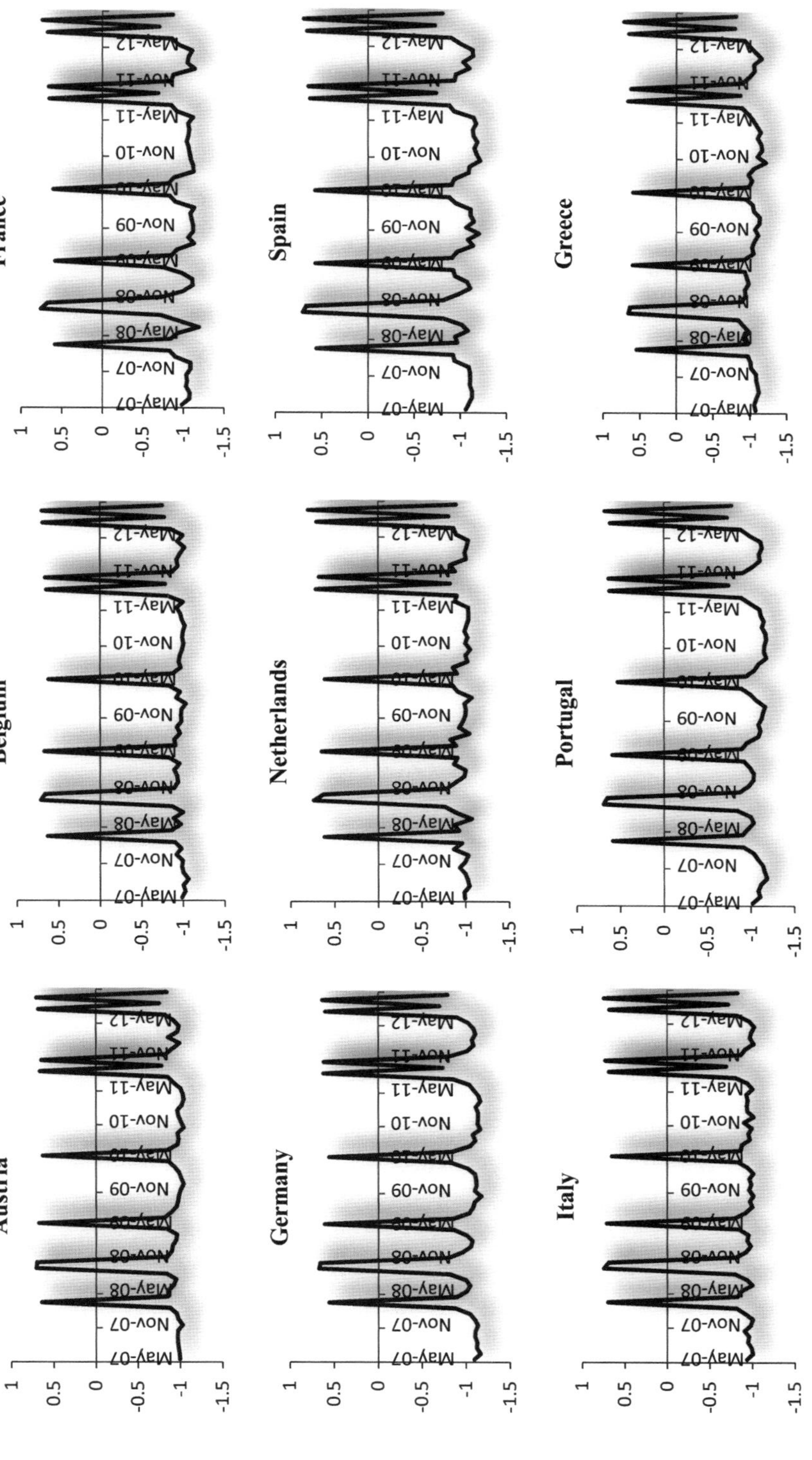

Fig. 2. ECB announcements (shaded) and latent propensity for ECB unconventional monetary measures (dash line) for Eurozone countries, ICE_BCO.

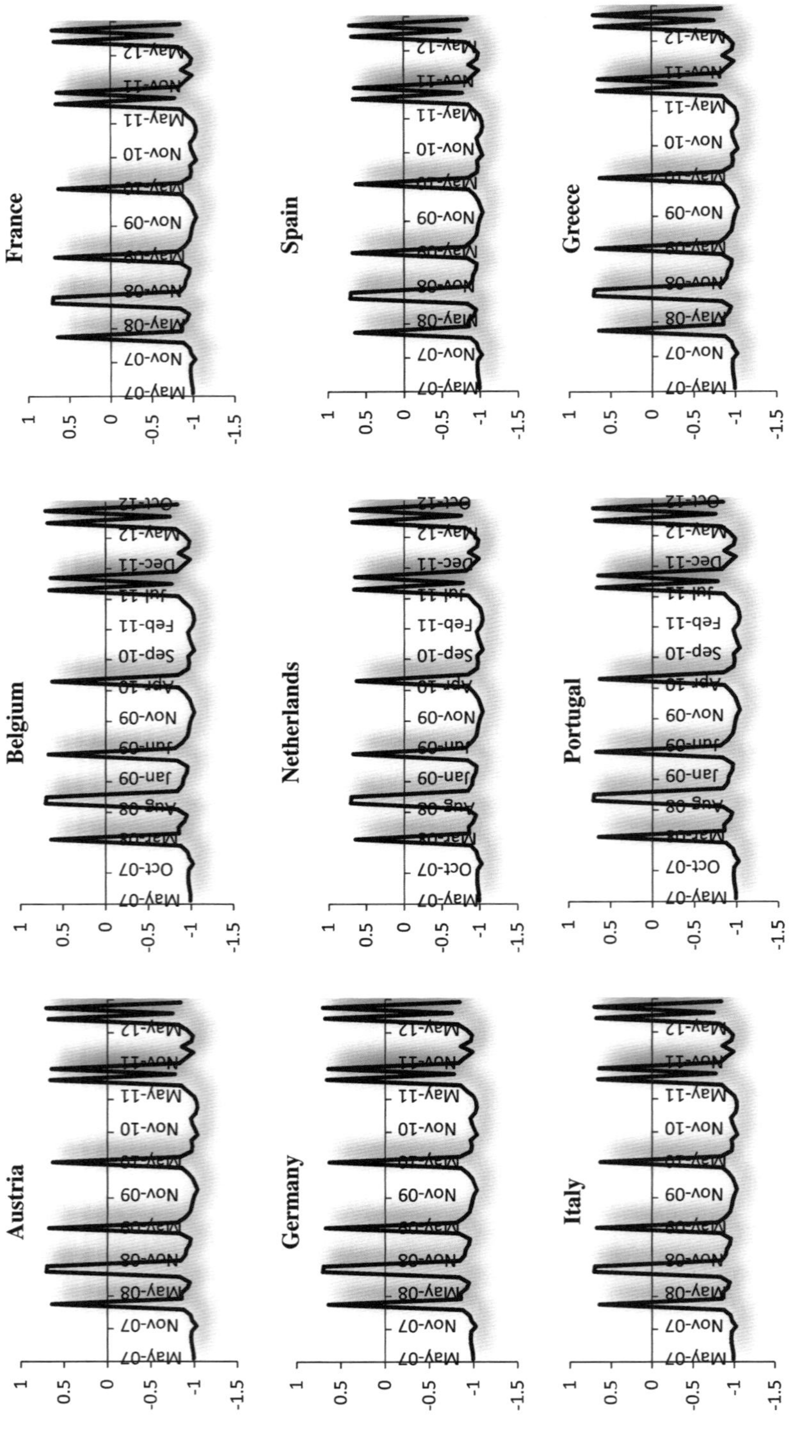

Fig. 3. ECB announcements (shaded) and latent propensity for ECB unconventional monetary measures (dash line) for Eurozone countries, NYM_LCO.

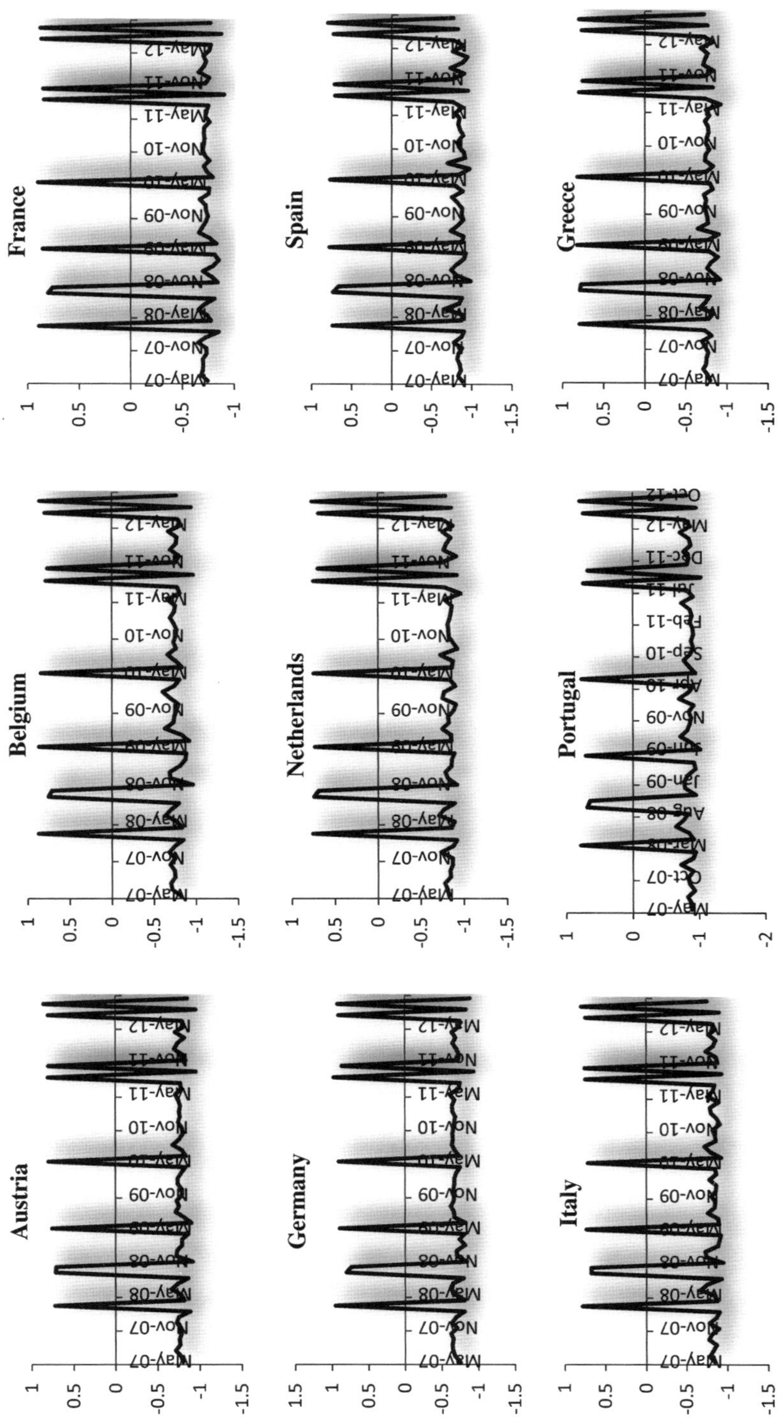

Fig. 4. ECB announcements (shaded) and latent propensity for ECB unconventional monetary measures (dash line) for Eurozone countries, ICE_NG.

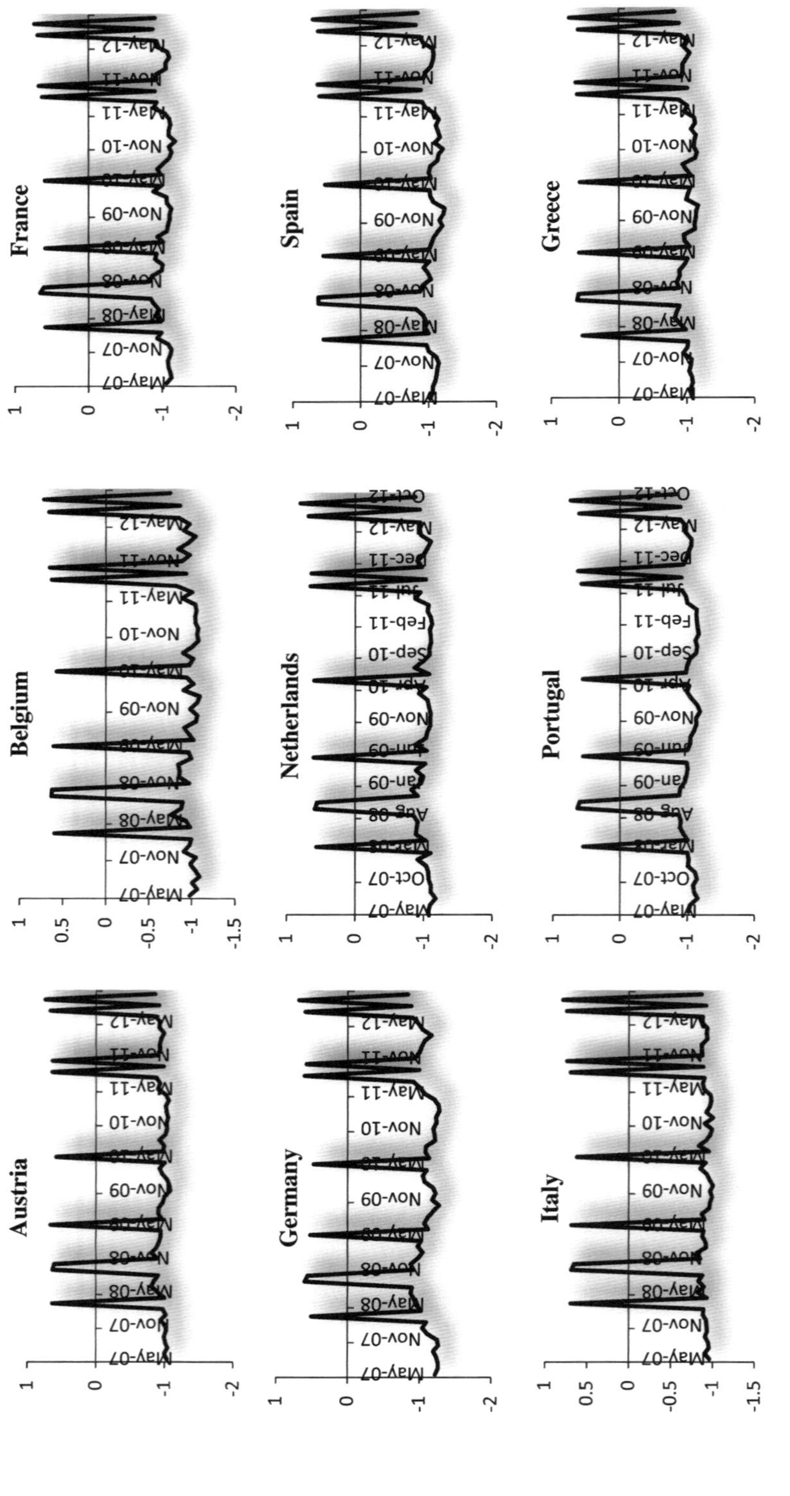

Fig. 5. ECB announcements (shaded) and latent propensity for ECB unconventional monetary measures (dash line) for Eurozone countries, GSCI.

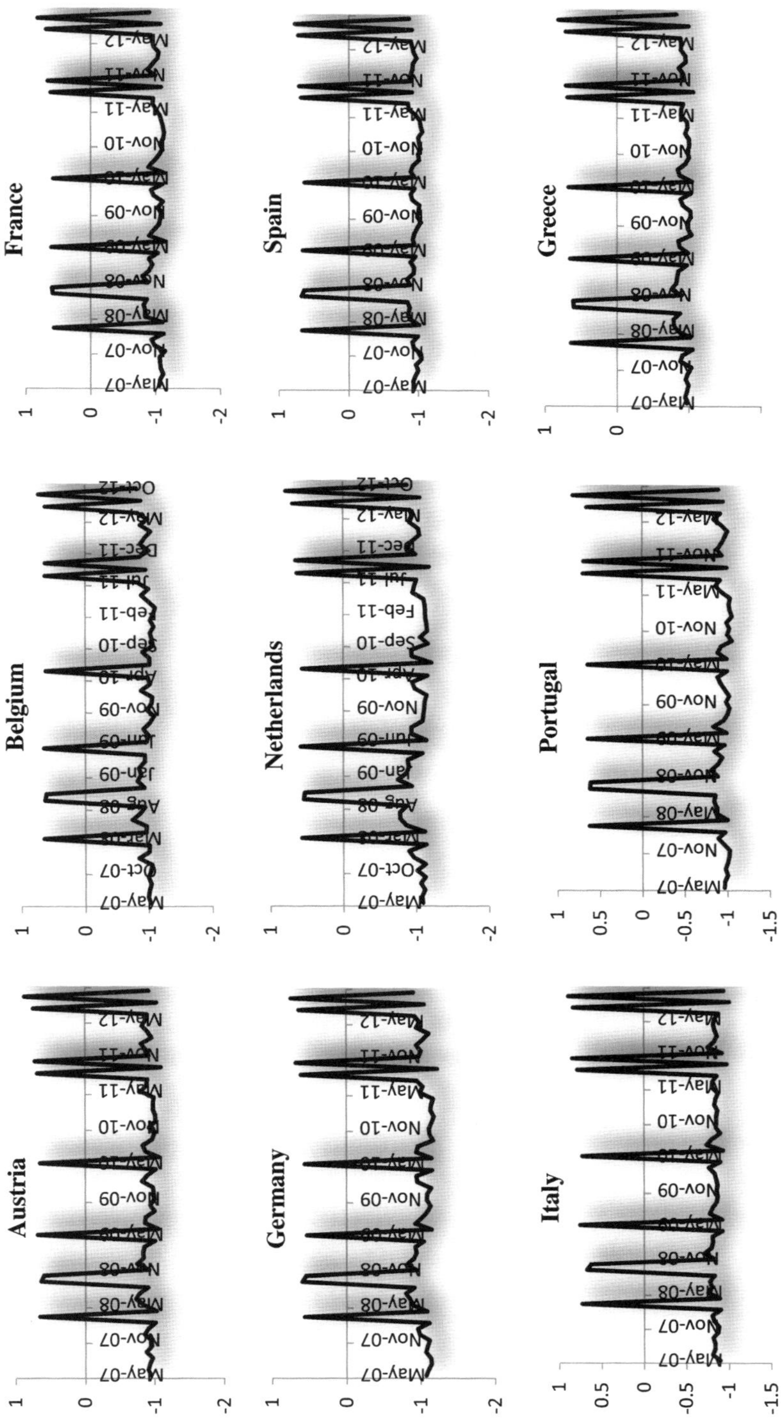

Fig. 6. ECB announcements (shaded) and latent propensity for ECB unconventional monetary measures (dash line) for Eurozone countries, BCOM.

Table 2. Panel-VAR and FEVDs with latent variable from qual var.

Panel A
(Brent futures prices)

Impulse variable / ystar	Response variables					
	ICE_BCO	IP	HICP	ystar	Stock_Ret	ESI
Europe	6.78	5.04	9.18	80.75	12.92	3.28

Panel B
(Light crude oil futures prices)

Impulse variable / ystar	Response variables					
	NYM_LCO	IP	HICP	ystar	Stock_Ret	ESI
Europe	10.06	4.44	8.5	76.68	11.53	2.28

Panel C (Natural gas futures prices)

Impulse variable / ystar	Response variables					
	ICE_NG	IP	HICP	ystar	Stock_Ret	ESI
Europe	7.92	5.97	5.76	74.7	12.6	9.71

Panel D
(Standard and poor's GSCI index)

Impulse variable / ystar	Response variables					
	GSCI	IP	HICP	ystar	Stock_Ret	ESI
Europe	6.56	5.82	11.57	81.58	11	4.73

Panel E
(Bloomberg commodity index)

Impulse variable / ystar	Response variables					
	BCOM	IP	HICP	ystar	Stock_Ret	ESI
Europe	8.42	6.16	10.15	83.04	14.6	5.46

Notes: The table presents results (four lags) for the contribution of ECB's latent propensity to unconventional measures (ystar) to the variance in each column variable (OIL, IP, HICP, ystar, Stock_Ret and ESI) for the Eurozone countries. The results are computed from a panel VAR with four lags. Note that we report here only the results for the response variables after a ystar shock (the rest of the results are available upon request).

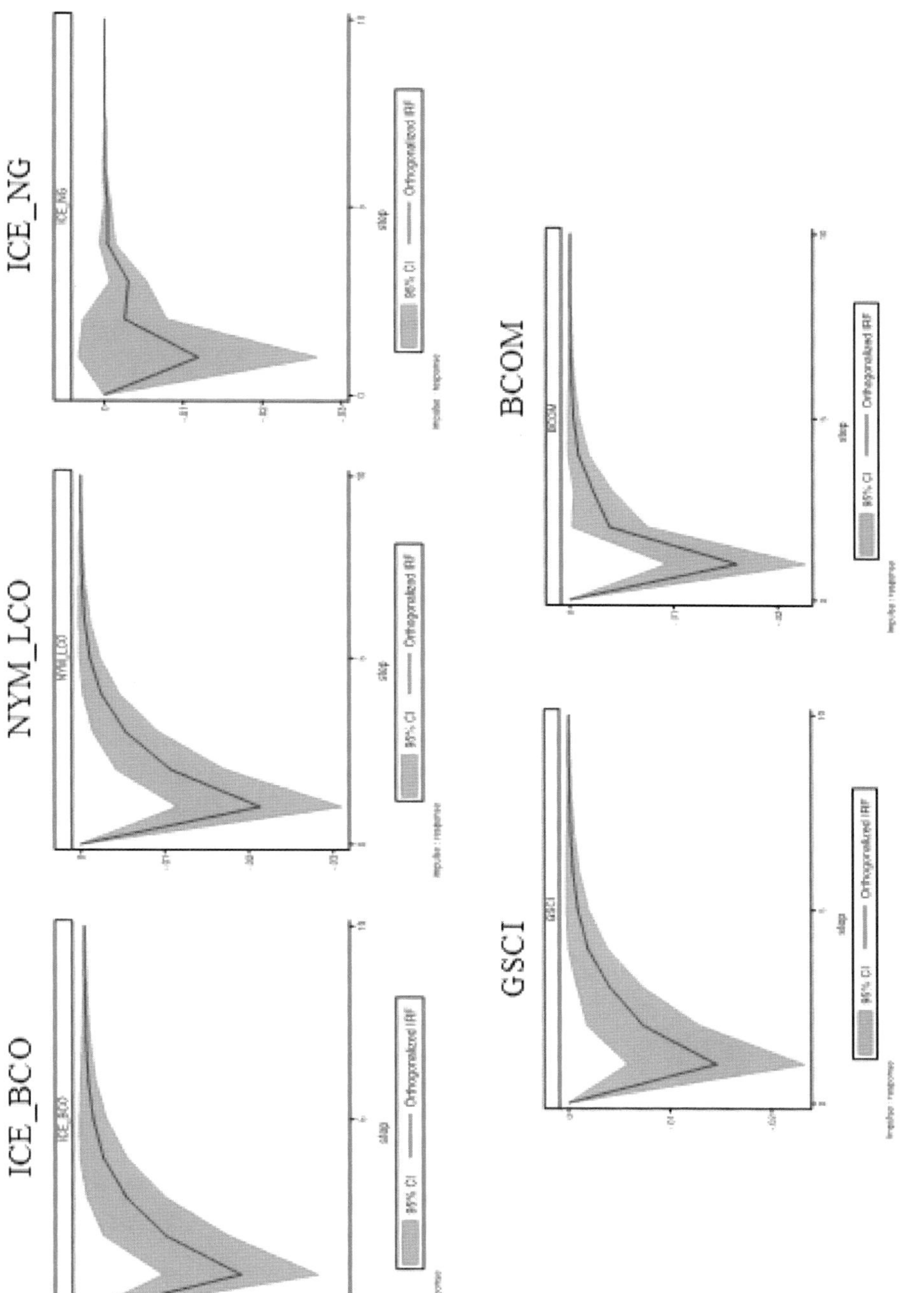

Fig. 7. The effect of a shock of ECB's unconventional policy stance on energy prices.

is similar for all energy price proxies, that is, there is a negative response to a shock in ECB's unconventional monetary policy. More specifically, the results indicate that an increase in the ECB's propensity to unconventional monetary policy decreases energy prices for all five energy price proxies during the first 2 months after the monetary shock.

4. Conclusion

In order to deal with the financial crisis in the US (2007–2009) and the financial crisis in the EU (2010–2013), many central banks implemented a number of unconventional (non-standard) monetary measures, since standard policies were not adequate to tackle the magnitude of these crises. Many previous studies suggest that monetary conditions affect energy and commodity prices (see, among others, Barsky and Kilian [2004], Taghizadeh and Yoshino [2014], Frankel [2008], Anzuini *et al.* [2010]). Most of these studies, however, examined conventional monetary policies. Only recently, Rosa [2014] examined the impact of both Fed's standard and non-standard policy measures on energy futures prices [see also Basistha and Kurov, 2015].

In this chapter, we address a gap in the relevant literature, and examine the effect of ECB's unconventional monetary policy measures on energy prices; that is, we examine if, and to what extent, ECB's expansionary unconventional monetary policy shocks affected energy prices. We propose an alternative way to estimate the effects of unconventional monetary policy on energy prices, which combines binary information about ECB's announcements with an otherwise standard monetary policy VAR. We produce dynamic forecasts and employ a Qual VAR [Dueker, 2005] model that is based on the single-equation dynamic ordered probit model of Eichengreen *et al.* [1985] and Dueker [1999]. The main advantage of the Qual VAR is its capability to handle a binary variable as endogenous, allowing the use of unconventional monetary policy announcements as an endogenous factor of the system, after modeling the interaction with business cycle variables.

Our results indicate that the non-standard ECB monetary policies during the recent financial crises had a significant and negative impact on energy prices. For example, we find that these policies accounted for approximately 10% of Light Crude Oil Futures price variance during the crises. The second more important contribution has been to the Bloomberg Commodity Index where 8.42% of price volatility is explained. In addition, IRFs suggest that an increase in the ECB's propensity to unconventional monetary policy decreases energy prices for all five energy price proxies during the first 2 months after the monetary shock.

Since unconventional monetary policies have now become part of a central bank's arsenal during financial turmoil and crisis, and thus may be used in future crises, these results shed light on the potential impact of these policies on important economic variables, such as energy prices.

Acknowledgments

Spyros Spyrou acknowledges financial support from the Research Centre at Athens 7 University of Economics and Business (RC-AUEB). Spyros Spyrou: This paper was prepared during a Sabbatical leave at Audencia Business School, France. I would like to thank colleagues at Audencia Business School for comments and suggestions on an earlier draft of this paper. Panagiota Makrychoriti acknowledges financial support from the General Secretariat of Research and Technology (GSRT, Greece) and the Research Centre at Athens University of Economics and Business (Action II, EP-2882).

Appendix

Table A.1. Press coverage of ECB actions.

Date	Event	Financial Times Headline	Headline Article	Front Page	VIX	Dummy
28/3/2008	6 month SLTROs	*US back-up for Iraqi offensive*	No	No	−0.17	AN_SLTROs
4/9/2008	Roll over of the outstanding 6 month SLTROs	*US stock s suffer on fear for economy*	No	No	2.6	AN_SLTROs
15/10/2008	6 month SLTROs and other measures	*Fresh squall rattles mark ets*	No	No	14.12	AN_SLTROs
7/5/2009	12 month SLTROs and other measures (including covered bond purchases)	*Us banks must add $74.6bn in equity*	No	Text	0.99	AN_SLTROs
4/6/2009	Details for the purchase programme of covered bonds	*Obama appeal to muslims*	No	No	−0.84	
10/5/2010	SMP and other measures	*Markets rally on EU bail-out*	Main text	—	12.11	AN_SMP
30/6/2010	Completion of covered bond purchases	*EU bank bonus rules sow confusion*	No	No	0.41	
4/8/2011	SLTROs and other measures	*Stock markets plunge worldwide*	Main text	—	8.28	
7/8/2011	SMP reactivation	*Traders braced for more turmoil*	Main text	—	16	AN_SMP
6/10/2011	12 month SLTROs and covered bond purchases	*ECB raids policy cupboard*	Title	—	−1.54	AN_SLTROs
8/12/2011	36 month VLTROs and other measures	*European banks' shortfall at €115bn*	—	—	1.92	
26/7/2012	Mr. Draghi's Speech "whatever it takes"	*Nomura axe falls on top staff*	No	Title	−1.81	AN_OMT
6/9/2012	Details for the OMT	*ECB signals resolve to save euro*	Title	—	−2.14	AN_OMT

Notes: Column "Event" describes the policy announcement; "Financial Times Headline" indicates the title of the "top story" on the front page of the *Financial Times*; "Headline Article" indicates where the ECB action is mentioned in the top story on the front page of the *Financial Times* (title, subtitle or text); "Front page" indicates where the ECB action is mentioned on the front page of the *Financial Times*, if not in the "top story" (title, subtitle, main text).

References

Andrews, D. W. K., Lu, B. (2001). Consistent model and moment selection procedures for GMM estimation with application to dynamic panel data models. *Journal of Econometrics* **101** (1), 123–164.

Anzuini, A., Lombardi, M. J. and Pagano, P. (2010). The impact of monetary policy shocks on commodity prices. Working paper. The European Central Bank.

Assenmacher-Wesche, K. and Dueker, M. (2010). Forecasting macro variables with a Qual Var business cycle turning point index. *Applied Economics* **42** (23), 2909–2920.

Barsky, R. B. and Kilian, L. (2004). Oil and the macroeconomy since the 1970s. *Journal of Economic Perspectives* **18**, 115–134.

Basistha, A. and Kurov, A. (2015). The impact of monetary policy surprises on energy prices. *Journal of Futures Markets* **35** (1), 87–103.

Bernanke, B. S., Gertler, M. and Watson, M. (1997). Systematic monetary policy and the effects of oil price shocks. *Brookings Papers on Economic Activity* **1**, 91–142.

Christiano, L., Eichenbaum, M. and Evans, C. (1999). Monetary policy shocks: What have we learned and to what end? *Handbook of Macroeconomics* **1** (A), 65–148.

Dueker, M. (1999). Conditional heteroscedasticity in qualitative response models of time series: A Gibbs-sampling approach to the bank prime rate. *Journal of Business & Economic Statistics* **17** (4), 466–472.

Dueker, M. (2005). Dynamic forecasts of qualitative variables: A Qual VAR model of US recessions. *Journal of Business & Economic Statistics* **23** (1), 96–104.

Eichengreen, B., Watson, M. W. and Grossman, R. S. (1985). Bank rate policy under the interwar gold standard: A dynamic probit model. *The Economic Journal* **95** (379), 725–745.

Fawley, B. W. and Neely, C. J. (2013). Four stories of quantitative easing. *Federal Reserve Bank of St. Louis Review*, January/February 2013, **95** (1), 51–88.

Frankel, J. A. (1986). Commodity expectations and commodity price dynamics: The overshooting model. *American Journal of Agricultural Economics* **68**, 344–348.

Frankel, J. A. (2008). The effect of monetary policy on real commodity prices. In J. Y. Campbell (ed.), *Asset Prices and Monetary Policy* (University of Chicago Press, Chicago) pp. 291–333.

Fratzscher, M., Lo Duca, M. and Straub, R.(2013). On the international spillovers of US quantitative easing. ECB Working Paper No. 1557.

Fratzscher, M., Duca, M. L. and Straub, R. (2014). ECB Unconventional Monetary Policy Actions: Market Impact, international Spillovers and Transmission Channels. Paper presented at the 15th Jacques Polak Annual Research Conference Hosted by the International Monetary Fund, Washington, DC, November 13–14.

Galariotis, E., Makrichoriti, P. and Spyrou, S. (2018). The impact of conventional and unconventional monetary policy on expectations and sentiment. *Journal of Banking and Finance* **86**, 1–20.

Love, I. and Zicchino, L. (2006). Financial development and dynamic investment behavior: Evidence from panel VAR. The *Quarterly Review of Economics and Finance* **46** (2), 190–210.

Lütkepohl, H. and Poskitt, D. H. (1991). Estimating orthogonal impulse responses via vector autoregressive models. *Econometric Theory* **7** (4), 487–496.

Lutz, C. (2015). The impact of conventional and unconventional monetary policy on investor sentiment. *Journal of Banking & Finance* **61**, 89–105.

Meinusch, A. and Tillmann, P. (2016). The macroeconomic impact of unconventional monetary policy shocks. *Journal of Macroeconomics* **47**, 58–67.

Rosa, C. (2014). The high-frequency response of energy prices to US monetary policy: Understanding the empirical evidence. *Energy Economics* **45**, 295–303.

Taghizadeh, H. F. and Yoshino, N. (2014). Monetary policies and oil price determination: An empirical analysis. *OPEC Energy Review* **38**, 1–20.

Yoshino, N. and Taghizadeh, H. F. (2014). Monetary policy and oil price fluctuations following the subprime mortgage crisis. *International Journal of Monetary Economics and Finance* **7** (3), 157–174.

Chapter 30

Chaos Versus Stochastic Paradigm in Energy Markets

Loretta Mastroeni* and Pierluigi Vellucci†

Department of Economics, Roma Tre University, Via Silvio D'Amico 77, 00145 Rome, Italy

**loretta.mastroeni@uniroma3.it*

†pierluigi.vellucci@uniroma3.it

The purpose of the chapter is to gain a better understanding of energy market movements and dynamics by examining two competing theories: deterministic chaos theory and stochastic paradigm. We advocate that feature of both worlds may coexist in the same phenomenon. In particular, we reassess the chaotic paradigm, by considering the advances that have been made in the design of estimation tools. We illustrate all the methodologies exploited in the energy finance literature and the related results.

Keywords: Chaos; butterfly effect; energy futures; time series analysis; energy prices; sensitive dependence on initial conditions; predictability; determinism; noise; self-similarity.

1. Introduction

1.1. *Uncertainty in energy market*

Uncertainty is assuming a major role in the energy markets: several factors (like temperature or macroeconomic events, for example) drive the demand for electricity, natural gas, heating oil, crude oil, whose prices are subject to frequent price fluctuations on a short- and long-term basis.

The constant changing of the markets can make it difficult to model the price process correctly. In particular, the liberalization of energy markets has produced the need to build suitable tools and models and the choice of importing the dominant paradigm of the financial markets (related to the random walk hypothesis). Over the years, several (stochastic) models have been introduced, taking into account the properties observed in the historical database of spot prices.

More specifically, starting from the basic stochastic models based on arithmetic and geometric Brownian motions, and introducing adjustments — like the mean reversion property, the regime switching, and others — many attempts have been made to take into account the characteristics and peculiarities of the various energy markets (see for instance [Geman, 2009; Pilipovic, 2007]). Such models are all rooted in the random walk model and therefore in the noise theory, which is constrained by the weak form of the Efficient Market Hypothesis (EMH) — the cornerstone of the efficiency paradigm. The EMH states that present security prices fully reflect all information consisting of past prices: an "efficient market" is one in which assets are fairly priced according to the information available, and neither buyers nor sellers have an advantage. From a mathematical point of view, the EMH states that market is a martingale or a "fair game".

Crashes in financial markets have resulted in considering the possibility to explore other roads, in particular, deterministic chaos theory, which seems to be endowed with more explicative power in some financial contexts. The adoption of chaos theory entails that the EMH does not apply, in full or in part, which leads to the use of nonlinear analysis tools.

As for the chaos approach, an important reason to be interested in it is that chaotic behavior could potentially explain fluctuations in many time series which appear to be random. The question is whether such random-looking data are really random or completely/partially deterministic. If they are completely random, then their behavior is hard to be predicted anyway; otherwise, it is possible to predict a deterministic system in short periods of time (whereas long prediction is impossible, due to instability of chaotic systems). Hence, this distinction provides the predictability degree of the analyzed system.

In particular, in energy markets, evidence of deterministic chaos would have important implications for both regulators and short-term trading strategies.

1.2. *The chaotic paradigm*

In this chapter, we wish to reassess the chaotic paradigm by considering the main estimation tools existing in the literature and the advances that have been made in their design. We illustrate all the methodologies exploited in the energy finance literature and the related results.

We consider in particular the problem of future prices forecasting in energy markets, whose behavior has been the subject of many research efforts. Though the large mainstream of activities has revolved around the use of statistical tools, an alternative approach emerged at the end of the eighties, which adopted a nonlinear deterministic paradigm (chaos) instead of a stochastic one. A steady streak of papers has been published since then to assess whether the chaotic approach could replace the stochastic one [Adrangi *et al.* 2001; Barkoulas *et al.* 2012; Chwee, 1998; Kyrtsou *et al.* 2009; Matilla-Garcia, 2007; Moshiri and Foroutan, 2006; Panas and Ninni, 2000; Serletis and Gogas, 1999].

All studies relied on the analysis of the time series of prices as observed on the major markets, and all arrived at a sharp conclusion: either support or reject the chaotic paradigm.

However, this dichotomy does not need to be a strict rule. Actually, we advocate that feature of both worlds may coexist in the same phenomenon. In addition, all the papers mentioned above adopted tools that were based on the assumption that either paradigm is present, but not both, which may lead to strong biases in the results [Mastroeni *et al.* 2018a, 2018b].

1.3. *A controversial matter*

The presence of chaos in the time series of energy markets is a controversial matter. In the literature on energy markets, one finds that the evaluations performed over the years show contrasting results, which, on the other hand, might also be due to a misunderstood application of the theoretical aspects of chaos theory. In this connection, we draw attention to the role, among others, of butterfly effect in the Devaney's chaos definition, giving emphasis on the misleading results about ostensible chaoticness of the time series.

As mentioned above, we also highlight the coexistence of chaotic and stochastic behavior. In Mastroeni *et al.* [2018a, 2018b], we rely on the use of an analysis tool for chaotic phenomena that incorporates the presence of noise (a stochastic feature) rather than ignoring it. This tool will be presented, behind the others, in the section devoted to methodologies.

1.4. *Outline of the paper*

The chapter is organized as follows: In Section 2, we present the features of one of the most popular properties of chaos, in the framework of energy literature. In Section 3, we introduce the definition of chaos. Section 4 is devoted to the methodologies of chaos theory applied to the framework of energy and commodity markets. The reader less interested in the mathematical aspects of our analysis can skip Section 4 and go to Section 5 which deals with the existing applications in energy markets literature.

2. "Butterfly Effect" in Energy Markets

In the literature, chaos is considered as an alternative to randomness for systems of complex behavior. One of the most famous (and simplest) example of chaotic system is the *logistic map*:

$$x_{n+1} = r\, x_n(1 - x_n)\,,$$

where x_n could represent the ratio of existing population to the maximum possible population, and is comprised between zero and one. The parameter r takes values in the interval $(0, 4]$. The logistic map is *chaotic* (later, we will focus on the meaning of "chaos") for a particular range of r.

Another notable system that allows for chaotic solutions (for certain parameter values and initial conditions) is the *Lorenz system*, a simplified mathematical model for atmospheric convection. The model is described by a system of three ordinary differential equations:

$$\frac{\mathrm{d}x}{\mathrm{d}t} = \sigma(y - x),$$

$$\frac{\mathrm{d}y}{\mathrm{d}t} = x(\rho - z) - y,$$

$$\frac{\mathrm{d}z}{\mathrm{d}t} = xy - \beta z.$$

Here, x, y and z represent the system state, t is time and σ, ρ, β are the system parameters. Both logistic map and Lorenz system show a very complex dynamics even if they are deterministic. From a technical standpoint, in both cases we start from a mathematical model (of one or more equations). Nevertheless, in many practical situations a mathematical model might not be available, which make it necessary to work with time series.

Nonlinear dynamics may be able to explain a large set of time series behaviors. In particular, it might be useful to investigate whether the nonlinearities are consistent with chaotic time paths, whose properties could be of special interest for commodity market observers. Among the others, let's mention the property that deterministic time series may show an apparent stochastic behavior.

That issue is strictly connected with the problem of unpredictability. Unpredictability is one of the features of chaotic systems. If we consider a chaotic system in the phase space (i.e. a space in which it is possible to represent the system state) the distance between two close trajectories increases exponentially over time. Thus, the knowledge of one of the two trajectories gives no information on the other one. Such a phenomenon is also known as "sensitive dependence on initial conditions" or "butterfly effect".

The trajectories divergence (and so the unpredictability) can be quantified through the Lyapunov exponents, which will be defined later.

The interest in possible chaotic behavior of commodity price series is related to the time series forecasting in the short run. In fact, a couple of decades ago, several studies showed that this (nonlinear) analysis may provide good results in predicting the price behavior in many financial contexts. See for instance, among others, [Osler and Chang, 1995; Clyde and Osler, 1997] and references therein.

The possibility of forecasting, even if limited to the short period, represents at any rate a basic theoretical motivation for the search of tools based on nonlinear methods.

There is a basic theoretical motivation underpinning the possibility of forecasting in the short time. Let us consider the time series y_n and assume that there exists a system (g, f, x_0) such that $y_n = g(x_n)$, $x_{n+1} = f(x_n)$, where x_0 is the initial condition at the initial time $n = 0$, g maps the m-dimensional phase space $\mathbb{R}^m$ to $\mathbb{R}$, and f maps $\mathbb{R}^m$ to $\mathbb{R}^m$. The function f maps an unknown (to the econometrician) dynamics that governs the evolution of the unknown (to the econometrician) state x_0. The econometrician observes y_n. The task is to uncover information about (g, f, x_0) from observations y_n. The time series y_n, which we will assume as the data time series under analysis, has a chaotic explanation if x_n is chaotic. The question is whether it is possible to forecast a chaotic series. Intuitively, the butterfly effect usually does not allow long-term forecasting of chaotic series. If we slightly change the value of the initial point: $x_0 \mapsto x_0' = x_0 + \delta x_0$, the point x_n at discrete time n will also be changed (see Fig. 1).

It may happen that, when time becomes large, the small initial distance δx_0 grows anyway, and it may grow exponentially fast: $\delta x_n \sim \delta x_0 e^{\lambda n}$, for some $\lambda > 0$. The term δx_n represents the uncertainty induced by perturbations. Hence, with given δx_0 and λ, it is bounded if $e^{\lambda n}$ is bounded and so if n is as small as possible ($n = 1$ or $n = 2$, for instance): this is the short-term forecasting of chaotic series, which is possible because δx_n is amplified at a finite rate $e^{\lambda n}$. Accordingly, for chaotic time series, if one knows (g, f) and could measure x_n without error, one could perfectly forecast x_{n+i} and, thus, y_{n+i} in the short time (let us say a few days when dealing with daily data).

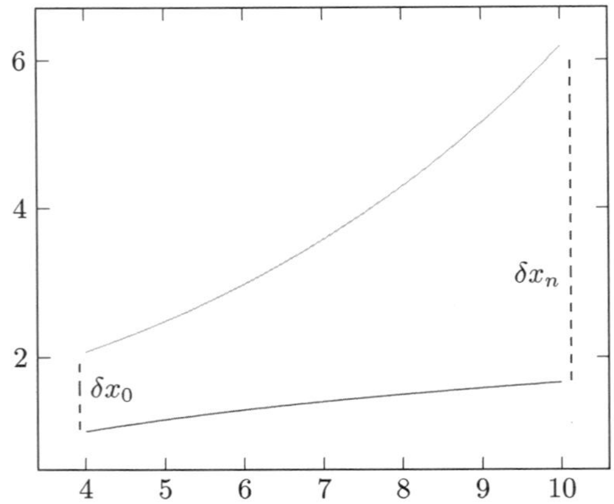

Fig. 1. Effect of a small change of initial condition.

3. Definition of Chaos

The theory of dynamical systems [Devaney *et al.*, 1989] is devoted to understand the asymptotic behavior of an iterative process. When this process is a differential equation with respect to an independent variable t (time), the theory attempts to predict the ultimate behavior of the solutions of the equation for large values of time ($t \to \infty$). However, in several practical applications, one frequently works on time series which can be thought to be derived from a discrete dynamical system, i.e. from the iteration of the function (map) f, introduced in Section 2. In this case, the theory aims to detect the eventual behavior of the points x, $f(x)$, $f^2(x), \ldots, f^n(x)$ as the discrete time n becomes large.

In this context, a notion of *chaotic behavior* naturally arises, i.e. roughly speaking, something which has to do with *unpredictability* and *sensitive dependence on initial conditions*. Among the several possible definitions of chaos, in this chapter we will focus on the Devaney's definition:

Definition 1 (Devaney's Definition). Let X be a set. $f : X \to X$ is said to be chaotic on X if

(1) f has sensitive dependence on initial conditions;
(2) f is topologically transitive;
(3) periodic points are dense in X.

A map possesses sensitive dependence on initial conditions if there exist points arbitrarily close to x which eventually separate from x by at least δ under iteration of f, i.e. if there exists $\delta > 0$ such that, for any $x \in X$ and any neighborhood N of x, there exist $y \in N$ and $n \geq 0$ such that $|f^n(x) - f^n(y)| > \delta$.

If a map possesses sensitive dependence on initial conditions, then for all practical purposes, the dynamics of the map cannot be obtained with numerical computations. This is due to the fact that small errors in computation, introduced by round-off, may magnify upon iterations [Devaney *et al.* 1989].

A topologically transitive map has points which eventually move under iteration from one arbitrarily small neighborhood to any other. In a certain sense, transitivity is an irreducibility condition because the dynamical system cannot be decomposed into two disjoint open sets which are invariant under the map.

Devaney wrote: "To summarize, a chaotic map possesses three ingredients: unpredictability, indecomposability, and an element of regularity. A chaotic system is unpredictable because of the sensitive dependence on initial conditions. It cannot be broken down or decomposed into two subsystems (two invariant open subsets) which do not interact under f because of topological transitivity. And, in the midst of this random behaviour, we nevertheless have an element of regularity, namely the periodic points which are dense" [Devaney *et al.* 1989].

In the works of Banks *et al.* [1992], Assaf and Gadbois [1992] and Vellekoop and Berglund [1994], the self-consistency of Devaney's definition is investigated. It is proven that (2) and (3) imply (1) in any metric space X, but, for general maps, this is the only redundancy: (1) and (2) do not imply (3), and (1) and (3) do not imply (2).

In the literature, there also exists an "experimental" definition of chaos, widely used by many non-mathematicians, particularly physicists, engineers and economists, and it consists of condition (1) of Definition 1, the sensitive dependence on initial conditions. There are a lot of numerical tests for this property, but this definition of chaos, as we already said, is not satisfactory. See, for instance, the counterexample 3.3 in the paper by Martelli *et al.* [1998].

The importance of the "experimental" definition of chaos is motivated by its widespread diffusion in the literature. Some papers [Matilla-Garcia, 2007; Panas and Ninni, 2000; Serletis and Gogas, 1999] claim to have discovered the evidence of "chaos", but this term is actually abused: all the papers mentioned above investigate the butterfly effect that, as we just said, is only one of the properties of a chaotic system. It is not a negligible particular. As they rightly say, "the theory is practice", to mean that the effectiveness of a theory is based on its ability to generate a knowledge of phenomena so accurate as to allow for the formulation of reliable forecasts. This also means that an insufficient regard to theoretical aspects might yield unreliable results. The contrasting results about the presence of butterfly effect (chaos) in commodity futures markets — which seem to be clear from the energy literature (see [Mastroeni and Vellucci, 2017]) — may be generated, for example, by this misunderstanding.

4. Methodologies

By way of the following sections, we explain step by step the methodologies of chaos theory applied to the framework of energy and commodity markets. We will see in the next section how these methodologies are employed in the literature.

4.1. *State space reconstruction and the embedding dimension m*

Let the price of a commodity at time t be denoted by p_t, then log returns are measured as $r_t = \ln \frac{p_t}{p_{t-1}}$. A scalar time series $\{r_t, t = 1, 2, \ldots, n\}$, $n \in \mathbb{N}$ represents the markets' observations, which can be used to reconstruct the state space (the so-called "phase space") [Packard *et al.*, 1980]. The phase space is defined as the multidimensional space whose axes consist of variables of a dynamical system. The asymptotic behavior of the dynamical system is related to an *attractor*, whose dimension will provide a measure of the minimum number of independent variables able to describe the dynamical system. The state space reconstruction is the fundamental step for recovering the properties of the original attractor from a scalar time series. In this respect, it is possible to prove that an attractor, which is topologically equivalent to the scalar time series, can be reconstructed from a dynamical system of N variables by using a method of time delay coordinate [Takens, 1981; Ruelle, 1989]. The reconstructed attractor of the original system is given by the vector sequence

$$\mathbf{s}_i = \left(r_i, r_{i+\tau}, r_{i+2\tau}, \ldots, r_{i+(m-1)\tau}\right), \tag{1}$$

where τ is an appropriate time delay, m is the embedding dimension and index i varying on $\{1, 2, \ldots, n - (m - 1)\tau\}$. Time delay and embedding dimension play a relevant role in the representation of the state vectors of the unknown original underlying system. Such representation is an accurate picture of the system dynamics, in the sense that it shall keep the information contained in *dynamical invariants* — which are defined as the conserved quantities along the phase space reconstruction and will be introduced in the next sections.

The implementation of Eq. (1) requires the correct choice of proper embedding parameters τ and m. An approach might be to select first τ and then m.

As documented in the literature, since τ plays no role in the mathematical framework, there exists no rigorous way of determining its value; in the literature, the issue of how to estimate τ has been extensively analyzed, and several methods have been suggested [Kantz and Schreiber, 2004]. We focus on the mutual information method. In particular, Fraser and Swinney [1986] proposed to use the first minimum of the mutual information between r_t and $r_{t+\tau}$ as the optimal embedding delay. The expression to be computed is based on Shannon's entropy. Here, we will not enter into details of the concept of entropy and its relation with information, but instead will just present the recipe for the computation of the mutual information.

We build a histogram of resolution ϵ for the probability distribution of the data, denoting by p_i the probability that $\{r_t\}_t$ assumes a value inside the ith bin, and by $p_{ij}(\tau)$ the probability that r_t is in bin i and $r_{t+\tau}$ is in bin j of the histogram. Then, the mutual information for time delay τ is defined as

$$I_\epsilon(\tau) = \sum_{i,j} p_{ij}(\tau) \ln p_{ij}(\tau) - 2 \sum_i p_i \ln p_i .$$

The first minimum of $I_\epsilon(\tau)$ characterizes the time lag where $r_{t+\tau}$ adds maximal information to the knowledge contained in r_t and so the redundancy is minimum. For a discussion of the controversial theoretical reasons for the existence of the minimum and of the advantages introduced by the method, see [Kantz and Schreiber, 2004, Section 9.2].

Estimation of the smallest sufficient embedding dimension has been performed through the method of the *false nearest-neighbours algorithm* (FNN algorithm) [Kennel *et al.*, 1992]. This method solves the problem of dummy overlappings caused by the projection of vectors $\mathbf{s}$ into a space of dimension m, with an m less than that required for a correct reconstruction. Such overlappings imply that the proximity of two points in the wrongly reconstructed space does not correspond to an actual proximity in a correctly reconstructed space (false nearest-neighbours).

In the FNN algorithm, the minimum embedding dimension is such that any further increase in the dimension does not significantly increase the distance between any two neighboring points in the trajectory. If we use the maximum norm, the statistics providing the fraction of false neighbors is [Kantz and Schreiber, 2004]

$$\mathrm{FNN}(r) = \frac{\sum_{i=1}^{n-m-1} \Theta\left(\frac{|\mathbf{s}_i^{(m+1)} - \mathbf{s}_{k(i)}^{(m+1)}|}{|\mathbf{s}_i^{(m)} - \mathbf{s}_{k(i)}^{(m)}|} - r\right) \Theta\left(\frac{\sigma}{r} - |\mathbf{s}_i^{(m)} - \mathbf{s}_{k(i)}^{(m)}|\right)}{\sum_{i=1}^{n-m-1} \Theta\left(\frac{\sigma}{r} - |\mathbf{s}_i^{(m)} - \mathbf{s}_{k(i)}^{(m)}|\right)}, \tag{2}$$

where r is the threshold on the distance between two neighboring points, $\Theta(\cdot)$ is the Heaviside step function

$$\Theta(x) = \begin{cases} 0, & x < 0 \\ 1, & x \geqslant 0, \end{cases} \tag{3}$$

$\mathbf{s}_{k(i)}^{(m)}$ is the closest neighbor to $\mathbf{s}_i$ in m dimensions, $k(i)$ is the index $k \neq i$ of the time series element for which we have the minimum $|\mathbf{s}_i - \mathbf{s}_k|$, and σ is a parameter such that we remove from counting all the pairs of points whose initial distance is already large (precisely larger than σ/r). It is possible to use some packages built for the R programming language; in particular: *timeLag* from package "nonlinearTseries", which gives a criteria for estimating a proper time lag τ; *false.nearest* from package "tseriesChaos", which performs the method FNN to help deciding the smallest sufficient embedding dimension m_d. The TISEAN package (see [Hegger *et al.*, 1999]) is also very popular.

The percentage of false nearest-neighbours estimated by the method will decrease with increasing m and, starting from its maximum at $m = 1$, it will become ideally zero at the correct embedding dimension. What we do in practice is to set a threshold FNN* establishing, as embedding dimension, the minimum value of m such that FNN $<$ FNN*. A very common choice is a threshold FNN* $= 0.5\%$ (as done, for example, in [Mastroeni and Vellucci, 2017; Mastroeni *et al.* 2018a, 2018b]).

Remark 1. We have to point out that the results of reconstruction are invariant under reasonable changes in the embedding procedure (the choices of τ and m). For a detailed discussion on how to make such reasonable choices we refer to [Kantz and Schreiber, 2004, Section 3.3].

Some authors, among those considered in the literature, do not even look for optimal embedding dimension and rather select a certain range of m, performing their estimations on that range. A similar approach does not allow to select an appropriate value for m. In fact, as explained in [Packard *et al.* 1980; Takens 1981; Kennel *et al.* 1992; Ruelle 1989], the FNN procedure identifies the number of "false nearest-neighbours", which correspond to points that appear to be the nearest neighbours because the embedding space is too small. When the number of false nearest-neighbours drops to zero, we have embedded the attractor in an m-dimensional Euclidean space. This is a rather delicate matter. If we choose $\bar{m} < m$, i.e. a dimension smaller than the appropriate embedding dimension m, we are viewing the attractor in a too small embedding space. Consequently, the estimation of the maximal Lyapunov exponent (MLE) might yield misleading results about the sensitive dependence on initial conditions of the analyzed time series. The same conclusion might occur in the case $\bar{m} > m$, even if, from a pure mathematical point of view, it does not matter whether one uses the minimum embedding dimension m or any $\bar{m} > m$ (see [Takens, 1981]). Actually, in more realistic terms, working in any dimension larger than the minimum one required by the data, leads to the problem of contamination by round-off or instrumental errors. In fact, this "noise" will affect the additional $\bar{m} - m$ dimensions of the embedding space, where no dynamics is operating (see [Kennel *et al.*, 1992]).

4.2. *Correlation dimension*

The correlation dimension was introduced by Grassberger and Procaccia [1983a, 1983b] and Kantz and Schreiber [2004]. It is based on the *correlation sum* of the time series, given by

$$C_m(\epsilon) = \frac{2}{N(N-1)} \sum_{i=1}^{N} \sum_{j=i+1}^{N} \Theta\left(\epsilon - \|\mathbf{s}_i - \mathbf{s}_j\|\right), \tag{4}$$

where $\mathbf{s}_i$ and $\mathbf{s}_j$ are two different points in the reconstructed phase space, as shown in (1), N is the number of sample points in the reconstructed phase space, and Θ is the Heaviside step function (3). For small ϵ and $N \to \infty$, we expect C to scale like a power law ϵ^D, and we can define the *correlation dimension* D by

$$d(N,\epsilon) = \frac{\partial \ln C(\epsilon)}{\partial \ln \epsilon}, \quad D = \lim_{\substack{\epsilon \to 0 \\ N \to \infty}} d(N,\epsilon).$$

The above definitions of the correlation sum and dimension involve phase space vectors. Thus, from a given scalar time series, we first have to reconstruct the phase space, for example by means of the embedding procedure described in Section 4.1.

The correlation dimension is a way to quantify the self-similarity[1] of a geometrical object and, in particular, of a data time series. When it is known that self-similarity is present in data time series, the correlation dimension is a tool to quantify it. Instead, if self-similarity still has to be established, it is not known whether the data are low dimensional deterministic, and so this concept is much less suited.

[1]The self-similarity is the property of an object to be exactly or approximately similar to a part of itself. It is also a typical property of fractals, which are of particular importance in the framework of chaos theory, since the graphs of most chaotic phenomenon are fractal.

When we try to describe some properties of a system compressing them into a number, we have to guarantee that such a quantity does not depend significantly on the measurement procedure, chosen coordinates, etc.: this property is called *invariance*. According to their definition, several quantities may fulfill such invariance requirement. For instance, the correlation dimension is invariant. However, the correlation sum at a given scale ϵ_0 is not. Thus, it is inadvisable to take $d(N, \epsilon_0)$ as an estimate for D.

The correct estimation of the correlation dimension from a time series is done in three steps: The first step reconstructs the attractor of the original system, given by the vector sequence (1). The second calculates the correlation sum expressed in (4), for several embedding dimensions m and for the available range of ϵ. Third, we look for a signature of self-similarity inspecting $C_m(\epsilon)$ and can compute a value for the correlation dimension when this signature is convincing enough.

As a signature of self-similarity, it is assumed the power law behavior of $C_m(\epsilon)$, which can be found by plotting the slope $D_m(\epsilon)$ of a double logarithmic plot of $C_m(\epsilon)$, i.e. $D_m(\epsilon) = \frac{\partial \ln C_m(\epsilon)}{\partial \ln \epsilon}$. Let us repeat this procedure in few dimensional embeddings (for example, $2-7$ is a common choice). If the choice of the dimensional embeddings number turns out to be insufficient, the computation goes on for higher values.

If it exists, that power law $C \propto \epsilon^D$ leads to $D_m(\epsilon) \propto D$. This means that, on the graph of $D_m(\epsilon)$, we are looking for a *plateau* (i.e. a range of ϵ for which the function $D_m(\epsilon)$ is approximately constant) which need not change with m. The height of that plateau — which will be, in general, an approximate value or a range of convincing values because of the imperfect flatness of the plateau — gives an estimation of the correlation dimension D.

Some authors (see [Panas and Ninni, 2000; Adrangi *et al.*, 2001; Barkoulas *et al.*, 2012]) estimate the correlation dimension employing methods based on Grassberger–Procaccia algorithm.

As for codes see, for instance, [Hegger *et al.*, 1999] and the TISEAN package.

4.3. *Maximal Lyapunov exponent*

As we have seen in the previous sections, initially close paths could end far apart and the knowledge of one of the two trajectories gives no information on the other one (the sensitive dependence on initial conditions).

Measuring for sensitive dependence on initial conditions can be done by a mathematical operation using what are called Lyapunov Exponents. Let $\mathbf{s}_{n_1}$ and $\mathbf{s}_{n_2}$ be two points in state space with distance $\|\mathbf{s}_{n_1} - \mathbf{s}_{n_2}\| = \delta_0 \ll 1$. Denote by $\delta_{\Delta n}$ the distance some time Δn ahead between the two trajectories emerging from these points, $\delta_{\Delta n} = \|\mathbf{s}_{n_1+\Delta n} - \mathbf{s}_{n_2+\Delta n}\|$. Then, the MLE λ is determined by

$$\delta_{\Delta n} \simeq \delta_0 e^{\lambda \Delta n}, \quad \delta_{\Delta n} \ll 1, \quad \Delta n \gg 1. \tag{5}$$

If λ is positive, which corresponds to an exponential divergence of nearby trajectories, then there is the butterfly effect. Naturally, two trajectories cannot split up farther than the size of the attractor, so that formula (5) is only valid during times Δn for which $\delta_{\Delta n}$ remains small. Otherwise, a saturation of the distance occurs and therefore (5) is violated. As a consequence, a more rigorous mathematical definition will have to involve a first limit $\delta_0 \to 0$ such that a second limit $\Delta n \to \infty$ can be performed without involving saturation effects. In this way, the exponent λ becomes a well-defined and invariant quantity. For further details, see [Kantz and Schreiber, 2004, Sec. 11.2].

To calculate λ, there exist several codes for different program languages. We mention, as examples, the routine R *lyap_k* from package "tseriesChaos" — which performs the algorithm proposed in [Rosenstein *et al.* 1993] — and the TISEAN package [Hegger *et al.* 1999].

The magnitudes of the Lyapunov exponents quantify a system's dynamics in information theoretical terms. The exponents represent the rate at which the system creates or distorts information [Shaw, 1981]. For example, consider a unit measuring error in two different commodity futures series, and denote with λ_1 and λ_2 their MLEs; then the error in the first series turns out to be amplified (or attenuated) $\frac{\lambda_1}{\lambda_2}$ times faster than in the second series.

The estimation of MLE is widespread in the energy markets literature (see [Barkoulas *et al.* 2012; Chwee, 1998; Kyrtsou *et al.* 2009; Matilla-Garcia, 2007; Panas and Ninni, 2000; Serletis and Gogas, 1999]).

4.4. *Kolmogorov entropy*

In addition to the MLE, the sensitive dependence on initial conditions can also be checked by the Kolmogorov entropy test. The definition of Kolmogorov entropy (or Kolmogorov–Sinai entropy [Kolmogorov, 1958], [Sinaĭ, 1959] or metric entropy) K can be found, for example, in [Farmer, 1982, eq. 7, p. 370]. In particular: (i) $K \geq 0$; (ii) K is infinite for random systems; and (iii) $K \neq 0$ for systems which show butterfly effect.

In [Pincus, 1991], the ApEn method is introduced to numerically quantify the (Kolmogorov) entropy content of a finite time series, as a measure of the regularity of the series itself. The regularity of the series clearly reflects in the predictability of the series. The ApEn computations are conceptually simple and detect the likelihood of repetitive patterns of fluctuation in a time series — the presence of such patterns rendering the series more predictable than in the case of their absence. ApEn needs two input parameters to be specified in order to evaluate the approximate entropy of a given time series: a block or run length m, and a tolerance window r. Then, the ApEn procedure first measures the logarithmic frequency with which runs of patterns that are close (within the tolerance window r) for m contiguous observations remain close (within the same tolerance r) in the subsequent incremental comparison. More in details, the ApEn algorithm can be formalized as described in [Benedetto *et al.*, 2016] and references therein, where a time series $x(n)$ of length N (i.e. with $n = 1, 2, \ldots, N$) sampled at time intervals T_s is considered. The length N can also be related to a time scale $T = N\,T_s$. Let us now select two m-dimensional sequence vectors, $u(i)$ and $v(j)$, defined as follows:

$$\mathbf{u}(i) = (x(i), x(i+1), \ldots, x(i+m-1));$$
$$\mathbf{v}(j) = (x(j), x(j+1), \ldots, x(j+m-1)),$$

with $i \neq j$, $i \geq 1$, and $j \leq Nm + 1$. The distance between these two sequences is defined as:

$$d_{u,v}(i, j) = \max\{\mathbf{u}(i+q) - \mathbf{v}(j+q)\}, \tag{6}$$

where $0 \leq q \leq m - 1$. If the distance expressed by (6) is smaller than a specified tolerance r, the two vectors are called similar. Then, for each of the $Nm + 1$ vectors $\mathbf{u}(i)$, the number of similar vectors $v(j)$ is given by measuring their respective distances. Now, if NV_i is the number of vectors $\mathbf{v}(j)$ similar to $\mathbf{u}(i)$, then the relative frequency $f_i(m, r, T)$ of finding a vector $\mathbf{v}(j)$ which is similar to $\mathbf{u}(i)$ within a tolerance level r and in the time scale T, is given by

$$f_i(m, r, T) = \frac{NV_i}{N - m}, \tag{7}$$

where $N - m$ is the number of vectors $\mathbf{v}(j) \neq \mathbf{u}(i)$ that are potentially similar to $\mathbf{u}(j)$. Now, we look at the relative frequency of the logarithm of (7), defined as

$$\phi(m, r, T) = \frac{1}{N - m + 1} \sum_{i=1}^{N-m+1} \ln f_i(m, r, T). \tag{8}$$

Finally, the approximate entropy is estimated by the following statistics [Martina *et al.* 2011]:

$$AE(m, r, T) = \frac{1}{T_S}[\phi(m, r, T) - \phi(m+1, r, T)]. \tag{9}$$

Widely used values for the first two input parameters are $m = 1, m = 2$ and $r = 20\%$ of the standard deviation of the analyzed time series.

In [Benedetto *et al.* 2015a, 2016] the predictability of commodity market time series is investigated by estimating their entropy (for a survey on the topic see [Benedetto *et al.* 2015b). The Kolmogorov entropy is also employed in [Adrangi *et al.* 2001; Panas and Ninni, 2000].

4.5. *Determinism test*

Even if the results obtained with the MLE may indicate the presence of butterfly effect, it is anyway important to compare the reliability of the results obtained about sensitive dependence on initial conditions. As we already said, some stochastic systems may show such sensitive dependence on initial conditions [Ikeguchi and Aihara, 1997; Tanaka *et al.* 1996, 1998]; thus, we propose to assume the results concerning a determinism coefficient as the reliability level (in percentage) of the MLE.

For this purpose, we explain the determinism test introduced by Kaplan and Glass [1992], referring to a package developed in the paper by Kodba *et al.* [2004].

The test is based on the reconstruction of the state space from the observed variable. To construct an approximate vector field of the system, the phase space is covered by equally sized boxes with the same dimension m as the reconstructed space. For each box, the average direction of the trajectory through the box during a particular pass is estimated. Each pass i of the trajectory through the kth box generates a unit vector, and the approximation for the vector field $\mathbf{V}_k$ in the kth box of the phase space is defined as the average vector of all passes. In [Kaplan and Glass, 1992], κ is defined as the weighted average of $\mathbf{V}_k$ with respect to the average displacement per step, R_k^m, of a random walk. In this way, the determinism coefficient κ is equal to one for a deterministic system, while $\kappa = 0$ for a random walk. Then, for the intermediate cases, κ measures the distance of the time series from a deterministic system and from a stochastic process. The idea is to take the *determinism coefficient* κ, obtained by the Kaplan and Glass test, as a measure of the reliability level (in percentage) of the test on sensitive dependence on initial conditions — as described in Mastroeni and Vellucci [2017]. Actually, it has been noted that time series generated from stochastic systems also may show positive MLE [Ikeguchi and Aihara, 1997; Tanaka *et al.* 1996, 1998].

A package of the test can be downloaded from M. Perc's Web page,[2] as described in [Kodba *et al.* 2004].

---

[2]M. Perc Web Page, http://www.matjazperc.com/ejp/time.html.

In the aforementioned literature, [Matilla-Garcia, 2007] (in addition to the above-mentioned [Mastroeni and Vellucci, 2017]) is the only paper which estimates the determinism coefficient. The approach followed in [Matilla-Garcia, 2007] employs a test developed by Kaplan [1994], which introduces a coefficient K. The non-zero value of K is interpreted as the level of non-determinism in the data. However, a range $K \in (0, \infty)$ is not very specific. For instance, it does not detect the level of determinism in the analyzed time series, it only assesses its order when compared with others.

4.6. *BDS statistic*

A popular assumption made in financial studies is that the log returns r_t of an asset are *iid* (independent and identically distributed) as a normal distribution with mean μ and variance σ^2. To detect the *iid* assumption of a time series, Broock *et al.* [1996] and Tsay [2005] propose a test statistic, commonly called *BDS test*.

The basic idea of the BDS test is to make use of the correlation sum (4) and proceed as follows. Fix, for example, an embedding delay $\tau = 1$ and consider the point (1) $\mathbf{s}_i$ in the m-dimensional space. If $\{r_t\}_{t=1}^n$ are actually *iid* random variables, then $\{\mathbf{s}_i\}_{i=1}^N$, where $N = n - m + 1$, should show no pattern in the m-dimensional embedding space. Accordingly, the correlation sum should satisfy the relation $C_m(\epsilon) = C_1^m(\epsilon)$. Let $C_m(\epsilon) = C_m(\epsilon, N)$; under the null hypothesis that $\{r_t\}_{t=1}^n$ are *iid* with a non-degenerated distribution function, the paper by Broock *et al.* [1996] shows that

$$\lim_{N\to\infty} C_m(\epsilon, N) = C_1^m(\epsilon) \text{ with probability 1,}$$

for any fixed m and ϵ. Let $C_1^m(\epsilon) = C_1^m(\epsilon, N)$. The BDS test statistic is defined as

$$D_m(\epsilon, N) = \frac{\sqrt{N}}{\sigma_m(\epsilon, N)} \left[C_m(\epsilon, N) - C_1^m(\epsilon, N)\right],$$

where

$$\sigma_m^2(\epsilon, N) = 4\Bigg[S^m(\epsilon, N) + 2\sum_{j=1}^{m-1} (S(\epsilon, N))^{m-j}\, C_1^{2j}(\epsilon, N) + (m-1)^2 C_1^{2m}(\epsilon, N) - m^2 S(\epsilon, N)\, (C_1(\epsilon, N))^{2m-2}\Bigg]$$

$$S(\epsilon, N) = \frac{6}{N(N-1)(N-2)} \sum_{t<s<u} \Theta\left(\epsilon - |r_t - r_s|\right) \Theta\left(\epsilon - |r_s - r_u|\right).$$

Finally, before applying the BDS test, it might be important to remove linear dependence, if any, from the data. The BDS test is employed by Panas and Ninni [2000] and Adrangi *et al.* [2001].

4.7. *Recurrence plots*

The method of recurrence plots (RPs) has been introduced in [Eckmann *et al.* 1987] to display the *recurrences* of dynamical systems. They can be viewed as approximate repetitions of certain events. Suppose we have a trajectory $\{\mathbf{s}_i\}_{i=1}^N$ (delay vectors of some embedding dimension) of a system in its phase space. Then, the corresponding RP is based on the following recurrence matrix:

$$R_{ij} = \Theta\left(\epsilon - |\mathbf{s}_i - \mathbf{s}_j|\right),$$

where $\Theta(\cdot)$ is the Heaviside step function and ϵ is a tolerance parameter to be chosen. The matrix compares the system states at times i and j. If the states are similar, this is indicated with $R_{ij} = 1$. On the contrary, if the states are rather different, the corresponding entry in the matrix is $R_{ij} = 0$. So, the matrix tells us the occurrence of similar states in the underlying system. The visual result is a plot consisting of points, diagonal lines as well as vertical and horizontal lines and their combinations (for example, the combination of vertical and horizontal lines forms rectangular patterns). In [Marwan *et al.* 2007], starting from several kinds of plot patterns, a qualitative interpretation of corresponding observations is provided: long and non-interrupted diagonals denote periodic motions, many single black points denote uncorrelated stochastic signal, while diagonal lines in the RP correspond to the predictability of the system, and so on. Among the references mentioned here, the RPs are used only in [Barkoulas *et al.* 2012; Mastroeni *et al.* 2018b].

Among others, the TISEAN package [Hegger *et al.*, 1999] offers to us also a practical implementation of RPs.

4.8. *Other methods*

The Kolmogorov–Sinai (KS) entropy can be approximated by the correlation entropy (CE) and, as we already said, it can be used to identify the presence of butterfly effect in a nonlinear dynamical system. Hence, CE gives an evaluation of the predictability of the time series. But the signal of the time series is blurred by the presence of noise, which introduces errors in the calculation of the correlation sum (4). To overcome this problem, Jayawardena *et al.* [2010] introduce a new quantity, the *modified correlation entropy* (MCE). It is an approximation of the KS entropy. For noise-free data, MCE and CE are equivalent. For noisy chaotic data, instead, the MCE represents a better approximation of the KS entropy, with respect to the general CE. Moreover, Jayawardena *et al.* [2008] present a method of estimating the noise level in a deterministic time series using a linear least-squares method. In two submitted papers by Mastroeni *et al.* [2018a, 2018b], we apply these methods to address the problem of noise in the copper and energy commodity price time series.

5. Applications to Energy Markets

The presence of butterfly effect in commodity futures markets is a controversial matter, as can be deduced from the literature reviewed below: some papers claim they have detected the presence of chaos (butterfly effect), while others state the opposite.

Chwee [1998] tests for the presence of butterfly effect using the NYMEX 1-month, 2-month, 3-month and 6-month daily natural gas settlement prices, from April 1990 to September 1996. The results fail to provide significant evidence of butterfly effect. Serletis and Gogas [1999] test for butterfly effect in seven Mont Belview, Texas hydrocarbon markets, using monthly data from 1985:1 to 1996:12 (for the markets of ethane, propane, normal butane, iso-butane, naptha, crude oil and natural gas) and find evidence of butterfly effect.

Panas and Ninni [2000] investigate butterfly effect in daily price data for two major petroleum markets, namely those of Rotterdam and of Mediterranean. The sample consists of the daily prices of different oil products from 4 January 1994 to 7 August 1998, resulting in 1161 observations, all collected from OPEC. The authors claim that their results, as summarized in Table 5 of their paper, show strong evidence of butterfly effect in a number of oil products considered.

Adrangi *et al.* [2001] investigate the presence of butterfly effect in crude oil, heating oil and unleaded gasoline futures prices from the early 1980s. Daily returns data from the nearby contracts are diagnosed by employing correlation dimension test, the BDS test and Kolmogorov entropy. They find strong evidence of nonlinear dependence in the data, but no consistency with chaos.

Moshiri and Foroutan [2006] examine daily crude oil futures prices from 1983 to 2003, listed in NYMEX and their test provides negative evidence of butterfly effect. Matilla-García [2007] studies the butterfly effect nature of three energy futures series — natural gas, unleaded gasoline and light crude oil — finding evidence in futures returns.

Kyrtsou *et al.* [2009] analyze five energy products (crude oil, gasoline, heating oil, propane and natural gas) over the period from 1994 to mid-January 2008, rejecting the null hypothesis of butterfly effect behavior.

Table 1. Datasets employed for energy prices analysis in the literature.

Market	Period start	Period end	Sampling	Reference
NYMEX	April 1990	Sept 1996	Daily	[Chwee, 1998]
Unspecified	Jan 1985	Dec 1996	Monthly	[Serletis and Gogas, 1999]
Unspecified	Jan 1994	August 1998	Daily	[Panas and Ninni, 2000]
NYMEX	Oct 1983	March 1995	Daily	[Adrangi *et al.* 2001]
NYMEX	Apr 1983	Jan 2003	Daily	[Moshiri and Foroutan, 2006]
NYMEX	Apr 1990	Jan 2006	Daily	[Matilla-Garcia, 2007]
Unspecified	Jan 1994	Jan 2008	Daily	[Kyrtsou *et al.* 2009]
Unspecified	Jan 1986	August 2011	Daily	[Barkoulas *et al.* 2012]

Table 2. Survey of methodologies employed in the literature.

Methods	[Chwee, 1998]	[Serletis and Gogas, 1999]	[Panas and Ninni, 2000]	[Adrangi *et al.* 2011]	[Moshiri and Foroutan, 2006]	[Matilla-Garcia, 2007]	[Kyrtsou *et al.* 2009]	[Barkoulas *et al.* 2012]
FNN	✗	✗	✗	✗	✗	✓	✗	✓
Correlation dimension	✗	✗	✓	✓	✓	✗	✗	✓
MLE	✓	✓	✓	✗	✓	✓	✓	✓
Kolmogorov entropy	✗	✗	✓	✓	✗	✗	✗	✗
Determinism test	✗	✗	✗	✗	✗	✓	✗	✗
BDS Statistic	✓	✗	✓	✓	✓	✓	✗	✗
RPs	✗	✗	✗	✗	✗	✗	✓	✓

Barkoulas *et al.* [2012] consider a data set which consists of daily oil spot prices covering the period 2 January 1985–31 August 2011. They do not find butterfly effect tendencies in the oil market, suggesting that "oil spot prices are the measured footprint of a stochastic rather than deterministic system" [p. 585]. See Tables 1 and 2 where a survey of datasets and methodologies employed in the literature of energy markets is shown.

6. Conclusions

A look at the literature of the last years would suggest that interest in the application of chaos theory in energy economics has progressively weakened. This might be due to many factors:

- insufficient regard to theoretical aspects, producing unreliable results (e.g. the abuse of term "chaos" in the "experimental" investigations);

- difficult replicability of the published results, hampered by inaccessible data and codes;
- complexity of the employed methods, not always accompanied by sufficient attention in their application (e.g. in the choice of optimal embedding dimension, in the consideration of noise possibly blurring the correlation dimension, in the interpretation of the slope $D_m(\epsilon)$ of the double logarithmic plot of $C_m(\epsilon)$, and so on);
- the sensitivity to the initial conditions shown by some stochastic systems, which may lead to biased or distorted results in the absence of the estimation of the determinism rate in the analyzed time series.

Nevertheless, paying attention to the issues raised by the above points, we think that chaos theory still plays a relevant role for the predictability of the energy markets time series. Indeed, chaotic behavior can potentially explain fluctuations in many time series which appear to be random. In particular, the presence of deterministic chaos would have important implications for regulators and short-term trading strategies in energy markets. Moreover, if the random walk model does not provide a proper account of market behavior, the relevance for the latter of the debated Efficient Market Hypothesis, with its basic role in financial markets, would also drop.

In other words, the basic question is whether random-looking data are really random or completely (or partially) deterministic. Its importance lies in the fact that while the behavior of completely random data is hard to be predicted anyway, it is possible to predict a deterministic system, although only on short periods of time, long prediction being instead impossible due to instability of chaotic systems.

References

Adrangi, B., Chatrath, A., Dhanda, K. K. and Raffiee, K. (2001). Chaos in oil prices? Evidence from futures markets. *Energy Economics* **23** (4), 405–425.

Assaf, D. and Gadbois, S. (1992). Definition of chaos. *American Mathematical Monthly* **99** (9), 865–865.

Banks, J., Brooks, J., Cairns, G., Davis, G. and Stacey, P. (1992). On Devaney's definition of chaos. *The American Mathematical Monthly* **99** (4), 332–334.

Barkoulas, J. T., Chakraborty, A. and Ouandlous, A. (2012). A metric and topological analysis of determinism in the crude oil spot market. *Energy Economics* **34** (2), 584–591.

Benedetto, F., Giunta, G. and Mastroeni, L. (2015a). A maximum entropy method to assess the predictability of financial and commodity prices. *Digital Signal Processing* **46**, 19–31.

Benedetto, F., Giunta, G. and Mastroeni, L. (2015b). Signal processing for financial markets. In *Encyclopedia of Information Science and Technology, 3rd Edn.* IGI Global. pp. 7339–7346.

Benedetto, F., Giunta, G. and Mastroeni, L. (2016). On the predictability of energy commodity markets by an entropy-based computational method. *Energy Economics* **54**, 302–312.

Broock, W. A., Scheinkman, J. A., Dechert, W. D. and LeBaron, B. (1996). A test for independence based on the correlation dimension. *Econometric Reviews* **15** (3), 197–235.

Chwee, V. (1998). Chaos in natural gas futures? *The Energy Journal* **19** (2), 149–164.

Clyde, W. C. and Osler, C. L. (1997). Charting: Chaos theory in disguise? *Journal of Futures Markets* **17** (5), 489–514.

Devaney, R. L. *et al.* (1989). *An Introduction to Chaotic Dynamical Systems*, vol. 13046. (Addison-Wesley Reading).

Eckmann, J. P., Kamphorst, S. O. and Ruelle, D. (1987). Recurrence plots of dynamical systems. *EPL (Europhysics Letters)* **4** (9), 973.

Farmer, J. D. (1982). Chaotic attractors of an infinite-dimensional dynamical system. *Physica D: Nonlinear Phenomena* **4** (3), 366–393.

Fraser, A. M. and Swinney, H. L. (1986). Independent coordinates for strange attractors from mutual information. *Physical Review A* **33**, 1134–1140.

Geman, H. (2009). *Commodities and Commodity Derivatives: Modeling and Pricing for Agriculturals, Metals and Energy*. (John Wiley & Sons).

Grassberger, P. and Procaccia, I. (1983a). Characterization of strange attractors. *Physical Review Letters* **50** (5), 346.

Grassberger, P. and Procaccia, I. (1983b). Measuring the strangeness of strange attractors. *Physica D: Nonlinear Phenomena* **9** (1), 189–208.

Hegger, R., Kantz, H. and Schreiber, T. (1999). Practical implementation of nonlinear time series methods: The Tisean package. *Chaos: An Interdisciplinary Journal of Nonlinear Science* **9** (2), 413–435.

Ikeguchi, T. and Aihara, K. (1997). Lyapunov spectral analysis on random data. *International Journal of Bifurcation and Chaos* **7** (06), 1267–1282.

Jayawardena, A. W., Xu, P. and Li, W. K. (2008). A method of estimating the noise level in a chaotic time series. *Chaos: An Interdisciplinary Journal of Nonlinear Science* **18** (2), 023115.

Jayawardena, A. W., Xu, P. and Li, W. K. (2010). Modified correlation entropy estimation for a noisy chaotic time series. *Chaos: An Interdisciplinary Journal of Nonlinear Science* **20** (2), 023104.

Kantz, H. and Schreiber, T. (2004). *Nonlinear Time Series Analysis*, vol. 7. (Cambridge University Press).

Kaplan, D. T. (1994). Exceptional events as evidence for determinism. *Physica D: Nonlinear Phenomena* **73** (1), 38–48.

Kaplan, D. T. and Glass, L. (1992). Direct test for determinism in a time series. *Physical Review Letters* **68** (4), 427.

Kennel, M. B., Brown, R. and Abarbanel, H. D. I. (1992). Determining embedding dimension for phase-space reconstruction using a geometrical construction, *Physical Review A* **45**, 3403–3411.

Kodba, S., Perc, M. and Marhl, M. (2004). Detecting chaos from a time series. *European Journal of Physics* **26** (1), 205.

Kolmogorov, A. N. (1958). A new metric invariant of transient dynamical systems and automorphisms in Lebesgue spaces. In *Dokl. Akad. Nauk SSSR (NS)*, vol. 119, pp. 861–864.

Kyrtsou, C., Malliaris, A. G. and Serletis, A. (2009). Energy sector pricing: On the role of neglected nonlinearity. *Energy Economics* **31** (3), 492–502.

Martelli, M., Dang, M. and Seph, T. (1998). Defining chaos. *Mathematics Magazine* **71** (2), 112–122.

Martina, E., Rodriguez, E., Escarela-Perez, R. and Alvarez-Ramirez, J. (2011). Multiscale entropy analysis of crude oil price dynamics. *Energy Economics* **33** (5), 936–947.

Marwan, N., Romano, M. C., Thiel, M. and Kurths, J. (2007). Recurrence plots for the analysis of complex systems. *Physics reports* **438** (5), 237–329.

Mastroeni, L., Vellucci, P. and Naldi, M. (2018a). A reappraisal of the chaotic paradigm for energy commodity prices. To appear on Energy Economics.

Mastroeni, L., Vellucci, P. and Naldi, M. (2018b). Co-existence of stochastic and chaotic behaviour in the copper price time series. Resources Policy 58, 295–302.

Mastroeni, L. and Vellucci, P. (2017). "Chaos" in energy and commodity markets: a controversial matter? Working paper n. 218, Department of Economics, University of Roma Tre.

Matilla-Garcia, M. (2007). Nonlinear dynamics in energy futures. *The Energy Journal* **28** (3), 7–29.

Moshiri, S. and Foroutan, F. (2006). Forecasting nonlinear crude oil futures prices. *The Energy Journal* **27** (4), 81–95.

Osler, C. L. and Chang, P. (1995). Head and shoulders: Not just a flaky pattern. Technical Report 4, Federal Reserve Bank of New York.

Packard, N. H., Crutchfield, J. P., Farmer, J. D. and Shaw, R. S. (1980). Geometry from a time series. *Physical Review Letters* **45** (9), 712.

Panas, E. and Ninni, V. (2000). Are oil markets chaotic? A non-linear dynamic analysis. *Energy Economics* **22** (5), 549–568.

Pilipovic, D. (2007). *Energy Risk: Valuing and Managing Energy Derivatives*. (McGraw Hill Professional).

Pincus, S. M. (1991). Approximate entropy as a measure of system complexity. *Proceeding of the National Academy of Sciences of the United States of America* **88** (6), 2297–2301.

Rosenstein, M. T., Collins, J. J. and De Luca, C. J. (1993). A practical method for calculating largest lyapunov exponents from small data sets. *Physica D: Nonlinear Phenomena* **65** (1–2), 117–134.

Ruelle, D. (1989). *Chaotic Evolution and Strange Attractors*, vol. 1. (Cambridge University Press).

Serletis, A. and Gogas, P. (1999). The North American natural gas liquids markets are chaotic. *The Energy Journal* **20** (1), 83–103.

Shaw, R. (1981). Strange attractors, chaotic behavior, and information flow. *Zeitschrift für Naturforschung A* **36** (1), 80–112.

Sinaĭ, J. (1959). On the concept of entropy for a dynamic system. In *Dokl. Akad. Nauk SSSR*, vol. 124, pp. 768–771.

Tanaka, T., Aihara, K. and Taki, M. (1996). Lyapunov exponents of random time series. *Physical Review E* **54** (2), 2122.

Tanaka, T., Aihara, K. and Taki, M. (1998). Analysis of positive lyapunov exponents from random time series. *Physica D: Nonlinear Phenomena* **111** (1), 42–50.

Takens, F. (1981). Detecting strange attractors in turbulence. In *Dynamical Systems and Turbulence, Warwick 1980*. Springer pp. 366–381.

Tsay, R. S. (2005). *Analysis of Financial Time Series*, vol. 543. (John Wiley & Sons).

Vellekoop, M. and Berglund, R. (1994). On intervals, transitivity= chaos. *The American Mathematical Monthly* **101** (4), 353–355.

Index

D

E

L

M

N

O

P